ANNUAL REVIEW OF IRISH LAW 2014

Annual Review of Irish Law 2014

Raymond Byrne
BCL, LLM, Barrister-at-Law
Director of Research, Law Reform Commission

William Binchy
BA, BCL, LLM, FTCD, Barrister-at-Law

ROUND HALL

THOMSON REUTERS

Published in 2015 by
Thomson Reuters Ireland Limited
(Registered in Ireland, Company No. 416940.
Registered Office and address for service:
43 Fitzwilliam Place, Dublin 2, Ireland)
trading as Round Hall

Typeset by
Gough Typesetting Services
Dublin

Printed by
CPI Group (UK) Ltd, Croydon, CRO 4YY

ISBN 978-0-41405-449-3
ISSN 0791-1084

A catalogue record for this book
is available from the British Library

Table of Contents

Preface

This is the 28th volume in the Annual Review series and our purpose continues to be to provide a review of legal developments, judicial and statutory, that occurred in 2014. As with the previous volumes, we endeavour to discuss those Acts and Statutory Instruments enacted and made during the year. In terms of case law, this includes those judgments delivered in 2014 and which were available to us and our contributors by mid-2015 (whether through online sources or in the law reports).

Once again it is a pleasure to thank those who made the task of completing this volume less onerous. For this 28th volume of the Annual Review series, we are delighted to have had the benefit of specialist contributions on Asylum and Immigration Law, Company and Insolvency Law, Constitutional Law, Contract Law, Criminal Law, Electricity, Energy and Natural Resources, Employment Law, Equity, Evidence, Information Law and the Ombudsman, Land Law, Planning and Development Law, Practice and Procedure, Probate and Succession Law, Social Welfare, and Whistleblower Protection included in this volume. We continue to take final responsibility for the overall text as in the past, but are especially grateful for the contributions of Patricia Brazil in Asylum and Immigration Law; Noel McGrath in Company and Insolvency Law; Oran Doyle and Estelle Feldman in Constitutional Law; Fergus Ryan in Contract Law; John P. Byrne in Criminal Law; Dr Eva Barrett in Electricity, Energy and Natural Resources; Desmond Ryan in Employment Law; Lucy-Anne Buckley in Equity; Aoife Beirne in Evidence; Estelle Feldman in Information Law and the Ombudsman, and Whistleblower Protection; Helen McCarthy and James Cross in Land Law; Garrett Simons in Planning and Development Law; Sam Collins in Practice and Procedure; Albert Keating in Probate and Succession Law; and Gerry Whyte and Mel Cousins in Social Welfare Law.

Finally, we are again very grateful for the ongoing support we receive from Round Hall (in particular Frieda Donohue, Martin McCann, Terri McDonnell, Orla King and Maura Smyth) and from Gough Typesetting Services (who have been involved in each volume of the Annual Review series). We are indebted to them for their assistance and professionalism, which ensures the continued production of this series.

Raymond Byrne and William Binchy
November 2015

Table of Cases

IRELAND

EUROPEAN

ENGLAND AND WALES

OTHER

Table of Legislation

CONSTITUTION OF IRELAND

IRISH STATUTES

Pre-1922 Acts

Post–1922 Acts

COURT RULES

IRISH STATUTORY INSTRUMENTS

BILLS

EUROPEAN

Directives

Regulations

GERMANY

NEW ZEALAND

INTERNATIONAL TREATIES AND CONVENTIONS

OTHER

Administrative Law

APPROPRIATION

The Appropriation Act 2014 (the "2014 Act"), which came into effect on its signature by the President on 19 December 2014, provided as follows. For the year ended 31 December 2014, the amount of supply grants in accordance with the Central Fund (Permanent Provisions) Act 1965 was €42,657,904,000. Reflecting the continuing depth of the fiscal difficulties for the State since 2009 (see also the *Annual Review of Irish Law 2013*, p.1), for the sixth successive year (and the only years in the 28 volumes of the *Annual Review of Irish Law*) this was less in actual terms than the corresponding figure in the Appropriation Act 2013, which was €43,736,835,000 (2012: €45,550,779,000; 2011: €46,374,724,000; 2010: €47,306,286,000; 2009: €47,868,895,000; 2008: €50,049,646,000). By 2014, however, reflecting some growth momentum in the economy, the State's finances were approaching equilibrium, so that the gap between spending and expenditure had narrowed considerably. This must be considered against the background of enormous borrowings that had to be continued in those years in order to maintain some level of the State's essential services and supports, including most social welfare payments (assisted by the EU-IMF Agreement for Financial Support, discussed in the Commercial Law chapter, below) (and bearing in mind that these borrowings did not maintain the level of spending that had been in place up to 2008, so that these years also involved cutbacks in State services and payments associated with the austerity linked to bringing the State's finances towards equilibrium).

Under the Public Accounts and Charges Act 1891, the sum for appropriations-in-aid was €3,582,708,000, slightly lower than the figure for 2013 of €3,804,859,000 (2012: €4,099,509,000; 2011: €4,041,379,000; 2010: €6,280,413,000; 2009: €5,978,112,000; 2008: €4,472,799,000).

The 2014 Act also provided, in accordance with s.91 of the Finance Act 2004, for carrying over into the year ending 31 December 2015 undischarged appropriations for capital supply services totalling €79,044,000, significantly lower than the equivalent 2013 figure of €132,596,000 (2012: €107,237,000; 2011: €115,160,000; 2010: €16,500,000; 2009: €125,717,000; 2008: €128,453,000). This in effect allowed this amount, which had not been spent on, for example, infrastructure projects in 2014, to be carried over into 2015.

Section 4 of the 2014 Act also amended s.3 of the Appropriation Act 1999 to reflect the changed financial allocation for the Health Service Executive (HSE), provided for in the Health Service Executive (Financial Matters) Act 2014 (discussed in the Health and Health Services chapter, below).

COMMISSIONS OF INVESTIGATION

The Commission of Investigation (Ronan MacLochlainn) Order 2014 (S.I. No. 346 of 2014), made under the Commissions of Investigation Act 2004, provided for the establishment of a Commission of Investigation to investigate matters relating to the fatal shooting of Ronan MacLochlainn by members of An Garda Síochána in the course of an armed robbery in Ashford, Co. Wicklow in May 1998. Public hearings in connection with the Commission began in 2015.

JUDICIAL REVIEW

The case law under Ord.84 of the Rules of the Superior Courts 1986 (S.I. No. 15 of 1986) that arose in 2014 is discussed in the various chapters in this *Annual Review of Irish Law* where the substantive subjects arising are detailed, notably in the Immigration and Planning Law chapters. Further reference may also be obtained through the Table of Statutory Instruments under the entry for the Rules of the Superior Courts 1986.

PUBLIC PROCUREMENT

Screening of tenders In *Gaswise Ltd v Dublin City Council* [2014] IEHC 56, the High Court (Finlay Geoghegan J.) granted the applicant a declaration that its exclusion from the screening of a public procurement tender had been invalid. The applicant challenged a decision made by the respondent Council to exclude it from a procurement process seeking to allocate four ranked places in a framework agreement for the maintenance and repair of boilers in public housing owned by the respondent Council. The Invitation to Tender ("ITT") was published by the respondent on 18 April 2013. The deadline for the submission of tenders was 28 May 2013. The applicant submitted a tender on that date. The tenders were subject to a two-stage evaluation process by the Council. The first stage involved screening tenders based on a number of pass/fail selection criteria. Tenders which failed to meet one or more of these selection criteria were excluded at that stage. The second stage involved evaluation of the surviving tenders based on the service offered, price and contract management procedures. Four successful tenders were to be chosen and ranked in the framework based on the results of the second-stage evaluation. The evaluation committee decided to exclude the applicant from the procurement process on the basis of its alleged failure to meet a criterion related to replacement parts. The applicant was informed of this decision by letter dated 23 July 2013. On 13 August 2013, the applicant instituted these proceedings. Pursuant to the European Communities (Public Authorities Contracts) (Review Procedures) Regulations 2010 (S.I. No. 130 of 2010) (the "2010 Regulations"), the applicant sought reliefs setting aside the respondent's decision to exclude it from the procurement process, and any decision relating to the award of the contract. At the commencement of the hearing, it was agreed that the case would proceed by way of modular trial. The first module would be confined to the applicant's challenge to the decision to exclude it from the procurement process.

In granting the relief sought, the High Court (Finlay Geoghegan J.) held that the interpretation of the ITT was a matter for the court. That interpretation must be carried out in a manner which gave effect to the core principles of equal treatment and transparency. Regulation 17 of the European Communities (Award of Public Authorities Contracts) Regulations 2006 (S.I. No. 329 of 2006), which implemented art.2 of Directive 2004/18/EC, the 2004 Directive on public works contracts, public supply contracts and public service contracts, provides that contracting authorities "shall treat economic operators equally and non-discriminatorily and shall act in a transparent way."

The court cited the following decisions in this context: *Universale-Bau AG v Entsorgungsbetriebe Simmering GesmbH* (C–470/99) [2002] E.C.R. I–11617, *SIAC Construction Plc v Mayo County Council* (C–19/00) [2001] E.C.R. I–7725, *Commission v Netherlands* (C–368/10) [2012] E.C.R. 1–284, and *Clinton (t/a Oriel Training Service) v Department for Employment and Learning* [2012] N.I.Q.B. 2 (although the decision of the Northern Ireland Court of Appeal in *Clinton* [2012] NICA 48, which broadly upheld the High Court decision in that case, was not cited). Applying the "SIAC test," the question for the court was whether the ITT would be interpreted by all reasonably well informed and normally diligent tenderers as including and espousing in a clear, precise and unequivocal manner the requirement that all tenderers submit a replacement parts statement. The court concluded that the requirement to submit a replacement parts statement was not expressed with sufficient clarity and precision in the ITT in the present case and it had, therefore, been unlawful for the respondent to exclude the applicant by reason of its failure to attach a replacement parts statement.

The ITT had contained a criterion that a statement confirming a turnover over a three-year period of €250,000 was required. The applicant had argued that one of the successful tenderers failed to comply with this requirement, and this also fell within the grounds pleaded in the case. Citing the decisions in *Uniplex v NHS Business Services Authority* (C–406/08) [2010] E.C.R. I–817 and *Baxter Healthcare Ltd v Health Service Executive* [2013] IEHC 413, the court held that time for commencing legal proceedings in respect of this matter started to run when the applicant had knowledge of the facts sufficient to enable it to consider that it had reasonable grounds to challenge the respondent's decision. Using this test, the claim was not time-barred under the 2010 Regulations.

As the applicant had an interest in being awarded the contract, it was eligible, under the 2010 Regulations, to challenge the respondent's decision. The court noted that it had a wide discretion regarding the remedy to be granted to the applicant, but as required by the European Court of Justice in *Unibet (London) Ltd v Justitiekanslern* (C–432/05) [2007] E.C.R. I–2271, it must apply the powers conferred upon it by the 2010 Regulations in a manner that ensured effective judicial protection of EU rights. The remedy granted must be proportionate and, in considering what is proportionate, the court had to consider the position of the respondent and other participants in the tender process. Against this background, the court concluded that the applicant was entitled to an evaluation of its tender by a fresh evaluation team, thus requiring that the tender be run from the beginning again.

Agriculture, Food and Forestry

ANIMAL HEALTH AND WELFARE

Detailed Regulations made in 2014 under Animal Health and Welfare Act 2013 A series of detailed Regulations and Orders were made in 2014 under the Animal Health and Welfare Act 2013 (the "2013 Act") (*Annual Review of Irish Law 2013*, pp.11–15). The number and range of these Statutory Instruments indicate the extent to which the 2013 Act introduced a significant number of reforms which required this level of new requirements. Many of the Statutory Instruments made in 2014 also revoked a large number of pre–2013 Statutory Instruments, thus indicating the extensive consolidation of the statutory landscape in this area at the level of secondary legislation, which mirrors the consolidation effected by the 2013 Act at the level of primary legislation. Further Statutory Instruments were made in 2015 under the 2013 Act, and we will return to these in the *Annual Review of Irish Law 2015*.

The Regulations and Orders made under the 2013 Act in 2014 were: African Horse Sickness Regulations 2014 (S.I. No. 116 of 2014); African Swine Fever (Restriction on Movements of Pigs and Pig Products) Regulations 2014 (S.I. No. 501 of 2014); Animal Health (African Swine Fever) (Non-EU Countries) Regulations 2014 (S.I. No. 115 of 2014); Animal Health and Welfare (Bovine Movement) Regulations 2014 (S.I. No. 521 of 2014); Animal Health and Welfare (Bovine Tuberculosis) Regulations 2015 (S.I. No. 58 of 2015); Animal Health and Welfare (Operations and Procedures) Regulations 2014 (S.I. No. 123 of 2014); Animal Health and Welfare (Operations and Procedures) (No.2) Regulations 2014 (S.I. No. 127 of 2014); Animal Health and Welfare (Restriction on Horned Cattle) Regulations 2014 (S.I. No. 111 of 2014); Animal Health and Welfare (Restriction on Horned Cattle) (No.2) Regulations 2014 (S.I. No. 224 of 2014); Animal Health and Welfare (Revocation) Regulations 2014 (S.I. No. 126 of 2014); Animal Health and Welfare (Section 17) Regulations 2014 (S.I. No. 107 of 2014); Animal Health and Welfare Act 2013 (Application to Tuberculosis in Non-Ruminant Animals) Order 2014 (S.I. No. 109 of 2014); Animal Welfare (Electro-immobilisation) Regulations 2014 (S.I. No. 108 of 2014); Bovine Viral Diarrhoea Regulations2014 (S.I. No. 118 of 2014); Control on Animal Vaccines Regulations 2014 (S.I. No. 193 of 2014); Control on Animal Vaccines (Amendment) Regulations 2014 (S.I. No. 590 of 2014); Control on Places where Poultry Are Kept Regulations 2014 (S.I. No. 114 of 2014); Control On Places Where Horses Are Kept Regulations 2014 (S.I. No. 113 of 2014); Equidae (Transfer of Ownership) Regulations 2014 (S.I. No. 189 of 2014); Equidae (Transfer of Ownership) (No.2) Regulations 2014 (S.I. No. 601 of 2014); Foot and Mouth Disease (Non-EU Countries) Regulations 2014 (S.I. No. 502 of 2014); Notification and Control of Animal Diseases Regulations 2014 (S.I. No. 110 of 2014); Pet Passport Regulations 2014 (S.I. No. 119 of 2014);

Pet Passport (No.2) Regulations 2014 (S.I. No. 602 of 2014); Prohibition on Tail-docking (Bovines) Regulations 2014 (S.I. No. 117 of 2014); Prohibition on Tail-docking (Bovines) (No.2) Regulations 2014 (S.I. No. 225 of 2014); Prohibition on Tail Docking (Dogs) Regulations 2014 (S.I. No. 125 of 2014); and Tail Docking and Dew Claw Removal (Dogs) Regulations 2014 (S.I. No. 128 of 2014).

Overlap between 2013 Act and EU-derived requirements Notwithstanding the considerable consolidation effected by the Animal Health and Welfare Act 2013 (the "2013" Act), the interaction with and overlap between such legislation and the relevant EU law, which of course also forms part of Irish law, is illustrated by the making in 2014 of a number of Regulations under s.3 of the European Communities Act 1972 (the "1972 Act") in order to give effect to EU law in the area of animal health and welfare. Ideally, these EU-derived Regulations would be brought within the Regulation-making power in the 2013 Act, rather than being made under s.3 of the 1972 Act. Indeed, Sch.3 to the 2013 Act, paras 46 and 47, provide that Regulations may be made under the 2013 Act in respect of:

> 46. Requiring compliance with, or prohibiting a contravention of, an act adopted by an institution of the European Union.
>
> 47. Any other matter relating to an animal, animal product, animal feed or disease or animal health and welfare the subject of an act adopted by an institution of the European Union.

It may be noted that similar provision has been made in other areas where EU-derived law is a significant feature, such as the Safety, Health and Welfare at Work Act 2005 (*Annual Review of Irish Law 2005*, pp.604–618) and the Chemicals Act 2008 (*Annual Review of Irish Law 2008*, pp.564–567). Thus, there would appear to be no reason why Regulations under s.3 of the 1972 Act continue to be required; and if the 2013 Act did not, over time, become the sole Regulation-making source for animal health and welfare matters, the significant effort involved in consolidating this area runs the risk of being degraded. For the time being, we note here the 2014 Regulations made under s.3 of the 1972 Act.

In the context of equidae, that is, horses, the European Union (Identification of Equidae) Regulations 2014 (S.I. No. 207 of 2014) gave administrative effect to Commission Regulation (EC) No.504/2008 and also implemented Council Directive 90/427/EEC and Commission Decision 92/353/EEC, and thus provided for the strengthening of the powers of the Minister for Agriculture in relation to the approval process for stud books and issuing bodies for equine identification documents and to the seizure and detention of animals and documents. They also revoked the provisions of the European Communities (Equine) Regulations 2011 (S.I. No. 357 of 2011) (the "2011 Regulations") to the extent that these related to equine identification. Regulations dealing with equine semen collection centres and ova or embryo collection and production teams contained in the 2011 Regulations remain in force.

Similarly, the European Communities (Control of Avian Influenza) Regulations 2006 (Amendment) Regulations 2014 (S.I. No. 223 of 2014) provide that an authorised officer, within the meaning of the Animal Health and Welfare Act 2013, is also an authorised officer under the European Union (Control of Avian

Influenza) Regulations 2006 (S.I. No. 701 of 2006) (the "2006 Regulations"), and may exercise the functions of an authorised officer under the 2013 Act for the purposes of the 2006 Regulations.

In the same way, the European Union (Protection of Animals at the Time of Killing) Regulations 2013 (S.I. No. 292 of 2013), as amended by the European Union (Protection of Animals at the Time of Killing) (Amendment) Regulations 2014 (S.I. No. 290 of 2014) put in place the administrative arrangements to give effect to Council Regulation (EC) No.1099/2009 (the "2009 EU Regulation") on the protection of animals at the time of killing. The 2009 EU Regulation and these Statutory Instruments, whose purpose is to avoid pain and to minimise the distress and suffering of animals at the time of slaughter, clearly also overlap with the general purposes of the Animal Health and Welfare Act 2013.

FORESTRY

The Forestry Act 2014 (the "2014 Act") provided for a modern and reformed legislative framework for forestry in the State, and in the process provided for the repeal and replacement of the Forestry Act 1946 (the "1946 Act"). The purpose of the 2014 Act was to support the development of a modern forest sector which operates in accordance with the principles of good forest practice. At the time of writing (July 2015), the 2014 Act had not yet been brought into force.

It was noted during the Oireachtas debates on the 2014 Act that, among the key changes in this era since the enactment of the 1946 Act was the recognition that forests are a multi-functional resource that provide significant economic, social and environmental benefits. It was noted that by the early 1900s, forest cover in Ireland had been reduced to 1 per cent of the land area of the country. This contributed to the need to regulate felling through the introduction of the Forestry Acts 1928 and 1946, which ensured that forest cover was maintained. By 2014, the area of the national forest estate in Ireland was over 730,000 hectares or almost 11 per cent of the total land area. While this had expanded significantly since the early 1980s with the introduction of grant schemes aimed at encouraging private landowners, mainly farmers, to become involved in forestry, it was accepted that this was still relatively low compared to other EU member states given that almost 40 per cent of total land in the European Union is under forest cover.

It was noted that in 2014 more than 54 per cent of the national forest estate was in public ownership, mainly through Coillte Teo (established under the Forestry Act 1988: see *Annual Review of Irish Law 1988*, p.5), with the remaining 46 per cent in private ownership. This contrasted with the position in the 1990s when 70 per cent was in public ownership and only 30 per cent was in private ownership. In 2014, there were more than 19,000 private forest owners throughout Ireland, the majority of whom were farmers and the sector employed a further 12,000. Exports of wood products in 2012 were just over €300 million, with wood-energy and processing also expanding as forests enter the production phase. Ireland's forests were also widely used by the public for amenity and recreation, with an estimated 18 million recreational visits to Irish forests each year.

Part 2 of the 2014 Act (ss.5–10) outlines in some detail the functions of the Minister for Agriculture, Food and the Marine, both general and specific. The general functions in s.5 include a range of promotional responsibilities relating to forestry, including afforestation, good forest practice that maintains the biological diversity of forests, the promotion of knowledge and awareness of forestry through education and training, and the development and marketing of a quality based processing sector. The Minister's general functions also include the regulation and monitoring of forest operations to ensure that forests are properly managed and protected from harmful pests, diseases and invasive species. The specific functions of the Minister are set down in s.6, and include the granting of licences for felling, afforestation, forest road works and approval of forest management plans, and the attaching of conditions to such licences and approvals. Regulation of forestry activities is essential both to avoid environmental damage and to maintain the existing forest estate so as to protect the investment by the State in the afforestation programme. The Minister may also give legislative effect to guidelines and standards covering a range of environmental considerations, from water quality to the protection of species such as the red squirrel and the freshwater pearl mussel.

Section 7 provides that the Minister may set conditions in licences, the extension of such licences and approvals and their suspension or revocation. Section 8 empowers the Minister to appoint committees to assist and advise in the performance of his or her functions. Where advantageous, this may include the delegation to a committee of certain functions, subject to the Minister retaining overall responsibility and accountability. Issues concerning the confidentiality of the work of the committee and the responsibility of members are set down in s.9.

Section 10 enables the Minister to require forest owners to submit a forest management plan in support of applications for consented activities. Such plans would cover felling, including thinning, reforestation, forest road works and other forestry-related activities such as amenity and recreational use of forests. The forest management plan will also provide a mechanism whereby an application for a felling licence may be incorporated within the plan thus allowing for a flexible, responsive and timely system for dealing with activities such as thinning.

Part 3 of the 2014 Act (ss.11–15) provides for protection of the environment when any forestry activity is being planned. The licensing of forestry activities must have regard to the continued protection of the environment. There are consultation processes in place with a range of stakeholders, including the Department of Arts, Heritage and the Gaeltacht, Inland Fisheries Ireland, An Taisce, local authorities and the public. There are also guidelines on matters such as water quality, landscape, biodiversity, archaeology, and protected flora and fauna. In 2014, approximately 18 per cent of the land area of Ireland was designated under EU law as Special Areas of Conservation (SACs) or Special Protection Areas (SPAs). There are also additional national designations, such as natural heritage areas and national parks. Forestry activities may be restricted in these designated areas.

Section 11 requires the Minister to have regard to the social, economic and environmental functions of forestry; and to follow good forest practice and to take particular account of the potential impact of forestry activities on different habitats and species in forests. Activities occurring within designated areas or affecting protected species, or activities that have the potential to impact on such areas or species, must be assessed for any adverse impact. Where it is considered that the activity has the potential to impact adversely on the designated area or protected species, the Minister will require the completion of an assessment of the impact of the forestry activity on the habitat, plant life, birds or animals so affected. Such assessments could also include proposals to avoid, mitigate or ameliorate any potential impact and if acceptable, these would then allow the proposed activity to proceed in an appropriately controlled and measured fashion.

Sections 12 and 13 place an onus on forest owners to notify the Minister if their forest is damaged or destroyed, and also give the Minister the power to require information from forest owners and wood-processing businesses for statistical or investigative purposes. Section 14 empowers the Minister to serve a notice on a landowner to remove vegetation from uncultivated land that is posing a threat to an adjoining forest or to authorise persons to enter the land and remove the vegetation. This was intended as a means to prevent forest fires where possible.

Section 15 deals with the control of species such as grey squirrels and rabbits where they pose a threat to forests, and empowers the Minister to serve a notice on a landowner requiring him or her to take specified action to protect neighbouring forests from damage. Where land is unoccupied, or the owner fails to comply with such notice, the Minister may authorise a person to enter the land and deal with the particular species.

Part 4 of the 2014 Act (ss.16–21) deals with felling licences. The previous licence system operated under the 1946 Act was considered cumbersome in the context of the needs of a modern forest sector and wider society. The 2014 Act simplified the process by replacing the two pre–2014 licences with a single felling licence. As a result, there will no longer be a requirement for a person to lodge an application for a felling licence at the nearest Garda station. The licence will be valid for a period of up to 10 years with the possibility of an extension for a further five years. When the Minister grants a licence, he or she may impose conditions, including whether or not the land should be replanted. Unlicensed felling will continue to be an offence with penalties, on summary conviction, of €200 for every tree removed or imprisonment for up to six months, or both. On conviction on indictment, penalties ranging to a maximum of €1 million or imprisonment for a term not exceeding five years, or both, may be imposed. These penalties were, it was noted during the Oireachtas debates on the 2014 Act, at the higher end of the scale (and created an arrestable offence), and this was intended to reflect the seriousness of the offence and the need for dissuasive measures to ensure that the forest estate is protected.

Section 19 provides for exemptions to the requirement for a felling licence. These include all trees within an urban area; trees that must be removed for public safety reasons or to prevent the spread of fire, pests or disease; and trees outside a forest that are within 10m of a public road which the owner considers to be posing a danger to road users. An important exemption from the licensing requirement is that landowners will be able to remove trees on their own holdings for their own use, up to a limit of 15m of wood in any period of 12 months, provided the trees are outside a forest and do not form part of a decorative avenue or ring of trees on the holding, or are within the environs of national monuments or archaeological sites, trees within designated European sites and trees which are more than 150 years old. Notwithstanding the exemptions, s.20 of the 2014 Act also enables the Minister to issue an order prohibiting the felling or removing of any tree, with penalties for those who do not comply.

Section 21 empowers the Minister to notify the Property Registration Authority of the imposition of a replanting order on land where trees have been felled without a licence or in contravention of a condition of a licence so that these can be registered as a burden on the land until the replanting order has been complied with. This is to ensure that trees which have been illegally cut down are replaced and also to protect prospective purchasers of forestry land. Once the conditions of the licence or the order are satisfied, the Minister, on such notification by the owner, will inform the registering authority of the discharge of the burden or compliance with the conditions.

Part 5 of the 2014 Act (comprising s.22 only) sets out the requirements for licensing of afforestation and forest roadwork projects and aerial fertilisation of forests. Section 22 expands on the application process and empowers the Minister to impose conditions on the grant of licences; it provides for the imposition of penalties where unlicensed development, or development that does not comply with the conditions of a licence, takes place; and also provides for the making of regulations governing the issuing of licences.

Part 6 of the 2014 Act (ss.23–25) deals with enforcement. Section 23 empowers the Minister to appoint authorised officers to enforce the various statutory provisions. These officers are normally departmental forestry inspectors but members of An Garda Síochána are also authorised officers for the purposes of the 2014 Act. The powers of authorised officers are set out in detail in s.24 and include the power of entry onto lands to inspect and remove, if necessary, any material considered a risk to trees and to remove records or other information relevant to the inspection or investigation. Section 25 empowers the Minister to charge for licences and other services provided by the legislation.

Part 7 of the 2014 Act, comprising s.26 only, empowers the Minister, in a case where illegal felling has occurred, to impose an order on the offender compelling him or her to replant the area or an equivalent area within his or her ownership. Section 26 also makes it an offence if the offender fails to comply with the order.

Part 8 of the 2014 Act (ss.27–29) deals with offences and penalties. Section 27 contains a list of offences, which include submitting false or misleading information in support of an application for approval or for a licence, failure to comply with notices or other conditions or requirements, causing irremediable damage to a tree and, as referred to above, intentional or reckless setting of fire to trees. The penalties in s.27 range from €200 on conviction for damaging or removing a tree to fines of up to €1,000,000 or five years imprisonment (or both) on conviction on indictment of felling or removing trees without a licence. Section 29 provides that where the offence is committed by a body corporate, the Minister may prosecute both the body corporate and officers of the body corporate.

Part 9 of the 2014 Act, comprising s.30 only, empowers the Minister to make Regulations relating to the range of forestry activities, including afforestation, forest protection, forest roads, training and education. Such Regulations may also include provisions to prevent the entry into the State, or for the control or extermination within the State, of insects, pests or invasive species that might threaten trees—an important provision having regard to the recent outbreak of ash dieback disease.

Part 10 of the 2014 Act (ss.31–34) includes s.31, which provides for the repeal of the 1946 Act. Section 32 provided for payment of compensation in certain limited circumstances where applications for licences are refused.

Part 11 of the 2014 Act, comprising s.35 only, amends the Agriculture Appeals Act 2001 (*Annual Review of Irish Law 2001*, p.4) to extend its remit to a number of forestry activities and to provide for the establishment of a forestry appeals committee.

JOHNSTOWN CASTLE ESTATE

The Johnstown Castle Agricultural College (Amendment) Act 2014 amended the Johnstown Castle Agricultural College Acts 1945 to 1996 in order to enable Teagasc, the Agriculture and Food Research Agency, to develop part of the Johnstown Castle estate in County Wexford, comprising the castle and gardens, as a visitor attraction and to permit the sale of a small area of land to the local community for a burial ground.

It was explained during the Oireachtas debates on the 2014 Act that Johnstown Castle estate was gifted to the State by private owners as provided for in the Johnstown Castle Agricultural College Act 1945. The gift was subject to a restriction that it be used exclusively for the purposes of a "lay agricultural college" and no other purpose. The Johnstown Castle Agricultural College (Amendment) Act 1959 extended use of the estate for the conduct of "agricultural research" and transferred ownership from the Minister for Agriculture to An Foras Talúntais, the statutory predecessor of Teagasc. The 1959 Act also included a provision preventing An Foras Talúntais from disposing of any part of the estate. The estate was transferred to Teagasc under the Agriculture (Research, Training and Advice) Act 1988 which also established Teagasc (*Annual Review of Irish Law 1988*, pp.39–40), with all related provisions remaining intact in terms of the disposal of estate land. The Johnstown Castle Agricultural College (Amendment) Act 1996 (*Annual Review of Irish Law 1996*, p.5) eased the statutory prohibition on a disposal of the estate, and it provided for the disposal of up to 5 per cent of the estate for "environmental, heritage, amenity or recreational purposes."

It was also noted during the Oireachtas debates on the 2014 Act that Johnstown Castle estate extends to 980 acres and consists of a protected 19th century castle surrounded by gardens and farmland. The estate is of historic and cultural significance. The castle was built in 1840 and is the most significant surviving country house in Wexford. The Irish Agricultural Museum Society operates a museum on the estate, displaying local agricultural heritage artefacts. The walled gardens and grounds remain open to the public and the Department of Agriculture, Food and the Marine and the Environmental Protection Agency (EPA) occupy offices adjoining the estate.

Teagasc is obliged to maintain the estate at substantial cost to the organisation and, as of 2014, it had been used for many years for farming and agricultural research purposes. The castle and gardens, comprising 120 acres, are no longer used for agricultural education or research. It was noted that Teagasc had been exploring the possibility of transforming the castle and gardens into a visitor attraction for the south-east. A conservation plan prepared in 2007, with support from the Heritage Council, recommended conservation works to ensure the significance of the property was maintained. A report commissioned in 2009 by Teagasc, the Heritage Council and the Irish Heritage Trust proposed phased interventions to transform the estate into a high quality visitor destination. Since then, a local steering group led by Teagasc commissioned a business plan to develop a range of visitor and amenity attractions that would attract a substantial number of visitors each year. In

2014, the estate had approximately 35,000 visitors a year, but it was thought that that figure could be increased significantly with the right investment.

Separately, it was stated that the local community in the village of Murrintown urgently required land for a burial ground and had identified 2.8 acres on the estate that would be suitable. Teagasc wished to facilitate the request, but the pre–2014 legislation, limiting disposal to "environmental, heritage, amenity or recreational purposes" prevented it from doing so. The 2014 Act therefore amended the 1945 Act to permit Teagasc to dispose of land for burial purposes. It was noted in this respect that the bequest of the estate was a substantial gift to the State by private owners, with certain conditions attached that restrict its use to agricultural education and research. Following examination of the pre–2014 legislation governing the estate, the Office of the Attorney General had confirmed that enabling legislation along the lines provided for in the 2014 Act could be introduced to extend use of the castle and gardens and facilitate the transfer of land for a burial ground.

Section 2 of the 2014 Act amended s.1 of the Johnstown Castle Agricultural College (Amendment) Act 1959 to define Teagasc by reference to the 1988 Act which established it. It also defined the map detailing that portion of the estate known as the castle and gardens for which a change of use was provided (the map was deposited with Ordnance Survey Ireland where it is available for public inspection). Section 3 of the 2014 Act amended s.3 of the 1959 Act, including provision for the inclusion of "burial ground" in the list of specific purposes for which land on the estate may be disposed of. The 2014 Act made no change to the pre–2014, 5 per cent limit on land disposals.

Asylum and Immigration Law

Patricia Brazil BL, Lecturer in Law, Trinity College Dublin

CASE LAW

Anonymity of asylum seekers in judicial review proceedings In *MARA (Nigeria) v Minister for Justice and Equality* [2014] IESC 71; unreported, Supreme Court, 12 December 2014, the Supreme Court addressed the entitlement of asylum seekers to anonymity in the context of judicial review proceedings. Charleton J. delivered the judgment of the court, and commenced his analysis of this issue with reference to the constitutional context, namely Art.34 of the Constitution and the case law thereunder including *In re R Ltd* [1989] I.R. 126, *Irish Times Ltd v Ireland* [1998] 1 I.R. 359 and *Doe v Revenue Commissioners* [2008] 3 I.R. 328.

Charleton J. summarised the principles derived from the Constitution in this regard as follows:

> "In the overall conduct of proceedings, the courts are required under the Constitution to pursue the aim of public hearings provided for in Article 34.1 and are also obliged to have regard to the other rights that may be thus affected. These include the right to litigate and the right to privacy. These rights are provided for by law under the terms of the Constitution itself. Since privacy is a broad right that encompasses situations from embarrassment to business confidence to professional secrecy, it has to be recognised that the preponderance of court cases are a source of stress and of sensitivity to litigants. Those who come to court and seek any restriction, due to their right to litigate, on the admission of the public or the untrammelled reporting of the facts and the identity of those involved will need to go considerably beyond merely arguing privacy in urging an exception under Article 34.1. It is only if the right asserted results, as a matter of proven fact, in undermining the entitlement to litigate due to a threat to life or safety or where the nature of the aspect of the case sought to be restricted means that if the court does not intervene the litigation will be practically impossible, or futile, that there should be any restriction on the open nature of access to the courts. Even there, in the absence of express legislative requirements, any restriction should be as limited as the protection of these rights necessarily demands; targeting particular pieces of testimony rather than an entire hearing, unless this is necessary, and favouring restrictions on anonymity over a completely closed hearing, unless this is essential."

Charleton J. then proceeded to consider the specific legislative context in the case of asylum seekers, namely s.19 of the Refugee Act 1996 (the "1996 Act") (as amended by s.11(1)(m) of the Immigration Act 1999 and s.7(k) of the Immigration Act 2003) which provides as follows:

> (1) The Commissioner, the Board, the Tribunal, the Minister, the Minister for Foreign Affairs and their respective officers shall take all practicable steps to ensure that the identity of applicants [for refugee status] is kept confidential.
>
> (2) Subject to sections 9(15) and 26, no matter likely to lead members of the public to identify a person as an applicant under this Act shall be published in a written publication available to the public or be broadcast without the consent of that person.

Applying the approach required under Art.34.1, Charleton J. noted that "a restriction, such as that in section 19 of the Act of 1996, should be given as narrow an interpretation as its wording requires consistent with Art.34.1." In that regard, it was noted that the definition of who is an applicant for refugee status in s.1(1) was surprisingly wide, insofar as it was "unlimited as to time or as to result." Section 1(1) provides:

> "'applicant' means a person who has made an application for a declaration [of refugee status] under section 8;"

Charleton J. thus noted that once a person has:

> "made an application claiming to be a refugee, on a literal construction of the legislation, they are thereafter an applicant. It may be argued that the end of that process with failure to achieve a recommendation of refugee status, as described above, ends their status as an applicant for refugee status. That might be the logical construction, absent the definition in section 1(1): but the clear terms of that definition mean that the status of applicant and the consequent restriction on publication of any identifying features such as name or address or particular circumstances unique to their identity is prohibited."

The prohibition on publication of any identifying features thus extends to situations where a person applies for judicial review of a decision of the Refugee Appeals Tribunal, or indeed a person who has applied for subsidiary protection, as they remain a person who has "made an application for a declaration under section 8" of the 1996 Act. Charleton J. noted that:

> "In legislating in this way, the Oireachtas must be thought to have had good reason to provide that anyone who applies for refugee status, no matter how apparently outlandish or incredible the grounds put forward, or no matter whether the person has thought the better of it and withdrawn the application, should retain anonymity as to anything to do with the fact that they had applied, notwithstanding any subsequent litigation in public as to the validity of refusal. The plain and unambiguous result of the wording is, clearly, that once a person has applied for refugee status that they retain anonymity with regard to any litigation relevant thereto in perpetuity."

It was noted that even in the event of unrelated litigation, such as a factory accident, that protection remains and, while the tort case may be reported normally, any mention of any prior failed application for refugee status may not be reported publicly. Charleton J. concluded specifically in relation to the case before the court that "[a]ny judicial review … which concerns a person who has once applied for refugee status, must preserve the anonymity of the litigant." However, it was noted that where questions of deportation arise as a result of overstaying a tourist or student visa, and where that person has not then applied for refugee status, the protection of s.19 of the 1996 Act does not apply. The court dismissed the application for an appeal against the refusal of judicial review on its merits but confirmed that as the applicant and her mother had applied for refugee status, albeit unsuccessfully, they remained entitled to anonymity in the judgment of the court and in any report of the court proceedings pursuant to s.19 of the 1996 Act.

Article 8 analysis in deportation orders At issue in *CIT v Minister for Justice and Equality* [2014] IEHC 447; unreported, High Court, Mac Eochaidh J., 31 July 2014, was the Ministerial examination of art.8 ECHR rights in the context of deportation decisions. In each of the deportation orders under challenge, the examination of file accepted that the making of a deportation order could constitute an interference with the applicants' rights to respect for private life within the meaning of art.8(1) of the ECHR. However, it was not accepted that that interference would have consequences of such gravity as potentially to engage the operation of art.8, and accordingly the examination concluded that the decision to make a deportation order did not constitute a breach of the right to respect for private life under art.8 of the ECHR. In so finding, the examination of file relied on the decision of the House of Lords in *R. (Razgar) v Secretary of State for the Home Department* [2004] 2 A.C. 368 which set out five questions to be addressed when considering art.8 rights in the context of a proposal to remove an individual:

> "(1) Will the proposed removal be an interference by a public authority with the exercise of the applicant's right to respect for his private or (as the case may be) family life?
>
> (2) If so, will such interference have consequences of such gravity as potentially to engage the operation of art.8?
>
> (3) If so, is such interference in accordance with the law?
>
> (4) If so, is such interference necessary in a democratic society in the interests of national security, public safety or the economic well being of the country, for the prevention of disorder or crime, for the protection of health or morals, or for the protection of the rights and freedoms of others?
>
> (5) If so, is such interference proportionate to the legitimate public ends sought to be achieved?"

On behalf of the applicants, it was contended that the examination of file erred in law in concluding that art.8 was not engaged, having regard to the level of integration achieved by the applicants into Irish society. It was submitted that rather, the examination should have concluded that the proposed removal would engage art.8 rights, and then proceeded to consider the following questions concerned with whether the interference could be justified in accordance with the *Razgar* formulation.

The respondent submitted that the Minister was correct in holding that the removal of the applicants would not have consequences of such gravity as potentially to engage the operation of art.8. In particular, reliance was placed on the decisions of the European Court of Human Rights in *Bensaid v United Kingdom* (2001) 33 E.H.R.R. 10 and *Nnyanzi v United Kingdom* (2008) 47 E.H.R.R. 18 which established that the general approach of the Strasbourg court was that any private life developed in a state by non-settled migrants would not be sufficient to come within the ambit of art.8.

Commencing his analysis, Mac Eochaidh J. noted a "peculiar feature" in the examination of file, namely that the analysis commences the art.8(1) analysis at question two of the *Razgar* questions, rather than at question one. Mac Eochaidh J. accepted that the series or hierarchy of questions as set out by Lord Bingham in *Razgar* was merely a recommendation, but noted that it appeared that the decision maker was attempting to follow the *Razgar* questions and the language in the decision was taken directly from the judgment of the House of Lords in *Razgar*. Mac Eochaidh J. noted:

> "Where a *Razgar*-type analysis starts at question two and accepts that rights are or might be engaged, one then anticipates that the decision maker will then ask if the interference is in accordance with law, and then whether a measure is necessary in a democratic society and, if so, whether it complies with the principles of proportionality. That is not what happens in this first decision under analysis. The decision maker, having indicated engagement of art.8 rights then goes back one step to the first of the *Razgar* questions, which, it is to be recalled, asks whether the proposed removal will be an interference by a public authority with the exercise of the applicant's right to respect for his private or family life? In the hands of the author of this decision, that question seems to be answered by conceding that the deportation order, if confirmed, 'may constitute an interference' with rights under art.8(1) of the Convention."

Mac Eochaidh J. held that such equivocation in relation to the first *Razgar* question was inappropriate, noting that either the proposed interference will amount to an interference with family/private life rights, or it will not. Turning to the treatment of the second *Razgar* question in the examination of file, Mac Eochaidh J. noted that no reason was given as to why interference would not have consequences of such gravity as to engage the operation of art.8, and that the consequences of the removal were not identified at all in the examination. Mac Eochaidh J. concluded:

> "It [sic] simply not enough for a decision maker to say, without anything else, that deportation will not have consequence of such gravity as to engage the operation of art.8. It is difficult to discern why the removal of the children from their school would not constitute a grave consequence sufficient to engage art.8. The consequences of the removal of the children from an environment which they know is a matter which should be addressed by the decision maker–but only for the purpose of identifying whether rights under art.8 are engaged. The obvious consequence of removal from the State

> is that the life of the deportee in Ireland will be terminated. How could this not be an interference with private life of the most extreme type?"

However, he noted:

> "The mere engagement of a right under art.8 does not mean the State's proposed action will breach that right, nor does it mean that the State's proposed action will not be protected by the rule of necessity established in art.8(2) of the Convention or by the principles of proportionality which may protect a decision, however negative the consequences might be for its addressee."

The proper meaning of the phrase "consequences of such gravity" in the second *Razgar* question was considered by Mac Eochaidh J. in *AMS v Minister for Justice and Equality* [2014] IEHC 57, where he summarised in *CIT* as follows:

> "Effectively, the question asks whether the interference can be described as merely technical or inconsequential. If the interference is of this order, the rights to respect for private and family life under art.8(1) will not be engaged by the proposed removal of the persons from the State. Where it is accepted that a proposed deportee has a private life, it seems to me that the answers to questions 1 and 2 can never be anything but affirmative. The removal of the applicant from Ireland will comprehensively end the private life experienced by the applicant in Ireland. This could never be anything other than an interference with that private life. In most cases this will be an interference which is greater than inconsequential and something other than merely technical. In other words deportation will always engage the right to respect for private life once it is established that private life as understood in Convention terms was experienced in the state."

Similarly, Mac Eochaidh J. suggested that the answers to the second and third *Razgar* questions in the deportation context were also likely to be affirmative, and citing the decision of Lord Bingham in *Huang v Secretary of State for the Home Department* [2007] UKHL 1, noted that "save in the most unusual of cases, an adjudicator or a decision maker will ultimately spend much of the analysis on the issue of proportionality", and concluded:

> "Decision makers are not required to find that a deportation measure offends proportionality because it comprehensively interferes with established private life in Ireland. Given that it is lawful for the State to regulate the presence of non-nationals on its territory and that immigration control does not per se offend rights protected by the Convention, something other than the natural consequence of deportation involving, as it does, the cessation or termination of private life in the deporting state, will be required if the proportionality analysis is to yield a positive result for an applicant. As for family life, the same sort of approach is appropriate, but because persons other than the proposed deportee may be affected, the consequences of the deportation for persons other than the deportee and the possibility of

relocating family life in another State are matters which may be appropriate to weigh in the balance in conducting a proportionality analysis where this point is reached."

The decision in *CIT* offered a useful guide to decision-makers in the deportation context. However, it should be noted that the decision was subsequently appealed and by judgment delivered on 30 July 2015 ([2015] IECA 192) the Court of Appeal allowed the appeal.

Challenge to constitutionality of s.3 of the Immigration Act 1999 A number of decisions during 2014 concerned challenges to the constitutionality of s.3 of the Immigration Act 1999 (the "1999 Act") on the ground that once a proposal to deport is issued and the person concerned chooses to make representations as to why a deportation order should not be made, there is no possibility of leaving the State voluntarily after the representations have been made but before a deportation order issues. The lead judgment appears to be *AL v Minister for Justice and Equality* [2014] IEHC 503; unreported, High Court, Barr J., 1 October 2014 but similar arguments were made in *QL v Minister for Justice and Equality* [2014] IEHC 507; unreported, High Court, Barr J., 1 October 2014 and *Javed v Minister for Justice and Equality* [2014] IEHC 508; unreported, High Court, Barr J., 1 October 2014.

In *AL* Barr J. summarised the core of the applicant's case:

> "that the absence of a gap between the considering of the representations made by the applicant leading to the rejection of those representations and the making of a deportation order, without an opportunity for the applicant to leave the country voluntarily without a deportation order being made, was an impediment to the applicant's rights to make representations pursuant to Art.41 of the Constitution and art.8 of the European Convention on Human Rights."

The applicant submitted that this point was considered in the Supreme Court decision in *Nawaz v Minister for Justice* [2012] IESC 58 which came before the court on a procedural point as to whether the challenge to s.3 of the 1999 Act should have been brought by plenary summons, or by judicial review subject to the requirements of s.5 of the Illegal Immigrants (Trafficking) Act 2000. The Supreme Court accepted the Minister's contention that a person challenging the section was in substance challenging each of the steps taken under s.3, and so that s.5 therefore applied. In the course of his judgment in *Nawaz,* Clarke J. held that any of the steps taken under s.3 were open to challenge together with a challenge to the validity of the section, and in particular stated:

> "I can see no reason why, on the facts of this case, a single challenge, brought by judicial review, to any of the measures adopted or to be adopted under s.3 of the 1999 Act coupled with a challenge to the validity of that section could not have been brought. For example a judicial review proceeding in which a declaration was sought that the Minister was obliged to provide for a suitable gap between the notification of an adverse decision on humanitarian leave and the making of a deportation order could have been brought. Such a

> proceeding could have sought a declaration that any deportation order made without providing for such a gap would be invalid. The application could further have suggested that a constitutional construction of s.3 required that such a gap necessarily be implied but that if, contrary to that assertion, the section mandated that no such gap be allowed, the section was inconsistent with the Constitution. Variations on that theme could also, of course, have been contemplated."

It was submitted that the applicant was married to a non-national who was residing in the State and that she was therefore part of a family unit with rights protected under Art.41 of the Constitution and art.8 of the European Convention on Human Rights. The applicant relied on the length of time in the State, in this case 10 years, in which time she started a family and married. The applicant relied on *EB (Kosovo) v Secretary of State for the Home Department* [2009] 1 A.C. 1159 as authority for the proposition that delay in the decision making process (in her case, a period of four and a half years had passed between the date of making representations and the decision to make a deportation order) might be relevant to a decision in that the applicant might during the period of delay have developed closer personal and social ties and developed deeper roots in the community than she could have shown earlier, and that the sense of impermanence with which relationships might have been imbued might have failed. It was stated that the applicant wished to make representations to the Minister that she fulfilled the criteria set out in the *EB (Kosovo)* case and that her rights could be vindicated only by permitting her to reside in the State.

The applicant contended that she had a right inhering under the Constitution and the Convention to apply to remain based on human rights grounds (a) in order to render the substantive rights to family life effective and/or (b) as a freestanding right under Art.40.3.1° of the Constitution and/or (c) as a right to remain based on the passage of time. The applicant submitted that the existence of a substantive right carries with it a right to apply to the appropriate forum to vindicate that right, and that in the case of the Convention the principle of effectiveness was expressly guaranteed by art.13. It was submitted that the guarantee of family life in art.8 implied a right to apply to the appropriate forum to vindicate that right. The applicant further submitted that s.3 of the 1999 Act disproportionately interfered with the applicant's rights to make a human rights based application for leave to remain. It was contended that the absence of a gap between the rejections of representations and the making of a deportation order was arbitrary and unfair, and that it impaired the right significantly by making her decide whether to gamble on not having a permanent deportation order issued so she could return to the State in which she has spent over a third of her life for the possibility of having her representations accepted by the Minister.

On behalf of the respondent, it was denied that the applicant enjoyed an entitlement to reside in the State pursuant to either Art.41 of the Constitution or art.8 of the European Convention on Human Rights, citing *AO v Minister for Justice* [2003] 1 I.R. 1, *TC v Minister for Justice* [2005] 4 I.R. 109 and *Abdulaziz v United Kingdom* (1985) 7 E.H.R.R. 471. In relation to the adequacy of the procedures pursuant to s.3 of the 1999 Act, the Minister submitted that because no constitutional or Convention rights of the applicant were engaged, the applicant could not point to any constitutional right which might be breached by the alleged inadequacies in s.3 of the 1999 Act and she therefore had no standing to challenge its constitutionality on the basis of such rights. Without prejudice to the generality of this statement, the respondent submitted that s.3 of the 1999 Act was concerned with the making of deportation orders and identified the procedures to be employed and, in line with the principles identified in *East Donegal Co-Op v Attorney General* [1970] I.R. 317, those provisions are supplemented by such procedures as are required to observe the principles of natural and constitutional justice.

Having summarised the competing arguments, Barr J. concluded that he was satisfied that there was a constitutional right to make representations to the Minister in advance of his taking a decision to make a deportation order, and that the applicant had a right under Art.41 of the Constitution and art.8 of the European Convention on Human Rights to have her circumstances considered by the Minister prior to his making the deportation order. Barr J. noted that this was catered for in s.3 of the 1999 Act which provides that a person can make written representations within 15 days of receiving notification that the Minister intends making a deportation order. Barr J. was satisfied that:

> "The fact that, if unsuccessful in her representations, the Minister will then go on to make a deportation order without any further option allowing the applicant to voluntarily leave the State, is not an impediment to the applicant's right to make representations to the Minister. While it is a possible consequence of the making of representations, and while it may operate as a deterrent to some applicants and may be a deterrent to the applicant in this case, it is not an unconstitutional or unlawful interference in the exercise of her right to make representations to the Minister as to why a deportation order should not be made in her case."

Accordingly, Barr J. concluded that the scheme provided for in s.3 of the 1999 Act safeguarded the right of the applicant to make representations to the Minister prior to any deportation being made, and that this was a sufficient protection to the applicant to make representations under Art.41 of the Constitution and art.8 of the European Convention on Human Rights. Barr J. held that the absence of a gap between the considering of the representations and if unsuccessful, the making of the deportation order, was not a breach of the applicant's constitutional rights or rights under art.8 of the ECHR. The applicant's application for judicial review was therefore refused. The challenges in *QL v Minister for Justice and Equality* [2014] IEHC 507; unreported, High Court, Barr J., 1 October 2014 and *Javed v Minister for Justice and Equality* [2014] IEHC 508; unreported, High Court, Barr J., 1 October 2014 were also refused by Barr J. on the same basis.

Challenge to system of direct provision In *CA v Minister for Justice* [2014] IEHC 532; unreported, High Court, Mac Eochaidh J., 14 November 2014 the High Court considered a challenge to the lawfulness of the system of direct provision and whether the system breaches human rights. The applicants were a mother and son who unsuccessfully sought refugee status in Ireland and at the time of the High Court decision were awaiting the outcome of their applications for subsidiary protection. The applicants instituted judicial review proceedings in respect of the absence of formal permission to be in the State during the subsidiary protection process, unlawful procedures for determining subsidiary protection and the prohibition on employment and receipt of social welfare, inter alia, but ultimately the focus of the case was on the alleged illegality of what the parties referred to as "direct provision". Mac Eochaidh J. noted that the term "direct provision" generally refers to the (cashless) provision of material support by the State to protection applicants to meet their basic needs. This support comprises accommodation, food, education for those under 18, healthcare and a small weekly allowance (known as Direct Provision Allowance or "DPA"). The applicants also sought to challenge the prohibition on the payment of mainstream social welfare to protection applicants, the prohibition on employment and the detailed rules applied in accommodation centres in which protection applicants live.

The applicants did not allege that direct provision was per se unlawful, nor did they say that the State was prohibited from operating a cashless system of material support for protection applicants (though it was said that prohibition on social welfare and employment were unlawful). The applicants' case concerned whether the direct provision system, as currently operated, was in breach of the principle of the separation of powers, whether it breached and/or disproportionably interfered with constitutional and fundamental rights, whether or not the direct provision allowance system was unlawful or ultra vires and/or whether the denial by statutory ban of access to social welfare benefits and/or the labour market for protection applicants was unlawful.

Mac Eochaidh J. commenced with a discussion of the background to the introduction of the system of direct provision in 1999 in the context of a rapidly growing number of people applying for asylum in the State. The court referred to the establishment of the Reception and Integration Agency (hereafter "RIA") which had overall responsibility for establishing and administering the scheme of accommodation, changes to the social welfare system including the introduction of the Direct Provision Allowance of £16, the prohibition on asylum seekers working provided for by s.9(4) of the Refugee Act 1996 and the RIA House Rules about which complaint was made by the applicants. Mac Eochaidh J. noted that he would adjourn the issues raised in relation to the legality of the prohibition on employment and the requirement to consider the best interests of the child as these had been the subject of separate proceedings before McDermott J. in respect of which judgments were pending.

Having summarised the declaratory reliefs sought, Mac Eochaidh J. then turned to consider the evidence, noting that no oral evidence was heard as the applicants had opted to pursue their complaints by way of judicial review and not plenary proceedings. On behalf of the applicants, emphasis was placed on the fact that it was the length of time for which they were exposed to the negative conditions in direct provision which formed a large part of the complaints they brought before the court. The first applicant asserted that the fundamental and far reaching nature of "direct provision" was clear, inter alia, from the RIA rules. It was submitted that the invasive nature of the system was further evidenced by the control exerted over housing, privacy, food and diet, freedom of movement, monitoring of individuals, social interaction, financial support and personal welfare. In particular, the first applicant claimed that direct provision impacted on the well-being, nurture, care and upbringing of children living within the system and interfered with parental autonomy. The respondents denied the applicants' account of an anonymous, isolated and degrading accommodation system and asserted that the applicants had been provided with a reasonable standard of accommodation and services which included educational and leisure facilities. The respondents denied that direct provision restricted freedom of movement, created isolation or segregation from society or that it removed residents' control over their own lives.

Mac Eochaidh J. noted that the applicants sought to rely upon numerous reports by a variety of governmental organisations, non-governmental organisations, international organisations and institutions to support their case that direct provision was unlawful, including reports from the UN Human Rights Committee, Irish Human Rights Commission, the Special Rapporteur on Child Protection and FLAC. The respondents argued that the statements in these documents were hearsay and must be excluded, and further pointed out that they had no opportunity to cross-examine the persons who made the statements. Mac Eochaidh J. agreed that statements in the exhibited documents sought to be relied upon as evidence as to fact should be excluded as inadmissible hearsay. Mac Eochaidh J. noted that the evidence from the first applicant's affidavit had discharged the burden of proof with respect to basic and important facts such as where she lived, her diet, her daily routine, her son's educational environment, all the physical characteristics of her accommodation and the content of RIA rules etc. The first applicant had also given clear evidence as to how she felt about her circumstances and the court had no hesitation in accepting that she had very negative feelings about her circumstances. However, in circumstances where the respondents trenchantly denied the existence of these negative effects, Mac Eochaidh J. noted that the court was faced with a significant dispute as to fact and that the court had not been offered the means to resolve this dispute because of the absence of oral evidence or cross-examination. Mac Eochaidh J. concluded that the applicants had thereby failed to discharge the burden of proof to establish that direct provision had the negative effects alleged.

Against that background, Mac Eochaidh J. summarised the three issues arising for determination as follows:

> "(a) Does 'direct provision', either in part or because of cumulative effect, breach the applicants' fundamental human rights?
> (b) Is Art.15.2 of the Constitution breached because 'direct provision' is an administrative scheme without legislative basis (apart from the prohibitions on work and social welfare)?
> (c) Is the weekly cash payment (adults €19.10 and children €9.50) known as the Direct Provision Allowance ultra vires the Social Welfare Consolidation Act 2005 or otherwise unlawful?"

On the first issue, described by the court as the "human rights" issue, having regard to the evidential deficits identified by Mac Eochaidh J., the court rejected the applicants' case that direct provision was a form of inhuman and degrading treatment either within the meaning of the Constitution or European Convention on Human Rights. This finding appears to have been made both in general and in respect of the specific complaint regarding duration of stay in direct provision. Mac Eochaidh J. also rejected the applicants' claim that direct provision breached their right to family life on evidential grounds. However, Mac Eochaidh J. concluded that a number of specific aspects of direct provision did violate the applicants' right to respect for private life pursuant to art.8 of the ECHR, including the rules regarding room inspections, monitoring of presence by way of daily signing-in, the requirement to notify of intended absence and the prohibition on overnight guests. Furthermore, Mac Eochaidh J. upheld the applicants' complaint regarding the absence of an independent complaints mechanism within the direct provision system.

In relation to the second issue, described by the court as the "separation of powers" argument, Mac Eochaidh J. dismissed the applicants' complaint that the absence of a legislative basis for the system of direct provision was in breach of Art.15.2.1° of the Constitution. Mac Eochaidh J. held:

> "The Constitution does not require that the legislature must establish principles and policies in order for the Government to exercise its executive powers. The Government may exercise executive powers independently of the legislature. In exercising its constitutional executive powers, the Government may not trespass upon the exclusive law making function of the legislature. If the Government establishes a scheme in pursuit of a policy which contains rules and conditions, though the rules may be regarded as a form of 'laws', this would not involve the executive usurping the law making function of the legislature within the meaning of Article 15 of the Constitution. For example, if the Government wished to promote the preservation of thatched cottages by paying grants for their restoration, a Minister could ask the Oireachtas to approve a fund for the scheme and rules for this scheme could be established on a purely administrative basis. It could not be said that rules in such a scheme (as to grant amounts, use of certified trades persons etc) would be regarded as a form of laws such that the scheme would trespass on the legislative function and violate the separation of powers."

Mac Eochaidh J. concluded that the mere fact that direct provision could have been placed on a legislative footing did not mean that this must happen, and concluded that the Government was entitled to establish and implement a system of direct provision of material support for protection applicants without policy input or legislative input from the Oireachtas (with the exception of approval for expenditure).

Finally, on the third issue, namely the lawfulness of the Direct Provision Allowance, Mac Eochaidh J. rejected the contention on behalf of the applicants that payment of the weekly Direct Provision Allowance was ultra vires the Social Welfare Consolidation Act 2005 (as amended) and unlawful by reason of the lack of any statutory basis for said payments. The respondents submitted that the Direct Provision Allowance was part of an administrative scheme established by the Government pursuant to its executive power, and it appears to be implicit in the decision of Mac Eochaidh J. that he accepted this characterisation. In any event, the court held that the applicants did not have locus standi to challenge the legality of the Direct Provision Allowance because of the failure to establish any injury arising from the alleged illegality.

The decision in *CA* is currently under appeal before the Court of Appeal. The decision is significant insofar as it held that aspects of the "house rules" in direct provision accommodation are unlawful, but the decision is limited insofar as the court held there was an evidential deficit in respect of many of the human rights complaints. It remains to be seen whether the court's conclusions on the separation of powers and Art.15.2.1° are consistent with the Court of Appeal's own decision in *Bederev v Ireland* [2015] 1 I.L.R.M. 301.

Conscientious objectors and refugee status In *AM v Refugee Appeals Tribunal* [2014] IEHC 388; unreported, High Court, McDermott J., 29 July 2014, the High Court considered a challenge to a refusal of refugee appeals by the Refugee Appeals Tribunal in relation to the possibility of conscientiously objecting to military service in Israel and whether the applicants had exhausted domestic remedies in that regard. The applicants were born in Kazakhstan; they were Orthodox Christians, Russian-speaking and of Russian ethnicity. They moved to Israel in 2006 with their parents and subsequently acquired Israeli citizenship. The family claimed that they were subject to severe forms of discrimination because of their Russian ethnicity and Christian faith while in Israel. They were also apprehensive that the two applicants would have to submit to compulsory military service for a period of two years in respect of the first applicant and three years in respect of the second applicant, once they reached the age of 18 years. The first and second applicants had a conscientious objection to military service. They each expressed the apprehension that if compelled to join the army they would have to kill and injure other people, which they did not wish to do. They also feared that they might be killed or wounded. Both intended to refuse to join the army as a result of which they might be exposed to prosecution and sentences of imprisonment. In 2007 the family left Israel and ultimately arrived in Ireland where they claimed asylum.

Although the Refugee Appeals Tribunal accepted that the applicants had a genuine and absolute objection to military service, their refugee appeals were refused on the basis that Israeli law permitted exemption from military service on grounds of conscientious objection. The Tribunal set out its understanding of Israeli law in relation to conscientious objection. The Tribunal was satisfied that the only question to be considered was whether as genuine absolute objectors the applicants were entitled to and in need of international protection. It accepted that a "genuine and absolute" objector may be entitled to status, but that the right was not absolute. It acknowledged that disproportionate penalties attaching to those who refuse to serve on the basis of conscientious objection may be regarded as persecutory. It stated that the obligation to provide protection only arose where the applicants' home state was unable or unwilling to discharge its duty to protect its own nationals. It stated in the first applicant's decision that:

> "Therefore, if the appellant was likely to be without relief in Israel, and could not find any relief from or assistance to resist her call up to the army, then she would be entitled to the protection of the international community. As there is statute law, case law, and a right to genuine absolute objection in Israel, with relief through the Supreme Court where there are now several precedents, and where the court is guided by human rights law, this application cannot succeed. The appellant must exhaust remedies which are available before fleeing the country of origin. This she did not do."

In the second applicant's case the Tribunal repeated what was stated in the first applicant's decision and added:

> "There is relief in Israel available through several organisations, and the courts. The law requires that domestic remedies be first exhausted before flight where that is possible. As such remedies are available and no attempt was made to access any of them, then the claim is premature. Although persecution can be a forward looking process, it must be realistically assessed where the actual threat of serious harm has not yet arisen, and it is uncertain whether it will arise. If it does, and the Tribunal supposes for the purposes of this decision that it will, then there is a remedy within the state which must first be exhausted. This is not a situation…which defines persecution as a serious threat of harm without remedy by the state."

McDermott J. commenced with a review of Israeli law in order to determine whether a person who establishes a genuine absolute conscientious objection to military service was protected by Israeli law in maintaining that belief and stance if he or she refuses to comply with the obligation to perform military service in the Israeli defence forces. Having reviewed the relevant provisions of Israeli law as well as the country of origin information before the Tribunal, McDermott J. was satisfied that Israeli law permits a person to claim exemption as a "full" conscientious objector and that the Tribunal was justified on the evidence available to it in reaching that conclusion. Accordingly, McDermott J. held that the Tribunal did not err in law or fact in finding that "there is a right to genuine absolute objection in Israel" and was also satisfied that when viewed in context, the Tribunal's determination clearly acknowledged the limitations on the right to seek an exemption from military service.

Notwithstanding the view taken by the Tribunal and the grounds upon which leave was granted, counsel on behalf of the respondents sought to maintain at the hearing that the applicants as "full conscientious objectors" were not entitled to claim refugee status pursuant to the terms of the Geneva Convention or s.2 of the Refugee Act 1996 (the "1996 Act"), and/or art.9 of the Qualification Directive. It was argued that a conscientious objector was not specifically included in the definition of a refugee under the Geneva Convention or s.2 of the 1996 Act, and that a state may apply a compulsory military service requirement on its citizens which was not in itself persecutory. McDermott J. therefore addressed this issue, which is of interest as it appears to be the first substantive engagement by the Irish courts with the entitlement to claim refugee status on the basis of conscientious objection (albeit that engagement was obiter dictum). McDermott J. referred to paras 170-174 of the UNHCR Handbook and Guidelines on Procedures and Criteria for Determining Refugee Status, art.9 of the Qualification Directive as well as the decision of the House of Lords in *Sepet & Bulbul v Secretary of State for Home Department* [2003] UKHL 15, in which it was held that there was no international consensus recognising a right to refuse to undertake military service on the grounds of conscience. However, McDermott J. also referred to Art.44.2.1° of the Constitution which guarantees freedom of conscience and religion, as well as art.10 of the Charter of the Fundamental Rights of the European Union which guarantees freedom of conscience including the right to conscientious objection.

Noting that the provisions of s.2 of the 1996 Act must be interpreted in a manner that is consistent with the Constitution, the European Convention on Human Rights and the EU Charter of Fundamental Rights, McDermott J. concluded:

> "The provisions of Article 9.2 and the Directive are minimal standards and it is open to any state in its laws to grant wider protection to refugee applicants. I am, therefore, satisfied that s.2 of the Refugee Act 1996, must be interpreted in accordance with the right to freedom of conscience under Article 40.3 of the Constitution and requires that international protection must be accorded to a full conscientious objector who has a well founded fear of persecution."

Citing the decision of the Grand Chamber of the European Court of Human Rights in *Bayatyan v Armenia* (2012) 54 E.H.R.R. 15, McDermott J. stated:

> "I am satisfied that the proper interpretation of s.2 of the Refugee Act 1996, and the application of the Qualification Directive in a manner compatible with the state's obligations under art.9 of the Convention and art.10 of the Charter of Fundamental Rights necessitates an interpretation of those provisions which permits a 'full' conscientious objector to apply for international protection and claim refugee status on the basis of a well founded fear of persecution for that belief… I am also satisfied that such an interpretation of s.2 of the Refugee Act 1996, is in accordance with the right to freedom of conscience as provided under Art.40.3 of the Constitution."

On the facts of this case McDermott J. held that the Tribunal member had not acted unreasonably in determining that the applicants should have had recourse to the local remedy seeking an exemption from military service and therefore dismissed the applications for judicial review. Whilst McDermott J.'s comments on persecution and conscientious objectors are therefore obiter, they are nonetheless significant insofar as they recognise the potential for a conscientious objector to be recognised as a refugee through the application of a human rights analysis derived from the Constitution, the European Convention on Human Rights and the European Union Charter on Fundamental Rights.

Credibility Once again a number of decisions of the High Court during 2014 concerned credibility findings by refugee decision makers. In *MAI v Minister for Justice and Equality* [2014] IEHC 623; unreported, High Court, Faherty J., 19 December 2014, Faherty J. addressed the important issue of adequate interpretation at appeal hearings, in particular where disputed credibility findings are subsequently made. The applicant was a Kurdish-speaking Iraqi national; his interview with the Refugee Applications Commissioner was conducted with the assistance of an interpreter speaking Kurdish-Badini (the Kurdish dialect spoken by the applicant). The hearing before the Refugee Appeals Tribunal was conducted with the assistance of an interpreter who spoke Kurdish-Sorani, a different dialect; an application for an adjournment of the Tribunal hearing was made by the applicant's solicitor at the outset of the appeal hearing but was refused on the basis that the Tribunal Member was satisfied that "the appellant was able to tender his evidence to the Tribunal fluently and easily through the Kurdish interpreter and any slight nuances in dialect were not such as to impinge on the ability of the appellant to be understood."

Commenting on the importance of adequate interpretation, Faherty J. noted:

> "Central to the ability of a decision maker to make a rational and informed assessment of evidence tendered in the course of a hearing is the decision maker's ability to receive that evidence through the clearest and most direct channel. This is routinely achieved where both the person giving evidence and the decision maker speak the same language. However, even where there is a shared language, difficulties may from time to time arise where a particular dialect is unfamiliar to either and this imposes on the decision maker an obligation to be vigilant to ensure the witness is understood. Where the person giving evidence does not speak the language of the decision maker, either adequately or at all, the service of an interpreter (who is versed in the languages of both) becomes a necessary and indeed mandatory tool. Interpretation services are a routine requirement in asylum cases before the Refugee Applications Commissioner and the Tribunal and indeed prior. I agree with the proposition, advanced in Goodwin-Gill and McAdam's *The Refugee in International Law* that:
>
> > '... the use of interpreters in a manner which will best elicit the narrative of the claimant is something of an art. Translation is not a mechanical process, but a two- way, sometimes three way street, that places particular responsibilities on every participant in the refugee determination process. The interpreter is both link and obstacle; link, because he or she facilitates an oral dialogue; and obstacle, because the questioner's intentions may be misunderstood, either because of a failure to communicate clearly and coherently, or because both parties do not possess a common basis of understanding and values. What the applicant says comes across filtered and then has to pass by the decision maker's own baggage of preconceptions.'"

In relation to the Tribunal member's statement that he was satisfied the applicant could give his evidence fluently and easily notwithstanding "slight nuances in dialect", Faherty J. noted that:

> "in the absence of the Tribunal Member's own proficiency or fluency in both Kurdish-Badini and Kurdish-Sorani, of which there is no evidence, I cannot accept that the decision to proceed with the oral hearing satisfied the Tribunal's obligation, either pursuant to s.16 (11) (d) of the Act or pursuant to the requirements of fair procedures to afford the applicant a proper hearing."

Noting that the applicant had had the benefit of a Kurdish-Badini interpreter before the Commissioner, Faherty J. noted that three of the eight negative credibility findings made by the Tribunal member concerned purported discrepancies in the applicant's evidence which could have arisen through an error in interpretation. Faherty J. concluded that:

> "In circumstances where it is not possible to discern the weight given by the Tribunal Member to that particular finding viz a viz the other credibility examples, the infirmity in the interpretation assistance provided on 4 May warrant the quashing of the Tribunal Member's decision."

The decision of Faherty J. in *MAI* is an important and timely reminder of the importance of adequate interpretation in refugee hearings. The absence of any qualification or accreditation system for interpreters in the State can give rise to issues in practice and it is vital that refugee decision makers are aware of the importance of ensuring appropriate standards are maintained.

In *RC (Zimbabwe) v Minister for Justice, Equality and Law Reform* [2014] IEHC 609; unreported, High Court, Barr J., 11 December 2014, Barr J. quashed a decision of the Refugee Appeals Tribunal on the ground of the Tribunal's failure to direct a s.16(6) investigation by the Refugee Applications Commissioner in relation to a matter central to the applicants' credibility. The applicants were Zimbabwean citizens who claimed asylum in the State on the basis of political opinion; as part of this claim they informed the Refugee Applications Commissioner that the second applicant's brother was an opposition politician who had also been forced to flee Zimbabwe and that he had subsequently been recognised as a refugee in the United Kingdom. The Refugee Applications Commissioner rejected their refugee applications on credibility grounds, and in relation to the documentation concerning the second applicant's brother, merely stated that it was "unable to verify the authenticity of these documents". The Refugee Applications Commissioner also made a finding pursuant to s.13(6) of the Refugee Act 1996 (the "1996 Act") on the basis that the applicants had lied about the period of time they spent in the United Kingdom before claiming asylum in Ireland. The effect of the s.13(6) finding was to deprive the applicants of an oral hearing on appeal.

During the course of their appeal before the Refugee Appeals Tribunal, the applicants' solicitor referred to the duty of co-operation provided in art.4 of the Qualification Directive and submitted that the Tribunal ought to direct the Commissioner to conduct an investigation pursuant to s.16(6) of the 1996 Act in relation to the documents concerning the applicants' family members who had been granted asylum abroad. Section 16(6) provides:

> The Tribunal may, for the purposes of its functions under this Act, request the Commissioner to make such further inquiries and to furnish the Tribunal with such further information as the Tribunal considers necessary within such period as may be specified by the Tribunal.

The Tribunal did not make any such request of the Commissioner and ultimately dismissed the applicants' appeals. Barr J. noted that the core of the applicants' claim for asylum was that the husband's family members had been granted asylum in the UK and other countries, on account of persecution suffered at the hands of the Mugabe regime. In this regard, the applicants claimed that they faced a similar risk of persecution and serious harm if repatriated because of these family and political connections. Barr J. concluded that:

> "while the Tribunal did not accept the narrative as told by the applicants

> that they had suffered persecution in Zimbabwe due to their relationship with TM in the period from 2002 to 2007, it was still obliged to assess the core claim made by the applicants that they would suffer persecution if returned to Zimbabwe due to their relationship to TM and their perceived support for the MDC.
>
> … To this end, the Tribunal was obliged to assess whether the applicants were related to TM and, if so, how they might be perceived in Zimbabwe and whether on account of such perception they might face persecution. The Tribunal did not carry out this inquiry, which it ought to have done. To this extent, the Tribunal was obliged to carry out a forward-looking test…
>
> … The RAT's failure to even refer to the applicants' request pursuant to s.16(6) that the documents concerning the applicants' family members be remitted to ORAC for further investigation, and for failing to provide reasons for its decision not to do this, constitutes a defect in the Tribunal's decision. The applicants are entitled to an order for certiorari on this account. In addition, the Tribunal failed to carry out any adequate forward looking test as to whether the applicants would be persecuted if returned to Zimbabwe due to their claimed relationship to T.M. and their perceived support for the MDC."

Accordingly, Barr J. quashed the decision of the Refugee Appeals Tribunal refusing the applicants' refugee appeals. The decision in *Refugee Convention (Zimbabwe)* is an important affirmation of the heightened duty of fair procedures in relation to a "papers only" appeal.

Perhaps the most striking decision of the High Court during 2014 in relation to credibility is the decision of Clark J. in *AAMO v Refugee Appeals Tribunal* [2014] IEHC 49; unreported, High Court, Clark J., 17 January 2014. The applicant arrived in the State in April 2009 and subsequently applied for asylum claiming a fear of persecution at the hands of the Sudanese authorities owing to his work in Darfur for the NGO Medicins Sans Frontières, as a result of which he had been targeted. According to Clark J., the applicant's claim "was documented and supported to an unusual level but was nevertheless refused on credibility grounds." The applicant applied for judicial review of the Tribunal's dismissal of his refugee appeal, and the Tribunal decision was ultimately quashed by Clark J. in a judgment that was unusually forceful in its criticisms of the decision maker. This is reflected in the opening paragraph of the judgment, which states:

> "Sometimes the court is called upon to review a decision which is so unfair and irrational and contains so many errors that judicial review seems an inadequate remedy to redress the wrong perpetrated on an applicant. This is such a case."

Having recited the extensive supporting documentation submitted by the applicant in the course of his refugee application, as well as the key facts grounding the claim, Clark J. noted that the Tribunal member had refused the appeal on a number of credibility grounds. Clark J. proceeded to analyse these findings, noting at the outset:

> "As previously stated, at the hearing of this application the Court expressed

> its deep concern at the fundamental nature of the many errors identified which infect the legality, fairness and constitutionality of the decision as a whole … when reviewing this quite extraordinary decision on the day of the hearing, the only conclusion which the Court could draw for the Tribunal's decision not to recommend that the applicant should be declared a refugee is that the Tribunal Member simply did not like the applicant. This can be the only explanation for doubting the applicant's well-documented name and occupation and rejecting his description of how he was known by his nickname–described in pejorative terms as an alias–and his background in human rights work as a doctor …
>
> Personal dislike is not a valid reason for any legal decision and certainly not a reason for ignoring numerous documents relevant to a claim which appear to emanate from reliable sources. If a decision maker finds that an applicant is a person who had gone to great lengths to set up a false claim, then his reasons and conclusions must be soundly based on the evidence presented which has been properly and fairly assessed. That unfortunately is not the case here."

Concluding that the credibility findings made were unsustainable, Clark J. stated that:

> "The decision in this case lacked justice and understanding in breach of the basic criteria identified in the UNHCR Handbook on Procedures and Criteria for Determining Refugee Status and was also in fundamental breach of Sections 11B(i) and 16(16) (d) and (e) of the Refugee Act 1996 and Regulations 5 and 7 of the Protection Regulations."

Accordingly, Clark J. quashed the decision of the Tribunal and remitted the appeal for rehearing. It is difficult to disagree with Clark J.'s comment that "the system failed the applicant in this case."

Damages for breach of EU law in relation to refusal of residence The decision in *Ogieriakhi v Minister for Justice and Equality (No.2)* [2014] IEHC 582; [2015] 1 I.L.R.M. 344 demonstrates the potentially significant consequences for the State of an unlawful decision to refuse permission to reside in the State pursuant to EU law. The plaintiff was a Nigerian national who arrived in Ireland in 1998 and applied for asylum. In 1999 he withdrew his asylum claim and instead applied for permission to reside in the State on the basis that he had married a French national; he was subsequently granted a residence permit by the Minister for Justice. The plaintiff's marriage ended two years later, and he subsequently formed a relationship with an Irish national; having obtained a divorce from his French wife in 2009, he subsequently married his Irish partner. In 2012 he was granted Irish citizenship by naturalisation.

The plaintiff sued the State in a *Francovich*-style action for damages claiming that the State failed properly to transpose the provisions of Directive 2004/38/EC (the "2004 Directive") into domestic law. This arose from the fact that in 2007 he was dismissed from his employment as a postal sorter with An Post, the State-owned postal company, on the sole ground that he had no right to work without a work permit. It was contended by the plaintiff that he did not require a work permit, as by that time he had already acquired permanent residence under the 2004 Directive. This claim was based on the fact that his French wife had remained in the State, and exercising her EU Treaty Rights, for over five years. Hogan J.in the High Court reviewed the evidence available regarding her activities in the State (noting certain evidential difficulties arose in circumstances where the marriage was long over and the plaintiff had lost contact with his ex-wife), but based on her records from the Department of Social Protection in relation to her status as an employee and job-seeker, the court had no difficulty accepting that the plaintiff's wife had resided in the State, and exercised her Treaty rights, for a continuous period between October 1999 and October 2004.

There then followed a series of proceedings by the plaintiff aimed at challenging the Minister's refusals to grant him a residence permit and/or permanent residence, including an unsuccessful action for *Francovich* damages. Following the decision of the Court of Justice in Case C-162/09 *Secretary of State for Work and Pensions v Lassal* [2010] E.C.R. I-9217 where it was held that continuous periods of five years' residence completed before the date of transposition of the 2004 Directive, in accordance with earlier European Union law instruments, must be taken into account for the purposes of the acquisition of the right of permanent residence pursuant to art.16(1) of the Directive, the Minister for Justice agreed to review his earlier refusal. In November 2011 the Minister concluded that the plaintiff was entitled to permanent residence, and the plaintiff subsequently instituted proceedings claiming damages for breach of his rights under the Directive in respect of the period when the Minister refused to recognise his entitlement to permanent residence.

Notwithstanding the decision to grant permanent residence, in defending the damages action the Minister nonetheless maintained that the plaintiff did not in fact meet the conditions of art.16(2) because, applying C-325/09 *Secretary of State for Work and Pensions v Dias* [2011] E.C.R. I-6387 and Case C-424/10 *Ziolkowski v Land Berlin* [2011] E.C.R. I-14035, the plaintiff had not demonstrated that his pre-April 2006 residence satisfied the requirements of the 1968 Regulation which was then extant immediately prior to April 2006. This was based on the Minister's contention either that the plaintiff's ex-wife had not been a "worker" at all material times between October 1999 and October 2004, or alternatively that she had not supplied or made available to the plaintiff housing following her departure from the family home.

Arising from these issues, Hogan J. decided to refer a number of questions to the Court of Justice (CJEU), namely:

> "Question 1
> Can it be said that the spouse of an EU national who was not at the time himself a national of a Member State has 'legally resided with the Union citizen in the host Member State for a continuous period of five years' for the purposes of Article 16(2) of Directive 2004/38/EC, in circumstances where the couple had married in May 1999, where a right of residency was granted in October 1999 and where by early 2002 at the absolute latest the parties had agreed to live apart and where both spouses had commenced residing with entirely different partners by late 2002?

Question 2
If the answer to Question 1 is in the affirmative and bearing in mind that the third country national claiming a right to permanent residence pursuant to Article 16(2) based on five years continuous residence prior to April 2006 must also show that his or her residency was in compliance with, inter alia, the requirements of Article 10(3) of Regulation (EEC) No. 1612/68, does the fact that during the currency of that putative five year period the EU national left the family home and the third country national then commenced to reside with another individual in a new family home which was not supplied or provided for by (erstwhile) the EU national spouse mean that the requirements of Article 10(3) of Regulation 1612/68 are not thereby satisfied?"

In relation to the plaintiff's application for *Francovich* damages, Hogan J. asked a further question as follows:

> "Question 3
> If the answer to Question 1 is in the affirmative and the answer to Question 2 is in the negative, then for the purposes of assessing whether a Member State has wrongfully transposed or otherwise failed properly to apply the requirements of Article 16(2) of the 2004 Directive, is the fact that the national court hearing an action for damages for breach of Union law has found it necessary to make a reference on the substantive question of the plaintiff's entitlement to permanent residence is [sic] itself a factor to which that court can have regard in determining whether the breach of Union law was an obvious one?"

The CJEU answered the first and second questions together, applying Case 267/83 *Diatta v Land Berlin* [1985] E.C.R. 567 and Case C-40/11 *Iida v Stadt Ulm* [2013] 1 C.M.L.R. 47, concluding that:

> "a third-country national who, during a continuous period of five years before the transposition date for that directive, has resided in a Member State as the spouse of a Union citizen working in that Member State, must be regarded as having acquired a right of permanent residence under that provision, even though, during that period, the spouses decided to separate and commenced residing with other partners, and the home occupied by that national was no longer provided or made available by his spouse with Union citizenship."

On the third question relating to the assessment of damages, the CJEU emphasised that "the principle of State liability for loss and damage caused to individuals as a result of infringements of EU law for which the State can be held responsible is inherent in the system of the Treaty", and restated the three conditions to be met for a right to reparation to arise, namely (i) the rule of law infringed must be intended to confer rights on individuals; (ii) the infringement must be sufficiently serious; and (iii) there must be a direct causal link between the breach of the obligation resting on the State and the damage sustained by the injured parties. In relation to the second condition, the court noted that whilst the decisive test for finding that an infringement of EU law is sufficiently serious is whether the Member State concerned manifestly and gravely disregarded the limits of its discretion, amongst the criteria national courts may take into account were the degree of clarity and precision of the rule infringed. The court concluded that:

> "in relation to a claim for damages for infringement of EU law, [the fact that] a national court has found it necessary to seek a preliminary ruling on a question concerning the EU law at issue in the proceedings on the substance must not be considered a decisive factor in determining whether there was an obvious infringement of that law on the part of the Member State."

The matter then returned to Hogan J. in the High Court who, in applying the CJEU's answer to the first and second questions, was in no doubt that the State had "failed properly to apply Union law insofar as Mr Ogieriakhi was wrongly refused residency on the basis that such residency had concluded prior to 30 April 2006." The focus then turned to the entitlement to, and assessment of, damages.

Applying the conditions as set out by the court, Hogan J. noted there could be "very little doubt" but that art.16(2) conferred rights on individuals; it was:

> "not only obvious from the context, structure and language of Article 16 itself, but it is, in any event, confirmed by the reasoning of the Court of Justice itself on the Article 267 reference which I made in this case".

As to whether the breach was sufficiently serious, Hogan J. accepted that all the relevant decision-makers within the Department of Justice and An Post had acted honestly by reference to their understanding of the law at the time, but nonetheless concluded that it was "impossible to avoid the conclusion that, viewed objectively, the breach of art.16(2) which took place in the present case was a very serious one with grave consequences for Mr Ogieriakhi."

On the third condition regarding a causal link between the breach and the damage suffered, again Hogan J. found there could be "little doubt" that there was a causal link between the breach of EU law and the damage suffered by the plaintiff:

> "Mr Ogieriakhi was dismissed from his employment simply because it could not be established that he had the right to work or reside here. Yet the reason why his entitlement to reside here was not acknowledged rested entirely on the Minister's pre-*Lassal* interpretation of the scope of application of art.16(2) of the 2004 Directive ratione temporis, i.e., that periods of five year residency completed prior to 30 April 2006 simply did not count for this purpose."

Concluding that the plaintiff had satisfied all three conditions prescribed in the *Francovich* test, and was therefore entitled to damages for breach of European Union law, Hogan J. awarded €107,905 in *Francovich* damages, comprising four years' full salary and two years at half salary to reflect a finding that the plaintiff had failed to mitigate his loss during this period by failing to take up an offer to return to employment with An Post in 2008. Hogan J. also awarded the plaintiff the sum of €20,000 damages in respect of the breach of his constitutional right to a good name in relation to his dismissal from employment with An Post. The total sum awarded to the plaintiff was thus €127,905 against Ireland and the Attorney General. The decision in *Ogieriakhi* is a salutary lesson in the costly consequences of failure to give proper effect to the provisions of the 2004 Directive.

Delay in determination of refugee appeal In *SKT (DRC) v Refugee Appeals Tribunal* [2014] IEHC 572; unreported, High Court, Barr J., 27 November 2014, the High Court considered a challenge to a Refugee Appeals Tribunal decision on the basis of a 28-month delay between the initial hearing of the appeal and issuing of the final decision. The oral hearing of the appeal was commenced on 17 November 2008 but was not completed on that date. Some seven months later, the Tribunal wrote to the applicant's solicitors enclosing translated documents which had been received by the Tribunal on 19 and 27 November 2008 on foot of a s.16(6) request to the Refugee Applications Commissioner. The appeal was scheduled to resume on 26 January 2010 but owing to a scheduling error was listed before a different Tribunal Member. Accordingly, the appeal was once again adjourned, and ultimately concluded before the correct Tribunal Member on 18 February 2010. The decision of the Tribunal did not issue for a further 12 months, on 3 March 2011.

The applicant thereafter commenced judicial review proceedings challenging the decision on a number of grounds, including delay. On behalf of the applicant it was contended that when determining asylum applications, the Refugee Appeals Tribunal was implementing EU law, and that the failure to conduct the hearing and give its decision within a reasonable time breached Ch.II, art.10 of the Procedures Directive. The applicant further contended that the Tribunal's delay in rendering its decision deprived the applicant of an effective remedy within the meaning of art.39 of the Procedures Directive. Barr J. recited the relevant provisions of the Directive, including recital (11) and arts 2(e), 10(d) and 23(2). Barr J. noted that these provisions appeared only to apply to the first instance decision maker, namely the Refugee Applications Commissioner, but stated:

> "Nevertheless, the court is mindful of the general applicability of the provisions of the Charter of Fundamental Rights to the implementation of asylum law. Article 41 provides that: 'Every person has the right to have his or her affairs handled impartially, fairly and within a reasonable time by the Institutions, bodies and agencies of the Union.' Article 47, which provides for the right to an effective remedy, states: 'Everyone is entitled to a fair and public hearing within a reasonable time by an independent and impartial tribunal previously established by law.'"

Turning to the provisions of Irish law, Barr J. noted that the duty of the Refugee Appeals Tribunal to act expeditiously is set out in s.16(8) of the Refugee Act 1996 (the "1996 Act"), which provides:

> The Tribunal shall ensure that an appeal against a recommendation of the Commissioner to which section 13(5) or 13(8) applies shall be dealt with as soon as may be and, if necessary, before any other application for a declaration.

Reference was also made to para.14 of the Second Schedule to the 1996 Act, which states:

> The chairperson shall endeavour to ensure that the business of the Tribunal is managed efficiently and that the business assigned to each division is disposed of as expeditiously as may be consistent with fairness and natural justice.

Distinguishing the previous decisions of Dunne J. in *FKS v Refugee Appeals Tribunal* [2009] IEHC 474 and Cooke J. in *QFC v Refugee Appeals Tribunal* [2012] IEHC 4 where the court had held that delays of eight months and 15 months respectively were not so egregious or prejudicial as to warrant the quashing of the Tribunal decisions, Barr J. held on the facts of this case:

> "It is stretching belief that the Tribunal Member would be able to recall the demeanour of the applicant when giving her answers 13 months and 28 months previously. The time period was simply too long to expect that the impressions made by the applicant in her evidence would not have faded considerably, if not completely, in the period which had elapsed. With a delay of such magnitude, particularly where the Tribunal's findings turned on the applicant's credibility and demeanour, it is understandable that she should feel that she did not get a fair hearing and determination of her asylum application."

Barr J. was satisfied that the delay in this case between the time when the appeal hearing began in November 2008 and the final delivery of the decision in March 2011, was too long, such that there must be valid concerns as to the fairness of the decision which emerged at the end of this process. He considered that the delay in this case fell within that exceptional category of cases, as referred to by Dunne J. in *FKS* and Cooke J. in *QFC*. In the circumstances, Barr J. quashed the decision of the Tribunal.

Duty to give clear reasons for decision A number of judgments of the High Court during 2014 concerned the duty to give clear reasons for a decision, both within the refugee context and the general immigration context. In *KB v Refugee Appeals Tribunal* [2014] IEHC 239; unreported, High Court, McDermott J., 2 May 2014, McDermott J. quashed a decision of the Refugee Appeals Tribunal on the basis of a failure to express clear findings on credibility and past persecution. McDermott J. noted that:

> "in the short analysis of the case by the respondent, he failed to make findings in respect of the applicant's account of past events of persecution, his perception of those events and the factual basis upon which he claimed to have a well founded fear. It is completely unclear what aspects, if any, of the claim were accepted by the first named respondent...
>
> The applicant was entitled to have his claim of a well-founded fear of persecution analysed on the basis of whether he subjectively held that fear

> and whether it was objectively justifiable pursuant to s.2 of the Refugee Act 1996 (as amended).
>
> …Insofar as it is suggested that a number of the findings made by the Tribunal are vague and non-specific, the court is satisfied that the decision is unclear as to what elements of the applicant's story were determined to be true or lacking credibility. Consideration of the issue of internal relocation, while assisted in many cases by the availability of country of origin information must also take account of the circumstances or events outlined by the applicant that are deemed credible. In this instance, it is not at all clear what element, if any, of the applicant's case was considered to be credible so that a proper assessment could then be made of whether it was possible for him to relocate in Nigeria."

McDermott J. noted that a number of submissions made by counsel for the respondents sought to explain what were said to be a number of findings that were clearly implicit in the decision of the Tribunal or sought to explain the decision as rational and reasonable by reference to the evidence (including country of origin information) and to certain aspects of the applicant's testimony. McDermott J. commented in this regard:

> "I am satisfied that to adopt some of these submissions would be to expand the basis of the decision as expressed by the Tribunal and to speculate as to the underlying reasons for the decision. There may well be reasonable grounds upon which the same result might have been delivered but it is not for the court to re-write the decision. The reasons for the decision must be made clear by the Tribunal in fairness to the applicant and in order for this Court to exercise jurisdiction by way of judicial review. The decision is unclear and somewhat cryptic in its statement of credibility findings and fails to address core elements of the applicant's claim."

Concluding that the applicant had established that the decision was fundamentally flawed, McDermott J. quashed the decision and remitted the appeal for hearing by a different Tribunal member.

In *TAR v Minister for Justice and Equality* [2014] IEHC 385; unreported, High Court, McDermott J., 30 July 2014, McDermott J. quashed a refusal of a visit visa for an Iraqi family whose son was a naturalised Irish citizen on the basis of a lack of clear reasons for the decision, while in *Parhiar v Minister for Justice and Equality* [2014] IEHC 445; unreported, High Court, Noonan J., 14 October 2014, the court quashed the refusal of an application for permission to reside in the State under the INIS Guidelines for Victims of Domestic Violence on the basis of a failure to give any reasons at all for the decision, contrary to *Meadows v Minister for Justice* [2010] 2 I.R. 701; [2011] 2 I.L.R.M. 157.

Furthermore, in *AP v Minister for Justice and Equality (No.2)* [2014] IEHC 241; unreported, High Court, McDermott J., 2 May 2014, McDermott J. quashed a decision of the Minister to refuse to grant the applicant a certificate of naturalisation for failure to give adequate reasons. The Minister contended that it would be "inimical to the interests of the State" to provide specific grounds for the refusal. McDermott J. held that the respondent had not adequately complied with the obligation to furnish the reason for the refusal in this case notwithstanding the exigencies under which the respondent was operating. The court accepted that the Minister is entitled to withhold material on the basis of public policy as recognised in *Mallak v Minister for Justice* [2012] 3 I.R. 297; [2013] 1 I.L.R.M. 73 and *AP v Minister for Justice and Equality* [2014] IEHC 17; unreported, High Court, McDermott J., 17 January 2014, but held that the Minister should make the earliest possible disclosure of reasons underlying the decision consistent with that duty. McDermott J. noted that it was "essential to the fairness of the process that the withholding or furnishing of reasons is determined carefully with due regard to the facts and requirements of each case."

EU Treaty Rights and removal or deportation In *Igunma v Governor of Wheatfield Prison* [2014] IEHC 218; unreported ,High Court, Hogan J., 29 April 2014 it was held that the removal procedure under the European Communities (Free Movement of Persons) (No.2) Regulations 2006 (S.I. No. 656 of 2006) applies to a spouse of an EU citizen and not the deportation power contained in s.3 of the Immigration Act 1999, even where that person has been refused permission to reside in the State because the marriage has broken down. Effectively, Hogan J. held that "once the 2006 Regulations apply to [a person] he can thereafter only be physically removed from the State in accordance with the procedures prescribed by Article 27 et seq. of the 2004 Directive and the corresponding provisions of the 2006 Regulations." A similar conclusion was reached by Barr J. in *Irshad v Minister for Justice and Equality* [2014] IEHC 167; unreported, High Court, Barr J., 6 March 2014 albeit that both decisions appear to have been arrived at independently insofar as neither Hogan J. nor Barr J. referred to the decision of the other.

EU Treaty Rights and self-employment In *Edos v Minister for Justice and Equality* [2014] IEHC 168; unreported, High Court, Barr J., 6 March 2014, the High Court quashed the Minister's refusal of an application for permission to reside in the State pursuant to the Citizens Directive (Directive 2004/38/EC) which application was made on the basis of self-employment in the State. The Minister refused the application on the ground of a failure to show that the business was a viable trading concern. Citing Case 139/85 *Kempf v Staatssecretaris van Justitie* [1986] E.C.R. 1741, Case 53/81 *Levin v Staatssecretaris van Justitie* [1982] E.C.R. 1035 and Case 196/87 *Steymann v Staatssecretaris van Justitie* [1988] E.C.R. 6159, Barr J. held that the Minister had applied the wrong test in assessing the application for residence within the State by requiring evidence that the business was a "viable trading concern" rather than asking whether there was self-employed activity that was effective and genuine. Barr J. noted that in accordance with the settled jurisprudence of the Court of Justice, it did not matter that the remuneration for that work was less than the minimum industrial wage, or less than the minimum amount of social welfare payments under Irish national law or that the applicants may have to rely on social assistance or other support to survive. Provided that the work carried out was effective and genuine then there was an exercise of the right of establishment within the State giving rise to a right of residence.

Family reunification As in previous years, decisions refusing family reunification were once again the subject of judicial scrutiny in 2014. In *AMS v Minister for*

Justice and Equality [2014] IEHC 57; unreported, High Court, Mac Eochaidh J., 13 February 2014; [2014] IESC 65; [2015] 1 I.L.R.M. 170 the applicant was born in 1985 and was a citizen of Somalia. He came to Ireland as an asylum seeker in May 2007 and was declared to be a refugee on 8 January 2009. In 2009 the applicant applied to the Minister pursuant to s.18 of the Refugee Act 1996 (the "1996 Act") for family reunification in respect of his wife, mother, daughter, two sisters and two brothers. The questionnaire was considered by the Refugee Applications Commissioner and a report was prepared and forwarded to the Minister for decision on 1 September 2009. In February 2010, the applicant was informed that his daughter and one of his brothers had been killed in a bomb attack in January 2010. The applicant subsequently engaged the assistance of solicitors who entered into correspondence with the Minister and provided documentation and further information in support of the applicant's application. Almost one year later, solicitors for the applicant wrote to the Minister, on 10 January 2011, requesting a decision within 28 days. In response the Minister requested further information to assist in the decision-making. Thereafter, the applicant's application for reunification with his wife, under s.18(3) of the 1996 Act, was granted on 4 May 2011. However, a decision to refuse the applications in respect of the remaining family members was issued, under s.18(4) of the 1996 Act, on 6 July 2011.

The applicant subsequently instituted judicial review proceedings in respect of the decision of 6 July 2011. This decision was quashed by order of Cross J. of 14 February 2012 ([2012] IEHC 72). Thereafter, on 5 April 2012, the applicant renewed his application for reunification with his mother and remaining siblings (one brother and two sisters), and in this respect, made additional submissions to the Minister. The second decision concerning the applicant's application for reunification issued on 20 July 2012, and again contained a refusal. The applicant instituted judicial review proceedings confined to seeking orders designed to quash the refusal in respect of his application for reunification in respect of his mother and one of his female siblings who was a minor. By decision of 13 February 2014 ([2014] IEHC 57) the decision of 20 July 2012 was quashed by Mac Eochaidh J. Mac Eochaidh J. held that it was unlawful for the Minister to refuse an application for family reunification pursuant to s.18(4) of the 1996 Act on the basis that the family members would be financially dependent on the State, and also on the basis that the decision to refuse the applicant's application for family reunification was disproportionate. The Minister appealed against this decision.

The Supreme Court (Denham C.J., Murray, Hardiman, Clarke and Dunne JJ.) held that s.18(4) of the Refugee Act 1996 confers a wide discretion on the Minister in deciding whether to allow family reunification in respect of those family members who do not enjoy an automatic entitlement. However, it was noted that that discretion is not absolute. Noting that the legislation is sparse as to the criteria to be applied by the Minister, Clarke J., delivering the judgment of the court, held that:

> "the proper inference to draw from the absence of detailed criteria is that the Oireachtas was mindful of the fact that the range of circumstances which might properly be taken into account in any individual case could vary enormously from one situation to another. Any attempt to impose specific criteria would run a real risk of unintended consequences which

could have unfortunate and unanticipated results both for the State and for meritorious applicants."

On the basis that the Oireachtas has conferred a wide discretion on the Minister, Clarke J. held that it would be necessary, in order that a factor might be ruled out from the Minister's proper consideration, for such a factor to be outside the scope of matters which could properly be taken into account, under the 1996 Act, in a family reunification application. It was held that the legitimate economic interests of the State could not be so classified. Clarke J. held that it would require clear language in the legislation which either expressly provided or necessarily inferred that such economic interests were not to be taken into account in order that it would be proper to interpret s.18 of the 1996 Act in a way which prevented the Minister from having regard to such economic interests in reaching an overall conclusion in an application under s.18(4).

However, Clarke J. noted that s.18 of the 1996 Act is designed in the interests of facilitating the reception of refugees and ensuring their personal wellbeing while in the State but accepted that it must also be taken into account that the section distinguishes between those on whom an automatic entitlement is conferred (s.18(3)) and those in respect of whom the Minister is entitled to exercise a discretion (s.18(4)). It was held that while significant weight must thus be placed on the undoubted statutory intention to facilitate family reunification, the fact that the discretion under s.18(4) exists at all clearly implied that there may be countervailing factors which must also be taken into account.

It was held that while the trial judge was correct to identify that the principal purpose of the relevant provisions of the 1996 Act was to facilitate the position of refugees by enabling them to be unified both with those close members of their family on whom automatic rights are conferred and other dependent relatives, nonetheless the Act did not confer an automatic right of reunification in respect of those more remote family members even though they be dependent. Clarke J. commented that the 1996 Act contemplates the possibility that persons, even though they may be dependent on a refugee, may not succeed in obtaining reunification. Accordingly, it was held that Mac Eochaidh J. was not correct to infer from the general purpose of the 1996 Act that the Minister could never have regard to financial considerations involving the State in determining how lawfully to exercise the discretion conferred by s.18(4).

On the other hand, it was recognised that significant regard must be had to the fact that s.18 as a whole was clearly intended to confer a benefit on a refugee, and through the refugee on dependent family members, in the form of an enhanced possibility of persons being permitted into the State as a result of a family reunification application being successful. The question of the potential cost to the State of meeting its obligations to members of the family of a refugee was a factor which could properly be taken into account in the overall assessment of the case. Clarke J. stated:

> "It equally follows, however, that some significant weight has to be given to the fact that the Oireachtas has chosen to confer a special entry status on dependent members of the extended family of a refugee and has also determined to confer, on such persons if they are admitted into the State,

> the same social welfare and health benefit entitlements as apply to a citizen of the State. In that context it is difficult to see how, without more, the mere fact that there may be some limited cost to the State of admitting a dependent member of the extended family of a refugee to enter the State could be decisive."

Turning to an assessment of proportionality, it was held that the correct approach was to assess whether, having regard to the extent of any interference with the rights or interests of the respondent and his family members, such interference was justified on the basis of the legitimate aims sought to be advanced. It was accepted that the court should accord a reasonable margin of appreciation to the views of that decision maker. However, Clarke J. held that where an applicant discharges the burden of demonstrating that the proportionality judgment of the decision maker was unreasonable in the sense identified by Fennelly J. in *Meadows v Minister for Justice* [2010] 2 I.R. 701; [2011] 2 I.L.R.M. 157, then the court must intervene, but the court should only interfere where the Minister's consideration of that balancing exercise was so clearly wrong that it was demonstrated that the Minister could not reasonably have come to the view that the balance should be proportionately exercised in the way in which it was.

On the facts of this case, Clarke J. held that the Minister's balancing exercise was clearly wrong:

> "In light of the fact that special and enhanced application status is given to dependent family members, the weight to be attached to the general entitlement of the State to exercise immigration control must be significantly less in a case such as this than in an ordinary case. Likewise, in the absence of any consideration of the broader economic consequences of family reunification applications, the financial consequences for the State on the facts of this case are extremely limited. In those circumstances it does not seem to me that it could reasonably be held that those factors outweigh, in a proportionate fashion, the family and other rights which must be balanced on the other side."

Lack of effective remedy where no independent appeal mechanism In *NM v Minister for Justice and Equality* [2014] IEHC 638; unreported, High Court, Barr J., 18 December 2014, the High Court held that the lack of an independent appeal in respect of an application for readmission to the asylum process pursuant to s.17(7) of the Refugee Act 1996 (the "1996 Act") was in breach of the "effective remedy" provisions in art.39 of the Procedures Directive.

The procedure under s.17(7) of the 1996 Act (as amended by the European Communities (Asylum Procedures) Regulations 2011 (S.I. No. 51 of 2011)) provided that a representative of the Ministerial Decisions Unit would carry out a preliminary examination to see if the applicant for readmission to the asylum process had provided new elements or findings relating to the examination of whether the person qualifies as a refugee. The Minister's consent would then be given if following the preliminary examination new elements or findings arose or were put forward by the applicant which significantly added to the likelihood of the applicant qualifying as a refugee. Section 17(7D) provided that the applicant must establish that she was, through no fault of her own, incapable of presenting these elements or findings for the purpose of her previous application for a declaration. It was further noted that the procedure under the amended s.17(7) provides that the initial decision was to be taken by an official of the Ministerial Decisions Unit of the respondent. If this decision was against the applicant, there could be a review of the application carried out by a more senior official in the Ministerial Decisions Unit.

Barr J. noted that art.39 of the Procedures Directive provides that Member States shall ensure that applicants for asylum have the right to an effective remedy before a court or tribunal against a decision not to examine further the subsequent application pursuant to arts 32 and 34 of the Directive. The applicant maintained that the review provided for in the statutory instrument did not constitute an effective remedy before a court or tribunal. The respondent agreed in part with this contention. The respondent accepted that the review decision taken by the more senior official in the Ministerial Decisions Unit did not constitute an effective remedy before a court or tribunal. However, the respondent stated that the remedy of judicial review before the High Court constituted the effective remedy for the purpose of art.39 of the Directive. The applicant argued that the remedy of judicial review could not be seen as an "effective remedy" due to the limitations on the jurisdiction of the court when considering a judicial review application, including the fact that the court cannot reverse the earlier decision and substitute its own findings of fact on the substantive issues, and the fact that the court is precluded from referring to more up to date country information. Barr J. noted:

> "There is no doubt that the court in exercising its judicial review jurisdiction is limited in the role that it plays. It has been stated on many occasions that the courts can only review the process leading to the impugned decision, rather than review the merits of the decision itself. The court is not an appeal court and is not free to substitute its own substantive findings for those of the decision maker. The court cannot reverse the decision of the decision maker; it can only annul its decision. The court can only interfere if it is satisfied that there was an error of law, or an error of fact on the face of the record, or there was some unfairness in the procedure adopted or if the decision was irrational in that there was no evidence supporting the finding made by the decision maker.
>
> Under the system put forward by the respondent, the applicant, if dissatisfied with the decision made by the higher official, can only apply to the court if she can point to some fault in the decision making process on the part of the decision maker. She cannot simply appeal to the High Court. She is only permitted to seek annulment of the decision on one of the grounds on which certiorari is granted by the court."

Barr J. distinguished Case C-175/11 *HID v Refugee Appeals Tribunal*, unreported, Court of Justice of the European Union, 31 January 2013, on the basis that the CJEU in that case found that the Tribunal was a court or tribunal for the purposes of art.39 of the Procedures Directive and that its independence was safeguarded by the availability of judicial review. In the present case, however, in the context of a s.17(7) refusal, whether at first instance or on internal review, Barr J. noted that neither the first instance decision maker nor the internal review decision maker was a court or tribunal. Accordingly, he was of the view that the combination of remedies, even taken as a whole in respect of s.17(7), did not at any stage provide for a remedy to a court or tribunal which was capable of reversing the first instance refusal. In the circumstances, the court was satisfied that the review procedure under the statutory instrument and the supervisory role of the High Court in exercising its judicial review jurisdiction did not constitute an "effective remedy" before a court or tribunal as required by art.39 of the Directive.

The decision of Barr J. in *NM* has potentially significant ramifications for a number of other areas of immigration law. The decision is under appeal, and it is hoped that the decision of the Court of Appeal will clarify the law on this important issue as a matter of urgency.

Particular social group There are relatively few decisions of the Irish courts to date that engage with the particular social group category. In *SJL v Refugee Appeals Tribunal* [2014] IEHC 608; unreported, High Court, Barr J., 10 December 2014 and *LRC v Refugee Appeals Tribunal* [2014] IEHC 500; unreported, High Court, Barr J., 1 October 2014, the High Court considered claims on behalf of a husband and wife that they were members of a particular social group by reason of the fact that they had breached the "one child" policy in China. The applicants argued that if they were returned to China they would suffer persecution in that the husband might be forcibly sterilised (which had already happened to the wife), that they would face heavy fines, and would suffer adverse effects in relation to employment as well as discrimination in respect of access to medical and educational benefits. Both applications were refused by the Refugee Applications Commissioner and on appeal by the Refugee Appeals Tribunal, and the applicants subsequently instituted judicial review proceedings challenging the Tribunal decisions.

Barr J. commenced by examining the provisions of s.2 of the Refugee Act 1996, reg.10(1)(d) of the European Communities (Eligibility for Protection) Regulations 2006 (S.I. No. 518 of 2006) and the UNHCR Guidelines on International Protection: Membership of a particular social group (7 May 2002.) Barr J. conducted an extensive review of jurisprudence from a number of other jurisdictions, including the Canadian cases of *Cheung v Canada (Minister of Employment and Immigration)* [1993] 2 F.C. 314, and *Chan v Canada (Minister of Employment and Immigration)* (1995) (128) D.L.R. (4 Ed.) 213, the decision of the New Zealand Refugee Status Appeals Authority in *In re ZWD* 20 October 1992, the Australian decision of *A v Minister for Immigration and Ethnic Affairs* [1997] H.C.A. 4 and the English decisions of *Liu v Secretary of State for the Home Department* [2005] 1 W.L.R. 2852, *Fornah v Secretary of State for Home Department* [2007] 1 A.C. 412 and *R. v Immigration Appeal Tribunal, Ex p. Shah* [1999] 2 A.C. 629.

Applying the various dicta in these cases, Barr J. held that it was arguable that the applicants could be seen as being part of a particular social group, defined as "people who, contrary to the one child policy in China, have had more than one child without permission." Barr J. identified the shared characteristic that they were parents of more than one child born in China without official permission, which characteristic could not be changed by the applicants. It was held that it was arguable that they faced persecution in the form of forced sterilisation (already carried out on the wife and threatened against the husband); large fines; loss of employment; and discriminatory treatment, such as discrimination in relation to medical and educational benefits. Barr J. noted that there was a large amount of country of origin information submitted on behalf of the applicants, both to the Refugee Applications Commissioner and on appeal to the Refugee Appeals Tribunal. However, the Tribunal appeared only to have had regard to one piece of country of origin information on the basis that it dealt with Fujian province. Barr J. noted that where country of origin information documentation is submitted, it must be looked at and incorporated into the decision of the Tribunal, even if only to reject the documents, but the reasons for so rejecting the documentation should be clearly stated. In this case, the remainder of the country of origin information documentation was ignored by the Tribunal. Accordingly, Barr J. held that it was necessary to refer the matter back to the Tribunal for further consideration of the applicants' claims in light of all the documentation submitted, in order to allow the Tribunal decide whether the applicants were refugees owing to the fact that they feared persecution by reason of their membership of a particular social group.

Right of residence for non-citizen spouse The question of the entitlement of an Irish citizen to reside in the State with his or her non-citizen spouse was addressed in *Gorry v Minister for Justice and Equality* [2014] IEHC 29; [2014] 2 I.L.R.M. 302. The first Nigerian applicant was refused asylum in Ireland and was the subject of a deportation order in June 2005. She subsequently met the second named Irish applicant and later married him in Nigeria. The first applicant then applied for the revocation of the deportation order made in respect of her, which was refused. After the second applicant suffered health problems in Ireland, the first named applicant reapplied for revocation of the June 2005 deportation order on the basis that the second applicant's health prevented him from travelling to and living with the first applicant in Nigeria. The first applicant was informed of the refusal of this reapplication by letter dated 20 July 2012. The respondent did not accept that the applicants' rights under art.8 of the European Convention on Human Rights and Art.41 of the Constitution merited the revocation of the deportation order and found that there were no new exceptional circumstances justifying the revocation of the deportation order. The applicants challenged the decision to refuse revocation by way of judicial review.

Mac Eochaidh J. commenced his decision by noting:

> "Decisions to remove or exclude from the state non-nationals married to Irish nationals require the balancing of the public interest in maintaining immigration control and the private interests of the individuals to live together in Ireland. There are many decisions, from the common law jurisdictions and international courts which have described the balancing exercise required to be undertaken and the principles which apply to this exercise. Ultimately, as Bingham L.J. said in *EB (Kosovo) v Secretary of State for the Home Department* [2009] 1 A.C. 1159 at 1188:
>
> > 'The search for a hard-edged or bright-line rule to be applied to the generality of cases is incompatible with the difficult evaluative exercise which article 8 [ECHR] requires.'"

It was noted that while these comments were made in respect of the balancing of rights arising under the Convention, the same could readily be said in respect of the balancing of rights arising under the Constitution. Mac Eochaidh J. also noted that the applicants and the respondent agreed that marital, family and private life rights were not absolute, in that frequently such rights must surrender to the countervailing right of the State to assert immigration control and permit serious interference with those rights. The issue for decision in this case was whether the State authorities lawfully engaged in a balancing exercise of the competing rights which resulted in a refusal to revoke the deportation order made in respect of the first named applicant.

Having reviewed the jurisprudence on art.8 including *R. (Mahmood) v Secretary of State for the Home Department* [2001] 1 W.L.R. 840, *EB (Kosovo) v Secretary of State for the Home Department* [2009] 1 A.C. 1159 and *VW (Uganda) v Secretary of State for the Home Department* [2009] EWCA Civ. 5, Mac Eochaidh J. held that the proper test under art.8 to decide the contest between state rights and family rights, and in particular to decide whether a national of a deporting or excluding state should join his or her partner in a third country, was whether it was reasonable to expect a spouse to join the removed or excluded spouse in his or her country of residence. It was held that the test was not whether the spouse could demonstrate an insurmountable obstacle to joining the removed or excluded spouse. Accordingly, Mac Eochaidh J. held that the respondent had erred in law by refusing the application through the deployment of an "insurmountable obstacles" test.

In relation to the constitutional principles, the decision-maker in this case had commenced the analysis by stating that there was no authority which supported the proposition that an Irish citizen or a person entitled to reside in the State had a right under Art.41 of the Constitution to reside with his or her spouse in this jurisdiction. Mac Eochaidh J. held that this was:

> "a mistaken understanding of the law. The starting point in any consideration where a mixed Irish and non-Irish nationality couple seeks to live in Ireland is that they have a prima facie right to do so by virtue of Art.41 of the Constitution. It is recalled that Art.41.3 pledges the State to guard with special care the institution of marriage. The circumstances of the marriage will indicate whether that right is engaged. If engaged, the State is entitled to supervise the right by requiring an entry visa for the non-national, for example. The mere fact that it is engaged does not mean that it cannot be trumped by a lawful countervailing purpose which must ensure that the denial of the right of residence is proportionate to the policy objective sought to be achieved."

It was further noted that a person seeking revocation of a deportation order was required to advance new circumstances justifying revocation, but that they were not required to demonstrate "exceptional new circumstances." To the extent that the respondent had referred to an absence of exceptional circumstances in the applicants' case, Mac Eochaidh J. held that this was irrational. Accordingly, Mac Eochaidh J. quashed the decision of the Minister refusing to revoke the deportation order in respect of the first applicant.

The decision in *Gorry* is significant as it is the first decision which recognises a prima facie right of residence for Irish citizens and their non-citizen spouses, albeit clearly stating that such right is not absolute and can be trumped by countervailing circumstances provided that the decision is proportionate. The decision in *Gorry* is under appeal.

Whether best interests of the child must be considered in deportation decisions In *Dos Santos v Minister for Justice* [2014] IEHC 559; unreported, High Court, McDermott J., 19 November 2014, the High Court considered whether there is a requirement to consider the best interests of a non-citizen child in a decision to make a deportation order. The applicants were a Brazilian family of two parents and five children who had resided unlawfully in the State for a number of years before deportation orders were made against them. It was argued that the deportation orders were unlawful inter alia for failing to respect and vindicate the personal rights of the minor applicants pursuant to Art.40.3 of the Constitution and further failed to make a reasoned assessment of the interference with their rights pursuant to art.8 of the European Convention on Human Rights and/or their Charter rights and/or their rights pursuant to the United Nations Convention on the Rights of the Child. It was also contended that in making the deportation orders the Minister acted in breach of the principle of the best interests of the child. Leave to seek judicial review was granted on 30 May 2013.

McDermott J. commenced his judgment on the substantive application for judicial review with a summary of the factual background to the case as well as a review of the jurisprudence concerning parental responsibility and Art.41 of the Constitution, in particular *AO & DL v Minister for Justice* [2003] 1 I.R. 1. McDermott J. then turned to the arguments concerning the personal rights and best interests of the children, referring to a number of decisions including *North Western Health Board v HW* [2001] 3 I.R. 622, *G v An Bord Uchtála* [1980] I.R. 32 and *Oguekwe v Minister for Justice, Equality and Law Reform* [2008] 3 I.R. 795. McDermott J. concluded:

> "39. The court is not satisfied on the basis of these authorities, that a non-national child illegally in the state has a right under Article 40.3 to a private life consisting of a right to remain in the state and/or participate in community life whether at national or local level. No authority was cited in support of the existence of such a right. It is clear from *Oguekwe* and earlier authorities that Irish citizen children have a right to reside in the state by virtue of that status. Non-national children do not have a constitutional right to be and/or to remain illegally within the state or a right to be reared and educated in the state. It is well settled that the state is entitled to deport non-nationals who are illegally in the state, whether they be adults or children. Though non-nationals are entitled to the protection of the fundamental rights provisions of the Constitution, the state is entitled as a matter of state sovereignty to regulate the entry and stay of non-nationals (*Re Illegal Immigrants Bill 1999* [2000] 2 I.R. 36 and *Pok Sun Shun v Ireland* [1986] ILRM 593). The decision in *Oguekwe* dealt with the proposed deportation of the non-national parents of Irish citizen children and did not extend any further protection from deportation or a right to reside to non-national children. Non-national children do not have a constitutional right not to be deported."

McDermott J. accepted that non-national children are entitled to avail of other fundamental rights under the Constitution including the rights accruing to them as members of a family under Arts 41 and 42, and the right to fair procedures embracing constitutional and natural justice. It was in that context that the submission that the respondent failed to consider the consequences of the removal of the children to Brazil for their welfare fell to be considered. It was claimed that the failure by the respondent to consider the best interests of each child and, in particular, the disruption to their social and educational ties that would be occasioned by their deportation to Brazil, vitiated the respective deportation decisions. McDermott J. commented in this regard that he was satisfied that:

> "the consideration by the Minister of the children's welfare or best interests is not an isolated issue. It is an important element of the decision-making process which must be considered as a matter of fair procedures under s.3 of the Immigration Act 1999, and in accordance with and appropriate to the relevant personal and family rights of the children under the Constitution and art.8 of the European Convention on Human Rights. This includes the presumption that the best interests of the child lie in maintaining the unity of the family."

McDermott J. then turned to consider the provisions of s.3 of the Immigration Act 1999 (the "1999 Act") on the power to make deportation orders, the jurisprudence in relation to that power, and the provisions of the United Nations Convention on the Rights of the Child, in particular art.3(1) which provides:

> "In all actions concerning children, whether undertaken by public or private social welfare institutions, courts of law, administrative authorities or legislative bodies, the best interests of the child shall be a primary consideration."

Having regard to Art.29.6 of the Constitution which provides that "[n]o international agreement shall be part of the domestic law of the State save as may be determined by the Oireachtas", McDermott J. concluded that the United Nations Convention on the Rights of the Child did not form part of domestic law. Turning to art.8 of the European Convention on Human Rights and the best interests principle, McDermott J. held that:

> "It is clear from the European Courts [sic] jurisprudence that a distinction is drawn between the consideration given to the expulsion of long settled non-nationals and foreigners who had no right to be or remain in the contracting states. The applicants had a history of deliberate breaches of immigration law. No evidence of any or any insurmountable obstacles to the return of the family to Brazil was adduced or that they could not enjoy educational, social and personal development in their home country. The elements of private life relied upon were created during a period of unlawful residence in Ireland. The parents were aware that the continuance of private and family life within the host country would be precarious from the time they decided to bring the children into the country."

McDermott J. was satisfied that the appropriate principles derived from constitutional and Convention jurisprudence had been applied in this case with due and proper regard for and emphasis upon factors relevant to the welfare and best interests of the children and the fairness of procedures to which they were entitled under Art.40.3 of the Constitution and the provisions of s.3 of the 1999 Act. The court was also satisfied that the rights to private and family life were properly and adequately considered in the examinations of file and the making of the deportation orders, and accordingly dismissed the applications for judicial review.

LEGISLATION

Civil Registration (Amendment) Act 2014 The Civil Registration (Amendment) Act 2014 (the "2014 Act") also includes some provisions of relevance to the asylum and immigration field. Section 18 of the 2014 Act amends s.58 of the Civil Registration Act 2004 to provide that:

> A registrar who—
> (a) in the performance of his or her functions under this Part forms the opinion that an intended marriage would constitute a marriage of convenience, or
> (b) receives under subsection (1) an objection the stated reason for which is that the intended marriage would constitute a marriage of convenience, and forms the opinion that grounds for the objection possibly exist and need to be investigated,
>
> shall refer the matter to the Superintendent Registrar of the registration area where the registrar who formed the opinion is assigned, for a decision…

Effectively, this allows for suspension and investigation of intended marriages based on a suspicion that it is a marriage of convenience. While there are clearly justifiable policy concerns in relation to marriages of convenience, particularly in the context of trafficking of human beings, it remains to be seen whether these provisions are compatible with the Constitution having regard to the decision of Hogan J. in *Izmailovic v Commissioner of An Garda Síochána* [2011] 2 I.L.R.M. 442. Much will depend on the application of the registrar's new powers in practice in relation to the formation of opinions as to marriages of convenience, and the application of fair procedures in any investigation that follows.

Employment Permits (Amendment) Act 2014 The most significant legislative change in the area of asylum and immigration law in 2014 was the provisions of s.34 of the Employment Permits (Amendment) Act 2014 (the "2014 Act") which replace the provisions of s.5 of the Illegal Immigrants (Trafficking) Act 2000 (the "2000 Act") concerning applications for judicial review which are subject to the statutory scheme of judicial review. Section 34(1) provides:

> A person shall not question the validity of—
> (a) a notification under section 3(3)(a) of the Immigration Act 1999,
> (b) a notification under section 3(3)(b)(ii) of the Immigration Act 1999,
> (c) a deportation order under section 3(1) of the Immigration Act 1999,

(d) a refusal under Article 5 of the Aliens Order 1946 (S.R. and O. No.395 of 1946),
(e) a refusal under section 4 of the Immigration Act 2004,
(f) an exclusion order under section 4 of the Immigration Act 1999,
(g) a recommendation of the Refugee Applications Commissioner under section 13 (as amended by section 7 (h) of the Immigration Act 2003) of the Refugee Act 1996,
(h) a decision of the Refugee Appeals Tribunal under section 16 (as amended by section 7(i) of the Immigration Act 2003) of the Refugee Act 1996,
(i) a refusal under section 17 (as amended by Regulation 34 of the European Union (Subsidiary Protection) Regulations 2013 (S.I. No. 426 of 2013)) of the Refugee Act 1996,
(j) a decision under section 21 (as amended by section 11(1)(o) of the Immigration Act 1999) of the Refugee Act 1996,
(k) a removal order under Regulation 20(1) of the European Communities (Free Movement of Persons) (No.2) Regulations 2006 (S.I. No. 656 of 2006),
(l) an exclusion order under Regulation 23(1) of the European Communities (Free Movement of Persons) (No.2) Regulations 2006 (S.I. No. 656 of 2006),
(m) an order under section 3(11) of the Immigration Act 1999,
(n) a recommendation of the Refugee Applications Commissioner referred to in Regulation 6(2)(b) of the European Union (Subsidiary Protection) Regulations 2013 (S.I. No. 426 of 2013),
(o) a decision of the Refugee Appeals Tribunal referred to in Regulation 8(22)(a) of the European Union (Subsidiary Protection) Regulations 2013 (S.I. No. 426 of 2013), or
(p) such other decision, determination, recommendation, refusal or order as may be prescribed by the Minister under subsection (9),

made on or after the date on which section 34 of the Employment Permits (Amendment) Act 2014 comes into operation, otherwise than by way of an application for judicial review under Order 84 of Rules of the Superior Courts (S.I. No. 15 of 1986) (hereafter in this section referred to as 'the Order').

The new s.5 statutory scheme of judicial review now extends to a range of decisions previously subject to the normal scheme of judicial review; such decisions include refusals to revoke deportation orders, removal orders under the European Communities (Free Movement of Persons) (No.2) Regulations 2006 (S.I. No. 656 of 2006) and decisions to refuse subsidiary protection (whether at first instance or on appeal). While s.34 of the 2014 Act brings certain previously excluded decisions within the remit of the statutory scheme of judicial review, somewhat curiously it omits any reference to decisions under the Dublin Regulation which were included within the original terms of s.5 of the 2000 Act. The time limit for institution of judicial review proceedings under the statutory scheme of judicial review is extended from 14 days to 28 days (with further provision for extensions of time for good and sufficient reason), which is to be welcomed as a more realistic provision which finally implements the recommendations of the Law Reform Commission in its Consultation Paper and *Report on Judicial Review Procedure*. Furthermore, the new statutory scheme of judicial review in immigration and asylum matters provides that the application for leave shall be ex parte, albeit subject to a higher threshold of substantial grounds; the court retains a discretion to direct that an application for leave be put on notice to the State where appropriate, such as where the High Court considers that an application involves a point of law of exceptional public importance or it is in the interests of justice to do so.

European Union (Dublin System) Regulations 2014 (S.I. No. 525 of 2014) The European Union (Dublin System) Regulations 2014 (S.I. No. 525 of 2014) were made for the purpose of supporting the operation in the State of the Dublin III Regulation (Regulation (EU) No 604/2013 of the European Parliament and of the Council of 26 June 2013 establishing the criteria and mechanisms for determining the Member State responsible for examining an application for international protection lodged in one of the Member States by a third-country national or a stateless person (recast)).

Immigration Act (2004) Visas Order 2014 (S.I. No. 473 of 2014) The Immigration Act (2004) Visas Order 2014 (S.I. No. 473 of 2014) revokes and replaces the Immigration Act 2004 (Visas) Order 2012 (S.I. No. 417 of 2012) and sets out classes of visa required and non-visa required nationals as well as requirements for persons required to be in possession of a transit visa when arriving at a port in the State for purposes of passing through the port in order to travel to another state.

Commercial Law

AGENCY

Self-employed commercial agent In *Bushell Interiors Ltd v Liecht Kuchen AG* [2014] IEHC 3, the High Court (Moriarty J.) held that the plaintiff had not established that it was a self-employed commercial agent within the meaning of Directive 86/653/EC on self-employed commercial agents (the "1986 Commercial Agents Directive"), which had been implemented by the European Communities (Commercial Agents) Regulations 1994 (S.I. No. 33 of 1994) (*Annual Review of Irish Law 1994,* pp.25–35). The plaintiff supplied the defendant with kitchens for distribution and claimed that it acted as agent for the defendant in Ireland (the defendant was a company registered in Germany). The plaintiff sought damages for alleged breach of contract and interference with its economic interests and compensation pursuant to art.17(3) of the 1986 Commercial Agents Directive. The defendant brought a motion to dismiss the proceedings for want of jurisdiction.

The High Court (Moriarty J.) granted the defendant's application and dismissed the plaintiff's proceedings. The court held that the plaintiff had not made out a stateable case that it was the agent of the defendant for the purposes of the 1986 Commercial Agents Directive, as no written agreement had been entered into between the parties. The court also held that the plaintiff had not discharged the onus on it to demonstrate that art.5 of the Brussels I Regulation, Regulation (EC) No.44/2001, should apply; the court pointing out that the parties were bound by a clause in the contract which stated that German law was the applicable law for the purposes of any disputes.

ARBITRATION

Stay of proceedings In *Franmer Developments Ltd v L&M Keating Ltd* [2014] IEHC 295, the High Court (Ryan J.) referred proceedings to arbitration in accordance with s.6 of the Arbitration Act 2010 (*Annual Review of Irish Law 2010*, pp.48–52), which implemented art.8 of the UNCITRAL Model Law on International Commercial Arbitration. The background to the case was that the plaintiff was a developer and the first defendant was a building contractor. In 2007, the parties entered into a building contract for the construction of an apartment block in the standard Royal Institute of Architects of Ireland (RIAI) form. The contract incorporated the UNCITRAL Model Law (the Model Law) and contained a clause providing for disputes to be referred to arbitration. A dispute arose as a result of alleged sub-standard building work and the plaintiff claimed damages from the first, second and third defendants for alleged loss and damage arising out of breach of contract, negligence, breach of duty and/or breach of professional duty, as well as breach of retainer. Damages were also sought against the fourth and fifth defendants. The other defendants were as follows: the second defendant was the architect; the third defendant was the quantity surveyor; the fourth defendant was a windows and doors domestic sub-contractor (who had been retained by the first defendant); and the fifth defendant was the consulting engineer (engaged by the second defendant) in connection with the fire alarm system. The architect and the quantity surveyor were both nominated in the building contract.

The first defendant applied to stay the court proceedings pending the arbitration of the dispute between itself and the plaintiff. The plaintiff resisted the application on the basis that the arbitration clause contained in the standard building contract did not bind the second, third, fourth or fifth defendants. The plaintiff contended that it would be unsatisfactory if only the portion of the dispute relating to the first defendant was sent to arbitration, and it would be artificial as the liability of the first defendant could not be determined without reference to the other defendants. On that basis, the plaintiff alleged that the only forum which could effectively deal with each party's liability was the court. While the plaintiff did not dispute that the arbitration clause was binding or that art.8 of the Model Law, as implemented by s.6 of the Arbitration Act 2010, applied, it was claimed that one or other of the exceptions contained in art.8(1) of the Model Law applied in the circumstances of the case to deprive the contractor of the entitlement to have the matter referred to arbitration. Thus, the court had to consider whether the agreement was "null and void, inoperative or incapable of being performed" under art.8 of the Model Law, such that the matter did not require to be referred to arbitration.

The High Court (Ryan J.), as already indicated, referred the matter to arbitration in accordance with the contract's arbitration clause. The court held that, having regard to the application of art.8(1) of the Model Law, the difficulty or complexity of the arbitration was not a relevant consideration. Article 8(1) provides that a party is entitled to an order referring the matter to arbitration unless the court finds "that the agreement is null and void, inoperative or incapable of being performed." It is not that the court finds that the arbitration is inconvenient or even incapable of being performed but, rather, that the agreement for arbitration is incapacitated. The court held that it was difficult to see in what circumstances an arbitration agreement that was otherwise legitimate could be null and void or inoperative or incapable of being performed merely because it would be complex, difficult or inconvenient. The court held that the present case contained no features to make the agreement to arbitrate incapable of being performed within the meaning of art.8. Neither was the matter so complex or difficult that it would make arbitration impracticable. The court noted that it was common in building cases to find multiple defendants or technical and complicated issues. If the arbitrator were to decide that the first defendant contractor was liable and made an award, it was a separate matter from whether any of the other defendants had a liability to the plaintiff. While it would be convenient to have all of the relevant parties before the court in the one proceeding, the court concluded that it did not follow that it was the only way of resolving the dispute.

COMPETITION AND CONSUMER PROTECTION

The Competition and Consumer Protection Act 2014 (the "2014 Act") amended the Competition Acts 2002 and 2012 (*Annual Review of Irish Law 2002*, pp.24–30, and *Annual Review of Irish Law 2012*, pp.39–45) and the Consumer Protection

Act 2007 (*Annual Review of Irish Law 2007*, pp.152–164) in order to provide for the merger of the National Consumer Agency and the Competition Authority into the Competition and Consumer Protection Commission. The 2014 Act therefore formed part of the general public service reform plan that has been developed since 2011 (see also the Acts discussed under the heading "Enterprise and Industrial Development" in this chapter, below). The 2014 Act also provided for significant reforms to substantive competition law and related enforcement provisions. The 2014 Act came into force on various dates between 1 August 2014 and 31 October 2014: see the Competition and Consumer Protection Act 2014 (Commencement) Order 2014 (S.I. No. 366 of 2014).

Competition and Consumer Protection Commission Part 2 of the 2014 Act (ss.8–46) deals with the merger of the National Consumer Agency and the Competition Authority into the Competition and Consumer Protection Commission (CCPC). The CCPC was established on 31 October 2014: see the Competition and Consumer Protection Act 2014 (Establishment Day) Order 2014 (S.I. No. 367 of 2014). Part 2 contains standard provisions on the establishment of a new body and the dissolution of existing bodies. In terms of structure and corporate governance, the CCPC comprises a chairperson and between two and six members, who will act in a collegiate manner. This structure is modeled on that of the Competition Authority and, consequently, there is no board of the CCPC. The initial members of the CCPC were the outgoing members of the Competition Authority and the outgoing CEO of the National Consumer Agency. Appointments in the future can only be made by the Minister for Jobs, Enterprise and Innovation, following an open recruitment process undertaken by the Public Appointments Service. As was the case with the two bodies it replaced, the 2014 Act provides that the CCPC shall be independent in carrying out its functions such as enforcement, investigations and merger determinations. The CCPC is accountable to the Oireachtas and to the Minister in line with standard accountability and governance procedures and practices.

Section 10 of the 2014 Act sets out the key functions of the CCPC. Section 10 consolidates, into the CCPC, the functions that had applied to the Competition Authority and the National Consumer Agency under the Competition Acts 2002 and 2012 and the Consumer Protection Act 2007, respectively. These functions include the promotion of competition; promotion and protection of the interests and welfare of consumers; enforcement of and ensuring compliance with relevant statutory provisions; investigating suspected breaches of relevant provisions (including breaches of arts.101 and 102 of the Treaty on the Functioning of the European Union); setting the strategic objectives of the CCPC; advising the Government, the Minister for Jobs, Enterprise and Innovation and any other Minister or public body in relation to any matter (including legislation) which is likely to impact on consumer protection and welfare or competition; promotion through public awareness and information campaigns; promotion of the development of alternative dispute resolution procedures as a means of resolving disputes arising out of certain consumer transactions; preparation of guidelines; reviewing and approving certain codes of practice; promotion of the interests of consumers of financial services; co-operation with similar bodies (either in the State or beyond); undertaking relevant research; supporting (if deemed appropriate by the CCPC) voluntary bodies whose activities cover consumer protection and welfare or competition, and carrying out studies on any issue relating to consumer protection and welfare or competition (either at the request of the Minister for Jobs, Enterprise and Innovation or on its own initiative). Section 10 also provides that the Minister for Jobs, Enterprise and Innovation may request the CCPC to carry out studies or analyses into issues that come under its remit. Finally, s.10 provides that the CCPC may only delegate certain functions.

Enforcement powers As well as the additional enforcement powers already provided for in the amendments made to the Competition Act 2002 by the Competition (Amendment) Act 2012 (*Annual Review of Irish Law 2012*, pp.39–45), the 2014 Act conferred further powers on the CCPC by extending the provisions of the Criminal Justice Act 2011 (*Annual Review of Irish Law 2011*, pp.284–289) to serious competition law offences. In addition, some elements of the Criminal Justice Act 2007 have been incorporated into the powers of the CCPC. Section 37 provides for the powers of CCPC authorised officers concerning their functions relating to competition law offences and largely replicates many of the powers set out in the Competition Act 2002. It also provides that an authorised officer may attend, with a member of An Garda Síochána, any questioning of a suspect and participate in any such questioning. Section 37 also provides for the power to use recordings as evidence in trials, analogous to those powers set out in ss.56 and 57 of the Criminal Justice Act 2007. Somewhat less extensive enforcement powers are provided for in s.36 of the 2014 Act in respect of CCPC authorised officers when they are enforcing consumer protection legislation.

Merger notifications Part 3 of the 2014 Act (ss.47–73) amended the Competition Act 2002 (the "2002 Act") in order to align it with the establishment of the CCPC. A number of sections also amended the 2002 Act in respect of the procedures to be operated by the CCPC on merger notifications generally. Many of these emanated from a public consultation process held by the Competition Authority in 2007 and 2008.

Briefly, the CCPC merger review process involves two phases. Phase 1 is a review period, following which a determination must be made by the CCPC either to clear the merger or to proceed to Phase 2, a full investigation, discussed below. The CCPC's deadline to make a Phase 1 determination is 30 working days after the "appropriate date" (as defined in s.19(6) of the 2002 Act, as amended by s.56(c) of the 2014 Act) or 45 working days after the "appropriate date" if any of the undertakings that made the notification submits proposals to the CCPC. If, after the Phase 1 investigation, the CCPC is unable to conclude that the proposed transaction will not lead to a substantial lessening of competition in any market for goods or services in the State, the CCPC proceeds to Phase 2, a full investigation. The CCPC's deadline to make a Phase 2 determination is 120 working days after the "appropriate date". Within this deadline, the CCPC must determine whether to clear the merger (with or without conditions) or prohibit the merger.

The appropriate date from which the above deadlines are calculated is normally the date of notification. However, this changes to a later date if the CCPC issues, within 30 working days from the date of notification, a formal requirement for the merging parties to provide further information. In addition, the CCPC's deadline of 120 days for making a Phase 2 determination will stand suspended for a certain period if, within 30 working days from the date of opening its Phase 2 investigation, the Commission issues a formal requirement for the merging parties to provide further information.

Media mergers Part 4 of the 2014 Act, which consists of a single section (s.74) amended the 2002 Act by inserting a new Part 3A on Media Mergers, which comprises 15 new sections (ss.28A–28O of the 2002 Act). This implemented the recommendations made in the 2010 Report of the Advisory Group on Media Mergers (the "Sreenan Report"). Under the pre-2014 system, if the Competition Authority determined that a media merger failed the competition test, the matter was closed and the issue was not referred to the Minister for Jobs, Enterprise and Innovation for a determination in the public interest. If the Competition Authority decided that the merger could comply with competition rules, the Minister could direct the Authority to carry out a full investigation based on the notification and analysis from the Competition Authority of its decision and the details of the merger, as presented. As part of this pre-2014 process, the Authority was required to give an opinion as to how the application of the relevant public interest criteria (for example, the strength and competitiveness of media businesses indigenous to the State and the extent to which ownership or control of media businesses and control of particular types of media business in the State are spread among individuals and other undertakings) should affect the exercise of the Minister's powers. If the Minister did not make a decision counter to the original Competition Authority determination, no further action was required. However, if the Minister made a decision counter to the original Competition Authority determination, this decision had to be confirmed through the making of an order, which had to be laid before the Houses of the Oireachtas.

The recommendations in the Sreenan Report, as implemented in the 2014 Act, were aimed at modernising the system for regulating media mergers to reflect international best practice. However, the broad three-step process in place for media mergers prior to the 2014 Act will continue to operate. First, a determination will be made by the CCPC that a merger has taken place. Secondly, a decision will be taken by the CCPC on whether the merger should be permitted to proceed on competition grounds. Thirdly, in the event that the CCPC allows the merger to proceed on competition grounds, a decision will be taken by the relevant Minister on whether the merger should be permitted to proceed on the grounds of the public interest aspect. There is no provision for, nor did the Sreenan Report recommend, an ongoing regulatory function in respect of media ownership. The power only falls to be exercised in the event that a media merger takes place as defined and that merger is permitted to proceed on competition grounds. The key concept relating to the definition of a merger remains the concept of "effective control" and no changes are provided for in this respect.

The changes made to the 2002 Act by the 2014 Act added two elements that went beyond those proposed in the Sreenan Report. The first is a change in the relevant Minister for such public interest considerations from the Minister for Jobs, Enterprise and Innovation to the Minister for Communications, Energy and Natural Resources, with a major role for the Broadcasting Authority of Ireland in drawing up a report for the Minister to consider prior to making a decision in the matter from a public interest aspect. The second change relates to designating the relevant Joint Oireachtas Committee as a notifiable body when the Minister for Communications, Energy and Natural Resources is considering any proposed media mergers from the public interest aspect. It may be noted that some further minor amendments to the 2002 Act on media mergers were subsequently made by s.4 of the Intellectual Property (Miscellaneous Provisions) Act 2014, whose main provisions are discussed in the Intellectual Property heading in this chapter, below. Each of the amendments to the 2002 Act were incorporated into the Revised Act version of the Competition Act 2002, available at lawreform.ie.

Consumer protection Part 5 of the 2014 Act (ss.75–82) made a number of amendments to the Consumer Protection Act 2007 (the "2007 Act"). Section 76 inserted a new s.24F into the 2007 Act (as amended by the Central Bank Reform Act 2010) to enable the CCPC to request certain information which may be required in relation to the calculation of levies to be imposed on financial institutions in connection with the funding of its financial education and information function. It also inserted a new s.24G into the 2007 Act to provide for arrangements for the secondment of certain Central Bank employees to the CCPC.

Section 77 of the 2014 Act amended s.55 of the 2007 Act to clarify the prohibited commercial activity that traders shall not engage in, relating to the language of any interaction with the consumer concerned.

Grocery goods sector Part 6 of the 2014 Act (ss.83–86) addresses certain practices in the grocery goods sector, which has been an ongoing feature of competition law regulation in the State for over two decades (see, for example, the discussion of the ban on below-cost selling in the context of the enactment of the 2002 Act in *Annual Review of Irish Law 2002*, p.30). During the Oireachtas debates on the 2014 Act, a number of national and EU initiatives to ensure good practices in the retail sector (particularly in the food supply chain from farm to retail outlets) were noted. These included unsuccessful attempts made in 2010 and 2011 to secure a voluntary code of practice (detailed in the Travers Report); a 2013 Report on the grocery goods sector by the Joint Committee on Agriculture, Food and the Marine and an EU-wide voluntary initiative in 2013 on principles of good practices in the food supply chain which had been adopted by some (not all) relevant European trade associations. At the time of the Oireachtas debates on the 2014 Act, the European Commission had published a Green Paper on unfair trading practices in the business to business food and non-food supply chain in Europe in 2013 and had commenced a public consultation on the Green Paper with a view to publishing a Communication on the topic. During the debates on the 2014 Act it was also indicated that statutory Regulations to deal with certain practices in this area, rather than a code of conduct, would be made, and that the CCPC would be responsible for overseeing and enforcing these Regulations.

ENTERPRISE AND INDUSTRIAL DEVELOPMENT

A series of Acts enacted in 2014 and 2015 that emanated from the Department of Jobs, Enterprise and Innovation formed part of the general public service reform plan that has been in place since 2011. These reforms involved the merger of the

National Consumer Agency and the Competition Authority into the Competition and Consumer Protection Commission (see the Competition and Consumer Protection Act 2014, discussed above); restructuring the enterprise support model for micro and small businesses (including the dissolution of the 35 County Enterprise Boards (CEBs), the transfer of their functions to Enterprise Ireland and the creation of local enterprise offices in city and county councils (see the County Enterprise Boards (Dissolution) Act 2014, discussed below)); the restructuring of transport and enterprise development bodies in the Shannon region (see the State Airports (Shannon Group) Act 2014, also discussed below); and the reform of five workplace relations bodies into two organisations (under the Workplace Relations Act 2015, which will be discussed in the *Annual Review of Irish Law 2015*).

Enterprise Ireland taking over functions of County Enterprise Boards The County Enterprise Boards (Dissolution) Act 2014 (the "2014 Act") provided for the transfer to Enterprise Ireland of the enterprise support model for micro and small businesses previously carried out by 35 County Enterprise Boards (CEBs). The 35 CEBs were dissolved by the 2014 Act, which also provided for the creation of local enterprise offices (LEOs) in city and county councils. The 2014 Act came into operation between 2–9 April 2014: see the County Enterprise Boards (Dissolution) Act 2014 (Commencement) Order 2014 (S.I. No. 160 of 2014).

The intention behind the 2014 Act was that city and county councils would merge the enterprise support elements of their business support units with the LEOs to provide an integrated micro and small enterprise support service at local level. It was noted during the Oireachtas debates on the 2014 Act that CEBs had had an impressive track record in job support over the 20 years up to 2014. The LEO structure in the 2014 Act would draw and build on the positive enterprise culture of the successful CEB model. On average, CEBs had assisted approximately 1,000 micro-enterprise projects each year through direct grant assistance, in addition to providing soft supports including training, mentoring and management. In 2013, just over €9.5 million was provided by the CEBs to micro-enterprises by way of capital grant support, with just under €8.5 million spent in providing soft supports. It was indicated that, in 2013, more than 26,000 participants were on CEB training courses and more than 6,500 participants were on management programmes, while almost 6,000 clients received mentoring support.

The creation of the LEOs under the 2014 Act was intended as a local first-stop-shop for new entrepreneurs and existing micro and small business owners. Other services would include those previously provided by the business development units of local authorities, the Department of Social Protection, the Department of Education and Skills, Microfinance Ireland, the Credit Review Office and enterprise-focused supports from the Revenue Commissioners. It was anticipated that the services to be provided by the LEOs would fall under four main areas: business information and advisory services; enterprise support services; entrepreneurship services; and local enterprise development services.

Section 4 of the 2014 Act empowered the Minister for Jobs, Enterprise and Innovation to appoint, by ministerial order, the day on which the CEBs were dissolved. This was designated as 15 April 2014: see County Enterprise Boards (Dissolution) Act 2014 (Dissolution Day) Order 2014 (S.I. No. 175 of 2014).

Section 5 enabled the Minister to dissolve the CEBs on the appointed day, that is, 15 April 2014.

Section 6 provided for the transfer of the functions of the CEBs to Enterprise Ireland; provided for the transferred functions to be performed by a local authority, in the functional area of a local authority, on behalf of Enterprise Ireland; and amended s.10 of the Industrial Development Act 1995 by deleting the words "subject to the prior consent of the Minister" as Enterprise Ireland already had the enabling powers specified.

Section 7 provided for all land and other property, including assets, previously vested in a CEB to be transferred to Enterprise Ireland; and for all rights, powers and privileges relating to or connected with such land to be vested in Enterprise Ireland without the need for a conveyance or assignment. Section 8 provided for the transfer of rights and liabilities of a CEB to Enterprise Ireland. It also provided that in the event of an action to sue, recover or enforce, Enterprise Ireland may do so in its own name without the need to give notice of the transfer to the person whose right or liability is transferred. It also provided that any lease, licence, wayleave or permission granted by a CEB shall continue in force as if granted by Enterprise Ireland.

Section 9 allowed any claim in respect of loss or injury alleged to have been suffered during the performance of CEB functions to lie against Enterprise Ireland, and empowered Enterprise Ireland to take the place of a CEB in any legal proceedings to which a CEB was a party immediately prior to the transfer. Section 10 ensured that anything commenced by a CEB, for example, loan agreements, grants or equity investments did not lapse on the transfer to Enterprise Ireland of the functions, assets and liabilities of the CEBs. Section 11 empowered the Minister to designate staff of a CEB to Enterprise Ireland or a local authority. Section 12 provided for Enterprise Ireland or the local authority to accept staff into their employment that were previously employed by a CEB on terms and conditions no less favourable in relation to remuneration and superannuation; and the amendment of the Second Schedule to the Industrial Development Act 1993 in relation to the secondment of staff; and the protection of pension entitlements to existing staff and pensioners. Section 13 set down the provisions regarding the preparation and submission by Enterprise Ireland of final accounts and final reports of the CEBs.

Forfás functions integrated into Department of Jobs, Enterprise and Innovation The principal purpose of the Industrial Development (Forfás Dissolution) Act 2014 (the "2014 Act") was to give effect to the government decision to dissolve Forfás and to integrate its research and policy advisory functions into the Department of Jobs, Enterprise and Innovation. A consequential purpose was to incorporate into the Health and Safety Authority the Irish National Accreditation Board (INAB), which had been established as a committee of Forfás (this aspect is discussed in the Safety and Health chapter, below). The 2014 Act came into effect on various dates in July 2014: see the Industrial Development (Forfás Dissolution) Act 2014 (Commencement) Order 2014 (S.I. No. 304 of 2014).

Forfás was established in 1994, under the Industrial Development Act 1993 (the "1993 Act") (*Annual Review of Irish Law 1993*, pp.8–9), as an agency of the then Department of Enterprise, Trade and Employment. The agency's core functions were to advise the Minister on matters relating to the development of industry in the State; to encourage the development of industry and technology in the State; to advise on the development and co-ordination of policies across the agencies supporting enterprise; to provide independent research in the areas of enterprise and science policy; to evaluate enterprise policy interventions; and to provide research and administrative support to a number of independent advisory groups, including the National Competitiveness Council, the Expert Group on Future Skills and the Advisory Council for Science, Technology and Innovation.

Under the 1993 Act and related legislation, Forfás was statutorily the employer of staff in IDA Ireland, Enterprise Ireland, Science Foundation Ireland and some staff in the National Standards Authority of Ireland. Forfás also had responsibility for pensions of enterprise agency staff and staff of a number of former agencies, including the Industrial Development Authority, Eolas, the National Board for Science and Technology, the Irish Goods Council and An Bord Tráchtála. Forfás also carried out a range of shared services on behalf of IDA Ireland, Enterprise Ireland and SFI, including the administration of pensions, property management and other central functions. The Irish National Accreditation Board (INAB) operated as a committee of Forfás and was supported by Forfás staff.

Part 5 of the 2014 Act (s.14) provides for Forfás staff seconded to, or working under the direction of, the National Standards Authority of Ireland (NSAI) to transfer to the NSAI on terms and conditions of service relating to remuneration and superannuation no less favourable than those applying before the transfer.

Part 6 of the 2014 Act (ss.15–27) provides for the dissolution of Forfás on a day to be appointed by the Minister. This occurred on 1 August 2014: see the Forfás (Dissolution) Order 2014 (S.I. No. 341 of 2014). Section 17 provides that references in any enactment to Enterprise Ireland, IDA Ireland or SFI as an agency of Forfás shall be construed as a reference to those bodies, as appropriate. Section 18 provides for the transfer of functions vested in Forfás to be transferred to Enterprise Ireland and IDA Ireland, as appropriate, in accordance with the Schedule to the 2014 Act. Section 19 provides for the transfer of functions vested in Forfás other than those referred to in ss.18 and 28 to be transferred to the Minister for Jobs, Enterprise and Innovation.

Section 24 provides that the staff of Forfás, other than those who are transferring to become employees of Enterprise Ireland, IDA Ireland, SFI, the NSAI or the HSA, will be appointed to an unestablished position in the civil service on terms and conditions of service relating to remuneration and superannuation no less favourable than those applying before the transfer. These staff will subsequently be designated as established civil servants.

Section 25 provides that superannuation schemes administered by Forfás prior to dissolution shall continue in force as if made by the Minister. Section 26 provides for the administration of superannuation schemes or arrangements referred to in s.25 or those referred to in s.12(5)(c) of the County Enterprise Boards (Dissolution) Act 2014 (discussed generally above) to be undertaken by a relevant body on behalf of the Minister and sets out arrangements to apply in regard to the administration of these schemes.

Section 27 provides for the preparation of final accounts for Forfás no later than one year after the dissolution date and for the preparation of a final annual report within six months of dissolution.

Strategic policy division in Department replacing Forfás Under the 2014 Act, the core policy advisory and research functions of Forfás were incorporated into a strategic policy division established within the Department. The strategic policy division will be tasked with a significant range of policy evaluation, co-ordination and planning activities on behalf of the Minister and for the Department's agencies. The key elements of the role of the strategic policy division will be in the areas of enterprise policy, competitiveness, horizon scanning, tax policy, development of the Government's annual Action Plan for Jobs, trade and innovation policies, education, skills and labour market analysis, and key policy surveys and research. The staff of Forfás who were previously engaged in delivering these functions were transferred into the division within the Department, together with relevant support staff from the agency. The strategic policy division will continue to provide support and secretariat services for a number of independent advisory groups, including the National Competitiveness Council and the Expert Group on Future Skills Needs.

National Competitiveness Council The National Competitiveness Council (NCC) reports to the Minister on key competitiveness issues facing the Irish economy and offers recommendations on policy actions required to enhance Ireland's competitive position. In the context of the changes made by the 2014 Act, the membership of the NCC was expanded to incorporate industry partners appointed to assist with disruptive reforms (under "An Action Plan for Jobs") and to broaden the range of Departments attending NCC meetings in an advisory capacity. The Government approved revised terms of reference for the NCC to give it greater flexibility to prepare and publish reports on issues it considers important, thereby copper-fastening its independence within the organisational structure provided for in the 2014 Act. The revised terms of reference also provide for a specific role for the council in respect of preparation of the competitiveness chapter of "An Action Plan for Jobs".

Enterprise Ireland Part 2 of the 2014 Act (ss. 5–7) provides (in s.5) for Enterprise Ireland and its subsidiaries to employ staff subject to the consent of the Minister and the approval of the Minister for Public Expenditure and Reform. Section 6 provides for the transfer to Enterprise Ireland of staff currently seconded from Forfás on terms and conditions of service relating to remuneration and related matters which are no less favourable than those applying before the transfer. Section 7 provides for Enterprise Ireland to establish a superannuation scheme in respect of persons referred to in s.6.

IDA Ireland Part 3 of the 2014 Act (ss.8–10) replicates the provisions of ss.5–7, inclusive, in respect of staff of IDA Ireland.

Science Foundation Ireland Part 4 of the 2014 Act (ss.11–13) deals with Science Foundation Ireland. It replicates the provisions of ss.5–7, inclusive, in respect of Science Foundation Ireland.

Irish National Accreditation Board Part 7 of the 2014 Act (ss.28–36) deals with the incorporation of the Irish National Accreditation Board (INAB) into the Health and Safety Authority. This was done by way of amendments to the Safety,

Health and Welfare at Work Act 2005 (discussed further in the Safety and Health chapter, below).

Consequential amendments Part 8 of the 2014 Act (ss.37–42) contains consequential amendments to a number of Acts as a result of the integration of Forfás into the Department of Jobs, Enterprise and Innovation. This included amendments to the Industrial Development Act 1993, the Metrology Act 1996, the Industrial Development (Enterprise Ireland) Act 1998 and the Industrial Development (Science Foundation Ireland) Act 2003.

Enterprise and transport development bodies in Shannon region The State Airports (Shannon Group) Act 2014 (the "2014 Act") provided for the restructuring of transport and enterprise development bodies in the Shannon region. The 2014 Act established a new commercial State company, Shannon Group plc, which incorporated the Shannon Airport Authority (SAA) and Shannon Development. The establishment of the Shannon Group plc completed the foundations to support a new future for Shannon and the mid-west region, as envisaged in the 2012 *Report by the Shannon Aviation Business Development Task Force* (the "Report"). In the Report, the task force stated it was satisfied that an independent Shannon Airport, coupled with a restructured Shannon Development, could develop and grow passenger traffic and the route network. It also anticipated that this could create new employment opportunities in aviation-related services in and around the airport. The Report pointed to the opportunities to develop and grow an internationally recognised centre for aviation services, known as the international aviation services centre (IASC) at Shannon, which could draw on its geographical location, good airfield facilities and ample adjacent land.

Shannon Group plc Under the 2014 Act, Shannon Group plc is the parent or holding company for Shannon Airport Authority and the restructured Shannon Development, and acquired all the shares of these two companies from the Minister for Public Expenditure and Reform. Both maintain their separate legal identities as wholly-owned subsidiaries of Shannon Group plc. The restructured Shannon Development was renamed Shannon Commercial Enterprises Ltd, which has a commercial remit.

Part 2 of the 2014 Act provides for the establishment of Shannon Group plc under the Companies Acts, the issuing of 38,100 shares in the company to the Minister for Public Expenditure and Reform and the issue of one share, to be held in trust for that Minister, to each of the subscribers to the Memorandum of Association of the company. These latter are standard minimum requirements for a public limited company under the Companies Acts. Section 9 provides for the payment of dividends to the Minister for Public Expenditure and Reform and for such dividends to be disposed of for the benefit of the Exchequer. The remainder of Pt 2 sets down the purpose, functions and general duties of Shannon Group and provides power for the company to borrow, subject to ministerial consents. An aggregate borrowing ceiling of €100 million for Shannon Group and its subsidiaries is specified in s.13, but this can be varied subsequently, if necessary and justified, by ministerial order.

Part 3 of the 2014 Act deals with the administration of Shannon Group and corporate governance arrangements. The board of the company will have ten members, including the chairman, the chief executive and two employee representatives. The chief executive of Shannon Group will also be appointed as chief executive of each of the group's two main subsidiaries, the SAA and Shannon Development. On staffing matters, provision is made in s.18 to confirm that the transfer of ownership of the SAA and Shannon Development to Shannon Group will not operate in a way that would worsen the conditions of service, or remuneration, of staff working in these two bodies. Section 20 provides that the members of the board of any subsidiary of Shannon Group should be appointed by the group board rather than solely by the chairman. However, subject to notifying the Shannon Group board, the Minister may specify any subsidiary for which he or she wishes his or her consent to be obtained for board appointments.

Part 4 of the 2014 Act (s.28) provides that, following the establishment of Shannon Group, all shares held by or on behalf of the Minister for Public Expenditure and Reform in the SAA and Shannon Development will be transferred to Shannon Group. The SAA and Shannon Development will then be wholly-owned subsidiaries of Shannon Group and provision is made for the SAA to be re-registered as a private limited company, similar to Shannon Development. Simultaneously with this transfer of ownership, the existing directors on the boards of the SAA and Shannon Development will cease to hold office. This will allow the board of Shannon Group to make appointments to the boards of these subsidiaries under s.20 of the 2014 Act.

State airport authorities, including superannuation schemes Part 5 of the 2014 Act contains a number of provisions that are relevant to State airports. Section 31 provides for the dissolution, for the time being, of Cork Airport Authority plc, but it also provides the power to reincorporate the authority at a later date. Essentially, the provisions in the State Airports Act 2004, which would facilitate the separation of Cork Airport from the DAA (if and when such a decision is made), were preserved. Cork Airport Authority plc was incorporated in 2004, the then Government's intention being to move relatively quickly towards the separation of Cork Airport from the DAA. However, that never happened and it was never envisaged that the company would remain in existence for a decade without the airport being separated from the DAA. By 2014, the board of the Cork Airport Authority had only existed in skeleton form for some time. Even in the period before that, when a board was in place, there were significant corporate governance concerns on the part of directors about their being on a board in such circumstances. The 2014 Act therefore brought this situation to an end, while preserving the Minister's power to incorporate the company again at a future date.

Section 32 provides for the renaming of the Dublin Airport Authority as "DAA". Each of its two airports, Dublin and Cork, will be branded separately. Since 2004, the name DAA had been used extensively across infrastructure, systems and other assets of the Authority.

Section 33 contains a series of technical amendments to existing airports legislation, in particular, the Air Navigation and Transport (Amendment) Act 1998 and the State Airports Act 2004, which arise as a consequence of the renaming of the Dublin Airport Authority, the dissolution of the Cork Airport Authority and the power in s.31 to reincorporate the Cork Airport Authority at a future date.

Section 34 of the 2014 Act provided for amendment to the statutory provisions governing superannuation schemes in State airport authorities. Section 34 also facilitated changes, by the trustee, to the Irish Airlines (General Employees) Superannuation Scheme (IASS). Section 34 was enacted against the background of attempts to resolve a dispute over a significant funding deficit in the IASS, which were only finally resolved in 2015 in the context of the sale of Aer Lingus to International Airlines Group, IAG (the holding company for British Airways).

Insolvency regime for aircraft under Cape Town Convention Part 8 of the 2014 Act provided for the adoption of the special insolvency regime applicable to aircraft, known as "Alternative A" under the Cape Town Convention on International Interests in Mobile Equipment (the "Convention"). Ireland was among the first countries to ratify the Convention through the enactment of the International Interests in Mobile Equipment (Cape Town Convention) Act 2005 (the "2005 Act"). The Convention and the 2005 Act provide an international legal framework for the financing of high value moveable or mobile assets such as aircraft, trains and satellites. It was noted during the Oireachtas debates on the 2014 Act that the Convention has no meaning or effect unless and until a Protocol is agreed and comes into force for each of the three asset types covered by the Convention. Until 2014, only one Protocol, the Aircraft Protocol, was operational. The 2005 Act gave effect to the Aircraft Protocol in national law. Essentially, the Convention and Protocol provide protection for creditors of aircraft assets in countries that have signed up to the Convention. The "Alternative A" insolvency regime for aircraft assets under the Convention and Protocol essentially replicates the insolvency regime in the United States where enhanced equipment trust certificates (EETCs) have been successfully issued since the 1990s. These are an aviation-specific form of asset-backed security, where the secured asset is the aircraft and they have proved popular for both airlines and investors in the United States. It is a matter for individual countries to specify the waiting period in the protocol following which, if a default is not rectified, the creditor is entitled to the automatic repossession of the aircraft.

The vast majority of countries that have adopted the "Alternative A" regime have opted to replicate the 60-day period applicable in the United States. Under the 2014 Act, Ireland also adopted a waiting period of 60 days. Since Ireland has a particularly strong foothold in the aircraft leasing business with nine of the top ten global leasing companies located in Ireland, adoption of the "Alternative A" insolvency regime for aircraft will support the development of aviation finance in Ireland and help maintain Ireland's leading global position in aircraft leasing where there is already growing competition from other jurisdictions that had already adopted the "Alternative A" regime.

An exemption from stamp duty was provided by the Minister for Finance in the Finance Act 2013 to facilitate the successful issuing of enhanced equipment trust certificates in Ireland and make this form of financing more attractive to investors. Together with the implementation of the "Alternative A" insolvency regime in the 2014 Act, it was suggested in the Oireachtas debates on the 2014 Act that these measures would enable airlines and leasing companies to access finance on more competitive terms and will help sustain and develop the leasing and aviation finance sectors within Ireland.

EURO AREA LOAN FACILITY AND ESM TREATY

As noted in the *Annual Review of Irish Law 2008*, pp.61–62, the *Annual Review of Irish Law 2009*, pp.112–116, the *Annual Review of Irish Law 2010*, pp.54–57, the *Annual Review of Irish Law 2011*, pp.92–97, the *Annual Review of Irish Law 2012*, pp.52–59, and the *Annual Review of Irish Law 2013*, pp.61–67, a series of Acts beginning in late 2008 were enacted in response to the international and national economic and fiscal crisis that emerged in 2008, and in response to the catastrophic banking failure in Ireland. As noted in the *Annual Review of Irish Law 2010*, by the end of 2010, for the first time in its history, the State was obliged to apply for direct financial assistance from the European Financial Stability Facility (EFSF) (now replaced by the European Stability Mechanism, ESM) and the International Monetary Fund (IMF). Further legislative activity, continued in this respect in 2013. As noted in the *Annual Review of Irish Law 2013*, in December 2013, the State completed the EU-IMF "bailout" although continued surveillance of the State will continue for the foreseeable future under the enhanced EU supervision of all eurozone national budgets which were agreed in the wake of the financial crisis. The rate of legislative activity in 2014 directly related to these events was, by comparison with previous years, relatively modest.

Euro Area Loan Facility to Greece Section 2 of the Central Bank Act 2014 made provision for certain payments out of the Central Fund to an account established by the European Stability Mechanism (ESM) as agent on behalf of euro area members. This account is to receive payments for the purpose of providing financial assistance to Greece under what is described as the Securities Market Programme (the "Programme"). This formed part of a series of measures agreed by euro area finance Ministers on 27 November 2012 to provide additional help to Greece. Section 2 of the 2014 Act facilitated the State's participation in the Programme. Member states under a full financial assistance programme are not required to participate in the scheme while in a programme. As Ireland successfully exited its programme in December 2013, the State was therefore liable to make payments under this process, beginning in 2014, with the transfer date being 1 July 2014 when the State was expected and required to make its first payment of €31 million for 2014 by that date. The Oireachtas was therefore required to enact the 2014 Act by 1 July 2014, which it did. As no payment was required from Ireland for 2013 while the State was in a programme, the total amount that the State would have paid was reduced by €35 million. The remaining total is €126 million. This will be paid annually, in decreasing amounts, between 2014 and 2025, with the last payment (covering the years 2025 to 2038) being €1.85 million. See also the discussion of s.1 of the 2014 Act under the heading "Financial Services" in this chapter, below.

FINANCIAL SERVICES

Implementation of 2013 Capital Requirements Directive and Regulation ("Basel III") The European Union (Capital Requirements) Regulations 2014 (S.I. No. 158 of 2014) implemented Directive 2013/36/EU, the 2013 fourth Capital Requirements Directive, ("CRD IV"). The European Union (Capital Requirements) (No. 2) Regulations 2014 (S.I. No. 159 of 2014) implemented the necessary administrative arrangements to give effect to the directly applicable companion Regulation (EU) No. 575/2013 on Capital Requirements ("CRR").

The combined effect of the CRD IV and the CRR was to implement in EU law "Basel III", which is a voluntary, but highly influential, framework on bank capital adequacy, stress testing and market liquidity risk agreed by the members of the Basel Committee on Banking Supervision in 2010–2011. Basel III was developed in response to the failures in financial regulation revealed by the global financial crisis of 2007–2008. The intention of Basel III is to strengthen bank capital requirements by increasing bank liquidity and decreasing bank leverage, which was regarded as a key element of the banking crisis that emerged in 2007–2008. The two sets of national implementing Regulations therefore constitute a significant legislative response to the failures of financial service regulations leading up to 2008. They should also be seen as complementing the "six pack" of EU laws on macroeconomic policy agreed at the end of 2011, including budgetary surveillance, intended to strengthen the EU Growth and Stability Pact (discussed in the *Annual Review of Irish Law 2012*, pp.53–55). This EU-based framework also includes the Single Supervisory Mechanism (SSM): see the European Union (Single Supervisory Mechanism) Regulations 2014 (S.I. No. 495 of 2014), discussed under the sub-heading "Single Supervisory Mechanism (SSM) enforcement arrangements" below.

It may be asked why some elements of the Basel III framework were implemented in an EU Directive and other elements in an EU Regulation. The explanation may be that the elements in the CRD IV require that account be taken of national supervisory and enforcement requirements, thus necessitating tailored national implementing legislation. By contrast, the CRR deals with detailed and highly prescriptive provisions on calculating capital requirements, liquidity, leverage, credit operational and market risks. These elements do not depend on matters of national supervision and enforcement and could therefore be dealt with in a directly applicable EU Regulation.

Given their importance, it is unfortunate that neither S.I. No. 158 of 2014 nor S.I. No. 159 of 2014 merited even a brief Explanatory Note to accompany them, a standard formality that is usually attached to even the least significant Statutory Instrument. It is to be noted, however, that the Central Bank, as the national regulator in this area, has published a considerable amount of the explanatory material in the aftermath of the making of the statutory Regulations, which is available at centralbank.ie. Bearing in mind the detailed content of the CRD IV Directive and of the CRR, what follows below is a brief overview.

Overview of CRD IV Directive The CRD IV Directive prescribes detailed rules relating to corporate governance, including remuneration policies, capital buffers and sanctions. It strengthens the requirements with regard to corporate governance arrangements and processes and introduces new rules aimed at increasing the effectiveness of risk oversight by boards, improving the status of the risk management function and ensuring effective monitoring by supervisors of risk governance.

In order to tackle excessive risk taking, the previous remuneration framework has been further strengthened with regard to the requirements for the relationship between the variable (or bonus) component of remuneration and the fixed component (or salary). From 2014 onwards, the variable component of the total remuneration must not exceed 100 per cent of the fixed component of the total remuneration of material risk takers. Exceptionally, and under certain conditions, shareholders can increase this maximum ratio to 200 per cent.

CRD IV also introduced a number of diversity requirements, in particular as regards gender balance on boards. Diversity in board composition should contribute to effective risk oversight by boards, providing for a broader range of views and opinion and therefore avoiding the phenomenon of "group think." CRD IV also sought to improve transparency regarding the activities of banks and investment funds in different countries, in particular, as regards profits, taxes and subsidies in different jurisdictions. This is considered essential for regaining the trust of EU citizens in the financial sector.

CRD IV also introduced new capital buffers. These include a new "capital conservation buffer", a capital buffer of 2.5 per cent of total exposures of a bank that needs to be met with an additional amount of the highest quality of capital (referred to as CET1 capital), which is in addition to a general 4.5 per cent CET1 capital requirement. The buffer's objective is to conserve a bank's capital. When a bank breaches the buffer, that is, when its CET1 capital ratio falls below 7 per cent, automatic safeguards kick in and limit the amount of dividend and bonus payments a bank can make. The further the bank "eats" into the buffer, the stricter the limits become. This prevents the bank's capital from being further eroded by such payments.

A second new capital buffer is the "countercyclical buffer". As its name indicates, it is intended to counteract the effects of the economic cycle on banks' lending activity, thus making the supply of credit less volatile and possibly even reduce the probability of credit bubbles or crunches. It works as follows: in good times, that is, where an economy is booming and credit growth is strong, it requires a bank to have an additional amount of capital (as in the case of the capital conservation buffer, CET1 capital). This is intended to prevent that credit becoming too cheap (there is a cost to the capital that a bank must have) and to prevent banks lending too much. If a bank does not have enough capital to fill this buffer, the same restrictions as in the case of the capital conservation buffer kick in. When the economic cycle turns, and economic activity slows down or even contracts, this buffer can be "released" (that is, the bank is no longer required to have the additional capital). This allows the bank to keep lending to the real economy or at least reduce its lending by less than would otherwise be the case.

Finally, the new rules seek to reduce to the extent possible reliance by credit institutions on external credit ratings by: (a) requiring that all banks' investment decisions are based not only on ratings but also on their own internal credit opinion, and (b) that banks with a material number of exposures in a given portfolio develop internal ratings for that portfolio instead of relying on external ratings for the calculation of their capital requirements.

Overview of the CRR It may be asked why some elements of the CRR deal with the detailed and highly prescriptive provisions on calculating capital requirements, liquidity, leverage, credit, operational and market risks. These elements do not depend on, for example, matters of national supervision and enforcement and could therefore be dealt with in a directly applicable EU Regulation. The CRR provides for a "Single Rulebook" which will contain for the first time a single set of prudential rules for banks and other financial service firms that will be directly applicable in all EU Member States. In this way it is hoped that all EU Member States will apply the rules in Basel III in a consistent manner. The content of the "Single Rulebook" will be set out in a series of detailed delegated European Commission directly applicable Regulations, made under the general authority of the CRR.

Single Supervisory Mechanism (SSM) enforcement arrangements The European Union (Single Supervisory Mechanism) Regulations 2014 (S.I. No. 495 of 2014) (the "2014 Regulations") formed another element of the Single Supervisory Mechanism (SSM) under the aegis of the European Central Bank (ECB), which was established at EU level in the wake of the financial services collapse that emerged in 2007–2008. The 2014 Regulations provided for the necessary administrative arrangements in the State to give full effect to Regulation (EU) No.1024/2013, conferring specific tasks on the ECB concerning policies relating to the prudential supervision of credit institutions, under the general superintendence of the ECB. The 2014 Regulations also gave administrative effect to Regulation (EU) No.468/2014 establishing the framework for co-operation within the SSM between the ECB and national competent authorities and with national designated authorities.

Financial Services Ombudsman Two High Court decisions in 2014 indicate the preference of the courts that the Financial Services Ombudsman (FSO) carry out an oral hearing in any instance where a conflict of fact arises. It is likely that these decisions reflect a growing desire by the High Court to see less appeals from the FSO dispute resolution regime, which have been growing significantly in recent years–notably in the wake of the banking and financial services crisis that emerged in 2007–2008. At the same time, it indicates the burden of investigative responsibility placed on the FSO to deal with such complaints in an oral manner, which may not have been envisaged when the FSO was established in 2004. In any event, the two High Court decisions in 2014 indicate that a considerable number of individual financial services disputes are likely to continue for the foreseeable future.

In the first case, *O'Neill v Financial Services Ombudsman* [2014] IEHC 282, the High Court (Hogan J.) remitted a case to the FSO against the following background. The appellant had made a complaint to the FSO to the effect that his insurance company, Zurich Insurance Plc, had wrongly failed to indemnify him in respect of flood damage to his diesel engine Mercedes van. The appellant's vehicle had been submerged for over five hours following a flood event. It was brought to a garage, where the appellant was informed that the vehicle had severe water damage to the engine and would be written off. The appellant contacted Zurich who appointed an assessor. The assessor requested that the engine be stripped down and rebuilt. The vehicle was subsequently written off and sold for scrap at a fraction of its true value. Zurich only agreed to pay a portion of the significant costs associated with the cost of dismantling the engine. A number of reports were compiled with conflicting conclusions as to the existence of flood damage to the vehicle. Zurich's assessor concluded that there was no real damage caused by the flooding, while the report prepared by the appellant's assessor reached the opposite conclusion. There were also significant factual issues raised by the report prepared by Zurich's assessor, as well as that prepared by the garage, on questions such as whether damp was present in the passenger compartment and whether any of the engine parts had in fact suffered flood damage. In arriving at its conclusions on the merits of the appellant's insurance claim, the FSO referred to the various reports before stating that it was satisfied Zurich was entitled to decline the claim on the grounds that the damage was not caused by flood damage based on the two reports provided by the company's motor assessor. The FSO stated that the case did not present such a conflict of fact such as would require the holding of an oral hearing to resolve any such conflict.

The High Court (Hogan J.), as already indicated, allowed the appeal and remitted the appellant's complaint to the FSO for rehearing, noting that there was a clear conflict of fact central to the resolution of the appellant's complaint. The court pointed out that s.57CI(2)(e) of the Central Bank Act 1942 (the "1942 Act"), as inserted in 2003, provides that "[a] complaint may be found to be substantiated or partly substantiated only on one or more of the following grounds… (e) the conduct complained of was based wholly or partly on a mistake of law or fact." The court held that in a case of this kind, any such mistake of fact would have to be regarded as so fundamental as to engage the supervisory functions of the FSO. If this is so, then the FSO must be prepared to adapt its procedures in order to properly exercise this statutory supervisory power. This means that the claimant must be given an adequate opportunity to demonstrate why the FSO should exercise these powers in aid of his claim on the ground of material error of fact.

The court noted that the FSO process was designed to be a less formal and expeditious method of dispute resolution, operating separately from the ordinary commercial courts and law of contract by reference to criteria almost akin to those applied to public bodies in judicial proceedings. In addition, the FSO's decisions were binding (subject to appeal to the High Court), and that the criteria for review under s.57CI of the 1942 Act were clearly inspired by public law principles rather than standard private law orthodoxies and (citing *Gallagher v ACC Bank* [2012] IEHC 396) that any attempt to re-litigate the same matters would normally be regarded as an abuse of process when it is not otherwise *res judicata*.

The court went on to hold that the power conferred by the 1942 Act, as inserted in 2003, was a classic example of where, by reason of the presumption of constitutionality (as set out in *East Donegal Co-Operative Ltd v Attorney General* [1970] I.R. 317), it is assumed that proceedings, procedures, discretions and adjudications which are permitted, provided for, or prescribed by an Act of the Oireachtas are to be conducted in a manner which conforms to the constitutional guarantee of basic fairness of procedures. As an agent of the State, the FSO was bound (as reaffirmed in *Dellway Investments Ltd v National Asset Management Agency* [2011] IESC 14) to uphold the constitutional right to fair procedures.

Where, as in this case, there was a stark conflict of fact and the resolution of a conflict was central to the fair disposition of the complaint, it was impossible to avoid the conclusion that some form of oral hearing was objectively necessary in order to give effect to this constitutional guarantee. In the circumstances, the requirements of fair procedures compelled the holding of an oral hearing before the FSO. In this respect, the court approved and applied the approach taken in comparable cases such as *Lyons v Financial Services Ombudsman* [2011] IEHC 454, *Hyde v Financial Services Ombudsman* [2011] IEHC 422 and *Smith v Financial Services Ombudsman* [2014] IEHC 40.

Similarly, in the second such case in 2014, *Carty-Doyle v Financial Services Ombudsman* [2014] IEHC 352, the applicant complained to the FSO that an investment she had made in 2005 in the Northern Ireland Property Fund (the "Fund"), carried out through the notice party, was inappropriate on a number of grounds. She alleged that the Fund borrowed over £222 million (500 per cent greater than envisaged) and that this borrowing was raised either via bank loan or via mezzanine finance. She also alleged that the fund was highly leveraged and the risk of loss of capital was increased. It was also alleged that representations had been made to her that the Fund would only be used to invest in commercial property, when, in fact, 70 per cent of the Fund was invested in residential property. She also claimed a management fee of 0.5 per cent of gross assets paid quarterly in arrears created a conflict of interest for the respondent by allegedly encouraging it to increase the gross assets through reckless borrowing to the detriment of investors. In response, the notice party argued information documents on the Fund described it as "high risk" and said it believed it was appropriate for her to invest all her funds in the Fund because, it alleged, she described herself to its representative as a "seasoned" and "successful" investor. The FSO held that there was no conflict of fact such as would require the holding of an oral hearing and that a finding could be made in the absence of an oral hearing. The applicant appealed the finding of the respondent to the High Court pursuant to s.57CL of the 1942 Act, as inserted in 2003.

The High Court (Herbert J.) set aside the finding of the FSO and remitted the matter back to the FSO for review, as had been done in the *O'Neill* case, above. The court held that it had not been open to the FSO to conclude that an oral hearing was not necessary. Regarding the notice party's argument that the applicant was a "seasoned" and "successful" investor, the FSO had concluded that the appellant's prior investment experience did not accord with the description of her as a "seasoned investor." However, the FSO made no finding at all as to whether or not the appellant had, in fact, described herself in discussion in this way, or whether she made the other statements regarding her investment experience. Therefore, the FSO was faced with a clear conflict of fact as to what had been said in discussions between the applicant and the notice party, and the FSO had therefore erred in principle in failing to exercise the discretion to hear oral testimony.

Regarding the risk, the notice party had argued that the applicant had been sent information about the investment and was fully aware of the risk involved. The documents alone did not provide an answer to the question as to why the notice party believed it was appropriate for the appellant to invest all her funds in the Fund, which they identified to be a high-risk investment. The FSO had found that a moderate level of risk was the appellant's "original intention". The court held that the FSO had erred in assuming that the appellant must simply have changed her mind about the degree of risk she was prepared to accept, and there was a very serious and material conflict evident on the face of the documents before the FSO. Consequently, fair procedures clearly required that the FSO should have heard oral testimony from the parties before reaching a conclusion. The FSO, having identified a conflict of fact between the parties as to whether or not the appellant had sought and had been given oral assurances that the Fund would invest in commercial property only, dismissed this claim by the appellant on the basis that there was no independent evidence to support it, when, in fact, there was. The court held that the FSO had therefore erred in fact in not considering properly or at all the appellant's complaint that the impugned investments did not come within the category of potential commercial development opportunities and there was a strong prima facie case that the finding of the FSO was vitiated by serious and significant error in this regard. The court stressed that it did not make any finding whatsoever on the merits or otherwise of the appellant's complaints.

Building society transfers Section 1 of the Central Bank Act 2014 (the "2014 Act") amended the Central Bank Act 1971 (the "1971 Act") in order to permit the transfer of assets and liabilities from what, in 2014, was the only one building society remaining in Ireland, ICS Building Society, to the holder of a banking licence, Bank of Ireland. This facilitated both the State and Bank of Ireland in fulfilling their respective commitments to the European Commission as part of Bank of Ireland's amended restructuring plan.

It was noted during the Oireachtas debates on s.1 of the 2014 Act that, in July 2013, Bank of Ireland agreed an amendment to its restructuring plan, which had previously been agreed by the European Commission in respect of State aid received by the bank. This allowed the bank to retain its life insurance subsidiary, New Ireland Assurance Company. As part of this amendment, the bank committed to certain substitution measures, including the sale of the ICS distribution platform together with, at the option of a purchaser, up to €l billion of mortgages and up to €1 billion of matching deposits. The purpose of the ICS substitution measure was to support new entities in entering the Irish market, thereby increasing competition to the ultimate benefit of the consumer.

Bank of Ireland was not required, under the substitution measures agreed, to sell ICS, but rather to offer for sale the distribution platform together with, at the option of the purchaser, certain assets and liabilities of ICS. The ICS distribution platform includes the ICS brand, the IT system and the broker network. Prior to the 2014 Act, Pt III of the 1971 Act could be used by banks to transfer between one another, their assets and liabilities under a scheme of transfer. The effect of the amendments to the 1971 Act in 2014 was to expand the scope of Part III of the 1971 Act to enable building societies to transfer assets and liabilities to banks using Pt III transfer schemes. The Minister for Finance stated during the Oireachtas debates on the 2014 Act that Pt III transfer schemes had been used successfully by banks many times in the past, and after the enactment of the 2014 Act, a building society would also be able to transfer its assets and liabilities in accordance with the 1971 Act, as amended. Any transfer of assets and liabilities pursuant to the 1971 Act is subject to the approval of the Minister for Finance after consultation with the Central Bank.

It was expected that ICS would apply, pursuant to Pt III of the 1971 Act, to transfer the bulk of its assets and liabilities to Bank of Ireland; and that an onward transfer of some of those assets and liabilities, to a third party, would subsequently be effected. This onward transfer might include up to €l billion of the €6 billion mortgage book held by ICS. The restructuring plan, which had been agreed between Bank of Ireland and the European Commission, requires that the Commission approve the purchaser of the ICS platform. The primary purpose of this condition in the restructuring plan was to encourage competition in the mortgage intermediaries market.

Strategic Banking Corporation of Ireland The Strategic Banking Corporation of Ireland Act 2014 (the "2014 Act") provided for the establishment of the Strategic Banking Corporation of Ireland (the SBCI). The general intention of the 2014 Act was that by increasing the availability of longer term flexible debt finance (appropriately priced), the establishment of the SBCI would provide SMEs with access to the type of "patient intelligent capital" that would increase productive investment, encourage growth and generate additional employment opportunities. In this way the SBCI would play a key role in reinforcing the State's economic recovery. The SBCI would not provide this capital investment directly to SMEs but would instead provide it to licensed banks, who would in turn provide it to SMEs. The important role of SMEs in the economy, employing nearly 70 per cent of the total labour force, was recognised during the Oireachtas debates on the 2014 Act.

Section 2 of the 2014 Act sets out the purposes of the SBCI, that is, to improve the availability of credit to enterprises and other persons in a manner that benefits the economy and the economic well-being of the State. This is achieved by the establishment of a new company, SBCI, which will avail of credit and make credit available through on-lending to enterprises, in particular SMEs. The 2014 Act empowers the Minister for Finance to guarantee the borrowings of the SBCI and to provide funding to it, although it was hoped that in time the SBCI would be able to fund itself without the need for either further loans from the Government or the need to guarantee all of its borrowings.

Part 2 of the 2014 Act (ss.5–10) provides for the establishment of the SBCI. It provides for the formation of the SBCI and group entities. It sets out the functions of the SBCI and outlines the composition of the SBCI board and the SBCI's relationship with the National Treasury Management Agency (the NTMA). Section 5 enables the formation of a private company under the Companies Act, called the Strategic Banking Corporation of Ireland (the SBCI). The SBCI will be independent in carrying out its functions under the Act. Section 5 allows the company to use the word "banking" in its name by disapplying ss.7(1), 8 and 15 of the Central Bank Act 1971 and exempts the SBCI's name from having to end in the suffix "Limited."

Section 6 provides for the SBCI to be able to form, promote or take shareholding in various types of subsidiaries, such as companies or joint ventures, and sets out the terms on which this can be done. These will be known collectively as SBCI group entities. The SBCI is not permitted to guarantee the borrowings or liabilities of any of its subsidiaries without the approval of the Minister for Finance. A definition of the SBCI's group entities is given in s.3. Section 7 provides that the memorandum and articles of association of the SBCI will be consistent with provisions of the legislation. It establishes that no alterations to the documents will be valid without the prior approval of the Minister.

Section 8 sets out the functions of the SBCI. The main functions of the SBCI will be to provide and promote, in a prudent manner, the availability of additional credit in the State suitable to the needs of borrowers, in particular SMEs. The SBCI will encourage more competition in the provision of credit in the State and greater diversity in the types of finance available. The functions of the SBCI will also include sourcing international and domestic funding to facilitate lending and providing finance to projects that contribute to national economic development. Section 9 provides for the SBCI to have a board of not more than nine members including its chairperson. It sets out that the first directors on incorporation will be appointed by the Minister and that subsequent boards and the position of a company secretary will be appointed by the SBCI in accordance with the terms and conditions of appointment set out in the memorandum and articles of association of the SBCI. The Minister will continue to appoint a chairperson from within the board.

Section 10 provides for the SBCI's relationship with the NTMA. It sets out that the NTMA will provide the SBCI and any of its subsidiaries with business and support services and systems that are considered necessary for the SBCI to perform its functions. It will allow these services to be provided either directly or indirectly. Section 10 also provides for the NTMA to assign staff to the SBCI to enable it to perform its functions under the 2014 Act. Under this section, the NTMA may also supply the SBCI with treasury services and advice in connection with debt securities and borrowings of the SBCI. The NTMA may also enter into transactions of a normal banking nature as an agent of the SBCI. The NTMA will be reimbursed by the SBCI for the costs incurred under this section. The NTMA will be also able to perform similar functions for subsidiaries of the SBCI.

Part 3 of the 2014 Act (ss.11–17) sets out the funding arrangements of the SBCI. Section 11 provides for the determination of the authorised share capital of the SBCI by the Minister for Finance, and for the initial issue of shares in the new company to the Minister. It also provides that the SBCI will issue shares to the value of €10 million to the Minister. This €10 million of equity capital will come from the National Pensions Reserve Fund (the NPRF).

The authorised share capital will be €250 million or a higher amount as the Minister may decide. However, the authorised share capital may never go above €1 billion. If the SBCI determines that further equity is required to meet its financial obligations as they fall due, it may issue further share capital to the Minister in exchange for the conversion of the outstanding loans from the NPRF, the Central Fund or a combination of both. Any change to the share capital will be laid before the Oireachtas. As already noted, it was not intended that all borrowings of the SBCI will need to be guaranteed by the State.

The 2014 Act provides flexibility around the value of the SBCI's share capital and gives the Minister the power to pay in authorised share capital at the request of the SBCI. This was done to facilitate a flexible capital structure known as callable capital. It is used by the European Investment Bank (the EIB), among others, to facilitate funding of an institution without the need to guarantee all borrowings. This model will be beneficial in the medium term but will not be used in the initial start-up phase of the SBCI. Callable capital involves an agreement with the lenders to a company that, should a certain balance sheet position be reached, the borrowing company will increase the amount of its issued and paid-in capital to a pre-agreed level. In the interim, the lender will lend to the borrower on the basis that the authorised share capital has been set to at least that level, and it is usually happy to lend even if the paid-in capital is a fraction of the authorised capital. This has a potential benefit in that there is no need to issue a guarantee for further borrowings.

Section 12 of the 2014 Act provides that the Minister can dispose of shares in the SBCI as he or she sees fit. Any fund received in respect of the shares will go to the Exchequer, for example, proceeds of sales or redemptions of shares. If the Minister is disposing of shares in the SBCI, the reasons for the disposal must be given to the Oireachtas. It is not intended that the Minister for Finance will sell shares, but flexibility to do so has been included.

Section 13 provides that the SBCI may borrow money in any currency through any type of debt it sees as appropriate. Section 13 limits the amount of borrowings that the SBCI can have outstanding at any particular time to €4 billion. If the SBCI were to borrow in a foreign currency, those borrowings would be valued using the European Central Bank's published exchange rates. Section 13 also allows the SBCI to engage in transactions of a normal banking nature for the purposes of carrying out its functions.

Section 14 amended s.54 of the Finance Act 1970 to allow the Minister to engage in normal banking transactions with the SBCI. Under this section, the Minister may issue funds from the Exchequer for the purposes of those transactions and any associated cost arising out of them. Broadly speaking, this is an enabling provision and is common when introducing a State entity that involves borrowing.

Section 15 provides for the Minister to give directions to the National Pensions Reserve Fund Commission with which the Commission must comply. Section 15 empowers the Minister to direct the Commission to provide credit to the SBCI and to provide funding to same to fund the subscription of the Minister's shares in the company. The Minister may also exercise any right based on a direction or terminate the terms of a direction.

Section 16 sets out the maximum amount of funding that the SBCI can be given by the State, which is €5 billion. It explains that the funding of the SBCI includes any loan, investment, exchange of assets, subscription for securities, debt securities, issued share capital and callable capital.

Section 17 allows for the SBCI board to decide what dividends are to be paid to the Minister. It also provides that any money received by the Minister in respect of his share in the company, including dividends, shall be paid into the Exchequer in such a manner as the Minister directs.

Part 4 of the 2014 Act provides for issuing guarantees by the Minister. Section 18 empowers the Minister to guarantee any money borrowed by the SBCI up to a maximum of €4 billion aggregate of all guarantees outstanding. Accrued interest does not count towards this maximum amount. The details of any guarantee provided for by s.18 shall be laid before the Houses of the Oireachtas as soon as may be after it is given. Guarantees would only be used when specifically required to enable borrowings from external providers of loans to the SBCI.

Part 5 sets out the procedures for ensuring the public accountability of the SBCI. Section 19 provides that the SBCI must submit its accounts to the Comptroller and Auditor General for audit within two months of the financial year to which they relate. The audited consolidated accounts will also be presented to the Minister and laid before each House of the Oireachtas. Section 20 provides that a senior member of the staff of the SBCI nominated by its chairperson will, whenever required by the Committee of Public Accounts, give evidence to that committee on the accounts and reports of the Comptroller and Auditor General into the SBCI.

Part 6 of the 2014 Act contains two miscellaneous provisions. Section 21 provides that the Minister, the National Treasury Management Agency (NTMA) and the NTMA's employees and staff are not to be considered either shadow directors under s.27(1) of the Companies Act 1990 or de facto directors of the SBCI. It is intended that the board of the NTMA be covered in this respect, ensuring that the Minister and the NTMA can carry out their various other functions without their involvement with the SBCI being a block to that work.

Section 22 provides that certain provisions of the Companies Acts will not apply to the SBCI. These provisions ensure that the Minister's relationship with the SBCI does not prevent him from carrying out any of his other functions and avoids redundant reporting requirements in the administration of the SBCI.

Part 7 of the 2014 Act, comprising s.23, sets out a number of tax exemptions that will apply to the SBCI and any subsidiary wholly owned by same. This is a standard provision for all companies and subsidiaries wholly-owned by the Minister for Finance. It is valid as long as the Minister remains the sole shareholder and, therefore, is the sole beneficiary of such tax exemptions. Section 23 also provides that income and gains arising to the SBCI or a wholly-owned subsidiary of same will be exempt from dividend withholding tax, corporation tax, DIRT, interest withholding tax, capital gains tax and stamp duty.

INDUSTRIAL AND PROVIDENT SOCIETIES AND FRIENDLY SOCIETIES

The Friendly Societies and Industrial and Provident Societies (Miscellaneous Provisions) Act 2014 (the "2014 Act") amended the Industrial and Provident Societies Act 1893 and the Friendly Societies Act 1896, both of which are regulated by the Registrar of Friendly Societies. It was noted during the passage of the 2014 Act that industrial and provident societies had developed in the late 19th century in rural areas, with an emphasis on farming co-operatives and agricultural banks; whereas friendly societies were largely an urban phenomenon, many offering insurance-type services, making payments and offering support at times of death, illness or inability to work.

It was also noted that co-operatives had played a significant role in the State's economic and social development during the years, particularly in the agrifood sector through groups such as Kerry Group, Glanbia and Dairygold. Co-operatives also played significant roles through the livestock marts that operate in nearly every county or even more directly through their group water schemes which account for more than one third of all registered co-operatives. Housing co-operatives also play a significant role in the provision of group and affordable housing for people with modest incomes through a mix of renting and ownership.

It was noted that the picture was somewhat different nowadays on the friendly societies side. While these societies had done great good in their day and, in the context of the small number that remained in 2014, continued to do, it had become clear in recent years that this was not a corporate model of choice in the 21st century. In fact, just three of the existing 47 societies had registered in between 2005 and 2014. It could be argued that the friendly society model had been a victim of its own success. As many of the activities carried out under the friendly societies umbrella developed, they became independently regulated sectors, for example, insurance and medical benefits societies, or were replaced by State-provided welfare systems.

In this context, there was concern about a "prudential supervision gap." While the Central Bank regulates savings, loan and insurance activities carried out by entities involved in the provision of financial services with a view to protecting the financial interests of members of the public doing business with the provider of the financial services, it did not do so where these activities were carried out by friendly societies. This was a source of some concern, given the potential risk to the interests of certain members of the public who may not be aware of their exposure and believe they are protected by the general regulatory activity of the Central Bank. As such, it was in the public interest to restrict the operation of new entities. However, the Registry of Friendly Societies had no expertise in this regard and there was no existing legal basis for such supervision, nor would it be practical, given the number of societies involved, to develop a dedicated supervisory regime within the existing registry. The most realistic institutional option for introducing an appropriate system of supervision was the Central Bank, which is at the center of financial supervision and financial stability oversight. The Central Bank also has a responsibility to provide, in a fully integrated and coordinated manner, for the prudential supervision and stability of all types of financial service within the financial system as a whole. To avoid the possibility of other bodies moving into this unregulated space, it had therefore been decided to close registrations to new friendly societies, and the 2014 Act provided for this.

The reasons given for amending the friendly societies legislation instead of introducing a new Act or Acts were twofold. First, this was to avoid diverting effort and resources away from the work on what was enacted as the Companies Act 2014. Secondly, the Companies Act 2014 will, to a certain extent, impact on how related issues in the co-operatives area will operate. There is no principled reason for the approach taken by the Companies Act 2014 on matters such as registration and financial reporting not to apply to friendly societies and co-operatives in due course also.

The 2014 Act is therefore aimed primarily at easing the regulatory burden on co-operative societies and making it easier to start up and run a co-operative as an alternative form of enterprise organisation. It addresses particular problems that have been identified in the co-operative sector and helps to ensure this model will thrive and grow to its potential. The 2014 Act also recognises the changing environment in which friendly societies operate and the lack of prudential supervision governing activities that, if carried out by other entities, would be subject to regulatory oversight and seeks to address these issues. Once the Companies Act 2014 was enacted, the intention was to prepare modern legislation to cater for the co-operative sector and existing friendly societies.

Part 2 of the 2014 Act (ss.4–8) relates to the operation of the Friendly Societies Act 1896 (the "1896 Act"). Section 5 provides for a significant change to the 1896 Act, that is, the termination of registration of societies under the 1896 Act. As already noted, only 47 societies remained in existence in 2014, of which just three were new entrants between 2005 and 2014; giving a clear indication that the friendly society model was no longer favoured by newly establishing organisations. This change will mean, in effect, that the friendly society model will continue only for a closed group of societies.

Section 6 places a restriction on existing societies establishing a loan fund, as provided for in s.46 of the 1896 Act, where they do not already have such a fund in place. This has been a little used provision–just three societies had a fund in place and this change will not impact on them.

Section 7 removes the role of the Minister in relation to cancellations of friendly societies. Under the 1896 Act, the Registrar of Friendly Societies must receive the prior approval of the Minister before cancelling societies. Section 7 removed this role in relation to friendly societies and also later in the 2014 Act to industrial and provident societies. It was noted that the Minister has no such role in relation to a company strike-off and that "such a role for a political authority is inappropriate in modern times."

Section 8 removes the restriction in the 1896 Act providing that the registrar must be physically absent for the powers, functions and duties to be exercised and performed by such other person as the Minister may authorise and allows another person to act alongside the registrar.

Part 3 of the 2014 Act (ss.9–12) relates to the operation of the Industrial and Provident Societies Act 1893 (the "1893 Act"). Section 10 sets out a number of amendments to the 1893 Act. It was explained that these relate to issues which were identified through a consultation process as being practical and immediate difficulties being experienced by co-operative societies in relation to the 1893 Act and that the amendments would ease the administrative burden for the co-operative sector.

Section 10(a) provides for the removal of the upper limit on the interest in a society which an individual society member may hold, where a society so specifies in its rules. The pre-2014 limit was €150,000, or 1 per cent of the total assets of the society, which had been set in 2005. This was generally suitable for all categories of society, although there was a risk that it may deter the formation of new societies having small memberships but high capital requirements, for example, wind farms. The original rationale for having a statutory limit on individual shareholdings is believed to be connected with the notion of equal participation by the members of a co-operative enterprise. This objective, however, can be fully achieved by co-operatives themselves through the medium of their own rules and without the need for legislative intervention.

Section 10(b) provides that an appeal from a refusal by the registrar to register a society, or to register a society's rules, may be made to the Circuit Court, rather than the High Court, as was the case prior to 2014. This should reduce costs for societies.

Section 10(c) made two amendments, including providing for the removal of the requirement for the Minister to approve the cancellation of a society's registration.

Section 10(e) provides that annual returns to the registrar may be submitted on one of two dates during the year, depending on the date of a society's financial year, that is, the date to which their balance sheet is made up. This allows societies freedom regarding their choice of year-end and extends the timeframe for the submission of the return. The pre-2014 system was restrictive and caused difficulties for societies, the annual business cycles of which do not accord with the dates set down in the 1893 Act, such as dairy societies which wish to bring their reporting year into line with the dairy production year.

Section 10(f) extends the right of members or persons having an interest in the funds of the society to inspect the books containing the names of members to include their holdings in the society, whether in shares or loans. This was, it appears, already the practice among many co-operative societies.

Section 10(g) provides for a right for non-members to inspect the books containing the names of members and their holdings in shares at reasonable hours at the registered office of the society. This section was modelled on a similar provision in the Companies Acts. Without this amendment, non-members would have no ability to access the membership or holding details of a society, because the requirement to make a triennial return, which contained that information, was repealed by the 2014 Act.

It was noted that the co-operative sector had sought the abolition of the requirement for societies to submit, at least once in every three years, a return, known as a triennial return, of the members and their holdings to the registrar. The sector had argued that the information is out of date too quickly to be useful and imposes an unnecessary administrative burden on societies. Section 11, therefore, in accordance with what proved to be general agreement that this return served no useful purpose, abolishes this requirement. Section 10(g) provides that both members and non-members will now be able to access information on members and their shareholdings directly through the co-operative society.

Section 12 of the 2014 Act provides for a number of amendments to the Industrial and Provident Societies (Amendment) Act 1978. It provides for an increase in the amount which a society may raise by way of subscription for shares, without the written permission of the registrar, from €12,697 (£10,000) to €30,000. It also extends the provision whereby certain funding sources are excluded from the requirement to obtain the written permission of the registrar to include moneys advanced by a public body to a registered society. This will remove the need for societies to seek the prior permission of the registrar before they can accept funds from a public body or where the amount of share capital raised in any period of six months does not exceed €30,000. The change meets the concerns of some societies affected, particularly building co-operatives, that the current restrictions are excessive.

Part 4 of the 2014 Act (ss.13–25) provides for the examinership provisions of the Companies (Amendment) Act 1990, as amended (the "1990 Act"), to be made available to co-operative societies. Examinership is a mechanism used to enable companies in financial difficulties to be put back on a sound footing and avoid liquidation. Prior to 2014, this mechanism was not available to industrial and provident societies. The practical effect is to limit the restructuring options available to a co-operative society in the event that it gets into financial difficulties.

A small number of sections or parts of sections of the 1990 Act are, for various reasons, disapplied for the purpose of the Act's application to industrial and provident societies. For example, s.6A is disapplied, as the provisions of the Companies Acts in relation to receivers do not apply to industrial and provident societies. Section 15 construes phrases in the 1990 Act which apply specifically to companies to the nearest equivalent definition or meaning for industrial and provident societies.

Section 16 applies s.2 of the 1990 Act, as amended by the Companies (Miscellaneous Provisions) Act 2013, which allows certain private companies to initiate proceedings in the Circuit Court, rather than the High Court. This also establishes what is meant by a "small society" which was not an existing concept in terms of co-operative societies. The criteria used to define a "small society" are similar to those used to define a "small private company."

Section 17 deals with the issue of who may petition for protection of the court, with certain modifications needed with regard to industrial and provident societies. It specifies the number of members of the society required to present a petition. The number equates with the existing proportion of members who are permitted by the Industrial and Provident Societies Act 1893 to request the registrar to investigate a society. For ease of reference, the section also restates and updates the references to the list of societies comprehended by s.3(2)(c) of the 1990 Act. By restating the list in the 2014 Act, the necessity to refer to Acts other than the 1990 Act is avoided. Additionally, as the list is not directly applicable to all industrial and provident societies, non-relevant elements are excluded. Section 17 also expands the definition of "director" to include the committee of management or other directing body of an industrial and provident society.

Section 20 substitutes the reference in ss. 7, 18 and 24 to the Companies Acts with the Industrial and Provident Society Act 1893 to reflect the fact that the Industrial and Provident Societies Acts rather than the Companies Acts provide the governing legislation for societies. Section 21 removes the reference to "shadow director" which is not a term which has an equivalent meaning in the context of an industrial and provident society. Section 25 restates the offences in the 1990 Act and was updated to equate with the provisions in the Companies Act 2014. It also provides that summary proceedings in relation to an offence under this section may be brought by the Registrar of Friendly Societies.

INTELLECTUAL PROPERTY

Patents and trade marks The Intellectual Property (Miscellaneous Provisions) Act 2014 amended the Patents Act 1992 (*Annual Review of Irish Law 1992*, pp.41–46) in order to give additional legal protection for medical research carried out prior to obtaining regulatory approval for new or generic drugs for human and veterinary use. The 2014 Act also amended the Trade Marks Act 1996 (*Annual Review of Irish Law 1996*, pp.68–76) to enable the State to ratify the Singapore Treaty on the Law of Trademarks, which is intended to reduce the administrative burden on trademark applicants worldwide.

Intellectual property law and international competitiveness During the Oireachtas debates on the 2014 Act the Minister for Jobs, Enterprise and Innovation noted that the amendments provided for in the 2014 Act were to be considered against the general background of supporting innovation and business. It was pointed out that patents add enormous economic value to new inventions by granting them a 20 year monopoly and enabling the commercial exploitation of novel ideas in the marketplace; while trade marks ensure businesses can promote brand identity and safeguard hard-won reputations for quality products and services by protecting brands from illegal imitation. The Minister stated that the pace of legislative change had accelerated in the area of intellectual property (IP) in recent years and that it was no longer sufficient simply to update IP legislation once every decade or so. It was stated that IP protection was a key factor in attracting foreign direct investment and that Ireland scored strongly in this area. He referred to a Grant Thornton Report published in 2014 which had highlighted that key decision-makers involved in making investment decisions stressed the importance of an effective and responsive IP regime, combined with research and development benefits, rating this even more highly than tax incentives. A 2013 international study carried out jointly by the European offices overseeing patents and trademarks pointed to the fact that, in Ireland, IP intensive industries accounted for almost 49 per cent of Irish GDP and 22 per cent of employment.

Patents and research preceding placing medicinal products on market Section 2 of the 2014 Act inserted a new s.42(h) into the Patents Act 1992 (the "1992 Act"), which expanded the limitation of effect of a patent for acts done in order to satisfy the application requirements for marketing authorisation for a medicinal product or a veterinary medicinal product in any State, whether an EU Member State or otherwise. This amendment owes its origin to Directive 2001/82/EC and Directive 2001/83/EC on the placing of human medicinal and veterinary medicinal products on the market, as amended by Directive 2004/27/EC (the "2004 Directive"). The 2004 Directive had provided for protection of medical researchers from patent infringement for acts done while seeking regulatory approval in the course of developing a generic drug. The 2004 Directive had been implemented in Irish law by the European Communities (Limitation of Effect of Patent) Regulations 2006 (S.I. No. 50 of 2006) (the "2006 Regulations"), which had inserted s.42(g) into the 1992 Act. Section 42 of the 1992 Act, as originally enacted, had protected certain acts such as those done privately for non-commercial purposes or acts done for experimental purposes from prosecution as patent infringements. Section 42(g), as inserted by the 2006 Regulations, broadened the scope of s.42, with the effect that since then any acts done in conducting studies and tests necessary for regulatory approval for medicinal products were also not regarded as patent infringements. This allowed generic drug manufacturers to carry out the various studies and tests necessary for regulatory approval or marketing authorisation to place generic drugs on the market.

The 2006 Regulations had correctly implemented the 2004 Directive but the Minister noted that several EU member states, including Germany, had taken a more expansionist approach and had adopted a broader research exemption. The Minister stated that this enhanced legal certainty for the pharma sector had been cited by the industry as an incentive to undertaking medical research and testing in those jurisdictions which introduced it; and that the broader research exemption had grown in popularity among EU member states and was valued by the pharma sector when investment options in Europe were considered.

The Minister noted that the United Kingdom had also implemented similar changes to its research exemption. The expanded research provision in s.42 of the 1992 Act, as amended by the 2014 Act, would therefore assist the pharma sector to continue to invest and undertake important research and development activities in Ireland within a legal framework that provided greater clarity as to what is possible without fear of infringing existing patents. In this respect the Minister noted that Ireland exported more than €21 billion of medicinal and pharmaceutical products in 2013.

Trade marks and Singapore Treaty on the Law of Trademarks Section 3(1) of the 2014 Act amended ss.29(3) and 29(4) of the Trade Marks Act 1996 (the "1996 Act") in order to ensure compliance with art.19(2) of the Singapore Treaty on the Law of Trademarks by allowing unregistered trade mark licensees to join the registered proprietor in infringement proceedings and by requiring the registration of the licence for the sole purpose of claiming costs arising in the course of those proceedings. These changes enabled the State to accede to the treaty.

It was noted during the Oireachtas debates on the 2014 Act that the Singapore Treaty was adopted in 2006 under the auspices of the World Intellectual Property

Organization. It revised and updated the previous 1994 Trade Mark Law Treaty, which Ireland had already ratified. The key objective of the Singapore Treaty is to create a modern and dynamic international framework, to harmonise administrative trademark registration procedures.

It was noted that, by 2014, there were 38 contracting parties to the Singapore Treaty, including 17 EU member states, and that much of the legislative requirements to accede to the treaty were already in place in Irish law. Prior to 2014, the 1996 Act had imposed an excessively high penalty on licensees who failed to register their details with the Irish Patents Office within the prescribed time period. The amendments made to the 1996 Act by the 2014 Act provided that an unregistered trade mark licensee may join a registered proprietor in infringement proceedings against a third party and receive part of the proceeds of damages following a successful infringement action. This is in line with the provisions of the Singapore Treaty.

NATIONAL TREASURY MANAGEMENT AGENCY

The National Treasury Management Agency (Amendment) Act 2014 (the "2014 Act") involved four principal elements. First, it established the Ireland Strategic Investment Fund (the ISIF). The ISIF will take over the assets of the National Pensions Reserve Fund (the NPRF) and use the discretionary assets of the fund, which stood at €6.9 billion in March 2014, for investment in the Irish economy in order to promote economic growth and help foster employment. Secondly, it placed the New Economy and Recovery Authority (NewERA) on a statutory basis. NewERA was established as a business unit of the NTMA, providing financial and commercial advice on commercial semi-states to shareholding Ministers. Thirdly, it will restructure the corporate governance of the National Treasury Management Agency (the NTMA) and its associated entities. The NTMA governance structures had become relatively complex as a result of the assignment of additional functions to the NTMA since it was established under the National Treasury Management Agency Act 1990 (the "1990 Act"). Under the amendments to the 1990 Act, made by the 2014 Act the NTMA, in addition to its core function of borrowing on behalf of the Exchequer and managing the national debt, will be directly responsible for the ISIF, NewERA, the functions of the National Development Finance Agency (the NDFA) and the State Claims Agency. Fourthly, the 2014 Act provided a statutory basis for the Legal Costs Unit within the State Claims Agency, which deals with claims against State bodies. The Legal Costs Unit was established to deal with third-party costs arising from certain tribunals of inquiry.

The NTMA was established under the 1990 Act, to borrow on behalf of the Exchequer and to manage the national debt. The agency was established outside normal public sector structures, with operational freedom to negotiate market-competitive salaries. This business model was designed to enable the NTMA to compete with the private sector and attract and retain specialists in mid-career who would not normally be attracted to working in a public sector environment.

Over the years, the NTMA's remit has been considerably extended. The principal additional functions are as follows. The agency is the manager of the National Pensions Reserve Fund, which was established in 2001. The investment of the fund is the responsibility of the NPRF Commission. The agency is the body through which the National Development Finance Agency performs its functions. The NDFA was established in 2003. Its role is to provide financial advice to State bodies undertaking major public investment projects and to procure and deliver public private partnership projects (PPP) in sectors other than transport and local authorities. It also procures non-PPP schools on behalf of the Department of Education and Skills. The agency, acting through its NewERA unit, provides advice to shareholding Ministers in relation to commercial semi-states. The agency is responsible for providing risk management advice and claims management assistance to State authorities with the aim of ensuring that the State's liabilities and expenses are contained at the lowest achievable level. The agency is known as the State Claims Agency when dealing with claims against State bodies. The agency also provides business services and staff to NAMA.

The NTMA does not have a board, although it does have an advisory committee whose role is to advise on matters referred to it by the agency. The chief executive of the NTMA is directly responsible to the Minister for the performance of the functions of the agency. The chief executive reports directly to the Minister on the NTMA's funding and debt management, State Claims Agency and NewERA functions. To that extent the NTMA is more like a government department than a State agency.

The NPRF, NDFA and NAMA were established under their own governing legislation and each has its own governing body. The NTMA acts as the executive in respect of the NPRF and the NDFA. It assigns staff to NAMA and also provides it with business and support services and systems. The NTMA chief executive is ex officio a member of the NPRF Commission and the board of NAMA and the chairman of the NDFA. A director of the NTMA acts as CEO of the NDFA.

The governance structure under which the NTMA operated had become unwieldy and complex as new functions had been bolted on. As NewERA, the ISIF and the Legal Costs Unit were put on a statutory footing, the opportunity was taken in the 2014 Act to simplify and streamline the governance structures of the NTMA and its associated entities. The 2014 converted the NTMA into a body with members, effectively a board. It will have a total of nine members; six members appointed by the Minister for Finance, serving a five-year term, and, ex officio, the chief executive officer of the NTMA, the Secretary General of the Department of Finance and the Secretary General of the Department of Public Expenditure and Reform. The Minister for Finance will nominate one of the appointed members as chairperson. The reconstituted NTMA will continue to be directly responsible for the borrowing and debt management functions, as well as the State Claims Agency and various other functions such as the Central Treasury Service, just as it had been prior to 2014. In addition, it will be directly responsible for the Ireland Strategic Investment Fund and NDFA functions, rather than acting on behalf of other statutory bodies, and it will have NewERA. No changes were included in the 2014 Act to the pre-2014 arrangements in respect of NAMA.

On foot of the changes in the 2014 Act, the NTMA advisory committee and the NDFA and its board will be dissolved, as will the State Claims Agency policy committee. The NPRF Commission will also be dissolved.

Part 3 of the 2014 Act established NewERA on a statutory basis. NewERA had already been established on an interim basis as part of the NTMA, for the purposes of providing financial and commercial advice on commercial semi-states to shareholding Ministers. Financial and commercial advice covers advice on a wide range of matters: a Minister's statutory role, exercising rights as a shareholder, governance, expected rates of return, dividend policy, corporate and investment strategy, acquisitions and disposals, as well as appointments and the remuneration of directors and the chief executive. NewERA will not have an executive role in its own right. It is a dedicated source of commercial advice for relevant Ministers who will continue to carry out their executive functions. NewERA will also be able to provide project management services and oversight in respect of acquisitions, disposals and restructurings, at the request of a relevant Minister.

The 2014 Act sets out the designated commercial semi-state bodies on which NewERA will provide advice. They are the ESB, Ervia (formerly Bord Gáis Eireann), Irish Water, Bord na Móna, Coillte Teoranta, EirGrid and any other State body specified by order. The 2014 Act provides that NewERA may provide financial and commercial advisory functions relating to other bodies if requested by the Minister with responsibility for the body.

The 2014 Act empowered the Minister for Public Expenditure and Reform to give directions to NewERA as to the performance of its functions. He or she must first consult the Minister for Finance and any relevant shareholding Minister. This mirrors the ministerial power of direction over other NTMA functions. Any such directions must be published. NewERA will be required to submit a report on the financial performance of each of the commercial semi-States under its remit to the Minister for Public Expenditure and Reform and relevant Ministers each year.

The 2014 Act also provides that NewERA, in consultation with relevant Ministers, may develop proposals for investment in order to support economic activity and employment in energy, water, telecommunications and forestry and any other sector that is specified by Order.

Part 4 of the 2014 Act confers on NewERA responsibility for the role in relation to infrastructure projects previously carried out by the National Development Finance Agency, NDFA. The NDFA was established in 2003 to provide a financial advisory service to State authorities in respect of capital projects over a certain size, at present €20 million. The NDFA and its board will be dissolved and its functions will be assigned to NewERA.

Part 5 of the 2014 Act established a legal costs unit within the State Claims Agency to oversee third-party costs awarded by certain tribunals of inquiry. The NTMA, as the State Claims Agency, manages personal injury claims, including bullying and harassment and third party property damage claims against specified State authorities, as well as associated risks. On foot of a Government decision, the State Claims Agency had already begun to advise on costs awarded by the Mahon Tribunal of Inquiry on planning matters and the Moriarty Tribunal of Inquiry on payments to politicians. The 2014 Act placed this function on a statutory basis. This was done to minimise the State's exposure and deliver significant savings to the Exchequer because third party costs represent the bulk of Tribunal costs. These costs are awarded in principle by tribunals and their amounts are determined in retrospect.

Part 6 of the 2014 Act established the Ireland Strategic Investment Fund, ISIF. The assets and the liabilities of the NPRF, just over €20 billion at the end of March 2014, became the assets and liabilities of the ISIF. The NPRF was set up as an investment fund to supplement Exchequer resources from 2025, when the burden of social welfare and public service pensions is expected to have increased considerably. The NPRF was invested on a global basis accordingly. A portion of the fund was used to recapitalise the banks during the financial crisis that emerged in 2008. These investments were worth some €13 billion at the end of March 2014 and were held at the direction of the Minister for Finance. The balance in the fund, €6.9 billion at the end of March 2014, will be used by the NTMA for investment on a commercial basis in a manner designed to support economic activity and employment in the State. The intention is to make funding available across the board for infrastructure, SMEs and other matters. It was noted during the Oireachtas debates on the 2014 Act that while the issue of the future cost of pensions had not gone away, it was considered that fostering economic activity and employment in Ireland was a greater priority in the circumstances of 2014 and that the resources of the NPRF should be redeployed accordingly.

The NTMA will set the overall investment strategy for the NPRF and in so doing will consult the Minister for Finance and the Minister for Public Expenditure and Reform and have regard to views expressed by them. An investment committee will be established by the NTMA, which will be responsible for individual decisions in line with the investment strategy and within parameters set by the agency. The 2014 Act carried over from the National Pension Reserve Fund Act 2009 the power of the Minister to direct that the NPRF be used to recapitalise the banks. This was done as a pragmatic precautionary measure and it was stated during the Oireachtas debates that it was not envisaged that the provision would ever be used. However, if for whatever reason, the Government needed to provide funding for the financial system, the likelihood is that it would need to be in a position to do so quickly.

Part 7 of the 2014 Act dissolved the National Pensions Reserve Fund Commission, the National Development Finance Agency, the NTMA Advisory Committee and the State Claims Policy Committee.

Part 8 contains two provisions. Section 54 allows Ministers to provide guarantees or indemnities in respect of borrowings by State authorities in respect of public private partnerships, PPPs. Section 55 allows the NTMA to use the Personal Public Service Number (PPSN) as a unique identifier for its State savings retail investment products.

Company and Insolvency Law

NOEL McGRATH
Lecturer in Law, Sutherland School of Law, UCD

DISQUALFICITION

In *Director of Corporate Enforcement v Walsh; Re Wallfab Engineering Ltd and Re RPB Products Ltd* [2014] IEHC 365 the High Court considered an application for the restriction of directors. The respondents were the directors of two companies which had jointly engaged in a metal fabrication business. The businesses had been profitable for many years but fell into financial difficulties as a consequence of the general downturn in the construction sector of the economy following the 2008 economic crash. Both companies were struck off the registrar under s.12 of the Companies (Amendment) Act 1982 for failing to file an annual return. The Director of Corporate Enforcement then sought an order disqualifying the respondent directors under s.160(2)(h) of the Companies Act 1990 (the "1990 Act") for failure to file the annual return.

The court began by recalling the decision in *Re Clawhammer Ltd* [2005] 1 I.R. 503 at 510 in which it was held that failure to file annual returns should be seen as a merely 'technical' breach of the companies' legislation as there may be practical consequences for both members and creditors if a company is struck off rather than liquidated in the normal course of events. Barrett J. then reviewed the existing authorities on the making of restriction orders under s.160 of the 1990 Act, citing inter alia, *Business Communications Ltd v Baxter*, unreported, High Court, Murphy J., 21 July 1995 and *Re Newcastle Timber Ltd* [2001] 4 I.R. 586. The court considered that these authorities clearly establish that the making of a disqualification order is discretionary and that the court should not exercise that discretion lightly. In exercising its discretion, Barrett J. suggested that the court should consider a number of factors:

Scale of the enterprise and qualification of the directors The court may have regard to the "personal circumstances and social background" of those who appear before it in order to "dispense measured justice and avoid unmerited harshness of treatment." In particular Barrett J. noted that two of the respondent directors were metal fabricators by profession and were not professionally qualified directors who had served at the helm of publically quoted companies. The third respondent was the wife of one of the other directors and took no active part in the operation of the company. Barrett J. found that she had been appointed "perhaps to satisfy the minimum two-director requirement that arises under law."

Context in which director transgressions occur The court should view the failure to file annual returns against the background of an unprecedented economic collapse. The court emphasised the serious nature of the failures which had occurred in this case, noting that the conduct of the directors might be classed as foolish or unwise, but held that their conduct had to be considered in light of the fact that the directors were faced with "economic challenges of such a scale and swiftness that customary practices such as the filing of returns may not have had the priority … that legal requirements ought generally to have."

Past behaviour of the respondents Barrett J. cited the decision in *Re Kentford Ltd* [2011] 1 I.R. 585 at 601, in which O'Donnell J., giving the judgment of the Supreme Court, held that s.160 "directs attention to that past conduct as certainly the best, if not the only, guide to the necessity for disqualification." On the facts the court noted aside from the failure to submit the annual returns which led to the striking off of the companies concerned, the court's attention had not been drawn to any other misbehaviour on the part of the directors over an extended period in office.

Having regard to the above factors the court declined to exercise its discretion to make an order disqualifying the directors. Barrett J. then considered whether it was appropriate to make, in the alternative, an order restricting the directors under s.160(9A) of the Companies Act 1990.

Barrett J. held that the effect of this section is to create a further discretion for a court to consider whether a s.150 order is appropriate in circumstances where it has already rejected an application for disqualification under s.160. Once the court has decided to go "down the path of considering whether a s.150 declaration falls to be made, … the court is trammelled by all the requirements of s.150, most notably that if the criteria set by that provision are satisfied the issuance of a restriction order is mandatory." Barrett J. did not expressly explain why the court opted to consider making an order to restrict the directors. Instead, he continued by considering whether the directors had acted honestly and responsibly and whether they had acted in a manner which made it just and equitable to justify making a s.150 order against them. On the basis of the facts already considered earlier in the judgment, Barrett J. declined to make any order against the directors, finding that though their conduct in failing to make annual returns and acquiescing in the striking off of the company was reproachable, when viewed in context the "respondents' various actions [were] not of such a category as would merit their being described as less than responsible."

Disqualification for Failure to File Accounts and Annual Returns In *Director of Corporate Enforcement v Liwosz and Brown; Re Aventine Resources plc* [2014] IEHC 611 the High Court considered an application from the Director of Corporate Enforcement to disqualify the two respondent directors under s.160(b) and (f) of the Companies Act 1990. The application focused on the failure by the directors to finalise the company's accounts over a period of several years and the fact that the company was in breach of two High Court orders requiring it to file outstanding annual returns. The court found the following facts:

(a) The 2008 and 2009 accounts and financial statements were filed late and were subsequently disclaimed by the company's auditors on the basis that they had insufficient audit evidence to justify their forming an opinion as to the appropriateness of the going concern basis in preparing the financial statements;

(b) The 2010, 2011 and 2012 accounts and financial statements had not been finalised and had not been laid before an AGM of the company;
(c) The annual returns for these years had not been filed with the CRO;
(d) The company had been in breach of two High Court orders made under s.371 Companies Act 1963, as amended, requiring the accounts and financial statements for 2010 and 2011 to be laid before an AGM and for it to complete its annual return for those years.

The first respondent had been a non-executive director of the company from 2005 to February 2008 and was re-appointed to the board in July 2008. His evidence explained that the failures to comply with the company's obligations arose from its impecunious financial position which prevented the commissioning of the necessary professional advice. He also averred that he had received no remuneration from the company for his activities between 2011 and 2013. The second respondent had been a non-executive director in October 2011 and as such disclaimed responsibility for the events which had occurred prior to his appointment. He further averred that he had received no remuneration as a director and believed himself to have been naïve in accepting the appointment.

The court adopted the test set out by O'Donnell J. in *Director of Corporate Securities v McCann; Re Kentford Securities Ltd* [2011] 1 I.R. 585 to the effect that the court should first consider whether a ground of disqualification has been made out and then move on to consider whether a disqualification order should issue in the individual case. On the facts the court had no difficulty in concluding that the directors had shown "blatant disregard not only of their duties as directors … but also for the express terms of two court orders directing them to comply." The court disqualified the first respondent for a seven year period and imposed a six year term of disqualification on the second respondent in light of his shorter period of involvement with the company.

RESTRICTION

Spousal Directors The High Court considered the position of a person who has consent to act as a company director in order to ensure that the company complies with the statutory minimum of two directors. In *McCoy v Courtney and Courtney; Re Zuccini Café and Restaurant Ltd* [2014] IEHC 369 and *McCoy v Courtney and Courtney; Re Mint Restaurants Ltd* [2014] IEHC 370 Barrett J. considered a husband and wife who had acted as directors of two companies which operated Dublin restaurants. The first respondent indicated to the court that he had no objection to a declaration being made against him. The second respondent claimed that she had merely acted as a "helpful spouse" in order to satisfy the statutory requirement for a second director.

Barrett J. began by suggesting that there is "a possible surfeit of judicial guidance on the criteria that are relevant to determining a s.150 application." He then considered the well-known authorities in the area beginning with *La Moselle Clothing Ltd v Souahli* [1998] 2 I.L.R.M. 345 and its subsequent 'amplification' in *Re Tralee Beef and Lamb Ltd* [2005] 1 I.L.R.M. 34 (HC); [2008] 3 I.R. 347 (SC). In a passage which might be viewed as representing a departure from the position in *Tralee Beef and Lamb,* Barrett J. questioned whether it was possible for a director to be thought of as having acted responsibly in circumstances "where he or she had complied with the Companies Acts but was in breach of his or her common law duties" or where he or she had breached "his or her common law duties [but] was not guilty of any breach of, or exposed to any penalty under, the detailed and comprehensive code established by the Companies Acts." Barrett J. then suggested that the position in *Tralee Beef and Lamb* had been further modified by the decision of the Supreme Court in *Re Mitek Holdings Ltd* [2010] 3 I.R. 374, citing in particular a dictum of Fennelly J. in which the learned judge emphasised the importance of avoiding standardised judicial criteria in favour of identifying the issues which are of importance in a particular case. Barrett J. went on to formulate the test for imposing a section 150 order in the following terms:

> "In deciding whether each of [the directors] has acted honestly and responsibly the court may of course have regard to their respective obligations as directors, to general commercial practice and to prior case-law but perhaps more to anchor than to determine any decision of the court as to the responsibility or otherwise of their respective actions."

On the facts, Barrett J. held that there was insufficient evidence to justify making a restriction order against the first respondent; however, the second respondent, though she had presented as a mere nominee director, had used a company credit card to finance non-business expenditure without having provided an explanation as to why this had been done. The court held that this was indicative of a lack of responsibility on her part and accordingly made an order against her.

Barrett J. delivered a judgment in nearly identical terms in *Hughes v Caffery and Caffery; Re Gleneagle Woodcrafts Ltd* [2014] IEHC 366 in which the liquidator sought a restriction order against two directors who were a married couple and who acted as directors of a company which manufactured wood products. The company ceased trading in 2008 after its business decline owing to a change in consumer spending patterns and an increase in cheap imported products competing in the Irish market. The liquidator's affidavit expressed the view that the directors had acted irresponsibly in failing to take measures in respect of the company between 2008 and the examinership in 2011. The liquidator also criticised the failure to file an annual return and abridged accounts for 2009, noting that the obligation to do so persisted despite the fact that the company was not trading. Finally, the liquidator suggested that the directors were culpable in failing to take action to prevent the accumulation of debts in associated companies, a factor which the liquidator identified as being one of the reasons for the company's insolvency.

Having set out the law in relation to s.150 in terms materially identical with those used in *Re Zuccini Café and Restaurant Ltd* [2014] IEHC 369 and *Re Mint Restaurants Ltd* [2014] IEHC 370, Barrett J. went on to consider the role of the liquidator in s.150 petitions. He acknowledged that in such proceedings the liquidator bears only a limited burden of proof in satisfying the court of the insolvency of the company and that the directors held office at an appropriate time. Thereafter, it falls to the directors to establish the existence of a relevant defence. Nevertheless Barrett J. held that:

> "there is no suggestion in the applicable case law that insofar as a liquidator

is concerned he or she can simply identify certain facts, make unreasoned assertions about a respondent director and then 'exit stage left'. It appears to the court that if a liquidator is to discharge his or her role of information provider fully and properly, the information provided to the court by such liquidator must be of meaningful assistance to the court in discharging its role under s.150."

The court went on to emphasise that the duty of the liquidator to act as a provider of information does not amount to a change in the burden of proof. On the facts the court declined to make an order against either director.

Excessive Directors' Remuneration Leading to Restriction The decision of the High Court in *Kelly v Monson* [2014] IEHC 573 concerned an application for the restriction of a husband and wife who had acted as directors of a small company. The husband was principal actor in the operation of the business with the wife adopting a passive role. The directors' remuneration had been increased by 60 per cent over the last four years of the company's operation at a time when the company's turnover was falling; the company also ceased to be tax compliant in the penultimate years of its operation and director remuneration increased further during this period. Barrett J. had no difficulty in making a restriction order under s.150 of the Companies Act 1990 against the husband, finding that he had demonstrated a lack of commercial probity / a want of proper standards in allowing director remuneration to increase as it did at a time when the company's business was in decline. The court refused to make a restriction order against the wife, finding that there was no evidence that any "real moral blame" attached to her. In doing so Barrett J. made a number of general observations about the nature and operation of the s.150 regime:

a. s.150 applies the same sanction to all directors against whom a restriction order is made regardless of the nature of their conduct, such a regime is capable of producing results which the court described as seeming unfair;
b. Barrett J. noted the existence of a pattern of s.150 applications in which the respondent directors consent to the making of restriction orders against them. The court suggested that in many such cases the respondent's consent may be explained by the fact that the respondents may not be in a position to fight an application rather than by the fact that "directors are satisfied that their alleged wrongdoings are such that they merit sanction." Barrett J. drew specific attention in this regard to the fact that the burden of proof to establish "that no blame attaches to them" rests with the respondent directors (citing *Business Communications v Baxter,* unreported, High Court, Murphy J., 21 July 1995). In this context Barrett J. suggested that s.150 applications involve "a certain intrinsic imbalance that may be conducive to an unfairness of outcome, something to which the court must ever be alive;"

   Barrett J. also pointed out that in consent cases, the court has frequently been presented with letters from the respondent directors to the effect that the respondent consents to the making of a s.150 order against them. Barrett J. suggested that as a matter of prudence such letters might in future contain language advising that the respondent directors seek independent legal advice before giving their consent; and

c. the court further pointed out that many of the s.150 applications heard in recent years concern companies whose insolvencies are attributable to the economic crash of 2008 and subsequent years. Barrett J. cited his earlier judgment in *Director of Corporate Enforcement v Walsh* [2014] IEHC 365 and suggested that the court must assess the conduct of company directors in light of developments in the wider economy, explaining that the "court must sometimes be prepared to countenance, as legitimate behaviour, that which at another time and in another context might fall to be treated, say, as wanting in responsibility, or to offer a basis on which it would otherwise be just and equitable to issue a declaration of restriction."

d. Finally Barrett J. repeated his view, expressed in *Director of Corporate Enforcement v Slattery* [2014] IEHC 363 that the decision in *Re Hunting Lodges Ltd* [1975] I.L.R.M. 75 does not require a restriction order simply because a person has consented to become a nominee director as a result of a spousal relationship or other ties of affection to another director.

Restriction – Costs In *Taite v Breslin; Re Shellware Ltd* [2014] IEHC 364 the High Court considered an application seeking an award of costs against a liquidator arising from a failed application for a restriction order against the directors. The court, citing with approval the earlier decision of Finlay Geoghegan J. in *Re KranksKorner* [2008] IEHC 423, summarised the test for costs in such cases in the following terms:

- first, s.150 itself makes no provision as to costs;
- secondly, the court in s.150 proceedings enjoys the general discretion as to costs that pertains under Order 99 of the Rules of the Superior Courts 1986, as amended;
- thirdly, it is not the case that when persons against whom a failed s.150 application is brought satisfy the court that they acted honestly and responsibly, that the normal rule is that they be, or that they not be, awarded their costs against the applicant liquidator;
- fourthly, there is no normal rule as to costs in such cases; the court must exercise its discretion in each case, having regard to the relevant facts and the statutory scheme; and
- fifthly, there does not generally appear to be any justification for making an order for costs against a liquidator where the following circumstances pertain: (i) there is no dispute that s.150 applied to the company in liquidation and to the respondents as directors thereof; (ii) the liquidator put all relevant facts to the Director for Corporate Enforcement when making his s.56 report(s); and (iii) the respondent directors had an opportunity either to comment on those facts in

> advance or to furnish the liquidator with relevant information in response to queries.

On the facts, the court declined to make an order in the applicant's favour.

OPPRESSION

Minority Share Valuation *Donegal Investment plc v Danbywiske and ors; Re Elst Ltd* [2014] IEHC 615 involved a trial in the High Court on a discreet issue as to the proper valuation of the petitioner's shares as an aspect of wider proceedings in which the petitioner had alleged various acts of oppression on the part of the majority shareholders. The company had been formed as a top level corporate vehicle in the merger of two businesses. There was dispute as to the size of the petitioner's shareholding in the company but for the purposes of trying the discreet issue the petitioner was assumed to have a 35 per cent shareholding and it was admitted for the purposes of the proceedings that the petitioner had suffered "a non-specified ground of oppression" so as to ground the court's jurisdiction to make an order for the purchase of the petitioner's shares at a specified price.

The principal dispute between the parties was to identify the correct approach to the valuation of the petitioner's shares. Expert evidence was adduced from three expert witnesses each of which differed as to whether and to what extent a discounted cash flow methodology should be used in valuing the petitioner's shares. The court identified three legal issues:

(a) whether a discount should be applied to the value of the petitioner's shares to reflect the fact that the petitioner was a minority shareholder in the company;
(b) whether the use of discounted cash flow methodology was appropriate as a matter of law in valuing the petitioner's shares; and
(c) whether the court should apply a marketability discount to the share price.

Dealing with the first issue the court considered the decision in *Re Skytours Ltd* [2011] 4 I.R. 651 in which Laffoy J. held that unless the company is a quasi-partnership, the court should ordinarily apply a discount reflecting the minority nature of the petitioner's shareholding in valuing the petitioner's shares. The court held that the company could be regarded as a quasi-partnership in that it was formed out of a joint venture between two earlier businesses which had been in difficulty prior to their merger. Secondly, the court noted that the relations between the parties were the subject of a shareholder's agreement which did not envisage shares in the company being bought out on the basis of a minority discount and which established a relationship of equality, mutuality, trust and confidence between the partners.

On the question on the discounted cash flow methodology, the court noted that this methodology has been criticised before both English and American courts as being unreliable and subjective, particularly in cases where future returns cannot be predicted with confidence. The court described the use of this approach as unsafe and suggested that it should only be used as a means of cross-checking more conventional market-based approaches to valuation.

Finally the court declined to apply a marketability discount holding that such an approach would be to ignore the fact that the respondent would hold 100 per cent of the shares in the company after the proposed purchase and in any event the question did not arise in attempting to determine how much the respondents, as distinct from another market purchaser, might be prepared to pay for the shares.

EXAMINERSHIP

Appointment of an Examiner *Re Pelko Holdings Ltd* [2014] IEHC 226 concerned a petition to appoint an examiner to the company which was opposed by a secured creditor of the company on the grounds that the application was premature and that the costs of an examinership were likely to be both excessive and disproportionate. The court held that s.2 of the Companies (Amendment) Act 1990 afforded discretion to refuse to appoint an examiner even where a company has a reasonable prospect of survival and is not already being struck out. The existing case law (*Re Traffic Light Group Ltd* [2008] 3 I.R. 253 and *Re Gallium Ltd* [2009] 2 I.L.R.M. 11) established that the discretion to refuse to appoint an examiner is to be cautiously exercised and should only be used in cases where there was no real danger of prejudicing the company's employees and the examinership petition amounts to a fraud on the company's creditors. Hogan J. summarised the concerns of the secured creditor, as involving (a) a dislike of the examinership process; (b) in particular a concern that an examinership might jeopardise the creditor's security; and (c) a concern that the costs of examinership are often, in practice, borne by the secured creditor. The court held that such concerns were not sufficient to warrant the refusal of an examinership petition where the statutory threshold tests where otherwise satisfied.

Discharge of an Interim Examiner for Material Non-Disclosure in the Petition In *Re O'Flynn Construction Company and ors* [2014] IEHC 458 the High Court considered an application to discharge an interim examiner appointed to the applicant companies at the petition of Carbon Finance Ltd ("Carbon"). The application was grounded on three allegations: (a) that the petition for the appointment of an interim examiner contained a material non-disclosure; (b) that the conditions necessary for the appointment of an interim examiner did not exist and (c) that the petition was actuated by an improper motive and other than in good faith. Having conducted an extensive review of the evidence Irvine J. found that there had been a number of non-disclosures in the petition and grounding affidavits presented to the court.

The applicant argued that the consequence of the non-disclosure should be the discharge of the examinership. Counsel for the respondent cited *Re Traffic Light Group Ltd* [2007] IEHC 446 and argued that the need to protect employment supported the adoption of a pragmatic approach to non-disclosure. Irvine J. rejected the respondent's argument, holding instead that *Traffic Light* could be distinguished on the basis that there the material non-disclosure was discovered only at the point when confirmation was being sought of a scheme of arrangement. This meant that the court was in a position to limit the benefits those responsible for the non-disclosure could obtain from their conduct, and secondly, it did not involve the obtaining of an ex parte order. The court went on to note that as the petitioners were also the company's major creditors any argument based on the possible consequences of a discharge of the interim examiner for the company's employees was to no avail as it would be open to the petitioners as creditors to choose not to pursue any course of action which would imperil the company's survival.

Extension of Time Period for Examinership In *Re JP Transpeed Express Portlaoise Ltd* [2014] IEHC 544, the High Court considered an application to extend the time period for an examiner to make his report under s.18 of the Companies (Amendment) Act 1990. The company operated a freight and haulage business and owed significant amounts to the Revenue Commissioners. The Revenue Commissioners opposed the application to extend time for the preparation of the examiner's report on the basis that the company's tax liabilities had been significantly understated when the petition to appoint an examiner was presented to the court. The Revenue Commissioners argued that the effect of this understatement was that the examinership process had become tainted with illegality with the consequence that the court lacked jurisdiction to further extend the process.

Section 4A of the Companies (Amendment) Act 1990 gives the High Court a discretionary power to decline to hear, or to continue to hear a petition for examinership in circumstances where the petitioner or independent accountant has failed to disclose material information or has otherwise failed to exercise the utmost good faith. Barrett J. rejected the Revenue Commissioners' argument that the misstatement had tainted the examinership with illegality, suggesting that this argument overlooks the discretionary nature of the power under s.4A. The court also held that in exercising the discretion provide by s.4A it is necessary to distinguish between a deliberate concealment of known facts (which would lead to an automatic discharge of the examinership) and an error in the facts as stated.

Barrett J. further distinguished the decision in *Re Belohn Ltd* [2013] IEHC 157 in which the High Court held that a material non-disclosure, even if the result of bona fide error, is a relevant factor when considering whether or not to appoint an interim examiner. *Re Belohn Ltd* was distinguished on the basis that the appointment of an interim examiner, involving as it does, ex parte proceedings, requires an especially high-level of scrutiny. The court also noted that on the facts there had been no failure to disclose in that the independent accountant's report presented at the time of the petition had expressly suggested that additional sums might be due and owing to the Revenue Commissioners.

Finally, Barrett J. stated that in deciding whether or not to extend the time for the examinership the court should have regard to the position of the company's employees should the examinership fail. Citing *Re Traffic Light Group Ltd* [2007] IEHC 446 and *Re Missford Ltd* [2010] IEHC 11 Barrett J. suggested that the court should regard the preservation of employment as being a second objective of the examinership proceedings, alongside the objective of preserving the company's enterprise as a going concern.

Confirmation of a Scheme of Arrangement and the Duties of an Examiner In *Re Camden Street Investments Ltd & Ors* [2014] IEHC 86 confirmation was sought of a scheme of arrangement proposed by an examiner who had been appointed to three related companies involved in the running of a pub. Finlay Geoghegan J. confirmed the scheme and approved a statement from Courtney's *Law of*

Companies, 3rd edn (London: Bloomsbury, 2012) to the effect that an examiner "must act honestly, reasonably, and with the fullest candour to the court in respect of all matters which, on objective criteria, could be material." The court emphasised the need for an examiner to inform the court where a scheme of arrangement involves fresh investment in the company from a person who has previously been a shareholder or director of the company. The court noted that while such investment is not objectionable per se it does give rise to special considerations and always requires disclosure. The court further noted that the duty of disclosure extends to the solicitor for the examiner as well as to counsel involved in settling the report of the examiner and its accompanying affidavits.

The court held that the examiner had breached his duty of disclosure to the court in several respects and exercised its discretion to confirm the scheme in the interests of preserving the position of the company's employees.

Unfair Prejudice and the Confirmation of a Scheme of Arrangement *Re SIAC Construction Ltd & Ors* [2014] IESC 25 involved a Supreme Court appeal by Polish appellants from the decision of Kelly J. in the High Court to confirm a scheme of arrangement proposed for a group of construction companies. The appellants and the companies concerned had been involved in the construction of a section of motorway in Poland. Litigation arising out of this relationship was pending before the Polish courts at the time of the examinership proceedings and the appellants claimed that the scheme of arrangement was unfairly prejudicial to their interests in that it purported to prevent them from pursuing certain claims arising from the Polish project.

Giving the unanimous judgment of the Supreme Court, Fennelly J. set out a two-part test for establishing that a scheme of arrangement is unfairly prejudicial to a creditor. First, the scheme must be prejudicial to the creditor in the sense that his or her interests as a creditor are adversely affected. Secondly, the prejudice to the creditor must be shown to be unfair. Unfairness can be satisfied by showing that the proposals are in a generalised sense unjust and that they expose the creditor to an inequality of treatment. The court held that judges considering whether a particular scheme is unfairly prejudicial should conduct a broad assessment of the effect of the proposals and should also consider the company's factual position. The court also held that judges must consider whether any particular interested party is treated differently from other similarly situated parties and if so, whether there are aspects of each party's individual position which place it at an unfair advantage or disadvantage. On the facts, the court upheld the decision of the High Court that the appellants were not unfairly prejudiced by the proposals in the scheme and dismissed the appeal.

LIQUIDATION

Fraudulent Disposition of the Company's Property In *Kirby v Petrolo Ltd and Stokes; Re Citywest Hire Ltd* [2014] IEHC 279 the High Court considered an application by the liquidator of a company for an order that the respondents deliver up a sum of €63,048.25 to the liquidator under s.139 of the Companies Act 1990 and for a declaration that the second respondent was guilty of misfeasance and/or breach of duty within the meaning of s.298 of the Companies Act 1963 (fraudulent trading). The company operated a restaurant. In order to receive payments from its customers it operated two credit card machines which were located on its premises and were linked to the company's bank account. The company ceased to trade on 10 June 2013 when its landlord repossessed the premises from which it operated. The landlord passed to the company's liquidator a credit card machine found on the premises which was subsequently found to be linked to the bank account of the first respondent. No credit card sales were recorded in the company's bank account for a number of days prior to the cessation of its trade. The liquidator claimed, based on an analysis of till receipts, that sales made by the company's restaurant during this period had been lodged to the account of the first respondent.

Finlay Geoghegan J. adopted the approach of Murphy J. in *Le Chatelaine Thudichum Ltd v Conway* [2010] 1 I.R. 529 in which he held that s.139 of the Companies Act 1990 can be invoked wherever "the company, its creditors or members be deprived of something to which it is, or to which they are, lawfully entitled."

The court held that the transfer of the proceeds of sales to the bank account of the first respondent amounted to a disposition of the company's property to the first respondent and that the effect of that disposition was to deprive the company of funds to which it was entitled. Accordingly the court held it had jurisdiction to make an order under s.139 against the first respondent if it was satisfied that it was just and equitable to do so. The court further found that the second respondent had had "at minimum control over the monies transferred" and accordingly could also be made the subject of an order under the section.

The respondents argued that it would not be just and equitable for the court to make an order against them on the basis that the monies received by the first respondent were used for the benefit of the company. In particular, the respondent claimed that the monies had been applied in paying wages of the company's staff and its other creditors. The court accepted that €41,999.23 of the money received had been applied in this manner and accordingly ordered repayment under s.139 of the amount of €21,049. The court declined to consider the liquidator's second application under s.297 of the Companies Act 1963 holding that resolution of this issue was unnecessary in light of the order made under s.139.

Fraudulent Disposition and Fraudulent Preference *Kennington v McGinley; Re Leo Getz Trading Ltd* [2014] IEHC 356 involved an allegation of a fraudulent preference under s.286 of the Companies Act 1963 (the "1963 Act") and s.139 of the Companies Act 1990. The company was established in 2006 and commenced trading in classic cars in 2007. The defendant was a director and secretary to the company until his resignation in June 2007. An official liquidator was appointed to the company in July 2009 on foot of a petition from the Revenue Commissioners. The liquidator, from the partial books and records available to him formed the view that the company was insolvent as of January 2008.

The court noted that the defendant, as a brother of the company's sole director from June 2007 onwards was a connected person for the purposes of s.286 of the 1963 Act and that as such any disposition to him in the two years prior to July 2009 could be deemed a fraudulent preference provided that the company was unable to pay its debts at the date of the transfer and that there was evidence of an intention to give him a preference over other creditors. The court held that the requisite intention may be established by circumstantial evidence particularly where, as in this case, several years after the transaction, direct evidence is not available. The court cited *Re M Kushler Ltd* [1943] Ch. 248 as providing guidance as to the correct approach in such cases, which Charleton J. summarised in the following terms:

> "[F]irstly, dominant intention is required; secondly, hindsight may suggest such an intention but that is not enough since the circumstances seen in the light of what subsequently happened may mislead and instead an intention to prefer must be proven as of the time of the relevant disposition; thirdly, circumstantial evidence is to be assessed as to its probability, the fact that there might be another explanation for a payment is to be assessed as to the competing proofs and is not necessarily an answer; fourthly, since what is involved here is a fraudulent preference, solid grounds are needed since what is required is an inference of something which has the taint of dishonesty about it at the very least and which in extreme cases may be very much more than that."

The court noted that where a transaction can be explained by both a favourable and an unfavourable inference the court should lean against the party bearing the burden of proof and that what is required is that the court "seek out the state of mind of the officer or officers of the company making the disposition judged from the circumstances as a whole and drawing such inferences as are appropriate."

In interpreting s.139 of the Companies Act 1990, Charleton J. noted that in contrast to s.286 of the 1963 Act there is no requirement for proof of an intention to prefer the defendant. Rather the section requires that the liquidator establish that the company's property has been disposed of in circumstances where the effect has been to perpetrate a fraud on the company. The principal difference between the two sections is that s.286 is focused on intent whereas s.139 is focused on effect.

On the facts the court found that there had been a series of cash transactions between the company and the defendant under which the defendant lent working capital to the company which was subsequently repaid. The court held that these transactions were explicable on the basis that the defendant represented the company's sole source of working capital and that the repayment of these loans was done with the dominant intention of ensuring that fresh working capital would be available to the company. Accordingly the court did not find that the requisite intention for an order under s.286 had been present, nevertheless the effect of these payments was to prefer the defendant at the expense of the payment of fiduciary taxes to the central fund. Charleton J. held that such an effect was caught by s.139 and made an order for the repayment of €102,100 to the liquidator.

COMPULSORY WINDING UP

Winding Up on Just and Equitable Grounds In *Re Fuerta Ltd* [2014] IEHC 12, the circumstances in which the High Court will order a company to be wound up on just and equitable grounds pursuant to s.213(f) of the Companies Act 1963 were explored. The company had been established in 2006 to participate along with other investors in an investment scheme for the development of a nursing home. The other investors were attempting to acquire the company's interest in the home under a tax efficient structure which required that the acquisition close promptly and within a particular time period. The sale of the company's interest in the nursing home was supported by its bankers; however the directors of the company were non-cooperative and its bank adduced evidence that the directors had not responded to a series of approaches in respect of the sale of the company's investments and the enforcement of the bank's security. In order to ensure that the company's investment could be promptly realised in the planned manner its bank sought an order for the winding up of the company on just and equitable grounds with a view to the liquidator exercising the company's corporate personality to secure an orderly and tax efficient disposal of the company's assets. The application was grounded on the fact that the company was in default of its obligations to make annual returns to the Companies Registration Office.

In the High Court, Charleton J. noted that applications for a winding up on just and equitable grounds are normally associated with situations where there has been deadlock or oppression within the company. Nonetheless, the judge held that both English commentary and previous Irish authority (citing *Re Irish Tourist Promotions Ltd*, unreported, High Court, Kenny J., 22 April 1974) establishes that the just and equitable ground can encompass a far broader range of situations including: (a) cases where the company was fraudulently promoted; (b) cases in which the company's substratum has gone; (c) cases of deadlock in the company; (d) cases in which there is a constitutional and administrative vacuum; (e) cases in which the management and conduct of the company are such that it is unjust and inequitable to require the petitioner to continue as a member; and (f) cases where a quasi-partnership has broken down. The court also noted that the official liquidation of a company is not a step which should be undertaken lightly but one which should be undertaken only where there has been a lack of compliance of the most serious nature coupled with the absence of reasonable alternative steps in the context of serious or impending prejudice.

On the facts, the court held that the requisite elements were present in this case in that the company was in persistent default of its obligations to make annual returns and the correspondence between the company and the applicant made clear that all reasonable steps had been taken by the bank to attempt to resolve the situation in advance of presenting its petition for the winding up of the company.

Liquidator's Power to Continue Plenary Proceedings *Re Hibernian Therapeutics Global Ltd* [2014] IEHC 41 involved an application for leave to continue aspects of plenary proceedings which were pending against the company at the time a winding up petition was granted and an official liquidator was appointed. The applicant sought leave to continue with a counterclaim against the company seeking a declaration that they were the legal or beneficial owners of certain shares in the company and an order rectifying the company's register of members. The company was insolvent and its major assets had been disposed of by the liquidator at the time this application was brought. The liquidator opposed the application on the basis that it would, if granted, increase the costs of the liquidation and would delay its completion. The applicant's evidence explained that they were engaged in defending litigation in the United States and that they had been advised by their American lawyers that they would have a good defence to the American litigation if they were able to establish that they were entitled to be registered as members of the company.

Finlay Geoghegan J. adopted the approach of Laffoy J. in *Wright-Morris v Irish Bank Resolution Corporation Ltd (In Special Liquidation)* [2013] IEHC 385 in which the learned judge had adopted English authorities suggesting that s.222 of the Companies Act 1963 gives the High Court a wide discretion "to do what is fair and reasonable in the circumstances" but that the court generally refuses leave "if the action proposed raised issues which can conveniently be decided in the course of the winding up." She also relied on her earlier decision in *Re MJBCH Ltd* [2013] IEHC 256 in which she had noted that the requirement to seek leave under s.222 represents a restriction on the constitutional right of access to the courts and exists to ensure that all proceedings relating to a company which is the subject of an official liquidation remain under the supervision of the court.

On the facts, the court held that the applicants had established that a potential prejudice to their position might arise if leave were refused. In addition, as submissions from the applicant had pointed out, the concerns of the liquidator in respect of costs and delay could be dealt with by giving leave to proceed subject to conditions. The court granted the application subject to the giving of an undertaking by the solicitors for the applicant to the effect that no costs would be sought against the company by the applicant arising from the contemplated proceedings and that any additional costs incurred in the liquidation would be discharged by the applicant.

LEGISLATION

Companies Act 2014 The Companies Act 2014 was signed into the law by the President of Ireland on 23 December 2014 and commenced on 1 June 2015. The Act repeals the entirety of the existing legislative corpus of company law in Ireland and replaces it with a revised scheme. The major change introduced by the Act is the establishment of the company limited by shares as a dominant corporate form in Ireland. The company limited by shares is designed to discharge the role previously played by the private limited company under the Companies Acts 1963–2013. The company limited by shares is governed by Pts 1–15 of the Companies Act 2014 (the "2014 Act") and has unlimited contractual capacity under s.38. The company limited by shares has a single document constitution which replaces the memorandum and articles of association required under the pre-existing regime. The contents of the former articles of association have been re-enacted (with significant amendments) as Pt 4 of the Act, though much of the contents of this part can be modified or dis-applied in respect of particular companies by making appropriate provision in the company's constitution.

The 2014 Act makes significant changes to the role, functions and duties of directors. The requirement for a company to have two directors has been dispensed with in favour of a single director regime (see s.128), though where a company has only one director a separate corporate secretary must be appointed (see s.129(6)). Part 5 of the Act partially codifies the fiduciary duties of directors with s.228 establishing a list of eight fiduciary duties owed by directors to the company.

Part 7 of the Act introduces major changes to the law of company charge registration. These include the replacement of the list of registrable charges with a general obligation for all charges to be registered, a new procedure allowing the particulars of an intended charge to be registered up to 21 days in advance of the completion of the transaction as well as significant revisions to the particulars which must be registered. Part 8 largely restates the existing law of receivers and adds a new statutory statement of the powers of a receiver (though additional powers may be conferred on a receiver in a debenture). Part 9 of the Act provides new procedures for the restructuring of companies limited by shares including new procedures for the merging of two such companies and the division of a company limited by shares into two or more companies.

Parts 10 and 11 restate the law of examinership and the law of winding-up and make significant changes to the process of court-ordered winding up while Pt 12 restates in a single form the law of voluntary and involuntary strike-off. Part 13 enacts the law of company investigations with minor amendments. Part 14 provides for compliance, restriction and disqualification orders and establishes a categorisation scheme for company law offences. Part 15 renews the legislative basis of the Registrar of Companies, the Company Law Review Group, the Director of Corporate Enforcement and the Irish Auditing and Accounting Supervisory Authority.

Parts 16–24 make special provisions for companies other than the company limited by shares. Part 16 establishes a new form of entity—the designated activity company ('DAC'). Unlike the company limited by shares the DAC retains a two document constitution in the form of a memorandum and articles of association. The memorandum of association will continue to contain an objects clause which sets out the objects and capacity of the company. Section 973 provides that the memorandum of association of a DAC does not limit the contractual capacity of the company but goes on to provide that a member of a DAC may restrain the commission of an *ultra vires* act by injunction. The section also provides that the directors of a DAC are under a duty to observe any limitation on their powers imposed by the constitution of the DAC. The remaining parts of the Act deal with the public company (Pt 17), guarantee companies (Pt 18), unlimited companies (Pt 19), external companies (Pt 21), unregistered and joint-stock companies (Pt 22) and investment companies (Pt 24). Part 20 sets out the process whereby a company of one type may be re-registered as another type of company. Part 25 makes provision for the recognition of foreign corporate insolvency proceedings.

Conflict of Laws

JURISDICTION

Exclusive jurisdiction In *Bushell Interiors Ltd v Liecht Kuchen AG* [2014] IEHC 3, Moriarty J. showed little hesitation in holding that art.23 of the Brussels 1 Regulation applied where the parties were in a commercial relationship alleged to involve, at a minimum, the supply of "high end kitchens" by the Irish-domiciled plaintiff to the German-domiciled defendant, as well as a principal-agent relationship in which the plaintiff acted as agent for the defendant. Clause 14 of the defendant's General Terms of Sale, Delivery and Payment provided as follows:

> "Place where a Contract is to be fulfilled- Venue- Validity of Laws:
> 1. For all disputes arising from business relations, directly or indirectly, including payment problems with bills of exchange, acceptance or cheques, the involved parties agree, as merchants to the exclusive jurisdiction of the courts in Schwabisch Gmund. Moreover, the plaintiff is also entitled to sue/bring an action at the defendant's headquarters.
> 2. German law is exclusively valid for all sales and deliveries and all legally founded relations. The Vienna UN Agreement on contracts for international sales/purchase of goods of April II, I980 cannot be applied.
> 3. Place of fulfilment of all mutual obligations is the head office of our company in Waldstetten."

At the commencement of their business relationship, the defendant wrote to the plaintiff setting out buying, payment and delivery terms, stating: "Thank you for your recent orders for the supply of a showroom display kitchen and an end customer's kitchen. We now write to confirm the trading terms agreed and enclose a copy of our Terms and Conditions of Sale." A further letter was furnished on 10 March 2009, setting out renewed trading terms and stating: "This supersedes and invalidates all previous Typelists and Agreements. Our Terms and Conditions of Sale remain unchanged."

Moriarty J. considered it "abundantly clear" that the parties were bound by the provisions of Clause 14 (the "Clause"), insofar as it related to the contracts for sale and delivery of kitchen units. The plaintiff had urged the court to hold that the Clause should not be taken as applying to the entirety of the trading relationship between the parties, but only to the contracts for sale of kitchen units and that the words "in relation to a particular legal relationship" should be strictly construed as limiting the application of the Clause to the General Terms of Sale, Delivery and Payment. Moriarty J. did not agree. A plain reading of the terms of the Clause stated that it applied to "disputes arising from business relations, directly or indirectly".

The plaintiff had not sought to contest the efficacy of the Clause, but merely to suggest that its application should be limited. However, the plain and unambiguous language of the Clause simply did not permit such an interpretation. Having regard to the trading terms and letters, the interpretation proposed by the plaintiff was likewise unsustainable and flew in the face of business common sense:

> "The letters were in the first instance furnished alongside a copy of the General Terms of Sale Delivery and Payment, and subsequently explicitly affirmed the latter's applicability. It is clear on the evidence before me that the letters and the terms must be read in conjunction and represent the totality of the agreement between the parties. In assessing the dealings between the parties in this regard, I am fortified in the view I have taken by the robust words of Steyn LJ in *Continental Bank NA v. Aeokos Cia Naviera SA* [1994] 2 All ER 540, as approved by McGuinness J in *Clare Taverns v. Gill*, [[2000] 1 I.R. 286]."

Accordingly, Moriarty J dismissed the proceedings for lack of jurisdiction.

Related actions In the *Annual Review of Irish Law 2012*, pp.112–114, we analysed *Websense International Technology Ltd v Itway SpA* [2012] IEHC 446, in which McGovern J., guided by the judgments of the Court of Justice in *Tatry v Maciej Rataj (Case C-406/920)*, the House of Lords in *Sarrio S.A. v Kuwait Investment Authority* [1999] 1 A.C. 32 and Finlay Geoghegan J. in *Popely v Popely* [2006] 4 I.R. 356, adopted a broad interpretation of art.17 of the Brussels 1 Regulation in holding that Irish proceedings relating to a complicated distribution arrangement should give way to proceedings initiated earlier in Italy, on the basis that they were "related proceedings". We noted that McGovern J. was unmoved by the existence of a provision in the distribution agreement choosing Dublin for arbitration, backed up by an exclusive jurisdiction clause in favour of Irish jurisdiction. The Court of Justice, in *Erich Gasser GmbH v Misat Srl (C116/02)* [2003] E.C.R. I-4207, had made it clear that, where the parties had declined to invoke the jurisdiction clause, it was incumbent on the court first seised of the matter to verify the existence of the agreement and to decline jurisdiction if it was established that the parties had actually agreed to designate the court second seised as having exclusive jurisdiction. The Court of Justice had also expressed its view on an issue that had been raised by the plaintiff in the instant proceedings, concerning the question of delay in the legal procedures of the court first seised of the matter. The plaintiff complained that, if the Italian court were permitted to deal with the matters in dispute before it, it would take a great deal longer than would be the case in Ireland and that the plaintiff would thereby be prejudiced.

In the *Gasser* case, the Court of Justice had stated that it was not compatible with the philosophy and the objectives of the Brussels Convention for national courts to be under an obligation to respect rules on *lis pendens* only if they considered that the court first seised would give judgment within a reasonable period. Nowhere did the Convention provide that courts might use the pretext of delays in procedure in other contracting States to excuse themselves from applying its provisions. The Court of Justice had gone on to express the view that delays in proceedings which might be such as to seriously affect a litigant could be examined by the European

Court of Human Rights, but that the national courts could not substitute themselves by recourse to the Regulation.

The Supreme Court affirmed McGovern J.: [2014] IESC 5. Guided by the decisions of *Tatry* and *Sarrio,* MacMenamin J. (Clarke and Dunne JJ. concurring) observed:

> "When one asks oneself the first question–is there a connection between these two set [sic] of proceedings–the answer must undoubtedly be 'yes'. The next question is whether there must inevitably be a significant overlap between the witnesses in the two cases? The answer must be 'yes' also. Finally, one might ask whether a determination in one case would have a significant bearing on the ultimate outcome of the two cases, having regard to claims and potential counterclaims? Here, the answer is 'yes' again. The real issue then is, whether on these transactions, Websense owes Itway money or *vice versa*? To my mind, the answers to the three key questions above point one way. They lead inexorably to the conclusion that it is expedient that the actions should be heard and determined together by the same court. This conclusion does not, of course, detract from the fact that it will be necessary for the Italian Court to make an initial determination on the choice of jurisdiction clause contained in the contract. But it is impossible to escape the conclusion that the issues, and the source of the *inter partes* litigation, emanate from the distribution agreement."

MacMenamin J. was of the view that *Gasser* remained "strong authority on the manner in which the Court of Justice would approach this question, not just in relation to Article 27 but also, even though there may be a discretion, in relation to Article 28". Advocate General Lenz in Case C-129/82 *Owens Banks Ltd v Bracco* [1994] Q.B. 509, had addressed the question of the nature of the discretion to be exercised in determining whether to grant a stay and had stated that it would "be appropriate in case of doubt for a national court to decide to stay its proceedings." MacMenamin J. noted that the Advocate General had gone on to identify three factors which might be relevant to the exercise of the discretion vested in national courts. These were, first, the extent of the relatedness and the risk of mutually irreconcilable decisions; secondly, the stage reached in each set of proceedings; and, thirdly, the proximity of the courts to the subject matter of the case. But, nonetheless, "as a general rule", MacMenamin J. thought that a stay should be granted by the second court, noting "for a case to be clear, the facts would have to very clearly indeed point to a refusal of a stay. The Advocate General's observations must be seen in light of the judgments of the Court of Justice."

Forum non conveniens In *DF v EM* [2014] IEHC 510, Baker J. considered that she did not have to determine the question of the operation of the doctrine of forum non conveniens in the context of the Brussels II *bis* Regulation as it could not yet be said that there were two competing jurisdictions. The dispute concerned the custody of the parties' children. The mother had initiated proceedings in Ireland, the father in Rhode Island. The Rhode Island court had indicated that the first issue that it was going to address was that of jurisdiction. The husband sought a stay of the Irish proceedings. Baker J. was of the view that, until the Rhode Island court determined the jurisdictional issue, which it was scheduled to do within a few days, it was premature for her to decide whether to order a stay. She stated:

> "The Court of Rhode Island is first seised. If it declines jurisdiction, the Irish proceedings will progress. If it assumes jurisdiction, the question of a stay of the Irish proceedings, pending a determination of the substantive matter, may come to be made in Ireland, and a consideration of that application will undoubtedly involve the complex questions of law identified by counsel in their submissions, in particular, the question of whether this Court has a jurisdiction to refuse to hear a case in the light of the implementation of Brussels II *bis*. A consideration of that substantive application for a stay must await the answer by the Court of Rhode Island of the jurisdictional question now to be considered by it. That question is logically prior to the hearing of the application to this Court for a stay, whether that application will be made under the inherent jurisdiction of the Court, under Brussels II *bis* or under the Hague Convention.
>
> There is at present no interlocutory application before this Court which is now to be stayed. What is sought is that the Mother be precluded from further progressing the proceedings in Ireland.
>
> For the reasons above, I make an order staying any further proceedings in the Irish courts pending the determination by the Court of Rhode Island and Providence Plantations of the question of whether it has and will assume jurisdiction to hear the issues relating to the custody, access and living arrangements of these children. Only after that matter has been determined can the Court in Ireland properly know whether there is a genuine and extant dispute between competing jurisdictions. The Court expresses no view as to whether this Court has a jurisdiction to stay the proceedings pending a determination of the substantive case. This application is made in the unusual circumstances where the jurisdictional question has yet to crystallise.
>
> In the circumstances, the order I make is limited in time and effect and the parties have liberty to bring a motion for a permanent or indefinite stay, depending on the conclusion of the jurisdictional issue before the Court of Rhode Island."

It thus appears that Baker J. did order a stay, but one of an inherently temporary character, leaving completely open the issue in regard to the Brussels II *bis* Regulation. It could perhaps be argued that that issue was capable of being determined once a court in another state had become seized. There would be significant difficulties in cases where that court was not going to consider the jurisdictional issue for some time. There seems no reason in principle why the Irish court should not confront the issue regarding stays and the Brussels II *bis* Regulation before the foreign court determines its jurisdictional competence.

The Lugano Convention and Maintenance Regulation The Circuit Court Rules (Lugano Convention and Maintenance Regulation) 2014 (S.I. No 597 of 2014) amend the interpretation of terms, orders and forms of the Circuit Court Rules, to facilitate the operation of the 2007 Lugano Convention on jurisdiction and the recognition and enforcement of judgments in civil and commercial matters (see the *Annual Review of Irish Law 2012*, pp.64–69, analysing the Jurisdiction of Courts and Enforcement of Judgments (Amendment) Act 2012) and the European Communities (Maintenance) Regulations (S.I. No. 274 of 2011), giving effect to the Council Regulation (EC) 4/2009 on jurisdiction, applicable law, recognition and enforcement of decisions and cooperation in matters relating to maintenance obligations.

CHILD ABDUCTION

Habitual Residence In *AJ v LJ* [2014] IEHC 92, Finlay Geoghegan J. gave a valuable review of the courts' approach to the determination of a child's habitual residence. In this case, the child who was the subject matter of the proceedings was an American citizen, born in one of the United States in 1998. Her parents were also American citizens. Their son had been born in 1991. The parents and their children lived in the state of their daughter's birth until 2003, when they moved to another state of the Union. They resided there until 2010, when they went to live in a third state of the Union. In 2008, the mother had spent a time working in Brazil, travelling back and forth for visits to her family. All of the changes of residence had been related to the mother's employment.

From 2010, the father travelled regularly for periods to Nigeria. He was in Nigeria in October 2012 when the mother took her daughter to Ireland, on the basis that her employment needed this. The father returned to the third state and, in due course, went to live in a fourth state of the Union, where he and the mother had resided between 1989 and 1996; having married there in 1992. Their daughter had been baptised in that state and had spent holiday periods of two to three weeks there with members of her extended family including her paternal grandmother. She had also attended summer camp there but otherwise had never resided there. For the purposes of the judgment, Finlay Geoghegan J. called this state "State A".

There was a dispute as to the precise basis on which the mother had gone to Ireland. The mother claimed that it had been for an agreed period of two years but the father denied this. In 2013, he initiated proceedings in State A, seeking the return of his daughter. For the case to fall within the terms of the Hague Convention, he had to be able to establish that his daughter's habitual residence in October 2012, at the time of the allegedly wrongful taking, was in State A. Finlay Geoghegan J. noted that it was "settled law for many years in this jurisdiction and other jurisdictions, including England and Wales", that the determination of habitual residence for the purposes of the Hague Convention was a matter of fact to be decided on the evidence in the case . She cited Fennelly J.'s observations in *S. (P.A.) v. S.(A.F.)* [2004] IESC 95 and McGuinness J.'s observations in *C.M. and O.M. v. Delegacion Provincial de Malaga & Ors.* [1999] 2 I.R. 363 at 381 in support. Finlay Geoghegan J. referred to the recent judgment of the United Kingdom Supreme Court in *In the matter of A (Children) (A.P.)* [2013] UKSC 60, [2014] 1 A.C. 1, where Baroness Hale set out a series of principles, the first of which she noted: "All are agreed that habitual residence is a question of fact and not a legal concept such as domicile. There is no legal rule akin to that whereby a child automatically takes the domicile of his parents."

Finlay Geoghegan J. went on to observe that, subject to the fundamental principle that habitual residence was a question of fact, the courts in England and Ireland had set out "certain principles" in relation to the determination of habitual residence, particularly of young children. One such principle was that the habitual residence of young children in the care of parents who were living together was the same as the habitual residence of the parents themselves and neither parent could change it without the express or tacit consent of the other or an order of the court. Waite J. had so stated in in *Re B: (Minors: Abduction)(No. 2)* [1993] 1 F.L.R. 993 at 995 and his remarks had been cited with approval in *S.(P.A.) v. S. (A.F.) and A.S. v. C.S.* [2010] 1 I.R. 370. However, it was important to emphasise that these were not legal principles, but rather were, as put recently by Baroness Hale in *Re L (A Child) (Custody: Habitual Residence)* [2013] 3 W.L.R. 1597 at 1607, para.21, to be regarded as "a helpful generalisation of fact, which will usually but not invariably be true, rather than a proposition of law."

The case law also disclosed that the court's approach to determining the habitual residence of a child would vary depending upon the age of the child: Finlay Geoghegan J. cited another recent English decision, *In re L.C. (Children)* [2014] 2 W.L.R. 124, in support. Where the evidence disclosed that a child had been resident in a particular country, the court had then to consider whether that residence had acquired the necessary degree of stability or integration to become habitual. The court would look at the integration of the child in a social and family environment in the relevant country. There was potentially a further relevant matter in relation to adolescent children such as the child in the instant proceedings, who was 15 years old, namely, the state of mind of the child.

Applying these principles to the facts of the case, Finlay Geoghegan J. concluded that the child had not been habitually resident in State A in October 2012. She had never resided there, save for short holiday periods. She had never resided with her parents in State A in a settled home environment since birth and never gone to school in State A, save for summer camp.

Whilst the court reached its conclusion on the question of the habitual residence on the basis of these undisputed facts, Finlay Geoghegan J. considered it appropriate to record that that conclusion was consistent with the child's state of mind as disclosed in the report of the interview conducted by a court-appointed clinical psychologist.

Exercising rights of custody The Hague Convention is drafted in a way that raises a difficulty of interpretation as to where the onus of proof lies. Article 3 provides that a removal or retention of a child is considered wrongful where it is in breach of the rights of custody of the applicant and at the time of removal or retention those rights "were actually exercised, either jointly or alone, or would have been so exercised but for the removal or retention." Viewed in isolation, art.3 clearly places the onus on the applicant to establish these requirements. Article 13(a), however, gives the court jurisdiction to refuse to order the return of a child where the person who opposes the child's return "establishes that…the person… having the care of the person of the child was not actually exercising the custody rights at the time of removal… ." This appears to place on the respondent the onus of establishing the non-exercise of the applicant's custody rights. What is the position, therefore, where an applicant does not adduce sufficient evidence to establish such exercise? Is the court entitled, or required, to refuse to order the child's return? And, in either case, why does art.13(a) appear to impose a burden on the respondent to prove non-exercise where the failure by the applicant to prove exercise has the effect of preventing, either absolutely or on a discretionary basis, an order for return of the child?

In *MJT v CC* [2014] IEHC 196, Finlay Geoghegan J. addressed the issue. The father of a girl born in 2005 initiated proceedings in November 2013, seeking his daughter's return to England. The child's mother had taken her to Ireland in 2011; the mother had died in December of the following year. The child was now living with her maternal grandmother. The father had last exercised his rights of access in 2008 but had stopped doing so when limited to supervised access. He had, however, continued to pay maintenance until shortly after the mother's death.

Finlay Geoghegan J. noted that, in para.73 of her Explanatory Report on the Hague Convention in 1982, Elisa Perez-Vera had stated that art.3 "requires that the applicant provide only some preliminary evidence that he actually took physical care of the child, a fact which normally will be relatively easy to demonstrate." Finlay Geoghegan J. observed:

> "An applicant for an order for the summary return of a child to its State of habitual residence pursuant to the Convention must, in my judgment put before the Court *prima facie* or preliminary evidence that the removal or retention of the child was wrongful within the meaning of the Convention. This follows from the purpose and wording of the Convention and underlined by the above explanations. Where the allegation is that the removal was in breach of the applicant's rights of custody (as in these proceedings), Article 3 requires such evidence of the applicant's *de jure* rights of custody and also that, as a matter of fact, the applicant was actually exercising his rights of custody."

Finlay Geoghegan J. considered it possible to discern from the limited jurisprudence on the issue that, "firstly, the courts take a very liberal view as to what will constitute the exercise of custody rights, and, secondly, that it does require the demonstration by an applicant/parent that he either did or attempted to maintain contact or a relationship with his child." In *Re H; Re S (Minors) Abduction: Custody Rights* [1991] 2 A.C. 476 at 500, Lord Brandon had expressed the view that: "article 3(b) must be construed widely as meaning that the custodial parent must be maintaining the stance and attitude of such a parent, rather than narrowly as meaning that he or she must be continuing to exercise day to day care and control."

In *Friedrich v. Friedrich* 78 F. 3d 1060 (6th Cir. 1996) in the U.S. Court of Appeals for the Sixth Circuit, Boggs J had stated:

> "Enforcement of the Convention should not to [sic] be made dependent on the creation of a common law definition of 'exercise'. The only acceptable solution, in the absence of a ruling from a court in the country of habitual residence, is to liberally find 'exercise' whenever a parent with *de jure* custody rights keeps, or seeks to keep, any sort of regular contact with his or her child."

In Ireland, the matter had been considered in the Supreme Court decision of *MSH v LH* [2000] 3 I.R. 390, analysed in the *Annual Review of Irish Law 2000*, pp.71

– 74, where the applicant was held to have been exercising his rights of custody while a prisoner as the children had visited him in prison and he had communicated with them by letter.

In the instant case, Finlay Geoghegan J. was not satisfied that the applicant had put before the court prima facie or preliminary evidence that he was exercising his rights of custody during a significant period of time prior to the removal of his daughter to Ireland.:

> "The authorities to which I refer simply require him to show that he kept or sought to keep regular contact or a relationship with his child. There is no evidence he did this during the three years prior to [his daughter]'s removal from England. In circumstances where the applicant was living in the same country as [her], the payment of maintenance ... does not in my judgment suffice. In the words of Lord Brandon in *Re H*, he was not maintaining the stance and attitude of a custodial parent. The definition in Article 5 of the Convention of rights of custody as including *'care of the person of the child'* underlines the requirement for personal contact or seeking to maintain contact or a relationship as part of the exercise of rights of custody. There may, of course, be factual situations where there is evidence that personal contact is precluded by court order or other reason, despite attempts made. There is no such evidence herein."

The wishes of the child Article 13 of the Hague Convention provides in part that "[t]he judicial or administrative authority may ... refuse to order the return of the child if it finds that the child objects to being returned and has attained an age and degree of maturity at which it is appropriate to take account of its views." In *CA v CA (otherwise C McC)* [2010] 2 I.R. 162, Finlay Geoghegan J. followed the three-stage approach to consideration of a child's objections, which Potter P. had set out in *Re M (Abduction: Child's Objections)* [2007] 2 F.L.R. 72 at 87:

> "The first question to be considered is whether or not the objections to return are made out. The second is whether the age and maturity of the child are such that it is appropriate for the court to take account of those objections (unless that is so, the defence cannot be established). Assuming a positive finding in that respect, the court moves to the third question, whether or not it should exercise its discretion in favour of retention or return."

In the Supreme Court decision of *AU. v. TNU (Child Abduction)* [2011] 3 I.R. 683, Denham C.J. (concurring) expressed agreement with the approach adopted by Baroness Hale in *In re M. (Abduction: Rights of custody)* [2008] 1 A.C. 1288 at 1308 that:

> "[i]n child's objections cases, the range of considerations may be even wider than those in the other exceptions. The exception itself is brought into play when only two conditions are met: first, that the child herself objects to being returned and second, that she has attained an age and degree of maturity at which it is appropriate to take account of her views. These days, and especially in light of article 12 of the United Nations Convention on

> the Rights of the Child, courts increasingly consider it appropriate to take account of a child's views. Taking account does not mean that those views are always determinative or even presumptively so. Once the discretion comes into play, the court may have to consider the nature and strength of the child's objections, the extent to which they are: 'authentically her own' or the product of the influence of the abducting parent, the extent to which they coincide or are at odds with other considerations which are relevant to her welfare, as well as the general Convention considerations referred to earlier. The older the child, the greater the weight that her objections are likely to carry. But that is far from saying that the child's objections should only prevail in the most exceptional circumstances."

Baroness Hale of Richmond had earlier observed in respect of these "Convention considerations" that, in cases falling within the Hague Child Abduction Convention:

> "there are general policy considerations which may be weighed against the interests of the child in the individual case. These policy considerations include, not only the swift return of abducted children, but also comity between the contracting states and respect for one another's judicial processes. Furthermore, the Convention is there, not only to secure the prompt return of abducted children, but also to deter abduction in the first place. The message should go out to potential abductors that there are no safe havens among the contracting states."

Denham C.J. in *AU v TNU* echoed this concern, stating that:

> "in interpreting and applying article 13 of the Convention, courts should not lightly exercise a discretion to refuse to return a child to his or her country of habitual residence since that would risk undermining the effectiveness of the Convention in both remedying and deterring the wrongful removal of children from the jurisdiction of the courts in such country. Furthermore, those courts are normally best placed to determine the respective rights of parents and in particular where the best interests of a child lie, which is of primary importance...The circumstances in which children would not be returned are exceptional. As article 13 states, in considering the circumstances in which an exception may be made to returning a child to such country, the court may take account of information provided to it from a competent authority concerning the child's social background. As was pointed out in *In re M. (Abduction: Rights of custody)* [2007] UKHL 55, [2008] 1 AC 1288, the extent to which the child's objections 'coincide or are at odds with other considerations which are relevant to his or her welfare are also relevant.'"

In *EJ v ED* [2014] IEHC 466, in "highly unusual" Hague Convention proceedings, Finlay Geoghegan J. deferred to a later stage in the proceedings the matter of ascertaining the wishes of the child, who was nearly eight years old where there was nothing in the evidence before the court which suggested that he had maturity less than his chronological age. The allegedly wrongful removal had occurred four years previously. This meant that the question whether the child had settled into his new environment would fall for consideration. The removal had taken place pursuant to the express terms of an order of the Californian courts. In addition to the reliefs under the Hague Convention, the applicant was seeking other reliefs, some of which sought his return to California and others of which sought the enforcement of access and other provisions of the Californian court order pursuant to which he had come to Ireland. Finlay Geoghegan J. explained the reason for the deferral, stating:

> "It must … be recalled that an application for the return of a child under the Hague Convention is in the nature of a summary application. There is no full welfare assessment of the child prior to the Court reaching its decision and making if so decided an order for return. The welfare assessment is a matter for the Court of habitual residence. This is an important underlying principle. It is therefore particularly important in such cases that a child is only required to be interviewed on one occasion, if at all possible.
>
> It appears to me that the matters upon which the Child should be given an opportunity to be heard will not be established until there has been some determination of one or more of the legal issues arising on the claims made and defences thereto. If I were now to make an order for the interview of the Child and direct questions relating to what I would term 'standard Hague issues', there is a considerable risk that these would not address matters which may form part of the consideration of a trial judge. As I have indicated if a wrongful removal is established it is inevitable that the question of settlement will arise and the trial judge may want to hear the Child on matters relating to his current life in Ireland. Similarly if the Court decides it has jurisdiction upon a basis other than the Hague Convention , to make, without a full welfare assessment an order for the return of the child to California there may be matters in relation to which the trial judge would decide the Child should be given an opportunity to be heard. If, on the other hand, it is determined that there is no legal basis for an order for return without a full welfare assessment but the Court has a discretion to enforce the Californian order here, the Court may wish to give the Child an opportunity of being heard in relation to the matters concerning his contact with the applicant.
>
> In all those circumstances to avoid the possibility of multiple interviews I decided it was in the best interests of the Child that the question of the Child being heard should be left over until the trial and until a trial judge has had an opportunity of considering at least some of the legal issues raised in these unusual Hague proceedings. At that time the Court will be able to identify the matters about which the Child should be heard and specify same in the order for interview."

CMH v JPD [2014] IEHC 261 related to an unmarried father of a 13 year old boy, who wrongfully removed him from England and brought him to Ireland in February 2014. By the end of April, the boy was attending school in Ireland. The mother initiated proceedings in the English courts. In proceedings under the Abduction of Children Act 1991 before Finlay Geoghegan J., the only defence raised on behalf of the father against the application to return the boy to his mother was that this would be contrary to the boy's wishes. In this regard, art.11 of Council Regulation (EC) No. 2201/2003 (the "Brussels II *bis* Regulation") is of some significance as it gives a role, in cases falling under the scope of that Regulation, for the courts of the child's habitual residence to order the return of the child notwithstanding the fact that the courts of the country to which the child has been wrongfully removed or where the child is wrongfully retained have declined to order the child's return. In *C.A. v. C.A.* (otherwise *CMcC*), Finlay Geoghegan J. expressed the view that:

> "it does not appear that the potential for the court of habitual residence to make an enforceable order for return pursuant to art. 11(8) takes away from the requirement that this court take into account the policy of the Convention, not only to secure the prompt return of abducted children, but also to deter abduction in the first place, and to respect the judicial process of other contracting states. Nevertheless, it is a factor to be taken into account and the weight to be attached would depend upon the facts of the particular application. Care must be taken that the policy of the Convention to deter abduction is not undermined by giving an advantage in any subsequent hearing to a parent who wrongfully removed children. If the court of the jurisdiction of habitual residence is required to consider custody issues, including an issue of return in the context of the court of another member state having made an order for non-return, there may be such an advantage or a perceived advantage."

In essence, Finlay Geoghegan J. was there signalling that an Irish court should not be tempted by s.11 into exercising too broadly its discretion not to return the child in the confident knowledge that the courts of the child's habitual residence can have another look at the case. By the time they do so, the psychological evidence relating to the child's welfare may have moved in the direction of not disturbing the existing arrangements and that would be to give the wrongdoing parent a strategic advantage.

In *EJ v ED*, the clinical psychologist who interviewed the child reported that he would like to go to school in Ireland and continue to live with his father. He never felt that he fitted in with his peer group in England. He enjoyed his friends in Ireland, where he also saw his grandmothers. In relation to his reasons for objecting to returning to England, the clinical psychologist reported that "he would like to be close to his relatives" and that he "would like to stay in Ireland with his Father. He is happy to retain contact with his Mother through visits, calls, etc. but does not wish to live in England". On the question as to whether the boy appeared capable of forming his own views, the report stated:

> "He is, in my opinion, capable of forming his own views as to where he would like to live. He has sampled life in various countries and feels comfortable in Ireland. He worries about his Dad's health and is happy to be with him, whereas he feels that his Mother has her sisters for company and support. Sporting involvement features large in his pastimes and he does not seem to have engaged with any team or specific sport while in the UK... I believe he has come to these conclusions independently. He states

> that his Father has told him that he 'just wants what [his son] wants'. I found no evidence of undue influence on [the boy]'s views."

Finlay Geoghegan J. found on the totality of the evidence that the boy objected to being returned to England and that this was his own view. Overall, his reasons for objecting related to his wish to have his principal place of residence in Ireland such that he could do his schooling in Ireland and play his main team sports in Ireland rather than by reason of negative views about England. He had no objection to visiting England and appeared not to object per se to living with his mother, noting "the objection is rather to living with his Mother in England because that prevents him continuing to live and go to school in Ireland."

Finlay Geoghegan J. concluded that she should exercise the discretion given to the court under art.13 of the Hague Convention in favour of making an order for the boy's return to England. She had taken his views fully into account but they were not determinative of the order that the court should make. Irrespective of whether the court made or refused an order for his return, by reason of arts 11(6) to (8) of Reg. 2201/2003, the ultimate decision as to with which parent and in which country he might now live would be taken by the English courts, following a full welfare assessment as to what is in his best interests. Finlay Geoghegan J. observed:

> "I must have regard to the fact that [the boy] was taken from England to Ireland by his Father, wrongly, within the meaning of the Hague Convention amounting to what is commonly referred to as abduction. If I were now to refuse to make an order for [his] return ...., it appears that the Father might obtain a significant advantage to the further decision to be taken by the English courts, as [his son] would probably have spent a longer time in Ireland and would not have attended secondary school in Birmingham which is his Mother's plan for his continued living in England prior to the taking of any decision pursuant to Articles 11(6)–(8) of the Regulation. It is clearly contrary to the policy of the Convention to permit an abducting parent obtain such an advantage."

PARENTAL RESPONSIBILITY

In *F v G* [2014] IEHC 152, in a judgment delivered on 15 January 2014, Keane J. provided a most important analysis of the impact of the enactment of the Protection of Children (Hague Convention) Act 2000 (the "2000 Act") on Irish private international law. The 2000 Act implements into Irish law the 1996 Hague Convention on Jurisdiction, Applicable Law, Recognition, Enforcement and Co-operation in respect of Parental Responsibility and Measures for the Protection of Children (the "1996 Hague Convention"). Ireland has ratified the Convention; the United States of America has not.

In the instant case, the mother of a boy, born in 2011, had taken him from California to Ireland, pursuant to an order of a Californian court, subject to two conditions: first, that she should file the Californian order in the appropriate court in Ireland as a "mirror" order, if that was permissible in Ireland, or, if not permissible, that she should seek to have an order filed in an Irish court specifying that only California had jurisdiction to modify the Californian order and that Ireland only had jurisdiction to enforce the Californian order; and, secondly, that she should retain legal counsel in Ireland to assist the father in obtaining a legal guardianship for the child pursuant to the Guardianship of Infants Act 1964 (the "1964 Act") (as amended).

When the mother sought an order on these lines from the High Court, the father opposed her application on a number of grounds. One of these was that any jurisdiction to make a "mirror" order that there might once have been, either at common law or in exercise of the power conferred under s.11 of the 1964 Act, had been entirely displaced by the commencement of the provisions of the 2000 Act, because the United States of America was not yet a contracting state to the 1996 Hague Convention. The father argued specifically that the 2000 Act expressly excluded and extinguished any other jurisdictional basis upon which recognition, enforcement and co-operation in matters of parental responsibility or the protection of children could previously have been ordered by the courts in Ireland. Keane J. gave short shrift to this argument, having regard to the unambiguous language of s.12 of the 2000 Act. He stated:

> "[F]ar from amounting to a complete delineation of the relevant jurisdiction in respect of rights of custody and access (as exclusively that established in respect of a contracting state under the 1996 Convention), the 2000 Act expressly preserves any separate jurisdiction of the court there may be in relation both to a child who is not habitually resident in a contracting state and in relation to the recognition and enforcement of measures that have been taken by the authorities of a non-contracting state in respect of a child. It is, therefore, this express saver in respect of any such separate jurisdiction there may be that represents a conscious choice by the legislature and that choice is, as might be expected, to preserve rather than extinguish it."

Even if the 2000 Act had not preserved that separate and additional jurisdiction in express terms, it would not be possible, in Keane J.'s view, to accept the father's argument that certain jurisprudence of the Supreme Court impelled the conclusion that, by necessary implication, no such jurisdiction could have survived the commencement of that Act. The decision of the Supreme Court in *GMcG v DW (No. 2)(Joinder of the Attorney General)* [2000] 4 I.R. 1 was distinguishable. In the instant case, the mother had not invited the court to identify and apply an inherent jurisdiction to make a "mirror" order. She had sought orders under s.11 of the 1964 Act or under the existing common law. Moreover, it did not seem to Keane J. to follow that a specific legislative measure designed to give the force of law in Ireland to a Convention governing questions of jurisdiction and enforcement in a specific field of private international law between contracting states had to be construed as repealing, *sub silentio*, any and all pre-existing jurisdictional principles in that field between Ireland and a non-contracting state, whether by reference to the principle *expressio unius est exclusio alterius* or any other principle. Keane J. commented:

> "It seems to me that the [mother]'s argument is based upon the proposition that the creation and implementation of a specific statutory regime for contracting states under the 2000 Act not only supplanted any pre-existing jurisdictional rules that applied between such states (which it plainly did),

> but also, by necessary implication, extinguished any and all pre-existing jurisdictional rules as applied by this State to non-contracting states (which, in my view, it plainly did not). It seems to me that the latter proposition is a *non sequitur.*"

On the basis of McGuinness J.'s judgment in *CM v Delagación de Malaga* [1999] 2 I.R. 363, Keane J. was satisfied that the court had jurisdiction to protect the rights and welfare of any child who was an Irish citizen (and who was not habitually resident in a contracting state to the 1996 Convention or a Member State under the Brussels II *bis* Regulation), regardless of where he or she might be living or present at the time of the proceedings, although it was reasonable to do so "only with caution or circumspection". Keane J. contrasted the position in the instant case to that in *C.M. v. Delagación de Malaga*:

> "[T]he California Court has itself directed that the jurisdiction of this Court should be invoked, insofar as that is possible, in aid of that relocation order. In those circumstances, there is little or no risk of inconsistent orders being made in relation to the child in the two jurisdictions involved. Shortly put, in this case the Court is being asked to exercise a jurisdiction in support of, rather than in opposition to, the jurisdiction claimed by the court in the other jurisdiction concerned with the child's welfare."

Keane J. provided an extended analysis of the nature and present status of "mirror" orders in Ireland and England. He found that, whereas the Irish courts, when making orders authorising relocation abroad of a custodial parent and child, often required the custodial parent to seek a "mirror" order in the new country, they had not yet substantively addressed the possible basis for the making of mirror orders themselves. He concluded as follows:

> "In considering an application for 'mirror orders', in the guise of an application for a direction (or directions) on a question affecting the welfare of a child, pursuant to the provisions of section 11 of the 1964 Act, the Court is constitutionally and statutorily mandated to have regard to the welfare of the child as the first and paramount consideration, and that principle applies not only in Irish cases involving no foreign element but also in cases where one or both parties is of foreign nationality, domicile or residence, and even in cases where a foreign court has already made a guardianship or custody order.
>
> The nature and scope of the jurisdiction to make 'mirror' orders, pursuant to the terms of section 11 of the 1964 Act, falls to be considered by reference to first principles in the absence of any directly applicable governing authority. Of most obvious and direct relevance are the general legal principles governing the recognition or enforcement of foreign custody orders as a matter of private international law. The fundamental principle in that regard is that the existence of a custody order made by a court to which neither Brussels II *bis* nor any other international law instrument recognised by the law of the State applies does not prevent a court in this jurisdiction from making such orders in this jurisdiction as, having regard to the child's welfare, it thinks fit.

Subject to that general rule, a number of factors are relevant to the exercise of the Courts [sic] discretion in that regard. Those factors include the following:

(a) The custody order of a foreign court deserves grave consideration but the weight to be given to it must depend on the circumstances of the case.

(b) An order made very recently, no relevant change of circumstances being alleged, will carry great weight. Its persuasive effect is diminished by the passage of time and by a significant change in circumstances, for example the removal of the child to another country or the supervening illness of one of the claimants.

(c) The status of the foreign court, and the nature of the proceedings in and the legal approach taken by the court, may all be taken into account. The effect of the foreign order will be at its weakest when it was made many years ago and has since been modified by consent and the child has nearly attained his majority and so can decide for himself with which parent he wishes to live."

In the instant case, the order of the Californian court was entitled to grave consideration. It had been made comparatively recently. A full contested hearing had preceded the judgment. The relevant laws of the two jurisdictions were fundamentally similar, being directed to the ascertainment and protection of the best interests of the child. There had been no evidence before the court of any significant change of circumstances during the intervening period. The child was still of tender years and there was no suggestion that he was in a position to make his own meaningful decision about where he wished to reside. While it was perfectly clear that the court had to form an independent judgment on what was required to protect the welfare of the child, and that it must not blindly follow an order made by a foreign court, it was appropriate to give weight to a foreign judgment and order. Keane J. stated:

> "The present application comes before this Court within a very short time of the foreign judgment and, as there is no significant new circumstance to be considered, I accord very substantial weight to the judgment and orders of the California Court, and I conclude that, insofar as the jurisdiction of this Court under section 11 of the 1964 Act permits them to be made, orders broadly equivalent to those made by the California Court should be made in the best interests of the child in this case to protect the custody, access and visitation rights of the respondent as the child's father in the event of the child's relocation in the State. I prefer to use the term 'equivalent' order rather than the term 'mirror' order, as it seems to me that the latter carries overtones suggesting the mechanical transcription (or blind application) of the terms of the foreign court order, which is not the exercise upon which the Court has been engaged in this case."

In a subsequent judgment in the case ([2014] IEHC 153), delivered on 7 March 2014, Keane J. stated that he considered that it would be "entirely inappropriate" to make an order directly mirroring every operative part of the Californian judgment, as the mother had urged. Instead, the court should seek to identify those parts of the order of the foreign court concerned, and the equivalent orders available to the High Court to make, that offered the necessary auxiliary or ancillary protection for the welfare of the child and which were in the interests of the parties (and, in particular, the father) while the child was transiently present within the State. In Keane J.'s view, the court should not make orders relating to the respective rights or interests of the parties that were more properly the subject of the proceedings before the Californian court.

Keane J. went on to state that the court would make an order pursuant to s.11(2)(a) of the 1964 Act granting custody of the child to the parties jointly and directing that the mother was to exercise primary care and control of the child. The court would also make orders, again pursuant to s.11(2)(a), in respect of the father's electronic and physical access with the child once the mother and child had relocated to Ireland. Those orders reflected as closely as possible the equivalent orders set out under the headings "Electronic Visitation" and "Physical Visitation" in the judgment and order of the Californian court.

The issue of the proposed relocation of a parent, which underlay *F v G*, is a difficult one for the courts. At its heart is a normative competition between the right of a custodial parent (usually the mother) to choose to reside abroad, away from the non-custodial parent, with the probable effect of damaging the child's relationship with the non-custodial parent over time. In England, in *Payne v Payne* [2001] Fam. 473, the Court of Appeal emphasised the right to relocate. In Ireland, a greater emphasis has been placed on the welfare of the child, with the consequence that it may be harder for a custodial parent to convince the court that relocation is appropriate: see MacMenamin J.'s judgment in *UV v VU* [2011] IEHC 519, analysed in the *Annual Review of Irish Law 2011*, pp.394 – 395. For a comprehensive analysis of the policy issues, see Carruthers, "International Family Relocation: Recent UK Experience" [2012] *Juridical Review* 187.

In *RL v Her Honour Judge Margaret Heneghan* [2014] IEHC 664, Abbott J. touched on the issue, in a judicial review application which was unsuccessful on all of several grounds. One of these grounds related to the entitlement of the Circuit Court judge to deal with the issue of relocation on an appeal from the District Court. Abbott J., in the course of addressing the separate issue of the applicant's lack of candour, observed:

> "Where the applicant may have been misled by reason of her connections with English law is by reason of the toxic affect [sic] of the proposition in *Poel* [*v Poel* [1970] 1 W.L.R. 1469] as affirmed in *Payne*, that the custodial parent could selfishly pursue their interest in location without having regard to the interest of the child. The judgment of MacMenamin J. [in *UV v VU*] has clarified (if clarification were needed) that this position is not accepted in Ireland and the paramountcy principle or the best interests of the child is the ultimate criterion by which all the circumstances, including the desire of the custodial parent to relocate are considered. Indeed, the term 'custodial parent' has become somewhat of a misnomer in the context of what, in modern times, the courts seek to achieve as a mediating and cooperative system of co-parenting in the context of relocation of the child."

In *Child and Family Agency v CJ* [2014] IEHC 669, O'Hanlon J. granted a declaration under art.17 of Council Regulation (EC) 2201/2003 (the "Brussels II *bis* Regulation") that the courts of Ireland had no jurisdiction under the Regulation in respect of matters concerning parental responsibility for the child who was the subject of the proceedings before the court. It was a matter for the Scottish courts to consider and decide all welfare issues arising in the case. O'Hanlon J. also held that the High Court was the appropriate forum to discharge the functions under the Regulation. The District Court did not have any power to make declarations under the Regulation. The Court of Appeal reversed O'Hanlon J's judgment in part, treating her observations on the position of the District Court as obiter: [2015] IECA 86. We will be analysing this important decision of the Court of Appeal in the *Annual Review of Irish Law 2015*.

ADOPTION

Discovery In *SH v Udaras Uchtala na hEireann* [2014] IEHC 82, the applicants, who were seeking to have a child registered in the Register of Adoptions, sought discovery of "all documents relating to any entry of particulars by the respondent in the Register of Inter Country Adoptions since the commencement of the Adoption Act 2010 (the "2010 Act"), and of entry Inter Country Adoptions effected in Mexico and/or Inter Country Adoptions of children who were habitually resident in Mexico, including any documents relating to the applications for such entries". This broad application had been provoked by the failure of the respondent to register the child in circumstances where the child appeared to fall outside the terms of the legislation in a way that would be hard to justify on policy grounds.

The arguments between the parties drew the attention of the court to the distinction between the best interests of the child to whom the application related and the best interests of the child to whom the records (whether register or documents) related. Abbott J. was persuaded by the judgment of Macken J. in *DC v DM* [1992] 2 I.R. 150 that the distinction made in the 2010 Act was in favour of the paramountcy principle applying to the child "to whom the register or documents related". Abbott J. went on to state:

> "For the sake of completeness, I have examined the relevant provisions of the 2010 Act and find that the use of the words 'any child' might arguably suggest either applicant in a case such as this or the child described in the register or documents. The context in which these words appear clearly point to the meaning of 'any child' being the child to whom the entry in the register or the documents relate, and named therein. I have firmly come to this conclusion having considered the affect [sic] of the provisions of s.86(1) which states:-
>
> > 'An t-Ard Chláraitheoir shall keep an index to make traceable the connection between each entry in the Adopted Children Register and the corresponding entry in the Register of Births.'
>
> The use of the word 'each' in relation to entry [sic] which is to correspond to an entry in the Registry of Births clearly relates to one child – not just any child – and when s.88 of the Act of 2010 relating to privacy of adoption records states 'unless the court is satisfied that it is in the best interest of

any child concerned to make the order', the position becomes clear. That is because the use of the word 'concerned' after child has no meaning of itself, as, its use in the context of the section is that of a qualifying word. What word does it qualify in this context? It might be argued (looking at para.(b)), that it could relate to any child – anywhere–to whom discovery or inspection of documents etc might relate. However, looking at para.(a) of s.88 the context for the word to be qualified is set by the words 'referred to in s.86(2)'. This relates clearly to the register of 'each' child. The use of the word "concerned" as a qualifier plainly relates to the records of each child in s.86(2), and to posit any other qualifying role in para.(b) of s.88 would be to introduce a contradiction, or anomaly, in the face of the plain meaning of s.88, when read in conjunction with s.86(2)."

Transitional provisions In *O'C v Udaras Uchtala na hEireann* [2014] IEHC 580, Abbott J. held that a couple who were in the process of adopting a Mexican child when the 2010 Act came into effect had such vested rights as would warrant the court's exercise of its power under s.92(2) of the 2010 Act to direct the respondent to register the adoption, even though there had not been compliance with s.23. The Mexican law and judicial authorities had rendered such compliance impossible.

CONTRACT

Place of performance Article 5.1 of the Brussels 1 Regulation (Council Regulation (EC) 44/2001) provides that a person domiciled in a Member State may be sued in another Member State, in matters relating to a contract, in the courts for the place of performance of the obligation in question. Unless otherwise agreed, in the case of the provision of services, this is "the place in a Member State where, under the contract, the services were provided or should have been provided." In *McCoy v McFeely* [2014] IEHC 289, the plaintiff, resident in Northern Ireland, was injured by a tackle when he was playing a game of football in the Republic of Ireland. He later sued his solicitor, also resident in Northern Ireland, for breach of contract and negligence, alleging that the solicitor had undertaken to sue in the Irish High Court the tackler and the owners of the ground where the match took place. The solicitor contested these allegations, maintaining that the tackler was a person without means who resided in Northern Ireland, who would not be a mark for damages. Moreover, counsel had advised that a claim against the organisers of the game would not be successful. All that had occurred was the giving of advice, which took place in Northern Ireland and that advice had been received by the plaintiff in Northern Ireland. The plaintiff had accepted the advice and, as a result, there had never been any question of taking any steps to institute proceedings in the Irish High Court. The defendant maintained that the courts in Ireland did not have jurisdiction to deal with the matter as the firm was domiciled in Northern Ireland and as the advice which was given was imparted to the plaintiff in Northern Ireland. Barr J. remitted the latter for plenary hearing. He observed:

"If the defendants' version is accepted, then it would appear that no part of the contract, was to be performed within this State. Consequently, this Court would not have jurisdiction to hear the proceedings. If on the other

> hand, the plaintiff's version is accepted, then it would appear that the court would have jurisdiction under Art. 15.1 of Regulation 44/2001. It is not possible to resolve this conflict on the basis of the affidavit sworn by the solicitors acting for the parties in these proceedings. I am of opinion that it would be necessary to hear from the parties themselves."

Consumer contracts Article 16 of the Brussels 1 Regulation gives consumers the choice of suing the other party to the contract either in the courts of the Member State of the consumer's domicile or in the courts of the Member State of the other party. A consumer contract is defined (in part) by art.15(1)(c) as one involving a contract concluded by a person (the consumer) for a purpose which can be regarded as being outside his trade or profession and the contract has been concluded with a person who pursues commercial or professional activities in the Member State of the consumer's domicile "or, by any means, directs such activities to that Member State or to several States including that Member State, and the contract falls within the scope of such activities".

McDonald v AZ Sint Elizabeth Hospital [2014] IEHC 88 involved a claim alleging that a hospital in Belgium had breached its contract by negligently carrying out a medical operation on the plaintiff, an Irish domiciliary. The plaintiff had consulted a UK-based English language website, where he learned of the facilities offered by the hospital. The web-based promotional material was clearly directed at both the UK and Ireland. The literature was written in English and not in Flemish or French. Part of the promotional brochure stated: "SOS is a totally independent organisation of surgeons, health providers and caretakers. We are based in Belgium with clinics in the UK and Ireland. As part of our team, we have co-workers in the UK and Ireland, all of whom are well qualified, and who endeavour to offer you the very best possible service."

The brochure gave a consultation address in Dublin at a named medical centre. The prices for the initial consultation were offered in both sterling and euro. Prospective customers were supplied with an Irish telephone number and they were told to "use this Irish phone number to dial the clinic directly." The brochure also contained a testimonial from an Irish-based patient. The plaintiff twice telephoned the second named defendant, a consultant retained by the hospital, to discuss the proposed procedure, the costs involved and the making of the appropriate appointments. He later went to the hospital, paid the appropriate invoice and had the operation. Hogan J. had little doubt that the plaintiff was a "consumer". Applying the principles stated by the Court of Justice in Case C-269/95 *Benincasa v Dentalkit Srl* [1997] E.C.R. I-3767, Hogan J. was satisfied that the plaintiff had been acting outside his own trade or profession when he availed himself of the medical services supplied by the hospital and that these were also clearly services the provision of which was personal to him.

On the question whether the hospital had directed its activities to Ireland, Hogan J. had no difficulty in distinguishing the decision of Kearns P. in *Harkin v. Towpik* [2014] 1 I.L.R.M. 51. In that case an Irish-domiciled plaintiff had travelled to Poland for the purposes of certain cosmetic surgery. Having examined the judgment of the Court of Justice in Case C-144/09 *Hotel Alpenhof GmbH v Oliver Heller* [2010] E.C.R. I-12527, Kearns P. concluded on the facts of that case that the services in that case had not been "directed" to this jurisdiction. We analyse Kearns P.'s decision in the *Annual Review of Irish Law 2013*, pp.84–87. Hogan J. stated:

> "While the facts of *Harkin* are not dissimilar in many respects from the present case, there are nonetheless important if subtle differences. It is true that just as in *Harkin* the plaintiff travelled abroad .... for this procedure and there met the consultants for the first time. Just as in *Harkin*, the operation was also performed abroad and the plaintiff discharged the bill when he arrived at the Hospital. But it is equally clear that in contrast to the position in *Harkin* the website in question in the present was also unequivocally directed to customers in Ireland. Thus, the prices for the procedures were advertised in Euro (and not merely in sterling); an Irish telephone number was provided for Irish patients; the testimonials included one from an Irish patient and reference was made to the possibility of pre-travel consultations in Dublin and Cork.
>
> In this respect, therefore, the plaintiff in the present case comes within the *Hotel Alpenhof* test in that the Hospital clearly envisaged doing business with patients domiciled in Ireland. This was in contrast to the position in *Harkin* where the relevant website was *exclusively* directed at patients domiciled in the United Kingdom. Moreover, as Kearns P noted in his judgment, the plaintiff in that case had simply happened to come across the website following an internet search."

TORT

Place of harmful event Article 5 of the Brussels I Regulation gives the victim of a tort the choice of taking proceedings, not only in the state of the defendant's domicile, as art.2 provides, but also in the state where the harmful event allegedly occurred. In *McDonald v AZ Sint Elizabeth Hospital* [2014] IEHC 88, an Irish domiciliary claimed that he had received negligent treatment by a consultant retained by a hospital in Belgium. The plaintiff had discussed the proposed procedure and the costs involved with the consultant but his contract was with the hospital, not the consultant. Hogan J. held that, whereas the plaintiff was entitled to sue the hospital in Ireland for alleged breach of its consumer contract with him, he could not sue the consultant in Ireland alleging tort. Hogan J. held:

> "It is clear that the plaintiff had no contract with [the consultant] at such. He was merely a consultant employed or otherwise retained by the Hospital. It is true that the evidence suggests that [the plaintiff] personally paid [the consultant], but in effect the latter received the payment on behalf of the Hospital. Insofar, therefore, as [the plaintiff] has a claim against [the consultant] it is a claim in negligence only and there is no contractual relationship between the parties.
>
> As [the consultant] is domiciled in Belgium for the purposes of Article 2 and is [sic] there is no suggestion that the 'harmful event' for the purposes of Article 5(3) giving rise to the action in negligence occurred in Ireland, this Court accordingly lacks jurisdiction to entertain any claim as against

[the consultant]. It could only have jurisdiction if there was a consumer contract for the purposes of Article 15, but as there was no contract between these parties, the issue does not arise."

INSOLVENCY

Opening of secondary proceedings In *Rathville Ltd v McArthur Group Ltd (in Administration)* [2014] IEHC 355, Charleton J., in an ex tempore judgment, authorised the opening of secondary insolvency proceedings in respect of a British company which had for a number of years had a branch in Ireland which it had very recently shut down. Article 3(2) of the EU Insolvency Regulation provides:

> Where the centre of a debtor's main interests is situated within the territory of a Member State, the courts of another Member State shall have jurisdiction to open insolvency proceedings against that debtor only if he possesses an establishment within the territory of that other Member State. The effects of those proceedings shall be restricted to the assets of the debtor situated in the territory of the latter Member State.

Article 33(1) provides in part:

> The court, which opened the secondary proceedings, shall stay the process of liquidation in whole or in part on receipt of a request from the liquidator in the main proceedings, provided that in that event it may require the liquidator in the main proceedings to take any suitable measure to guarantee the interests of the creditors in the secondary proceedings and of individual classes of creditors. Such a request from the liquidator may be rejected only if it is manifestly of no interest to the creditors in the main proceedings… .

Charleton J. did not consider that the initiation of secondary proceedings would involve an unnecessary duplication. He noted that a provisional liquidator had already been appointed by the High Court and that this appointment had "proven not to be a wasted exercise" in the sense that a potential debt of nearly half a million euros of public money in terms of fiduciary taxes had been uncovered due to his efforts. This debt had "not been known of in the United Kingdom proceedings". There was a serious issue as to how the collection of fiduciary taxes in Ireland would be ranked in terms of priority in the United Kingdom proceedings. Charleton J. refused a stay, as it was clear to him that it was "manifestly of interest to the United Kingdom creditors that this process should continue".

FOREIGN JUDGMENTS

Public policy The EU system of private international law places great emphasis on the free movement of judgments. Once the jurisdictional grounds have been complied with, and the defendant properly notified of the proceedings, the judgment that follows should be recognised in other states more or less automatically. Public policy is retained as a ground for non-recognition, but it is accepted that it should be applied sparingly.

In *Celtic Salmon Atlantic (Killary) Ltd v Aller Acqua (Ireland) Ltd* [2014] IEHC 421, the Irish-domiciled plaintiff sued the Danish-domiciled defendant for breach of contract and negligence in respect of fish feed that it had supplied, which the plaintiff alleged was defective. The plaintiff's case depended on a report produced by an expert some time previously, the disputed fish feed being no longer in existence. The defendant had already obtained from a Danish court a judgment declaring that the fish food that it had supplied was not defective. The plaintiff had chosen not to participate in the Danish proceedings. The defendant sought to have the Irish proceedings dismissed as they were inconsistent with the judgment from the Danish court. Hogan J. declined to dismiss the Irish proceedings in respect of this claim. He stated:

> "[I]n the very special circumstances of this present case, recognition of the Danish judgment in respect of claim 2 would be manifestly contrary to public policy for the purposes of Article 34(1) of the Brussels Regulation. This is because the operation of the Danish Administration of Justice Act meant that the expert report prepared by Celtic Atlantic's expert would probably not be admissible in evidence or, if admissible, would not be given any weight. The practical consequence of this was that Celtic Atlantic could not effectively advance its claim that the fish feed was unsuitable for this type of fish, since the success of this claim was entirely contingent on the admissibility of an expert report. Celtic Atlantic could not have foreseen in June and July 2008 that it would have been necessary to apply to the Danish courts to have such a report commissioned. The tests which [the expert] conducted in the early summer of 2008 could not now be readily duplicated, even if an application to the Danish courts for the appointment of an expert under the Danish Administration of Justice Act were to be successful."

The decision raises the large question as to whether the fact that different rules of procedure apply in different European states which can have differential implications for the success of a claim if taken in one or other state can generate a public policy barrier to recognition of a judgment. The plaintiff in this case was fully entitled to advance its case in the Danish courts in accordance with the Danish rules of procedure. The fact that it did not, and possibly could not, have anticipated that it would be litigating in Denmark some time in the future was perhaps unfortunate. Whether public policy should justify its suing in Ireland inconsistently with the principle of recognition of prior judgments is more debatable.

Constitutional Law

ORAN DOYLE, Trinity College Dublin
and
ESTELLE FELDMAN, Trinity College Dublin

ACCESS TO JUSTICE

Champerty The issue referred by the Supreme Court back to the High Court in *Greenclean Waste Management Ltd v Leahy (No.2)* [2014] IEHC 314 was whether after the event (ATE) legal costs insurance is illegal in this jurisdiction by reason of the tort of champerty or other analogous public policy considerations. Hogan J. observed that the common law torts of maintenance and champerty long pre-dated the coming into force of the Constitution and, accordingly, were carried over by Art.50.1. Furthermore, in contrast with the position in England and Wales, the scope of these torts has not been directly affected or altered by legislation. At para.10 he defined maintenance as the improper provision of support to litigation in which the supporter has no direct or legitimate interest. Hogan J. continued:

> "Champerty, on the other hand: 'is an aggravated form of maintenance and occurs when a person maintaining another's litigation stipulates for a share of the proceeds of the action or suit': *Camdex International Ltd. v. Bank of Zambia* [1998] Q.B. 22, 29, per Hobhouse L.J. Champerty may thus be described with only a little exaggeration as a secular form of simony within the legal system, for, as Hobhouse L.J. aptly put it in *Camdex International*, what 'is objectionable is trafficking in litigation.'"

Nevertheless, Hogan J. acknowledged that since the torts were first recognised diverse concepts such as legal aid, representative actions, pro bono work, "no foal, no fee" arrangements and the involvement in litigation of community and voluntary groups and trade unions in support of their members had become common practice. Thus, he found, at para.11 that "the scope of application of the law of champerty must thus accommodate itself to modern social realities and must be interpreted accordingly." He analysed the nature and scope of ATE insurance and construed the policy concluding:

> 26. In truth, the real objection to ATE insurance is to the size of the premium and the fact that it is normally payable only after a positive court decision or settlement. At one level it is easy to represent this as simply a disguised method of investing in litigation and recovering a share of the proceeds of the action under the guise of a handsome premium. If ATE coverage was confined to this, then I think the argument that it savoured of champerty and was therefore void as contrary to public policy would be almost unanswerable.

> 27. Yet there is more to ATE than this. There are certainly some cases – even if doubtless a minority of cases–where ATE is payable to cover the insured's legal costs even where the insured has lost the litigation. The premium is also payable where the coverage is terminated in advance of the determination of the proceedings. It should also be borne in mind that ATE also serves important needs within the community by facilitating access to justice for persons and entities who might otherwise be denied this. In that regard, ATE insurers provide a legitimate service by providing access to justice and this service cannot properly be regarded as simply regarded as either investing in or trafficking in litigation."

Ad hoc legal aid scheme effectively a right The respondent in *Minister for Justice and Equality v O'Connor* [2014] IEHC 640 failed in his challenge to the constitutionality of the European Arrest Warrant Act 2003. The plaintiff had claimed that in failing to make provision for statutory-based legal aid the Act contravened the equality guarantee in Art.40.1. Edwards J. in his comprehensive judgment held that the presumption of constitutionality had not been rebutted and that the court had no reason to believe that the Act was constitutionally deficient in any respect. Inter alia he relied on *Minister for Justice, Equality and Law Reform v Olsson* [2011] 1 I.R. 384 (*Annual Review of Irish Law 2011*, pp.314, 315 and 333). His description of the non-statutory Attorney General's Scheme, since renamed as The Legal Aid – Custody Issues Scheme, is informative:

> "In the case of a person arrested on foot of a European arrest warrant, effective access to justice is in fact afforded by the guarantees provided in s.13(4) of the Act of 2003, coupled with the possibility, which exists for persons unable to fund legal representation from within their own resources, of seeking a recommendation under the Attorney General's Scheme / the Legal Aid (Custody Issues) Scheme that such representation should be paid for by the State. The evidence given in this Court by Mr. Gilheaney, which mirrors that given to the Supreme Court by Mr. Jevon Alcock in the Olsson case, was that where a judicial recommendation is granted the Legal Aid Board invariably follows that recommendation. In reality, the discretion, such as it is, is only ever exercised one way, that is in favour of the applicant under the scheme, save, of course, and as provided for in the published scheme, in those relatively rare cases where fraud is suspected based upon evidence of substantial non-disclosure, or misrepresentation, concerning the applicant's financial means.
>
> The Court completely accepts that the Attorney General's Scheme / the Legal Aid (Custody Issues) Scheme is not law, that it is non-statutory in origin, and that it has not otherwise been established by law. It is simply an ad hoc administrative scheme. However, in this Court's view there is no requirement for it to be a statutory scheme or otherwise established in law. The important thing is that that for which it provides, which I am satisfied on the evidence before me is effectively available as of right, should not be contrary to law or prohibited by law."

Relative prior knowledge of litigants In judicial review proceedings in

Harrington v The Environmental Protection Agency [2014] IEHC 307 Barrett J., in assessing whether there were extenuating circumstances for delay in commencing proceedings, observed at para.6: "The court does not consider that it is reasonable to expect Mr. Harrington or individuals in the exact same position to purchase the *Irish Times* or continuously to consult the EPA website so as to determine the EPA's position from time to time on various matters." This might be considered a more contemporary although less evocative version of Kennedy C.J.'s 1935 obiter when he found that the essentials of common justice had been disregarded by an officially published determination of the Land Commission about "matters involving rights of specific interest and importance to individuals, some of whom, if not all, are poor men, tenants of poor holdings, men moreover unlikely in the course of a lifetime to see a copy of *Iris Oifigiúl*" (*In re Estate of Earl Mountcharles* [1935] I.R. 163 at 167).

ADMINISTRATION OF JUSTICE

Admonishment for abuse of process Edwards J. was required to consider whether it was unconscionable for the applicant to seek rendition of the respondent for a second time in *Minister for Justice and Equality v J.A.T* [2014] IEHC 320. The respondent claimed multiple breaches of rights inter alia the right to fair procedures, art.6 of the European Convention on Human Rights and/or Arts 38 and 40 of the Constitution; the rights to life, liberty, bodily integrity and human dignity, arts 2, 3 and 5 ECHR and/or Arts 40.3 and 40.4 of the Constitution; the right to respect for, and enjoyment of, family life, art.8 ECHR and/or Art.41 of the Constitution. It was accepted that due to his medical adversities the respondent was a vulnerable person, likely to find the proceedings against him more burdensome than a person in the whole of their physical and mental health. However, Edwards J. noted that to seek the extradition of such a person is not per se abusive of the process. He continued by describing the circumstances of the case which included the fact that there had been previous proceedings which had failed; the reasons why the first proceedings failed; the justification, if any, for the applicant seeking to come again; the procedural history of the case including the total time involved to date; the alleged delay and if delay was indeed a factor, the degree to which such delay had been culpable; the public interest in the respondent's extradition; and finally, the respondent's personal circumstances including his particular vulnerabilities.

> "It is a fact beyond dispute that the first set of proceedings failed for reasons that could have been addressed within the scope of those proceedings if the defects, or problems, had been identified and/or correctly engaged with, in time. It is also correct to say that no specific explanation is proffered as to why appropriate steps were not taken. In the Court's view it is regrettable that the applicant has not risen to the challenge of engaging with this issue in the course of the present proceedings. With due respect to counsel for the applicant the reason is not 'blindingly obvious' as he suggests. Yes, it was necessary to seek to come again because the first proceedings failed, and it is indeed obvious why those proceedings failed. What is not at all obvious, however, is why they were allowed to fail in circumstances where the defects were capable of being addressed at a relatively early stage."

On balance, Edwards J. was satisfied that the respondent had suffered unjust harassment on account of the manner in which his rendition had been pursued to date, and that cumulatively the proceedings in *Minister for Justice, Equality and Law Reform v J.A.T* [2010] IESC 61; unreported, Supreme Court, Hardiman J., nem diss, 21 December 2010 ("T. (No. 1") and the present proceedings, had subjected the respondent in particular, but also his family, to oppression. He therefore found that the proceedings must be regarded as being de facto abusive of the court's process. However, following his comprehensive and careful analysis, he did not consider that he would be justified in refusing surrender, notwithstanding that the manner in which the respondent's rendition had been pursued had been abusive of the process. Edwards J. reasoned as follows:

> "It is a matter of significance that nobody has set out to deliberately abuse the Court's process or by underhand and despicable means to secure an unfair advantage. That said, a duty of care was owed both to the court and to the respondent, which has ostensibly been breached. This is not a case, however, where irremediable ongoing prejudice has been caused to the respondent by the unjustifiable prolongation of the rendition efforts. The respondent's medical conditions were pre-existing and were not caused by the additional oppressive stress to which he has been subjected. Moreover, his medical conditions, though they remain ongoing, have fortunately not significantly worsened with the effluxion of time. Indeed, there has been some improvement. The many risk factors for self harm and suicide identified by Dr. M. in his report existed at the time of the first proceedings. Though Dr. M. has stated that the stress of being surrendered to the United Kingdom authorities may potentially have a negative impact on both the respondent's mental health and that of his son, I am satisfied on the evidence that that was always going to be the case given the vulnerabilities of those parties. Accordingly, while oppression has occurred, and it is very regrettable, it may be regarded as an historical prejudice at this time in the sense that the case is now at the point that it ought to have been at in January 2009, when the High Court gave judgment in *T. (No 1)*, had the initial rendition request been addressed with due diligence. However, any surrender that may happen hereafter, with all its direct and indirect consequences, is something that the respondent and his family would have to have faced in any event even if the first case had been properly conducted. Moreover, the court is entitled to take account of the fact that the respondent, and others affected, may possibly have legal remedies open to them to pursue in respect of any suffering which they have been caused to experience unnecessarily.
>
> In this Court's view the abuse of process that has occurred in this case can be appropriately addressed by admonishment of the parties responsible for it, and particularly of the applicant who had carriage of the proceedings in this jurisdiction at all stages. The Court wishes to deprecate in strong terms the fact that the respondent has been unjustly harassed and oppressed and unnecessarily twice vexed with litigation. That having been recorded, I consider that the abuse that has occurred has not been so egregious that the mere fact of going forward in the light of it would be offensive. On

balance, taking into account all of the circumstances of the case, I believe that it should still be allowed to proceed in the overall interests of justice."

Constitutional jurisdiction of High Court Art.34.3.1 confers the High Court "a full original jurisdiction in and power to determine all matters and questions whether of law or fact, civil or criminal." In *Wicklow County Council v Fortune* (No.4) [2014] IEHC 267 Hogan J. observed at para.11 that if "this Court [sic] not grant a declaration of right in an appropriate case, it is hard to see how this constitutional mandate 'to determine all matters and questions' could properly be fulfilled and this is so even when this Court is sitting (as here) in its appellate capacity". He held that this was distinct from any statutory provision.

In *Dunne v Mahon* [2014] IESC 24, Clarke J. (MacMenamin and Dunne JJ. concurring), inter alia, held that the High Court has a jurisdiction to dissolve an unincorporated association or club where no appropriate machinery exists for securing its proper winding up.

CONSTITUTIONAL AND NOMINATE TORTS

> "The governing question in essence is identical in all of these particular cases: can it be said that the nominate tort provides an adequate or complete mechanism for the vindication of individual rights?" (Hogan J. in *D.F. v Garda Commissioner (No.3)* [2014] IEHC 213 at para.20).

False imprisonment and assault and battery For those who anticipate in a judgment of Hogan J. comprehensive reasoning, detailed in-depth knowledge of constitutional, common law and statutory precedents and nuances from both within and without the jurisdiction, *D.F. v Garda Commissioner (No.3)* [2014] IEHC 213 is no disappointment. It is a tour de force. The previous judgments in *D.F.* have been analysed in *Annual Review of Irish Law 2013*, and the factual background may be found there.

The plaintiff was claiming damages in respect of the nominate torts of false imprisonment and assault and battery as well as for negligence and breach of duty. In addition, damages were claimed for breaches of constitutional rights and for breach of rights under the European Convention of Human Rights Act 2003. Further, damages were claimed for breaches under the Charter of Fundamental Rights of the European Union and under the United Nations Convention on the Rights of Persons with Disabilities 2006. Finally, the plaintiff sought declaratory relief in relation to the illegality of the arrest. In the instant proceedings the defendants contended that some of these claims should be struck out as either unsustainable in their own right or as otherwise merely replicating claims for damages in respect of nominate torts of assault and false imprisonment.

Considering the constitutional claims, Hogan J. found it convenient to break down the individual claims and to assess the claims based on specific nominate torts by reference to the individual constitutional guarantees.

Right to liberty Art.40.4.1 Regarding the tort of false imprisonment Hogan J. relied on the summary by Fawsitt J. in *Dullaghan v Hillen* (1957) Ir. Jur. Rep. 10

at 15 and affirmed the observation of McMahon and Binchy in their "magisterial textbook" *Law of Torts*, 4th edn (Dublin: Bloomsbury, 2013), p.911 that these comments represent "'an admirably succinct statement of the principal features of the tort.'" He found it clear from this exposition of the parameters of the tort of false imprisonment that

> "it may accordingly be regarded as a complete and full vindication of the guarantee of personal liberty in Article 40.4.1. Liability for false imprisonment is strict and is not based on notions of fault or negligence. By providing a mechanism for the protection of individual liberty in this fashion the common law may thus be said to give full effect to this particular constitutional guarantee" (at para.22).

By reason of unnecessary duplication he struck out the claim for damages for breach of the constitutional right to liberty as being simply another way of claiming the same relief.

Rights to the person, bodily integrity and privacy Art.40.3.2° Hogan J. then considered whether the claims in assault and battery were similarly duplicated by the claims for breach of the constitutional rights to the person, bodily integrity and privacy as guaranteed by Art.40.3.2°. He agreed with Baker J.'s obiter in *P.R. v K.C.* [2014] IEHC 126 (also see elsewhere in this chapter) that the nominate torts of assault and battery may generally be regarded as a realisation of the constitutional command in Art.40.3.2 to protect the person. The question which arose in the instant case was whether there are any circumstances at all in which these constitutional guarantees can be called in aid in order to supplement these torts.

Since the tort of assault requires a prior apprehension of a battery before it actually takes place, absent this apprehension, no tort of assault is committed. Hogan J. observed that this factor could be relevant given the plaintiff's mental condition. He did stress the assertion of the Gardaí that they had acted lawfully at all times. Nevertheless, he refused to strike out this element of the constitutional claim because

> "it is just possible that the plaintiff will be able to demonstrate at the full hearing of the action that these nominate torts of assault and battery will insufficiently vindicate these constitutional rights to the integrity of the person so far as the manner of his arrest by members of the Gardaí are concerned" (at para.32).

Arts.40.3.1° and 40.3.2° protections Applying the test of duplication to the other claims for damages he dismissed those under the European Convention of Human Rights Act 2003 having already held, at para.39, that as expressed they were non-justiciable under s.3 of that Act. His obiter in para.41 is nonetheless constitutionally significant:

> "Insofar as the common law torts of assault and battery offered inadequate protection to the plaintiff's rights in the present case, every protection in respect of the guarantee against torture and inhuman and degrading treatment is necessarily and by definition subsumed in the concomitant

protection of the person in Article 40.3.2 and the protections of bodily integrity in Article 40.3.1."

For completeness it should be added that Hogan J. at paras 42–49 struck out as unsustainable the claim based on the Charter of Fundamental Rights of the European Union as the matters at issue were wholly internal to the State, at paras 42-49. He held the claim under the United Nations Convention on the Rights of Persons with Disabilities 2006 non-justiciable, at paras 50-55. The claims for declaratory relief were also struck out as being inappropriate and potentially confusing in what would be a jury case, at paras 56-61.

Reckless lending In *Healy v Stepstone Mortgage Funding Ltd* [2014] IEHC 134 Hogan J. rejected the existence of a tort of reckless lending observing that inventing a new category of torts is reserved to the Oireachtas by Art.15.2.1. He did, however, elucidate on the incremental development of the common law system, stating at para.9 that the courts can generally only develop or supplement the law of torts where this corpus of law has been shown to be "basically ineffective" to protect constitutional rights in a particular case. He cited as examples *Meskell v Coras Iompair Éireann* [1973] I.R. 121, *Hanrahan v Merck, Sharp & Dohme Ltd.* [1988] I.L.R.M. 629 at 636, per Henchy J., *Herrity v Associated Newspapers Ltd.* [2008] IEHC 249, [2009] 1 I.R. 326 and *Sullivan v Boylan* [2013] IEHC 104.

Statutory dependants' wrongful death action *Hewitt v Health Service Executive* [2014] IEHC 300 considered whether a separate cause of action for wrongful death lay for statutory dependants which was within the statutory time limits in contrast to the action taken by the personal representative of the deceased which was statutorily time barred. Baker J. observed that tort is an important tool for the vindication of constitutional rights, citing Hogan J. in *D.F. v Garda Commissioner (No.3)* [2014] IEHC 213 and her own judgment in *P.R. v K.C.* [2014] IEHC 126, both cases considered elsewhere in this chapter. She also cited Hardiman J.'s judgment in *Grant v Roche Products (Ireland) Ltd.* [2008] IESC 35 in which he had affirmed Henchy J.'s judgment in *Hanrahan v Merck Sharpe & Dohme (Ireland) Ltd.* [1988] I.L.R.M. 629, and had pointed to the role of the law of torts in implementing the State's duty under Art.40.3 and the Personal Rights Articles of the Constitution. In *Hewitt* the constitutional imperative required a broad construction of s.48 of Civil Liabilities Act 1991 so as not to exclude the persons entitled to bring a claim under the section by events which occurred before the cause of action could have accrued. There is also a constitutional requirement of fairness to the defendant. Thus, in arriving at this decision Baker J. held that the action under s.48 may be brought only if a causative connection can be shown between the death and the alleged wrongful act of a defendant. This would be tested by the evidence and the likely success of the legal action lessened the longer the time that passed between the death and the action alleged to have caused death.

COURT PROCEEDINGS AND PROCEDURES

Anonymity in court proceedings In *MARA (Nigeria) (infant) v Minister for Justice and Equality* [2014] IESC 71, Charleton J. gave detailed consideration to the circumstances in which court proceedings might be heard otherwise than in public or not openly reported. Art.34.1 requires that justice be administered in public "save in such special and limited cases as may be prescribed by law." Legislation might require an *in camera* hearing, reporting restrictions, or a prohibition on the identification of the parties. Courts have a discretion to direct that proceedings be heard otherwise than in public, but this should only be exercised in the most exceptional cases. A concern for privacy was not sufficient, since most court cases are a source of stress and anxiety for the litigants. Only in circumstances that would thwart the right to litigate or make litigation virtually impossible – due for example to threats to personal safety – should a court exercise the discretion to direct that proceedings be heard otherwise than in public. In the context of asylum seekers, the statutory basis for restricting identifying asylum seekers was s.19 of the Refugee Act 1996, as amended, which provides that no matter likely to lead members of the public to identify a person as an applicant under this Act shall be published in a written publication available to the public or be broadcast without the consent of that person. This meant that, although proceedings could be conducted in public, no identification of persons could occur in any written report of those proceedings.

The plaintiff in *ABC v DEF* [2014] IEHC 680 was granted an interim injunction preventing the defendant from issuing defamation proceedings which would identify her. The plaintiff, of fragile mental health and with frequent suicidal ideation (at paras 5 and 15), had accused the defendant of child sexual abuse (at para.6) as a consequence of which he had been suspended from his ministry and become subject to media attention. White J. noted at para.36 that the matter had been referred to the DPP and that if the defendant were charged, s.7 of the Criminal Law Act 1981, as amended, would apply and the complainant could not be named. She had not sought a hearing in camera but to restrict disclosure of her name or identity. In weighing up the balance of convenience White J. considered it an important factor that the plaintiff did not seek to publish nor was the plaintiff responsible for the decisions which had led to the unnecessary publicity for the defendant. Whilst understanding "the defendant's anger and frustration where innocence is maintained but compromised when suspension from ministry occurred" he held that in the hierarchy of constitutional rights, the undoubted risk to the plaintiff's life took precedence.

Entry to the Commercial Court list In *Morrissey v National Asset Management Agency* [2014] IEHC 343, Kelly J. rejected an application to have the proceedings transferred into the Commercial Court list. The plaintiffs owed considerable sums of money to NAMA and other parties. In their plenary summons they sought declarations and damages largely on constitutional and ECHR grounds. The judge managing the Commercial Court list has a wide discretion whether to admit cases to that list: it is not limited to 'commercial law' cases but rather concerns cases that have a commercial character. However, in *PJ Carroll Ltd v Minister for Health and Children* [2005] 1 I.R. 294, Geoghegan J. in the Supreme Court had commented obiter that caution should be exercised in admitting "fundamentally constitutional" cases into the Commercial Court list, as distinct from commercial cases with a constitutional dimension. Kelly J. placed considerable weight on this comment in coming to the conclusion that the proceedings in question were fundamentally constitutional and ought not be admitted to the list.

PIAB authorisation In *PR v KC* [2014] IEHC 126, Baker J. held that an action for breach of constitutional rights did not require an authorisation from the Personal Injuries Assessment Board before it could proceed to court. The plaintiff sued for breach of his right to bodily integrity arising out of alleged sexual abuse. Section 4(1)(iii) of the Personal Injuries Assessment Board Act 2003 excludes from that Act "any action intended to be pursued in respect of an alleged breach by a person of a provision of the Constitution." Baker J. rejected the argument of the defendant that this would allow people to avoid the application of the Act simply by recharacterising their claim in terms of a breach of constitutional rights. In each case, such a claim would have to be scrutinised to see whether the constitutional element was merely an ancillary claim or another way of seeking the same relief. In this case, the constitutional element was not ancillary in that sense. Accordingly, no PIAB authorisation was required before it could go to court.

In a subsequent case, however, the Supreme Court took a different approach. In *Clarke v O'Gorman* [2014] IESC 72, O'Donnell J., with whom the other members of the court agreed, held that the reference to "any action intended to be pursued in respect of an alleged breach by a person of a provision of the Constitution" must be understood to refer to the sort of residual cases where the law of torts was not adequate and horizontal constitutional rights might have some effect. Therefore, any case that could be characterised in terms of traditional tort law was subject to the need for a PIAB authorisation.

Joinder of party to proceedings In *Waterville Fisheries Development Ltd v Aquaculture Licenses Appeals Board* [2014] IEHC 248, Hogan J. considered an application that the judicial review of a decision by the Aquaculture Licences Appeal Board should be dismissed *in limine* because the applicant had failed to serve two statutorily prescribed notice parties within the requisite time limit. Both notice parties were subsequently served and indicated that they had no interest in participating in the proceedings. Hogan J. held that the statutory requirement could not be read in a narrowly literal manner but rather must be construed in a manner that reflects fundamental constitutional values, such as the right of access to the courts. The section should therefore be read as if it referred to "relevant parties who had a real interest in the outcome of the proceedings." The board and the grantee of the licence were necessary parties to the judicial review proceedings; other parties were not.

Financial Services Ombudsman In *O'Brien v Financial Services Ombudsman* [2014] IEHC 268, Hogan J. rejected a claim that the FSO had unduly delayed in making a determination of the applicant's claim. Although the delays were unfortunate, they were not so manifestly excessive as to be inexcusable. He paid particular regard to the resource constraints under which the FSO operated. However, he also considered a preliminary objection by the FSO to the fact that FLAC, the applicant's solicitors, had published a report critical of the FSO that included reference to an earlier stage of the applicant's claim and that more or less coincided with the High Court hearing. Although Hogan J. could understand how "a conscientious public officer such as [sic] Ombudsman would be anxious to uphold the independence of his office against perceived slights of this kind," he considered the complaint to be unfounded. FLAC's report was "a sober and well informed critique of recent legislative and judicial developments in an area in which there are doubtless a wide variety of views." In his view, FLAC was endeavouring to educate public opinion in the sense provided for in Art.40.6.1° of the Constitution. The Ombudsman and others might object to the claim that he was pro-industry, but constitutional guarantees would be wholly undermined if such views could not be freely voiced. This was especially so in the context of criticism of those, such as politicians, judges and statutory office-holders, who were privileged to hold high office in the name of the People of Ireland.

CRIMINAL PROCESS RIGHTS

Right of access to a solicitor *People (DPP) v Gormley* [2014] IESC 17 provides probably the most significant instance of the courts adjusting their understanding of Irish constitutional law in response to developments at ECHR level. This case involved two joined appeals from the Court of Criminal Appeal on grounds certified as being of exceptional public importance. The cases both revolved around claims of rights of access to solicitors while in Garda custody. Mr Gormley, suspected of rape, made inculpatory statements before his solicitor arrived. Mr White, suspected of murder, provided physical samples pursuant to the Criminal Justice (Forensic Evidence) Act 1990, prior to the arrival of his solicitor. Both were subsequently convicted, with reliance being placed in both cases on the evidence obtained in this way.

The courts had previously established that a right of reasonable access to a solicitor is constitutionally protected. In *People (Director of Public Prosecutions) v Madden* [1977] I.R. 336, the Court of Criminal Appeal had held that this right did not impose any obligation on the Gardaí to proffer the assistance of a legal adviser without request. In *People (Director of Public Prosecutions) v Healy* [1990] 2 I.R. 73, the Supreme Court held that the right of reasonable access to a solicitor required the Gardaí to inform the accused immediately of the arrival of the solicitor and, if the accused requested it, to grant access to the solicitor without any delay. The only basis for refusing such a request would be reasons which objectively viewed from the point of view of the interest or welfare of the detained person, would be viewed by a court as being valid. In *People (Director of Public Prosecutions) v Buck* [2002] 2 I.R. 268, Keane C.J. held that the questioning of an accused person prior to the arrival of her solicitor did not breach any constitutional right of reasonable access to a solicitor, in such a way as to bring into play the exclusionary rule. Instead, the trial judge should address the admissibility of that evidence in her discretion, having regard to fairness to the accused and to public policy. In *People (Director of Public Prosecutions) v O'Brien* [2005] 2 I.R. 206, the right of reasonable access was breached where the Gardaí recommended a particular solicitor consciously knowing that there would be a delay in his arrival. However, this was held not to affect the admissibility of statements made after he had arrived and consulted with his client. In *Lavery v Member in Charge, Carrickmacross Garda Station* [1999] 2 I.R. 390, the Supreme Court held that the right of reasonable access did not extend to allowing the accused have his solicitor present during questioning. In *People*

(Director of Public Prosecutions) v Creed [2009] IECCA 90, the Court of Criminal Appeal held that as there was no *conscious and deliberate* breach of the right of the accused to reasonable access to a solicitor, it was a matter for the discretion of the trial judge whether to admit in evidence a hair sample that the accused had been under an obligation to provide. One interesting feature of this case law was that the breach of a right of reasonable access to a solicitor was held to vitiate the legality of the detention of the accused. That rendered the accused in unlawful, and hence unconstitutional, detention, with the result that any evidence had to be excluded. However, one side-effect of this constitutional device was that an accused could drift in and out of lawful custody depending on the reasonableness of the actions of the Gardaí in allowing the accused access to her solicitor. A further side-effect is that a breach of the right would have the same outcome, in evidentiary terms, for physical samples as for statements, since both would occur when the accused was in unlawful custody.

The Supreme Court placed considerable reliance on the case law of the European Court of Human Rights, as applied in the United Kingdom by its Supreme Court, in reaching its conclusion as to the meaning of the Constitution. In *Salduz v Turkey* (2009) 49 E.H.R.R. 19, the applicant had been convicted partly on the basis of a statement taken by the police while he was interrogated in the absence of a lawyer. Mr Salduz challenged his conviction before the European Court of Human Rights on the basis that it infringed art.6(3) of the ECHR, which provides that everyone charged with a criminal offence has the right to defend himself in person or through legal assistance of his own choosing or, if he has not sufficient means to pay for legal assistance, to be given it free when the interests of justice so require. The Grand Chamber held in favour of Mr Salduz. Reviewing the importance of fair trial rights, the way in which pre-trial events can affect trials, and the increasing complexity of criminal law such as to increase the need for legal advice, the court, at para.55, stated the general principle as follows:

> "in order for the right to a fair trial to remain sufficiently "practical and effective" (see paragraph 51 above) Article 6 § 1 requires that, as a rule, access to a lawyer should be provided as from the first interrogation of a suspect by the police, unless it is demonstrated in the light of the particular circumstances of each case that there are compelling reasons to restrict this right. Even where compelling reasons may exceptionally justify denial of access to a lawyer, such restriction – whatever its justification – must not unduly prejudice the rights of the accused under Article 6 …. The rights of the defence will in principle be irretrievably prejudiced when incriminating statements made during police interrogation without access to a lawyer are used for a conviction."

In *Cadder v Her Majesty's Advocates* [2010] UKSC 43, a majority of the UK Supreme Court held that the implication of *Salduz*, and other cases applying it, was that contracting states were under an obligation to organise their systems in such a way as to ensure that, unless in the particular circumstances of the case there are compelling reasons for restricting the right, a person who is detained has access to advice from a lawyer before he is subjected to police questioning.

Clarke J. also noted case law of the ECtHR which distinguishes between the right of access to a lawyer and its consequences for the taking of statements and taking of samples: unless there are circumstances amounting to cruel and degrading treatment in breach of art.3, the taking of physical samples before an accused person has access to a lawyer does not raise concerns under the ECHR.

Having reviewed this case law, Clarke J. proceeded to consider what he referred to as "the international jurisprudence." Clarke J. emphasised, at para.7.9, the limited circumstances in which foreign jurisprudence could be relevant:

> "Foreign jurisprudence which turns, not on general principles or on rights expressed in the same or similar terms, but on the specifics of foreign constitutional or legislative documents, will only be of true assistance if the Irish regime under consideration is sufficiently similar."

These caveats are fairly standard, but it is noteworthy that he did not apply the same caveats in respect of the ECHR case law from Strasbourg and London. Clarke J. reviewed fairly quickly the position in the USA, Canada, New Zealand and Australia. He characterised the first three of these jurisdictions as holding that questioning could not proceed after an accused requested a lawyer, although there were differences in terms of whether the accused had to ask for a lawyer.

Clarke J. formulated the question facing the Supreme Court as follows at para.8.1:

> "The first real question of principle which this Court, therefore, now has to consider is as to whether the entitlement to a trial in due course of law, guaranteed by Article 38(1) of Bunreacht na hÉireann, encompasses an entitlement to have access to legal advice prior to the conduct of any interrogation of a suspect arrested and/or prior to the taking of any forensic samples from such a suspect."

Clarke J. noted that the current state of Irish law did not guarantee any such right, but noted the intermittent dicta of the courts to the effect that the Constitution is a living document that requires to be interpreted from time to time in accordance with prevailing norms. He first accepted that pre-trial matters could be covered by Art.38.1, given that arrest represents the coercive power of the State being used against a suspect and is an important juncture in a criminal process. He distinguished this stage of the process from that, pre-arrest, where the police could be said to be engaged in an investigative process. From the time of arrest, a fundamental requirement of basic fairness applies and any breach of that requirement can lead to an absence of a trial in due course of law.

Addressing the specific question, Clarke J. observed at para.9.1:

> "As already analysed, the consistent international position is that any entitlement to have access to a lawyer at an early stage after arrest necessarily carries with it an entitlement not to be interrogated after such access is requested and before access to such a lawyer is obtained. The reasoning of the ECtHR and the Courts of the United States, Canada and New Zealand which lead to such a conclusion has already been analysed. I am persuaded that like reasoning applies to the interpretation of the

> constitutional entitlement to a trial in due course of law of an arrested suspect under Bunreacht na hÉireann."

Clarke J. accepted that access to a lawyer serves many purposes; however, advice on what can happen to the accused immediately after arrest, including questioning, is one of the most important functions. As such, the right would be undermined if questioning could continue before the accused got to consult with her solicitor. For these reasons, basic fairness required an entitlement not to be interrogated after a request for a lawyer has been made and before the lawyer has been able to give advice. He later formulated this as the incorporation within the entitlement not to self-incriminate of an entitlement to legal advice in advance of any mandatory questioning of a suspect in custody.

Clarke J. then identified a number of reasons as to why the state authorities should not be surprised by the judgment of the court. He referred first to the ECtHR decision in *Salduz*, as well as the fact that the possibility of *Salduz* itself was foreseeable. He referred to the judgment of the Court of Criminal Appeal in *People (DPP) v Ryan* [2011] IECCA 6, in which the court adverted to the need for a uniform practice for the treatment of accused people in custody, including access to a solicitor, ensuring conformity with the ECHR. Clarke J. later observed that the development being made by the court had been anticipated in the judgments of foreign courts traditionally found persuasive by the Irish Supreme Court. Clarke J. explained the relevance of all this at para.9.7:

> "The likelihood that the State would be required, as the UK Supreme Court put it in *Cadder*, to organise its systems to take account of such rights has been on the agenda for a sufficient period of time that a finding that the constitutional right to a fair trial encompasses the right to access to legal advice before questioning can hardly come as a surprise. If it be the case that the State has not, to date, organised itself in a manner sufficient to allow such questioning to take place in conformity not just with the Constitution but also with the well established jurisprudence of the ECtHR, then it is those who are in charge of putting such provisions in place who must accept responsibility."

Of course, the facts of the cases before the court predated the ECtHR judgment in *Salduz*. Moreover, the Irish courts had never been persuaded before on this issue by the position pertaining in the USA, Canada and New Zealand. Nevertheless, one suspects that the purpose of these comments was not to address any complaints of injustice in *White* and *Gormley* but instead to preempt any complaints from the State of the type made when the Supreme Court last declared unconstitutional a crucial aspect of the State's evidence-gathering apparatus in *People (DPP) v Damache* [2012] IESC 11. Still and all, what is of more importance here is that, while it is reasonable to say that the State should have anticipated a conclusion against it under the European Convention on Human Rights Act 2003 (the "ECHR Act 2003"), it goes a further step to say that the state authorities should have anticipated a finding against them under the Constitution. That depends on an elision of constitutional and ECHR principles. Of course, the consequences of the constitutional finding were far more significant than the consequences of any finding under the ECHR Act 2003.

For all of these reasons, Clarke J. concluded that Mr Gormley's conviction had been in breach of the right to a trial in due course of law. He reached a different conclusion in respect of Mr White's argument in relation to the taking of physical samples. The difference was that such samples were objective and did not depend on a choice being made by the accused in respect of which legal advice could be beneficial. If the law were to give a suspect a choice in this matter, basic fairness might require a different result.

From a substantive viewpoint, this result is probably to be welcomed. Hardiman J., in a separate concurring judgment, graphically described the way in which suspects are treated by Gardaí before being questioned. Ensuring that the suspect has access to legal advice is a good way of redressing the balance of power prior to interrogation. This approach also provides a clear rule for the Gardaí: this is preferable than a case-by-case inquisition into whether the Gardaí were taking the necessary steps to ensure reasonable access to a solicitor. In this regard, the location of the right within Art.38.1, rather than mediated through the making of detention unlawful and a consequent infringement of the right to personal liberty, is a doctrinal improvement for two reasons. First, it allows the court to distinguish between statements and samples; secondly, it removes the need for the dangerous legal fiction of an accused drifting in and out of lawful custody. The lawfulness of custody should be clearly identifiable and not dependent on the reasonableness of actions taken by the Gardaí. What is also significant about this is that it sidesteps the exclusionary rule. Evidence is included or excluded based on a direct assessment of whether the trial would be otherwise than in due course of law. This assessment turns on basic fairness. This leaves some discretion for the courts although it would seem to follow from Clarke J.'s judgment that it would not be a trial in due course of law for any reliance to be placed on incriminatory statements made prior to the opportunity to consult with a solicitor. At the same time, it immunises the outcome of the case from any retrenchment of the exclusionary rule.

Implications of *Damache* In the *Annual Review of Irish Law 2012* and the *Annual Review of Irish Law 2013*, we considered a number of cases in which the courts addressed the implications for criminal proceedings of the Supreme Court's declaration in *Damache v DPP* [2012] 2 I.R. 266 that s.29 of the Offences Against the State Act 1939, as amended, was unconstitutional. The general position reached by the courts was that criminal defendants who had appeals in being could rely on the finding in *Damache* provided that they had raised an issue about the constitutionality of s.29, or at least about evidence obtained pursuant to it, during their trial. In *O'Connor v Governor of Midlands Prison* [2014] IEHC 46, the applicant sought to use habeas corpus proceedings to rely on *Damache* in circumstances in which he had raised no issue about the validity of the search warrant at trial. Indeed, the Court of Criminal Appeal had refused leave to allow him add a new ground of appeal based on the decision in *Damache*. In the habeas corpus proceedings, Hogan J. held that he was bound by the decisions of the Court of Criminal Appeal that delineated the parameters of those who could benefit from *Damache*. Habeas corpus proceedings were not appropriate for ventilating what was really a ground of appeal against conviction.

In *McKevitt v DPP* [2014] IECCA 19 the Court of Criminal Appeal refused to certify a question of law of exceptional public importance for the Supreme Court.

The applicant had failed to satisfy the court that the *Damache* judgment constituted a "newly discovered fact" for the purposes of allowing the Court of Criminal Appeal to quash his conviction on the basis of a miscarriage of justice. The court then refused to certify this question as a point of law for the consideration of the Supreme Court. Even if the judgment in *Damache* could be considered to be a newly discovered fact, the Supreme Court's previous judgment in *A v Governor of Arbour Hill Prison* [2006] 4 I.R. 88 made it clear that the effects of a declaration of unconstitutionality did not apply retrospectively.

In *DPP v Patchell* [2014] IECCA 9, the Court of Criminal Appeal likewise refused to certify a question of law of exceptional public importance for the Supreme Court. In this case, not only had the accused not previously raised any point about the validity of the search warrant, he had conceded at trial that the prosecution did not need to cover by evidence the arrest and detention of the accused. This concession, no doubt thought to be in the best interests of the accused at the time, precluded him from now seeking to rely on the finding in *Damache*.

Habeas corpus In *Farrell v Governor of St Patrick's Institution* [2014] IESC 30, the Supreme Court allowed an appeal against an order for habeas corpus. The High Court had granted an order of habeas corpus on the basis that a District judge had breached the terms of a stay on criminal proceedings by making an order remanding an accused in custody. That stay had been issued by another High Court judge in judicial review proceedings. Denham C.J., with whom the other judges agreed, held that the stay did not terminate the proceedings before the District Court: it prevented those proceedings being advanced or progressed but did not preclude the District judge from making orders that essentially preserved the status quo. The order remanding the accused in custody was of that type. Denham C.J. rejected the argument that the Supreme Court should not hear the appeal on the grounds that it was moot. In her view, the appeal raised significant issues for other cases. O'Donnell J. questioned whether the appeal was even moot in the first place: the accused had been released but if that rendered an appeal moot, no appeal could ever be taken by a respondent against an order of habeas corpus. O'Donnell J. also made some interesting observations on the place of Art.40.4.2° as a constitutional guarantee of liberty. In particular, he queried whether the proceedings were the best way in which to secure the liberty of the applicant in this case:

> "The liberty of the citizen is vital to the constitutional order and something which the courts and every other institution are bound to vindicate without fear or favour but it should be said, that in practical terms the liberty of this citizen could have been achieved without the drama of these proceedings. First, he had been remanded in custody it is true, but with consent to bail in the sum of €300 and an independent surety in the same amount. It was not suggested that securing of this bail posed any insuperable difficulty for him and there was ample time to have any surety approved before the expiry of the sentence so that he would not have to be remanded in custody in these proceedings. Accordingly, the applicant could, with the assistance of his representatives, have secured his own release by the 4th of July and before the swiftest lawyer could have brought proceedings and the most conscientious judge made any order. Second, while the focus of this case

has been the validity of the order of the District Court ... the key to that validity lay in the interpretation of the [stay] granted by the High Court. If there was real doubt or controversy as to what was meant by that order it could have been addressed with the High Court before the launching of an inquiry under Article 40."

In *McKevitt v The Governor of Portlaoise Prison* [2014] IEHC 442, Barton J., following an ex tempore judgment of the Supreme Court, held that habeas corpus proceedings were an inappropriate vehicle for a claim that the applicant's detention was illegal on the ground that the Minister for Justice had wrongfully refused to order remission of the applicant's sentence.

In *FX v Clinical Director of the Central Mental Hospital* [2014] IESC 1, the Supreme Court considered an appeal from the judgment of Hogan J. on a habeas corpus application, considered in the *Annual Review of Irish Law 2012*. The court clarified two important points about the habeas corpus jurisdiction. First, the High Court's jurisdiction does lie in respect of detention orders made by courts of coordinate jurisdiction. Secondly, although the Constitution does not allow for stays to be placed on orders of habeas corpus, orders can be made for controlling the release of persons who are incapable of protecting themselves.

In *Cirpaci v Governor of Mountjoy Prison* [2014] IEHC 76, Hogan J. considered a habeas corpus application in circumstances in which it was effectively conceded that a District judge had erred in law by failing to inform an accused person of his right to elect for jury trial. However, the Governor argued that habeas corpus applications should be limited to circumstances where the error was patent on the face of the record. In this regard, the Governor relied on comments from Denham C.J. in *FX* to the effect that if an error is good on its face, the appropriate remedy is generally an appeal or a judicial review. Hogan J., however, considered that the Governor was placing too much reliance on that comment and interpreting it out of context. He therefore rejected the contention that an error had to be patent on the face of the record in order for an applicant to avail of the habeas corpus procedure. The defect in the current case was fundamental to the legality of the detention of the applicant. Exercising his right to appeal could not have cured the defect, since that would not provide his right to jury trial. As the accused had been convicted without jurisdiction, it followed that his detention was necessarily otherwise than in accordance with law.

Constitutional right of access to the Gardaí In *Boden v The Commissioner of An Garda Síochána* [2014] IEHC 371, the applicants alleged that the Governor of the Midlands Prison had breached their constitutional right of access to the Gardaí to make complaints against the Governors of the Midlands Prison and of Arbour Hill Prison. They argued that it would be a breach of Art.40.1 not to allow them access to the Gardaí on the same basis as those who were not incarcerated. Barr J. rejected the claim on the basis that it was not factually sustainable: the applicants had been permitted to write to the Commissioner of An Garda Síochána, who had passed on their complaints to the Assistant Commissioner with responsibility for policing in the Laois area.

Right to privacy In *DPP v Lawel* [2014] IECCA 33, the Court of Criminal Appeal considered a situation where customs officials had intercepted a package addressed to a Mr Tony Tuto and found it to contain cocaine. Mr Tuto did not exist. Mr Lawel lived at the address given for Mr Tuto and accepted the package, claiming to be Mr Tuto. He subsequently claimed that his right to privacy had been infringed through interception of the package. MacMenamin J. held that it was not open to Mr Lawel to assert this right. Such an argument could only be asserted on behalf of Mr Tuto, who did not exist. Moreover, Mr Lawel could not assert a proprietary right to the package as the very possession of it constituted the criminal offence in question.

Disqualification of drivers In *People (DPP) v Sweeney* [2014] IECA 5, the Court of Appeal upheld an appeal against a sentence. The accused pleaded guilty to two offences under the Criminal Justice (Theft and Fraud Offences) Act 2001, involving the sale of a stolen Ford Transit van to a third party. He received a sentence of two years imprisonment, suspended on the basis that he would make full recompense to the duped purchaser. However, the trial judge also relied on s.27(1)(a) of the Road Traffic Act 1961 to disqualify the accused from driving for four years. That section allows such orders where an accused is "convicted of an offence under this Act or otherwise in relation to a mechanically propelled vehicle." In *Conroy v Attorney General* [1965] I.R. 411, the Supreme Court held that disqualification orders were a "secondary punishment" that did not alter the character of an offence as a minor offence. In the view of the Supreme Court, at 441, a disqualification order was "essentially a finding of unfitness of the person to hold a driving licence." In the view of Hogan J., delivering the judgment of the Court, the implication of *Conroy* was that a disqualification order could only be imposed where the facts disclosed by the offence indicated that an accused was unfit to drive. The trial judge had therefore erred in making that order in the present case.

Language rights In *Ó Maicín v Ireland* [2014] IESC 12, the Supreme Court considered whether the applicant had a right to a trial before a jury that could understand evidence given in Irish directly, without the aid of an interpreter. It is established that there is a general right for people to conduct their business with the State through Irish. This follows from the status of the Irish language in Art. 8 as the national language and the first official language. There is also a clearly established right to jury trial, in the circumstances set out in Art.38 of the Constitution. The members of the court were agreed that the right to jury trial could not of itself generate a right to trial before a jury that could understand the evidence in your own language. That would be impractical in the case of languages other than Irish and English. Speakers of other languages would – of course – have an entitlement to translation facilities but their trials could not be precluded simply on the basis that there were not jurors who spoke their language. The question for consideration, therefore, was whether Art.8 generated the right for which Mr Ó Maicín contended. A majority of the Supreme Court held that it did not.

Clarke J., who delivered the leading majority judgment, held that the State had a general obligation to encourage the use of the Irish language. In respect of a citizen who wishes to conduct her business with the State through Irish, however, the State has a specific constitutional obligation to respect the language wishes. Clarke J. noted, at para.3.6, that this obligation was not absolute:

> "The fact that the State has such a constitutional obligation does not, however, mean that, at a constitutional level, there is an absolute obligation on the State to ensure that persons wishing to so do can conduct all official business through Irish without translation. An assessment of whether, in any particular circumstance, the State has complied with its obligations in respect of the Irish language, will, therefore, necessarily involve an analysis of the rights of those who wish to conduct their affairs through Irish but also the language rights of those wishing to use English and, where appropriate, any competing interests or constitutional obligation that may arise."

For Clarke J., the relevant competing considerations were the language rights of those who wanted to conduct their business with the State through English, their entitlement to sit on juries, and the constitutional obligation that a jury be representative. He did not consider an argument, canvassed by the State, that resource constraints could limit the State's obligations. Reviewing the previous case law on the right to jury trial, he held that there was an obligation that juries be broadly representative or represent a fair cross-section of the community. In deciding how to define the parameters of a jury panel, the Oireachtas has a certain discretion to exclude categories of persons but it would be unconstitutional to impose restrictions that would render the jury panel not broadly representative.

In *MacCárthaigh v Éire* [1999] 1 I.R. 200, the Supreme Court had rejected a similar claim to that advanced by Mr Ó Maicín. The principal issue was whether the fact that Mr Ó Maicín lived in the Gaeltacht should lead to a different result. Clarke J. noted evidence that showed that in a broad Gaeltacht area, approximately two thirds of people speak Irish on a daily basis, while in some narrowly drawn areas that proportion could be as high as 90 per cent. However, he considered that there would be a significant difference between the numbers who spoke Irish on a daily basis and the numbers who would be competent to understand a case in Irish. There was no real evidence of what proportion of people would be able to understand Irish to the requisite standard.

Clarke J. held that it would not be possible to establish a jury panel based on those small electoral districts with the highest proportion of Irish-speakers. Such a panel would run the risk of being non-representative; a significant proportion of people would have to withdraw from the panel due to some knowledge of the case or the defendant and other witnesses. Conversely, if a broad Gaeltacht panel were established, so many people would have to be excluded due to their lack of competence in Irish that it would not be broadly representative.

Hardiman J. delivered a lengthy dissenting judgment. He did not consider that the language obligations on the State could be balanced in the manner suggested by Clarke J. He was also more accepting that those who spoke Irish on a daily basis would be able to serve on juries. There was a general practice of court service staff identifying potential jurors who could not speak English; this could equally be applied to jurors who could not speak Irish. This could be applied in a Gaeltacht-wide district without difficulty.

The Special Criminal Court In *Murphy v Ireland* [2014] IESC 19, the Supreme Court considered a constitutional challenge to s.46(2) of the Offences Against the State Act 1939 (the "1939 Act"), which allows the DPP to certify that, in respect of non-scheduled, indictable offences, the ordinary courts are in his opinion "inadequate to secure the effective administration of justice and the preservation of public peace and order in relation to the trial of such person on such charge." In those circumstances, the District Court must send the accused for trial in the Special Criminal Court, without a jury. This reflects Art.38.3 of the Constitution which allows for the establishment of special courts in those circumstances. The plaintiff argued that this section breached Art.40.1 by discriminating between two classes of persons charged with the same offence, some of whom were tried by juries and others of whom were not. O'Donnell J., delivering the judgment of the court, emphasised the importance of Art.40.1 in setting the republican and egalitarian character of the Constitution. He characterised Art.40.1 as having two main concerns. On the one hand, following the approach of Walsh J. in *Quinn's Supermarket v Attorney General* [1972] I.R. 1, discrimination reflecting prejudice based on human attributes, such as race, gender, religion, etc, "while not prohibited must be demonstrated to comply with the principles of equality." This appears similar to the Supreme Court's conclusion in *re Article 26 and the Employment Equality Bill 1996* [1997] 2 I.R. 321 that some grounds of classification are presumptively proscribed. On the other hand, significant differentiations on other grounds may be unconstitutional if they cannot be justified. O'Donnell J. held that the plaintiff did not have a sound anti-discrimination claim: he was treated differently because an officer of the State, exercising a constitutionally envisaged function, had determined that he was differently situated. The plaintiff's constitutional challenge to s.46 of the 1939 Act was never likely to have succeeded. What is more interesting is O'Donnell J.'s general account of Art.40.1. This suggests that constitutional protection of equality has not been ended by the Supreme Court's decision in *D v Ireland* [2012] IESC 10, as we suggested in the *Annual Review of Irish Law 2012*. However, until the courts next address an equality claim involving one of the presumptively proscribed characteristics, it will not be possible to know the force of constitutional equality protection.

Exclusionary rule In *Criminal Assets Bureau v Murphy* [2014] IEHC 583, Birmingham J. considered the application of the exclusionary rule to proceeds of crime cases. He considered that the issue was not determined by previous decisions of the courts – notably the Supreme Court in *Kennedy v The Law Society of Ireland (No 3)* [2002] 2 I.R. 458 and the High Court in *Competition Authority v Irish Dental Association* [2005] 3 I.R. 210. The contention in this case was that cash had been found during a search of a dwelling that was unconstitutional on account of the *Damache* decision. Birmingham J. rhetorically questioned whether, if the Gardaí had instead discovered property that demonstrably belonged to another (such as a unique piece of art), that should be disregarded on the basis of an exclusionary rule. For this reason, he concluded that the exclusionary rule did not apply to criminal asset cases. This conclusion does not so readily follow. It is quite possible that a person could retain another's property where knowledge of the state of affairs only came about through an unconstitutional procedure. That Birmingham J. was not prepared to countenance this possibility suggests that the countervailing interest of an individually wronged property owner counts for more than the countervailing interest of a wronged victim of crime. This is further evidence of the general unease with the exclusionary rule, culminating in the Supreme Court decision in *DPP v JC* [2015] IESC 31, which will be considered in next year's *Annual Review*.

Witness protection programme In *Mooney v Commissioner of An Garda Siochána* [2014] IEHC 155, Gilligan J. held that a claim by the plaintiff that he be admitted into the witness protection programme should be heard otherwise than in public. As the Oireachtas had not put the programme on a statutory basis, there was no legislative authorisation for the proceedings to be held in camera. However, Gilligan J. considered that courts held a very limited discretion under Art.34.1 to direct that proceedings not be held in public. This was not a question of balancing constitutional rights but rather concerned the administration of justice. An order could be made if it was not possible otherwise to administer justice fairly. Given the fears that the defendants had in this case about exposing the workings of the witness protection programme, they would not be able to conduct their defence properly if the case was held in public. Gilligan J. therefore directed that it be heard otherwise than in public.

Appeal against activation of suspended sentences In *McCabe v Ireland* [2014] IEHC 435, Hogan J. considered a constitutional challenge to the scheme for the activation of suspended sentences under s.99 of the Criminal Justice Act 2006 (the "2006 Act"). The Circuit Court, on appeal from the District Court, had imposed a six-month sentence on Mr McCabe but suspended it for two years. Within that period, Mr McCabe was convicted of another offence in the District Court, which remanded him back to the Circuit Court, which activated the suspended sentence. Mr McCabe's challenge to the reactivation on non-constitutional grounds failed. If the District Court had imposed the suspended sentence on Mr McCabe, he would have had a right of appeal against the activation of the sentence. However, the statutory scheme made no such provision in respect of suspended sentences imposed by the Circuit Court as an appellate court from the District Court. Hogan J. held that this infringed Art.40.1 of the Constitution: there could be no justification for such an arbitrary distinction, particularly as it bore on the liberty of Mr McCabe. Separately, Hogan J. held that Art.34.3.4° required a right of appeal for all such decisions. The decision to activate a suspended sentence is not automatic but requires consideration by the court of new facts and circumstances. It is not a technical or procedural decision, such as a decision about the venue of a trial, but instead bears directly on the liberty of the accused. Therefore, a right of appeal was constitutionally required. In terms of remedy, this case raised the issue of how courts should address an unconstitutional gap in a legislative scheme. Hogan J. adopted the approach taken by the Supreme Court in *Carmody v Minister for Justice* [2010] 1 I.R. 365. Rather than declare s.99 of the 2006 Act unconstitutional, he ordered that Mr McCabe's suspended sentence could not be reactivated unless there were a statutory mechanism in place to allow him to appeal that reactivation.

Vague criminal offences In *McInerney v Director of Public Prosecutions* [2014] IEHC 181, Hogan J. followed his judgment in *Douglas v DPP* [2013] IEHC 343, considered in last year's *Annual Review*. In that case, Hogan J. considered that s.18 of the Criminal Law (Amendment) Act 1935 created three separate criminal offences. He held that the two offences of which Mr Douglas had been charged were unconstitutionally vague, leading him to sever the underlined sections in s.18:

> Every person who shall commit, at or near and inside of any place along

> which the public habitually pass as of right or by permission any act in such a way as to offend modesty *or cause scandal or injure the morals of the community* shall be guilty of an offence under this section and shall on summary conviction thereof be liable to a fine not exceeding [IR£500] or, at the discretion of the court to imprisonment for any term not exceeding [six months].

In *McInerney*, the issue was whether the remaining offence of offending modesty was likewise unconstitutionally vague.

Hogan J. reasoned that Art.5 and Art.15.2.1° impose an obligation on the Oireachtas, when creating criminal offences, to specify the principles and policies that map out the contours of any offence. In this regard, Hogan J. placed reliance on the courts' case law about the delegation of legislative power, in particular the *Cityview* test, which is formulated in identical terms. This constitutional parallel is not convincing. The reason for the principles and policies test in the context of the delegation of legislative power is that prima facie any delegation of legislative power is unconstitutional. Conversely, providing principles and policies within criminal offences scarcely provides the level of certainty that should be constitutionally required. The Oireachtas routinely grants to delegated legislators the power to create criminal offences. It has never been suggested that such delegations are per se unconstitutional, although of course each delegation must conform with the principles and policies test. This means that the articulation of principles and policies still leaves considerable discretion to the delegated decision-maker whether to criminalise types of behaviour. But it could scarcely provide sufficient certainty for the delegated legislator simply to repeat those policies and principles in the criminal offence that it creates. In short, the factors that are relevant to the delegation of legislative power are different from the factors that are relevant to the issue of certainty in the criminal law. We should not confuse these by subsuming them within the same category of 'principles and policies.' It is sufficient to test the rule against vagueness on general rule of law principles, clearly supported by the constitutional prohibition on retroactive penal sanction in Art.15.5.1°, as also noted by Hogan J.

The State argued that it was legitimate to criminalise offending modesty: this term was to be assessed with reference to right-thinking members of the community. Hogan J. considered, however, that this remained elusive. There was not a shared community sense of what constituted immodest behaviour. The actus reus was hopelessly and irremediably vague, failing the test laid down in *King v Attorney General*. It intrinsically invited arbitrary and inconsistent application and could not withstand constitutional scrutiny. The entirety of s.18 has therefore been declared unconstitutional.

Sentence imposed in absentia In *Quilligan v Kilrane* [2014] IEHC 116, Hogan J. held that the applicant's rights under Art.38.1 had been infringed where he was sentenced in absentia to a term of imprisonment of five months for dangerous driving. Summonses had been sent to a number of addresses but the applicant maintained that he had not received them and Hogan J. held that it had not been established that proper notice had been given. While there might be circumstances in which a sentence could be imposed in absentia, Hogan J. followed *O'Brien v*

Coughlan [2011] IEHC 330 to hold that the accused must be present where the District judge is considering the imposition of something more than a short-term custodial sentence.

Prosecutorial delay In *O'Donoghue v Director of Public Prosecutions* [2014] IEHC 23, Baker J. considered an application to prohibit a trial for possession of illegal drugs on the grounds of undue delay. Four years elapsed between the date of the alleged offence and service of the summons. This was largely due to difficulties in locating the applicant, although the efforts of the Gardaí could perhaps have been more strenuous in that regard. The applicant did not allege that he had suffered any specific prejudice; nevertheless, he maintained that his right to an expeditious trial was breached. He claimed that the delay was greater than should be permitted for a summary trial. In Baker J.'s view, there were two periods of blameworthy delay: first, a period of one year between the first attempt to serve the summons and the applicant leaving for Australia; secondly, a period of four months after the applicant's return from Australia. Baker J. placed some weight on the fact that the applicant had made admissions to two of the charges when questioned by the Gardaí. Baker J. refused to prohibit the trial. She also emphasised the judgment of O'Donnell J. in *Byrne v DPP* [2010] IESC 54 to the effect that something exceptional is required for the High Court to prohibit a trial in judicial proceedings: the District judge bore the constitutional obligation of ensuring a fair trial and could strike out proceedings for prosecutorial delay.

Privacy and searches In *Director of Public Prosecutions v McDonnell* [2014] IEHC 35, O'Malley J. considered the implications of a search of the clothing of an accused person carried out while the accused was in hospital receiving medical treatment. The accused had been involved in a car accident and brought to hospital. He was coherent and responded to the name that matched the registered owner of the car involved in the accident. Nevertheless, a Garda searched the pocket of his jeans, which had been cut off him, for the purpose of confirming his identity. When she did so, she found two bags of suspicious white powder and came to the view that the accused was under the influence of an intoxicant. She made a statutory demand of the accused to provide a blood sample, which he refused to do. O'Malley J. concluded that the Garda had neither the consent of the accused nor any lawful authority to search his jeans. They were his property and protected by his privacy rights. There was no question of any emergency situation here that could have justified the search. However, the fact that evidence was unconstitutionally obtained did not, in O'Malley J.'s view, vitiate the lawfulness of the demand to the accused to provide a blood sample. Following the Supreme Court decision in *DPP v Cash* [2010] 1 I.R. 609, O'Malley J. compared the evidential basis required for a lawful arrest to the evidential basis required for a lawful statutory demand. The exclusionary rule applied to the admission of evidence in proceedings but this principle did not extend to the issuing of the statutory demand.

Segregation of prisoners In *Killeen v Governor of Portlaoise Prison* [2014] IEHC 77, Hedigan J. upheld the continued segregation of three prisoners from the general prison population, emphasising that the courts' role was not to micromanage prisons. He was satisfied that the segregation, although a curtailment of their rights, was proportionate in circumstances in which the three posed significant threats to other prisoners. It was a concern that the segregation had continued for so long. Hedigan J. read a requirement into the prison rules that the segregation must be subject to periodic review by the Director General of the Prison Service.

Missing evidence *Stirling v Collins* [2014] IESC 13 provides a very rare example in recent years of a trial bring prohibited due to missing evidence. The accused was charged with a number of public order and criminal damage offences. A Garda had observed him, through CCTV, allegedly damaging a phone-box. At various court hearings before the trial commenced, the prosecution had assured the court that the videotape was available for the accused to view. However, shortly before the trial, it became clear that the tape had been mislaid. The trial before the District Court commenced with an account being given of the usual procedures for preserving evidence. The High Court refused an application to prohibit the trial, largely on the basis that the trial had commenced and the continuity of the trial should be respected. On appeal, however, MacMenamin J., with whom the other members of the court agreed, held that this was an appropriate case for an order of prohibition. Although the superior courts should not be called on to micromanage criminal proceedings in lower courts, this was not a case of probable prejudice but unavoidable prejudice to the accused: the only evidence that could sustain a conviction was missing. Moreover, although the trial had commenced, all that had occurred was an explanation of how the evidence might have gone missing.

Remission of sentences and executive power In *Farrell v Governor of Portlaoise Prison* [2014] IEHC 392, Hogan J. considered a challenge to a refusal to grant remission to a prisoner. Of relevance for our purposes is Hogan J.'s characterisation of this power. He held that the power to remit a sentence is entirely an executive function, but Art.13.6 implies that the exercise of the power can be regulated by law. Once there are such statutory provisions, any exercise of the power—whether by a member of the Government or otherwise—must comply with those provisions. This reflects the way in which the executive power—unlike the judicial and legislative powers—is subject to control by another organ of government.

District Court Poor Box Whilst none of the issues in *Kennedy v Gibbons* [2014] IEHC 67 were of a specifically constitutional nature, Hogan J. held that there was no discretion to replace a statutory requirement for the imposition of penalty points with a donation to the poor box. He declared at para.4 that the poor box system operated by the District Court was so widespread and inveterate throughout the State both before and after 1922

> "that it must accordingly be regarded as part of the common law which was carried over into our modern legal system by Article 50.1 of the Constitution, its obscure and uncertain origins notwithstanding. Although, moreover, the existence of such a jurisdiction is not to be found in any of the acknowledged sources–such as textbooks or decisions of venerable judges of some antiquity–referencing the pre-1937 common law which was carried over on the coming into force of the Constitution, its existence is nonetheless such an embedded feature of our legal system that it must

> be now regarded as part of that common law, if only by reference to the principle *communis error, facit jus*."

FAMILY

Surrogacy In *MR v DR* [2014] IESC 60, the Supreme Court allowed an appeal from the judgment of the High Court (see *Annual Review of Irish Law 2013*, pp.133-135) that declared the genetic mother was the mother of twins born as a result of a surrogacy arrangement. A married couple were the genetic parents of two twins fertilised *in vitro*. The zygotes were implanted in the womb of the genetic mother's sister who subsequently gave birth to the twins. The genetic parents agreed with the gestational mother that the twins would be brought up as the children of their genetic parents, and this occurred. The genetic parents instituted legal proceedings challenging the decision of the Registrar to register the genetic father and gestational mother as the parents of the children. The Registrar had acted pursuant to his legal advice that the legal principle *mater semper certa est* (the mother is always certain) had to be followed: the person who gave birth to the child necessarily was the child's mother.

Denham C.J., with whom O'Donnell J. agreed, reasoned that there was no constitutional, statutory or common law rule that could be applied to the case. In terms of the Constitution, whereas Art.40.3.3° clearly related to the gestational mother in the abortion context, the reference to mothers in Art.41.2 could apply to genetic, gestational or adoptive mothers. The Oireachtas, unlike legislatures in other jurisdictions, had not intervened to regulate the area. In terms of the common law, she did not accept that the maxim *mater certa est* (motherhood is always certain) had ever been part of the common law. Any statements that appeared to imply such a maxim were merely statements of fact made in the time before scientific advances in relation to artificial human reproduction (AHR). In her view, the law was quite simply silent, and it was a matter for the Oireachtas, not the courts, to fill the gap:

> "113. Any law on surrogacy affects the status and rights of persons, especially those of the children; it creates complex relationships, and has a deep social content. It is, thus, quintessentially a matter for the Oireachtas.
>
> 114. As stated earlier, there is no definitive definition of "mother" in the Constitution. Nor is there anything in the Constitution which would inhibit the development of appropriate laws on surrogacy.
>
> 115. The words mater semper certa est, upon which the appellants laid much stress, is not the basis of Irish law on the issue before the Court. The words simply recognise a fact, which existed in times gone by and up until recently, that a birth mother was the mother: both gestational and genetic. This was the factual situation until scientific and medical advances enabled persons to avail of assisted human reproduction.
>
> 116. There is a lacuna in the law as to certain rights, especially those of the children born in such circumstances. Such lacuna should be addressed in legislation and not by this Court. There is clearly merit in the legislature addressing this lacuna, and providing for retrospective situations of surrogacy."

It would appear to follow from Denham C.J.'s judgment that it would be wrong for the Civil Registrar to register either the gestational mother or the genetic mother. Murray J. was similarly wary of judicial intervention but did provide a definite resolution to the proceedings. In his view, it was a matter of simple statutory interpretation. Section 19 of the Civil Registration Act 2004 (the "2004 Act") requires the Registrar to register the particulars of birth, including the name of the child's mother. Therefore, only one mother can be registered. In Murray J.'s view, it was most unlikely that the Oireachtas had intended to make a radical alteration to the existing law and provide that only a genetic mother could be registered, rather than the gestational mother.

Hardiman J. likewise strongly stated the view that any change to the law on this case was a matter for the Oireachtas, not the courts. It raised questions of attitude and values so deep that it should, on a similar basis to judgments in *Sinnott v Minister for Education* [2001] 2 I.R. 545 and *TD v Minister for Education* [2001] I.R. 259, be reserved to the elected organs of government.

O'Donnell J., with whom Hardiman J. agreed, was critical of the fact that there had been no legislative response to the issues raised by AHR. The questions were of huge direct concern to infertile couples and to any children born as a result of AHR, as well as to society in general. It should be addressed through the Oireachtas rather than through the courts, who of necessity could only resolve the case before them in a binary fashion. O'Donnell J., similarly to Murray J., treated the case primarily as one of statutory interpretation. In his view, s.19 of the 2004 Act required that one mother be registered, and that be the gestational mother. This was not an unconstitutional choice on the part of the Oireachtas. However, this decided no more than that precise point and did not preclude the Oireachtas from taking other measures that might provide recognition for genetic mothers.

MacMenamin J. agreed with Denham C.J., Hardiman and O'Donnell JJ.

Clarke J. held similar doubts about the legitimacy or effectiveness of the courts taking on a role to design a system of regulation for AHR. However, in his view, it did fall to the courts to interpret the word 'mother' in the 2004 Act, particularly given the failure of the Oireachtas to act since encouraged by the Supreme Court to do so in *Roche v Roche* [2010] IESC 10. In his view, both common law and statutory law left open the question of whether 'mother' in the 2004 Act meant birth mother or genetic mother. He likewise considered that the Constitution did not offer further guidance. Therefore, the correct reading of the Act was that both the genetic and the birth mother should be registered as the mother of the child. Although this might appear odd, it was no more odd than denying the motherhood of either party.

Although there was a difference between the judgments of Clarke J. and the other judges, they all agreed that the Oireachtas retained a wide discretion to regulate issues of AHR. This is consistent with the approach previously adopted by the Supreme Court in *Roche v Roche.* Whether the Oireachtas eventually acts on this invitation to legislate remains to be seen.

Divorce In *A v A* [2014] IESC 49, the Supreme Court considered the issue of proper provision for spouses in divorce proceedings and, in particular, whether a court order could be reopened in subsequent proceedings. Ms A argued that her former husband had not made full disclosure of his financial assets in the original divorce proceedings. Clarke J., with whom Hardiman and MacKechnie JJ. agreed, noted that Art.41.3 of the Constitution required that a court could only grant a dissolution of marriage where it was satisfied that "such provision as the Court considers proper having regard to the circumstances exists or will be made for the spouses, any children of either or both of them and any other person prescribed by law." It followed that there was an added constitutional dimension to any failure by a spouse to make full and frank disclosure in relation to her assets. This justified the departure, in this case, from the normal rule that new proceedings should be instituted in order to set aside a previous judgment on the basis of fraud. It was permissible to raise the issue by way of motion in the previous divorce proceedings. Clarke J. also held that the constitutional dimension was relevant to the level of disclosure required of a spouse: such disclosure was necessary to allow the court fulfil its function of ensuring that proper provision could be made for the other spouse and children. In this case, Clarke J. upheld the finding of the trial judge that there had been a deliberate failure to make disclosure. This could be rectified by the court, without affecting the decree of divorce, making an order for further provision – not on the basis of changed circumstances, but rather to reflect the provision that would have been made in the first instance.

Habeas corpus In *W v Health Service Executive* [2014] IEHC 8, Peart J. repeated the view that habeas corpus proceedings, in the context of child care issues, unless there is a fundamental want of jurisdiction for the court's order.

FAIR PROCEDURES

***Dellway* Principles** *Disappointed interview applicant Grange v Commission for Public Service Appointments* [2014] IEHC 303 considered whether certain decisions of the Commission are amenable to judicial review and if so, whether those in respect of the plaintiff, a disappointed applicant for a civil service position, should be allowed stand. Barrett J. held it unquestionable that there was a public law dimension to the proceedings before the court. He distilled from a "comprehensive body of law" a number of key principles regarding judicial review. Ultimately, he held the decisions justiciable relying, at para.25, on *Dellway Investments Ltd. v National Asset Management Agency* [2011] IESC 14; [2011] 4 I.R. 1 (see *Annual Review of Irish Law 2011* pp.168–172; 612) that "it suffices that rights 'could' be impacted by a particular process for that process to be justiciable." He cited Denham J. (as she then was), at para.148:

> "'This judgment addresses the issue of fair procedures. The decision in this case is based on a fundamental constitutional principle. When an order could affect the rights of a person in that it might restrict his existing right to trade or his right to enjoy some benefits contracted for, such a possible result is sufficient to require that the procedure which can lead to that result must conform to the principles of constitutional justice, which includes the right to be heard.'"

Barrett J. noted at para.44 that nowhere in the applicable case law is there any suggestion that procedural perfection is a pre-requisite to a finding of fairness.

"In an imperfect world, some imperfection of process is to be expected and when it arises, as it almost inevitably shall, it will not necessarily be a bar to a finding that there was nonetheless basic fairness of procedures: a flawed process may still be entirely fair". He could perceive nothing in the processes of the Commission that were impugned "that is so wrong as to have denied or even been capable of denying Mr. Grange that basic fairness of procedures to which he is entitled under the Bunreacht and which, the court finds, he received" (at para.44).

Policy exemption from Dellway principles In *Rehab Group v Minister for Justice & Equality* [2014] IEHC 312, O'Malley J. noted that she was dealing with an area of law which appears to be in the process of development. The plaintiffs had claimed that they had been entitled to a right to make representations and a right to a hearing, prior to the respondent's 2012 decision to phase out a non-statutory scheme, sometimes referred to as the Charitable Lotteries Fund or CLF. This had been a scheme to alleviate the impact on charities which were adversely affected in their fund-raising efforts by the establishment of the National Lottery in 1986. She found the decision at issue to be one of policy:

> "93. The 'policy' category is closely identified with the category of cases to do with legislation, where the *audi alteram partem* rule is generally considered to be inapplicable for reasons both of principle and practicality. The reasons of principle relate to the fact that the area of legislation is within the domain of the elected representatives of the people, and therefore not generally a matter for the courts."

Nevertheless, in finding which decisions attract the rules of natural justice and which lie within the policy exemption O'Malley J. observed, at para.94, that all of the authorities make it clear that the analysis must be based on the facts and circumstances of each individual case. With regard to the scheme she accepted that it had been an effort made by the executive, after years of lobbying by the applicants and others, to ameliorate the difficulties faced by a specific group of charities.

> "98. In this context, it would certainly have been the case that while the scheme operated, the beneficiary charities would all have had certain rights in respect of its administration. They would have been entitled to demand that it be operated fairly and in accordance with the set criteria. If the responsible Minister at any given time had decided to drop an individual charity from the scheme–for example, because of a perceived deficiency in financial accounting–that body would undoubtedly have been entitled to reasons and to an opportunity to be heard. However, it is accepted that at all times the scheme was to be subjected to periodic review and that the beneficiaries have no legal right to its continuance. There was never a representation, express or implied, that a decision to terminate the scheme would not be taken without consultation."

She concluded, therefore, that this was a case where the applicants could assert a legal right to the payments, or make a claim that the termination of the payments interfered with any other legal right of theirs other than, perhaps, their right not to be wrongly damaged in their reputation. Given the circumstances, O'Malley J. rejected the decision in *Dellway Investments Ltd. v National Asset Management Agency* [2011] IESC 14; [2011] 4 I.R. 1, as aiding the applicants:

> "[105] It is clear that at least some of the members of the Supreme Court adopted a formulation in regard to the right to be heard which does not depend on assertion of a risk of interference with specific, enforceable legal rights. However, the context of that case was such that I do not consider it possible to say that the traditional exemption of policy decisions from the application of the rules of natural justice has been abrogated."

FREEDOM OF ASSEMBLY

Hyland v Dundalk Racing (1999) Ltd trading as Dundalk Stadium [2014] IEHC 60 is one of a series of cases dealing with very complex issues arising in the ongoing dispute between some bookmakers and the owners and operators of Dundalk racecourse. In 2007 the first all weather racetrack in Ireland was opened in Dundalk and the plaintiff with a number of other bookmakers and their supporters had protested outside the entrance to the new stadium on a number of occasions after it had first opened. The bookmakers' protests related to matters peculiar to them and to their professional interests, namely, the failure by Dundalk to honour what the bookmakers considered was their contractual due, namely, the 1945 seniorities recognised by the Pitch Rules. The defendants claimed that these protests amounted to illegal picketing. Inter alia Hogan J. had to consider "the rather difficult question of where peaceful protest begins and ends and, specifically, at what point is the line crossed from peaceful protest into illegal industrial action" (at para.74). He observed that this line could be especially difficult to draw where, as in the instant case, the protests did not relate to classic political grievances, but rather related to issues not entirely dissimilar to those which might otherwise arise in an industrial relations context.

Art.40.6.1.ii guarantees:

> The right of the citizen to assemble peaceably and without arms. Provision may be made by law to prevent or control meetings which are determined in accordance with law to be calculated to cause a breach of the peace or to be a danger or nuisance to the general public and to prevent or control meetings in the vicinity of either House of the Oireachtas.

Hogan J. noted that the protests had been carried out on a public road immediately outside the stadium and were prima facie entitled to the benefit of the constitutional guarantee. Further, no law has been enacted to prevent or control meetings of this kind and there was no suggestion that the protests amounted in themselves to a breach of the peace or a danger or nuisance to the general public. He construed the term "nuisance" as follows:

> "Of course, those patrons attending the race-meeting might have regarded the protesters as something of a nuisance in the colloquial sense of that term, but that is not the sense in which the Constitution uses this concept.

> 'Nuisance' in this sense refers to activities which make it difficult or impossible for the general public to use their own amenities, by, e.g., blocking access to a private dwelling or by holding late night protests in a purely residential area."

He considered the context and nature of the protests to be of importance:

> "78. In the first place the protestors had a strong interest in communicating their message, especially to the sporting public. They believed – with deep conviction – that they had been wrongly deprived of their contractual rights and that they had been most unjustly treated by Dundalk as a result and that the sporting public would support them if they – the bookmakers – could only inform and educate them in relation to the background facts. These accordingly were views the expression of which were fully was protected by the parallel free speech guarantee contained in Article 40.6.1.i. It followed thus that the protestors had the right to seek to persuade public opinion of the justness of their cause in the sense envisaged by Article 40.6.1 itself: see, by analogy, my own comments to this effect in *Cornec v. Morrice* [2012] IEHC 376, [2012] 1 I.R. 804 at 818-825.
>
> 79. Second, it is true that the protests were outside a racecourse stadium. While admittedly sporting and entertainment venues are not forums normally associated with public protest, neither is this unknown. Just to take a well known historical example, it could not have been said, for instance, that the protests which took place in January 1970 outside the Lansdowne Road stadium by reason of the fact that Ireland were playing (in the then apartheid era) South Africa in a rugby test match were not the manifestations of constitutionally protected rights of free speech and peaceable assembly.
>
> 80. It must also be recalled that substantial amounts of public money were used to fund the stadium project, so that the stadium cannot be realistically regarded as a purely private venture. The present case is accordingly very different from a case involving the picketing of a private dwelling with menaces, where the constitutional rights of the occupier or owner of a private home to the protection of the inviolability of that dwelling as guaranteed by Article 40.5 would otherwise be engaged: see *Sullivan v. Boylan* (No.2) [2013] IEHC 104.
>
> 81. Third, the most important feature of all is that the protestors sought only to persuade and to rest their case on an appeal to the sporting public to acknowledge the justness of their cause while remaining within the law. …. Given that the free exchange of ideas, arguments and views is central to the operation of the democratic State envisaged by Article 5 and is at the heart of the protections of free speech and peaceable assembly contained in Article 40.6.1, the public expression and manifestation of different and dissenting views must–in general, at least–be tolerantly accepted by all."

Not industrial action Hogan J. distinguished this protest and industrial action which is regulated by the Industrial Relations Act 1990, a law which does not apply to self-employed persons such as bookmakers and, consequently, a law from which they could derive no benefit had they, indeed, been picketing. He held that the subtle difference between these protests and industrial action involving picketing is that the latter is premised on the express or implied threat of collective action on the part of the trade union concerned and its individual members to dissuade others from exercising certain legal and contractual rights, most notably to attend at a workplace. In this case not only was there no evidence of any such express or implied threat but it was not so regarded by the sporting public who seem to have largely ignored the protest. However, insulting and abusive language had been directed by some of the protesters at other bookmakers. Hogan J. at para.86 held that this conduct "was quite unlawful and – depending on the exact language used – might have potentially constituted a breach of the peace."

With regard to the possibility of the defendants having applied for an injunction to prohibit the protests his judgment was nuanced:

> "87. Provided that the protestors otherwise refrained from any overt actions against individuals and the protest remained peaceable and without any acts of trespass and otherwise remained within the law, then if Dundalk had applied for an injunction at the time it would not have been entitled to any such relief, since the core of the protestors' activity was fully protected by the guarantees contained in Article 40.6.1.i (free speech) and Article 40.6.1.ii (peaceable assembly) of the Constitution.
>
> 88. Dundalk would, however, have been entitled to have obtained an injunction restraining the use of jeering, insulting language and verbal abuse which was personally directed – and I emphasise these words–at those bookmakers (such as Mr. McCartan) and others who entered the stadium."

Proportionality Of critical importance is the introduction of the concept of proportionality into this section of the judgment:

> "This does not mean in and of itself that the protest thereby became unlawful. The right of free speech and free assembly are critical constitutional rights and they are vital to the functioning of the free and democratic society posited by Article 5 of the Constitution. The principle of proportionality comes into play here and the right of protest is not to be lost merely because of the regrettable lapses on the part of an undisciplined minority."

Applying Non-Fatal Offences against the Person Act 1997 Hogan J. also held that s.9 Non-Fatal Offences against the Person Act 1997 (the "1997 Act") did not apply. It was his opinion that the protesters merely attended "at or near" Dundalk Stadium, while not actually trespassing thereon. As they had attended simply for the purposes of communicating information, in the circumstances this conduct did not amount to the act of "watching or besetting" within the meaning of s.9(2) of the 1997 Act. He concluded:

> "91. For all of these reasons, I am satisfied that the protesters had engaged in the constitutionally protected activities of free speech and free assembly without engaging in any overt acts to dissuade others or to commit acts of trespass or other illegal acts. It follows, therefore, that, subject to the important qualification in respect of the jeering and verbal abuse of

individuals – which was unlawful–the protests outside the stadium were otherwise perfectly lawful. "

FREEDOM OF SPEECH

Hyland v Dundalk Racing (1999) Ltd trading as Dundalk Stadium [2014] IEHC 60 is considered in greater detail elsewhere in this chapter under the heading FREEDOM OF ASSEMBLY. The following obiter of Hogan J. at para.81 is of relevance with regard to freedom of speech:

> "Given that the free exchange of ideas, arguments and views is central to the operation of the democratic State envisaged by Article 5 and is at the heart of the protections of free speech and peaceable assembly contained in Article 40.6.1, the public expression and manifestation of different and dissenting views must–in general, at least–be tolerantly accepted by all."

He did include a caveat in the event that there is jeering or verbal abuse of individuals which is unlawful.

IMMIGRATION

Each year, the courts consider a large number of challenges to deportation decisions. Following the Supreme Court's decision in *Dimbo v Minister for Justice, Equality and Law Reform* [2008] IESC 26, constitutional and ECHR rights function as matters to be considered in the decision-making process, rather than as substantive fetters on the ministerial power to issue deportation decisions. The proportionality standard recognised in *Meadows v Minister for Justice and Equality* [2010] 2 I.R. 710 provides a further constraint. The immigration cases are considered more fully in the Asylum and Immigration Law chapter of the *Annual Review of Irish Law 2014*, p.12. In this sub-section, we confine our attention to those cases that suggest a refinement or development of the constitutional principles that apply to this area of law.

Direct provision In *CA v Minister for Justice and Equality* [2014] IEHC 532, the High Court rejected a challenge to the system of direct provision to those awaiting immigration decisions. Direct provision is the cashless provision of material support by the State in the form of accommodation, food, education, etc. The applicants, a mother and her son, had been living in direct provision for a number of years, her son for the entirety of his life. Their applications for asylum were refused. While awaiting decisions on their subsidiary protection applications, the applicants challenged the lawfulness and constitutionality and compatibility with the ECHR of the direct provision system. Two fundamental procedural issues arose in the case. The first concerned the admissibility of various reports about the legality, proportionality and quality of direct provision that had been exhibited by the applicants' solicitor in an affidavit within the proceedings. Mac Eochaidh J. held that it would be inappropriate to have regard to such reports as they could not properly be evidence of the truth of their contents. Oral testimony had not been given and there was no opportunity for the Minister to cross-examine the authors of the reports. The second fundamental procedural issue again concerned the consequences of the applicants' decision to proceed by way of judicial review rather than plenary proceedings. Although Mac Eochaidh J. was prepared to accept the affidavit evidence of the applicant as to her experience of direct provision and her feelings about it, there was a fundamental dispute on the affidavits as to whether direct provision had the negative effects contended for by the applicants. The applicants could have filed affidavits by expert witnesses or sought to cross-examine the deponents of affidavits filed on behalf of the Minister, but had elected not to do so. In the circumstances, Mac Eochaidh J. held that the applicants had failed to discharge the burden of proof to establish that direct provision had negative effects. This had significant implications for the applicants' claims that their human rights were breached by the system of direct provision.

The applicants' claims that direct provision breached their rights to freedom from torture and inhuman or degrading treatment, whether under the Convention or the Constitution, were rejected on the grounds that the applicants had not provided the evidential basis to substantiate the claim. However, Mac Eochaidh J. reviewed a number of discrete privacy challenges to the rules that apply in detention centres under the direct provision system. He held that while the authorities were entitled to carry out room inspections, it was a disproportionate interference with privacy rights to allow unannounced inspections without the consent of residents, particularly given that such inspections could occur when residents were absent. Moreover, the applicants' accommodation constituted their dwelling and benefited from constitutional protection under Art.40.5. The requirements that the applicant should daily sign in to indicate her presence in her home and notify any intended absences were likewise a disproportionate interference with private life. Mac Eochaidh J. reached the same conclusion in respect of the absolute prohibition on guests during both day and night. Mac Eochaidh J. held that the complaints handling procedures breached constitutional justice insofar as it infringed the principle of *nemo iudex in causa sua*. It was inappropriate that the Reception and Integration Agency should write the house rules, be in a commercial relationship with the operators of the centres, and then be the adjudicator on complaints against those operators. Mac Eochaidh J. rejected the applicants' contention that the ban on private cooking breached the applicants' rights. This was a necessary incident of communal living, which itself was a reasonable choice open to the Minister.

Mac Eochaidh J. rejected the more fundamental challenges to the system of direct provision. The applicants had conceded that some scheme of direct provision might be lawful but had failed to establish the factual basis to support the constitutional claim that their family life was affected by this scheme. Mac Eochaidh J. appeared to hold out the possibility that it might have been possible to provide evidence that would ground such a constitutional claim.

Finally, the applicants challenged the scheme of direct provision on the basis that it breached Art.15.2 of the Constitution as there was no legislative basis for it. Mac Eochaidh J. rejected the premise of this argument. The power to control immigration was an aspect of the executive power. The Minister did not need statutory authorisation to establish the direct provision system. This was not a case, such as *Laurentiu v Minister for Justice* [1999] 4 I.R. 26, in which the Oireachtas had asserted control of an area of policy and then made an unrestricted delegation to a Government Minister, nor a case, such as *O'Neill v Minister for Agriculture* [1988] I.R. 539, in which a Minister chose to operate an administrative scheme instead of a statutorily prescribed scheme. Rather, it was an area in respect of which the Oireachtas had never asserted its legislative power. The fact that the scheme amounted to a prima facie infringement of constitutional rights did not mean that legislation was required. In this regard, following an interesting exegesis on the possible differences between the English word 'executive' and the Irish word *comhallach*, Mac Eochaidh J. concluded that there was no difference of meaning between the Irish and English versions of the Constitution. The scheme of direct provision was a legitimate exercise by the Government of the executive power of the State.

Right to freedom of conscience In *AM v Refugee Appeals Tribunal* [2014] IEHC 388, McDermott J. held that the right to freedom of conscience was protected by Art.40.3.1 as an unenumerated right:

> "Freedom of individual conscience underpins many of the democratic values and fundamental rights of the Constitution. The right to vote, to participate as a candidate in any form of election, the rights to freedom of expression, association and assembly and religious freedom are all dependent on the freely exercised will and conscience of the individual. Though it is not recognised as a separate fundamental right under the Constitution, it is clearly part of the constitutional fabric and, as such, is, I am satisfied, an unenumerated right guaranteed by Article 40.3 of the Constitution. Its recognition in this case is entirely in accordance with assuring the 'dignity and freedom of the individual' as outlined in the Preamble and the democratic nature of the state as defined by Article 5."

This is a rare recognition of a new unenumerated right. However, it employs the least contentious method of recognising new constitutional rights (implication from the constitutional text) and is therefore not inconsistent with the general scepticism towards this doctrine that has pertained since at least 2000. That said, it is an important constitutional development given that the Supreme Court in *McGee v Attorney General* [1974] I.R. 284 concluded that non-religious freedom of conscience was not constitutionally protected by Art.44 of the Constitution.

Right to make representations prior to a deportation decision In *Javed v Minister for Justice and Equality* [2014] IEHC 508, Barr J. held that the applicant had a constitutional right to make submissions to the Minister in respect of how a proposed deportation decision would affect her constitutional and ECHR rights. However, this constitutional requirement was met by s.3 of the Immigration Act 1999, which provides that a person can make representations within 15 days of receiving notice that the Minister proposes to issue a deportation order. Barr J. rejected the applicant's contention that this process is unsatisfactory as it removes the opportunity for a person to depart the State voluntarily rather than be the subject of a deportation order. While this might deter someone from making representations, this was not an unconstitutional interference with the right. In this regard, Barr J. compared it to the costs penalty that might apply to a person who chose to commence legal proceedings: this did not amount to an unconstitutional interference with the right to litigate. This comparison does not seem apt. There is a difference between a financial disincentive that applies through operation of market forces and the choice of the Oireachtas to structure the deportation process in such a way that a person who exercises the right to make representations loses the right to leave the State voluntarily. This is particularly the case given that a deportation order is indefinite, unless the Minister accedes to a request to revoke it. Barr J. came to the same conclusion in *AL v Minister for Justice and Equality* [2014] IEHC 503 and *QL v Minister for Justice and Equality* [2014] IEHC 507.

Consideration of rights and proportionality As noted above, the rights that apply in the deportation context are procedural in character: consideration must be given to whether, for example, the family rights of a deportee would be unconstitutionally affected by the deportation. However, those rights do not act as substantive fetters on the decision-maker constrained by a court in judicial review proceedings. The proportionality requirement recognised in *Meadows v Minister for Justice* had the potential to transform the procedural right into a substantive right. This was the application of *Meadows* taken by Hogan J. in cases such as *Efe v Minister for Justice Equality and Law Reform* [2011] IEHC 214. However, Cooke J. took a narrower approach, treating *Meadows* as a requirement that the decision-maker ensure that there was no disproportionate interference with constitutional rights, a decision that would then be reviewed on a rationality basis by the High Court. See, for instance, *ISOF v Minister for Justice, Equality and Law Reform* [2010] IEHC 386. This is stronger protection than *Dimbo* as it structures the form of consideration (proportionality analysis) that the Minister must give to constitutional rights. Nevertheless, it retains the basic *Dimbo* position in that the rights are not substantive fetters on the decision-making process, to be enforced by the reviewing court.

The Supreme Court now appears to favour the approach of Cooke J. In *AMS v Minister for Justice and Equality* [2014] IESC 65, Clarke J., with whom the other members of the Supreme Court agreed, held at para.7.12 that the court should afford a reasonable margin of appreciation to the decision-maker but intervene "where an applicant discharges the burden of demonstrating that the proportionality judgment of the decision maker was unreasonable." In this case, the court held that the applicant had discharged that burden. This case concerned family reunification, a special class of applicants. It was difficult to see how the general state interest in controlling immigration could outweigh the family circumstances in a case such as this. On this basis, the court disallowed the appeal against the judgment of Mac Eochaidh J., who had held that no proper proportionality exercise had been undertaken. See *AMS v Minister for Justice and Equality* [2014] IEHC 57.

The *Dimbo/Meadows* division of responsibility between decision-maker and reviewing court is apt to mislead decision-makers as to the extent of consideration that they must give to constitutional rights. An example of this can be seen in *Gorry v Minister for Justice and Equality* [2014] IEHC 29. Mac Eochaidh J. was critical of a deportation decision where the assessor held that there was no authority to support the proposition that an Irish citizen might have a right under Art.41 of the Constitution to reside with her or his spouse in the jurisdiction. The assessor considered that the law only required a consideration of the position of the couple. Mac Eochaidh J. held that this was mistaken; the starting point was that the couple have a prima facie right to live together in Ireland. This is incorrect insofar as it implies that the decision-maker is circumscribed by the married couple's right to live together in Ireland. Instead, the courts are content to review deportation decisions on the basis that the decision-maker must consider the right (the formulation adopted by the assessor in this case) not on the basis that there is a substantive fetter circumscribing the scope of the assessor's discretion. The mistake of the assessor was to omit to refer to the consideration as a 'right.' The failure to do so led Mac Eochaidh J. to quash the decision. It is to be hoped that the Supreme Court's decision in *AMS* may clarify this issue.

Rights of non-marital family In *KI v Minister for Justice and Equality* [2014] IEHC 83, McDermott J. held that non-marital families did have rights that should be considered in a deportation process. Where parents are not married but the family demonstrates all the other attributes of family relationships and life, similar consideration should be given to the impact of deportation on the interests of children. Broadly following the Supreme Court's view in *JK v VW* [1990] 2 I.R. 437 on the rights of interest or concern that might lead to an order of guardianship in favour of an unmarried father, McDermott J. held that the decision-maker should consider the nature and extent of the father's relationship with his children. Ultimately, McDermott J. upheld the validity of the Minister's decision to refuse to revoke the deportation order.

INVIOLABILITY OF THE DWELLING

Deprivation of home In *Lattimore v Dublin City Council* [2014] IEHC 233 O'Neill J. affirmed that where a person is to be deprived of their home, within the meaning of art. 8 of the European Convention of Human Rights (right to respect for private and family life), they are entitled to have the proportionality of that decision determined by an independent tribunal. The housing authority could not be such a tribunal. *Inter alia* a breach of Art.40.5 had been claimed. O'Neill J. held that the decision taken had not been disproportionate and as such there had been no breach of Art.40.5 of the Constitution. The substantive issues in the case were considered in terms of European law with the constitutional provision appearing as something of an afterthought.

LEGISLATIVE POWER

Non-delegation doctrine The courts considered the delegation of legislative power in two cases in 2014. In *Bederev v Ireland* [2014] IEHC 490, Gilligan J. rejected a challenge to the constitutionality of s.2 of the Misuse of Drugs Act 1977 (the "1977 Act"). Section 2 of the 1977 Act defines a controlled drug and therefore effectively determines the applicability of all the other sections of the Act. A substance is a 'controlled drug' either if it is listed in the Schedule to the Act or it is declared to be so by the Government pursuant to s.2(2):

> The Government may by order declare any substance, product or preparation (not being a substance, product or preparation specified in the Schedule to this Act) to be a controlled drug for the purposes of this Act and so long as an order under this subsection is in force, this Act shall have effect as

> regards any substance, product or preparation specified in the order as if the substance, product or preparation were specified in the said Schedule.

The reason for this approach is that new drugs emerge very quickly and it is difficult for primary legislation to keep up with new dangerous substances. The plaintiff was charged with offences under the 1977 Act in relation to the possession of and possession with intention to sell methylethcathinone. This drug had been prescribed as a controlled drug by the Misuse of Drugs Act 1997 (Controlled Drugs) (Declaration) Order 2011 (S.I. No. 551 of 2011). Gilligan J. considered that the policy of the Oireachtas was clear from various provisions in the legislation and the schedule itself: "to control and regulate those substances which are subject to misuse and which would cause harm to human health and to society as a whole if not controlled." It was also significant that the Oireachtas had a power to annul any regulations under s.38 of the 1977 Act. Gilligan J. rejected the plaintiff's claim that alcohol could be prescribed under s.2. In his view, the legislative context, historical perspective and the scheme of the Act all made it clear that this legislation aimed "to control substances which would have negative and detrimental effects on human health and society and is limited to those substances which are likely to be universally harmful to those who misuse them." Gilligan J. therefore rejected the constitutional challenge. In 2015, however, the Court of Appeal granted the plaintiff's appeal and declared s.2(2) unconstitutional: *Bederev v Ireland* [2015] IECA 38. This case will be considered in next year's *Annual Review*.

In *O'Connell v The Turf Club* [2014] IEHC 175, McGovern J. considered a challenge to the constitutionality of sections of the Irish Horseracing Industry Act 1994 that allowed the Turf Club to make and amend the Rules of Racing. The Turf Club was conducting an inquiry into the applicants and alleged infringements of those rules at a race meet. McGovern J. held at para.30 that the *Cityview* test had been satisfied:

> "The Acts set out ample principles and policies which enable the respondent to make and enforce the Rules. These principles and policies are not only to be found within the Acts, but are also discernible by reference to the Rules of Racing as laid down by the respondent at the date of the enactment of the 1994 and 2001 Acts. The Oireachtas was aware of the existence of those Rules because they are defined in the Act of 1994 as meaning, inter alia, '*... in relation to flat racing, the Rule of Racing as laid down by the Irish Turf Club*' [emphasis added]. The principles and policies are also provided by and/or are discernible by reference to the inherent nature and attributes of the sport of competitive horseracing."

In the unusual circumstances of this case, it was not unreasonable for McGovern J. to rely on the existing Rules of Racing, acknowledged by the Oireachtas, as evidence of the principles and policies in the Act that should guide the exercise of any delegated legislative power. However, it does not seem appropriate to rely on the characteristics of the object of regulation as evidence of the principles and policies that are to guide how that object should be regulated.

NATURAL RESOURCES AND NORTH-SOUTH RELATIONS

In *Barlow v Minister for Agriculture* [2014] IEHC 471, the plaintiffs challenged the constitutionality of the arrangement whereby vessels registered in Northern Ireland could fish for mussels in Irish territorial waters. In the mid-1960s, the British, Irish and Northern Irish Governments had—through a series of letters and undertakings—formed a Voisinage agreement that effectively allowed Irish and Northern Irish fishing boats reciprocal rights in each other's waters. The plaintiffs challenged the validity of this agreement on a number of grounds.

First, they contended that it breached Art.10 of the Constitution. Article 10.1 provides that all natural resources within the jurisdiction of the State belong to the State subject to all estates and interests therein for the time being lawfully vested in any person or body. Article 10.3 allows provision to be made by law for the management of the property which belongs to the State and for the control of the alienation, whether temporary or permanent, of that property. Birmingham J. held that this provision was inapplicable to the facts of the case. Although mussel seed on the seabed within Irish territorial waters could be classified as a natural resource, it was not a natural resource that *belonged* to the State. Historically, wild animals were considered the property of no-one. They could be managed by the State but were not owned by the State. A fortiori, the Voisinage agreement did not amount to the alienation of a natural resource owned by the State.

Secondly, the plaintiffs argued that the constitutional commitment to the rule of law required that there be legal authorisation for the Voisinage agreement. Birmingham J. rejected this contention. The Voisinage agreement was an exercise of the Government's foreign policy power, in the particularly fraught context of relations between Ireland, Northern Ireland and Great Britain. While it might be justiciable, the courts should grant a wide margin of appreciation to the Government. In constitutional terms, it was an agreement or convention of a technical or administrative kind that did not require to be laid before the Dáil.

PARLIAMENTARY PRIVILEGE

Legislative immunity extends to statutory committee A bench of seven sat in the Supreme Court for the appeal in *Callely v Moylan & Ors* [2014] IESC 26, a claim by a committee of the Oireachtas that its proceedings were non-justiciable. This was an appeal from *Callely v Moylan & Ors* [2011] IEHC 2; [2011] 2 I.L.R.M. 339 in which O'Neill J. had quashed the Seanad *Report of the Results of an Investigation into Complaints Concerning Senator Ivor Callely* dated 14 July 2010, and a resolution of Seanad Éireann adopted by Seanad Éireann on 14 July 2010, to the effect that Senator Ivor Callely be censured and suspended from the House without pay for 20 days. This had been in respect of complaints made under the Ethics in Public Office Act 1995 and the Standards in Public Office Act 2001 that Senator Callely had abused the Seanad system of reimbursement for travel expenses by claiming a residence in Bantry as his normal residence for reimbursement purposes. Two issues had been considered, justiciability and the application of fair procedures. The pertinent details of the case were considered in *Annual Review of Irish Law 2011*, pp.166–168; 181–190 and are not repeated here.

In the Supreme Court five judgments were delivered. The majority opinion granting the appeal and setting aside the High Court order was a lengthy and extensive joint judgment of O'Donnell J. and Clarke J., Denham C.J. concurring. In this judgment a comprehensive analysis of the justiciability issue had been presented under two separate headings, a broad and a narrow approach. Fennelly J., in a brief judgment, concurred with the broad approach of justiciability but not with the narrow approach issuing his own short decision. The majority held that there was no error of law or breach of fair procedures on the part of the Seanad committee despite the committee's failure to acknowledge that Senator Callely's claim had been in compliance with the Department of Finance interpretation of normal residence. The minority of Murray J., Hardiman J. and McKechnie J. each issued a judgment, the last two of some length. Murray J. concurred with McKechnie J.'s opinion on the fair procedures issue and Hardiman J. concurred with certain of McKechnie J.'s arguments in that regard. The judgments included what might be considered classic presentations of the theory of the separation of powers and the role of the different organs of the State as inferred from Art.6 as well as citing from authorities referred to in detail in the High Court judgment. As such this consideration of the Supreme Court decision concentrates on what appear to be the more significant or potentially novel aspects of the varied judgments.

Immunity qualified by absence of rules in standing orders The joint judgment of O'Donnell J. and Clarke J. noted that Senator Callely had sought relief against individual members of Seanad Éireann and in doing so had relied upon statements made by them in the course of proceedings in Seanad Éireann. This brought into account specific immunities as expressed in Art.15.12 and O'Donnell J. and Clarke J. noted, at para.54, that even if persuaded that the proceedings before the committee and in the Seanad were justiciable, they would not be prepared to make orders in the form sought by the respondent and would have required careful argument as to the relief which it would be appropriate to have granted without contravening the Constitution. They concluded this section as follows at para.56:

> "In the case of members of the Oireachtas, they have very significant privileges in respect of their individual and collective utterances, and are given significant exemption from criminal law in the shape of privilege from arrest. At a minimum therefore it should not be surprising if the law attaching to the incidence of their membership of the most important collected body in the State, is itself distinct."

They continued:

> "57. It follows that the Constitution defines areas within the exclusive competence of each of the powers of government which go beyond the narrowest definition of those powers and includes areas which are either inherently part of the function concerned by virtue of being inextricably linked to that function or must properly be said to fall within the function concerned because of the terms of the Constitution itself. In that context we have no doubt but that determining travel and subsistence expenses and putting in place a regime to ensure that they are properly policed falls within

> the legislative power conferred on the Oireachtas. That is not, however, an end to the matter. As noted earlier, the fact that a particular function lies within the sphere of one or other organ of government does not necessarily mean that the exercise of that power may not be subject to some degree of interaction with or scrutiny by another power of government. The fact, for example, that a particular function can properly be characterised as part of the executive function conferred on the government itself does not mean that it may not be subject to review in the courts or subject to a requirement to abide by legislation properly passed by the Oireachtas, scrutinised, if necessary, for its consistency with the Constitution by the courts. While the imposition of a policing regime with appropriate penalties in respect of funding made available to members of the Oireachtas to enable them to perform their functions is clearly part of the legislative function contemplated by the Constitution, the real question which is at the core of these proceedings is whether it is a function which is exclusively conferred on the Houses of the Oireachtas or rather while conferred on the Houses, is amenable, nonetheless, to judicial review."

They noted at para.61 that the scrutiny of judicial review is available to a citizen who is not a member of either House and who may be subjected to aspects of the legislative power. The real issue of controversy was whether the same principle applies to the exercise of similar aspects of the legislative power over members of the Houses. They were critical of the High Court decision:

> "76. It was suggested in the judgment of the High Court that the distinction between members and non-members in this regard creates an impermissible discrimination contrary to Article 40.1 of the Constitution. However, and with respect, this reasoning cannot be supported. There can be few better examples of a difference in social, and indeed constitutional, function justifying a difference in treatment in the law. Members of the Oireachtas are given unique duties powers and privileges by the Constitution. It is hardly surprising that that role also involves some limitation of the rights otherwise afforded to citizens in a different context. As already observed, there are other examples in the Constitution where citizens appointed or elected to particular posts are given different privileges, obligations, duties, and on occasions, liabilities."

They concluded their analysis of the broad approach to the issue as follows:

> "80. It is important to note that this reasoning does not mean that all the proceedings of the Oireachtas are immune from scrutiny or that members lose their constitutional rights. As already observed, it is emphatically the function of the courts to determine the proper boundaries of the exercise of the legislative power in each case, which, pursuant to the separation of powers requires that their proceedings be non-justiciable. This cannot be a matter for the Oireachtas, or either House. Therefore, it seems to us that the real test in each case is whether the actions sought to be subjected to review form an important and integral part of the exercise of the legislative power

and does not directly affect persons outside the Houses of the Oireachtas. In that context, it is important to note that the 'specified act' which can be the subject of an inquiry under s.4(1) of the 2001 Act must be an act which interferes with the ability of a member of the relevant House to carry out his constitutional function as such member. The definition of 'specified act' in substance, provides for as much. Purely private activity which could not impact on the carrying out of the constitutional legislative function is expressly excluded. It is true that such activity is not confined directly to the act of legislating but, for the reasons already analysed, the legislative function seems to us to go beyond the core activity of participating in deliberations leading to the adoption of legislation. We are, therefore, satisfied that the sort of activity which can be considered to be a 'specified act' is closely associated with the core legislative function and comes within an area which can legitimately be governed by rules and orders.

81. Furthermore, the fact that the Constitution requires that there remain an area of activity in the legislature which is non-justiciable, does not mean that that area is beyond the reach of the Constitution. The Oireachtas is itself required to uphold the Constitution and to respect the rights of citizens, whether members or not. This indeed, is no doubt why the Oireachtas has adopted rules to protect individuals in the context of the exercise of freedom of speech within the Oireachtas which is guaranteed by the Constitution and why there is elaborate provision for fair procedures in the legislation providing for committee hearings under the ethics in public office legislation. The fact that there cannot be immediate recourse to the courts places, if anything, a heavier onus on the Oireachtas to ensure that constitutional rights are respected in proceedings which are themselves non-justiciable. Finally, and on a related point, the fact that the area of non-justiciability is itself derived from the principle of separation of powers under the Constitution, is itself a limitation on the manner in which the powers may be exercised. A principle which is derived from the Constitution and intended to maintain constitutional equilibrium, could not be used to subvert the order and values protected by the Constitution. Accordingly, proceedings which amounted to a fundamental departure from the dictates of the Constitution, which was neither prevented nor remedied by the Oireachtas itself then (as indeed was perhaps contemplated in passing in cases such as *Finn v. The Attorney General* [1983] I.R. 154, *Slattery v. An Taoiseach* [1993]1 I.R. 286, and *O'Malley v. An Ceann Comhairle* [[1997] 1 I.R. 427]) the Courts could be obliged to act to maintain the Constitutional balance. It is however, neither necessary nor perhaps desirable to speculate on the precise circumstances in which it could be said that the principle of separation of powers no longer required that the proceedings of the legislative power be beyond judicial scrutiny. No such case is alleged here and nor does it appear to have arisen as a matter of history since the foundation of the State. It is not to be readily assumed that such an occasion would arise in the future.

82. Thus, we conclude that the separation of powers, at least in principle, means that internal disciplinary proceedings of the Oireachtas which are properly within the scope of the legislative power, are non-justiciable. If

therefore, the proceedings had been brought pursuant to rules or standing orders, we conceive that they could not be challenged in these proceedings. We apprehend that this is the view of the majority of the Court. A further question however, remains as to whether the fact that the Oireachtas has chosen to legislate rather than adopt rules and orders can have any effect on the justiciability of decisions made in a case such as this."

O'Donnell J. and Clarke J. then considered the narrow basis of analysis. As this was grounds for dissent by Fennelly J. and as it is quite technical the discussion is repeated in full:

> "83. It is necessary to consider if the decision of the High Court can be justified on the narrower ground of the absence of formal rules or orders. There are, it seems to us, a number of reasons why this is not possible. First, it is apparent from some of the matters cited above that the principle of non-justiciability does not solely depend upon the words of Article 15.10 but also, and perhaps more importantly, is derived from the separation of powers. Second, it is important to consider why it was necessary to provide explicitly for a power to make rules and standing orders. It seems to us that the purpose of Article 15.10 resides in the word 'each'. In other words, each House of the Oireachtas, independent of the other, and of anyone else, can adopt its own rules which have the force of law. It does not require the concurrence of the other House or the President. It is therefore an important expression of the autonomy of each House, something which is indeed relevant to the larger issue in this case.
>
> 84. As Geoghegan J. observed in *Howlin v. Morris*, the main purpose of Article 15.10 is 'to dispense with the necessity for legislation' (para. 93). But it does not follow from this that, if the rules are contained in legislation, they lose the protection of the Constitution. The function of Article 15.10 is to ensure that each House has the independent capacity to adopt its own rules and it does not have to acquiesce in rules formulated by any other body including the other House. It is worth asking why it was thought necessary to introduce legislation in this case at all. In the first place it was necessary because there were financial consequences to the machinery being established. Perhaps even more importantly, legislation was necessary because, in respect of an inquiry, whether by a committee of the Oireachtas or the Commission established by the Act, it was necessary to confer powers to summon witnesses and compel the production of documents. This is something that requires legislative authority and is beyond the competence of either House whether by rule or standing order. Finally, the Act applies of course to many persons other than members of the Oireachtas but applies the same substantive standard to all those within its scope. It was certainly convenient therefore to put all of the provisions in the same piece of legislation.
>
> 85. If each House of the Oireachtas independently and autonomously adopts the legislation including that portion of the legislation establishing both the mechanism for procedure and the substantive standard of behaviour, we cannot see any reason to say that it has not adopted its 'own' rule, even

if it happens to be the same rule as that applying to the other House of the Oireachtas.

86. In any event, the matter does not end there because by standing order 90 the Seanad, in our view, adopted, by standing orders, the procedures contemplated in the Act. Standing order 90 (of the 2007 Standing Orders of the Seanad) provides:

'There shall stand established at the commencement of every Seanad, a Select Committee of Seanad Éireann which shall be called the Select Committee on Members' Interests of Seanad Éireann, to perform the functions conferred on it by the Ethics in Public Office Act, 1995.'

87. Thus, if there was any doubt about it, it seems that the Seanad, by creating a committee to operate the Act has, by standing order, adopted the rule of behaviour in the Ethics in Public Office Act 1995 (as amended). Indeed, in the High Court, the High Court judge acknowledged this and conceded that 'Standing Order 90 does draw the respondents' inquiry within the ambit of Seanad standing orders' (para.78). However, he considered that could not be conclusive because he considered the subject matter of the investigation manifestly fell outside the 'normal sphere of parliamentary activity' (para. 78). This was undoubtedly, so he said; 'where the subject matter of the inquiry and the potential findings of fact were likely to cause great damage to the good name and reputation and, perhaps, livelihood of the Member under investigation.' (para.78). This distinction cannot be sustained. The narrow ground is essentially a formal and technical one: the objection was to the absence of standing orders and the High Court's (correct) acknowledgement that standing order 90 brings the proceedings within the realm in which standing orders ought to be fatal to the narrow ground. Furthermore, for the reasons set out above we do not agree that the subject matter of this inquiry fell outside the legislative function.

88. Finally, and in any event, the non-justiciability of the internal operations of the Oireachtas is not solely dependent on the existence of Article 15.10 rules; it is derived from the separation of powers. If something falls within an area of non-justiciability mandated by the separation of powers, essential to Constitutional equilibrium, it does not lose that status by the introduction of legislation which facilitates the performance of the function. Accordingly we would allow the appellants' appeal and set aside the order of the High Court."

However, the judgment continues by stating at para.89 that "a majority of the court takes the view that the absence of rules adopted by standing orders means that the proceedings of the Committee and Seanad are justiciable." In looking at the actions of the committee O'Donnell J. and Clarke J. held that there were no unfair procedures regarding Senator Callely but the question was whether or not there had been an error of law. They concluded:

"114. It is true that the Committee did not frankly acknowledge in its conclusions that Senator Callely was in compliance with the Department of Finance interpretation. The first occasion on which this was acknowledged was in the Statement of Opposition referred to above. Whether this reticence

> was due to a desire not to expose the officials to criticism for proffering that interpretation, or a less high minded desire to avoid public attention and criticism of the Oireachtas expenses regime more generally, may be a matter of speculation and comment, but it cannot resolve this case. In truth the principal complaints about the Committee are directed, with some merit, not to what the Committee did, but rather what it said (or did not say) in its Report and more particularly in the documents filed in defence of these proceedings. But the only issue for this Court is one of law. In our view the Committee was correct in rejecting as erroneous the 1994 interpretation and was entitled to conclude that Senator Callely had indeed misrepresented his normal place of residence and thereby committed a specified act which was inconsistent with the maintenance of public confidence in the performance by him of his office."

Judgment of Fennelly J. As noted above Fennelly J. agreed with the joint judgment of O'Donnell and Clarke JJ. that, in principle, decisions made in internal disciplinary proceedings by either House of the Oireachtas are non-justiciable and that any proceedings conducted pursuant to rules or standing orders may not be challenged by way of judicial review (para.82 of the joint judgment). He expressed his agreement with the statement, at para.81 of the joint judgment

> "that a 'principle which is derived from the Constitution and intended to maintain constitutional equilibrium, could not be used to subvert the order and values protected by the Constitution.' Thus, if it should transpire that a House of the Oireachtas was either generally or in a particular case disposed to ignore and not observe the constitutional imperatives, the courts, as the ultimate guardians of rights, would be bound to intervene. It is not easy to imagine such circumstances or to devise a standard."

He disagreed with O'Donnell and Clarke JJ.'s analysis of the narrow approach on the following grounds:

> "12. The Ethics in Public Office Act, 1995 and the Standards in Public Office Act, 2001 establish a statutory scheme for the investigation of and reporting on complaints against members of the Houses of the Oireachtas. Section 8 of the Act of 1995 provides that each House is to appoint a select committee. In the case of the Seanad it is to be the Committee on Members' Interests of Seanad Eireann. Section 8(2) provides:
>
>> "A person (other than a member) who considers that a member (other than a member who is or, at the relevant time, was an office holder) may have contravened section 5 or 7 or done a specified act may make a complaint in writing in relation to the matter to the Clerk and, subject to subsection (3), the Clerk shall refer the matter to the Committee and shall furnish a copy of the complaint to the Committee." …
>
> 13. Section 4(1) provides the definition of a 'specified act.' The machinery of investigation and report created by these two acts is entirely statutory. The notion of 'specified act' as a subject of complaint is statutory. No rule or standing order of the Seanad adopted it as a subject of complaint. This is

> not, in my view what was envisaged by Article 15.10 of the Constitution. In order to enjoy the benefit of any immunity from judicial review, at the very least the Seanad would have had to have adopted the notion of 'specified act' as the subject of a rule governing members.
>
> 14. I am of opinion that the decision of the Select Committee was not, therefore, immune from judicial review. It follows that the respondent is entitled to the benefit of normal judicial review and that he was entitled to have fair procedures followed by the Select Committee."

No havens of immunity: Constitution requires safeguard of judicial review In his short, and succinct, dissenting judgment Murray J. held that there cannot be havens of immunity from judicial scrutiny.

> "17. If the appellants were correct in their contention for constitutional immunity it would concentrate in the hands of a Committee absolute power over the constitutional fate of one elected citizen.
>
> 18. In short, it seems to me that to adopt the view that the courts have no such jurisdiction would be the antithesis of respect for the separation of powers denying, as it would, the role accorded to the judiciary to safeguard personal rights and to ensure that powers are exercised lawfully and constitutionally."

He held that having regard to the *East Donegal* principles, the courts must also have jurisdiction to review the manner in which powers were exercised under the Ethics in Public Office Act 1995. "Any other approach would give a constitutionally impermissible immunity from scrutiny of an Act of the Oireachtas and the use of its powers" (at para.20).

East Donegal principles must apply In a hard-hitting and forthright judgment Hardiman J. gave no quarter to the submission of the committee. The committee had found that Senator Callely had misrepresented his normal place of residence for the purpose of claiming allowances. The Senator had challenged this decision on the basis that the evidence showed clearly that he had adhered to the definition of the Department of Finance. Hardiman J. remarked:

> "The Committee's substantive defence to this claim by Mr. Callely was, in the words of the learned High Court judge 'quite remarkable.' Notwithstanding the unambiguous finding, quoted above, that Senator Callely 'has done a specified act, as contemplated by s.4 of the Act of 2001, by misrepresenting his normal place of residence for the purpose of claiming allowances', in their defence to these proceedings the Committee denied that it had found that the applicant had misrepresented his normal place of residence within the meaning of the Act of 1938. They also asserted that the Department of Finance's interpretation of the phrase 'normal place of residence' was 'erroneous and ultra vires the Act of 1938'. But the Committee then made a central concession."

In its "Statement of Grounds of Opposition", in effect the defence to Mr. Callely's proceedings, the committee said as follows:

> "(10) Without prejudice to the foregoing, if the Committee concluded that the applicant misrepresented his normal place of residence within the meaning of s.4(1)(e) of the Act of 1938 (*which is denied*), it was entitled not to apply the Department of Finance 1994 interpretation of that phrase, as communicated to the applicant by letter dated the 2nd October 2008. The latter interpretation of the 'normal place of residence, was erroneous and ultra vires the Act of 1938. *For the avoidance of doubt, the respondents acknowledge that the applicant's claim for expenses came within the scope of the interpretation given by the Department of Finance.*" (Emphasis added by Hardiman J.)
>
> This is a most remarkable pleading. First, it denies that the Committee made a finding that the applicant had misrepresented his normal place of residence whereas it is quite clear that it had made precisely that finding in so many words. The terms of paragraph 10 of the Statement of Opposition are wholly inconsistent with the plain words of paragraph (1) of the Committee's 'findings and determinations' of 14 July 2010, which is quoted in full above."

Later on in the judgment Hardiman J. stated:

> "The first thing that requires to be said about this concession is that it was entirely novel. At no stage during the hearings before the Committee or in the Committee's findings was it stated or accepted by the Committee that Mr. Callely's claim for expenses came within the interpretation given by the Department of Finance. The Committee appears simply to have ignored this issue."

Further on he stated:

> "The Committee's concession was repeated, and the Committee's scene-shifting defence re-stated, at para.(4.2) of the Committee's written submissions in the High Court as follows:
>
> > '*The [Committee's Members] acknowledge that, having regard to [Mr. Callely's] evidence as to his use of his house in Kilcrohane, that house constituted a normal place of residence within the meaning of the Department of Finance 'definition'*. However, the Committee was not deciding whether the applicant's claim came within the Department of Finance definition. Rather, the Committee was deciding whether the applicant had done a 'specified act' within the meaning of s.4(1)(a) of the Act of 2001.' [Emphasis added by Hardiman J.]
>
> This submission at first sight appears to dance on the head of a pin, and to be wholly artificial, not to say contrived."

Subsequently Hardiman J. characterised the committee's representations in the following terms:

> "The distinction made in the pleadings is jesuitical in the worst sense of that term.
>
> I am unable to understand why, in their written submissions, the Committee refers to the Department of Finance 'definition' with this last word in inverted commas. This usage plainly suggests that the Department's statement is <u>not</u> a definition." (Emphasis added by Hardiman J.)

Hardiman J. failed to see the relevance of Art.15.10 since it had not been alleged that Senator Callely had breached any "Rule or Standing Order" made by the Seanad. "I can find nothing in that Standing Order to support the view that there is some sort of haven, quite outside the law and the Constitution of Ireland for politicians to make destructive findings in relation to other politicians." He, too, held that the committee was a creature of statute and thereby subject to the *East Donegal* principles. He concluded as follows on the justiciability issue:

> "The fact that the Houses of the Oireachtas must have complete freedom, and immunity from judicial scrutiny, in the conduct of their legislative function does not mean that the politicians who compose it can establish for themselves an area of immunity, quite outside the restraint of the law or even the Constitution. The Constitution would be subverted if the legislators could, by conferring a particular function on an Oireachtas Committee, create total immunity in the discharge of an adjudicative function. There is no comparative support either, in the law of countries similar to ours, for the view that fundamental rights can be rendered incapable of assertion in court simply because the adjudicating body is a parliamentary Committee."

Art.15.10 does not afford immunity McKechnie J. began by referring to the fact that by reason of Senator Callely's membership of a House of the Oireachtas

> "[1] …it is said that the High Court could not, and thus on appeal this Court cannot, exercise the very functions for which the courts exist, namely, in a case such as this, the vindication of core constitutional rights, such as the right to one's good name, the right to earn a livelihood and – as part of a process which is claimed to have irreparably eroded such rights – the right to fair procedures. In short, the Superior Courts must stand aside even if otherwise satisfied that what is asserted would justify their intervention. Such an outcome, surprising as it must be to a great number, is said to be mandated by the Constitution of Ireland, 1937 itself ('the Constitution' or 'the 1937 Constitution'), so as to give due recognition to the legislative power, when exercising a sub-set of that power, namely parliamentary privilege. In essence it is essential to and demanded by the separation of powers."

Thus, he set the tone of his lengthy, comprehensive and reasoned judgment considering those rights, at para.2, which are

> "at the highest level of our constitutional order, not only from the viewpoint of the administration of justice but also from the perspective of the very

> Constitution itself. Thus, any mandatory disablement of the judicial system of government solely because of his Oireachtas position, is a matter of grave significance which each member of the public will have a great interest in. It will therefore be necessary to inform them in the clearest manner possible if this is so."

The judgment was structured in two parts: Part A deals with the justiciability issue considering first the separation of powers point and secondly the political standards point. Part B addresses the substance of the judicial review application.

McKechnie J. found that the allegations against Senator Callely would be a significant matter for any individual and to so accuse the holder of such a public position must indeed be serious. To determine and make findings as the Committee on Members' Interests of Seanad Éireann (CMI) did, is an extremely grave matter.

> "[70] …Not only did the Committee find that the applicant committed the misrepresentation as alleged, but it further held that such misrepresentation was on-going, was of a serious and grave nature and was done intentionally. In addition it held that the Senator had also, in effect, acted in bad faith. Moreover, to have the House of which one is a member, adopt a report and pass a resolution of censure and suspension without pay, must surely be a matter of the highest gravity.
>
> 71. In these circumstances it would require little evidence to conclude that such a determination, including the sanction and its endorsement by the House, could cause serious damage to a person's good name and livelihood, both generally and in particular as a public representative, as well as in many other respects. There is no reason whatsoever to question the affidavit evidence of Mr. Callely to the effect that he was pilloried in the media, reviled by the public, ostracised by colleagues and acquaintances and abused by strangers. If ultimately those findings should stand, it is almost certain that irreparable damage will have been caused.
>
> 72. Whether such state of affairs is justified or not is entirely beside the point: what is to be noted is that the applicant was investigated by the CMI, which was empowered by legislation to make adverse findings which could be very damaging to his good name and reputation and to his right to earn a livelihood. In all other circumstances of which I am aware, where such a possibility exists, one would expect that the guarantee of fair procedures and constitutional justice would apply, and that for the vindication of such rights, an aggrieved person, if necessary, would have access to the courts. These are the cornerstone issues in this case. Despite the undoubted importance of the separation of powers, it is crucial not to lose sight of this point. Accordingly, it must follow, at least presumptively, that the constitutional rights of the applicant are engaged and that the issues relative to such rights, are amenable to judicial review."

With regard to the immunities provided for in Arts.15.10, 15.12 and 15.13 McKechnie J. observed:

> "106. The justification for such privileges and immunities is undoubtedly

> substantial and must be both acknowledged and respected. However, the effective and unfettered exercise of the duties and functions of the legislative arm would not be unduly affected if the parameters of such immunities are viewed strictly. In such way, that organ of the State can perform its functions in a manner entirely compatible with the Constitution whilst the judicial arm can ensure that its role, as the administrator of justice serving those who seek recourse to it, is not restricted, limited, or indeed even ousted any more so than is necessary."

The respondents had not argued that what is covered by Art.15.10 is deserving of absolute immunity.

> "127. So judicial access at different levels is permitted but apparently as here, where the 'complained of' is a member of Seanad Éireann and where the 'complaint' relates to expenses, it is not.
>
> 128. What is highly interesting about this point, indeed far more so than the acknowledgement that absolute privilege does not exist, is that even when intervention can take place, the courts' jurisdiction to involve itself was said to be highly circumscribed. It was contended that access, in most of the examples above given, is permitted only on the basis of the courts' role as the ultimate adjudicator of what is included in or excluded from the remit of the legislative power. The scope of review does not exist beyond this parameter and does not succumb to provisions of the Constitution which are not directly relevant to such exercise. It therefore follows that intervention is not permitted because of the court's obligation to vindicate rights, but rather and solely, on the basis of determining whether the legislative branch has exceeded its powers, as duly conferred. It is therefore only those provisions of the Constitution which relate to the separation of powers that can form part of this analysis. These do not involve provisions such as Articles 40 to 44 of the Constitution.
>
> 129. I would entirely reject this submission: what is the exclusive domain of the legislative arm remains solely a matter for it. There is no question of this, or, I suspect, the executive arm, either now or indeed ever, attempting to exercise a function which is exclusively that of another branch of government. Hardiman J. went to very considerable length in *Howlin v. Morris & Ors.* [2006] 2 I.R. 321 to emphasise this point (p. 366). However, when judicial intervention is permitted by the Constitution there is no basis, at any level of justification, for the imposition of such restrictions. The courts either can or cannot intervene but when they do, the basis for their authority in so doing derives from their obligation, as the ultimate guardian of constitutional rights, to uphold and protect such rights, when called upon. Therefore when appropriate to do so, the exercise by the judicial organ of its constitutional powers, cannot be trammelled, in the manner suggested."

In deciding on the extent of immunity McKechnie J. asked the following questions:

> "in what way will the efficiency and efficacy of the House be curtailed if the breadth of parliamentary privilege as claimed, is found not to exist:

how would the House be obstructed in the discharge of its functions or frustrated in the conduct of its core and essential business? No answer of any real substance has been given to these critical questions: certainly none that resonates with me. It is not suggested nor could it be, that the process of legislation itself would be interfered with or that such immunity is a necessary feature of that process. Nor is it claimed that freedom of debate is impaired, nor that full deliberation is curtailed, nor that the Seanad's role, relative to matters covered by rules and standing orders, would be compromised. At its height, it is said that the House must have disciplinary control over its members, when expenses are involved, and that such must be a necessary adjunct to its powers. Whilst Mr. Callely was obviously a member of the House at the time and whilst expenses relate to his attendance at the House, those factors in themselves are not sufficient to carry this submission. In the absence of an express immunity provision, it becomes necessary to establish, if such is to be inferred, that its constitutional role will otherwise be critically impaired. I cannot see how this would result or follow if the actions of the respondents are subject to judicial review. How such might impact on good governance or why the suggested immunity is central to the form of governance required by the Constitution, have never been satisfactorily answered. Consequently, I do not believe, at the level of principle, that the immunity argued for can be inferred either as a constitutional imperative or otherwise to achieve some overriding constitutional objective."

He concluded Part A of his judgment as follows:

> "I would entirely agree with the views of the learned High Court judge and would reject at first instance any suggestion that the Court would be incapable of reviewing the political judgment or ethical standard element of s.4, because of some intrinsic disability on its part or otherwise. Conduct which may bring a profession, organisation, grouping or entity into disrepute is an issue which falls to be determined in a variety of ways, virtually on a daily basis by the courts. If the standard, wherever it sits, can be appreciated by the reasonable man or woman, as is acknowledged, it is very difficult to see how the courts could be regarded as being so inept to that end. I therefore consider this submission as made in this regard, to be unsustainable."

McKechnie J. held at para.174 that the CMI's enitire process is subject to the overriding principles of constitutional justice and fair procedures. He found at para.185 that there are two essential ingredients within the relevant statutory provision, first the requirement that a "specified act" has been committed and second the application to that act, of the political criteria. Unless and until both steps have been satisfied he failed to see how a conclusion that a breach of its provisions has occurred could be reached:

> "187. This point can be looked at in another way. Let's assume that the statement of contravention makes no mention of a preceding 'act

> or omission'; if this were the case it must be asked to what, in such circumstances, could the ethical standard apply? What could be condemned or exonerated? Indeed how could the standard itself be set or formulated? In respect of what activity or conduct could a member's action be found to have been flawed, inappropriate or substandard, or how and why could public confidence be said to have been undermined? In my view the existence of a 'specified act' is critical to the operability of the section. It follows therefore that if the act or omission asserted against a member is not established, his/her conduct must be exonerated and a violation of the section cannot be found."

He concluded:

> "214. It is undoubtedly the case that the Committee had ultimate control over what activity it would specify as constituting the 'specified act', provided of course that the essence of the public complaints were included. That left open the possibility of accepting that the expense claims as made, fell within the Department's definition, but that nevertheless the behaviour of the member concerned and the circumstances of its occurrence, were such as could amount to a 'specified act' and could thereby give rise to a s.4 breach. A further possible alternative which could have been adopted is that, irrespective of whether the expense claims were or were not within that definition, the conduct of the applicant likewise fell to be considered. However, neither of these possibilities grounded the allegation against Mr. Callely. A decision was made to centre the misrepresentation allegation at the heart of the charge levelled against him. Having made that decision, the respondents must abide by its consequences."

Justiciability The minority judgments dissented inter alia on the basis that as the matters affecting Senator Callely were rooted in legislation, by definition they came within the *East Donegal* principles and are, as a consequence, justiciable. The three dissenting judges were of the opinion that where the constitutional rights of individuals are concerned be they, or be they not, members of the Oireachtas, there can be no haven from judicial scrutiny. It also seems that Fennelly J. was inclined towards this view in his observation that constitutional principles may not be used to subvert the Constitution. However, he was not specific as to the standard that would allow the courts to intervene. In summary, the dissenting view seems to be the more attractive proposition.

PROPERTY RIGHTS

Compensation for total loss in seizure The Supreme Court was required to interpret the word "compensation" in s.17 of the Diseases of Animals Act 1966, as amended, in *Rafferty v Minister for Agriculture, Food and Rural Development* [2014] IESC 61. Denham C.J. (Murray, Hardiman, O'Donnell, McKechnie JJ. concurring) observed that analysing the term "compensation" may be very statute specific. In construing legislation whereby property has been seized by the State fundamental constitutional principles must be borne in mind. She held that a person who has been compulsorily deprived of his or her property or property interests by the State is entitled, in principle, having regard to the constitutional protection of property rights from unjust attack, to compensation for the total loss caused or resulting as a consequence of compulsory deprivation of those interests. Denham C.J. noted at para.45 that as the case law indicated:

> "there are circumstances in which it may be, for legitimate reasons, constitutionally permissible to limit the compensation to an amount less than the total loss including consequential loss. Any such exception would be subject to strict scrutiny by the courts as to the legitimacy of the grounds limiting full compensation for loss actually sustained, and subject also to the principle of proportionality."

O'Donnell J., in a short ancillary judgment, strongly criticised, at para.3, a wholly inadequate and confusing statutory regime which leaves the person appointed by the Minister

> "without guidance in the assessment of compensation in an area which may be factually complex and occurs in a context that involves a difficult intersection between constitutional rights and the public interest. Leaving the assessment of compensation without any statutory guidance must significantly increase the chances that the compensation assessed will be unfair to the citizen, the public, or possibly both."

NAMA Act ss.84 and 147 constitutional The plaintiff in *National Asset Loan Management Ltd v McMahon & ors; National Asset Loan Management Ltd. v Downes* [2014] IEHC 71 had brought two distinct causes of action against the defendant, Séamus Downe, the sole remaining defendant of a partnership of solicitors. The debts and obligations of the defendants, all relating to property, had been acquired from AIB Bank pursuant to the plaintiff's duty under s.10 of the National Asset Management Agency Act 2009. Multiple defences had been raised including a challenge to the constitutionality of ss.84 and 147 of that Act. The points advanced in support of these challenges were outlined at para.39 as:

> "that the principles of constitutional and natural justice guaranteed under Article 40.3 are set at naught; that the defendant's property rights under that article and under Article 43.1 and 2 are unjustly attacked; that the defendant has a right to earn a living, which means an entitlement to keep the income stream generated from property; that the equity of redemption can be, and is, part of the property rights in question and is not respected; and that the bundle of the defendant's contractual rights can be unjustly torn apart by the legislation."

Charleton J. granted judgment to the plaintiff. He followed, at para.40, the Supreme Court decision in *Re Health (Amendment) (No.2) Bill 2004* [2005] 1 I.R. 105 at 201 which, in an analysis of any unjust attack on property rights, requires the court first, to examine the nature of the property rights at issue; secondly, to consider whether the impugned sections consist of the regulation of those rights in accordance with the principles of social justice and whether the legislation seeks to delimit those rights in accordance with the exigencies of the common good; and, thirdly, having considered these issues, to determine whether injustice is the touchstone of the result, which may emerge in the lack of balance as between the common good and the necessary vindication of the relevant rights. Recalling the purposes of the Act, he agreed with the submissions of the Attorney General that were there to be a declaration of unconstitutionality it would defeat the prime purpose which was to address the serious threat to the economy and the stability of credit institutions in the State.

Restricting his analysis to the arguments advanced, Charleton J. focused on s.84(3):

> "For the avoidance of doubt, NAMA may, subject to Chapter 1 of Part 7 , take steps to acquire an eligible bank asset even though the participating institution concerned has indicated in information provided to NAMA under section 80 that it does not consider the bank asset to be an eligible bank asset and that it objects to its acquisition."

He commented on the eloquent argument put forward by counsel for the defendant conjuring up the spectre of the plaintiff agency "as a kind of monster enabled by legislation to gobble up performing loans and to subject borrowers to authoritarian rigour." Charleton J. continued, at para.42:

> "The reality has not turned out that way: far from it. Further the legislation neither enables nor permits that kind of despotic burden on those holders of loans transferred to the agency and nor is the section capable of being used in such a way. In *The State (Lynch) v. Cooney* [1982] I.R. 337 at 380, Henchy J. stated in relation to the exercise of discretion conferred by statute:
>
> > 'It is to be presumed that, when it conferred the power, Parliament intended the power to be exercised only in a manner that would be in conformity with the Constitution and within the limitations of the power as they are to be gathered from the statutory scheme or design.'"

Charleton J. was eloquent in his criticism of the behaviour of banks which had led to the current situation:

> "[42] ....
> It would be contrary to the experience of this nation over the last decade were bank management to be given a final decision as to whether a loan must be transferred into the agency. As a matter of historical reality, it has emerged clearly in multiple cases before this division of the High Court, that Anglo Irish Bank plc, now in liquidation as Irish Bank Resolution Corporation, led a charge of ill-considered lending which was so successful in capturing what was called 'market share' as to cause panic among competing lenders and spook them into charging into imprudent lending. That bank exercised false leadership at a time when the policy of restraint, so necessary because of the temptations inherent in the profit motive, seemed to defer to the market. Anglo Irish Bank's chimeral pursuit of profit was temporarily

> apparently profitable. By following chase, other banks exacerbated the property overvaluation that crashed like a giant wave on the Irish taxpayer from September 2008. Social anguish has been the result. Since persons involved in banking at the highest level seem most responsible for this, it would be astonishing were the Oireachtas to give a final decision to any participating bank as to what assets should be transferred to the agency. To have done so would have been to have undermined the very scheme of the Act. Furthermore, what is alleged to be the unjust purpose and result of the section simply cannot be read into the legislation. There is nothing in the text of the section which requires the balance between rights to property and exigency of the common good to be construed in so lopsided a way as to lead to a finding of unconstitutionality."

He relied on *McDonald v Bord na gCon* [1965] I.R. 217 and its core principle of the presumption of constitutionality and held as a matter of fact that, neither in its text, nor in its application nor in any reasonably open interpretation is there any constitutional infirmity to the section.

With regard to s.147, Charleton J. was guided by *Dellway Investments Ltd. v National Asset Management Agency* [2011] IESC 14; [2011] 4 I.R. 1 at 360-377 citing Finnegan J. who had made it clear that the special treatment of mortgagees and the commercial consequences of the transfer of a mortgage to the agency gave rise to a right to be heard on the part of the borrower. This interpretation was based on the principles of constitutional justice as elucidated in *East Donegal Co-operative Livestock Mart Limited v Attorney General* [1970] I.R. 317. Thus, he held at para.45 that there is no aspect of this section which gives rise to any real risk that the rights of a citizen would be interfered with in an unjust manner due to an absence of a fair approach. He concluded:

> "There has been no property right of the defendant that has been unjustly attacked. The defendant's has [sic] a right to earn a living does not necessarily mean an entitlement to keep the income stream generated from property where those legal rights have been signed away in debt or guarantee obligations. The Court regards the equity of redemption in mortgage contracts as among the most important of property rights. Such rights are like other property rights: entitlements that can be exchanged for value or which can be altered or lost in consequence of legal instruments validly entered into. The property rights in question are respected when proper consideration is given by a lending institution to whether a debt is sustainable and whether the equitable title that remains with a mortgagor can be salvaged by some reasonable arrangement. But here there has been no unjust tearing apart of property rights because the debt burden was overwhelming and the obligations entered into at arms length and in the clear hope of advantage."

Misleading reasons deny right to be heard The National Asset Management Agency (NAMA) and the National Asset Loan Management (NALM) company had acquired loans from Anglo Irish Bank (now IBRC) in respect of a commercial property known as Belfield Office Park. Four investor groups were involved and during a review of the loans, all members of the investor groups bar Mrs Leona Flynn of the Flynn Family group had, on request, provided a statement of affairs. Mrs Flynn had refused to present a statement of affairs as she denied that she was an obligor of NAMA/NALM. NAMA/NALM had called in the loan of the Flynns, a sum of €21.9 million. In the first instance it had been decided in *Flynn v National Asset Loan Management Ltd.* [2014] IEHC 408 that Mrs Flynn was, indeed, an obligor of NAMA/NALM. In the second stage of the case, Cregan J. was required to consider the claims of the Flynns that they had been treated so unfairly by NALM that it amounted to a breach of their natural and constitutional rights to fair procedures and amounted to a breach of statutory duty by NALM.

Two specific arguments were:

> "[239] …1. That in calling in the loans (and in the correspondence leading to the calling in of the loans) NALM gave misleading reasons for calling in the loan and failed to disclose the real reason for calling in the loan. In so doing NALM deprived the Flynns of their right to be heard. 2. That NALM, in calling in the loans of Flynns, but not the loans of all of the other investor groups in Belfield Office Park, unlawfully targeted the Flynns'."

Based on the evidence Cregan J. concluded, at para.276, that the only reason NALM had, in fact, for calling in the Flynns' loans was because Mrs Flynn had denied the debt and refused to provide a statement of affairs.

> "277. The complaint made by the Flynn family is that the real reason why the loan was called in was because Mrs. Flynn was refusing to give a statement of affairs. Therefore, the Flynns say, this letter of 5th February, 2013, was entirely misleading. It sets out misleading reasons, which purport to relate to the business plan and it did not set out the real reason, (namely that NAMA was concerned that Mrs. Flynn was refusing to provide a statement of affairs). In my view, this objection by the Flynns to the NALM Letter of Reasons is well founded.
>
> 278. I am of the view therefore, that the reasons put forward by NALM in its Letter of Reasons of the 5th February, 2013, were inaccurate and misleading. The letter was, as Mr. McDowell S.C. submitted, 'a smokescreen'. If NALM was truly dissatisfied with the business plan put forward by all investor groups for Belfield Office Park Limited it would have decided to call in the loans of all four investor groups in Belfield Office Park Limited. The fact that it did not decide to call in the loans of all four investor groups leads inexorably to the conclusion, in my opinion, that this was not the real reason for calling in the loans. Mr. O'Brien under cross examination could not put forward any cogent explanation as to why, if NALM were truly concerned about the business plan, the loans of all four investor groups were not called in."

With regard to dissatisfaction with the business plan, Cregan J. stated further that if NAMA did have a genuine difficulty with the Belfield Office Park business plan, which is entirely within their statutory powers and prerogative, then the logic of that position would demand that they would move against all four members of the investor group. He observed that the corollary is also true:

> "[287] … if NAMA had genuine concerns about the Belfield Office Park business plan, then it would not be a lawful, proportionate or justifiable action only to call in the loans of the Flynn group. This would amount, in my view, to an unlawful 'targeting' of one investor group – unless NALM can put forward some objective justification for so doing."

Cregan J. found that the reasons relating to the business plan put forward by NALM as justification for calling in the Flynn loans was without substance. However, he found the second argument of NALM more substantive:

> "[289] …This argument is that NALM was entirely justified in moving against the Flynns and calling in the Flynn loans because one of the borrowers–Mrs. Flynn–denied all liability for the loan, denied that she was an obligor of NAMA and refused to provide a statement of affairs to NAMA. NALM was therefore suspicious of her behaviour and believed that Mrs. Flynn might have assets which she did not want to make available to NALM in respect of her debt. In other words, NALM argued, all things being equal, NALM must treat all four investor groups in Belfield Office Park equally; however if there is an issue, which is significant, by which one investor differentiates himself from the other investors then NALM is justified in treating that person differently from the others."

Having reviewed the evidence, Cregan J. considered the legal principles applicable. With regard to the NAMA Code of Practice he found that, absent an objective justification for treating one member of the group differently, NAMA has a statutory duty and an obligation enshrined in the code to treat all investor groups in Belfield Office Park equally.

Section 11(6) of the National Asset Management Agency Act 2009 imposes a duty of transparency on NAMA in the performance of its functions. Cregan J. found that NAMA had breached this statutory duty:

> "301. When one considers the application of this statutory duty of transparency to the facts of this case, it is clear that the Letter of Reasons of 5th February, 2013 (which accompanied the letter of demand) did not accurately set out the real reasons for calling in the loan. In particular as set out above, the letter of 5th February 2013 set out reasons which were not the real reasons for calling in the loan. Moreover the said letter does not include the real reason for the decision to call in the loan."

Relying on Finlay Geoghegan J.'s judgment in *Treasury Holdings v NAMA* [2012] IEHC 297 (*Annual Review of Irish Law 2012*, p.482), and the evidence from NALM's letters which referred to "statutory objectives," Cregan J. held that NALM had been exercising public power. As such two principal rights flowed from such a finding: (a) The right to be heard prior to the taking of the decision and (b) The duty on the part of NALM to act fairly and in a reasonable manner. He reviewed the additional authorities of *Dellway Investments v NAMA* [2011] IESC 14 and *Mallak v Minister for Justice Equality and Law Reform* [2012] IESC 59 (*Annual Review of Irish Law 2012* pp.23, 24, 179, 363) and noting that the Flynns had complained that they had been deprived of the right to be heard, Cregan J. observed:

> "[323] … The right to be heard is expressed in the Latin maxim 'audi alteram partem'. The verb 'audi' is expressed in the imperative mood. It is a command, a direction, to the court or tribunal: hear the other side, listen to the other side. This duty to hear gives rise to a corresponding right: the right to be heard. The right to be heard is a powerful and important right. Although it is expressed in the passive voice, it is in fact, an active right: a right to speak or a right to make representations to the court, tribunal or statutory body which seeks to make a decision which affects the person concerned. It is a right which is at the heart of our legal system. For if a person is denied a right to be heard, they are shut out of participation in the vital process which affects their interests. This right to be heard has been recognised for hundreds of years. It has been recognised and protected in our constitution since 1937 and it has been articulated and applied in numerous cases of the High Court and Supreme Court over the last few decades.
>
> 324. The right to be heard necessarily means that the person affected must know the action which is being proposed and the reasons for that action. This gives them an opportunity to make representations on the issue and to rebut, if they can, the reasons for the action. It follows therefore that the person affected must be informed of the real reasons for the proposed action and not be given misleading or spurious reasons. If a person is not given the real reasons for a proposed decision and/or if he is given misleading or spurious reasons, then his representations cannot deal with the actual reasons. In such a case the right to be heard is not vindicated. It becomes a nullity. That is the case here.
>
> 325. Moreover if a statutory body such as NAMA does not give full substance to the right to be heard it creates insidious and undesirable effects. If the real reasons are not set out, it creates a suspicion in the eyes of the affected person that he has not been told of the real reasons for the decision. This leads to a further suspicion that there are other 'unspoken reasons', that there is 'another agenda' or in this case that NAMA was out 'to target' the Flynns.
>
> 326. It is in this atmosphere of unspoken, reasons that suspicion of government agencies thrives. That is not in the public interest. It is not conducive to public trust in a vital state body such as NAMA. I am of course conscious that NAMA is exercising an important statutory function on behalf of the citizens of Ireland. But it must exercise those functions in accordance with the principles of fairness and natural and constitutional justice."

Cregan J. gave a specific instance of the consequence of this suspicion:

> "327. This concern about suspicion breeding suspicion is not merely conjecture. In this case, James Flynn gave evidence that the first time he

> was told by NAMA of the real reason why the loan was being called in, was at a meeting with NAMA on 28th February, 2013 some three weeks after the letter 5th February, 2013 calling in the loan. Such was his level of suspicion of NAMA's behaviour at this time that he secretly recorded the meeting on his mobile phone without telling NAMA. He did so, he said 'because he wanted to get a handle on what was going on. We were very much in the dark as to what was going on.' Whilst this action was the subject of justifiable criticism by NALM, it is precisely to avoid this sort of behaviour that there is a duty to provide reasons, and thus to give substance to the right to be heard."

The final issue considered was whether NALM was under a duty to act fairly and reasonably in taking a decision to enforce and if so, whether it did, in fact act fairly and reasonably. Finding that NAMA is under an obligation to act fairly and reasonably Cregan J. added:

> "333. Moreover, another appropriate legal principle to apply in this case is the NAMA code of practice adopted pursuant to section 35 of the NAMA Act 2009 referred to above. This code in effect imposes an obligation on NAMA also to act in a reasonable manner and in particular it imposes an obligation on NAMA 'to endeavour to deal with stakeholders reasonably vis-à-vis other peers/competitors in similar circumstances. It is of course hedged about with the qualification about NAMA's responsibility to the tax-payer and also the debtor's corresponding obligations to NAMA. It does however mean that NAMA must seek to deal with debtors reasonably vis-à-vis other debtors in similar circumstances. On the facts of this case therefore, it is necessary for NAMA or NALM to deal with the Flynns reasonably vis-à-vis other debtors in similar circumstances which on the facts of this case means the other investor groups in Belfield Office Park. Therefore NALM must deal with all the debtors in Belfield Office Park in a similar fashion unless there is some objective justification not to do so."

He held that in this instance there had been objective justification in that Mrs Flynn had denied that she had a liability and had refused to provide a statement of affairs whereas all other members of all investor groups did so. In summary, Cregan J. held inter alia that the Flynns had been denied the right to be heard but had not been targeted unlawfully. He set aside the letter of demand given that the real reasons for calling in the loan were not stated in the letter.

Money laundering *Cassidy v Commissioner of An Garda Síochána* [2014] IEHC 386 confirmed that when a freezing order is made over certain accounts on foot of the Criminal Justice (Money Laundering and Terrorist Financing) Act 2010, the onus is on the owner of the accounts to show that the funds, subject of the freezing order, are not being used as part of a money laundering operation or are not funds used for the financing of terrorist activities. Barr J. observed at para.28 that, in the absence of weighty and countervailing factors, the prevention of a criminal offence must be regarded as a warranted justification for the interference with property rights.

Regulating unapproved developments *McGrath Limestone Works Ltd v An Bord Pleanála* [2014] IEHC 382 is a lengthy judgment in which Charleton J. refused an application for judicial review which inter alia challenged the constitutionality of s.261A of the Planning and Development Act 2000, as amended. This provision was necessitated by Ireland's membership of the European Union and the aftermath of the decision of the European Court of Justice in *Commission v Ireland* (C-215/06) [2008] E.C.R. I-4911. He observed at para.10.9 that primary legislation was properly regarded as necessary to rectify a glaring, though unwitting, deviation from Ireland's duty in European law whereby major projects could proceed unknown to local planning authorities but could be, and were, despite having potentially major effects on European sites of conservation, or despite having major impacts on local environments, could simply be approved in retrospect by a retention permission without any assessment being conducted or any environmental impact statement being submitted.

REFERENDUM LITIGATION

Thirty-First Amendment ... Children's Rights Few outside the ivory towers of academe and beyond the protagonists and their supporters are likely to be aware that arising from continuing litigation the provisional status of the Thirty-First Amendment to the Constitution (see *Annual Review of Irish Law 2012* pp.128-43) continued during 2014. In *Jordan v Minister for Children and Youth Affairs* [2014] IEHC 327 McDermott J. dismissed the challenge to the constitutionality of the Referendum Act 1994 (the "1994 Act"). Previously, in *In the Matter of the Referendum on the Proposal for the Amendment to the Constitution contained in The Thirty First Amendment to the Constitution (Children) Bill 2012* [2013] IEHC 458 he had dismissed a petition presented under s.42 of that Act requesting an order to annul the result of the Thirty-First Amendment, the 2012 Children's Rights referendum (see *Annual Review of Irish Law 2013*, pp.168–170). In both judgments he relied on *Hanafin v Minister for the Environment* [1996] 2 I.R. 321 in which the Supreme Court had considered the nature, scope and rationale of the relief available under ss.42 and 43 of the 1994 Act, in respect of the unconstitutional use of public funds in the course of a referendum campaign. In the hearing on costs in *Jordan v Minister for Children and Youth Affairs* [2013] IEHC 625 McDermott J. had noted at para.19 that the Supreme Court decision in *Hanafin* was entirely distinguishable from *Jordan* insofar as it was the first case concerning the conduct of a referendum petition in the face of unconstitutional conduct by the government in the course of a referendum campaign and clearly involved novel issues of law. He found no novel issues in the instant case. In *Jordan v Minister for Children and Youth Affairs* [2014] IEHC 327 McDermott J. held inter alia at para.57 that it is entirely reasonable, rational and proportionate that a petitioner who seeks to set aside what is, prima facie, the will of the people properly expressed and freely given should bear the onus of proof of doing so. He declared himself satisfied at para.66 that the provisions of ss.42 and 43 "embody a rational and proportionate onus and standard of proof which may, on occasion, be difficult, but is not inherently impossible to discharge."

Both judgments have been the subject of appeal to the Supreme Court which in *Re. Referendum Act & re. Jordan and Jordan v Minister for Children and Youth Affairs* [2015] IESC 33 unanimously upheld the High Court dismissals of the actions. The substance of these decisions will be considered in next year's Annual Review.

RIGHT TO ASSOCIATE

Closed shop policy The facts as described by Ryan J. in *O'Connell v Building & Allied Trades Union* (BATU) [2014] IEHC 360 illustrate why, in the general run of things, industrial relations problems between management and trade unions are within the jurisdiction of the specialist tribunals rather than the High Court. However, it is clear that this dispute went way beyond customary trials and tribulations even of the construction industry. Ryan J., finding for the plaintiff, held at para.133 that it was and is wrongful both under the Constitution and at common law for a trade union to operate a closed shop policy but then refuse a qualified person membership which, thus, prevented him from working. He stated:

> "138. The plaintiff was wrongfully excluded from the Union which then put him out of work because he was not a member. In the result BATU and its officers breached the plaintiff's constitutional rights and engaged in a campaign against the plaintiff that constituted the torts of intimidation and conspiracy by excluding him from membership and threatening builders who employed him."

Club members' rights What is a club? What keeps it alive and when can it be said, as a matter of law, to come to an end? These were the fundamental questions which arose in *Dunne & ors v Mahon* [2014] IESC 24, a successful appeal to the Supreme Court against a decision of the High Court to permit the dissolution of the Roadstone Sports & Social Club ("the Club") and distribute its assets. Much of Clarke J.'s judgment (MacMenamin and Dunne JJ. concurring) related to construing the rules of the Club, essentially matters of contract law. However, Clarke J.'s observation on club members' rights to associate and dissociate are of interest especially in the context of the desire of some members to dissolve the Club. Citing, at para.6.7, *National Union of Railwayman v Sullivan* [1947] I.R. 77, that freedom of association is recognised under the Constitution and that the corollary right to disassociate is constitutionally protected, he did not see that the right to disassociate carries with it, even on the part of a majority, a right to have the relevant unincorporated association dissolved. He continued:

> "True it is that members have a stake in any club or organisation and, in particular, have a financial stake in an organisation which owns valuable assets. But their primary stake, indirectly held, in those assets is to have the assets concerned used in furtherance of the purposes of the association or club concerned. It is to that that they committed when joining the body. The mere fact that they no longer wish those assets to be deployed in that way does not, of itself, give them a right to deprive others (even a minority) of their entitlement to have those resources applied for the common purpose for which the resources were allocated in the first place.
>
> 6.8 The primary solution to a party's right to disassociate is fulfilled simply by their resignation from the body concerned. Of course, there may

> be cases, such as *Education Co. of Ireland v. Fitzpatrick (No. 2)* [1961] I.R. 345, where the consequences of not being or not remaining a member of an association may be such as lead to the conclusion that a person is being coerced to join or remain in the association concerned. To the extent that it might be said that, in suggesting that a person can resign from a club, such a person might, thereby, be deprived of what would otherwise be their interest in the club's assets, it can also, and with greater force, be said that the only reason why such a person has an interest in those assets in the first place is because that person joined an organisation which was committed to the use of those assets for a specified purpose. If that purpose is no longer capable of being fulfilled then, for reasons which I will shortly address, there is ample jurisdiction to have the Court intervene. However, if, albeit only with the support of a minority of its existing members, the club or association remains both financially viable and capable of fulfilling its purpose, then it seems to me that there is no infringement of the right to disassociate by indicating that it can be achieved at the price of giving up one's interest in the club or association concerned and allowing a minority who wish to carry on with its activities to use the resources which were designed to that end for that purpose. On that basis, it does not seem to me that there is any implied entitlement on the part of a simple majority either to alter the rules of a club or to require its dissolution in the absence of express rules providing for such alteration or dissolution."

RIGHT TO GOOD NAME

Balancing rights to good name and to freedom of speech *Leech v Independent Newspapers (Ireland) Ltd* [2014] IESC 79 was a successful appeal against the award of €1,872,000 libel damages. Dunne J. (Murray and McKechnie JJ. concurring) having referred to the various authorities e.g. *Barrett v Independent Newspapers Ltd.* [1986] I.R.13, *de Rossa v Independent Newspapers Plc* [1999] 4 I.R. 432, concluded

> "that an appellate court will be slow to interfere with the verdict of a jury on the assessment of damages but nevertheless awards by juries are subject to scrutiny and if an award is so disproportionate in the circumstances of the case having regard to the respective rights of freedom of expression on the one hand and on the other hand the requirement under the Constitution to protect the good name of every citizen that no reasonable jury would have made such an award then the award will be set aside on appeal."

She noted that it was accepted that the role of compensatory damages in defamation cases is not on all fours with the role of compensatory general damages in personal injuries cases. There is a "vindicatory" element to damages in defamation cases which is not a factor in general damages in a personal injuries case. The nature of the defamation suffered by Ms Leech attacked both her moral character and her professional reputation. "Overall, it would be no exaggeration to say that the series of articles published by the Newspaper in respect of Ms Leech had a profound effect on her in every aspect of her family and professional life."

Dunne J. considered the defendants' argument that extremely large awards of damages in cases such as the instant case have a chilling effect on the freedom of the press and should, therefore, be subject to careful scrutiny. She cited O'Flaherty J. in *Dawson v Irish Brokers Association*, unreported, Supreme Court, 27 February, 1997:

> "' ... The jury were entitled to award damages for loss of reputation, as well as for the hurt, anxiety, trouble and bother to which the plaintiffs had been put. However, the defendants in defamation cases should never be regarded as the custodians of bottomless wells which are incapable of ever running dry. The opposite has proved true in the publishing sphere in this and other countries – with sad consequences for those who lost employment as a result of untoward awards. Further unjustifiably large awards, as well as the cost attendant on long trials deals a blow to the freedom of expression entitlement that is enshrined in the Constitution.'"

Dunne J. held that an award of damages must be fair to the plaintiff and to the defendant.

> "However, freedom of expression is not an entirely unrestricted freedom. In the context of defamation proceedings it must be balanced by the provisions of Article 40.3.2 of the Constitution which provides that the State 'shall, in particular, by its laws protect as best it may from unjust attack and, in the case of injustice done, vindicate the life, person, good name and property rights of every citizen'. The matter was expressed trenchantly by Hamilton C.J. in the de Rossa case when he said at page 456:'Neither the common law nor the Constitution nor the Convention give to any person the right to defame another person.'"

She further affirmed Hamilton C.J.'s ratio that there must be "a due balancing of the constitutional right to freedom of expression and the constitutional protection of every citizen's good name."

Accordingly, Dunne J. held that an award of damages cannot be so disproportionate as to have the effect of not just vindicating the good name of the citizen but of restricting the freedom of expression of a newspaper. Desirous of bringing an end to the litigation between the parties the court set aside the verdict of the jury on damages and substituted a sum of €1,250,000 for damages.

Open-ended suspension invalid In *McMahon v Irish Aviation Authority* [2014] IEHC 431 the plaintiff who had held the position of Club Chief Instructor (CCI) with the Irish Parachute Club (IPC) at Clonbullogue Airfield, County Offaly successfully challenged his suspension from that post by officials of the Irish Aviation Authority (the "Authority") in February 2013. The decision of Hogan J. centred on whether or not the Authority had exercised fair procedures consistent with its obligation to exercise its statutory power in a manner which respected the principles of *East Donegal Co-Operatives Ltd. v Attorney General* [1970] I.R. 317. He stated that this means that the Authority must generally respect fair procedures and ensure that its decisions are (i) bona fide, (ii) factually sustainable and (iii) not unreasonable. Referring to the considerable volume of case law which attests to this point he gave the examples of *The State (Lynch) v Cooney* [1982] I.R. 337 at 361 per O'Higgins C.J. and *Mallak v Minister for Justice and Equality* [2012] IESC 59, [2013] 1 I.L.R.M. 73 at 91–99, per Fennelly J. (para.32). He observed the following regarding suspensions:

> "33. The extent to which a person is entitled to fair procedures prior to the imposition of a suspension will generally depend on the overall circumstances and the context in which the action has been taken. The necessity for urgent action, the nature of the suspension, its implications for the good name of the person concerned and, above all, its duration are critical factors. If the suspension is in the nature of a purely 'holding' suspension which has been imposed to enable an urgent inquiry to take place, then any obligation to abide by fair procedures prior to its imposition may be attenuated or may even not apply at all: see, e.g., the comments of Keane C.J. in *Deegan v. Minister for Finance* [2000] E.L.R. 190. 198-199."

Referring to the plaintiff specifically Hogan J. noted that the suspension meant that Mr McMahon was obliged to stand down from a prestigious position which meant everything to him and given that the position has had to have been filled in the meantime, his prospects of being appointed again to that post could not be regarded as high. Hogan J. continued:

> "35. There is equally no doubt but that a suspension of this kind has considerable implications for the good name of the person affected. Many might reasonably think that the Authority imposed the suspension because of concerns that Mr. McMahon had taken a casual or even irresponsible attitude to the vital question of air safety or that he improperly yielded to commercial pressures in allowing flights to take off where the weather conditions for sport parachuting were doubtful or even hazardous. As I pointed out in *Wallace v. Irish Aviation* Authority [2012] IEHC 178, [2012] 2 I.L.R.M. 350, 351, often the 'very fact of suspension is enough, in this valley of squinting windows, to expose the employee to the decidedly unpleasant prospect of calumny and detraction at the hands of the unforgiving and the uncharitable.' Here it must be recalled that Article 40.3.2 of the Constitution requires the State by its laws to protect that right to good name 'as best it may from unjust attack' and in the case 'of injustice done' to vindicate that right."

He acknowledged that the Authority had been in a difficult position. As the regulatory authority of a hazardous activity such as parachuting, it must be allowed "the widest possible degree of flexibility when it comes to taking urgent action in the interests of safety." It had been presented with three serious complaints and, if these complaints were ultimately substantiated, then those who participated in parachute jumping at Clonbollogue might face unacceptable risks (at para.37). He found at para.38 that the perceived need to take urgent action to investigate these complaints and, above all, to ensure that air safety was not compromised, meant that "the State's capacity fully to protect and vindicate Mr. McMahon's right to a good name was circumscribed in the first instance". He considered that the hearing that had resulted in the suspension "was less than perfect" at para.39; nevertheless, he held:

> "40. In view, however, of the fact that the Authority must have the necessary freedom to take urgent action in the interests of public safety and having regard to the hazardous nature of the activities which it regulates, it was entitled in the first instance, in line with the comments of O'Higgins C.J. in *Lynch*, to take urgent action and to suspend the applicant in these circumstances."

However, the duration of the suspension, which was not a purely holding suspension pending an early hearing, was a cause of concern, as the suspension had lasted from February 2013 until the date of the hearing in June 2014. He found at para.43 that a suspension of that duration "cannot realistically be regarded as a purely holding mechanism, not least given that the underlying facts were not – at least so far as the question of whether Mr. McMahon was fit to remain in his position as CCI is concerned – unduly complex". Hogan J. noted that there is clear authority to the effect that a lengthy suspension will be rendered invalid, especially if that delay is prejudicial to the applicant and cited *Flynn v An Post* [1987] I.R. 68. He found that the delay:

> "[45] …has been considerable, stretching well beyond any period necessary to get to the bottom of the basic facts of the matter so as to allay any possible safety concerns. It is also true that while the suspension has not had the same extensive financial implications for the applicant as it did for the plaintiff in *Flynn* (where the suspension had been without pay), it is plain nonetheless that the suspension has had some financial implications for the plaintiff. But most of all this long suspension has had the effect of seriously affecting Mr. McMahon's constitutional right to a good name and dashing a cherished ambition of his."

Hogan J. held these matters to be prejudicial in themselves. In addition, the reasons given for the suspension had to be factually sustainable which he found not to be the case in respect of one key reason. He was prepared to excuse this non-compliance with the necessity to give reasons which are factually sustainable given the imperative need for urgency on the part of the Authority but it was a further reason why the need for an early hearing which was procedurally completely fair and which produced conclusions which are factually sustainable was all the more imperative. Whilst it could not be said that the suspension per se was invalid from the inception, a lack of factually sustainable reasons was a further basis by which it can be said that an open ended suspension of this kind became invalid. He concluded:

> "59. One can put all of this another way: the Authority is entitled to act in a summary fashion in order to protect public safety, as indeed happened in this case. But if it so acts by, for example, suspending an individual, then it is obliged to ensure that there is a fuller hearing which complied with the requirements of fair procedures (including adequate notice to all concerned) within a relatively short space of time. The proper protection

of the constitutional right to a good name will generally demand no less. This did not happen in the present case."

Damages for breach of constitutional rights In *Ogieriakhi v Minister for Justice and Equality* (No.2) [2014] IEHC 582, inter alia, the plaintiff sued for damages for breaches of his constitutional rights to a good name and to his property rights as protected by Art.40.3.2 of the Constitution. This was by reason of the circumstances in which he came to be dismissed. Hogan J. noted at para.75 that this was the principal claim in so far as general damages were concerned. Further, this appeared to be "the first case in which this Court has been required to determine whether a person who has been dismissed in this or similar fashion can sue for breach of his constitutional right to a good name by reason of the injury to his reputation resulting in that dismissal."

With regard to the manner of the dismissal, the plaintiff had been an auxiliary postal worker when he had been dismissed by An Post on the sole ground that he did not have a valid work permit. However, at that time the plaintiff had, in fact, acquired a right of residence by virtue of art.16 of the Free Movement Directive (Directive 2004/38/EC). In a detailed judgment based on reference to the *Francovich* principles (*Francovich v Italian Republic* (C-6/90 and C-9/90) [1991] E.C.R. I–5357) Hogan J. awarded the plaintiff damages for breach of European Union law (see paras 5 to 73).

In considering the constitutional claim Hogan J., at para.74, totally accepted "the evidence of Mr. Ogieriakhi and that of his wife, Ms. Madden, that his dismissal from employment had serious financial and reputational consequences for him and his family. It brought about serious financial strain." Hogan J. acknowledged that damages for inconvenience, upset and distress falling short of a cognisable psychiatric injury are not recoverable in an action for negligence. However, in relation to the claim for property rights, he held, at para.83, that:

> "the *Francovich* remedy provides the plaintiff with an effective and adequate protection of the property rights which are associated with his employment and the right to earn a living. In other words, the award of €107,905 may be taken to represent an adequate and just compensation for the wrongful interference with his property rights in respect of the loss of income which he might fairly have anticipated had he not been dismissed."

However, he took a different view in respect of the protection of the plaintiff's constitutional right to a good name.

Inadequacy of rule in Addis Hogan J. observed that the common law has traditionally declined to award damages for loss of reputation following dismissal from employment citing the classic examples of *Addis v Gramophone Co. Ltd.* [1909] A.C. 488 and *Johnson v Unisys Ltd.* [2003] 1 A.C. 518. *Addis,* which "held (or, at least, appears to have held)" that damages are not recoverable in contract for the manner in which an employee has been dismissed from his employment, "has cast a long shadow over this branch of the law of contract" (at para.86). He stated:

> "90. So far as our courts are concerned, the question of whether damages

could be awarded in an action in contract for breach of reputation was left over by Gilligan J. in *Carey v. Independent Newspapers (Ireland) Ltd.* [2004] 3 I.R. 52 (although his judgment contains an exceptionally helpful and insightful summary of the law in this area) and by Laffoy J. in *Nerney v. Thomas Crosbie Holdings Ltd.* [2013] IEHC 127. The *Addis* principle was, however, applied by McWilliam J. in *Garvey v. Ireland (No.2)* [1979] I.L.R.M. 266."

McWilliam J., as cited by Hogan J. at para.92, had endorsed the principle in *Addis* ([1979] I.L.R.M. 266 at 268):

> "'I accept the decision in this case. Accordingly, unless some injury was occasioned by the plaintiff as a result of the wrongful removal from office of the plaintiff which could reasonably have been foreseen by the defendants, I am of the opinion that he is not entitled to any general damages under this heading.'"

Hogan J. continued his scrutiny of *Garvey (No. 2)* and of the reliance on the *Addis* principle which he found deficient in vindicating the constitutional rights guarantee. As such his analysis is quoted in full:

> "94. There are a number of features of *Garvey (No.2)* which invite comment. First, the summary and very public removal of an office-holder in this fashion is something which will inevitably cause the holder immense personal distress, given its humiliating circumstances. Contrary to what McWilliam J. seemed to imply, it is very hard to see that this type of injury is not foreseeable. Second, the decision in *Addis* did not turn on questions of foreseeability, as such, but rather that the additional injury caused to the plaintiff's reputation by reason of the circumstances of his dismissal was simply not recoverable in an action for damages for breach of contract–as distinct from tort – precisely because (as the House of Lords saw it) of the nature of the cause of action in contract. Third, it is notable that McWilliam J. awarded damages (albeit reduced) for arbitrary conduct on the part of the Government, even though this was precisely the kind of damages for breach of contract which *Addis* seems to exclude. Fourth, McWilliam J. reduced the damages because he thought that the plaintiff would have suffered a similar injury had he in fact been lawfully removed from office. But this, with respect, surely begs the question as to whether the plaintiff could lawfully have been removed had due process been properly observed. In any event, even if this were so, the extent of the public humiliation suffered by the plaintiff would surely have been less had he been removed after due process rather than being removed in the arbitrary fashion which in fact occurred: this, after all, had been a key feature of the reasoning of Henchy J. in *Garvey (No.1)*.
>
> 95. One other important issue which did not feature at all in *Garvey (No.2)* – even though, as we have seen, it was a critical element of the judgment of Henchy J. in *Garvey (No.1)* – was the protection of the plaintiff's good name in Article 40.3.2, as informed by the Preamble's

commitment to the objective of securing the dignity of the individual. This is, however, a central feature of the instant case which presents this question, apparently for the first time.

96. It may be immediately observed that a rule which provides that damages for loss of reputation are excluded from recovery would be *prima facie* incompatible with express terms of the guarantee imposed on the State by Article 40.3.2 to protect the good name of every citizen, as informed by what Henchy J. described in *Garvey (No.1)* ([1981] I.R. 75, 99) as the 'broad motivating and purposive considerations' of the Preamble's commitment to human dignity. After all, employment is not just simply a means of earning a living. Employment gives dignity to what otherwise would be for many a soulless existence and our occupation may be said to be one of the key defining features of our life. The twin constitutional guarantees of dignity and good name would accordingly be purely hollow and emptied of any substance if the law did not provide an adequate remedy to compensate for loss of reputation in this kind of case and the affront to the dignity of the individual which such a humiliating unlawful removal from office entails. After all, as O'Byrne J. said in *Buckley v. Attorney General* [1950] I.R. 67, 81, it is the duty of the courts to ensure that these constitutional guarantees are given 'life and reality.'

97. So far as the present case is concerned, it is therefore sufficient to say that as the *Addis* rule would be 'basically ineffective' (to use the words of Henchy J. in [*Hanrahan v. Merck, Sharpe & Dohme Ltd.* [1988] I.L.R.M. 623]) to protect the constitutional right to a good name in the circumstances of this case, the plaintiff is accordingly entitled to sue directly for damages for breach of his constitutional rights. This is particularly so given the highly unusual feature of this claim where the dismissal of the plaintiff from his employment was brought about not by reason of his conduct or the financial situation of the employer, but rather because of the application of immigration rules in a manner which has been subsequently found by the Court of Justice to be contrary to the requirements of EU law."

Inadequacy of tort remedy With regard to the circumstances of the present case, *Ogieriakhi*, Hogan J. found it unnecessary to examine the extent to which the rule in *Addis* might have to suffer modification by reason of Art.40.3.2 so far as the generality of employment disputes governed by private law are concerned. Having found that the plaintiff's constitutional right to a good name was not protected by employment contract law, he held that neither would it be protected by the principal remedy provided by law for the vindication of the constitutional right to a good name, namely an action for the tort of defamation.

"[98] ….As the employment cases themselves tacitly recognise, the vindication of the employee's right to a good name following dismissal must normally come through either the mechanism of contract law or not at all. This is because defamatory words or conduct will not normally accompany the act of dismissal and, even if they do, the uttering of such words will generally be protected by privilege in the manner now contemplated by s.18 of the Defamation Act 2009.

> 99. It is, moreover, the very of [sic] act of dismissal which often sends the signal to future employers that the employee is not fit to be re-hired. The gist of the damage to the plaintiff's good name was the immediate and unlawful termination of his contract of employment with An Post. This was not capable of being remedied either by the tort of defamation (for the reasons just stated) or by an action for breach of contract (by reason of the rule in *Addis*). It might have been capable of being remedied by means of proceedings under the Unfair Dismissal Acts 1977 to 2007, but, as we have seen, the Employment Appeals Tribunal rejected the claim that this dismissal was unfair."

Therefore, he held, at para.100, that existing law did not adequately vindicate the plaintiff's constitutional right to a good name, at least in the unusual and special circumstances of the present case.

In assessing damages for injury and loss of reputation at €20,000 Hogan J. described the circumstances of the dismissal:

> "[101] There is no doubt but that An Post sought to minimise the loss and disruption which the plaintiff suffered. Nor could it be said that An Post acted in an arbitrary or high-handed fashion. Yet the plaintiff nonetheless suffered a grievous injustice: he was summarily dismissed over his protests that he had a legal entitlement to work here in circumstances that must have been personally humiliating and undignified. To make matters worse, his dismissal was totally unrelated to his work or performance or the necessity for the company to re-structure its business. The summary nature of the dismissal created the impression that he was not lawfully entitled to work and perhaps worse."

Finally, he considered that it could be argued that this particular loss should also have been dealt with as part of the main *Francovich* claim and not just simply as a separate head of loss for breach of constitutional rights.

> "104. I am not sure that very much turns on this. It suffices to say that if Irish domestic law affords a plaintiff a remedy in a case of this kind for damage to his good name (as I have held that it does, at least in a case of this kind), the principle of equivalence requires that a similar remedy be made available even where the claim is exclusively regarded as a claim for damages arising from a breach of European law."

RIGHT TO LIFE OF THE UNBORN

Brain death and pregnancy Once again fault lines were exposed in the legal landscape of Art.40.3.3, the right to life of the unborn, when a family suffering the most tragic circumstances were obliged to engage in court proceedings in *P.P. v Health Service Executive* [2014] IEHC 622. N.P., a pregnant young mother of two had been transferred to a Dublin Hospital suffering from headaches and vomiting. When the plaintiff, her father, arrived at the hospital on 29 November 2014 he was told his daughter had died. "He was taken to see her remains in the ICU Unit and noted she was on a life support system. He was told by the medical staff that, for legal reasons, they felt constrained to put his daughter on life-support because her unborn child still had a heart beat." On 3 December 2014 a medical clinical determination had been made that N.P. had suffered brain stem death and the plaintiff was so advised on that date. On 8 December 2014 N.P. had been transferred to the medical care of the clinical staff at the hospital outside Dublin where she was

> "in the intensive care unit of the hospital where she is being supported by mechanical ventilation and being fed by a nasogastric tube. She has been maintained on very heavy doses of medication for a number of conditions including pneumonia, fungal infections, high blood pressure, fluid build-up and fluctuations in the production of urine. She has been receiving physiotherapy twice daily for secretions from her chest and her joints and muscles are being cared for. On the 17th December, 2014 a tracheostomy operation was carried out on N.P. to facilitate the continuation of maternal organ supportive measures in an attempt to attain foetal viability."

The plaintiff had been advised by the medical staff at the hospital that "it was intended to maintain this regime of treatment for the duration of the pregnancy". The plaintiff, who had the support of his family and of his daughter's fiancé, the acknowledged father of the unborn, believed that such measures were unreasonable and should be discontinued. He believed further that the prolonged somatic support measures were experimental in nature and that they had no proper basis in medical science or ethical principle. The matter first came to the High Court on 15 December 2014 and full hearing took place with a Divisional High Court, Kearns P., Baker J., Costello J., on 23 December 2014. The court issued its decision on 26 December 2014 that somatic support of N.P. should be withdrawn at the discretion of the medical team.

Expert evidence The court heard expert evidence from a number of experienced clinicians. It noted in the evidence of Dr Peter Boylan, consultant obstetrician, that he had:

> "adverted to the discussions which had taken place between the members of the multi-disciplinary medical team within the Dublin hospital, all of which emphasised and were focussed on the difficulties for medical practitioners as a consequence of the absence of medico-legal guidelines and because of difficulties arising from the 8th Amendment to the Constitution."

The evidence of Dr Frances Colreavy, intensive care consultant, was described as "devastating":

> "She had trained in Ireland and Australia but said she had never experienced a case of this nature before where somatic treatment had been applied for 20 days to a person who is brain dead. She examined N.P. on the evening of the 22nd December and noticed the presence of eye and face make up which were used as the above mentioned two children visited their deceased mother for the first time that day. However, the whites of the eyes were so swollen that the eyelids could not close properly. There was evidence of

> ongoing infection with high fever, high white cell count, fast heart rate and evidence of a high output circulation. There was evidence of pus which required evacuation from a drain site on the right side of the head. This site has not closed and on examination there is a hole in the skull with brain tissue extruding. There was also evidence of a fungal infection at this site. There were huge amounts of fluid in the lungs with additional evidence of a urinary tract infection and the lower abdominal wall was noted to be inflamed. Serious infection is inevitable in this case due, in the opinion of Dr. Colreavy, to the presence of a rotting brain which is leaking to the outside, together with the drips, catheters and tubes required to extend somatic support, the administration of steroid therapy, liver dysfunction and prolonged stay in the ICU environment which is colonised with resistant bacteria. There is also evidence of cardiovascular instability requiring high doses of medication. There is evidence of hypertension relating to fluid overload with an attendant risk to placental perfusion. There is total body oedema (puffiness) abnormal function and a build up of fluid in the body. There were six syringe pumps beside the woman's bed for her various treatments. N.P. needed nutrition, bowel support, drugs for infections, a head wound needed to be dressed and she had to be turned to avoid pressure sores. Dr. Colreavy said that the pregnant abdomen looks unlike any other she had seen and she was worried that indicated an infection underneath. All the sources of infection had not been identified. In her view, continuing the somatic support was not appropriate and amounted to 'experimental medicine'. She had found the mother's temperature to be 38.5 and previously even higher at 39°. She would expect the temperature in the uterus to be even higher, perhaps 40. The striae, the stretch marks of pregnancy, are very abnormally discoloured in this case and the abdomen itself looks very boggy and filled with fluid indicating that there could be inflammation or infection in the abdomen itself. There is also evidence of urinary infections and evidence of fungus at the tip of one of the tubes that are inserted into a vein to support the blood pressure and the circulation. She also has high blood pressure and is receiving very high doses of drugs to address this worrisome feature. Some of the infections are very resistant to antibiotics and some of the drugs being administered are not licensed for use in pregnancy situations. She did not believe it was realistic to consider that somatic support for the mother could continue to be provided until the foetus reached viability."

As part of the evidence of Dr Stephen McNally, consultant neurosurgeon and national lead in neuro-oncology in the hospital to which N.P. had been transferred in Dublin, the court recorded as follows:

> "Having had to deal with the family of N.P., he found their frustrations and their humanity both touching and humbling. While he had seen some dreadful things in neurosurgery he had never seen this. It was very difficult not to be able to follow the wishes of the family because of uncertainty as to the legal standing with regard to the unborn child. Legal advice had been sought but no opinion in writing had been received prior to the time

> for a transfer back to the hospital outside Dublin. He believed that, having regard to N.P.'s condition when admitted to hospital in Dublin, that she was '*probably gone*' by the time she arrived in their door." (emphasis in original).

In assessing the evidence the court paid tribute to the plaintiff and to N.P.'s partner for their immense courage and fortitude in dealing with the catastrophe which had befallen them and which had been compounded by the necessity of coming to court to give evidence. With regard to that evidence the court found that the:

> "entire medical evidence in this case goes one way only, and that is to establish that the prospects for a successful delivery of a live baby in this case are virtually non-existent. The medical evidence clearly establishes that early gestation cases have a much poorer prognosis for the unborn child than those cases where brain death of the mother occurs at a later stage, usually improving after 24 weeks."

Findings The court found as fact that brain stem death had occurred on 3 December 2014 and that N.P.'s pregnancy was at 15 weeks gestation. It found

> "no realistic prospect of continuing somatic support leading to the delivery of a live baby. While there have been instances where lengthy somatic treatment has led to the birth of a live baby, the evidence in this case, and, in particular, that of Dr. Colreavy, is persuasive to a conclusive degree that the ongoing somatic support for the mother is causing her body increasingly to break down and that overwhelming infection from various sources will, as a matter of near certainty, bring the life of the unborn to an end well before any opportunity for a viable delivery of a live child could take place.
>
> The Court emphasises that, having regard to its finding that the unborn child will not be born alive, this is not a case where the Court's view is to any degree influenced by any consideration that if the unborn child were to be born alive, it might nonetheless be impaired to a greater or lesser degree. This is not a case where the Court on the evidence is required to consider that possibility. This case turns on its own particular facts which are centred entirely on whether the unborn child can survive at all.
>
> The Court is further satisfied on the evidence that, in addition to the ongoing trauma and suffering experienced by the family and partner of N.P. through the continuance of somatic support, such continuing support will cause distress to the unborn child in circumstances where it has no genuine prospect of being born alive. It would be a distressing exercise in futility for the unborn child. That consideration is important when it comes to considering what in this case is in the best interest of the unborn child."

Relevance of Art.40.3.3° The parties represented in the case had differed in their submissions on the relevance of Art.40.3.3° and also on the interpretation of the phrase "as far as practicable." The Article states: "The State acknowledges the right to life of the unborn and, with due regard to the equal right to life of the mother, guarantees in its laws to respect, and, as far as practicable, by its laws to defend and vindicate that right." The court relied on precedent holding as follows:

> "It is the view of the Court that, while the ordinary common understanding of what in context was involved in the referendum which led to the present wording of Article 40.3.3, particularly insofar as it mandates due regard to the equal right to life of the mother, was to protect the legal position created in Ireland by s.58 of the Offences Against the Person Act 1861, the provision, in its plain and ordinary meaning may also be seen as acknowledging in simple terms the right to life of the unborn which the State, as far as practicable, shall by its laws defend and vindicate. This does not mean that the Court discounts or disregards the mother's right to retain in death her dignity with proper respect for her autonomy with due regard to the grief and sorrow of her loved ones and their wishes. Such an approach has been the hallmark of civilised societies from the dawn of time. It is a deeply ingrained part of our humanity and may be seen as necessary both for those who have died and also for the sake of those who remain living and who must go on. The Court therefore is unimpressed with any suggestion that considerations of the dignity of the mother are not engaged once she has passed away."

With regard to the last point made counsel representing the unborn had argued that, given that N.P. had died:

> "the rights of the unborn child must take precedence over the understandable grief of the family of N.P. and her entitlement to a death with dignity. There were no 'equal rights' to be placed in the balance in this case and therefore the overriding obligation was to vindicate the right to life of the unborn as far as practicable. It was accepted, however, that in attempting to vindicate the unborn child's right to life in this case, the Court must consider what is in the best interests of the unborn."

Counsel representing N.P. had also argued that "given what had occurred, a death without indignity was not possible and thus greater weight should be given to the continuance of the pregnancy than striving to achieve the lost opportunity of a dignified death."

Death and indignity Having upheld the need for dignity of the mother the court nevertheless held that "when the mother who dies is bearing an unborn child at the time of her death, the rights of that child, who is living, and whose interests are not necessarily inimical to those just expressed, must prevail over the feelings of grief and respect for a mother who is no longer living." The court took guidance from *In re a Ward of Court (witholding medical treatment) (No. 2)* [1996] 2 I.R. 79, *Airedale NHS Trust v Bland* [1993] A.C. 789, *Re A (A Minor)* [1993] 1 Med L Rev 98. Specifically in relation to the issue as to whether continuing the artificial measures maintaining the bodily functions of the mother and of the unborn child had a realistic prospect that the child will be born alive the court considered Sheikh and Cusack, "Maternal Brain Death, Pregnancy and the Foetus: The Medico-Legal Implications" *2001 Medico Legal Journal,* Farragher, Marsh and Laffey, "Maternal Brain Death – An Irish Perspective" *Irish Journal of Medical Science*, Vol. 174–No. 4 and *S.R. (A Ward of Court)* [2012] 1 I.R. 305. The court concluded:

> "Given that the unborn in this jurisdiction enjoys and has the constitutional guarantee of a right to life, the Court is satisfied that a necessary part of vindicating that right is to enquire as to the practicality and utility of continuing life support measures. Seen in this way, the facts of this case are even stronger than those in the *S.R* case. This unfortunate unborn has suffered the dreadful fate of being present in the womb of a mother who has died, and in which the environment is neither safe nor stable, and which is failing at an alarming rate. We accept the evidence of the medical witnesses that–from a medical viewpoint–normal bodily parameters are maintained within extraordinarily fine limits, and that in this case there is no real prospect of maintaining stability in the uterine environment, having regard to the degree of infection, the fluctuating temperatures in the body of the mother, the difficulty in maintaining a safe blood pressure and the amount of toxic medication being administered to the mother which is not licenced for pregnancy. The somatic support being provided to the mother is being maintained at hugely destructive cost to both her remains and to the feelings and sensitivities of her family and loved ones. The condition of the mother is failing at such a rate and to such a degree that it will not be possible for the pregnancy to progress much further or to a point where any form of live birth will be possible. As Dr. Mortell put it, while the unborn child is not yet in distress, it is facing into a 'perfect storm' from which it has no realistic prospect of emerging alive. It has nothing but distress and death in prospect.
>
> To maintain and continue the present somatic support for the mother would deprive her of dignity in death and subject her father, her partner and her young children to unimaginable distress in *a futile exercise which commenced only because of fears held by treating medical specialists of potential legal consequences*. Highly experienced medical practitioners with the best interests of both mother and unborn child in mind do not believe there is any medical or ethically based reason for continuing with a process which Dr McKenna described as verging on the grotesque on the particular facts in this case". (emphasis added)

The court mentioned that under cross-examination the plaintiff had agreed that his daughter had never executed any living will or advance direction as to what might happen if she were to sustain serious illness or become incapable of communicating her wishes. One might wonder what, if any, difference such stated wishes of a woman in this situation would have. Apart from reporting the lack, the court was silent on the matter. It seems likely that if such wishes expressed the view that no extreme measures should be taken to preserve life they might not be respected. Equally, it might be said that if such wishes expressed the view that the life of the unborn should be maintained at all costs, these, too, might not be respected. The brutally honest, if not brutish, submission of counsel for the unborn that the pregnant woman was not entitled to dignity after death was rejected by the court. The submission may have been rejected but the reality had been evident for some 27 days after the father had been first told that N.P. was dead. Irrespective of the court's opinion it is difficult to ascribe the term "dignity" to any aspect of N.P.'s desperate condition as reported in the judgment. Moreover, the court was quite clear that "when the mother who dies is bearing an unborn child at the time of her death, the rights of that child, who is living, and whose interests are not necessarily inimical to those just expressed, must prevail over the feelings of grief and respect for a mother who is no longer living."

This case arose because doctors were unsure of their legal position if they had allowed N.P. a dignified and respectful death having declared her brain dead. As observed by the court, they had engaged in a futile exercise which commenced only because of fears held by the treating medical specialists of potential legal consequences. If such an appalling scenario should recur and even if the clinical specialists and the family were united in a wish to permit natural death, little has been clarified in the legal scenario. The period of gestation and the prolongation of the pregnant mother's somatic health will remain in question and will require a High Court rather than an expert clinical determination. The uncertainty of the legal implications for medical specialists remains unresolved.

RIGHT TO PRIVACY

Mass data surveillance The proceedings in *Schrems v Data Protection Commissioner* [2014] IEHC 310 arose as a consequence of the revelations of Edward Snowden, the United States whistleblower. Hogan J. upheld the decision of the Data Protection Commissioner that Mr Schrems' complaint was unsustainable in law holding, at para.76, that the Commissioner had "demonstrated scrupulous steadfastness to the letter of the [the Data Protection Directive, Directive 95/46/EC of the European Parliament and of the Council of 24 October 1995 (O.J. L281/38)] and the 2000 Decision." This decision of the European Commission set up the Safe Harbour regime which held that the data protection regime in the United States is adequate and effective where the companies which transfer or process the data to the United States self-certify that they comply with the principles set down in this decision. Hogan J. noted that one of the many issues arising was whether the Safe Harbour principles are still effective and functional some 14 years after that decision and finding. He adjourned the proceedings pending the outcome of an art.267 of the Treaty on the Functioning of the European Union reference in which he asked the following questions:

> "Whether in the course of determining a complaint which has been made to an independent office holder who has been vested by statute with the functions of administering and enforcing data protection legislation that personal data is being transferred to another third country (in this case, the United States of America) the laws and practices of which, it is claimed, do not contain adequate protections for the data subject, that office holder is absolutely bound by the Community finding to the contrary contained in Commission Decision of 26 July 2000 (2000/520/EC) having regard to Article 7 and Article 8 of the Charter of Fundamental Rights of the European Union (2000/C 364/01), the provisions of Article 25(6) of Directive 95/46/EC notwithstanding? Or, alternatively, may the office holder conduct his or her own investigation of the matter in the light of factual developments in the meantime since that Commission Decision was first published?"

In the course of his judgment Hogan J. made some significant observations, which underlie his decision, about privacy especially in the era of electronic surveillance and heightened secrecy. Given the importance of this context it is considered most reliable to quote extensively from his judgment.

The context of the Snowden revelations The full text of this section of Hogan J.'s description of the implications of Snowden's disclosures, paras 4-8, is included in the chapter on Whistleblower Protection in this Annual Review, p.708. In the context of privacy Hogan J. summarised as follows:

> "8. On the other hand, the Snowden revelations demonstrate a massive overreach on the part of the security authorities, with an almost studied indifference to the privacy interests of ordinary citizens. Their data protection rights have been seriously compromised by mass and largely unsupervised surveillance programmes."

The PRISM programme and the FISA court Based on the extensive exhibits contained in affidavits filed in the proceedings Hogan J. concluded that personal data transferred by companies such as Facebook Ireland to its parent company in the United States is thereafter capable of being accessed by the United States National Security Agency (NSA) in the course of a mass and indiscriminate surveillance of such data. Underpinning this conclusion were quotations from both *The Washington Post* and *The Guardian.* The former had published details concerning the PRISM programme which apparently enables the NSA to collect personal data such as emails, photographs and videos from major internet providers such as Microsoft, Google and Facebook. This is conducted on a mass scale in accordance with orders made by the US Federal Intelligence Court sanctioning such activities. Hogan J. considered, at para.13, that the denials from official sources, such as they have been, "were feeble and largely formulaic, often couched in carefully crafted and suitably ambiguous language designed to avoid giving diplomatic offence." He found that the accuracy of much of the Snowden revelations does not appear to be in dispute.

Hogan J. then described the Foreign Intelligence Surveillance Court as provided for by a federal statute, the Foreign Intelligence Surveillance Act 1978 ("the FISA Court").

> "[14] …The FISA Court is a specialist court consisting of federal judges enjoying standard constitutional guarantees in relation to tenure and independence. This Court entertains applications by the NSA for warrants in relation to foreign surveillance and interception of communications.
>
> 15. It would seem, however, that the FISA Court's hearing are entirely conducted in secret, so that even the court orders and its jurisprudence remain a closed book. The US security authorities are, in effect, the only parties who are or who can be heard in respect of such applications before the FISA Court. One of the striking features of the Snowden revelations was the disclosure of (hitherto secret) orders of the FISA Court which effectively required major telecommunication companies to make disclosure of daily telephone call records on a vast and undifferentiated scale, while the company in question was itself prevented from disclosing the existence

> or the nature of the order. Yet the essentially secret and *ex parte* nature of the FISA Court's activities makes an independent assessment of its orders and jurisprudence all but impossible. This is another factor which must – to some degree, at least–cast a shadow over the extent to which non-US data subjects enjoy effective data protection rights in that jurisdiction so far as generalised and mass State surveillance of interception of communications is concerned."

Mr. Schrems and the Data Protection Commissioner The applicant is an Austrian post-graduate law student at the University of Vienna who had already made 22 other complaints to the Commissioner concerning Facebook Ireland. The current judicial review proceedings solely concerned the 23rd dated 25 June 2013 arising directly out of the Snowden revelations and, specifically, the PRISM programme. Hogan J. noted that the Commissioner had formed the view that as Facebook had self-certified under the Safe Harbour regime and as there was a Community finding that the Safe Harbour regime provided adequate data protection, there was nothing left for him to investigate. Accordingly he had exercised his power not to investigate the matter further under s.10(1)(b) of the Data Protection Acts 1988–2003, on the basis that the complaint was "frivolous and vexatious". He continued :

> "33. It should also be pointed out that the Commissioner had, in any event, raised the question of the PRISM allegations with Facebook Ireland in advance of receiving Mr. Schrem's complaint. In the course of those discussions, Facebook Ireland confirmed that its parent, Facebook, did not provide access to US security agencies to subscriber data, save by means of targeted requests which were properly and lawfully made. The Commissioner had satisfied himself on the basis of an audit which he had carried out of Facebook Ireland that it had appropriate procedures in place for the handing of access requests received from security agencies generally."

As noted above, Hogan J. did find that the Commissioner had acted correctly. With regard to the terminology used he observed at para.39:

> "It is certainly true that in the ordinary sense of these words the present complaint – raising as it does weighty issues of transcendent importance in relation to data protection – is neither 'frivolous' nor 'vexatious'. While in this respect the actual language of s.10(1)(b) of the 1988 Act is somewhat unfortunate and perhaps even unhelpful, nevertheless, as Birmingham J. pointed out in *Novak* [*v. Data Protection Commissioner* [2012] IEHC 449, [2013] 1 I.L.R.M. 207] in this particular statutory context these words also apply to a case where the claim is considered to be unsustainable in law. In fairness, the Commissioner has also been most anxious to stress ... that it is in this particular sense that the terms have been used in the present case and that they described the Commissioner's conclusion that the complaint cannot succeed."

Data privacy The Commissioner had challenged the locus standi of the applicant contending that as there was no evidence by which he could have concluded that the Safe Harbour Principles were in fact being violated in the case of data transfers between Facebook Ireland and Facebook. It had been submitted that these complaints were essentially hypothetical and speculative in nature. It had also been submitted that no evidence had ever been adduced to suggest that there was an imminent risk of grave harm to Mr Schrems or that any of his data had been or was likely to be accessed by the NSA.

Hogan J. acknowledged that such evidence should not be shown. However, he stated that that was not really the gist of Mr Schrem's objection. The Snowden revelations had demonstrated that the US security services can routinely access the personal data of European citizens which has been so transferred to the United States and, in these circumstances, he considered it a fair question to ask whether US law and practice in relation to data protection and State security provides for meaningful or effective judicial or legal control. He continued:

> "43. The essence of the right to data privacy is that, so far as national law is concerned and by analogy with the protection afforded by Article 40.5 of the Constitution, that privacy should remain inviolate and not be interfered with save in the manner provided for by law, i.e., by means of a probable cause warrant issued under s.6 of the Interception of Postal Packets and Telecommunications Messages (Regulation) Act 1993, on the basis that the interception of such communications involving a named individual is necessary in the interests of either the suppression of serious crime or the protection of national security.
>
> 44. This is also clearly the position under EU law as well, a point recently confirmed by the Court of Justice in Case C-293/12 Digital Rights Ireland in a case where the Data Retention Directive, Directive 2006/24/EC was held to be invalid by reason of the absence of sufficient safeguards in respect of the accessing of such data by national authorities....
>
> 45. The same reasoning applies here. Quite obviously, Mr. Schrems cannot say whether his own personal data has ever been accessed or whether it would ever be accessed by the US authorities. But even if this were considered to be unlikely, he is nonetheless certainly entitled to object to a state of affairs where his data are transferred to a jurisdiction which, to all intents and purposes, appears to provide only a limited protection against any interference with that private data by the US security authorities."

Hogan J. held it to be manifestly obvious that the case raised issues of both national and EU law, although, given the central importance of the Commission decision of July 2000, the issue is largely governed by EU law.

Accessing private communications under Irish law This section of the judgment is quoted in its entirety. As can be seen in para.56 Hogan J. held that under Irish law the Commissioner would have been obliged to investigate Mr Schrems' complaint further.

> "47. As far as Irish law is concerned, the accessing of private communications by the State authorities through interception or surveillance directly engages

the constitutional right to privacy: see, e.g., *Kennedy v. Ireland* [1987] I.R. 587; *People v. Dillon* [2003] 1 I.L.R.M. 531 and *People v. Idah* [2014] IECCA 3 [see below in this chapter]. As Hamilton P. noted in *Kennedy,* this constitutional right is underscored by the Preamble's commitment to the protection of the 'dignity and freedom of the individual' and the guarantee of a democratic society contained in Article 5 of the Constitution.

48. One might add that the accessing by State authorities of private communications generated within the home – whether this involves the accessing of telephone calls, internet use or private mail – also directly engages the inviolability of the dwelling as guaranteed by Article 40.5 of the Constitution. As it happens, by one of those accidents of legal history, these very same words are also contained in Article 13(1) of the German Basic Law ('inviolability of the dwelling') ('unverletzlichkeit der Wohnung'). It is, accordingly, of interest that the German Constitutional Court has held that the accessing by state authorities of otherwise private communications within the home also engages that more or less identically worded guarantee of inviolability of the dwelling which is contained in Article 13(1) of the Basic Law. Indeed that Court went further and found that legislation providing for the interception and surveillance of communications partly unconstitutional because it provided for a disproportionate interference without adequate safeguards with that very guarantee of inviolability of the dwelling in Article 13(1) of the Basic Law: see *Anti-Terrorism Database Law decision* (1 B v R 1215/07)(April 24, 2013) at paras 93 *et seq*.

49. Naturally, the mere fact that these rights are thus engaged does not necessarily mean that the interception of communications by State authorities is necessarily or always unlawful. The Preamble to the Constitution envisages a 'true social order' where the 'dignity and freedom of the individual may be assured', so that both liberty and security are valued. Provided appropriate safeguards are in place, it would have to be acknowledged that in a modern society electronic surveillance and interception of communications is indispensable to the preservation of State security. It is accordingly plain that legislation of this general kind serves important – indeed, vital and indispensable–State goals and interests: cf. by analogy the decision of the German Constitutional Court in the *Anti-Terrorism Database* case (at paras 106, 131 and 133, passim) and the comments of the Court of Justice in Case C-293/12 *Digital Rights Ireland Ltd.* [2014] E.C.R. I-000 at paras 42-44.

50. The importance of these rights is such nonetheless that the interference with these privacy interests must be in a manner provided for by law and any such interference must also be proportionate. This is especially the case in respect of the interception and surveillance of communications within the home. While the use of the term 'inviolable' in respect of the dwelling in Article 40.5 does not literally mean what it says, the reference to inviolability in this context nonetheless conveys that the home enjoys the highest level of protection which might reasonably be afforded in a democratic society: see, e.g., *Wicklow County Council v. Fortune* (No.1) [2012] IEHC 406.

51. By safeguarding the inviolability of the dwelling, Article 40.5

provides yet a further example of a leitmotif which suffuses the entire constitutional order, namely, that the State exists to serve the individual and society and not the other way around.

52. In this regard, it is very difficult to see how the mass and undifferentiated accessing by State authorities of personal data generated perhaps especially within the home – such as e-mails, text messages, internet usage and telephone calls – would pass any proportionality test or could survive constitutional scrutiny on this ground alone. The potential for abuse in such cases would be enormous and might even give rise to the possibility that no facet of private or domestic life within the home would be immune from potential State scrutiny and observation.

53. Such a state of affairs – with its gloomy echoes of the mass state surveillance programmes conducted in totalitarian states such as the German Democratic Republic of Ulbricht and Honecker–would be totally at odds with the basic premises and fundamental values of the Constitution: respect for human dignity and freedom of the individual (as per the Preamble); personal autonomy (Article 40.3.1 and Article 40.3.2); the inviolability of the dwelling (Article 40.5) and protection of family life (Article 41). As Hardiman J. observed in *The People v. O'Brien* [2012] IECCA 68, Article 40.5

> "... presupposes that in a free society the dwelling is set apart as a place of repose from the cares of the world. In so doing, Article 40.5 complements and re-inforces other constitutional guarantees and values, such as assuring the dignity of the individual (as per the Preamble to the Constitution), the protection of the person (Article 40.3.2), the protection of family life (Article 41) and the education and protection of children (Article 42). Article 40.5 thereby assures the citizen that his or her privacy, person and security will be protected against all comers, save in the exceptional circumstances presupposed by the saver to this guarantee."

54. One might accordingly ask how the dwelling could in truth be a 'place of repose from the cares of the world' if, for example, the occupants of the dwelling could not send an email or write a letter or even conduct a telephone conversation if they could not be assured that they would not be subjected to the prospect of general or casual State surveillance of such communications on a mass and undifferentiated basis.

55. That general protection for privacy, person and security in Article 40.5 would thus be entirely compromised by the mass and undifferentiated surveillance by State authorities of conversations and communications which take place within the home. For such interception of communications of this nature to be constitutionally valid, it would, accordingly, be necessary to demonstrate that this interception of communications and the surveillance of individuals or groups of individuals was objectively justified in the interests of the suppression of crime and national security and, further, that any such interception was attended by appropriate and verifiable safeguards.

56. If this matter were entirely governed by Irish law, then, measured by these constitutional standards, a significant issue would arise as to whether the United States 'ensures an adequate level of protection for the privacy

and the fundamental rights and freedoms' of data subjects, such as would permit data transfers to that country having regard to the general prohibition contained in s.11(1) of the 1988 Act and the constitutional principles I have just set out. Certainly, given what I have already described as the (apparently) limited protection given to data subjects by contemporary US law and practice so far as State surveillance is concerned, this would indeed have been a matter which the Commissioner would have been obliged further to investigate.

57. It is, however, agreed, that the matter is only partially governed by Irish law and that, in reality, on this key issue Irish law has been pre-empted by general EU law in this area. This is because s.11(2)(a) of the 1988 Act (as substituted by s.12 of the Data Protection (Amendment) Act 2003) effects a *renvoi* of this wider question in favour of EU law. Specifically, s.11(2)(b) of the 1988 Act provides that the Commissioner must determine the question of the adequacy of protection in the third State 'in accordance' with a Community finding made by the European Commission pursuant to Article 25 of the 1995 Directive. It is accordingly for this reason that we must therefore turn to a consideration of the position at EU law."

Safe Harbour regime Hogan J. observed that the position under EU law is equally clear and, indeed, parallels the position under Irish law. However, he considered that the safeguards for data protection under the EU Charter of Fundamental Rights are perhaps even more explicit referring to art.7 (respect for private and family life) and art.8 (protection of personal data). He noted that in *Digital Rights Ireland* the Court of Justice held that the Data Retention Directive was invalid, precisely because not only did it not contain appropriate safeguards, but it failed to provide for the retention of the data within the European Union with supervisions by an independent authority in the manner required by art.8(3) of the Charter. He concluded:

"62. Judged by these standards, it is not immediately apparent how the present operation of the Safe Harbour Regime can in practice satisfy the requirements of Article 8(1) and Article 8(3) of the Charter, especially having regard to the principles articulated by the Court of Justice in *Digital Rights Ireland.* Under this self-certification regime, personal data is transferred to the United States where, as we have seen, it can be accessed on a mass and undifferentiated basis by the security authorities. While the FISA Court doubtless does good work, the FISA system can at best be described as a form of oversight by judicial personages in respect of applications for surveillance by the US security authorities. Yet the very fact that this oversight is not carried out on European soil and in circumstances where the data subject has no effective possibility of being heard or making submissions and, further, where any such review is not carried out by reference to EU law are all considerations which would seem to pose considerable legal difficulties. It must be stressed, however, that neither the validity of the 1995 Directive nor the Commission Decision providing for the Safe Harbour Regime are, as such, under challenge in these judicial review proceedings.

63. The Safe Harbour Regime was, of course, not only drafted before the Charter came into force, but its terms may also reflect a somewhat more innocent age in terms of data protection. This Regime also came into force prior to the advent of social media and, of course, before the massive terrorist attacks on American soil which took place on September 11th, 2001. Outrages of this kind – sadly duplicated afterwards in Madrid, London and elsewhere–highlighted to many why, subject to the appropriate and necessary safeguards, intelligence services needed as a matter of practical necessity to have access to global telecommunications systems in order to disrupt the planning of such attacks."

He summarised the proceedings in his conclusions:

"69. The applicant's objection is, in reality, to the terms of the Safe Harbour Regime itself rather than to the manner in which the Commissioner has actually applied the Safe Harbour Regime. There is, perhaps, much to be said for the argument that the Safe Harbour Regime has been overtaken by events. The Snowden revelations may be thought to have exposed gaping holes in contemporary US data protection practice and the subsequent entry into force of Article 8 of the Charter suggests that a re-evaluation of how the 1995 Directive and 2000 Decision should be interpreted in practice may be necessary. It must be again stressed, however, that neither the validity of the 1995 Directive nor the validity of the Commission's Safe Harbour decision have, as such, been challenged in these proceedings."

Surveillance of criminal activity The Court of Criminal Appeal considered whether covert police activity involving aural and video devices amounts to an interference with private life in *DPP v Idah* [2014] IECCA 3. This was in the context of undercover activity by members of An Garda Síochána under the provisions of the Criminal Justice (Surveillance) Act 2009 and consideration of the differences between authorisation by a District judge and, arising from the unavailability of a District judge, approval by a senior Garda officer for the use of surveillance equipment. MacMenamin J. (Herbert J. and de Valera JJ. concurring) referred, at para.36, to *Ludi v Switzerland* (1992) 50 E.H.R.R. 173 in which the European Court of Human Rights had stated that the closer one is to pure criminal activity then the less is the reasonable expectation of privacy. There is a continuum ranging from outright participation in crime to fringe, and perhaps unwitting, involvement. Albeit *Ludi* did not directly address electronic means of covert surveillance it recognised that intelligence gathering is vital to the work of police forces. McMenamin J. observed that, in general, there is a discernible qualitative difference between a face-to-face encounter between a suspect and a member of the Gardaí on the one hand, and carrying out surveillance on the other. He continued:

"37. There can be no doubt that the State may make incursions into the right of privacy in accordance with law. This is particularly the case in circumstances where the State is seeking to provide in relation to 'the investigation of arrestable offences, the prevention of suspected arrestable offences and the safeguarding of the State against subversive and terrorist

> threats'. Nevertheless that law must be sufficiently clear in its terms to give individuals an adequate indication as to the circumstances in which public authorities are entitled to resort to such covert measures and it must provide necessary safeguards for the rights of individuals potentially affected. In the view of this court, that is precisely the intent and purpose of the Act of 2009.
>
> 38. Indeed, in the particular circumstances of this case, where one is dealing with an alleged plot to import large quantities of controlled drugs, the common good must weigh heavily in the balance. It cannot be said that the accused's reasonable expectation of privacy extends to involvement in any such alleged illegal enterprise. That is not to say that this accused is left without protection; but to acknowledge that the safeguards granted under the 2009 Act adequately vindicate his rights in this regard."

McMenamin J. distinguished the Supreme Court judgment in *DPP v Peter Byrne* [2003] 4 I.R. 423:

> "54. The statutory position in *Byrne* differs from this case in one important particular. Section 8(2) of the Criminal Justice (Drug Trafficking) Act 1996, which was in issue in *Byrne* is not accompanied in the other sections of the 1996 Act by a section in similar terms to s.14(4) of the 2009 Act, granting a discretion to trial judge to admit evidence obtained where there has been non-compliance."

It was held at para.55 that this discretion is limited to the admission of evidence of information or material obtained where there has been a failure to comply with a requirement of that authorisation or approval. It does not extend to information or materials obtained under an invalid authorisation or approval. In the circumstances the admission of evidence obtained under an approval now deemed invalid should not have been permitted and a re-trial was ordered.

Contract Law

FERGUS RYAN
Maynooth University

BREACH OF CONTRACT

Murphy v O'Toole and Sons Ltd and Bank of Scotland (Ireland) Ltd. [2014] IEHC 486 This case primarily addresses the Statute of Limitations and when a cause of action is deemed to arise in respect of an alleged breach of contract. The issue was a preliminary matter, to be determined before the claim of breach of contract was considered. The plaintiff in this case, Mr Murphy, was an agricultural contractor. In April 2002 he entered into an oral contract for the purchase of an Amazone Sower. This was delivered to him in October 2002. Financing for the machine was provided through a hire-purchase agreement with the second defendant, Bank of Ireland (Scotland), and was received in October 2002. In early 2003 Mr Murphy was stopped by the Gardaí, who informed him that the Sower was not suitable for road transportation in conjunction with his tractor, and that he was in breach of road traffic laws. While the plaintiff returned the machine to the first defendant in October 2003, he did not commence proceedings until July 2008.

The plaintiff claimed that the first defendant (O'Toole and Sons) was in breach of contract in that the machine was not suitable for transport on the public highway in combination with a tractor, and therefore was not fit for the purpose for which it had been bought. The plaintiff also asserted that the defendant had negligently advised him that the machine was fit for transportation by road.

The first defendant, however, claimed that the plaintiff's case was statute-barred. In contract cases, s.11(1)(a) of the Statute of Limitations 1957 requires that proceedings be commenced within six years of the date on which the cause of action accrued. The first defendant claimed that time began to run in April 2002, when the contract was made. The plaintiff, in addition to disputing that the agreement was made in April 2002, counter-argued that time only began to run in October 2002 at the point in time when the machine was delivered. In the alternative he claimed that the contract was conditional upon hire purchase finance being obtained from the second defendant, which did not happen until October 2002.

Baker J. found as a matter of fact that an oral agreement for the sale of the machine was made on 8 April 2002, despite the plaintiff's contention that the agreement was made later in the year. Although there was no order form or written evidence of agreement and no deposit paid, Baker J. accepted the defendant's evidence, based in part on diary entries, that the plaintiff and first defendant had orally agreed the sale in April. She also relied on evidence that an additional part for the machine was ordered in May 2002, which was consistent with an April agreement. In particular, she accepted the defendant's evidence that the deal was sealed by a handshake, which was common in the particular trade.

Baker J. also rejected the plaintiff's proposition that the agreement was conditional upon loan finance being provided. The plaintiff maintained that he could not have paid for the expensive machine out of his own funds, and that it was not credible that he would have agreed to buy the machine until he was sure he could pay for it. He therefore asserted that the contract was either subject to a condition precedent that it would not come into force until loan finance was obtained or, in the alternative, that the agreement was a tripartite one that came into being only when finance was drawn down.

The judge characterised the contract as an 'agreement to sell' under s.1(3) of the Sale of Goods Act 1893 (the "1893 Act"). Under ss.27 and 28 of that Act, the seller has a duty under such agreements to deliver the goods, and the buyer a concurrent obligation to pay for them.

While accepting that a contract could be made subject to a condition precedent, and in particular could be made conditional on obtaining loan finance, Baker J. concluded that there was no such condition precedent in this case. While the defendant knew that finance would be required, the parties had not discussed such a condition, and there was no express agreement on the point. For a contract to be subject to a condition precedent, the judge noted, "such a condition must be express between the parties." The court would not imply such a term. Nor was such a term necessary to give the contract business efficacy. Mere silence on the point did not suffice to supply such a condition. Notably, in this case, O'Toole and Sons had ordered the machine in April 2002, just after the agreement was made. As a matter of probability, the judge observed, had the agreement been conditional he would not have placed the order until financing was in place.

As a matter of fact, the judge concluded that Mr Murphy had agreed to buy the machine in April 2002, before finance was in place, and without reference to any condition as to financing. Notably, she accepted the first defendant's evidence that buyers of machines usually were able to secure finance to complete orders made previously; in cases where financing fell through, the first defendant was usually able to sell on the machines to other buyers. The contract, she concluded, was made in April 2002, and fell within the definition of an agreement to sell under s.1(3) of the 1893 Act, with the corresponding obligations on the seller to deliver the goods and the buyer to pay for them. It was not conditional on loan finance being secured. Baker J. also rejected the proposition that an agreement came into operation only when the loan finance was secured.

The question that then arose was whether the Statute of Limitations 1957 statute-barred the claim. Baker J. concluded that the cause of action in this case accrued on the date the goods were delivered in October 2002. In contract, the general rule is that the cause of action accrues from the date of breach of contract and not the date on which the damage is suffered. As the agreement was an agreement to sell, the breach occurred in this case not when the agreement was made but rather "on the date when the goods come into possession of the buyer, and it is when the buyer takes custody of goods and it is then that the seller is in breach of the warranties and conditions as to quality or fitness for purpose as in the contract." Notably, the buyer could not have pleaded breach of contract between April and October 2002 because "until performance it could not be said that there had been a breach of the obligations of the seller."

She concluded:

> "When time separates the agreement for sale from the performance of the conditions in that agreement, the contract is not breached until it can be said that the contract was not fully performed or performed in compliance with the conditions on the part of the seller."

This meant that, as a matter of law, the breach (if there was a breach) occurred on the date of delivery of the machine to the plaintiff, October 2002, which was within the six year period of limitations for claims based on contract. Proceedings were commenced in July 2008. As such, the cause of action in contract was not statute-barred.

The plaintiff had also sued in tort for negligence and negligent misstatement, claiming that he had been induced to enter into the contract on the basis that the Sower was suitable for road transport using a tractor. In case she was wrong on the first issue in this case, Baker J. proceeded also to consider this point. Again the Statute of Limitations was invoked. In tort, time begins to run when damage has been caused by a wrong (*Hegarty v O'Loughran* [1990] 1 I.R. 148). The plaintiff claimed that the damage only arose when he became liable to pay for the goods, and pay back the finance loan. The judge noted, however, that a representation is actionable only where it induced a party to enter into the contract. Such a representation, of necessity, must have been made before the contract is made.

Therefore, assuming such a representation was made, it must have been made before the contract was entered into on 8 April 2002. In *Gallagher v ACC Bank* [2012] IESC 35, Fennelly J. observed that "once a party relies on advice to his detriment by entering into a transaction whereby he fails to get that to which he is entitled, the cause of action is complete, notwithstanding the fact that quantification of the loss may be difficult." If the case was based solely on negligent misrepresentation, therefore, the cause of action would have crystallised on the day the contract was made and therefore would (if this were purely a tort-based action) have been statute-barred by the time proceedings began. This was because only representations that induced him to enter into the contract were actionable and these of necessity could only be made before the contract was entered into.

Nonetheless, the court concluded that the core of the cause of action in this case was contract-based. Relying on *Gallagher v ACC Bank,* Baker J. was satisfied that she should not artificially decouple the claims in tort and contract. As O'Donnell J. observed in *Gallagher*, the courts should seek to reduce the differences in limitation periods for causes of action arising in both contract and tort, essentially from the same fact scenario. Where possible, he said, "the policy of the law should thus be to minimise, rather than expand, the disparity between the running of time in contract and tort cases, at least where the wrongdoing alleged was identical." On the facts of the case, Baker J. observed, the central and primary claim made here was one of contract and therefore the cause of action accrued at the date of the breach of contract. As a result, the court ruled that the claim was not statute-barred.

COLLATERAL CONTRACTS

Irish Banking Resolution Corporation v McCaughey [2014] IESC 44 This case concerns a request for summary judgment in respect of loan monies owing to the plaintiff bank. It further addresses controversies arising from the defendant's investment in funds that sought to develop and run US-based hotels. These investments were the subject of a Supreme Court judgment in *McCaughey v Irish Banking Resolution Corporation* [2013] IESC 17, reported in the *Annual Review of Irish Law 2013* (pp.221-225).

The defendant, Mr McCaughey, owed the plaintiff bank substantial sums of money that had been extended to him and that he had, in turn, invested in a series of investment schemes involving a number of US-based hotels. These projects had been spearheaded by the plaintiff's predecessor in title, Anglo Irish Bank, but had run into significant financial difficulties. The terms of the relevant loan facilities required the loan monies to be repaid on demand or, at the latest, by March 2008. The defendant did not dispute that he owed the monies. Nonetheless, he claimed, in defence, that he had a collateral contract with the bank to the effect that the loans would not be repayable until such time as the investment projects had come to an end, or had been liquidated. He also alleged that he had been misled as regards certain aspects of the investment projects.

The bank sought summary judgment for the sums owed. In the High Court, [2014] IEHC 230, Kelly J. concluded that there was an arguable defence in respect of some but not all of the loans. He agreed that there was at least an arguable defence as to the existence of a collateral agreement. It was clear, he said, that "in appropriate circumstances the terms of a written agreement may be affected by the existence of a collateral contract or warranty made between the parties." He concluded, however, that some of the investment funds had in fact come to an end. Therefore, even if the collateral agreement had been made, it would not have provided a defence, as the investment schemes had in fact expired.

Kelly J. concluded that the allegations of negligence, misrepresentation, negligent misstatement, breach of duty and breach of contract were statute-barred. Even on the merits they did not disclose an arguable defence. The defendant "had not demonstrated, even on the low threshold of proof required, the basis for a counterclaim in respect of the various complaints." There was no evidence, he said, to support the claims made. Notably, some of the assertions had already been addressed in previous litigation. Therefore he concluded that summary judgment should issue in respect of some of the loans, including those relating to two specific schemes, the New York Hotels Fund and the Woolgate Fund.

On appeal to the Supreme Court, Mr McCaughey contended that these funds had not in fact come to an end. He noted that he was an investor in the New York Hotels Fund. That fund, a US limited partnership, owned 100 per cent of two further US limited partnerships, which in turn each owned one of two hotels. While one of the hotels had been transferred to another unrelated entity, the fund still had a stake in the second hotel. Therefore, there remained at least some prospect, albeit minimal, of a return on the New York Hotels Fund. Clarke J. (with whom Laffoy J. and Dunne J. concurred) thus concluded that there was in fact at least an arguable defence to the effect that the New York Hotels Fund had not yet been terminated. Given that there was some prospect of a return (however minimal) the Supreme Court agreed that the defendant had an arguable defence on this specific point, though whether the fund had or had not ended awaited conclusive determination at plenary trial.

Clarke J., however, refused to permit the defendant to raise as a counterclaim or defence, allegations of misselling in respect of the New York Fund. He noted that substantially the same allegations had been considered and dismissed as part of previous litigation involving the parties (*McCaughey v Irish Banking Resolution Corporation* [2013] IESC 17) and that it would be an abuse of process to allow Mr McCaughey to resurrect these claims.

In respect of the Woolgate Fund, the Supreme Court upheld the High Court decision to the effect that there was no arguable defence that the fund had not ended. As part of the complex investment structure, the defendant had acquired unit-linked policies with an assurance company. That assurance company held shares in Woolgate Exchange SA, which in turn held equity in a limited partnership that owned the relevant investment property. Woolgate Exchange SA, however, had become insolvent and had been liquidated. As a result, there was "no prospect of any monies being paid by [Woolgate Exchange] into the united linked fund." There were, therefore, no arguable grounds to suggest that the fund was not at an end. Even on the most generous of interpretations, it was clear the fund had expired.

Mr McCaughey had also alleged misselling on the part of Anglo in respect of the Woolgate Fund. He claimed that the debt level associated with the property at the time of investment was 87.5 per cent, when he had been told it was 83.6 per cent. The loan covenant required that the loan-to-value ratio not exceed 84 per cent, which meant that the lender could call in the loan if it exceeded that ratio and if no steps were taken to reduce the ratio. He also alleged that Credit Suisse, senior financiers to the fund, had agreed to fund the project for five years, when in fact the fund was expected to run for at least five and up to seven years.

Clarke J. noted, however, that Mr McCaughey had not claimed that he had been induced to invest on the basis of these representations or that had he known the true facts he would not have invested. It was clear also, given the "truly disastrous performance" of the investment project, the loans would have been called in whether the initial loan to ratio value was 87 per cent or 84 per cent and regardless of the length of time Credit Suisse intended to invest. The differences might have been relevant had the fund performed somewhat less well than was expected, but in the disastrous circumstances that befell the fund, they "could not have made any conceivable difference." There was, therefore, no basis for claiming that the allegedly inaccurate representations affected the performance of the fund in any way. Mr McCaughey, notably, had not asserted that, had he known of these marginal differences, he would not have invested.

Clarke J. thus concluded that the High Court was correct in finding that there was no arguable basis for the claim of missselling in respect of the Woolgate Fund.

In the course of his decision, Clarke J. made some interesting comments about the summary judgment jurisdiction. For summary judgment to issue, he noted, it had to be clear that the defendant had no arguable defence. As he had observed in *McGrath v O'Driscoll* [2007] I.L.R.M. 203 at 210, the court should only grant summary judgment "where the issues which arise are relatively straightforward and where there is no real risk of an injustice being done by determining those questions within the somewhat limited framework of a motion for summary judgment.". While case law suggests that the defence should be 'credible' Clarke J. stressed that the use of that term in this context has "a very narrow meaning.". "A defence is not incredible", he observed, "simply because the judge is not inclined to believe the defence. It must … be clear that the defendant has no defence.". For the purpose of determining whether there is an arguable defence, he added, the court must accept the facts as asserted by the defence, though a mere assertion unsupported by any evidence will not be sufficient.

CONDITIONS PRECEDENT

Maloney v Danske Bank A/S [2014] IEHC 441 This case concerned the legal status of a 2008 floating charge entered into between RQB Ltd and Danske Bank. The former company was now in liquidation and the official liquidator applied to court claiming that the floating charge was not valid or enforceable. The bank disputed this, claiming it was valid. While this is a company law case, some aspects of contract law arise, in particular the operation of conditions precedent, the court's power to imply terms, and the role of consideration in making a contract enforceable.

In 2005, National Irish Bank (the predecessor of Danske Bank) gave RQB Ltd an overdraft facility of €12 million on agreed terms. The overdraft was subject to a joint and several guarantee for €12 million signed by three guarantors in December 2005. In September 2008, with a view to restructuring the 2005 overdraft, the bank offered a loan facility for €8 million, and an additional overdraft facility of €2 million. The company agreed and signed and accepted this offer, with a contract coming into being on 10 September 2008.

Arising from this scenario, there were two related and largely similar agreements, one concerning the loan and one addressing the overdraft. Clause 5 of the loan agreement required that the loan facility be secured by personal joint and several guarantees for €8 million by three guarantors (which were executed in September 2008) together with a first fixed and floating charge over the assets and undertaking of the company. A floating charge was executed on 10 September 2008. In it, the parties agreed that, in exchange for the credit facilities, the company would charge its undertaking and all its property in favour of the bank "as a security for all monies the payment whereof is intended to be hereby secured[,] such charge to be a floating security… ."

The agreements stipulated that the new loan and overdraft would remain open until 30 September 2008, and would be subject to renegotiation if the funds were not used by that date. The facilities would be made available, however, only when certain security arrangements were completed.

Clause 8 of the loan agreement required that the guarantors provide personal asset statements that were to be satisfactory to the bank. While the guarantors had provided personal assets statements, the bank was not satisfied with these. As a result, it refused to advance the loan and overdraft facilities to the company. Further negotiations proved to be fruitless, and despite ongoing discussions, the facilities anticipated by the 2008 agreements were never drawn down.

In the meantime, the company's financial position had worsened. The bank made formal demands for the repayment of the monies it had lent under the 2005 facility, totalling around €8.5 million. The bank asserted that, in default of payment, it would rely on the securities provided in the 2008 facility letters.

In 2009, the bank obtained judgments against the company and two of the guarantors in respect of the monies owed to it. In November 2009, the company was wound up on the petition of a creditor. In 2010, McGovern J. granted judgment in favour of the bank against one of the guarantors on foot of his personal guarantee.

(See *Danske Bank T/A National Irish Bank v RQB Limited & Ors* [2010] IEHC 347, discussed in the *Annual Review of Irish Law 2010* at pp.243–246).

The parties agreed that the principles set out in *ICDL GCC Foundation v European Computer Driving Licence Foundation Ltd* [2012] IESC 55 applied to the interpretation of the loan and overdraft contracts, both of which were to be construed together.

The liquidator claimed that the floating charge was not enforceable. It had been signed in the context of the 2008 loan agreement. As the monies under that agreement had never been advanced, the bank could not, he claimed, rely on the floating charge. If the new loan and overdraft had never been extended, he argued, the security therefore could not be realised. The loan and overdraft agreements, he asserted, were contingent on a condition precedent that had never been satisfied. No loan facilities or overdraft had been advanced to the company on foot of the 2008 agreements. Thus, he claimed, the agreements lapsed on 30 September 2008. He therefore argued that the floating charge itself also lapsed. The liquidator claimed further that it was an implied term of the floating charge that it would come to an end if the bank failed to advance funds as anticipated by the 2008 agreements. The liquidator also asserted that there was no consideration for the floating charge, though the bank countered that no consideration was required as the charge was made under seal.

The bank, for its part, claimed that the floating charge was a stand-alone security and that it was not subject to any condition precedent but, instead, could be invoked against the defendant. The bank's continued forbearance in respect of the existing 2005 loans was sufficient consideration, it maintained, to support the floating charge. At any rate, it claimed, the charge had been made under seal and did not require consideration. It had, moreover, been validly registered with the Companies Registration Office.

A "condition precedent", Cregan J. observed, is a condition that must be fulfilled before other conditions are fulfilled, such that, if this condition is not fulfilled "then the other conditions fall away or become unenforceable." Some authorities, he noted, distinguished between a condition precedent to the contract (claiming that there is no contract until the condition is met) and a condition precedent to performance where the contract exists but obligations thereunder are suspended. Cregan J., however, considered this distinction "illogical". The creation of a condition precedent presupposed that the parties had reached agreement. A condition precedent, as a matter of logic, could not "prevent the coming into being of a contract at all":

> "There is either a contract in being or there is no contract. The very concept of a 'condition precedent' means that the parties have agreed on a condition precedent. *If they have agreed on a condition precedent then they have reached an agreement.* Thus *there is a contract in being.* If that is so, the concept of a condition precedent which prevents a contract coming into existence is meaningless." (Emphasis added).

Effectively, he observed, if the parties agree that a certain condition must be fulfilled before the rest of the contractual conditions can be fulfilled or performed, this is a "condition precedent". Before the other contractual obligations become enforceable, this condition must be satisfied.

Therefore, as a matter of logic, a condition precedent means, Cregan J. noted, "that the parties have agreed that the obligations in the contract must occur in a certain sequence over a certain period of time…[I]f the earlier condition is not fulfilled then the other conditions do not have to be fulfilled or are unenforceable.". He thus concluded that:

> "…the essence of a condition precedent is that it is a condition which precedes other conditions or contractual obligations contained in the contract. By calling it a condition precedent the parties intend to mean that if this condition is not fulfilled then the other conditions of the contract are unenforceable."

Applying these principles to the present case, Cregan J. ruled that the floating charge had lapsed as of 30 September 2008, and was no longer enforceable. Under the loan agreement, the bank had agreed to lend the company €8 million and the company agreed to repay this money. The parties in turn agreed that the personal guarantees and floating charge would be security for the 2008 loan and overdraft. Critically, Clause 8 of the loan agreement required that before the facilities could be used, personal asset statements that were satisfactory to the bank had to be provided, but these were never forthcoming. This meant that the condition precedent was never fulfilled, with the result that the bank did not advance the loan.

Under Clause 12 of the loan agreement, if the loan facilities were not drawn down by 30 September 2008, the agreement would be subject to renegotiation. As utilisation had not in fact commenced by that date, the judge ruled, the agreements effectively had come to an end and had lapsed due to the failure to provide satisfactory personal asset statements.

The bank claimed that although the 2008 loan was never advanced, the floating charge remained as security in respect of the prior 2005 loan. In other words, the bank argued, the charge was a free-standing security for any monies owing to it. This was, in Cregan J.'s view, "completely unsustainable":

> "It is clear–both as a matter of logic and as a matter of common sense,–that if no loan has been advanced there is therefore no obligation on the company to repay a non-existent loan. It must also follow–again as a matter of logic and of common sense–that, if no loan has been advanced, there can be no enforceable security in respect of a non-existent loan.".

The wording of the loan agreement itself supported this view. Clause 5 thereof specifically expressly stated that the "loan facility" is secured by the floating charge. The loan in question clearly is that anticipated by the 2008 agreement: "There is no express or implied language to the effect that the floating charge would be a charge for the 2005 loan facility." The floating charge, he noted, only came into being as a security under the 2008 loan agreement: "It did not come into being for any independent reason." As a matter of construction of the contract, the floating charge was intended to provide security for the 2008 loan facility only "and was not in any way intended to be a stand alone security." While the floating charge did not make reference to the 2008 agreement, the latter agreement had referenced the floating charge. Notably, the charge had been signed the same day as the 2008 loan agreement and guarantees. The three documents stood to be construed together.

As the condition precedent had not been complied with, the 2008 agreement lapsed, and with it the security also lapsed. This meant, the judge concluded, that the floating charge was unenforceable.

Notably, Clause 5 of the loan agreement had stated that: "Any security held now or at any future time shall be security for all the Borrower's liabilities to the Bank (actual or contingent) and whether as principle or surety." The judge noted, however, that the floating charge was no longer valid and enforceable as, though valid at the time it was made, it had lapsed due to the non-fulfilment of a condition precedent.

The judge also rejected the proposition that the floating charge "had an independent and stand-alone existence". This was, he believed, unsustainable. It was clear, he said, that the parties intended to grant the floating charge as security for the 2008 loan, not the 2005 loan. The 2008 agreement expressly stated that it was the 2008 loan facility and overdraft that were to be secured by the floating charge. The bank was, moreover, getting additional security for the 2008 loan; the 2005 loan was secured only by the personal guarantees. There was no evidence that the company ever agreed to apply the floating charge retrospectively to cover the 2005 loan. Clear and unambiguous language would have been required to have given the agreement such effect, and this was lacking here.

The liquidator had also argued that it was an implied term of the 2008 loan agreement "that if the loans were not advanced then the security would not be maintained." A court may imply terms into a contract either by reference to custom or by law or as a matter of fact. Cregan J. referred, in particular, to the business efficacy and officious bystander tests, both of which seek to determine the presumed, though unexpressed, intention of the parties. Terms may be implied either where it is necessary to give the contract business efficacy or where the term would have been so obvious to the parties that it did not need stating. The purpose of so doing is to give effect to the parties' true intention. It was not the court's role to seek to improve upon the contract.

In this case, however, Cregan J. concluded it was not necessary to imply a contractual term as the contract was "clear on its face." In particular, Clause 5 of the loan agreement "specifically provides that it is the [2008] loan facility which is to be secured by the floating charge." The contract itself thus clearly indicated the floating charge only covered the 2008 loan. As that loan facility had never been advanced, the floating charge too had lapsed. It would be wholly unsustainable to maintain that the floating charge applied also to the 2005 loan. As such, it was unnecessary for the court to imply any terms.

The judge rejected, however, the liquidator's claim that the floating charge was unenforceable for lack of consideration. The bank for its part had agreed to loan €8 million and extend the overdraft in exchange for the company's promise to repay the loan and provide the relevant security, including the floating charge. As such, the judge was satisfied that there was consideration for the loan agreement: "The floating charge itself constituted part of the consideration for the loan agreement." The consideration for creating the floating charge, in turn, was the bank's agreement to loan the monies. Therefore, the floating charge validly came into existence on

10 September 2008, but it lapsed once the condition precedent failed. Given this conclusion, the judge did not have to consider whether the contract was validly made under seal.

While agreeing that the charge had been validly created and properly registered with the Companies Registration Office (CRO), the judge again pointed out that the 2008 agreement had lapsed and therefore the floating charge also lapsed. It was, therefore, unenforceable. Whether the charge had been validly registered at the CRO was irrelevant in determining its current enforceability.

Notably, in previous proceedings in *Danske Bank T/A National Irish Bank v RQB Limited & Ors* [2010] IEHC 347) McGovern J. had determined that Mr Niall McFadden's personal guarantee in respect of RQB was enforceable. In that case, however, Cregan J. noted, "different considerations applied in relation to the wording and extent of the personal guarantees given in 2005 and 2008." Thus, it was not necessary for Cregan J. to consider that case in coming to any conclusions in the present case.

Cregan J. therefore concluded that the floating charge was unenforceable.

CONSIDERATION

See *Moloney v Danske Bank A/S* [2014] IEHC 441, discussed above under CONDITIONS PRECEDENT and *Allied Irish Banks Plc v McKenna, Donlon and Copeland* [2014] IEHC 122, discussed below under GUARANTEES.

CONSUMER PROTECTION

Competition and Consumer Protection Act 2014 This Act replaces the former Competition Authority and National Consumer Agency with a new Competition and Consumer Protection Commission. This step is in line with Government policy to reduce the number of independent state agencies. The Act also makes some amendments (inter alia) to the Competition Act 2002 and the Consumer Protection Act 2007.

The Act in its entirety is now in force. Parts 1-3 (other than s.8) and 5-7 of the Act came into operation on 31 October 2014. (Competition and Consumer Protection Act 2014 (Commencement) Order 2014 (S.I. No. 366 of 2014)). Part 4 was separately brought into operation also as of 31 October 2014 by the Competition and Consumer Protection Act 2014 (Commencement) (No. 2) Order 2014 (S.I. No. 401 of 2014). 31 October 2014 was also deemed to be the establishment day for the new Commission. Section 8 of the Act came into force on 1 August 2014 (Competition and Consumer Protection Act 2014 (Commencement) Order 2014 (S.I. No. 366 of 2014).)

Establishment and functions of Competition and Consumer Protection Commission Notably, s.38 of the Act abolishes the Competition Authority and National Consumer Agency with effect from 31 October 2014. All functions of the former Authority and Agency are transferred to the Commission. Statutory references to the former Authority and Agency are deemed to refer henceforth to the Commission (s.39). Staff, assets, rights and liabilities of the dissolved bodies are also transferred to the new Commission.

The powers and functions of the new Commission are set out in Pt 2 of the Act.

Subject to the relevant Acts, the Commission is independent in the performance of its functions (s.9(5)). Section10 stipulates that the Commission's functions will include promoting competition and promoting and protecting the interests and welfare of consumers. The Commission may also carry out investigations, at its own initiative or on foot of a complaint, into any alleged breach of the relevant statutory provisions addressing competition and consumer protection, or of arts 101 or 102 of the Treaty on the Functioning of the EU (TFEU). It may enforce relevant statutory provisions relating to consumer and competition law. It is also permitted to encourage statutory compliance, including through the publication of guidance notices. The Commission is further empowered to advise the Government and Ministers and other public bodies in relation to competition and consumer law, and may make recommendations for law reform and comment on proposals for legislative change. The Commission is also enabled to engage in research, awareness raising and to provide information, education and guidance to traders and the public at large on matters within its remit. Provision is made for cooperation with other prescribed statutory bodies, with a view to ensuring consistency and avoiding duplication of efforts. The Commission may promote quality assurance schemes, review and approve codes of practice under s.88 of the Consumer Protection Act 2007, and publish guidelines for traders under s.90 of that Act.

The Act also grants the Commission powers and functions in respect of financial services to consumers (s.11). In particular, the Commission may carry out studies, surveys and analyses of financial services and for this purpose may require persons to release information or records to the Commission or to come before the Commission to provide such information in person. It is an offence intentionally to prevent the Commission from exercising these specific functions or to obstruct or hinder their exercise. It is also unlawful to fail to comply with the Commission's requirement to attend before it or to fail to supply information or records, or to provide information to the Commission that the person knows or ought reasonably to know is false or misleading in a material respect. The Commission itself is empowered to bring summary proceedings for an offence under s.11, attracting up to 12 months in prison, a class A fine (up to €5,000), or both. Conviction on indictment attracts a fine of up to €30,000 or five years' imprisonment or both.

The Act makes provision for the membership and staffing of the Commission, as well as the appointment of authorised officers by the Commission. It further empowers the Commission to carry out investigations (s.18). For this purpose it may summon witnesses before it, and examine them on oath. It may also require a witness to produce to the Commission books, documents and records in the witness' power or control. Failure to cooperate with the Commission, including failing to attend when summoned, refusing to answer questions or failing to supply information, books, documents or records, or providing false or misleading information all constitute offences under the Act. The penalties for the commission of these offences are severe: on indictment, for instance, the maximum fine is €250,000 or a five-year prison term or both.

The Act also empowers the Commission to appoint authorised officers to enforce relevant statutory provisions, and confers extensive powers thereon, the powers in question being largely equivalent to those conferred by the 2002 and 2007 Acts. For the purpose of enforcing relevant consumer protection provisions, for instance, the authorised officer may enter a trade or business premises and secure or remove and retain books, documents and records relating to the trade or business. (Entering a private dwelling, however, requires a District Court warrant or the occupier's consent). An officer may also require a person carrying on a trade, business or activity or an employee thereof to provide books, documents or records or other information relating to a business. It is an offence to obstruct or impede the authorised officer in the performance of his or her duties, or to fail to comply with a lawful request or requirement thereof.

Notably, s.4 of the 2014 Act allows summary proceedings for an offence under the Act to be commenced within two years of the alleged date of the offence, notwithstanding s.10(4) of the Petty Sessions (Ireland) Act 1851 which ordinarily sets a limit of six months for the commencement of most summary criminal proceedings.

Media Mergers The Act makes various amendments to the Competition Act 2002, based on the recommendations of the Advisory Group on Media Mergers (2008) (The "Sreenan Report"). In particular, it introduces a new Pt 3A specifically relating to media mergers, the broad purpose of which is to ensure plurality in the media and diversity of ownership. Effectively, Pt 3A requires the Minister for Communications, Energy and Natural Resources to determine whether a media merger is in the public interest. For this purpose the Minister may commission an examination by the Broadcasting Authority of Ireland, following which he or she may determine whether to permit or block the media merger, or allow it subject to conditions.

Amendments to the Consumer Protection Act 2007 Part 5 makes a number of amendments to the Consumer Protection Act 2007 (the "2007 Act"), discussed at length in this chapter in the *Annual Review of Irish Law 2007* (at pp.152–164). The Act repeals Pt 2 of the 2007 Act, with the exception of ss.24A to 24E. Part 2 dealt with the establishment and operation of the National Consumer Agency.

A number of definitions in the 2007 Act are altered. The original definition of "consumer" in the 2007 Act is amended such that to be treated as a consumer, a natural person (whether in the State or not) must be "acting wholly or mainly for purposes unrelated to the person's trade, business or profession." The innovation in the 2014 Act lies in the addition of the words "wholly or mainly". The definition of goods is enhanced by an extended definition of computer software to include "content stored in a digital format or content stored electronically in a format which is not digital." The 2014 Act also extends and updates the definition of "relevant statutory provisions" specifically to include a series of relevant statutory instruments listed in a new Sch.9 to the 2007 Act. These include a variety of statutory instruments addressing consumer protection passed since 2005. The definition of a "transaction decision" in the 2007 Act is also amended such that it now applies whether or not a transaction is completed. The definition of "relevant statutory provisions" is also amended to include the recently enacted European Union (Consumer Information, Cancellation and Other Rights) (Amendment) Regulations 2014 (S.I. No. 250 of 2014).

The Central Bank Reform Act 2010 had invested the National Consumer Agency with new powers in relation to providing advice and information to consumers in relation to financial services. To fund this, the Act empowered the Agency to levy businesses in the financial services sector. Section 76 of the 2014 Act empowers the Commission to collect information with a view to calculating the levy. For this purpose, s.77 allows for the secondment of staff from the Central Bank to the Commission.

Section 55 of the 2007 Act sets out a series of prohibited commercial practices in which traders may not engage. As enacted, s.55(1)(o) prohibited a business from "providing after-supply service to a consumer in a language that is not an official language of the relevant State in which the trader is located, nor is it the language in which the trader and consumer communicated prior to the agreement to supply." According to s.55(2), however, s.55(1)(o) did not apply where either, "prior to the agreement to supply, the trader clearly discloses to the consumer the language or languages in which the after-supply service is available" or "the primary language in which the trader and consumer communicated prior to the agreement to supply is the official language of the relevant State in which the trader is located but is not the official language of the relevant State of the consumer." Section 77 of the 2014 Act now replaces s.55(1)(o) and s.55(2) with a simplified provision requiring that a trader may not undertake "to provide after-sales service to consumers with whom the trader has communicated prior to a transaction in a language which is not the official language of the relevant State in which the trader is located and then [make] such service available only in another language without clearly disclosing this to the consumer before the consumer is committed to the transaction." Subsection 2 is deleted.

Section 87 of the 2007 Act provides protections for whistle-blowers reporting breaches of consumer law to the Commission. In particular, it ensures that those reporting breaches will be protected against liability in tort or for breach of contract, and from victimisation by their employers. The protection, however, only applied where the person acted "reasonably and in good faith." Section 78 of the 2014 Act removes the words "and in good faith" in both s.87(1) and s.87(3) though the whistle-blower must still be shown to have acted reasonably. This brings the Act into line with the wording of the Protected Disclosures Act 2014, which requires that the person making a disclosure must reasonably believe the disclosed information to be true. [816 *Dáil Debates* Cols 413–414.]

Regulation of Grocery Goods Undertakings Part 6 of the 2014 Act inserts a new Ch.5 in Pt 3 of the 2007 Act, allowing for the regulation of various practices carried out between grocery goods undertakings. The broad purpose is to eliminate various unfair trading practices allegedly carried out by larger producers, wholesalers and retailers to the detriment of smaller suppliers. This includes requiring 'hello money' as a prerequisite to positioning a product favourably on the retailer's shelves and various practices that require suppliers to foot the bill for in-store promotion of products and for shrinkage and wastage of products or to accept unilaterally imposed contract terms. The measures are largely directed at preventing more powerful players from exploiting inequalities in bargaining power to the detriment of smaller grocery undertakings. As the Minister for Jobs, Enterprise and Innovation pointed out in the Committee Stage debate in the Dáil, "[t]he purpose of this legislation is to deal with abusive practices that are essentially related to market power." While the Minister had originally hoped to address these issues by voluntary code (see the draft Code of Practice for Designated Grocery Goods Undertakings (2011)), this ultimately proved not to be possible. (See also the "Travers Report", Travers, *Exploration of the Possibilities of the Agreement of a Voluntary Code of Practice for Grocery Goods Undertakings* (DJEI, 2011)).

For this purpose, a 'grocery goods undertaking' is defined as an undertaking engaged for gain in the production, supply, distribution, wholesale or retail of grocery goods, whether or not it sells these good directly to the public. 'Grocery goods' include food and drink intended for human consumption, including additives, ingredients and processing aids, as well as intoxicating liquors, though it does not include food or drink sold by an undertaking in the course of catering, restaurant or take-away services, or alcohol sold for consumption on-premises. 'Grocery goods' also includes household cleaning products, toiletries, garden plants and plant bulbs.

Section 63B of the 2007 Act, as inserted by the 2014 Act, empowers the Minister for Jobs, Enterprise and Innovation, having consulted with the Commission, to make regulations in relation to particular aspects of the commercial relationships between relevant grocery goods undertakings and other grocery goods undertakings in relation to the sale or supply of grocery goods. A 'relevant grocery goods undertaking' is effectively a large, well-resourced producer, supplier, distributor, wholesaler or retailer, and is defined as a grocery goods undertaking engaged in the production, supply, distribution, wholesale or retail of grocery goods in the State where its annual worldwide turnover exceeds €50 million (or where it is one of a group of related undertakings with such a turnover). Effectively, therefore, these measures are largely targeted at major players in the market, and are designed to address potential abuse of unequal bargaining power. The Minister may make such regulations where he or she considers it to be appropriate, with a view to promoting competitive trade between grocery goods undertakings, safeguarding the interests of consumers (in particular, in having value for money and choice), making sure trading relationships are conducted in good faith and in a fair, open and transparent manner, ensuring freedom of contract and reasonable certainty in respect of the risks and costs associated with trading, and maintaining strong, innovative, efficient and competitive production and supply bases. Notably, the measures are not designed to address price – which will still be the subject of negotiations inter partes – but rather various types of potentially oppressive conduct.

Without prejudice to the Minister's general power to make regulations, s.63B(2) allows the Minister to make regulations specifically to address (inter alia) the following matters:

- The form contracts for sale, supply, receipt, or purchase of grocery goods to be entered into between relevant grocery goods undertakings and other grocery goods undertakings may take, and the manner in which such contracts may be varied, terminated or renewed;
- How arrangements for supply and delivery may be varied;
- How certain terms and conditions relating to payment for grocery goods, the promotion of goods, liability for negligence and responsibility for customer complaints may be incorporated into contracts;
- Limits on the circumstances in which the relevant grocery goods undertaking may seek payment for shrinkage, wastage or marketing costs;

- The circumstances in which the relevant grocery goods undertaking may or may not seek payment from a grocery goods undertaking for buying grocery goods for resale;
- How forecasts for supply of grocery goods are prepared;
- Whether and in what circumstances a relevant grocery goods undertaking may seek payment from a supplier to retain shelf space or provide better positioning on shelves for the supplier's grocery goods;
- Prohibiting relevant grocery goods undertakings from directly or indirectly compelling a grocery goods undertaking to make a payment or grant an allowance in respect of a promotion of the latter's grocery goods in the former's premises, for advertising or display of the grocery goods in those premises, or to retain shelf space or better positioning or more space for those goods;
- Limiting the obligation of grocery goods undertakings to participate in promotions by relevant grocery goods undertakings;
- Prohibiting practices whereby a relevant grocery goods undertaking requires a grocery goods undertaking to obtain goods or services from a third party where the relevant grocery goods undertaking profits from this arrangement; and
- The timeframe within which payments for grocery goods supplied to relevant grocery goods undertakings are to be made.

Relevant grocery goods undertakings may also be required to prepare annual compliance reports detailing their compliance with regulations made under s.63B, and provide information and documents and maintain records for this purpose. The Minister may also require training for staff in relevant grocery goods undertakings to ensure compliance with the relevant regulations.

In making regulations, the Minister may prescribe certain classes of relevant grocery goods undertakings or grocery goods undertakings to which certain regulations shall apply, and may for this purpose distinguish between retailers, suppliers and wholesalers.

Notably, however, regulations made under s.63B are prospective in effect only, and do not apply to contracts made or renewed before the date on which the regulations come into operation (though they do apply to contracts entered into or renewed on or after that date).

For the purpose of enforcing these regulations the Commission is empowered to inspect relevant grocery goods undertakings and, where it has reasonable grounds to believe that regulations have been breached, to investigate complaints regarding compliance. Where, following an investigation, the Commission uncovers a contravention of a regulation made under s.63B, the Commission may serve a contravention notice. Such a notice shall, inter alia, direct the relevant grocery goods undertaking to remedy the contravention by a specific date. Such a notice may be appealed to the Circuit Court within 21 days of its service, the Circuit Court being empowered to confirm, vary or cancel the notice. In the absence of compliance with a notice, the relevant grocery goods undertaking may be found guilty of an offence and made subject to the penalties set out in s.79 of the 2007 Act. A relevant grocery goods undertaking may also commit an offence where, without reasonable excuse, it contravenes a provision in a regulation made under s.63B that is expressed to be a penal provision. Additionally, any person who is aggrieved by a failure to comply with the regulations or with a contravention notice is deemed to have a right of action for relief against the relevant grocery goods undertaking, though, unless otherwise agreed, damages may not exceed the limit of the Circuit Court's jurisdiction in a tort action. The 2014 Act also amends the 2007 Act to allow the Commission to publish a 'name and shame' list of grocery goods undertakings fined or penalised under these provisions, or that are the subject of a contravention notice.

Proposed new Consumer Rights Bill In the course of his second stage speech on the Competition and Consumer Protection Bill in the Dáil, the Minister for Jobs, Enterprise and Innovation makes reference to further consumer law proposals that are at an advanced stage of preparation. In particular, he noted his plans to bring forward "a further consumer rights Bill in 2015 that will update sales law and build on the experience of the Consumer Protection Act." Indeed, in May 2015 a general scheme of a Consumer Rights Bill was published and opened up for consultation, and is available on the website of the Department of Jobs, Enterprise and Innovation: *www.djei.ie/en/consultations/consultations-files/scheme-of-a-proposed-consumer-rights-bill-May-2015.pdf*. This Consumer Rights Bill proposes to consolidate and update various existing consumer rights laws. The Bill is prompted largely by recommendations made by the Sales Law Review Group's *Report on the Legislation Governing the Sale of Goods and Supply of Services* (2011).

European Union (Consumer Information, Cancellation and Other Rights) (Amendment) Regulations 2014 (S.I. No. 250 of 2014) This short amending Statutory Instrument makes a relatively minor technical amendment to the European Union (Consumer Information, Cancellation and Other Rights) Regulations 2013 (S.I. No. 484 of 2013) (the "2013 Regulations") discussed in last year's *Annual Review of Irish Law 2013* (pp.218–221). Regulation 1 (2) of the 2013 Regulations states that "These Regulations come into operation on 13 June 2014 and apply to contracts concluded after that date." The 2014 amendment replaces this provision with the following: "(2) These Regulations come into operation on 14 June 2014 and apply to contracts concluded on or after that date." The purpose of this amendment appears to be to prevent a gap emerging between the coming into force of the 2013 Regulations and the expiry of those older regulations they replaced (namely the European Communities (Cancellation of Contracts Negotiated Away from Business Premises) Regulations 1989 (S.I. No. 224 of 1989) and the European Communities (Protection of Consumers in Respect of Contracts Made by Means of Distance Communications) Regulations 2001 (S.I. No. 207 of 2001)). The risk otherwise was that contracts concluded on 13 June 2014 would potentially be subject to neither the new nor the old rules, as the old regulations expired as of that date. The amendment means that contracts concluded on that date will be subject to the old rules, with contracts concluded on 14 June 2014 and thereafter having to comply with the 2013 Regulations.

European Communities (Unfair Terms in Consumer Contracts) (Amendment) Regulations 2014 (S.I. No. 336 of 2014) The European Communities (Unfair Terms in Consumer Contracts) (Amendment) Regulations 2014 make a small amendment to the European Communities (Unfair Terms in Consumer Contracts) Regulations 1995 (S.I. No. 27 of 1995) (the "1995 Regulations"), deeming the Commission for Communications Regulation to be an authorised body for the purpose of reg.2. This gives the Commission power to apply to the Circuit or High Court for the purpose of enforcing the 1995 Regulations, for instance by declaration or injunction. A person appointed as an authorised officer under s.39 of the Communications Regulation Act 2002 will also be an authorised officer for the purposes of the 1995 Regulations. For the purpose of the 1995 Regulations, the authorised officer shall have all the powers of an authorised officer appointed under s.39.

European Union (Protection of Consumers in respect of Timeshare, Long-term Holiday Product, Resale and Exchange Contracts) (Amendment) Regulations 2014 (S.I. No. 400 of 2014) These Regulations make a small amendment to the European Union (Protection of Consumers in respect of Timeshare, Long-term Holiday Product, Resale and Exchange Contracts) Regulations 2011 (S.I. No. 73 of 2011) (the "2011 Regulations") which gave effect to Directive 2008/122/EC of the European Parliament and of the Council of 14 January 2009.

As enacted, reg.17(3) of the 2011 Regulations states that a consumer may (without prejudice to other rights of cancellation)

> "… without incurring any penalty, terminate a long-term holiday product contract, at any time after he or she *makes* the second instalment payment under that contract, by giving notice to the trader within 14 calendar days of receiving a request from the trader to make an instalment payment under the contract." (Emphasis added).

As amended, the Regulation allows the consumer to terminate the contract "at any time after he or she *receives a request from the trader to make* the second instalment payment". In other words, it is not necessary for the person to pay the second instalment as a prerequisite to exercising the right to terminate. It is sufficient that a request for a second instalment has been made. This ensures the consumer's right to end the contract after receiving a request for the second instalment payment. The amendment came into force on 8 September 2014.

CREDIT AGREEMENTS

McCarthy, Bevan and Hughes v Bank of Scotland Plc and Cotter [2014] IEHC 340 This case offers an illuminating example of some of the more creative approaches being taken to avoid liability for overdue loans. Ultimately, however, Hogan J. struck out the proceedings on the basis that they were frivolous and vexatious, as permitted by Ord.19 r.28 of the Rules of the Superior Courts.

In 2006, the three plaintiffs had borrowed approximately €2.2 million from the defendant bank's predecessor in title, with a view to investing in two commercial properties. The properties were mortgaged as security for the loans. The project was financially unsuccessful and the bank called in the loans. A receiver was appointed for this purpose.

The plaintiffs made an extensive variety of claims against the defendant bank, including claims for damages for allegedly stolen property, "damages for theft, deception, breach of duty, misrepresentation, causation, fraud, deceit, non-performance, breach of contract, breach of promise, attempted damage by perjury, dishonest and insolvent trading and counterfeiting."

The plaintiffs, representing themselves, effectively contended that the defendant bank had not in fact loaned real money, but was engaged in creating and loaning illegal currency. The plaintiffs had, they argued, not received loans of real money but, rather, a fictitious credit created by the bank. They maintained that a loan was only valid where it was made in the form of notes or coin, effectively something concrete and tangible. Therefore, they argued, the loan agreement in this case was invalid.

A similar argument had been made in *Dempsey v Enviston Credit Union* [2006] BCSC 750 where the plaintiff claimed that banks lack real money but instead create money "out of thin air" in the form of credit. The banks, he alleged, "do[ ] not place hard currency in the hands of the debtors." The court in *Dempsey,* however, dismissed this argument as "fanciful" and "completely devoid of merit." (See also *Freeman v Bank of Scotland Ireland* [2013] IEHC 371).

Birmingham J. had dismissed a similar argument in *Kearney v KBC Bank Ireland plc* [2014] IEHC 260, noting that: "Quite simply the plaintiff drew down funds and thereby took on the responsibility to repay. What the source of these funds was matters not a whit."

Hogan J., likewise, observed that the plaintiffs' line of argument "lack[ed] any relationship to contractual or other legal realities." The source of the bank's money was irrelevant; the obligation to repay the loans, he said, remained. He also rejected the claim that a loan must be made in the form of coin or notes: "this runs entirely contrary to modern realities." The claim of fraud was, he ruled, unfounded. The plaintiffs had, the judge concluded, drawn down and used the funds, and were now obliged to repay them.

The judge also rejected the claim that the bank was insolvent when it made the loans and that therefore the loans were invalid. Even if the bank had been insolvent (which was denied) the validity of the loans, he said, would not have been affected by such insolvency.

The plaintiffs had also claimed that the bank had monetised their promissory notes and securitised their mortgages (sold them on to other investors). In fact, the mortgages had not been securitised. The judge dismissed both arguments as "entirely unmeritorious and lacking in any substance whatever."

While sympathetic towards the plaintiffs' financial plight, the judge concluded that the loans were perfectly valid, and that the arguments to the contrary were "spurious and foolish." Hogan J. thus struck out the proceedings as frivolous and vexatious.

DAMAGES

ADM Londis Plc v Ranzett Ltd., Dolan and McConnell (No. 2) [2014] IEHC 659 This case concerns the quantum of damages to be awarded where a franchisor unlawfully ends its contract with a franchisee. It provides a cautionary tale for franchisors who too hastily terminate a franchise, without allowing the franchisee to trade out of its difficulties, or to minimise its losses in an orderly fashion.

Ray Dolan and Annaliese McConnell, a married couple, ran a Londis shop in

Drogheda, through their company Ranzett Ltd. By late 2008, the business was in financial difficulty, having run up significant debts to Londis. In December 2008, ADM Londis plc ("Londis") abruptly terminated Ranzett's Londis franchise.

In *ADM Londis plc v Ranzett Ltd (No 1)* [2013] IEHC 63, Hogan J. found that the company owed €561,283 in unpaid invoices, and ruled that Dolan and McConnell were liable as personal guarantors in respect of the company's debts. He also ruled, however, that the plaintiff was in breach of contract in that it had abruptly and, the judge concluded, unlawfully terminated the franchise agreement and debranded the Drogheda premises. These breaches effectively destroyed the value of the couple's business and precipitated the forfeiture of the lease on the premises.

While the plaintiff had urged that any losses were those of the company and not of the couple, the judge was satisfied that under the contractual relationship between the parties, Mr Dolan and Ms McConnell "have primary obligations" in respect of the contract. The "fate of the three defendants [was] entirely intertwined for the purpose of this damages claim."

The defendants claimed for losses under three heads: those arising from the termination of the franchise and consequent inability to trade; the losses flowing from the subsequent forfeiture of the lease on the business premises and the losses that arose when goods over which Londis had retention of title were separated out from non-Londis goods.

While Ranzett Ltd was admittedly "heavily under-capitalised" and facing into a difficult financial future, the breach of contract led to the forfeiture of the lease on the premises, with disastrous consequences. The defendants were unable to stay open and trade and in particular were unable to seek an alternative wholesale supplier.

While it was still likely that the defendant company would have eventually gone into liquidation, the judge was satisfied that the termination of the franchise deprived the company of critical breathing space. The very abrupt manner in which the franchise was terminated precipitated a financial catastrophe, leading to a "cascade of claims against the defendants." Given more time, Hogan J. believed, the defendants may well have been able to wind down their business in a more gradual manner. In particular, they may have been able to sell or assign their lease. Notably, the landlord was able to secure a new tenant soon after the forfeiture, a fact demonstrating that the lease had some value, though admittedly unknown. Given more time, the defendants would also have been in a position to dispose of specialist equipment leased from Friends First. The latter had repossessed the equipment and sold it in a fire sale, leaving Mr Dolan with an outstanding debt to Friends First of €155,000.

Hogan J. noted that calculating the company's value was made particularly difficult by the fact that the contract had been terminated in financially precarious times, with property values and retail sales in sharp decline. The company's lease and good location were important assets. Had the company continued trading into 2010, it would likely have struggled. The defendants valued the company based on weekly turnover as worth €900,000. They noted also a proposal to buy the company for €1.4 million, made in 2007 (though ultimately withdrawn). Nonetheless, Hogan J. was satisfied that, given the radical deterioration in economic conditions by the end of 2008, the company was in far worse shape by that stage. Using a multiplier of 10 times weekly turnover, the judge estimated the value of the business at

€420,000. He therefore proposed to award €420,000 in damages for the destruction of the business and forfeiture of the lease.

Londis had reserved title in respect of some of the stock supplied by it to the defendants. It had sought to recover this stock, but had decided not to exercise this right in respect of €65,000 of stock held by Ranzett Ltd. By the time Mr Dolan was made aware of this decision, however, he was unable to sell that stock. Hogan J. concluded that the defendants were entitled to claim for the plaintiff's failure "to exercise its contractual powers of retention of title in a manner which was also consistent [with] its fiduciary obligations under the trading terms agreement, so that these contractual entitlements were exercised in a manner which also took account of the defendants' interests."

The court found, however, that Mr Dolan was at fault as he had not promptly allowed Londis to repossess the stock on 4 December 2008. The plaintiff had been entitled to do so under the contract. In *McCord v Electricity Supply Board* [1980] I.L.R.M. 153, referring to s.34(1) of the Civil Liability Act 1961, the Supreme Court ruled that "damages for breach of contract may be reduced – or even entirely negatived – where the plaintiff has been guilty of fault or contributory negligence." Because Mr Dolan had, objectively speaking, been at fault in preventing Londis from repossessing the stock promptly, the judge reduced damages in respect of this heading by one-third, from €65,000 to €44,000.

There was insufficient evidence to determine losses in respect of the repossession of specialist equipment. While the re-possession was the "natural and foreseeable consequence" of the store's abrupt closure, Hogan J. was unable to quantify that loss and invited the parties to adduce evidence on this point. If the value of the equipment would likely have been higher than that obtained by Friends First in the fire sale, the difference would be credited to the defendants and set off against the amount owed to the plaintiff.

Hogan J. thus awarded the defendants €420,000 in respect of the value of the company and the forfeiture of the lease, and €44,000 in respect of the value of the goods which were not re-possessed following the retention of title exercise. This totalled €464,000. Hogan J. ruled that this be set off against the award of €561,283.91 previously made to the plaintiff.

See also *ADM Londis Plc v Ranzett Ltd (No 3)* [2014] IEHC 660 and *ADM Londis Plc v Ranzett Ltd (No 4)* [2015] IEHC 69, where Hogan J. considered outstanding matters and the issue of costs.

GUARANTEES

Allied Irish Banks Plc v McKenna, Donlon and Copeland [2014] IEHC 122 This case addresses a number of points in relation to the enforceability of guarantees, and, in particular, the operation of the defence of non est factum. It also examines whether or not independent legal advice is required for a commercial guarantee.

The plaintiff, AIB, sought summary judgment for €168,345 against the second and third defendants in respect of a 2007 guarantee limited to €250,000. The question that arose was whether the defendants had an arguable defence or, put another way, whether there was a "fair and reasonable probability of the defendants having a real or bona fide defence." (*Aer Rianta cpt v Ryanair (No 1)* [2001] 4 I.R.

607). Jurisdiction to grant summary judgment should be used sparingly (*Zurich Bank v McConnon* [2011] IEHC 75).

In 2007, the three defendants entered into a guarantee in which they jointly and severally guaranteed loans and an overdraft extended to Kapada Ltd, a company in respect of which they were directors and shareholders. A second guarantee was entered into in December 2007, limited to €250,000.

The second defendant, Mr Donlon, claimed he had not received independent legal advice prior to signing the guarantee. He also asserted that his signature thereon had not been witnessed and that the guarantee was not under seal. He also contended that AIB was in breach of the Consumer Protection Code 2006.

Addressing the absence of independent legal advice, Birmingham J. observed "there is no requirement in law that an adult entering into a guarantee on behalf of a company of which he is a director and shareholder should have independent legal advice." (See *O'Hara v Allied Irish Banks* [1985] BCLC 52). The lack of independent advice, therefore, did not in this case give rise to an arguable defence. (Different considerations potentially apply where the guarantor is not a director or shareholder but rather is a person in an intimate relationship with such a person. Here, however, this scenario did not arise. The guarantor was a director, and the purpose of the guarantee was clearly to secure the commercial interests of the company of which he himself was a director).

The second defendant had also alleged that the guarantee was not properly witnessed and was not made under seal. Birmingham J. rejected both propositions. Mr Donlon claimed that the solicitor who witnessed the guarantee had pre-signed it before Mr Donlon (and may not have been present when the defendants signed it). The judge observed, however, that it was not legally necessary for a guarantee to be witnessed. He also ruled that as the guarantee was supported by consideration (in the form of the extension of loan and overdraft facilities to the company) it was not necessary for it to be made under seal.

Nor did the Consumer Protection Code 2006 apply, as Mr Donlon was not acting as a consumer for this purpose. This was a commercial loan guaranteed by its directors; as such, consumer law and policy did not apply.

While Mr Donlon asserted a potential counterclaim based on how the bank operated Kapada's bank account, this appeared to be no more than a vague assertion. Simply asserting that you may have a counterclaim, without more detail, is not sufficient to avoid summary judgment. While the threshold for being granted leave to defend is low, the judge observed, "it has not been crossed by Mr Donlon." It was thus "very clear" that the second defendant had no defence. Summary judgment was granted in respect of the second defendant.

The third defendant, Mr Copeland, raised a possible defence of non est factum. Mr Copeland effectively argued that he had not realised the consequences of assuming joint and several liability in respect of the debt. Instead, due to a misunderstanding on his part, he thought that he would only be liable for one third of Kapada's debt if the guarantee were to be enforced.

The principles relating to non est factum were set out in *Tedcastle McCormack and Company v McCrystal*, unreported, High Court, Morris J., 15 March 1999. In order to invoke non est factum, a person must show:

> "(a) That there was a radical or fundamental difference between what he signed and what he thought he was signing;
> (b) That the mistake was as to the general character of the document as opposed to the legal effect;
> (c) That there was a lack of negligence i.e. that he took all reasonable precautions in the circumstances to find out what the document was."

While he understood he had signed a guarantee, Mr Copeland assumed that he would only be liable thereunder for one-third of the debt and not for the whole debt. He noted that he suffered from depression and doubted his ability at that time to understand fully what he had signed. He claimed that he understood the word 'joint' in the guarantee to refer to the fact that there were three guarantors and did not realise it meant he could be made personally liable for the entirety of up to €250,000 in company debt.

Even accepting this evidence as true, and bearing in mind the low threshold for obtaining leave to defend, Birmingham J. did not accept that this defence was arguable. Mr Copeland knew he was signing a guarantee, but claimed he misunderstood its legal effect. The second limb of the test in *Tedcastle* rules out mistakes as to legal effect. While it was arguable, the judge said, that "there was a radical or fundamental difference between what he signed and what he thought he was signing" (satisfying the first limb of that test), Birmingham J. nonetheless concluded that "it still seems to me that there was such a degree of carelessness on the part of Mr. Copeland in signing the document that he cannot now repudiate what he signed."

Mr Copeland was a company director. He acknowledged he had read parts of the guarantee document but was not sure if he had read para.20 thereof. He claimed, however, that even if he had read it, he would still have misunderstood its legal effect. Paragraph 20 stated that liability under the guarantee was joint and several and continued to apply even if it was held no longer binding on other guarantors. In particular, it stipulated that "this guarantee shall operate not only as a joint and several guarantee by all of the Guarantors, but also a separate guarantee by each of them."

While acknowledging that the clause "would not receive an award from the Campaign for Plain English", Birmingham J. did not consider the language thereof "exceptionally technical." Its meaning, he said, "would have been apparent to any businessman." The average businessperson would at least have appreciated that "on one interpretation there was an exposure to €250,000, which was after all the only figure mentioned in the guarantee…" If unclear on the point, the guarantor should have realised that it would have been prudent to seek advice. He could, the judge observed, possibly have consulted the solicitor who witnessed the guarantees for clarification.

In similar circumstances, in *ACC Bank plc v Kelly* [2011] IEHC 7, Clarke J. noted:

> "I am not satisfied that any person taking the trouble to read the clause in question could have any difficulty in understanding what it meant. Even if

> someone had such difficulty then it is incumbent on such a person to take advice."

He further observed that if a person signed without reading they "must accept the consequences." If he or she reads it and does not understand it, he or she should not sign without advice. If he or she is willing to sign the document without understanding it fully "then again they must accept the consequences."

Mr Copeland claimed that he had not realised he had misunderstood the document's meaning, and therefore did not know that he needed to seek advice. Yet Birmingham J. concluded that where

> "a businessman signs documents of a legal and technical nature without fully understanding their meaning and without taking advice that he must accept the consequences. It also seems to me that the position extends to the situation where the document is such that it would be widely understood by businessmen, if the individual called on to sign is for one reason or another, in a position where unlike the generality of businessmen he would fail to understand the document or is at risk of misunderstanding the nature of the document. If that is the situation, then he must take advice or suffer the consequences of not doing so."

Birmingham J. observed that pleas of non est factum rarely succeed and that judges should entertain the defence sparingly. As Donovan L.J. observed in *Muskham Finance Limited v Howard* [1963] 1 Q.B. 904 at 912, the plea must be

> "... kept within narrow limits. Much confusion and uncertainty would result in the field of contract and elsewhere if a man were permitted to try to disown his signature simply by asserting that he did not understand that which he had signed."

The defence, the judge concluded, did not apply where a businessman claims not to remember whether or not he read the full guarantee document but had he done so he would have misinterpreted it. Having failed to make out an arguable defence, summary judgment was also granted against the third defendant.

Northern Bank Ltd. t/a Danske Bank v Michael and Bridget Quinn [2014] IEHC 311 This case concerns guarantees entered into by the defendants, Michael and Bridget Quinn. The plaintiff bank sought summary judgment against the defendants, which they in turn opposed, claiming they had a number of arguable points of defence.

The plaintiff bank claimed that the defendants had given a guarantee limited to UK£500,000 in respect of the debts of Cloughvalley Stores Northern Ireland Ltd. The latter company having defaulted on its debts, the bank sought to enforce the couple's guarantee.

The fundamental question in a case for summary judgment, based on well-settled authority, was whether the defendants had a "fair or reasonable probability of ... having a real or bona fide defence." (See for instance *Danske Bank v Durkan*

New Homes [2010] IESC 22). The bank maintained that the defendants in this case had no bona fide defence.

Hedigan J. first noted that the defendants had also commenced proceedings in Northern Ireland challenging the appointment of an administrator. They claimed that they had been denied access to certain documents. These documents, however, had no relevance to the case before Hedigan J., which concerned solely the enforceability of the guarantee. The Northern Irish proceedings and the claim for discovery therein were, he said, entirely separate from the claim in the instant case and were not relevant to the motion for summary judgment in respect of the guarantee. Should the defendants wish to seek discovery of the relevant documents, they would have to do so in the Northern Irish proceedings.

The defendants relied on a number of other defences.

1. They claimed that the case should have been taken in Northern Ireland. In response, Hedigan J. noted that while they could have entered a conditional appearance and challenged jurisdiction at an earlier juncture in these proceedings, it was now too late to do so. They had accepted the jurisdiction of the Irish courts. Given, moreover, that they were resident in Ireland, the Irish courts clearly had jurisdiction to hear the case.
2. They also maintained that there was no privity of contract as the guarantee was, they claimed, with "Northern Tailored Solutions", and not the bank. The judge, however, noted that the guarantee clearly stated that it was "between Northern Bank Ltd. trading as Danske Bank and themselves." While the facility letter admittedly contained the heading 'Northern Tailored Solutions', this was, the judge said, "of no significance."
3. They claimed also that there was no consideration given in respect of the guarantee, but again, the judge rejected this contention. The bank had, he said, provided consideration by affording credit and banking facilities to the company. This was, he said, "good and valuable consideration."
4. The defendants also claimed that they did not have independent legal advice. Hedigan J. noted, however, that the defendants were adults possessed of their full faculties and not infirm or compromised in any way. The lack of independent legal advice did not afford them an arguable defence. Indeed, while the bank had advised them to seek independent legal advice, they had chosen not to do so.
5. The judge also rejected the assertion that the claim was statute-barred. The guarantee was an 'on-demand facility' in respect of which "time runs from the date of demand", namely October 2011. The proceedings having commenced in December 2012, the plaintiff was well within time.
6. The judge also ruled that the proceedings commenced in Northern Ireland had "no bearing on these proceedings and may continue independently in that jurisdiction."
7. Hedigan J. also rejected the purported defence that the claim was not properly particularised, the particulars in the endorsement of claim

having been "sufficient to enable the defendants to know whether they should defend or not."

8. He further refuted the claim that the bank had not made a formal demand for payment in respect of the debts. The bank had, indeed, formally issued a written demand in November 2011, calling for immediate payment of UK£4.7 million. The company's property was sold to satisfy the debt in part, but a balance of UK£3.9 million nonetheless remained owing.
9. The defendants also claimed that the affidavits of employees of the bank, detailing the debts of the bank, contained hearsay. The judge however rejected this claim. The employees had offered prima facie evidence that was admissible before the court.

Hedigan J. thus concluded that there was no arguable defence, and that the guarantee was clearly valid. The plaintiff was entitled to summary judgment for UK£500,000 plus interest.

IMPLIED TERMS

See *Maloney v Danske Bank A/S* [2014] IEHC 441, discussed above under CONDITIONS PRECEDENT.

INCORPORATION OF TERMS/IMPLIED TERMS

See also *James Elliott Construction Ltd. v Irish Asphalt Ltd.* [2014] IESC 74 discussed below under SALE OF GOODS.

Noreside Construction Limited v Irish Asphalt Ltd. [2014] IESC 68 This Supreme Court decision upholds the previous High Court decision of Finlay Geoghegan J. reported in the *Annual Review of Irish Law 2011* (at pp. 262-265). The case involves a 'battle of the forms' type scenario where the question arises as to which of two rival sets of terms and conditions formed part of a contract. The overriding message emanating from the judgment is that one should not depend on general references to terms and conditions in invoices and delivery documents as a means of incorporating those terms and conditions into a contract. (This point is also emphasised in the Supreme Court decision in *James Elliott Construction Ltd. v Irish Asphalt Ltd.* [2014] IESC 74 discussed below under SALE OF GOODS). If a party wishes to ensure that an exclusion or limitation clause makes it into a contractual agreement, the best strategy is to negotiate an express clause to that effect forming part of a formal written agreement. In the alternative, the specific terms and conditions should be given directly to the client's managers, in documents expressly containing those conditions.

The defendant/appellant in this case had supplied infill material (aggregate) to the plaintiff/respondent construction company for use in a construction project. It later transpired that the aggregate contained pyrite and was not suitable for use as under-floor infill. The aggregate had in fact been used for this purpose, as a result of which serious structural damage was caused to various buildings.

In the High Court the plaintiff had asserted that its particular terms and conditions—which included a requirement that the defendant indemnify Noreside against losses and damage arising from the use of the aggregate—had been incorporated. These terms and conditions were said to have been printed on the back of a purchase order form. Noting that the front of the order form made no reference to the terms on the reverse and had not been brought to the defendant's attention before the agreement was concluded, Finlay Geoghegan J. ruled that these terms did not form part of the contract.

The defendant claimed that its liability for damage and losses was limited by a clause in its standard terms and conditions which, it claimed, had been incorporated into the contract by signature, reasonable notice and/or custom in the trade. The defendant specifically claimed that its delivery dockets had been signed by the plaintiff's staff on delivery of the aggregate. These dockets contained the following statement at the foot of the page: "This material is sold subject to the terms and conditions available on request." Clause 8 of Irish Asphalt's terms and conditions purported to limit its liability for defective product to the cost of its replacement. The company would not, it asserted, otherwise accept any liability for losses arising from the supply or use of defective materials.

The High Court rejected the defendant's assertion. Finlay Geoghegan J. concluded that the delivery dockets were not contractual documents and their signature did not serve to incorporate the terms and conditions referred to thereon. Finlay Geoghegan J. further ruled that the reference in the delivery dockets did not constitute sufficient notice of the terms and conditions. Nor was there enough evidence of a well-established custom in the trade limiting a quarry's liability for defective aggregate.

The Supreme Court agreed, dismissing the appeal. In a decision in which O'Donnell and MacMenamim JJ. concurred, Dunne J. concluded that the defendant's terms and conditions had not been incorporated. In this case, a concluded 'master contract' was reached on 26 March 2003. Each subsequent order and delivery gave rise to a separate and distinct contract but each new contract, the court ruled, was on the same terms and conditions as originally negotiated in the master contract. While the parties were free to vary the originally agreed terms and conditions, the dockets did not, Dunne J. found, have the effect of altering the original agreement or adding new terms.

The question that arose was whether the delivery dockets had played a role in making the contract—in its formation—or whether they simply acted as a record of its execution or performance. In short, were they contractual or post-contractual documents? While not dismissing outright the possibility of delivery dockets having contractual effect in appropriate cases, Dunne J. concluded, given the particular facts of this case, that the dockets' role was to record the particular order and delivery. These were not 'contract-making' documents. The dockets, in other words, had the primary purpose of recording the performance of an already concluded contract. While they "had a contractual purpose in the execution of the contract, they did not have a contractual effect in the sense of making or varying the contract." In other words, they did not play a role in the contract's formation.

As Auld L.J. noted in *Grogan v Robin Meredith Plant Hire* [1996] C.L.C. 1127 in order for a document to give rise to a variation in contractual terms, the critical test was whether the document came "within the class of a document which the party receiving it knew contained, or which a reasonable man would expect to contain, relevant contractual conditions."

Dunne J. placed particular emphasis on the fact that the dockets did not in fact expressly list or contain the relevant terms and conditions, nor did they refer to specific terms and conditions that would have been well known in the industry. Notably, they made no reference to price. Rather "they were created for the purpose of recording the type and amount of aggregate delivered and whether that aggregate was collected or delivered on site."

Dunne J. also agreed that the actions of the parties were not sufficient to give reasonable notice of the conditions. In particular, she observed that the plaintiff had never received a copy of Irish Asphalt's conditions, nor were they "identified in any shape or form or specified by reference to any known industry-wide terms and conditions." The vagueness of the reference on the docket was instrumental in this context. Had the proviso specifically referred to well-known industry terms and conditions, or had specific terms and conditions been listed or set out on the document, the situation might have been different. Instead, the docket contained a bald and vague statement, lacking specificity or substance, referring to unspecified conditions available elsewhere, without any elaboration. While noting that a party may rely on terms and conditions even where the other side has not read them, Dunne J. noted that: "the document relied on by the party asserting the terms and conditions should *actually contain either the conditions themselves or in some other way identify the terms and conditions relied on.*" (Emphasis added).

The onerous nature of the limitation clause in this case appears to have played a significant role in the judge's ruling (as it did in *James Elliott Construction*, discussed below.) The limitation clause, Dunne J. noted, "could only be described as onerous." The more onerous the clause, she added, the greater the onus on the person relying on it to show that sufficient steps were taken to give reasonable notice thereof. In this case, she concluded, the steps taken were not sufficient to give reasonable notice.

Dunne J. also rejected the contention that the terms and conditions had been incorporated by course of dealing:

> "The fact that the proviso is contained in a large number of delivery dockets does not assist Irish Asphalt in circumstances where Irish Asphalt has never given any reasonable notice of its terms and conditions to Noreside … The fundamental problem in this case for Irish Asphalt is that over the entire period of dealing between the parties, Irish Asphalt never supplied its terms and conditions to Noreside …"

Nor was there sufficient evidence of incorporation by custom or practice. According to McDermott, *Contract Law* (Dublin: Round Hall, 2001) at para.7.07, for this to occur, the term in question would have to be certain, reasonable and of "sufficient notoriety that the parties must be taken to have known of it and intended it should form part of the contract." Dunne J. concluded that there was insufficient evidence of a custom well known within the trade that the liability of quarry owners would, in the absence of an express exclusion or limiting clause, automatically be limited.

While the judgment does not rule out the possibility of including terms and conditions in a contract by means of a delivery docket, it certainly underlines that such a strategy may be very risky indeed. It also emphasises that simply referring to unspecified terms and conditions in a document will not be sufficient to ensure their incorporation, unless they are well-known industry standard conditions and expressly identified as such. The better approach, therefore, is to expressly list the relevant terms and conditions in documentation directed to the client, preferably at senior decision-making level. Dunne J.'s decision exhibits a strict approach to incorporation, and suggests that parties would be best served negotiating for express conclusion of such terms in a written, signed master contract. If terms and conditions are to be referenced in a document, either they should be expressly listed thereon or the document should make reference to specific industry-standard terms and conditions that are well known to the parties. Vague references to 'terms and conditions available on request' will not, it appears, be sufficient for incorporation. The judgment also underlines the risks involved in making reference to terms and conditions in documents where those documents might not be regarded as having contractual effect.

MISREPRESENTATION

See also *Irish Banking Resolution Corporation v McCaughey* [2014] IESC 44, discussed above under COLLATERAL CONTRACTS.

PRIVITY OF CONTRACT

Murphy v Allianz Plc [2014] IEHC 692 This case concerns an application to strike out proceedings on the basis that they disclosed no reasonable cause of action. The case has some interesting contract law points, and provides a good example of the application of the doctrine of privity of contract. It also illustrates the operation of s.62 of the Civil Liability Act 1961, which allows a person to lay claim to insurance monies in cases where an insured party is bankrupt or an insured company has been wound up.

The plaintiff in this case was a sub-contractor working for a Mr McShane, who in turn worked for a contractor Bri-Mo Ltd. In early 2004, the plaintiff was injured on site when bricks fell on his foot. A year later, the incident was reported to the defendant insurance company, Allianz, which subsequently asked for further information. In particular, it had repeatedly asked Bri-Mo for an auditor's certificate regarding wages that was required under the policy, but which was never forthcoming. As a result of this failure, Allianz refused to indemnify the company and repudiated liability in respect of the claim. In 2010, Bri-Mo was struck off the register of companies for failing to make corporate returns. In 2011, the High Court ruled in favour of the plaintiff, in default of defence, in an action taken against Bri-Mo in respect of the injury.

The plaintiff sought various reliefs for damages for breach of statutory duty, breach of contract, negligence, negligent misstatement, misrepresentation, and breach of duty. He also claimed that under s.62 of the Civil Liability Act 1961, damages and costs payable to the plaintiff "constitute monies payable to the plaintiff in discharge of a valid claim which the defendant is obliged, under the terms of an insurance policy between it and Bri-Mo Ltd., to pay the plaintiff."

Section 62 states that where an insured person has effected a policy of insurance in respect of liability for a wrong, and that person

> "if an individual, becomes a bankrupt or dies or, if a corporate body, is wound up or, if a partnership or other unincorporated association, is dissolved, moneys payable to the insured under the policy shall be applicable only to discharging in full all valid claims against the insured in respect of which those moneys are payable, and no part of those moneys shall be assets of the insured or applicable to the payment of the debts (other than those claims) of the insured in the bankruptcy or in the administration of the estate of the insured or in the winding-up or dissolution, and no such claim shall be provable in the bankruptcy, administration, winding-up or dissolution."

In other words, in the particular circumstances laid out in that section, it requires that the insurance monies be paid directly to meet the claims of the wronged party.

Section 62 requires that, when a corporate body is involved, it must have been wound up. Crucially, however, while Bri-Mo had been struck off the register of companies, it had never been wound up. Allianz also maintained that it was entitled to refuse the indemnity and repudiate liability as the auditor's certificate had not been supplied to it, as required by a precondition in the insurance contract. The defendant further argued that there was no contract or contractual nexus between the parties. It maintained that there was no duty of care between an insurance company and a person claiming against an insured party.

Gilligan J. agreed to strike out proceedings. Under Ord.19 r.28 of the Rules of the Superior Courts, a court may strike out proceedings where they disclose no reasonable cause of action. An action may also be stayed or dismissed where it is shown to be frivolous or vexatious. The court, furthermore, has an inherent jurisdiction to stay proceedings to avoid an abuse of the process of the court. In *Barry v Buckley* [1981] I.R. 306, Costello J. observed that "[t]his jurisdiction should be used sparingly and only in clear cases." The purpose of this jurisdiction is to avoid injustice where continuing the proceedings "cannot be justified and is manifestly causing irrevocable damage to a defendant." In *Sun Fat Chan v Osseous Ltd* [1992] 1 I.R. 425, McCarthy J. repeated that the courts should be slow to entertain such an application and that if an amendment to the statement of claim would save the action from foundering, then the action should be allowed to proceed.

The key issue according to Gilligan J. was the interpretation of s.62. For s.62 to apply in this case the insured company must first be wound up. It was quite clear, however, that Bri-Mo had not been wound up or liquidated. On that basis alone, the judge observed, the plaintiff's case was "doomed to failure."

Even if Bri-Mo had been wound up, he added, the plaintiff would have to have shown that he was entitled to the monies payable to the insured under the policy. The judge was satisfied, however, that the claim had been validly repudiated over seven years previously, a fact of which the plaintiff's solicitors had been aware from at least 2010. Bri-Mo had never challenged this repudiation.

Additionally, even if Bri-Mo had been wound up, the plaintiff's claim was not a valid one against the insured, in particular because the quantum of liability had not yet been determined.

Gilligan J. ruled, moreover, that the defendant owed no legal duty to the plaintiff under contract, statute or tort. Citing *Hu v Duleek Formwork Ltd. (in liquidation) and Aviva* [2013] IEHC 50, the judge also concluded that there was no privity of contract in this case between the defendant and plaintiff. The plaintiff could not, therefore, seek to enforce a contract of insurance between Bri-Mo and Allianz.

The judge thus determined that the circumstances merited striking out proceedings on the basis that the proceedings disclosed no reasonable cause of action and (employing the court's inherent jurisdiction) that the case was bound to fail.

RESTRAINT OF TRADE

Levinwick Limited v Hollingsworth [2014] IEHC 333 This case illustrates the high threshold that must be satisfied in order to enforce a restraint of trade clause in an employment contract. The plaintiff owned a chain of pharmacies, including Blake's pharmacy in Celbridge, Co. Kildare. The defendant, Mr Hollingsworth, a pharmacist, had worked as pharmacy manager in Blake's pharmacy from August 2007 to March 2013, at which point he left to work in pharmacies in North Dublin and then South Kildare. In January 2014, however, Mr Hollingsworth returned to Celbridge to work as a pharmacy manager in a rival local pharmacy.

When Mr Hollingsworth commenced work with Blake's pharmacy in 2007, he had entered into an employment contract, clause 15 of which purported to restrict his choice of employment were he to leave the plaintiff's employ. Under clause 15, Mr Hollingsworth had agreed not to work in, manage, own or run a pharmacy or a business trading in similar goods within a two mile vicinity of Blake's pharmacy. This restriction was to run for two years after his employment with the plaintiff ended. The covenant also required that Hollingsworth not solicit any person who had been one of the plaintiff's customers in the 12 months before Hollingsworth left employment. The clause further stipulated that he agreed "that all of the above restrictions are reasonable in all the circumstances and are no more than is necessary for the protection of the interests of the Pharmacy." If the restrictions were found to be unreasonable in relation to the area, duration or type of service, the covenant would still apply in relation to such area, duration or type of service as a court considered reasonable.

A covenant in restraint of trade, prima facie, is unenforceable at common law but can be enforced provided it (a) protects a legitimate business interest and (b) is no wider than is reasonably necessary for the protection of that business interest. The burden of proving the covenant's reasonableness lies on the person who seeks to rely on it.

As Clarke J. explained in *Murgitroyd & Co. Ltd. v Purdy* [2005] 3 I.R. 12 at 21, the relevant restriction must be "reasonable to protect the goodwill of the employer", having particular regard to its nature and extent. Clauses preventing the solicitation of former customers should not be "excessively wide." (21). An employee may also be prevented from setting up business within the employer's catchment area. The prohibition's temporal and geographical scope is particularly relevant in determining its reasonableness. Clarke J. noted that a more restrictive view is adopted when covenants in employment contracts are considered when compared with restrictions in contracts for the sale of a business. Restrictive covenants in employment contracts are "never reasonable as such" and will only be approved in very specific circumstances where an employee holds personal knowledge or influence over customers such that he could take advantage of the employer's trade (21).

The plaintiff argued that, in the absence of the restriction, its customers would likely follow the defendant to another Celbridge pharmacy. It asserted that it normally took up to two and a half years for a new pharmacy manager to become established in a new area, and to forge new customer relationships.

The plaintiff did not claim that the defendant had in fact solicited former customers or used any trade secrets but contended that the clause was nonetheless necessary to safeguard its goodwill. It claimed, moreover, that the pharmacy's business had declined in recent years and asserted that 75 per cent of that decline was caused by the defendant's departure.

The plaintiff relied in part on a letter sent in March 2010 to the Independent Pharmacy Ownership Scheme (IPOS) in which the defendant had placed particular emphasis on the pharmacy's strong bonds with its customers and its exceptional customer service. The judge noted, however, that the context in which the letter was written had to be considered. The IPOS ran a scheme to help young pharmacists buy their own businesses, and the defendant was seeking their assistance. The letter, moreover, stressed the strong relationship between the staff as a group and their customers, and had not singled out the defendant as having any particularly strong relationship with customers.

The defendant noted that he had left Celbridge for 10 months before returning, and was unlikely to have had such a strong bond with customers. He claimed that the plaintiff had overstated customer loyalty to him as a pharmacist: customers were, he said, more likely to attend the pharmacy because it was close by or had good parking and maintained that it would be unusual to follow a pharmacist to another business.

McGovern J. noted that clause 15 was in restraint of trade. Thus, it could only be enforced "if it protects a legitimate business interest of the plaintiff and is no wider than is reasonably necessary for the protection of that interest." For this purpose, if the clause is to be enforceable the plaintiff had to demonstrate that "both the nature of the restriction and its extent must be reasonable to protect the goodwill of the employer ...". The plaintiff had not sought to show that a less onerous clause would not have been effective in protecting its goodwill.

The judge rejected the proposition that Hollingsworth was, before his departure, the face of the pharmacy, or that customers viewed him as such. He also rejected the proposition that the decline in Blake's pharmacy's fortunes was attributable mainly to the defendant's departure therefrom. Pharmacy retailers had faced various significant challenges in the years since 2008. Between 2009 and 2013, turnover at Blake's pharmacy had declined by 26.5 per cent, this decline having commenced long before the defendant's departure. Increased local competition from new pharmacies and reduced prescription fees played a significant part in this decline. Notably, the plaintiff could, the judge observed, have determined empirically whether and if so how many customers had followed the defendant by examining customers' patient records, but had failed to do so. There was, in other words, insufficient evidence of the claimed impact of the defendant's departure.

The judge also noted that the pharmacy had "a substantial number of employees." At the time Hollingsworth was employed there, Blake's pharmacy had two full-time pharmacists, including the defendant, and two locums, as well as eight or nine assistant staff. As pharmacy manager, much of Hollingsworth's work involved behind-the-scenes administrative and managerial tasks that would normally have kept him away from customers. The other pharmacist ran the dispensary and had more personal contact with customers.

The judge thus concluded that the restraint of trade clause was not enforceable. In particular, the plaintiff had not demonstrated that the nature of the defendant's role and work was such that clause 15 was necessary to protect its goodwill. He therefore refused the plaintiff's claim for an injunction and/or damages.

SALE OF GOODS

James Elliott Construction Ltd. v Irish Asphalt Ltd. [2014] IESC 74 This is a Supreme Court appeal from the High Court decision of Charleton J., [2011] IEHC 269, reported in the *Annual Review of Irish Law 2011* (pp. 274-280). It concerns a number of important issues relating to the meaning of the implied terms of merchantability and fitness for purpose in Sale of Goods legislation. Additionally, the judgment provides an extensive examination of the rules relating to the incorporation of contractual terms, in particular, of limitation clauses, and the effect of documents such as delivery dockets and credit notes in a contractual context. The verdict highlights the great care required in ensuring incorporation of a business' preferred terms, and emphasises that general references to unspecified and unknown terms and conditions will not usually suffice to ensure incorporation thereof. Together with the Supreme Court in *Noreside Construction Limited v Irish Asphalt Ltd.* [2014] IESC 68, discussed above under INCORPORATION OF TERMS, the decision possibly signals a harder line on the incorporation of exclusion and limitation clauses. Ultimately, however, the Supreme Court referred certain questions of EU law to the Court of Justice of the European Union, the outcome of which may have profound implications for the laws relating to liability for defective goods.

The plaintiff, Elliott Construction, was involved in building a youth centre in Ballymun. In its construction, it had used infill material (aggregate or crushed rock) supplied by the defendant, Irish Asphalt, from the latter's quarry. It turned out, however, that this material contained pyrite, which expanded on contact with water, seriously damaging the building and requiring extensive remediation works costing €1.55 million. James Elliott carried out the remedial works at its own expense, and sought compensation from Irish Asphalt for damage arising from the pyrite heave. After exhaustive examination of the complex evidence, the High Court determined that the damage caused was due to the presence of pyrite in the material supplied by the defendant, and thus found against the latter.

In its appeal, the defendant accepted that the pyrite heave had caused the relevant damage. The fundamental question, therefore, was whether it was the plaintiff or defendant that was liable for the cost of remediation.

The High Court decision In an extensive, thorough and forensic High Court judgment, Charleton J. had found that the pyrite contained in the aggregate had expanded causing serious damage to the building. He also concluded that the contract between the parties included a requirement that the infill comply with the national standard IS EN13242:2002 (based on an EU standard) for what is termed 'clause 804' aggregate. He determined that the aggregate in fact supplied did not meet that standard. The contractual conditions as to the merchantability of goods and their fitness for purpose (inserted by the Sale of Goods Act 1893 (the "1893 Act"), as amended by the Sale of Goods and Supply of Services Act 1980 (the "1980 Act")) meant, he said, that clause 804 aggregate should be sufficiently inert, strong and durable so that it did not move or heave or otherwise cause damage to the building. The implied terms as to fitness for purpose and merchantability required that the aggregate should not be subject to chemical changes, should be durable, should not break down due to unusually high or low temperatures or contact with moisture within reasonable limits, and should be strong enough to serve its purpose.

The material supplied by Irish Asphalt, the High Court found, had in fact failed to meet the required standards for clause 804. The material was "poor quality aggregate" and failed several quality tests. In particular, its susceptibility to water absorption rates was high (good quality aggregate should have low water absorption values). It was also less resistant to expansive and weathering forces, and more prone to heave. The material, in short, failed the required clause 804 standard, and meant that the defendant had breached the contract.

The High Court also determined that the parties' contract contained implied conditions as to merchantability and fitness for purpose, implied by ss.14(2) and (4) of the 1893 Act. These terms had been breached, the court found, as the aggregate was not sufficiently inert, strong and durable. Charleton J. rejected the proposition that a limitation clause had excluded liability for the damage, concluding that the defendant's terms and conditions had not been validly incorporated into the contract.

The Supreme Court appeal On appeal, Irish Asphalt denied that there had been a breach of the implied terms as to merchantability and fitness for purpose. It also contended that liability for breach was limited by clause 8 of its terms and conditions of sale, which purported to limit liability for defective products to the cost of replacing them. If this limitation were to apply, it could make a significant difference to the extent of liability. Remediation had cost the plaintiff €1.55 million. The aggregate, by contrast, had cost €25,000, including VAT.

The defendant also claimed that a breach of the clause 804 standard had not been properly established. It further contended that by making a finding that there was a breach of implied terms as to inertness, durability and strength, the High Court had created a new domestic law standard that was impermissible under EU law.

The Supreme Court (O'Donnell, MacMenamin and Dunne JJ.) issued a joint ruling of the court. It rejected the defendant's attempt to challenge the High Court's findings of fact: there was evidence, the court found, to allow the High Court judge to find as he did. It is well established that the Supreme Court will be very slow to unsettle findings of facts and inferences of fact made at trial at first instance. (See *Hay v O'Grady* [1992] 1 I.R. 210).

The defendant claimed, however, that the tests carried out on the aggregate in 2009 were not legally effective, as EU and national standards required such material to be tested at the time of delivery, when the product was placed on the market, and not thereafter. Requiring that the materials meet the standards at a later point in time after delivery was incompatible, it said, with the existing EU and national standards, and thus in breach of EU law. It claimed, also that there had been no breach of the implied terms as to merchantability and fitness for purpose or, if there had been, such a conclusion was not compliant with EU law.

The Supreme Court concluded that the contract required that clause 804 aggregate be supplied, and that the aggregate supplied should have complied with this standard. Compliance with this standard was to be assessed first at the time of delivery of the product, but the court ruled that it was also possible, by subsequent testing, to show that the product, as a matter of probability, had not complied with that standard as of the time of delivery. The Construction Products Directive 89/106/EEC required that goods met its essential requirements "during an economically reasonable working life". As such, testing during the product's lifetime was permitted in order to determine compliance. The court thus rejected the proposition that the testing methods set out in the appendix to the relevant standard were the only methods of testing that could be used. The tests used, the court ruled, were sufficient to show that the product could not have satisfied the standard as of the date of delivery. On the evidence, it was very improbable, the court added, that the product had complied with the standard as of that date.

Merchantable Quality The court noted that as this was a sale in the course of business, s.14 of the 1893 Act (as amended by the 1980 Act) implied conditions into the contract that the supplied goods must be of merchantable quality and fit for purpose. As amended by s.10 of the 1980 Act, s.14(2) of the 1893 Act requires (subject to exceptions that are not relevant here) that "Where the seller sells goods in the course of a business there is an implied condition that the goods supplied under the contract are of merchantable quality...". Under s.14(3), goods are defined as being of merchantable quality

> if they are as fit for the purpose or purposes for which goods of that kind are commonly bought and as durable as it is reasonable to expect having regard to any description applied to them, the price (if relevant) and all the other relevant circumstances, and any reference in this Act to unmerchantable goods shall be construed accordingly.

The phrase 'merchantable quality', the court observed, is rather archaic in form and origins. The law developed, it noted, such that the concept gradually moved from one focussed on the vendor's perspective, which emphasised the saleability of the item (where it did not matter if the goods were of good or bad grade provided they were sellable) towards a greater focus on the acceptability of the item to the average purchaser. In *Australian Knitting Mills v Grant* (1933) 50 C.L.R. 387, Dixon J. observed that goods are of merchantable quality if they are "in such an actual state that a buyer fully acquainted with the facts and, therefore, knowing what hidden defects exist and not being limited to their apparent condition would buy them without abatement of the price...and without special terms."

The question that arose therefore was whether it was sufficient for a good to be of merchantable quality that it be suitable for *some* purposes for which it is normally used, even if it was not suitable for some or all *other* purposes. The defendants relied on *Aswan Engineering Establishment Co. v Lupdine Ltd* [1987] 1 W.L.R. 1 as support for the proposition that if goods are sold under a general description and are normally used for several purposes, they are merchantable if they are fit for any of these purposes, even if they are not fit for all those purposes. The defendant argued that while the aggregate was not fit for the purpose of being used under the load-bearing cement floors of the youth centre, it was normally sold for several purposes, including for road construction, and for car parks and open areas. As the product was suitable for some of those purposes, the defendant maintained, it must be taken that the product was of merchantable quality.

Yet the court noted that other cases such as *Rogers v Parish (Scarborough) Ltd.* [1987] Q.B. 933 cast doubt on this view. In *Cavalier Marketing (Australia) Pty Ltd v Rasell* (1990) 96 A.L.R. 375, in the Supreme Court of Queensland, Cooper J. pointed out at p.400that "goods may have more than one normal purpose" and where that was so "all normal purposes for which goods are commonly bought [should] be brought into consideration. Fitness is tested against each of these purposes and none are to be excluded."

In fact, the Supreme Court in this case was not satisfied that the aggregate was suitable for some of the purposes for which it had been used; this, it concluded, had not been demonstrated. The court was not satisfied that the particular aggregate was necessarily fit for these other purposes. The evidence "did not demonstrate that a purchaser with knowledge of the defect would nevertheless pay a similar price for such material for use even under a car park and in open space areas."

Assuming, however, that it had been suitable for some purposes to which it was put, and that it was saleable to a purchaser who knew it contained pyrite and that it was liable to swell and heave, the court concluded that this fact alone would not be sufficient for the product to be merchantable. While the common law concept of merchantability focussed on saleability, and therefore leaned towards the interests of merchants, modern legislation places greater emphasis on the experiences of the customer. Notably, the court observed, the purpose of the 1980 Act had been to change the law in favour of the purchaser, and in particular to lock in certain protections for consumers. The provisions of s.14(3) of the 1893 Act, as amended, were clear and unambiguous. It refers to the "purpose or purposes" for which goods of that kind are commonly bought.

The court therefore believed the approach in *Rogers v Parish* was the most sensible. It noted that sellers would be more knowledgeable about the product and the purposes to which it might be put. A buyer, by contrast, may not be aware that the good had multiple uses and may well assume that the purpose he or she has in mind is the product's sole purpose. Following the reasoning in *Aswan* would require the court to find the product merchantable even though it was unfit for the purpose for which it was bought (possibly the product's most obvious purpose) on the basis that it is fit for a purpose of which the buyer may be ignorant. An interpretation of s.14(3), the court concluded, that placed the risk on the seller was "sensible and logical." Sellers are normally more aware than buyers of the likely uses to which their products will be put. The court thus found that the High Court was correct in finding that the goods were not of merchantable quality. It was, in short, not sufficient that the goods be suitable for some purposes but not all purposes for which they are normally is bought.

Fitness for a specified purpose The Supreme Court, however, overruled the High Court's parallel conclusion that there had been a breach of the specific and separate condition implied by s.14(4) as to fitness for a purpose made known to the seller, either expressly or impliedly. S.14(4) stipulates that where

> the seller sells goods in the course of a business and the buyer, expressly or by implication, makes known to the seller any particular purpose for which the goods are being bought, there is an implied condition that the goods supplied under the contract are reasonably fit for that purpose, whether or not that is a purpose for which such goods are commonly supplied, except where the circumstances show that the buyer does not rely, or that it is unreasonable for him to rely, on the seller's skill or judgement.

While there is some overlap between this condition and that implied by s.14(2) there are important differences. In particular, s.14(4) presupposes that the buyer will make the particular purpose known to the seller, either expressly or implicitly. S.14(4) also presupposes reliance on the seller's skill and judgment and can be displaced by evidence that there was no such reliance.

While the High Court was satisfied that the material was not reasonably fit for a purpose that had been notified to the seller under this particular subsection, the Supreme Court disagreed. S.14(4), it said, may be triggered in cases where "the particular purpose has been made known by implication", but it is not sufficient under s.14(4) that the seller simply knows the purpose for which the product is intended. There must, the court said, be some evidence that the buyer made that purpose known to the seller. In this case, the defendant probably knew that the aggregate was to be used under the building, "but there is no evidence from which it can be said that it was made known to the seller by the buyer as envisaged by s.14(4)." Nor had the buyer relied on the seller's knowledge, skill and judgment; it had instead followed its own advisors' instructions that clause 804 should be used. Therefore, no implied condition arose under s.14(4) (though this mattered little in practice, as the court had already found that there had been a breach of s.14(2) as to merchantable quality).

Did the delivery dockets have contractual force? The court proceeded to consider the status and effect of certain delivery dockets that the defendant claimed had served to incorporate the defendant's terms and conditions into the parties' contract. With each delivery of aggregate, the plaintiff's foreman signed a delivery docket supplied by the defendant confirming the receipt and quantity of the delivery. The delivery docket stated that the aggregate was "sold subject to the terms and conditions" of the defendant, which were "available on request." Crucially, while the docket referred to those conditions, available on request, it did not expressly contain or set out those terms and conditions. Clause 8 of those terms and conditions purported to limit liability for defective goods to the cost of their replacement, and to disclaim further liability for damage. The question that arose was whether this was sufficient to incorporate the limitation clause into the contract.

The court accepted that there was an overarching master contract together with separate contracts for supply. Did the delivery dockets have contractual force? The question that arose was whether each delivery docket acted as a document making or varying the contract, that is, affecting the *formation* of the contract, or whether it was, instead, a post-contractual document, simply confirming *performance* of contractual obligations, or recording the fact of delivery or quantity of goods supplied. As *Treitel on the Law of Contract*, 12th edn (London: Sweet and Maxwell, 2007) para.7-006 observes, a clause is not incorporated into a contract if the document in which it is contained "is not intended to have contractual force." For instance, a document that is intended simply as a receipt for payment is not contractually binding (though describing a document as a 'receipt' does not necessarily deny it contractual effect in every case). The document, the court agreed citing *Treitel*, will have contractual effect if the person to whom it is given knew or ought reasonably to have known it was intended as a contractual document or was given reasonable notice that it contained conditions. Documents of a type that generally contains contractual terms will have contractual effect, though whether a document falls into this category "depends on commercial practice, which may vary from time to time."

According to *Chitty on Contracts*, 31st edn (London: Sweet and Maxwell, 2012), para.12-009, in order to have contractual force a "document must be of a class which either the party receiving it knows, or which a reasonable man would expect, to contain contractual conditions...."

While agreeing that a delivery docket could, depending on the circumstances, have contractual effect, the court ruled in this case that the particular delivery docket used by the defendant was not sufficient to have the effect of incorporating new terms into the contract. Crucially, the dockets did not contain or set out the relevant terms and conditions, but simply referred vaguely to unspecified terms and conditions available elsewhere. It was clear from precedent, the court said, that the document in question, to successfully incorporate the relevant terms, had to contain, "in one form or another, the terms and conditions actually relied on", or in the alternative it had to refer to specific terms and conditions well known in the relevant industry. In other words, the specific terms and conditions need to be spelt out clearly on the relevant document or clearly identified as well-known industry-wide conditions. The general reference in this case to unspecified terms and conditions not set out on the docket but available elsewhere (and not being standard or well-known industry terms), the court concluded, did not suffice.

Moreover, the delivery dockets in this case had, the court observed "...the purpose of recording the type of material delivered, the date of delivery and quantity delivered, and did not set out the terms and conditions of the contractual arrangement between the parties." They were not documents that contained contractual terms or of a type that the plaintiff or any reasonable person would have expected to contain contractual conditions. Therefore, the delivery dockets did not, the court ruled, have the effect desired by Irish Asphalt and had not incorporated the latter's limitation clause into the contract.

Incorporation by Signature? The clause had not been incorporated by the foreman's signature on the delivery notes, the court ruled. The court had already found that the dockets did not have the effect of making or varying the contract, and were more in the nature of records of delivery, evidence of the performance of the contract as opposed to its formation: "a party will only be found to have incorporated terms and conditions by signature or a contractual document.". The delivery dockets were not contractual documents in the sense that they played no role in the formation of the contract. Notably, the dockets did not contain specific terms and conditions but instead, made general reference to unspecified conditions available elsewhere. The party to be bound by signature, the court said, must be in a position to determine what the terms and conditions are (even if he had not in fact read what he had signed). This meant that the document either had to set out the specific conditions or at least make reference to well-known conditions. "A bland reference to terms and conditions alone cannot suffice", the court concluded. "How is one supposed to know what the terms and conditions are?" This seems to suggest that signature of a document that makes general reference to conditions available elsewhere may not normally be effective to incorporate those conditions unless they are well-known in the relevant industry. The terms were not incorporated by signature. The safer bet, therefore, is to set out the terms explicitly in the signed document.

Incorporation by Actual Notice? Likewise, the Supreme Court rejected the proposition that either Elliott Construction had actual notice of the exclusion clause or that Irish Asphalt had taken reasonable steps to bring the clause to the plaintiff's attention. Upholding the trial judge's analysis, the court noted that a letter sent by the defendant did not in fact contain the terms and conditions, as the defendant had alleged. The trial judge had also rejected the proposition that because the defendant's systems would normally have operated to notify the client of its terms and conditions, that he should accept that actual notice of those terms had issued. On the evidence, it was not clear, he concluded, that the systems in fact were systematically followed. Instead, they were, the evidence established, quite "random" and, it seemed, unreliable.

Credit notes that contained the terms and conditions and issued to the plaintiff's accounts office were "not a reasonable context" in which to notify the plaintiff of a clause as critical as the limitation clause, the court found. The credit notes, the trial judge observed and the Supreme Court agreed, did "not concern the formation of a contract but the true performance of an existing obligation by reference only to price and perhaps, on occasion, to quantity." The court thus upheld the fact, as established at trial, that actual notice of the limitation clause had not been given.

Incorporation by reasonable notice? The court also upheld the finding that the defendant had not taken reasonable steps to notify the plaintiff of its standard terms. In doing so, the court endorsed the view that as well as the quality of notice, the particular quality of the *clause*, and in particular whether or not it is substantively onerous, is also relevant in determining whether reasonable steps have been taken to bring terms to a client's notice. This was, the trial judge had concluded, an onerous limitation clause, liable to "leave the builder to lose his reputation and possibly his profit, and more", even if use of the material turned out to be "actively dangerous". If the defendant's systems had been functioning reliably, such notice as was required might have issued, but there was no evidence here that reasonable notice was ever given to the plaintiff. Although the terms and conditions had been listed on some documentation such as credit notes, this documentation was not of a type, Charleton J. observed, that one would reasonably expect to be considered by persons at decision making level.

The Supreme Court agreed. The limitation clause was not actually set out on the delivery dockets, and "there is nothing to suggest that the actual terms and conditions and, in particular, clause 8, were ever brought to the attention of anyone in Elliot Construction". The fact that the term was an onerous term added "additional force", the court said, to this conclusion. Nor was there sufficient evidence that the provisions of clause 8 set out in credit notes were ever brought to the attention of any representative of Elliot Construction, still less any person at managerial level, with authority to make and vary contracts.

The trial judge had placed particular emphasis on the fact that the employees dealing with the delivery dockets and credit notes were not senior managerial staff. Charleton J. had found that reasonable notice to a company required "notification at a level within the corporation which might reasonably be expected to be effective in terms of bringing the clause to the attention of the appropriate decision making level within that corporation." In particular, the foreman and accounts staff, while experienced and skilled, did not have authority to negotiate contractual terms. It was logical, the Supreme Court concluded, that notice should be provided at the level at which decision-making occurred, in this case, at senior management level. Notice to staff in the accounts department or to a foreman was not, in this case, reasonable notice (though the court stressed that each case turns on its particular facts.)

Incorporation by course of dealing? The court also rejected the proposition that the defendant's terms and conditions had been incorporated by a consistent course of dealing. Although 1,119 delivery dockets had been signed in the course of the parties' dealings, these dockets did not set out the defendant's terms and conditions and were not, for the reasons summarised above, contractual documents in the sense that they did not play a part in the formation of the contract. The court also discounted the claim that credit notes sent to the plaintiff amounted to a consistent course of dealing. Only three of the relevant credit notes set out the terms and conditions. Others contained no conditions. This did not, the court concluded, amount to a course of dealing either sufficient in quantity or consistency to incorporate the relevant terms into the contract.

There was thus, the Supreme Court concluded, no basis on which the defendant's limitation clause been incorporated into the contract. Accordingly, it was not necessary to consider whether the clause was 'fair and reasonable' as required by s.55(4) of the 1893 Act, as inserted by s.22 of the 1980 Act.

Compliance with European Standards Therefore, as a matter of national law, the plaintiff succeeded; the defendant was liable for the cost of remediation. The Supreme Court, however, agreed that as certain points of European Union law arose, these issues should be referred to the Court of Justice of the European Union under art.267 TFEU, for clarification of points of EU law. In particular, the defendant had claimed that the determination that the aggregate breached the allowable standard for clause 804 and was not of merchantable quality breached the terms of the Technical Standards Directive (98/34/EC). The defendant asserted that there was a European standard in place and protocols for testing thereunder, and that the High Court decision had not placed sufficient weight on that standard and the testing protocols set out therein. The defendant, in particular, claimed that the manner and time of testing in this case were in breach of the EU standard and thus not compliant with EU law. It also claimed that in setting out a test that the product be inert, durable and strong, the High Court had introduced new standards that were not in keeping with the required standards, and had not been notified to the EU, as required by the Technical Standards Directive.

This gives rise to an interesting question; does compliance with an established European standard for the placement of goods on the EU market necessarily mean that the goods are automatically fit for purpose and of merchantable quality for the purpose of contract law? If this were so, the Supreme Court observed, it would lead to a "dramatic shift" in Sale of Goods law. It is well accepted as a matter of contract law that liability for a defective product does not require fault on the part of the seller or supplier. Once the product is found not to be fit for purpose or not of merchantable quality, the supplier is liable, regardless of the degree of care he has taken. Yet, if Irish Asphalt was found to be correct, a product made in compliance with the relevant standard would be presumed fit for purpose, a presumption that could be displaced only by showing that the goods did not satisfy the relevant standard. If this argument was accepted, therefore, all claims would be "reduced to a question of whether the product complied with the standard" and would be determined by reference to testing at the time of supply rather than when the defect becomes evident to the consumer.

The Supreme Court doubted that such a radical change was intended. It rejected the proposition that the High Court was under any obligation to notify new standards to the EU, given that it is not a national standardisation body, and concluded that the 1980 Act cannot be considered a standard for these purposes. While the court considered it doubtful whether Irish Asphalt would ultimately benefit from the reference, it nonetheless considered that it had raised a number of issues "that cannot be said to be so clear or self evident as to not require a reference." The Court could not rule out the possibility of an answer from the CJEU that might affect the outcome of the case. The court thus considered itself obliged to make a reference of these points of EU law to the Court of Justice of the European Union.

SET-OFF, RIGHT OF

Stapleford Finance Ltd v Peter Courtney [2014] IEHC 668 In this case, the plaintiff claimed summary judgment in respect of an outstanding loan, the balance on which was €117,666.80 plus interest. The plaintiff had taken over the loan formerly owed to the Irish Banking Resolution Corporation (which in turn, had previously been owed to Anglo Irish Bank). It asserted that the defendant had no bona fide defence in respect of the claim.

Starting in 1999, Anglo Irish Bank (IBRC's predecessor in title) had provided the defendant with loan facilities for the purpose of investing in a portfolio of shares. As a precondition to granting the loan, the bank had required a first legal charge to be made over the shares as security for the loan facility. For this purpose, the defendant executed a letter of pledge over the stocks and shares in favour of the bank. Clause 4 of that letter allowed the bank to sell the securities to realise the debt. The parties had also agreed that repayments and payments by the borrower were to be made without set off or counter claim. The facility letters required that the total value of security not fall below 1.25 times the loan amount outstanding to the bank.

The share values, however, subsequently dropped, such that the value of securities fell below the minimum required levels. Attempts to get the defendant to provide further security failed. In October 2011, the bank sought repayment of the amount outstanding. In November 2011 the bank sold the shares. Together with dividends, this realised €109,140, which it put towards satisfying part of what was owed to it. A sum of €116,533.96 plus interest was left owing. The defendant, however, refused to make further payments until the bank restored the share portfolio.

The defendant acknowledged that it owed the money, but he was unable to pay the debts. The plaintiff sought summary judgment in its favour, claiming that the defendant had no arguable defence to the claim. For summary judgment to be granted, the court has to be satisfied that there is no fair or reasonable probability of the defendant having a real or bona fide defence (*Aer Rianta cpt v Ryanair Ltd.* [2001] 4 I.R. 607). It is not necessary to weigh up the merits of each side's arguments or to show that the defence is likely to succeed at plenary trial. As Hardiman J. put it in *Aer Rianta*, the question that arises is whether it is "very clear" that the defendant has no case (at p.623). If either there is no issue to be tried or there are only issues that are straightforward and easily determined or if the defendant's affidavits fail to disclose even an arguable defence, summary judgment may be granted. It is well established, however, that it should not be granted lightly.

Where the defendant has made a counter claim, somewhat more complex considerations apply. These have been considered in *Prendergast v Biddle*, unreported, Supreme Court, 31 July 1957, and more recently in *Moohan v S. & R. Motors (Donegal) Ltd* [2008] 3 I.R. 650. In *Prendergast*, Kingsmill Moore J. noted that, in such cases, a judge may consider the strength of the counter claim and the answer thereto, the parties' conduct and how promptly they have made their claims, the nature of the claims, and the parties' financial position. If a counterclaim is lodged where the plaintiff is in "embarrassed circumstances", summary judgment might not be granted as there would be a risk that the plaintiff might spend any winnings following judgment (for instance, clearing debts), thereby diminishing the prospect of recouping the funds following a successful counterclaim.

In *Moohan*, Clarke J. summarised the relevant principles. Where a counterclaim is lodged, the court must first determine whether the cross-claim gives rise to a defence in equity to the proceedings. This in turn depends on whether the cross claim arises from the same fact scenario (for instance, in the context of the same contract) as gives rise to the plaintiff's claim. If it does, then an equitable set-off may be available. If, however, the cross claim "arises from some independent set of circumstances" the claim will be allowed, and the counter claim will have to be pursued separately, in distinct proceedings.

Notably, where the parties have agreed as part of their contract that there is to be no counter claim or set off or at least that any payments to be made under the contract are to be made without set-off or counter claim, a set-off in equity in respect of the counterclaim will not be available, even if it arises from the same contractual scenario.

The defendant raised a number of defences and counterclaims. He first claimed that an affidavit by the bank was inadmissible as hearsay on the grounds that the bank official making the affidavit "had no personal involvement in any of the dealings between the bank and the defendant." Barton J., however, rejected this claim. The bank was, he said, "entitled to adduce evidence from an employee of the bank itself for the purposes of proving an amount due in proceedings against a customer .... [T]he sworn testimony of an officer or partner employed by the bank is sufficient to prove an amount due by a customer to a bank." (See also *Bank of Scotland v Stapleton* [2012] IEHC 549). In *Moorview Developments Ltd and Others v First Active plc* [2010] IEHC 275, for instance, Clarke J. dismissed as "fanciful", "the idea that a bank wishing to prove its case in debt against a customer has to produce a separate bank official who was personally involved in each individual transaction which gives rise to the customer's current debt." A witness from the bank, he concluded, may provide evidence of the bank's records showing the amount the customer owed.

Barton J. also rejected the defendant's contention that the bank had broken the terms of the Investment Intermediaries Act 1995 (the "1995 Act"). Section 2(6)(h) of the 1995 Act, (as substituted by s.16(2) of the Insurance Act 2000) expressly indicated that an investment firm "shall not include credit institutions which provide investment business services or investment advice." Thus, the bank was not covered by the relevant Act. The letter of pledge had, at any rate, allowed the bank to dispose of the shares. The mandate signed by the defendant was also an "execution only" mandate.

The judge also dismissed the defendant's claim that the summary judgment process involved "an abuse of the process of the court" saying "this submission has no basis in law." Given that the defendant did not seek to challenge the loan facility letters, the letter of pledge, or the computation of amounts owing, the plaintiff was well within its rights to seek summary judgment.

The defendant also claimed that in liquidating the shares the bank had acted in breach of the 2006 Consumer Protection Code. Barton J. noted, however, that a breach of the code does not vitiate the bank's contract with the consumer. In *Zurich Bank v McConnon* [2011] IEHC 75 and *McCaughey v Anglo Irish Bank Corporation Ltd.* [2011] IEHC 546 Birmingham J. concluded that a breach of the code neither relieved the borrower from having to repay the loan, nor did it nullify the relevant loan agreement. Likewise, in *Friends First Finance v Cronin* [2013] IEHC 59, Herbert J. noted that there was nothing in the Consumer Credit Act 1995, as amended

> "which expressly or impliedly would render the loan agreements illegal, invalid or unenforceable because of a breach by the plaintiff of any of these statutory provisions or of the Consumer Protection Code 2006."

Thus Barton J. concluded that the alleged breaches of the code did not give rise to an arguable defence. (See also *AIB v Smith* [2012] IEHC 381.)

The defendant had claimed that the bank sold the portfolio "at the worst possible time in the market causing a loss and consequently a greater liability of the defendant than he might otherwise have had." The bank should have held onto the shares, the defendant argued, and not sold them so quickly. He maintained that forecasts at the time predicted a rise in the share values; indeed some of the share values did in fact subsequently recover.

Should the bank have waited for an improvement in market conditions? On foot of the letter of pledge, the judge concluded, the bank was within its rights to realise the security and apply the process to set off the debts. At the time the shares were sold, the defendant was unable to service his loans. The bank was not required to sit it out and "gamble on the market" in the hopes of an improvement in the share price.

In *Bula Ltd. (in receivership) v Crowley* [2003] 2 I.R. 430, Denham J. (citing *Re Charnley Davies Ltd* [1990] B.C.L.C. 760) ruled that a receiver did not have a general obligation to wait before going to the market. She concluded that the receiver's first duty is to secured creditors and, in proceeding to sale, may put their interests first: "The receiver was not under a duty to wait for the market to rise." For instance, in *China and South Sea Bank Ltd. v Tan Soon Gin* [1990] 1 A.C. 536 a creditor delayed selling shares which had been pledged as security, by which point they had become worthless. The Judicial Committee of the Privy Council held that the creditor had no duty towards the surety or mortgagor and could sell when it wanted to.

Barton J. concluded that while the bank was required to exercise reasonable care in obtaining the best value for shares at the time they were sold, it had been entitled to decide when they were sold. These shares had been sold on the open market; given that fact, the judge could not see how the defendant could validly maintain that the bank failed to take reasonable care.

The defendant had effectively claimed that the bank owed him a duty of care and that it should have waited for the market to recover; in failing to do so, the defendant asserted the bank had been negligent. Despite the case law to the contrary, the judge was not satisfied that this claim was entirely unarguable.

The defendant claimed that his portfolio was primarily comprised of Irish bank shares (including Anglo, AIB and Bank of Ireland) and asserted that Anglo's reckless lending had led to the collapse in these share values. He maintained also that Anglo had engaged in "illegal market manipulation of its share price by making very large loans to customers and staff for the acquisition of its own shares" and had misled the market as to its true worth. He asserted that he would not have invested €80,000 in bank shares in April 2008 were it not for the bank's actions. Had he known of the true state of affairs back in 2008, he could have sold his shares and repaid the loans with a surplus of €107,000.

The judge agreed that these are "unquestionably serious allegations". Whether the defendant might succeed in this claim "would have to be established in any proceedings as may be instituted by the defendant." While such claims may have been arguable, however, they did not constitute a defence or a defence by way of counter-claim and set off to the bank's claim but instead had to be treated as independent cross claims to be pursued separately. Likewise, the bank's exercise of its power of sale was a matter that gave rise to an independent cross claim.

The judge observed that the bank and defendant had agreed, as part of their contract, "that all repayments on foot of the facilities were to be made without counter claim or set off". The court was obliged to give effect to this term, particularly given that the defendant had not challenged the facility letters or letter of pledge.

Nonetheless, given that the defendant may be able to prove these serious allegations, Barton J. concluded that, in the interest of justice, it was both necessary and appropriate to stay proceedings on the execution of judgment in favour of the plaintiff. The court had, Barton J. noted, a well-settled inherent jurisdiction to grant a stay of execution on a judgment or court order whenever justice so required, though the court should not stay proceedings where this would work an injustice.

Taking into account the position of the parties, including the defendant's financial situation, the judge concluded that justice would best be served

> "by granting the plaintiff an order giving it liberty to enter a final judgment against the defendant for the amount claimed but with a stay of execution of the judgment on certain conditions in relation to the prosecution of a counter claim or such other proceedings as the defendant may now decide to pursue against the bank."

Admittedly, the plaintiff in this case was not party to the matters complained of by the defendant, the plaintiff having bought out the loans. Yet, the plaintiff could not, the judge said, be put in a better position than the bank in relation to the realisation of the debts.

The stay was therefore made conditional on the defendant prosecuting his cross claims with due diligence. The court thus gave the plaintiff liberty to enter a final judgment against the defendant for the amount due but with a stay on execution of the judgment on the conditions stated herein.

UNDUE INFLUENCE

Bank of Scotland v Anne Hickey [2014] IEHC 202 This case involves a successful motion for summary judgment, but also raises a number of interesting points around undue influence and the effect it has on third parties.

In 2001, the bank entered into a loan agreement with the defendant, Ms Hickey and her then partner, Mr Porter, with whom she was in a relationship at the time. Under the agreement, the bank lent IR£212,000 for the purchase of a property and another IR£100,000 for the refurbishment of an adjoining premises. As security, the bank obtained an equitable mortgage over a number of properties. By 2009, however, the loan had fallen into arrears, with €155,842 owing to the plaintiff bank. The bank sought repayment of the loan and took steps to realise its security.

The plaintiff sought summary judgment. In order for summary judgment to be granted (and a plenary trial denied) the judge has to be satisfied that the defendant has no arguable defence to make. It is not necessary to show that the defendant would be likely to succeed at trial or that the defence is particularly compelling. All that is required is that, assuming what the defence claims is true, there is "an arguable defence" that there is (as Ackner L.J. put it in *Banque de Paris v de Naray* [1984] Lloyd's Law Report 21) "a fair or reasonable probability of the defendants having a real or bona fide defence" (p.23). It is not enough, however, that the defence merely asserts a given situation in its defence, without more.

In her defence, Ms Hickey claimed that very little of the money earmarked for the two properties was in fact spent on either property. Mr Porter, she alleged, had spent the majority of the loan monies for other purposes. She claimed, moreover, that she had obtained no benefit from such spending. Ryan J., however, rejected this defence, noting that Ms Hickey had agreed in writing that she and Mr Porter would be jointly and severally liable for the debt. It was no defence to show that the borrowed money had not been spent as intended. It was irrelevant whether she or Mr Porter had misspent the money; she was equally liable to repay it.

Ms Hickey also alleged that in executing the loan agreement she had acted "at the behest and direction of Mr Porter" and effectively under his undue influence. Ryan J., however, concluded that the evidence of undue influence comprised no more than the mere assertion that she had acted at Mr Porter's behest and direction, with no concrete evidence or example of pressure or coercion being presented. Such an assertion alone was "hopelessly inadequate as evidence and goes nowhere near establishing the case". There was, he observed, "no proof or detail of any fact or circumstances to suggest that Mr Porter had exerted undue influence …". In short, there was no detail and there were no examples of the alleged coercion beyond the "bald and brief statement" that she had acted at his behest. The judge noted that she had been represented by a solicitor in relation to the loan agreements and mortgages.

Ms Hickey alleged that because she and Mr Porter had been in an intimate relationship at the time, the bank had a duty to take steps to ensure that her decision was made independently. In this case, however, the judge was satisfied that the alleged duty to take such steps did not arise as this was purely a commercial loan. In the loan documentation, Ms Hickey had described herself as a company director and had confirmed that she was acting in a business capacity, in the course of her business or trade. The loans were advanced not solely to benefit another, but to advance her business interests. (See also *ACC Bank plc v McEllin* [2013] IEHC 454).

As Clarke J. noted in *Ulster Bank v Roche* [2012] 1 I.R. 765 at p.780 (following *Royal Bank of Scotland v Etridge (No 2)* [2001] UKHL 44), "a bank is placed on inquiry where it is aware of facts which suggest, or ought to suggest, that there may be a non-commercial element to a guarantee". In this case, however, Ryan J. noted, Ms Hickey had acted as a company director for the purposes of her business or trade. There was no suggestion that the loans were advanced otherwise than to promote her commercial interests. Ryan J. noted that where two people jointly borrow and act together as part of a joint commercial venture in obtaining and using these borrowings, the bank is not put on enquiry, and the principle set out in *Ulster Bank v Roche* (which in turn is based in part on the House of Lords decision in *Royal Bank of Scotland v Etridge (No 2)* [2001] UKHL 44) does not apply. Whether independent legal advice should be sought was thus a matter for the defendant in this case and not the plaintiff. The particular circumstances were not such as to put the bank on enquiry as to Ms Hickey's independent decision making capacity.

The judge added, finally, that insofar as Ms Hickey had signed the loan documents, she was bound by their terms. Citing *Irish Bank Resolution Corporation v Quinn* [2011] IEHC 470, he observed that "a person who signs a legally effective document without properly considering it or understanding it, will be prima facie bound to accept any consequences which may later arise".

Ryan J. thus concluded that the existence or potential existence of any defence had not been established. Summary judgment was thus granted in respect of the reliefs sought by the plaintiffs.

Bank of Ireland v Cochrane and Cochrane [2014] IEHC 605 This case concerns an allegation of actual undue influence in the context of an execution of guarantee agreements. The defendants in this case were the owners and managers of two companies. In July 2010, they had personally entered into contracts of guarantee and indemnity in respect of loans made to the companies by the plaintiff bank. The defendants claimed that these guarantees were vitiated by actual undue influence. The companies in question were in a perilous financial condition at the time of the guarantee agreements.

The defendants signed the guarantees at a meeting with bank officials in July 2010. They claimed that the atmosphere at that meeting was intimidating, threatening and unsettling. The defendants claimed that the bank, knowing of their precarious financial situation, had extracted the guarantees from them in circumstances where they had no effective choice but to sign up. They claimed that the bank had threatened that finance to allow stocking of their businesses would not be forthcoming unless they signed the guarantees. They asserted, furthermore, that they had no opportunity to seek independent legal advice; indeed they said they were required to sign documents waiving their entitlement to seek such advice.

The bank for its part vigorously disputed the defendants' account of the meeting, asserting that the meeting had taken place in a professional and friendly atmosphere, and had ended pleasantly. No complaint had been made to the manager at the relevant time; indeed the bank asserted that relations between it and the defendants remained pleasant even after the meeting. Indeed in 2011, the bank claimed, Mr Cochrane had complimented the bank's staff on the manner in which they had managed the couple's account.

Barr J. refused summary judgment, which had been sought by the bank. There was, he concluded, a fundamental dispute as to what had transpired at the July 2010 meeting. While the defendants accepted that they had signed the loan offers, guarantees, and waivers of independent legal advice, they claimed that they had done so under enormous pressure. The bank, for its part, rejected this claim, maintaining that the meeting had been conducted in a professional and amicable manner.

Given the "stark conflict of fact" in the affidavits, Barr J. was satisfied that summary judgment should be refused. Determining the truth required a plenary trial, at which witnesses could be examined and cross-examined. Noting the jurisprudence on summary judgments, Barr J. remarked that summary judgment should only be granted where the affidavits (per Hardiman J. in *Aer Rianta cpt v Ryanair Ltd.* [2001] 4 I.R. 607 at 623), "fail to disclose even an arguable defence".

The judge, nonetheless, appeared sceptical of the defendants' prospects of success. Noting that the defendants were "experienced business people, who had a long history of doing business with the bank" he expressed "considerable doubt" about their chances of succeeding in establishing this defence. That said, a judge need not be satisfied that the defendants' arguments are likely to succeed in order to refuse summary judgment. Unless it is clear that the defendants had no arguable defence, the judge should incline towards permitting a plenary trial to proceed. Summary judgment was thus declined.

Criminal Law

JOHN P. BYRNE, BCL, LLM, Barrister-at-Law, PhD

INTRODUCTION

The Court of Criminal Appeal issued three important sentencing decisions on 18 March 2014 which set out guidelines for matters of sentencing in respect of different types of offence: *DPP v Z* [2014] IECCA 13, *DPP v Fitzgibbon* [2014] IECCA 12, [2014] IECCA 25 and *DPP v Ryan* [2014] IECCA 11. These cases are significant as they go further than previous decisions of the Court of Criminal Appeal in matters of sentencing by setting out a range of sentence, and, in the case of *Z*, by placing, effectively, a duty on counsel for the DPP to draw the sentencing judge's attention to any appropriate sentencing guidelines. This particular aspect proved controversial with the Office of the Director of Public Prosecutions who sought further guidance from the court on the extent of the obligation which arose in circumstances where judges in Circuit Criminal and Central Criminal Courts began to seek guidance from her counsel at sentencing hearings.

There are different reasons why the Court of Criminal Appeal may have issued its judgment in *Z*, including: the court may have felt it was incongruous for the DPP to fail to offer any assistance on sentencing at trial, and then appeal the sentence imposed if it was consequently not satisfied with the outcome (the word "unfair" was later used by the court in *Fitzgibbon*); also, appeals on grounds of undue leniency may have been viewed by the court as largely avoidable if such a procedure was in place—especially in circumstances where there was already a backlog of cases before the court.

Following submissions by the DPP to clarify the extent of its obligation, particularly in circumstances where it was unclear if it should be best practice for counsel to always proffer the maximum sentence (something which the Bar Council had advocated against in the past), the Court of Criminal Appeal addressed the issue again in its second hearing in *Fitzgibbon*. The court made a distinction between "guidance" and "assistance"—the latter was permitted but the former was prohibited. "Assistance" was simply drawing the sentencing court's attention to ISIS (Irish Sentencing Information System), or cases such as *Fitzgibbon* and *Ryan*, cases where a range was set down, and indicating where counsel for the DPP considered the matter fell on that range. It did not amount to "guidance", which was indicating to the judge that the appropriate sentence fell between *x* and *y* years—that was not permitted (para.3.4):

> "It is not for any outside party to give guidance to a sentencing judge as to what the sentence in a particular case should be. But there is a very real difference between guidance, on the one hand, and assistance, on the other. What this Court suggested in *Z* was that counsel for the D.P.P. should be of assistance in drawing to the attention of the Court, any relevant materials

> which, it might be suggested, the Court should take into account in imposing sentence."

There was another point of contention in *Z*. The court placed a burden on the DPP in respect of assessing factors in mitigation of sentence when it ruled that it must inform defence counsel if it does not accept a matter advanced in circumstances where it can "prove to be wrong" the matter advanced. The prosecution then has a duty to invite the court to put the defence on proof if it continues to advance the matter. The reason for this approach was explained further in the second *Fitzgibbon* hearing when the Court of Criminal Appeal stated (para.6.6):

> "it is frequently the case that prosecuting counsel, while acknowledging that certain mitigating factors are present, nonetheless argues that the sentence is unduly lenient ... in those circumstances it seems to this Court that there is an obligation on the D.P.P. to deal with such matters at a sentencing hearing for to address them on appeal without having made submissions at the sentencing hearing is unfair."

This makes sense. If counsel for the DPP has evidence to hand at the sentencing hearing that a particular factor in mitigation is incorrect, then it should indicate that concern at the hearing by informing the defence counsel to withdraw that factor. If defence counsel continues to assert the matter as a factor in mitigation and the prosecution either has evidence the factor is incorrect, or, has no evidence one way or the other, then it should invite the court to put the defence on proof of that issue. The ruling seeks to prevent prosecution counsel from "hedging their bets" by narrowly maintaining silence at trial and allowing the matter to be addressed instead on appeal if the sentencing outcome is unsatisfactory.

In any event, considering the matter broadly, it is to be commended that the Court of Criminal Appeal would seek to set down sentencing guidelines. In doing so, surely, the court is cognizant of the day-to-day concerns of victims, their families, and ordinary citizens who have, often vocally, expressed their frustrations at inconsistencies in the sentencing system in Ireland. No court system, or indeed, government, should be deaf to such considerations. Whether this particular system proves to address all of those concerns remains to be seen but it is still a very useful starting point, and, moreover, the newly constituted Court of Appeal appears to be carrying the baton as it has already indicated its willingness to consider setting down guidelines in respect of other types of offences. (*D.P.P. v Casey*, *The Irish Times*, 23 June 2015)

In other matters, the Supreme Court made an important distinction in 2014 between two different types of cases involving access to a solicitor by an accused while in Garda custody: *DPP v Gormley* and *DPP v White* [2014] 1 I.L.R.M. 377; [2014] IESC 17. Gormley's conviction hung significantly on interrogation evidence he gave after requesting access to his solicitor but before his solicitor had arrived. In *White*, a sample provided before his solicitor arrived constituted significant inculpatory evidence against him. White saw his conviction upheld while Gormley's was overturned.

In *Minister for Justice v Connolly* [2014] IESC 34, a 2012 High Court ruling which held a European Arrest Warrant issued by Spain was defective on its face—it referred variously to "an offence" and then on a separate page to "2 offences"—was appealed to the Supreme Court by the Minister and rejected. In *DPP v Daniels* [2014] 11 J.I.C. 0401; [2014] IESC 64, the Supreme Court, in an "extraordinary, chilling and frightening" case, upheld a discretionary life sentence imposed for a first time offender, in circumstances where mitigating factors were present, including age.

The newly constituted Court of Appeal issued several notable decisions on sentencing including *DPP v McMenamy* [2014] IECA 47, where the defendant had showed "callous disregard for the health of the injured victim" (his fiancé). In *DPP v Brett* ex tempore, [2014] IECA 48, the court substituted a sentence for time already served (seven weeks) and suspended the balance, in circumstances where the accused had caused the death of a victim after driving with a blood alcohol reading of 266mg. per litre. In *DPP v O'Brien* [2014] IECA 36, the court restored parity of sentence between two offenders tried in relation to the same incident in different counties.

DELAY

Blameworthy prosecutorial delay In *Donoghue v DPP* [2014] IESC 56, the Supreme Court ordered that an injunction should be granted preventing the Director of Public Prosecutions from further prosecuting the case against Mr Donoghue in circumstances where there had been prosecutorial delay. One consequence of that delay was that Mr Donoghue found himself facing prosecution as an adult when he could and should have been prosecuted at a time when the provisions of the Children Act 2001 applied to him, had the prosecution been conducted in a timely manner.

On 29 March 2010, just three days after his sixteenth birthday, members of the Gardaí called to his home. Heroin with a value of €7,560 was found together with weighing scales. On the discovery of those items, Mr Donoghue immediately took responsibility and he signed an admission to this effect in the notebook of the prosecuting Garda.

On 16 April 2012, an order was made in the High Court granting leave to seek relief by way of judicial review (Peart J.). The matter came for hearing before the High Court on 29 January 2013 and Birmingham J. granted the relief sought, namely an injunction by way of judicial review restraining the DPP from prosecuting Mr Donoghue.

One of the reasons for the delay in prosecuting Mr Donoghue was attributable to a delay in obtaining statements from two members of An Garda Síochána in relation to the detention of Mr Donoghue in Coolock Garda Station. The Supreme Court considered there was nothing to suggest that their statements would have been anything other than straightforward, and it was difficult to understand why it took so long. The court indicated there was a partial explanation for the delay in respect of one member, but no explanation whatsoever for the delay in respect of the other.

Giving judgment, Dunne J. said:

> "The special duty of State authorities owed to a child or young person over and above the normal duty of expedition to ensure a speedy trial is an important factor which must be considered in deciding whether there has been blameworthy prosecutorial delay. That special duty does not of

itself and without more result in the prohibition of a trial. As in any case of blameworthy prosecutorial delay, something more has to be put in the balance to outweigh the public interest in the prosecution of offences. What that may be will depend upon the facts and circumstances of any given case. In any given case, the age of the young person before the courts will be of relevance. Someone close to the age of eighteen at the time of an alleged offence is not likely to be tried as a child no matter how expeditious the State authorities may be in dealing with the matter. On the facts of this case, had the prosecution of Mr. Donoghue been conducted in a timely manner, he could and should have been prosecuted at a time when the provisions of the Children Act 2001 would have applied to him. The learned trial judge correctly identified a number of adverse consequences that flowed from the delay. Accordingly, I am satisfied that the learned trial judge was correct in reaching his conclusion that an injunction should be granted preventing the Director of Public Prosecutions from further prosecuting the case against Mr. Donoghue."

Enough time had elapsed to Proceed with Prosecution The passage of time was considered from a different perspective in the Supreme Court case of *Breifne O'Brien v DPP* [2014] IESC 39. Here the appellant argued that he was at risk of an unfair trial in circumstances where the State's case against him had been the subject of considerable media coverage and not enough time had passed since the bulk of that publicity to guarantee him a fair trial.

The appellant, a former businessman, was charged with 45 counts of theft and deception contrary to ss.4 and 6 of the Criminal Justice (Theft and Fraud Offences) Act 2001. It was alleged that the appellant operated a pyramid or ponzi-type scheme during the course of which he sought and received large sums of money on the basis of fictitious investment opportunities. His alleged modus operandi was to seek money from one investor and, having promised that investor a return, when the time came for the return of the investment, if he was not able to convince the investor to reinvest in another further bogus transaction, he would seek a different investor and would use the new investment to pay off the first investment and its bogus return. This process is alleged to have been repeated over a 10 to 15-year period, but in December 2008 it became apparent that the appellant was in financial difficulty and was unable to repay sums allegedly invested.

Most of the sensational articles printed in relation to the matter were published between 2009 and 2012. A book was published in 2010 and a television documentary was screened twice in 2012, while the repeat in January 2013 on the 3e channel was described by the court as having low audience figures.

The Supreme Court, Denham C.J., giving judgment against the appellant, ruled (para.77):

> "In the circumstances of this case, the fact that years have passed since the bulk of the publicity, the application of the fade factor, the fact that a trial judge sitting in a criminal court will be in a position to give directions to the jury, and to ensure that there is a fair trial, leads this Court to the conclusion that there is no longer a real risk of an unfair trial, and that the

> appellant enjoys the constitutionally protected presumption of innocence in any trial. The Court would dismiss the appeal."

EUROPEAN ARREST WARRANT

Warrant Defective In *Minister for Justice and Equality v Connolly* [2014] IESC 34, Mr Connolly's delivery to Spain on foot of a European arrest warrant was refused by the High Court, on 19 December 2012, on the basis that the warrant was deficient in that it did not contain a clear or satisfactory statement of the offence. The Minister appealed that decision to the Supreme Court.

In the translation supplied by the Spanish authorities, the warrant stated

> "ordering prosecution and issuance of an arrest warrant for Michael Martin Connolly for **an** alleged offence of endangerment of public health, as set forth in Articles 368 and 369 of the Spanish Penal Code".

Notwithstanding the reference to "**an** offence", the third page of the document stated that it referred in total to "2 Offences". Giving judgment for the Supreme Court, Hardiman J., dismissing the appeal by the Minister, said (para.65):

> "I consider it to be an imperative duty of a court asked to order the compulsory delivery of a person for trial outside the State to ensure that it is affirmatively and unambiguously aware of the nature of the offences for which it is asked to have him forcibly delivered, and for which he may be tried abroad, and of the number of such offences."

Parity of process not necessary under the European Arrest Warrant In the Supreme Court decision in *Minister for Justice and Equality v Busby* [2014] IESC 70, a European arrest warrant was issued by the United Kingdom on 13 July 2012 for the surrender of the appellant. On 17 July 2012, it was endorsed before the High Court and the appellant was brought before the High Court on 18 July 2012. The warrant sought the surrender of the appellant for prosecution for offences which were identified by the ticking of the box marked "terrorism" on the warrant and it certified "the offences are not extra-territorial offences". On 31 July 2013, the High Court (Edwards J.) certified one point of law of exceptional public importance, namely, where an offence is deemed extra-territorial for the purposes of s.44 of the European Arrest Warrant Act 2003, is it necessary to show that the executing state could prosecute the act or omission of which the offence consists on a similar basis to the jurisdiction asserted by the issuing state?

Section 44 states:

> A person shall not be surrendered under this Act if the offence specified in the European arrest warrant issued in respect of him or her was committed or is alleged to have been committed in a place other than the issuing state and the act or omission of which the offence consists does not, by virtue of having been committed in a place other than the State, constitute an offence under the law of the State.

The case turned on the question whether parity of process is necessary under the European Arrest Warrant; in other words, whether it is necessary to show that the executing state could prosecute the act or omission of which the offence consists on a similar basis to the jurisdiction asserted by the issuing state.

The Supreme Court, in its judgment, set out the background as follows (para.6):

> "Adam Busby is the self-proclaimed leader of an extremist group called the Scottish Liberation Army. His conduct giving rise to the offences is that:
>
> 1) On 27 November 2009 at the Scottish Sun Newspaper, the Guild Hall, 57 Queen Street, Glasgow he did, by means of telephone communication sent to Nicholas Sharp, an employee of the Scottish Sun Newspaper, Guild Hall, 57 Queen Street, Glasgow utter threats to said Nicholas Sharpe, did purport to represent an organisation called the Scottish National Liberation Army, and did threaten to contaminate the drinking water supplies of major English towns and cities with a noxious substance, with 'the intention of inducing in said Nicholas Sharpe, and others, a belief that there would be danger to human life and a serious risk to human health.
>
> 2) On 20 December 2009 at the Scottish Sun Newspaper, Guild Hall, 57 Queen Street, Glasgow he did by means of telephone communication send to the Scottish Sun Newspaper, Guild Hall, 57 Queen Street, Glasgow a text message, the content of which he knew or believed to be false, with the intention of inducing in employees of said Scottish Sun Newspaper a belief that various packages containing caustic, poisonous or other noxious substance had been sent to a number of political figures, including the then Prime Minister of the United Kingdom, Gordon Brown, which was capable of endangering human life or of creating a serious risk to human health:
>
> Contrary to the Anti-terrorism, Crime and Security Act 2001, Section 114(2)
>
> 3) On 15 April 2010 at the Press Association, 1 Central Quay, Glasgow he did communicate, by telephone, information to Victoria Mitchell, Deputy Editor of the Glasgow branch of the Press Association with the intent of inducing in her the false belief that a bomb, or other thing liable to explode or ignite, was present at the bridge at the Argyle Arcade in Glasgow.
>
> Contrary to The Criminal Law Act 1977, Section 51(2) and (4).
>
> 4) On 15 April 2010 at the Glasgow branch of the Samaritans, 210 West George Street, Glasgow, he did communicate, by telephone, information to another person namely Margaret Foley, with the intent of inducing in her the false belief that a bomb, or other thing liable to explode or ignite, was present at The Hilton Hotel, Glasgow. Contrary to The Criminal Law Act 1977, Section 51(2) and (4).
>
> 5) On 9 June 2010 at the Edinburgh Evening News, Edinburgh he did communicate, by telephone, information to another person namely Simon Lyle, a Reporter there, with the intent of inducing in him the false belief that a bomb, or other thing liable to explode or ignite, was present at the Forth Road Bridge.
>
> Contrary to The Criminal Law Act 1977, Section 51(2) and (4).
>
> 6) On 9 June 2010 at the Scottish Daily Express Newspaper, Glasgow, he did communicate; by telephone, information to another person namely

> Tom Martin, Executive News Editor, with the intent of inducing in him the false belief that a bomb, or other thing liable to explode or ignite, was present at the Erskine Bridge, Glasgow. Contrary to The Criminal Law Act 1977, Section 51(2) and (4).
>
> 7) On 9 June 2010 at the Scottish Sun, Guild Hall, 57 Queen Street Glasgow he did communicate, by telephone information to another person, namely Gail Cameron, a News Reporter there, with the intent of inducing in her the false belief that a bomb, or other thing liable to explode or ignite, was present at the Erskine Road Bridge, Glasgow.
>
> Contrary to The Criminal Law Act 1977, Section 51(2) and (4).
>
> Incidents 2–7 were hoaxes: no noxious substances or bombs were found."

Giving judgment for the court, Denham C.J. answered the certified question in the negative and stated the European arrest warrant system is based on the principle of mutual recognition of the judicial decisions of the legal systems of other Member States, and of mutual trust. The court considered the appropriate approach was that set out by Murray C.J. in *Minister for Justice Equality and Law Reform v Brennan* [2007] 3 I.R. 732, where he stated:

> "The sole matter which I wish to make clear here is that the mere fact that a trial or sentence may take place in a requesting state according to procedures or principles which differ from those which apply even if constitutionally guaranteed, in relation to a criminal trial in this country does not of itself mean that an application for surrender should be refused … ."

Equally, the judgment of Fennelly J. in *Minister for Justice Equality and Law Reform v Stapleton* [2008] 1 I.R. 669 was referred to where the court stated: "Extradition does not demand that there be parity of criminal procedures between contracting states."

PROCEDURE

Access to Solicitor In *DPP v Gormley* and *DPP v White* [2014] 1 I.L.R.M. 377; [2014] IESC 17, the Supreme Court dealt simultaneously with two cases which involved the right of access to a solicitor while in Garda custody, or, more generally, that a person should not be tried on any criminal charge save in "due course of law" as set down in Art.38.1 of the Constitution. Both of the defendants were convicted of serious criminal offences. On 7 November 2007, Mr Gormley was convicted in the Central Criminal Court of attempted rape, contrary to s.4 of the Criminal Law (Rape) (Amendment) Act 1990. He was later sentenced to six years' imprisonment with five years' post-release supervision. Mr White was convicted at the Central Criminal Court of murder on 29 July 2009, and was sentenced to mandatory life imprisonment. Both separately appealed to the Court of Criminal Appeal and subsequently, that court separately certified questions for determination in respect of both cases to the Supreme Court.

In the case of Mr Gormley, his conviction was substantially based on admission evidence made during interrogation in custody during a period after he had requested the presence of a solicitor and before that solicitor had arrived to advise him. In the case of Mr White, forensic samples were taken from him at a time after he had requested the presence of a solicitor and before the arrival of the solicitor concerned.

Clarke J., giving judgment for the court, distinguished between the two defendants. In the case of Mr White, he was legally obliged to provide samples and they were taken in an unobtrusive way. In the case, however, of Mr Gormley, his conviction, which significantly hung on the interrogation evidence he gave after requesting his solicitor, and before his solicitor arrived, had suffered a breach of his constitutional guarantee of fair process—a trial otherwise than in due course of law—and consequently, his appeal was allowed.

Hardiman J., obiter, concurred with Clarke J. in distinguishing between a detention for questioning and a detention solely for the purpose of taking a scientific sample about whose taking there is no option for the defendant. He continued (para.26):

> "I should like to add, however, that the distinction between these two types of custody must be fully and properly explained in ordinary language by the gardaí. There can be no question of taking a sample under compulsory process and then going on to directly question the defendant about a crime, or even to 'chat' about it, without the defendant's quite different rights in this area being fully and accurately explained."

Arrest may only be exercised with the use of such force as is reasonable In *DPP v Cullen* [2014] IESC 7, the question for the Supreme Court, via case stated, was whether the use of unreasonable force in carrying out an arrest renders the arrest unlawful. Mr Cullen was arrested on suspicion of drunk driving and immediately handcuffed in circumstances where the arresting sergeant had a policy of handcuffing all such suspects irrespective of the circumstances but had also formed the necessary opinion to enable an arrest under the provisions of the Road Traffic Acts. Mr Cullen was subsequently subjected to an evidential breath test under s.13(1)(a) of the Road Traffic Act 1994, as amended. That breath test resulted in a reading of 71ml of breath which is in excess of the permitted amount.

On cross-examination, the relevant sergeant stated that Mr Cullen had co-operated with the Gardaí at all times during the interaction between Mr Cullen and the Gardaí prior to and subsequent to his arrest. The sergeant further accepted that Mr Cullen had not used or threatened force in order to avoid arrest, nor had the sergeant formed the opinion that there was anything in the conduct of the accused which might lead him to suspect that the accused might resist arrest unless restrained. The sergeant stated it was his policy to place any person arrested for an offence under s.49 of the Road Traffic Act—driving while under the influence of intoxicating liquor or a drug—in handcuffs irrespective of the circumstances as it was his experience that such persons might become abusive and resist arrest either immediately prior to or following communicating the reason for arrest to them.

The issue which arose at his trial concerned the lawfulness of the actions of the relevant sergeant in immediately handcuffing Mr Cullen and the consequences for the charges brought against Mr Cullen for drunk driving.

Fennelly J. (Hardiman J. concurring) stated the power of arrest, whether exercised by a police officer or by a citizen, may only be exercised with the use of such force as is reasonable in all the circumstances. An error of judgement by an officer in applying force which he genuinely believes to be necessary will not either render the arrest invalid or expose the officer to legal remedy, whether criminal or civil. He stated (para.25):

> "I would entirely accept that any individual member of An Garda Síochána is fully entitled to and may well be obliged to apply handcuffs to an arrested person, where he or she genuinely believes that it is necessary to do so in the particular case. The decision must be left to the individual Garda dependant [sic] on his or her own appreciation of the requirements of the individual case. The nature of the offence, the prevailing circumstances, the personality and character of the individual to be arrested must be taken into account. The law is realistic. It is appreciated that decisions on the necessity for an arrest, the appropriate amount of force and the need for the use of handcuffs are often made under pressure of circumstances of urgency, of danger of flight, and of violence and the threat of violence. Ordinarily, courts are slow to review decisions of Garda officers made in the wide range of situations which they confront in the course of their duty."

However, in the instant matter, the Supreme Court considered the decision as to whether to apply handcuffs was pre-ordained. It did not depend on any evaluation of the circumstances and it left no room for the case of the entirely peaceful and co-operative suspect. Therefore, on that basis, the arrest was unlawful and that was enough to determine the case.

Clarke J., dissenting, held the arrest was lawful on the basis the placing of the handcuffs affected the manner of his arrest rather than the entitlement to arrest him and, thus, did not affect the lawfulness of his arrest or his custody thereafter. On that basis, he next moved to consider the evidence obtained. He noted the question turned on the exclusionary rule of evidence which, ultimately, governed whether subsequent inculpatory evidence should be excluded. He noted the Supreme Court was set, at that time, to consider the issue of exclusionary evidence in another case. As that matter was pending, it was viewed by the judge that it should not be considered in the instant case. The decision he referred to, the landmark case of *DPP v JC* [2015] IESC 31 where the exclusionary rule of evidence set down in *DPP v Kenny* [1990] 2 I.R. 110 was overturned in a majority decision, will be covered in the *Annual Review of Irish Law* next year.

Criminal Justice (Forensic Evidence and DNA Database System) Act 2014 Aside from case law, the most significant development within the realm of criminal procedure in 2014 was the enactment of the Criminal Justice (Forensic Evidence and DNA Database System) Act 2014 (the "2014 Act"). Its long-awaited enactment follows a reference in 2003 by the Attorney General to the Law Reform Commission (LRC) (made under the Law Reform Commission Act 1975) requesting it to consider whether a DNA database should be established, and to address the constitutional and human rights issues associated with that question. The publication in 2005 of the LRC's *Report on the Establishment of a DNA Database* (LRC 78-2005) followed a 2004 Consultation Paper on the issue. The 2014 Act was built on the edifice of the Criminal Justice (Forensic Evidence and DNA Database System) Bill 2010 which lapsed on dissolution of the 30th Dáil.

The 2014 Act replaces existing statutory and common law arrangements governing the taking of samples for forensic testing from suspects for use as evidence in criminal investigations and proceedings. It replaces them with, effectively, a "codified" statute-only regime; repeals the Criminal Justice (Forensic Evidence) Act 1990; and, significantly, it provides for the establishment of a DNA database system for use by An Garda Síochána as an intelligence source for criminal investigations and to assist in finding missing persons and unknown persons.

The Act is notable in that it affords powers variously to different parties, aside from the Minister, namely: (i) the Director of the newly established Forensic Science Ireland (FSI); (ii) a System Oversight Committee, both of which report to the Minister; (iii) the Commissioner of An Garda Síochána who can, in certain circumstances, extend the period for retaining a sample or DNA profile when it would otherwise be removed; and (iv) a staff member of FSI in the sense that searches of the newly established DNA Database System may only be conducted by a staff member—defined in s.2 of the Act as "an officer of the Minister who is assigned to perform duties in FSI".

This chapter will consider this significant Act under three headings: The DNA Database System and its administration; the taking of samples for the DNA Database System; and the Removal and Retention of samples from the DNA Database System. What follows is a brief analysis of some of the more salient aspects, but practitioners are encouraged to consult the instrument directly for a more complete understanding of its provisions.

The DNA Database System and its Administration Section 59 of the 2014 Act provides that Forensic Science Ireland (FSI) shall establish the DNA Database System (the "System"). FSI is the new name for the Forensic Science Laboratory of the Department of Justice and Equality. Section 67 gives power to the Director of FSI to establish and operate the System and s.70 obligates him or her to make an annual report to the Minister. Section 71 says a committee, known as the DNA Database System Oversight Committee (the "Committee"), is established. The Committee oversees the management and operation of the System for the purposes of maintaining the integrity and security of the System and shall, for those purposes, satisfy itself that the provisions of this Act in relation to the System are being complied with (s.72). Section 73 says the Director and the other members of the staff of FSI "shall cooperate with the Committee" in relation to the performance by the Committee of its functions under the Act. Similar to the obligation which falls on the Director of FSI, the Committee, likewise, must make an annual report in writing to the Minister (s.74).

Section 60 restricts the purposes for which the System may be used for the investigation of criminal offences and the finding or identification of missing persons; the identification of seriously ill, or severely injured persons; persons who are unable to indicate their identity; or the identification of the bodies of unknown deceased persons.

The DNA Database System shall comprise two divisions: the investigation division and the identification division (s.59). The investigation division contains the crime scene index, the reference index and the elimination indexes. The identification division contains the missing and unknown persons index (Pt 6).

The crime scene index is dealt with in s.61 and contains DNA profiles generated from samples of biological material found at, or recovered from, crime scenes. "DNA profile" is defined in s.2, and, in relation to a person, is confined to information derived from the non-coding part of DNA which refers to the chromosome regions of an individual's DNA which are not known to provide any functional properties of the person, are clearly identifiable as relating to the person and are capable of comparison with similar information derived from an examination and analysis of another sample of biological material for the purpose of determining whether or not that other sample could relate to that person.

Section 62 provides for the reference index and this contains DNA profiles generated from samples pursuant to various sections of the Act dealt with below in this chapter.

The elimination index is broken down into two subcategories, the Garda Síochána index and the crime scene investigators index. In both cases, the index contains DNA profiles generated from samples taken from, either, certain Garda personnel, or civilian crime scene investigators. It covers members/trainee members of An Garda Síochána and civilian staff members who are assigned to duties relating to the investigation or technical examination of crime scenes or anything found at or recovered from a crime scene (s.41). Section 43 makes provision for taking samples from staff members of FSI who are considered to be at risk of contaminating crime scene samples in the execution of their duties. Section 44 makes provision for taking samples from other categories of persons including staff members of the State Pathologist's Office and the Ombudsman Commission.

Section 68 specifies the rules in accordance with which a DNA profile entered in an index may be compared with another profile in that index or with a DNA profile in another index. A profile entered in an index may be compared with other profiles in the same index. As regards comparisons between profiles entered in different indexes: a profile in the crime scene index may be compared with a profile in the reference index and with profiles in the elimination indexes under certain conditions; a profile in the reference index may be compared with a profile in the crime scene index or in the missing and unknown persons index; a profile entered in the missing and unknown persons index may be compared with a profile in the reference index or the crime scene index but only for the purposes of identification. Searches of the System may only be conducted by a staff member of FSI.

The Taking of Samples for the DNA Database System Section 2 of the Act differentiates between intimate and non-intimate samples. An intimate sample refers to a sample of blood, pubic hair or urine, or a swab from a genital region or a body orifice other than the mouth, or a dental impression. Conversely, a non-intimate sample refers to a sample of saliva; hair, other than pubic hair; a nail, or any material found under the nail; a swab from any part of the body including the mouth (but not from any other body orifice or a genital region); and a skin impression, such as a footprint.

The section specifies, at subs.3, that in the case of a person (other than a deceased person) only "non-intimate" samples, namely, a sample of hair other than pubic hair, or a swab from the mouth, can be taken for the purposes of the DNA Database System.

Section 4 provides that samples taken under Pt 2 or 4 of the Act, including any DNA profile generated by those samples, may be transmitted outside of the State pursuant to a request under either: Ch.3, Pt 5 of the Criminal Justice (Mutual Assistance) Act 2008 (which concerns requests for identification evidence); or a request by the International Criminal Court pursuant to s.50 of the International Criminal Court Act 2006. A DNA profile, but not a sample, may be provided to Europol as per ss.8 and 9 of the Europol Act 2012.

Part 2 of the Act makes provision for the taking of a sample, or samples, from persons in Garda custody who are suspected of being involved in the commission of criminal offences but have not been charged.

Section 9 provides three categories of sample can be taken—a sample for the purposes of the DNA Database System (s.11), an intimate sample (s.12), or a non-intimate sample (s.13)—in circumstances where a person is detained pursuant to any of the existing Garda Síochána detention powers, namely: s.30 of the Offences Against the State Act 1939, s.4 of the Criminal Justice Act 1984, s.2 of the Criminal Justice (Drug Trafficking) Act 1996, s.50 of the Criminal Justice Act 2007, or s.16 or 17 of the Criminal Procedure Act 2010. Section 42 of the Criminal Justice Act 1999 is also included, which covers a sample taken from a person who is arrested and detained for the purposes of the investigation of an offence other than the offence in respect of which he or she is imprisoned.

The rationale for linking the taking of a sample to the detention powers under those provisions is that, generally speaking, the taking of a sample is limited to offences which carry a sentence of five years or more, subject to limited exceptions in the case of the Offences Against the State Act 1939 and the Criminal Justice (Drug Trafficking) Act 1996 which contain a small number of offences which do not meet a threshold of five years.

Section 11 permits a member of An Garda Síochána to take a sample from a detained person for the purpose of generating a DNA profile for entry in the reference index of the DNA Database System; the sample is not taken for evidential purposes. A member not below the rank of sergeant must authorise the taking of the sample. Notwithstanding that the consent of the person to the taking of the sample is not required, the person is to be informed of various matters before the sample is taken, including (where applicable) that reasonable force may be used in the event that he or she fails or refuses to allow the sample to be taken (s.11(3)(c)). Protected persons and children under 14 years of age are excluded from the application of this section. The Minister, by order, shall exclude certain offences from the scope of this section because their nature is such that evidence relating to DNA would not assist with their investigation or prosecution.

Section 12 permits a member of An Garda Síochána to take, or cause to be taken, an intimate sample from a person who is detained under any of the provisions referred to in s.9(1) for the purposes of forensic testing and, if appropriate, the generation of a DNA profile in respect of the person to be entered in the DNA Database System. A sample of this type may only be taken if a member of An Garda Síochána not below the rank of inspector has authorised it and the appropriate written consent has been given by the detained person concerned. Before giving the necessary authorisation, the member must be satisfied that there are reasonable grounds for suspecting the involvement of the person in the offence in respect of which the person concerned is detained and for believing that the sample will tend to confirm or disprove the involvement of the person in the offence. Before the detained person is requested to consent, he or she must be informed of various matters including the consequences of not consenting which are detailed in s.19. The appropriate level of consent under this section is dealt with in s.15. Section 18 sets out who can take a sample under this section, stating that medical practitioners and nurses are permitted to take samples in the case of a sample of blood or pubic hair or a swab from a genital region or a body orifice other than the mouth, and shall, in so far as practicable, be a person who is of the same sex as the person from whom the sample is being taken.

Section 13 gives authority to take non-intimate samples. If the sample taken is one which may be used to generate a DNA profile in respect of the person, then the sample may also be used for the purpose of the DNA Database System. A sample of this type may only be taken if a member of An Garda Síochána not below the rank of inspector has authorised it. Unlike in the case of intimate samples under s.12, the consent of the person concerned is not required.

Section 19 is significant. It says a refusal to consent or a withdrawal of consent without reasonable cause may give rise to an adverse inference being drawn in subsequent criminal proceedings. Such an adverse inference may be treated as corroborating any evidence to which it is relevant; it may not be the sole or main basis of a conviction. The adverse inference may not be drawn if certain steps have not been followed, including, that the person was told in ordinary language that a failure to consent or a withdrawal of consent could give rise to such an inference being drawn.

Section 24 deals with the use of force for the purposes of taking a sample under s.11 (DNA Database System) or s.13 (non-intimate samples). Reasonable force must be authorised by a member of An Garda Síochána not below the rank of superintendent. The detained person must be informed in advance of the intention to use reasonable force and that the necessary authorisation has been given. The use of reasonable force must be observed by a member not below the rank of inspector who is to determine the number of members necessary. The taking of a sample with the use of reasonable force must be recorded by electronic means.

Section 26 abolishes the common law power of a Garda to take samples from a suspect in custody with his or her consent.

Part 3 of the Act governs the taking of a sample from a volunteer for the purposes of generating a DNA profile in respect of that person. The Part does not govern the taking of samples for other purposes from a volunteer, e.g. the lifting of material from the victim of an offence that may have been left by the perpetrator. The Part also sets out the circumstances in which a mass screen (an intelligence-led screen of a class of persons) may be conducted. The samples that may be taken under this Part are limited to mouth swabs or head hair (s.2(3)).

Section 27 provides that a member of An Garda Síochána may request a person, i.e. a volunteer, to have a sample taken for the purpose of generating a DNA profile in respect of him or her in relation to the investigation of a particular offence or an incident that may involve the commission of an offence.

In the event that the DNA profile of a victim or a person reasonably considered to be a victim is required in relation to the investigation of an offence or incident, this section applies, i.e. he or she is to be treated as a volunteer. Before seeking the consent of a volunteer to the taking of a sample, the member or authorised person must inform the volunteer of certain matters including that he or she is not obliged to provide the sample.

The volunteer's consent must be in writing. If a volunteer consents but then withdraws it (or withdrawal can reasonably be inferred from the conduct of the volunteer) before or during the taking of the sample, the withdrawal will be treated as a refusal. The withdrawal must be recorded in writing. The section states that a refusal to consent to the taking of a sample shall not of itself constitute reasonable cause for a member to suspect the person of having committed the offence concerned for the purpose of arresting and detaining him or her under any of the detention powers listed in s.9 in connection with the investigation of that offence.

Section 28 says DNA profiles generated from a sample taken under s.27 may be entered in the reference index of the DNA Database System. Such profiles will not be entered in the System routinely. Their entry will instead be subject to the specific written consent of the volunteer, which is a separate consent from that under s.27 required for the taking of a sample under that section.

Section 29 sets out the circumstances in which a mass screening of a class of persons defined by certain characteristics may be conducted. It provides that a mass screening must be authorised by a member not below the rank of chief superintendent. In order to authorise a mass screening, the member must have reasonable grounds for believing that the mass screening of the target class is likely to further the investigation of the offence and is a reasonable and proportionate measure to be taken in the investigation of that offence. A mass screening may only be conducted in respect of a relevant offence which is defined in s.2(1) as an offence in respect of which a person may be detained under any of the Garda detention powers listed in s.9(1); these offences, as stated previously, are generally offences which attract a maximum sentence of five years or more.

The target class may be determined by sex, age, kinship, geographic area, time, or any other matter which the authorising member considers appropriate. A person who comes within the target class is a volunteer and therefore is not obliged to accede to a request to provide a sample.

His or her written consent is required. As is the case with all volunteers, he or she must be informed of certain matters before his or her consent is sought. If the person consents but then withdraws it (or withdrawal can reasonably be inferred from his or her conduct) before or during the taking of the sample, the withdrawal will be treated as a refusal. The withdrawal must be recorded in writing. A sample taken as part of a mass screening may not be used for the purposes of the DNA Database System—it is tested and retained for the purposes of the investigation of the relevant offence in respect of which it was taken. The section states that a refusal to consent to the taking of a sample shall not of itself constitute reasonable cause for a member to suspect the person of having committed the offence concerned for the purpose of arresting and detaining him or her under any of the detention powers listed in s.9 in connection with the investigation of that offence.

Part 4 provides for the taking of samples for the purposes of the DNA Database System from offenders (adult and child), former offenders and from the bodies of deceased persons who are suspected of having committed an offence. The samples that may be taken under this Part are limited to mouth swabs or head hair in the case of persons and to any biological material that may be used to generate a DNA profile in the case of deceased persons.

Section 31 concerns adult offenders. It provides that a sample may be taken for the purpose of generating a DNA profile in respect of the person for entry in the reference index of the DNA Database System. The section is limited to offenders who, on commencement of the section, are still subject to sentence in connection with a relevant offence; or are sentenced after commencement (whether convicted before or after commencement) in respect of a relevant offence; or are serving sentences of imprisonment in the State following transfer (whether before or after commencement of the section) under the Transfer of Sentenced Persons Act 1995 or the Transfer of Execution of Sentences Act 2005 in respect of an offence that corresponds to a relevant offence; and persons who (on or after commencement of the section) are subject to the registration requirements of Pt 2 of the Sex Offenders Act 2001.

The sample is to be taken as soon as practicable after a person comes within one of the eligible categories and in any event before expiry of the sentence or the notification requirements. Where the offender is in prison, the sample will be taken by a prison officer following authorisation by the prison governor. Where the offender is not in prison, the sample may be taken by a member of An Garda Síochána where an authorisation to do so has been given by a member not below the rank of sergeant and the offender attends at a station for that purpose pursuant to "a notice to attend" issued by a member not below the rank of inspector. Non-compliance with the notice to attend without reasonable cause may result in the offender being prosecuted summarily. The section specifies the information that is to be given to the offender by the prison officer or the member, as the case may be, before the sample is taken.

Section 32 sets out the rules in respect of taking a sample from a child offender and it mirrors s.31.

Sections 33 and 34 concern the circumstances in which former offenders may be required to provide samples for the purpose of generating a DNA profile for entry in the reference index of the DNA Database System.

Section 33 contains the criteria that must be met before a person comes within the term "former offender". A former offender is a person who is no longer subject to a sentence for a relevant offence or, in the case of a sex offender, is no longer subject to notification requirements under the Sex Offenders Act 2001. A person is not a former offender for the purpose of this section: if his or her DNA profile is already entered in the reference index of the DNA Database and a member of An Garda Síochána or a judge of the District Court is not satisfied having regard to a range of specified factors that it is appropriate that a sample be taken under s.33; the person concerned is not ordinarily resident in the State or does not have his or her principal residence in the State; and a period of 10 years has elapsed since the expiry of the last sentence for a relevant offence of which the person was convicted or, in the case of a sex offender, since the end of the last notification period to which he or she was subject. Only certain convictions handed down when the person was a child are eligible for consideration—those triable by the Central Criminal Court and any other offences prescribed having regard to the nature and seriousness of the offence.

Section 34 sets out the procedures to apply in the case of former offenders.

Where a member not below the rank of superintendent is satisfied that a person is a former offender and that it is in the interests of the protection of society and desirable for the purpose of assisting in the investigation of offences to have a sample taken from the person under this section, the member may authorise the taking of the sample. Where such an authorisation has been given, a member may request the former offender concerned to attend at the station for the purpose of having the sample taken. The person shall be put on notice that if he or she does not attend, an ex parte application may be made to a District Court judge for an order authorising the sending of a notice to attend, failure to comply with which is a summary offence. Should an application to a District Court judge be necessary it must be made by a member not below the rank of superintendent. In the event that the person is prosecuted for not complying with the court order, it shall be a defence for him or her to show that he or she is not a former offender. Before a sample is taken under this section the former offender must be given certain information.

Section 35 allows a sample to be taken from the body of a deceased person for the purpose of generating a DNA profile in respect of the person to be entered in the reference index of the DNA Database System. The taking of such a sample must be authorised by a District Court judge on the application of a member not below the rank of superintendent. An application may be made where the member has reasonable grounds for suspecting that the person, prior to his or her death, has committed a relevant offence and that the taking of a sample will further the investigation of the offence concerned. The judge may make further orders in relation to entry, search and seizure on the application of the member in order to allow the order to take the sample to be executed.

Samples under this section are to be taken by registered medical practitioners or any other prescribed persons. A profile entered in the reference index of the System in accordance with this section may be compared with the other profiles in that index and with the profiles contained in the crime scene index of the System in accordance with s.68(3). Once this exercise has been completed, the profile is to be removed from the System and the sample destroyed unless the member in charge of the investigation of the offence concerned is satisfied that the sample and profile should be retained for the purposes of that investigation. This section does not authorise the exhumation of a body.

Removal and Retention of Samples from the DNA Database System Part 10 deals with the important issue of removal of samples and DNA Profiles from the DNA Database System. Generally speaking, the Act prescribes an indefinite retention arrangement for the samples and DNA profiles of convicted persons entered in the DNA Database System. There is an exception in the case of child offenders—other than those convicted of offences triable by the Central Criminal Court—which permits their profile to be removed after a number of years. Those suspected but not convicted of any offence shall have any samples, or DNA profile, removed, but the Commissioner of An Garda Síochána can extend the period either is retained for 12 months renewable in the case of samples, and 12 months renewable, up to six years, in the case of the DNA Profile of an adult. The period of six years can be extended on application by the Commissioner to the District Court under s.93.

Former offenders can apply to the Commissioner to have their profile removed in circumstances where a conviction has been quashed or declared to be a miscarriage of justice. Exceptional circumstances, such as a case of mistaken identity, may lend themselves to having samples destroyed, but, again, this is, effectively, at the discretion of the Garda Commissioner insofar as he or she must be satisfied that exceptional circumstances exist. An appeal to the District Court from a decision under this Act by the Garda Commissioner is available in certain cases. Volunteers may apply to have any sample and any profile generated destroyed (s.87). Pursuant to the request, the sample/profile is to be destroyed within three months subject to s.93.

Section 76 sets out the circumstances in which an intimate or non-intimate sample taken from a person is to be destroyed. Where the section applies, the sample concerned is to be destroyed before the expiry of a period of three months from the date on which the applicable circumstance first applied. The circumstances are that: the person was not proceeded against within 12 months for a relevant offence, or if proceeded against was acquitted or the proceedings were dismissed or discontinued; the person is subject to an order under s.1 of the Probation of Offenders Act 1907 and has not been convicted of a relevant offence during a period of three years from the making of the order; or the person's conviction was quashed or declared to be a miscarriage of justice. In the case of a person who was not proceeded against, the failure to institute proceedings must not be due to the fact that the person absconded or could not be located. The period between the taking of the sample and the expiry of the three-month period is called the "retention period". This section is expressed as being subject to s.77.

Section 77 provides a procedure by which the retention period referred to under s.76 may be extended in certain circumstances and permits the Commissioner of An Garda Síochána to authorise the retention of the sample for a period of 12 months from the expiry of the retention period. The 12-month period is renewable.

Section 78 provides that an intimate or non-intimate sample shall be destroyed (other than as permitted by s.76) where the Commissioner is satisfied that exceptional circumstances exist. These include cases where it is established that no offence was committed, a person was detained in a case of mistaken identity, or the detention of the person, during which the sample was taken, is declared by a court as unlawful.

Section 80 sets out the circumstances in which a DNA profile generated from a sample taken from a person under s.11, 12, 13, 31 or 32 and entered in the reference index of the System is to be removed. Where a profile comes within the section, it must be removed before the expiry of a period of three months from the date on which the applicable circumstance first applied. The circumstances are that: the person was not proceeded against within 12 months for a relevant offence, or if proceeded against was acquitted or the proceedings were dismissed or discontinued; the person is subject to an order under s.1 of the Probation of Offenders Act 1907 and has not been convicted of a relevant offence within a period of three years from the making of the order; or the person's conviction was quashed or declared to be a miscarriage of justice. In the case of a person who was not proceeded against, the failure to institute proceedings must not be due to the fact that the person absconded or could not be located. The period between the generation of the DNA profile from the sample and the expiry of the three-month period is called the "retention period". This section is expressed as being subject to s.81 as that section permits an extension of the retention period in certain circumstances.

Those circumstances (s.81) are where the Commissioner of the Garda Síochána determines that it is necessary to retain the DNA profile concerned in the reference index of the System to assist in the investigation or prosecution of offences.

The circumstances in which the Commissioner may determine that the profile is to be retained are either: (i) a decision on whether to institute proceedings against the person has not been taken or the investigation concerned has not been concluded; or (ii) having regard to specified factors the Commissioner believes it is necessary.

The specified factors include whether the person has any previous conviction for an offence similar in nature or gravity, the nature and seriousness of the offence, whether the victim or intended victim was a child, a vulnerable person or a person associated with the person (as defined in s.75) and the age of the person at the time the sample was taken.

The length of the permitted extension period varies depending on the ground on which the extension is authorised. However, in all cases it is subject to a maximum of six years in the case of an adult or three years in the case of a child or protected person from the date on which the sample from which the profile concerned was generated or, if appropriate, the date on which the sample is deemed under s.86 to have been taken from the person concerned.

Section 83 concerns former offenders. It provides that a person from whom a sample was taken under s.34 may apply to the Commissioner to have the profile generated from that sample removed from the System in the event that a conviction has been quashed or declared to be a miscarriage of justice. A right of appeal lies to the District Court.

While an indefinite retention arrangement is in place for the DNA profiles of convicted persons entered in the system, s.84 makes an exception in the case of child offenders other than those convicted of offences triable by the Central Criminal Court or prescribed by the Minister having regard to their nature and seriousness. A retention period of four years or six years applies depending on whether the sentence imposed was non-custodial or custodial. The application of these reduced retention periods is subject to certain qualifications such as the child offender not being convicted of an offence within the default period.

Disclosure in Criminal Cases The Law Reform Commission (LRC) published its report on *Disclosure and Discovery in Criminal Cases* (LRC 112 –2014). It noted the prevailing background of uncertainty in respect of the operation in practice of the prosecution's duty of disclosure in criminal cases. It pointed out that case law has consistently noted the duty of disclosure forms a central part of the right of the accused to a fair trial in accordance with Art.38.1 of the Constitution. The case law has emphasised that the general duty is to disclose any material that may help the defence case, help to damage the prosecution case or give a lead to other evidence.

The LRC noted that, nonetheless, difficulties have emerged particularly in relation to the precise scope of the duty of disclosure, the absence of a clear procedure for ensuring that disclosure is made, and made in a timely fashion. Also noted by the LRC was the absence of a formal procedure for disclosure of material held by third parties, not the prosecution, and the absence of rules for dealing with claims of privilege or confidentiality which may arise in relation to those materials.

The LRC recommended that legislation be enacted to provide a clear framework to address those difficulties and the report included a draft Criminal Procedure

(Disclosure) Bill, which includes, among its provisions, a section which requires disclosure as soon as practicable and in any event not later than the date on which the book of evidence is served, in the case of trial on indictment. It also provides that objective material, such as CCTV footage, should be disclosed at an early stage of an investigation.

The report calls for introduction of a pre-trial preliminary hearing, in which the defence, the prosecution, a third party or any person affected by a request for disclosure are provided with an opportunity to have a judicial determination of the disclosure of prosecution material, including where a claim for privilege or confidentiality is made.

Gardaí question suspect about an offence other than the one for which he was arrested In *DPP v MC* [2014] IESC 28, the respondent was acquitted by order of the Special Criminal Court on an interpretation of s.30(3A) of the Offences against the State Act 1939 (the "1939 Act"). He had been tried in the Special Criminal Court on a single count of unlawful possession of an explosive substance. The only evidence against him was a statement of admission made in answer to garda questions while he was detained. The reason for the decision of the court to acquit him was that, in the opinion of the court, the respondent had been in unlawful custody when he made the statements of admission.

On 11 September 2010, the respondent was arrested by a member of An Garda Síochána pursuant to s.30 of the 1939 Act on suspicion that he was a member of an unlawful organisation contrary to the provisions of s.21 of that Act. This arrest followed a search of the respondent's home during which the Gardaí discovered an electrical grinder and a quantity of ammonium nitrate, an explosive material. The respondent was taken to Monaghan Garda Station. He was introduced to the member in charge and detained. The member in charge was informed that the respondent had been arrested on suspicion of membership of an unlawful organisation.

At first the respondent was questioned in relation to the membership charge. At a certain stage during his detention, he was informed that he was then going to be questioned in relation to the explosives that had allegedly been found at his home. Having initially declined to answer any questions, he changed his position and made a statement in which he accepted responsibility for possession of both the electric grinder and the explosive (ammonium nitrate). This was the evidence on which the prosecution relied.

Counsel on behalf of the respondent argued that his detention had become unlawful at the point at which the Gardaí commenced to question him about an offence other than the one for which he had been arrested. The DPP referred a question of law on the issue to the Supreme Court. It was not disputed that any statements of admission made by the respondent while he was in unlawful custody would be inadmissible in evidence against him. The question was whether the custody was lawful.

Clarke J. (dissenting) held the Special Criminal Court had erred in ruling the custody was unlawful. He said it was clear that questioning for an offence other than the one in respect of which the suspect was arrested can occur but that the admissibility of any evidence consequently obtained is dependent on the suspect remaining in lawful custody. That issue turned on whether a bona fide suspicion remained in being in respect of the offence for which the accused was originally arrested, applying *DPP v Howley* [1989] I.L.R.M. 629.

Fennelly J., giving judgment of the Supreme Court, held the Special Criminal Court was correct: it could not apply *Howley*, on the basis that decision had not interpreted the subsequently enacted s.30(3A) of the 1939 Act as amended by s.21 of the Criminal Justice (Amendment) Act 2009, which states:

> (3A) If at any time during the detention of a person pursuant to this section a member of the Garda Síochána, with reasonable cause, suspects that person of having committed an offence (the "other offence") referred to in subsection (1) of this section, being an offence other than the offence to which the detention relates, and—
>
> (a) the member of the Garda Síochána then in charge of the Garda Síochána station, or
>
> (b) in case the person is being detained in a place of detention, other than a Garda Síochána station, an officer of the Garda Síochána not below the rank of inspector who is not investigating the offence to which the detention relates or the other offence,
>
> has reasonable grounds for believing that the continued detention of the person is necessary for the proper investigation of the other offence, the person may continue to be detained in relation to the other offence as if that offence was the offence for which the person was originally detained, but nothing in this subsection authorises the detention of the person for a period that is longer than the period which is authorised by or under the other provisions of this section.

In the court's ruling, that amended section "clearly requires the intervention" of the member in charge before the detained person can be questioned in relation to another offence. While Fennelly J. accepted he could "see a possible argument that, if the original suspicion persists, that could, on a narrow reading, suffice to justify the detention and that no further authority is required", he continued that regard must be had to the fact that the person is being detained on the authority of the State for the purpose of investigating a crime of which he is suspected, but must be presumed innocent. He held that as s.3A did not exist, it was not interpreted in *Howley*. As there had been no intervention by the member in charge in the circumstances of the instant case then the detention was, he considered, unlawful and the Special Criminal Court was correct in arriving at the same conclusion.

ROAD TRAFFIC

The Road Traffic Act 2014 introduces the offences of failure to display an N-Plate on a mechanically propelled vehicle driven by a novice driver, and interference with the odometer of such a vehicle.

N-Plate Section 4 says it is an offence for a driver who is the holder of a first driving licence for the period of two years from the date of its issue (a "novice") to drive a mechanically propelled vehicle in a public place unless there is displayed an N-Plate. An N-plate is a rectangular plate or sign bearing the letter "N", not less than 15 centimetres high in red on a white ground, in clearly visible vertical positions to the front and rear of the vehicle. A novice driver is defined in s.3.

Interference with Odometer Section 14 introduces into Irish law the offence of interference with the odometer of a mechanically propelled vehicle—known colloquially as "clocking". The offence was enacted following considerable lobbying—by industry commentator *cartell.ie* and others—amid concern over the rise of the practice and consequent requirement to better protect consumers. "Clocking", effectively, means the odometer of the vehicle misrepresents, usually understates, the true mileage the vehicle has travelled. This impacts on the vehicle's open market selling price and gives rise to other concerns such as repair and maintenance schedules for the vehicle and passenger safety.

A person commits an offence under the section where he or she interferes, or attempts to interfere, with the odometer and cannot show subs.4 applies, namely: the person was acting in good faith in order to test, repair or replace the odometer. Subsection 2 makes it an offence for a person to "procure another person to contravene" the section, meaning it would be an offence for a person to request another to use, for instance, mileage correction equipment to alter the odometer to reflect anything other than the true actual mileage. A person is liable on conviction to a class C fine or to imprisonment for a term not exceeding three months, or to both.

SENTENCING

Sentencing Guidelines In *DPP v Z* [2014] IECCA 13, *Z* pleaded guilty to 14 sample counts of rape and child cruelty against four of his daughters in circumstances where he had initially pleaded not guilty to 271 counts of rape and cruelty and changed his plea the day before the trial. He was sentenced by Carney J. to life imprisonment on each of the counts of rape and two and seven years respectively (being the maximum sentence permitted in each case) on the counts of cruelty. The remaining counts were, after a discussion with counsel, taken into consideration.

The sentencing judge had available to him a comprehensive account of the appalling and depraved abuse, both physical and sexual, inflicted by Mr Z on his four daughters over a prolonged period of time. In all the circumstances, as pointed out, the sentencing judge imposed the maximum sentence permitted in respect of each of the offences and in particular imposed a sentence of life imprisonment in respect of each of the counts of rape. It was against those sentences, and in particular the imposition of the life penalty, that Mr Z appealed.

During the course of the sentencing hearing, a discussion had occurred between the sentencing judge and counsel for the DPP concerning the appropriate approach to sentencing in a case such as this. Initially, counsel for the DPP submitted that the case was, on its facts, at the top end of the range. The CCA agreed with that assessment, saying, there could be little doubt, on the basis of the evidence, that counsel was correct and it would "frankly be difficult to overestimate the severity of the many cruel and depraved crimes committed by Mr. Z against his own children".

Thereafter, however, the trial judge sought further assistance from counsel for the DPP in relation to the actual range of sentences which might be considered appropriate for a case of this type being one at the top end of the range. Having taken instructions, counsel submitted that the top end of the range, even in cases where there has been a plea of guilty, permitted either a very lengthy determinate sentence or a life sentence.

In its judgment, the CCA commented on this exchange saying, for many years it was the practice in criminal courts for the prosecution not to offer any view on sentence as such, but, whatever may have been the merits of such a practice in the past, such a practice can no longer be justified. The CCA stated (para.2.4):

> "It seems to this Court that it is incongruous that the DPP should be entitled to criticise on appeal, on the basis of undue leniency, a sentence imposed by a sentencing judge without having first suggested to the sentencing judge the sentence or range of sentences which it was submitted ought be considered appropriate."

The court continued saying there were developments which ought to assist the DPP in giving guidance to the court. It cited cases such as *DPP v Carl Loving* [2006] 3 I.R. 355 (child pornography offences); *DPP v Derrick Stronge* [2011] IECCA 79 (dangerous driving causing death); and *DPP v Brian Wall* [2011] IECCA 45 (offences under s.15A of the Misuse of Drugs Act 1977), saying these were cases where the CCA had endeavoured to conduct an analysis of the case law in relation to sentences for those particular types of offences and give some general guidance as to the type of sentences which might be appropriate for offences with a particular level of seriousness along the spectrum. The court also mentioned the ISIS (Irish Sentencing Information System) project, which provides details as to the range of sentences which are typically imposed by sentencing judges for particular types of offences. The court stated (para.2.5):

> "There is no reason why the attention of a sentencing judge should not be drawn to such decisions and submissions made as to where, in the light of the analysis by this Court, the offence in question is said to lie along a spectrum of severity. In many of the cases this Court had endeavoured, as it will do in this case, to identify the principal factors which will ordinarily influence a decision as to where along the spectrum of seriousness of the offence concerned a particular offence might lie. In some cases, this Court may endeavour to provide further guidance as to how such factors may convert into actual sentences. For example, in a judgment delivered today in *Director of Public Prosecutions v. Ryan*, a formation of this Court (differently constituted in part) sought to give such guidance in relation to sentencing for certain firearms offences. Likewise in a further judgment delivered today in *Director of Public Prosecutions v. Fitzgibbon* similar guidance is given in respect of assault causing serious harm."

In a significant passage the court stated (para.2.7):

> "In this Court's view, there is now an obligation on the prosecution to draw to the attention of a sentencing judge any guidance, whether arising from an analysis carried out by this Court or from ISIS or otherwise, which touches on the ranges or bands of sentences which may be considered appropriate

to any offence under consideration and the factors which are properly, at least in ordinary cases, to be taken into account. In many cases, this should not impose any significant burden on the prosecution for the sources ought be easily recognised. In addition, it seems to this Court that it is incumbent on the prosecution to suggest, where such guidance is available, where the offence under consideration fits into the scheme of sentencing identified and why that is said to be the case. Finally, the prosecution should indicate the extent to which it is accepted that factors urged in mitigation by the defence are appropriate and give at least a broad indication of the adjustment, if any, in the overall sentence which it is accepted ought to be considered appropriate in the light of such mitigation."

The court then moved to directly address the issue of appeals on the grounds of undue leniency when it stated (para.2.8):

"Without engaging in such an exercise, it is unfair that the sentencing judge should be capable of being criticised on appeal by the DPP for undue leniency where the DPP has not suggested to the trial judge the sentence or range of sentences which is said to be appropriate in the first place. If a sentencing judge imposes a sentence outside the range suggested by the DPP, then it is, of course, open to the DPP to appeal, provided that the divergence from what is said to be an appropriate approach to sentencing involves an error of principle. But that right of appeal carries with it an obligation to indicate, in advance, to the sentencing judge, what the DPP considers the proper approach should be in the first place."

This ruling, even confined to that specific extract, is particularly significant as, in effect, the CCA is stating it was incongruous for the DPP to fail to offer assistance on sentencing at trial, and then appeal the sentence imposed if it was consequently not satisfied with the outcome. The new approach is clear: counsel for the DPP should draw the sentencing judge's attention to any guidance, whether pursuant to previous decisions of the CCA or ISIS; then indicate where the offence under consideration fits into the scheme of sentencing there identified; say why that is said to be the case; and give its assessment on mitigating factors—those which are considered appropriate—and to what extent, in the view of the DPP, they should impact on the sentence imposed.

The court clarified aspects of the process which the DPP considered might raise difficulties in its decision in *DPP v Fitzgibbon* [2014] IECCA 25. That decision is not to be confused with the original court decision in *Fitzgibbon*, delivered the same day as *Z*, but was, instead, a related hearing on the matter of sentence after finding an error in principle in the original *Fitzgibbon* case [2014] IECCA 12. In *Fitzgibbon*, the court emphasised its intention in *Z* was to achieve consistency in sentencing:

"[I]t is important to note that an important factor behind the views expressed by this Court in *Z* is a desire, while recognising the significant range of different factors which may be relevant to the sentencing process in any individual case, to bring about the maximum level of consistency in

> sentencing which is compatible with giving proper weight to … individual factors."

The CCA ruled in *Z* the sentencing judge is in no way bound by the submissions of the DPP, and it is open to defence counsel to put forward any matters which are urged in mitigation. This was re-emphasised in *Fitzgibbon* when the court re-iterated:

> "It is clear that the question of sentencing is purely a judicial matter. It is not for any outside party to give guidance to a sentencing judge as to what the sentence in a particular case should be. But there is a very real difference between guidance, on the one hand, and assistance, on the other. What this Court suggested in *Z* was that counsel for the D.P.P. should be of assistance in drawing to the attention of the Court, any relevant materials which, it might be suggested, the Court should take into account in imposing sentence."

The court explained its distinction between "guidance" on the one hand and "assistance" on the other: it was not for the DPP to indicate to the judge the appropriate sentence is between *x* and *y* years. However, it was appropriate for counsel for the DPP to "draw the Court's attention to the fact that this Court has given guidance as to the appropriate ranges of sentences for crimes of a particular type and to submit, on the facts and having regard to appropriate sentencing principles, that the case in question falls into a particular part of that range".

In the matter before the court in *Z*, the CCA upheld the sentence imposed by the court at trial. The court noted Criminal Justice Act 1999, s.29 which provides that a court is not precluded from passing the maximum sentence in respect of any offence, notwithstanding a plea of guilty, if the court is satisfied that there are "exceptional circumstances relating to the offence which warrant the maximum sentence". The CCA stated s.29 requires the court to balance the exceptional nature of the offence (if that be found) with such mitigating factors as are present and clearly permits the court, in an appropriate case, to take the view that the exceptional nature of the offence outweighs any mitigation present so that the maximum sentence can still be imposed. The CCA stated the exceptional circumstances in cases of the type before the court in the instant case "are to be found in the nature of the offences themselves".

The CCA also stated (para.4.1 to 4.3):

> "The test is as to whether there are exceptional circumstances surrounding the offence which would warrant the imposition of the maximum penalty of life imprisonment notwithstanding such mitigating factors as there may be. While it may always be possible to envisage a worse case (abuse might have gone on for a longer period or involved more children or had different, and arguably more depraved, features), nonetheless, in order that it might be said that there are exceptional circumstances relating to the offence, it is not necessary that it be impossible to envisage an even more serious offence of the type concerned. What is required is that the particular offence not only be of a very serious type of the offence concerned but be so in an exceptional way.

> While it might have been preferable for the sentencing judge to have identified the features which he considered rendered these offences exceptional, this Court has no doubt that a fair reading of the sentencing judge's ruling as a whole makes it clear that he considered that the evidence which he had heard placed this case in the exceptional category. It seems clear from the first two paragraphs of the transcript of the trial judge's ruling on sentence that he considered the facts as had been recorded on the transcript of the sentencing hearing as in indicating a range of offending 'both as regards multiplicity of offences and the heinousness of the acts making up the constituent parts of each individual crime' as giving rise to exceptional circumstances. This view is confirmed by the fact that, in the first part of the final sentence in para.2, the sentencing judge states that he is satisfied that 'a life sentence [is] warranted on the facts of the case'. This Court is strongly of the view that the sentencing judge was more than entitled to come to such a conclusion on the evidence before him."

The court considered there were striking similarities between the instant case and the Supreme Court decision in *DPP v R McC* [2008] 2 I.R. 92; it was clear to the court that both fell into an exceptional category which involves prolonged and depraved sexual and physical violence against persons who are entitled to place their trust in the perpetrator.

As regards mitigating factors, the court considered the plea of guilty, so late in the day, was not to be factored in mitigation. The court considered a late plea "of little value". It also considered whether the sentencing judge had taken adequate account of the dysfunctional background of Mr Z and his abuse problems. The court made reference to a decision of a differently constituted Court of Criminal Appeal, delivered the same day as *Z*, in *DPP v Adam Fitzgibbon* (see below), where it made clear that drink or drugs abuse and a dysfunctional background can be a mitigating factor. The court in *Z* stated it "agrees with the analysis of that issue in *Fitzgibbon.* It is clear, therefore, that there may be cases where either or both, or particularly a combination of, a dysfunctional background and substance abuse, can be a factor which needs to be materially taken into account." However, turning to the instant case, the court was of the view that, on the facts, any mitigation which might derive from background or substance abuse could not possibly outweigh the exceptional nature of the offences themselves.

Finally, the court addressed the issue of rehabilitation, saying such a prospect is a matter which the court must always take into account. However, the weight to be attached is dependent on the facts of the individual case. Where a cogent basis is put forward for suggesting that there is a real prospect of rehabilitation, it may carry significant weight so far as mitigation is concerned. In contrast, where any hope of rehabilitation is purely speculative, little weight may attach. The court stated (para.4.10):

> "In addition, it must be noted that any such speculative hope of rehabilitation will be present in virtually every case. The whole point of s.29 of the 1999 Act is that it may nonetheless be permissible to impose the maximum sentence notwithstanding limited mitigation. Mitigation which would be present in virtually any case cannot, therefore, of itself, necessarily exclude

> the imposition of the maximum penalty in an exceptional case. If it could, it would have the effect of rendering the section largely inoperative."

The court upheld the maximum sentence of life imprisonment and dismissed the appeal. Such mitigating factors as were present were not sufficiently weighty to preclude a sentencing judge from imposing the maximum sentence given the horrific and exceptional nature of the crimes at issue.

Sentencing Guidelines in Assault Causing Serious Harm Cases (section 4) The second significant decision delivered by the Court of Criminal Appeal on matters of sentencing was *DPP v Fitzgibbon* [2014] IECCA 12. In this case, a serious assault took place at an Applegreen service station in Corbally, Co. Clare in full view of CCTV cameras, tapes from which were played to the court. The victim was aged 16 at the time of the assault which was described as "unprovoked, sustained and vicious".

The appellant pleaded guilty to a charge of assault causing serious harm contrary to the Non-Fatal Offences Against the Person Act 1997 (the "1997 Act"), s.4, and was sentenced by Carney J. to a term of 15 years imprisonment with the final three years suspended. He appealed against severity of that sentence. Counsel for the appellant presented two principal arguments: the sentence was not consistent with other assaults of a similar nature, and insufficient weight was given to mitigating factors.

The background to the case is relevant and so it will be set out in further detail. On the evening of the offence, the appellant was under the care of two workers from the HSE who had arranged to collect him from the city centre of Limerick. The evidence was that when he was picked up he appeared to be under the influence of drink and drugs, (he later said he was "stoned out of his head on vodka and tablets") was agitated and was hyperactive. He was being driven back to a residential home when he shouted to the driver to pull in and, just as the car was parked, got out saying "you have no idea what I am capable of". He then walked towards his victim who was sitting on a window sill outside of a pharmacy at the filling station.

He then launched what the court considered was a vicious and frenzied attack on his victim involving 26 punches to the head, 65 stamps on the head and two stamps to the chest. The attack lasted over four minutes during which time the victim was for the most part lying motionless on the ground and offering no resistance. One witness (there were 11 in all, including the two care workers) indicated that Adam Fitzgibbon had said that the victim "had got my friend 35 years, the scumbag c..t". Brain scans afterward demonstrated that the victim suffered a left sided subdural haematoma and right-sided fracture of the orbit.

The appellant was 17 years old at the time of the offence. He had, what was described as, an unfortunate upbringing: unavailable parents; ineffective parenting strategies; multiple disruptions in relation to his sense of home; a father who was coming and going in his life; difficult father-son relationship; problems at school from primary level; undiagnosed learning disability; ineffective identification of specific learning difficulties; early drug use; association with older peer group; involvement in petty criminal activity; expulsion from school; psychoactive drug dependence; alcohol abuse; conflict orientated and defensive in interpersonal relations; acceptability of violence in peer group; absence of life goals and planning; and, situational variables in relation to group rivalries.

The sentencing judge at trial first held that the influence of drink and drugs "affords no defence but also no mitigation in one's responsibility to society."

He went on to say (para.5.1):

> "I take account of 1) the unprovoked nature of the attack; 2) the ferocity of the attack; 3) the sustained nature of the attack; 4) the fact that only the intervention of a third party saved Kevin Meaney from worse; 5) the nature of the injuries inflicted; and 6) the effects on the victim and his family."

He considered the appropriate sentence was one of 15 years' imprisonment before turning to consider mitigating factors. As regards the accused's dysfunctional background he considered "this affords little, if any, mitigation". The mitigating factors the judge expressly referred to were: the accused's plea of guilty; the accused's lack of previous convictions prior to the date of the instant offence; the age of the accused and an obligation to provide him with a tunnel of hope for the future and rehabilitation.

Taking those factors into account, the trial judge suspended the final three years of Adam Fitzgibbon's sentence on condition he enter a bond in the sum of €1,000 to stay away from the victim and his family in perpetuity.

Giving judgment the CCA first addressed some general principles. The court made reference to a decision of a differently constituted Court of Criminal Appeal, delivered the same day as *Fitzgibbon*, in *DPP v Ryan*, (see below) where the court set out the proper approach in assessing sentence prior to the adjustment, if appropriate, of the sentence to reflect any mitigating factors. On the facts of that case, a detailed analysis was engaged in of the appropriate ranges of sentences to be imposed in respect of the possession of firearms in suspicious circumstances. In addition, the factors which were likely to properly influence the placing of a particular offence along the relevant scale were identified. The court in *Fitzgibbon* said it agreed with the broad approach adopted in *Ryan* and proposed, insofar as it was possible, to engage in a similar exercise in the instant case.

The court said it was only appropriate for the court to seek to give guidance on the range of appropriate sentences in circumstances where the court has available to it sufficient materials to enable it to make an appropriate assessment. It followed that the extent to which guidance could be given was dependent on the adequacy of such information and the degree to which it can be regarded as comprehensive. The CCA in the instant case considered it did not have the same degree of information available to it as the court dealing with *Ryan* and, thus, the guidance given in *Fitzgibbon* was described as being necessarily, "more tentative".

The court proceeded to summarise the salient decisions. In *DPP v Osborne*, unreported, Court of Criminal Appeal, 29 May 2003, the CCA upheld a sentence of eight and a half years. The sentencing judge accepted the accused may have been under an initial misapprehension on coming on the scene of an event. However, by the time the serious assault which was at the heart of that case occurred, the sentencing judge was satisfied that the accused could have been under no misapprehension but that the victim was an innocent party. The assault was particularly serious and caused the victim to suffer from significant permanent disability. There was some debate in that case about potential comparison between sentences for serious assaults and those for manslaughter. In that context, Geoghegan J., delivering judgment, said:

> "The sentence appropriate to the permanent destruction of a young man's life may not necessarily in all circumstances be less than the sentence which would have been appropriate for manslaughter if death had resulted from the same crime."

In *DPP v Hogan*, unreported, Court of Criminal Appeal, 28 April 2003 the CCA upheld a sentence of 12 years in a case which involved the accused bursting in on the victim in the victim's dwelling house with such force that the door burst from its hinges. The victim was stabbed multiple times with a Stanley knife including a significant mark being cut into his back. The assault required 99 stitches. Giving judgment, Hardiman J. said there were no mitigating factors of any substance.

In *DPP v McMahon* [2011] IECCA 94, the accused, following a discussion as to the continuing need to take certain medication, stabbed his treating consultant psychiatrist a total of eight times on various parts of his body. He then stabbed another doctor who had responded to the commotion. The stab wounds caused a life-threatening haemorrhage in his treating consultant, who as result of the attack, suffered from a severe form of Post-Traumatic Stress Disorder with superimposed depression. The wounds to the responding doctor could also have been life-threatening. The accused in this case was charged with assault causing serious harm contrary to s.4 of the 1997 Act in respect of the attack on his treating psychiatrist and assault causing harm (s.3 of the 1997 Act) in respect to his actions relating to the responding doctor. Amongst the relevant factors were the facts that the accused had a previous conviction for manslaughter, and had been released from prison eight months prior to the offences. He pleaded guilty and was sentenced to 10 years' imprisonment for the section 4 offence, and three years on the section 3 offence to run concurrently. Those sentences were not backdated to take into account time spent in custody, which in effect meant a sentence of over 11 years.

The DPP appealed on the grounds of undue leniency, arguing that the threat which the accused posed to society necessitated a life sentence. The CCA, in its judgment, stated (para.8.3):

> "On this appeal the Director of Public Prosecutions did not argue that the sentence imposed was outside the permissible range of sentences for what might be described, however inaccurately, as an ordinary offender who committed an offence contrary to s.4 of the 1997 Act shortly after serving a prison sentence for manslaughter. This Court considers that the sentence imposed was at the lower end of that spectrum, and that a heavier sentence could have been imposed."

In *DPP v Cahill* [2008] IECCA 84, the accused, during an unprovoked attack, lunged at his victim with a six-inch blade causing a very severe injury. The medical report in the case confirmed that the injuries sustained were life-threatening and that the victim required emergency procedures on admission to hospital. Mr Cahill had a number of previous convictions, some for similar offences. He was initially sentenced to three years' imprisonment with two years of that sentence suspended. On appeal, this was increased to eight years' imprisonment with the final three years suspended.

In *DPP v Anthony McDonagh* [2010] IECCA 127, the accused was charged and convicted of three counts in relation to a shooting incident: possession of a firearm with intent to endanger life contrary to s.15(a) of the Firearms Act 1925, as substituted and inserted by s.43 of the Criminal Justice Act 2006, and as amended by s.35 of the Criminal Justice Act 2007; possession of a firearm with intent to endanger life contrary to s.15(a) of the Firearms Act 1925, as amended; and assault causing serious harm contrary to s.4 of the Non-fatal Offences Against the Person Act 1997. He was sentenced to 12 years' imprisonment on each count, all to run concurrently. However, the aggravating factor of possession of a firearm was present in that case.

The court cited O'Malley, *Sentencing Law and Practice*, 2nd edn (Dublin: Round Hall, 2006), where the author notes in Ch.16 the decision in *DPP v O'Brien*, unreported, Central Criminal Court, 28 April 2003 where a man who left his victim brain-damaged following an attack, necessitating full-time care, was sentenced to eight years' imprisonment with the final two years suspended.

The cases reviewed by the court all involve serious assaults and left serious consequences for the victims. All could be said to be, in the opinion of the court, to a greater or lesser extent, at the upper end of the range in terms of severity. The court noted the difficulty in relation to sentencing under the Non-Fatal Offences Against the Person Act, s.4, in that the range of sentences available—from a suspended sentence to life imprisonment—was broad. The CCA stated (para.8.7):

> "When faced with such a broad range, it is important that some attempt be made to identify both the factors which are properly taken into account when determining the severity of the offence and the culpability of the accused, and also that guidance be offered on the appropriate ranges of sentence (depending on the severity of the offence in question). As with all criminal offences, the primary focus must be on the extent of wrongdoing and culpability on the part of the accused."

The court said it was true the criminal law does have regard to consequences in distinguishing connected criminal offences. For example, murder is distinguished from attempted murder even though the reason why the intended victim was not killed may have nothing to do with the blameworthiness of the culprit. Likewise, the variety of offences involving assault are categorised by reference to the harm done. However, notwithstanding that characterisation, the primary focus must remain on the actions of the guilty party. The court stated (para.8.8):

> "In the context of section 4 offences, it must, of course, be acknowledged that, in order for such an offence to be committed, serious harm must be caused. In the vast majority of cases that serious harm will be at least a possible or predictable outcome of the assault. Even where the consequences might be somewhat more severe than might have been predicted in the light of the nature of the assault concerned, it will not ordinarily lie in the mouth of a person guilty of assault to place too great reliance on the fact

> that the consequences were more severe than might have been reasonably predicted. To a significant extent those who commit significant assaults take a chance on the consequences. However, there will always be cases where the unfortunate consequences of an assault are wholly disproportionate to the severity of the relevant assault and, thus, the blameworthiness of the guilty party. For those, or other unusual reasons, there will always be cases where, even without significant mitigation, and notwithstanding the serious consequences of the relevant assault, a non-custodial sentence would still be the appropriate starting point."

Having addressed sentences at the upper end of the range, the court moved to consider "tentatively" the lower end of the range. In the absence of unusual factors, a sentence of between two and four years was considered appropriate, before any mitigating factors are taken into account, for offences at the lower end of the range, and, a middle range sentence of between four and seven and a half years seemed appropriate to the court. The appropriate sentence for offences of the most serious type is seven and a half to 12 and a half years. The court said there were cases which would warrant, without mitigation, a sentence above 12 and a half years up to and including, in wholly exceptional cases, the maximum sentence of life imprisonment. The court referred to its decision in *DPP v Z* (see above) in relation to imposition of a maximum sentence.

In an important passage the court stated (paras 8.12 to 8.14):

> "First, it must be emphasised that the severity or viciousness of the assault by virtue of which a victim has suffered injury must always be a highly significant factor. Subject to the earlier comments made in that regard, the injuries suffered must also be taken into account. It does, of course, have to be acknowledged that there is not always an exact correspondence between the severity of an attack and the degree of injury suffered. Sometimes, although no thanks to the assailant, a person who is subjected to a particularly vicious attack luckily escapes with relatively minor injuries. Likewise, a relatively minor attack can have severe consequences. A single blow can, unfortunately, lead to serious injuries. While some regard must, nonetheless, be paid to the consequences of the assault much greater weight will obviously attach to those consequences where they are such as might reasonably be expected to flow from the nature of the assault concerned or at least are not wholly disproportionate to that assault.
>
> The degree of culpability of the accused is also an important factor. An entirely unprovoked attack will, ordinarily, be regarded more seriously than an assault which arises out of an incident, most particularly one which is not, or at least not only, of the perpetrators making. Factors such as provocation can be a legitimate factor to take into account in assessing the seriousness of an assault.
>
> The general circumstances surrounding the assault, including whether it was committed in the context of other criminality, can also be a factor. The use of weapons or other objects likely to make more severe the injuries caused can also be an important factor. As pointed out earlier, there will, doubtless, on the facts of any individual case, potentially be other factors which may need to be taken into account."

In respect of the instant case, the court said no true explanation has ever been given as to why the assault took place. The court said there could be little doubt that the video evidence in the case shows an appalling and vicious assault which could only be placed at the upper end of the range. The court continued (para.8.16):

> "However, it does need to be taken into account that many assaults do not occur in the full glare of video cameras. In such cases, all a sentencing judge has to go on are eye witness accounts which may not demonstrate the full ferocity and viciousness of an assault in quite the same way as a video camera can. Sentencing should not, however, be excessively influenced by reference to the extent to which there was graphic evidence available. While the Court agrees that this case is properly placed at the top end of the most serious part of the range, the Court is, nonetheless, not satisfied that this is one of those cases which is so severe or so serious that it must go beyond that range. In those circumstances, it seems clear to this Court that, before considering any question of mitigation, the initial indicative sentence proposed by the trial judge of 15 years was out of line with the generality of sentences reviewed in this judgment which relate to severe assaults with often catastrophic consequences for victims. On that ground alone, this Court is satisfied that the appeal would have to be allowed."

The court next considered mitigating factors. As regards the evidence, the accused was under the influence of drink and drugs and the court accepted that the mere fact an offence is committed by a person who is under the voluntary influence of drink or drugs does not, of itself, offer any significant mitigation. If people get drunk and commit offences while they are drunk, then they cannot be heard to use their drunkenness as a mitigating factor. However, the court considered that the situation was different for persons who suffer from a persistent problem of addiction or substance abuse who should have, in an appropriate case, that factor taken into account. The court stated (para.9.3):

> "There is a world of difference between a case in which a person seeks to rely on the fact that they were drunk to provide some partial mitigation for an offence and one where a person who suffers from substance abuse and, in particular, may be seeking to take steps to deal with their problem although not yet successfully, may seek to offer that as part of the general circumstances which ought to be taken into account."

The court also noted the cases where unfortunate elements in a person's background are put forward as factors in mitigation, saying, those cannot, of itself and by itself, amount to a significant mitigating factor. The court referred to its judgment, delivered by Geoghegan J., in *DPP v Stafford* [2008] IECCA 15, where it says (para.9.4):

> "The learned trial judge correctly points out that in the case of numerous offenders appearing before him there is a dysfunctional history. That of itself and by itself cannot really differentiate the case from many others. There are sound public policy reasons why minimal importance can be

> attached to mitigating arguments based on drink or drugs. Furthermore, many law abiding families suffer a series of unfortunate bereavements and that cannot be an excuse for crime. What the court thinks is important in this case, however, and given the nine year supervision order which the learned trial judge imposed, the court believes the trial judge was of the same view is the concrete evidence of genuine attempts at self-rehabilitation with particular reference to drugs. This seems clear from the reports which were before the judge. In considering whether the sentence is unduly lenient or not, the nine year supervision order should not be ignored. Clearly, it was thought out carefully by the learned judge and in a context that rehabilitation appeared viable."

The court emphasised the judgment delivered by Geoghegan J. in *Stafford* is not authority for the proposition that a dysfunctional background, no matter how severe, cannot be a potentially significant factor to be properly taken into account in the sentencing process, as appeared to be the interpretation of the sentencing judge at trial. The court stated (paras 9.6 to 9.7):

> "This Court went no further than to say that drink, of itself, or drugs, of itself, cannot be a mitigating factor. Likewise, some degree of dysfunctionality in background is not likely to provide a mitigating factor. However, that being said, a sentencing court is required to consider, as part of the overall circumstances, whether a persistent problem with substance abuse, most particularly if it could be said to stem from a particularly difficult upbringing, can amount to a factor which can weigh significantly in an appropriate sentencing process on the facts of a particular case. This will be so, as Geoghegan J. pointed out, especially if there are attempts at rehabilitation or, in the view of this Court, where the accused was particularly young at the time of the offence and where there may be a realistic prospect of rehabilitation in the future."

Giving judgment, on the issue of mitigating factors, the CCA said it was satisfied there was, likewise, an error in principle on the part of the trial judge.

After adjourning the matter, the court resumed (*DPP v Fitzgibbon* [2014] IECCA 25) to give sentence. The court substituted a sentence of 12 and a half years with three years suspended to take account of "all mitigating factors properly identified".

Sentencing Guidelines in Firearms Offences In *DPP v Ryan* [2014] IECCA 11, the Court of Criminal Appeal set down—for the third time in the same day—guidelines on matters of sentencing. Mr Ryan pleaded guilty to two firearms offences. The first concerned possession of a Browning semi-automatic pistol in such circumstances as to give rise to a reasonable inference that he did not have it in his possession for a lawful purpose. As noted by counsel, this offence is frequently referred to colloquially as "suspicious possession" of a firearm. The second offence concerned the possession of ammunition suitable for use in the Browning semi-automatic pistol in suspicious circumstances.

The evidence was that Mr Ryan was one of four occupants in a car which left the suburbs of Limerick heading in the direction of Ballyneety. The car turned onto a side road and stopped at the entrance to a field. Members of An Garda Síochána were carrying out surveillance in the area. At various stages, two of the occupants of the car got out of the car and searched undergrowth in a field. Eventually, Mr Ryan got out of the vehicle and pointed to a spot inside the fence into the field. As a result, a package was picked up and wrapped in a cloth bag which was returned to the car. The car, which was owned by Mr Ryan, then began to drive back towards Limerick City at which point it was stopped by Gardaí attached to the Special Detective Unit and the Regional Support Unit. The firearm and ammunition which were the subject of the charges were found in the cloth bag.

Under questioning Mr Ryan admitted his involvement but stated he did not intend to use the firearm in question. He stated that he was simply asked to collect a weapon and pass it on to a third party, whom he declined to name as he was in fear. There was a background issue of a feud amongst criminal gangs.

The prosecution, at the sentencing hearing, sought to link the firearms offences with the feud already mentioned. The only evidence proffered to that effect was a statement that the gun and ammunition were in Mr. Ryan's possession as part of the feud and evidence of a previous conviction for violent disorder in 2004 which was said to have also stemmed from his involvement in the feud.

The Court of Criminal Appeal stated the sentencing judge had been "careful" in how he dealt with the issue (para.4.8):

> "Now, the two accused were caught red-handed, so to speak. That's the case for the prosecution, and there seems to be a basis to make that argument. Now, there is a challenge to the admissibility of the evidence as to why they had the gun and the ammunition and maybe that objection is well based. But what can be ... asserted was that they were in possession of a gun, that ... Kieran Ryan has a previous conviction for an offence of violent disorder which was connected with the what's called, if I may call it, the main feud in the city. It cannot be said that this possession of this gun was connected with that feud but it can be said that he has a previous conviction for an offence related to the same feud. I think that's the safest way of approaching this. And the other matters, which are hearsay and which have been challenged by the defence ... I'll disregard, forget and will not take into account."

The CCA said the sentencing judge had formed the view the gun and ammunition could not be shown to be connected to the feud but the previous conviction of violent disorder – described by the DPP as a pitched battle between two factions in a car park in Limerick – was connected to the feud.

The CCA ruled the trial judge was entitled to take those circumstances into general account, but, was not entitled to re-punish Mr Ryan for the earlier offence. The CCA considered the trial judge had handled the matter well and no criticism could be directed at his approach.

In relation to sentencing, a number of factors were taken into account by the sentencing judge: Mr Ryan had pleaded guilty at a very early point, but had been caught "red-handed"; he had made a number of admissions at an early stage which would have facilitated his conviction; the tragic circumstances in which the father of Mr Ryan came to lose his life as part of the feud to which reference has already been made; his family circumstances where, having, it was said, "gone off the rails" after the death of his father, he had re-established himself, in family terms, with a child and partner.

The sentencing judge indicated that, were it not for any relevant mitigating factors, most particularly the early plea of guilty, he would have considered a sentence "very near the maximum. I would have been thinking of a sentence of 12 years". However, in the light of the early plea of guilty, a sentence of eight years on both counts was imposed.

On appeal, counsel for Mr Ryan suggested that, in the light of various decisions of the CCA, a starting point of 12 years, before applying an appropriate deduction for mitigating factors, was sufficiently out of line with what might be described as the going rate as to render it an error in principle.

The court next considered the case law:

In *DPP v Eoin Barry* [2008] IECCA 93, the accused had been sentenced to four years for the suspicious possession of firearms and ammunition but also in circumstances where there was, as in the instant case, an early plea coupled with a very early admission of responsibility when being questioned by An Garda Síochána. The accused and members of his family were subjected to significant threats.

In *DPP v James Melia* [2008] IECCA 106, the case had a complicating factor by virtue of certain offences being committed while on bail. There were also a number of separate offences. Ultimately, the CCA concluded that the sentences imposed by the trial court were unduly lenient and imposed a series of sentences which had the effect of cumulatively requiring the accused to serve a sentence of six years.

In *DPP v Darren Larkin* [2008] IECCA 138, the CCA varied sentences imposed by the sentencing judge to provide for a sentence of 15 years for attempted murder and 10 years for each of the relevant firearms offences. The accused had pleaded not guilty and had appealed his conviction. As the conviction for attempted murder demonstrates, this was a case where the firearms were actually used rather than one where they were simply being transported.

In *DPP v Denis Dwyer* [2009] IECCA 12, the CCA increased a sentence of four years to the presumptive minimum of five years where the accused had pleaded guilty to a count of possession of a Kalashnikov rifle together with relevant ammunition. That was also a case where the accused had, in the view of the CCA, been caught red-handed.

In *DPP v Owen Clail* [2009] IECCA 13, the accused had again pleaded guilty to offences relating to the possession of firearms and ammunition. One of the relevant weapons was a non-functioning Glock semi-automatic pistol. The CCA was, however, satisfied that, although non-functioning, the firearm was intended for criminal purposes. The second firearm was a revolver which was effective. It is also the case that the circumstances surrounding the finding of the weapons in question involved not just the weapons but also paramilitary paraphernalia. The CCA, before going on to consider any relevant mitigating factors, considered the appropriate range to be "7 to 8 years". In the light of certain mitigating factors, the last 18 months of a sentence of seven and a half years was suspended.

In *DPP v Martin Walsh* [2009] IECCA 150, the accused was found, as a result of surveillance, in a car with a sawn-off shotgun. In delivering the judgment of the CCA, Finnegan J. noted the nature of the weapon was a significant factor in determining the seriousness of the offence and considered the sawn-off shotgun in that case should come to the top end of such a hierarchy. The sentencing judge had imposed a term of five years which Finnegan J. described as "certainly at the very lowest end of what is appropriate in all the circumstances of the case".

In *DPP v Dermot O'Callaghan* [2010] IECCA 52, the Director of Public Prosecutions appealed on the basis of undue leniency. The sentences were imposed in respect of a series of offences including firearms offences. However, that was a case where the trial judge accepted, and the CCA agreed, that there were exceptional circumstances. It was considered "not particularly relevant to this case".

In *DPP v Garrett Fitzgerald* [2010] IECCA 53, the accused was sentenced for possession of a firearm and ammunition, the firearm in question being an automatic shotgun. There was again a very early indication of a plea of guilty. In delivering the judgment of the CCA, Denham J. indicated that "8 years would be the appropriate starting point". That was said to be the case by virtue of the nature of the gun and the fact that it was brandished in a crowded bar. In the light of a plea of guilty, the sentence was reduced to six years.

In *DPP v Christopher Curtin* [2010] IECCA 54, the accused was sentenced to seven years' imprisonment for possession of a firearm and ammunition. The CCA dismissed an appeal brought by the Director of Public Prosecutions on the basis of undue leniency. It was noted the relevant accused had a previous conviction for possession of a firearm with intent to endanger life. The CCA concluded the sentence might be considered to be lenient but nonetheless was satisfied that the Director of Public Prosecutions had failed to establish a sufficient error to warrant allowing the appeal.

Finally, in *DPP v Frank Ward* [2012] IECCA 15, the accused was sentenced in respect of offences which involved the shooting of the well-known publican, Mr Charlie Chawke. While a number of the offences with which the sentencing judge was concerned, relating to possession of a firearm, had attracted a sentence of 12 years, some of the more serious offences had attracted life imprisonment. The judgment of the CCA was principally concerned with whether a lengthy, although determinate, sentence was more appropriate than the life sentence.

Counsel for the DPP brought the court's attention to *DPP v Geasley*, unreported, Court of Criminal Appeal, 10 June 2013. In that case, the CCA heard an appeal brought by the accused against sentence. The sentencing judge had imposed a sentence of seven years. The offence related to the possession of glock pistols. The CCA increased the sentence (notwithstanding the fact that it was the accused's appeal) to one of 10 years with one year suspended. The court described the possession of the glock pistol as being "the enormous crime of possessing a lethal weapon" and stated that its judgment was necessary for the protection of the community and the deterrence of the prisoner.

Having reviewed the case law, the court summarised the position that the principal factors which will normally require to be taken into account in assessing the seriousness of an offence of possession of a firearm in suspicious circumstances are: (i) the nature and quantity of the firearm or firearms concerned; (ii) the extent to which any firearm was either actually used or brandished in a way which would have caused people to be concerned that it might be used; (iii) the extent that the offence arose or might be inferred to have arisen out of criminality generally (and if so the seriousness of same) or out of specific and personal circumstances; and

(iv) any circumstances concerning the culpability of the accused, such as the extent of the involvement of the accused or the extent to which it might be said that the accused was operating under a threat.

In the absence of exceptional and specific circumstances, there was a minimum presumptive, although non-mandatory, sentence of five years, according to the CCA. Before considering any appropriate adjustment to reflect mitigating factors, the court said it seemed in general terms, an offence at the lower end of the range ought attract a sentence of five to seven years, an offence in the middle of the range ought attract a sentence of seven to 10 years and an offence at the top of the range a sentence of 10 to 14 years.

Against that background, it is argued on behalf of Mr Ryan that an indicative sentence of 12 years, before any mitigating factors were taken into account, wrongly placed the offence in the middle of the most serious end of the range.

The CCA said in order for it to interfere with a sentence, it must, first, find there was an error in principle. The court stated (para.8.2):

> "Where the contention made on behalf of an appellant is, as here, that the sentencing judge's view of where the offence lies, in all the circumstances of the case, on the spectrum of seriousness, and the sentencing judge's decision as to how that assessment converts into an actual sentence, is incorrect, then, in order to regard the case as involving one in which an error of principle is established, it must necessarily be that this Court views the divergence from what would have been an appropriate assessment of the seriousness of the offence and the culpability of the accused and the appropriate sentence to be imposed in that context to be sufficiently significant to warrant a finding of error of principle. The fact that this Court might, had it been the sentencing court, have imposed a slightly lower or slightly higher sentence or assessed the case at a slightly lower or higher point on the spectrum of seriousness, would not, of itself, be sufficient to justify such a finding. However, in this Court's view the disparity just identified in this case is sufficiently significant to justify finding that the initial assessment of the trial judge, as to the seriousness of this offence and the sentence which it ought carry in the absence of mitigating factors, amounts to an error in principle."

Turning to the issue of mitigating factors, the CCA considered the deduction made by the sentencing judge was excessive. This was particularly so in the light of the fact that Mr Ryan had a very serious previous conviction for violent crime which would, in substance, have deprived him of any material entitlement to a reduction in sentence by reason of previous good character or relatively good character punctuated only by much less serious wrongdoing. The CCA stated (para.9.2):

> "In a number of the cases already analysed, a reduction of the order of 2 years or, perhaps, of one-quarter, seems to have been considered appropriate to reflect early admissions and an early plea of guilty. Given that there were no other significant mitigating factors identified by the trial judge in this case, it is difficult to see how a reduction of 4 years or one-third was appropriate."

In all the circumstances, the CCA was of the view that a sentence of eight years was excessive and substituted a sentence of seven years—applying a starting point of nine years with a deduction of two years for mitigating factors.

Rare case in which the maximum sentence is permissible In *DPP v Daniels* [2014] 11 J.I.C. 0401; [2014] IESC 64, the Court of Criminal Appeal certified a question for the consideration of the Supreme Court, namely, whether it is lawful to give an accused person the maximum term of imprisonment for the offence with which he is charged even where there are significant mitigating factors such as a guilty plea, a first offence, and age. The trial judge imposed a discretionary life sentence and that sentence was upheld by the Court of Criminal Appeal having regard to the obvious gravity of the case.

The facts of the case are disturbing. At 18 years of age, the applicant attempted to murder a young girl aged approximately 10 years of age. She was a neighbour of the applicant and he lured her to a field near their homes on the pretext of looking for some puppies that he said he had seen earlier on in the field. While they were engaged in the search for the puppies, the applicant took a lace out of his pocket, put it around the girl's neck and tried to strangle her. She tried to scream and he pushed her down on the grass. The lace was around her neck and she pretended that she was dead. The applicant took the lace off her neck and shortly afterwards, she was able to make her escape and ran home. There, she alerted a babysitter. The applicant was subsequently arrested and then charged. On the third day of his trial for attempted murder, the applicant pleaded guilty to the charge. A *nolle prosequi* was entered in respect of three other counts on the indictment.

In the course of the sentence hearing, evidence was given by Sergeant Tom O'Dwyer who described a number of admissions made by the applicant in the course of his interviews with the Gardaí following his arrest. Amongst other things he said: "I was just trying to inflict pain. I just wanted to see what it was like" and "I got the lace around her neck. When I did this it was my intention to choke her. I wanted to see what it would be like to kill somebody."

Aside from the issue of whether a life sentence was appropriate in light of mitigating factors, such as age, the Supreme Court was also asked to consider whether the sentence imposed amounted, effectively, to one of preventative detention—a sentence which sought to incarcerate the defendant for the future in order to prevent him from committing further offences—and whether this was permissible under Irish law.

Giving judgment the Supreme Court, Dunne J., upholding the maximum sentence, held the sentence imposed should not be longer than is necessary to punish the offender for the offence concerned. The court stated (para.13):

> "it is beyond doubt that a case in which a maximum sentence is imposed notwithstanding mitigating factors will be exceptional. Such a situation is, of course, provided for by the provisions of s.29 of the Criminal Justice Act 1999 in respect of guilty pleas and expressly provides at s.29(2) as follows:
>
> > 'To avoid doubt, it is hereby declared that subsection (1) shall not preclude a court from passing the maximum sentence prescribed by law for an offence if, notwithstanding the plea of guilty, the court is

> satisfied that there are exceptional circumstances relating to the offence which warrant the maximum sentence.'"

The court ruled that in order to reach the conclusion that a sentence included an element of preventative detention, it would be necessary to show that no court acting properly could have imposed the sentence. The facts of the case were, as described by Hardiman J., "extraordinary, chilling and frightening". It was described by the Supreme Court as one of those rare cases in which the maximum sentence permissible under the law was appropriate. Dunne J. stated (para.21):

> "it necessarily does have a preventative effect in that the applicant is not at liberty to commit further offences whilst in custody and thus society has the benefit of that protection but insofar as there is a preventative element achieved by the sentence I think it is fair to say as Hardiman J. said in the case of *The People (Director of Public Prosecutions) v. Duffy*:
>
> > 'The preventative effect is incidental to this: the sentence does not exceed what is required for purely penal purposes in so aggravated a case.'"

Dunne J. concluded (para.23):

> "When a sentence imposed on an individual is a proportionate sentence having regard to the seriousness of the offence and the personal circumstances of the offender, it could not be said that the sentence imposed was one which contained an element of preventative detention even in the exceptional circumstances that a maximum sentence has been imposed notwithstanding the existence of some mitigating circumstances. Some offences are so grave that a maximum sentence will be the appropriate sentence."

CCA Appropriate Court to Revoke a Suspended Sentence it imposed In *DPP v Foley* [2014] IESC 2, the Supreme Court considered a point of law referred to it from the Court of Criminal Appeal, namely: where the Court of Criminal Appeal has varied a sentence by wholly or partly suspending it, is the Court of Criminal Appeal the appropriate court vested with jurisdiction to consider the revocation of that suspended sentence?

On 19 April 2007, the Court of Criminal Appeal heard an appeal against alleged undue leniency brought by the Director of Public Prosecutions and allowed the appeal.

On 19 April 2007, the CCA (Kearns, Murphy, MacMenamin JJ.) said it would not interfere with a sentence of seven years' imprisonment consecutive to a 12-month sentence imposed for an earlier offence. The total that was arrived at was eight years and the sentencing trial judge suspended the entirety of the eight years, but, varying the sentence, after a finding of undue leniency, the CCA suspended five of the eight years and the suspension was to be on the same conditions as those fixed by the Circuit Court judge.

The appellant subsequently committed further offences after his release from custody, and, as he was in breach of the conditions attached to the five-year suspended term of imprisonment, he was remanded "to the next sitting of the Court that made the said order" (s.99(9) of the Criminal Justice Act 2006). The DPP, relying on the wording of that section, considered the appropriate court in the circumstances was the CCA.

On 19 October 2011, the CCA (Finnegan, Budd, O'Keeffe JJ.) delivered a reserved judgment holding that the CCA was the appropriate court to deal with the revocation, in whole or in part, of the five-year suspended portion of the appellant's sentence which had been imposed by the CCA on 19 April 2007.

It was that decision which the Supreme Court had to consider. Upholding the decision of the CCA, Denham C.J., giving judgment for the court said where the CCA has quashed a sentence pursuant to s.2 of the Criminal Justice Act 1993, by wholly or partly suspending it, the CCA is the appropriate court vested with jurisdiction to consider the revocation of the suspended sentence pursuant to s.99 of the Criminal Justice Act 2006.

Under the Court of Appeal Act 2014, the Court of Criminal Appeal was abolished.

Mitigating Factors adequately taken into account In *DPP v Byrne* [2014] IECA 45 the Court of Appeal (ex tempore) considered an appeal on severity of sentence imposed upon the appellant, a 77 year old, convicted of four counts of indecent assault on an indictment as sample counts on the understanding that remaining counts (15 counts total) would be taken into consideration.

The applicant was sentenced to two years' imprisonment on each of the counts with the other counts taken into account to two years' imprisonment, i.e. the maximum sentence of imprisonment on those four counts, totalling eight years' imprisonment. The learned trial judge then suspended the last or the latter four years of that, leaving a custodial sentence of four years and a suspended sentence of a further four years. There were mitigating circumstances in the case: the accused's personal circumstances, his family circumstances, the illness of his wife, and a plea of guilty.

The court was not satisfied there was any error in principle by the sentencing judge and it rejected the appeal as to the severity of sentence.

The President of the Court of Appeal, giving judgment, stated (paras 13 to 14):

> "What the judge did in the end was to total the various counts to come to eight years and then to make an allowance for various mitigating features. ... The plea of guilty, even though it came somewhat late in the day, it is not as early as it might have come, it is still of significant value ... Ultimately, having reached the total of eight years imprisonment, the learned trial judge applied a generous reduction of a full half of that period of time. That seems to this Court to represent an allowance that adequately covers all the points that might be made in mitigation."

Quite extraordinarily unusual circumstances Extraordinary mitigating factors were not taken adequately into account in another Court of Appeal decision, *DPP v Brett* (ex tempore) [2014] IECA 48. Here, the appellant, a man of previously unblemished character, caused the death of a victim while driving with a measured blood alcohol reading of 266mg per litre.

The accused pleaded guilty, and showed genuine remorse; those were described as normal mitigating factors by the court. There were also, in the view of the court, extraordinary mitigating factors, namely his health condition: he has very serious kidney trouble which requires dialysis three times every week. He also has eye problems. It was argued by counsel on his behalf that if he were to be sentenced to a jail sentence, his renal difficulties, with the need for regular dialysis three times a week for three and a half hours on each occasion, plus his vision impairment would cause him particular difficulties. He had very limited options for haemodialysis access. His mode of dialysis carried with it a significant risk of infection that was life-threatening.

In light of what the court described as "quite extraordinarily unusual circumstances that obtain in this case", it formed the view (the President giving judgment) that the sentencing judge at trial fell into error by insufficiently appreciating and evaluating the unusual health issues. The court suspended the balance of the sentence over and above what Mr Brett had already served in prison (seven weeks) on condition that he keeps the peace and be of good behaviour and not apply for a driving licence.

Probation Report should have been sought In *DPP v Doolan* [2014] IECA 22 the appellant, Mr Doolan, appealed against the severity of a sentence of two years imprisonment, with the final year suspended in respect of the offence of robbery at Hacketts Bookmakers on 5 December 2013. The appeal was firmly framed such that this was a case, it was argued, that should have been dealt with by way of a community service order or by way of an entirely suspended sentence. The judge at trial did not seek a probation report, and there were mitigating factors: first time offence, a good work record, and an early plea of guilty.

Birmingham J. giving judgment stated (paras 11 to 12):

> "The court's view is that the case that the learned trial judge was required to consider was a difficult one and a sensitive one. It was difficult because the offence of robbery is inherently a serious offence, but on the other side of the coin, the judge was being asked to proceed to sentence somebody who was a first time offender, somebody with the family background and circumstances described, somebody with a good work record, somebody who had pleaded at an early stage and had provided very meaningful cooperation indeed to the extent that he made possible the prosecution that was brought against him, which would otherwise have been impossible.
>
> It seems to the court in that situation where the case was, as we would identify it, quite finely balanced as to what the outcome should be, that the judge erred in not seeking a probation report and in not maximising the amount of information that would be available to him when it came to performing the difficult and sensitive task of sentencing in this particular case."

The Court of Appeal (ex tempore) requested a probation report, unavailable at trial, and, on reviewing the report substituted for the term of imprisonment a sentence of 200 hours of community service.

Callous disregard for the health of the injured victim In *DPP v McMenamy* [2014] IECA 47, the DPP applied to the Court of Appeal for review of a sentence of six years' imprisonment with the final year suspended on conditions for an assault occasioning serious harm on the victim, his fiancé.

The parties were living together. At the time of the episode, there were two boys in the house, the children of the victim. A third child was elsewhere. The two adults went out for some drinks; they came back; they let the babysitter go and there followed an episode involving considerable violence which lasted some time that was noticeable and noticed by the neighbours. In this altercation, the victim sustained, inter alia, a subdural haematoma, and bruising of her face and body.

The defendant, after inflicting those injuries, left her in a comatose or semi-comatose condition and did not ring an ambulance, or, when he rang an ambulance service he then changed his mind, and did not follow it up. It was clear that the victim was in grave need of hospital treatment.

When the victim did arrive at the hospital, she was admitted for months and gradually made a recovery to the extent that she has recovered but she was left with significant sequelae of a long-term, probably permanent, nature. These include a change of personality.

The court said this was not the first time Mr McMenamy had attacked a girlfriend. Two previous victims had been the subject of assault by him—one woman on two occasions and another woman on one occasion. On one occasion, he got a suspended sentence and on another he got a jail sentence with a part of it suspended.

The defendant had pleaded guilty and the sentencing court had a number of testimonials and references available to it before passing sentence. Giving judgment, the court stated (the President, ex tempore, para.9):

> "The sentence imposed by the learned Circuit judge fits the category of being located in the zone of acceptability as being a sentence that was legitimately open to the trial judge. However, in view of the serious aggravating features in this case, specifically two, the previous convictions for similar offences and the callous disregard for the health of the injured [victim] in the aftermath of the attack, those are very serious aggravating features."

The court substituted a sentence of 10 years' imprisonment with the final two years suspended.

Man had not met his case appropriately In *DPP v O'Keeffe* [2014] IECA 24, the appellant appealed against severity of sentence imposed in the Circuit Criminal Court in respect of an offence of assault causing harm contrary to s.3 of the Non-Fatal Offences Against the Person Act 1997. He was sentenced to four years' imprisonment with one year suspended. The assault in question arose out of an incident which occurred in the Anchor Bar in Dungarvan when the appellant was involved in an unprovoked glass attack on a victim which caused him severe and permanent injury described as "truly horrific". He sustained a significant laceration to his face, running from his right upper eyelid, down along his cheek, along the side of his nose, culminating in a deep laceration through his upper lip.

The victim was part of a group that was socialising with, and saying farewell to, one of their number who was about to go to Australia. They had been out for a meal and were having a few drinks after the meal and ended up at the Anchor Bar at about 23.00 on the night in question, which was 10 May 2008. They had just arrived in the Anchor Bar and were proceeding towards the bar. The appellant was also present in the Anchor Bar and he was part of another group that were participating in a stag party. As the injured party's group entered the Anchor Bar, it appeared that somebody in that group may have brushed off a member of the other group. The injured party turned around and as he turned around he was suddenly, and without any provocation offered by him, struck with a glass in the face by the appellant. Although the details were somewhat vague, the evidence before the court indicated there may have been a prior altercation of some sort involving other persons in the two respective groups, but if there had been it had had nothing to do with the injured party and he was not involved in any such incident.

Affirming the sentence imposed, the Court of Appeal, Edwards J. (ex tempore) accepted the appellant did offer an apology and he did express remorse and he did offer compensation, albeit late in the day, in the sum of €15,000 which was raised at considerable cost to him. There were, however, factors which went the other way such as giving a false name, evading apprehension, not offering a guilty plea at the earliest stage, and his offer of compensation and remorse was also not advanced at the earliest stage. The court stated (para.13):

> "Clearly, if this man had met this case appropriately, if he had not given a false name, if he had not evaded apprehension, if he had offered a plea of guilty at the earliest stage, if he had paid compensation at an early stage when it would have represented a clear indication of his remorse and his desire to make restitution, he would have been entitled to a very substantial credit and it might well have been the case that he would have been dealt with much less severely... ."

The court found no error of principle in respect of the sentence imposed by the Circuit Criminal Court and it was affirmed.

Sentence more severe in Dublin than Wicklow Finally, in *DPP v O'Brien* [2014] IECA 36 the appellant appealed against the severity of a sentence of six years imprisonment imposed in respect of a charge of violent disorder in circumstances where he stood trial at the Circuit Court in Dublin while another individual, involved in the same incident, had received a sentence of four years in the Circuit Court in Wicklow.

The background facts were extremely serious, involving a number of people participating in what the court described as "a quite outrageous assault and a quite outrageous incident at the home of the injured party". During the course of the incident, the injured party was struck with sticks and golf clubs, lost consciousness, suffered two fractures of the skull and various other fractured bones, rib injuries, a fractured wrist and many other injuries.

Counsel for the DPP argued there was a basis for the different sentences imposed in that there was a suggestion that the appellant had produced a knife in the course of the incident or brought a knife to the incident and held it in proximity to the face of the victim. Counsel for the appellant argued that it appeared a knife was subsequently substituted in evidence for a slash hook. The court was not impressed with the distinction, saying (para.7):

> "If it is the case that a slash hook was used or threatened as distinct from a knife, it certainly does not seem to the court that that improves matters from the point of view of Mr. O'Brien. However, the essential point and the heart of this case is the disparity between how Mr. O'Brien was dealt with in Dublin and how Mr. Nealon was dealt with in Wicklow."

The court, Birmingham J. (ex tempore), substituted a sentence of four years so as to achieve parity with the sentence that was imposed in Wicklow Circuit Court on the other individual involved.

Electoral Law

BANKRUPTCY DISQUALIFICATION REPEALED IN FULL

The Electoral (Amendment) Act 2014 (the "2014 Act") repealed the bankruptcy disqualifications for election to and membership of Dáil Éireann and of the European Parliament. By virtue of Art.18.2 of the Constitution, which provides that for a person to be eligible for election to Seanad Éireann he or she must be eligible to be elected to Dáil Éireann, the effect of the 2014 Act was that the bankruptcy disqualification for membership of the Seanad was also removed.

It was noted during the Oireachtas debates on the 2014 Act that its enactment owed much to High Court proceedings which were at that time pending, *Godsil v Ireland and Attorney General*. In the *Godsil* case, the plaintiff wished to stand for election to the European Parliament in the elections to be held in May 2014, but as she had been declared bankrupt in February 2014 she was barred from standing under the legislation as it stood at that time. The plaintiff claimed that the exclusion of bankrupts from standing for election breached the guarantee of equality before the law in Art.40.1 of the Constitution, that it constituted discrimination on the grounds of social and economic status, and that it interfered with her right to a free choice as a voter on her own behalf and on behalf of the electors in the constituency in which she wished to stand. The effect of enacting the 2014 Act was that the plaintiff became eligible to stand in the European Parliament election in May 2014, which she duly did.

It is worth noting that the plaintiff withdrew her High Court proceedings after the 2014 Act was enacted. The High Court (Kearns P.) subsequently held that the plaintiff was not entitled to the full costs of her claim, but only to the administrative outlay, including stamp duty on filing documents. On appeal by the plaintiff, the Supreme Court (McKechnie, Dunne and Charleton JJ.) held, in *Godsil v Ireland and Attorney General*, unreported, Supreme Court, 24 February 2015 (not available on the Courts Service website at the time of writing, but a report of which was published in *The Irish Times*, 25 February 2015), that the plaintiff was entitled to her full costs in both the High Court and the Supreme Court. The defendants had opposed her application for costs on the grounds that she had "waited until the last minute" to bring her proceedings, and that the Government had moved expeditiously to bring the 2014 Act through the Oireachtas. The Bill that was enacted as the 2014 Act had been published on 7 April 2014 and, having passed through both Houses, it was signed by the President on 16 April 2014. The plaintiff had argued that, prior to the introduction of the Bill, the Government had given no indication that it would rush through a change in the law or that it was considering such a change. As a result, she argued that she was required to initiate her proceedings. She had also argued that costs should also be awarded to her because the case had been taken in the public interest.

Delivering the Supreme Court's judgment, McKechnie J. was reported to have stated that the plaintiff had been "directly instrumental" in bringing about a change in the law relating to bankruptcy which had stood since 1923; and that while such a result was not without precedent, it must surely be unusual. McKechnie J. stated that he could not see why "costs should not follow the event." Given the facts of this case, and the absence of any disqualifying conduct or factors, he could not find anything which "either in justice or in logic would justify anything less than a full cost order in this regard." He added that it was not therefore necessary to address the plaintiff's argument that she should be awarded costs because the case was brought in the public interest.

Returning to the Oireachtas debates on the 2014 Act, it was also noted that the plaintiff would have been entitled to stand in the local elections to be held in May 2014 (and, in fact, the plaintiff did so), because the disqualification of an undischarged bankruptcy had been removed by the Local Elections (Petitions and Disqualifications) Act 1974. It was also pointed out that, as of 2014, bankruptcy was not a disqualification for elections to the national parliaments or European Parliament in at least 18 EU Member States. In addition, the pre-2014 position gave rise to the following anomalies: an Irish citizen adjudicated bankrupt in another jurisdiction was eligible for election to the Dáil, or to the European Parliament to represent Ireland, but an Irish citizen adjudicated bankrupt in Ireland was not eligible for election to either; similarly, where a TD or an MEP was adjudicated bankrupt in Ireland, they ceased to be a TD or MEP, but if a person was adjudicated bankrupt in another jurisdiction a vacancy in the Dáil or the European Parliament would not arise. The same anomalies applied to membership of the Seanad.

It was accepted that it was difficult in the 21st century to identify a valid reason for retaining this disqualification, particularly having regard to the enactment of the Personal Insolvency Act 2012 (*Annual Review of Irish Law 2012*, pp.69–80) which had altered the view of bankruptcy to one of protection or remedy rather than punishment. It was accepted that, in the past, the disqualification from election to or holding elected public office by virtue of being an undischarged bankrupt partly reflected a concern that a person in such circumstances could be more susceptible to inappropriate influence. This, it was noted, might have had some validity when the provision was originally conceived in a previous era, but it had to be considered in the context of the current (and pending) legislative framework in place to uphold ethics in public office, to restrict the potential for inappropriate influence of private and corporate political funding and to guard against corruption. This legislative framework included the Ethics in Public Office Act 1995, the Standards in Public Office Act 2001, the Electoral (Amendment) (Political Funding) Act 2012 and the planned Criminal Justice (Corruption) Bill (of which the Scheme of a Bill had been published by the Department of Justice and Equality in 2012, and which would, when enacted, consolidate and reform the Prevention of Corruption Acts 1889 to 2010).

Section 1 of the 2014 Act provided for the removal of the disqualification of bankruptcy for election to the Dáil by repealing s.41(k) of the Electoral Act 1992 (the "1992 Act"), and for removal of the disqualification of bankruptcy for membership of the Dáil by repealing s.42(3) of the 1992 Act. Section 2 of the 2014 Act provided for the repeal of the bankruptcy disqualification for election to the European Parliament by removing the reference, in s.11(2)(a) of the European

Parliament Elections Act 1997 (the "1997 Act"), to s.41(k) of the 1992 Act. No statutory amendment was required to remove the bankruptcy disqualification for membership of the European Parliament because s.11(5)(a) of the 1997 Act simply provides that a person shall cease to be a member of the European Parliament if he or she becomes subject to any of the disqualifications referred to in s.11(2)(a) of the 1997 Act. No amendments were required to the Seanad Electoral (University Members) Act 1937 (the "1937 Act") because of the combined effect of Art.18.2 of the Constitution, referred to above, and because (mirroring Art.18.2), s.16(2) of the 1937 Act provides that "No person who is for the time being disqualified from or incapable of being elected as a Member of Dáil Éireann shall be a candidate at an election in a university constituency." Having regard to these cross-references to the Dáil provisions, the bankruptcy disqualification was, therefore, also in effect removed for the Seanad as a consequence of the amendments in the 2014 Act.

CLERKS OF DÁIL ÉIREANN AND SEANAD ÉIREANN

The Electoral (Amendment) (No.2) Act 2014 (the "2014 Act"), which comprises three sections only, provides that the Clerk-Assistant of Dáil Éireann may perform the functions of the Clerk of Dáil Éireann under the Electoral Acts whenever the Clerk of the Dáil is not available through illness, absence or other cause; and that the Clerk-Assistant of Seanad Éireann may perform the comparable functions of the Clerk of Seanad Éireann in similar circumstances. Section 1 of the 2014 Act provides that if and so long as the office of Clerk of Dáil Éireann is vacant or the holder of that office is unable through illness, absence or other cause to perform his or her functions under the relevant statutory provisions the Clerk-Assistant of Dáil Éireann shall perform those functions; and that the statutory provisions are those in the relevant sections of the Seanad Electoral (University Members) Act 1937, the Seanad Electoral (Panel Members) Act 1947 (the "1947 Act"), the Electoral Act 1992, the Presidential Elections Act 1993, the Referendum Act 1994 and the European Parliament Elections Act 1997. Section 2 contains comparable provisions in respect of the Clerk and Clerk-Assistant of Seanad Éireann.

During the Oireachtas debates on the 2014 Act, it was explained that many sections of the Electoral Acts provide that where the office of Clerk of the Dáil is vacant, the Clerk-Assistant of the Dáil shall perform the duties of the Clerk of the Dáil. For example, s.39 of the Electoral Act 1992, which deals with the issue and return of writs at Dáil elections, provides that the Clerk-Assistant of the Dáil shall carry out the duties of the Clerk of the Dáil if the office of Clerk of the Dáil is vacant or if the Clerk is unable to fulfil the duties through illness, absence or other cause. Another example is in Rule 101 of the Second Schedule to the European Parliament Elections Act 1997, which provides that the Clerk-Assistant of the Dáil shall perform the functions of the Clerk of the Dáil in respect of the filling of casual vacancies in the European Parliament whenever the office of Clerk of the Dáil is vacant or the Clerk is unable to fulfil the relevant duties through illness, absence or other cause.

It was noted, however, that prior to the enactment of the 2014 Act the Electoral Acts were not consistent in making such provision and the 2014 Act addressed this anomaly. It was also noted that the anomaly had come to notice when consideration was being given to the making of the by-election order to fill the vacancy in the Seanad arising from the election of Senator Deirdre Clune to the European Parliament in May 2014. Prior to the 2014 Act the legislative provisions on filling the vacancy were set out in Pt 5 of the 1947 Act, which requires the Clerk of the Dáil to perform specific functions in the by-election process. These include sending to the Seanad returning officer a "statement of the names, addresses and descriptions of all the members of the Dáil who are then entitled to sit and vote in that House." On receipt of that statement, the Seanad returning officer prepares a list which forms part of the electoral roll for the by-election.

As the office of Clerk of the Dáil was, in 2014, vacant and as there was no provision in the 1947 Act for a person other than the Clerk of the Dáil to furnish the necessary statement to the Seanad returning officer in respect of the electoral role, the by-election could not proceed in accordance with the 1947 Act. In addition to dealing with this specific difficulty of the Seanad by-election, the 2014 Act addressed all provisions in the Electoral Acts, that is, the entire electoral code where similar difficulties could arise in the future, in respect of both the Clerk of the Dáil and the Clerk of the Seanad.

During the Oireachtas debates on the 2014 Act, it was noted that the reason for the vacancy in 2014 in the office of Clerk of the Dáil (who is Secretary General of the Houses of the Oireachtas Commission and, therefore, the most senior civil servant in the Oireachtas) was an ongoing impasse as to the procedures to be put in place for the appointment of a new Clerk of the Dáil to replace the previous Clerk, Mr Kieran Coughlan, who had retired in 2013. This impasse was to be resolved when the Houses of the Oireachtas (Appointments to Certain Offices) Bill 2014 was enacted. At the time of writing (July 2015), the 2014 Bill had passed all stages in the Dáil and was at Committee Stage in the Seanad; and we will return to it in the *Annual Review of Irish Law 2015* if it is enacted in 2015.

EUROPEAN PARLIAMENT CONSTITUENCIES

The European Parliament Elections (Amendment) Act 2014 (the "2014 Act") implemented the recommendations in the *Report on European Parliament Constituencies 2013* and provided for the election of 11 MEPs in Ireland for the 2014 to 2019 parliamentary term. In 2012, the Constituency Commission had recommended no change to the State's constituencies for the European Parliament elections due to be held in 2014. However, with the impending accession of Croatia to the European Union, the European Council decided in June 2013 on a new allocation of seats to Member States in the European Parliament, the effect of which was to reduce Ireland's allocation of seats from 12 to 11.

The Electoral, Local Government and Planning and Development Act 2013 provided for the amendment of electoral law to allow for the setting up of a Constituency Commission in the circumstance that the allocation of seats to the European Parliament had been changed but a census was not held or due to be held. The European Parliament Constituency Commission was duly set up and reported in September 2013.

It was noted during the Oireachtas debates on the 2014 Act that the State's allocation had at one time been 15, and that the reduction to 11 would result in sprawling constituencies; and that the workload of the Irish representation would be even more thinly spread across 20 committees where, it was noted, the majority of the European Parliament's work is done.

The 2014 Act amended the European Parliament Elections Act 1997 (the "1997 Act") by replacing the Third Schedule to the 1997 Act with a new Third Schedule which set out the name of each constituency, the counties and cities that each constituency will be comprised of and the number of members that will be elected for each constituency in European elections held after 1 January 2014.

The major change from the pre-2014 configuration was that the 2014 Act provided for three constituencies instead of four. The reason for this change was that the Electoral Act 1997 specifies that there shall be three, four or five members in a European Parliament constituency. Given that 11 members were to be elected for the 2014 to 2019 parliamentary term, having four constituencies was not a viable option since it was not possible to allocate 11 seats across four constituencies of three, four or five members. The population per MEP in the three constituencies as of 2014 ranged from 409,276 to 424,356. By contrast, a broader range in terms of the variance of population is permitted for Dáil Éireann constituencies by Art.16.2.4° of the Constitution: see *Annual Review of Irish Law 2013*, pp.275–276.

The three-seat Dublin constituency remained unchanged, which comprises the counties of Fingal, Dún Laoghaire-Rathdown and South Dublin, along with the city of Dublin. The effect of this was that the Dublin constituency saw its representation closely aligned with the other constituencies in the State.

The 2014 Act provided for a new four-seat Midlands-North-West constituency. This comprises the counties of Cavan, Donegal, Galway, Kildare, Laois, Leitrim, Longford, Louth, Mayo, Meath, Monaghan, Offaly, Roscommon, Sligo and Westmeath, along with the city of Galway. In effect, this new constituency consists of the current North-West constituency, along with five counties which were in the former East constituency, but it will not contain County Clare.

The new South constituency comprises the current South constituency along with four counties from the former East constituency and County Clare. It contains the counties of Carlow, Clare, Cork, Kerry, Kilkenny, Limerick, North Tipperary, South Tipperary, Waterford, Wexford and Wicklow, along with the cities of Cork, Limerick and Waterford.

Electricity, Energy and Natural Resources

DR EVA BARRETT, Faculty of Law,
Maynooth University Department of Law

ELECTRICITY

Annual levies applied to entities involved in the electricity sector to fund the independent operation of the Irish energy regulator, the Commission for Energy Regulation On 31 December 2014, the Electricity Regulation Act 1999 (Electricity) Levy Order 2014 (S.I. No. 550 of 2014) came into effect. This Order provides for specific levies to be applied to entities involved in the electricity sector, i.e. the transmission system operator, the transmission system owner, the distribution system operator, the distribution system owner, generators, suppliers, interconnector operators and those permitted to construct electricity lines pursuant to art.37 of the Electricity Regulation Act 1999. Section 5 sets out the specific payments required.

ESB (the semi-state electricity provider) given a legal basis to engage in the installation and operation of electronic communications networks and services While still a bill, the ESB (Electronic Communications Network) Act 2014 was described by the former Minister for Communications, Energy and Natural Resources, Pat Rabbitte, as a relatively short legislative proposal, designed to provide an explicit legal basis to enable the ESB to engage in the installation and operation of electronic communications networks and services, either alone or by agreement with one or more other companies and to provide for consequential matters. As such, it contains just nine short sections. The central sections are ss.2, 3, 4, 5 and 8 (which relates to the gas sector and accordingly, is dealt with under that heading). Section 2 gives the ESB permission to engage in electronic communications networks and electronic communications services. It provides an explicit legal basis to allow the ESB to engage in the electronic communications market. Section 3 allows ESB to provide other companies with access to its electricity infrastructure. Section 4 re-defines the term "electric line" in the ESB Acts 1927–2004 and the Electricity Regulation Act 1999 to provide a single definition. It extends the definition of electric line to also include electronic communications infrastructure which is suspended from the electricity network and includes a retrospective element to maintain the status of the existing electronic communications network following this amendment. Section 5 extends the statutory way-leave rights provided to the ESB (which allow it to cross private lands subject to the payment of compensation where appropriate) to any company authorised by the ESB to install electronic communications infrastructure along its electricity network. The extension of these rights is subject to the approval of the Commission for Energy Regulation. The Act was brought into operation by the ESB (Electronic Communications Networks) (Commencement) Order 2014 (S.I. No. 286 of 2014) on 19 June 2014.

ENERGY CONTRACTS

Energy contracts, jurisdiction and enforcement of International Court of Arbitration (ICC) awards On 13 March 2014, in *Yukos Capital SARL v OAO Tomskneft VNK* [2014] IEHC 115, the High Court held that for it to recognise and enforce an ICC award (made pursuant to s.7 of the Arbitration Act 1980 and s.41 of the Arbitration Act 1954), jurisdiction first had to be demonstrated. In *Yukos Capital SARL*, Kelly J. found this had not been demonstrated. This High Court case concerned an application by the respondent, OAO Tomskneft VNK, to set aside an order granting the applicant leave to serve these proceedings outside the jurisdiction. The applicants sought the enforcement of the ICC award.

The substantive proceedings concerned an award made by a single arbitrator, the late Dr Robert Briner, in respect of three loans made by the applicant, Yukos Capital SARL (a Luxembourg company) to the respondent, OAO Tomskneft VNK (a Russian open joint stock company, jointly owned by OAO Rosneft, one of the biggest international oil companies in the world, which is owned by the Russian Federation, and OAO Gazprom, the large global energy company which employs over 400,000 people and accounts for 15 per cent of global gas output). The High Court case, which appeared before Kelly J., was the fourth attempt to enforce this award. Previous attempts had been made in Russia, France and Singapore (which were still ongoing at the time).

In finding for the respondent, Kelly J. stated that while the presence of assets within the jurisdiction was not a pre-requisite to grant leave to serve Irish proceedings outside the jurisdiction, the absence of assets in, or likely to be in this State, raised a question mark over the "solid practical benefit" that would ensue if the award was enforced in Ireland. In analysing the various arguments raised, he further stated, "the desire or entitlement to obtain an award from a 'respected' Court has already been exercised in France and is underway in the courts of Singapore". The respondent had already had to defend proceedings in Russia and in France and (to date) had been successful in doing so. It would be unjust to require the respondent to defend its position again. Accordingly, it was not appropriate to assume jurisdiction. Academic commentators (in particular Professor Geert van Calster) considered the case to be a good illustration of the attraction and uncertainty of forum shopping.

ENERGY EFFICIENCY

National Energy Efficiency Targets and the Transposition of the Energy Efficiency Directive (Directive 2012/27/EU) into Irish law The EU's Energy Efficiency Directive (Directive 2012/27/EU on energy efficiency [2012] OJ L 315/1) was published in the Official Journal on 14 November 2012 with a transposition deadline of 5 June 2014. Under the Directive, Member States are required to establish indicative national energy efficiency targets for 2020, based on either primary or final energy consumption. The Directive also sets legally binding obligations for end-users and energy suppliers. Member States are free to make these minimum requirements more stringent as they strive to save energy. The Directive's main requirements are outlined below.

Article 3 requires Member States to set an indicative national energy efficiency target, based on either primary or final energy consumption, primary or final energy savings, or energy intensity. This target was to be notified to the Commission by 30 April 2014. The Directive provides Member States with a choice. Under art.7, they can either require distribution system operators (the operators of the lower voltage electricity lines) and/or retail energy sales companies to achieve energy savings of 1.5 per cent of the annual energy sales to final customers each year from 1 January 2014 to 31 December 2020 or they can opt to take other policy measures to achieve equivalent energy savings among final customers.

Articles 5 and 6 require the renovation of at least 3 per cent of the total floor area of buildings owned by central governments each year from 2014, and the purchase of buildings, services and products with high energy-efficiency performance, with the public sector thus leading the way in energy efficiency. Article 15 requires each Member State to carry out an assessment of the potential for the application of high-efficiency cogeneration and efficient district heating and cooling in their territory by 31 December 2015. Article 8 requires mandatory regular energy audits for large companies to be conducted at least every four years, with the exception provided for companies with certified energy and environmental systems. Article 9 requires the rollout of smart grids and smart meters and the provision of accurate information on energy bills, to empower consumers and encourage more efficient energy consumption.

On 23 July 2014, the European Commission published a Communication reporting on the outlook for the attainment of the 2020 energy efficiency target. It stated that the EU was expected to achieve energy savings of 18–19 per cent by 2020—missing the 20 per cent target by 1–2 per cent. However, if EU countries implement all of the existing legislation on energy efficiency, the 20 per cent target could still be reached without additional measures. The Communication also put forward a target of 25 per cent increased energy efficiency by 2030.

In 2014, Ireland submitted its third National Energy Efficiency Action Plan (NEEAP). Two Action Plans had previously been submitted under the preceding EU energy efficiency legislation. Ireland's third NEEAP was the first plan submitted pursuant to the Energy Efficiency Directive. In the NEEAP, the Irish Government pledged to save 31,925 GWh (primary energy savings) or 20 per cent of the average of unadjusted final energy consumption between 2001 and 2005, expressed as "primary energy equivalent" by 2020. This national target covers the whole economy, excluding aviation and marine bunker fuels. Ireland had also set a 33 per cent target for the public sector (requiring a saving of 3,240 GWh) by 2020 determined using the same methodology. The NEEAP showed that by the end of 2012, Ireland had achieved 39 per cent of the national target and was making steady progress towards achieving the 33 per cent public sector target. (In April 2014, Ireland also submitted an Energy Efficiency Directive Annual Report, in fulfilment of reporting requirements outlined in art.24 of the Energy Efficiency Directive.) The NEEAP described eight areas targeted by specific policies designed to ensure achievement of Ireland's targets. In addition, the plan detailed the choice taken by the Irish Government to fulfil the requirements of art.7 of the Energy Efficiency Directive. The Irish energy distribution system operator and retail energy sales companies are now required to achieve energy savings of 1.5 per cent of the annual energy sales to final customers each year from 1 January 2014 to 31 December 2020 under an Energy Efficiency Obligations Scheme, introduced by the European Union (Energy Efficiency Obligation Scheme) Regulations 2014 (S.I. No. 131 of 2014).

The European Union (Energy Efficiency Obligation Scheme) Regulations 2014 (S.I. No. 131 of 2014) provide the Minister for Communications, Energy and Natural Resources with the power to issue an Energy Efficiency Notice to an energy supplier or class of energy suppliers setting out the measures, standards, conditions, thresholds, timescales and targets to be achieved by an energy supplier or class of energy supplier in respect of the year or years to which the notice relates. Those targeted by an Energy Efficiency Notice can either meet their requirements in full or contribute to the Energy Efficiency National Fund at a rate determined by the Minister, in partial lieu of the energy savings required. Monies from the Energy Efficiency National Fund may be used to support the objectives stated in the Regulations: (i) supporting the delivery of energy efficiency improvement programmes and other energy efficiency improvement measures; and (ii) promoting the development of a market for energy efficiency improvement measures. Penalties for non-compliance with the requirements of an Energy Efficiency Notice are contained in reg.7.

The remaining requirements of the Directive were transposed by the European Union (Energy Efficiency) Regulations 2014 (S.I. No. 426 of 2014) which are divided into seven parts (Pt 1 providing general provisions; Pt 2 on the public sector; Pt 3 on energy audits; Pt 4 on metering and billing; Pt 5 on combined heat and power and district heating; Pt 6 on energy transformation, transmission and distribution; and Pt 7 on energy efficiency information, services, incentives and financing). Part 1 places a range of obligations on public bodies relating to the efficient use of energy so that the public sector can demonstrate an exemplar role, including in the areas of energy audits, energy efficient public procurement and the purchase or leasing of energy efficient buildings. Part 3 requires the publication of minimum criteria for energy audits and the establishment of a National Registration Scheme for the registration of energy auditors to be established, maintained and operated by the Sustainable Energy Authority of Ireland (SEAI), which was set up pursuant to the Sustainable Energy Act 2002, primarily to promote renewable energy. The SEAI is also given responsibility for assessing the availability of qualification, accreditation and certification schemes for energy audits.

Part 4 places the Commission for Energy Regulation (CER) under an obligation to ensure that final customers for electricity and natural gas are provided with competitively priced smart metering systems that accurately reflect the final customer's actual energy consumption and that provide information on actual time of use. The distribution system operator, ESB Networks, is placed under an obligation to provide a final customer with a competitively priced individual meter where a new connection is made in a new building or a building undergoes major renovations. Regulation 19(2) provides the CER with the power to require energy suppliers to apply time-of-use tariffs to a class or classes of customer. The CER is also obliged to ensure that specific requirements for smart meters (covering security, privacy, advice and information) which are listed in regs 19(4)(a)–(e) are met.

Part 5 lays out a range of requirements in the promotion of energy efficiency in the combined heat and power sector. These require the SEAI to carry out a comprehensive assessment and cost-benefit analysis of the potential for the application of high efficiency combined heat and power and district heating and cooling in Ireland. Part 5 also sets out a range of obligations regarding the co-ordination, supervision and issuance of guarantees of origin. Part 6 requires the CER to direct the transmission and distribution system operators to undertake an assessment of the energy efficiency potential of the electricity and gas transmission and distribution systems in the State and submit such assessments to the CER no later than 30 June 2015. Part 7 requires the SEAI to: (i) ensure that information on available energy efficiency mechanisms and financial and legal frameworks is transparent and widely disseminated to all relevant market actors; and (ii) encourage the provision of information to banks and other financial institutions on the possibilities of participating in the financing of energy efficiency improvement measures. The Minister for Communications, Energy and Natural Resources, the Minister for the Environment, Community and Local Government and the SEAI are also required to evaluate and, if necessary, take appropriate measures to remove regulatory and non-regulatory barriers to energy efficiency, without prejudice to the basic principles of property and tenancy law, in particular as regards the split of incentives between the owner and the tenant of a building or among owners.

ENERGY LABELLING

Update of products subject to Energy Labelling Requirements The Energy Union (Energy Labelling) (Amendment) Regulations 2014 (S.I. No. 351 of 2014) were made to implement Directive 2010/30/EU on the indication by labelling and standard product information of the consumption of energy and other resources by energy-related products (recast) [2010] OJ L 153/1. These Regulations amended the European Union (Energy Labelling) Regulations 2011 (S.I. No. 366 of 2011) to insert a new Sch.1, adding products to the list of those already subject to EU labelling requirements. The complete list of products now subject to labelling requirements is as follows: household refrigerators and freezers; household washing machines; household tumble dryers; household combined washers and dryers; lamps and luminaires; air conditioners; domestic ovens and range hoods; televisions; space and combination heaters; water heaters and storage tanks; vacuum cleaners; and energy related products on the internet. Schedule 1 to the Energy Union (Energy Labelling) (Amendment) Regulations 2014 (S.I. No. 351 of 2014) also includes the EU legislation stipulating the specific labelling requirements for each product.

ENERGY PRICES

The SEAI obliged to report on the gas and electricity prices charged to industrial consumers as required by Eurostat (the statistical office of the European Union) The European Communities (Reporting of Electricity and Natural Gas Prices Charged to Industrial Consumers) Regulations 2014 (S.I. No. 578 of 2014) transposes EU Directive 2008/92/EC (which seeks to improve the transparency of gas and electricity prices charged to industrial end-users by obliging Member States to ensure that these prices and the pricing systems used are communicated to Eurostat twice a year) into Irish law.

Under the Irish Regulations, the SEAI has been designated as the body responsible for providing information on the average prices and terms of sale of electricity and gas to industrial consumers to Eurostat. The Regulations oblige electricity and gas suppliers to provide the requisite data and information to the SEAI on prices charged by them to their business customers twice yearly by 31 January and 31 July. The SEAI is provided with powers to direct suppliers it considers have not complied, or are not complying with data reporting obligations, to provide requisite data. Section 11 places an obligation on the SEAI to preserve the confidentiality of commercially sensitive information received by it including data and information used for calculating weighted average prices.

Public Service Obligations for 2014 Electricity Regulation Act 1999 (Public Service Obligations) (Amendment) Order 2014 (S.I. No. 603 of 2014). As noted by the CER, which is responsible for calculating and administering the Public Service Obligation (PSO) in line with government policy, the PSO is a subsidy charged to all electricity customers in Ireland (Commission for Energy Regulation, Public Service Levy 2014/2015 CER/14/361). It consists of various subsidy schemes to support the Government's policy objectives related to renewable energy, indigenous fuels (peat) and security of energy supply. The proceeds of the levy are used to contribute to the additional relevant costs incurred by PSO-supported electricity generators which are not recovered in the electricity market. The PSO is applied from 1 October 2014 to 30 September 2015. For the 2014/2015 period it is €335.4 million. Twenty-eight per cent of this went directly to renewable; 35 per cent to peat; 31 per cent to ensure security of supply; and 0.05 per cent for ancillary costs. This compared with a €210.9 million PSO levy for the 2013/2014 period. The biggest drivers for the increase in costs are: lower wholesale electricity prices; lower running of Tynagh (a 400 MW gas plant provided with a PSO for security of supply reasons); and more renewable generation coming on-stream.

GAS

Change of name of Bord Gáis Éireann (the semi-state company previously responsible for the supply of Irish gas) or The Irish Gas Board to Ervia Section 8 of the ESB (Electronic Communications Network) Act 2014 changes the name of Bord Gáis Éireann, or The Irish Gas Board, to Ervia. The Change of Name of Bord Gáis Éireann to Ervia (Appointed Day) Order 2014 (S.I. No. 287 of 2014) which brought this change came into effect on 20 June 2014, following the sale of Bord Gáis Éireann's energy business to Centrica plc for €1.1 billion (*Annual Review of Irish Law 2013*, pp.279–281). As part of the sale, the Bord Gáis name transferred to the new owners. The rebranding project has an estimated cost of €2.9 million.

Commencement Orders for Various Sections of the Gas Regulation Act 2013 During the course of 2014, commencement orders were made for various sections of the Gas Regulation Act 2013, which provided for the sale of Bord Gáis Éireann's energy business, while retaining the gas sector's strategic assets (the infrastructure including the transmission network which consists of transmission pipes which are used to transport large volumes of natural gas) in state ownership (*Annual Review of Irish Law 2013*, pp.279–281). The Gas Regulation Act 2013 Commencement Order 2014 (S.I. No. 41 of 2014) brought the following parts into effect: Pt 1 (the preliminary and general provisions); Pt 3 (the provisions on the transfer of the energy business to the energy company); and s.38(d) (on the superannuation of officers and servants of the Board). The Gas Regulation Act 2013 (Commencement) Order 2014 (S.I. No. 229 of 2014) brought ss.5–12 (on the network company; the memorandum and articles of the network company; the directors of the network company; the conditions governing disqualification for office of director of network company; the ban on members of either House of the Oireachtas or the European Parliament simultaneously acting as directors or staff members of the network company; the requirement for members of staff of the network company to disclose material interests; and the ban on network staff or directors disclosing confidential information) into effect. Finally, Gas Regulation Act 2013 (Commencement) Order 2014 (S.I. No. 538 of 2014) brought ss.13–20 (on the requirement for Bord Gáis Éireann and Gaslink to prepare and submit a network transfer plan to the Minister; the procedure for Ministerial approval of that network transfer plan; the network transfer date; the network transfer itself; the issue of a proof of title certificate; the right to production of proof of title documents; and annual reports and accounts) into effect.

Annual levies applied to entities involved in the gas sector to fund the independent operation of the Commission for Energy Regulation On 31 December 2014, the Electricity Regulation Act 1999 (Gas) Levy 2014 (S.I. No. 551 of 2014) came into effect. This Order provides for specific levies to be applied to entities involved in the gas sector, i.e. any person engaged in the transmission or distribution or as a shipper of natural gas. Section 5 sets out the specific payments required.

Judicial review challenge to Commission for Energy Regulation Decision to restrict the ability of shippers on the Irish gas transmission system to buy and sell the necessary rights to use the gas transmission system to ship gas Following recent changes to the gas sector, while Bord Gáis Éireann continues to own the Irish gas transmission network, Gas Link, a wholly owned independent subsidiary of Bord Gáis Éireann now acts as the operator of the transmission network. Bord Gáis Éireann and Gas Link are remunerated for the ownership and operation of the gas transmission system through the payment of regulated tariffs for the purchase and use of entry capacity to, and exit capacity from, the gas transmission system. Gas capacity that is acquired directly from Gas Link is known as "primary capacity", the price of which is regulated. Primary capacity can be booked on an annual, month ahead, day ahead or within day basis. Primary capacity which is acquired but not needed can be sold on and is then known as "secondary capacity", the price of which is not regulated.

On 21 August 2013, the CER (acting under s.13 of the Gas (Interim) (Regulation) Act 2002) adopted a Decision entitled "Access Tariffs and Financing of the Gas Transmission System" (CER13/191). This Decision sought to respond to changes in the patterns of gas transmission system usage, which had resulted in a drop off in the booking of primary capacity and the consequent erosion of transmission tariff revenues. The original plan was for the Decision to be implemented as soon as possible in 2013/2014. In the Decision, the CER noted that the drop-off in primary capacity bookings by power generators and large industrial and commercial users was due to a number of well-documented developments which were unlikely to be a short term phenomenon. These included growing wind energy penetration, the East-West Electricity Interconnector (500 MW High Voltage Direct Current (HVDC) link between the electricity transmission grids of Ireland and Great Britain) coming on stream, the re-emergence of coal-fired generation as well as difficult economic circumstances. Consequently, in taking the Decision, the CER had two aims: to prevent certain parties from shifting the burden of remunerating the costs of their network access onto other parties and to remove within day sales of short-term capacity purchasing options (which allowed certain categories of users to avoid committing to primary capacity bookings, again shifting the burden of remunerating the costs of their network access onto other parties). Thus, the Decision: (i) removed the possibility for shippers to sell secondary capacity at exit from the gas transmission system from 1 October 2013; and (ii) sought to remove the possibility for shippers (including large daily metered customers) to buy within-day capacity at exit (from 10 January 2014).

The applicants, Viridian Power Ltd (which owns a power station in Finglas, Dublin known as "Huntstown 2" and holds a shipping licence allowing it to transport gas for use at the power station) and Huntstown Power Company Ltd (which also owns a power station in Finglas, Dublin known as "Huntstown 1" and holds a shipping licence allowing it to transport gas for use at the power station) applied for judicial review of both the Decision and the Direction to Gas Link to take steps to give effect to the Decision. In addition, in *Viridian Power Ltd v Commission for Energy Regulation* [2014] IEHC 614, an application was also made to: (i) place a stay on the aspects of the Decision which related to within day capacity at exit; and (ii) restrain the CER and Gas Link from taking action to give effect to those aspects of the Decision. This application was unsuccessful.

In his consideration of the application, McGovern J. noted that both the applicants and the respondents agreed that the principles outlined in *Okunade v Minister for Justice, Equality and Law Reform* [2012] IESC 49, and *Curust Financial Services Ltd v Loewe-Lack-Werk* [1994] 1 I.R. 450 applied. Accordingly, he used a test (derived from *Okunade* and *Dowling v Minister for Finance* [2013] IESC 37 and put forward by the applicants) to find that the requirements necessary to grant a stay in judicial review proceedings had not been satisfied. McGovern J. took the "unnecessary delay" of the applicants in making their application into account, noting that the ex parte application was brought some six weeks after the first part of the Direction came into effect. He stated that while this delay did not defeat the application, it was sufficient to weigh in the balance of whether or not the reliefs should be granted, when considered with the other points raised in argument.

In considering these points, McGovern J. placed a considerable degree of emphasis on the following arguments made by the respondent. First, if a stay were granted, significant financial benefits to other users of the gas system and, in particular, to residential customers would not be realised. Secondly, considerable financial and practical inconveniences would result for third parties if the reform package was stalled from progressing to its complete implementation. This was because the tariffs for 2013/2014 had already been determined on the basis of the Direction taking effect. Therefore, further adjustments would be required to resolve the inevitable revenue recovery shortfall in the short-term. Thirdly, if a stay were granted, the existing inequitable distribution of the burden of providing Gas Link's revenue would continue. Finally, the reforms had been designed to work together and should not be treated in isolation.

He determined that the applicants had failed to establish that there was a real risk of injustice to them if a stay or injunction were to be refused. In coming to his decision, he took the applicants' delay into account and stated that while the applicants asserted that they might suffer loss and damage, the loss and damage to the users and the public, which would result from the grant of a stay, was both real and substantial.

Commission for Energy Regulation decide to rescind the part of the Decision challenged in *Viridian Power Ltd v Commission for Energy Regulation* [2014] IEHC 614 On 20 February 2014, the Commission for Energy Regulation notified industry that the "Within Day Capacity Direction" aspect of its decision on "Access Tariffs and Financing the Gas Transmission System" (CER/13/191) had been rescinded by the Commission and therefore would not be implemented. The central reason given for this was that market circumstances had changed; there had been material progress towards realising the key objective of the Decision and so the reason to implement the "Within Day Capacity Direction" had disappeared. Following this, on 28 November 2014, McGovern J. handed down his decision on Viridian Power Ltd's application for the costs arising from their application for judicial review *(Viridian Power Ltd v Commission for Energy Regulation* [2014] IEHC 614). The judge accepted that market circumstances had changed, removing the need to implement this aspect of the Decision and rendering the proceedings moot by the actions of one party, due to external events. Consequently, he determined the fact pattern was similar to that which had arisen in *Cunningham v President of the Circuit Court* [2012] 3 I.R. 222 and ordered both sides to bear their own costs.

Definition of Classes of Liquefied Petroleum Gas Incidents On 11 February 2014, the Liquefied Petroleum Gas Safety (Liquefied Petroleum Gas Incident) Regulations 2014 (S.I. No. 77 of 2014) (the "2014 Regulations") were published in Iris Oifigiúil. Liquefied Petroleum Gas (LPG) is defined as gas having the characteristic of being easily liquefied by the application of pressure, provided as commercial butane and commercial propane or mixtures thereof (Electricity Regulation Act 1999 (Liquefied Petroleum Gas Works) Regulations 2011 (S.I. No. 299 of 2011)). The 2014 Regulations were made by the CER exercising the power to make regulations relating to the reporting and investigation of LPG incidents conferred on it by s.9JG of the Electricity Regulation Act 1999, as amended. They provide for the definition of classes of LPG incidents. In summary, the Regulations state that the following incidents are LPG incidents where they are the consequence of the misuse, abuse, leakage, combustion or explosion of LPG: (i) the death of any person; (ii) the injury of any person (which requires medical attention other than as an outpatient); or (iii) the loss or damage to any building, land or other property, where in the opinion of the LPG undertaking concerned the aggregate value of such loss or damage is in excess of €6,500.

Reporting and Investigation of LPG incidents On 31 March 2014, the Liquefied Petroleum Gas Safety (Liquefied Petroleum Gas Incident Reporting and Investigation) Regulations 2014 (S.I. No. 78 of 2014) came into operation. These Regulations provide for the reporting of LPG incidents by LPG undertakings that made, or may have made, available to a domestic or commercial final customer the LPG involved in the LPG incident concerned.

An "LPG undertaking" is defined by the 2014 Regulations as meaning

> any person who imports LPG or purchases LPG directly from a refinery within the State and makes LPG available to individual domestic or commercial final customers by way of LPG cylinder, bulk tank or via a piped LPG distribution network.

The report must be in writing and the Regulations provide for the investigation of LPG incidents by a gas safety officer appointed by the CER.

INFRASTRUCTURE

Reporting Obligations on Infrastructure Investment projects in oil, gas, electricity, biofuel and carbon dioxide On 26 February 2014, the EU adopted Regulation (EU) No. 256/2014 of the European Parliament and of the Council concerning the notification to the Commission of investment projects in energy infrastructure within the European Union [2014] OJ L84/61. This Regulation was designed to replace Council Regulation (EU, Euratom) 617/2010, which had been annulled by the Court of Justice of the European Union as having been adopted on an inappropriate legal basis (*Parliament v Union* (C-490/10) [2012] E.C.R. I-0000). Its objective is to obtain an overview of the process of investment in energy infrastructure in the European Union by generating better data through reporting.

As such, the Regulation establishes a common framework for the notification to the Commission of data and information on investment projects in energy infrastructure in the petroleum, gas, electricity and bio-fuel sectors and related to carbon dioxide produced by these sectors. Under its provisions, Member States (or the entity they delegate the task to) are required to collect and notify data and information on investment projects concerning production, transport and storage from 1 January 2015 and every two years thereafter. Member States are exempt from the requirement if they already provide the information required, as outlined in art.3.

The EU legislation was transposed into Irish law by the European Union (Notification of Investment Projects in Energy Infrastructure) Regulations 2014 (S.I. No. 579 of 2014), which came into operation on 1 January 2015. The Irish Regulations concern infrastructure investment projects for oil, gas, electricity, biofuel and carbon dioxide and place an obligation on undertakings planning or implementing investment projects to provide the Minister for Communications, Energy and Natural Resources with project specific data and information, outlined in s.3, e.g. the volume of capacity planned or under construction; the type and main characteristics of infrastructure; the likely year of commissioning; the type of energy sources used; the installations capable of responding to security of supply crises; the equipment of carbon capture storage systems or retrofitting mechanisms for carbon capture and storage. Investment decisions relating to the decommissioning of energy infrastructure in the same categories must also be reported. This data and information is to reflect the position at 31 March of the reporting year. The

Regulations also give the Minister the power to issue directions where he or she is of the opinion that an undertaking has failed to comply with s.3 and to apply to the High Court for an order directing the undertaking to comply.

Powers and responsibilities of ESB and EirGrid to enter land to survey land, uprate and repair transmission lines considered in *Electricity Supply Board v Killross Properties Ltd* [2014] IEHC 635 In this case, the plaintiffs sought injunctions, orders and declarations to restrain the defendants from preventing them entering the defendant's lands to uprate and repair a number of 110kv lines and the construction of a temporary line diversion. This case is interesting as it provides a full and careful consideration of the powers of ESB (the semi-state electricity company group which includes ESB Networks, the transmission asset owner) and EirGrid (the Irish transmission system operator) to access and repair electricity lines and their responsibilities in this regard (along with a consideration of the case-law relevant to compulsory purchase orders). In his decision, Hedigan J. noted that pursuant to s.53(1) of the Electricity Supply Act 1927 (the "1927 Act"), ESB is statutorily entitled to place any electric line above or below ground but must serve notice (stating its intention and giving a description of the nature of the line and the position and manner in which it is to be placed) seven days before doing so. The right is subject to the right of the owner or occupier to be paid compensation and once ESB is authorised to place a line, it may at any time enter on the lands for the purpose of placing, repairing or altering a line.

He further noted the power of ESB and EirGird to survey land under s.20(4) of the 1927 Act and reg.8(2) of the European Communities (Internal Market in Electricity) Regulations 2000, respectively. In its submissions, the defendant argued that the notice which was served was ineffective as the notice had been drafted, signed and served by an officer of ESB Networks (a company independent of ESB). It was argued that for the notice to be valid, the decision to serve must be made by the Board of ESB. This argument was rejected by the court, which distinguished a notice served in relation to work to uprate lines and the making of an order such as a compulsory purchase order. The court held that the first was an ordinary administrative act, which an officer of ESB was authorised to do whereas the second could only be made by the Board of ESB.

PETROLEUM

Updated Petroleum Safety Framework The Electricity Regulation Act 1999, as amended, inter alia by the Petroleum (Exploration and Extraction) Safety Act 2010 gives the Commission for Energy Regulation (CER) responsibility for the safe regulation of petroleum exploration and extraction activities in Ireland. The Act requires the CER to establish a risk-based petroleum safety framework to regulate the safety of petroleum activities and in particular designated petroleum activities carried out by petroleum undertakings (Commission for Energy Regulation, *Guidance for Notification of Petroleum Incidents*, CER/14/015). For this purpose, the CER was given the power to make a number of specific regulations by the Petroleum (Exploration and Extraction) Safety Act 2010. Accordingly, the CER made the Petroleum Safety (Petroleum Incident) Regulations 2014 (S.I. No. 4 of 2014) (the "2014 Regulations") to update the existing regime.

Under s.13S of the existing Act (the Petroleum (Exploration and Extraction) Safety Act 2010) where a petroleum incident occurs, the petroleum undertaking or undertakings concerned notify the CER as soon as possible after the incident. The Act lists six categories of events as petroleum incidents. The 2014 Regulations update, subdivide and provide further detail on these categories which have been divided into 15 subcategories (not intended to be mutually exclusive) as follows:

i. an uncontrolled fire or explosion;
ii. an uncontrolled release of petroleum gas that could have resulted in a fatality or a serious injury;
iii. an uncontrolled release of petroleum liquid that could have resulted in a fatality or a serious injury;
iv. an uncontrolled release of a non-petroleum hazardous substance that could have resulted in a fatality or a serious injury;
v. loss of mooring, stability or buoyancy of a vessel;
vi. a collision by a vessel, vehicle, crane, helicopter or aircraft with any petroleum infrastructure;
vii. an instance of a stand-by vessel not being in a position to provide rescue to persons on offshore petroleum infrastructure;
viii. a person falling into the sea;
ix. mustering on onshore or offshore petroleum infrastructure, other than for planned drills;
x. evacuation of onshore or offshore petroleum infrastructure, other than for planned drills;
xi. activation of a blow-out prevention or diversion system, or activation of any other emergency shutdown device, in each case to provide well control;
xii. a positive flow indication from a well as a result of an unplanned fluid influx;
xiii. the detection of hydrogen sulfide in the course of operations at a well or in samples of well-fluids from a well where the presence of hydrogen sulfide in the reservoir being drawn on by the well was not anticipated;
xiv. failure to maintain a planned minimum separation distance between two or more wells;
xv. the collapse, overturning, or failure of any load-bearing part of any lift, hoist, crane, or derrick;
xvi. failure of any equipment associated with a well being worked on whose purpose is to prevent or limit the effect of the unintentional release of fluids from the associated well or reservoir, or whose failure would cause or contribute to such a release;
xvii. any incident that leads to third party property damage outside the boundary fence of the relevant onshore petroleum infrastructure or within 500 metres of the relevant offshore petroleum infrastructure; or
xviii. the dropping of an object that could have resulted in an outcome specified in (a) to (e) of the definition of petroleum incident

> contained in section 13A(1) of the Act of 1999 or could have resulted in an occurrence specified in (i) to (xvii) of the definition of prescribed occurrence under these Regulations.

The 2014 Regulations also require the notification of petroleum incidents to be in writing. However, in the case of a petroleum incident resulting in loss of human life or a missing person, they require the petroleum undertaking or undertakings to supply the Commission with the name of the deceased or missing person(s), brief particulars and the location of the petroleum incident by the quickest practicable means. Failure to notify the CER of a petroleum incident is an offence under the Act and can result in a fine of up to €5,000 on summary conviction, or a fine of up to €1,000,000 on conviction on indictment. (Further details on how to report an incident are contained in the CER's *Guidance for Notification of Petroleum Incidents*, CER/14/015).

Levy on undertakings carrying out or proposing to carry out a petroleum production or well activity The Electricity Regulation Act 1999 (Petroleum Safety) Levy Order 2014 (S.I. No. 558 of 2014) imposes a levy on undertakings (carrying out or proposing to carry out a petroleum production or well activity) to allow the CER to cover the costs incurred in establishing, implementing and operating the petroleum safety framework. For 2014, the establishment costs of the petroleum safety framework for 2014 were €1,900,000, while the operational costs were €2,215,632.

RENEWABLE ENERGY

The EU's Renewable Energy Directive and Ireland's second report on its progress towards reaching its legally binding renewable energy target The Renewable Energy Directive (Directive 2009/28 on the promotion of the use of energy from renewable sources [2009] OJ L140/16), a complex and detailed piece of legislation, was adopted by the EU as part of its Climate and Energy Legislative Package and it came into force on 25 June 2009. It places various legal obligations on Ireland in the period between 2009 and 2020 (some of which either became applicable, or were implemented in 2014) and so its main provisions are briefly outlined below.

The main objectives of the Renewable Energy Directive are to:

> [establish] a common framework for the promotion of energy from renewable sources … [and set] mandatory national targets for the overall share of energy from renewable sources in gross final consumption of energy (art.1).

Accordingly, Annex I of the Directive allocated overarching national renewable energy targets to Member States, to be achieved by 2020. For Ireland, the target was to achieve 16 per cent renewable energy by 2020. To ensure the development of renewable energy at an appropriate pace to meet the 2020 targets, art.3(2) provided interim indicative targets for the four two-year periods leading up to 2020. The monitoring and enforcement of targets were to be further supported by national renewable energy action plans along with arts 4(4) and 4(5) of the Renewable Energy Directive. These will each be dealt with in turn.

National renewable energy action plans were required from each Member State by 30 June 2010, to provide detail on how specific national targets were to be achieved by describing existing and additional measures to be put in place to ensure renewable energy developed at an appropriate pace to reach both the 2020 and indicative interim targets. In its national renewable energy action plan, the Irish Government broke down the 16 per cent target into sub-targets to be achieved by specific sectors to contribute to the achievement of the final overall target. The plan divided the overarching target into sub-targets to be achieved in the three sectors: (i) transport; (ii) heating and cooling; and (iii) electricity (using wind, wave, hydro, and biomass for electricity production). It outlined how the majority of the final target could be reached by increasing the amount of renewable energy consumed in electricity production to 40 per cent, to be primarily generated from onshore wind (with lesser contributions to be made by offshore wind and biomass).

Article 4(4) of the Renewable Energy Directive requires a Member State whose share of renewable energy falls below the indicative trajectory to submit an amended plan to the Commission by June of the following year. Article 4(5) states that the Commission may make a recommendation to a Member State in relation to a national renewable energy action plan or an amended national renewable energy action plan. In addition to these overarching requirements, art.13 of the Renewable Energy Directive also placed an obligation on Member States to ensure that the

> national rules concerning the authorisation, certification and licensing procedures that are applied to plants and associated transmission and distribution network infrastructures for the production of electricity, heating or cooling from renewable energy sources, and to the process of transformation of biomass into biofuels or other energy products, are proportionate and necessary.

Member States are also obliged to ensure that they were in a position to guarantee the origin of electricity, heating and cooling produced from renewable energy sources. Article 15 requires the information contained in these guarantees to be standardised and recognisable in all Member States to provide consumers with information on the composition of the different electricity sources. Article 16 requires Member States to build the necessary infrastructures to support the secure operation of the electricity system as it accommodates the further development of electricity production from renewable energy sources. Article 17 sets out the criteria to be met for biofuels to be permitted to count towards national renewable energy targets and art.18 sets up a system to allow Member States to verify that the required criteria for biofuels can be met. Article 22 requires Member States to submit a report to the European Commission on the national progress made in renewable energy development by 31 December 2011, and every two years thereafter.

Ireland's second progress report on its national renewable energy action plan was submitted on 19 December 2014. It provided detail on the levels of renewable energy in use in Ireland in 2011 and 2012, Ireland's revised trajectory to meet its 2020 targets and the 51 laws and policies which had either existed, were in place, or were planned to increase future renewable energy consumption in Ireland. It noted that in 2011 the total estimated annual cost of supporting renewable energy was: (i) €51.27 million in the electricity sector and (ii) €300,000 million in the heating sector.

It stated, on p.30, that Ireland had exceeded its renewable energy target by 270 MW in 2012 and was projected to exceed its pledged targets each year until 2020. These figures are surprisingly good given that Ireland's previous progress report (which was submitted a year after the deadline) showed that Ireland had failed to reach the interim electricity targets which were set for 2009 and 2010 (to attain 20.4 per cent renewable electricity by producing 4140 MW of energy from wind). For 2010, Ireland had installed just 1389 MW of wind (with just 25 MW produced from offshore resources). Moreover, on 27 March 2013, the former Irish Minister for Communications, Energy and Natural Resources, Pat Rabbitte, gave a speech which described the gap that existed between the 3,521 MW renewable electricity target pledged (the estimated 40 per cent target, based on projected demand) and the then present level of wind development (1,826.5 MW) to state:

> "In terms of the 2020 renewable electricity target, [Ireland is] 630MW behind where the National Renewable Energy Action Plan has outlined [it] should be in 2012. The target will not be achieved without an increase in wind energy build from an historic average of 180MW per year to at least 250MW per year."

From the second progress report, Ireland now appears to be back on track, however the Irish Government noted in the report that: "All sectors require considerable effort to achieve the three fold increase in renewable energy that is required to meet the legally binding target of 16% under Directive 2009/28/EC". The report revises the earlier projections of the contributions to be made from each renewable energy resource. Accordingly, the final 16 per cent target is now expected to be made up of 9.1 per cent renewable electricity (which will mainly be provided by achieving a 40 per cent renewable electricity consumption share in the Irish electricity market); 4.0 per cent renewable heating and 2.9 per cent renewable transport. It also revises its previous position in relation to offshore wind stating,

> "the Government has decided that in meeting our legal obligation to deliver the 2020 renewables target, onshore rather than offshore wind should be pursued in the first instance, in order to minimise any support scheme costs borne by electricity consumers."

Furthermore, additional emphasis is to be placed on biomass to contribute in a much more substantial way to the achievement of the final target. Following the submission of the first progress report, a draft bioenergy plan was published in October 2014.

The transposition of the EU's Renewable Energy Directive into Irish law On 21 January 2014, the European Commission published a press release detailing how Ireland had been referred to the Court of Justice of the European Union for failing to transpose certain provisions of the Renewable Energy Directive (specifically the provisions relating to: the national 10 per cent target for renewables in transport;

the streamlining of administrative procedures; the management of grid access for electricity from renewable sources; and sustainability criteria for biofuels and bioliquids) into Irish law. It stated that a letter of formal notice had been sent to Ireland in January 2011, followed by a reasoned opinion in June 2012.

To remedy the situation, the European Union (Renewable Energy) Regulations 2014 (S.I. No. 483 of 2014) (the "2014 Regulations") were made on 28 October 2014. The 27 regulations cover: the exemplary role of public bodies concerning public buildings; access to and operation of the grid; guarantees of origin; the calculation of the share of energy produced from renewable energy (for the purposes of reporting under the Renewable Energy Directive) and bioliquids. The main regulations are briefly discussed below.

Regulation 4(1)(a) requires the transmission system operator and distribution system operator to ensure that electricity generated from renewable sources can be transmitted and distributed; reg.4(1)(b) requires the transmission system operator to give priority to generating units using energy from renewable sources in so far as the secure operation of the electricity system permits and reg.4(1)(c) states that subject to certain restrictions a generator of electricity from renewable sources that is connected to the electricity system shall be able to sell and transmit such electricity at all times, whenever the source becomes available. Regulation 4(3) could be of particular importance. It directs the CER to ensure that the transmission system operator or the distribution system operator, as appropriate, takes appropriate grid and market-related operational measures in order to minimise the curtailment of electricity from renewable sources on the electricity system. (Curtailment is when electricity generated by an electricity producer is reduced due to system reasons such as the "System Non-Synchronous Penetration" (SNSP) limits being exceeded or for frequency control). While wind developers may find it good to see this clearly stated in Irish legislation, the question of how curtailment is to be reduced is still primarily dependent on the successful implementation of EirGrid's *DS3 programme*, which aims to address the various factors that influence the SNSP limit, with the ultimate aim of increasing the limit from non-synchronous sources (such as wind and HVDC interconnector imports) from 50 per cent to 75 per cent. The issue of how curtailment should be treated, e.g. on pricing and how decisions should be taken as to which generator to curtail, was previously the subject of much discussion and debate during the consultations undertaken by the Single Electricity Market Operator for Ireland (consisting of the CER and Utility Regulator for Northern Ireland) in 2012 and 2013.

Regulations 5–8 concern guarantees of origin. Guarantees of origin are to be issued by the Single Electricity Operator for Ireland. The CER is required to establish a supervisory framework for the issuance, registration, transfer and cancellation by electronic means, of guarantees of origin to generators of electricity from renewable energy sources. Regulation 6 states unequivocally that a guarantee of origin has no function in terms of the State's compliance with the targets set in the Renewable Energy Directive. Regulation 6(3) states that a supplier can use a guarantee of origin as proof of the share or quantity of energy from renewable sources in its energy mix for the purposes of providing reliable information on its fuel mix to customers (as required by reg.25 of European Communities (Internal Market in Electricity) Regulations 2005 (S.I. No. 60 of 2005)). Regulation 7 provides some detail on the characteristics of a guarantee of origin, e.g. a guarantee of origin applies to the standard size of 1MW hour; it shall have a unique identification number, etc. Regulation 8 states that a guarantee of origin shall be issued by SEMO in response to a request from a generator of electricity from renewable energy sources; however, a guarantee of origin may not be requested for electricity generated outside the State. It also provides detail on the information which must be received before a guarantee of origin may be issued and the circumstances which would lead to a guarantee of origin being revoked. Regulation 13 states that the Regulations do not apply in respect of guarantees of origin for high efficiency CHP. Regulation 17 covers the sustainability criteria for biofuels. Biofuels and bioliquids meet the sustainability criteria if they fulfil the criteria in paras 1–7 of Sch.3 to the 2014 Regulations.

Conferral of additional functions on the SEAI concerning certification schemes The Sustainable Energy Act 2002 (Conferral of Additional Functions—Renewable Energy) (Amendment) Order 2014 (S.I. No. 482 of 2014) conferred additional functions on the SEAI concerning certification schemes for installers of small-scale biomass boilers and stoves, solar photovoltaic and solar thermal systems, shallow geothermal systems and heat pumps.

Wind Energy: Decision granting permission for wind farm close to Natura 2000 sites in Roscommon quashed due to a failure to complete lawfully conducted appropriate assessments and to provide sufficient reasoning to support the decisions taken On 25 July 2014 in *Kelly v An Bord Pleanála* [2014] IEHC 400, Finlay Geoghegan J. quashed a decision to grant two planning permissions for wind developments in Roscommon. The permission for the first development was for 16 wind turbines with a hub height of 85m, rotor diameter of 100m, to be developed within 10km of 10 conservation sites, including three Natura 2000 sites, (Lough Croan SAC, Four Road Turlough CSAC and the River Suck Callows SPA) which are host to important numbers of wetland and water birds listed in Annex I of the EU's Wild Birds Directive as being in danger of extinction. The permission for the second development was for: (i) 19 wind turbines with a hub height of 85m, rotor diameter of 100m and overall height of 135m; (ii) an 85m anemometer mass; and (iii) a 110kv substation. Within 15km of the second site, there are 14 Natura sites including the three Natura 2000 sites already mentioned.

In the initial appeal against the grant of planning permission, two separate inspectors appointed by An Bord Pleanála recommended the refusal of planning permission. However, on 8 August 2013, planning permission was granted to both developments by a majority of 4:1. The applicant (the chairman of a group of local residents called the Wind Turbine Action Group South Roscommon) initially challenged the decisions and the procedures leading to the decisions to grant permission to both developments on eight separate grounds. Two arguments relied on by the applicant were discussed in depth by the court. The Board had failed to carry out an appropriate assessment of the proposed developments and the Board erred in failing to have any proper regard to the inspectors' recommendations and, in particular, the scientific doubt expressed in these recommendations.

In considering the nature of appropriate assessment, Finlay Geoghegan J. cited *Waddenzee* (C-127/02) [2004] E.C.R. I-7405, para.61; *Commission v Spain*

(C-404/09) [2011] E.C.R. I-11853, paras 99 and 100; and *Sweetman v An Bord Pleanála* (C-258/11) [2013] E.C.R. I-0000 with approval to state that:

> "Section 177V(1) must be construed so as to give effect to Article 6(3) of the Habitats Directive, and hence, an appropriate assessment carried out under the section must meet the requirements of Article 6(3) as set out in the CJEU case law. If an appropriate assessment is to comply with the criteria set out by the CJEU in the cases referred to, then it must, in my judgment, include an examination, analysis, evaluation, findings, conclusions and a final determination."

She then provided the following very clear explanation of the requirements for an appropriate assessment to be found to have been lawfully conducted, stating that it:

> "(i) Must identify, in the light of the best scientific knowledge in the field, all aspects of the development project which can, by itself or in combination with other plans or projects, affect the European site in the light of its conservation objectives. This clearly requires both examination and analysis.
>
> (ii) Must contain complete, precise and definitive findings and conclusions and may not have lacunae or gaps. The requirement for precise and definitive findings and conclusions appears to require analysis, evaluation and decisions. Further, the reference to findings and conclusions in a scientific context requires both findings following analysis and conclusions following an evaluation each in the light of the best scientific knowledge in the field.
>
> (iii) May only include a determination that the proposed development will not adversely affect the integrity of any relevant European site where upon the basis of complete, precise and definitive findings and conclusions made the Board decides that no reasonable scientific doubt remains as to the absence of the identified potential effects.
>
> 41. Hence in my judgment the full appropriate assessment required by s.177V(1) must include all of the above elements and not just the determination expressly referred to in the sub-section."

She also distinguished the determination which must be made by the Board in areas where an appropriate assessment is necessary from a "planning decision", stating that while the Board has a very wide discretion in exercising its jurisdiction for planning decisions, the determination which must be made as part of an appropriate assessment is considerably narrower and legally constrained.

In applying this to the facts of the present case, she determined that the Board had failed to carry out an appropriate assessment to meet these requirements for both developments. Furthermore, Finlay Geoghegan J. determined that the findings made and conclusions reached by the inspector in relation to the second development did not support the determination reached by the Board.

With regard to the extent of the reasons which must be provided (pursuant to s.177V(5) of the Planning and Development Act 2000, as amended) for a determination made under art.6(3) of the Habitats Directive, she stated that the essential principle was that the reasons must be such as to enable an interested party to assess the lawfulness of the decision and in the event of a challenge being brought, to give the court access to sufficient information to enable an assessment as to lawfulness to be made. Interestingly, she stated,

> "the Board could not make a lawful decision to grant planning permission unless it had reached a lawful determination, in an appropriate assessment lawfully conducted, that the proposed development would not adversely impact on the European sites in question. In accordance with the CJEU decision in Sweetman, it is for the national court to determine whether the appropriate assessment (including the determination) was lawfully carried out or reached, and to do so, it appears to me that the reasons given for the Board's determination in an appropriate assessment must include the complete, precise and definitive findings and conclusions relied upon by the Board as the basis for its determination. They must also include the main rationale or reason for which the Board considered those findings and conclusions capable of removing all scientific doubt as to the effects of the proposed development on the European site concerned in the light of the its [sic] conservation objectives. In the absence of such reasons, it would not be possible for a court to decide whether the appropriate assessment was lawfully concluded or whether the determination meets the legal test required by the judgments of the CJEU."

The Board was found to have failed to give adequate reasons to support either decision.

On 28 July 2014, there was a short further hearing relating to the precise form of order and costs and in *Kelly v An Bord Pleanála* [2014] IEHC 400 costs were awarded against the Board. In addition to the orders of certiorari granted in the main proceedings, Galetech (a notice party to the original proceedings) sought an order remitting each appeal to the Board for determination in accordance with the law. The Department of Arts, Heritage and the Gaeltacht (also a notice party) supported by the applicant, requested the court to give further directions as part of the remittal. This request was granted and an order made (i) directing the Board to invite all parties to make a further submission before conducting its appropriate assessment and (ii) directing the Board that where further information was to be sought in either appeal, it was to make clear in which appeal or appeals the requested information was to be considered and to give any appropriate notice required by the Planning and Development Act 2000, as amended.

Wind Energy: grid connections and proposed wind developments to be considered together in planning permission applications following the decision of the High Court in *O Grianna v An Bord Pleanála* [2014] IEHC 632 In this case the applicants sought a Declaration that the respondent had failed to carry out an environmental impact assessment in accordance with the provisions of s.172 of the Planning and Development Act 2000, as amended, as interpreted in accordance with the EU Environmental Impact Assessment Directive (Council Directive 2011/92 on the assessment of the effects of certain public and private projects on the environment [2011] OJ L26/1). The main argument put forward by the applicants was that the Board had failed to carry out an environmental impact assessment in relation to the overall project. There were two phases in the project: first, the construction of the wind turbines, and secondly, the works necessary to connect the wind farm to the national grid. It was submitted by the applicants that the cumulative effect of the entire development on the environment should have been the subject of the Board's environmental impact assessment, and that an impermissible "project-splitting" had occurred, thereby invalidating the decision-making process. Peart J. found in favour of the plaintiffs. He cited Clarke J. in *Arklow Holidays Ltd v An Bord Pleanála* [2006] IESC 15 with approval, stating:

> "I am satisfied that the second phase of the development in the present case, namely the connection to the national grid, is an integral part of the overall development of which the construction of the turbines is the first part."

The impact of this decision on wind development should not be underestimated. Prior to the judgment, "project-splitting" of this nature was a widely used practice. What this judgment ultimately means is that wind developers will have to wait longer before submitting their applications for planning permission to ensure that they have detailed proposals for connection to the national grid from ESB Networks. These details can take a number of years to materialise. Consequently, the judgment is likely to increase the length of time (and probably also the risk and cost) of wind development in Ireland.

Following this judgment, the question of whether the matter should be remitted to the Board was raised before Peart J., who remitted the matter to the Board, stating that where the situation could be reasonably expected to be remedied if remitted, and particularly where the Board was of opinion that this was the case, then the court ought to remit the matter (*O'Grianna v An Bord Pleanála* [2014] IEHC 632).

WHOLESALE ENERGY MARKETS

Regulation of wholesale market manipulation and abuse regulation updated In 2011, the EU adopted the REMIT Regulation (Regulation 1227/2011 of the European Parliament and of the Council on wholesale energy market integrity and transparency [2011] OJ L326/1) to prohibit market abuse on wholesale markets in electricity, gas and related products. While the EU REMIT Regulation was adopted in 2011, many of its provisions are becoming applicable and so the central among these will be discussed below.

The overarching objective of the REMIT Regulation is to address potential problems specific to energy markets, which can arise due to the sensitivity of energy prices to the availability of production and transmission capacities. This sensitivity makes prices easy to influence either by: (i) creating a false impression as to the availability of capacities, or (ii) reducing actual production. As Europe's wholesale energy markets have become increasingly cross-border in nature, price setting occurs through the interaction of supply and demand across national boundaries and, as a result, transactions are frequently concluded outside the country to which the trades relate. All of this creates ways of committing market abuse transcending national borders.

The REMIT Regulation applies to "wholesale energy products", a term defined to include the following contracts and derivatives, irrespective of where and how they are traded:

> (a) contracts for the supply of electricity or natural gas where delivery is in the Union;
> (b) derivatives relating to electricity or natural gas produced, traded or delivered in the Union;
> (c) contracts relating to the transportation of electricity or natural gas in the Union;
> (d) derivatives relating to the transportation of electricity or natural gas in the Union.

Contracts for the supply and distribution of electricity or natural gas to final customers with a consumption capacity greater than 600 GWh per year are also considered to be wholesale energy products. The rules place clear prohibitions on trading on insider information, and market manipulation. They do not apply to financial instruments which are already covered by the Market Abuse Directive (Directive 2003/6/EC on insider dealing and market manipulation (market abuse) [2003] OJ L96/16) or contracts for the supply and distribution of electricity or natural gas for the use of final customers below the 600 GWh threshold.

Inside information is defined as "information of a precise nature which has not been made public, which relates directly or indirectly to one or more wholesale energy products, and which if made public would be likely to significantly affect the prices of those wholesale energy products". As noted by Ms Valerie Lawlor, McCann Fitzgerald (in her presentation on REMIT to a recent Energy Law Ireland—Electricity Association of Ireland breakfast seminar), while a general definition for "inside information" is provided by the REMIT Regulation, greater clarification on what the term encompasses and also what is meant by the term "information of a precise nature" can be gleaned from CJEU discussions of the Market Abuse Directive in *Lafonta v Autorité des Marchés Financiers* (C-628/13) [2015] E.C.R. I-0000 and *Geltl v Daimler* (C-19/11) [2012] E.C.R. I-0000. Further analysis is also provided by the three editions of non-binding guidelines on the REMIT Regulation (2011, 2012 and 2013) provided by the Agency for the Cooperation of Energy Regulators (ACER) on its website. Overall, the REMIT Regulation:

- prohibits the use of inside information when selling or buying at wholesale energy markets. Exclusive and price-sensitive information are to be disclosed before trades can take place;
- outlaws manipulative transactions or the spreading of incorrect information that give false or misleading signals about the supply, demand or prices;
- obliges energy traders to report their wholesale energy product transactions to ACER either directly or through a third party, e.g. a broker or trade reporting system. This data includes the price, volumes, date and time of the transaction, the name of the seller and the buyer and the beneficiary. This particular obligation became applicable through the Commission Implementing Regulation (Regulation 1348/2014 on data reporting implementing Article 8(2)

and 8(6) of Regulation No.1227/2011 on wholesale energy market integrity and transparency [2014] OJ L363/121), which was published in the official journal on 18 December 2014;

- requires those entering into wholesale energy product transactions (which are reportable to ACER) to register with the national regulatory authority in the Member State in which they are established or resident or, if they are not established or resident in the Union, in a Member State in which they are active;
- makes ACER responsible for independent monitoring of all the trades and checks to determine whether the rules are followed. On the basis of the data received, ACER is to conduct its own analysis. If its initial assessment confirms a suspicion of market abuse, it will request national regulators to investigate the case on the spot. In the case of cross-border manipulations it will co-ordinate the investigations. If regulators establish that there has been a breach of rules, they will apply appropriate penalties which have to reflect the damage caused to consumers;
- requires the sharing of information between national regulatory authorities, competent financial authorities of the Member States, national competition authorities, ESMA (the EU authority which contributes to safeguarding the stability of the European Union's financial system) and other relevant authorities and the co-operation of these entities as outlined in art.16;
- obliges any person professionally arranging transactions in wholesale energy products who reasonably suspects that a transaction may contain elements of insider trading or market manipulation to notify the national regulatory authority without further delay; and
- requires Member States to put effective, dissuasive and proportionate penalties in place to help stop and prevent market manipulation.

As noted by ACER, the market abuse provisions of the REMIT Regulation apply to "any wholesale energy product which is a financial instrument, including those listed in Section C of Annex I of MiFID [the Markets in Financial Instruments Directive, Directive 2004/39/EC as amended] but which is not admitted to trading on a regulated market in a Member State and for which a request for admission to trading on such a market has not been made" (ACER, *Guidance on the application of REMIT* [2013] 3rd edn).

To provide further detail on the REMIT Regulation's reporting requirements, on 18 December 2014, the EU adopted the Commission Implementing Regulation to lay down rules for the provision of data to ACER and further define the details of reportable wholesale energy products and reportable data. Article 3 provides a list of contracts which must be reported to ACER; art.4 provides a list of contracts (and details of transactions) which are reportable at the request of ACER. Article 7 provides details of the deadlines for reporting each transaction type. The Regulation also outlines when the requirements begin with:

- reporting obligations for standard contracts in the supply of electricity or gas (as described in art.6(1)) to apply from 7 October 2015;

- reporting obligations for the European Network for Transmission System Operators (ENTSO) for gas (as described in art.9(1)) to apply from 7 October 2015;
- reporting obligations for ENTSO for electricity (as described in art.8(1)) to apply from 7 October 2015 (subject to the proviso contained in art.12(2)); and
- reporting obligations for the remaining contracts to apply from 7 April 2016.

The Irish European Union (Wholesale Energy Market Integrity and Transparency) Regulations 2014 (S.I. No. 480 of 2014) were published on 24 October 2014. The Regulations designate the CER as the national body responsible for fulfilling the requirements of the EU's REMIT Regulation. The Irish Regulations state that those convicted of failing to publish inside information (as required under art.4 of the EU REMIT Regulation) or guilty of market manipulation (in violation of art.5 of the EU REMIT Regulation) are liable on summary conviction to a class A fine (to a maximum of €5,000) or on conviction on indictment (i) to a fine not exceeding €50,000 where the party in question is an individual, or (ii) to a fine not exceeding €500,000 where the party in question is a body corporate. Regulation 7 makes it an offence: to fail to provide ACER with a record of wholesale energy market transactions, including orders to trade (as required by art.8 of the EU REMIT Regulation); or for those entering into wholesale energy product transactions (which are reportable to ACER) to fail to register with the national regulatory authority in the Member State in which they are established or resident or, if they are not established or resident in the Union, in a Member State in which they are active (as required by art.9 of the EU REMIT Regulation). Either offence can result in a class A fine where it is on summary conviction, or a fine not exceeding €50,000, where it is on indictment. Regulation 8 gives the CER the power to appoint officers to facilitate the implementation of the prohibitions against market abuse.

Authorised officers have the right to

- have access to any relevant document in any form, and to receive a copy of it;
- demand information from any relevant person, including those who are successively involved in the transmission of orders or conduct of the operations concerned, as well as their principals, and, if necessary, the right to summon and hear any such person or principal;
- carry out on-site inspections;
- require existing telephone and existing data traffic records;
- require the cessation of any practice that is contrary to the EU REMIT Regulation or delegated acts or implementing acts adopted on the basis thereof;
- request a court to freeze or sequester assets; and
- request a court or any competent authority to impose a temporary prohibition of professional activity.

Authorised officers are also obliged to inform ACER without delay in as specific a manner as possible where they have reasonable grounds to suspect that acts in breach of the EU REMIT Regulation are being, or have been, carried out either in that Member State or in another Member State. They may also request ACER to exercise its powers of investigation, investigation initiation, or information gathering under the EU REMIT Regulation.

Person or persons who (a) obstruct or impede an authorised officer in the exercise of these powers, (b) fail to comply with the requirement of an authorised officer acting in exercise of these powers, (c) knowingly alter, suppress or destroy any books, documents or records which the person concerned has been required to produce, or may reasonably expect to be required to produce, or (d) knowingly give the CER or an authorised officer information which is false or misleading, in a material respect, are guilty of an offence and liable on summary conviction to a class A fine.

WATER

Delay placed on the implementation of domestic water charges; caps placed on domestic water charges and a referendum required where a proposal is made to alienate shares in Irish Water to any person other than a Government Minister The water sector has undergone significant change in the past few years including the establishment of a basis for the introduction of domestic water charges by the Water Services Act 2013 and the Water Services (No. 2) Act 2013 (*Annual Review of Irish Law 2013*, pp.281–285) and the delay and capping of the domestic water charges by the Water Services Act 2014, which was signed into law on 28 December 2014. The reasons behind the transformation of the sector are interesting and originate at European level and particularly from the EU Water Framework Directive (Directive 2000/60/EC of the European Parliament and of the Council of 23 October 2000 establishing a framework for Community action in the field of water policy [2000] OJ L 327/1).

The EU Water Framework Directive came into force on 22 December 2000 with the objective of promoting sustainable water use based on a long-term protection of available water resources. The central article (from the point of view of water charges) is art.9, which provides the basis for water charges in the EU. It required Member States to take account of the principle of recovery of the costs of water services by ensuring that water-pricing policies were established by 2010, to provide adequate incentives for users (including industry, households and agriculture) to use water resources efficiently, and thereby contribute to the environmental objectives of the Directive. Article 9.4 provided a limited exemption. Member States could decide not to apply water charges for a given water-use activity, where this was determined not to compromise the purposes and the achievement of the objectives of this Directive. The Department of the Environment, Heritage and Local Government's *River Basin Management Plan 2008* (June 2008) provided details on Ireland's plan to avail of this exemption, which former MEP Kathy Sinnott stated was brokered by the Irish Government in 2000 (*Irish Times*, 21 November 2014). Page 51 of the Government's *River Basin Management Plan* states:

> "The Government's National Water Pricing Policy adopted in 1998 requires the charging of non-domestic customers for water and waste water services to recover the full costs of providing such services to these customers. This

> is in line with … Article 9 of the EU Water Framework Directive. The installation of meters on the supply of non-domestic customers will facilitate the equitable, transparent and efficient implementation of water pricing policy. Metering of all non-domestic uses is due to be completed in 2008. Capital, operational and maintenance costs in relation to the domestic sector are met from public funds. This is permitted for a 'given water activity' under Article 9(4) of the Directive where it is 'within established practice' and 'where this does not compromise the purposes and the achievement of the objectives of the Directive.'"

Subsequent to this, in the Memorandum of Understanding on the EU/IMF programme of support for Ireland in 2010 the Irish Government committed itself to re-organising the sector around a fully publicly owned national utility (Irish Water) and to introducing charges for domestic users to incentivise a more sensible use of the resource and ensure more sustainable financing for the sector. In particular, it stated that water charges would be introduced by 2012/2013, by which time metering was also to have been installed across the State. Both projections have since been revised. The introduction of the Water Services Act 2014 means that the introduction of the water charges will not be levied against domestic dwellings before 1 January 2015 and the Commission for Energy Regulation (CER) has indicated that water metering is expected to continue until the end of 2016 (by which time it is expected that 1.05 million households will be metered).

While resentment against water charges is universal (as was evident from the public protests of October and November 2014), there are strong justifications for their introduction for social and legal reasons. From a social perspective, water charges will save government funds and force households to think conservatively about water usage. Until Irish Water was set up in January 2014, the water sector was run by 34 local authorities each operating over small geographic areas and running their own investment programmes, financed mainly from general government funds. Water charges were imposed on non-domestic users but collection rates were low, and domestic users were not charged. As a result, investment in water supply and treatment infrastructure was insufficient. It has been estimated that almost 50 per cent of clean water is currently wasted through leaks (Environmental Protection Agency, *Focus on Urban Waste Water Treatment 2013* (2014)).

From a legal perspective, arguments have previously been made that Ireland's water policies do not further the objectives of the EU Water Framework Directive and do not comply with EU law. For instance, on 24 November 2011, the European Commission issued a press release (MEMO/11/824) stating that it was concerned that Ireland had incorrectly implemented the concept of water services as described in EU water legislation, leading to inappropriate water pricing. The release stated that the Commission was sending Ireland a Reasoned Opinion to ask it to adjust its national legislation. It is against this backdrop that the Irish water sector is being reformed, with the latest reforms introduced by the Water Services Act 2014 primarily designed to abate public discontent on water charges.

The Water Services Act 2014 was signed into law on 28 December 2014. It contains 16 sections, the most salient of which are discussed below. Section 2 of the Act requires a referendum to allow the alienation of Irish Water shares to any person other than a Minister of the Government. Section 2 provides that existing non-domestic water charges will continue to apply. (See *Commission for Energy Regulation Water Charges Plan Non-Domestic Water and Wastewater Charges, New Connection Charges, 8 October 2014,* CER/14/453). However, it also provides that Irish Water will not impose water charges on dwellings until after 1 January 2015 and that for the time period running from 1 January 2015 until 31 December 2018, the following maximum charges will apply to the following categories of dwellings:

- €160 will be the maximum charge applied to a dwelling occupied by one adult as his or her principal private residence;
- €260 will be the maximum charge applied to a dwelling occupied by two or more adults as their principal private residence; and
- €260 will be the maximum charge applied to either a dwelling occupied by a person as a private residence but not as the principal private residence, or a dwelling which is unoccupied or a dwelling but no more.

Section 3(4) provides that households with either a sole water supply service or a sole waste water service will pay 50 per cent of these rates. Subject to limitations outlined by the section, s.3(7) places caps on the amount which may be charged by Irish Water during the period to run from 1 January 2015 until 31 December 2018. During this period, Irish Water may not charge more than €1.85 for each 1,000 litres of water supplied by it, and not more than €3.70 for each 1,000 litres of water supplied and waste water removed by it. Section 3(14) provides that where the occupant fails to register with Irish Water before 31 December 2014, that occupant will be liable to annual water charges of €260 in respect of that dwelling until 31 December 2018 or such time as registration occurs. Where the occupant registers, a lower amount can be charged.

Section 4 contains the late payment provisions. It provides that where a customer had not paid any charges owed within 12 months of the date of the first demand and has not entered into a payment plan with Irish Water (with which the customer is complying), the customer can be charged arrears, along with the following maximum annual penalties:

- €30 for a dwelling occupied by one adult as his or her principal private residence;
- €60 for a dwelling by two or more adults as their principal private residence; and
- €60 for either a dwelling occupied by a person as a private residence but not as the principal private residence, or a dwelling which is unoccupied or a dwelling but no more.

Again (similar to s.3(4)), where a household only has a sole water supply service or a sole waste water service, then 50 per cent of the appropriate annual penalty rate (listed above) can be applied. Section 5 makes provision for an annual grant made in respect of a dwelling for water conservation or a water conservation grant to be made available in 2015. Details of eligibility for the grant are contained in s.5(2). Section 5(5) gives the Minister the power to make regulations to provide further details on the grant scheme.

Section 7 states that the CER shall establish a Public Water Forum to consist of between 12 and 60 members to perform the following functions:

- represent the interests of the customers of Irish Water;
- provide Irish Water with comments and suggestion in relation to its performance of its functions;
- provide the CER with comments and suggestions in relation to Irish Water's performance of its functions;
- comment on any policy document produced by Irish Water, when requested to do so by Irish Water;
- comment on any consultation document produced by the CER when requested to do so by the CER; and
- carry out such other activities in respect of other matters as the Minister by order specifies.

Section 8 obliges the CER to provide a dispute resolution service to any customer of Irish Water having an unresolved complaint relating to Irish Water, the details of which are required to be published on its website. Section 11 abolishes the controversial power of Irish Water to require PPS numbers from its customers.

Annual levy applied to Irish Water, as Ireland's water service provider, to fund the independent operation of the Irish energy regulator, the Commission for Energy Regulation On 1 March 2014, the Electricity Regulation Act 1999 (Water) Levy Order 2014 (S.I. No. 101 of 2014) came into effect. This Order provides for an annual levy to be imposed on Irish Water to ensure the independent operation of the CER. For 2014, the levy amount was €2,733,830.

Commencement Order for various sections of the Water Services (No. 2) Act 2013 The Water Services (No. 2) Act 2013 (Commencement) Order 2014 (S.I. No. 76 of 2014) set 7 February 2014 as the appointed day for ss.22 (on water charges plan), 23 (on the agreement in relation to water charges), 44 (amending the Electricity Regulation Act 1999) and Pt 5 (on the role and powers of the CER in relation to the water sector) to come into effect.

Commencement Order for various sections of the Water Services (No. 2) Act 2013 The Water Services (No. 2) Act 2013 (Commencement) (No. 2) Order 2014 (S.I. No. 422 of 2014) set 1 October 2014 as the appointed day for the remaining parts of s.4(1) and (3) (on repeals), Pt 3 (on water charges) and s.41 (on the CER's strategy statement) to come into operation.

Employment Law

DR. DES RYAN, Lecturer in Law, Trinity College, Dublin

INTRODUCTION

The focus of this chapter is on 2014 developments in Irish employment law. As ever, employment law continued to develop at a remarkable pace in 2014. Following the approach adopted in previous years in this chapter of the *Annual Review of Irish Law*, a number of specific areas are selected here for detailed analysis. The five areas considered this year are those concerning: (i) employment status and the contract of service/contract for services distinction; (ii) injunctions and restrictive covenants; (iii) injunctions restraining dismissal in the context of "no-fault" termination; (iv) case law relating to bullying, harassment and stress at work; and (v) the introduction of the Protected Disclosures Act 2014. This range of topics enables an assessment of key developments to have taken place in 2014 in both the statutory and common law contexts. This selection also enables an analysis of well-established areas of litigation alongside the new and potentially very far-reaching area of protected disclosures. It is also worth noting in introducing this year's chapter that, as is well known, progress continued apace in 2014 on the introduction of the Workplace Relations Act 2015 and this will be the subject of detailed analysis in next year's chapter of the *Annual Review of Irish Law*.

EMPLOYMENT STATUS

The High Court Decision in *Murphy v Grand Circle Travel* [2014] IEHC 337 The complex question of when an individual will be categorised as an employee or an independent contractor was the subject of an important High Court judgment (Moriarty J.) in the case of *Murphy v Grand Circle Travel* [2014] IEHC 337. The fact-sensitive nature of these cases was well captured by Moriarty J. when he observed (at [4]):

> "It is well settled from the Irish and English case-law cited that controversies of this nature can rarely be resolved by an aggregation of documentation all pointing utterly unequivocally to one conclusion or the other."

Murphy arose from an unfair dismissal claim in which a preliminary issue as to employment status had been raised. The Employment Appeals Tribunal found the plaintiff to be an independent contractor but the Circuit Court reversed, and the matter was then appealed to the High Court. The relevant factual background concerned an "Independent Contractor's Agreement" which contained several terms consistent with the occupation by the plaintiff of that status; as against this, it was conceded that other documentation did make reference to "employment". The plaintiff complained that her signing of the Independent Contractor's Agreement occurred in circumstances where it was effectively thrust upon her after the commencement of her engagement with the defendant, with the plaintiff having no adequate opportunity to consider its full content, or take independent legal advice, and under a degree of pressure from the defendant's head office to have this done. Weighing the balance of the evidence before him, Moriarty J. concluded:

> "Overall, while I have not addressed sequentially all the agreed criteria by way of formal and informal documentation, mutuality or the lack of it, and other criteria referred to in the decided cases, I have come to the view that the overall probabilities, including my feeling that the Plaintiff's work over the three years involved a degree of engagement by tourism entities other than the Defendant in excess of the small incidence she referred to in evidence, warrant a finding that the relationship was that of an independent contractor. I have also had full regard to all that was heard in relation to the matter of gratuities or 'tips'."

Analysis It is, with respect, noteworthy that notwithstanding the very strong emphasis laid in previous case law on the importance of mutuality of obligation (see, for example, the comments of Edwards J. in *Minister for Agriculture v Barry* [2008] IEHC 216, [2009] 1 I.R. 215), the judgment in *Murphy* does not examine this criterion at any length. As an aid to legal clarity in this perennially difficult but fundamental body of case law, it is respectfully submitted that a strong focus on the question of whether the mutuality of obligation criterion is satisfied would lend greater consistency to this jurisprudence. That this consistency and clarity is badly needed is revealed in the procedural history of *Murphy* itself, which was after all decided in the context of an unfair dismissals claim but which nevertheless was the subject of scrutiny by the Employment Appeals Tribunal, the Circuit Court and the High Court.

INJUNCTIONS AND RESTRICTIVE COVENANTS

The High Court decision in *Levinwick Limited v Hollingsworth* [2014] IEHC 333 It is frequently the case that restrictive covenants contained in contracts of employment will be deemed to be unenforceable by the courts as being in restraint of trade. A good example of this was seen this year in *Levinwick Limited v Hollingsworth* [2014] IEHC 333, where the impugned clause arose in a pharmacy context. The impugned clause read as follows:

> "You undertake that during the term of your employment but for a period of 24 months after the termination of your employment, for any reason, you will not be employed or engaged by, do locum work, manage, own or part-own, a pharmacy or other retail business which trades in cosmetics or gifts or which provides photography services within a two-mile radius of the Pharmacy, you will not solicit in competition with the Pharmacy the business of any person, firm or company who is at the time of termination of your employment or was during the preceding 12 months a customer of the Pharmacy and you will not, in competition with the Pharmacy, solicit any person who was during your employment with the Pharmacy employed

> or engaged by the Pharmacy within 12 months prior to the termination of your employment, and who by means of such employment, is likely to be in possession of confidential information relating to the Pharmacy or its business.
>
> You agree that all of the above restrictions are reasonable in all the circumstances and are no more than is necessary for the protection of the interests of the Pharmacy.
>
> You agree that, in the event that any of the above restrictions is held to be unreasonable by reason of the area, duration or type or scope of service covered by such restriction, then effect will be given to such restriction in such reduced form as may be decided by any court of competent jurisdiction."

In deeming the above clause to be unenforceable, McGovern J. started with the proposition that the clause, as one in restraint of trade, was consequently only enforceable if it protected a legitimate business interest of the plaintiff and was no wider than was reasonably necessary for the protection of that interest. McGovern J. further emphasised that, in order for such clauses to be enforceable, both the nature of the restriction and its extent must be reasonable to protect the goodwill of the employer. He concluded:

> "The plaintiff has not established that the nature of the defendant's position and his work in Blakes Pharmacy gave rise to such a personal connection with customers of the Pharmacy that the restriction imposed by [the clause] was necessary to protect the goodwill of the plaintiff. Therefore, the plaintiff is not entitled to the injunctive relief or damages or other relief".

Levinwick thus serves as a salutary reminder to employers about the difficulties which may be encountered in seeking to rely on such clauses in the courts, and of the consequential need to scrutinise closely such clauses so as to ascertain the necessity and proportionality of the restrictions they impose.

NO-FAULT TERMINATION: ASSESSMENT OF THE *SHEEHY V RYAN* POSITION

High Court clarifies legal position on no-fault termination The High Court this year handed down two significant judgments in the context of injunction applications in which attempts were made to restrain the termination of the plaintiffs' employment on grounds not alleging any fault. This factual matrix, of course, raises the difficult questions brought up in considering the long-established common law position, confirmed by the Supreme Court in 2008 in *Sheehy v Ryan* [2008] 4 I.R. 258, that an employer may dismiss an employee for good, bad or no reason as long as notice is properly provided. It is interesting to analyse each of these judgments with a view to assessing the implications of *Sheehy v Ryan* for injunction applications seeking to restrain "no-fault termination" of employment.

***Hughes v MonGodb Ltd* [2014] IEHC 335** In *Hughes v MonGodb Ltd* [2014] IEHC 335, the plaintiff sought a number of injunctions arising from the termination of his employment which was stated to be on the basis that he was "not a good fit for the company". The defendant expressly stated that the plaintiff had not been dismissed by reason of being found guilty of any misconduct or poor performance, a position that was challenged by the plaintiff, who alleged that "performance related issues" had been raised but never resolved. Keane J. summarised the plaintiff's case at para.15:

> "The plaintiff appears to be making the case that modern developments have modified the law to the extent that the defendant here was not entitled to give notice in accordance with the relevant term of the contract between the parties if his reason for doing so was bad."

On behalf of the plaintiff, it was argued that the court should consider a "diluted approach" to the test in *Maha Lingam v Health Service Executive* [2006] 17 E.L.R. 137, based on the decision of Hogan J. in *Wallace v Irish Aviation Authority* [2012] IEHC 178. In his judgment in *Hughes*, Keane J. provided valuable analysis of the status of *Wallace* and its impact on other employment injunction applications when he said:

> "[I]n *Wallace*, Hogan J. was presented with what he described as a net issue of construction concerning the express use of the term '*[d]isciplinary action will not be taken pending the outcome of the appeal*'.... Second, in that context it is not at all clear to me that the effect of the decision in *Wallace* is to dilute the test in *Maha Lingam* in any way, nor of course could it do so as a matter of *stare decisis*. I do not understand *Maha Lingam* as authority for the proposition that the court should inflexibly refuse (or 'wash its hands of') any claim for a mandatory injunction to specifically enforce a contract of employment. Rather, I view [it] as authority for the principle that such mandatory injunctions are exceptional and that applicants must satisfy a strong or clear case test, instead of the *prima facie* case test normally applicable as part of the *Campus Oil* principles."

***Wallace* distinguished** It is clear from the above passage that, in the view of Keane J., *Wallace* is a decision to be interpreted very much on its own facts, and will not lightly be invoked so as to avail a plaintiff in an employment injunction application who makes claims of potential reputational damage. It will be recalled that, in *Wallace*, Hogan J. had referred to what he termed a "valley of squinting windows", thereby explaining why it would sometimes be necessary for a High Court judge to grant injunctive relief to protect a plaintiff from the reputational fall-out flowing from a decision taken by an employer. Analysing the above passage in the judgment in *Hughes*, however, it seems clear that such a broad invocation was not one which the High Court was prepared to countenance, with *Wallace* being distinguished on the specific procedural mis-step taken by the employer in that case of purporting to place the employee on administrative leave whilst her appeal against dismissal was pending.

Reliance placed on *Bradshaw v Murphy* [2014] IEHC 146 In his judgment in *Hughes*, Keane J referred to another 2014 judgment that is relevant to the question of no-fault dismissal, which is the decision of Finlay Geoghegan J. in *Bradshaw v Murphy* [2014] IEHC 146. In that case, as in *Hughes*, the employee sought an injunction to restrain the termination of his employment, arising against the backdrop of certain allegations that the employer had made regarding the plaintiff's conduct. Crucially, however, the defendant in *Bradshaw* specifically indicated to the High Court that it would not terminate the plaintiff's employment on grounds of the said misconduct – seeking instead to rely upon its common law power to terminate without reason as long as notice was observed. Finlay Geoghegan J accepted that the defendant employer did indeed still have such a power. As she summarised matters (at para.15): "The fact that the [employer] previously threatened to dismiss, for the reasons [of alleged misconduct] does not preclude the [employer] from terminating in accordance with the contractual provisions".

Implications of these judgments for injunctions restraining dismissal In both *Hughes* and *Bradshaw*, then, the High Court has this year confirmed the orthodox common law rule that the employer can dismiss without reason as long as notice is properly observed. In considering the extent to which this is appropriate and just, it is worthwhile to reflect on the observation of Keane J. in *Hughes* when he effectively queried (at para.22) whether a fixed boundary can ever be drawn between "mutual incompatibility" and "individual fault" in any area of unsuccessful human interaction. Because of such difficulty, Keane J. apparently regarded the orthodox position as justifiable. Further justification was to be found in an assessment of precedent, with Keane J. commenting (at para.25) that he did not believe there was any authority for the proposition that a bad reason that informs, but which is not relied upon to justify, the termination of an employment contract in accordance with its terms, renders that dismissal wrong in law. In this regard, it is also important to note that Keane J. distinguished the decision of the High Court in *Naujoks v Institute of Bioresearch* [2007] E.L.R. 25, on which the plaintiff in *Hughes* sought to rely as authority for the proposition that dismissals based on allegations of poor performance attract the same requirement for disciplinary procedures conducted in accordance with natural and constitutional justice as dismissals based on misconduct. In *Hughes*, Keane J. distinguished *Naujoks* in very clear terms:

> "It seems to me that the decision of the High Court in *Naujoks* was based very firmly on the draughtsmanship of the contract at issue whereby 'failure to properly discharge duties' was treated with the same gravity–and made subject to the same procedural consequences–as 'dishonesty', thereby leading to the conclusion that the invocation of the particular form of dismissal under the relevant term of the employment contract applicable to both circumstances should attract the requirements of fair procedures in either case. It does not seem to me that the case is authority for the much broader proposition that a dismissal on grounds of performance is to be treated as equivalent to a dismissal on grounds of misconduct in every case thereby attracting an entitlement to fair procedures in either case that is to be implied into every contract of employment."

BULLYING, HARASSMENT AND STRESS AT WORK

There were two significant decisions of the High Court this year concerning bullying, harassment and stress at work, in which the legal principles in this area have been further clarified.

***Glynn v Minister for Justice, Equality and Law Reform* [2014] IEHC 133** Although a case in which the plaintiff's claim was unsuccessful, the High Court decision in *Glynn* provides a significant addition to the case law in this area, not least because of the lengthy analysis provided in the judgment of Kearns P. as to the legal definitions of bullying and stress and the nature and meaning thereof. It is worth setting out in full the analysis of Kearns P. in this regard. He said:

> "Workplace stress and occupational stress are all things which, conceptually at least, are quite different from each other, though on occasion they can overlap and coincide. Occupational stress is not actionable given that occupational stress is something which every employed person may experience at some stage of his or her working life and can occur for reasons quite distinct from and unrelated to bullying. Workplace stress on the other hand may be actionable if certain legal criteria are met. It can be the result of behaviour which falls far short of bullying. It can be the result of negligence where excessive demands are made of an employee or where complaints about shortcomings in the workplace go unheeded. It lacks however that degree of deliberateness which is the hallmark of bullying. It follows that the first question that must be asked in every bullying case is whether the behaviour complained of, by reference to an objective test, imports that degree of calibrated inappropriateness and repetition which differentiates bullying from workplace stress or occupational stress.
>
> The legal definition of bullying as recommended by the Report by the Task Force on the Prevention of Workplace Bullying (Stationery Office, March, 2001) is set out in the Industrial Relations Act 1990 (Code of Practice Detailing Procedures for Addressing Bullying in the Workplace) (Declaration) Order 2002 (S.I. No. 17 of 2002) as:
>
>> [R]epeated inappropriate behaviour, direct or indirect, whether verbal, physical or otherwise, conducted by one or more persons against another or others, at the place of work and/or in the course of employment, which could *reasonably* be regarded as undermining the individual's right to dignity at work. An isolated incident of the behaviour described in this definition may be an affront to dignity at work but, as a once off incident, it is not considered to be bullying. (Emphasis added)
>
> This wording must be taken as requiring an objective test to determine if bullying has occurred. The test must, for reasons of common sense also, be an objective one given that any other would leave every defendant vulnerable to allegations of bullying based on purely subjective perceptions on the part of a plaintiff who might contend that straightforward situations at work or otherwise were construed by him/her as amounting to bullying."

On the facts before him, Kearns P. found that the incidents of which the plaintiff complained were incidents which fell 'far short' of the definition of workplace bullying referred to in the above-quoted passage. In summary, the plaintiff had argued that over a period of four days she suffered significant stress as a result of being hounded and harassed by a superintendent to whom she was reporting in relation to the need to complete certain account tasks quickly and in relation to an issue of an individual cheque which the superintendent had drawn in relation to his expenses. Kearns J. rejected the proposition that these facts could meet the legal test for bullying and did so in the following terms:

> "[The] events upon which the plaintiff relies to mount her claim turn on the events of a few short days in May, 2005 a time span more identifiable with a once-off or single incident rather than the kind of 'repetitive' and 'inappropriate' conduct which constitutes the wrong of workplace bullying or harassment. Even if events were as described by the plaintiff, they are more synonymous with the kind of 'isolated incident' excluded from the definition of bullying by S.I. No. 17 of 2002."

The very short timeframe involved in the *Glynn* case is indeed remarkable, but the overall impression gained from studying the judgment in *Glynn* is that the bar to be surmounted for a plaintiff to succeed in a bullying, stress and/or harassment claim is indeed a high one. That such a bar can be surmounted on appropriate facts is, however, amply demonstrated by another High Court decision this year, to which my analysis now turns.

***Ruffley v The Board of Management of St Anne's School* [2014] IEHC 235** The decision of O Neill J. in *Ruffley* marked a further significant contribution to the case law in 2014 on bullying, harassment and stress at work. Here, the High Court awarded substantial damages including loss of earnings for workplace bullying which the plaintiff was found to have suffered in the course of her employment as a special needs assistant in the defendant's primary school. Of particular interest about the factual matrix in *Ruffley* is the fact that the injuries were occasioned to the plaintiff arising from, *inter alia*, what was found to be a mis-application of the defendant's disciplinary procedures. The relevant factual background arose due to a particular incident relating to the locking of a door in a sensory room in which the plaintiff carried out part of her duties. The principal of the school took issue with the plaintiff's actions in this regard and consequently set in train the disciplinary procedures applicable in the school. The manner in which these procedures were used, and the subsequent treatment of the plaintiff which – in contrast to the *Glynn* case analysed above – occurred for in excess of one year, were found by O Neill J. to be "grossly unfair" and he was satisfied that foreseeable injuries were occasioned to the plaintiff as a result, leading him to award a very substantial sum in compensation of in excess of €255,000.00 (which sum included damages for loss of earnings). The implications of this judgment are potentially very significant, particularly because of the criticism levelled against the employer for the manner and extent to which it invoked the machinery of its disciplinary procedures. This important aspect of *Ruffley*, coupled with the high level of compensation awarded, would suggest that it will be a frequently-cited authority in this area in future cases.

PROTECTED DISCLOSURES ACT 2014

Significant new protective regime introduced this year Without doubt, a highlight in developments in Irish employment law this year was the introduction of the long-awaited Protected Disclosures Act 2014 (the "2014 Act"). This extremely significant legislative regime ushers in an entirely new range of protections for whistleblowers and will likely have radical implications for employment law in this jurisdiction. It is therefore timely to examine some of the key aspects of this legislation and to clarify its main parameters and key provisions.

The scope of persons protected under the whistleblowers legislation in Ireland A striking feature of the 2014 Act is the very broad range of persons who enjoy protection. Unlike a great many pieces of protective employment legislation in Ireland, the 2014 Act affords its protections to "workers" rather than "employees" and the definition of worker contained in s.3 of the Act is extremely broad, being a person who is an employee; a person who entered into or works or worked under any other contract, whether express or implied and (if it is express) whether oral or in writing, whereby the individual undertook to do or perform (whether personally or otherwise) any work or services for another party to the contract for the purposes of that party's business; a person who works in circumstances in which the individual is introduced or supplied to do the work by a third person, and the terms on which the individual is engaged to do the work are or were in practice substantially determined not by the individual but by the person for whom the individual works or worked, by the third person or by both of them.

The range of persons afforded legal protection under the 2014 Act is further considerably widened by virtue of s.13, which enshrines a new cause of action in tort for persons who have been adversely treated as a result of a protected disclosure made either by them or by another:

> "If a person causes detriment to another person because the other person or a third person made a protected disclosure, the person to whom the detriment is caused has a right of action in tort against the person by whom the detriment is caused."

This potentially very significant provision is another new protection for employees and non-employees alike and could be of potential relevance to, for example, persons who encourage or affirm the disclosures made by the whistleblower.

What kind of behaviour is protected under the 2014 Act? Under s.5 of the 2014 Act, a worker may make a protected disclosure of "relevant information". Information is relevant if, in the reasonable belief of the worker, it tends to show one or more "relevant wrongdoings", and it came to the attention of the worker in connection with the worker's employment. Very significantly, the protection for the whistleblower remains available even if the information disclosed, on examination, does not in fact reveal wrongdoing. This constitutes a very important illustration of the level of protection afforded in Ireland to whistleblowers who are making allegations erroneously or in the face of an uncertainty of the relevant facts. It is important to note in this regard, however, that deliberate false reporting will fail the "reasonable belief" test and is not protected under the 2014 Act.

It is also noteworthy that under the new regime, the motivation for making a disclosure is irrelevant to whether or not it is a protected disclosure: s.5(7) of the 2014 Act.

The 2014 Act sets out, in s.5, a list of "relevant wrongdoings". These include the commission of an offence; failure to perform a legal obligation (other than one arising under a worker's contract of employment); a miscarriage of justice; endangerment of people's health and safety; environmental damage; improper use of public money; oppressive, discriminatory or gross negligence or gross mismanagement in the context of a public body; and concealment of any of these wrongs.

The 2014 Act seeks to encourage the making of the vast majority of disclosures to the employer or another responsible person in the first instance.

Under s.6 of the 2014 Act, the worker is permitted to disclose to a responsible person where the worker reasonably believes that this person has legal responsibility for the relevant wrongdoing or the wrongdoing does not relate solely or mainly to the worker's employer.

The 2014 Act provides (in s.6(2)) that a disclosure will be treated as a disclosure to an employer where it is done in accordance with a procedure authorised by the employer, such as, for example, an internal whistleblowing procedure.

Alternatively, s.7 of the 2014 Act provides that a worker may make a protected disclosure to a "prescribed person". The Minister for Public Expenditure and Reform may, by order and taking into account defined criteria, prescribe certain appropriate persons to be recipients of disclosures of relevant wrongdoings. Section 7(1)(b) of the 2014 Act provides that, in making the disclosure to the prescribed person, the worker must hold a reasonable belief that the wrongdoing falls within the description of matters over which the prescribed person has responsibility and the worker must also reasonably believe that the information disclosed and any allegations therein are substantially true.

Section 8 of the 2014 Act provides that, in the context of public bodies, a worker may make a protected disclosure to a Minister exercising any function relating to the public body.

A protected disclosure may be made by a worker in the course of obtaining legal advice from a barrister, solicitor or trade union official (or official of a statutorily identified body): s.9 of the 2014 Act.

Under s.10 the 2014 Act, a worker may make a protected disclosure in other circumstances if the worker "reasonably believes" that the information disclosed and any allegation contained in it are substantially true. The disclosure must not, however, be made for personal gain (although this excludes any reward payable under or by virtue of any enactment). In all the circumstances of the case, it must be reasonable for the worker to make the disclosure. One or more of the following conditions must also be satisfied:

- at the time the worker makes the disclosure, the worker reasonably believes that he or she will be subjected to penalisation by the employer if a disclosure is made in circumstances other than to a legal adviser;

- where no relevant person is prescribed in relation to the relevant wrongdoing, the worker reasonably believes that it is likely that evidence relating to the relevant wrongdoing will be concealed or destroyed if the worker makes a disclosure to an employer or responsible person;
- the worker has previously made a disclosure of substantially the same information other than to a legal adviser; and
- the relevant wrongdoing is of an exceptionally serious nature.

Section 10(3) of the 2014 Act also sets out certain criteria which may be considered in determining whether it was reasonable in all of the circumstances of the case for the disclosure to be made.

These include:

- the identity of the recipient of the disclosure;
- the seriousness of the relevant wrongdoing;
- whether the wrongdoing is continuing or likely to occur again;
- any breach of confidentiality;
- in respect of a previous disclosure, any previous action taken or which might reasonably be expected to have been taken by the recipient of the disclosure; and
- whether a worker complied with any procedures authorised by an employer when making a disclosure to that employer or another responsible person.

A subsequent disclosure may be regarded as a disclosure of substantially the same information as that disclosed by a previous disclosure even though the subsequent disclosure extends to information about action taken or not taken by any person as a result of the previous disclosure: s.10(4) of the 2014 Act.

Section 16 of the 2014 Act provides that a person to whom a protected disclosure is made, and any person to whom a protected disclosure is referred in the performance of that person's duties, shall not disclose to another person any information that might identify the person by whom the protected disclosure was made. There are various qualifications to this provision, but it does demonstrate an important identity protection for whistleblowers under the new legislation.

Redress provided for under the 2014 Act The legislation affords a substantial range of redress options for employees who are adversely affected as a result of whistleblowing. An important feature of the 2014 Act is that it amends the Unfair Dismissals Acts 1977–2007, in three key respects. First, it expressly deems a dismissal to be unfair where that dismissal flows from the employee's having made a protected disclosure. As with regular unfair dismissal cases, the onus is on the employer to satisfy the relevant body (currently the Rights Commissioner Service or Employment Appeals Tribunal) that it can justify the dismissal: the employee does not have any onus in this respect, save where the fact of dismissal is in issue.

Secondly, the 2014 Act amends and significantly enhances the redress which could otherwise be awarded for unfair dismissal by allowing an employee who is dismissed for having made a protected disclosure to obtain compensation of up to a maximum of five years' remuneration. This is a striking development in the law on unfair dismissal and one that sits in marked contrast to other unfair dismissal cases in which the financial redress available is capped at two years' remuneration.

The third key change brought about by the 2014 Act to the existing unfair dismissals regime in this jurisdiction is that the qualifying service requirement which applies to most unfair dismissal cases—whereby employees must have one year's continuous service before they may bring an unfair dismissal claim—is expressly waived in the context of protected disclosures.

Another very significant feature of the 2014 Act is that Sch.1 to the Act empowers the Circuit Court to grant interim reliefs restraining the termination of a person's employment in the context of having made a protected disclosure—a provision which seems likely to be tested in the very near future.

Quite apart from the protection against dismissal, the employee who is a whistleblower in Ireland is also protected against penalisation. Penalisation is very broadly defined in s.3 of the 2014 Act and includes any act or omission that affects a worker to the worker's detriment (to include inter alia, suspension, lay-off, dismissal, demotion and loss of opportunity for promotion, transfer of duties or alteration of terms and conditions; unfair treatment; coercion, intimidation or harassment; discrimination, disadvantage, injury, damage or loss or threat of reprisal). Pursuant to Sch.2 to the 2014 Act, the very strong redress of up to five years' remuneration is again possible here.

As already set out above, the 2014 Act (s.13) creates a new tort action open to a person who sustains 'detriment' as a result of whistleblowing, with detriment being defined to include coercion, intimidation, harassment, discrimination, disadvantage or adverse treatment in relation to employment (or prospective employment), injury, damage or loss, and threat of reprisal.

Conclusions It is clear, therefore, that the 2014 Act provides a robust and far-reaching range of legal protections for whistleblowers. The implications of this Act will doubtless be assessed by the courts and tribunals tasked with interpreting it and it thus seems highly likely that its provisions will be the subject of further detailed analysis in the pages of the *Annual Review of Irish Law* in future years.

Equity

DR LUCY-ANN BUCKLEY,
National University of Ireland Galway

TRUSTS

Charitable Trusts The most significant development in the law of trusts arose in the context of charitable trusts, as many of the remaining sections of the Charities Act 2009 ("the 2009 Act") were finally brought into force. The most noteworthy aspects of the 2009 Act are outlined in the Equity chapter for that year (Tobin, "Equity", in Byrne and Binchy (eds), *Annual Review of Irish Law 2009* (Dublin: Round Hall, 2010), p.447). However, although the Act itself was highly significant, only a few sections, largely dealing with definitions and the sale of mass cards, were initially brought into force. These were ss.1, 2, 5, 10 (except subss.(3) and (4)), and 99, which were brought into force from 1 September 2009 by the Charities Act 2009 (Commencement) Order 2009 (S.I. No. 284 of 2009). The delay in implementation has now largely been rectified by two new statutory instruments. The first, the Charities Act 2009 (Establishment Day) Order 2014 (S.I. No. 456 of 2014), provides that 16 October 2014 is the Establishment Day for the purposes of the 2009 Act, thereby establishing the Charities Regulatory Authority (the CRA). The Board of the CRA was appointed on 30 April 2014, and the current focus of the CRA is on establishing itself as an agency and compiling an initial register of charities (see further O'Beirne, "Recent Developments in Charities Regulation" (2014) 6 Bar Rev. 122). The CRA will then begin to implement its regulatory functions. The second statutory instrument, the Charities Act 2009 (Commencement) Order 2014 (S.I. No. 457 of 2014), effectively provides that the remainder of the 2009 Act shall come into force from 16 October 2014, with the exceptions of s.4 (dealing with Ministerial orders and regulations), Pt 4 (dealing with the protection of charitable organisations) and Pt 7 (miscellaneous provisions).

Cy-près jurisdiction In the case law, the issue of cy-près jurisdiction arose in the High Court in *In the Matter of Charities Act 1961 v Jordan* [2014] IEHC 678. The case concerned a residuary gift in the will of the testator, Patrick Jordan, in favour of a number of boys' clubs in London, including, as ultimate residuary legatee, "the Derek Jordan Memorial Fund". Derek Jordan, the testator's son, had died at a tragically young age. As he had been involved with a charitable organisation known as the London Federation of Boys Clubs (later the Federation of London Youth Clubs), his parents had wished to set up a memorial fund with the Federation in their son's memory. Unfortunately, the intended memorial fund was never established, and did not exist at the time of the testator's death. The question therefore arose as to whether the gift in favour of the memorial fund could be applied cy-près, given that the memorial fund itself had never existed. It has previously been established that a gift to a non-existent institution may be applied cy-près, where it can be shown that the settlor had a general charitable intention, and it has been suggested that the court is particularly ready to infer such an intention in this context (see, e.g., the remarks of Buckley J. in *Re Davis* [1902] 1 Ch. 876 at 881). However, such an inference is not invariably drawn (see, e.g., *Re Goldschmidt* [1957] 1 W.L.R. 524), and on the facts, White J. held that the testator in this case could not be said to have a general charitable intention, as the purpose of the gift was specifically to honour the memory of his son. The gift therefore could not be applied cy-près, even if the point regarding the memorial fund's existence did not arise.

Constructive trusts In the Supreme Court, the case of *O'Donnell v Bank of Ireland* [2014] IESC 77 raised interesting equitable issues on constructive trusts, knowing receipt and dealing, and the doctrine of notice. The case concerned an appeal brought by the four children of Mr Brian O'Donnell and Mrs Mary Patricia O'Donnell, claiming they were beneficially entitled to the family home, a property known as Gorse Hill in Co. Dublin. McGovern J., in the High Court, had rejected the appellants' claim to various reliefs sought, and had awarded costs against them and ordered them to vacate the property (*O'Donnell v Governor & Company of the Bank of Ireland* [2013] IEHC 375).

Gorse Hill had been acquired through a very complex legal structure. The legal and beneficial title to the property were vested in a company, Vico Ltd, and the paid up share capital in the company was held on a discretionary trust for the appellants. McGovern J. had held that the appellants were beneficially entitled to the shares in Vico Ltd, under the terms of a discretionary trust, but not to Gorse Hill itself. In the Supreme Court, the appellants relied on the decision of the UK Supreme Court in *Prest v Petrodel Resources Ltd* [2013] 3 W.L.R. 1 to argue that Gorse Hill was clearly purchased and held by Vico Ltd for the benefit of the appellants, and that the company had no other purpose. Accordingly, the appellants contended that Vico Ltd effectively held Gorse Hill on trust for the appellants, as they were beneficially entitled to the shares in the company. However, Laffoy J., writing for the Supreme Court, held that "the ordinary principles and presumptions of equity", as Lord Sumption had described them in *Prest,* could not be stretched to justify such a finding (para.108).

The appellants also relied on the principle of "knowing receipt" to argue that the Bank of Ireland ("the Bank"), which had acquired its interest in Gorse Hill under securities given to it by Vico Ltd, should be found liable as a constructive trustee of that interest. In this regard, the appellants relied on the first class of "knowing receipt" set out by Millett J. in *Agip (Africa) Ltd v Jackson* [1989] 3 W.L.R. 1367. Under this category, a person who receives trust property for his own use and benefit, with actual or constructive notice that it is being transferred in breach of trust, is liable as a constructive trustee. Although the traditional notice requirements continue to apply in Ireland (as set out in *Re Frederick Inns Ltd* [1994] 1 I.L.R.M. 387), it was acknowledged that the test for knowing receipt now differs in the UK, following the decision of the Court of Appeal of England and Wales in *Bank of Credit and Commerce International (Overseas) Ltd v Akindele* [2001] Ch. 437. That case established that, in England and Wales at least, the question now is simply whether the recipient had sufficient knowledge of the circumstances surrounding the transfer to render it unconscionable for him to retain the benefit. In the event, Laffoy J. noted that the court did not have to address this divergence, as it had not been contended that the UK approach should be accepted in Ireland. It therefore remains unclear whether the Irish courts are likely to move from their current, well-established approach. This is regrettable, as the current approach has been criticised by Keane as "clearly unsatisfactory, since there is little, if any, analysis of the degree of knowledge required to establish liability in cases of alleged knowing receipt" (Keane, *Equity and the Law of Trusts in the Republic of Ireland*, 2nd edn, (Dublin: Bloomsbury Professional, 2011) at para.13.30). Furthermore, the current approach may lead to the imposition of liability even where there is no unconscionable behaviour on the part of the recipient, as occurred in *Frederick Inns* itself.

On the facts, the Bank had received a transfer of an interest in Gorse Hill, and had done so for its own benefit. However, it had received the transfer from Vico Ltd, not from the trustee of the discretionary trust ("the Trustee"). Furthermore, since it had been found as fact that Vico Ltd was the legal and beneficial owner of Gorse Hill, and that the appellants had no beneficial interest in it, it followed that the Bank had not acquired an interest in trust property. The most that the appellants could establish was that the Trustee had approved the giving of various guarantees and securities by Vico Ltd to the Bank, but this was a far cry from transferring trust property to the Bank, and entirely ignored the separate corporate personality of Vico Ltd. Laffoy J. concluded:

> "The proposition advanced is simply incorrect; there was no transfer of trust property, or of an interest in trust property, to the Bank because what the Bank got from Vico Ltd was an interest in Gorse Hill which Vico Ltd, as the sole legal and beneficial owner of Gorse Hill, had capacity … and power to pass to the Bank" (para.123).

Although Laffoy J. considered this to be "the end of the constructive trust argument" (para.123), she nevertheless went on to address the remaining criteria for knowing receipt. On the question of whether the transfer to the Bank was in breach of trust, Laffoy J. noted that the essential argument was that, by approving the guarantees given by Vico Ltd, the Trustee was effectively benefiting Mr and Mrs O'Donnell, in breach of the express terms of the discretionary trust. Despite the lack of direct evidence from the Trustee, Laffoy J. concluded that a breach of trust had not been established, since the legal and beneficial interest in Gorse Hill was never trust property, and therefore could not have been transferred in breach of trust. Even had there been such a transfer in breach of trust, the trial judge had found as fact that the Bank had no actual or constructive notice of the terms of the discretionary trust, and these findings were supported by credible evidence and could not be disturbed. Accordingly, as the appellants had not satisfied any of the criteria for knowing receipt derived from the first category in *Agip*, it followed that this claim could not be made out.

Powers and duties of trustees A detailed analysis of the duties of trustees was provided in *Greene v Coady* [2014] IEHC 38. The plaintiffs, who were beneficiaries or potential beneficiaries of a pension fund, claimed damages against the defendant trustees of the fund for alleged breach of trust. The claim arose out of the acceptance by the trustees of an offer of €23.1 million (plus another €14 million outside of the fund) from the employer contributor of the fund to close its liability to contribute. The plaintiffs alleged that the trustees should have demanded a contribution of at least €129.2 million to make up the fund's deficit, and that this failure amounted to a wilful default by the trustees. The plaintiffs contended that the trustees' decision could not have been taken by a reasonable body of properly informed trustees, that the trustees' vote to accept the employer's offer was vitiated by a conflict of interest, and that the trustees had ignored relevant matters while taking notice of irrelevant ones.

Of particular interest is the issue which arose in the case regarding the standard for the review of decisions by pension trustees. In general, as Charleton J. noted:

> "In making any decision as to the liability of trustees it is not for the court to be cleverer or better informed or more astute or more enquiring or better in its judgment than the trustees. The court must also avoid the temptation to listen to the evidence and to make its own conclusion as to what should have been done by the trustees on the date of the impugned decision. The hot seat of a trustee is where the court should place itself and on the basis of what the trustees knew or ought to have known and should look at the decision through the vision of the trustees informed by the same material and by the same relevant considerations that were properly to have been then considered. A measure of appreciation is by law to be applied. Trustees must take all relevant matters into account; trustees must exclude irrelevant matters; trustees must direct themselves properly in law and in interpreting the provisions of a trust deed and rules" (at para.3.0).

This was already well established.

However, as Charleton J. noted, there was some doubt as to whether a decision by trustees could only be set aside if it could be demonstrated that the trustees would have acted differently, had they taken account of certain relevant factors, or if it was sufficient that the trustees *might* have acted differently, had they been aware of the factors in question. This uncertainty is noted by Keane (*Equity and the Law of Trusts in the Republic of Ireland*, 2nd edn, (Dublin: Bloomsbury Professional, 2011) at 10.49–10.50, cited by Charleton J. at para.3.0). Keane notes English authority suggesting that where trustees are obliged to exercise a discretion (as in a pension trust), it is sufficient that they might have acted differently, had they not been under a mistake of fact. Keane further suggests that "it would seem reasonable that the threshold for intervention should be lower in cases such as pension trusts where the right to benefit has been hard earned". Keane also notes successful challenges to the decisions of pension trustees on grounds of perversity in English case law, but suggests that similar principles, based on public law concepts such as "natural justice" or "fair procedures", might not necessarily apply in Ireland.

In this case, no argument was made to distinguish between a pension trust and trusts of other kinds, even though it might have been argued, as suggested by Keane, that the beneficiaries of a pension trust are not in receipt of a gratuitous benefit, but have earned their benefits and have relied on certain pension entitlements as part of their remuneration package. Charleton J. held that there was "no warrant" for drawing such a distinction, which "would effectively enable the court to substitute its own judgment for that of the trustees" (para.3.1). Hence, "once trustees are shown to have acted honestly and in good faith after having taken account of all relevant considerations and excluded all the irrelevant considerations … only decisions which are properly to be characterised as being ones that no reasonable body of trustees could have made may in law be condemned", and there was no place for retrospective "counsels of perfection" (para.3.1). Charleton J. considered that all trusts were important, and "all are subject to the same rules" (para.3.1).

Charleton J. also clarified that, once a consideration is relevant, it is for the trustees to determine how much weight should be accorded to that particular factor, and how the relevant factors should be balanced overall. Noting that: "It is easy to rebalance factors so that the result can be different", Charleton J. emphasised that: "It is not the task of a court to do that" (para.4.0). He continued that

> "once the standard of interference is set at the test of perversity, shorthand for where the decision is identified as one which no reasonable body of trustees properly informed and considering the decision could have made, the court should not decide that too much or too little weight had been given to a particular factor unless this is, firstly, based on tenable evidence and not mere speculation and, secondly, the measure of appreciation inherent in the reasonableness test brings that decision outside those parameters" (para.4.0).

While Keane, as noted above, had suggested that an approach to reasonableness based on the principles of judicial review might not be appropriate in the trusts context, Charleton J. considered that it was appropriate to have regard to public law principles. This was because trustees are selected for their reasonableness, were entitled to receive representations from the beneficiaries, and might have expert advice, paid for by the fund. Charleton J. therefore cited the public law decision of *Kildare County Council v An Bord Pleanála* [2006] IEHC 173, where MacMenamin J. emphasised that any consideration of the weight to be accorded to a particular factor was a matter for the decision maker, except where a factor was perversely inflated or deflated. Charleton J. commented that

> "as it is appropriate not to interfere save for decisions which are plainly unreasonable, it must remain within the ambit of the powers of trustees to weigh one factor more heavily and another less. To otherwise analyse a decision of trustees would be for the court to substitute its own judgment" (para.4.1).

Charleton J. also addressed the scope of the fiduciary duty owed by trustees. It is, of course, well established that trustees may not place themselves in a position which may entail a conflict of interest with the duty they owe to the beneficiaries of the trust. In the pension trust context, a potential conflict might arise between duties owed to the company and the duty owed to the beneficiaries of the pension scheme. In this case, the trustees contended that the rule against conflicting interests might be overcome by informed consent; by the fact that the conflict arose through the natural operation of the trust scheme itself; and through express provision in the trust deed. Charleton J. emphasised that there was one "fundamental obligation" that could "never be departed from", namely, "that the trustees will pursue the aims of the trust honestly and in good faith" (para.5.6). This applied irrespective of the terms of the trust deed, with the result that a decision guided by an "improper motive" would always be a breach of trust (para.5.6).

Accordingly, while

> "an exemption may be provided under a trust deed … the purpose of entering into the office of trustee is to fulfil the objects of the trust; and this cannot happen if a conflict of interest or duty is such as to paralyse or even influence any trustee so that he or she cannot rationally and objectively approach and decide on a problem" (para.5.6).

However, an allegation of such a conflict and its effects must be proven as fact. For this purpose:

> "Conflicts of duty are to be equated to conflicts of interest as the duty does not arise without the interest and the genesis of the rule in the frailty of human nature requires that both are equally to be treated." (para.5.8)

The most interesting point in this section of the decision was Charleton J.'s confirmation that, where it is implicit in the nature of the trust that particular decisions involving trust business will affect the trustees personally, there is an exception to the rule that trustees cannot act in a situation where a conflict of interest arises (para.5.11). However, for this to apply, "the necessary exercise of the decision-making power of trustees notwithstanding conflict must be inevitable" (para.5.11), and the exception does not apply beyond the scope of what is inherently contemplated by the trust deed.

In other points of note, Charleton J. elaborated, at para.7.1, on the circumstances in which an application to the court for directions, currently provided for in the Rules of the Superior Courts, Ord.54, r.1, may properly be made by the trustees of a trust. However, he noted that trustees could not be liable for failing to make such an application unless they were unable properly to make the decision in question, which was not the case here. Charleton J. also clarified that the phrase "willful default" could not encompass a situation where trustees, having considered the matter, opted not to pursue a particular course of action (para.8.1), in this case, serving a notice of contribution. Instead, "willful default" arises "only where that default can be truly characterised as a conscious breach of duty or a reckless breach of duty, in the sense of conscious awareness that is dismissed" (para.8.8). Finally, Charleton J. confirmed that the trustees could have regard to more than the financial considerations under the trust deed, when considering how to act, and could legitimately consider other potential detriments to the members of the fund, such as the potential loss of employment (para.16.13).

PROMISSORY ESTOPPEL

In *Cavey v Cavey* [2014] IESC 16, the parties were all children of Maurice Cavey, who died in 2006. The respondents ("the executors") were named as executors of their father's will, and were granted probate in 2008. The plaintiff, Francis Cavey ("Mr Cavey"), brought an unsuccessful application under s.117 of the Succession Act 1965. He subsequently brought a second action in promissory estoppel, claiming that both of his deceased parents had represented to him that he would inherit the family home, and that he had relied on this to his detriment. The executors sought to have these proceedings dismissed on the grounds, inter alia, that they were statute barred under s.9 of the Civil Liability Act 1961 (the "1961 Act"). This order was granted at trial by Herbert J., and Mr Cavey appealed.

The key point of the appeal was raised by the court, rather than by Mr Cavey, who was a litigant in person. This concerned the nature of a claim for promissory estoppel, rather than the elements of such a claim, which were not addressed by the court. Specifically, given that s.9 of the 1961 Act governs the limitation period in respect of a cause of action which "has survived against the estate of a deceased person", does a claim for promissory estoppel constitute such an action? Giving the judgment of the court, Clarke J. noted that a promise to make a testamentary gift was technically not breached until a person died without doing so, as he might have made a will in compliance with his promise at any time prior to his death. If so, it followed that the cause of action was based on the deceased's failure to act during his lifetime. This in turn suggested that, since the claim arose only on death, it would not fall within the ambit of s.9 of the 1961 Act, and would not be statute-barred.

The question had previously been addressed in a number of decisions by the High Court, most recently by O'Keeffe J. in *Prendergast v McLaughlin* [2011] 1 I.R. 102, but had not been examined by the Supreme Court. In *Prendergast*, O'Keeffe J. concluded, in accordance with one line of previous High Court authority, that the cause of action was completed immediately prior to the death of the deceased, rather than at the moment of death. The action therefore survived against the deceased's estate, and was subject to the 1961 Act. However, in a second line of authority, Barron J. had taken a different view, holding that it could not be determined that the testator had failed to comply with his promise until he actually died, unless he had expressly repudiated the promise while still alive (*Reidy v McGreavey*, unreported, High Court, Barron J., 19 March 1993).

Clarke J. concluded that there was a

> "significant distinction … between a cause of action which results from an act or omission of the deceased, on the one hand, and a cause of action which may exist against those in charge of the administration of the estate of the deceased, on the other" (para.4.6).

If Mr Cavey had a cause of action in promissory estoppel at all, it could only be because his father had, during his life, failed to fulfil a legally enforceable promise to leave the family home to him. This would amount to a failure by his father, rather than a failure by his father's estate, even though the subsequent action was brought against the estate. Clarke J. therefore concluded that

> "such a claim necessarily comes within the scope of the phrase 'a claim surviving against the estate of the deceased' even if it is true that a deceased could have avoided such a claim being capable of being brought by complying with their promise to bequeath the relevant property up to the moment before their death" (para.4.7).

Accordingly, the claim fell within the scope of s.9 of the 1961 Act, and was statute-barred.

Promissory estoppel was also addressed by the High Court in *National Asset Loan Management Ltd v McMahon; National Asset Loan Management Ltd v Downes* [2014] IEHC 71. The key issue was whether certain securities, which had been acquired by NAMA, were enforceable against the defendant. Although the decision did not raise any new points regarding estoppel, it nevertheless provides a useful summary of the key elements of the doctrine, and of their practical application in a situation where the defendant's claim was essentially based on the legal advice he had received, and the assumptions he had made based on that advice.

Charleton J. noted that definitions of estoppel had developed since the seminal decision of Kenny J. in *Revenue Commissioners v Moroney* [1972] I.R. 372. However, it still "clearly requires some action or behaviour or representation by the party who is to be bound" (para.20), and could not be based on unilateral assumptions, although it might be based on a clear mutual understanding or assumed state of fact or law, where this could be proven. To this extent, Charleton J. approved (at para.21) the doctrine of estoppel by convention, as stated by Treitel (*The Law of Contract*, 13th edn (London: Sweet & Maxwell, 2011) at 3.094).

Apart from this limited possibility, Charleton J. emphasised that: "Estoppel is based either on representations or on situations of behaviour that, reasonably construed, clearly withdraw or alter the strictures of legal obligations in such a way that it would be unfair to later enforce these" (para.20). He added:

> "Where the matter is one of representation, it should be easy to identify the legal term supposedly altered and the representation directed in this regard. Where it is a matter of both parties proceeding on the basis of a common understanding, the mutual convention of the parties may suffice as a foundation for estoppel" (para.20).

The test for estoppel is objective, as Charleton J. noted that "whether such a situation amounts to an unambiguous and unequivocal retreat from insistence on full legal rights is to be construed according to the perceptions of reasonable people" (para.21). However, in the present case, there was no representation or behaviour by the party to be estopped, which could reasonably be interpreted as giving rise to expectations. On the contrary, the claim was "based on empty assumption" (para.22). Charleton J. concluded that: "In no sense would it be reasonable to conclude on the evidence heard that a mutually binding and differing state of affairs had come into being and in alteration of the legal relationship between the parties" (para.22). In particular, Charleton J. noted that: "No one can rely on advice from their own lawyer as founding an estoppel" (para.23), at least where such advice was purely a matter of professional opinion and did not stem from any representations made by the opposing party.

Charleton J. concluded that:

> "What is needed in any form of estoppel is 'a clear and unequivocal promise or assurance'. While, perhaps, some authorities might take the approach that it is the unfairness of allowing the party with the legal rights to go back on their stated position, there must still be a stated representation or

> underlying shared circumstance giving rise to the other party, at a minimum reasonably, concluding that relevant legal rights have been set aside. The proof of any such alleged representation through words or circumstances is on the party seeking to rely on it" (para.23).

A mere assumption was insufficient, unless there was "proof that the assumption is shared by both sides or is made by one and acquiesced in by the other" (para.23).

EQUITABLE MAXIMS

Equity looks on that as done which ought to be done; the rule in *Walsh v Lonsdale* An interesting application of the rule in *Walsh v Lonsdale* (1882) 21 Ch. D. 9 occurred in *North Quay Developments Ltd v Carty* [2014] IEHC 444. The case concerned a lease that had been delivered into escrow, pending the fulfilment of a condition precedent. The question was whether the lease was binding on the parties once the condition was satisfied, even though the lease was never formally released from escrow.

The lease in this case was entered into in 2007 by the lessor, North Quay Developments Ltd, and the intended tenant, Iverwell Ltd ("Iverwell"). The mutual intention of the parties was that Iverwell would fit out the premises as a shoe shop. However, Iverwell went into liquidation in 2012. The defendant, Mr Carty, who was the principal director of Iverwell, was also a party to the lease and had guaranteed the payment of rent by Iverwell. The question raised was whether the defendant was now liable to pay that rent. This depended on whether the defendant was bound by the lease, which in turn depended on whether Iverwell was bound by it. The defendant contended that the lease was executed in escrow, and that Iverwell had entered into possession of the property under an agreement for an occupational lease, which had terminated in 2008 once certain conditions were satisfied. At this point, the actual lease should have been released from escrow and handed over to Iverwell. As it was not (apparently due to an oversight), the defendant contended that the lease was never effective and could not ground the plaintiff's claim.

Hogan J., in the High Court, concluded that the lease was in fact effective, due to the operation of the rule in *Walsh v Lonsdale* (stating that an agreement for a lease is as good as a lease itself), and the separate but connected equitable maxim that equity regards that as done which ought to be done. Although there were exceptions to the rule in *Walsh v Lonsdale*, they did not apply here. Accordingly, once the condition precedent had been satisfied, the lease ought to have been formally released from escrow and delivered to Iverwell, and equity would treat the parties as if this had in fact been done. The defendant could therefore not object to the application of the terms of the agreement, particularly as neither Iverwell nor the defendant had, on the facts, been prejudiced by the failure to deliver the actual lease.

RECEIVERSHIP BY EQUITABLE EXECUTION

A conflict in the case law on equitable execution may finally have been resolved in the High Court decision in *Start Mortgages Ltd v Doheny* [2014] IEHC 656. The case raised the issue of whether a receiver could be appointed by way of equitable execution over any settlement proceeds or award of damages that might in future be made to the defendant in an action for personal injuries.

The plaintiff obtained a consent judgment against the defendants, which remained almost entirely unsatisfied. The plaintiff secured the judgment against land belonging to the first named defendant, and subsequently became aware that the second defendant had issued personal injury proceedings against a third party, and that these proceedings had been transferred from the Circuit Court to the High Court. The plaintiff contended that these proceedings might be settled for a considerable sum, or might lead to a significant award of damages in favour of the second defendant, and that, if so, the plaintiff should be entitled to an equitable interest in the sum realised. The plaintiff therefore sought to appoint a receiver over the potential proceeds of the action, arguing that the second defendant's right to damages amounted to an equitable interest, though not yet a legal right, and that the potential for recovery must be significant, given that the case had been transferred to the High Court. In support of its application, the plaintiff relied on the decision in *O'Connell v An Bord Pleanála* [2007] IEHC 79, where Peart J. appointed a receiver by way of equitable execution over a claim by the judgment debtor to potential damages in a personal injuries action, which had not yet been heard.

It was argued for the second defendant that, since the action had not yet been heard, and no award had yet been made, there was no legal or equitable property that could be subject to the order. Counsel also highlighted two cases preceding *O'Connell*, namely, the decision of the Supreme Court in *National Irish Bank Ltd v Graham* [1994] 1 I.R. 215, and the later High Court decision in *Honniball v Cunningham* [2010] 2 I.R. 1.

In *Graham,* the Supreme Court refused to grant an order for equitable execution over a herd of cattle, on the grounds that the plaintiff could execute its judgment in the ordinary way by the seizure of the herd. In its judgment, the Supreme Court stated that "the jurisdiction to appoint such a receiver is confined to cases in which a debtor enjoys an equitable interest in property which cannot be reached by legal process". The requirement of an equitable interest in the property was subsequently confirmed in the High Court by Laffoy J. in *Honniball.* Neither case was opened properly to the court in *O'Connell*, and indeed, the decision in *O'Connell* was criticised by Keane on the grounds that: "Since there was no property of any sort to which the judgment debtor was entitled, either immediately or in the future, it is difficult to understand over what equitable interest in property the execution process could attach" (Keane, *Equity and the Law of Trusts in the Republic of Ireland*, 2nd edn, (Dublin: Bloomsbury Professional, 2011), para.21.09, cited by Donnelly J. in *Start Mortgages* at para.11). The divergence in authority was noted in subsequent case law, but had not yet been resolved.

Noting that a claim for damages is not a due debt, Donnelly J. concluded that it did not constitute property to which the second defendant was entitled, in law or in equity, either now or in the future. A bare right of action for damages for personal injuries is not assignable (*Law Society of Ireland v O'Malley* [1999] 1 I.R. 162), and the damages themselves were "uncertain, unliquidated and unascertainable at present" (para.22). Concluding that the decision in *O'Connell* was essentially based on the view that a receiver by way of equitable execution could be appointed in respect of future debts, Donnelly J. nevertheless felt, following detailed analysis, that there were strong reasons for departing from *O'Connell*, as the decision in that case did not contain any significant review of the previous decisions in *Graham* and *Honniball*. Donnelly J. therefore felt obliged to follow the previous principle laid down by the Supreme Court in *Graham*.

INJUNCTIONS

Interlocutory injunctions There were no significant doctrinal developments with regard to injunctions. However, a number of cases raised interesting points regarding application, and one, *Baínne Aláinn Ltd v Glanbia Plc* [2014] IEHC 482, provided a thorough analysis of the general principles and policy considerations underlying the case law on interlocutory orders, which is well worth reading.

The plaintiff in *Baínne Aláinn* sought an order to prevent the defendant from altering a distribution agreement for dairy products. Of particular interest was Barrett J.'s emphasis on the limits of judicial guidelines. Barrett J. stressed that, under the Rules of the Superior Courts 1986, the court has an underlying jurisdiction to grant an interlocutory order where it considers it just or convenient to do so, and may grant the order either conditionally or unconditionally. He also emphasised that

> "while there are obvious advantages to the court complying with such recognised guidelines as may be drawn from case-law in this area, not least in terms of ensuring certainty and avoiding arbitrariness, that case-law has long been informed by the common-sense recognition … that the question as to whether or not to grant an interlocutory injunction is one in respect of which the court ultimately retains a degree of flexibility and discretion that is unconstrained by strict criteria, though subject of course to the rules of precedent" (para.23).

This flexibility was essential because even apparently similar facts might in practice require dissimilar treatment.

With regard to the balance of convenience, Barrett J. noted that there were at least two good reasons for requiring an undertaking as to damages. The first, referenced in *American Cyanamid v Ethicon Ltd* [1975] A.C. 396, was that it assists the court to avoid expressing any opinion on the merits of the case until the final hearing of the action. The second reason is to reduce the risk of unfairness to the respondent, in the event that the plaintiff is unsuccessful at trial. Barrett J. noted the potential for inequality, since wealthier plaintiffs are more likely to be in a position to give the undertaking as to damages, and are therefore better placed to avail of interlocutory relief. However, he emphasised that

> "there are a number of bases on which, if presented with the right set of conditions, a court could, by reference to, and in conformity with, existing law and precedent, grant injunctive relief to an applicant of limited or middling means without imposing a requirement as to an undertaking for damages" (para 26).

He suggested that there were at least three such possible bases. First, the court had an inherent jurisdiction under the Rules of the Superior Courts to grant an order where it appears "just or convenient to do so", even if the applicant was not in a position to provide or make good the usual undertaking as to damages. Secondly, following from the comments of O'Higgins C.J. in *Campus Oil v Minister for Industry (No. 2)* [1983] I.R. 88, endorsing Lord Diplock's comments in *American Cyanamid*, special factors may be taken into account in particular cases. Barrett J. suggested that: "Presumably this would extend to the injustice that could result through undue insistence on the requirement as to an undertaking in damages in a case where an applicant has substantial cause but not especially substantial means" (para.26). Thirdly, Barrett J. suggested that several factors identified by McMenamin J. in *Whelan Frozen Foods Ltd v Dunnes Stores* [2006] IEHC 171 as relevant to the issue of whether an interlocutory order should be granted, might also justify not requiring an undertaking as to damages in some cases. These were: "(1) the '*general rule*' that a court should where possible strive to maintain the *status quo ante* between the parties; (2) the relative financial standing of the parties; and (3) the balance of the risk of doing an injustice" (para.26; emphasis in original). Barrett J. emphasised that he was not saying that an undertaking as to damages should never be required in interlocutory applications, but rather that "just because something is typically done does not mean that it must always be done" (para.27). This was essential for policy reasons, as: "In this way the courts can ensure that the levelling influence of the law invariably pertains and that equitable relief is not unfairly denied to those whom the Fates have perhaps treated inequitably" (para.27).

The principles espoused in *American Cyanamid* are of course well settled, and will not be repeated here. However, it is worth noting Barrett J.'s emphasis on the "rich substance" (para.29) of the guidance provided in that case, which Barrett J. felt should prompt a detailed series of queries in an interlocutory application (listed at para.29 of the judgment).

The judgment of Barrett J. also provides very useful guidelines on evaluating the adequacy of damages in interlocutory applications. In *Curust Financial Services Ltd v Loewe-Lack-Werk* [1994] 1 I.R. 450, Finlay C.J., in the Supreme Court, had stated that difficulty in assessing damages was not the same as impossibility in doing so. Analysing this, Barrett J. stated that there were cases where an estimate of damages might essentially be meaningless, due to the degree of guesswork involved, and that when Finlay C.J. had spoken of "impossibility" in assessing damages, he had meant "damages that are completely impossible to calculate with such a degree of accuracy as to represent the probable loss that a person will suffer absent injunctive relief" (para.32). Similarly, when Finlay C.J. referred to the fact that quantifiable damages amounted to a commercial loss, Barrett J. considered that he was again referring to the fact that some estimates of damages were so based on assumptions and guesswork "that they can no longer be said to be damages that the plaintiff would be likely to suffer as a matter of probability were the actions or events that it is sought to injunct allowed to transpire" (para.35). In such cases, although it was technically possible to quantify the probable damages in some sense, they "are not capable of quantification to a degree that would suggest they were likely to arise as a matter of probability and so are not commercial losses of the type to which Finlay C.J. intended to refer" (para.35). Accordingly, it was Barrett J.'s view that the consideration of the adequacy of damages in an interlocutory application should involve a detailed series of queries (summarised at para.36 of the judgment).

With regard to the adequacy of damages, Barrett J. also distinguished between personal and business reputation. Hence, previous authority suggesting that damages were adequate compensation for the loss of reputation was not applicable to the present facts.

Subsequently, analysing the comments of McMenamin J. in *Whelan Frozen Foods,* Barrett J. considered that McMenamin J.'s judgment again suggested a series of queries relevant to interlocutory applications (summarised at para.42 of the judgment).

Ultimately, Barrett J. amalgamated the queries prompted by the judgments in *American Cyanamid*, *Curust* and *Whelan*, suggesting that together they raised the following non-exhaustive and potentially overlapping queries for consideration in interlocutory applications (summarised at para.43 of the judgment):

> "(1) Does the material available to the court at the hearing of the application fail to disclose that the plaintiff has any real prospect of succeeding in his claim for a permanent injunction at the trial? (*American Cyanamid*)
>
> (2) If the plaintiff were to succeed at the trial in establishing his right to a permanent injunction, (a) would he be adequately compensated by an award of damages in the measure recoverable at common law for any loss arising to the time of trial from the non-issuance of the interlocutory injunction and (b) would the defendant be in a financial position to pay them? (*American Cyanamid*)
>
> (3) If such damages aforesaid would not provide an adequate remedy for the plaintiff in the event of his succeeding at trial, and the defendant were to succeed at the trial in establishing his right to that which was sought to be enjoined, (a) would the defendant be adequately compensated under an undertaking by the plaintiff as to damages for such loss as the defendant would sustain by virtue of the issuance of the interlocutory injunction against the defendant, and (b) would the plaintiff be in a financial position to pay them? (*American Cyanamid*)
>
> (4) Is there any doubt as to the adequacy of the respective remedies in damages available to either party or to both? (*American Cyanamid*)
>
> (5) Do the various factors that present in a case appear to be evenly balanced? (*American Cyanamid*)
>
> (6) Is it the case that the extent of the uncompensatable disadvantage to each party would not differ widely? (*American Cyanamid*)
>
> (7) Is the loss arising clearly and exclusively a commercial loss and so typically capable of being assessed in damages under the heading of loss actually suffered up to the point when damages fall to be assessed and also under the heading of probable future loss? (*Curust*)
>
> (8) Does such challenge as may arise in the assessment of damages reflect a difficulty, as distinct from a complete impossibility, in the assessment of same; a mere difficulty not being a ground for characterising the award of damages as an inadequate remedy? (*Curust*)
>
> (9) Is it contended that damages would not constitute an adequate remedy by reason of a real risk that the postponement of their payment until after the determination of the action would lead to the collapse, from a financial point of view, of the party so contending? (*Curust*)
>
> (10) If the injunction were refused, is it the case that the party seeking same would (a) be shut out from a market in which it has previously

participated or (b) merely be obliged to share that market with another, with situation (a) justifying further enquiry as to the balance of convenience and situation (b) pointing to the possible adequacy of damages? (*Curust*)

(11) If it is contended that damages would not constitute an adequate remedy by reason of a real risk that the postponement of their payment until after the determination of the action would lead to the collapse, from a financial point of view, of the party so contending, is there evidence before the court, such as evidence regarding the general position of the parties with regard to their indebtedness or net assets or the probable result of increased competition, whereby the case so advanced has been established as a matter of probability? (*Curust*)

(12) Is there any doubt as to the capacity of the party against whom an injunction is sought to pay any damages awarded against them? (*Curust*)

(13) Is there a new/expanding business dimension to the facts presented before the court that would make the quantification of damages particularly difficult? (*Curust*)

(14) Is the court's assessment of damages predicated, as it must be, on the continued existence of the parties as going concerns to the trial of the full action? (*Whelan*)

(15) In its determination as to where the balance of convenience lies is the court attaining insofar as possible the maintenance of the *status quo ante*? (*Whelan*)

(16) In its determination as to where the balance of convenience lies has the court had regard to (a) the financial standing of each of the parties and (b) the effect of the absence of an injunction on the respective positions of the plaintiff and the defendant, and (c) the justice of the case, bearing in mind the evidence as to points (a) and (b)? (*Whelan*)

(17) In its determination as to where the balance of convenience lies has the court had regard to the balance of the risk of doing an injustice? (*Whelan*)

(18) In its determination as to where the balance of convenience lies has the court had regard to the degree of uncertainty as to when the hearing of the plenary action will take place, even having regard to the desire of both parties to achieve an early hearing, it not being open to the court to ignore the difficulties which may arise in the preparation of discovery or the assignment of a date when the court calendar will be free? (*Whelan*)".

Applying these criteria to the facts of the case, Barrett J. held that it was appropriate to grant interlocutory relief to the applicant. Stating that relief would have been appropriate in the circumstances even without an undertaking as to damages, Barrett J. noted that this was not necessary as the applicant was willing to give the usual undertaking, and it appeared that there was substance to this offer. Barrett J. found that the balance of convenience was clearly in the applicant's favour, and that the order was just and convenient.

Challenges to legislative measures The decision of Peart J. in *Garda Representative Association v Minister for Public Expenditure & Reform* [2014] IEHC 237 again contained some interesting comments on the balance of convenience. The applicant (the GRA) had been granted leave to challenge the lawfulness of the Public Service Management (Sick Leave) Regulations, 2014 (S.I. No. 124 of 2014, hereafter "the Regulations") on the ground that they were ultra vires the respondent Minister. The Regulations introduced a radically different sick leave scheme for almost all public servants, and particularly impacted members of An Garda Síochána, who had historically enjoyed especially favourable terms on sick leave. The GRA contended that the Regulations were brought into effect in breach of fair procedures and/or its legitimate expectation. In a separate application, the GRA applied for an interlocutory order to restrain the Minister from operating the Regulations in respect of the GRA's members (though not in respect of other public servants), pending the determination of its action for judicial review.

On the facts, Peart J. was not satisfied that the GRA had sufficient locus standi for the application. However, he also added some detailed comments on an obiter basis, regarding the balance of convenience in cases involving challenges to legislative measures. Noting the judgment of Finlay C.J. in *Pesca Valentia Ltd v Minister for Fisheries and Forestry* [1985] I.R. 193, Peart J. distinguished that case insofar as it involved penal provisions, which the Regulations did not. However, Peart J. also noted Finlay C.J.'s emphasis on the presumption of constitutionality, insofar as it related to whether the plaintiff had established a fair question to be tried. Finlay C.J. had also commented that impeding the Executive in performing its functions under an Act that enjoyed the presumption of constitutionality was relevant to the balance of convenience, though he stated that he was not satisfied that any special principle applied in this regard in interlocutory applications. Peart J. also noted the detailed comments of Clarke J. on this point in *D v Ireland* [2009] IEHC 206. Clarke J. emphasised that granting interlocutory orders restraining the implementation of legislation could lead to legislation that was prima facie valid effectively being sterilised for prolonged periods, and that this was an important consideration for the balance of convenience. Hence, courts should only grant interlocutory orders in this context where there were "significant countervailing factors" or it was possible to minimise the interference with the legislative objective. Clarke J. subsequently re-emphasised this point in his judgment in *Okunade v Minister for Justice, Equality and Law Reform* [2012] 3 I.R. 153, albeit in a different context.

In the present case, Peart J. noted that the Regulations had been introduced for two key reasons, namely, to reduce the cost of public service sick leave arrangements to the taxpayer, and to meet national financial obligations arising from the Memorandum of Understanding signed by the Government and the Troika. Commenting that this must be regarded as "a pressing need in the national interest" (para.24), Peart J. noted that this would not necessarily "trump the interest of any particular litigant" challenging a statutory measure, but "must weigh heavily in the balance" when considering the balance of convenience (para.24). Even if an individual were ultimately found to have suffered a wrongful loss due to the operation of the Regulations, this could be addressed retrospectively by an award of damages, and there was no risk that such damages would be irrecoverable. Even if damages might not be adequate in some circumstances, Peart J. concluded that he had "no doubt" that "barring some truly exceptional circumstances in an individual and exceptional case, the balance of convenience must lie against prohibiting the operation of measures which are prima facie lawful pending a determination of the issues arising" (para.25).

Peart J. also referred to the role of the strength of the plaintiff's case in situations "where the risk of injustice may be evenly balanced" (as expressed by Clarke J. in *Okunade* at para.95). Clarke J. had distinguished between cases of judicial review and other types of proceedings, suggesting that there could be "greater scope" in judicial review cases to take account of the strength of the plaintiff's case (para.95). While not exactly expressing a similar view, Peart J. noted that, if he had had to resort to considering the strength of the applicant's case as part of the evaluation of the balance of convenience, he would not have considered the applicant's case to be particularly strong. However, on the facts, he did not consider the question of the greater injustice to be evenly balanced.

In the context of trade disputes The decision in *Dublin Airport Authority Plc v Services Industrial Professional Technical Union* [2014] IEHC 644 offered nothing new from the perspective of equitable doctrine, but is nevertheless of interest because it addresses the operation and effects of industrial relations provisions in the interlocutory context.

The defendant in this case was the trade union SIPTU, which planned to engage in industrial action further to a complex dispute regarding a pension scheme. The planned action took the form of a four-hour work stoppage at Dublin and Cork Airports by SIPTU members of the pension scheme. The plaintiffs, Dublin Airport Authority Plc (the DAA) and Ryanair Ltd, sought a range of interlocutory orders preventing SIPTU from embarking on the action. The primary arguments were made on behalf of the DAA, which alleged that there was no valid trade dispute within the meaning of the Industrial Relations Act 1990 (the "1990 Act"). The dispute related to a broad pensions crisis involving multiple parties, and as the DAA had satisfied all its contractual obligations, it contended that the dispute could not be said to concern the terms or conditions of or affecting the employment of any person, as required by the 1990 Act. This interpretation was strongly contested by SIPTU.

Even if there were a valid trade dispute, the DAA alleged that the ballot for industrial action conducted by SIPTU was flawed, as SIPTU had not balloted all of its members employed by the plaintiffs, but only those who were involved in the disputed pension scheme. The DAA contended that it was unreasonable to expect that other SIPTU members, who worked with the members affected by the dispute, would pass the picket line and continue to work as normal. As not all members of the union who might be expected to participate in the action had been balloted, it followed that the ballot did not comply with the requirements of the 1990 Act. In response, the defendant contended that only those affected by the outcome need be balloted.

It was also alleged that some of the employees who had been balloted were governed by agreements which expressly prohibited the taking of industrial action for the duration of those agreements. The DAA further alleged that the work stoppage, scheduled to take place on one of the busiest days of the year, would cause it irreparable loss and damage, as both Dublin and Cork Airports would have to be closed.

Gilligan J. considered that the plaintiffs had raised two significant issues in relation to the defendant's compliance with the 1990 Act. On the issue of whether there was a valid trade dispute within the meaning of the 1990 Act, Gilligan J. commented that the fact that negotiations had been so lengthy and extensive, involving multiple parties (including employers, trade unions and the Labour Court) over several years, tended to support the view that a genuine trade dispute existed. However, having reviewed the authorities, Gilligan J. concluded that he did not have sufficient information to determine whether or not a serious issue arose to be determined in this regard. This point therefore fell to be determined on a full hearing, and was not a basis for granting interlocutory injunctive relief against SIPTU.

However, with regard to the composition of the ballot, Gilligan J. considered that there was a serious question to be tried as to whether some of those balloted should have been excluded. There was also a serious question as to whether SIPTU should have included all of its members employed by the plaintiffs in the balloting process, particularly as it had not been disputed that those members would be called on to support the industrial action. After considering the authorities, Gilligan J. found that onus lay upon SIPTU to show that it had complied with the statutory requirements on balloting, and that it had adduced no evidence in this regard. Accordingly, it could not rely on the statutory restriction of the right to an injunction under s.19(2) of the 1990 Act, and the normal *Campus Oil* principles applied. Gilligan J. concluded that damages would not be an adequate remedy, in light of the disruption to third parties and the potential losses to the plaintiffs, for which SIPTU was unlikely to be a "mark". Accordingly, he held that the balance of convenience favoured the granting of injunctive relief.

The decision in this case was arguably inevitable, since it is well established that a ballot for industrial action should include all members whom it was reasonable at the time for the union to believe would be called upon to engage in that action (*Daru Blocklaying Ltd v Building and Allied Trades Union* [2003] 1 I.L.R.M. 164). It is also clear that the onus is on the union to show proper compliance with the balloting procedure. Indeed, in *Nolan Transport (Oaklands) Ltd v Halligan* [1999] 1 I.R. 128, 161, Murphy J. expressed confidence that unions would take steps to ensure that ballots would be professionally and independently supervised, to ensure that compliance with the statutory requirements could easily be demonstrated. It was therefore surprising that the union in this case had not taken greater care to include all members working at Dublin Airport, who might feel obliged to refuse to pass the picket line, thereby leaving itself open to interlocutory proceedings. The question of whether some of those balloted should have been excluded is, however, more difficult to evaluate.

Mandatory interlocutory injunctions A useful review of the principles applicable to mandatory interlocutory orders was provided in *Tola Capital Management LLC v Linders* [2014] IEHC 316. The defendants in this case wished to enter into an agreement with Ulster Bank to buy back loans which they owed to Ulster Bank, and which were secured on certain properties. To do this, the defendants needed to obtain finance. They signed an option agreement with the plaintiff, as a possible financier, but subsequently obtained finance elsewhere, as they alleged they were contractually entitled to do. The plaintiff sought a number of orders, including orders restraining the defendants from completing a debt purchase agreement with Ulster Bank in respect of the properties, other than in trust for the plaintiff, and from disposing of, or dealing with, the properties otherwise than in accordance with a loan structure specified under the option agreement.

Having considered submissions, Cregan J. concluded that the first order sought by the plaintiff, restraining the defendants from completing a debt purchase agreement other than in trust for the plaintiff, was essentially mandatory in nature. Cregan J. commented: "This does not simply restrain the defendants from doing what they intended to do; it means that they must take active steps at the closing of their debt buy back agreement with Ulster Bank to ensure that these properties are held in trust for the plaintiff" (para.33). This would clearly amount to "a dramatic alteration in the contractual relationship" between the parties, and "could also clearly have a significant and damaging effect on the agreement which the defendants have with their new financier" (para.33). The ultimate effect would be "to frustrate the contract which the defendants have entered into with Ulster Bank", which the court would be "very slow" to do (para.33). The second order sought, restraining the defendants from dealing with the properties other than in accordance with the option agreement, would effectively frustrate the debt purchase agreement the defendants had entered with Ulster Bank, which was due to complete shortly, and compel the defendants to contract with the plaintiff. Again, therefore, this order was essentially mandatory in nature.

There followed an extensive review of the authorities, from which Cregan J. concluded that the "pure" *Campus Oil* test had been refined or varied in the context of applications for mandatory interlocutory orders (para.47), and must show a strong case that he is likely to succeed at trial. Furthermore, in applications for mandatory orders, "the court should also particularly adopt 'whatever course would carry the lower risk of injustice'" (para.48).

Cregan J. also noted that the main relief ultimately sought by the plaintiff was specific performance of the option agreement entered into by the parties, which was effectively a loan agreement. In general, the courts lean against specific performance in this context, although it was unclear whether there was an absolute rule in this regard. This issue could not be determined at the interlocutory stage, but Cregan J. held that it was appropriate to consider the traditional reluctance in this regard, when evaluating the strength of the plaintiff's case. He therefore concluded that the plaintiff had not demonstrated that it was likely to succeed at trial.

Cregan J. went on to discuss whether damages were an adequate remedy for the plaintiff. Counsel for the plaintiff had contended that, although damages would be adequate compensation for the alleged loss, the defendant was not a "mark" for those damages. This was disputed by the defendants, who also contended that the plaintiff had made unsubstantiated general claims of loss, which were unquantified, and simply alleged that the defendants could not meet whatever these substantial losses turned out to be. Cregan J. commented,

> "given that it has accepted that damages are an adequate remedy, it follows as a matter of logic that the plaintiff should be in a position to assess at least a range of what those damages might be. The burden of proof is on the plaintiff so to do if they wish to argue that the defendants are not in a position to meet such an award. However, given that it has not done so in this case, it seems to me that it cannot argue, that the defendants cannot meet an award of damages when that amount is an unknown" (para.68).

In the event, Cregan J. accepted that the defendants were likely to be able to meet any award of damages to the plaintiff.

Finally, with regard to the balance of convenience, Cregan J. stated that he was entitled to consider the nature of the relief sought, which in this case would effectively undermine the agreement of the defendants and Ulster Bank. Cregan J. commented: "The court should be extremely slow to grant orders which could have such an effect" (para.72). He also considered that the adequacy of damages should be regarded as an aspect of the balance of convenience, which in this case militated against the granting of an injunction. He further relied on the reluctance of the court to make orders requiring constant supervision, in a context where all trust between the parties had broken down. Finally, Cregan J. examined the consequences for both parties, if the order were granted or refused, and held that the consequences for the defendants would be catastrophic if the order were granted, while the plaintiffs could be compensated by an award of damages. He therefore refused the orders sought.

In the employment context The decision in *Hughes v Mongodb Ltd* [2014] IEHC 335 again involved an interlocutory application, this time in an employment context. The applicant was employed as technical director for the respondent's operations in Europe, the Middle East and Africa, in the company's Ireland office. The detailed letter originally offering the applicant employment stated that a full employment contract would be presented on acceptance of the offer, but this never occurred. However, the letter of offer itself stated that the applicant's contract could be terminated by one month's notice by either party, with the respondent reserving the right to furnish pay in lieu of notice. No disciplinary process was referred to in the letter.

In May 2014, as he was returning from a business trip, the applicant was informed over the phone, by his immediate superior, that his employment was being terminated. This was confirmed by an email later that day, which stated that the applicant's employment was terminated with immediate effect, that one month's salary would be paid in lieu of notice, and that the applicant would be provided with a standard reference. The applicant contended that the manner of his termination breached his right to fair procedures and seriously damaged his good name. The defendant contended that the plaintiff's employment was terminated because he was not a good fit for the company, and that he had not been found guilty of any misconduct or poor performance. The applicant contested this, alleging that that his superior, when calling to dismiss him, had raised performance-related issues. However, the applicant contended that he had never been given a chance to address these issues, and had not been provided with any support or mentoring. The applicant issued proceedings seeking a declaration that he remained employed by the defendant and various associated orders, as well as contractual and other damages. Pending the hearing of the action, he sought interlocutory relief.

As the case related to an employment contract, the applicant was required to demonstrate, following *Maha Lingam v Health Service Executive* [2006] 17 E.L.R. 137, that he had a strong case and was ultimately likely to succeed at trial. However, Keane J. also noted that the employment contract in this case specifically stated that either party was entitled to end the contract on one month's notice, and that the defendant could pay the applicant in lieu of the notice period. The applicant was therefore essentially arguing that the defendant was not entitled to act on his contractual entitlements with regard to notice, if his reason for doing so was bad. This entailed two further contentions: first, that the defendant's stated, "no fault" reason for terminating the contract was false; and secondly, that "poor performance", as the real ground for termination, necessarily implied a contractual term with which the relevant rules of fair procedures and natural justice would be complied.

Keane J. stated that *Maha Lingam* was "authority for the principle that such mandatory injunctions are exceptional and that applicants must satisfy a strong or clear case test, instead of the *prima facie* case test normally applicable as part of the *Campus Oil* principles" (para.17). Although the applicant contended that he had an implied contractual right to fair procedures prior to dismissal in connection with performance-related grounds (as opposed to grounds related to misconduct), Keane J. held that there appeared to be no authority for this proposition, and strong authority to the contrary, in the decision of Finlay Geoghegan J. in *Bradshaw v Murphy* [2014] IEHC 146.

Furthermore, the defendant made no allegation that the applicant's dismissal was at all based on fault, and was in fact willing to provide a written reference affirming the contrary. In this regard, Keane J. commented:

> "Even if it were assumed, for the purpose of argument, that the defendant is (as the plaintiff appears to suggest) being disingenuous in the reason it gives for the termination of the plaintiff's employment, I do not believe that there is any authority, and certainly none has been produced to me, for the proposition that a bad reason that informs, but which is not relied upon to justify, the termination of an employment contract in accordance with its terms, renders that dismissal wrong in law" (para.25).

Keane J. concluded that the applicant had not shown that he had a strong case, and was likely to succeed at trial, and the application for interlocutory relief was therefore rejected.

Evidence

AOIFE BEIRNE LLB (Dub.), LLM (Cantab.), Barrister-at-law

LEGISLATIVE DEVELOPMENTS

Criminal Justice (Forensic Evidence and DNA Database System) Act 2014 The Criminal Justice (Forensic Evidence and DNA Database System) Act 2014 was enacted on 22 June 2014. However, the vast majority of the sections of the Act have not yet been commenced. As well as providing for the establishment of a DNA database, the Act will replace the existing statutory and common law arrangements governing the taking of samples for forensic testing for use as evidence in criminal investigations and proceedings and will repeal the Criminal Justice (Forensic Evidence) Act 1990. The Act, when commenced in full, is likely to throw up interesting issues concerning the admissibility of evidence and the exclusionary rule. In the meantime, it is sufficient to mention some of the salient features of the Act.

Section 11 provides that where a person is arrested and detained, a member of the gardaí may take or cause to be taken a sample for the purpose of generating a DNA profile to be entered in the reference index of the database system, where a sergeant so authorises. Sections 12 (intimate samples) and 13 (non-intimate samples) are the main provisions providing for the taking of forensic samples and are similar to the pre-existing provisions. Section 19 provides that inferences may be drawn from the refusal to consent at the trial of the person, providing they were informed of the potential consequences and had the opportunity to consult their solicitor.

Section 26 effectively prohibits the taking of samples other than in accordance with the Act. Section 27 puts the Supreme Court decision in *DPP v Boyce* [2008] IESC 62 on a statutory footing and provides that a Garda may take a sample from a volunteer (to include a victim) in respect of an investigation of a specific offence. The volunteer must be informed that a DNA profile may be generated for use in the investigation of the specific offence and must consent in writing to give the sample; this consent must specify the offence which is being investigated. A refusal to consent or a withdrawal of consent shall not of itself constitute reasonable grounds for suspecting that person of the offence in question.

Section 163 seeks to provide a certificate procedure for the various authorisations required under the Act other than an authorisation to take a DNA sample under s.11. The certificate, with authorisation or a copy thereof, is evidence of the matters stated in the certificate. A judge may, if it is considered to be in the interests of justice, direct that oral evidence be given and adjourn the proceedings to a later date to receive that evidence. Under s.20, if the results of the analysis of a s.11 sample were to be given in evidence, direct evidence of the sergeant's authorisation under s.11 may be required.

Sections 169 and 170 create presumptions in respect of the handling of intimate, non-intimate and crime scene samples. There is a presumption that a relevant sample was placed in a tamper-evident, numbered container on the date and by the member whose name is affixed thereto and was forwarded for forensic testing where that appears to be the case. A certificate from a member of staff of FSI stating that the tamper-evident container appeared to be intact, stating the date upon which they opened the container, shall be proof of those facts. A judge may direct that oral evidence be called "in the interests of justice" and the proceedings may be adjourned for that purpose. Section 170 substitutes a new certificate procedure in drug cases in the place of s.10 of the Misuse of Drugs Act 1984.

Road Traffic Act 2014 Section 38(2) of the Road Traffic Act 2010 provided:

> In any proceedings in respect of a fixed charge offence a document purporting to be a certificate or receipt of posting or delivery issued by An Post or another postal service is admissible in evidence as proof of the posting or delivery, as the case may be, of a fixed charge notice, until the contrary is shown.

Section 21 of the Road Traffic Act 2014 amends s.38(2) by, inter alia, deleting the words "until the contrary is shown". This was a response to the legal loophole that had emerged whereby persons accused of driving offences were escaping conviction by claiming they never received the fixed penalty notice in the post. The burden of proof in relation to the serving or non-serving of the penalty notice now rests on the vehicle owner.

CASE LAW—CRIMINAL EVIDENCE

Relevance In *DPP v MJ* [2014] IECCA 21, the Court of Criminal Appeal made some general comments about relevance in the context of admissibility of evidence. McKechnie J., for the court, held that, first, relevance was a necessary precondition to the admissibility of any piece of evidence in a criminal trial (or for that matter in a civil action) and evidence that is irrelevant is not admissible. Secondly, "relevance", at least in a general sense, will be established where the evidence tends to prove or disprove, or renders it more or less probable, that the accused person did or did not commit the act in question. Thirdly, even if this threshold is met, evidence, although relevant, may not be received if any of the exclusionary rules—either common law or statute-based—are applicable to it. Fourthly, such evidence may also be excluded if fairness of procedure or the vindication of constitutional or ECHR rights requires it. In essence therefore, the court held that evidence is at least prima facie admissible if relevant, material and probative, but may be excluded on any of the grounds indicated. The court also reiterated that the probative force or cogency of any piece of evidence is a matter of weight; inconsistencies go to weight and both are firmly within the remit of the tribunal of fact.

Burden of proof In *DPP v Perennial Freight Ltd* [2014] IEHC 323, Kearns P. in the High Court accepted that a reversed burden of proof could apply in determining whether an offence was committed under the Finance (Excise Duties) (Vehicles) Act 1952. Section 3 of that Act adopted the Roads Act 1920, s.13(3) of which states:

> If in any proceedings under this section any question arises as to the number of vehicles used or as to the character, weight or horse power of any vehicle or as to the number of persons seated by a vehicle or as to the purpose for which any vehicle was used the burden of proof in respect of the matter in question shall lie on the defendant.

Therefore, Kearns P. accepted the argument made by the prosecution that where the prosecution raises a prima facie case that the vehicle is improperly licensed due to the weight of the vehicle, the evidential burden of proof with respect to the actual weight of the vehicle transfers to the accused. It is a matter for the District judge what weight he or she gives to the evidence. The defendant must prove that the vehicle was not outside the scope of his or her licence.

Presumptions *Sweeney v Fahy* [2014] IESC 50 provides a useful exposition of the law relating to presumptions. The appellant had been convicted of drink driving contrary to s.49, subss.(1) and (6)(a), of the Road Traffic Act 1961 (the "1961 Act") as inserted by s.10 of the Road Traffic Act 1994. Section 19(1) of the Road Traffic Act 1994 (as amended) (the "1994 Act") provided that:

> As soon as practicable after it has received a specimen forwarded to it under section 18, the Bureau shall analyse the specimen and determine the concentration of alcohol or (as may be appropriate) the presence of a drug or drugs in the specimen.

Section 19(3) provided that:

> As soon as practicable after compliance with subsection (1), the Bureau shall forward to the Garda Síochána station from which this specimen analysed was forwarded a completed certificate in the form prescribed for the purpose of this section and shall forward a copy of the completed certificate to the person who is named on the relevant form under section 18 as the person from whom the specimen was taken or who provided it.

The appellant complained that there was undue delay between the respective dates of two certificates received by him, the first of which showed a nil concentration and the second one, received almost three months later, which showed traces of cocaine.

In any prosecution taken under s.49 of the 1961 Act, the DPP could rely on the presumptions contained in ss.19(4) and 21(3) of the 1994 Act. Section 19(4) provided that:

> In a prosecution for an offence under this Part or under sections 49 or 50 of the principal Act, it shall be presumed until the contrary is shown that subssections (1) to (3) have been complied with.

Section 21(3) of the 1994 Act also provided that:

> A certificate expressed to have been issued under section 19 shall, until the contrary is shown, be sufficient evidence in any proceedings under the

> Road Traffic Acts, 1961 to 1994, of the facts stated therein, without proof of any signature on it or that the signatory was the proper person to sign it, and shall, until the contrary is shown, be sufficient evidence of compliance by the Bureau with the requirements imposed on it by or under this Part or Part 5 of the Act of 1968.

In dismissing the appeal, McKechnie J. commented that presumptions are designed, at least for the most part, to ease the evidential burden on a party to either civil or criminal proceedings. They feed on proof of some basic fact or proposition, which once established compels or allows a court to assume the existence of some other fact or proposition. In this way, what can be inferred does not have to be established in a primary way, as the basic fact or proposition has to be.

The judge noted that presumptions which are in statutory form and exist in the area of criminal prosecution, such as the ones at issue in this case, must be strictly construed but will be influenced by the relevant rules of constitutional justice and fair procedures, as well as other principles such as the presumption of innocence and where the burden of proof rests. In this regard, the court referred to *Hardy v Ireland* [1994] 2 I.R. 550 which dealt with s.4 of the Explosive Substances Act 1883 and *O'Leary v The Attorney General* [1995] 1 I.R. 254 which dealt with s.21 of the Offences Against the State Act 1939.

The court noted that, as made clear in both *Hardy* and *O'Leary*, the proper construction of those provisions, given the constitutional context in which they arose, was to regard them as evidentially focused, thus leaving untouched the legal burden with regard to the guilt or innocence of the accused. McKechnie J. added that, while *Hardy* and *O'Leary* dealt with specific statutory provisions, he had no doubt but that, unless clearly mandated by its specific wording, all such presumptions should likewise be construed.

It was therefore the case that, once the basic fact is established, the onus shifts to the opposing party to negative the existence of the presumed fact, proposition or state of affairs; one can do so by producing evidence as to their non-existence. If successful to that end, the result is that the presumption does not apply and in such circumstances, the party in whose favour the presumption existed must establish the presumed fact in the normal way.

While not relevant to the case at hand, as the shifting of the evidential burden did not relate to the question of guilt or innocence, McKechnie J. did offer some additional obiter views on the question of the standard of proof. McKechnie J.'s view, which was applied in *Hardy*, was that the standard should not exceed the civil standard. He was not even convinced that contrary proof to such a level is required. It may be that evidence, of a credible and plausible nature, which creates a reasonable doubt, would be sufficient to negative a presumption.

He added that all presumptions that impact on the exercise of judicial power are rebuttable. Presumptions that compel a judge to arrive at a conclusion by a process that dictates how judicial power should be exercised are contrary to Art.34.1 of the Constitution.

McKechnie J. concluded by setting out the following helpful summary of his findings regarding presumptions at para.50:

> "(i) Presumptions are creatures which assist a party, in either civil or

criminal cases, in discharging the proof upon him, in respect of matters covered, and to the level as provided.

(ii) These are variable in both substance and form: some follow from the establishment of basic facts: some have added requirements: the wording of any particular one may differ from another: some directly address the court 'the court shall ...': some do not '... it shall be presumed ...': the nature of what may be inferred can also vary, and they may arise either at common law or by statutory provision.

(iii) In the criminal context, almost all must be interpreted in light of basic legal and constitutional principles such as fair procedures and constitutional justice and what these may give rise to, in the context of any given case, for example the presumption of innocence, burden of proof, etc.. When so viewed, there will be very few indeed, if any, which are not confined to the evidential burden of proof: those which are suggested as affecting the legal burden will be scrutinised with great care as to their compatibility with such provisions.

(iv) When the onus shifts the standard of rebuttal is not at the criminal level: at most it is on the balance of probability: arguably an even less standard such as creating a reasonable doubt, could be sufficient.

(v) When that standard has been satisfied, the presumption is disapplied with the result that the obligation reverts to he upon whom the general onus of proof rests.

(vi) Any presumption, which forecloses on the exercise of judicial power, such as one being described as 'conclusive' as to guilt, will be considered as an infringement on that power. It will, as a result, be stood down."

Presumption of innocence In *DPP v Piotrowski* [2014] IECCA 17, a complaint was made that a trial judge did not adequately address the presumption of innocence in his charge to the jury. The trial judge, when he had finished dealing with the burden of proof in some detail, commenced to deal with the presumption of innocence and put the burden of proof (and indeed the standard of proof) which lies on the prosecution in the context of the presumption of innocence by going on, in the same passage, to indicate that there is no desired result in the case other than that there be a verdict "on whether the prosecution have proved their case beyond reasonable doubt on each of these charges."

Clarke J. distinguished this scenario from the decision in *DPP v D O'T* [2003] 4 I.R. 286, where the trial judge had omitted to make any reference to the presumption of innocence. It was held that the presumption of innocence was fully dealt with and the burden and standard of proof on the prosecution was put in the context of the importance of the presumption of innocence. The substance of the requirements for a proper charge in relation to those matters were all present and there was nothing in the form of the charge which could have confused the jury or left them with an inadequate understanding of the proper approach to be adopted.

In *O'Brien v DPP* [2014] IESC 39, the applicant had brought an application by way of judicial review seeking to prohibit his criminal trial on grounds that he could not now, or in the future, receive a fair trial by reason of substantial and ongoing adverse publicity. The Supreme Court dismissed the appeal by the applicant of the decision of Kearns P. in the High Court (discussed in detail by Dr Daly in the *Annual Review of Irish Law 2013*) wherein Kearns P. had refused to prohibit the trial, but directed that the criminal proceedings be stayed for a period of 12 months.

The Supreme Court held, inter alia, that comments made by Kelly J. in the course of prior civil proceedings in the Commercial Court involving the plaintiff did not infringe his presumption of innocence in a later criminal trial where he stood accused of theft and deception offences. It was held that while the statements of Kelly J. in the Commercial Court were strong, and were reported widely, they arose in a civil case where the appellant had not opposed the applications of his creditors in relation to facts indicating a type of ponzi scheme. Kelly J. made no decision in relation to any criminal trial, other than to refer papers to the Garda Bureau of Fraud, so that consideration could be given as to whether an investigation was warranted and Kelly J. would not be a judge on any criminal trial of the appellant. It was for the DPP to determine if there is to be a prosecution, and if she so determined, there would be a criminal trial, at which a basic principle is the presumption of innocence.

Cross-examination In *DPP v Piotrowski* [2014] IECCA 17, Clarke J. held that a trial judge has an important role during cross-examination in ensuring that the case is confined to questions which are at least of sufficient relevance to the issues which the jury has to decide to make their pursuit material. It appears that a trial judge is entitled to exercise a greater degree of control over the extent to which general issues of credibility can be pursued, as opposed to during cross-examination which is directly relevant to the facts of the case, in the sense of the facts which are alleged to constitute the offence charged, or the guilt of the accused in respect of that offence.

In *McCann v Halpin* [2014] IEHC 276, in the context of an application for judicial review, it was held by Cross J. in the High Court that, despite the fact that the respondent District Court judge had clearly interrupted counsel on a number of occasions, and in particular during cross-examination, the interruptions were not themselves such as to render the trial unsafe or unsatisfactory or to warrant intervention by way of judicial review.

Cross-examination—the rule in *Browne v Dunn* In *DPP v Burke* [2014] IEHC 483, a question arose as to whether the rule in *Browne v Dunn* (1893) 6 R. 67 constituted part of Irish law. This rule establishes that a party who intends to call evidence to contradict the testimony given by a witness on examination-in-chief is required to put that evidence to him or her in cross-examination so that he or she has an opportunity of providing an explanation in relation to that evidence. If a party fails to do this, then the trial judge has a discretion as to whether to admit the contradictory evidence (see, in this regard, McGrath, *Evidence*, 2nd edn (Dublin: Round Hall, 2014), paras 3-139–3-134).

The two accused argued that if they could point to the fact that a witness who gave exculpatory statements was not challenged on any part of her evidence which excused the accused, that this fact alone, without any requirement for the trial judge to weigh the evidence, must lead to an acquittal. Baker J. disagreed.

As alluded to by Baker J., *Browne v Dunn* was itself a defamation case, but the judgment had become the *locus classicus* of rules relating to the conduct of a case. She noted that the rule had been followed in England and some other jurisdictions. She stated that there appeared to be two aspects to the rule: first, the status of evidence not put to a witness for the other party and, secondly, how to treat evidence not challenged in cross-examination.

Baker J. held that, in a criminal context in particular, to impose a duty on an accused person to cross-examine the witnesses for the prosecution could impact on the right to silence at trial, and could displace the burden of proof in practice, and prevent an advocate from making tactical choices in the conduct of defence. She held that this must be the case having regard to the higher standard of proof, and the fact that the burden lies on the prosecution, which gives effect to the presumption of innocence.

Baker J. did not accept that the ratio of *Browne v Dunn* was that a court must accept uncontroverted evidence, and held that there was no rule of law that requires a party to enter upon cross-examination of a witness. Baker J. set out a helpful summary of her conclusions at para.52:

> "(a) In closing submissions or argument a party may not impeach the credibility of a witness if that witness's evidence has not been tested in cross-examination;
> (b) *Ipso facto* a person who does not cross-examine evidence is faced with the prospect that the evidence is heard by the trial judge or the jury and is untested.
> (c) There is no requirement that evidence be cross-examined, but by not cross-examining evidence the evidence goes to the fact finder as untested and uncontradicted evidence.
> (d) Untested and uncontradicted evidence carries greater weight than tested contradictory evidence.
> (e) It is not the function of any rule of law to direct the court to accept evidence merely on account of the fact that it has not been tested. The court must hear all of the evidence before it and is entitled to weigh the evidence, including unchallenged evidence, against the evidence as a whole adduced at the trial.
> (f) A trial judge or a jury is not compelled as a matter of law to accept evidence because it is not challenged. Unchallenged evidence is part of the evidence at trial and the fact that it is unchallenged gives it somewhat greater weight, but does not direct a particular result."

In so finding, Baker J. made it clear that the rule (although she expressed her reluctance to characterise it as such) was to some extent authority on the requirement of fairness in the conduct of a trial.

Admissibility of photographs In keeping with previous decisions of the Court of Criminal Appeal such as *People (DPP) v Carney* [2011] IECCA 53, the court held in *DPP v Hussain* [2014] IECCA 26 that photographs of a victim's injury were admissible. Their admission was objected to by the appellant on the grounds that such evidence was more prejudicial than probative. The court held that it was principally a matter for the trial judge to form a judgment, in the light of the state of the evidence as a whole and the issues which have emerged at the trial, as to whether a particular piece of evidence should be admitted where an objection of that type is raised. The trial judge was in the best position to make a judgment on such issues and this court should only interfere with a trial judge's decision in that regard in a very clear case. In this case, there were issues before the court as to the precise way in which the injuries to the victim had occurred. It was, therefore, open to the trial judge to form the view that, broadly speaking, contemporaneous photographs of the injuries might be of assistance to the jury in addressing those questions and it refused to allow the appeal on this basis.

Corroboration In *People (DPP) v D* [2014] IECCA 20, the court quashed the appellant's convictions for sexual assault and directed a retrial in circumstances where it held that the judge's charge was deficient in that he failed to give a corroboration warning and a warning in relation to delay.

MacMenamin J. in the Court of Criminal Appeal considered previous authorities such as *People (DPP) v JEM* [2001] 4 I.R. 385 and *People (DPP) v PJ* [2003] 3 I.R. 550 and approved the decision in *DPP v Gentleman*, unreported, Court of Criminal Appeal, 25 February 2002, and stated that if a corroboration warning is given, it should be "clear, unmistakable and contextualised." The court emphasised that it is unnecessary for a trial judge to deliver an elaborate ruling, but, whatever decision is made, it must be one which is susceptible to analysis on the basis of whether it is, indeed, a decision judicially made.

While MacMenamin J. did not consider that it is necessary for a trial judge to set out precisely a form of words which he or she intended to use, nonetheless, it was highly desirable that counsel should at least know the position as to how the judge's discretion will be expressed and the reasons therefore, prior to embarking on their closing speeches. In this case, both the prosecution and the defence were left uncertain as to whether a corroboration warning would be given.

It was held that a corroboration warning must contain sufficient elements in order to ensure that a jury has a clear understanding of its duties. While the warning in this case did reflect that there was no corroboration of the complainant's account, it was lacking in a number of respects and it could not be said that the warning was "clear and unmistakable": (i) there was no mention of the fact that the alleged incidents happened approximately 20 years prior to the trial; (ii) the charge did not draw attention to the view that experience has demonstrated that the passage of time can do strange things to people's recollection of events so long in the past; and (iii) the charge did not advert to the fact that the complaint was made many years after the date of the alleged offences.

There was also no explanation to the jury of the function that corroborating evidence may serve in any given case, or that it might be dangerous to convict in the absence of such evidence. There was no indication that the jury might be slower, or more careful, to convict, on the basis of an uncorroborated account given by the complainant, nor was the jury informed that the absence of corroboration was a factor which they should consider in deciding whether or not it was safe to convict the accused.

The court again emphasised that there was a distinction between a corroboration warning, and the warning that is necessary in cases where there has been a considerable lapse of time. This type of warning has two elements: (i) it consists of general illustrations as to the difficulties which may generally arise in dealing with cases where there has been a long lapse of time; and (ii) there is a direct contextualisation; that is to say that the general illustrations of the difficulties which can arise in defending such cases were not only explained, but brought home to the jury by illustrating how those difficulties arose in the case before it.

In *DPP v Buck* [2014] IECCA 45, McKechnie J. in the Court of Criminal Appeal made some general comments concerning corroboration. The trial judge had given a warning pursuant to s.10 of the Criminal Procedure Act 1993. The Court of Criminal Appeal again endorsed the decision in *The People (DPP) v Connolly* [2003] 2 I.R. 1 and restated at para.77 that all trial judges should remain acutely conscious, not only of these statutory provisions, but also of the wider jurisprudence dealing with corroboration in general. The judge is not bound to use any particular form of words, however:

> "What the charge must achieve however, is that the jury be given a clear explanation as to what corroboration is, told whether there is or is not evidence in the particular case capable of amounting to corroboration, and if so, what that evidence is: further, if there is, they must also be informed that it then becomes a matter for them to decide whether such evidence is, as a matter of fact, corroborative. The judge will continue, by the use of phraseology commensurate with the degree or level of warning which he intends, to say that even if there is no corroboration the jury nonetheless is entitled to convict if satisfied as to the accused's guilt beyond a reasonable doubt."

Right of access to a solicitor Undoubtedly the most significant decision of 2014 has to be *People (DPP) v Gormley & White* [2014] IESC 17, [2014] 1 I.L.R.M. 377. The issues in these two cases were whether the gardaí are obliged to postpone questioning when a detainee requested access to a solicitor and whether inculpatory statements made and real evidence obtained after such a request but before the solicitor arrived were admissible.

It was remarked by Clarke J. that the question of recognition of a right to access to a solicitor had been a real possibility for some time, and that it should not come as a surprise to anyone with an interest in the area, not least of all the authorities.

The facts relating to Mr Gormley were as follows. The appellant was convicted of attempted rape, contrary to the Criminal Law (Rape) Amendment Act 1990, in 2007. He was alleged to have committed the offences in the early hours of 24 April 2005. He was arrested at 13.47 that day and arrived at the Garda station at 14.00. He was informed of his rights and given the names of two solicitors at 14.15. Efforts were made to contact both solicitors and eventually one agreed to attend. Before the solicitor arrived, the appellant was interviewed at 15.10 during which interview a number of inculpatory statements were made. The solicitor arrived at 16.48 and another interview took place subsequent to a meeting with the solicitor. The inculpatory statements made during the first interview were deemed admissible by the trial judge and the appellant was found guilty.

Mr White had been convicted of murder. His case was similar to Mr Gormley's, except that forensic evidence had been taken in the form of swabs and hairs were taken from him after a request for a solicitor was made but before the solicitor arrived. Mr White was arrested at 07.45 on 13 February 2008, and was taken to the Garda station. At 07.58, he made a request for his nominated solicitor. This solicitor could not be reached at her usual business number at this time, but a recorded message provided an alternative number for emergencies. This information was conveyed to Mr White and he was asked whether another solicitor could be contacted. Mr White was also told that efforts would continue to be made to contact the nominated solicitor. At 08.15, a message was left on the emergency phone number as a call to that number was not answered. However, the call was returned within one minute and the solicitor confirmed that she was coming "immediately" to the Garda station. The solicitor declined the opportunity to speak to Mr White via the phone. Mr White was informed of this development. The solicitor arrived at the Garda station at 09.42. In the meantime, permission had been requested and granted for the taking of various forensic samples from Mr White under the Criminal Justice (Forensic Evidence) Act 1990. The various samples had all been taken by 08.30.

Both failed in their appeals to the Court of Criminal Appeal, the CCA in each case citing the right of "reasonable access" to a solicitor (see, in this regard, *DPP v Raymond Gormley* [2009] IECCA 86 and *DPP v Craig White* [2011] IECCA 78).

The Supreme Court allowed Mr Gormley's appeal, with Clarke J. giving the main judgment. Clarke J. began by considering a number of Irish authorities (*People (DPP) v Madden* [1977] I.R. 336; *People (DPP) v Healy* [1990] 2 I.R. 73; *People (DPP) v Buck* [2002] 2 I.R. 268; *People (DPP) v O'Brien* [2005] 2 I.R. 206; *Lavery v Member in Charge Carrickmacross Garda Station* [1999] 2 I.R. 390; *People (DPP) v Creed* [2009] IECCA 90) and noted that the current state of the law in Ireland was that the right to have access to a lawyer while in custody was a constitutionally recognised right. A failure to provide reasonable access after a request from a suspect in custody can, on that basis, render the custody unconstitutional and thus lead to any evidence obtained on foot of such unconstitutional custody becoming inadmissible. The jurisprudence had not, however, gone so far as to require that advice from a requested solicitor actually be made available to the relevant suspect prior to questioning or the taking of samples.

Clarke J. began his analysis by reviewing the jurisprudence of the European Court of Human Rights. In *Salduz v Turkey* (2009) 49 E.H.R.R. 19, the Grand Chamber had found that the guarantee of a fair trial in art.6 of the ECHR required that a suspect was entitled to access to a lawyer from the commencement of his detention. The Grand Chamber found specifically that "access to a lawyer should be provided as from the first interrogation of a suspect by the police, unless it is demonstrated in light of the particular circumstances of each case that there are compelling reasons to restrict this right" (para.55).

Clarke J. then considered decisions from the US, Canada and New Zealand and concluded that, consistent with the ECHR position, there is, at a minimum, an obligation in most circumstances (possibly subject to some exceptions) on investigating police to refrain from interrogating a suspect at a time after the suspect has requested a lawyer and before that lawyer has arrived to advise the suspect concerned. He referred to *Miranda v State of Arizona* 384 U.S. 436 (1966) where it had been held that not only was there a right to consult a lawyer prior to questioning but also to have a lawyer present during questioning. The Canadian position, after *R v Sinclair* [2011] 3 S.C.R. 3, was that s.10(b) of the Canadian Charter of Rights and Freedoms requires that there is a duty on the police to hold off questioning until the detainee has had a reasonable opportunity to consult counsel. The position in Australia was that there was a right to "try to communicate with a lawyer" and that the current practice is that before questioning commences, police are required to inform suspects that they may communicate or attempt to communicate with a lawyer. In New Zealand, s.23(1)(b) of the Bill of Rights Act 1990 provided that "everyone who is arrested or who is detained … shall have the right to counsel and instruct a lawyer without delay and to be informed of that right."

The first question for the Supreme Court was whether the entitlement to a trial in due course of law guaranteed by the Constitution encompasses an entitlement to have access to legal advice prior to the conduct of any interrogation of a suspect arrested and/or prior to the taking of any forensic samples from such a suspect. In this regard, Clarke J. was convinced that once the power of the State had been exercised against a suspect in the form of an arrest, it was proper to regard the process thereafter as being intimately connected with a potential criminal trial rather than being one at a pure investigative stage. Therefore, it followed that the requirement that persons only be tried in due course of law required that the basic fairness of process, identified as an essential ingredient of that concept in *State (Healy) v Donoghue* [1976] I.R. 325, applied from the time of arrest of a suspect.

The next question which arose for consideration was as to whether that requirement of basic fairness involves an entitlement not to be interrogated (or not to have forensic samples taken) without having first had access to legal advice. Clarke J. had no difficulty in finding, in accordance with the consistent international position, that the guarantee of a trial in due course of law carried with it an entitlement not to be interrogated after a request for a lawyer had been made and before that lawyer had become available to give advice. He referred to the fact that there may be many reasons why access to a lawyer may be required at an early stage and "there can be little doubt but that advice on the immediate events which often occur on the arrest of a suspect (such as questioning) is one of the most important aspects of the advice which any suspect is likely to require as a matter of urgency."

Clarke J. went on to state:

> "There would be little point in giving constitutional recognition to a right of access to a lawyer while in custody if one of the principal purposes of that custody in many cases, being the questioning of the relevant suspect, could continue prior to legal advice being obtained. At a minimum any such right would be significantly diluted if questioning could continue prior to the arrival of the relevant lawyer. In those circumstances, it seems to me that the need for basic fairness, which is inherent in the requirement of trial in due course of law under Article 38.1 of the Constitution, carries with it, at least in general terms and potentially subject to exceptions, an entitlement not to be interrogated after a request for a lawyer has been made and before that lawyer has become available to tender the requested advice."

Interestingly, Clarke J. also stated that the right was designed to provide support for the right against self-incrimination, which is consistent with the position in the United States in *Miranda*.

Turning to Mr White's case, Clarke J. found that there was a distinction to be made between a situation where incriminating statements were made after the request for a solicitor had been made and where real evidence had been obtained. Results of forensic testing are objective. Those results do not depend on the will of a suspect. Neither do they depend on comments made by the suspect in circumstances where the right to self-incrimination could have been invoked or where interrogation in the absence of advice led to the suspect being unfairly prejudiced.

Clarke J. was not satisfied that the mere fact that otherwise lawful forensic sampling was properly taken prior to the attendance of a legal adviser rendered any subsequent trial, at which reliance is placed on the results of tests arising out of that forensic material, unfair. He was also not satisfied that there was any fair trial constitutional prohibition on the taking, without prior legal advice, of a sample in a minimally intrusive way which is justified in law. He did, however, acknowledge that the position might be different where the suspect had a genuine legal choice available in respect of the taking of samples and where it would be reasonably necessary for the suspect concerned to have access to legal advice before making such choices.

There was little consideration of the implications of the *Gormley & White* judgment subsequently in 2014. In *Donoghue v DPP* [2014] IESC 56, Dunne J., giving the judgment of the Supreme Court, observed that the appellant in that case had made admissions in his home prior to an interview at a Garda station in the absence of any information that he was entitled to access to a solicitor. While the decision of the Supreme Court was concerned solely with prosecutorial delay, Dunne J. was acutely aware that the issue of the right of access to a solicitor might arise for consideration in an appropriate case.

In *DPP v Parker* [2014] IEHC 652, Donnelly J. considered *Gormley & White* and held that earlier cases concerning the results of forensic testing on samples in drink driving cases taken in the absence of access to a solicitor, which were authority for the proposition that such samples are admissible, were not overturned by *Gormley & White*. She concluded that since the decision *Gormley & White*, the mere fact that a forensic sample was taken prior to the attendance of a legal advisor as had been requested by the accused having been told of his rights, does not of itself render a trial which relies on the results of tests of those samples, unfair. The question of admissibility of evidence remains for the determination of a trial court, and will be determined on a case-by-case basis.

Guidelines for gardaí on the questioning of suspects have been set out in the *Code of Practice on Access to a Solicitor by Persons in Garda Custody*, dated April 2015.

Improperly obtained evidence In *DPP (McConnell) v McDonnell* [2014] IEHC 35, O'Malley J. applied *DPP v Cash* [2010] 1 I.R. 609 in the context of a demand under the Road Traffic Acts. The accused had been involved in a single vehicle accident and had been brought to hospital. In an attempt to ascertain the identity of the accused, a member of the gardaí searched his belongings. She discovered two bags of a suspicious white powder and formed the opinion that the accused was under the influence of an intoxicant. She made a demand of the accused under s.15 of the Road Traffic Act 1994 for the accused to provide a specimen of his blood or at his option a specimen of urine in accordance with s.15(1)(b) of the Road Traffic Act 1994. The accused refused to give a sample. He was later charged in the District

Court with failing to give a sample, dangerous driving and possession of cocaine, and the District judge stated a case to the High Court as to, first, whether the search was unlawful, and if so, whether the gardaí could rely on such an opinion and form a lawful opinion that the accused had consumed an intoxicant and in consequence make a lawful demand of the accused to provide a sample.

Having answered both questions in the affirmative, O'Malley J. held, having considered *Cash*, that the evidence required to prove a lawful demand is comparable to that required for a lawful arrest. While the demand must be authorised by law and must be lawfully made, and the opinion grounding the demand must be genuinely and reasonably held, there is no requirement that the opinion be based upon matters that would in themselves be admissible. O'Malley J. further held at para.37 that "[t]o rule otherwise would be to import the rules of evidence into the process of investigation, and to require the prosecution to establish that no part of the material revealed by the investigation were tainted by illegality." It appeared to O'Malley J. that the logic of *Cash* lay in the analysis of the difference between investigation and trial. In the context of this case, the crucial difference was that the rules governing admissibility of evidence cannot simply be transferred to the formation of suspicions and opinions.

Confessions—the Judge's Rules In *DPP v Buck* [2014] IECCA 45, the appellant challenged, inter alia, the admission into evidence of an alleged confession on the grounds that rr.4, 6, and 9 of the Judge's Rules had not been complied with. It was submitted on behalf of the appellant that given his anxious and agitated condition, a caution should have been administered before the admission was made, as the Garda must have known that some inculpatory statement was about to be offered, it being irrelevant whether it related to the crimes under investigation or to some other form of criminality.

Rules 4, 6, and 9 of the Judge's Rules read as follows:

> "4. If the prisoner wishes to volunteer any statement, the usual caution should be administered. It is desirable that the last two words of such caution should be omitted, and that the caution should end with the words 'be given in evidence'.
>
> 6. A statement made by a prisoner before there is time to caution him is not rendered inadmissible in evidence merely because no caution has been given, but in such a case he should be cautioned as soon as possible.
>
> 9. Any statement made in accordance with the above rules should, whenever possible, be taken down in writing and signed by the person making it after it has been read to him and he has been invited to make any corrections he may wish."

McKechnie J., in dismissing the appeal, reiterated that the Judge's Rules are rules of good administration and their purpose is to offer guidance in promoting procedural fairness and in preventing confessions being obtained inappropriately. He stated that even if such rules are not rules of law, they have nonetheless obtained a status of real significance, recognised as such by the common law world. It was held that a statement, whether exculpatory or inculpatory, obtained in violation of the rules, is a matter of deep concern to the judicial power and will always require searching analysis. He held at para.22:

> "[A]ny non-observance of the rules will require both an appropriate explanation and an adequate justification for what occurred. However, any breach thereof will not be subject to the same strict exclusionary rule, as is evidence obtained in deliberate and conscious violation of one's constitutional rights; rather it has always been the situation that such a statement, howsoever described, once voluntary, is admissible at the discretion of the trial judge."

McKechnie J. made some brief comment in respect of each of the particular rules at issue at para.32:

> "(i) Rule 4 has several purposes to it; as well as underpinning the fundamental value against self-incrimination, it is designed to impress upon the mind of the subject person, the full implications of that person volunteering a statement or of answering questions put to him: as has been said, 'the sense of the caution and every limb of it must be conveyed to the mind of the person to whom it is addressed' (Kennedy C.J. on behalf of the Court of Criminal Appeal in *The Attorney General v. Cleary* [1934] 1 Frewen 14 at p. 17). Equally so what the Court of Criminal Appeal stated in *The Attorney General v. Durnan (No. 2)* [1934] I.R. 540 (*'Durnan'*), remains as valid today as it was when stated, namely that this caution, 'is no idle formulae' (p. 548). Finally, it is also worthy of note that the Court in *Durnan* case also observed that the caution, despite not being ideal, 'enshrines the result of long experience'. (p. 548)
>
> (ii) Rule 6: even if a statement has been made before there was an opportunity to issue a caution, such caution must be given as soon as possible thereafter. A careful consideration of the facts of each individual case will be critical to determine if this rule, in any of its several elements, has been breached.
>
> (iii) Rule 9, which for obvious reasons has the qualification mentioned by the trial judge ... is more focused on statements rather than on interviews conducted by way of questions and answers (O'Malley, *The Criminal Process* (Dublin; Round Hall; 2009), p. 771). The purpose of this rule was outlined in *D.P.P. v. Pringle* .... The proviso, 'whenever possible' will find concrete expression only on an evaluation of particular circumstances and may result in the exclusion of a statement as occurred in *The People (DPP) v. McNally* (1981) 2 Frewen 43. Finally, this rule does not require the gardaí to write down everything said by the accused, only 'statements' must to [sic] be noted down (*The People (Director of Public Prosecutions v. McKeever* [1994] 2 I.L.R.M. 186 (*'McKeever'*)."

McKechnie J. held that on the facts of this case the Judge's Rules did not apply.

However, it was held that the essence of the rules remains relevant, in any consideration of "fundamental fairness." The argument on this basis was held to fail also. In this particular case, the Garda had asked some questions of the appellant, but it was established on the facts that he did not know that the accused was about to confess to a crime. The case was thus distinguishable from *The People (DPP) v Breen*, unreported, Court of Criminal Appeal, 13 March 1995. McKechnie J. did indicate that the boundary line might be crossed where, in the process of purporting to ask clarifying questions, the involvement of the gardaí becomes such as to suggest an interrogation rather than clarification or where the volunteered information indicates that an arrest, at that point, should be made.

Right to silence In *DPP v MJ* [2014] IECCA 21, the trial judge, in the context of explaining where the burden of proof rests, informed the jury that there was no obligation on an accused person to give evidence, and that he has an absolute right "to remain silent", if he so wished. The appellant claimed that the reference to "silence" may have caused the jury to overlook or misunderstand the import of the direction which was that an accused person does not have to give evidence and that nothing adverse can be taken from the exercise of his right, in not doing so. The Court of Criminal Appeal was entirely satisfied that those concerns were quite misplaced and that it was abundantly evident what circumstances the judge was addressing. The court also held that in that context any distinction between the phrase, "the right to remain silent" and that of "the right not to give evidence", may be more philosophical than practical. Some of the case law demonstrated that the use of either expression is interchangeable. Therefore, the court held that once the substance of the right was clearly and accurately put, the use of the impugned expression may be unobjectionable.

In *DPP v Bolger (No. 2)* [2014] IECCA 1, a contention that inferences should not have been drawn (under ss.18 and 19 of the Criminal Justice Act 1984 as substituted by ss.28 and 29 of the Criminal Justice Act 2007 and s.19A of the Criminal Justice Act 1984 as inserted by s.30 of the Criminal Justice Act 2007) was rejected by the Court of Criminal Appeal. The trial judge had admitted a memorandum of interview so that inferences could be drawn from the appellant's silences. On the facts of that case the court was satisfied that: (a) the appellant was advised by the gardaí that they intended to invoke the statutory provisions; (b) the appellant consulted with his solicitor; (c) the gardaí explained the sections of the statute to him in layman's language; (d) the appellant indicated that he understood the caution; (e) the appellant engaged with the gardaí; and (f) this was recorded on videotape, and that the evidence was properly admitted.

Photographs in custody A power to take photographs is granted under s.12 of the Criminal Justice Act 2006. A member of An Garda Síochána not below the rank of sergeant may authorise the photograph of an arrested person to be taken as soon as may be after his or her arrest for the purpose of assisting with the identification of him or her in connection with any proceedings that may be instituted against him or her for the offence in respect of which he or she is arrested.

In *DPP v Parker* [2014] IEHC 652, Donnelly J. held, in the context of a consultative case stated from the District Court, that the mere fact that the gardaí took a photograph of the accused while he was detained, other than in accordance with s.12, did not make the detention of the accused unlawful or unconstitutional such as to render the evidence acquired thereafter inadmissible in subsequent proceedings and warrant the dismissal of the prosecution against the accused. The photograph had been taken with the written consent of the accused. Donnelly J. held that the photograph issue had no substance, and was not a matter which prolonged the accused's detention or which gave rise to any other evidence. She did say that, if there had been the gratuitous taking of an indecent or obscene photograph, such that in the circumstances of a particular case might constitute such an outrage, a District judge in pursuance of his or her constitutional duty may be required to stay or dismiss the proceedings, and she cited *Keating v Governor of Mountjoy Prison* [1991] 1 I.R. 61 in this regard.

***Damache* implications** In *DPP v McKevitt* [2014] IECCA 19, the Court of Criminal Appeal refused to certify as matters of exceptional public importance whether the decision in *Damache* could amount to a "newly discovered fact" within the meaning of s.2 of the Criminal Procedure Act 1993. MacMenamin J., giving the judgment of the court, referred to his earlier judgement in *DPP v McKevitt* [2013] IECCA 22 in which it had been held that the decision in *Damache* did not constitute a "newly discovered fact" and that there was no miscarriage of justice in Mr McKevitt's case. It could not be said then that an application to the Supreme Court was "in the interests of justice" and it could not be suggested that what arose was a matter of "exceptional public importance". The Supreme Court had already held in *A v Governor of Arbour Hill Prison* [2006] 4 I.R. 88 that when an Act is declared unconstitutional, a distinction is made between the making of such a declaration on the one hand, and its potential retrospective effect on cases which have been already been determined by the court.

Surveillance *DPP v Idah* [2014] IECCA 3 concerned the operation of the Criminal Justice Surveillance Act 2009 (the "2009 Act"). The Court of Criminal Appeal quashed a conviction for drugs offences and ordered a retrial in circumstances where inadmissible surveillance evidence was put before the jury.

The appellant was convicted of soliciting another to commit the offence of unlawful importation of a controlled drug, and soliciting another to commit the offence of the unlawful importation of a controlled drug having a value in excess of €13,000. The appellant was accused of soliciting two undercover gardaí to import controlled drugs into the State from Brazil. Twenty-four contacts between the undercover gardaí and the appellant were recorded. During the course of the contacts, it is said the appellant gave the undercover gardaí money to pay for their hotel, to feed themselves, and supplied two airline tickets to Brazil, together with $1,000 in cash. It was said discussions took place as to the amount of drugs to be ingested, the form and weights in which the drugs would be packaged, the hotel where they were to stay, what both carriers would do on the journey, and how they would liaise on their return to this jurisdiction. Audio recordings and transcripts of these contacts were put in evidence at the trial and verified by the undercover gardaí in their evidence. Neither of the undercover gardaí gave viva voce evidence of the entirety of the conversations between themselves and the accused at the trial.

It was stressed by the MacMenamin J., giving the decision of the Court of Criminal Appeal, that the judgment did not determine any issue regarding the admissibility otherwise of viva voce evidence from members of the gardaí involved in interactions with the appellant, since such viva voce evidence was not adduced at the trial.

The central issue in the case was therefore whether the gardaí were engaged in surveillance at the time it is said they had conversations with the appellant relating to the importation.

"Surveillance" is defined in s.1 of the 2009 Act as meaning:

> (a) monitoring, observing, listening to or making a recording of a particular person or group of persons or their movements, activities and communications, or
> (b) monitoring or making a recording of places or things, by or with the assistance of surveillance devices.

A "surveillance device" is defined in s.1 of the 2009 Act as follows:

> "Surveillance device" means an apparatus designed or adopted for use in surveillance, but does not include—
> (a) an apparatus designed to visual acuity or night vision, to the extent to which it is not used to make a recording of any person who, or any place or thing that, is being monitored or observed,
> (b) a CCTV within the meaning of s.38 of the Garda Síochána Act 2005, or
> (c) a camera, to the extent to which it is used to take photographs of any person who, or anything that, is in a place to which the public have access.

Section 4 of the 2009 Act authorises a superior officer of, inter alia, the gardaí to apply to a judge for authorisation on a number of specified grounds. Section 7(2) of the 2009 Act provides that a member of the gardaí can apply to a superior officer for the grant of an approval to carry out surveillance in specified cases of urgency. These include absconsion, obstruction of justice, and destruction of evidence or the security of the State.

Section 14(4) of the 2009 Act provides:

> (a) Information or documents obtained as a result of surveillance carried out under an authorisation or under an approval granted in accordance with section 7 or 8 may be admitted as evidence in criminal proceedings notwithstanding any failure by any member of the Garda Síochána, member of the Defence Forces or officer of the Revenue Commissioners concerned to comply with a requirement of the authorisation or approval concerned, if the court, having regard in particular to the matters specified in paragraph (b), decides that –
> (i) the member or officer concerned acted in good faith and that the failure was inadvertent, and
> (ii) the information or document ought to be admitted in the interests of justice.
> (b) The matters referred to in paragraph (a) are the following:

(i) whether the failure concerned was serious or merely technical in nature;
(ii) the nature of any right infringed by the obtaining of the information or document concerned;
(iii) whether there were circumstances of urgency;
(iv) the possible prejudicial effect of the information or document concerned;
(v) the probative value of the information or document concerned.

On the facts of this case, an authorisation pursuant to the 2009 Act was obtained from a judge of the District Court permitting the installation/use of a "surveillance device" within a hotel room for the period of 14–18 September 2010. The authorisation did not permit the use of the recording device in any other location. The conversations and meetings did not in fact take place in the hotel room although that authorisation was specific to that location. Some were outside the hotel in the immediate vicinity; some were elsewhere. Some were on the telephone. This judicial authorisation obtained from the District Court covered the period from 14 September 2010 to 18 September 2010, and expired at midnight on 18 September 2010. The following day, 19 September 2010, was a Sunday. An approval was granted by a senior member of the Gardaí on the morning of 19 September 2010, said to be in circumstances of urgency. The evidence disclosed that no attempt was made on 17, 18 or 19 September 2010, to obtain further judicial authorisation.

The issue in this case was the admissibility of recordings of face-to-face meetings which took place between the appellant and the undercover gardaí on 15, 17 and 19 September 2010.

The trial judge had held that the covert recording by An Garda Síochána of meetings held between the appellant and undercover members did not constitute "surveillance" within the meaning of the Criminal Justice (Surveillance) Act 2009. Therefore, he had held that evidence of transcripts of the recordings were admissible.

MacMenamin J. remarked that any incursions into the right to privacy must be in accordance with law and the intent and purpose of the 2009 Act was that the law must be sufficiently clear in its terms to give individuals an adequate indication as to the circumstances in which public authorities are entitled to resort to such covert measures and it must provide necessary safeguards for the rights of individuals potentially affected.

MacMenamin J. held that the essential nature of surveillance is that it is covert and at a remove from the subject. "Surveillance" would not traditionally have been considered to include the obtaining or recording of information actually disclosed to and in the presence of an undercover garda by a person or persons unaware of the covert purpose of the personal contact. Therefore, the effect of s.1 of the 2009 Act was to enlarge the traditional and well understood meaning of "surveillance". The court held that the express terms of the 2009 Act seek to confine surveillance to specified activities carried out "by or with the assistance of surveillance devices." If such devices are not used, then the Act does not apply. It, therefore, had no application to other investigative techniques.

The court then had to examine the actions of the gardaí to determine whether they fell under the 2009 Act. It was held that the admissibility of evidence obtained directly by gardaí through their own senses, without any assistance in the form of a surveillance device, was unaffected by the 2009 Act. Therefore, face-to-face communications between the undercover gardaí and the accused did not amount to surveillance. Even if the 2009 Act had not been enacted, it was held that it would not be unlawful for an undercover member of An Garda Síochána in the course of such an investigation to make personal contact with, or to speak to another person for the purpose of obtaining information where that other person is entirely unaware of the covert purpose of the meeting. The court considered that it was not the intention of the legislature to include within the definition of "surveillance", investigative practices and procedures which did not require the protection of the Act in order to be lawful. It held that to bring such practices and procedures, already subject to legal control, within the terms of the 2009 Act, could well lead to a substantial reduction in the benefits to the public good and the security of the State which the legislature was seeking to achieve in enacting the 2009 Act.

However, simultaneous to those interactions, it was held that surveillance was being conducted through the use of a surveillance device worn by one of the undercover gardaí. Other officers were or could have been "listening to" the transmitted exchanges. Neither activity would have been possible without the use of a surveillance device. The recordings of these exchanges were later transcribed and the transcripts were given to the jury at the trial. It was held that the admissibility of these recordings and transcripts fell to be decided within the ambit of the 2009 Act.

MacMenamin J. held that s.14(4) clearly demonstrated that a failure to comply with the requirements of an authorisation or approval does not, in itself, render evidence inadmissible. Here, there had been non-compliance with the authorisation, as detailed above.

MacMenamin J. refused to interfere with the trial judge's decision to admit the transcripts of the recordings of 15 and 17 September 2010 as he was not convinced that there was a manifest error in the judge's reasoning. There was evidence of confusion in the ranks of senior officers of An Garda Síochána as to the scope and administration of the provisions of the 2009 Act, which was then a relatively new Act.

The court, however, did deem the approval granted for the 19 September 2010 to be invalid as there was no evidence that any circumstances of urgency, as prescribed by s.7(2) of the 2009 Act, were present. MacMenamin J. considered the case of *DPP v Peter Byrne* [2003] 4 I.R. 423, which concerned s.8(2) of the Criminal Justice (Drug Trafficking) Act 1996 to be on point in this regard.

MacMenamin J. stressed the distinction between an authorisation and an approval under the 2009 Act. He stated that the gardaí are not free to choose whether they will apply for an authorisation to a judge or an approval from a superior officer. They must apply to a judge, unless identified circumstances of urgency are present when an approval may be valid. When there is no evidence that any attempt was made to apply to a District judge for variation or renewal of an authorisation, and where there is no clear evidence of one of the exceptions provided for in the section, the State has failed to demonstrate that the approval was validly granted. He also held that the discretionary power of the trial judge under s.14(4) did not extend to evidence obtained where there has been no valid authorisation or approval.

Therefore, the court concluded that the admissibility of the recordings from that date should not have been permitted.

Character evidence In *DPP v Piotrowski* [2014] IECCA 17, the appellant had been convicted of a number of offences including aggravated burglary, assault causing harm, false imprisonment, aggravated sexual assault and rape of his former partner. He appealed on a number of grounds. In relation to one of the grounds, it was held that certain background evidence relating to an alleged blackmail attempt, assaults and threats to kill made by the appellant prior to the incidents was admissible to show the attitude of the appellant to the breakdown of his relationship. The Court of Criminal Appeal held that it was not simply evidence of previous misconduct. It was evidence that was referable to the events that were alleged to constitute the offence. As the evidence was undoubtedly prejudicial, the court emphasised the need for the trial judge to execute his adjudicative role in determining whether, on balance, such prejudicial evidence was sufficiently probative to warrant its admission. The court was satisfied that it was within the range of decisions which were open to the trial judge, in all the circumstances of the case, to form the view that the probative nature of this evidence was sufficient to warrant its admission notwithstanding its prejudicial character and dismissed the appeal on that ground.

In this case, the trial judge had also given the appellant leave pursuant to s.3(1) of the Criminal Law (Rape) Act 1981, as substituted by s.13 of the Criminal Law (Rape) (Amendment) Act 1990, for leave to cross-examine the victim about her prior sexual history. The Court of Criminal Appeal emphasised that there was a clear obligation on a trial judge to ensure that any permitted cross-examination on previous sexual history is kept within the bounds of what is relevant to the case. In addition, a judge is entitled to ensure that cross-examination on collateral issues is kept within reasonable bounds.

In *DPP v Dumbrell* [2014] IECCA 22, the Court of Criminal Appeal considered the still relatively new s.1(f)(iiia) in the Criminal Justice (Evidence) Act 1924 (the "1924 Act") (inserted by s.33(a) of the Criminal Procedure Act 2010 (the "2010 Act")). It will be recalled that this section provides that the accused's shield will be lost where he or she has personally or by his or her advocate, "asked questions of any witness for the purpose of making, or the conduct of the defence is such as to involve, imputations on the character of a person in respect of whom the offence was alleged to have been committed and who is deceased or so incapacitated as to be unable to give evidence." Section 1A of the 1924 Act (as inserted by s.33(b) of the 2010 Act) introduces a notice requirement which stipulates that, where a person charged with an offence intends to adduce such evidence, at least seven days notice to the prosecution or leave to adduce such evidence without giving the period of notice is required. If such evidence is led, then under s.1A(b) the prosecution can cross-examine the accused or ask any other witness questions that: (i) would show that the accused has been convicted of any offence other than the one wherewith he or she is then charged, or is of bad character, or (ii) would show that the person in respect of whom the offence is alleged to have been committed is of good character.

The two appellants had been convicted of murder. The first appellant in the course of the trial had served notice of his intention to adduce evidence that would cast imputations on the character of the deceased victim. He did not adduce this evidence as the trial judge had made clear that this would lead to him losing his shield. However, in the course of cross-examination, the second appellant volunteered that the deceased has a number of convictions. This led to the introduction into evidence of the previous convictions of the second appellant but not of the first appellant. Both appellants appealed their convictions and one of the first appellant's grounds of appeal was that the trial judge had erred in failing to afford him the opportunity to adduce the previous convictions of the deceased and thereby deprived him of the opportunity to put the previous convictions of the deceased to prosecution witnesses.

Denham C.J., sitting in the Court of Criminal Appeal, explained that the section must be applied fairly by the court. Its purpose, she said, was to correct a potential imbalance in the trial process whereby an accused may attack the credibility of a victim through information on previous convictions.

In dismissing the appeals, it was held that the first appellant had received a fair trial. The first appellant did not have the opportunity to cross-examine on the deceased's previous convictions as a consequence primarily of a decision that he made that he did not wish to drop his own shield. The court considered that that the first appellant got the best of the situation as there was disclosure of the previous convictions of the deceased, with no consequential information provided of the first appellant's convictions. The court left open the question of whether it would be unfair to allow a situation whereby an accused, who has elected not to adduce evidence as to a deceased's victim's previous convictions by reason of an unwillingness to have his own previous convictions put in evidence, could subsequently benefit from a co-accused dropping his shield, and then proceed to cross-examine witnesses in relation to a deceased's previous convictions to demonstrate a proclivity for violence.

This case demonstrates that a co-accused may benefit without losing their shield where the other accused casts imputations on the character of a deceased or victim of the offence.

DPP v Hawkins [2014] IECCA 38 concerned an appeal by Ms Hawkins of her conviction on 181 counts of theft against U2 member Adam Clayton. Charleton J., in the Court of Appeal, having referred to *McNeill*, held that background evidence of an encounter between the appellant and Mr Clayton was highly relevant, as it demonstrated that there were clear limits set to the legitimate spending power of the appellant on his bank accounts. It demonstrated, in addition, that the appellant was aware of these limits and that she did not have authority, and therefore could not honestly, purchase holiday excursions for herself and her children. Therefore the evidence constituted a fact from which dishonesty could be inferred in relation to the counts of theft before the jury.

Identification evidence In *DPP v McNulty* [2014] IECCA 34, the central issue, in the context of an application for leave to appeal to the Supreme Court on a point of law, was whether the jury ought to be charged to the effect that if they reject alibi evidence put forward by the defence, this does not automatically lend support to the identification evidence put forward by the prosecution. It being settled law that there was a requirement to give a warning to the jury in respect of identification evidence (*People (Attorney General) v Casey (No. 2)* [1963] I.R. 33) and alibi evidence (*People (DPP) v Burke & O'Leary* [1986] 3 Frewen 92), the applicant contended that there must be an obligation on a trial judge to give a direction on the relationship between the two. MacMenamin J., for the Court of Criminal Appeal in refusing leave to appeal, found that no such requirement existed and that a trial judge enjoyed a large amount of discretion in this regard as long as the principles were correctly applied and the issues explained clearly.

Chain of evidence In *DPP v Hawkins* [2014] IECCA 38 Charleton J., in the Court of Appeal, held that the chain of evidence was dependent on the standard of proof in criminal cases, that the jury should be satisfied of the provenance of relevant exhibits beyond reasonable doubt and that such facts are proven beyond reasonable doubt. It was held that it was not subject to a requirement of mathematical certainty, as was contended for by the appellant, despite the fact that the prosecution may wish to exercise a counsel of prudence in very many cases.

Charleton J. remarked that there could be some instances where the writing of an appropriate name and number on a bag may suffice to establish its provenance to that standard. However, calling a chain of evidence to explain to the jury how physical evidence came to be in one place when it was found to be in another may not always be necessary. If there are gaps in the chain of evidence these may be a ground upon which the jury can find that the prosecution has not proved its case beyond reasonable doubt. He did not believe that there was any distinction to be drawn in this regard between items of physical evidence, such as a murder weapon, and documentary evidence, such as bank statements, while acknowledging that physical items may require more care. Charleton J. held at para.35:

> "A bank account statement of transactions by a particular named person can, of course, be printed out again and again since the actual record will consist of electrical activity in computers. A bank account statement is, of its nature, referable to any named person on a named account with a particular bank in a particular location. It therefore follows, that proof beyond reasonable doubt that a bank statement relates to a particular individual, and if the same bank statement is produced earlier in the trial, is somewhat easier of proof."

CASE LAW—CIVIL EVIDENCE

Civil burden of proof It has been established that the civil burden of proof may shift where the matter is "peculiarly within the range of the defendant's capacity of proof" (*Rothwell v Motor Insurers Bureau of Ireland* [2003] 1 I.R. 268 and *Hanrahan v Merck Sharp & Dohme* [1988] I.L.R.M. 629). This is sometimes known as the "peculiar knowledge" principle.

Jordan v Minister for Children and Youth Affairs [2014] IEHC 327 involved a petition challenging the Children's Referendum on the grounds of unconstitutional conduct. The petitioner contended that the burden of proof should shift to the respondents as the Referendum Act 1994 imposed "an excessively onerous burden on a petitioner" in establishing that the referendum result had been materially affected by the unconstitutional conduct. McDermott J. in the High Court rejected this where he held that the application of the civil onus and standard of proof was entirely in accordance with the constitutional supremacy of the will of the people as evidenced by the provisional referendum certificate.

McDermott J. held that it was entirely reasonable, rational and proportionate that a petitioner who seeks to set aside what is, prima facie, the will of the people properly expressed and freely given should bear the onus of proof of doing so. He did not consider that evidence as to whether unconstitutional conduct "affected materially" the result of the referendum as a whole is a matter that is either within the peculiar knowledge of the defendants or exclusively within their capacity to prove or disprove. He was satisfied that a shifting of the burden was not warranted on the well-established principles by which such a reversal of onus may occur or is otherwise required because of a right to "due process" or fair procedures under Art.40.3 of the Constitution. There was no constitutional basis for a legal presumption that the constitutional wrongdoing established could be regarded as having "affected materially" the result of the poll as a whole or a shifting of the burden of proof. He also held that ss.42 and 43 of the Referendum Act 1994 embodied a rational and proportionate onus and standard of proof which may, on occasion, be difficult, but was not inherently impossible to discharge. He thus rejected the proposition that they were unconstitutional.

Weight It is well-established that the weight to be attributed to evidence which is admitted is a matter for the tribunal of fact. In *Lopes v Minister for Justice Equality & Law Reform* [2014] IESC 21, the Supreme Court held that a court was not obliged to accept uncontradicted evidence. Clarke J. remarked at para.7.9 that it was the duty of any court to assess the credibility of any evidence presented. It was particularly important to emphasise that, in cases where there could not be, or is unlikely to be, contradictory evidence, there was a particular duty on the court to carefully scrutinise such evidence with a view to forming a conclusion as to whether it can be regarded as sufficiently credible to satisfy the requirement that the facts be established on the balance of probability.

Bankers Books Evidence Acts In 2014, a number of decisions handed down sought to ensure strict compliance with the Bankers Books Evidence Acts 1879–1959 (the "Acts"). These Acts, as alluded to by Cregan J. in *ACC Bank Plc v Byrne* [2014] IEHC 530, are "difficult, convoluted and opaque" and a court is required to consider developments in commercial life having regard to legislative provisions from a bygone age.

The decision in *Ulster Bank Ireland Ltd v Dermody* [2014] IEHC 140 imposed a stricter burden of proof on banks in enforcement proceedings. The bank in that case was pursuing the defendant on foot of guarantees. An employee of the bank's parent company that was dealing with its debt collection swore the grounding affidavit.

Section 4 of the Bankers Books Evidence Act 1879 provides as follows:

> A copy of an entry in a banker's book shall not be received in evidence under this Act, unless it be first proved that the book was at the time of the making of the entry one of the ordinary books of the bank, and that the entry was made in the usual and ordinary course of business, and that the book is in the custody and control of the bank.
>
> Such proof may be given by a partner or officer of the bank, and may

> be given orally or by affidavit sworn before any commissioner or person authorised to take affidavits.

O'Malley J. in the High Court dismissed the claim on foot of certain guarantees because the grounding affidavit was sworn by an employee of the bank's parent company, rather than by an employee of the bank itself. As the deponent was not an "officer" of the bank, the bank had not met the requirements of the Act. Accordingly, the individual was not able to give evidence substantiating the claim despite the fact that the bank had authorised him under a power of attorney to do so.

The issue for the court was whether the records in this case were admissible by way of a common law exception to the rule against hearsay, and if they were not, whether there had been compliance with the Acts. O'Malley J. declined to follow the previous decisions of Clarke J. in *Moorview Developments v First Active plc* [2010] IEHC 275, Finlay Geoghegan J. in *Bank of Scotland plc v Fergus* [2012] IEHC 131 and Ryan J. in *Bank of Ireland v Keehan* [2013] IEHC 631 which were of the view that business records of this nature were admissible as prima facie evidence of the truth of their contents. She felt bound to follow the Supreme Court decision in *Criminal Assets Bureau v Hunt* [2003] 2 I.R. 168 and held that in the instant case, the evidence of the bank's deponent was not admissible to prove the truth of the contents of the records unless it came within the provisions of the Acts.

As to whether there had been compliance with the Acts, O'Malley J. held that, while an employee can be an "officer" within the meaning of the Acts, an employee of a separate legal entity could not be. The fact that the two companies were closely related did not alter their separate legal existence. Therefore, the evidence supporting the claim was inadmissible hearsay. In so holding, O'Malley J. approved the decision of Peart J. in *Bank of Scotland v Stapleton* which held that an employee of Certus (who manage Bank of Scotland's loan portfolio in Ireland) could not prove the evidence required under the Acts.

It should be noted that McGovern J. in *Permanent TSB v Beades* [2014] IEHC 81 had reached a similar conclusion earlier, but this was not cited in *Dermody*.

As to whether *Dermody* had retrospective effect, Baker J. in *Ulster Bank Ireland Ltd v Kavanagh trading as Barony B&B* [2014] IEHC 299 held that it did not and refused to set aside a judgment where the affidavit grounding the application for judgment was sworn by someone other than an officer of the plaintiff bank. Such retrospective effect, Baker J. found, would offend against the principle of certainty and finality in litigation.

In *ACC Bank Plc v Byrne* [2014] IEHC 530, Cregan J. found that the bank's affidavit evidence was lacking as there has been no compliance with s.4 of the 1879 Act, which related to formal proof.

In *Flynn v National Asset Loan Management Ltd* [2014] IEHC 408, Cregan J. also held that the effect of s.191 of the National Asset Management Agency Act 2009 is that it is only an officer of NAMA or a NAMA group entity who is entitled to give evidence of proof of a debt. Section 191(3)(c) provided that the Bankers Books Evidence Acts have effect in relation to the books and records of NAMA if certain requirements are met.

These requirements are likely to be impractical for banks, and if followed, could lead to mere technical objections as to proof defeating an otherwise straightforward debt recovery claim.

Expert evidence At one stage, there existed a well-established rule of evidence that expert witnesses were not permitted to give opinion evidence as to the ultimate issues in the case. This was clear from cases such as *AG (Ruddy) v Kenny* (1960) 94 I.L.T.R. 185. The rule can now be said to be obsolete in civil cases, and indeed this is evident from the decisions of Barron J. in *McMullen v Farrell* [1993] 1 I.R. 123 and, more recently, Charleton J. in *Condron v ACC Bank Plc* [2012] IEHC 395, [2013] 1 I.L.R.M. 113.

In *Karen Millen Fashions Ltd v Dunnes Stores* [2014] IESC 23, the Supreme Court was required to address the admissibility of evidence as to the impact of a design upon witnesses called upon to address questions of novelty and individual character. What was at issue in this case was whether Karen Millen had acquired any unregistered design rights in relation to particular items which Dunnes had copied, and in particular whether the designs had the requisite individual character under Community Regulation (EC) No. 6/2002 of 12 December 2001. The High Court had honoured the ultimate issue rule, in refusing to admit evidence as to individual character given by certain witnesses. O'Donnell J. in the Supreme Court did not think that a court errs if it adheres to the traditional rule. However, he did state the following at para.23:

> "For my own part, I can see how it is at least convenient to permit experts to give evidence in general as to their conclusions, so long as it is very clearly understood that what is important are the reasons leading the expert to that conclusion rather than the fact of the conclusion itself. Anything else is somewhat artificial. It is a matter of near certainty that the only expert witnesses called by either side will have formed an opinion favourable to that side and their evidence can often be best understood when both the reasons and conclusions are stated so long as it is understood and appreciated that the reasons leading an expert to a particular conclusion are the important matters for the court to consider."

Legal professional privilege In *University College Cork v Electricity Supply Board* [2014] IEHC 135, Finlay Geoghegan J. provided some useful comments about legal professional privilege in the context of the plaintiff's application for inspection of certain documentation. The defendants claimed privilege over the same documentation.

Finlay Geoghegan J. noted that it was not in dispute that there existed two categories of legal professional privilege: legal advice privilege and litigation privilege. In this regard, she cited Malek (ed.), *Phipson on Evidence*, 17th edn (London: Sweet & Maxwell, 2010) and McGrath, *Evidence*, 1st edn (Dublin: Round Hall, 2005), wherein the latter stated at para.10-08:

> "The existence of these two sub-categories of legal professional privilege, commonly termed 'legal advice privilege' and 'litigation privilege' respectively, is now generally recognised, though some uncertainty about their precise parameters and degree of overlap remains. In particular, it is uncertain whether communications between a client and his or her legal adviser regarding litigation in being or anticipated are protected only by legal advice privilege or by both. For the reasons articulated below, the

better view is that such communications are more properly protected by legal advice privilege alone and that litigation privilege should be regarded as applied to third party communications and work product only."

Finlay Geoghegan J. summarised the relevant principles regarding litigation privilege as follows at para.4:

"(i) Litigation privilege constitutes a potential restriction and diminution of a full disclosure, both prior to and during the course of legal proceedings which is desirable for the purpose of ascertaining the truth and rendering justice. As such, it must be constrained. *Smurfit Paribas v. AAB Export Finance* [1990] 1 I.R. 469 per Finlay C.J. at p. 477.

(ii) The purpose of litigation privilege is to aid the administration of justice, not to impede it. In general, justice will be best served where there is candour and where all relevant documentary evidence is available. *Gallagher v. Stanley* [1998] 2 I.R. 267 per O'Flaherty J. at p. 271.

(iii) The document must have been created when litigation is apprehended or threatened.

(iv) The document must have been created for the dominant purpose of the apprehended or threatened litigation; it is not sufficient that the document has two equal purposes, one of which is apprehended or threatened litigation. *Gallagher v. Stanley* [1998] 2 I.R. 267 at p. 274 approving the test propounded by the House of Lords in *Waugh v. British Railways Board* [1980] A.C. 521.

(v) The dominant purpose of the document is a matter for objective determination by the Court in all the circumstances and does not only depend upon the motivation of the person who caused the document to be created. *Gallagher v. Stanley* and *Woori Bank & Hanvit LSP Finance Ltd. v. KDB Bank Ireland Ltd.* [2005] IEHC 451.

(vi) The onus is on the party asserting privilege to prove, on the balance of probabilities, that the dominant purpose for which the document was brought into existence was to obtain legal advice or enable his solicitor prosecute or defend an action. *Woori Bank* and *Downey v. Murray* [1988] N.I. 600."

The defendant claimed privilege over three reports on the basis of litigation privilege arising from apprehended, threatened or then existing litigation relating to earlier floods. Finlay Geoghegan J. held that a 1990 report attracted litigation privilege as its dominant purpose was Circuit Court proceedings brought by an individual against the ESB. However, she held that two reports dating from 1997 and 2000 did not attract litigation privilege, as they did not satisfy the dominant purpose test. Rather, it appeared to the judge, that from the nature of the reports that as a matter of probability, they were reports prepared in normal course, to detail the precise facts relating to the flood events at the relevant periods.

The plaintiff then challenged the claim to privilege over the 1990 report on the basis that privilege no longer subsisted. In response, the defendant claimed that the maxim "once privileged, always privileged" whilst applying to legal advice privilege, does not apply to litigation privilege.

Finlay Geoghegan J. declined to follow previous High Court authorities such as *Bord na Móna v Sisk* [1990] 1 I.R. 85 and *Quinlivan v Tuohy*, unreported, High Court, Barron J., 29 July 1992, which had held that litigation privilege subsisted. In those decisions, the judge found, there appeared to have been an absence of consideration of earlier authorities, such as *Kerry County Council v Liverpool Salvage Association* [1904] 38 I.L.T.R. 7, and of the purpose of litigation privilege as distinct from legal advice privilege. She instead was persuaded by the approach of the Canadian Supreme Court in *Blank v Canada* 2006 S.C.C. 39, [2006] 2 S.C.R. 319. It was held that the analysis, reasoning and conclusions in the lead judgment of Fish J. in that case in relation to the distinctions in the purpose of legal advice privilege and litigation privilege was convincing and consistent with the judgments of the Supreme Court in *Smurfit Paribas Bank v AAB Export Finance Ltd* [1990] 1 I.R. 469. She approved Fish J.'s conclusion that litigation privilege "is neither absolute in scope nor permanent in duration" and cited the following dictum of Fish J. at para.31 with approval at para.33 of her judgment:

> "Though conceptually distinct, litigation privilege and legal advice privilege serve a common cause: The secure and effective administration of justice according to law. And they are complementary and not competing in their operation. But treating litigation privilege and legal advice privilege as two branches of the same tree tends to obscure the true nature of both.
>
> Unlike the solicitor-client privilege, the litigation privilege arises and operates even in the absence of a solicitor-client relationship, and it applies indiscriminately to all litigants, whether or not they are represented by counsel: see *Alberta (Treasury Branches) v. Ghermezian* (1999), 242 A.R. 326, 1999 ABQB 407. A self-represented litigant is no less in need of, and therefore entitled to, a 'zone' or 'chamber' of privacy. Another important distinction leads to the same conclusion. Confidentiality, the *sine qua non* of the solicitor-client privilege, is not an essential component of the litigation privilege. In preparing for trial, lawyers as a matter of course obtain information from third parties who have no need nor any expectation of confidentiality; yet the litigation privilege attaches nonetheless.
>
> In short, the litigation privilege and the solicitor-client privilege are driven by different policy considerations and generate different legal consequences.
>
> The purpose of the litigation privilege, I repeat, is to create a 'zone of privacy' in relation to pending or apprehended litigation. Once the litigation has ended, the privilege to which it gave rise has lost its specific and concrete purpose—and therefore its justification. But to borrow a phrase, the litigation is not over until it is over: It cannot be said to have 'terminated', in any meaningful sense of that term, where litigants or related parties remain locked in what is essentially the same legal combat.
>
> Except where such related litigation persists, there is no need and no reason to protect from discovery anything that would have been subject to compellable disclosure but for the pending or apprehended proceedings which provided its shield. Where the litigation has indeed ended, there is

> little room for concern lest opposing counsel or their clients argue their case 'on wits borrowed from the adversary'...".

Finlay Geoghegan J. recognised that the approach in Canada was consistent with that adopted by the High Court of Northern Ireland in *Porter v Scott* [1979] N.I. 6 and Fitzgibbon J. in *Kerry County Council v Liverpool Salvage Association* [1904] 38 I.L.T.R. 7.

She concluded, at para.46, that the objective of litigation privilege, which is "in the public interest in the proper conduct of the administration of justice", is the creation of what has been referred to as a "zone of privacy" in the interests of the efficacy of the adversarial system to permit a party in litigation to prepare its position without adversarial interference and without fear of premature disclosure. This objective, she held, did not require such privilege to automatically continue beyond the final determination of either that litigation or closely related litigation. She further held that:

> "Where the second proceedings are not closely related to the first proceedings, there is no objective of the proper conduct of the administration of justice which can be said to outweigh the disadvantage arising from the restriction of disclosure of all the facts."

Accordingly, Finlay Geoghegan J. was not satisfied that the defendant was entitled to claim privilege over the 1990 report as there was no substantive or close connection between the plaintiff's claim in the proceedings arising out of the 2009 flood and other claims arising out of the 1990 flood.

Public interest privilege In *AP v Minister for Justice and Equality* [2014] IEHC 17, which concerned an application for judicial review of the refusal of an application for naturalisation, the respondent Minister resisted inspection of three documents on the basis that they attracted public interest privilege on the grounds of national security. It was held that there was no doubt that the documents were clearly relevant to a consideration of the refusal and the applicant's ability to challenge it.

The respondent contended that rigorous checks are carried out in applications for certificates of naturalisation which include the obtaining of information from external agencies, including security agencies. It was also contended that this information was received on a strictly confidential basis from external sources which it would not otherwise be able to obtain, and may relate to issues of national importance including national security. O'Malley J. considered the decisions of *Murphy v Dublin Corporation* [1972] I.R. 215 and *Keating v Raidió Teilifís Éireann* [2013] IESC 22 in noting that it was important to recognise the State's legitimate interest in this area.

O'Malley J. recognised that the respondent was clearly concerned that the maintenance of confidentiality was in furtherance of a purpose which is in the public interest, namely the State's interest in ensuring that it continues to receive information related to issues of national importance, including national security, relating to individual applicants for certificates of naturalisation as part of the rigorous examination of each case. She recognised that the use of confidential information or intelligence reports obtained from informants or otherwise has been an accepted tool in the administration of justice in this jurisdiction for many years and was widely used in the investigation and prosecution of organised crime and counter-terrorism. She held that the sharing of information between police forces and other agencies necessarily requires confidence by the donor that the recipient agency will maintain an appropriate degree of confidentiality and protection in respect of the information received and its source.

Accordingly, O'Malley J. refused disclosure of one document in its entirety and allowed inspection of another, subject to redactions, on the grounds that there was a public interest in maintaining the confidentiality of the information. She ordered full inspection of one other document on the grounds that it was a relevant document and she was not satisfied that there is any risk to the public interest presented by its inspection by the applicant or his legal team, and it was, in addition, a document which the court would expect to be furnished as a matter of fair procedures to the applicant.

Parliamentary privilege Article 15.12 of the Constitution provides:

> All official reports and publications of the Oireachtas or of either House thereof and utterances made in either House wherever published shall be privileged.

Callely v Moylan [2014] IESC 26 concerned the investigation by the Committee on Members' Interests of Seanad Éireann into claims that the applicant had misrepresented his normal place of residence for the purpose of claiming expenses. The applicant had sought relief against individual members of Seanad Éireann and relied upon statements made by them in the course of proceedings in Seanad Éireann. Under Art.15.13 such persons are not amenable to any court or authority other than the House itself for utterances made. This is an individual privilege in addition to the privilege attached to the utterance itself wherever published, pursuant to Art.15.12.

In a judgment given jointly by O'Donnell and Clarke JJ., the Supreme Court discussed the combined effect of Arts 15.10, 12, 13 and 15 of the Constitution. It was held that those provisions combined to place the Houses of the Oireachtas and the members for the time being thereof, in a distinct and special legal position. Members of the Oireachtas have very significant privileges in respect of their individual and collective utterances, and are given significant exemption from criminal law in the shape of privilege from arrest.

Informer privilege *Re Dunne, a Bankrupt* [2014] IEHC 285 established that informer privilege could be available in the context of s.28 of the Bankruptcy Act 1988 (as amended). That section provides for a search warrant to be issued "where it appears to the Court that there is reason to believe that any other property of the bankrupt is concealed in any house, building, room or other place not belonging to the bankrupt." The bankrupt challenged the validity of the warrant obtained under s.28. McGovern J. considered authorities such as *Director of Consumer Affairs v Sugar Distributors* [1991] 1 I.R. 225 and *Marks v Beyfus* [1890] 25 Q.B.D. 494 which established that, in criminal matters, police informers need not be disclosed as otherwise the information to enable the police to deter and detect crime might not be forthcoming. Having approved a statement of Lord Diplock in *D v NSPCC* [1978] A.C. 171, it appeared to McGovern J. that the Official Assignee was entitled to maintain informer privilege when he makes an application for a section 28 warrant. McGovern J. did add that if the question of ownership of the contents at the premises remained in issue, then that evidence would have to be tendered in the usual way to establish, on the balance of probabilities, whether or not the bankrupt is the owner of such property.

Family Law

FINANCIAL PROVISION

JK v RK [2014] IEHC 451 presented the court with the challenge of identifying the proper approach to financial provision in a case where the husband was a high earner, there were no children to care for, there was paid domestic help, the husband was expected to do his share of the housework, and the wife "was free to pursue qualifications that interested her, and to engage in commercial and voluntary enterprises and part-time work related to those qualifications". There was no evidence before the court of any significant income or resources generated by the wife's activities during the marriage, but the wife submitted that she had given up her career to support the husband in his. The husband's evidence was that the wife had not enjoyed the particular employment that she gave up after marrying and that, by agreeing to prioritise his corporate career and the income it generated, the wife was thereby enabled to pursue her own interests and educational opportunities. It is not disputed that the wife had supported the husband in his career progression, had agreed to the various relocations required by his career and had taken primary responsibility for looking after the home. Keane J. acknowledged that "[i]n those ways, amongst others, the wife undoubtedly contributed to the husband's income, earning capacity and property and financial resources."

Keane J. found both parties to be truthful and sincere witnesses. The conflict between them appeared to arise from the manner in which their individual perspectives had altered since the commencement of their marriage. The husband's view was that, as time went on, he became more focussed on a mainstream corporate career whereas the wife continued, perfectly understandably, to value a different work/life balance. The wife's view was that she had given up the best years of her life to supporting her husband and unsuccessfully attempting to start a family with him, with the result that her career and pension prospects had become weak.

Keane J. went on to observe:

> "While I have concluded that wife's role in the home, while by no means that of the traditional homemaker, has diminished her earning capacity to some extent … I do think that a person with the number and range of qualifications held by the wife is capable of earning a reasonable livelihood in the future."

The husband's net income was more than €217,000. Keane J. ordered that he continue to pay his wife €6,000 gross per month. He also stated that he would make an appropriate pension adjustment order granting the wife the entirety of the husband's first pension fund and so much of his second pension fund as was necessary to bring the overall value of the pension fund available to the wife up to €500,000, equating to 40 per cent of the current aggregate value of those two funds.

In *O'C v O'C* [2014] IEHC 698, where the spouses, of late middle age, both had health difficulties, the husband objected to the sale of the family home and equal division of the proceeds, arguing that his wife had not contributed financially to its acquisition and had retained the proceeds of the sale of an earlier family home. O'Hanlon J. nonetheless ordered the sale and division. She considered that the husband was "tak[ing] a very narrow view of the role of the [wife] in terms of her child rearing function and also her function as wife and homemaker to the family."

FLS v XXL [2014] IEHC 663 is but one of many instances of the High Court making orders relating to foreign land owned by one or both of the spouses in the exercise of its wide-ranging powers to make orders for financial provision on granting a judicial separation or divorce. In this case, Abbott J. ordered the transfer of the husband's interest in German property to his wife as part of a series of orders relating to financial provision and maintenance. In deciding what orders to make, courts in Ireland (as also in England), in stark contrast to their civil law counterparts, tend not to be greatly troubled by the conflict of laws dimension. They have power to vary settlements relating to foreign property governed by foreign law. Whilst prudence may act as a restraint, the legislation does not expressly limit the court's powers to override spousal entitlements arising under a foreign matrimonial regime. Other decisions in 2014 in which the court made similar orders are *JK v RK* [2014] IEHC 451, *KC v TC* [2014] IEHC 667 and *H v H* [2014] IEHC 673.

KC v TC [2014] IEHC 667 involved findings of serious wrongdoing against a husband, whom O'Hanlon J. found to be "grossly irresponsible" and "grossly in breach of his duties to disclose to this court the full extent of his financial circumstances". O'Hanlon J. commented:

> "This Court has had the opportunity of observing the demeanour of the [husband], and, while he was polite and courteous, he failed to answer in a candid manner the questions put to him … . His affidavits failed to refer to [a number of] payments. He admitted that the failure to disclose these payments prior to the settlement of the interim maintenance order was non-disclosure, and that his affidavits of means filed prior to the interim maintenance order … . were both untruthful and inaccurate … . The continuous and deliberate conscious decisions of the [husband] not to disclose the existence of [several] payments and not to use these monies to reduce the mortgage attaching on the family home was reprehensible in the extreme."

A further non-disclosure on the husband's part was characterised by O'Hanlon J. as amounting to serious litigation misconduct. The husband was found to have made reviewable dispositions for the purposes of s.35 of the Family Law Act 1995, which were accordingly set aside.

In *SQ v TQ* [2014] IEHC 389, Keane J. gave useful guidance on the approach to be adopted in determining the scope of the power of the High Court to order one spouse in matrimonial proceedings to provide information or documentation to the other spouse and to the court concerning the financial circumstances of a company in which the former holds a majority shareholding. The wife in this case was seeking more information of this kind than her husband had provided.

After a comprehensive analysis, including extended discussion of the case law in Ireland and England, Keane J. concluded that a somewhat broader approach than that adopted in the decisions of the Supreme Court in *Johnston v Church of Scientology* [2001] 1 I.R. 682 and *Thema International Fund plc v HSBC Institutional Trust Services (Ireland) Limited* [2013] IESC 3 was appropriate on the basis of the particular jurisdiction engaged in the instant case, the specific facts before the court and the *sui generis* nature of the relief sought in the instant application.

As to the particular nature of the underlying proceedings , Keane J. noted that :

> "[t]hey involve the determination of the appropriate ancillary relief in judicial separation proceedings where proper provision is in issue, which means that the Court has a quasi-inquisitorial role and an obligation to inquire into the relevant matters of its own motion if necessary. It also means that the parties have a specific duty, not only to one another but also to the court, to make full and frank disclosure of all the material facts which are relevant to the exercise of the court's powers, including the nature and extent of the resources available to them. Accordingly, in this case the obligations of the Court, and the duties of the parties, go significantly further than they would in respect of the question of discovery in adversarial litigation generally."

As to the specific facts of the instant case, the husband had already demonstrated an ability to secure the company's unqualified co-operation with the forensic accountants retained on his behalf to prepare a valuation of the company and, by extension, of his shareholding in it for the purpose of the proceedings. The court was thus dealing with documentation and information that it was reasonable to believe could be obtained for the asking (as in *Northern Bank Finance Ltd v Charlton*, unreported, High Court, Finlay P., 26 May 1977), or which must be regarded, prima facie, as being available to the defendant if requested (as in *Yates v Ciba Geigy Agro Ltd*, unreported, High Court, Barron J., 29 April 1986).

As to the third factor, Keane J. commented:

> "This is not strictly an application for discovery at all. It is primarily an application for an order pursuant to Section 38(8) of the [Family Law] Act [1995], requiring the husband to give to the wife such particulars of his property and income as may be required for the purposes of the proceedings. It need hardly be re-emphasised that the conduct of these proceedings entails a consideration of the ancillary relief necessary to make proper provision not only for the parties, but also for the dependent members of the family concerned."

Keane J. accordingly ordered the husband to furnish the particulars sought by the wife.

In *In the matter of the Judicial Separation and Family Law Reform Act 1989, AA and BA and In the matter of the Family Law (Divorce) Act 1996 BA and AA and by order CD* [2014] IESC 49, the Supreme Court affirmed, with a minor modification, Irvine J.'s judgment giving a series of financial reliefs to a divorced wife whose former husband had been guilty of a deliberate failure to disclose the full extent of his assets during the divorce proceedings in 2001. On the question whether the proceedings should have been by way of plenary summons rather than motion, it seemed to Clarke J. that

> … the key question which arises concerns the constitutional obligation of the court to ensure that proper provision is made. This is not simply an *inter partes* case in which a final order or settlement is reached. It is a case where the court has its own constitutional obligations. In those circumstances, it seems to me that the court retains a discretion, at least in divorce cases, to decide the appropriate procedure whereby any issue concerning a deliberate failure to disclose resources can be resolved. While there is no doubt but that plenary proceedings are the proper means for bringing any claim to have a court order set aside, I am satisfied that, at least so far as divorce cases are concerned, the court retains a discretion to permit such a claim to be brought by any procedural means which the court considers fits the needs of the case. It is, therefore, unnecessary to consider what the situation might be in, for example, ordinary *inter partes* proceedings.
>
> Given that the court has a discretion, it seems to me that it was within the jurisdiction of Abbott J. to direct and Irvine J. to uphold the decision that these proceedings, in all the circumstances, be brought by a motion. It might well be that had, from the beginning, [the husband] maintained that the proceedings should have been brought by plenary summons, the proper course of action for the court to have adopted would have been to direct that the proceedings be brought in that way. However, [the husband] made no such application at any realistic time. In those circumstances, I am satisfied that Irvine J. was more than entitled to continue with the proceedings in the form with which [the husband] had acquiesced.

SA v BA [2014] IEHC 452 raised the question whether a farm should be sold. The spouses were in their early sixties. The husband, who had certain physical infirmities, wanted the farm to be sold. The wife preferred that only part of the property be sold and she indicated her desire to establish an "art and healing" centre on the part of the farm property that she proposed to retain. She had studied for a year in art college, given art lessons until 2008, and held an exhibition of her work in the library in a nearby town in 2013 at which she had sold two paintings for €200 and €150 respectively. Some years previously, she had converted part of one of the outbuildings into an art studio or exhibition space with her husband's assistance. A single art exhibition had been held there in 2008. The wife had done a course in the spiritual practice of Reiki or "hands-on healing". She hoped to do a course in reflexology in a nearby town and, perhaps, one in aromatherapy. She believed that these interests could be intertwined in a viable form of commercial enterprise based on the farm. She also hoped that some of the more modern farm buildings could be rented out as warehouse space for shops or businesses in the nearby town and that other farm buildings and the parkland that she proposed to retain could be let out for agricultural purposes and that she could, in consequence, retain a portion of the Single Farm Payment. The remaining unused outbuildings would simply be closed up and secured.

Keane J. decided to order the sale of the farm. He acknowledged that it had been skilfully argued that the wife had shown herself to be a practical and pragmatic person over the course of the parties' marriage and that this should lend credibility to the proposals she was making concerning the family farm. Keane J. was, however, unable to overlook the fact that the wife had prepared no business plan in respect of any aspect of her complex and multi-faceted proposal. There were no projections. There was no market research:

> "The letting of agricultural land and buildings; the leasing of warehouse space; the demand for art studio space, art classes, Reiki healing and reflexology; and the market for art work locally—all of these things remain imponderables—subject only to certain optimistic predictions and hopeful comparisons ventured by the wife or by others on the wife's behalf. The wife has, at best, a very limited track record in the various commercial areas that are the subject of her proposed venture"

Moreover, the evidence indicated that the wife's proposed solution was likely to have a negative impact on the value of the remaining lands, which might lead to a significant diminution in the value of the overall pool of matrimonial assets out of which the court was obliged to make proper provision for each of the parties.

PRESUMPTION OF ADVANCEMENT

In *GR v JJD* [2014] IEHC 665, the present status of the old doctrine of the presumption of advancement was raised in legal argument but not resolved by Abbott J. as he held against the husband's claim to entitlement of the disputed property on another ground. The husband had contended that the doctrine was incompatible with the constitutional principle of equality between the spouses and art.5 of Protocol 7 of the European Convention on Human Rights.

Abbott J. rejected the husband's assertion that a resulting trust had been established. He stated:

> "I am of the view that the status of the registered ownership of the folio concerned should be governed by the principles set out in *Tinker v Tinker* [1970] 2 W.L.R. 331 … . This is on the basis that the court should take, as a separate exercise, the position of the [husband] as an honest man, who intended in the face of some apprehended (but not present) financial collapse of his business, to protect his assets for his wife. In these circumstances the authority of *Tinker v Tinker* [1970] 2 W.L.R. 331 would indicate that there is a clear intention to be inferred that the [husband] intended a clear gift and the presumption of advancement is not required to save it … ."

CHILDREN

In the Constitutional Law chapter, above p.119, Oran Doyle and Estelle Feldman discuss the decision of *MR and DR (suing by their father and next friend OR) v An tArd Chlaraitheoir* [2014] IESC 60, where the Supreme Court, reversing Abbott J., held that the birth mother rather than the gestational mother was the person who should be registered as mother under the Civil Registration Act 2004.

In *RS v TS* [2014] IEHC 257, the clinical psychologist appointed by the court to produce a report under s.47 of the Family Law Act 1995 concluded that it would be in the best interests of the children emotionally and psychologically if they were to continue living with their mother and have access with their father every second weekend. He based this on the view that, "[w]hile spending equal time with each parent can work for children following marital separation, it requires a high level of co-operation and mutual respect between the separating parents and this is clearly not the case here."

Keane J. was not persuaded by this clinical conclusion, which he forensically demolished in the following passage:

> "The Court's reasons for rejecting that conclusion are as follows. First, the older child has expressed the wish that he should spend equal time with each of the parties. Second, where there are high levels of conflict and low levels of mutual trust between parents, as appears to be the position in this case, there is no logical connection that the Court can identify between that fact and any need to divide custody of the children unequally, rather than equally, between the parents. Third, there is no logical basis that the Court can identify for the proposition that the equal division of custody between parents on alternate weeks provides less regularity and predictability of access for the children concerned than an arrangement whereby primary custody of the children is awarded to one parent and the other is given limited access to the children.
>
> Fourth, as far as the Court is aware, there is no basis for the suggestion that an equal division of custody will provide less stability for the children in this case than granting primary custody to the wife and limited access to the husband. The husband has acquired a home in the same area as the existing family home in order to ensure that there will be no disruption to the children's school or social activities when they are in his care … .".

Keane J. awarded the spouses joint custody of the children, with shared access equally on a week-on/week-off basis.

In *CQ v IMcG* [2014] IEHC 699, O'Hanlon J., varying an order for joint custody made by the Circuit Court, ordered that the mother should have sole custody of the two younger children. O'Hanlon J. was concerned about the father's propensity for abusive and threatening behaviour. She also ordered that, prior to the commencement of any further access, the father should undergo six sessions of psychotherapy, with the precondition that the psychotherapist confirm to the court that safe access could take place.

Section 6 of the Civil Registration (Amendment) Act 2014 requires mothers of children born outside marriage to register the name of the father. The mother may, however, furnish a statutory declaration that one of three specified "compelling reasons" justifies her not doing so. These are:

> (a) That she does not know the identity of the father of the child;
> (b) That she does not know the whereabouts of the father;
> (c) that she believes that providing the information is not in the best interests of the safety of the child.

In case (c), the statutory declaration must contain and, as necessary, exhibit information, particulars and evidence relating to that belief.

PRACTICE AND PROCEDURE

Conflict of interest In *MM v GIM* [2014] IEHC 687, White J. declined to accede to an application for an injunction taken by a husband in family law proceedings, seeking to have his wife's solicitor no longer represent her in the proceedings. The wife's solicitor had advised the husband on legal matters in regard to his relationship with his wife (who had not yet married him) between 16 and 11 years previously. The solicitor had no recollection of having done so. White J. was satisfied that the husband would not be prejudiced by the solicitor's continuing to represent the wife on appeal to the Supreme Court in the family law proceedings, which would be heard on the transcript of the High Court proceedings.

Contempt of Court In *R v R* [2014] IEHC 648, O'Hanlon J. made an order attaching a husband for contempt of court in failing to comply with a previous order to make maintenance payments to his wife. O'Hanlon J. recorded in her judgment that the husband, a lay litigant, had declined to apply for legal aid or accept the services of a solicitor who was willing to offer legal services on a pro bono basis. O'Hanlon J. placed a stay on the order of attachment and committal to prison for 28 days, to allow the husband to purge his contempt and make the necessary payment of the outstanding sum.

Media reports In *AB v CD* [2014] IEHC 180, Keane J. refused an application made by a mother under s.40(3A) of the Civil Liability and Courts Act 2004, as inserted by s.5 of the Courts and Civil Law (Miscellaneous Provisions) Act 2013, to exclude bona fide representatives of the press from the court during family litigation relating to the custody and care of her children. The litigation had been going on between the father and mother for more than a decade and extended to other matters. The father was seeking to have struck out an earlier order made by Abbot J., whose judgment had contained a paragraph that had attracted considerable media attention:

> "I asked [the mother] if, after the making of the High Court order [of 21st July 2010] but before the furnishing of reasons [in a judgment delivered on 26th July 2011], she asked a Dáil Deputy to make enquiries for her in relation to the matter from the judge, and that the Dáil Deputy sought the services of a Circuit Court judge to ask me was it a fact that [one of the parties' minor children] had been sent away to the primary care of the father. She agreed that she had made that approach to the Dáil Deputy and apologised on the basis that it was at a time when she was unrepresented. I informed the court that on being asked the question by the Circuit Court Judge (quite improperly), I replied that a judgment would issue on the web in due course in relation to the matter."

The thrust of the mother's argument was that, while the desirability of promoting public confidence in the administration of justice might militate in favour of permitting the press to report upon the husband's application to set aside Abbott J.'s Order, the fact that the parties and their children had already been publicly identified, at least in their own locality, made it necessary to conduct the remainder of the proceedings in camera. The nature and scope of the exception being contended for would apply, by analogy, to no more than 5 per cent of the cases of this sort that came before the court.

Keane J. identified two difficulties with this proposition. The first was that:

> "some degree of local identification must be closer to the norm than to the exception in family law litigation. Parties may confide their problems or difficulties in close friends or family members who may in turn confide in others, creating a ripple effect. Certain pivotal incidents involving family members may be witnessed by other persons who may in turn describe them to others. For these reasons, the sphere of personal or family privacy is rarely, if ever, entirely impermeable and few families, if any, are immune from local gossip, reprehensible as that may be."

The second difficulty related to the fact that, in the words of counsel for the mother, "everybody knows that this case relates to the judges talking in the yard, and the allegation about [a named politician], and to pretend otherwise is wholly unreal." It seemed to Keane J. that this characteristic, far from tilting towards excluding the press, lent particular weight to the countervailing consideration in the case, namely, the desirability of promoting public confidence in the administration of justice:

> "In a case that raises an issue of attempted interference with the administration of justice, the importance of the general principle enshrined in section 40(3A)(a) of the 2004 Act whereby *bona fide* representatives of the Press are entitled to report on proceedings of this sort appears to me to take on greater, rather than lesser, significance."

In a subsequent decision, *AB v CD* [2014] IEHC 450, Keane J. rejected the husband's claim of bias against Abbott J. and his claim that there had been a breach by the mother of the in camera rule on the basis, in the latter instance, that that issue had already been raised by the court in the course of the appeal hearing and accordingly the court was "now *functus officio* on that point."

In *ABC v DEF* [2014] IEHC 680, White J. granted an interlocutory injunction against the publication of the name of the applicant, the defendant in defamation proceedings taken against her by a cleric against whom she had made to the appropriate authorities allegations of sex abuse. Evidence was given to the effect that there was a risk that, if identified publicly in the defamation proceedings, the applicant might end her own life. White J. observed:

> "In weighing up the balance of convenience it is an important factor that the [applicant] did not seek to publish nor was [she] responsible for the decisions which led to the unnecessary publicity for the [respondent]. I fully understand [his] anger and frustration where innocence is maintained but compromised when suspension from ministry occurred. In the hierarchy

of constitutional rights, the undoubted risk to the [applicant]'s life takes precedence."

Costs of Section 47 Assessor In *BCMcM v JCMcM* [2014] IEHC 688, White J. reduced by €22,000 an invoice for almost €80,000 presented by a court-appointed assessor for his preparation of reports under s.47 of the Family Law Act 1995. He commented that, "[o]bjectively it would never be contemplated by a family court that s.47 reports and attendance in court by the assessor would reach the level of €80,000." There was no question that the assessor had wrongly inflated the amount: White J. referred approvingly to his "exceptional" work. It emerged, however, that he had not availed himself of secretarial assistance, which would be costed at €20 per hour rather than his hourly charge of €150.

Fisheries and Harbours

FISHERIES

Confiscation and proportionality In *Montemuino v Minister for Communications, Marine and Natural Resources* [2013] IESC 40, the Supreme Court gave important guidance on the confiscation regime under the Fisheries (Consolidation) Act 1959 (the "1959 Act"). Section 224B(3) of the 1959 Act, as inserted by s.5 of the Fisheries (Amendment) Act 1983, provides:

> A person who fishes or attempts to fish in contravention of regulations under this section shall be guilty of an offence and shall be liable on conviction on indictment to a fine not exceeding [EUR 253,947.62], and, as a statutory consequence of the conviction, to forfeiture of all or any of the following found on the boat to which the offence relates:
> (a) any fish,
> (b) any fishing gear.

The appellant was alleged to have breached the Sea Fisheries (Control of Catches) Regulations 2003 (S.I. No. 345 of 2003), which were introduced in order to create an offence for the infringement of Regulation (EC) No.2807/83 on the recording of information on Member States' fish catches. The appellant was therefore charged on indictment with an offence contrary to s.224B(3) of the 1959 Act. The appellant challenged the constitutionality of s.224B(3), on the grounds that the mandatory and non-discretionary nature of the penalty of forfeiture imposed by s.224B(3) was disproportionate. On appeal before the Supreme Court, an issue was raised as to whether, on its true construction, the section did truly require a forfeiture of all fish and all fishing gear, or rather whether s.224B(3) afforded a sentencing judge discretion to impose a forfeiture of whatever amount of fish and fishing gear, or both, deemed appropriate to meet the gravity of the offence. The Supreme Court answered this in the affirmative.

Delivering the only judgment, Clarke J. (with whom Denham C.J., Hardiman, Fennelly and MacMenamin JJ. concurred) held that s.224B(3) of the 1959 Act was to be construed as conferring a discretion on a sentencing judge to determine the appropriate degree of forfeiture that was to apply in respect of any fish and/or fishing gear found on a relevant vessel. He stated that, before applying the double construction rule of statutory interpretation identified in *McDonald v Bord na gCon* [1965] I.R. 217 and *East Donegal Co-Op Ltd v Attorney General* [1970] I.R. 317, it was first necessary to ascertain what the legislation meant by reference to the ordinary canons of construction. Citing with approval the court's decision in *DPP v Moorehouse* [2005] IESC 52, [2006] 1 I.R. 421, Clarke J. noted that as a penal statute, s.224B(3) of the 1959 Act must be construed strictly, and any ambiguity was to be resolved in favour of the person charged with the criminal offence. He went on to state that the use of the phrases "a statutory consequence", together with "all or any" in s.224B(3), gave rise to an ambiguity in that it was unclear whether or not the section intended the mandatory forfeiture of all fish and all fishing gear. Citing the decision of the EU Court of Justice in *Kamer van Koophandel en Fabrieken voor Amsterdam v Inspire Art* (C–167/01) [2003] E.C.R. I–10155, Clarke J. considered that on either construction of s.224B(3) of the 1959 Act, the penalty to be imposed was an effective one for the purposes of EU law. He added that, in imposing an appropriate penalty, a sentencing judge was required to have regard to the importance of ensuring compliance with EU legislation while ensuring that any penalty imposed was proportionate. Since, on the ordinary principles of construction, no question as to the compatibility of the impugned section with the Constitution arose, Clarke J. concluded that it was not necessary to apply the double construction rule, and the specific reliefs sought by the plaintiff were therefore refused.

The decision in the *Montemuino* case should also be seen against the background of other amendments made to the confiscation regime in s.224B of the 1959 Act by the Sea-Fisheries and Maritime Jurisdiction Act 2006 (*Annual Review of Irish Law 2006*, pp.391–392).

EU fishing quotas for 2014 The Sea-Fisheries (Quotas) Regulations 2014 (S.I. No. 161 of 2014), made under the Sea-Fisheries and Maritime Jurisdiction Act 2006 (*Annual Review of Irish Law 2006*, pp.391–392), were made to give full effect to Regulation (EU) No.43/2014, which fixed for 2014 the fishing quotas for certain fish stocks and groups of fish stocks, applicable in EU waters and to EU fishing vessels in certain non-EU waters. They also revoked the Sea-Fisheries (Quotas) Regulations 2013 (S.I. No. 183 of 2013).

Health and Health Services

GENERAL PRACTITIONER SERVICE

Free GP care for under 6s The Health (General Practitioner Service) Act 2014 (the "2014 Act") provided for a general practitioner (GP) service to be made available without fees to all children aged five years and younger. The 2014 Act therefore formed the first element of the policy to introduce, on a phased basis, a universal GP service without fees for the entire population. The 2014 Act came into force on different dates in 2015: see Health (General Practitioner Service) Act 2014 (Certain Provisions) (Commencement) Order 2015 (S.I. No. 267 of 2015).

It was noted during the Oireachtas debates on the 2014 Act that, in 2014, just over 40 per cent of the population had access to a publicly-funded GP service through a General Medical Services card (GMS card); and that the balance of the population, almost 2.5 million people, paid the market rate for a GP consultation, which was in the region of €55 per visit. It was also noted during the Oireachtas debates on the 2014 Act that the 2013 *Report of the Expert Advisory Group on the Early Years Strategy* had recommended providing access to GP care without fees to all children in the age group covered by the 2014 Act, as the identification of health issues at an early age can mitigate or reduce the impact of ill-health later in life. It was also noted that the *Growing Up in Ireland* survey had reported that, in 2014, almost one in four children in Ireland were either overweight or obese, which was likely to lead to significant health issues later in life.

The 2014 Act provided an entitlement for all children aged five years and younger (the "under 6s") to a GP service without fees; it removed the need for children aged five years and younger to have a medical card or a GP visit card under the general medical services, GMS, in order to qualify for a GP service; it provided that the HSE may enter a contract with GPs for the provision of this GP service to children; and it provides that the Minister may set the rates of fees payable to GPs for this service.

Section 2 of the 2014 Act amended s.47 of the Health Act 1970 (the "1970 Act") to provide for the extension of the HSE appeals process to decisions on the operation of the GP service provided for in the 2014 Act and for the director general of the HSE to appoint persons to carry out appeals. The pre-existing provision in the 1970 Act empowering the Minister to make Regulations in respect of the appeals process was restated without change.

Section 3 of the 2014 Act amended s.47A of the 1970 Act concerning the requirement that a person be "ordinarily resident" to reflect the changes made to s.47 of the 1970 Act by s.2 of the 2014 Act. It also extended the "ordinarily resident" requirement to include the GP service provided for in the 2014 Act.

Section 4 of the 2014 Act amended s.58 of the 1970 Act to remove children under 6 years from the pre-existing GP service under the medical card scheme, as provided for in s.58 of the 1970 Act; this is because they were to be covered by the GP service provided for in the 2014 Act, as inserted into the 1970 Act by s.5 of the 2014 Act, below. This did not alter or affect those families who already had, or were eligible for medical cards (including those with children under the age of 6), who would continue to receive their medical card entitlements.

Section 5 of the 2014 Act provided for the insertion of two new sections into the 1970 Act, ss.58B and 58C. Section 58B of the 1970 Act provides that the HSE shall make available a GP service without fees to all children aged five years and younger. It provides that a parent or guardian of a child seeking access to this service should provide to the HSE such evidence as it considers necessary to demonstrate their entitlement to the service and where such evidence is not provided the HSE may treat the child as if he or she is not entitled to the service. Where possible, the HSE will offer a choice of GP to those accessing this service.

Section 58C of the 1970 Act, as inserted by the 2014 Act, provides that the HSE may enter into a contract with any suitably qualified and vocationally trained general practitioner for the provision of GP services to all children aged five years and younger. The HSE may also enter into a contract for relevant services with any registered medical practitioner who already holds a GMS contract for the six-month period following commencement of s.58C. In addition, s.58C provides that the Minister for Health may, by Regulations, and with the consent of the Minister for Public Expenditure and Reform, fix the rates of fees and allowances to be paid to GPs for services provided under these contracts. Section 58C requires that the Minister, in making such Regulations, shall engage in consultation. It also prescribes the role of the Minister and the HSE, the nature and manner of the consultations and the considerations to which the Minister must have regard in making Regulations. This includes the need to have regard to agreements entered into with the representatives of GPs relating to such consultations.

HEALTH AND SOCIAL CARE PROFESSIONALS COUNCIL

Opticians Board subsumed into CORU, the Health and Social Care Professionals Council The two main purposes of the Health (Miscellaneous Provisions) Act 2014 (the "2014 Act") were as follows. First, it provided for subsuming the Opticians Board (Bord na Radharcmhastóirí) into CORU, the Health and Social Care Professionals Council, which had been established under the Health and Social Care Professionals Act 2005 (the "2005 Act") (*Annual Review of Irish Law 2005*, pp.424–429), which was achieved by amending the 2005 Act and repealing the Opticians Act 1956. Secondly, the 2014 Act made general amendments to the 2005 Act to ensure consistency with the legislation governing other health regulators, such as the Medical Council. The provisions required to subsume the Opticians Board into CORU came into force on 31 December 2014: see the Health (Miscellaneous Provisions) Act 2014 (Commencement) Order 2014 (S.I. No. 588 of 2014).

During the Oireachtas debates on the 2014 Act, on overview was provided of the extent to which the provisions in the 2005 Act concerning the 12 designated health care professionals listed in it, to which opticians and optometrists were added by the 2014 Act, had actually been implemented in practice. It was noted that regulation of the 13 health care professionals under the 2005 Act was primarily by way of the statutory protection of professional titles, by confining their use solely to persons granted registration by CORU.

The structure of the system of statutory regulation under the 2005 Act comprises a registration board for each profession, a committee structure to deal with disciplinary matters, with CORU, the Health and Social Care Professionals Council, having overall responsibility for the regulatory system. These bodies are collectively known as CORU and are responsible for protecting the public by regulating health and social care professionals in Ireland.

The 2005 Act provides for a two-year transitional or "grand-parenting" period during which existing practitioners must register on the basis of specified qualifications. After this period, only registrants of a registration board (who will be subject to the 2005 Act's regulatory regime) will be entitled to use the relevant designated title. As the optical professions had already been regulated under the Opticians Act 1956, no transitional period applied to them in their transfer to the regulatory system under the 2005 Act.

By 2014, the registers of four professions had been established: dietitians, radiographers, social workers and speech and language therapists. The register for occupational therapists was expected to be open in 2015. At the time of writing (July 2015), the CORU website, coru.ie, stated that registration boards for all 13 professions (including the optical professions) were being established on a phased basis, and that all professions would be regulated by the end of 2017.

In preparing for full implementation of the 2005 Act, the 2014 Act amended Pt 6 of the 2005 Act, which deals with the CORU fitness to practice regime. As amended by the 2014 Act, Pt 6 of the 2005 Act is similar to that applicable to medical practitioners, nurses and midwives.

It was also noted during the Oireachtas debates on the 2014 Act that other professions were seeking designation under the 2005 Act, including audiologists, counselors, creative arts therapists and psychotherapists. It was stated that priority would first be given to establishing the regulatory regimes for the 13 professions already designated under the 2005 Act, as amended. When all the registers had been established (at the time of writing, July 2015, likely to take place towards the end of 2017), it was stated that the Department of Health would request CORU to prepare a risk assessment, in terms of public protection, of the principal health and social care professions seeking designation and to make recommendations concerning options for their possible future regulation.

Part 1 of the 2014 Act (ss.1 – 3) includes s.2, which provides for the repeal of the Opticians Act 1956.

Part 2 (ss.4 – 40) contains the main provisions of the 2014 Act, which relate to the amendments to the 2005 Act, in order to apply the 2005 Act provisions to the professions of optometrist and dispensing optician. Sections 6, 12 and 21 of the 2014 Act also provide for dividing, for the purposes of the 2005 Act, the designated profession of radiographer into the two designated professions of radiographer and radiation therapist. Sections 6, 12, 13 and 16 of the 2015 Act amend the 2005 Act to permit a registration board to regulate two or more designated professions, and these amendments apply to all professions regulated under the 2005 Act.

Provisions in 2005 Act for CORU on governance, fitness to practice, registration and offences As already noted, the other main purpose of the 2014 Act was to align the provisions of the 2005 Act on governance, fitness to practice, registration and offences with those in the Medical Practitioners Act 2007 (the "2007 Act") and the Nursing and Midwives Act 2011 (the "2011 Act"). As to governance, the principal amendments relate to the election of a deputy chairperson of the Health and Social Care Professionals Council, the role of the council's chief executive officer, quorums and the holding of certain meetings of the council and registration boards by video link or the circulation of papers. In terms of CORU's fitness to practice regime, the changes made to the 2005 Act by the 2014 Act allow for the following: the cancellation of the registration of a registrant convicted of an indictable offence if it is in the public interest to do so; the appointment of persons to assist in investigating complaints against a registrant; the application for immediate suspension of the registration of a registrant on an ex parte basis; and the publication of the transcript of the proceedings of a committee of inquiry.

As to registration, the 2005 Act, as amended by the 2014 Act, provides for the charging of fees for approving education and training programmes and for attaching conditions to the registration of a registrant with a relevant medical disability. The provisions in the 2005 Act relating to the prosecution of offences were amended to provide the Health and Social Care Professionals Council with new investigation powers similar to those of the Medical Council under the 2007 Act and the Nursing and Midwifery Board of Ireland under the 2011 Act.

HEALTH INSURANCE

Risk equalisation and lifetime community rating The Health Insurance (Amendment) Act 2014 (the "2014 Act") amended the risk equalisation scheme in the Health Insurance Acts 1994 to 2013 (*Annual Review of Irish Law 2012*, pp.351 – 353 and *Annual Review of Irish Law 2013*, pp.343–344) and also introduced a modified form of community rating called lifetime community rating from 1 March 2015. Unusually, the 2014 Act provided for its commencement on various specified dates between 25 December 2014 and 1 May 2015.

As noted during the Oireachtas debates on the 2014 Act, risk equalisation underpins the community-rated health insurance market. The main purpose of the 2014 Act was to specify the risk equalisation credits, the rate of the hospital bed utilisation credit (the "H book") and corresponding stamp duty levies required to fund the credits to apply from 1 March 2015. It was also noted that the private health insurance sector had experienced great difficulties since the economic downturn that emerged in 2007 and 2008. The ageing market, reductions in membership and a sustained growth in claims had resulted in premium increases since 2008. Coverage had fallen from a peak of just under 51 per cent of the population in 2008 to 44 per cent in June 2014. Average claim costs per insured person rose by 12.6 per cent between 2008 and 2012, although there was a reduction of 2 per cent in average claim costs in 2013. The size of the market contracted less in the year to July 2014 than it did during the previous 12 months. The reduction had improved from a fall of 63,460 members in the year to mid-2013, to a reduction of 36,538 in the year to mid-2014. The third quarter of 2014 recorded a small increase in the number of people with health insurance for the first time in many years.

The 2014 Act was therefore presented as part of a series of measures aimed to ensure health insurance would be affordable to as many people as possible in a sustainable, competitive market. The measures include lifetime community rating, reduced rates for young adults, a reduction in the levy which funds the Health Insurance Authority and no increase in the stamp duty levy for the risk equalisation scheme.

It was noted in the Oireachtas debates on the 2014 Act that lifetime community rating, which was introduced from 1 May 2015, is a modification of community rating to reflect the age at which a person first takes out health insurance. Its primary purpose is to encourage people to purchase health insurance at a younger age. Those who take out private health insurance earlier in life, and retain it, will pay lower premiums than those choosing to join when they are older. The 2014 Act amended the Health Insurance Acts 1994 to 2013 to provide that from 1 May 2015, there was a "late-entry loading" for people aged 35 years and over who purchase private health insurance for the first time, or renew after a break in cover of more than 13 weeks. The loadings are set at 2 per cent per year starting at age 35 years, up to a maximum loading of 70 per cent at age 69 and over. A "grace period" until 30 April 2015 was included in the 2014 Act to allow as many people as possible to take out health insurance. During this period no penalties applied. Following expiry of the grace period, there will be credits for previous periods of health insurance cover and credits of up to three years for unemployment since 2008, to reflect the impact of the recession.

The 2014 Act also removed the large step-effect increase in premiums that occurred prior to 2014 for most young adults after their 21st birthday, as for many, premiums could have doubled once they reached 21 years of age. The 2014 Act provided for the introduction of a young adult rate of premium, age-based rather than student-based, and designed to smooth out the rise in premiums between child and full adult rates. Insurers retained discretion with regard to whether to provide these rates. Where an insurer chooses to provide young adult rates, it must also provide the full range of rates within the specified bands. Thus, s.2 of the 2014 Act amended s.7(5)(b)(i) of the Health Insurance Act 1994 (the "1994 Act") to provide for a sliding scale of young adult rates for health insurance premiums up to and including age 25 years and remove the requirement that such persons be in full-time education or dependent on the policyholder to benefit. Section 2 also inserted a new s.7(5A) to provide that where a health insurer proposes to offer young adult rates, it must offer the full range of rates within the specified bands. Insurers will retain discretion as to whether or not to provide these rates.

Section 3 amended s.7A of the 1994 Act to empower the Minister to make Regulations to provide for lifetime community rating. With effect from 1 May 2015, late-entry loadings apply for those aged 35 years and over who purchase private health insurance for the first time or renew after a break in cover of more than 13 weeks. The amendments were two-fold: first, by amending s.7A(3) of the 1994 Act, it provided that the obligation to require the payment of late-entry loadings is subject to relevant Regulations; and, secondly, by replacing "may" with "shall" in s.7A it clarified that the obligation on insurers to impose lifetime community rating loadings as provided for by Regulations is mandatory.

Section 4 amended s.8(3) and (5) and deleted s.8(6) of the 1994 Act. The additional provisions in s.8(3) and the amendment of s.8(5) were to clarify that people transferring from one health insurance policy to another are not required to serve additional waiting periods other than those applying to an upgrade in cover. Section 8(5) of the 1994 Act was further amended to provide for the transfer of served waiting times for people transferring from restricted membership undertakings to open-market insurers without the application of any additional initial waiting period. As a result, s.8(6) was repealed.

Section 5 amended s.11(C) of the 1994 Act, to provide that 1 March 2015 was the effective date for revised risk equalisation credits to be payable from the Health Insurance Authority's levy-based risk equalisation fund. Section 6 amended Sch.3 to the 1994 Act to provide for the revised amount payable from the risk equalisation fund for the hospital bed utilisation credit. This covered health insurance contracts renewed or taken out from 1 March 2015.

Section 7 of the 2014 Act replaced Table 2 in Sch.4 to the 1994 Act with effect from 1 March 2015, under which the applicable risk equalisation credits payable from the risk equalisation fund for certain classes of insured persons were revised. Section 8 of the 2014 Act amended s.125A of the Stamp Duties Act 1999 (the "1999 Act") to specify the applicable stamp duty rates for the respective periods 1 January 2015 to 28 February 2015 and 1 March 2015 onwards.

HEALTH PRODUCTS REGULATORY AUTHORITY

The European Communities (Animal Remedies) (Amendment) (No.2) Regulations 2014 (S.I. No. 361 of 2014) amended the European Communities (Animal Remedies) (No. 2) Regulations 2007 (S.I. No. 786 of 2007) to give further effect to Directive 2001/82/EC on the approval, distribution and administration of animal remedies by transferring competency for the granting of research licences to the Health Products Regulatory Authority (formerly the Irish Medicines Board: see *Annual Review of Irish Law 2013*, p.351).

HEALTH SERVICE EXECUTIVE

Annual financial allocation reintegrated into Department of Health The Health Service Executive (Financial Matters) Act 2014 (the "2014 Act") formed part of the general reforms to the Health Service Executive (HSE) enacted in recent years, which have included the Health Service Executive (Governance) Act 2013 (the "2013 Act") (*Annual Review of Irish Law 2013*, pp.344 – 346). The 2014 Act provided for the "disestablishment" of the annual financial allocation, or Vote, for the HSE; that is, that rather than the HSE receiving its own separate annual financial allocation, its Vote from 2015 onwards would become part of the annual Vote of the Office of the Minister for Health. The HSE will continue to collect the income it generates through statutory charges (for example, hospital charges), superannuation contributions and other miscellaneous income. The 2014 Act also provided for a new statutory financial and service plan governance framework to align with the altered Vote arrangements in the 2014 Act. These changes complemented the changed governance arrangements enacted in the 2013 Act, under which the HSE directorate replaced the HSE board. The 2014 Act came into effect on the date of its enactment, 17 July 2014. Section 4 of the Appropriation Act 2014 (discussed in general in the Administrative Law chapter, p.1, above) also amended s.3 of the

Appropriation Act 1999 (the "1999 Act") to reflect the changed financial allocation for the HSE.

It was pointed out during the Oireachtas debates on the 2014 Act that the Health Act 2004 (the "2004 Act") (*Annual Review of Irish Law 2004*, pp.313 – 317), under which the HSE had been established, had provided that the HSE had its own Vote and that the Minister for Health had no legal role in setting its budget. This was intended to give the HSE greater operational autonomy from what, in the pre-2004 health board system (which the HSE replaced), was characterised as a politicised health decision-making system. The 2014 Act was enacted, however, to address what was regarded as a defect in this arrangement, namely, a weakening of the accountability of the HSE to the Minister for Health and the Department of Health, and, in turn, a weakening of accountability of the Minister and Department to the Oireachtas. The purpose of the 2014 Act, therefore, was to re-establish appropriate and proper accountability of the HSE to the Department of Health and, thus, of the Minister and Department to the Oireachtas.

Part 2 of the 2014 Act (ss.4 – 14) contains the bulk of its provisions and comprises various amendments to the 2004 Act. Section 4 amended s.5A of the 2004 Act, inserted by the Health Act 2007 (the "2007 Act") (which established the Health Information and Quality Authority, HIQA), and provides that expenses incurred by the HSE are payable out of moneys provided by the Oireachtas, subject to the approval of the Minister for Health and the sanction of the Minister for Public Expenditure and Reform. This amendment limited the application of this provision up to 1 January 2015 to take account of its replacement by s.33A of the 2004 Act, as inserted by s.11 of the 2014 Act, discussed below.

Functions of HSE Director General and general HSE governance arrangements Section 5 of the 2014 Act amended s.16G of the 2004 Act, inserted by the 2013 Act, which sets out the general functions of the HSE Director General. As originally inserted in 2013, s.16G provides that the director general is responsible to the HSE directorate, as the HSE's governing body, for the performance of his or her functions, except where he or she is acting as chairperson of the HSE directorate. As amended by the 2014 Act, s.16G provides an additional exception by which the director general is required to report to the Minister for Health if he or she is of the view that the actions of the HSE are likely to lead to a breach of its budget limits, which is provided for in s.34A of the 2004 Act as inserted by s.12 of the 2014 Act, discussed below.

Section 6 of the 2014 Act amended s.28 of the 2004 Act (the definitions section for Pt 7 of the 2004 Act), which sets out the accountability framework for the HSE, to take account of further definitions which are required arising from new provisions inserted into the 2004 Act by the 2014 Act.

Section 7 of the 2014 Act inserted a new s.30A into the 2004 Act, which enables the Minister to determine a net budget for the HSE, and sets out the process for doing so. The Minister is required to notify the HSE of its budget no later than 21 days after the publication of the Estimates for the Public Services, more commonly known as the abridged Estimates volume, (the "AEV"). It was stated during the Oireachtas debates on the 2014 Act that, in practice, it is likely that the net determinations will be issued on the day the AEV is published or the following day. Section 30A also allows the Minister to adjust a net determination for the HSE in the course of the year. Sections 8 and 9 made consequential amendments to the service plan provisions in ss.31 and 32 of the 2004 Act, arising from the new Vote and budget setting arrangements inserted by the 2014 Act.

Section 10 of the 2014 Act inserted a complete replacement section for the existing s.33 of the 2004 Act, which requires the HSE to manage services in a manner that is in accordance with the approved service plan. Section 33 was expanded to require the HSE to manage the services within the net determination notified to it by the Minister. Section 33(2) reintroduced into the 2004 Act the concept of the "first charge principle." Under this principle, if the HSE exceeds its budget in one year, the deficit is a first charge against the following year's approved budget. If the HSE has a surplus, it would be allowed to carry over the surplus into the following year, subject to the approval of the Minister for Health and with the consent of the Minister for Public Expenditure and Reform. These constraints in the carry-over of a surplus are necessary to ensure compliance with the provisions of the Ministers and Secretaries (Amendment) Act 2013 (*Annual Review of Irish Law 2013*, pp.1 – 3), which put the principle of ministerial expenditure ceilings on a statutory basis.

Section 11 inserted two new sections, 33A and 33B, into the 2004 Act. Section 33A, referred to above, empowers the Minister for Health to issue grants to the HSE with the agreement of the Minister for Public Expenditure and Reform and, as already noted replaces s.5A of the 2004 Act with effect from 2015. Section 11 also inserted s.33B into the 2004 Act, and provides for a separate process for approving a capital plan and provides for the governance arrangements regarding the approval of such a plan.

Section 12 inserted two new sections, 34A and 34B, into the 2004 Act, in connection with the functions of the director general of the HSE. Section 34A gives the director general the statutory responsibility of ensuring that the HSE operates within its budget in respect of capital and non-capital expenditure. It also obliges the director general to notify the Minister if actions being undertaken by the HSE are likely to lead to its breaching its financial limits. Section 34B provides that the director general shall be accountable to the Oireachtas Committee of Public Accounts in respect of the HSE's annual financial statements and any other reports made by the Comptroller and Auditor General. This provision is required because s.40G of the 2004 Act, as inserted by the 2013 Act, which makes the director general the accounting officer of the HSE, was amended by s.13 of the 2014 Act (see immediately below) so that he or she ceases to be the accounting officer with effect from 1 January 2015. As noted, s.13 of the 2014 Act amended s.40G of the 2004 Act and made the HSE director general the accounting officer for the HSE for the years 2005 to 2014, but not after that. The effect was that the director general remained accountable for the appropriation accounts for 2005 to 2014, and that the HSE was required to produce appropriation accounts for 2014.

Functions of audit committee of HSE Section 14 of the 2014 Act amended s.40L of the 2004 Act, as inserted by the 2013 Act, which sets out the functions of the audit committee of the HSE. These functions relate to advising the director general and the directorate of the HSE on financial matters. Prior to the 2014 Act, s.40L(3)(b) reflected the statutory position of the director general of the HSE as being the accounting officer. The 2014 Act amended s.40L(3)(b) to delete this reference and replaced it with an obligation on the audit committee to advise on matters relating to the HSE's and the director general's obligations in respect of the implementation of the service plan in accordance with the Vote arrangements in the 2004 Act, as amended by the 2014 Act.

Transitional arrangements Part 3 of the 2014 Act (ss.15 – 16) contained transitional arrangements to enable the changeover from the pre-2014 Act system to the Vote arrangements in the 2004 Act, as amended by the 2014 Act. Section 15 provided that the HSE's Vote shall be abolished on 1 January 2015 and that funding will be arranged through the Vote of the Minister for Health in 2015. It also provided funds in the Vote of the Minister for Health for 2015; this was to enable the Department to provide grants to the HSE pending Dáil approval of the Minister's Vote. This provision ceased to have effect after the Dáil approved the Estimate for the Minister for Health for 2015. Section 16 inserted a new paragraph 20 into Sch.4 to the Valuation Act 2001 (the "2001 Act") to ensure that the buildings of the HSE remain exempt from rates.

HEALTH SERVICES ELIGIBILITY

Hospital in-patient charges Part 3 of the Health (Miscellaneous Provisions) Act 2014 (the "2014 Act"), which is discussed in general terms above under the heading "Health and Social Care Professionals Council," addressed an unintended lacuna in s.19 of the Health (Amendment) Act 2013 (the "2013 Act") (*Annual Review of Irish Law 2013*, pp.348 – 350). The 2013 Act had modernised the contributions regimes in a wide range of residential settings so as to better reflect current models of residential care service provision in the disability, mental health and care of older people sectors. It was noted during the Oireachtas debates on the 2014 Act that a specific problem had come to light during the implementation planning phase for the 2013 Act, which the 2014 Act rectified.

It was explained during the Oireachtas debates on the 2014 Act that under the national disability strategy and the Government's mental health strategy, *A Vision for Change* (2006), available at *www.hse.ie*, there had been an ongoing drive towards community-based living in the disability and mental health sectors. In line with this, the increasing trend, in particular in the disability sector, was for accommodation needs to be met by the agencies of the State, such as local authorities, that are responsible for addressing the accommodation needs of citizens generally. However, the 2013 Act, unintentionally, had omitted situations where service-users are maintained, although not accommodated, in specified settings by or on behalf of the HSE. The primary purpose of Pt 3 of the 2014 Act was, therefore, to ensure that affordable contributions towards ongoing daily living costs would apply to those maintained in such settings, subject to appropriate safeguards. For example, the level of contribution could be reduced to reflect the extent to which service-users met their accommodation or maintenance costs themselves.

INDIVIDUAL HEALTH IDENTIFIERS

Background to and purpose of individual health identifiers ("IHIs") The Health Identifiers Act 2014 (the "2014 Act") provided the legislative framework for individual health identifiers ("IHIs"), for patients and for health service providers for use across the health service, both public and private. The 2014 Act thus implemented a recommendation in the 2008 *Report of the Commission on Patient Safety and Quality Assurance* that provision be made for such health identifiers. This recommendation was followed by two papers published by the Health Information and Quality Authority (HIQA) in *Recommendations for Unique Health Identifiers for Patients* and *Recommendations for Health Identifiers for Health Care Practitioners and Organisations*. The fundamental purpose of IHIs is to improve patient safety by providing that the right information is associated with the right patient at the point of care; and IHIs also have a part to play in advancing the State's e-health agenda.

The Health Identifiers Act 2014 (Commencement) Order 2015 (S.I. No. 294 of 2015) provided that the following provisions of the 2014 Act came into effect on 13 July 2015: ss.1 – 6, 7(1), 8, 9, 10(1)(b) and (4), 11(6)(a) (insofar as it relates to the purpose of the performance by the Minister for Health of a function conferred on him or her by the 2014 Act), 21-23, and 25-34. This brought into effect those provisions that deal with the initial implementation stage of the 2014 Act, which will focus on the IHIs and the establishment of the National Register of Individual Health Identifiers.

Broadly, the 2014 Act provides that an IHI for patients is to be used by health service providers on their patient records and in relevant communications. A National Register of Individual Health Identifiers will be established containing the IHIs and other identifying particulars relating to the individual. These identifying details are set out in the 2014 Act, but it was emphasised during the Oireachtas debates on the 2014 Act that the legislation contained two important elements to protect the privacy of patients. First, an IHI will be a number which, in itself, will contain no personal data, and secondly, no clinical information may be contained in the National Register of IHIs. Equally, from the perspective of health care provision, a health service cannot be refused merely because an individual does not have an IHI or does not provide information to help assign an IHI.

The 2014 Act also provides that a National Register of Health Services Provider Identifiers will be established. Thus, health professionals, health care organisations and some employees will also have a unique identifier and must use their identifiers on their patient records and in relevant communications. This will clearly identify the person and organisation involved at each stage of care. The National Register of Health Services Provider Identifiers will contain the provider identifier, name, business address and other relevant details and will be publicly accessible. (As noted, at the time of writing, July 2015, this element of the 2014 Act had not yet been brought into force.)

The 2014 Act sets out how the registers may be developed initially ("seeded") and maintained. In the case of the IHI, this will involve using information already in the health care system or asking the patient to provide the information. The 2014 Act sets out who may access the national IHI register and also the processing of identifying details contained in the register. Access to the national IHI register is mainly for health service providers and other specified persons set out in the 2014 Act. The 2014 Act provides that the Minister for Health must put measures in place to help ensure that the national IHI register is accessed only for relevant purposes and by people who are permitted to access it; and the 2014 Act provides that it is an offence for a person to access the register inappropriately.

The 2014 Act also provides that prescribed health service providers in other EU Member States may be allowed to use the IHI and access the IHI register. This is subject in each case to a detailed agreement between the Minister for Health and the provider, and subject to the Minister having consulted with the Data Protection Commissioner.

"Specified persons" Section 2 of the 2014 Act contains important definitions, including "specified person," "authorised disclosee" and "relevant purpose." A "specified person" is a health service provider, such as a medical practitioner, or any of the eight bodies listed in Sch.2, which are: the Chief Inspector of Social Services, the Child and Family Agency, the Health Research Board, the Irish Blood Transfusion Service, the Health Products Regulatory Authority (previously, the Irish Medicines Board), the Mental Health Commission, the National Cancer Registry Board and the State Claims Agency. Specified persons may access the IHI register and process the IHI and other identifying data on it for a relevant purpose.

"Authorised disclosees" Authorised disclosees do not have access to the IHI register, but they are persons to whom a specified person or the Minister may disclose an IHI and other identifying particulars for a particular secondary purpose. The 14 authorised disclosees are listed in Sch.1 and are: the Opticians Board (Bord na Radharcmhastóirí, which in accordance with the Health (Miscellaneous Provisions) Act 2014, discussed above, was subsumed into CORU, the Health and Social Care Professionals Council); the Central Statistics Office; a coroner; the Dental Council; the Health Information and Quality Authority; the Health Insurance Authority; the Inspector of Mental Health Services; the Medical Council; the National Treatment Purchase Fund Board; the Nursing and Midwifery Board of Ireland; the Pharmaceutical Society of Ireland; the Pre-Hospital Emergency Care Council; a registration board established by or under the Health and Social Care Professionals Act 2005 (the "2005 Act"); and an undertaking authorised to operate a scheme of health or health-related insurance under the Health Insurance Act 1994 (the "1994 Act"). The Minister may, by Regulations, add to the list of authorised disclosees and of specified persons where doing so is in the public interest and after consultation with the Data Protection Commissioner.

"Relevant purpose" The IHI may only be used for a relevant purpose. A relevant purpose includes a "primary purpose" and a "secondary purpose." Section 2 of the 2014 Act defines a "primary purpose" as the present, past or future provision of a health service to an individual. Section 2 defines a "secondary purpose" as follows:

> (a) the promotion of patient safety, including clinical auditing and the investigation and reporting of patient safety incidents,
> (b) the identification or prevention of a threat to public health,
> (c) the management of health services, including—
> (i) the planning, monitoring, delivery, improvement, auditing and evaluation of health services,

(ii) the investigation and resolution of complaints relating to health services, and
(iii) the management of national health systems,
(d) the carrying out of health research that is the subject of a research ethics approval (or any cognate expression) under an enactment or European act prescribed for the purposes of this paragraph,
(e) the performance of any function conferred on a person under this Act or another enactment for which the processing of identifiers is necessary,
(f) the provision of a scheme of health or health-related insurance operated by an undertaking authorised to so do under the Health Insurance Act 1994, or
(g) any—
(i) processing of relevant information (individuals) required to protect or prevent injury or other damage to the health or safety of an individual,
(ii) processing of relevant information (individuals) required by or under an enactment, rule of law or equity or order of a court,
(iii) processing of relevant information (individuals) that is in accordance with the Data Protection Acts 1988 and 2003 and required for—
(I) the purposes of obtaining legal advice,
(II) the purposes of, or in the course of, legal proceedings, or
(III) the purposes of, or in the course of, alternative dispute resolution procedures agreed between a service provider and an individual as a means of resolving a dispute,
or
(iv) subject to section 3 (4) and (8) [of the 2014 Act], processing of relevant information (individuals) relating to health that is prescribed for the purposes of this subparagraph.

This definition had been subject to a number of additions as it proceeded through the Oireachtas, including the insertion of the reference to the identification or prevention of a threat to public health.

IHIs and national IHI register Part 2 of the 2014 Act (ss.5 – 12) deals with IHIs and the IHI register. Section 5 provides that the Minister may assign an IHI to a living individual, whether he or she is ordinarily resident in the State, to whom a health service is being, has been or may be provided. An IHI may also be assigned to a deceased individual where that person has died on or after the coming into operation of s.5 without having been assigned an IHI when alive. Section 5(2) provides, as already noted, that an IHI will not contain any personal data. Section 5 also provides that the assigning of an IHI to an individual is not to be regarded in any way as indicating, in and of itself, an entitlement to, or eligibility for, the provision of a health service for the individual. Section 5 also provides that the Minister may put in place measures to assist in enabling an individual to have his or her IHI made known to him or her. The IHI may also, where appropriate, be made known to another person acting on behalf of the individual, for example, for reasons of the individual's age, capacity or if the individual has died.

Section 6 provides for the Minister to establish and maintain a national register of individual health identifiers, the IHI register. This IHI register will contain identifying particulars of each individual who has been assigned an IHI in so far as the identifying details are known. The identifying details are the fundamental details that allow an individual to be uniquely identified for the purposes of the IHI. The only information that can be contained in the IHI register for an individual is his or her IHI and these identifying particulars. The identifying details include the individual's name, address, date of birth and personal public service number. There is also provision for a signature and a photograph. Any addition to the list of identifying particulars can only be made by the Minister following consultation with the Data Protection Commissioner.

Sections 7 to 9 provide for developing and maintaining the accuracy of the national IHI register. Section 7 allows the Minister to use identifying particulars he or she has, or the HSE has, to develop and populate the IHI register in order that people are not asked for information they have already given. Section 7 provides that a health services provider may also ask a person for identifying particulars where the provider is, has or is proposing to provide a health service for the person. The health services provider must forward the information and any update to the Minister.

Section 8 allows another Minister of the Government to provide the Minister for Health with an individual's other identifying particulars but only where such provision is made solely for the purposes of establishing and maintaining the accuracy of the register. Section 9 provides for the General Registrar of Births, Marriages and Deaths (An tArd-Chláraitheoir) to provide information for the Minister for Health relevant to the Minister's functions under the 2014 Act.

Section 10 of the 2014 Act provides for access to the IHI register. Only the Minister, specified persons and persons covered by a section 12 agreement (see below) can access the national IHI register. This access can only be for a relevant purpose, with the Minister also being able to access the national IHI register for the purpose of performing a function conferred on him or her by the 2014 Act or another enactment. The Minister must put in place measures to enable the register to be accessed by specified persons for relevant purposes. The Minister must make the IHI register otherwise inaccessible.

Section 11 provides for the use of the IHI and information on the IHI register by health service providers, other specified persons and the Minister. A health service provider must request an individual to provide his or her IHI when the provider is providing a health service for him or her. Section 11 also takes account of patients who because of age or capacity may need the assistance of others in this regard. Where the health service provider is given the IHI or is able to establish it from the register from information provided by the individual, the provider must associate it with the patient's medical record, and use it in relevant communications with his or her own provider identifier as set out in s.20 of the 2014 Act. This would include, for example, where a GP writes a patient referral letter to a hospital consultant. Section 11(4) provides that no person can be refused a health service solely because he or she does not have an IHI or refuses to provide it. Section 11 also makes provision for disclosing an IHI and identifying particulars to an authorised disclosee for a particular secondary purpose.

Section 12 provides for the use of the IHI and access to the national IHI register in another EU Member State where a person receives health services in that other Member State. This deals with cases where the HSE has made an arrangement with a service provider outside the State to provide services for a significant volume of patients. Section 12 provides that the Minister may enter into an agreement with health service providers in another EU Member State, referred to as an "equivalent person," for the purposes of allowing that provider to obtain and use the IHI and to access the national IHI register. The Minister must consult the Data Protection Commissioner before entering into any such agreement.

Health services provider identifiers and national register of health services providers Part 3 of the 2014 Act (ss.13 – 20) deals with health services provider identifiers and the national register of health services providers. Section 13 provides for the assignment of health services provider identifiers. As noted above, health service providers are health practitioners, for example, doctors, dentists and nurses and also relevant bodies listed in Sch.2. Relevant employees and agents of health practitioners and relevant bodies are also included in the definition of "health service provider" and the Minister is empowered to facilitate a phased approach in assigning identifiers to these employees and agents through a process of prescribing, in Regulations, classes of employees and agents in this regard.

Section 14 provides for the establishment and maintenance of a National Register of Health Services Provider Identifiers. Sections 15 to 17 provide for the development and maintenance of the register; and, for this purpose, professional regulatory bodies, relevant bodies and health practitioners are required to provide specified information to the Minister. Section 18 empowers the Minister to use relevant information he, she or the HSE already has for the purpose of assigning a health services provider identifier and establishing and maintaining the register.

Section 19 provides for access to the National Register of Health Services Provider Identifiers. The provider register will be accessible to the public because it will be a register of organisations and persons involved in providing health services and the only information on the register identifying individuals will relate to them solely in their capacity as health services providers.

Section 20 provides for the use of the health services provider identifier and the National Register of Health Services Provider Identifiers. Health practitioners who are already required under other legislation to use the registration number given to them by their professional regulatory body can instead continue to use that number in the provision of the health service concerned.

Offences Part 4 of the 2014 Act (ss.21 – 25) provides for offences under the 2014 Act. Section 21 sets out the offences relating to assignment of individual health identifiers. Sections 22 and 23 provide for offences relating to accessing the National Register of Individual Health Identifiers and for an offence relating to processing an individual health identifier. Section 24 provides for offences relating to the assignment of health services provider identifiers. Section 25 provides for offences by bodies corporate.

Delegation of Ministerial functions Part 5 of the 2014 Act (comprising s.26 only) provides for the delegation of certain functions of the Minister. This is in recognition of the day-to-day operational realities associated with assigning the identifiers and maintaining the registers. Section 26 provides that the Government may, by order, delegate to the HSE any or all of the Minister's functions under the Act, except excluded functions. Excluded functions are the Minister's power to make Regulations and entering into section 12 agreements. Section 26 also provides that any function delegated to the HSE continues to be vested concurrently in the Minister, and the delegation does not remove or derogate from the responsibility of the Minister to Dáil Éireann or as a member of the Government for the performance of any functions that are delegated. For the list of delegated functions, see the Health Identifiers Act 2014 (Delegation of Relevant Functions) Order 2015 (S.I. No. 383 of 2015).

Data protection Part 6 of the 2014 Act (comprising s.27 only) deals with the relationship between the 2014 Act and the Data Protection Acts 1988 and 2003. Section 27(1) provides that a living individual's IHI will be considered personal data under the Data Protection Acts when held by the Minister, or by a specified person or by the HSE when acting in a s.26 delegated capacity under the 2014 Act. Section 27(2) provides that this shall not be construed to prevent a living individual's IHI held by any other person from being personal data in accordance with the Data Protection Acts. Section 27(3) contains an additional safeguard under the 2014 Act for information on the register relating to a deceased individual, who would not otherwise be protected under the Data Protection Acts, which are otherwise concerned with the protection of the personal data of living identifiable people. Section 27(3) thus provides that s.2(1)(d) and s.2C of the Data Protection Act 1988 (the "1988 Act"), which deal with security arrangements for personal data, will apply to the information in the IHI register in respect of a deceased individual as those sections apply to a living individual.

Investigations, data exchange and professional regulation Part 7 of the 2014 Act (ss. 28 – 39) deals with various miscellaneous matters. Section 28 provides that the Minister may arrange for investigations to be carried out in respect of the operation of any provision of the 2014 Act. Section 29 empowers the Minister to enter into an agreement with another person to carry out certain activities, such as specialist IT support services. Section 30 empowers the Minister to carry out measures to verify any information provided to him or her under the 2014 Act, or to establish the efficient and effective operation of the registers.

Section 31 provides for data exchange agreements between the Minister and other relevant persons specifying the procedures to be followed by each party with respect to the provision of personal data between them. The Minister must consult the Data Protection Commissioner in regard to a data exchange agreement. To underline the privacy considerations that run through the 2014 Act, s.32 provides that any processing of personal data by the Minister or the HSE, if designated under s.26, shall go no further than is reasonably necessary for the performance of those functions. Section 33 provides for the Minister's power to specify the form of documents required for the purposes of the 2014 Act. Section 34 empowers the

Minister to extend the period for providing information to him or her as required under the 2014 Act.

Sections 35 to 39 provide for the amendment of relevant legislation concerning health professionals regulatory bodies to provide for the Minister, or the HSE if delegated this function, to make complaints to the appropriate professional regulatory body where the professional concerned has failed to comply with a provision of the 2014 Act. For example, this could arise if the professional failed to comply with obligations under the 2014 Act by failing to attach the patient's IHI and his or her provider identifier to a patient record. Sections 35 to 39 therefore amended the following Acts for this purpose: the Dentists Act 1985; the Health and Social Care Professionals Act 2005; the Pharmacy Act 2007; the Medical Practitioners Act 2007; and the Nurses and Midwives Act 2011.

MISUSE OF DRUGS

Cannabis liquid on prescription The Misuse of Drugs (Amendment) Regulations 2014 (the "2014 Regulations") (S.I. No. 323 of 2014), made under the Misuse of Drugs Act 1977 (the "1977 Act"), amended the Misuse of Drugs Regulations 1988 (the "1988 Regulations") (S.I. No. 328 of 1988) in order to provide for authorised medicinal products containing a liquid extract of cannabis having a specified composition and presentation to be prescribed, supplied and possessed for the treatment of patients. They also removed the handwriting requirements in relation to certain details on prescriptions for controlled drugs specified in the Schedule to the Misuse of Drugs (Supervision of Prescription and Supply of Methadone) Regulations 1998 (S.I. No. 225 of 1998). The 2014 Regulations came into force on 11 July 2014. Complementing these, the Misuse of Drugs (Designation) (Amendment) Order 2014 (S.I. No. 324 of 2014), also made under the 1977 Act, amended the Misuse of Drugs (Designation) Order 1998 (S.I. No. 69 of 1998) by retaining cannabis in Sch.1 to the 1998 Order, while removing from the scope of the Order authorised medicinal products containing a liquid extract of cannabis having a specified composition and presentation. These 2014 Regulations also came into force on 11 July 2014.

NURSING HOMES SUPPORT SCHEME

Transferred assets Section 6 of the Health (General Practitioner Service) Act 2014 (the "2014 Act"), which is discussed generally above under the heading "General Practitioner Service," amended the Nursing Homes Support Scheme Act 2009 (the "2009 Act") (*Annual Review of Irish Law 2009*, pp.499 – 500) in order to put beyond doubt that assets which are transferred after an application for the scheme is made also come within the definition of "transferred assets." This was intended to prevent a situation arising where an applicant could transfer assets immediately after an application for State support is made on the basis of an argument that such asset transfer is not definitively captured by the definition of transferred assets in Sch.1 to the 2009 Act. The nursing homes support scheme is predicated on the principle that applicants must contribute according to their means. The 2009 Act provides that assets transferred within the five years prior to applying for the scheme are taken into account in the financial assessment. The amendment made by the 2014 Act does not affect a person's right to sell assets for full market value. Rather, it is intended to prevent people from depriving themselves of assets for the purposes of the financial assessment. If a participant in the scheme were to transfer assets immediately after an application for State support is made, or at any point subsequent to that, the pre-2014 definition meant that it might be possible that the asset could be excluded from a financial review. The amendment made to the 2009 Act by s.6 of the 2014 Act was intended to address that.

PATIENTS' RIGHTS

Patients' cross-border rights in EU health care The European Union (Application of Patients' Rights in Cross-Border Healthcare) Regulations 2014 (the "2014 Regulations") (S.I. No. 203 of 2014) implemented the three key provisions of Directive 2011/24/EU, the 2011 Directive on Patients' Rights in Cross-Border Healthcare (the "2011 Directive"). The 2014 Regulations came into force on 1 June 2014 (the 2011 Directive having come into force in October 2013).

The 2011 Directive sought to put into concrete legislation the case law of the EU Court of Justice that emerged in 1998 in the wake of the *Decker* and *Kohl* cases, Case C-120/95, *Decker v Caisse de Maladie des Employes Prives* [1998] E.C.R. I-1831 and Case C-158/96, *Kohll v Union des Caisses de Maladie*, [1998] E.C.R. I-1931. Subsequent case law included the joined cases *Geraets-Smits and Peerbooms*, Case C-157/99 *Geraets-Smits v Stichting Ziekenfonds* and *Peerbooms v Stichting CZ-Groepzorgverzekeringen* [2001] E.C.R. I-5473 and Case C-372/04, *R (Watts) v Bedford Primary Care Trust and Secretary of State for Health* [2006] E.C.R. 1-4325.

The first of the three key elements of the 2011 Directive, as implemented in the 2014 Regulations, was to provide for cooperation between healthcare systems, which involves the development of National Contact Points ("NCPs"), in Ireland, the Health Service Executive (HSE). The NCPs are, in essence, national information desks, which are intended to support patients in their reimbursement procedures or enable them to make well-informed choices among the possible solutions offered by other Member States healthcare systems, through European Reference Networks ("ERNs"). The ERNs aim to facilitate access to diagnosis and healthcare services in connection with highly specialised medical treatment, especially for patients affected by rare diseases.

Regulation 6 of the 2014 Regulations requires that the HSE shall, in so far as it considers it is necessary or desirable for the purposes of enabling patients resident in Ireland to exercise their rights in relation to access to cross-border healthcare provided in another EU Member State, to ensure that information about each of the following is available to, or accessible by, patients resident in the State and health professionals: (a) the rights and entitlements of patients resident in the State to receive healthcare in another Member State; (b) the procedures for accessing and determining those rights and entitlements; (c) the procedures for appeal and redress if patients consider that their rights have not been respected; (d) the terms and conditions for reimbursement of costs; and (e) the contact details of national contact points in other Member States.

Regulation 5 of the 2014 Regulations requires that the HSE shall, in so far as it considers it is necessary or desirable for the purposes of enabling patients resident in another EU Member State to exercise their rights in relation to access to cross-border healthcare provided in the State, ensure that information about each of the following is available or accessible: (a) healthcare providers; (b) patients' rights; (c) complaints procedures and methods of seeking remedies; and (d) legal and administrative options available to settle disputes, including in the event of harm arising from the provision of healthcare. Regulation 5 also provides that the HSE shall, in so far as it considers it is necessary or desirable for the purposes of enabling patients resident in another EU Member State to exercise their rights in relation to access to cross-border healthcare in the State, ensure that, on request, information about each of the following is made available: (a) a specific healthcare provider's right to provide services; (b) any restrictions on a specific healthcare provider's right to provide services; (c) standards and guidelines on quality and safety; (d) provisions on the supervision and assessment of healthcare providers; (e) healthcare providers who are subject to the standards mentioned in sub-paragraph (c); and (f) accessibility of hospitals for persons with disabilities.

The second element of the 2011 Directive implemented in the 2014 Regulations is the reimbursement of the costs of cross-border healthcare, which under reg.10 is to be done by the HSE.

The third element of the 2011 Directive implemented in the 2014 Regulations concerns a prior authorisation process for cross-border healthcare, that is, where certain forms of treatment are subject to prior approval by the relevant health care provider. Regulation 12 of the 2014 Regulations provides that this is also to be done by the HSE.

The Regulations, and the 2011 Directive, reflect the growing recognition of the role of patients in the health care setting, which in Ireland was fully explored in the 2008 *Report of the Commission on Patient Safety and Quality Assurance* (the "Madden Report"). The move from a health professional – especially doctor-centered approach (the "medical model") to a patient-centered approach (the "social model") has also for many years been recognised through the development of case law on informed consent in tortious medical negligence claims: see McMahon and Binchy, *Law of Torts*, 4th edn (Dublin: Bloomsbury, 2013). The wide-ranging recommendations in the Madden Report have not yet been implemented (but see the Health Identifiers Act 2014, discussed above). To some extent, the literature on the role of patients mirrors the debate on the role of victims in the criminal justice system, in respect of which it is notable that Directive 2012/29/EU, the 2012 Directive on Victims of Crime (the "2012 Directive"), is also likely to have significant effects in Irish criminal law and procedure when the Criminal Justice (Victims of Crime) Bill 2015 (which is intended to implement the 2012 Directive) is enacted.

SUNBEDS AND SKIN CANCER

Background to need for regulation of sunbeds The principal purpose of the Public Health (Sunbeds) Act 2014 (the "2014 Act") is to protect children from the risk of skin cancer by prohibiting the use of sunbeds on sunbed premises by those under 18 years of age and to regulate the use of sunbeds by those over 18 years of age. The overall aim of the 2014 Act is to contribute to the long-term goal of reducing skin cancer rates in the State. The 2014 Act was modeled on similar legislation enacted in the UK: the Public Health etc. (Scotland) Act 2008 (the

"2008 Act"), the Sunbeds (Regulation) Act 2010 (England and Wales) (the "2010 Act") and the Sunbeds Act (Northern Ireland) 2011 (the "2011 Act"). The vast majority of the 2014 Act's provisions (with the sole exception of s.14, concerning prescribed training for staff) came into force between July 2014 and March 2015: see the Public Health (Sunbeds) Act 2014 (Commencement) Order 2014 (S.I. No. 299 of 2014) and the Public Health (Sunbeds) Act 2014 (Commencement) Order 2015 (S.I. No. 37 of 2015).

In 2006, the European Commission's Scientific Committee on Consumer Products (the "SCCP") issued an opinion warning of the risks to health of sunbeds; noting that the risk of melanoma seemed particularly high when sunbeds were used at a young age. The SCCP recommended that those under 18 years should not use Ultra-Violet (UV) tanning devices. The EU adopted the opinion and the European Commission had called on Member States to ensure an appropriate use of sunbeds.

It was noted during the Oireachtas debates on the 2014 Act that in 2009 the World Health Organization's International Agency for Research on Cancer (a recognised leading expert scientific body charged with providing evidence-based science to underpin global cancer control policies) had reclassified UV-emitting tanning devices from a group 2A carcinogen (one that is probably carcinogenic to humans) to a group 1 carcinogen (one that is carcinogenic to humans). Also in 2009, the State's Chief Medical Officer (CMO) conducted a review of the international literature on health effects associated with the use of ultra-violet emitting tanning devices. The CMO found that the medical evidence justified a complete prohibition on the use of sunbeds by children up to 18 years of age, based on the significantly increased risks associated with exposure to ultra-violet radiation in early years. The CMO recommended that the issue of the increased risk posed by UV radiation for certain subgroups of the adult population could be dealt with by way of regulation and awareness raising.

It was also pointed out during the Oireachtas debates on the 2014 Act that skin cancer is the most common type of cancer in Ireland and that the number of new cases of melanoma diagnosed in Ireland has been steadily increasing since the National Cancer Registry began publishing data in 1994. The National Cancer Registry had stated that there were more than 10,000 cases of skin cancer in Ireland in 2011, and that the incidence of cancer in Ireland was projected to double by 2040. Based on 2014 trends, the number of women diagnosed with melanoma was projected to increase by a factor of between 93 per cent and 175 per cent in the period up to 2040 and, in the same period, the increase for men could be of the order of between 134 per cent and 327 per cent. As of 2014, there were approximately 150 fatalities per year from melanoma, with approximately 7,000 people living with this disease in Ireland. Data from the HSE indicated that the cost of treating skin cancer ranged from €6,000 to €10,000 per patient, depending on the complexity of the disease. New oncology drugs, such as ipilimumab, had become available and it was effective in a number of cases, however, in 2014, prices cost between €50,000 and €80,000 to treat each patient with it. In the years leading up to 2014, between 60 and 80 patients had presented with such advanced melanomas each year.

It was noted that for most people, the main source of exposure to UV radiation is the sun. UV radiation is responsible for up to 90 per cent of skin cancers and most UV damage is caused during childhood and adolescence. A child's skin is most sensitive to UV radiation and up to 80 per cent of a person's total life-time

UV exposure is accumulated in childhood. In addition, many people are exposed to high doses of UV radiation through artificial sources. Sunbeds and sunlamps used for tanning purposes are the main source of deliberate exposure to artificial UV radiation. All forms of such radiation contribute to skin cancer.

Ban on selling or hiring sunbed to person under 18 Against this background, s.4 of the 2014 Act provides (along the same lines as the 2008, 2010 and 2011 Acts enacted in the UK) that it is an offence to sell or hire a sunbed to a person aged under the age of 18 years, and s.5 of the 2014 Act provides that it is an offence to allow a person under 18 to use a sunbed on a sunbed premises. Section 6 of the 2014 Act prohibits unsupervised use of sunbeds in commercial premises.

Section 3(2) of the 2014 Act provides for an exemption to allow the use of ultraviolet radiation for the medical treatment of specific skin conditions such as dermatitis and psoriasis in both children and adults. This exemption is limited to treatment involving phototherapy provided under the supervision or direction of a relevant registered medical specialist such as a dermatologist. The treatment must be provided by a health care establishment.

Section 7 of the 2014 Act sets out mandatory requirements for protective eyewear, because eyes are particularly vulnerable to damage from ultraviolet radiation exposure. Section 8 of the 2014 Act also sets out certain hygiene requirements for sunbeds and sunbed premises.

Restrictions on marketing practices and health claims for sunbeds To protect public health, s.9 of the 2014 Act prohibits certain marketing practices such as allowing a customer who rents a sunbed for four weeks to get one week free, or offering "early-bird" deals. Prior to the enactment of the 2014 Act these offers had been commonplace and had incentivised clients to opt for a greater number of sessions than they might have originally intended. The detailed prohibitions are set out in the Public Health (Sunbeds) (Prohibition of Certain Marketing Practices) Regulations 2015 (S.I. No. 51 of 2015).

Similarly, s.10 of the 2014 Act prohibits the use of health claims other than those that may be prescribed by way of Regulations. Prior to the enactment of the 2014 Act, it had been common for sunbed operators to claim certain health benefits for sunbed use, including an increase in the production of vitamin D as a result of sunbed use. It was pointed out during the Oireachtas debates on the 2014 Act that the World Health Organization had commented that "incidental exposure to the sun, combined with normal dietary intake of vitamin D, provides adequate vitamin D for a healthy body throughout the year."

Section 11 of the 2014 Act also requires sunbed operators to display warning signs on sunbed premises and social media sites. The mandatory warning signs will inform the public of the health risks associated with sunbed use. The operator of a sunbed business will be required to provide information on the risks of sunbed use to potential sunbed users. This information will be required to be in written form. The operator must also ensure the potential client has read and considered the information and has signed the form before using the sunbed. See the Public Health (Sunbeds) (Warning Signs) Regulations 2015 (S.I. No. 53 of 2015).

Section 13 of the 2014 Act requires all sunbed operators, including sellers and hirers, to notify the Health Service Executive (HSE) stating they provide sunbeds for use, sale or hire. See the Public Health (Sunbeds) (Notification) Regulations 2015 (S.I. No. 52 of 2015).

Training for sunbed operators Section 14 of the 2014 Act provides that the Minister for Health may specify by Regulations the training required for those supervising the operation, sale or hire of sunbeds in accordance with the National Framework of Qualifications maintained by Quality and Qualifications Ireland ("QQI") under the Qualifications and Quality Assurance (Education and Training) Act 2012 (the "2012 Act") (*Annual Review of Irish Law 2012*, pp.293 – 297). The prescribed training will cover issues such as the risks of sunbed use, proper screening for potentially exposure-limiting conditions and emergency procedures in case of overexposure to ultraviolet radiation. As indicated above, at the time of writing (July 2015) s.14 of the 2014 Act was the only section in the 2014 Act that had not yet been brought into force.

Sunbed health information Section 15 of the 2014 Act provides that the Minister shall prescribe information on the health effects and such other information relating to the use of sunbeds as the Minister may consider appropriate. See the Public Health (Sunbeds) (Health Information) Regulations 2015 (S.I. No. 50 of 2015) as amended by the Public Health (Sunbeds) (Health Information) (Amendment) Regulations 2015 (S.I. No. 168 of 2015).

Inspections, investigations and offences Sections 16 to 19 of the 2014 Act empower HSE environmental health officers to carry out inspections and investigations to verify compliance with the 2014 Act. Section 20 of the 2014 Act provides for a regime for fixed payment notices (usually referred to as on-the-spot fines) for certain offences in order to allow HSE environmental health officers to deal quickly and effectively with non-compliance with the 2014 Act. See the Public Health (Sunbeds) (Fixed Payment Notice) Regulations 2015 (S.I. No. 60 of 2015). Section 21 provides that the HSE may also publish a sunbed non-compliance list that will, in effect, name and shame offenders.

Section 22 of the 2014 Act provides that, on conviction for an offence under the 2014 Act, a Class A fine (that is, a fine of up to €5,000) and/or imprisonment of up to 12 months may be imposed by the District Court. The 2014 Act did not create any indictable offences (this is also in line with the comparable UK Acts of 2008, 2010 and 2011).

TOBACCO SMOKING IN VEHICLES

Background to ban on smoking in vehicles with children The Protection of Children's Health (Tobacco Smoke in Mechanically Propelled Vehicles) Act 2014 (the "2014 Act") created an offence of smoking in a vehicle while children are present in the vehicle. It was noted during the Oireachtas debates on the 2014 Act that it began its legislative life as a Private Members Bill, the Protection of Children's Health from Tobacco Smoke Bill 2012 (the "2012 Bill"), sponsored by Senators Crown, van Turnhout and Daly. In June 2012, the Government approved the principle of prohibiting smoking in cars with children present and for the drafting of amendments to the Private Members' Bill. The Department of Health worked in consultation with the Senators, the Attorney General's Office, the Department of Justice and Equality, the Department of Transport, Tourism and Sport, and An Garda Síochána on the relevant amendments, which also involved changing its title. At the time of writing (July 2015), the 2014 Act had not yet been brought into force. It is notable that a similar ban in England and Wales was provided for by means of Regulations under s.5 of the English Health Act 2006 (the "2006 Act"), which were ultimately made in 2015, the Smoke-free (Private Vehicles) Regulations 2015 (the "2015 Regulations"), in force from 1 October 2015.

The 2014 Act prohibits smoking in vehicles (which are defined to have the same meaning as in the Road Traffic Act 1961 (the "1961 Act")) where children are present and it will be enforced by An Garda Síochána. It was noted during the Oireachtas debates on the 2014 Act that environmental tobacco smoke is a carcinogen and contains the same cancer-causing substances and toxic agents that are inhaled by the smoker and that there is no safe level of exposure to second-hand smoke. In children, exposure to second-hand tobacco smoke is a recognised risk factor for the development of asthmatic symptoms and increased risk of other illnesses such as pneumonia, bronchitis and middle ear infections. Exposure to tobacco smoke is particularly harmful in enclosed spaces, such as cars.

Prohibition on smoking in vehicles with children Section 2 of the 2014 Act sets out the prohibition on smoking tobacco products in mechanically propelled vehicles in which a child is present. It specifies that a person who smokes a tobacco product in a vehicle in which a child is present shall be guilty of an offence. This also applies in situations where the smoker himself or herself is under 18 years of age and is in the presence of another child. Where this offence is committed by someone who is not the driver, the driver shall also be guilty of an offence. Section 2 also contains a number of defences to a charge. A defence exists where the person smoking reasonably believed that others present in the vehicle were over 18 years of age. There are also defences for the driver. One defence is that the driver was unable to stop the other person from smoking because he or she did not wish to take any action which might compromise the safety of the passengers. Another defence is where it can be shown that the driver made all reasonable efforts to stop the other person smoking. Section 2 also provides that where a member of An Garda Síochána is of the view that a person present is a child, this presumption remains until the contrary is shown and proved.

Enforcement and offences Section 3 sets out the powers of An Garda Síochána under the 2014 Act. Where a member of An Garda Síochána believes that a person is smoking in a vehicle with a child present, he or she may ask the driver to stop the car, and demand the name and address of any person who may be committing an offence. Where a person fails to stop the car, or to give his or her name and address, or provides false information, he or she shall be guilty of an offence.

Section 4 provides for the issuing of a fixed charge notice in connection with offences under the 2014 Act. It specifies that a fixed charge notice may be served on a person where a Garda has grounds to believe that he or she has committed an offence under the 2014 Act. These provisions are based on the comparable fixed charge notice system in the Road Traffic Acts.

Section 5 provides that the Minister for Health may make Regulations for prescribed matters in the 2014 Act, for example, the form to be used for issuing a fixed charge notice under the Act, and the prescribed amount to be paid under the notice.

Section 6 provides that a person who is guilty of an offence under the 2014 Act shall be liable on summary conviction to a class D fine (currently under the Fines Act 2010 (the "2010 Act"), a fine not exceeding €1,000). This includes an offence of refusing to stop the vehicle, refusing to give a name or address, or giving false information.

Information Law and the Ombudsman

ESTELLE FELDMAN
Trinity College, Dublin

This chapter of the *Annual Review* considers significant issues relating to the Information Commissioner, to the Commissioner for Environmental Information, and to the Ombudsman, each of which are independent regulatory bodies with distinct roles and responsibilities. The Ombudsman has a senior function. Issues concerning the statutory sectoral ombudsmen, with the exception of the Pensions Ombudsman, are also considered. In addition, there is a section noting statutes and statutory instruments affecting information disclosure in general.

PUBLIC SERVICE NOT ACTING IN SERVICE OF PUBLIC

In 2014 some positives are recorded in the co-operation afforded to the principal regulators by most of the bodies they have been investigating on foot of complaints. Nevertheless, once again in this chapter we look at events during the calendar year, some of which are rooted in failures of common sense, inadequate control systems, and ineptitude in central government and public bodies as revealed in the process of legitimate oversight.

Lack of Appeal and Independent Oversight An area of public administration that continues to elude administrative oversight is the immigration and asylum services of the Department of Justice and Equality. The following is noted by the Ombudsman in *Passports for Irish-born children of non-EEA parents* (see analysis below in this chapter), an investigation under s.4 of the Ombudsman Act 1980 into the complex difficulties experienced by foreign nationals legitimately working in Ireland who had applied for passports for their Irish-born children. It notes at pp.36–37:

> "The actions of the immigration authorities in these matters are not under scrutiny in this investigation. They cannot be examined by this Office, for the reasons outlined [earlier]. It follows that this Office cannot make any findings or recommendations to the Department of Justice in relation to its administrative systems. As has been noted many times since the Office of the Ombudsman was established in 1984, Ireland is almost unique among countries with a public service Ombudsman in having the State's interactions with its immigrant non-EEA workers and asylum-seekers excluded from jurisdiction. This is exacerbated in these particular cases by the fact that the passport legislation allows for a right of appeal against decisions made on other grounds but does not allow for a right of appeal where the basis for the refusal relates to citizenship. Furthermore, there is

> no legal right to appeal decisions on citizenship made under the Immigration Act, 2004 either. Effectively, there is no independent oversight (other than by way of recourse to judicial review) of public administration in this area.
>
> In the absence of rights of appeal in any of these areas, it is important that the [Department of Jobs, Enterprise and Innovation] and [the Department of Foreign Affairs and Trade] work more closely with [the Department of Justice and Equality] to ensure that non-national workers in the State are treated fairly and are not disadvantaged or treated in a discriminatory manner by the agencies with which they interact."

We repeat our regular question, by what logic is any aspect of a public body excluded from an oversight regime the purpose of which is to ensure good administration?

Anomaly in Administration: Failure to Apply One Standard In the course of another of the Ombudsman's investigations, also analysed below in this chapter, disparities between different regions were discovered as to how the Health Service Executive (HSE) administers the statutory long-term illness (LTI) scheme. The Ombudsman's investigation *Local Rules for National Schemes Inequities in the administration of the Long Term Illness Card Scheme*, January 2014, p.16 notes:

> "This is the second investigation in recent times to uncover practises [sic] in one part of the country which are at variance with the rest. Given that one of the aims in establishing the HSE, more than seven years ago, was to promote consistency of approach and of standards, it is of great concern that such variation of approach could happen and could continue unchecked until this Office is alerted to the matter by a complainant and only then does it become an issue for the HSE." [footnote omitted]

Anomaly in Administration: All Assistance Withdrawn The first of the Ombudsman's investigations as referenced by the above quotation had been published in 2012, *Motorised Transport Grant*, which dealt inter alia with illegalities in the administration by the Department of Health and Children of travel subsidy schemes for disabled persons with mobility needs. Once the anomalies in administering the scheme had been publicly highlighted, instead of acting in an even-handed manner with all requiring this assistance, the scheme was cancelled in relation to the matters that had been investigated. The HSE initially acted in a similar fashion in respect of the LTI scheme. As described below in this chapter, the LTI scheme is now administered in a uniform manner. However, the Government's commitment of 11 June 2013 to introduce new statutory provisions in relation to financial supports for disabled persons with mobility needs remains unfulfilled. This is despite the fact that the Government had established an inter-departmental group, chaired by the Department of the Taoiseach, to develop proposals for a new scheme. The Ombudsman's observations from his Annual Report 2014 are presented below in this chapter. In the meantime, vulnerable older people who must suffer restrictions in their activities without the aid of the mobility allowance have been without the grants for over two years. The hope held out by promised leadership of the Department of the Taoiseach has been dashed by inactivity.

Incomprehensible Legislation The Department of Public Expenditure and Reform was responsible for two major items of legislation in 2014. The Protected Disclosures Act 2014 is considered in the Whistleblower Protection chapter of this Annual Review. The Freedom of Information Act 2014 (the "FOI Act 2014") is considered below in this chapter. Neither statute is written in plain language, and in many respects each is opaque, if not incomprehensible. By way of example the following clause from s.34(11) of the FOI Act 2014 has been selected at random:

> A Minister of the Government shall, in each year after the year in which this section comes into operation, cause to be prepared and furnished to the Commissioner a report in writing specifying the number of certificates issued by him or her in the preceding year and the provisions of section 32 or 33, as may be appropriate, by virtue of which, pursuant to section 13, the grant of the FOI request concerned was refused, or, pursuant to section 21, a decision to uphold a decision to refuse to grant, the FOI request concerned was made.

Moreover, inexplicably and inexcusably, even though most of the clauses are equivalent to a cut and paste from the pre-existing legislation namely the Freedom of Information Acts 1997–2003, the entire structure and section numbering system of the statute has been changed. For the foreseeable future this will add an immense burden to those who will have to navigate the Act, including the courts, since all of the legal precedents are based on the old numbering system. The FOI Act 2014 is discussed further below.

INFORMATION COMMISSIONER

Statutory references in this section continue to refer to the appropriate sections of the Freedom of Information Acts 1997 to 2003 unless otherwise stated. The freedom of information regime has been previously considered in *Annual Review of Irish Law 1997*, p.2 et seq. and in all editions of the *Annual Review of Irish Law* since 1999. In addition to hard copy, documents referred to may be found at the Information Commissioner's website *www.oic.gov.ie*. Since the Freedom of Information Act 1997 (the "FOI Act 1997") came into force, there have been three Information Commissioners, Mr Kevin Murphy (1997–2003), Ms Emily O'Reilly (2003–2013) and Mr. Peter Tyndall (2013 to date). As such, references to publications may refer to "he" or "she", depending on the date of publication. It may be noted that, in 2007, the separate role of Commissioner for Environmental Information was assigned to the office-holder.

FREEDOM OF INFORMATION ACT 2014

The Freedom of Information Act 2014 (No. 30 of 2014) (the "FOI Act 2014") commenced on 14 October 2014. According to the Explanatory Memorandum (the "Memo") at p.1, accompanying the Freedom of Information Bill 2013 Bill (No. 89 of 2013) the purpose of the legislation is:

> "to provide for the commitments in relation to freedom of information contained in the Programme for Government:—

- by removing the main substantive restrictions in access to official information introduced in 2003,
- extending FOI to all public bodies,
- providing a framework for the extension of FOI to non-public bodies in receipt of significant funding from the Exchequer,
- the legislation also provides an opportunity for a necessary consolidation modernisation and updating of the legislation."

The Memo noted, at p.1, the following in respect of the restrictions contained in the Freedom of Information (Amendment) Act 2003:

> "Amendments made in 2003 involving six sections of the FOI Act 1997 have been characterised as representing a significant curtailment of the principle of the right to access to records provided for in the original Freedom of Information legislation. This Bill essentially reverses those substantive restrictions. These relate mainly to the treatment of Government Records (Section 28), restrictions in relation to records under the deliberative process exemption (Section 29) and exemptions for categories of records relating to security, defence, international relations and Northern Ireland (Section 33). Details are contained in the individual section notes below."

The Information Commissioner (the "Commissioner"), in the *Annual Report of the Information Commissioner 2014*, at p.10, welcomed the Act:

> "The new Act contains a number of welcome improvements to the FOI regime, including a provision for FOI to apply to all public bodies unless specifically exempt. This means that a number of public bodies that were previously excluded from FOI are now under the scope of the legislation. Bodies such as An Garda Síochána, NAMA, the NTMA and the Central Bank are now included. My Office has been calling for the extension of FOI to such bodies for a number of years. The Act also provides for future application to non-public bodies that are in receipt of significant funding by the Exchequer and I look forward to developments in this area. In addition, when a new public body is established, it will automatically be subject to the provisions of the Act, although the Minister may make an order to specifically exclude certain bodies, in whole or in part."

Fees With regard to the fees regime the Commissioner in the *Annual Report of the Information Commissioner 2014*, at p.10, noted:

> "I am particularly pleased that the requirement to pay a fee for making a request has been removed and that there has been a substantial reduction in the fee payable for applications made to my Office for review of decisions made by FOI bodies. The fees applicable to search and retrieval costs have also undergone a significant overhaul. The new Act provides that fees will apply only where the preparation time for a request exceeds 5 hours, and the fees will be capped at €500."

The amounts of fees and charges have been prescribed by the Freedom of Information Act 2014 (Fees) Regulations 2014 (S.I. No. 484 of 2014). Under the original 1997 regime, fees were prescribed for search and retrieval but it was not until the 2003 amendments that charges were in force for initial requests (s.7), internal review (s.14), and for appeals to the Information Commissioner (s.34). Whereas the Commissioner noted the removal of fees for an initial request, now s.12 of 2014 Act, he failed to mention that a fee remains for a request for internal review, now s.21 of the 2014 Act, as well as for review by the Commissioner, now s.22 of 2014 Act. In this respect, consider the complicated language of s.4 of S.I. No. 484 of 2014 which renders both the Act and the Regulations as good as impenetrable:

> 4. (1) Subject to paragraph (3)(a), a fee of €30.00 is prescribed for the purposes of paragraph (a)(i) of section 27(13), in respect of a person who makes an application under section 21, not being
> (a) an application in relation to a decision under section 9 or 10, or
> (b) an application in relation to a decision to charge a fee or deposit, or a fee or deposit of a particular amount, under section 27.

Moreover, the Freedom of Information Act 2014 (Fees)(No. 2) Regulations 2014 (S.I. No. 531 of 2014) prescribe a reduced fee for medical card holders which is surely an acknowledgement by the Minister for Public Expenditure and Reform, the responsible Minister, that these fees can be oppressive. By retaining any fee for a review application, internal or by the Commissioner, the Government's promise to restore the pre-2003 status quo is breached.

Complex and Abstruse Legislation It can be seen from the references to fees that, as indicated in the introductory paragraph to this chapter, the legislation can be incomprehensible. This author comments on the FOI Act 1997 in "Openness, Transparency and Accountability" in *Freedom of Information: Law and Practice* (Dublin: FirstLaw, 2006) pp.177–255, pp.179–180 as follows:

> "[the] Long Title of the Freedom of Information Act describes it as: 'An Act to enable members of the public to obtain access, to the greatest extent possible consistent with the public interest and the right to privacy, to information in the possession of public bodies'. These words should be very familiar to anybody involved with the Act. However, how many are aware that this appears to be the only Act on the Statute Book that is directed at 'members of the public' and that has as its express object 'to enable members of the public'? Consequently, anyone who is unfamiliar with the Act might reasonably expect it to be in fairly clear and simple terms, even, perhaps, in a form that is accessible and transparent to those who are not experienced administrative and constitutional lawyers."

The change of structure, and most particularly the different numbering of sections in the 2014 Act only adds another layer of density to legislation that is already opaque and difficult to navigate.

False Information On the other hand, the FOI Central Policy Unit, Department of Public Expenditure and Reform has published a *Code of Practice for Freedom of Information for Public Bodies* (the "Code") under s.48 of the FOI Act 2014, available from *www.foi.gov*, last accessed 25 July 2015, which, with one major caveat, is in clear and in plain language. It reflects a practice of some government bodies to write codes and guidance notes as they would wish the legislation to be rather than ensuring that the legislation itself is written in an easily understood format. As always, it must be stressed that a code of practice/guidance notes are not the law.

The caveat in relation to the Code refers to the false impression contained at "Section 9 Engagement with the Office of the Information Commissioner" at pp.35–36. It states:

> "*Future role of the OIC*
> The OIC should consider identifying the public bodies which perform well, i.e. demonstrate a good understanding of the Act through effective use of exemptions, consideration of public interest and harm test factors, provision of well-argued cases and timely and good decisions which stand up under review. The OIC should showcase these on its website to promote good practice across the public sector.
>
> The OIC might contribute where appropriate, to the development of guidance notes by the CPU [Central Policy Unit]. As is the case in these other jurisdictions, this could be achieved without compromising the independence of the Information Commissioner in decision-making on appeal cases.
>
> In other jurisdictions, the OICs have a critical role in providing guidance to public bodies on the functioning of the Act. Serious consideration should be given by the OIC to adopting such a role as well as contributing, where appropriate, to the development of guidance notes by the CPU. As is the case in these other jurisdictions, this could be achieved without compromising the independence of the Information Commissioner in decision-making on appeal cases."

These comments tend to deny the extraordinary work in championing FOI of the late Kevin Murphy, first Information Commissioner, and his successors, Emily O'Reilly, and now, Peter Tyndall. The facts as contained in the Annual Reports of the Information Commissioner and as reported and analysed in this chapter of the *Annual Review of Irish Law* from 1999 to date give the lie to such a suggestion. Any difficulties the Commissioner may have had in being heard by the CPU or any other department of government has not been because of a lack of effort on the part of the Commissioner. It suffices to quote once again from Kevin Murphy's "Reflections" first published in Feldman (ed.), *Freedom of Information: Law and Practice* (Dublin: FirstLaw, 2006), pp.xi to xix and repeated in *Annual Review of Irish Law 2012*, pp.337–338:

> "The essence of a modern democracy is that there should be open, frank and informed discussion about all aspects of governance and that it should take place in a calm and professional manner especially in the Dáil and Seanad which have the sole and exclusive power of making laws for the State. When I decided to give a written commentary to each Deputy and Senator on how the proposed amendments to the FOI Act would affect the practical

> application and operation of certain provisions of the Act, I was accused, by the Minister for Justice, Equality and Law Reform, Michael McDowell, of getting involved in an area which was the preserve of the politicians. My commentary was, however, strictly in accordance with the provisions of Section 39 of the FOI Act. And when the then Minister for Finance Charlie McCreevy, who had responsibility for the amending legislation, was queried by a journalist about the need for rushing it through, his response was that the Government had made up its mind, did not intend to change it and, if people did not like it, they could show what they thought at the next general election. Shades of old Stormont and majority rule! To cap it all, a month after I had retired, a €150 fee was introduced for appeals to the Information Commissioner; an action likely to encourage public bodies to incline towards refusal rather than release and to discourage requesters from appealing even when their statutory right to information had been wrongly denied. As a result of this rather cynical action, my successor, Emily O' Reilly, has had to work in an environment in which public bodies are much more antagonistic to FOI. Emily continues to highlight the adverse effects of this excessive fee and of the other amendments to the Act."

The balance of this chapter section deals with matters under the Freedom of Information Acts 1997–2003 and, thus, refers to sections of the legislation with that numbering system. Where appropriate reference is made to the equivalent section of the 2014 Act as per the following e.g. appeal to the Information Commissioner is s.34 (now s.22 of the FOI Act 2014).

SUPREME AND HIGH COURT APPEALS

Section 42 of the 1997 Act (now s.24 of the FOI Act 2014) governs the right to take an appeal from a decision of the Information Commissioner on a point of law to the High Court. Such decisions issue consequent on a s.34 review (now s.22 of the FOI Act 2014) (*Annual Review of Irish Law 1999*, p.351 et seq.). The statutory barrier preventing appeals from the High Court to the Supreme Court was withdrawn by the Freedom of Information (Amendment) Act 2003 (*Annual Review of Irish Law 2003*, p.391). There were no s.42 Supreme Court judgments in 2014; one *ex-tempore* judgment and three written High Court appeal judgments are considered below. As in previous years we note other judgments in which a request under the Freedom of Information Act appears to have had a significant impact on proceedings.

Liberal Access in a Non-restrictive Manner The body of law now established has resulted in the High Court consistently referring to Fennelly J.'s judgment, albeit dissenting, in *Sheedy v Information Commissioner* [2005] 2 I.R. 272 (see *Annual Review of Irish Law 2005*, p.431 et seq.) and the finding of McKechnie J. in the High Court in *Deely v Information Commissioner* [2001] 3 I.R. 439 (see *Annual Review of Irish Law 2001*, p.405 et seq.) regarding the nature of the appeal to the High Court. It is no longer remarkable to refer to judgments as upholding the principles of the widest possible access to publicly held information, in light of Fennelly J.'s description of the Act:

"The passing of the Freedom of Information Act 1997 constituted a legislative development of major importance. By it, the Oireachtas took a considered and deliberate step which dramatically alters the administrative assumptions and culture of centuries. It replaces the presumption of secrecy with one of openness. It is designed to open up the workings of government and administration to scrutiny. It is not designed simply to satisfy the appetite of the media for stories. It is for the benefit of every citizen. It lets light in to the offices and filing cabinets of our rulers. The principle of free access to publicly held information is part of a world-wide trend."

Appeal Dismissed There was one *ex-tempore* judgment in 2014. Eagar J. relied on Ord.130 of the Rules of the Superior Courts which requires that a ground of appeal and point of law be stated. As no point of law had been identified by the applicant he dismissed the appeal in relation to Office of the Information Commissioner case *Mr X and the Health Service Executive* Case 120129 (4 April 2014) (see *Annual Report of the Information Commissioner 2014*, pp.38–39).

Discontinued review outside jurisdiction Section 34(9)(a) of the FOI Act 1997 states:

The Commissioner may refuse to grant an application under subsection (2) or discontinue a review under this section if he or she is or becomes of the opinion that—

(i) the application aforesaid or the application to which the review relates ("the application") is frivolous or vexatious.

The immediate background to *Kelly v The Information Commissioner* [2014] IEHC 479 was an appeal to the Commissioner based on seven applications to University College Dublin (UCD). These were deemed to be frivolous and vexatious and part of a long-running dispute between the appellant and UCD. As noted at para.64, the respondent had considered it pertinent that she had previously found the appellant's use of the Act to be an abuse of process:

"'I note, for example, that in 2003 I discontinued 12 separate review applications made by you to my Office on the ground that the applications or the applications to which the reviews related were frivolous or vexatious. In 2006, I refused to accept a further 26 separate review applications relating to Trinity College Dublin for the same reason. Similarly, in 2011, I discontinued 30 further review applications relating, yet again, to Trinity College Dublin.'"

It had earlier been noted in the judgment that as part of ongoing litigation between the appellant and UCD there were a number of written superior court judgments including an order from Hedigan J. of 29 January 2013 prohibiting the applicant from issuing further proceedings, at paras 11 and 12.

O'Malley J. held at para.98 that the court had no jurisdiction to entertain the appeal against the Commissioner's decision to discontinue her review as an appeal to the court is limited to a point of law arising from the decision of the Commissioner following a review as per s.42(1) (appeal to the High Court on a point of law). She described the Commissioner's statutory discretion as follows:

> "Pursuant to s.34(9)(a), if he or she 'is or *becomes* of the opinion' (emphasis added) that the application for a review, or the application to which the review relates, is frivolous or vexatious, he or she may then refuse to grant the application under subs.(2) -that is, an application for a review–or may discontinue a review. There are therefore two possible scenarios here. The Commissioner can decide, whether before or after receipt of submissions as to a 'proposed review', not to embark upon a review or may, having embarked upon it, decide to discontinue it for the reason stated. I agree with the appellant that one can only 'discontinue' a process if it is in being, but that is not the end of the matter.
>
> 'Following the review' the Commissioner may decide to affirm, vary or annul (and, in the latter case, effectively re-decide) the decision in question–s.34(2)(b). This, in my view, has to mean 'following the completion of a full process of review'. It would not, I believe, be open to the Commissioner to make any of these decisions on the basis of a partly completed process."

In the instant case there had been no decision and, thus, there could be no point of law arising for appeal.

Interregnum between Incumbents Inter alia the appellant had questioned, at para.74, the authority of the senior investigator in the respondent's office "in circumstances where the appeal had been lodged at a time when no Information Commissioner was in place and there was thus no person empowered to delegate this function to him." O'Malley J. dismissed this argument at para.77:

> "It is not the law that the staff of public service bodies or agencies necessarily lose the legal right to continue to do their jobs and to make the decisions that they were previously authorised to make every time there is an interregnum in the position of head of such agency. Such a rule would, inter alia, mean that any such body would present an open goal for litigants during such periods."

The Commissioner has reported that this case has been appealed to the Court of Appeal (see *Annual Report of the Information Commissioner 2014*, p.42).

Judicial Independence The appointment of a retired High Court judge by the Minister for Health to conduct a review, and the essential characteristic of judicial independence thereby inherent in the function carried out by that judge, is fundamental to the decision in *Minister for Health v Information Commissioner* [2014] IEHC 231. O'Neill J. set aside the decision of the Information Commissioner and held that records in the physical possession of the Department of Health for safe-keeping purposes did not amount to legal possession under s.2(5) of the FOI Act 1997. Section 2(5)(a) of that Act states "a reference to records held by a public body includes a reference to records under the control of the body."

The background to the appeal, as described at para.3 of the judgment, had been the appointment in 2010 of Smyth J. to conduct a review:

> "to examine and recommend to the Minister for Health and Children whether a further investigation into the procedures and practices operating at Our Lady of Lourdes Hospital, Drogheda, during the period 1964 to 1995, to protect patients from sexual abuse while undergoing treatment or care at the hospital and to deal with allegations of sexual abuse against Mr. Michael Shine, would be likely to provide additional information or insight which would be of significant public benefit."

Following the completion of the review, the judgment describes at para.4 how Smyth J. had delivered a number of boxes of documents and records to the offices of the Department with a letter attached detailing the basis on which these documents were being handed over:

> "Four boxes contained information which Mr Justice Smyth had received from the Department. One box contained records of the review which had been maintained by Ms. Mary Reynolds. It was stated that 'the only circumstance in which this may be opened, on notice to us, is if it is necessary for the verification of information relating to recoupment of personal expenses by individuals.' A box labelled 'G' was unaffected by any restrictions. The final category of boxes, which contains the documents relevant to these proceedings, contained a total of six boxes labelled A-F. In relation to these documents Mr. Justice Smyth stated that they:
>
> > '... may not be disclosed or opened in any circumstances except by court Order for Discovery, of which I wish to be notified. These contain information received by me on the assurance given by me to each participant that their communications with the review would be treated as confidential. In the absence of such assurance I am satisfied that many individuals would not have participated in the Review'."

The Department, inter alia, submitted to the court at para.29 that:

> "*Mr. Justice Smyth performed a quasi-judicial function and was specifically appointed to carry out the review by virtue of his independence and his status as a retired High Court Judge* [emphasis added]. At no point has he ceded control of the relevant documents to the Department, and his letter of 23rd September outlining the terms on which the documents were delivered to the Department, makes it expressly clear that the opposite is what is anticipated."

In upholding the appeal O'Neill J. was satisfied that it would give rise to absurd and wholly unintended consequences, albeit in rare circumstances, that mere lawful possession of a document was sufficient to make that document amenable to disclosure under the FOI Act 1997, on the basis that the document was "held" by the public body within the meaning of s.6(1) (right of access to record held by a public body). O'Neill J. says at paras 41–42:

"In my opinion, for a document to be "held" within the meaning of s.6(1) of the 1997 Act, it must be either lawfully created by the public body in question or lawfully provided to that public body or lawfully obtained by the public body, in connection with the functions or business of that public body and the document must not be subject to any prior legal prohibition affecting it's [sic] disclosure. For example, the use of documents discovered in legal proceedings can only be used in those proceeding and for no other purpose. Thus, documents which came into the possession of a public body by was [sic] of discovery in legal proceeding, could not subsequently be released by the public body in response to a request under the 1997 Act, unless the party in the legal proceedings, who had discovered the document consented to the disclosure under the 1997 Act.

Part III of the 1997Act containing ss.19 to 32 inclusive, deals with exempt records. Whilst s.32 creates an exemption from disclosure for certain records, the disclosure of which is prohibited by any enactment other than a provision specified in Column (3) of the Third Schedule to the Act, any legal prohibition on disclosure in private law, or generally, in common law, unless it falls within one of the exemptions set out in ss. 19 to 32, is not the subject of an exemption under Part III of the 1997 Act. The Act of 1997 does not make any express provision by way of a saver in respect of binding legal prohibition from disclosure, such as by expressly subjecting such legal prohibitions to the provisions of the Act in the future, and perhaps a saver for those existing on the coming into effect of the Act. In the absence of any provision in the Act in this regard, and to ensure harmony between the Act and other co-existing binding legal prohibition on disclosure, not contemplated in the Act, it is necessary, in my opinion, to construe the term 'held' in s.6(1) in the manner set out above."

The independence of Smyth J., a judge of the High Court, was undoubtedly decisive in arriving at the decision. The nature of his appointment and function was described by O'Neill J. at paras 43–46 as follows:

"[43] .. It is to be observed that the 'Drogheda Review' was clearly a convenient name or label attached to the function or process carried out by Mr. Justice Smyth, and as such, the 'Drogheda Review' did not have a distinct legal personality. The legal personality which was the 'Drogheda Review' was Mr. Justice Smyth.

44. The task undertaken by Mr. Justice Smyth was, as set out in the Terms of Reference for the review. The reason Mr. Justice Smyth was asked to carry out this review was because he was a retired judge of the High Court and therefore the primary and essential characteristic of the review was that it was to be an exercise conducted in an entirely independent and impartial way. Independent in this context means independent of all those who had an interest in the outcome of the review, and that included the Minister for Health, the Department of Health, staff members of Our Lady of Lourdes Hospital in Drogheda and former patients of that hospital and any interest groups formed by those patients.

45. Without that essential characteristic of independence, it is highly

> *probable that this review would not have been commissioned in the first place.* [emphasis added]
>
> 46. For Mr. Justice Smyth to conduct the review in this way, it was essential that he had unfettered control over every aspect of the review, including the documents to be procured and examined by him, the persons from whom statements were to be taken or with whom interviews were to be conducted, the terms upon which this would take place, including the manner in which the material assembled would be disposed of at the conclusion of the review. In this respect, one must bear in mind the highly sensitive nature of the subject matter of the review and the probable difficulties of gaining the necessary degree of cooperation from all those who could contribute to the review in circumstances where Mr. Justice Smyth did not have available to him the normal judicial powers of compellability."

O'Neill J.continued at para.49 by considering the nature of the relationship between Smyth J. and either the Minister or the Department of Health. This was not an employment relationship, nor that of an office holder, nor that of a principal and agent.

> "It is easy to say what the relationship between Mr. Justice Smyth and the Department was not, and in that respect, I am quite satisfied that whilst in a general sense, it could be said that Mr. Justice Smyth was providing a service in consideration of the payment of an agreed fee, the provision of this service cannot be considered as falling within the terms of s.6(9) because the application of s.6(9) in the circumstances would be wholly inconsistent with the independent nature of the function discharged by Mr. Justice Smyth."

Regarding the nature of the documents at issue, the judge commented at paras 50–51:

> "At issue in these proceedings is a transcript of a conversation or interview between Mr. Justice Smyth and the first notice party. In his letter of 23rd September 2010, and his subsequent letter of 5th July, 2012, Mr Justice Smyth sets out two reasons as to why a transcript of this interview is included amongst the boxes of material in respect of which there is to be no disclosure in any circumstances except by court order for discovery. His first reason in this regard was based upon an assurance of confidentiality given to all participants that their communications with the review would be treated as confidential, without which, Mr. Justice Smyth was satisfied, many individuals would not have participated in the review. Secondly, as outlined in his letter of 5th July 2012, the transcript of these interviews, and specifically, the first named notice party's, was brought into existence so as to avoid the necessity of Mr. Justice Smyth having to laboriously take a handwritten note of the conversation as it was taking place, thereby impeding the flow of the interview and perhaps inhibiting the interview by an excessively formalistic approach. Mr. Justice Smyth asserts that the transcript was his note of the interview. Mr. Justice Smyth states in this letter that these transcripts were prepared exclusively for his own use, that

> it was made clear to all of the participants that this was the position and that they would not be made available to anybody else.
>
> 51. No party to the proceedings has ever challenged these statements which are exhibits in the affidavit of Derek McCormack, and hence, evidence in these proceedings."

With regard to who owned and controlled the records at issue, O'Neill J. noted at para.52 that the Department itself vehemently asserted that it does not.

> "The Minister commissioned the Drogheda Review and did so on a basis which constituted Mr. Justice Smyth as the person carrying out the review, as entirely independent of the Department and the Minister. It would seem to me to be wholly inconsistent with the status of Mr. Justice Smyth in this regard, for the Department to, at the same time, claim that it either had a proprietorial interest or was entitled to exercise legal control over the material that was brought into existence by Mr. Justice Smyth it the conduct of the review. I am quite satisfied that the Minister or the Department is not the legal owner of these records, nor is there any basis upon which it could legitimately assert any form of control over these documents or records so that it could, against any other party, assert a legal entitlement to them, resulting in these documents being 'held' by the Department for the purposes of the Act of 1997."

O'Neill J. concluded at para.57:

> "As Mr. Justice Smyth was entitled to impose these terms and conditions, and as the Department accepted into their custody this document on those terms, unless Mr. Justice Smyth agrees otherwise, the Department is bound by those terms and lawfully prohibited from any disclosure, save as excepted by Mr. Justice Smyth."

Inadequate Inquiry by Commissioner *Westwood Club v Information Commissioner* [2014] IEHC 375 was a successful appeal against the decision of the Commissioner upholding the refusal of Bray Town Council, a notice party to the proceedings, to grant access to the appellant to any records held by the Council concerning Bray Swimming Pool and Sports Leisure Centre Ltd. known as Shoreline. Shoreline had been set up by Bray Town Council to operate leisure facilities and included a number of members of the Town Council on its Board. Over €10 million in funding was provided to Shoreline by way of a loan from the notice party. The leisure centre was built on the notice party's land and occupied by Shoreline originally without any lease and subsequently a lease was granted to Shoreline at an uneconomic rent, at paras 2–3.

The appellant's request for access to the financial records of Shoreline for 2008 and 2009 had been refused by Wicklow County Council on the basis that the records belonged to the company. In appealing this refusal to the Commissioner the appellant's submission noted that the notice party had built the facility at a cost of approximately €10.5 million and that the completed pool was then transferred to Shoreline. Further, as Bray Town Council owned 100 per cent of the share capital of Shoreline and as three of the directors of Shoreline were employees of the Council it was implausible for the Council to assert that it did not have records of Shoreline just because Shoreline had legal independence.

As part of the preliminary investigation the potential records being sought were divided into (a) the records of Shoreline; and (b) any records held by the Town Council in its capacity as a shareholder, a division which Cross J. found useful and followed, at para.14. He noted at para.27 that the respondent had accepted the arguments that the Council did not control the company or have any role in its day to day operation and that any records held by the company could not be deemed to be held by the Council further to s.2(5)(a) of the FOI Act.

With regard to records held by the Town Council in its capacity as a shareholder, the respondent relied on s.27, which protects commercially sensitive information, and applying the public interest test under s.27(3) found that it weighed in favour of withholding the records. Cross J. found that in relying on s.27 the notice party had failed to specify how the documents, if disclosed, could prejudice the financial position of the notice party. Moreover, the respondent had not properly inquired into the claim of potential detriment. He found at para.70 that the information as furnished by the notice party to the respondent and ultimately accepted by the respondent amounted "to little more than a restating of the Act and listing of the documents in saying that these documents were commercially sensitive etc."

Although finding error in relation to this first test under s.27, Cross J. accepted at para.81 the respondent's approach to the public interest test when she had stated "[in]sofar as there is a public interest in the release of commercially sensitive information regarding a limited company that is not subject to the FOI Act, I am satisfied that this has been adequately met by the various requirements of company legislation.".

Cross J. then considered the documents held by Shoreline and whether the notice party controlled Shoreline. He accepted the realistic point made by the respondent that she had no power to conduct "exhaustive investigation" into how a private company, which is being set up in accordance with company law, is operated in practice. Nevertheless, he found at para.95 that the respondent had not adequately considered all relevant matters in relation to the issue of control and indeed that some matters were not considered at all and some matters were given erroneous consideration. He continued at paras 96–98:

> "What was not considered was that the Notice Party provided a loan to Shoreline in a sum in excess of €10m. This was referred to erroneously by the Respondent as a 'payment of grant monies. The accounts of the company clearly referred to the fact that it has this debt to the Notice Party and clearly a company that is dependent upon the goodwill of the Notice Party might well be deemed to be controlled by that Notice Party. Clearly, this is an issue that ought to have been considered. The respondent gave no consideration at all to this issue and in fact, seems to have misconstrued this vast loan and debt which remains on Shoreline's books as being the payment of 'grant money'.
>
> Whatever about the day to day activities of Shoreline as long as they proceed to conduct the swimming pool and leisure facilities, I have no doubt that if the directors of Shoreline in their independent capacity deemed it

appropriate to change the swimming pool to a casino that the Notice Party would not be likely to approve of such a change and would be in a position, due to the loan, to prevent it if they so wished. I find that the Notice Party must be said to control Shoreline and indeed the conclusion to the contrary is irrational within the meaning of the O'Keeffe decisions on judicial review and the failure to even consider the issue is an error of law which must and did effect the final conclusion of the respondent.

In addition, the Respondent did not comment or take into account the fact that Shoreline was in possession of the property under a lease (which only came into existence a considerable length of time after the construction of the pool) which is not a commercially viable one. In other words, if the commercial relationship of two arms lengths corporations were to apply and an economic rent were to be charged, I am satisfied that Shoreline would in all probability not be able to meet such rent and would be insolvent."

The final point decided by Cross J. related to the burden of proof. He noted that all parties had accepted that the burden of proof lay in favour of disclosure and that the notice party at all times had carried the burden of demonstrating why the documents should not be released. He commented further that save in one significant matter, the respondent had at all times clearly accepted that that was the case, at paras 100–101. However, in the preliminary decision of the investigator the appellant had been informed erroneously that the onus lay on it to demonstrate why the record should be released. Cross J. observed at paras 104–105:

> "The decision of the Respondent did not refer to this shift in the onus of proof to the Appellant and whereas the language of the decision of the Respondent might well lead one who is reading that decision on its own to conclude that the Respondent at all times accepted that it was incumbent upon the notice party to demonstrate why the documents should not be released. I have, however, formed the view that the failure of the Respondent to repudiate the legally erroneous statement in the preliminary view (that it was now encumbent upon the Appellant to show why the documents should be released etc.) and indeed the incorporation of the reasoning of the preliminary decision maker into the final decision without such a repudiation, has fatally undermined the final decision itself. This error in the preliminary view is a significant error in the process of the decision making and the decision itself is tainted by that error.
>
> The final decision rests upon the preliminary view and this clearly and expressly requires the applicant to prove something that the applicant never is required to prove."

Of itself, this last error might not have resulted in upholding the appeal. In summary, Cross J. held at para.108 that the following were material errors by the respondent:

> "(a) in its failure to properly analyse the issue of confidentiality;
> (b) in its failure to properly analyse the issue of the control; and
> (c) in its reliance upon its preliminary view that was clearly tainted by illegality."

Non-FOI Appeal Cases *Decisive Evidence Obtained by FOI Request* In *B v Minister for Social Protection* [2014] IEHC 18 Barrett J. noted at para.9 that the applicant's solicitors had "utilised the freedom of information legislation to undertake some research into the decision-making process that pertains within the Department for Social Protection. This has yielded some statistical evidence that is of relevance to this application." Barrett J. said at para.21 that this evidence showed that "deciding officers within the Department of Social Protection do not just inform themselves fully as to the views of the medical assessors but, at least in the case of the initial deciding officer in B.'s case, appear invariably to conform with same, or at least did so in 3,806 out of 3,806 cases." This indicated that there was an impermissible fettering of discretion.

Refusal to Give Reasons by the Department of Justice, Equality and Law Reform In *A.P. v Minister for Justice & Equality [No.2]* [2014] IEHC 241 McDermott J., in quashing the refusal to grant a certificate of naturalisation to the applicant, referred to a cryptic general reference to provisions of the FOI Act 1997 being insufficient justification to refuse reasons. The respondent, by letter, had clearly stated that he had decided not to disclose the reasons for his decision to the applicant having considered his obligations under the Freedom of Information Act, with particular reference to ss. 18, 24, 25 and 26. In fact, no request under the FOI Act 1997 had been made, see para.19.

Calling the FOI Act 1997 in aid when there had been no request seems so peculiar that the court's reasoning is quoted *in extenso*, at paras 22 and 29:

> "The invocation of the sections in the letter and their enclosure with it does not assist in any way an understanding of the decision-making process or the reasons for the decision. The reader is invited to deduce whether or which reasons were withheld and upon what basis: it may or may not be the security of the State, the defence of the State, international relations of the State, matters relating to Northern Ireland, records containing information conveyed to the Minister in confidence on the basis that it would be treated by the Minister as confidential, information the disclosure of which would be likely to prejudice the giving to the Minister of further similar information from the same person and/or that the disclosure of the information concerned would constitute a breach of a duty of confidence provided for by an agreement of some kind. In any event, these matters are relevant to the refusal by the Minister acting under a request pursuant to s.7 of the Act.
>
> This is without prejudice to the entitlement of the respondent when justifying the withholding of reasons as to why the conclusion as to good character was reached, to rely upon any appropriate privilege of the type asserted in this case. However, the court is satisfied that the utmost transparency is required in such cases and that the respondent should have firstly, informed the applicant that the reason for the refusal of the certificate was that he had failed to fulfil the condition of "good character" under s.15(1)(b) of [Irish Nationality and Citizenship Act 1956, as amended]. Secondly, if it was considered appropriate to refuse to give any further reasons, a justification should have been furnished in

that regard based on the fact that the recommendation was made on the basis of information which was properly the subject of privilege: a cryptic general reference to provisions of the Freedom of Information Act 1997 was, in this case, insufficient. In that way, the applicant would be furnished with some understanding at the earliest possible opportunity and to the extent practicable, of the reason for the refusal and/or the justification, if any, for the withholding of the basis for that reason. It is important in this respect that each case is considered on its own merits and that all relevant matters are considered by the respondent at the time the decision is made. The court does not consider it to be appropriate that the reason for refusal of the certificate and/or the reasons for refusing to disclose the underlying basis for that decision were revealed for the first time after the initiation of judicial review proceedings. The limited but important information ultimately disclosed in Mr. Kelly's affidavit ought properly to have been furnished in the letter of 30th April together with the material which was the subject of the disclosure order."

Stock Instruction to Make FOI Request Unacceptable In *Egan v Governor of Wheatfield Prison* [2014] IEHC 613 McDermott J. rejected the practice of prison governors to require prisoners' solicitors to make FOI requests when seeking information. By affidavit the Prison Governor stated, at para.26:

"'Solicitors have been informed, by various Prison Governors on numerous occasions in the past, that the proper procedure for requesting documents pertaining to a prisoner is to make such an application through a Freedom of Information request to the Department of Justice, Equality and Defence. Such applications are dealt with in accordance with the provisions of the Freedom of Information Act 1997, as amended, which provides a timeframe within which such request must be dealt with and also provides an appeals process should the applicant be dissatisfied with the response. Fahy, Bambury & McGeever Solicitors persist in seeking documents directly from the prison. No Freedom of Information request has ever been received in respect of the items sought.'"

The solicitors had been acting on instructions received from their client concerning a deprivation of important access visits to his partner and children and loss of communication rights by letter and telephone for a period of 56 days. McDermott J. stated at para.26 as follows:

"If this is thought to be an explanation for the failure to answer the correspondence, it is entirely inadequate. It suggests that the explanation offered by Assistant Chief Officer Hickey is only part of the story, and that it was believed that the solicitors correspondence did not warrant the courtesy of a reply because they were going to get the stock answer that the matter should be dealt with under the Freedom of Information Act. It is an entirely inappropriate response to solicitors who have been communicating with their client who was operating under the restriction described following a disciplinary hearing, in respect of which he was entitled to seek legal advice."

NON-DISCLOSURE ENACTMENTS

Section 32 of the FOI Act 2014 refers to non-disclosure enactments, i.e. provisions in other statutes or in statutory instruments for the mandatory refusal of access to certain records whose disclosure is prohibited, or whose non-disclosure is authorised. The terms of the FOI Act 2014 apply to these provisions only where such a provision is listed in Sch.3 to the Act; in this circumstance the disclosure of records is assessed solely by reference to the other provisions of the FOI Act 2014. There is provision for review every five years by the Joint Committee on Finance, Public Expenditure and Reform of the operation of any enactments that authorise or require the non-disclosure of records, to determine whether they should be amended or repealed or be added to Sch.3. Section 32 has been previously considered in previous editions of *Annual Review of Irish Law* since 2001.

Delayed Reviews In 2012 the then Information Commissioner, Emily O'Reilly, had reported that the last review by the Joint Committee had been conducted in 2005 and a further review was, at that stage, several years overdue. In his 2014 Annual Report the Commissioner expressed disappointment that the Joint Committee's report remained outstanding. He found it noteworthy:

> "that the Houses of the Oireachtas saw fit to ensure that the requirement to review non-disclosure provisions would remain in place in the FOI Act 2014. Under section 41, all Government Ministers must furnish to the Joint Committee a report on the enactments within their respective areas of governance that contain provisions prohibiting the disclosure or authorising the non-disclosure of certain records. Under section 41(6), the first such report must be furnished within 30 days after the fifth anniversary of the day on which the last report, under section 32 of the Act of 1997, was furnished and subsequent reports must be furnished every five years thereafter. ....
>
> ...Had the provisions of the Act been strictly adhered to, the Ministers would have submitted their fourth reports by 21 May 2014 for consideration by the Joint Committee. As things stand, the third reports remain to be considered."

As a consequence the Commissioner suggested at p.35 of the *Annual Report of the Information Commissioner 2014* that:

> "rather than require Ministers to submit the fourth round of reports that were due in 2014, it may be preferable for the Joint Committee to report on its deliberations of the reports currently before it and to require the Ministers to submit their next reports by 21 May 2019 and every five years thereafter."

STATUTORY CERTIFICATES AND NOTICES

Certificates of Exemption *Section 19* As amended by the Freedom of Information (Amendment) Act 2003, s.19 became a mandatory exemption for records relating to certain communications of Government and also sought to expand the definition of Government. The Secretary General to the Government is required to report the number of certificates of exemption issued to the Information Commissioner. This amendment was strongly criticised in the *Annual Review of Irish Law 2003*, pp.133 et seq., not merely for its restrictive nature, but also for the probability that it is unconstitutional. Section 19(1) was considered in *Minister for Education and Science v Information Commissioner* [2008] IEHC 279 analysed in the *Annual Review of Irish Law 2008*, pp.127–128 and 350–352. No section 19 certificates were issued in 2014.

Section 20 Section 20 as amended by the Freedom of Information (Amendment) Act 2003 gives discretionary power to Secretaries General of Government departments to certify that a record of whatever nature relates to a deliberative process of Government and is thus exempt from release. Such a certificate is not amenable to internal review and cannot be appealed to the Information Commissioner. Section 20(1)(c) states, inter alia, that such a certificate shall be final. Effectively, this means that the decision is entirely in the hands of the senior civil servant and that all Ministers, not just the departmental Minister, are bound by this unreviewable decision. In 2006, the first such certificate was issued by the Secretary General of the Department of Justice, Equality and Law Reform. The constitutional implications of issuing a section 20 certificate were discussed in the *Annual Review of Irish Law 2006*, pp.236–237. No new certificate was issued under this section in 2014.

Section 25 Under s.25(1) (now s.34(1) of the FOI Act 2014) a Government Minister may exempt a record from the application of the Freedom of Information Act (*Annual Review of Irish Law 2000*, p.275). The annual details regarding the issuing and renewal of section 25 certificates have been noted in previous editions of the *Annual Review of Irish Law*.

In 2014 three section 25 certificates were renewed by the Minister for Justice and Equality and will fall for review in 2016. Another three certificates will fall for review in 2015. One certificate was issued by the Minister under the equivalent provision, s.34 of the FOI Act 2014. The new certificate will fall for review in 2016 (see *Annual Report of the Information Commissioner 2014*, p.30.)

In 2014 the Minister for Foreign Affairs and Trade issued three certificates under s.34 of the FOI Act 2014. These certificates will fall for review in 2016 (see *Annual Report of the Information Commissioner 2014*, p.30).

Copies of the statutory notifications to the Information Commissioner are reproduced in Appendix I of the *Annual Report of the Information Commissioner 2014*.

Section 25 Review: Notice from Department of the Taoiseach Section 25(7)(a) required that the Taoiseach review the operation of s.25(1) at regular prescribed intervals, first described in *Annual Review of Irish Law 2005*, p.468. Section 34(7) (a)(i) of the FOI Act 2014 has replaced this section. Previously the Taoiseach's office certified the review to the Information Commissioner and a copy was reproduced in an Appendix to the Annual Report. No certificate is noted in the Annual Report 2014.

As noted in *Annual Review of Irish Law 2010,* pp.421–422, a section 25 certificate can be the subject of a discovery order (see *Minister for Justice, Equality and Law Reform v McGuigan* [2010] IEHC 398).

Statutory Notices of Non-compliance with Information Commissioner Requests *Section 35 Notice* Section 35 of the FOI Act 1997 (now s.23 of the FOI Act 2014) provides that, where a statement of reasons for refusing a request is inadequate, the Commissioner may require the head concerned to furnish a further statement. In 2014 one section 35 notice was issued to the National Maternity Hospital (NMH). This was the first such notice issued since 2004.

In the course of a review the Office considered that the reply that had issued to the requester had not adequately addressed the request and had not complied with the stated requirements of an adequate internal review decision. See the *Annual Report of the Information Commissioner*, p.16:

> "In the circumstances, my Office issued a formal section 35 notification directing NMH to furnish to the requester, and to my Office, a written statement of reasons why access to the records requested was being refused and of any findings on any material issues relevant to the decision. While I am disappointed that it was necessary to issue such a notification, it is even more disappointing that I was compelled to issue a section 37 notification in respect of the same case."

Section 37 Notice The FOI Act 1997 provides for the issue of a notification under s.37 (now s.45 of the FOI Act 2014) to the head of the public body concerned requiring the production of information and/or records. Section 37(2) of the FOI Act 1997 (now s.45(2) of the FOI Act 2014) states:

> 2) The Commissioner may for the purposes of such a review or investigation as aforesaid enter any premises occupied by a public body and there—
>
> (a) require any person found on the premises to furnish him or her with such information in the possession of the person as he or she may reasonably require for the purposes aforesaid and to make available to him or her any record in his or her power or control that, in the opinion of the Commissioner, is relevant to those purposes, and
>
> (b) examine and take copies of, or of extracts from, any record made available to him or her as aforesaid or found on the premises.

Nine section 37 notices were served in 2014 and for the first time since the inception of the Office the Information Commissioner entered premises in accordance with s.37(2).

In his Annual Report, the Commissioner expressed disappointment noting that nine section 37 notices is a small number relative to the number of engagements between his Office and public bodies. Nevertheless, he was concerned to note a consistent pattern of non-compliance by some public bodies with their obligations under the FOI Act. He continued in the *Annual Report of the Information Commissioner 2014*, at p.13:

> "The public bodies in receipt of section 37 notices in 2014 are the Irish Greyhound Board (three notices), University College Dublin (two), Cork County Council (one), Tipperary County Council (one), the Department of Justice and Equality (one) and the National Maternity Hospital (one).
>
> It is a matter of some concern that four of the bodies in receipt of section 37 notices in 2014 were also the recipients of such notices in 2013. These are University College Dublin, the National Maternity Hospital, Cork County Council, and the Irish Greyhound Board. In fact, both University College Dublin and the National Maternity Hospital also featured in the 2012 Annual Report as recipients of section 37 notices."

University College Dublin (UCD) Access had been sought to records associated with two separate applications for review in December 2013. As the records had not been provided, the Office issued two notices under s.37 to the President of UCD and asked for the records for both reviews to be forwarded by 25 February 2014. The *Annual Report of the Information Commissioner 2014*, p.13 notes: "The notice letters were acknowledged but neither set of records was received. Consequently, on 28 March 2014, the Director General of my Office wrote again to the President of UCD and the records were eventually submitted in early April."

National Maternity Hospital (NMH) In his Annual Report for 2013 the Commissioner noted that the NMH had taken measures to resolve the matter of delays, see *Annual Report of the Information Commissioner 2013*, pp.11–13. The Commissioner expressed his frustration that a s.37 notice was again required during 2014 and that the NMH was also the recipient of a s.35 notice, see *Annual Report of the Information Commissioner 2014*, p.14.

Cork County Council The Commissioner expressed his frustration in relation to Cork County Council in the following terms in the *Annual Report of the Information Commissioner 2014*, p.14:

> "My Office has noted examples of poor practice by Cork County Council in the processing of some FOI requests and in their dealings with my Office. In one case, the Council did not provide either the decision making records or the subject records to my Office in a timely manner. In that same case, my Office decided to issue a section 37 notice in April 2014 following an unsuccessful attempt to obtain further information deemed relevant to the review. The Council acknowledged receipt of the notice and one week later a further acknowledgement was received which explained that the matter was only then being considered by staff of the Council, seven weeks after the initial request for information had issued. My Office eventually received a response to the request three months after it had been made.
>
> I am aware of other cases where the Council failed to adhere to statutory timeframes when processing FOI requests. While section 37 notices did not issue in those cases, it seem to me that there may be underlying issues

> concerning the attention afforded by the Council to the FOI regime. It remains a fact that the administration of FOI is a statutory function that should be afforded as much weight as any other statutory function. Indeed, it is noteworthy that the Code of Practice issued by the Department of Public Expenditure and Reform describes FOI as '...a core function of the work of public bodies'. I intend to ask my staff to visit the Council's Offices during the year to discuss its administration of the FOI process."

Irish Greyhound Board (IGB) In 2014 IGB was subject to three section 37 notices and was the first public body entered by the Commissioner's staff on foot of a s.37(2) notice. The seriousness of this decision by the Commissioner warrants quoting much of the report from the *Annual Report of the Information Commissioner 2014*, p.15:

> "While the former Commissioner came close to using her section 37(2) powers just once in her tenure, my Office had not previously found it necessary to actually enter a premises for the purposes of a review. However, this year, I have to report that circumstances left me with no choice but to use those powers for the first time. Consequently, I formally delegated responsibility to two of my staff to enter the premises of the IGB for the purposes of obtaining access to information that had been the subject of repeated requests from my Office.
>
> From the very beginning of the review, my Office experienced a considerable delay in obtaining records from the IGB to allow even an initial examination. In fact, it took in excess of six months, and a substantial amount of effort on the part of my staff, for my Office to receive a properly presented set of records and a related schedule. An investigator from my Office was appointed to examine the matter. The investigator's initial examination in this case and in another review concerning the IGB highlighted a number of issues, including delays by the IGB in dealing with requests, failing to provide records to this Office, poor decision making and case handling and failure to adhere to the provisions of the FOI Act.
>
> The investigator also noted that during the course of the review, the IGB had appointed no fewer than three members of IGB staff to act as FOI officer and liaise with my Office at various stages. It was apparent that there was no clear handover of responsibilities or exchange of information between the FOI officers, a situation which I am certain contributed to the delay in the review process. In addition, it was clear from the records provided that the IGB had not in fact identified all the relevant information and records that came within the scope of the applicant's original FOI request.
>
> A substantial amount of correspondence, in the form of emails, letters and personal meetings is recorded in this case. All of the correspondence, from March to September 2014, records the attempts of the investigator to elicit a satisfactory response from the IGB, to enable a proper investigation of the matter. However, in late August 2014 the CEO of the IGB contacted my Office and spoke personally with the investigator on several occasions, in order to help bring about a satisfactory resolution of the ongoing problem. Notwithstanding the intervention of the CEO, I concluded that the most effective method of progressing the matter was to issue a notice under

> section 37(2) as a prior notice under section 37(1) did not prove successful. My Office wrote to the CEO on 8 September 2014 to make arrangements for my staff to visit the offices of IGB in Limerick. That visit took place, by arrangement and with the cooperation of the IGB, on 25 September 2014, in accordance with the provisions of s.37(2)."

Two further section 37 notices were issued to the IGB during 2014.

COMMISSIONER FOR ENVIRONMENTAL INFORMATION

The role of the Commissioner for Environmental Information is to decide on appeals taken by members of the public who are not satisfied with the outcome of their requests to public authorities for environmental information. The Access to Information on the Environment Regulations (S.I. No. 133 of 2007) (the "AIE Regs") assigned this legally distinct role of Commissioner for Environmental Information to the holder of the Office of Information Commissioner. The Regulations give effect to Directive 2003/4 of the European Parliament and of the Council of 28 January 2003. The activities of the Commissioner for Environmental Information were considered in previous editions of the *Annual Review of Irish Law* since 2007. In addition to hard copy, documents referred to may be found at the Environmental Information Commissioner's website (*www.ocei.gov.ie)*. Part II of the Information Commissioner's *Annual Report 2014* (see p.73 et seq.) is devoted to the *Annual Report of the Commissioner for Environmental Information*.

The following details related to procedures involved in the regime are repeated from earlier Annual Reviews in order to facilitate knowledge of this underused and relatively unknown legislation.

Guidelines Article 14 of the AIE Regs allows the Minister to publish guidelines which, under art.14(2), a public authority "shall ... have regard to", in the performance of its functions under the AIE Regs (see *Annual Review of Irish Law 2007*, p.355). It is worth repeating that these Guidance Notes are not, nor do they purport to be, a legal interpretation of the AIE Regs. It should also be noted that, in appeals to the Commissioner for Environmental Information (CEI), to the extent relevant, he has regard to the guidelines. The Regulations and the Guidance Notes may be found on the Department of the Environment, Heritage and Local Government's website *www.environ.ie/en.*

Two Distinct Access to Information Regimes There have been statutory obligations to release environmental information since 1990 under European law and 1993 under domestic law. Since the enactment of the Freedom of Information Act in 1997, both legislative codes have operated in parallel, but as fully distinct and separate systems. It is important to note that there are significant differences between the two regimes (see *Annual Review of Irish Law 2007*, pp.355–359; *Annual Review of Irish Law 2008*, pp.366–386). However, there are strong similarities in the processes for making requests and appealing refusals.

Fees Article 15 concerns fees. There are no up-front fees for a request for environmental information, nor for an internal review. The public authority may, nonetheless, charge a fee for providing environmental information (art.15(1)), but must publicise details of those fees (art.15(2)). This section was subject to a decision of the CEI in 2008, see *Annual Review of Irish Law 2008,* pp.368–369.

The fee of €150 required for an appeal to the CEI has been amended by the European Communities (Access to Information on the Environment) (Amendment) Regulations 2014 (S.I. No. 615 of 2014) as follows:

> 4. (a) The Regulations of 2007, as amended by the Regulations of 2011 are amended by the substitution of the following for article 15(3):
> 'Subject to sub-article (4), a fee of €50 shall be charged for making an appeal to the Commissioner under article 12.'
> (b) The substitution of the following for article 15(4):
> 'In respect of an appeal pursuant to article 12 by—
> (a) a holder of a medical card,
> (b) a dependant of a holder of a medical card, or
> (c) a person referred to in article 12(3)(b), the fee charged shall be €15.'

Independent Resource Allocation For the first time since the establishment of the office in 2007 the CEI was granted an independent resource allocation in October 2014. Instead the Office had had to rely entirely upon the resources that could be made available from the Office of the Information Commissioner. This followed seven years of representations made by the office-holders to the responsible government department, currently the Department of Public Expenditure and Reform (see *Annual Report of the Commissioner for Environmental Information 2014*, pp.80–81).

SUPREME AND HIGH COURT APPEALS

There are no reported judgments in 2014.

DECISIONS OF THE COMMISSIONER FOR ENVIRONMENTAL INFORMATION

Decisions may be found on the Office of the Commissioner for Environmental Information's website, *www.ocei.gov.ie.* Three 2014 appeals are described in the Annual Report 2014.

Distinguishing Environmental and Distantly Related Information *Stephen Minch and Department of Communications, Energy and Natural Resources* Case CEI/13/0006, 18 December 2014, in which the CEI upheld the refusal to grant access to the report entitled *Analysis of options for potential State intervention in the roll out of next-generation broadband* on the ground that the information concerned is not environmental information within the meaning of the Regulations. He noted that the judgment of the European Court of Justice in *Ville de Lyon v Caisse des Depots et Consignations* (C-524/09) 22 December 2010, involving a request for access to trading data relating to greenhouse gas emission allowances, had held that not all information with a connection even to greenhouse gas emissions necessarily qualifies as environmental information within the meaning of the Directive. He also considered the question of whether the National Broadband Plan (NBP) may itself be a "measure" within the meaning of art.3(1)(c) such that the requested report could qualify under para.(e) of the environmental information definition. However, noting that the NBP is merely a high level strategy setting targets for the delivery of high speed broadband throughout Ireland, he found in the *Annual Report of the Commissioner for Environmental Information 2014*, pp.76–77 that:

> "the NBP is not itself a measure affecting or likely to affect the environmental elements and factors referred to in paragraphs (a) and (b) of the definition, as the link between the plan and any effect on the environment is simply too remote, unlike the measures and activities that may be adopted to implement the plan."

The applicant has appealed this decision to the High Court.

Irish Water *David Healy, Friends of the Irish Environment and Department of Environment, Community and Local Government* CEI/12/0007 (11 June 2014) This appeal was deemed as withdrawn by agreement with the applicant. This case was an appeal against a refusal by the Department to grant access to an unredacted version of the *Irish Water: Phase 1 Report* and its Appendices. During the course of the appeal, and following meetings between the CEI's Office and Department officials, the Department agreed to publish the report in full subject to Government approval. The report is available on the Departmental website. (see *Annual Report of the Commissioner for Environmental Information 2014*, pp. 77–78.)

CEI's Discretion to Deem Appeal Withdrawn *Damien McCallig and Eirgrid* CEI/12/0009 (8 July 2014) During the course of the CEI's review, Eirgrid agreed to release the requested information in full. The applicant refused to withdraw the appeal as requested and the CEI exercised his discretion under art.15(5) of European Communities (Access to Information on the Environment) Regulations 2007 to 2014 (S.I. No. 133 of 2007, S.I. No. 662 of 2011 and S.I. 615 of 2014) (the "AIE Regs") which states: "The Commissioner may deem an appeal to be withdrawn if the public authority makes the requested information available, in whole or in part, prior to a formal decision of the Commissioner under article 12(5)." (see *Annual Report of the Commissioner for Environmental Information 2014*, p.78.)

STATUTORY NOTICE OF COMPLIANCE

Article 12(6) Notice Article 12(6) of the AIE Regs states:

> The Commissioner may, for the purposes of this article, do any of the following:
> (a) require a public authority to make available environmental information to the Commissioner and, where appropriate —
> (i) require the public authority concerned to attend before the Commissioner for that purpose, and

(ii) where the public authority is a body corporate, require its chief officer to attend,

(b) examine and take copies of any environmental information held by a public authority and retain it in his or her possession for a reasonable period,

(c) enter any premises occupied by a public authority and there require to be furnished with such environmental information as he or she may reasonably require, or take such copies of, or extracts from, any environmental information found or made available on the premises.

The first notice was issued in 2010 (see *Annual Review of Irish Law 2010*, pp.434–435), with a further notice issued in 2011 (see *Annual Review of Irish Law 2011*, pp.427–428). No notices were issued in 2014 (see *Annual Report of the Commissioner for Environmental Information 2014*, p.76).

OMBUDSMAN

The Ombudsman is governed by the Ombudsman Act 1980 as amended by the Ombudsman (Amendment) Act 2012. In addition to hard copy, documents referred to may be found at the Ombudsman's website *http://www.ombudsman.ie*. Mr Michael Mills was appointed first Ombudsman in 1984. He was succeeded by Mr Kevin Murphy in 1994, who was succeeded by Ms Emily O'Reilly in mid-2003 who was succeeded by the present incumbent, Mr Peter Tyndall, in December 2013; hence references to publications may refer to "he" or "she" depending on the date of publication. The activities of the Ombudsman have been previously considered in all previous editions of the *Annual Review of Irish Law* since 2000.

Information Commissioner and Ombudsman Compared Both the Information Commissioner and the Ombudsman deal with matters of administrative accountability. However, there are differences in the statutory role and responsibility of each Office. One of the most significant is that whereas the Commissioner's decisions are binding subject to appeal to the High Court the Ombudsman functions on the basis of persuasive authority. The Ombudsman (Amendment) Act 2012 has introduced an element of compellability in that under s.10 the Ombudsman may apply to the Circuit Court to enforce requests made to public bodies in the course of investigations.

Ombudsman's Statement of Intent In the introduction to his second Annual Report the Ombudsman once again outlined a number of areas with potential for improvement (see *Annual Review of Irish Law 2013*, pp.384–386 and pp.388–389). These included the possible extension of his jurisdiction to include public services provided by private bodies; a role for the Ombudsman in implementing alternative dispute resolution (ADR) measures as prescribed by recent European Directives and Regulations; a standardised approach to complaint handling across the public sector and the introduction of a single portal for complaints.

Constitutional Recognition of the Ombudsman This remains an unresolved issue. As far back as 1996 the Constitution Review Group recommended constitutional status for the Ombudsman, see e.g. *Annual Review of Irish Law 2010*, p.417.

Mobility Allowance and Motorised Transport Grant Schemes In 2012, the then Ombudsman presented two s.6 Special Reports to the Oireachtas. These are *Too Old to be Equal? A Follow-up Investigation by the Ombudsman into the illegal refusal of Mobility Allowance to people over 66 years of age* and *Motorised Transport Grant*. Rather than bring these schemes in compliance with the law the Government's response was to discontinue these important schemes for vulnerable people, see *Annual Review of Irish Law 2012* p.385, and *Annual Review of Irish Law 2013*, pp.388–389. In the *Annual Report of the Ombudsman 2014*, p.27 the Ombudsman presented an update on the lack of progress in this matter:

> "The Annual Reports for 2012 (pages 33–36) and 2013 (page 31) outlined the background to the decision of the Department of Health to discontinue the Mobility Allowance (MA) and Motorised Transport Grant (MTG) schemes to new applicants and the subsequent developments arising from that decision.
>
> As previously outlined, in 2013 the Government decided to introduce a new statutory travel subsidy scheme for disabled persons with mobility needs. In the absence of any clear evidence of progress on the matter I wrote to the Secretary General of the Department of Health on 12 November 2014 asking for a progress update and some indication as to the likely timescale for the legislation. I also discussed the matter with the Department. I was given assurances that the matter was being actively pursued by the Department. I am keen to see progress being made as the lack of a scheme is undoubtedly having an adverse effect on potential beneficiaries."

OMBUDSMAN REPORTS

Casebook A key development in 2013 was the launch of the *The Ombudsman's Casebook*. The *Annual Report of the Ombudsman 2014*, p.8, notes:

> "By regularly publishing a digest of case summaries, it becomes possible for bodies in the jurisdiction of the Office to learn not just from their own mistakes, but from those of others. This approach can help to avoid mistakes being made in the first place."

The Ombudsman also noted at p.8 that as well as offering a useful perspective to service providers, "it helps my Office to be alert to any developing trends where there are clusters of complaints which might suggest systemic problems which need to be addressed."

End of life care In June 2014 the Ombudsman published *A Good Death A Reflection on Ombudsman Complaints about End of Life Care in Irish Hospitals.* In the Introduction to the Report the Ombudsman noted that many public bodies and voluntary groups have responsibility and interest in this area including the

Health Service Executive, the Health Information and Quality Authority, the Irish Hospice Foundation and the Forum on End of Life. With regard to his own role he continued, at p.3:

> "The Ombudsman too can play a role in the national debate and exploration about death. Despite the personal trauma involved, the experiences of most patients and their relations in care settings reflect a service which is caring, professional and dignified. However, over the years, the Office continues to receive many complaints relating to end of life events. The numbers may be low, but the experiences are unique and in many instances, had a profoundly disturbing effect on family members. We decided to reflect on some of the complaints we received in recent years and to draw from them common themes that may assist service providers and policy makers to improve practice. Some of the stories shared here are sad and reflect the intense emotion of those directly involved. However in order to improve the experiences of people in the future we need to tell their stories and learn from our mistakes.
>
> We hope these reflections will make a positive contribution to the national debate on end of life care and the campaign to make Ireland a good place to live in and to die in. If there is one message to be learned from complaints brought to us, it is that small things make a big difference. Those moments at the end of a loved one's life are extremely precious and will be re-lived again and again. Excellent communication and a positive, respectful attitude are required from all people associated with the care of the dying person and their loved ones. I hope that the stories related here will remind us to keep this in mind at all times."

INVESTIGATION REPORTS

The Ombudsman Act 1980 states at s.4(2):

> Subject to the provisions of this Act, the Ombudsman may investigate any action taken by or on behalf of a Department of State or other person specified in Part I of the First Schedule to this Act (being an action taken in the performance of administrative functions) where, upon having carried out a preliminary examination of the matter, it appears to the Ombudsman—
>
> (*a*) that the action has or may have adversely affected a person (other than a Department of State or other person specified in the First or Second Schedule to this Act), and
>
> (*b*) that the action was or may have been—
>
> (i) taken without proper authority,
>
> (ii) taken on irrelevant grounds,
>
> (iii) the result of negligence or carelessness,
>
> (iv) based on erroneous or incomplete information,
>
> (v) improperly discriminatory,
>
> (vi) based on an undesirable administrative practice, or
>
> (vii) otherwise contrary to fair or sound administration.

This section has been repeated in full to facilitate readers.

In 2014 the Ombudsman issued three reports under s.4(2). All Reports are referred to in the Ombudsman's *Annual Report* and may be accessed in full on the website, as may reports from earlier years.

Inequities in the National Scheme Justified by the Health Service Executive *Local Rules for National Schemes Inequities in the administration of the Long Term Illness Card Scheme* (*Long Term Illness Card Scheme*), (the "Report"), published in January 2014, was an investigation of a complaint about the refusal of the Health Service Executive (HSE) to award a Long Term Illness Card (LTI card) to a woman for her son who was diagnosed as having attention deficit hyperactivity disorder (ADHD) and autistic spectrum disorder (ASD). The Report notes at p.5:

> "The HSE acknowledged that there are variations around the country in the assessment of certain illnesses for the purposes of the scheme. These variations meant that applications for the card from people suffering from the same type of illness could be treated differently depending on where the applicants lived; in some parts of the country they would qualify for the card while in others, they would not qualify for it."

Different Classification Schemes In the course of the investigation the Ombudsman asked the following question: "How did it come about that Medical Officers in the HSE use different disease/illness classification systems for the purpose of administering a national scheme?" The Report continued, at p.9:

> "The answer probably lies in the historic separation of the former health boards into different functional areas. This however, is not a sufficient explanation. The LTI card scheme, from the time of its inception in 1971, was always a national scheme with a statutory basis. There should, therefore, always have been a uniform and standardised approach to its implementation."

HSE Statutory Authority to Administer Scheme The HSE in its submission to the investigation had sought to justify, at Appendix 1, p.20 of the Report, its failure to insist on uniform standards:

> "Medical Officers are clinicians; as such, the organisation expects them to carry out their work as professionals and they can legitimately expect to exercise clinical autonomy. This reasonably extends to their choice of internationally accepted diagnostic classification system. The fact that clinicians in the HSE elect to rely on one or other of two current systems is an inherent part of their clinical decision-making. Practice is not arbitrary; Medical Officers were consistent in their use of classification schemes, which formed a legitimate basis for their decision-making. The disparity arose because clinicians' choice of diagnostic scheme was not consistent across the country."

The HSE had sought direction from the Department of Health on the interpretation of the phrase "mental illness" as it applies to the scheme. The Ombudsman dismissed this approach at p.12 of the Report:

> "The LTI scheme is a statutory scheme administered by the HSE and for which it has responsibility. Under Section 7(8) of the Health Act 2004 'the Executive has all the powers necessary or expedient for it to perform its functions'. This means that the HSE has the authority in law and the competence to decide on the interpretation of the phrase 'mental illness'. It is not reliant on the Department (as is the case with administrative, non-statutory schemes) to give guidance on the implementation of the scheme. While it may be appropriate to seek guidance on particular issues, the scheme remains the statutory responsibility of the HSE to administer in a fair manner.
>
> The HSE has not developed a consistent approach on the question of whether the disorders of ASD and ADHD are regarded as mental illnesses for the purpose of the LTI scheme. It attributes the variations in approach to the fact that two different diagnostic classification systems are in use. Again, it is not at all clear that it is necessary for the HSE to choose between the two systems for the purpose of the scheme. It is only necessary to decide if the disorders in question come within the terms of the scheme."

Findings and Recommendations The findings of the Report, at p.17, are as follows:

> "1. That Ms Kelly [not her real name] was adversely affected by the refusal of her applications for a Long Term Illness card in July 2009 and in September 2010 and that the decisions to refuse her applications were based on erroneous or incomplete information, on irrelevant grounds and were improperly discriminatory.
>
> 2. That the decision to refuse to recompense Ms Kelly for her son's medication for the period of her application prior to March 2012 was taken on irrelevant grounds, erroneous or incomplete information and improperly discriminatory.
>
> 3. That the administration of the Long Term Illness card scheme by the HSE, treating children differently depending on their geographical location, is improperly discriminatory, an undesirable administrative practice and contrary to fair or sound administration.
>
> 4. That the HSE failed in its responsibility to ensure a uniform approach to the administration of the LTI card scheme and failed also to provide the HSE administrators of the scheme with adequate and clear guidance in relation to the scheme and that these failures were contrary to fair or sound administration.
>
> 5. That, in the light of the fact that the scheme is under review and the outcome of that review is not yet known, the HSE proposal to alter the approach of its Medical Officers who heretofore had accepted ASD and ADHD as conditions which conferred eligibility under the scheme, is contrary to fair or sound administration."

The Ombudsman found in favour of the complainant and made the following recommendations at p.18 of the Report:

- "that the HSE refund Ms Kelly the cost of medications for her son in the period from when she first made an application for him under the LTI scheme to the time when her application was granted. (The cost was approximately €3,000)
- that, as the outcome from the Review Group is awaited by the HSE and in the absence of any substantive amendments to the governing legislation, the HSE continues to administer the LTI scheme as it has done for many years in the greater part of the country, thereby including ADHD as constituting a mental illness which, in the case of persons under 16 years, gives entitlement to a LTI card.
- that steps be taken to ensure that the LTI Scheme, as a national scheme, is administered in a uniform fashion throughout the country.
- that all of these recommendations are implemented before the end of October 2013."

In June 2015, the time of the publication of his Annual Report 2014, the Ombudsman reported that the HSE had accepted the findings and recommendations had been accepted. Subsequent to a general policy review the HSE has developed new operational guidelines which take account of the available national and international clinical evidence. The new guidelines are described in the *Annual Report of the Ombudsman 2014*, at pp.29–30:

> "The new guidelines, directed that ADHD be regarded as a mental illness for the purposes of the LTI scheme. The guidelines outlined the factors which must be present in such cases. These set a clinical threshold which has to be met in order to establish eligibility in any given case. The guidelines have been implemented on a national basis to ensure consistency and clarity in the administration of the scheme."

Home Care Grant Denied This investigation report was published in February 2014. As the entire report, entitled *Home Care Grant Denied*, as presented on the Ombudsman's website is less than 500 words it is reproduced in full below:

> "This report examines why an application for a Home Care Grant (HCG), on behalf of an elderly, dependent woman, was refused by the HSE, even though it was submitted several weeks before the grant was abolished. The Ombudsman's investigation looked at how the HSE dealt with the application, how it communicated with the applicant, and how the decision to abolish the grant was communicated to key stakeholders. The Ombudsman found that the decision to abolish the grant was not communicated to all of the key stakeholders in a timely way, that no arrangements were in place to track applications received before the cut-off date, and that no appeals process was offered to the applicant.
>
> The HCG (a cash grant paid to assist older people to buy in extra care which could not be provided by the HSE) had been a feature of the Home

Care Package Scheme (HCPS) until December 2010. At that point, new national guidelines for the HCPS were published and the payment of cash grants was to be phased out. The HSE told the Ombudsman that training and briefing sessions for HSE staff about changes to the Scheme were held across each region and at local level with all of the key stakeholders. However, these briefing sessions did not take place until mid November 2010 which meant that the Public Health Nurse (PHN) was unaware that the grant was being abolished when she advised the woman to apply for it.

In this case, the woman applied for the cash grant in October 2010 and her application was being considered on financial and medical grounds. While she had been deemed eligible on means grounds, her application had to be signed off by the PHN and the woman's General Practitioner (GP) who had to verify that she was medically eligible as well. The form was signed by both PHN and GP on 10 November 2010 but, unfortunately, her application was not approved because the form was not returned by the GP until January 2011. At that stage, the grant had been abolished.

While the woman was offered some additional home help hours, which were provided by the HSE, her family considered that the cash grant should have been paid given that the delay in processing her application was not of her making.

The Ombudsman is pleased that the HSE accepted the findings and recommendations and apologised to the family. An *ex gratia* payment of €8,500 was made to them in settlement of their complaint. Sadly, the woman passed away in 2013."

Lack of Coherent Approach to Employment and Residency Permits This report is entitled *Passports for Irish-born children of non-EEA parents* (the "Report"), and was published July 2014. This was an investigation into three separate complaints from Brazilian men about the difficulties they faced in obtaining passports for their children born in Ireland. The Ombudsman summarised the process as follows at p.4 of the Report:

> "Such workers, to live and work in Ireland, must interact with two separate government agencies in maintaining their legal status here; the Department of Jobs, Enterprise and Innovation and the Department of Justice and Equality. The Department of Foreign Affairs and Trade has responsibility for processing passport applications. .... the Ombudsman found that, while the laws in relation to both the processing of passport applications and employment permits were being correctly applied in the cases of complaint to his Office, the administrative processes of the three agencies were likely to cause difficulties for members of the public that could amount to unfairness and unnecessary delay in individual cases."

In order to establish title to citizenship (and thereby, an Irish passport) as they apply to people born in the State to parents of non-EU nationality, one of the parents must have resided in the State for an aggregate of at least three out of the four years prior to the child's birth and any period of time in those four years not covered by a permission to be in the State given by the Minister for Justice may not be counted for this purpose.

No Independent Appeal Process The Ombudsman noted that it is clear that to have periods of unlawful residence is a serious matter for the people concerned. Such periods of time will negatively affect any future applications, not only for passports for Irish born children, but also applications for long-term residency status and citizenship. Although foreign nationals may have been living and working in the State for a considerable number of years, periods of unlawful residence will be subtracted from the years which are being reckoned for the purposes of any such applications. Periods of unlawful residence can arise for example because of delays in receipt of employment permits, or delays between the date on that permit and the actual date on which the non-national presented himself and his employment permit to the immigration office. The Report states, at p.24:

> "In other words, although the non-national presented himself at the immigration office with an employment permit which pre-dated his attendance, the "permission to remain" was not granted from that earlier date. The Department of Justice confirmed that this was the usual practice. Permissions to remain are not granted in retrospect by the immigration officer."

There is no independent appeals process for these matters.

Cooperation with Investigation The Ombudsman appears to have received full cooperation from the Department of Jobs, Enterprise and Innovation and the Department of Foreign Affairs and Trade, both under investigation. In addition, the Department of Justice and Equality, which for these purposes does not come within the Ombudsman's jurisdiction, was also helpful in supplying information and dealing with the Ombudsman's staff. The report is lengthy, some 58 pages, and reveals the difficulties caused by the system for the people involved. The Report, at p.5 states:

> "It is a complex system and there was little doubt that the people concerned had engaged with it to the best of their abilities. They had paid numerous fees for their residency permits over the years. Fees had also been paid by their employers for the employment permits. They were, in addition, engaged in full-time employment far from the capital, with little access to advice or services."

Whilst the investigation was underway, two of the cases were reviewed and passports issued for the children concerned. The third case resulted in the issue of a passport subsequent to the completion of the investigation.

"Permission to Remain" Anomaly Unjustified The Ombudsman could find no answer when the purpose of allowing disparity between employment permits and permission to remain periods was queried. He states at p.37:

> "It is important to note at this point that the State is not without responsibility to immigrant workers whose employers have successfully applied for employment permits for them. They have children born in the State and will, in time; have the right to apply for citizenship [footnote omitted]. In fact, in all of these cases, the men involved have amassed a sufficient period of lawful residence time to apply for citizenship. They had reasonable grounds to suppose their Irish-born children would have title to citizenship without the need—and cost—of a formal application process. They are employees and taxpayers and have various rights and obligations under, at a minimum, employment, social welfare, education and health legislation. They and their employers have paid fees for every 'permission to remain' and every employment permit. The fact that they do not have permission to be in the State for periods ranging in duration from a few days to a number of months for the same time as their presence here in State-approved employment appears to be an anomaly in our administration. The question arises; what purpose is served by allowing these gaps to appear in a person's lawful residence in the State and no answer is immediately apparent."

The Ombudsman's recommendations for closer co-operation between the State agencies involved have been accepted and are in the process of implementation.

STATUTORY NOTICES OF NON-COMPLIANCE WITH OMBUDSMAN REQUESTS

Section 7 A section 7 notice is a statutory demand under s.7 of the Ombudsman Act 1980 for the provision of information, required by the Office of the Ombudsman Office in examining a complaint and is normally only issued as a last resort, when there has been an unacceptable delay on the part of the public body in providing the requested information (see further, previous editions of the *Annual Review of Irish Law* since 2002).

In 2014 the Ombudsman recorded that two section 7 notices were issued, one in respect of the HSE and the other to Westmeath County Council. The Ombudsman was pleased to report that after issuing the notices the records were received, see *Annual Report of the Ombudsman 2014*, p.18.

SECTORAL OMBUDSMEN

Financial Services Ombudsman The relevant website is *www.financialombudsman.ie.*

High Court Appeals There were a number of High Court appeals in 2014 and some of the points in judgments which may have wider application are given below.

Construction of Contract Law not Reserved to FSO Hogan J. in *Millar v Financial Services Ombudsman* [2014] IEHC 434 acknowledged the novel powers of the Financial Services Ombudsman (FSO) which call for the application of specialist skill and judgment so far as financial dealing is concerned. However, he held that this principle does not apply so far as the ordinary application of the law of contract is concerned. He continued at para.17:

> "It was never the intention of the Oireachtas that a complainant should be disadvantaged by electing to make a complaint to the Ombudsman rather than by proceeding in the ordinary courts. Within the judicial system no appellate court would hesitate to correct what it considered to be legal error on the part of the first instance court. The Supreme Court would not hesitate, for example, to reverse what it considered to be an erroneous decision of this Court on a point of contract law, no matter how experienced or expert the trial judge was in matters of contract or commercial law. In these circumstances, it could not be correct that this Court should defer to the Ombudsman on matters of pure contract law, not least given that the Ombudsman's decision would create a *res judicata* on that very contractual point which would bar the re-litigation of the issue before the ordinary courts."

He held at para.20 that "the question of contractual construction is one which, generally speaking, at least, this Court is required to examine afresh in the course of determining a statutory appeal taken against a decision of the Ombudsman presenting such an issue."

Delays in Office of FSO *O'Brien v. Financial Services Ombudsman* [2014] IEHC 268 concerned an unsuccessful appeal against delays in the office of the FSO. The court considered a number of constitutional issues. The case is analysed in the Constitutional Law chapter of this Annual Review.

Oral hearings The issue of whether or not the FSO should or should not hold an oral hearing continued to feature in High Court appeals. Birmingham J. in *O'Driscoll v Financial Service Ombudsman* [2014] IEHC 462 helpfully listed the precedents for both sides of the argument at para.17.

In *O'Neill v Financial Services Ombudsman* [2014] IEHC 282 Hogan J. held at para.21 that where the conflict of fact between the appellant and the respondent "is a stark one and the resolution of this conflict is central to the fair disposition of the complaint, then it is impossible to avoid the conclusion that some form of oral hearing is objectively necessary" in order to give effect to the constitutional guarantee of basic fairness of procedures. Similarly, O'Malley J. in *O'Donoghue v. Financial Services Ombudsman* [2014] IEHC 620 stated at para.56:

> "It seems to me that in these circumstances there was a direct conflict on the factual accounts given by the different parties, which could not be resolved purely by reference to the documents in the case, and that the credibility of the appellant was squarely in issue. Accepting that the respondent has a broad discretion as to when he should hold an oral hearing, the fact that he did not appears to have produced a situation where conflicts of fact were resolved in different ways with no apparent reason for the differences. It is true that the appellant did not ask for a hearing. He stated that he would prefer instead that the matter be resolved by agreement. However, given that

he was not legally represented and given the respondent's own obligations to consider an oral hearing in cases of material conflict, the appellant's failure to ask for one cannot be conclusive."

Garda Síochána Ombudsman Commission (GSOC) The relevant website is *www.gardaombudsman.ie.*

The Garda Síochána Ombudsman Commission (GSOC) was mired in controversy during 2014. This was in part due to the continuing revelations regarding the Garda whistleblowers (see the Whistleblower Protection chapter in this Annual Review), and also due to apparent leaks from GSOC regarding unlawful surveillance of their offices. A series of press releases which illustrate the difficult year of GSOC can be accessed in the Media Room on the GSOC website.

The Guerin Report The *Report to an Taoiseach, Enda Kenny TD on a Review of the action taken by An Garda Síochána pertaining to certain allegations made by Sergeant Maurice McCabe* conducted by Seán Guerin SC (the *"Guerin Report"*) was highly critical of GSOC's failure to provide it with requested documentation. Mr Guerin noted at para.1.8:

> "Unfortunately, I have received no documentation from the Garda Síochána Ombudsman Commission. On 13 March 2014 Mr Simon O'Brien of GSOC wrote to me to indicate that the process of marshalling the relevant material was under way as a priority. On 26 March 2014, I wrote to a reminder to GSOC and referred to the very limited period of time available to complete this review. On 2 April 2014, GSOC wrote to say that the relevant material had been identified and, subject to approval by GSOC, would be forwarded in due course. The tight timescale for the review was acknowledged. A further reminder of the request for documents, and of the very limited time available to review them, was sent to GSOC on 10 April 2014. At 4.48 p.m. on 23 April 2014 I received a letter from Arthur Cox Solicitors on behalf of GSOC raising various preliminary legal and practical issues which might usefully have been raised at an earlier stage. Although the letter expressed an eagerness to co-operate and stated that GSOC had 'voluminous' relevant documents, I have not seen any of those documents, I do not understand why the obstacles to my seeing them were first identified to me in correspondence delivered shortly before close of business on the eve of the date upon which my report was due. Even if GSOC's concerns could have been immediately overcome, there was of course no practical reality to 'voluminous' documentation being reviewed at that late stage. I wish to acknowledge the courtesy with which GSOC dealt with my requests for documentation and GSOCs stated willingness to furnish documentation. I regret that the eagerness to cooperate that was communicated on behalf of GSOC by its solicitors did not find practical expression in an ability to make relevant documents available for examination in good time. That has, unfortunately, been an obstacle to any assessment as part of this review of the adequacy of the investigations conducted by GSOC. It did not, however, interfere with the other work of the review."

GSOC issued a press release, dated 9 May 2014, to provide clarification "where required" on references to it in the Report. In relation to comments that the *Guerin Report* was finalised in the absence of the documentation from GSOC, the press release stated as follows:

> "Under the Terms of Reference furnished to Mr Guerin, he was requested to conclude his review within 8 weeks 'or as soon as possible thereafter'. Therefore, while we were aware of the tight timescale, we were not aware of an exact fixed deadline date.
>
> GSOC had marshalled a good deal of documentation, and this was available prior to the Guerin report being finalised. GSOC did, upon concluding this job of work and reviewing the body of documentation to be provided, come to the decision that it would be, in our view, proper to request certain safeguards (Mr. Guerin refers to these as 'appropriate safeguards'), prior to releasing documentation, to assure the protection of the rights of people concerned by the cases in question."

Other matters referred to include a response to para.18.2 in the *Guerin Report* that the approach adopted by GSOC in described investigations was ultimately broadly similar to that of An Garda Síochána:

> We are unsure of whether this is a criticism of GSOC or simply an observation. So we take this opportunity to clarify that GSOC investigations are often conducted using policing powers conveyed by the Garda Síochána Act (2005). In such cases, in accordance with the Act, GSOC has 'all the powers, immunities and privileges conferred and all the duties imposed on any member of the Garda Síochána … . In other words, GSOC is subject to the same rules in conducting investigations as the gardaí, so it should not be surprising that the approach would be 'broadly similar'.
>
> The same section notes that the final disciplinary recommendation was 'consistent with the Garda approach i.e. that individual members of An Garda Síochána should bear responsibility for their conduct of their own investigations'.
>
> Here, we would draw attention to the fact that the Garda Síochána Act (2005), under which we operate, focuses on the conduct of individual members. GSOC agrees strongly that it may often be more appropriate to focus on potential issues within the system. In fact, in our recent submission to the Joint Oireachtas Committee on Justice, Equality & Defence recommending legislative amendments, we have proposed that there should be a re-focusing of the objectives of police oversight to place greater emphasis on resolving potential policy or systemic issues, rather than simply aiming to apportion blame on individuals for specific actions.
>
> In this regard, we would also draw attention to the fact that the report highlighted that 'GSOC did give express consideration to the possibility that disciplinary proceedings may be warranted against supervisory and management officers for neglect of their respective duties in those capacities'.

> It is regrettable that Mr Guerin's inquiry did not have sight of GSOC's documentation."

The press release continues by describing some of the content and quoting from the documentation.

Unlawful Surveillance of GSOC offices Inquiry into Reports of Unlawful Surveillance of Garda Síochána Ombudsman Commission (the "*Cooke Report*"). An article appeared in *The Sunday Times* on 9 February 2014, apparently arising from a deliberate leak in GSOC, asserting that the offices of GSOC had been targeted as part of a sophisticated surveillance operation which had used "government-level technology" (the Cooke Report, para.3.1). There was an inference that members of An Garda Síochána may have been involved. On 19 February 2014, following a resolution of Dáil Éireann, the Government appointed Cooke J., retired High Court judge, to conduct the inquiry which had led to the *Cooke Report*. The terms of reference, described at para.2 of the *Cooke Report*, were:

> "To establish a chronology and identify the sequence of events and facts leading up to and relating to the Public Interest Investigation pertaining to security concerns commenced by the Garda Síochána Ombudsman Committee pursuant to Section 102 (4) of the Garda Síochána Act 2005 on or about the 8th October 2013.
>
> To examine all reports, transcripts, records, minutes, correspondence and documentation and consider any oral or other evidence as is deemed relevant to the aforementioned Public Interest Investigation.
>
> To review and assess any evidence of a security breach or attempted security breach at the GSOC as informed by, inter alia, the chronology and facts established at (1) above or arising from the examination at (2) above, and as may have occurred at any time up to 18th February 2014.
>
> If appropriate, to make recommendations regarding measures to improve the existing security arrangements of GSOC for the purpose of addressing risks to data and communications identified in the course of this review and to ensure the integrity and security of their data and information in the interests of maintaining public confidence in the ability of GSOC to discharge its statutory functions in the public interest.
>
> To make any other recommendations, whether in regard to legislation or otherwise, as may be considered appropriate arising from the review aforesaid into this matter.
>
> To report on the above matters within eight weeks or as soon as may be thereafter."

The *Cooke Report* had concluded at para.11.1(1) that it was "impossible on the basis of the technical opinions and available information, categorically to rule out all possibility of covert surveillance" and continued that "it is clear that the evidence does not support the proposition that actual surveillance of the kind asserted in the Sunday Times article took place and much less that it was carried out by members of the Garda Síochána."

The Cooke Report was published on 4 June 2014. GSOC issued a Press Release dated 11 June 2014 in response to the Report stating inter alia:

> "The report has found that, while certain anomalies raised concerns about security within GSOC—one of which 'remains unexplained'— 'the evidence does not support the proposition that actual surveillance of the kind asserted in the Sunday Times article took place and much less that it was carried out by members of the Garda Síochána'. This in fact mirrors key findings of our own investigation which stated, as per our press release of 10th February, that GSOC was 'satisfied that our databases were not compromised' and that 'there was no evidence of garda misconduct.'"

On 24 September 2014 yet another media release from GSOC was entitled *Report by the Garda Síochána Ombudsman Commission following its fact-finding investigation into possible disclosure of confidential information*. The accompanying press release stated:

> "As stated in a press release of 10th September last, the Commission received a report following a fact-finding investigation by Mr Mark Connaughton SC into the possible disclosure of confidential information.
>
> The Commission remains of the view, supported by the opinion of Mr Connaughton, that the content of his report in terms of operational, investigative and personal detail renders publication extremely difficult.
>
> In the interests of transparency, the attached report gives as much detail from Mr Connaughton's report as is possible, having regard to the foregoing considerations, in order to alleviate any possible public concerns."

Ombudsman for Children The relevant website is *www.oco.ie*.

Ombudsman for the Defence Forces The relevant website is *www.odf.ie*. The Ombudsman for the Defence Forces website appears to have been inactive since June 2014 when the Annual Report for 2012 was posted on the site.

In *Annual Review of Irish Law 2013*, pp.403–405, it considered *Gorman v Ombudsman for the Defence Forces* [2013] IEHC 545, an unsuccessful challenge to the appointment of Patrick Anthony McCourt as Defence Forces Ombudsman. Mr McCourt a former member of the Defence Forces, served between 1963 and 2010. From February 2001, until his retirement in 2010, Mr McCourt served in roles outside of the military chain of command, first, as Judge Advocate and, latterly, as Military Judge. According to a report of April 2014 in the *Sunday Independent* the Permanent Defence Forces' Other Ranks Representative Association (PDFORRA) has lodged an appeal of this decision in the Supreme Court. (Cusack, "Shatter back in firing line over Ombudsman appointment", *Sunday Independent*, 20 April 2014.)

STATUTES AND STATUTORY INSTRUMENTS

Freedom of Information Act 2014 This Act enables members of the public to obtain access, to the greatest extent possible consistent with the public interest and the right to privacy, to information in the possession of public bodies, other bodies in receipt of funding from the State and certain other bodies. It enables persons to have personal information relating to them in the possession of such bodies corrected and, accordingly, to provide for a right of access to records held by such bodies. It also provides for necessary exceptions to that right and for assistance to persons to enable them to exercise it. It further provides for the independent review both of decisions of such bodies relating to that right and of the operation of the Act generally (including the proceedings of such bodies pursuant to the Act) and, for those purposes, to provide for the continuance of the office of Information Commissioner and to define its functions. It provides for the publication by such bodies of certain information about them relevant to the purposes of the Act, it repeals the Freedom of Information Act 1997 and the Freedom of Information (Amendment) Act 2003, it amends the Central Bank Act 1942, and the Official Secrets Act 1963. It also repeals certain other enactments, and provides for related matters. For analysis of the Act see above in this chapter.

Protected Disclosures Act 2014 This Act makes provision for and in connection with the protection of persons from the taking of action against them in respect of the making of certain disclosures in the public interest and for connected purposes. For analysis of the Act see the Whistleblower Protection chapter in this Annual Review, p.708.

S.I. No. 97 of 2014–Central Bank Act 1942 (Financial Services Ombudsman Council) Complaint Information Regulations 2014 These Regulations make provision for the form and manner in which information may be published concerning financial service providers who have had at least three complaints made against them which have been found to have been substantiated or partly substantiated. The Regulations also allow for sector-specific information to be included.

S.I. No. 137 of 2014–Central Bank Act 1942 (Financial Services Ombudsman Council) Levies and Fees (Amendment) Regulations 2014 These Regulations made by the Financial Services Ombudsman Council in accordance with ss.57BE and 57BF of the Central Bank Act 1942 (as amended) amend the Central Bank Act 1942—Financial Services Ombudsman Council—Levies and Fees Regulations 2013 (S.I. No. 477 of 2013) and provide for a scheme of levies on regulated entities to fund the operation of the Financial Services Ombudsman's Bureau for the year ended 31 December 2014.

S.I. No. 140 of 2014–Freedom of Information Act 1997 (Prescribed Bodies) Regulations 2014 These Regulations prescribe Irish Water as a public body for the purposes of the Freedom of Information Act 1997 (No. 13 of 1997) by its inclusion in subpara.(5) of para.1 of the First Schedule to that Act. In accordance with s.3(5) of that Act, these Regulations provide that the Freedom of Information Act 1997 shall apply to all functions of Irish Water.

S.I. No. 144 of 2014–Local Elections (Disclosure of Donations and Expenditure) Act 1999 (Period for Reckoning Election Expenses) Order 2014 This Order determines the period for the reckoning of election expenses incurred by or on behalf of a candidate, designated person, national agent of a political party, or third party at the local elections to be held on 23 May 2014, in accordance with s.12B of the Local Elections (Disclosure of Donations and Expenditure) Act 1999. Section 12A of the said Act specifies limits on electoral expenditure which may be incurred by a candidate, designated person and national agent during the period specified in the Order.

S.I. No. 164 of 2014–Central Bank Act 1942 (Financial Services Ombudsman Council) (Amendment) Regulations 2014 The purpose of these Regulations is: (a) to amend and clarify the definition of "consumer" to include (i) a natural person when acting in the course of or in connection with the carrying on of a business and (ii) sole traders; (b) to apply the limit of €3 million annual turnover to all persons, groups of persons and incorporated bodies; and (c) to provide for a definition of "turnover" in respect of a person/group of persons and in respect of a financial service provider.

S.I. No. 197 of 2014–Criminal Justice (Withholding of Information on Offences against Children and Vulnerable Persons) Act 2012 (Prescribed Organisations and Prescribed Persons) Order 2014 This Order prescribed Pieta House C.P.S.O.S. Ltd for the purposes of s.4 of the Criminal Justice (Withholding of Information on Offences against Children and Vulnerable Persons) Act 2012 (the "2012 Act") and specified each of the classes of persons in the Schedule employed or otherwise engaged by Pieta House C.P.S.O.S. Ltd for the purposes of s.4 of the 2012 Act.

S.I. No. 250 of 2014–European Union (Consumer Information, Cancellation and Other Rights) (Amendment) Regulations 2014 These Regulations amend reg.1 of the European Union (Consumer Information, Cancellation and Other Rights) Regulations 2013 (S.I. No. 484 of 2013) by substituting for para.(2) the following paragraph: "(2) These Regulations come into operation on 14 June 2014 and apply to contracts concluded on or after that date."

S.I. No. 310 of 2014–European Union (Branch Disclosures) (Interconnection of Business Registers) Regulations 2014 These Regulations give effect to the amendments of Council Directive 1989/666 of 21 December 1989, concerning disclosure requirements in respect of branches opened in a Member State by certain types of company governed by the law of another State by Directive 2012/17 of the European Parliament and of the Council of 13 June 2012 on the interconnection of central, commercial and companies registers.

S.I. No. 312 of 2014–Health Insurance Act 1994 (Determination of Relevant Increase under section 7A and Provision of Information under section 7B) Regulations 2014 These Regulations provide for premium loadings to be applied to in-patient indemnity health insurance contracts purchased on and from 1 May 2015 and require registered undertakings to set different premium prices depending on the age at which an individual takes out health insurance. The Regulations provide that the loading in respect of an insured person shall be his or her premium before tax relief multiplied by 2 per cent for each year by which his or her age at entry exceeds 34 years, subject to a maximum loading of 70 per cent. The specified date of 1 May 2015, on and from which loadings will apply, will facilitate a grace period from 1 August 2014 (nine months) during which time people who are not currently members of the health insurance market can join without incurring loadings. A nine-month grace period will also apply for anybody who has his or her principal residence outside the State on 1 May 2015 and who has, after 1 May 2015, his or her principal residence in the State.

The Regulations set out the circumstances when the loadings will be reduced, where the member has a qualifying "credited period". A "credited period" will apply where individuals previously had health insurance. A "credited period" of up to three years will also apply for individuals who previously had health insurance prior to the introduction of premium loadings and ceased to be an insured person on or after 1 January 2008 by reason of being in receipt of a relevant social welfare payment. The individual's "age of entry" will be reduced by the "credited period", in years and complete months, thus reducing the applicable level of loadings.

The Regulations also include a requirement for registered undertakings to provide another undertaking with a written statement of a person's previous period or periods of health insurance cover and to do so in as practicable a timeframe as possible, but in any event no later than 30 days after receiving the request. The Regulations also place a requirement on registered undertakings to retain relevant records for a period of not less than 20 years from the date of termination of the contract.

S.I. No. 319 of 2014–Personal Insolvency Act 2012 (Regulatory Disclosure Statement of a Personal Insolvency Practitioner) Regulations 2014 These Regulations are made for the purposes of s.161 of the Personal Insolvency Act 2012.

S.I. No. 327 of 2014–Protected Disclosures Act 2014 (Commencement) Order 2014 This Order appointed 15 July 2014 as the day on which the Protected Disclosures Act 2014 (No. 14 of 2014) came into operation. (see Whistleblower Protection chapter in this Annual Review, p.708)

S.I. No. 339 of 2014–Protected Disclosures Act 2014 (Section 7(2)) Order 2014 prescribed each person specified in column (2) of the included Schedule to be the recipient of disclosures of relevant wrongdoings falling within the description of matters specified in column (3) of the Schedule in relation to the person. (see Whistleblower Protection chapter in this Annual Review, p.708)

S.I. No. 484 of 2014–Freedom of Information Act 2014 (Fees) Regulations 2014 prescribe amounts of fees and charges for the purposes of ss.27 and 21(d) of the Freedom of Information Act 2014, in respect of requests made under s.12 of that Act and in respect of certain applications for review of decisions of FOI bodies under ss.21 and 22. (see above in this chapter)

S.I. No. 489 of 2014–Health (Provision of Food Allergen Information to Consumers in respect of Non-Prepacked Food) Regulations 2014 These Regulations concern the provision of food allergen information to consumers in respect of non-prepacked food. They provide for the means, expression and presentation through which allergen particulars are to be made available on non-prepacked food, as provided for under art.44 of Regulation (EU) No. 1169/2011 of the European Parliament and of the Council of 25 October 2011 on the provision of food information to consumers.

S.I. No. 531 of 2014–Freedom of Information Act 2014 (Fees) (No. 2) Regulations 2014 prescribe amounts of fees and charges for the purposes of ss.27 and 22(1)(d) of the Freedom of Information Act 2014 in respect of requests made under s.12 of that Act and in respect of certain applications for review of decisions of FOI bodies under ss.21 and 22. (see above in this chapter)

S.I. No. 556 of 2014–European Union (Provision of Food Information to Consumers) Regulations 2014 These Regulations give effect to Regulation (EU) No 1169/2011 of the European Parliament and of the Council of 25 October 2011 (as affected by Corrigendum to Regulation (EU) No 1169/2011), Commission Delegated Regulation (EU) No 1155/2013 of 21 August 2013 and Commission Delegated Regulation (EU) No 78/2014 of 22 November 2013 on the provision of food information to consumers.

These Regulations revoke and replace the European Communities (Labelling, Presentation and Advertising of Foodstuffs) Regulations 2002 to 2013 and the European Communities (Nutrition Labelling for Foodstuffs) Regulations 2009.

S.I. No. 615 of 2014–European Communities (Access to Information on the Environment) (Amendment) Regulations 2014 amend the European Communities (Access to Information on the Environment) Regulations 2007 to 2011 for the purpose of ensuring that Ireland complies with the provisions of Directive 2003/4 of the European Parliament and of the Council of 28 January 2003 on public access to environmental information, in particular the requirement that access to a review procedure is not prohibitively expensive.

Land Law

HELEN MCCARTHY BL and **JAMES CROSS** BL

Adverse possession The decision of Hogan J. in *Dooley v Flaherty* [2014] IEHC 528 is a useful statement of what may constitute a sufficient "act of possession" on the part of a "paper owner" in the defence of a claim for adverse possession.

The plaintiffs sought an order for vacant possession of a property they purchased at auction in May 2012. At the time of the auction they believed that the property was vacant, subject to a life tenancy in favour of one Paddy Flaherty. Mr Flaherty had died in December 1995. His brother, Michael Flaherty (senior), took over the life tenancy. On the death of Michael Flaherty (senior), his son, Michael Flaherty (the "defendant"), took over the tenancy. The defendant did not dispute the plaintiffs' title but alleged that he had acquired a right to the property through adverse possession.

In evidence, the predecessor in title stated that he had received rent from the defendant in September 1998 and again in 2004. He said that he did not meet the defendant in 2008 when he called to the property to collect rent. In 2007, his employees gained entry to the property to carry out repairs caused by dampness. Following complaints made by the owners of the adjoining property in October 2008, the predecessor in title arranged for one of his employees to repair the slates on the roof. The predecessor in title also had the property insured.

The defendant stated that he had spent all his life at the property. His family paid rent to the previous owners. He acknowledged paying the predecessor in title £5 in September 1998. He claimed that this was the only rent he had ever paid in relation to the property. The defendant claimed that he refused to sign a document acknowledging that rent was due in 2010. The defendant stated that he was unaware that the roof had been repaired.

It is well established that in order to establish adverse possession, the squatter must establish that he had continuous uninterrupted possession for a period of not less than 12 years. The defendant claimed that time started to run in his favour from September 1998.

It is also accepted that once title is extinguished by adverse possession, then no subsequent act of possession would be sufficient to reinstate it.

The condition of the premises is relevant to show whether the squatter had an intention of adversely acquiring the premises. If he or she did have such an intention, more care would have been taken of the property during the running of the limitation period. In this case, however, evidence was given to the effect that the defendant was a man of modest and frugal tastes who cared little for what the modern world regards as essential or necessary. This evidence rebutted the presumption that because the property was poorly-maintained the defendant did not have an intention of adversely possessing the property. The property must be capable of enjoyment. Despite the plaintiffs' assertion that the property was not suitable for human habitation, it had been the home of the defendant for his entire life. Hogan J. held that the role of the court is not to inquire into the subjective tastes and feelings of landowners for the purposes of assessing whether the law on adverse possession applied to a particular property. "Enjoyment" in the legal sense refers to the use of and obtaining benefit from the property and not simply to the act of deriving pleasure or satisfaction from ownership.

Hogan J. held that there were acts of possession by the predecessor in title in effecting repairs to the roof and to the slates. These repairs were carried out in October 2008 before the expiration of the limitation period. Further, the predecessor in title gave evidence that he had insured the property. Hogan J., following the judgment in *Powell v McFarlane* (1979) 38 P. & C.R. 452, held that this was a sufficient act of possession, as even the lightest acts done by or on behalf of the owner of the paper title will be sufficient to establish that he was not dispossessed.

Promissory estoppel – Statute of Limitations In *Cavey v Cavey* [2014] IESC 16, a decision of the Supreme Court delivered by Clarke J. (Murray and Dunne JJ. concurring) on 4 March 2014, the application of s.9 of the Civil Liability Act 1961 ("the Section") to a claim based on promissory estoppel was considered.

The plaintiff's father ("the Deceased") died on 18 December 2006 and the plaintiff claimed that during the course of his life, the Deceased had represented to him that he would inherit the family home. The plaintiff said that he had acted on that representation and claimed under the doctrine of promissory estoppel. The plaintiff commenced the proceedings on 23 July 2010.

Herbert J. found that the plaintiff's action was statute-barred pursuant to the Section which provides that no proceedings shall be maintainable in respect of any cause of action whatsoever which has survived against the estate of a deceased person unless the proceedings were commenced either within the relevant period and were pending at the date of his death or within a period of two years after his death, whichever period first expires.

The issue to be determined was whether a claim in promissory estoppel could properly be described as a cause of action which has survived against the estate of the Deceased. The question had previously been considered by the High Court, O'Keeffe J., in *Prendergast v McLaughlin* [2011] 1 I.R. 102. That case also involved a claim in promissory estoppel and O'Keeffe J. favoured the approach of Fennelly J. in *Corrigan v Martin* (unreported, High Court, Fennelly J., 13 March 2006) where it was held, at p.6, that

> "the obligation of the deceased was to perform the contract during his lifetime and not at the moment of his death. Hence the cause of action was completed immediately before his death … the cause of action, therefore subsisted at the moment of the death and survived against his estate …".

A different view had been taken by Barron J. in *Reidy v McGreavey* (unreported, High Court, Barron J., 19 March 1993) where it was found that a claim based on a failure to honour a promise could not have been taken until the death of the deceased, because it could not have been ascertained until then.

Clarke J. noted that there is a significant distinction made in the Section between a cause of action which results from an act or omission of the deceased, and one which may exist against those in charge of the administration of the estate. Clarke J. found that if the plaintiff had a cause of action in promissory estoppel, it can only be based on establishing that the Deceased was in breach of a promise during his lifetime. This involves an allegation of a failure on the part of the Deceased and not a failure of the estate itself and such a claim comes within the scope of the phrase "a claim surviving against the estate of the deceased". Clarke J. therefore concluded that the plaintiff's claim was statute-barred on the basis that,

> "on a proper interpretation of the effect of s.9 of the 1961 Act, a claim in promissory estoppel arising out of an enforceable promise by a person to leave property by will, is a claim which can properly be characterised as one which survives against the estate of that person …".

This decision provides some much needed clarity in light of the opposing approaches adopted by the High Court previously and clarifies that the fact that a will breaking the promise only becomes operative at the date of death, is of no relevance.

Landlord and tenant On 1 April 2014, Barrett J. delivered a judgment in the case of *Ronan McNamee and Jacqueline McNamee v Estherfield Ltd and Hickey's Pharmacy Ltd* [2014] IEHC 205. The judgment was handed down in the context of an application for summary judgment in respect of arrears of rent. Barrett J. followed the now well-established principle as set out by Clarke J. in *Dublin Docklands Development Authority v Jermyn Street Ltd and Black Tie Ltd* [2010] IEHC 217 and O'Neill J. in *Quarryvale Two Ltd and Quarryvale Three Ltd v Stephen Beere and Graeme Beere* [2012] IEHC 546, that a landlord can claim arrears of rent which have accrued after the issuing of a Summary Summons up to the date of the judgment, without the need to issue fresh proceedings.

The decision of Laffoy J. delivered on 1 July 2014 in *Ickendel Ltd v Bewley's Café Grafton Street Ltd* [2014] IESC 41 (Denham C.J., Murray, O'Donnell, Clarke, Laffoy JJ.) was much anticipated by landlords and tenants alike. The case was by way of appeal of the decision of Charleton J. in *Ickendel Ltd v Bewley's Café Grafton Street Ltd* [2013] IEHC 293 which had caused speculation in relation to the interpretation of upwards only rent review clauses by the courts.

The case concerned the construction of a phrase in a commercial lease dated 22 September 1987 ("the Lease") and Laffoy J. is very clear that the issue of construction is not of general application to rent review clauses.

In the High Court, it had been found that, for the purposes of a rent review carried out on 1 January 2012, the phrase "the rent payable hereunder during the preceding period" means the initial rents payable under the Lease in respect of the period 6 August 1987 to 31 December 1991. The landlord appealed this finding and sought a declaration that a proper interpretation of the phrase "the preceding period" means the rent payable during the five-year period immediately preceding the review under construction. The effect of the provision was that following the review, the tenant would be liable for a rent equal to the greater of (a) the rent payable during the preceding period, or (b) the revised rent.

The significance of the interpretation was that the initial yearly rent payable was €232,410, whilst the yearly rent payable for the five-year period leading up to the review was €1,463,964. If the landlord's construction was correct, the latter figure would have been payable from the review date.

Laffoy J., in allowing the appeal, held that

> "there is no ambiguity in or between the various provisions of the Lease … when, to adopt the words of McKechnie J. in *Marlan Homes Limited v Walsh* [[2012] IESC 23], the Court focuses its mind 'on the language adopted by the parties being that which they have chosen to best reflect their intentions'."

Laffoy J. went on to hold that the expression "the preceding period" must mean the period immediately preceding the relevant period of five years which is subject to review. The effect of this construction was to provide an upwards only rent and Laffoy J. stated that: "That outcome is what the parties bargained for in plain language. They did not bargain for a rent revision arrangement based on a 'market rent' that can rise and fall in respect of different review periods."

The decision of Kearns P. in *O'Shaughnessy v Private Residential Tenancies Board* [2014] IEHC 401 concerned whether a landlord was "an approved body" pursuant to s.6 the Housing (Miscellaneous Provisions) Act 1992 (the "1992 Act") and consequently whether the provisions of the Residential Tenancies Act 2004 (the "2004 Act") are applicable to properties they lease.

A tenant brought a motion seeking to set aside and to discharge the determination order of the Chairperson of the Private Residential Tenancies Board (PRTB).

The tenant resided at 25a Pembroke Gardens, Ballsbridge, Dublin 4 and Strand Trust Ltd is the landlord of the property (the "landlord"). A dispute arose between the tenant and landlord. The tenant submitted an application for dispute resolution services to the PRTB. The tenant alleged that the landlord had served an invalid notice of termination. The landlord made a separate application for dispute resolution.

The adjudicator determined that the landlord did not fall within the category of "an approved body" pursuant to s.6 of the 1992 Act, that the 2004 Act applied, and that the landlord had served a valid notice of termination.

The tenant appealed this decision to the Tribunal on the grounds that the adjudicator erred in finding that the landlord was not excluded from the provisions of the 2004 Act.

The landlord gave evidence that an organisation named "Protestant Aid" is a registered charity, founded in 1836. Strand Trust Ltd was formed in 1988 and is a separate registered charity. Both charities are administered from the same building. Strand Trust Ltd provides accommodation to those who have an urgent need for it in return for some rent. Accommodation for the tenant was organised following an approach from a concerned person. The tenant gave evidence to the effect that the company which employed him as a verger with select vestry of St Anne's Church, Dawson St was "one and the same" as Strand Trust Ltd. The tenant submitted that the PRTB does not have jurisdiction to deal with the dispute as the 2004 Act does not apply to a dwelling let by an approved body for the purposes of s.6 of the 1992 Act.

The Tribunal found that both parties intended that a landlord and tenant relationship would come into existence at the commencement of their relationship and further that the dwelling was not let by a housing body approved for the purposes s.6 of the 1992 Act. The Tribunal determined that the termination notice was valid and that the tenant should vacate the premises within seven days and that the tenant pay the arrears in rent.

The tenant appealed this determination to the High Court pursuant to s.123(3) of the 2004 Act.

Kearns P. held that whilst "Protestant Aid" and the "Strand Trust Ltd" are administered from the same building, share a telephone line, perform similar and overlapping functions and have a number of shared directors, this does not make them "one and the same." The landlord had not sought to obtain approved status. The court cannot circumvent the necessary procedural requirements for obtaining such approval. Further, the tribunal member provided comprehensive reasons for its findings as to why the landlord is not an approved housing body.

In *Murphy v Hooton* [2014] IEHC 266, the plaintiff, as statutory receiver appointed by the National Asset Management Agency over premises charged under a defaulting mortgage, sought an interlocutory injunction restraining the defendant, as occupant, from trespassing on the said premises and to deliver up possession.

The occupant claimed that she began a monthly tenancy with the borrower in February 2008 when she took over the running of a business, which provides emergency accommodation for the homeless, from her husband. As a term of her agreement with her husband in return for the monthly tenancy she would pay a rent of €3,250 in discharge of the mortgage payments payable by them to Irish Nationwide Building Society (now IBRC, in special liquidation). The occupant does not have a written tenancy agreement nor does she have written consent from the bank allowing the borrower to sublet the premises to the defendant.

Upon his appointment, the receiver requested that possession of the premises be secured. The receiver wrote to the occupant asking her to set out the basis of her claim, by which she maintained an entitlement to be in occupation of the property. The receiver did not receive a reply. It was only after the initiation of proceedings that the occupant set out her claim by way of a replying affidavit.

The occupant sought to resist the injunction, claiming that IBRC were fully aware of her tenancy and her control of the business. She claimed that she was entitled to a new tenancy under Pt II of the Landlord and Tenant (Amendment) Act 1980 as she had been carrying on a business at the premises for upwards of five years and had acquired a business equity.

The receiver argued that a tenancy between the owner/borrower and a tenant without the prior consent in writing with the mortgagee will, where there is a covenant against assignment or sub-letting, be void against the mortgagee.

Peart J. held that the receiver was entitled to an injunction to restrain the defendant's trespass on the grounds that the occupant had failed to establish an arguable case that the mortgagee consented to the borrower subletting the premises to the occupant. The evidence of acquiescence or consent must be clear. It must be clear exactly what are the terms which they are deemed to have accepted. The court followed the seminal decision in this area of Dunne J. in *Fennell & ACC Bank v N17 Electronics Ltd (in liquidation)* [2012] IEHC 228 which held that a covenant prohibiting the assignment or subletting of a property cannot be negated by stealth or accident. In this case there was no reasonable, proper and transparent engagement between the borrowers and the bank. The bank has a title which entitles them to recover possession. The balance of convenience favours the plaintiff as the plaintiff would be in position to compensate the occupant for her losses if they lose the substantive action. Peart J. postponed the perfection of any order to enable possession to be given up in an orderly fashion in light of the nature of the business being carried out at the premises.

Application to vacate *lis pendens* The registration of a *lis pendens* can be done by a party with relative ease; the consequences for a purchaser or vendor, however, can be far-reaching and tantamount at times to an injunction prohibiting the disposal of land. A number of applications to vacate a *lis pendens* came before the courts in 2014 and two judgments from Cregan J. provide a very useful analysis of this area.

In *Thomas Tougher v Tougher's Oil Distributors Ltd and John O'Regan (No.2)* [2014] IEHC 255, the plaintiff issued a Plenary Summons seeking a number of reliefs, including a declaration that he was the beneficial owner of a number of properties. The plaintiff also sought damages due to breach of contract and negligence arising from the failure of the defendants to honour contracts and agreements in place. The plaintiff registered a *lis pendens* against a number of properties.

The first-named defendant sought an Order pursuant to s.123 of the Land and Conveyancing Law Reform Act 2009 (the "2009 Act"), to vacate the *lis pendens* together with Orders to strike out the plaintiff's claim on the grounds that it was unsustainable/bound to fail and/or that it disclosed no reasonable cause of action.

Section 123 of the 2009 Act provides that:

> Subject to section 124, a court may make an order to vacate a *lis pendens* on application by—
> (a) The person on whose application it was registered, or
> (b) Any person affected by it, on notice to the person on whose application it was registered—
> (i) Where the action to which it relates has been discontinued or determined, or
> (ii) Where the court is satisfied that there has been an unreasonable delay in prosecuting the action or the action is not being prosecuted bona fide.

It became clear during the course of the submissions that the plaintiff had registered the *lis pendens* as he was concerned that the company would be engaged in a process of "asset stripping" and that it would not have any assets to satisfy any judgment, in damages, which he might obtain against the defendants. The plaintiff was also pursuing a claim that, by reason of an alleged agreement with the second defendant, he was entitled to become a shareholder under the alleged contract, and consequently, he was entitled to claim ownership over the company's properties.

The first-named defendant applied first to have the action "determined" in accordance with s.123(b)(i), by way of an application pursuant to Ord.19 r.28 of the Rules of the Superior Courts (RSC) and/or pursuant to the inherent jurisdiction of the court to strike out on the grounds that they were unsustainable and/or bound to fail, or that they disclose no reasonable cause of action against the defendant, or that they amount to an abuse of the process of the court.

First, Cregan J. considered Ord.19 r.28 of the RSC and the well-established principle that the jurisdiction which it confers is exercisable by reference to the pleadings only (*McCabe v Harding* [2004] 1 I.R. 506; *Barry v Buckley* [1981] I.R.

306; *Keane v Considine* [2010] IEHC 267; *Aer Rianta Cpt v Ryanair Ltd* [2004] 1 I.R. 506).

Cregan J. then went on to consider the court's inherent jurisdiction to strike out proceedings if they are frivolous or vexatious or bound to fail. The court noted that this jurisdiction is, however, to be exercised "sparingly and only in clear cases" (*Barry v Buckley* [1981] I.R. 306; *Sun Fat Chan v Osseous Ltd* [1992] 1 I.R. 435) and the dicta of Clarke J. in *McCourt v Tiernan* [2005] IEHC 268 that when exercising its jurisdiction a court "must treat the plaintiff's claim at its high watermark".

Cregan J. also cited the judgment of Ryan J. in *Kelly v IBRC* [2012] IEHC 402 wherein it was held that proceedings asserting an interest in land, such as to justify the registration of a *lis pendens*, constituted an abuse of process, and parts of the plenary summons were struck out together with an order that the *lis pendens* be vacated.

In the instant case, Cregan J. held that the plaintiff's claim for breach of contract was clearly stateable and not bound to fail.

The part of the plaintiff's claim to be legally or beneficially entitled to the assets of the company was, however, bound to fail as it is a "fundamental principle of company law that shareholders have a right to a share in the company but they do not have a direct right to have a share in any of the company's assets" (*Ciara Quinn v Irish Bank Resolution Corporation Ltd (in special liquidation)*, unreported, High Court, Finlay Geoghegan J., 20 December 2013). The court found support for this view in the plaintiff's own submission that he registered the *lis pendens* to ensure that the defendants did not engage in asset stripping pending the determination of his claim.

The part of the plaintiff's claim seeking declaratory orders that he was legally or beneficially entitled to the company properties was therefore struck out. The action in respect of such matters was therefore held to have been "determined" within meaning of s.123(b) of the 2009 Act, with an order made pursuant thereto vacating the *lis pendens*.

The following month, on 26 June 2014, Cregan J. handed down another judgment in the case of *Tola Capital Management LLC v Linders (No.2)* [2014] IEHC 324, wherein the defendants applied to have two *lites pendentes* registered against them vacated.

The High Court had previously granted the plaintiff an injunction prohibiting the defendants from completing a debt purchase agreement with Ulster Bank in respect of certain properties.

The defendants wished to enter into an agreement with Ulster Bank to buy back certain loans which they or their companies owed to Ulster Bank and which were secured on properties which either they, or companies controlled by them, owned. The plaintiff was to provide evidence of alternative funding during the defendants' renegotiations to refinance their loans with Ulster Bank. The parties entered into an option agreement. Under the terms of this agreement, the defendants granted the plaintiff an exclusive option to obtain certain properties. A holding company controlled by the plaintiff would purchase the loans. The bank would release all claims over the companies and properties. The properties would be transferred to and retained by the holding company.

The defendants entered into an agreement with Ulster Bank for the repurchase of their loans. The negotiations to agree a partnership structure pursuant to the option agreement failed. Following this failure the plaintiff, by notice, exercised its option to purchase the properties. The defendants gave notice of their intention to decline to proceed with the purchase of the properties. The defendants argued that they had obtained alternative financing which was comprised entirely of debt with no third party equity participation. The defendants wrote to the plaintiff stating that their sole remaining obligation under the option agreement was the payment of €500,000 to the plaintiff. The plaintiff maintained that there was a binding agreement for the purchase of the properties.

Two *lites pendentes* were registered against the defendants in the Central Office.

The plaintiff's statement of claim specifically pleaded that a separate company, of which the defendants are controlling shareholders, is the owner of the relevant properties and not the defendants themselves.

The defendants argued that the *lites pendentes* registered by the plaintiff were not proper *lites pendentes* within the meaning of s.121(2)(a) of the 2009 Act and consequently should be vacated. Section 121(2)(a) provides that:

> (a) any action in the Circuit Court or the High Court in which a claim is made to an estate or interest in land (including such an estate or interest which a person receives, whether in whole or in part, by an order made in the action) whether by way of claim or counterclaim in the action.

may be registered as a *lis pendens*.

Secondly, the defendants argued that the court should make an order to vacate the *lites pendentes* pursuant to s.123(b)(ii) of the 2009 Act as the action was not being prosecuted bona fide.

Cregan J. held that the plaintiff itself would never acquire the properties. The properties were to be transferred and held by a holding company which was not yet in existence. Therefore, at the date of the registration of the *lites pendentes*, the person who was claiming an interest over the lands did not exist. It was clear from the agreement that the new company would be 100 per cent controlled by the plaintiff. The properties would be owned by the plaintiff's subsidiary. It is a principle of company law that a shareholder does not have any proprietary interest in the property of the company in which he has that shareholding. Therefore, the plaintiff has no interest in the properties, the subject matter of the proceedings.

In addition, the defendants are not the owners of the properties but the controlling shareholders of the company that owns the properties. It was held that the defendants therefore had no interest in the properties, the subject matter of the proceedings. Consequently, the *lites pendentes* were not properly registerable against the defendants.

Further, Cregan J. held that the *lites pendentes* should be vacated because the plaintiff's action was not being prosecuted bona fide. The plaintiff should have reconsidered its position and realised that it was not appropriate to maintain the *lites pendentes* once they learned that the defendants were not the owners of the properties. Despite the knowledge of this fact, the plaintiff persisted in maintaining the *lites pendentes* and contested the application to vacate them. It should also have been apparent to the plaintiff that as the properties were to be transferred to the holding company that they lacked interest in the properties.

Both decisions illustrate a strict application of the grounds upon which a *lis pendens* is validly registrable and a strong message that registration should not be embarked upon lightly.

The rule in *Walsh v Lonsdale* In *North Quay Developments Ltd v Carty* [2014] IEHC 444 (Hogan J., 15 October 2014), North Quay Developments Ltd (the "landlord") sought, by summary summons, judgment in the sum of €156,888 in respect of arrears of rent on foot of a lease agreed in February 2007 but immediately held in escrow.

In February 2007, Iverwell Ltd (the "company") entered into possession of a retail premises owned by the landlord. It was contemplated that the company would fit out the premises as a shoe shop. The business failed due to high rents and a lack of consumer demand following the banking collapse of 2008. The company defaulted on its obligations to pay rent. The principal director of the company guaranteed the performance of the payments obligations.

The company argued that there was never an effective lease supplied by the landlord which would serve to release that lease from its provisional status in escrow. Consequently, the company cannot be held liable under the guarantee which is contained in the lease and in respect of which the principal director would otherwise be liable to the landlord as surety following the default of the company.

The landlord argued that the company's case had no relation to reality. The liquidator appointed to the company disclaimed the lease pursuant to s.290 of the Companies Act 1963 as an onerous contract. The landlord submitted that it was the intention of the parties that the agreement for the occupational lease would be supplanted by the actual lease once the architect's certificate of compliance was furnished by the company to the landlord. Following the fulfilment of this condition precedent, the obligation to supply the company with a duly-executed version of the lease was overlooked.

Hogan J. held that since the enactment of the Supreme Court of Judicature (Ireland) Act 1877, the courts have consistently held that an agreement for a lease is as good as a lease. In this case, even if no actual lease was formally delivered following the release of the lease from the suspensive form in which it was held in escrow, equity treats as done what ought to have been done. Once the certificate of compliance was furnished to the landlord's solicitors, the pre-condition to the operation of the lease was satisfied and the lease took effect in equity. The limitations to the rule in *Walsh v Lonsdale* (1882) 21 Ch. D. 9 do not apply in this case, as the enforcement of the lease would not be inequitable. In this instance, no third parties were purported to be bound by the lease. The company was not prejudiced by the failure to deliver the actual lease.

The court held that the lease became binding and operative once the condition precedent for the operation of that lease was fulfilled and that the condition precedent was fulfilled when the company's architect supplied the landlord with a certificate of compliance following the fit-out of the shop. Despite the fact that the lease was not formally delivered up to the company as agreed, the company was bound by the lease in equity. The company suffered no prejudice by the failure to deliver up the lease. Consequently, it would not be inequitable to give effect to the lease.

The court, having found that the company had not established any arguable defence, granted summary judgment in the sum of €156,888.

Law Reform

The Law Reform Commission's Report, *Disclosure and Discovery in Criminal Cases* (LRC 112-2014) addresses an aspect of criminal procedure of the most fundamental kind. Underlying the Report are perennial questions. Is a criminal prosecution a search for truth or for justice? Should the prosecution and defence be regarded as competing adversaries who dictate the scope of the evidence before the court or does the court have an independent entitlement—perhaps even an obligation—to establish the true position? Should regard be had to the fact that the resources of the State to acquire evidence tend to be greater than those of the accused? Is there an obligation of candour resting on the prosecution to reveal to the accused all relevant evidence, including evidence damaging to the prosecution's case? Is there a converse obligation resting on the accused to reveal what actually happened—in other words, an obligation to self-incriminate—or, more moderately, to disclose in advance of the trial the evidence that he or she proposes to adduce?

Speaking broadly, it may be said that the traditional approach was that the prosecution had only a limited duty to disclose evidence that damaged its case and the accused was not obliged to incriminate himself or herself or give advance notice of evidence intended to be adduced. Over the past few decades, matters have been changing. The constitutional guarantee of trial in due course of law is now regarded as imposing a clear duty of disclosure on the prosecution. In *McKevitt v Director of Public Prosecutions*, Supreme Court, 18 March 2003 (*ex tempore*, Denham, McGuinness, Murray and Hardiman JJ. concurring), Keane C.J. observed:

> "[T]he prosecution are under a duty to disclose to the defence any material which may be relevant to the case which could either help the defence or damage the prosecution and that if there is such material which is in their possession they are under a constitutional duty to make that available to the defence."

The jurisprudence of the European Court of Human Rights, focusing on the need for equality of arms, is in substantial accord. Directive 2012/13 of the European Parliament and of the Council of 22 May 2012 on the right to information in criminal proceedings reinforces this approach. The Director of Public Prosecutions has issued *Guidelines for Prosecutors*, revised in November 2010, setting out criteria for disclosure of evidence in advance of trial.

Conversely, the privilege against self-incrimination has been curtailed, albeit indirectly, by permitting inferences to be drawn from an accused's failure to have replied to police questioning in certain areas. Moreover, the accused must now give prior notice of proposed alibi evidence and the identity of expert witnesses, and a court may make an order under s.15 of the Criminal Justice Act 2011 requiring the provision of information in connection with "relevant offences" specified in that Act. Michael Mulcahy SC, commenting on this statutory initiative, made the point that it undermined the argument of mutuality underpinning the rationale against the availability of discovery for the accused in criminal cases, contained in *People (Director of Public Prosecutions) v Flynn* [1996] 1 I.L.R.M. 317 and *Director of Publications v Sweeney* [2001] 4 I.R. 102: "The Criminal Justice Act 2011, Criminal Discovery and *Egalite des Armes*" (2012) 17 Bar Rev. 21 at 24.

Ireland is not alone in modifying the traditional approach in recent times; a similar, and even more radical, trend is apparent in other common law jurisdictions and in Scotland. For a deeply reflective analysis of how best to understand and categorise this international phenomenon, see Ringnalde, "Procedural Tradition and Convergence of Criminal Procedure Systems: The Case of Investigation and Disclosure of Evidence in Scotland" (2014) 62 Am. J. of Comparative L. 1133.

The Law Reform Commission, in its Report, discusses these developments. It recommends that legislation be enacted, setting out the general scope of the prosecution's duty of disclosure, including the criteria to be employed when assessing the relevance of material of which disclosure is sought, and it contains a *Draft Criminal Procedure (Disclosure) Bill* to give effect to this.

The statutory statement of the duty of disclosure would be consistent with existing case law and would require the prosecution to disclose to the accused or his or her solicitor any prosecution material which:

(a) is in the possession or power of procurement of the prosecution;
(b) is relevant to the case;
(c) has not previously been disclosed by the prosecutor to the accused or his or her solicitor; and
(d) can help the case for the defence, damage the case for the prosecution or give a lead to other evidence.

Disclosure would have to be made as early as possible and in sufficient time as to allow the effective exercise of the rights of the defence. The statutory test of relevance would be supplemented by a list of factors set out in guidelines. The Commission considers that the current *Guidelines for Prosecutors* constitute a suitable vehicle for this purpose.

The statutory framework would provide for a scheduling system. The schedules would comprise:

(a) prosecution material that the prosecutor agrees to be disclosed;
(b) prosecution material that the prosecutor considers should not be disclosed on the ground that it:
    (i) is subject to a privilege from disclosure that is recognised by any enactment or rule of law, including public interest privilege and legal professional privilege, or,
    (ii) should not for other stated reasons, including that it is not relevant, be disclosed to the accused; and
(c) prosecution material of which the prosecutor is aware but which is not, at the time of completing the prescribed form, in the possession or power of procurement of the prosecutor.

Objective material, such as CCTV footage and forensic evidence, would have to be disclosed at an early stage, including at the point where a person is detained in Garda custody. Further disclosure of scheduled materials would occur after this.

In relation to summary prosecutions, the Commission proposes that the legislation should indicate that the duty of disclosure applies and should occur "as soon as practicable and in any event alongside the summons or charge sheet". A proportionality test, on the lines indicated in the Supreme Court decision in *Director of Public Prosecutions v Doyle (Gary)* [1994] 2 I.R. 286, would set out the factors to be considered with respect to disclosure in summary proceedings.

As regards prosecutions on indictment, the Commission recommends that disclosure should occur "as soon as is practicable and in any event not later than either the date on which the accused is put on his or her election or the date on which the book of evidence is served on the accused or the accused's solicitor".

The Commission considers that provision should be made for pre-trial preliminary hearings in which disputed questions concerning disclosure may be determined by the court on the application of the accused, the prosecution or any third party who may be affected by disclosure, including a potential third-party witness. The Scheme of a Criminal Procedure Bill 2014, published earlier in the year by the Department of Justice and Equality, already included such a mechanism.

The Commission recommends that, in such hearings, "it would be presumed, unless the contrary is established to the satisfaction of the court, that disclosure of the material is to be ordered in the interests of justice to ensure a trial in due course of law and to allow the preparation of the defence and the court should have regard to all the circumstances in determining whether to make an order for disclosure". The court should refuse to make an order for disclosure, provided this does not prejudice the right to a trial in due course of law, where:

(a) the material is subject to a privilege from disclosure that is recognised by any enactment or rule of law, including public interest privilege or informer privilege;
(b) access to the material may lead to a serious threat to the life or the fundamental rights of another person; or
(c) the refusal is strictly necessary to safeguard an important public interest, including where access to the prosecution material could prejudice an ongoing investigation or seriously harm the national security of the State.

When deciding on whether to order disclosure, a court should be required to take a number of factors into consideration including, but not limited to, the following:

(a) the probative value of the material;
(b) whether it is necessary for the accused's right to a trial in due course of law and the public interest in preserving the integrity of the criminal justice process;
(c) the rights of any person to whom the material held by the third party relates, including any reasonable expectation of privacy of that person, and any potential harm (whether physical or emotional), including the risk of secondary and repeat victimisation, which disclosure of the material held by the third party may cause to that person; and

(d) whether it is necessary to make an immediate order for disclosure and, in particular, whether it would be appropriate in the circumstances to postpone until the trial consideration of disclosure of the material, including having regard to other probative evidence that has already been disclosed concerning any person to whom the material held by the third party relates.

In a sexual offence case, the court would be required to take the following additional factors into consideration:

(a) society's interest in encouraging the reporting of sexual offences;
(b) society's interest in encouraging the obtaining of treatment by complainants of sexual offences; and
(c) the public interest in ensuring that adequate records are kept of counselling communications.

In such a disclosure pre-trial hearing, the Commission proposes that the complainant, a third party or any person affected by the making of a disclosure order should be on notice and should be entitled to be legally represented, free of any contribution, under the Civil Legal Aid Act 1995.

There is no doubt that the task of protecting the rights of the accused and, at the same time, protecting the separate rights of the complainant is formidably difficult. See Temkin, "Digging the Dirt: Disclosure of Records in Sexual Assault Cases" (2002) 61 Camb. L.J. 126; Cassim, "Seeking Access to the Confidential Records of a Third Party: The Accused's Right to a Fair Trial v the Third Party's Right to Privacy" (2009) 42 Comp. & Int'l L.J. of S. Africa 128; Raitt, "Disclosure of Records and Privacy Rights in Rape Cases" (2011) 15 Edinburgh L. Rev. 33. The three additional factors to which the Commission would require the court to have regard consist of constant values, applicable to all such cases. It is hard to see how their normative force could vary from case to case, though of course the factors against which they would be weighed would be different in every case.

Limitation of Actions

CONTRACT

In *Murphy v Joe O'Toole & Sons Ltd* [2014] IEHC 486, Baker J. gave useful guidance on the operation of the Statute of Limitations in the context of breach of contract. The plaintiff, a farmer and agricultural contractor, entered into an agreement in April 2002 for the sale to him of a piece of agricultural machinery, as a result of which the vendor incurred a legal obligation to deliver the machine in exchange for the concurrent obligation of the plaintiff to pay for it. The machine was delivered on 30 October 2002. Proceedings for breach of contract (and negligence: see below, p.475) were initiated in July 2008.

Baker J. held that the claim was not statute-barred. There was no precedent directly in point. Baker J. had resort to the Sale of Goods Act 1893, which distinguished between a sale where delivery takes place at the time of the contract and an agreement for sale, where delivery is to occur on a future date. Baker J. observed:

> "The date of the delivery of the goods may or may not be the date title in the goods passes, but in this particular case there is no reason to suppose, nor has it been argued before me, that title to the ... machine did or could have passed to the buyer before the goods were delivered and before he paid for them. What is clear, however, is that under s.1 of the Act of 1893 the delivery of the goods, and the concurrent obligation to pay for the goods, is the point at which the contract or agreement for sale becomes a sale, and breach, if there was one, occurred at performance or delivery when the contract was no longer executory but was executed."

Accordingly, Baker J. held that the limitation period of six years ran from the date of delivery of the machine.

PROFESSIONAL NEGLIGENCE

In *Haughey v J & E Davy, t/a Davy* [2014] IEHC 206, the plaintiff first sought investment advice from the defendant stockbroker in 2005, when he was 20 years old. The relationship continued for a number of years. The plaintiff, who lost substantially on contracts for difference, claimed damages for breach of contract and negligence. (We consider the successful outcome of that claim in the Torts Chapter, below, pp.648–650.) The defendant, as stockbroker, had a duty under the Rules of the Irish Stock Exchange 1997 to examine closely the particular circumstances of its clients. Charleton J. concluded that the defendant had not done this effectively and had culpably failed to identify a number of personal characteristics that made it dangerous for the plaintiff to invest as he did.

In regard to the question of the possible application of the Statute of Limitations, Charleton J. observed:

> "There was a complete failure to get to know James Haughey for what he was. There was a complete failure in that fundamental obligation under the rules of the Irish Stock Exchange. That obligation is not one which arises at one point in time only and is then completed; it is a continuing obligation. In this case, at no stage was that obligation met. While it may be met by a thorough introduction and analysis that maintains a profile over years or decades, failure to engage in that analysis means that there is an unfulfilled obligation throughout the entire of the relationship. That is why this case has nothing to do with the Statute of Limitations."

PURE ECONOMIC LOSS

In *Komady Ltd v Ulster Bank Ltd* [2014] IEHC 325, the plaintiffs, customers of the defendant bank, initiated litigation on 23 November 2012, claiming that the bank had been guilty of misselling by negligently advising them to enter Swaps agreements on 18 July 2006. The plaintiffs argued that it was only in 2012 that they first learned the true nature of the Swaps. The limitations question was taken as a preliminary issue.

Peart J. held that the claim was statute-barred, on the authority of *Gallagher v ACC Bank plc* [2012] 2 I.R. 620, where the Supreme Court had held that the cause of action for negligence accrued at the date of entry into a financial venture that was alleged to be damaging to the plaintiff rather than at some later time. *Gallagher* is analysed in detail in the *Annual Review of Irish Law 2012*, pp.414–421.

Counsel for the plaintiff in *Komady* had argued that, until actual loss had occurred, the tort was not completed and that it was not until such time in 2012 that the plaintiffs sought and were given advice from legal and financial experts that their damage became manifest or apparent. Peart J. responded:

> "The difficulty with that argument … is that it is in effect contending for a discoverability test, and that is something which has not been provided for by the Oireachtas in any amendment to the Act of 1957, except in relation to personal injury actions. In my view, as was the case in *Gallagher v. ACC*, the plaintiffs suffered their loss when in July 2006 they entered into the Swaps which were negligently mis-sold to them according to the assumed facts in that regard. As Fennelly J. stated [in *Gallagher*]: 'It is to my mind inescapable that the plaintiff's claim as pleaded is that that he suffered damage by the very fact of entering the transaction and purchasing the bond. The cause of action then accrued.'
>
> Even if one was to say that the date of accrual was the date on which the plaintiffs were first 'out of the money' and had to make a payment to the bank under the Swaps rather than 'in the money' and in receipt of a payment from the bank, that date was October 2006, and the plaintiffs did not commence their proceedings until 23rd November 2012. But I hold in any event that the date of accrual was the date on which they entered into

these Swaps. That is the date on which they were mis-sold the Swaps and the date therefore on which they suffered damage."

In *Murphy v Joe O'Toole & Sons Ltd* [2014] IEHC 486, the purchaser of an agricultural machine sued the vendor for breach of contract, negligence and negligent misstatement in respect of alleged defects in the machine. Baker J. held that the Statute of Limitations in the claim for breach of contract ran from the date of delivery: see above, p.473. With regard to the claims for negligence and negligent misstatement, she appeared to consider that the Statute ran from the time of the making of the allegedly negligent representations, which necessarily preceded the making of the contract, or the date of the making of the contract. She interpreted O'Donnell J.'s remarks in the Supreme Court decision of *Gallagher v ACC Bank plc* [2012] 2 I.R. 620 on the close connection that can occur between claims for breach of contract and claims for negligence as mandating the re-characterisation of the latter as claims for breach of contract. Perhaps O'Donnell J. did not intend to go so far but rather to ensure that claims for negligence tagged on to claims for breach of contract should not be permitted adventitiously to shield plaintiffs from the six-year limitation period applicable to claims for breach of contract.

FATAL ACCIDENTS

In *Hewitt v Health Service Executive* [2014] IEHC 300, Baker J. was called on to resolve a highly important question relating to the limitation period for fatal accident claims, which, curiously, had never previously been squarely addressed by an Irish court. May such claims be maintained where the person who has died failed to sue the defendant for the wrong done to him or her within the limitation period for that person's claim? In the instant case, the claim was one for professional negligence against medical personnel for alleged failure to diagnose cancer in a woman, resulting in her death some years later. The woman had learned of the failure but had not initiated any litigation within the two-year period following her acquiring that knowledge. Accordingly, any claim that she might have had no longer existed by the time of her death. Her family later took fatal accident proceedings.

The key provision is s.48(1) of the Civil Liability Act 1961. It provides:

> Where the death of a person is caused by the wrongful act of another such as would have entitled the party injured, but for his death, to maintain an action and recover damages in respect thereof, the person who would have been so liable shall be liable to an action for damages for the benefit of the dependants of the deceased.

Baker J. concluded that the fatal accident claim was not defeated by the failure of the deceased woman to have initiated litigation within the limitation period relevant to her claim. Baker J. observed:

> "It seems to me that the cause of action, being one that can only accrue at the date of death of the deceased, cannot be one that becomes statute-barred before the date of death. The action and the cause of action in s.48

> is one created by statute and is an action of a different type from one which may be maintained by a person arising from a wrongful act during his or her life. The claim under s.48 is a claim that may be maintained by the dependants of Mrs. Hewitt for *solatium* and damages insofar as they can show she would have provided either direct monetary or indirect service benefits to them during her life. Such an action may be maintained only if the person, making the contribution or whose death has caused the mental anguish, has died...
>
> As a matter of logic, the action under s.48 of the Act of 1961 is one that comes to exist in the dependants at the death of the deceased, and is not an action which could be barred by any time that might run before that date. The clear words of s.6 of the Statute of Limitations (Amendment) Act 1991 provide that time runs at the date of death, or knowledge of the dependants, and does not link limitation to the knowledge of the deceased, or to other factors that might have barred her. For the reasons I have outlined I am not persuaded that this clear limitation period is altered or supplemented by the interpretation canvassed by counsel for the defendant as to the meaning of s.48(1)."

Baker J. distinguished the decision of *Mahon v Burke and the Midwestern Health Board* [1991] 2 I.R. 495, where Lavan J. had held that the settlement by the deceased of his claim precluded a subsequent fatal accident claim. In Baker J.'s view, that case was concerned with preventing double recovery rather than the question that arose in the instant case.

Commentators generally favour the approach taken by Baker J., on the basis that the deceased may not have been aware of his or her entitlement to sue (Healy, *Principles of Irish Tort Law* (Dublin: Clarus Press, 2006), para.2.104) or that to deny the fatal accident claim is to bar the cause of action before it accrues (White, *Irish Law of Damages for Personal Injuries and Death*, Vol.1 (Dublin: Butterworth, 1989), para.8.3.08). Formally, the latter analysis may be contested. A fatal accident claim, where the deceased failed to initiate litigation during his or her lifetime within the relevant limitation period, is not "barred" before it accrues: it simply never comes into existence because a necessary precondition has not been fulfilled. The dependants had no claim at all prior to the enactment of the Fatal Accidents Act 1846. It is true that the dependants' claim is separate from that of the deceased, but as a historical and personal matter, it derives from the intimate relationship between the dependants and the deceased. A deceased may have chosen not to sue a defendant for one of a variety of laudable reasons. For the law to ignore an autonomous decision of the deceased is not always to advance the cause of justice.

COUNTERCLAIMS

Section 6 of the Statute of Limitations 1957 provides:

> For the purposes of this Act, any claim by way of set-off or counterclaim shall be deemed to be a separate action and to have been commenced on the same date as the action in which the set-off or counterclaim is pleaded.

In *Irish Bank Resolution Corporation Ltd v McCaughey* [2014] IEHC 230, the defendant's counterclaim alleged negligence, misrepresentation, negligent misstatement, breach of duty and breach of contract against the plaintiff bank. The defendant made what Kelly J. described as "a potential knock out point" in respect of the alleged counterclaim, to the effect that the limitation period had expired.

The plaintiff's proceedings had commenced in July 2013. Kelly J. noted that the last agreement in suit was on 28 March 2007, and, accordingly, any claim in respect of it should have been brought by March 2013. Thus, the purported counterclaim was time-barred. The defendant's allegations of wrongdoing in the management of the funds could be made only against the manager of the funds, which was not the plaintiff in the litigation.

EMPLOYMENT

In *Health Service Executive v McDermott* [2014] IEHC 331, Hogan J. was called on to interpret s.6(4) of the Payment of Wages Act 1991 (the "1991 Act"), which introduces a time limit for claims taken under the Act before the Rights Commissioner. It provides:

> A Rights Commissioner shall not entertain a complaint under this section unless it is presented to him within the period of 6 months beginning on the date of the contravention to which the complaint relates or (in a case where the Rights Commissioner is satisfied that exceptional circumstances prevented the presentation of the complaint within the period aforesaid) such further period not exceeding 6 months as the Rights Commissioner considers reasonable.

The plaintiff, a medical consultant employed at the defendant's hospital, in June 2011 sought compensation for the non-payment of a salary increase over the previous six months. The defendant argued that s.6(4) defeated the claim as the non-payment had commenced as far back as June 2009. Affirming the Employment Appeals Tribunal, Hogan J. rejected this argument. He reasoned as follows. Every distinct and separate breach of the 1991 Act amounted to a "contravention" of the Act. Thus, if an employee was paid monthly and the employer made an unlawful deduction in respect of salary for every month in a two-year period, "it might be said in the abstract that there ha[d] been 24 separate 'contraventions' of the 1991 Act during that period". The key question was the "date of the contravention to which the complaint relates". Hogan J. commented:

> "In other words, time runs for the purposes of the Act not from the date of any particular contravention or even the date of the first contravention, but rather from the date of the contravention 'to which the complaint relates'. As the EAT pointed out in its ruling on the matter, had the Oireachtas intended that time was to run from the date of the first contravention, it could easily have so provided."

Thus, in a case where the employer had been unlawfully making deductions for a three-year period, then, provided that the complaint which had been presented related to a period of six months beginning "on the date of the contravention to which the complaint relates", the complaint would nonetheless be in time.

Hogan J. acknowledged the possibility that, when enacting s.6(4), the Oireachtas had not fully appreciated that everything might turn for the purposes of time on the actual manner in which the particular complaint was actually framed by the employee, but he considered that the language of the sub-section "really admits of no other conclusion".

Hogan J. gave a stark example of the detrimental implications of the interpretation of the sub-section advanced on behalf of the Health Service Executive:

> "[A]n employer hires a young employee with little English and who perhaps has little familiarity with Irish labour rights legislation. The employer makes a series of unlawful deductions from the employee's wages and this state of affairs continues for many years due to the employee's vulnerability and lack of awareness of his statutory entitlements. Is to be said that in those circumstances the employer should be permitted to continue to make these unlawful deductions every month, more or less in perpetuity, even though this result would be precisely the logical consequence of the argument now advanced by the HSE?"

Hogan J. noted that, in *Moran v Employment Appeals Tribunal* [2014] IEHC 154, the parties had also canvassed many of the arguments which featured in *Health Service Executive v McDermott*, but that, in the event, Keane J. had not found it necessary to rule on them because the complaint as formulated by the claimant in that case related to a time period of alleged contraventions which was plainly time-barred.

CONSPIRACY

In *O'Connell v Building & Allied Trades Union* [2014] IEHC 360, Ryan J. dismissed a claim for conspiracy against the fifth named defendant, the Construction Industry Federation, which the Supreme Court had permitted the plaintiff to add as a defendant in 2012. The events which were alleged to support the claim had occurred between 1997 and 2001. Ryan J. observed that the claim against this defendant was "statute barred for a long time" and that there was no evidence of conspiracy or even agreement between the Confederation and other defendants. Although the plaintiff had maintained in his application to join the Construction Industry Federation that there had been more recent wrongful action by it, the evidence "fell hopelessly short of proving any such conduct".

PERSONAL INJURIES

In *Brennan v Mullan* [2014] IEHC 61, the plaintiff was born in 1971. He sued a religious congregation, claiming that he that he had been sexually abused by one of its members when he was a child. Cross J. held that he was out of time under the Statute of Limitations (Amendment) Act 1991. Cross J. noted, that, in contrast to the facts in *Delahunty v South Eastern Health Board* [2003] 4 I.R. 361, the plaintiff had been "aware that his significant psychological and psychiatric injuries were attributable to his abuse certainly from 1995".

In *Byrne v Heffernan* [2014] IEHC 424, Kearns P. held that a claim initiated in December 2009 for negligent diagnosis against a psychiatrist and the hospital that employed him was statute-barred. The plaintiff had been treated for schizophrenia for more than a decade as an in-patient, from around 1983, when she was 16 years old. She maintained that the actual cause of her distress was not mental illness but rather that she was the victim of ongoing sexual abuse. In 1992, she was told by another doctor that he considered that she was not suffering from mental illness. Having met with the hospital's Director of Services around December 2001 in relation to her alleged misdiagnosis, the plaintiff consulted a solicitor in 2002. She initiated, and settled, litigation alleging sexual abuse occurring while she was a patient.

Dismissing the claim against the hospital, Kearns P. stated:

> "It is clear from the various records that the plaintiff had serious concerns in relation to her diagnosis at a very early stage. Certainly by August 2001 the plaintiff was seeking an apology from [the psychiatrist who made the original diagnosis] and sought a meeting with the director of services in an attempt to gain answers to the many questions she had in relation to her treatment. She was also contemplating consulting a solicitor around this time and subsequently did so in November 2002.
>
> Based on the plaintiff's own evidence and the vast amount of records available, the Court cannot accept that the instruction to her solicitor in 2002 related solely to the sexual abuse claim while the misdiagnosis was simply a grievance at the 'back of her mind'. On the contrary, her evidence was that she informed her solicitor of her contention that she was misdiagnosed and it is clear from the records that the possibility of a negligent misdiagnosis was very much at the forefront of her concerns at that time and was integral to her decision to consult with a solicitor in an attempt to obtain the answers she was entitled to. While the sexual abuse aspect of her complaint duly proceeded in the ordinary way, no steps were taken in relation to the misdiagnosis until December 2008. This issue, to put it simply, was 'parked' ... The plaintiff made very clear in her evidence that she had made her solicitor fully aware of her belief that she had been misdiagnosed and that something had gone wrong in relation to her treatment. She described feeling frustrated that the 'system and her family' continued to disbelieve her and says she informed her solicitor in order to find out what legal options were available to her. It is clear that, at the very latest, the Statute began to run when the plaintiff consulted her solicitor in November 2002."

SEXUAL ABUSE

In *Brennan v Mullan* [2014] IEHC 61, where the plaintiff, born in 1971, alleged that he had been sexually abused as a child by a member of the defendant religious congregation, Cross J. rejected the defendant's argument that the effect of s.48A was "simply to introduce a once off extension of time, running for one year from 21st June, 2000". Cross J. stated:

> "[T]he effect of the 2000 Act was, in my view, to do two things. First of all, s.48A(1) stated that a person who satisfied its provisions would be considered to be a person under a disability within the meaning of the Statute of Limitations Act 1957, as amended, (i.e. have two years after the end of the disability period to bring the action) and further under s.(3), if the plaintiff were not under a disability in the case of an action claiming damages for sexual abuse *etc*. then that person had a once off period of one year after the passing of the 2000 Act to bring his proceedings provided certain conditions were met. It is clear that s.48A(1) and s.48A(3) are creating separate rights or entitlements to a victim of sexual abuse."

In order to qualify as being under a disability under s.48A(1), the plaintiff had to be suffering from a psychological injury caused by the act of sexual abuse or any other act of the person who committed the act of sexual abuse and that injury had to be of such significance that "his or her will, or his or her ability to make a reasoned decision to bring such action, is substantially impaired". It was clear that any disability that the plaintiff was suffering from had been caused by the act of a member of the defendant religious congregation. Accordingly, the issue before the court was whether the ability of the plaintiff to make a reasoned decision to bring the action was "substantially impaired".

The defendant had submitted that the plaintiff in 1995 had gone to see a solicitor and counsel. The only reason he did not actually institute the case at the time was because he had been legally advised that it would not succeed. The plaintiff had relied on the evidence of Dr Paul McQuaid, a child and adolescent psychiatrist, who established that the plaintiff suffered, inter alia, post-traumatic stress and depression, immature sexualisation, doubt and insecurity, personality trait disorder and feelings of isolation and rejection.

Cross J. had no hesitation following the judgment of Ryan J. in *Doherty v Quigley* [2011] IEHC 361 in holding that the plaintiff, prior to initiating of the proceedings, was suffering from psychological injury of such significance that his ability to make a reasoned decision to bring the action was substantially impaired, within the meaning of s.48A(1). Cross J. found that, after the 1995 advice, the plaintiff had continued to suffer from a disability which was still substantially impairing his ability to bring the proceedings. He was still "clearly psychologically considerably damaged". He had been unable to make a formal complaint to An Garda Síochána or to confront the Congregation. Accordingly, though he had been given much good advice in 1995 and later, he had been unable to follow that advice. He had not persisted with his counselling and his problems with relationships, friends and generally with his life had persisted. Even with the support of a loving wife and family and after the launching of proceedings, he still had not the capacity to inform his parents that he had been abused. He had to undergo a considerable regime of planned preparation before he could inform his siblings. Accordingly, Cross J. held that the defence of the Statute of Limitations failed.

In *Byrne v Heffernan* [2014] IEHC 424, Kearns P. dismissed a claim for negligence initiated in December 2009 against a hospital and one of its psychiatrists taken by a woman who alleged that she had been the victim of ongoing sexual abuse, which was negligently diagnosed as schizophrenia around 1983, resulting in extended periods of hospitalisation. Kearns P. held that the woman had had knowledge of the relevant ingredients specified by the Statute of Limitations (Amendment) Act 1991 by 2002 at the latest: see above, p.479. Although he set out in his judgment legal submissions as to the possible application of the Statute of Limitations (Amendment) Act 2000 (the "2000 Act"), Kearns P. did not specifically address that legislation when dismissing the claim. It must therefore be concluded that he considered it to have no application, as the resolution of the date of knowledge issue could not trump the issue as to the possible application of an extension of time permitted under the 2000 Act.

The present statutory dispensation regarding the relationship between the concepts of contributory negligence, vicarious liability and sexual abuse is one that may need reconsideration. In *Hickey v McGowan* [2014] IEHC 19, the plaintiff had been subjected to serious sexual abuse over a three-year period from 1969 to 1972, when he was a pupil at a school where the second named defendant, as a member of the Marist Order of Brothers, was a teacher. The school manager at the time had since died. The first named defendant was the head ("Provincial") of the Marist Brothers in Ireland. He was sued as being vicariously liable for the acts of the second named defendant. O'Neill J., after a detailed analysis of recent international developments in the law on vicarious liability, imposed liability on the first named defendant in respect of the second named defendant's tortious conduct. O'Neill J. also considered the question of the possible vicarious liability of the deceased school manager. If he was so liable, then s.35(1)(i) of the Civil Liability Act 1961 would come into operation as any claim against him was statute-barred. Section 35(1) provides in part as follows:

> For the purpose of determining contributory negligence—
>
> ...
>
> (i) where the plaintiff's damage was caused by concurrent wrongdoers and the plaintiff's claim against one wrongdoer has become barred by the Statute of Limitations or any other limitation enactment, the plaintiff shall be deemed to be responsible for the acts of such wrongdoer ...'

By way of contrast, the plaintiff would not have his damages reduced to take account of any vicarious liability of deceased or other members of the Marist Congregation against whom his claim might be statute-barred. This was on account of O'Neill J.'s holding that the Congregation was to be treated as a corporate body, in the instant proceedings represented by the first named defendant.

In estimating the extent of the school manager's vicarious liability, O'Neill J. was satisfied on the evidence that by far the greatest element of control over the teaching activities of the abusing Brother had rested with his superiors in the Marist Congregation. The manager of the school had had "little or no role to play in any of this". He had, however, retained his residual legal authority over the contractual arrangements between himself and the abusing Brother, an authority which could "not be treated as negligible or a nullity". O'Neill J. assessed the liability of the manager at 10 per cent of the overall liability, which was subtracted from the award of damages.

One must have some concerns as to how s.35(1)(i) will operate in future claims for sexual abuse where vicarious liability is in issue. The 2000 Act is premised on the fact that sexual abuse can have such a damaging psychological effect as to delay the making of a claim by the victim. In the instant case, the effect had been so strong as to block out all memory of the abuse for decades. If the victim sues Defendant A for vicarious liability and manages to withstand any defence under the Statute of Limitations or under the separate ground of undue delay, he or she will then have to run the gauntlet of Defendant A's producing another defendant—Defendant B—or, worse still, more than one other defendant, now deceased, against whom the plaintiff could, in theory have taken proceedings and the claim against whom is definitively defeated by s.9(2) of the Civil Liability Act 1961. The Supreme Court in *Moynihan v Greensmyth* [1977] I.R. 55 upheld the constitutionality of s.9(2) on the basis of the desideratum of winding up the estates of deceased persons with due expedition; but that surely is an easier question than whether it is constitutional to reduce the compensation for victims of sexual abuse during childhood on account of the early demise of their abusers. Frankly, the present law appears hard to reconcile with fundamental constitutional values relating to dignity, equal treatment, bodily integrity, the right to litigate, property rights and the rights and welfare of children.

LEGITIMATE EXPECTATION

In *Rossmore Properties Ltd v Electricity Supply Board* [2014] IEHC 159, the question of the limitation period appropriate to a claim for breach of legitimate expectation was raised, but not resolved. The plaintiff sought court authorisation for a "very radical" amendment to its statement of claim, by the substitution of completely new wording. The litigation concerned compensation for restrictions on development of the plaintiff's land. Whereas the original draft of the statement of claim had included a plea that, in Birmingham J.'s words, was "at least a nod in the direction of the doctrine of estoppel/legitimate expectation", the proposed amendment contained a specific plea that the plaintiff "has a legitimate expectation to be compensated by the defendant pursuant to an agreement between the ESB and the Irish Farmers Association called Code of Practice for Survey, Construction and Maintenance of Overhead Lines in Relation to the Rights of Land Owners of October 1985". The prayer claimed damages pursuant to that doctrine.

Birmingham J. authorised the amendment to the statement of claim, noting that the defendant would be free in the substantive proceedings to raise the limitation defence by way of preliminary issue. He considered that the defendant's assertions made in relation to the plaintiff's claim being statute-barred by the defendant were

> "far from straightforward and obvious ... The approach that I would take to situations where a defendant has concerns that he or she wishes to raise in relation to the statute of limitations is, that unless it is obvious that the claim is statute barred, so that no useful purpose would be served by permitting the amendment then the appropriate course of action is to permit the amendment while making it clear that the defendant is of course entitled to rely on the statute of limitations and is not in any way to be disadvantaged in that regard by the fact of the amendment."

The defendant had argued that the claim in legitimate expectation was a claim in tort and that, accordingly, a six-year time limit was applicable. The defendant relied on *Taite v The Minster of Social Welfare* [1995] I.R. 418, the case dealing with the State's failure to implement the EU Directive dealing with equal treatment for men and women in matters of social security, and *McDonald v Ireland* [1998] 1 I.R. 134, dealing with the position of an An Post employee deemed to have forfeited his post following upon his conviction of the offence of membership of an unlawful organisation in accordance with the provisions of s.34 of the Offences Against the State Act 1939, a section subsequently found unconstitutional. The plaintiff had contended that the claim was not one where the time limit referable to torts applied but rather that what was in issue was an equitable remedy. It accepted that delay defeats equity and said that, by seeking the amendment, it exposed itself to a more rigorous regime.

Birmingham J. did not give any indication of his views on this debate. The answer is by no means clear: see McMahon & Binchy, *Law of Torts* (Dublin: Bloomsbury Professional, 2013) 4th edn, paras 10.178–188, *Lett & Co Ltd v Wexford County Council* [2012] IESC 14.

PROMISSORY ESTOPPEL

In *Cavey v Cavey* [2014] IESC 16, the Supreme Court, affirming Herbert J.'s judgment in the High Court *sub nom C v C* [2012] IEHC 537, held that a claim against the plaintiff's late father's estate for promissory estoppel was statute-barred. For analysis of the Supreme Court judgment, see Karl Dowling, "Promissory Estoppel and the Statute of Limitations" (2014) (4) Ir. Probate L.J. 19. The essence of the claim was that the father had promised to leave his son property in his will. Clarke J. stated:

> "It seems to me that a significant distinction is made in s.9(2) [of the Civil Liability Act 1961], so far as claims against an estate are concerned, between a cause of action which results from an act or omission of the deceased, on the one hand, and a cause of action which may exist against those in charge of the administration of the estate of the deceased, on the other. If [the plaintiff] had a cause of action in promissory estoppel at all, it can only be because he might be able to establish that his late father was in breach of a legally enforceable promise in respect of bequeathing the family home to him. If such could be established it would be a failure, during his life, on the part of his late father to make an appropriate will to comply with his promise that gives rise to the claim.
>
> That involves an allegation of a failure on the part of his father rather than a failure by the estate itself. How otherwise could such a claim be brought? It necessarily involves a claim against the estate but arising out of a failure on the part of the deceased. It seems to me that such a claim necessarily comes within the scope of the phrase 'a claim surviving against the estate of the deceased' even if it is true that a deceased could have avoided such a claim being capable of being brought by complying with their promise to bequeath the relevant property up to the moment before their death.
>
> I am, therefore, satisfied that, on a proper interpretation of the effect

of s.9 of the 1961 Act, a claim in promissory estoppel arising out of an enforceable promise by a person to leave property by will, is a claim which can properly be characterised as one which survives against the estate of that person in the sense in which that term is used in the section. It follows that the claim brought in these proceedings could only be maintained by [the plaintiff] if it had been commenced within two years of his late father's death. The claim not having been so commenced, it is clearly statute barred."

SUCCESSION

In *LC (a Minor) v HS* [2014] IEHC 32, analysed by Dr Alan Keating, "The Interaction between Section 117 and Section 121 of the Succession Act 1965" (2015) Conveyancing & Prop L.J. 58 and in the Probate and Succession Law Chapter below, p.583, Clark J. held that the plaintiff's claim under s.121 of the Succession Act 1965, made almost four years after the death of her father in 2005, was statute-barred and not saved by the fact that the child had initiated a s.117 application within the appropriate limitation period for such application. It transpired that the father had in fact died intestate. Clark J. observed:

> "[W]hile it might be unnecessary to expressly seek a declaration under Section 121 in Section 117 proceedings, this does not equate to what happened in this case where more than three years elapsed between the time when the Plaintiff became aware of the disposition and the date on which the Defendant was first put on notice of the Section 121 claim by way of the 2009 proceedings. Although the Section 117 proceedings were brought within time they were not appropriate to an intestacy and they did not include a claim under Section 121 nor was any claim brought to amend the pleadings within a reasonable time after the Plaintiff was aware that [her father] had died intestate and that it had been asserted by the Defendant that his estate did not comprise any real property. In those circumstances it is clear that her claim falls to be dealt with under the intestacy rules under Section 67, and it would be unconscionable for the Court to exercise its inherent jurisdiction to make an order under Section 121. The Court is satisfied that the action is statute barred."

ADVERSE POSSESSION

In *Dooley v Flaherty* [2014] IEHC 528, Hogan J. gave useful guidance on aspects of the law on adverse possession. The property in question was a derelict house in Galway city, in a state of considerable disrepair, with no internal toilet and no hot water. The defendant, who was asserting an adverse title, was an elderly man. The plaintiffs pointed to the state of dereliction and the consequent impairment on the potential for enjoyment of living in the premises as evidence of an absence of an *animus possidendi* on his part. Hogan J. did not agree. He observed:

> "If the decrepit state of the premises serves to create a presumption that there was no real *animus possidendi* on the part of the squatter, such a presumption is, at best, a slight one which can be disproved on the facts of

> a particular case. Such is the position here. It is clear that Mr. Flaherty is a man of extremely modest and frugal tastes. It is also clear from his evidence that he is content with his work and his own company and that he cares little for that which the modern world seems to regards as essential or necessary. One may surmise that Mr. Flaherty would be quite content to live in this accommodation, irrespective of whether he owned it or not. In the present case, therefore, the state of the property has no relevance to the question of whether Mr. Flaherty's possession was adverse to the true owner."

Even though the property might not be suitable for human habitation, the fact remained that the defendant had derived enjoyment from it. It had been his home all of his life. In Hogan J.'s view, the term "enjoyment" in the context of adverse possession connoted the use and obtaining benefit from a property rather than the act of deriving pleasure or satisfaction from ownership. Hogan J. observed:

> "If ... the plaintiffs' submission were correct, it would mean that the courts might be required into inquire into the subjective tastes and feelings of landowners for the purposes of assessing whether the law on adverse possession applied to that particular property, thus adding needless complexity to an area of the law which is already beset with its own difficulties. Just as importantly, this would also unfairly weaken the legal rights of landowners. The owner of an ugly office block in a desolate industrial estate is nonetheless entitled to have her legal entitlements safeguarded by the law, even if she actually detested the place and derived no personal pleasure or satisfaction from that ownership."

The evidence established that the plaintiffs' predecessor in title had carried out some repairs on the roof of the property during the period in respect of which the defendant asserted adverse possession. This was fatal to his defence, since even minimal acts by the owner would suffice, as Clarke J. had held in *Dunne v Iarnrod Eireann* [2007] IEHC 314. The fact that the defendant was unaware of these acts was irrelevant and did not afford him a defence. Hogan J. ruminated on the possibility that an owner who claimed an act of possession by entering his own lands by stealth might not satisfy the *Dunne* test:

> "[W]here, for instance, certain farmland has been occupied adversely by a squatter, would it suffice to arrest the running of time if, for example, the owner could show that he had once walked the lands at night during the running of the 12 year period?"

Such a question had no relevance to the instant case, where the repairs had been carried out openly.

The fact that the plaintiffs' predecessor in title had insured the property throughout the period was a further reason for holding that the plaintiffs' *animus possidendi* had been established, in Hogan J.'s view.

MISTAKE

In *Edwards v Ark Life Assurance Co Ltd* [2014] IEHC 437, the plaintiff claimed that the defendant had been guilty of breach of contract and misrepresentation in respect of a contract of insurance made in 1999. He alleged that the defendant, its servants or agents had keyed the policy onto their system as a single life policy rather than as a joint life (last survivor) policy for his wife and himself. His wife had died in 2003. The proceedings were initiated more than six years after the date of her death but, on the defendant's motion for dismissal of the claim as being statute-barred, the plaintiff argued that s.72(1) of the Statute of Limitations 1957 (the "1957 Act") preserved the claim. Section 72(1) provides:

> Where, in the case of any action for which a period of limitation is fixed by this Act, the action is for relief from the consequences of mistake, the period of limitation shall not begin to run until the plaintiff has discovered the mistake or could with reasonable diligence have discovered it.

The plaintiff argued that he had not discovered the mistake until he received a letter in June 2006, from an employee on behalf of the defendant to the plaintiff. In a succinct judgment on the limitation question as a preliminary issue, White J. held that, by reason of s.72(1), the claim was not statute-barred. White J. noted, however, that it would be open to the judge hearing the substantive claim "to consider the statute, and to apply it or restrict the claim to six years premiums calculated from the date of issue of the proceedings".

BREACH OF TRUST

In *Komady Ltd v Ulster Bank Ltd* [2014] IEHC 325, where customers of a bank alleged that they had been missold Swap agreements by their bank in 2006, more than six years before they initiated the litigation against the bank, they asserted that, because the bank was in a fiduciary relationship with them, their claim might be seen as one more akin to a fraudulent breach of trust and, as such, a claim for which no period of limitation is provided in the 1957 Act. Section 44(a) of that Act provides:

> No period of limitation fixed by this Act shall apply to an action against a trustee or any person claiming through him where–
> (a) the claim is founded on any fraud or fraudulent breach of trust to which the trustee was privy ....

Mr Howard has referred also to Canny, *Limitation of Actions* (Dublin: Round Hall, 2010) where at para.13-20 the author states:

> "The Statute of Limitations 1957 contains no reference to actions for breach of fiduciary duty. A breach of fiduciary duty is a cause of action in equity rather than an equitable relief, but as the reliefs sought in action for breach of fiduciary duty will be equitable reliefs, s.11(9) of the Act of 1957 will still apply. This has the result that no limitation period will apply to an

> action for breach of fiduciary duty unless the courts would have applied a limitation period by analogy prior to the passing of the 1957 Act."

Peart J. did not agree. In his view, the facts of the present case, as assumed, were "just the sort of facts where a court would and should apply the limitation period by analogy, as it would have prior to the 1957 Act." Peart J. noted that, in *Knox v Gye* (1872) 5 App Cas 656, a case concerning the taking of an account, Lord Westbury had stated:

> "The general principle is that where a Court of Equity assumes a concurrent jurisdiction with Courts of Law no account will be given after the legal limit of six years, if the statute is pleaded. If it could be doubted whether the executor of a deceased partner can, at Common Law, have an action of account against the surviving partner, the result will still be the same, because a Court of Equity, in affording such a remedy and giving such an account would act by analogy to the Statute of Limitations. For where the remedy in Equity is correspondent to the remedy at Law, and the latter is subject to a limit in point of time by the Statute of Limitations, a Court of Equity acts by analogy to the statute, and imposes on the remedy it affords the same limitation. This is the meaning of the common phrase that a Court of Equity acts by analogy to the Statute of Limitations, the meaning being that where the suit in Equity corresponds with an action at Law which is included in the words of the statute, a Court of Equity adopts the enactment of the statute as its own rule or procedure. But if any proceeding in equity be included within the words of the statute, there a Court of Equity, like a Court of Law, acts in obedience to the statute."

Peart J. considered that there was nothing in the facts of the instant case to take it outside what had been stated by Lord Westbury:

> "The facts giving rise to the equitable claim by virtue of any fiduciary relationship are co-terminus with the facts giving rise to the claim in tort, even if fiduciary obligations are of an ongoing nature during the relationship. That relationship does not alter the fact that the plaintiffs are able to plead, as they have done, that in July 2006 they were negligently and in breach of duty (presumably including a breach of fiduciary duty) induced by the bank to enter into the Swaps."

Peart J. did not accept that the claim came within s.44. For the plaintiffs to assert that it was in the nature of a claim for fraudulent breach of trust, they would have to be able to rely also on the provisions of s.71(1)(a), where fraud is claimed, and the plaintiffs had stated unequivocally that they were not relying on fraud per se.

FRAUDULENT CONCEALMENT

Section 71(1)(b) of the Statute of Limitations 1957 provides that, where, in the case of an action for which a period of limitation is fixed by that Act, the right of action is concealed by the fraud of the defendant, the period of limitation shall not begin to run until the plaintiff has discovered the fraud or could with reasonable diligence have discovered it. In *Komady Ltd v Ulster Bank Ltd* [2014] IEHC 325, Peart J. held that s.71(1)(b) could not "serve as a *deus ex machina* to rescue the plaintiffs from the fatal effects of the six year limitation period". The plaintiffs claimed that they had been negligently advised by their bank to enter into Swaps agreements with the bank in 2006 and that they had not discovered the detrimental character of the Swaps until 2012. They argued that the defendant had concealed information from them that would have enabled them to know that they had a cause of action against the bank, or at least would have put them on inquiry; the bank knew that they had no separate legal advice and, being in a fiduciary relationship, had concealed the true nature of the Swaps. The plaintiffs contended there had been further concealment for the purpose of s.71(1)(b) because the bank had not complied with the Market in Financial Instruments Directive (MiFID) as it had failed to reclassify them as retail clients.

Peart J. set out his understanding of the meaning of s.72(1)(b) as follows:

> "It is agreed by all sides that the ordinary concept of criminal fraud is not a necessary ingredient for the purpose of section 71(1)(b) of the Act, as otherwise section 71(1)(a) would be superfluous. The correct meaning for the purpose of sub-section (1)(b) has been expressed in different ways on different occasions both here and in the United Kingdom, but it certainly means, in the light of the authorities opened that where the facts necessary to found a cause of action have been concealed from a plaintiff by the defendant so that it would be unfair for that plaintiff to be held to have had knowledge of them, or to be expected to have made inquiry in that regard, and where it would be unconscionable for the defendant to be permitted to rely upon the plaintiff's delay in discovering those necessary facts, time will not be considered to have commenced for the purpose of the Statute until the facts became known. It is clear also that no moral turpitude is required on the part of the defendant. But, as Lord Denning stated in *Kitchen v. Royal Air Force Association* [1958] 1 WLR 563 it is 'clear that the phrase covers conduct which, having regard to some special relationship between the parties concerned, is an unconscionable thing for the one to do towards the other'."

The plaintiffs had placed considerable reliance in their argument on the existence of the fiduciary relationship between the parties at the time the Swaps had been entered into. Peart J. was willing to agree that such a relationship could impose a greater obligation of disclosure upon the bank. But, in his view, the fact remained that everything that the plaintiffs needed to know in order to get any advice on the Swaps was known to them by 8 July 2006:

> "They had the Swap agreements they entered into. They knew what their conservative financial objectives were and that they had explained them to the bank. They knew also that the bank had not explained these Swaps to them. They knew that they thought that they were some sort of fixed rate interest agreement. By October 2006, if not sooner, they certainly knew that it was possible that they would have to pay money to the bank

> in circumstances where they were 'out of the money'. In my view if they had gone to a solicitor at any time after July 2006, and sought advice as to whether these Swaps met their conservative financial objectives, they would have been in a position to provide all the necessary information in order to get such advice, and to decide if the Swaps had been mis-sold. Instead, they did nothing until they ran into financial difficulties in 2012 whereupon a financial review was undertaken and they received advice to the effect that these Swaps had not been suitable for the purposes in July 2006. The fiduciary relationship does not add anything to those facts. The coming into force of the MiFID in November 2007 adds nothing of relevance to those facts. It did not suddenly reveal to the plaintiffs some vital fact that was not available to them from July 2006 and which was essential to their knowledge that they had a cause of action."

In Peart J.'s view, the plaintiffs were confusing the emergence of further facts during the course of an action with facts sufficient for the accrual of a cause of action. They had had ample facts at their disposal in order to commence an action for negligence in relation to these Swaps. A process of discovery might in due course have strengthened (or weakened) their hand in terms of their ultimate success at trial but it was not necessary that every fact be known in order to commence proceedings.

In *Vieira Ltd v Ulster Bank Ltd* [2014] IEHC 591, Keane J. expressed his agreement with Peart J.'s analysis in *Komady Ltd v Ulster Bank Ltd.*

PRACTICE AND PROCEDURE

The Personal Injuries Assessment Board Act 2003 In *Mulloy v Reid* [2014] IESC 4, the Supreme Court, affirming Ryan J., held that the date of an authorisation, for the purposes of s.50 of the Personal Injuries Assessment Board Act 2003 (the "2003 Act"), in a case where the document is issued to an individual by registered post under s.79, is the date on which that person would have received the document in the ordinary course of post. Accordingly, on the facts in the instant case, the plaintiff's case was not statute-barred. The pith of Clarke J.'s comprehensive analysis is contained in the following observations:

> "It seems to me that counsel for [the plaintiff] was correct when he drew attention both to the fact that two of the three methods by which documents may be either served, given or issued to persons (in accordance with s.79 of the PIAB Act) require actual delivery into the control of the recipient. Why then would the Oireachtas have allowed an authorisation to be considered to be 'issued to' a recipient by registered post in circumstances where, unlike the other two cases, the document could be said to have been 'issued to' the relevant claimant without it coming (or having been deemed to have come) under his or her control. I am also satisfied that counsel was correct when he suggested that *Freeney* [*v Bray Urban District Council*, High Court, O'Hanlon J., 16 July 1981] is authority for the proposition that the court should lean in favour of actual communication when interpreting statutory provisions which impose strict time limits affected by the communication of a notice or document. Where, as here, important rights (in particular the

> right of access to the court) can be interfered with by reason of a failure to comply with a time limit then the highest level of certainty and fairness in the operation of the relevant statutory regime is mandated. The situation might be different if there were clear statutory language which pointed only to a different interpretation. However, the view that time begins to run again against a claimant at a point when the claimant did not know of that fact is one which I would only come to if the statute clearly mandated such to be the case."

Clarke v O'Gorman [2014] IESC 72 is a most important decision on s.12 of the 2003 Act, to the effect that it does not extinguish a plaintiff's cause of action or exclude the courts' jurisdiction but rather affords the defendant a defence which the defendant may raise in its pleadings. The plaintiff alleged that, many years previously, she had been sexually assaulted by the defendant. She had not made any application to the Injuries Board under the provisions of the 2003 Act. The defendant had not raised the matter in its defence but, when the jury had been empanelled, challenged the jurisdiction of the court to hear the case in view of such failure. De Valera J. acceded to the defendant's challenge. The Supreme Court reversed.

The Supreme Court held, first, that a claim for damages for sexual assault, battery and trespass to the person required the plaintiff to seek the consent of the Injuries Board. This holding is contrary to the interpretation favoured by Baker J. earlier in 2014 in *PR v KC Legal Personal Representatives of the Estate of MC Deceased* [2014] IEHC 126. O'Donnell J. provided a most elaborate and searching analysis of the legislation. In a key passage, he stated:

> "[C]auses of action on the one hand, and claims for personal injuries on the other, are not similar concepts. In my view, it is wrong to pose the question whether this was an action for trespass to the person and assault *or*, a civil action for personal injuries, as if these were mutually exclusive categorisations. They are not. A cause of action is something logically and legally different from the type of damage suffered as a result of the facts giving rise to the cause of action. The fact that a claim can be described as one for personal injuries does not mean that it is not an action for assault, for example. Since they are different things, the description of the cause of action on the one hand and the damage alleged in consequence on the other, are not mutually exclusive categories of causes of action, but instead overlap and intersect. Some claims for trespass to the person and assault may not involve personal injuries (although that is rare), and there are obviously many actions for personal injuries that do not involve assault (although they may all be, at some technical level, a trespass to the person). But the vast bulk of actions for trespass to the person and assault will also be, and be properly described as, actions for personal injuries. That this is so is reinforced by the provisions of s.17 of the 2003 Act which permits, but does not require, the Board to refuse to provide an assessment in certain cases containing elements out of the ordinary. In particular section 17(1)(ii)(IV) permits this course:
>
> > '[I]n case the relevant claim arises out of a trespass to the person, because the making of an assessment of the claim by the means to

> which assessors are limited to employing by this Act would not respect the dignity of the claimant.'
>
> This provision, on its face, implies that claims arising out of trespass to the person are *prima facie* included in the Act and therefore are claims for personal injuries."

O'Donnell J. accepted that some confusion could be caused by the terms of s.4(1)(i) excluding claims where, in addition to a claim for personal injuries, it is bona fide intended to claim damages or other relief "in respect of any other cause of action":

> "This might be read as implying that a claim for personal injuries is itself a cause of action. But I think that it is clear that 'other cause of action' means here, other than the cause of action giving rise to the claim for personal injuries. Indeed a reading of s.4 as a whole makes this clear. A civil action is defined as an action for the purposes of recovering damages in respect of a wrong, for personal injuries. The term 'other cause of action' refers back to 'wrong' and not 'personal injuries'. The phrase 'Other cause of action' in s.4(1)(i) means therefore in my view a cause of action other than that in which personal injuries are claimed. Once this is understood much of the conceptual difficulties and complications disappear. The question then becomes whether this is one of those rare cases in which the claim is for damages for assault or trespass to the person not resulting in personal injury. Self-evidently this is not so. The claim for personal injuries is alleged to have been suffered as a result of an assault. The claim is accordingly one for personal injuries and consequently a civil action captured by the Act."

O'Donnell J. went on to consider the circumstances in which a claim for breach of constitutional rights would not need the authorisation of the Injuries Board to proceed. He stated:

> "[O]n the language of s.(4)(1)(iii) it can be argued that *any* claim which is either characterised, or perhaps is capable of being analysed, as a claim for breach of constitutional rights, is exempted from the statute. Such a conclusion would however, entirely subvert the operation of the statute. Thus a question arises as to whether such a broad interpretation should be given to s.(4)(1)(iii) since it is rare for a statute to provide an exception which swallows the entirety of the Act[.]
>
> The intersection between claims for damages for breach of constitutional rights and claims in tort was discussed in *Hanrahan v. Merck Sharp and Dohme Ireland Ltd* [1988] ILRM 629. The effect of that decision is that the existing torts and other causes of action known to common law are to be considered the method by which the State performs its obligation to vindicate the constitutional rights of the citizen. It is only therefore if it can be shown that the existing law does not adequately protect the constitutional rights of the citizen that a separate claim for breach of constitutional rights can be invoked. In my view, it is clear that it is this limited and residual sense that the Act refers to actions for breach of constitutional rights. This is also consistent with the internal logic and structure of the Act. The scheme

> of the Act is to deal with large numbers of routine claims which can be reduced to reasonably predictable valuations. Where there is any difficulty or complexity, the Act either excludes such claims *in limine*, or permits the Board to decline make an assessment. By definition, any claim for breach of constitutional rights not itself capable of being pursued within one or other of the established causes of action must be a matter of some novelty, and consequently difficult to assess. Furthermore, it is very unlikely that such claims, if dependent on a novel legal analysis, could result in a consensual settlement on a valuation provided by the Board. Such claims are better left to courts from the outset. It is therefore understandable that such novel claims would be excluded. The same cannot be said for a standard negligence action recast as a claim for interference with the constitutional protection of the person and bodily integrity. Consequently, in my view, quite apart from the pleading point, it is apparent that the plaintiff's claim does not fall within category contemplated here. It is a claim which if valid, can be fully met by the law of trespass to the person. It does not fall under s.4(1)(iii) of the Act."

The hearing in the High Court, following the lead of *Sherry v Primark* [2010] 1 I.R. 407, had proceeded on the assumption that the effect of s.12 of the 2003 Act was jurisdictional and that therefore the point did not require to be pleaded by the defendant, and could be taken at any time in the proceedings. O'Donnell J. disagreed with this approach:

> "In my view, s.12 does not operate as a jurisdictional provision. The very concept of jurisdiction is sometimes a broad one, but in this case, I think the word is used in its narrowest and purest sense. The defendant can only succeed here, given the manner in which the application was made and its timing, if the Act deprives the court of jurisdiction to hear and determine the claim. Section 12 is certainly significant. It imposes a legal prohibition. But it is significant that the prohibition is not directed towards the court, but rather towards the parties, and in particular the plaintiff. The operative part of the section provides that 'no proceedings may be brought' in respect of any such claim without an authorisation. Manifestly it is the plaintiff who brings proceedings to whom this prohibition is directed. If the section said, as it could have, that unless and until an application was made to the Board and an authorisation granted, a plaintiff or intending plaintiff could not bring proceedings in respect of any claim, the meaning of the section would, in my view, be identical, but it would be more difficult to contend that the impact of the section deprived the court of jurisdiction, rather than imposing a restriction on the right of a plaintiff to bring a claim."

O'Donnell J. considered that this reasoning was reinforced by a comparison with the various provisions of the Statute of Limitations, several of which used the phrase "shall not be brought". It was clear that these provisions had the effect, not of extinguishing the right, but of barring the remedy. Whilst s.12 of the 2003 Act was expressed in more emphatic terms, what was much more significant was the employment of the same verb; O'Donnell J. commented:

> "[I]t is the *bringing* of proceedings which is restricted in both cases. In using that formulation, the Oireachtas was employing a statutory formulation which was very well known. While distinctions between jurisdictional and procedural limitations are difficult both conceptually and in practice, the fact is that the legal consequence of the Statute of Limitations is one that is well recognised and was well known in 2003 when the Act was enacted..."

In concluding that the trial judge had been wrong to dismiss the plaintiff's claim, O'Donnell J. noted the lateness of the defendant's jurisdictional application to de Valera J. and the fact that there had been no application to amend the pleadings. These factors, in his view, "should weigh heavily" against any subsequent application in the proceedings to amend the defence to include any plea in relation to the 2003 Act.

In *Power v Personal Injuries Assessment Board* [2014] IEHC 480, O'Malley J. held that the Injury Board's issuance of an authorisation by DX tracked mail did not comply with the requirements of s.79 of the 2003 Act. O'Malley J. observed:

> "Having regard to the authorities on statutory interpretation ..., I am of the opinion that the purpose of the section is to ensure that a person who is entitled to an authorisation to issue court proceedings for personal injuries receives it. Given that a limitation period begins to run on the date of issue of the authorisation, and given the potentially serious consequences of failure to meet the deadline thereby imposed, certainty as to the receipt is of considerable importance. The constitutional right of access to the courts is in issue."

In *Farrell v Board of Management of St Kevin's CBS Arklow* [2014] IEHC 100, a dispute arose as to the date on which the Injuries Board had issued its authorisation under s.14. If the date for which the defendant contended was correct, the plaintiff's claim would be statute-barred. The plaintiff had been injured in an incident at the defendant's school on 5 December 2007. The Injuries Board had issued an authorisation dated 11 January 2012. This named the respondent as "St. Kevin's CBS". On 22 August 2012, the plaintiff's solicitors wrote to the Injuries Board, asking if it "would please issue a further Authorisation in favour of The Board of Management St. Kevin's CBS Arklow". With a letter of 14 November 2012, the Board issued what the letter described as an "amended authorisation, reflecting the correct respondent title". This "amended authorisation" continued to bear the same issue date as its predecessor: 11 January 2012.

The defendant contended that the date of issue remained 11 January 2012 and thus that the period for initiation of the plaintiff's action had expired on 30 August 2012. The plaintiff argued that the practical reality of matters was that the date on which the authorisation finally issued was 14 November 2012. This would have the result that the limitation period expired sometime in 2013. As the plaintiff had issued his personal injuries summons on 20 December 2012, the defendant contended that it had been issued out of time.

Guided by the principles applied in *Figueredo v McKiernan* [2008] IEHC 368, Barrett J. rejected the defendant's argument, stating:

> "[I]t would be harsh, to say the least, that despite [the plaintiff] and his solicitors taking every step that they could to commence proceedings, including requesting the Personal Injuries Assessment Board, a party over whom [the plaintiff] has no control, to amend the authorisation, [the plaintiff] should suffer detriment because of the Board's practice whereby (a) issuing an authorisation to proceed against a party who was differently identified in the initial authorisation is treated merely as an amendment of that initial authorisation, and (b) it is considered appropriate that an amended document should continue to bear the date of issuance of the original document notwithstanding that the amended document in fact issues on a later date …
>
> In the present case, the authorisation empowering the plaintiff to proceed against the correctly named defendant was sent under an accompanying letter on 14th November, 2012. The court considers that it is this later date and not 11th January 2012, the date which it bears, that should be treated as the relevant date for the purposes of calculating the limitation period arising."

Disputed issues of fact In *Brandley v Deane t/a Hubert Deane & Associates* [2014] IEHC 610, Barr J. declined the first named defendant's application to dismiss the plaintiffs' claim for negligence as being statute-barred, based on the affidavit evidence of the parties. The plaintiffs were developers who built and later sold three townhouses. The first named defendant was an engineer engaged by the plaintiffs to supervise and certify the construction works. The foundations were laid in early 2004. The first named defendant certified the works on 4 September 2004. The townhouses were in due course sold. Defects manifested themselves some years later in one of the houses. The plaintiffs initiated litigation against the first named defendant on 30 November 2010 claiming damages for negligence and breach of contract.

The first named defendant, in seeking to establish that the claim was statute-barred, submitted that, if he had been negligent in his supervision and certification of the works, the breach of contract and tort of negligence had occurred by 4 September 2004 at the latest. The limitation period of six years had elapsed nearly three months before the plaintiffs' plenary summons was issued. It was irrelevant that the damage to the property might not have become discoverable until some later date. He invoked the substantial case law on the question, culminating in Birmingham J.'s judgment in *Hegarty v D. & S. Flanagan Brothers Ballymore Ltd* [2013] IEHC 263.

The plaintiffs did not argue for the application of a different legal test. They submitted that, based on their expert evidence, the damage had occurred some time after completion of the property in December 2004, and probably in August 2005. They argued that, where there were disputed issues of fact, such as when the actual damage to the property had occurred, it was not appropriate to determine such conflicts on affidavit evidence.

Barr J. agreed with the plaintiffs' argument, holding that it would be necessary to hear oral evidence from the parties and their expert witnesses before reaching any conclusion on the Statute of Limitations point.

Local Government and Housing

LOCAL GOVERNMENT REFORM

Overview of Local Government Reform Act 2014 Because of its significance, we begin this chapter with an overview of the Local Government Reform Act 2014 (the "2014 Act"). The 2014 Act represented one of the most significant legislative reforms of local government structures since the foundation of the State, and implemented in legislative form *Putting People First: Action Programme for Effective Local Government* (2012), the Government's main proposals for local government reform. Among the most significant provisions in the 2014 Act were the abolition of town councils, thus leaving elected local government limited to the larger, mostly county-based, city and county councils. It also had the effect of reducing the number of elected councillors. This was presented as part of the Government's wider rationalisation and reduction of State bodies.

The 2014 Act made significant and far-reaching amendments to the Local Government Act 2001 (the "2001 Act") (*Annual Review of Irish Law 2001*, pp.46–450), which is now the "Principal Act" setting out the legislative framework for local government law in the State. The 2001 Act therefore represented the starting point for the modern legislative reorganisation of local government in the State, following the insertion into the Constitution in 1999 of Art.28A, which gave specific constitutional recognition to local government. The 2014 Act involved a further major step in this process.

The Minister for the Environment, Community and Local Government, in presenting the 2014 Act in the Oireachtas as a Bill, stated:

> "It represents change from outdated, inconsistent and, in some cases, almost redundant structures to a configuration that is rational and reflects modern life; a heavily managerial system of governance to one where the elected council assumes a proper position of leadership and responsibility; a primarily infrastructure-focused role to one that has social, economic and community development as a key priority; and a mindset of dependency on the part of local authorities to one of much greater self-reliance and accountable, democratic leadership. The reform process is facilitating this fundamental change through significant reforms across the entire spectrum of local government in the context of its structures, functions, funding, governance and operational arrangements."

In terms of the reorganisation of the structures of local government at county, sub-county and regional levels, Pts 2 to 6 and Pt 10 (and the related Schs 3, 4 and 5) of the 2014 Act provided for:

- the merger of six city and county councils in Limerick, Tipperary and Waterford into three local authorities;
- the dissolution of all 80 town councils and their replacement by municipal districts;
- the formulation of a new integrated county-to-sub-county relationship, with the establishment of a comprehensive system of municipal governance;
- the establishment of membership levels within the new structures;
- the replacement of the pre-2014 regional structures with new consolidated regional assemblies;
- the listing and assignment of local government reserved functions to each level, and provision for a range of new reserved functions for elected councils;
- wider provision for devolution of functions from central level to local government;
- provisions relating to local and community development, including the establishment of Local Community Development Committees within the local government system; and
- provision for a plebiscite in relation to the possible establishment of an office of a directly elected mayor for the Dublin metropolitan area and related governance options (which was to have been held in 2014 but did not occur).

In addition, Pts 7 and 8 (and related Sch.3) of the 2014 Act contained a range of provisions relating to the more efficient and effective governance and management of local authorities. This included:

- rebalancing of powers between the executive and the elected council, with much greater powers granted to the elected council to direct policy, oversee implementation, and actively review the actions of local authority management; and
- the elected council also have a power of decision over appointments to the new Council Chief Executive positions which replaced the pre-2014 City and County Manager positions (which will be derived from recommendations by the Public Appointments Service on foot of the selection process for the post).

The 2014 Act also contained the following provisions related to the management and governance of local authorities:

- the pre-2014 post of City or County Manager was replaced by a post of Chief Executive, providing more explicit statutory expression of the duty of the Chief Executive to assist the formation of policy by the elected council, to comply with that policy, to support its implementation and to account for action in that regard;
- the expansion of the role and remit of local authority Strategic Policy Committees, the establishment of a National Oversight and Audit Commission, and changes to local authority audit arrangements;
- the amendment of s.140 of the Local Government Act 2001, which gives elected members power to direct the Manager. As amended

by the 2014 Act, s.140 no longer applies to the planning functions (as recommended in the *2012 Report of the Tribunal of Inquiry into Planning Matters, the Mahon Tribunal*) or to any approval or decision involving the provision of a service, finance or other form of assistance (financial or otherwise) by the local authority;
- as amended by the 2014 Act, s.140 of the 2001 Act also no longer applies to functions of the Local Community Development Committees. However, these provisions were accompanied by streamlining procedures relating to the use of s.140 involving reduction in the number of elected members required to sign a notice of intention to propose a section 140 resolution from three to two and in the period of notice required for such a resolution from seven to five days.

The 2014 Act came into effect on various dates in 2014: see the Local Government Reform Act 2014 (Commencement of Certain Provisions) Order 2014 (S.I. No. 38 of 2014), the Local Government Reform Act 2014 (Commencement of Certain Provisions) (No. 2) Order 2014 (S.I. No. 146 of 2014), the Local Government Reform Act 2014 (Commencement of Certain Provisions) (No. 3) Order 2014 (S.I. No. 214 of 2014), the Local Government Reform Act 2014 (Establishment Day) Order 2014 (S.I. No. 215 of 2014), the Local Government Reform Act 2014 (Transfer Date) Order 2014 (S.I. No. 216 of 2014), the Local Government Reform Act 2014 (Dissolution of the County Tipperary Joint Libraries Committee and Transfer of Assets and Liabilities) Order 2014 (S.I. No. 232 of 2014) and the County and City Development Boards Dissolution Order 2014 (S.I. No. 233 of 2014).

Local Government Areas and Local Authorities: Limerick, Tipperary and Waterford Part 2 of the 2014 Act (ss.8 to 18) provided for the dissolution of existing city and county councils in Limerick, Tipperary and Waterford and the establishment of new amalgamated authorities as their successors, and for related matters. Section 8 provided for the Minister to fix a day to be the establishment day on which the arrangements in Pt 2 relating to local authority mergers in Limerick, Tipperary and Waterford will take effect. Section 9 provided for the amalgamation of the existing local government areas in Limerick, Tipperary and Waterford to form a single local government area in each case and that references in legislation to cities and counties and city councils and county councils will apply to the amalgamated areas and their councils. Section 10 defined the boundaries of the new local government areas of Limerick, Tipperary and Waterford as the combined boundaries of the existing areas in each case.

Section 11 provided for the preparation, deposit, availability, and evidential status of new maps for the amalgamated local authority areas by the Commissioner of Valuation under the Valuation Act 2001. Section 12 amended the provisions in the Local Government Act 2001 relating to local government areas to take account of the new amalgamated areas in Limerick, Tipperary and Waterford and the dissolution of town councils, including the substitution of a new s.10 and Sch.5 of the 2001 Act which specify local government areas, consisting of cities, counties and in the case of the amalgamated areas, cities and counties, and the associated local authorities. Section 13 provided for the establishment of a single local authority in each of the local government areas established by s.9 and for related matters. These new authorities are known as Limerick City and County Council, Tipperary County Council and Waterford City and County Council. Each of the new authorities have the same functions as are vested by law in county and city councils generally. Section 13(2) provided that the law which applied to the dissolved councils before the establishment day also applies to the local authorities established by s.13.

Local Government Areas and Local Authorities: General Section 14 amended s.11 of the Local Government Act 2001, which provides for the establishment, titles and administrative areas of local authorities generally, to take account of the local authority mergers and dissolution of town councils. Provision is made for the continued application of royal charters and letters patent relating to local authorities for ceremonial and related purposes in accordance with local civic tradition, notwithstanding dissolutions.

Section 15 provided for the substitution of a new s.21 and a new Sch.7 of the 2001 Act specifying revised membership for each county, city and the new merged local authorities established by s.13 based on the recommendations of the *Local Electoral Area Boundary Committee Report 2013*.

Section 16 established an office of Chief Executive in respect of each of the (merged) local government areas established by s.9. It also provided for the termination of interim dual manager provisions in respect of Limerick County and City Councils, North and South Tipperary County Councils and Waterford County and City Councils, for the two offices of manager in each case to be filled by the one person, and for persons holding such offices to be appointed Chief Executive for the merged authority.

Section 17 provided for the formal dissolution of Limerick City and County Councils; North and South Tipperary County Councils; Waterford City and County Councils and for the three new councils, Limerick City and County Council, Tipperary County Council and Waterford City and County Council, to be their successors for all purposes.

Section 18 provided that, consequential on the dissolution of local authorities and their replacement under s.14, all acts duly done and decisions duly made by or on behalf of a dissolved authority will continue to have force and effect as immediately before the dissolution. Further consequential provisions related to the dissolution of local authorities and their successors were contained in Pts 4 and 5 of, and Sch.4 to, the 2014 Act.

Municipal Districts and Dissolution of Town Councils Part 3 of the 2014 Act (ss.19 to 25) provided for a new system of municipal governance at sub-county level outside of the Dublin area, with the members for each municipal district performing specified reserved functions of the local authority in respect of their district and collectively at overall local authority level. Provision was made for the dissolution of all town councils and their incorporation in the relevant counties for all purposes, for the determination of the areas of municipal districts, and for related matters.

Municipal Districts Section 19 inserted a new Pt 3A in the Local Government

Act 2001 providing that: every county (other than the Dublin counties) and city and county will be divided into municipal districts consisting of specified local electoral areas, to be determined by Ministerial order, for the purposes of the 2014 local elections, and for the titles of districts; the elected members for the local electoral areas in each municipal district will be known as "the municipal district members" and will act in that collective capacity for the purpose of performing a range of reserved functions of the county council or city and county council in respect of the municipal district.

Section 20 amended s.23 of the 2001 Act in relation to local electoral areas and to the determination of municipal districts by Ministerial order, taking account of the dissolution of town councils and of other amendments made to the 2001 Act. Section 21 provided for the functions of the municipal district members. A new s.131A and a new Sch.14A (contained in Sch.3 to the 2014 Act) were inserted into the 2001 Act. Provision was made for certain reserved functions of a local authority to be performed in respect of each municipal district by the municipal district members concerned (mainly in Pt 1 of Sch.14A to the 2001 Act, as inserted by the 2014 Act), and others to be performed by either the municipal district members or by the overall local authority membership (mainly in Pt 2 of Sch.14A). Reserved functions listed in Pt 3 of Sch.14A to the 2001 Act, as inserted by the 2014 Act, can only be performed by members of the overall local authority. Provision was also made for:

- the overall local authority to delegate additional reserved functions to municipal district level subject to certain conditions;
- regulations and guidelines with a view to ensuring effective operation of the new governance arrangements, including such matters as avoidance of duplication, resolution of differences and disagreements, and consistency between the overall local authority and municipal district levels;
- a right of "call-in" by the overall authority in certain circumstances; and
- varying the assignment of reserved functions between county and district level.

Section 22 provided for regulations to apply, with or without modification, to municipal districts or to municipal district members, various provisions of the 2001 Act relating to a local authority or the council of a local authority. These include provisions relating to matters such as meetings, procedures, members, committees, expenses and ethics requirements (see also the Local Government (Application of Certain Provisions of the Local Government Act 2001 to Municipal District Members) Regulations 2014 (S.I. No. 230 of 2014)).

Dissolution of Town Councils Section 24 provided that on a date specified by order ("the transfer date") each town council stands dissolved and ceases to exist and the local authority for the county or a city and county in which the town is situated shall, for all purposes, be the successor to the town council, and the area of the town shall, for the purposes of all local authority functions, be included in and form part of the relevant county or city and county. The transfer date was specified as being not later than the day on which the term of office of local authority members ended following the 2014 local elections. Section 25 contained consequential provisions relating to the dissolution of town councils. These include that all acts and decisions in respect of a town council shall continue to have effect and that a function of a town council shall be read as a reference to a function of the local authority in whose administrative area a dissolved town council was situated. Regulations may be made providing for any matter necessary to give effect to the dissolution of town councils. Provision was also made for a number of consequential amendments and repeals of provisions of the 2001 Act arising from the dissolution of town councils, including the deletion of Sch.6 to the 2001 Act, which had set out towns as local government areas, and Pt 3 of Sch.7 to the 2001 Act which had set out the membership of certain town councils.

General provisions relating to dissolutions Part 4 of the 2014 Act (ss.26 to 28), in conjunction with Sch.4, provided for a wide range of consequential and other necessary matters to give effect to dissolutions and successions. Section 26 provided that Sch.4, which sets out detailed consequential and transitional provisions relating to local authorities, shall apply in relation to the dissolutions effected by Pts 2 and 3 and to each dissolved authority and its successor authority. Section 27 made provision in relation to actions by local authorities to facilitate implementation of the Act in anticipation of its commencement. Section 28 provided that specified provisions of the 2014 Act became effective on enactment specifically for the purpose of holding the 2014 local elections and made clear that elections would not be held in 2014 in the case of local authorities that were dissolved.

Financial provisions consequential on dissolutions Part 5 of the 2014 Act (ss.29 to 34) provided for the establishment of a single rating authority for each county, including harmonisation of commercial rates between towns and counties, for the standardisation of vacancy refunds across the country and a number of related matters such as the amalgamation of existing valuation lists arising from the creation of a single rating authority. Section 29 provided for the harmonisation of commercial rates between those existing in towns and counties forming new local authority areas. In order to ease the transition for ratepayers to a standardised rate, while avoiding a negative impact on overall local authority revenue, the harmonisation of rates will take place over a maximum of 10 years. An adjustment mechanism was provided to phase in increases and decreases. Decisions on relevant matters such as the Annual Rate on Valuation, the annual adjustment and the adjustment period will rest with the elected council.

Section 30 provided that the local funds of the councils of the counties and cities in Limerick, Waterford and Tipperary which were amalgamated under the 2014 Act shall continue to exist after the establishment day and shall be maintained by the appropriate successor authority.

Section 31 provided for the standardisation of vacancy refunds across the country. Prior to the 2014 Act, a separate refund regime entitling commercial property owners to a 50 per cent refund of their annual commercial rates liability in the event that a property is unoccupied operated in Dublin City, Cork City and Limerick City. Elsewhere in the country refunds were 100 per cent of rates liability. Section 31 standardised the refund rate at 50 per cent nationally. Section

32 provided for a duty to inform a rating authority of transfer of relevant property. Section 33 provided for the amalgamation of pre-2014 Act valuation lists arising from the creation of a single rating authority. Section 34 provided for clarification that the "county rate" is applicable to the new City and County Councils.

Community Development within Local Authority Areas Part 6 of the 2014 Act (ss.35 and 36) provided for the alignment of the local and community development sector with local government. It provided for Local Community Development Committees to be established as committees of the local authority in each local government area to enhance strategic planning and coordination in local and community development programmes, and for the dissolution of City and County Development Boards.

Section 35 provided for the dissolution of City and County Development Boards and for consequential and transitional matters arising from the dissolutions.

Section 36 inserted a new s.49A into the Local Government Act 2001 (the "2001 Act"), providing for the establishment of new Local Community Development Committees, which are independent in the performance of their functions subject to the relevant statutory provisions. Section 36 also amended the 2001 Act by inserting a new Ch. 2 into Pt 13, consisting of seven new sections, 128A to 128G, as follows. Section 128A contains relevant definitions. Section 128B provides for the functions of Local Community Development Committees, including the preparation by the committees of five year Local and Community Plans for the local and community development of their respective areas. Section 128C contains detailed provisions in relation to Local and Community Plans, including a requirement that the plan be consistent with both the core strategy and objectives of the development plan under the Planning and Development Acts and the procedures relating to the adoption of a Local and Community Plan by the committee, its consideration by the municipal district members and its approval by the elected council of the local authority. Section 128D provides for the membership of committees. Section 128E provides for staffing, management and administration of committees. Section 128F provides that the Minister may make regulations for the purposes of the Chapter generally or in relation to the Local Community Development Committees and may issue general policy guidelines with which the committees must comply. Section 128G sets out requirements in relation to relevant bodies, including a requirement to co-operate with the Local Community Development Committee and to ensure that their policies and programme are consistent with the objectives of the Local and Community Plan. The bodies required to cooperate with the committee are publicly funded bodies including those specified in Sch.5.

Local Authority Governance and Management Part 7 of the 2014 Act (ss.37 to 57) provided for a range of changes in local authority governance arrangements and in relation to the role of the executive within local government structures. There is provision for an enhanced policy making role for elected members, including in relation to economic development and enterprise support; stronger oversight powers for the elected council in relation to the implementation of policy; and increased obligations on the executive in relation to the elected council.

Section 37 amended s.32 of the 2001 Act dealing with alternative titles for Cathaoirleach and Leas-Chathaoirleach, in light of the dissolutions provided for in Pts 2 and 3. In particular, it provided that the titles of Lord Mayor and Deputy Lord Mayor may be used in respect of Cork and Dublin Cities, and that the titles of Mayor and Deputy Mayor may be used in Galway City, Limerick City and County, Waterford City and County, and certain municipal districts. Section 38 extended the provisions for the removal of the Cathaoirleach to include reasons related to the discharge of duties as chairperson of the Corporate Policy Group (CPG); extended the provisions for the removal of the chairperson of a Strategic Policy Committee (SPC); and provided that any such removal requires a two thirds majority of those present and voting. Section 39 inserted a new s.35A into the 2001 Act to ensure that the provisions relating to the election of Cathaoirleach and Leas-Chathaoirleach also apply to the municipal district members provided for in the 2014 Act.

Section 40 provided for the effective discharge of the business of committees established under Pt 7 and of meetings of committees and municipal district members. Section 41 amended s.48 of the 2001 Act to provide for the establishment of a Strategic Policy Committee (SPC) dealing with economic development and support for enterprise; provided that Ministerial guidelines in relation to the operation of SPCs may include requirements in relation to consultation of the SPC in the formulation of policy and the timeliness of presentation of policy papers; provided that an SPC may request attendance of a public authority at a meeting of the SPC to assist the SPC in regard to its functions to consider matters connected with the formulation, development, monitoring and review of policies which relate to the functions of local authorities, and procedures for non-attendance of the public authority; and placed an obligation on an SPC to have regard to the spatial and economic strategy of the appropriate regional assembly.

Section 42 amended s.50 of the 2001 Act to provide for area committees in: (a) Cork City Council; (b) Dublin City Council; (c) Dun Laoghaire-Rathdown County Council; (d) Fingal County Council; (e) Galway City Council; and (f) South Dublin County Council.

Section 43 amended s.66 of the 2001 Act to make more specific provision for the promotion of the interests of the local community and the general development of the area, including enterprise and economic development. Section 44 inserted eight new sections, ss.66A to 66H, into the 2001 Act to make more specific provision for the making and publication of local economic and community plans.

Section 45 amended s.72 of the 2001 Act to extend the provision in that section for the transfer of certain functions from Government Departments to local authorities to also apply to the transfer of functions of other public authorities.

Section 46 amended s.127 of the 2001 Act in connection with the duty of a local authority to "take such steps as it considers appropriate to consult with and promote effective participation by the local community in local government."

Section 47 amended s.132 of the 2001 Act to extend the obligation on the Chief Executive to assist and advise the council to include the municipal district members, the CPG, SPCs and the Local Community Development Committee. The Chief Executive will also have an obligation to report on the implementation of policy determined by the elected council. Where the elected council is not satisfied with the report of the chief executive or the actions contained therein, they may adopt, by resolution, a statement outlining their reasons for this view. The Chief Executive has 14 days in which to provide a comprehensive response indicating what new actions will be undertaken or why no alternative course is available. On foot of this report, or otherwise, the elected members can request the Chief Executive to advise on the review of policy, or the implementation of policy.

Section 48 amended s.133 of the 2001 Act to provide for the restructuring of the membership of the CPG from the pre-2014 Act membership composition of the Cathaoirleach and chairperson of each SPC, to include also the leader of each registered political party in the council representing at least 20 per cent (or such other percentage specified by Order) of the elected members, and where not included as one of these ex-officio members, a member from an unrepresented municipal district. Provision was made for the Minister to alter this percentage in the period between the poll and the first meeting of councils after the election up to a maximum of 25 per cent. It also provided for the CPG to promote greater coordination in the performance of local authority functions by municipal district members and for Ministerial guidelines on timely presentation of policy proposals.

Section 49 amended s.134 of the 2001 Act to provide that the local authority corporate plan includes activities relating to the functions of municipal district members and to provide that corporate plans will set out the policy of the local authority where not otherwise provided for in any other plan, statement, strategy, or similar document.

Section 50 inserted a new s.134A into the 2001 Act requiring each local authority to prepare a "service delivery plan" identifying the services intended to be provided by it to the public.

Section 51 inserted a new s.136 into the 2001 Act extending the obligation on the Chief Executive to provide information to the council and to provide information to the municipal district members, SPCs and the Local Community Development Committee. It provided for a monthly management report, prepared for the elected members by the Chief Executive, in relation to the performance of executive functions, the implementation of policy or other matters required by the council in the exercise of its reserved functions and the provision of services.

Section 52 provided that the power, under s.140 of the 2001 Act, for an elected council to direct the Chief Executive in the performance of executive functions, is no longer applicable in relation to planning functions or to a decision to provide, to any named person or group, any service, finance or other form of assistance or benefit, financial or otherwise. The number of members required to sign the notice of intention to propose a s.140 resolution and the time required for a meeting on the resolution to take place were reduced, from three to two members and from seven days to five days, respectively.

Section 53 amended s.141 of the 2001 Act to oblige local authority elected members to provide information on a quarterly basis to the local authority for inclusion on a public register on all attendance at meetings of other bodies arising from their membership of the council, and payments made to them by such bodies. It also provided for a public register of payments made to elected members in respect of attendance at conferences, seminars or other meetings or events. As well as other provisions around training, it provided regulatory powers for the Minister to require attendance at training and development courses, including powers to reduce the amount of expenses and allowances payable to members in the event of non-attendance.

Section 54 substituted a new Ch.2 of Pt 14 of the 2001 Act (Position of Chief Executive) which carried through the replacement of the position of county or city manager by a Chief Executive. Additional elements now included in this Chapter include:

- a provision in s.145 of the 2001 Act that, in future, it will be open to the elected members to decide on the appointment of a person recommended by the Public Appointments Service for a post of Chief Executive, on foot of a selection process. Where the nominee of the Public Appointments Service is not appointed, the selection process will recommence;
- a provision in s.149(7) of the 2001 Act placing an obligation on the Chief Executive to have regard to the views of elected members expressed at meetings of the council, municipal district members, committees and in written response to drafts of new or amended policies; and
- a new power in s.149(8) of the 2001 Act for elected members to request reports by the Chief Executive on actions taken or planned in exercise of executive functions or a review of the implementation of such actions.

Section 55 amended s.151 of the 2001 Act to extend the judicial recognition of copies of documents to include documents certified by delegated employees to be a true copy of an order made by a delegated employee.

Section 56 amended s.225 of the 2001 Act to provide for the Minster to meet with a delegation from an association of local authorities at least once a year in relation to the functions of such association provided for in the 2001 Act.

Section 57 amended Sch.10 to the 2001 Act to provide for the rationalising to a single date for the first meeting of councils after elections; that councils shall determine the date of the first meeting of municipal district members; and powers to councils to reduce, on a sliding scale, the allowances and expenses of members who persistently refuse to leave a meeting where it has been resolved that their behaviour has been disorderly.

Financial Procedures, Audit and Oversight Part 8 of the 2014 Act (ss.58 to 61) dealt with the financial relationship between county and municipal district levels and related procedures; the functions of municipal district members in respect of the local authority budgetary process; and amendments to the 2001 Act to reflect the dissolution of town councils. It also introduces new provisions in relation to audit procedures and regulations. In addition, Pt 8 also provided for the establishment of a National Oversight and Audit Commission for Local Government (NOAC). The NOAC will scrutinise local government performance, in fulfilling national, regional and local mandates, scrutinise value for money where State funds are channelled through local government, and will support the development of best practice and enhanced efficiency in the performance of local government functions.

Section 58 provided for amendments to Ch.1 of Pt 12 of the 2001 Act. It defined the financial relationship between county and municipal district levels and provided for amendments of the 2001 Act to reflect the dissolution of town councils. It provided that the Minister may, by regulation, set out the budgetary format and the process to formulate a local authority budget. Functions were provided to municipal district members in respect of the local authority budgetary process. Other consequential amendments were made along with provision for the Minister to prescribe by regulation the changes in budgetary timeframes whereby, from 2014, local authorities will be required to make draft budgets available to the public by early October and, under EU provisions, the final budget must be adopted by 31 December.

Section 59 amended s.122 of the 2001 Act to provide that local authorities will be required to establish an audit committee within three months of taking office, the functions of audit committees, and provision for the Minister to make regulations regarding matters such as membership, meetings and reports of audit committees. Section 60 substituted s.121 of the 2001 Act, containing provisions relating to attendance by the auditor at a meeting of the audit committee or the local authority, and provision for qualified legal privilege for an auditor attending a meeting under these provisions.

Section 61 inserted a new Pt 12A, comprising 12 sections (ss.126A to 126L), into the 2001 Act to provide for the establishment and functioning of the NOAC as follows. Section 126A provided for the interpretation of terms in the new Pt 12A. Section 126B provided for the establishment of the NOAC, whose members are independent in the performance of their functions. Section 126C set out the functions of the NOAC including to review local government performance in fulfilling national, regional and local mandates relative to performance indicators, to oversee financial performance, to oversee the implementation of national policy including public service reforms and to support the development and enhancement of best practice. Section 126D provided a mechanism for the Minister, or the appropriate Minister in respect of functions within his or her remit, to request the NOAC to prepare a report, and set out the methodology to be followed in preparing, submitting and publishing the report. In addition, this section required the local authority Chief Executive to prepare, within 28 days of receipt of a relevant NOAC report, an implementation plan setting out how the issues raised are to be responded to. It is a reserved function of the elected members to adopt any such implementation plan. Section 126E places a duty on local government bodies to provide requested information to the NOAC, and s.126F requires other public authorities to endeavour to supply the requested information. Section 126G provides that the NOAC may publicise its intention to prepare a report and may invite submissions from the public for consideration when preparing a report.

Section 126H sets out provisions concerning membership of the NOAC, including that members hold office for two periods not to exceed five years and s.126I lists the eligibility, including disqualification criteria, and tenure of office of members of the NOAC. Section 126J provides for procedural matters (meeting arrangements, quorum) and for holding oral hearings in relation to any of its functions, and s.126K provides for an annual report. Section 126L allows the Minister to make regulations in relation to the NOAC, and to determine whether a trust or other body or a class of such trust or other body is a "local government body" and therefore subject to the NOAC.

Regional Assemblies Part 9 of the 2014 Act (s.62) inserted a new s.43 into the Local Government Act 1991, which provided for the replacement of regional authorities by regional assemblies with the general purpose of co-ordinating, promoting or supporting strategic planning and sustainable development, and promoting effectiveness in local government and public services. The composition of regions and other detailed provisions relating to regional assemblies will be prescribed by Order. Provision is also made for more effective arrangements for the governance and administration of regional assemblies (see also the Local Government Act 1991 (Regional Authorities) (Amendment) Order 2014 (S.I. No. 228 of 2014), the Local Government Act 1991 (Regional Assemblies) (Establishment) Order 2014 (S.I. No. 573 of 2014) and the Local Government Act 1991 (Regional Assemblies) (Establishment) (Amendment) Order 2015 (S.I. No. 62 of 2015)).

Regional Assemblies and Regional Spatial and Economic Strategy Part 10 of the 2014 Act (s.63) amended the Planning and Development Act 2000 to provide for the making of Regional Spatial and Economic Strategies by the Regional Assemblies.

Proposed Plebiscite on a Directly Elected Mayor for Dublin Metropolitan Area Part 11 of the 2014 Act (ss.64 to 71) provided for the arrangements in relation to the holding of a plebiscite to consider future local governance arrangements for the Dublin metropolitan area, including options for the introduction of a directly elected mayor. Such a plebiscite was due to have been held alongside the 2014 local elections but for the reasons noted below, the necessary local authority resolutions for it were not passed. Nonetheless, we note here the relevant provisions of the 2014 Act.

Section 64 set out the definitions of the terms "Dublin local authority," "Dublin metropolitan area," "directly elected mayor"' and "plebiscite" for the purpose of Pt 10. Section 65 provided that, following a request from the Minister, the Lord Mayor of the City of Dublin shall convene a forum, representative of elected members of the four Dublin local authorities to discuss *inter alia* the establishment of an office of a directly elected mayor for the Dublin metropolitan area. Subsequent to its discussions, the forum shall submit a written report, including a draft resolution and a supporting statement, containing its deliberations and conclusions to the Minister.

Section 66 provided that once the Minister is satisfied with the resolution and supporting statement, it can be put before each of the Dublin local authorities. The resolution shall provide for the holding of a plebiscite on whether the office of directly elected mayor should be established for the Dublin metropolitan area. The resolution and supporting statement should also include details of the future functions, structures and governance for the Dublin metropolitan area; the changes that would arise in relation to the local authorities and in relation to the functions of other bodies; their relationships with the office of directly elected mayor; cost and resource implications; advantages and disadvantages arising; and measures to maximise efficiency, effectiveness and accountability and to avoid duplication. All four Dublin local authorities had to adopt the resolution no later than 31 March 2014, on the basis of an absolute majority in each local authority, to enable the plebiscite to be held. Such resolutions were not passed by the prescribed date.

Section 67 provides that, if the resolution provided for in s.66 had been adopted, a plebiscite would have been held to provide for the establishment of the office of a directly elected mayor and other such matters relating to local government in the Dublin area as the Minister considers appropriate. The plebiscite would have been held in tandem with the 2014 local government elections. This section also provides for the making of regulations setting out the arrangements for holding the plebiscite, including provision of information to the electorate. Section 68 set out the electorate entitled to vote at the plebiscite, which was the electorate for the local elections in the four Dublin authorities. Section 69 provided that, had the plebiscite been passed, the Minister would have been required, within two years of the date of the plebiscite, to submit to both Houses of the Oireachtas, a report, either setting out proposals for legislating for the establishment of the office of a directly elected mayor or containing a statement of the Minister's reasons for not making proposals for legislation for the establishment of the office of a directly elected mayor.

Section 70 provided for the apportionment of costs between the Dublin local authorities in respect of the holding of the plebiscite in proportion to their population at the last census of population. Section 71 provided that, where a forum as required under s.65 had been convened and actions commenced before the coming into force of the 2014 Act, then requirements in regard to the forum report and consultations in regard to the resolution and accompanying statement would have been met.

BUILDING CONTROL

Certification of Compliance The Building Control (Amendment) Regulations 2014 (S.I. No. 9 of 2014) (the "2014 Regulations"), made under the Building Control Acts 1990 to 2007, amended the Building Control Regulations 1997 (S.I. No. 496 of 1997) (the "1997 Regulations") (*Annual Review of Irish Law 1997*, p.557) and came into force on 1 March 2014. The 2014 Regulations also revoked and replaced the Building Control (Amendment) Regulations 2013 (S.I. No. 80 of 2013) (the "2013 Regulations") (*Annual Review of Irish Law 2013*, pp.441-442) which had also been due to come into force on 1 March 2014.

The main purpose of the 2014 Regulations, like the 2013 Regulations, is to provide for: statutory certification of the design and construction of building projects; lodgement of compliance documentation; mandatory inspections during construction and validation; and registration of certificates.

The Royal Institute of the Architects of Ireland had objected to some of the detailed elements of the 2013 Regulations, and the 2014 Regulations therefore modified these, especially in relation to the wording of the statutory certificates to give greater comfort to architects signing the certificates of compliance. The 2014 Regulations also recognise the online building control management system (available at: *localgov.ie/en/BCMS* [last accessed 14 July 2015]) as the preferred means of building control administration.

Article 9 of the 1997 Regulations, as amended by reg.7 of the 2014 Regulations, provides for a revised form of commencement notice which must be submitted to a building control authority (city or county council) prior to the commencement of construction works. From 1 March 2014, the commencement notice must be signed by the owner of the works.

Where the works involve the creation of a building (including a single dwelling unit), an extension greater than 40 square metres or require an application for a Fire Safety Certificate in accordance with Pt 3 of the Building Control

Regulations 1997 to 2014 the commencement notice and the appropriate fee must in addition be accompanied by the following: (a) general arrangement drawings; (b) a schedule of design documents as are currently prepared or to be prepared; (c) an assessment made through the online building control management system of the proposed approach to compliance with the requirements of the Building Regulations 1997 to 2013; (d) the preliminary inspection plan; (e) a certificate of compliance (Design); (f) notices of assignment in respect of the builder who will carry out the works and of the assigned certifier who will inspect and certify the works; and (g) certificates of compliance signed by the builder and the assigned certifier (a registered architect, registered building surveyor chartered engineer) undertaking to carry out their roles in accordance with the requirements of the Building Regulations 1997 to 2013.

The commencement notice and accompanying documentation must be filed electronically using the online building control management system (available at: *localgov.ie/en/BCMS* [last accessed 14 July 2015]). Where notices and documentation are submitted in written format, the building control authority will arrange for scanning and uploading of same for which an administrative charge will apply and statutory deadlines relating to such notices may be delayed by up to seven days.

Article 9 of the 1997 Regulations, as amended by reg.7 of the 2014 Regulations, also obliges a building owner to notify the building control authority of any changes of ownership of the works or of the persons assigned as builder or as assigned certifier and to provide the appropriate notices of assignment and forms of undertaking in respect of the new assignees. Failure to attend to any of these obligations, as well as being an offence in itself, would delay or inhibit inclusion of details of the final certificate on the statutory register.

Article 20A(2) of the 1997 Regulations, as amended by reg.10 of the 2014 Regulations, set out a revised form of seven day notice and otherwise changes the administrative arrangements that pertain to the seven day notice process in line with those changes described above in relation to the commencement notice process.

A completely new Pt 3C of the 1997 Regulations was inserted by reg.12 of the 2014 Regulations. This provides for new certificates of compliance on completion. A completion certificate must be sent to the building control authority and included on the statutory register maintained under Pt 4 of the 1997 Regulations before works or a building to which these regulations apply can be opened, occupied or used. The completion certificate must be signed by the builder and the assigned certifier and must be accompanied by plans and documentation showing how the completed building complies with the requirements of the Building Regulations 1997 to 2013 (and clearly indicating any differences to design documentation previously submitted to the building control authority at commencement or during construction) and by the inspection plan as implemented by the assigned certifier. It is important to emphasise that, after 1 March 2014, the certificate of compliance on completion must be validated and registered by the building control authority before the building it relates to may be opened, used or occupied. If the certificate of compliance is rejected by the building control authority within 21 days it is not valid. In February 2014 the Minister for the Environment published a *Code of Practice for Inspecting and Certifying Buildings and Works* (available at envion. ie, [last accessed 14 July 2015]) under art.20G of the Building Control Regulations

1997 to 2014 for the purposes of providing guidance with respect to inspecting and certifying work for compliance with the 1997 Regulations. Compliance with this Code of Practice indicates prima facie compliance with the relevant requirements of the 1997 Regulations, as amended by the 2014 Regulations.

HOUSING

Social housing The Housing (Miscellaneous Provisions) Act 2014 enacted a number of changes to the State's framework of social housing support. These included replacing one of the key pre-2014 State housing supports, the rent supplement system, with a Housing Assistance Payment (HAP). The 2014 Act also envisaged the creation of more social housing units than had been the case in the previous two decades, either through local authorities or the not-for-profit voluntary sector.

The balance between these two elements of social housing policy was recognised during the Oireachtas debates on the 2014 Act. Thus, in 2014 the Government had committed more than €200 million in funding that would be used to build, purchase or refurbish some 2,900 housing units between 2014 and 2016. This figure was contrasted with the reality that more than 70,000 households remained in receipt of rent supplement in 2014; and that a large number of households would, in the short to medium term, meet their housing needs in the private rented sector with State support.

Parts 2, 4 and 5 of the 2014 Act came into force on various dates between 2014 and 2015: see the Housing (Miscellaneous Provisions) Act 2014 (Commencement of Certain Provisions) Order 2014 (S.I. No. 404 of 2014) and the Housing (Miscellaneous Provisions) Act 2014 (Commencement of Certain Provisions) Order 2015 (S.I. No. 121 of 2015). Part 3 of the 2014 Act (on a housing purchase scheme) had not been brought into force at the time of writing (July 2015).

Rent supplement replaced by Housing Assistance Payment (HAP) and transferred to local authorities (housing authorities) Part 4 of the 2014 Act (ss.35 to 51) is the most significant element of the 2014 Act because it contained the statutory framework for the introduction of the HAP. The HAP scheme brought together all long-term social housing services provided by the State under the local authority system.

In addition, Pt 4 provided for the implementation of mandatory direct deduction of rental contributions due to housing authorities from the welfare payments of HAP recipients and local authority tenants, which was regarded as a key provision to avoid and combat the build-up of rent arrears that cause significant financial difficulty for local authorities, but more significantly for tenants. The HAP scheme was intended as an opportunity to improve standards and levels of compliance, remove employment traps and create a more equal and fair social housing system where the rights and opportunities available to tenants in different forms of social housing would be improved. Households that move onto the new HAP retain the ability to apply for other social housing options, including the traditional local authority house or a unit provided by the voluntary sector. As the household will be within the local authority system, they will do this by joining the relevant local authority's transfer list. The transfer list will reflect the specific priority or previous position the household had on the housing waiting list in the authority area in which they are resident. They will, therefore, be placed on a transfer list with no less favourable terms than if they had remained on the main housing waiting list. Following the enactment of the 2014 Act, the Ministerial powers in s.22 of the Housing Act 2009 (*Annual Review of Irish Law 2009*, pp.639-645) were used to require every local authority to provide access to the transfer list to households that transfer to the HAP scheme and also to reserve a proportion of allocations for households on the transfer list.

Under Pt 4 of the 2014 Act, the qualification of a household for social housing support will have to be determined by a housing authority through a statutory social housing assessment and the authority must be satisfied that assistance under the scheme is an appropriate form of support for that household. The provision of assistance under the scheme can include a path to alternative forms of support, where appropriate and where required. HAP beneficiaries will source their own accommodation in the private rented market (as happened prior to the 2014 Act with rent supplement) and will enter into a tenancy agreement with the landlord concerned. The housing authority will pay the rent for the accommodation directly to the landlord on behalf of the household, which will be required to pay a rent contribution to the authority calculated in accordance with the authority's differential rent scheme. To be included in the HAP scheme the accommodation must meet the statutory standards for rented accommodation and the landlord must be tax compliant. The framework in the 2014 Act was also intended to facilitate the removal of some existing barriers to employment by allowing HAP recipients to remain in the scheme if they gain full-time employment. The 2014 Act includes provisions detailing ineligibility for HAP, the cessation of a HAP payment and amendments to the Housing Acts 1966 to 2013 that are consequential on the introduction of HAP. During the Oireachtas debates on the 2014 Act, s.48 was inserted to provide for an internal review procedure for certain HAP decisions.

Part 5 of the 2014 Act (ss.52 to 58) includes a number of miscellaneous provisions, notably s.53, which provides for the implementation of mandatory, direct deduction of rental contributions due to housing authorities from the welfare payments of HAP recipients and local authority tenants. Part 5 also includes provisions for data sharing and exchange between housing authorities, the Department of Social Protection, the Department of the Environment and other relevant bodies for the administration of the housing functions of local authorities. This includes s.54, which made a range of amendments to the rent supplement provisions in the Social Welfare Consolidation Act 2005 that were required as a result of the introduction of the HAP.

ECHR-compliant procedure on termination of local authority tenancies Part 2 of the 2014 Act (ss.6 to 20) provided for significant reform of the termination of local authority tenancies. It was noted that the summary repossession procedure used by housing authorities under s.62 of the Housing Act 1966 (the "1966 Act") had withstood judicial scrutiny over many years, but that the enactment of the European Convention on Human Rights Act 2003 had resulted in a series of cases claiming that the s.62 procedure was incompatible with the European Convention on Human Rights (ECHR). It was noted that the Supreme Court, in *Donegan v Dublin County Council* [2012] IESC 18, which applied the analysis of the European Court of Human Rights in *Connors v United Kingdom* (2002) 35 (E.H.R.R.) 691 (which concerned comparable UK legislation), made a declaration under the 2003 Act that s.62 of the 1966 Act was incompatible with the ECHR where there is a factual dispute about the basis for the evictions as it did not provide for an independent hearing of the merits of the proposed eviction. Part 2 of the 2014 therefore repealed s.62 of the 1966 Act and replaced it with a revised procedure for repossessing local authority dwellings where serious breaches of tenancy agreements have occurred, including anti-social behaviour and breaches of rescheduling arrangements for rent arrears.

Sections 7 to 11 of the 2014 Act set out procedures for tenancy warnings and their review. In the case of non-compliance with tenancy warnings for anti-social behaviour housing authorities will have strengthened powers under ss.12 and 13 to either recover possession of the dwelling or seek an exclusion order, as appropriate. Sections 14 to 17 deal with abandoned local authority dwellings and recovery of property in the case of death of a tenant and certain other cases. Part 2 also provided a legislative mechanism to update all existing local authority tenancy agreements to reflect its provisions without the necessity to terminate all existing agreements for the purpose of entering into new agreements incorporating updated terms and conditions.

Incremental purchase scheme Part 3 of the 2014 Act (ss.21 to 34) provided for what was described in the Oireachtas debates as one of the measures most sought after by tenants, that is, an incremental purchase scheme for existing houses which will cover local authority houses other than newly-built or newly-acquired houses and local authority apartments, which were covered by the pre-2014 incremental purchase schemes under the Housing Act 2009. The incremental purchase scheme in ss.21 to 30 of the 2014 Act offers a number of key benefits. For families, the scheme offers the path to home ownership for those willing and able to undertake a house purchase. The scheme is structured to make it attractive for people to retain long-term roots in the community and to continue their commitment to an area, thereby contributing to more stable and integrated communities. During the Oireachtas debates on the 2014 Act, a requirement was removed from s.25 that would have required a tenant purchaser of an existing local authority house to obtain the prior written consent of the housing authority to carry out material improvements to the house during the period of the incremental purchase on the property. It was intended that this removal would make it easier for purchasers to improve their homes with consequent benefits for the construction sector generally.

The 2014 Act also provided for Regulations on specific aspects of the new scheme, including the qualifying conditions for applicants, calculation of discounts, the method used by local authorities to determine the purchase price and discount and the period of the charging order. The 2014 Act also includes provision for a claw-back to enable the State to benefit appropriately from any resale of the purchased property. As noted above, at the time of writing (July 2015), Pt 3 of the 2014 Act had not been brought into force.

Planning and Development Law

GARRETT SIMONS, S.C.

JUDICIAL REVIEW: PROCEDURE

Legal Costs Section 50B of the Planning and Development Act 2000 (the "PDA 2000") (as inserted by the Planning and Development (Amendment) Act 2010 and amended by the Environment (Miscellaneous Provisions) Act 2011) provides that special costs rules apply in respect of certain environmental litigation.

There is still some controversy as to the precise category of cases to which the new costs rules apply. The section provides that the new costs rules apply to proceedings taken pursuant to a law of the State which gives effect to three specified EU environmental directives. The High Court had previously given the section a purposive, as opposed to a literal, interpretation, and held that the new costs rules only apply where the proceedings concern a project or a plan which is subject to one of the three environmental directives: see *JC Savage Supermarket Ltd v An Bord Pleanála* [2011] IEHC 488, and *Kimpton Vale Developments Ltd v An Bord Pleanála* [2013] IEHC 442. More recently, however, the High Court in *Harrington v An Bord Pleanála* (Appeal 297/2014) has granted leave to appeal to the Court of Appeal on the question of whether the new costs rules apply more generally.

There is also some dispute as to whether the new costs rules apply to the Habitats Directive 1992/43 (the "Habitats Directive"). On a literal interpretation, the new costs rules are confined to the three directives specifically identified under s.50B, namely the Environmental Impact Assessment Directive 2011/92 (the "EIA Directive"); the IPPC Directive (now the Industrial Emissions (IPPC) Directive 2010/75); and the Strategic Environmental Assessment Directive 2001/42. It may be, however, that a purposive interpretation would extend the new costs rules to include the Habitats Directive also. The Court of Justice of the European Union (CJEU) has indicated that, in order to ensure effective judicial protection in the fields covered by EU environmental law, national law should be interpreted in a manner which is consistent with the objectives of the Aarhus Convention. See *Lesoochranárske zoskupenie VLK v Ministerstvo životného prostredia Slovenskej republiky* (C-240/09) [2011] E.C.R. I-01255.

Whereas there is no express provision made under the Habitats Directive itself for a review procedure before a national court, it is arguable that decision-making under art.6 of the Habitats Directive does come within the scope of the Aarhus Convention, i.e. as a decision to permit proposed activities which may have a significant effect on the environment. On this analysis, decision-making under the Habitats Directive should be amenable to a review procedure which meets the requirements of art.9 of the Aarhus Convention, including the requirement that the review procedure is not prohibitively expensive. If s.50B is open to an interpretation which would extend the new costs rules to a challenge based on an alleged breach of the Habitats Directive, then it seems that the national court would be required to adopt such a sympathetic interpretation.

It must be emphasised, however, that the interpretative obligation is qualified: national law need only be interpreted consistently with the Aarhus Convention to the fullest extent possible. The national courts are not required to interpret national law *contra legem*. It is certainly arguable that the fact that the legislature chose to specify three particular environmental directives under s.50B was deliberate, and that the list was intended to be exhaustive. On this argument, it would not be open to a court to "read in" a fourth directive, namely the Habitats Directive.

These issues may well have to be addressed by the Court of Appeal in *Harrington v An Bord Pleanála* (Appeal 297/2014) given that that case involves an alleged breach of the substantive requirements of the Habitats Directive.

Apportionment of legal costs The High Court in *McCallig v An Bord Pleanála (No. 2)* [2014] IEHC 353 has introduced a further gloss on the operation of s.50B. In particular, it seems that costs may have to be apportioned as between EU law issues and national law issues. The case concerned a challenge to the grant of planning permission for a wind farm subject to the EIA Directive, and thus satisfied the *JC Savage Supermarket Ltd/Kimpton Vale Developments Ltd* test. The High Court (Herbert J.) held that it was necessary to distinguish between (i) those grounds of challenge which raised issues under the EIA Directive, and (ii) those which raised national law issues. The court held that the new costs rules only applied to the former. On the facts, the applicant had failed on her challenge based on the EIA Directive, and, in accordance with s.50B(2), the court made no order as to those costs. The applicant had succeeded on certain national law issues, and the court ordered that An Bord Pleanála and the notice party be responsible for that portion of the costs.

As flagged above, it is not clear whether the new rules under s.50B extend to cases raising issues under the Habitats Directive. If the new costs rules do extend to such cases, then the *McCallig* formulation may need to be modified so as to include grounds based on the Habitats Directive, and not just the three directives specifically identified under s.50B.

In *McCallig v An Bord Pleanála (No. 3)* [2014] IEHC 354, the court had to rule on the costs of the costs application. (The costs application had taken three days). Herbert J. accepted, in principle, that where an otherwise successful party had raised issues improperly or unreasonably which added significantly to the length of, or to the costs of, proceedings, then that party may be deprived of some or all of the costs and, depending upon the circumstances, may even be directed to pay a part or all of the other party's costs. On the particular facts of the costs application in *McCallig*, however, the court decided that even the issues in respect of which the applicant was unsuccessful had been properly raised, and that the applicant should not have to pay those costs. The applicant was not, however, entitled to recover the costs of those issues as against the other parties. More specifically, the court rejected an argument that the applicant should be entitled to her costs on those issues because the legislation was uncertain and required to be clarified. See para.10:

> "I am unable to accept the argument made on behalf of the applicant that she should be awarded the costs of the claim that s.21 of the [Environment (Miscellaneous Provisions) Act 2011], applied retroactively, because the intention of the Legislature in that regard was uncertain and required to be

> ascertained. When an issue of this nature arises in the course of ordinary inter partes litigation and, the determination of the issue will result in a benefit to the party contending for a retrospective application and, a detriment to the party arguing for a prospective application or a statutory provision if the former is successful, (or vice versa), in my judgment the costs of this issue, like every other contentious issue in the proceedings, should be determined in accordance with the ordinary general rules as to costs."

Finally, the High Court in *McCallig v An Bord Pleanála (No. 2)* [2014] IEHC 353 ruled that the amendment introduced to s.50B by the Environment (Miscellaneous Provisions) Act 2011 (the "2011 Act") is not retrospective in effect. The proceedings in *McCallig* had been instituted prior to the commencement of the 2011 Act, but judgment was delivered subsequent to the commencement of the Act. The court held that the pre-amendment version of the new costs rules applied.

Time-limits The institution of judicial review proceedings under the PDA 2000 (as amended) is subject to an eight week time-limit. As a result of amendments introduced under the Planning and Development (Strategic Infrastructure) Act 2006, the time-limit runs from the date of the making of a "decision" or the doing of an "act". The statutory language suggests that it may not always be safe to await a final "decision" by a local planning authority or An Bord Pleanála before instituting proceedings. More specifically, if an earlier "act" on the part of the statutory body discloses the legal error which will ultimately be relied upon in the judicial review proceedings, then it may be necessary to challenge that "act" within eight weeks.

This dilemma is illustrated by two judgments in 2014. The first, *McGrath Limestone Works Ltd v An Bord Pleanála* [2014] IEHC 382, concerned a challenge to decision-making under s.261A of the PDA 2000 (as inserted in 2010). The decision-making process under s.261A is unusual in that the first-instance determination of the local planning authority is subject to a "review" rather than an "appeal". An Bord Pleanála, on review, may either confirm or set aside the planning authority's determination. The applicant for judicial review in *McGrath Limestone Works Ltd* had joined both the planning authority and An Bord Pleanála as respondents to the proceedings, and had sought orders quashing both determinations. The planning authority, Mayo County Council, argued that the proceedings were out of time insofar as its decision was concerned. This argument, if pursued to its logical conclusion, would mean that a successful challenge to An Bord Pleanála's determination would result in the planning authority's first-instance decision reviving. This would be so irrespective of whether the planning authority's decision disclosed precisely the same error of law as resulted in the board's determination being set aside.

The High Court (Charleton J.) rejected Mayo's argument, on the basis that, if accepted, it would lead to an "absurd" result.

> "Here, the decision that is challenged is that of Mayo County Council as reviewed by An Bord Pleanála. Both [legal challenges] were made by notice parties and the date of the decision of An Bord Pleanála is the date from which time runs because it is this decision and not any intermediate step with which the applicant McGrath Limestone Works has an issue. It would

> also be absurd for the legislature to provide for a review of a decision and when that might be successful on judicial review to have an applicant told: okay, you have won against An Bord Pleanála but now you are saddled with the local planning authority decision that you reviewed."

The second judgment, *Harrington v Environmental Protection Agency* [2014] IEHC 307, concerned a decision made under the Environmental Protection Agency Acts, rather than under the PDA 2000. As discussed below, the principal issue in the case was whether an earlier licence revived in circumstances where the subsequent grant of a revised licence had been set aside in judicial review proceedings. The Environmental Protection Agency (the "EPA") had indicated, in a non-statutory letter, that it intended to treat the earlier licence as continuing in force. Some months thereafter, the EPA carried out a statutory examination of the licence and made amendments thereto. Judicial review proceedings were then instituted challenging the decision to amend the licence, on the grounds that there was no licence in existence, i.e. that the earlier licence had not revived.

The developer argued, in effect, that this ground of challenge had crystallised at the time the EPA had sent the letter indicating that it intended to treat the earlier licence as continuing in force. The developer contended that, as the proceedings were instituted more than three months after the non-statutory letter had been sent, the proceedings were out of time.

A challenge to a licence or a revised licence is subject to an eight week statutory time-limit. It appears to have been assumed for the purpose of the proceedings, however, that this statutory time-limit did not apply to the *amendment* of a licence: the judgment is based on the general three month time-limit for judicial review proceedings under Ord.84 r.21(1) of the Rules of the Superior Courts.

The High Court (Barrett J.) held that the applicant was possessed of sufficient knowledge and information on receipt of the EPA's letter to commence judicial review proceedings against the EPA regarding its stance as to the continued subsistence of the original licence. The proceedings were brought outside the three months allowed under Ord.84 r.21(1), and the court ruled that the applicant had offered no convincing reason for his failure to do so.

With respect, it is difficult to understand how the time for the making of an application for certiorari can be said to have begun to run before the decision being challenged has actually been made. Order 84 r.21(2) provides that where the relief sought is an order of certiorari in respect of any judgment, order, conviction or other proceeding, then the date when grounds for the application first arose shall be taken to be the date of that judgment, order, conviction or proceeding. It is arguable that an administrative decision to issue an amended licence constitutes a "proceeding" for the purpose of this sub-rule. Even if the decision does not constitute a "proceeding", the sub-rule does indicate that some formal step is required before time begins to run. A non-statutory letter does not appear to fulfil this requirement for formality.

The High Court sought to rely on a judgment of the CJEU in respect of public procurement, *Uniplex (UK) Ltd* (C-406/08) [2010] E.C.R. I-817, in support of its finding. It is arguable, however, that a second judgment of the CJEU, which was delivered on the same day as *Uniplex (UK) Ltd*, provides a better comparator. The second judgment is *Commission v Ireland* (C-456/08) [2010] E.C.R. I-859. One of the issues in that case was whether the time-limit under Ord.84A of the RSC could be interpreted as applying to *interim* decisions made by a contracting authority. The CJEU held that legal certainty requires that if a time-limit is to apply not only to final decisions but also to interim decisions, then this had to be clear from the relevant national legislation. See para.63:

> "The extension of the limitation period under Order 84A(4) of the RSC to interim decisions taken by contracting authorities in public procurement procedures in a manner which deprives the parties concerned of their right of review satisfies neither the requirements of legal certainty nor the objective of effective review. Interested parties must be informed of the application of limitation periods to interim decisions with sufficient clarity to enable them effectively to bring proceedings within the periods laid down. The failure to provide such information cannot be justified on grounds of procedural rapidity."

It is not at all clear from the wording of Ord.84, r.21(2) that it is intended to capture interim decisions, still less a non-statutory letter of the type involved in *Harrington*. As noted above, the wording of r.21(2) suggests that some formality is required before time begins to run in respect of a decision. Moreover, the statutory time-limit which governs challenges to the grant of a licence or a revised licence provides that time runs from the date of the *grant* of the licence/revised licence. Even if this statutory time-limit does not capture the *amendment* of a licence (as opposed to the grant of a revised licence), it is nevertheless consistent with a requirement for a formal decision before time begins to run.

The decision-making process at issue in *Harrington*, namely the examination and amendment of existing licences, was intended to give effect to the Industrial Emissions (IPPC) Directive, 2010/75. Article 25 of the Directive obliges Member States to provide a "review procedure". Member States are required to ensure that practical information is made available to the public on access to administrative and judicial review procedures. It is at least arguable that the High Court's interpretation of the time-limit is inconsistent with legal certainty, and undermines the effectiveness of the "review procedure".

Time-limits and default planning permission The question of whether the statutory eight week time-limit applies to a claim for a default planning permission was considered by the Supreme Court in *Ryan v Clare County Council* [2014] IESC 67. The case concerned the earlier version of the legislation, i.e. prior to the amendments introduced to the default planning permission regime under the Planning and Development (Amendment) Act 2010. The Supreme Court ruled that the (earlier) legislation envisaged a two-step process: (i) a deemed *decision* to grant planning permission, and (ii) a subsequent *grant* of planning permission. The appropriate remedy where a planning authority declined to issue a grant of default planning permission was an order of mandamus directing the planning authority to do so. This remedy did not involve a challenge to the validity of a planning decision, and thus was subject to the general three month time-limit under Ord.84 of the RSC.

The Supreme Court found on the facts that it was reasonable for the claimant to have awaited the expiration of the four week time-limit for appealing the (default) decision to An Bord Pleanála before making a formal demand that the planning authority issue a grant. The judicial review proceedings had been instituted within three months of the planning authority's refusal of that demand, and were therefore within time.

Locus standi of companies The question of whether a discrepancy between the description of (i) the party making an administrative appeal, and (ii) the party instituting subsequent judicial review proceedings challenging the appeal decision, invalidates those proceedings was considered in *Waterville Fisheries Development Ltd v Aquaculture Licenses Appeals Board (No. 1)* [2014] IEHC 248. On the facts of the case, an appeal against a decision to grant an aquaculture licence had been expressed to be in the name of the Waterville Fisheries Development Group; in the notice of the appeal, the group had described itself as a community based group dedicated to the protection and enhancement of the salmon and seatrout fishery of the Lough Currane catchment. The subsequent judicial review proceedings were brought in the name of a company limited by guarantee, Waterville Fisheries Development Ltd.

The High Court held that on the (admittedly unusual) circumstances of the case, it was clear that both the group and company share the same interest in challenging the licence decision as they were to all intents and purposes the same entity. The court indicated that any concern that the company was being used to avoid any potential liability for legal costs could satisfactorily be addressed, where necessary, in the context of an application for security for costs.

Service of notice parties Prior to the Planning and Development (Amendment) Act 2010 (the "2010 Act"), an application for leave to apply for judicial review had to be made on notice to a number of prescribed parties. In the case of a planning appeal, these included the applicant for planning permission, the relevant planning authority, and An Bord Pleanála.

As a result of amendments introduced under the 2010 Act, the application for leave to apply for judicial review is now normally made on an ex parte basis. The court retains a discretion, however, to require that the application for leave be heard on an inter partes basis.

Somewhat surprisingly, the 2010 Act does not prescribe the parties to be served with the proceedings in the event that leave is granted. This appears to be an oversight. Express provision is made for the service of prescribed parties in circumstances where the High Court exercises its discretion to direct that the leave application be heard on an inter partes basis. These include the applicant for planning permission and the relevant planning authority. The legislation thus recognises that these parties have an interest in the proceedings. It would seem logical that, in the event of leave being granted on an ex parte basis, these parties should be served with the proceedings and afforded an opportunity to be heard at the full hearing. The 2010 Act is, however, silent on this issue. It seems anomalous that the legislature would go to the trouble of identifying the parties to be served in the event of an inter partes leave hearing, but say nothing as to which parties are to be heard at the full hearing. It is submitted that the legislation should be read as containing an implied obligation to serve the same parties in both scenarios.

One issue which sometimes arises in practice is whether it is necessary to serve proceedings on all parties who had participated in an appeal. In the case of a controversial development project, there may be a large number of individual appellants before An Bord Pleanála. If one appellant chooses to institute judicial review proceedings challenging An Bord Pleanála's decision, is it necessary to join all of his or her co-appellants to the legal proceedings? The judgment in *Waterville Fisheries Development Ltd v Aquaculture Licenses Appeals Board (No. 1)* [2014] IEHC 248 suggests that a requirement to serve each "party" to an appeal should be read as if it referred to relevant parties who have a real interest in the outcome of the proceedings. The court ruled, on the facts, that the late service of judicial review proceedings on a third party did not invalidate those proceedings. The third party had participated in the licence appeal process, and, on a literal interpretation, should have been served with the proceedings within the statutory time-limit. The court held, however, that the statutory requirements in relation to service should be looked at through the prism of the applicant's constitutional right of access to the courts. The court stated that an interpretation which required that proceedings be dismissed by reason of a failure to serve parties who were never necessary parties in the first place, even though this could have no real bearing on the real issues in the proceedings, would be manifestly at odds with the applicant's constitutional right of access to the courts.

The judgment in *Waterville Fisheries Development Ltd* concerned a challenge to a decision to grant an aquaculture licence, rather than a decision under the planning legislation, but similar constitutional principles would seem to apply to both legislative schemes.

Setting aside earlier decision In many instances, the planning legislation provides for a two-stage decision-making process, i.e. a first-instance decision by the local planning authority, with a right of appeal thereafter to An Bord Pleanála. Parties are generally expected to exhaust their right of appeal before having recourse to the courts by way of judicial review proceedings. In the event that a decision by the board is successfully challenged in judicial review proceedings, the first-instance decision of the planning authority does not revive. This is because a decision of An Bord Pleanála on a planning appeal annuls the planning authority's decision, even in circumstances where the board's decision is subsequently set aside. See *McCallig v An Bord Pleanála (No. 1)* [2013] IEHC 60.

This issue was considered in two judgments in 2014. The first, *McGrath Limestone Works Ltd v An Bord Pleanála* [2014] IEHC 382, concerned a challenge to decision-making under s.261A of the PDA 2000 (as inserted in 2010). The decision-making process under s.261A is unusual in that the first-instance determination of the local planning authority is subject to a "review" rather than an "appeal". An Bord Pleanála, on review, may either confirm or set aside the planning authority's determination. As discussed above, the High Court dismissed as absurd an argument that an order of certiorari quashing An Bord Pleanála's decision would have the legal effect of reviving the planning authority's decision of first instance.

The second judgment, *Harrington v Environmental Protection Agency* [2014] IEHC 307, concerned decision-making in respect of integrated pollution and prevention control licences ("IPPC licences") under the Environmental Protection Agency Acts. The legislation provides for the "review" of licences. The original licence had been subject to review, and a revised licence had issued. This revised licence was subsequently set aside in judicial review proceedings. The EPA adopted the approach that the original licence had revived, and some months later purported to make a number of technical amendments to the licence. The decision to amend the licence was challenged in a second set of judicial review proceedings. The applicant argued that the consequence of the setting aside of the revised licence in the first set of judicial review proceedings was that there was no licence in existence, and thus there was no licence capable of being amended. The applicant argued that the EPA had been in error in treating the original licence as having revived.

Relevantly, the language employed by the Environmental Protection Agency Acts differs from that under s.37 of the PDA 2000. In particular, there is no express statement to the effect that the issue of a revised licence "annulled" the original licence; instead, it is stated that a revised licence "shall have effect in lieu of" the original licence. It was argued on behalf of the developer that the grant of a revised licence had a suspensive effect insofar as the original licence was concerned, and that once the decision to grant the revised licence was quashed, the original licence was reinvigorated.

The High Court (Barrett J.) concluded that this was too strained an interpretation of the phrase "in lieu of". The court went on, however, to hold that a literal interpretation of the legislation, i.e. to the effect that the original licence did not revive, would produce an absurd result. The court stated that it would make no sense were the setting aside of a revised licence to have the "catastrophic consequence" of creating a legal vacuum in which no licence pertained. It was likely that the licensable activity would have to cease at least for a time, i.e. pending the making and determination of a fresh application for a licence.

Barrett J. held that the Oireachtas could not have intended that, in the event of a revised licence being quashed, a legal vacuum should pertain. In the court's view, the only logical and fair reading of the legislation was that the licensing arrangements which pertained before the revised licence was quashed should resume force. The court stated that such an interpretation did no violence to the language of the EPA Acts, and appeared entirely consistent with the purpose of the legislation.

The approach adopted in *Harrington* certainly has the benefit of being pragmatic. Such an approach may not be appropriate, however, where the original licence suffers from the same legal defect which resulted in the revised licence being set aside. For example, one of the circumstances in which it is mandatory to revise a licence is where there has been a change in the emission standards applicable. A revised licence may have been set aside because the EPA failed to properly apply an updated emission standard to the activity. To allow the original licence to revive might equally result in a breach of the updated emission standard. The time-limit for challenging the revived licence would, presumably, have long since expired, i.e. the time-limit would run from the date the original licence was granted, not from the later date of when the licence revived.

Another example is where the revised licence has been set aside because of a breach of the requirements of the EIA Directive. A development consent issued in breach of the EIA Directive should generally be set aside, and the requisite assessment carried out before a fresh consent is granted. See *Wells* (C-201/02) [2004] E.C.R. I-723. It would not be an effective remedy were the setting aside of the revised licence simply to result in the revival of the original licence unless the original licence was itself compliant with the EIA Directive. The bright line rule laid down in *Harrington* does not allow for any consideration of the validity of the original licence.

Collateral attack Section 50 of the PDA 2000 (as amended) provides that a person may not question the validity of a planning decision other than by way of an application for judicial review. Generally, an application for judicial review must be instituted within eight weeks of the impugned decision.

Occasionally, a respondent will seek to defend judicial review proceedings on the basis that the proceedings, although nominally directed to a recent decision, involve an indirect or collateral attack on an earlier decision. A recent example, from the environmental law context, is provided by *Harrington v Environmental Protection Agency* [2014] IEHC 307. The applicant sought to challenge a decision to amend an integrated pollution and control licence (IPPC licence). The original licence had been granted several years earlier. The court ruled that the proceedings involved an impermissible collateral attack on the original licence. The court went on to indicate that, in any event, the ground of challenge was not made out on the facts. In particular, the court held that the applicant's reliance on the judgment of the CJEU in *Commission v Ireland* (C-50/09) [2011] E.C.R. I-873 was misplaced. The legislative lacuna identified in that case did not arise on the facts of *Harrington* in circumstances where a copy of the environmental impact statement (EIS), which had been submitted during the planning application, had been forwarded to the EPA with the IPPC licence application.

There is some tension between the concept of impermissible collateral attacks and the case law of the CJEU in respect of multi-stage decision-making. The judgment in *Wells* (C-201/02) [2004] E.C.R. I-723 suggests that the decision-maker charged with determining an application for a later stage of a multi-stage development consent may be required to remedy any failure, at the earlier stages, to comply with the requirements of the EIA Directive. In principle, if the second decision-maker does not discharge this remedial obligation, then its decision might be open to challenge. In practice, however, it seems that any remedial obligation is subservient to the procedural autonomy of the individual Member States. Irish administrative law differs from that of certain civil law jurisdictions in that it does not allow a decision-maker, such as the EPA or An Bord Pleanála, to reopen earlier administrative decisions. In the circumstances, such decision-makers do not have legal competence to discharge a remedial obligation.

JUDICIAL REVIEW: SUBSTANTIVE

Relevant considerations An example of a planning decision being set aside because of the failure of the decision-maker to take into account a relevant consideration is provided by *Kerry County Council v An Bord Pleanála* [2014] IEHC 238. The case concerned an application for development consent pursuant to the Roads Acts 1993 to 2007. The proposed road development would have involved the improvement of the existing road and the provision of a cycleway.

An Bord Pleanála formed the provisional view that the road development, as proposed, would have an unacceptable detrimental impact on the visual amenities and landscape character of the area. The board, accordingly, exercised its statutory power to invite the roads authority to make alterations to the original proposal. In particular, the board suggested that a narrower overall road cross-section, omitting the cycleway, should be adopted. The roads authority made a submission in response, illustrating the challenges associated with potential alternative cycleway routes.

An Bord Pleanála ultimately refused development consent. The board concluded that the proposed design, including the cycleway, contributed significantly to the width of the proposed road alignment and the associated landscape impacts. The board was not satisfied that the cycleway justification was sufficient to overcome the landscape concerns.

The roads authority, Kerry County Council, then instituted judicial review proceedings challenging An Bord Pleanála's decision. The roads authority argued that the board had erred in failing to take into account the needs of cyclists and pedestrians, and, consequently, had failed to exercise its jurisdiction properly.

The High Court (Charleton J.) held that An Bord Pleanála had failed to consider the needs of cyclists and pedestrians in turning down a proposed road scheme which made express provision for them. The court therefore set aside the decision to refuse development consent. The court based its ruling on two statutory provisions, as follows. First, a roads authority is obliged, in carrying out its statutory function of maintaining and constructing national and regional roads, to consider the needs of all road users. See s.13(5) of the Roads Act 1993. The court held that, in considering whether proposed road development ought to be approved or not, the board must have regard to whether the roads authority has fulfilled this statutory obligation.

Secondly, under s.143 of the PDA 2000 (as amended) the board, in performing its functions, is obliged to have regard to the policies and objectives for the time being of the Government. The court held that, although expressed in statutory terms, it is the unequivocal policy of the Government, and of the Oireachtas as declared through legislation, that roads should be maintained and constructed in consideration not simply of cars, commercial vehicles and buses, but of all road users. This meant that the needs of cyclists and pedestrians must also be included for the proper formulation of plans. The court concluded that there was no evidence at all that these considerations played any part in the board's decision-making process.

Reasonableness The courts will generally only interfere with a planning decision on its merits where it can be demonstrated that the decision is irrational or unreasonable. This is a very high threshold, and requires that an applicant for judicial review demonstrate that there was no material before the decision-maker capable of supporting its decision. A rare example of a planning decision being set aside as "unreasonable" is provided by *Mahon v Cork County Council* [2014] IEHC 555. The planning authority had designated lands occupied by a dwelling house and curtilage as "public open space". The High Court held that there was no basis upon which the objectives of the development plan could be met by the inclusion of the dwelling house and its curtilage within the "public open space" zoning. The dwelling house and its curtilage could not be said to fall within the type of open space contemplated within the development plan.

Section 5 reference A procedure is provided under s.5 of the PDA 2000 whereby disputed questions as to whether or not a particular act constitutes "development" may be referred for determination. Generally, the determination will be made by the local planning authority, at first instance, with a right of review thereafter to An Bord Pleanála.

It is at least arguable that the question of whether a particular act constitutes development involves a question of law. This is especially so where the question turns on the correct interpretation of a planning permission. A permission is a public document, and falls to be interpreted in an objective, common sense way as it would be understood by a member of the public, i.e. it does not require any particular planning expertise. If a section 5 reference can properly be characterised as involving a question of law, then the High Court, in reviewing a determination under s.5, need not defer to An Bord Pleanála's view but should instead subject the decision to full-blooded review. In practice, however, the courts simply treat a decision on a section 5 reference as any other planning decision, and will only set aside An Bord Pleanála's decision if it is shown to be unreasonable or irrational. This approach is illustrated by the judgment in *Ógalas Ltd v An Bord Pleanála* [2014] IEHC 487, para.18.

> "It is not my function to substitute my decision for that of the Board and my role is confined to asking itself [sic] whether the decision of the Board was arrived at following improper considerations or as a result of a failure to take into account relevant considerations or as a result of an incorrect interpretation of the planning permission. [...]".

Baker J. expressly adopted the threshold for "reasonableness" as per *O'Keeffe v An Bord Pleanála* [1993] 1 I.R. 39; *Evans v An Bord Pleanála*, unreported, High Court, Kearns J., 7 November 2003; and *Weston v An Bord Pleanála* [2010] IEHC 255. These cases all involved a challenge to a decision to grant or refuse planning permission.

Duty to give reasons The recent judgment in *Kelly v An Bord Pleanála* [2014] IEHC 400 suggests that an enhanced duty to give reasons may arise in the context of the carrying out of an "appropriate assessment" for the purposes of art.6(3) of the Habitats Directive 92/43. On the facts, a local objector had sought to challenge a decision to grant planning permission for a wind farm. An Bord Pleanála had determined that the proposed development would not adversely affect any of the European sites in the vicinity. One of the grounds of judicial review was that An Bord Pleanála had failed to state adequate reasons for its determination in this regard. The board, in defending the proceedings, had sought to rely on earlier Irish case law on the duty to give reasons, and in particular, the suggestion that the duty to give reasons is a light one. The High Court in *Kelly* referred to more recent case law from the CJEU and from the Supreme Court, and, further, sought to draw a distinction between the decision to grant or refuse planning permission, and the specific determination required under the Habitats Directive. See paras 48 and 49 of the judgment:

> "On this issue, I have concluded that the submission made on behalf of the applicant and the Department is correct. First, the essential principle is that the reasons must be such as to enable an interested party assess the lawfulness of the decision and in the event of a challenge being brought, the

> court must have access to sufficient information to enable an assessment as to lawfulness to be made. On the facts of this judicial review, the challenged decisions are those to grant planning permissions. However, the grounds of challenge include the failure of the Board to carry out a proper or lawful appropriate assessment under Article 6(3) as implemented in Ireland. For the reasons already stated in this judgment, the Board could not make a lawful decision to grant planning permission unless it had reached a lawful determination, in an appropriate assessment lawfully conducted, that the proposed development would not adversely impact on the European sites in question. In accordance with the CJEU decision in *Sweetman*, it is for the national court to determine whether the appropriate assessment (including the determination) was lawfully carried out or reached, and to do so, it appears to me that the reasons given for the Board's determination in an appropriate assessment must include the complete, precise and definitive findings and conclusions relied upon by the Board as the basis for its determination. They must also include the main rationale or reason for which the Board considered those findings and conclusions capable of removing all scientific doubt as to the effects of the proposed development on the European site concerned in the light of the its conservation objectives. In the absence of such reasons, it would not be possible for a court to decide whether the appropriate assessment was lawfully concluded or whether the determination meets the legal test required by the judgments of the CJEU.
>
> Secondly, it appears to me that whilst the requirement for an appropriate assessment has been implemented in Ireland by amendment of the Planning Acts and requires to be carried out inter alia as part of the planning process, the determination which must be made by the Board as competent authority it is not a 'planning decision' in the sense used in the judgments relating to reasons relied upon by the Board. In such a planning decision, the Board is exercising a jurisdiction with a very wide discretion. By contrast, the determination it must make as part of an appropriate assessment is significantly narrower and legally constrained as explained in the CJEU cases cited. It also determines the Board's continuing jurisdiction to grant planning consent, and therefore a decision which goes to its jurisdiction. The application of the principles set out by Clarke J. in *Christian*, *Rawson* and *EMI* to the different types of decision results as envisaged therein in a requirement for reasons of a different order in relation to the different types of decision."

The practical effect of the judgment in *Kelly* would appear to be that An Bord Pleanála (or the local planning authority at first instance) will have to state the rationale for its Habitats Directive determination separately from its rationale for granting or refusing planning permission.

The High Court in *Waterville Fisheries Development Ltd v Aquaculture Licence Appeals Board (No. 2)* [2014] IEHC 381 has confirmed that a duty to give reasons arises even in the case of the exercise of what is described in legislation as an "absolute discretion". The case concerned a decision not to hold an oral hearing into an aquaculture licence appeal. The legislation provides that the decision-maker has an "absolute discretion" to hold an oral hearing. The court held that the decision-maker is required to give reasons for its decision not to hold an oral hearing or, at the very least, to be prepared to justify its failure to give such reasons. The court went on to say that these reasons need not be elaborate, but per *Mallak v Minister for Justice Equality and Law Reform* [2012] 3 I.R. 297, the reasons must nonetheless either be given or the failure to do so must be objectively justified.

Statutory guidelines A local planning authority, and An Bord Pleanála on appeal, are required to "have regard to" any statutory guidelines issued by the Minister pursuant to s.28 of the PDA 2000 (as amended). The case law suggests that this obligation is very difficult to enforce in practice. The High Court in *Ó Grianna v An Bord Pleanála* [2014] IEHC 632 reiterated that An Bord Pleanála is not obliged to slavishly or rigidly follow and apply the guidelines, and stated that it follows from this that the board may exercise some discretion in relation to the guidelines. The High Court went on then to say that there is no statutory obligation on the board to give reasons for not following or for departing from particular guidelines. The High Court had earlier ruled that the onus lies with the applicant for judicial review to establish that the board failed to have regard to the relevant guidelines. The court noted that the board's decision expressly stated that the board had regard to the guidelines.

> "I accept of course that a Board cannot simply in some purely formulaic way recite that it had regard to the Guidelines when there is clear evidence from the Decision that it cannot have done so, and still be considered to have complied with its obligations under section 28 of the Act of 2000. But we are not dealing with such an extreme and improbable situation as that. The Board in this case has stated that it had regard to the Guidelines, and it is evident from the materials before it, including the inspector's report relied upon heavily by the Board, and the Decision itself, that it did so. The fact that it has not slavishly followed the Guidelines does not indicate that it has not had regard to them as it is required to do."

With respect, the combined effect of, first, imposing the onus of proof on an applicant to establish a negative, i.e. that the board did *not* have regard to the guidelines, and, secondly, relieving the board of an obligation to state reasons, makes it almost impossible for an applicant to challenge a decision on the grounds of an alleged failure to have regard to relevant guidelines.

Oral hearings An Bord Pleanála has a statutory power to hold an oral hearing in respect of any of its decision-making functions under the PDA 2000 (see ss.134 and 134A of the PDA 2000 (as amended)). The legislation states that the board may decide to hold an oral hearing in its "absolute discretion". The High Court in *Waterville Fisheries Development Ltd v Aquaculture Licence Appeals Board (No. 2)* [2014] IEHC 381 has ruled, in the context of a similarly worded provision under the fisheries legislation, that an "entirely literal" interpretation of the phrase "absolute discretion" would be unconstitutional. Such a literal interpretation would purport to give the decision-maker an absolute power which, on this interpretation, could be exercised in a fashion which did not require objective justification by reference to principles of *vires*, reasonableness and fair procedures. The court ruled that the phrase should be given a constitutional interpretation. More specifically, the court held that the statutory provision must be read as if it merely vested the decision-maker with a "wide and flexible power" to decide whether to hold an oral hearing. It could not be read as granting the decision-maker any wider power, or as dispensing the decision-maker from the obligation to give reasons for its decision not to hold an oral hearing. The decision-maker is required to give reasons for its decision not to hold an oral hearing or, at the very least, to be prepared to justify its failure to give such reasons.

The court held that, in the particular circumstances of the case, the decision-maker was entitled to conclude that no oral hearing was necessary. The case concerned an appeal in respect of an aquaculture licence. The court found that there was no conflict of fact, central to the outcome of the licensing process, which necessitated an oral hearing. The court also ruled that the decision-maker's failure to give reasons for deciding not to hold an oral hearing did not vitiate its decision to grant the licence. There was no nexus between this procedural failure and the ultimate decision to grant the licence.

ENFORCEMENT PROCEEDINGS

Legal costs The judgment in *McCoy v Shillelagh Quarries Ltd (No. 1)* [2014] IEHC 511 confirms that the special costs rules under Pt 2 of the Environment (Miscellaneous Provisions) Act 2011 (the "2011 Act") are not confined to cases alleging a breach of planning permission, but extend to include cases of wholly unauthorised development. The proceedings concerned quarrying activities. The applicant brought a preliminary application, pursuant to s.7 of the 2011 Act, for a determination that the special costs rules applied to the proceedings.

The respondent contended that the quarry had the benefit of a pre-1964 user, and thus did not require planning permission. The respondent argued that the proceedings did not seek to "enforce compliance" with any planning permission, but rather involved an allegation that the quarrying activity was wholly unauthorised and was being carried out without the benefit of any planning permission at all. The High Court (Baker J.) followed the approach of Hedigan J. in *Hunter v Nurendale Ltd* [2013] 2 I.R. 373, and held that, as a matter of statutory interpretation, the special costs rules apply to proceedings which seek to enforce a statutory requirement that planning permission be in existence for a particular use of land.

The respondents had also argued that the application for a determination in respect of costs was "premature", and that the making, at a preliminary stage of the proceedings, of a determination in favour of the applicant would represent a "substantial fetter" on the discretion of the trial judge hearing the enforcement proceedings. Baker J. rejected this argument, stating that the legislature did not envisage any express restriction on the time at which an application under s.7 of the 2011 Act could be made. The judge continued to say that, having regard to the fact that an application can be made even *before* proceedings had commenced, the making of an application at a stage where substantial affidavits had been served, and where the matter was progressing to trial, seemed appropriate.

Baker J., again following the approach in *Hunter v Nurendale Ltd*, indicated that an applicant for a protective costs order must show that he or she has a reasonable prospect of success. As discussed in the *Annual Review of Irish Law 2013*, p.452, it is questionable whether Pt 2 of the 2011 Act requires such an elaborate assessment.

On the particular facts of *McCoy v Shillelagh Quarries Ltd (No. 1)*, the question of whether the quarrying activities at the site constituted unauthorised development had previously been considered by the High Court in earlier proceedings and by An Bord Pleanála pursuant to a section 5 reference. Baker J. held that the applicant had satisfied the "reasonable prospect of success" test, having regard to the litigation history of the site, and the fact that relevant planning decisions had been made in favour of the proposition that the user of the lands constituted unlawful quarrying. The judge went on to emphasise, however, that how the evidence would evolve, and how ultimately the substantive proceedings would be determined, were not matters for her to determine at this time.

It is a condition precedent to the application of the special costs rules that the breach of statutory requirements has caused, is causing, or is likely to cause, damage to the environment. Baker J. held that this test had been met, and that the test did not require the balancing of the possible evidence or assertions by the parties but merely that the court be satisfied that the proceedings relate to the general public interest in the environment and not to the private enjoyment of land.

Baker J. rejected an argument that the applicant had not provided sufficient information as to the level of legal costs. The judgment in *Hunter v Nurendale Ltd* had suggested obiter that an applicant ought to set out broadly what their financial situation is so as to assist the court in making an assessment. The applicant in *McCoy* had deposed that he was a full-time student and not a person of "substantial means". He had also drawn attention to the fact that the respondents had engaged junior and senior counsel. No estimate of the quantum of costs was provided, but the applicant did aver that the previous enforcement proceedings had been "very costly", and went on to say that it was "likely that the costs in these proceedings will be significant".

Baker J. suggested that it was not the intention of Hedigan J., in outlining the proofs in *Hunter v Nurendale Ltd*, to require that a person would disclose the intimate and private elements of his or her financial circumstances. Baker J. also ruled that there was sufficient evidence for her to extrapolate that the legal costs would be very high.

Finally, the High Court also rejected an argument to the effect that the recent joinder of the local planning authority, South Dublin County Council, to the proceedings as co-applicant meant that it would now be disproportionate and unnecessary to make a determination under s.7 of the 2011 Act. More specifically, the respondent had argued that the making of a section 7 determination in favour of one of two co-applicants would unnecessarily tie the hands of the trial judge in the exercise of his or her discretion, i.e. that if costs were to be awarded by the trial judge, same could only be ordered against the newly joined local authority applicant. The special costs rules do not apply to proceedings instituted by a statutory body, such as a local planning authority (see s.4(3) of the 2011 Act). Thus, if the High Court did make a determination that the special costs rules applied, same would be confined to the personal applicant, Mr McCoy, and would not extend to the local authority.

In rejecting these arguments, Baker J. held that the trial judge's discretion would be sufficiently wide to offer protection to the applicant and the respondents.

> "The order would protect the first personal applicant from an award of costs against him and equally protects the respondents from having to pay Mr. McCoy's costs, but does not prevent the trial judge in making a nuanced and reasoned judgment with regard to costs notwithstanding the existence of a declaration. Further, the court has the power under s.3(3) [of the Environment (Miscellaneous Provisions) Act 2011] to award costs against a party by reason of the manner in which the party has conducted the proceedings and also has power to award costs in favour of party in a matter of exceptional public importance or where 'in the special circumstances of the case' it is in the interest of justice to do so.
>
> It seems to me that the trial judge's discretion is sufficiently wide to offer protection to both the applicant and the respondents should a declaration be made at this stage in favour of Mr. McCoy, and indeed it seems to me that the making of such a declaration does not prevent an argument that the interest of justice may ultimately mean that a costs order be made in favour of or against Mr. McCoy especially in the context of the addition of an additional party. Thus the interests of the respondents are also protected."

The judgment of the High Court has since been upheld by the Court of Appeal: *McCoy v Shillelagh Quarries Ltd* [2015] IECA 28.

In a second judgment, *McCoy v Shillelagh Quarries Ltd (No. 2)* [2014] IEHC 512, the High Court awarded the costs of the first hearing to the applicant.

Section 5 determination The High Court in *Marine Terminals Ltd v Dublin City Council* [2014] IEHC 294 confirmed that the existence of judicial review proceedings challenging an earlier determination by a local planning authority on a section 5 reference does not preclude that authority from carrying out its statutory duties in respect of planning enforcement in the interim.

Declaration as to unauthorised development The High Court in *Wicklow County Council v Fortune (No. 4)* [2014] IEHC 267 confirmed that the court has a free standing and independent jurisdiction to grant a declaration which is distinct from the special jurisdiction under s.160 of the PDA 2000. On the facts, the court granted a declaration that the timber chalet, the subject-matter of the proceedings, is an unauthorised development.

PLANNING PERMISSION

Default planning permission A planning authority is, generally, required to make a decision on a planning application within eight weeks of the date of application. This time-limit is subject to extension in a number of circumstances, for example, where a request for further information has been served. Prior to the Planning and Development (Amendment) Act 2010, the sanction for failing to meet the time-limit was a deemed decision to grant planning permission. The rationale underlying this sanction seems to have been that a planning authority which delays in determining a planning application should forfeit the right to refuse planning permission. Of course, the fact that this sanction may adversely affect innocent third parties seems to have been ignored.

An attempt had been made in an earlier High Court judgment to restrict the availability of default planning permission to circumstances where the proposed development was of a type for which the planning authority would, in the normal course of events, have been prepared to grant permission. The Supreme Court in *Ryan v Clare County Council* [2014] IESC 67, citing its judgment in *Abbeydrive Developments Ltd v Kildare County Council* [2009] 3 I.R. 58, reiterated that there is no such restriction in the legislation. The Supreme Court held that it is not the business of the courts to have regard to substantive, merit-based planning considerations. The only restriction on the availability of default planning permission is that it cannot result in a grant of planning permission which would be ultra vires the planning authority. The most obvious example of this is where the proposed development would represent a "material contravention" of the statutory development plan. In such circumstances, a planning authority may only grant permission if a three-quarters majority of the elected members vote to do so. This statutory safeguard would be set at naught if the planning authority could bring about a default decision to grant planning permission, without a vote, by the simple expedient of allowing the eight week period to elapse without making a decision.

On the facts of *Ryan v Clare County Council*, it had been alleged that the proposed development would have involved a material contravention of the local area plan. The Supreme Court held that—on the version of the legislation then in force—there was no statutory restriction on a planning authority granting planning permission for development which would represent a material contravention of a local area plan (as opposed to a development plan). The Supreme Court went on to say that it was open to question whether the application would necessarily have contravened the local area plan at all.

On a separate point, the Supreme Court held that it was unnecessary, on the pleadings in *Ryan v Clare County Council*, to decide whether the legislative provision made for default planning permission involved a breach of the rights of third parties affected by the proposed development. The planning authority had sought to rely, in argument, on the European Convention on Human Rights Act 2003 (the "ECHR Act"). However, in the absence of a formal claim for a declaration that the planning legislation was incompatible with the European Convention, the only aspect of the ECHR Act relevant to the proceedings was the interpretative obligation under s.2. The Supreme Court considered that the wording of the relevant section of the planning legislation was clear, and made no provision for the notification of a deemed decision, nor for a right to be heard. The court held that it was not possible to construe the section so as to provide the form of procedural protection of potential rights contended for by the planning authority. To do so would have involved the court in a process of "statutory redrafting which would, in effect, fundamentally alter the effect and range of application of the sub-section".

Interpretation of planning permission Occasionally, a planning permission will incorporate, by reference, a definition from another document, such as, for example, statutory planning guidelines. The judgment in *Ógalas Ltd v An Bord Pleanála* [2014] IEHC 487 confirms that, where this happens, the planning permission falls to be interpreted principally by reference to the version of the guidelines in force as of the date the planning permission was granted, and not by reference to any updated or revised version of the guidelines.

On the facts of *Ógalas Ltd*, planning permission had been granted in 2004 for the development of a retail warehouse unit. Condition No.18 of the planning permission provided as follows.

> "The retail element of the proposed development shall be restricted to retail warehousing development only. In this regard, the range of goods to be sold in the retail units shall be restricted to bulky household goods and goods generally sold in bulk (as defined in Annex 1 of the Retail Planning Guidelines for Planning Authorities issued by the Department of the Environment and Local Government in December, 2000), including carpets and floor coverings, furniture, electrical goods, computers and DIY items including gardening equipment."

An updated version of the Retail Planning Guidelines was issued in April 2012. Relevantly, the definition of "bulky goods" had been amended. In particular, the revised definition omitted the earlier reference to goods which were not large individually, but would be bulky as part of a "collective purchase", e.g. wallpaper or paint.

A question was referred to An Bord Pleanála, pursuant to s.5 of the PDA 2000, as to whether the class and type of goods being sold represented a material change of use, and contravened the above condition. In particular, it was alleged that the unit was being used for the sale of non-bulky merchandise, such as, for example, kitchenware, cooking utensils, cleaning items, bathroom accessories, towels, candles, cushions, bed linen, clocks, and picture frames.

An Bord Pleanála's inspector, in her report, had attached weight to the revised definition of "bulky goods" under the 2012 version of the guidelines, and concluded that it tightened the scope of the definition, and removed ambiguity with regard to the type of goods which could be sold from retail warehouse units. The inspector recommended a finding that there had been a material change in use.

An Bord Pleanála made a determination that there had been a material change in use, and a material contravention of the terms of the planning permission and of the relevant condition. The board's decision included an express reference to the 2000 version of the guidelines. The board's decision contained inter alia a finding that the retailing activity carried out included the sale of a substantial amount of non-bulky household goods which did not come within the scope of the definition of activities of a "retail warehouse" as set out in the said guidelines, and was not restricted to the sale of bulky household goods and goods generally sold in bulk as defined.

The developer issued judicial review proceedings seeking to challenge An Bord Pleanála's determination. In particular, it was contended that the board's inspector had erred in placing reliance on the 2012 version of the guidelines, and that this error invalidated An Bord Pleanála's decision.

The High Court (Baker J.) accepted that the inspector had erred, but found that this error had not been replicated by An Bord Pleanála. See paras 26–28:

> "It seems to me that s.28 does not always require the Board to have regard to the most up to date Guidelines if other, or, as here, earlier, Guidelines are those applicable to the matter before it. The meaning of condition

> 18 is expressly limited to the Guidelines of 2000 and it is these which are relevant in the interpretation process. The requirement in s.28 that the Board and, ipso facto, an inspector carrying out a Board appointed function, have regard to the Guidelines cannot have the effect that the express words of condition 18 are to be read as containing a reference to the later Guidelines. This does not mean that the Guidelines of 2012 cannot inform the interpretative process, and it seems to me that the effect of s.28 is to mandate the Board to consider them, and in particular to take note of any clarification or interpretative assistance offered by them. But if an application of the Guidelines of 2012 leads to a result which differs from that which would result from the Guidelines of 2000 the latter must prevail. To hold otherwise would mean that the express language of the condition could be displaced or replaced by a later administrative act of the Minister in issuing new Guidelines.
>
> [...]
>
> Insofar as the inspector did come to her conclusion and recommendation based on what she perceived to be the less flexible test found in the Guidelines of 2012, she was applying, in my view, an incorrect or irrelevant test and the interpretative process had been guided primarily by the Guidelines of 2000 as these were the ones expressly identified as relevant in condition 18 itself. If the inspector's decision or her recommendation were substantially based on a view that the Guidelines of 2012 imported a tightening of the definition of bulky goods, she would have fallen into error. I accept the argument of the applicant that such an error would be an error of law were it to find its way into the decision making process."

In finding that An Bord Pleanála had not replicated this error on the part of the inspector, the High Court attached significance to the following. First, the board's determination expressly referred to the 2000 version of the guidelines, and the board's conclusion was linked to the definitions set out in Annex 1 of that version of the guidelines. Secondly, it was clear from the sequence of draft documents, and, in particular, from the matters which were omitted from the final draft, that the board did not regard the 2012 version of the guidelines as being determinative. More specifically, whereas the first draft of the board's decision had made reference to the definition of "retail warehouse", and "bulky goods" in the 2012 version of the guidelines, this was omitted in the final decision.

Finally, the High Court provided the following clarification as to what is entailed in the definition of "bulky goods" under the guidelines. See para.36:

> "I do not accept that the Retail Guidelines intended every item of household equipment or furnishing to qualify as bulky goods. Nor do I accept what is urged by counsel for the applicant that bulky goods must simply be read as items 'needed for the house and garden'. This interpretation ignores the simple fact that the Guidelines, whether they be the Guidelines of 2000 or 2012, clearly envisage that the goods either be individually bulky, in the sense that they are bulky or large in size, or that they be sold normally as part of a bulky purchase. A candle could not be defined as a bulky good in either sense, although on a broad interpretation a candle is an item of

> equipment for the house or garden. Equally, not all furniture is bulky and furniture could be distinguished from a fixture by reference to the fact that a fixture is not movable."

The High Court subsequently refused leave to appeal to the Court of Appeal: *Ógalas Ltd v An Bord Pleanála (No. 2)* [2015] IEHC 205.

ENVIRONMENTAL IMPACT ASSESSMENT

Project-splitting The concept of "project-splitting" refers to the practice whereby what is, in truth, a single project is divided into a number of separate consent applications. This is done with the intent of avoiding the requirement to subject the project to environmental impact assessment (EIA), by ensuring that each consent application is below the relevant threshold for EIA. The term "project-splitting" is sometimes used, in a secondary sense, to describe a scenario whereby the requirement for EIA is not avoided entirely, but where some aspect of the project is omitted from the consent application, or where the cumulative impact of the project with other projects is not properly assessed.

The High Court in *Ó Grianna v An Bord Pleanála* [2014] IEHC 632 had to determine whether, in assessing a proposed wind farm project, it was also necessary to assess the environmental impact of the connection between the wind turbines and the national electricity grid ("grid connection"). Planning permission had been granted for the erection of a number of wind turbines. One of the conditions stated that the permission was not to be construed as any form of consent or agreement to a connection to the national grid.

An Bord Pleanála argued that—in circumstances where the planning permission expressly stated that it was not to be construed as any form of consent for the grid connection—the wind turbines and the grid connection constituted *separate* projects for EIA purposes. The board further contended that when the (separate) project in relation to the grid connection became the subject of a consent application, the cumulative effects of that development would then be assessed, including by reference to its cumulative effect with the wind farm development.

The developer had sought to argue, by reference to art.5(1)(b) of the EIA Directive, that in circumstances where no proposals had yet been formulated by ESB Networks for the grid connection design, it simply was not possible for it (the developer) to include a consideration of same in its EIS, and, consequently, it was not possible for An Bord Pleanála to assess the potential environmental impact of the works associated with that phase of the development. (Article 5(1)(b) of the EIA Directive provides that a Member State may consider whether a developer may reasonably be required to compile particular information having regard, inter alia, to current knowledge and methods of assessment).

The High Court (Peart J.) rejected these various arguments. The court held that the grid connection was an "integral part of the overall development", and was "fundamental to the entire project".

> "I am satisfied that the second phase of the development in the present case, namely the connection to the national grid, is an integral part of the overall development of which the construction of the turbines is the first

> part. […] The wind turbine development on its own serves no function if it cannot be connected to the national grid. In that way, the connection to the national grid is fundamental to the entire project, and in principle at least the cumulative effect of both must be assessed in order to comply with the Directive."

The High Court ultimately concluded that no sensible developer would complete the first phase of the development project, i.e. the wind turbines, without having been granted permission for the connection to the national grid, or without having been assured that the connection phase is exempted development. In the court's view, there was no real prejudice in requiring the developer to hold off making an application for planning permission until an EIS for the entire project could be completed and submitted.

> "I appreciate that [the developers] have indicated that it simply is not possessed of the necessary information in this regard and could not include it in its EIS. But that does not mean that given more time and further contact with ESB Networks it could not be achieved so that it could be included in an EIS which addressed the impact of the environment of the total project 'at the earliest stage'. It may mean that the developer must wait longer before submitting its application for planning permission. But it seems to me likely at least that even if a phase 1 permission is granted with a condition such as Condition 4 contained therein, no sensible developer would complete phase 1 of the development without having been granted permission for the connection to the national grid, or without having been assured that the connection phase is exempted development. In that way, it is difficult to see any real prejudice to the developer by having to wait until the necessary proposals are finalised by ESB Networks so that an EIS for the entire project can be completed and submitted, and so that a cumulative assessment of the likely impact on the environment can be carried out in order to comply with both the letter and spirit of the Directive."

It is respectfully submitted that the approach adopted by the High Court is correct as a matter of EU law. Article 5 of the EIA Directive provides that a developer must supply certain minimum information, including inter alia a description of the project comprising information on the site, design and size of the project. Under Annex IV, the developer may also be required to provide a description of the physical characteristics of the "whole project", and the land-use requirements during the construction and "operational phases". It is submitted that the grid connection forms part of the "whole project" for EIA purposes, and is necessary for the "operational" phase of the wind farm. As stated by Peart J., the wind turbine development on its own serves no function if it cannot be connected to the national grid.

Alternatively, even if one accepts that the grid connection represents a distinct project, the EIA Directive nevertheless requires that it be assessed, as a cumulative impact, in the context of the consent application for the wind turbines. Under Annex IV of the EIA Directive, a developer may be required to provide a description of the "likely significant effects" on the environment resulting from the existence of the project, including indirect, secondary and cumulative effects. This requirement has been interpreted by the CJEU in *Commission v Spain* (C-404/09) [2011] E.C.R. I-11853 at para.80 as meaning that an EIA must also include an analysis of the cumulative effects on the environment which a project may produce if considered jointly with other projects, insofar as such an analysis is necessary in order to ensure that the assessment covers examination of all the notable impacts on the environment of the project in question. Wind farm projects will often be located in remote, ecologically sensitive areas, and the putting in place of a grid connection has the potential to have significant effects on the environment. The precise route of the line, and its form, i.e. overhead or underground, should therefore be assessed.

It is no answer to suggest—as An Bord Pleanála appears to have done—that the assessment can be carried out *after* development consent has been granted for the wind turbines. It is an objective of the EIA Directive, as recorded in the recitals, that effects on the environment should be taken into account at the *earliest* possible stage in all the technical planning and decision-making processes. The CJEU relied on this recital in *Wells* (C-201/02) [2004] E.C.R. I-723 to find that where national law provides that a consent procedure is to be carried out in several stages, one involving a principal decision and the other involving an implementing decision which cannot extend beyond the parameters set by the principal decision, the effects which the project may have on the environment must be identified and assessed at the time of the procedure relating to the principal decision. Although this statement was made in the context of an outline planning permission and an approval, it may also have resonance for consecutive planning permissions. The grant of planning permission may serve as a precedent for a subsequent planning application. In this regard, there is much force in the applicant's argument in *Ó Grianna* that if the wind turbines were erected pursuant to the impugned planning permission, it would be more difficult for the planning authority or An Bord Pleanála thereafter to refuse an application for a subsequent permission in respect of the connection to the national grid. The developer would, in the applicant's words, already have "a foot in the door".

Peat extraction Peat extraction is a licensable activity under Pt IV of the Environmental Protection Agency Act 1992 (as amended). The relevant category is defined as follows: "The extraction of peat in the course of business which involves an area exceeding 50 hectares". In *Environmental Protection Agency v Harte Peat Ltd* [2014] IEHC 308, the High Court (Barrett J.) ruled inter alia that this category: (i) included all activities that are directly associated with peat extraction, e.g. the use of access roads, the storage of harvested peat, the establishment of buffer zones and the creation of sedimentation ponds; and (ii) allowed for the aggregation of sites, for the purposes of calculating the 50 hectare threshold, where a business undertaking/entity carries out peat extraction at a number of different locations.

HABITATS DIRECTIVE

Appropriate Assessment Article 6 of the Habitats Directive 92/43 seeks to regulate plans or projects which might have a significant effect on the conservation objectives of designated sites. Article 6(3) prescribes a two-stage procedure. First, a project must be "screened" in order to determine whether the project is likely to have a significant effect on a designated site. The trigger here is a light one. Secondly, in the event that the screening determination is positive, then the competent authority must carry out an "appropriate assessment" of the project. The competent authority must determine whether the plan or project will adversely affect the integrity of the site concerned.

Article 6(3) of the Habitats Directive does not elaborate upon what is involved in an "appropriate assessment". This is in marked contrast with the EIA Directive, where a detailed procedure is prescribed.

The CJEU has considered what is required by an "appropriate assessment" in a number of judgments. In the *Mechanical Cockle Fishing* case (C-127/07 *Waddenzee*), the court stated that an "appropriate assessment" implies that all the aspects of the plan or project which can, by themselves or in combination with other plans or projects, affect the site's conservation objectives must be identified in the light of the best scientific knowledge in the field. In *Commission v Spain* (C-404/09) [2011] E.C.R. I-11853, the court held that an assessment cannot be regarded as "appropriate" if it contains gaps and lacks complete, precise and definitive findings and conclusions capable of removing all reasonable scientific doubt as to the effects of the proposed works on the site concerned. This requirement has been restated in more recent judgments, including *Sweetman v An Bord Pleanála* (C-258/11) 11 April 2013, para.44 and *Briels v Minister van Infrastructuur en Milieu* (C-521/12) 15 May 2014.

Where a project is subject to the requirement to obtain development consent under the planning legislation—as opposed to under some other specific legislation, such as, for example, the Gas Acts or the Foreshore Acts—then the "appropriate assessment" will be carried out in the context of the planning application. Part XAB of the PDA 2000 prescribes the procedure for the carrying out of an "appropriate assessment". The key elements include: (i) the submission by the developer of information in the form of a "Natura Impact Statement" ("NIS"); (ii) public consultation; and, (iii) the making of a formal determination by the decision-maker as to whether the project will adversely affect the integrity of the site concerned.

The judgment in *Kelly v An Bord Pleanála* [2014] IEHC 400 confirms that the carrying out of an "appropriate assessment" must include an examination, analysis, evaluation, findings, conclusions and a final determination. See para.39:

> "Section 177V(1) must be construed so as to give effect to Article 6(3) of the Habitats Directive, and hence, an appropriate assessment carried out under the section must meet the requirements of Article 6(3) as set out in the CJEU case law. If an appropriate assessment is to comply with the criteria set out by the CJEU in the cases referred to, then it must, in my judgment, include an examination, analysis, evaluation, findings, conclusions and a final determination."

The judgment in *Kelly* also confirms that the carrying out of the "appropriate assessment" must be evident from the decision itself. This can be achieved by setting out the assessment as part of the formal decision, or by the decision-maker adopting an assessment carried out by one of its officers or inspectors.

> "it appears to me that the reasons given for the Board's determination in an appropriate assessment must include the complete, precise and definitive

> findings and conclusions relied upon by the Board as the basis for its determination. They must also include the main rationale or reason for which the Board considered those findings and conclusions capable of removing all scientific doubt as to the effects of the proposed development on the European site concerned in the light of the its conservation objectives. In the absence of such reasons, it would not be possible for a court to decide whether the appropriate assessment was lawfully concluded or whether the determination meets the legal test required by the judgments of the CJEU.
>
> [...]
>
> In reaching that conclusion, I am not deciding that the findings and conclusions always have to be ones made by the Board itself. Where the Board appoints an inspector to prepare a report, and the inspector carries out an appropriate assessment as part of his or her report, it may be that if the Board, on consideration, accepts the relevant findings made and conclusions reached by its Inspector in his or her report, that the production of the report may satisfy some or all of the obligation of the Board to give reasons for its determination. This would depend upon the relevant facts."

Sites designated subsequent to development consent Under Irish law, the requirement to carry out an "appropriate assessment" applies not only to sites which have been formally designated as a "Special Area of Conservation" ("SAC") but also extends to sites which have been proposed for designation.

Occasionally, a scenario will arise whereby, by the time a site is proposed for designation, development consent will already have been granted for a project within the vicinity of the newly proposed site. A formal "appropriate assessment" will not normally have been carried out prior to the grant of development consent because, as of the date of the grant of the consent, the site had not yet been proposed for designation, and thus did not attract the legal requirement for "appropriate assessment". The question which arises in such a scenario is whether it is necessary to revisit the grant of development consent, i.e. in order to allow an "appropriate assessment" to be carried out retrospectively.

The case law of the CJEU—in particular *Commission v Spain* (C-404/09) [2011] E.C.R. I-11853—confirms that the procedural requirements under arts 6(3) and (4) of the Habitats Directive do not apply retrospectively. However, a Member State is subject to the overarching obligations of art.6(2), i.e. the Member State must avoid the deterioration of natural habitats and the habitats of species as well as significant disturbance of species for which those areas have been classified.

This issue arose tangentially on the facts of *Sandymount and Merrion Residents Association v An Bord Pleanála (No. 2)* [2013] IEHC 542. An Bord Pleanála had granted development consent for the extension of the existing waste water treatment works at Ringsend, Dublin. As part of the project, it was proposed to relocate the effluent outfall tunnel from the inner bay to the outer bay. This would involve the construction of a new nine kilometre tunnel.

The consent took the form of a foreshore approval under Pt XV of the PDA 2000 (as amended in 2006). A number of weeks after the foreshore approval had been granted, part of Dublin Bay had been proposed for designation as an SAC. The qualifying interests included intertidal and sub-tidal reefs, and the harbour porpoise. The proposed site included the area where the effluent outfall tunnel was to be located.

A residents association sought to challenge the decision to grant the foreshore approval. One of the arguments pursued at the hearing was that the relevant part of Dublin Bay should have been proposed for designation *earlier*, and that, as such, it was entitled to a form of interim protection under the Habitats Directive even before it was proposed for designation as a conservation site. The argument then ran to the effect that—even though the site had not been proposed for designation as of the date of its decision—An Bord Pleanála was nevertheless obliged to take appropriate protective measures in order to maintain the ecological characteristics of the site.

The facts of the case potentially gave rise to a difficult question of principle: what steps, if any, must a Member State take to comply with the Habitats Directive where a development consent has been granted *prior* to the proposed designation of a site? In the event, however, the High Court resolved the case on narrower grounds. First, the court held that the applicant had not met the burden of proving any lack of protection for the site: although the site had only been proposed for designation subsequent to the board's decision, the court held that the change in status of the relevant sea area and the reasons relating to harbour porpoises and reefs had appeared clearly in the environmental impact statement.

Secondly, it seems from the judgment that the foreshore approval was only one of a number of development consents which were required before the development project could be completed. In particular, the proposed relocation of the primary discharge point, i.e. the outfall tunnel, would require a review of the existing waste water discharge licence under the Waste Water Discharge (Authorisation) Regulations 2007. It also seems that a foreshore licence might be required from the Minister under the Foreshore Acts. The High Court was satisfied that an "appropriate assessment" for the purposes of the Habitats Directive could be carried out in the context of the decision-making in respect of these consents. See para.4.8 of the judgment.

> "In conclusion on the protection issue, it is beyond doubt that a planning consent authorises nothing more than construction of the sewage works and pipeline, in this instance, and that this is subject to stringent conditions for the protection of the environment. Where there is to be a modification in relation the existing licence for waste water, and the plan to discharge treated sewage effluent into the special area of conservation in Dublin Bay is such a modification, then the Environmental Protection Agency must consider the appropriate safeguards in the context of the obligations which arise under the relevant European and national legislation; in particular article 6 of the [Habitats] Directive. In granting or refusing a foreshore licence for the necessary works, the relevant minister of Government has a similarly onerous obligation."

There may be a question mark as to whether the High Court's approach is consistent with the case law of the CJEU in respect of multi-stage decision-making. This case law arises primarily in the context of the EIA Directive, but the principles would seem to apply equally to the Habitats Directive.

Recital (2) of the EIA Directive indicates that effects on the environment should be taken into account at the earliest possible stage in all the technical planning and decision-making processes. The CJEU has identified the objective of this as being to prevent the creation of pollution or nuisances at source, rather than subsequently trying to counteract their effects. See *Commission v Ireland* (C-215/06) [2008] E.C.R. I-4911 at para.58.

The CJEU has ruled that, in the context of multi-stage decision-making, the effects which a proposed project may have on the environment must normally be identified and assessed at the time of the procedure relating to the "principal" decision. See *Wells* (C-201/02) [2004] E.C.R. I-723 at para.52.

> "Accordingly, where national law provides that the consent procedure is to be carried out in several stages, one involving a principal decision and the other involving an implementing decision which cannot extend beyond the parameters set by the principal decision, the effects which the project may have on the environment must be identified and assessed at the time of the procedure relating to the principal decision. It is only if those effects are not identifiable until the time of the procedure relating to the implementing decision that the assessment should be carried out in the course of that procedure."

It is at least arguable that the decision to grant foreshore approval represents the "principal" decision in respect of the proposed waste water treatment works, and that the waste water discharge licence represents a mere "implementing" decision. In particular, it seems that the location of the effluent outfall tunnel will have been determined conclusively in the context of the decision to grant foreshore approval. If this is the case, then there is a respectable argument that the "appropriate assessment" for the purposes of the Habitats Directive must be carried out in the context of the decision to grant foreshore approval, i.e. this represents the earliest possible stage of the decision-making process, and the only stage at which meaningful consideration of alternative locations is open/possible. See, by analogy, *Commission v United Kingdom* (C-6/04) [2005] E.C.R. I-09017 where the Advocate General indicated that conservation objectives should be taken into account at an early stage (on the facts, at the stage of adopting land use plans). See Advocate General's opinion, at para.48.

Sites which have not yet been designated The legal protections under arts 6(2), (3) and (4) of the Habitats Directive only apply to a site once it has been formally adopted by the EU Commission as a "site of Community interest" ("SCI"). The CJEU has made it clear, however, in a number of cases that a form of interim protection applies to sites which have been proposed for designation but have not yet been formally adopted. A Member State may not authorise interventions which incur the risk of seriously compromising the ecological characteristics of a proposed site. See *Dragaggi* (C-117/03) [2005] E.C.R. I-167 and *Bund Naturschutz in Bayern* (C-244/05) [2006] E.C.R. I-8445.

Initially, this interim protection was said to apply only from the stage a site has been included in a list of proposed sites transmitted by a Member State to the EU Commission. In the more recent judgment in *Commission v Cyprus* (C-340/10)

15 March 2012, however, the CJEU has indicated that interim protection may also extend to sites which should have been, but were not, included in the list of proposed sites. On the facts of that case, the Republic of Cyprus did not dispute that the site satisfied the ecological criteria in art.4(1) of the Habitats Directive and, therefore, should have been included in the national list of SCIs sent to the Commission. Indeed, the Cypriot government undertook to include the site in a revised list of proposed sites, which it did, albeit more than 17 months after the reasoned opinion was issued.

In *Harrington v An Bord Pleanála* [2014] IEHC 232 an ambitious attempt was made to expand further on this line of case law. In brief, the applicant sought to argue (i) that any and all lands which contained a priority habitat type should have been proposed for designation, and (ii) that such lands attract interim protection pending the rectification of this alleged failure to designate. With respect, it is very difficult to reconcile these arguments with the wording of the relevant provisions of the Habitats Directive. In particular, the applicant's interpretation would deny individual Member States and the EU Commission any discretion to select representative samples of priority habitat type. This would be contrary to the case law of the CJEU which confirms that Member States enjoy a margin of discretion when making their site proposals. See *Commission v Ireland* (C-67/99) [2001] E.C.R. I-5757 at para.33.

Moreover, the applicant's arguments also appear to overlook the fact that art.5 of the Habitats Directive prescribes a very specific remedy in relation to non-designation of sites. The existence of this remedy would exclude the type of private enforcement which the applicant sought to pursue.

In the event, it was not necessary for the High Court to rule on these issues in *Harrington*, and the case was resolved on a narrower basis. The High Court ruled that the applicant had failed to make out any evidential basis for her argument that there had been a breach of the Habitats Directive. The court held that the applicant had failed to adduce any evidence whatsoever to support her contention that the site in question was a priority habitat. The applicant had thus failed to discharge the onus of proof resting on her to establish that An Bord Pleanála was required to carry out an "appropriate assessment".

> "I have come to the conclusion that the respondent did not fail in any way in its duty to conduct an appropriate inquiry, as required of them by statute, by failing to carry out their own independent ecological assessment. The applicant failed to adduce any evidence whatsoever to support her contention that the site in question was a priority habitat, warranting, on the basis of the "precautionary principle", the elimination of "scientific doubt" by the carrying out of an independent ecological assessment. Thus, in these judicial review proceedings, I am quite satisfied that the applicant has failed to discharge the onus of proof resting on her to establish that the respondent failed in its legal duty, as she contends, in that regard."

QUARRIES

Section 261A of the PDA 2000 The CJEU ruled in *Commission v Ireland* (C-215/06) [2008] E.C.R. I-4911 that the generous provision made under the original Planning and Development Act 2000 for retention planning permission was inconsistent with the EIA Directive. The CJEU indicated that a system of regularisation, such as that then in force in Ireland, might have the effect of encouraging developers to forgo compliance with the requirements of the EIA Directive. See, generally, *Annual Review of Irish Law 2008*.

As part of the legislative measures introduced to give effect to the judgment, local planning authorities were obliged to carry out an examination of the quarries in their functional area. If the planning authority determined that "development" had been carried out in breach of the requirements of either the EIA Directive or the Habitats Directive, then the authority was required either (i) to direct the quarry operator to apply for development consent ("substitute consent"), or (ii) to issue an enforcement notice. These provisions were set out in a new section, s.261A.

The lawfulness of the s.261A procedure was challenged in *McGrath Limestone Works Ltd v An Bord Pleanála* [2014] IEHC 382. The case concerned a quarry which had commenced operation prior to October 1964. The Supreme Court judgment in *Waterford County Council v John A Woods Ltd* [1999] 1 I.R. 556 indicates that, in the case of quarrying which commenced prior to October 1964, planning permission is not required for the completion of quarrying works which might reasonably have been anticipated as of that date.

On the facts of *McGrath Limestone Works Ltd*, An Bord Pleanála had determined that a lateral extension in the area of excavation, which had occurred post-1990, went beyond the works which might have been reasonably anticipated as of October 1964. The board, accordingly, confirmed the planning authority's determination directing that an application for "substitute consent" be made. The quarry operator challenged this determination in the judicial review proceedings.

The High Court dismissed the challenge to the validity of the board's determination. The court indicated that the appropriate standard of review was rationality, as per *O'Keeffe v An Bord Pleanála* [1993] 1 I.R. 39.

> "As in many of these cases, the matter has been argued as if it is within the power of the High Court to overturn a decision as unattractive. There is no such function vested in the High Court. Instead, what is considered in a judicial review is the procedure of the administrative body, its jurisdiction and whether in any administrative or quasi-judicial assessment of the facts determined flew in the face of fundamental reason and common sense."

The court held that the legal test as per *Waterford County Council v John A Woods Ltd* had been properly applied both by Mayo County Council and by An Bord Pleanála, and that their factual analysis was based on tenable material.

The judgment is very lengthy, and it is beyond the scope of this discussion to address all issues raised. Rather, the discussion will be confined to two aspects of the judgment which may have relevance for other cases, as follows.

First, the High Court judgment addresses the interaction between the provisions of s.261A and s.261. In brief, s.261 had provided for the registration of quarries during the period April 2004 to April 2005. Following registration, the local planning authority was empowered (i) to impose conditions on the continued operation of the quarry, or (ii) to direct that an application for planning permission (subject to environmental impact assessment) be made.

On the facts of *McGrath Limestone Works Ltd*, the planning authority had decided to impose conditions. The quarry operator sought to argue, in the judicial review proceedings, that the fact that the planning authority had, in 2006/2007, decided not to direct that an application for planning permission (subject to environmental impact assessment) be made gave rise to a legitimate expectation to the effect that the operation of the quarry was compliant with the EIA Directive. It was argued that it would be inconsistent with this (alleged) legitimate expectation to issue a direction to apply for "substitute consent" pursuant to s.261A.

The High Court rejected this argument. Charleton J. held that the planning authority had made no representation in 2006/2007 such as would found a "legitimate expectation" that development consent would never be required in the future. See para.4.3:

> "Nothing in the section [s.261] enables a local planning authority to make any binding determination that a quarry if registered subject to conditions would thereafter be exempt from the need to apply for planning permission if investigation or admission uncovered, for instance, that any unauthorised development had taken place or that any declared status by quarry owners that they were outside the scope of the planning code because of use existing in 1964 was optimistic."

The court ruled, on the facts, that Mayo County Council had made no representation in 2006/2007 that it had accepted the quarry owner's argument that an environmental impact assessment need not be carried out because of what the owner claimed to be high existing levels of environmental protection on site. See para.4.5:

> "If there is any ground upon which the principle of legitimate expectation might apply, there would first of all have to exist at least that level of unequivocal declaration that supports estoppel in private law. This is absent on the facts of this case. Reading the correspondence, all that is apparent is that McGrath Limestone Works argues that an environmental impact assessment need not be engaged because of what are claimed to be high existing levels of environmental protection on site and suggest conditions instead. Mayo County Council made no declaration such as that they accepted this or that they had inspected the site thoroughly and that no impact on the environment or on protected habitats could possibly arise either then or into the future. It would be hard to imagine any local planning authority being inspired into any such declaration. Such a decision would be astonishing. Further, there is nothing on the facts which could amount to declaration, much less an unequivocal representation, that the status of the quarry had been decided for ever and from that point on. Nothing changed in the former status of the quarry either because of registration or because of the imposition of conditions of operation on the quarry. [...]"

The judgment goes on to suggest that, even if a representation had been made, there could be no *legitimate* expectation that an unlawful state of affairs should continue unchecked. See para.4.5:

> "Any representation sufficient to have set up a legitimate expectation would, in this instance, have been a trespass into the sovereign authority of the State under Article 6 of the Constitution. It should be remembered that jurisdiction is both the conferring of power to act and is also a boundary to the exercise of that power. Under the Act of 2000, Mayo County Council had no such power as contended for here. Even were such a power exercised it would be outside the boundary of what would be legitimate. There can be no expectation that is legitimate that an unlawful state of affairs that is expressly subject to sanction under national legislation should continue unchecked. Nor can it be expected that the legal landscape will be frozen through administrative fiat and that what the Oireachtas may see as socially unacceptable may never be provided for in legislation in the future. Even less can such an expectation arise under European law, since the need for an assessment on the effect of a project on the environment arises from that source."

The second issue of general relevance arising from the judgment concerns the constitutional validity of s.261A. In brief outline, the quarry operator had made two principal complaints as follows. First, it was alleged that an ex post facto determination that development, which had been carried out in the past, had been carried out in breach of the EIA Directive and/or the Habitats Directive involved the *retrospective* imposition of criminal liability. Secondly, it was alleged that the quarry had the benefit of established pre-1964 use rights, and that the imposition of a requirement to apply for development consent (in the form of "substitute consent") was an unjust attack on those rights.

The High Court rejected each of these complaints. The court held that a determination that past quarrying activities had been carried out in breach of the two directives did not amount to a retrospective declaration of unlawful conduct. See para.10.2:

> "No person or enterprise can expect that, as regards the environment or the entitlement of the people of Ireland to participate in the planning of its built infrastructure and land use, the law will never change. It changed here. The result was remedial. Quarries had, firstly, to be registered, and partly regulated despite a pre planning code use and, secondly, as care for the environment became perceived as more important, impact on natural habitats was to be analysed, assessed, commented on through inclusive participation, and then regulated. None of that gave rise to retrospective criminal or civil liability. Mayo County Council in their actions on this matter made this as clear as could be. By the legislation, for the future, the environment is to be considered and conditions may be appropriately imposed or actions may be appropriately prohibited. That is entirely within the scope of the legislative power of the Oireachtas as limited by Article 15.5.1°."

At an earlier point in the judgment, the court had characterised a determination under s.261A(2) in the following terms. See para.5.10:

> "This was far from a finding that disreputable conduct had occurred, much less that a criminal offence had been perpetrated. All that was found was a state of facts following an appropriate enquiry. This does not amount to a declaration of unlawful conduct. It is, instead, recognition that a state of affairs that is not in conformity with European law requires rectification. That situation was always more than dubious given the absence of an appropriate environmental impact assessment and, as with any situation considered undesirable, the Oireachtas is entitled to legislate in respect of it even had no European obligation arisen."

Insofar as the alleged unjust attack on property rights was concerned, the court held that there is nothing unlawful in *prospective* developers being restricted as to how they will use their premises where that restriction is reasonably and fairly arrived at for the proper planning and sustainable development of a neighbourhood. The court also queried whether the refusal of planning permission for "sufficient and proportionate planning reasons" should give rise to a right to be compensated.

The High Court also ruled that even if there had been an interference with the quarry operator's constitutional rights, same was shielded from review under Art.29.4 of the Irish Constitution. The court ruled that a legislative response was necessary to rectify the deficiencies in the implementation of the EIA Directive identified by the CJEU in *Commission v Ireland* (C-215/06) [2008] E.C.R. I-4911. The amending legislation, namely s.261A, was thus "necessitated" by Ireland's membership of the EU and accordingly came within the scope of Art.29.4.

COMPULSORY PURCHASE ORDER

Notice to Treat The general rule under s.217(6) of the PDA 2000 is that a notice to treat must be served within 18 months of a compulsory purchase order becoming operative. It had been argued on behalf of An Bord Pleanála in *Flancrest Enterprises Ltd v An Bord Pleanála*, unreported, High Court, Peart J., 20 December 2013 that this 18 month time-limit did not apply to a railway order made pursuant to the Transport (Railway Infrastructure) Acts. In brief, it was argued that a railway order does not represent a compulsory purchase order within the meaning of s.217, and that the legislature intended that An Bord Pleanála should have a wide discretion to include in a railway order such provisions as the board considers necessary or expedient for the purpose of the order.

The High Court rejected these arguments, and held that on a literal interpretation the 18 month time-limit applies to a railway order.

> "On a literal construction a railway order is to have effect as a compulsory purchase order, and if one therefore treats it as such, then the procedures for a compulsory purchase order must be those to apply, and therefore section 217 (6) of the Act of 2000 is applicable. In my view this does not result in any absurdity. In fact it seems to make complete sense, and is consistent with a necessary requirement that where property rights are to be interfered with or adversely affected by legislation, the Oireachtas should do so to the least extent consistent with the objectives of the legislation. This is the so-called 'minimal restraint' test now more commonly referred to as a test

of proportionality, appearing in *Heaney v. Ireland* [1994] 3 I.R. 593 at 607 per Costello J. (as he then was)."

Practice and Procedure

SAM COLLINS

ABUSE OF PROCESS

Order 19 rule 28 of the Rules of the Superior Courts 1986 ("RSC") and the inherent jurisdiction of the courts to dismiss proceedings that are frivolous or vexatious or have no chance of success See generally Trevor Murphy, "To Strike or Not to Strike? A Review of the Jurisdiction to Dismiss Proceedings in the Superior Courts" (2014) 21(2) C.L.P. 33.

In *Lopes v Minister for Justice, Equality and Law Reform* [2008] 4 I.R. 743, the plaintiff commenced proceedings against the Minister, arising from alleged discrimination by the courts in personal injury and related professional negligence litigation. The Minister applied for an order striking out the plaintiff's claim under Ord.19 r.28 RSC, on the grounds that it disclosed no cause of action, or an order under the inherent jurisdiction of the court dismissing the plaintiff's claim as being an abuse of process and having no reasonable prospect of success, or being bound to fail. This application was succeeded in the High Court (Hanna J.) ([2008] 4 I.R. 743) and the plaintiff appealed ([2014] IESC 21).

Clarke J. (with whom Laffoy and Dunne JJ. concurred) explained the difference between applications made under Ord.19 r.28 and under the inherent jurisdiction of the court as follows:

> "If, even on the basis of the facts as pleaded, the case is bound to fail, then it must be vexatious and should be dismissed under the RSC. If, however, it can be established that there is no credible basis for suggesting that the facts are as asserted and that, thus, the proceedings are bound to fail on the merits, then the inherent jurisdiction of the Court to prevent abuse can be invoked."

Considering the nature of the plaintiff's claim, Clarke J. expressed the view that the case was more appropriately considered under the inherent jurisdiction of the court rather than under the RSC. He emphasised that the jurisdiction to dismiss must be exercised sparingly and that the plaintiff's evidence must be taken at its high water mark. Clarke J. had regard to the complexity of the legal issues involved in the plaintiff's claim (including judicial immunity from suit and potential vicarious liability on the part of the Minister) and expressed the view that, given that complexity, it would not be appropriate to dismiss the plaintiff's claim on a particular legal ground. Instead, Clarke J. considered whether the plaintiff's allegations of judicial bias, discrimination or corruption, on which his claim was based, were credible.

Clarke J. noted that a number of allegations which, individually, might have been insufficient to warrant a finding of bias might, cumulatively, warrant such a finding, but that the mere fact that there were multiple allegations did not of itself constitute credible evidence (quoting with approval the dictum of Denham J. (as she then was) in *Bula Ltd v Tara Mines (No.6)* [2000] 4 I.R. 412 at 462 that "seventeen noughts are still nothing"). Clarke J. proceeded to carefully examine each of the plaintiff's allegations and held that there was no basis for suggesting that there was any evidence, or any prospect of there being any evidence, to support his factual accusations. On that basis, the appeal was dismissed.

In *Clohessy v Legal Aid Board* [2014] IEHC 72, proceedings against three defendants (the Minister for Justice and Law Reform, Ireland and the Attorney General) were struck out in circumstances where no cause of action was pleaded, or reliefs claimed, against those defendants.

In *Murphy v Allianz plc* [2014] IEHC 692, the plaintiff, a bricklayer and sub-contractor, had suffered a personal injury at work. The main contractor, Bri-Mo Ltd, held a policy of insurance with the defendant. Bri-Mo was struck off the register of companies and the plaintiff issued proceedings against the defendant based primarily on s.62 of the Civil Liability Act 1961. The defendant applied to strike out the proceedings pursuant to Ord.19 r.28 RSC on the grounds that they disclosed no reasonable cause of action and were bound to fail. Gilligan J. acceded to this application in circumstances where s.62 of the Civil Liability Act 1961 did not apply (Bri-Mo having not been wound up), and where the plaintiff had no privity of contract with the defendant.

See also *Irish Bank Resolution Corporation v Purcell* [2014] IEHC 525, where a third party statement of claim, claiming damages and an indemnity or contribution from the Central Bank of Ireland (CBI) relating to an alleged breach of duty by CBI in, *inter alia*, authorising and approving a challenged delegation of powers by Irish Nationwide Building Society's board to its Chief Executive Officer, was not struck out.

Striking out proceedings—"illegal creation of currency" claims Arguments based on banks allegedly engaging in the "illegal creation of currency" did not prove fruitful before the courts in 2014: see Mary Donnelly, "Banking and Security Law Update" 22(4) C.L.P. 107, 110. In *Kearney v KBC Bank Ireland plc* [2014] IEHC 260, the bank had advanced six loans to the plaintiff (a property investor and developer). The loans were secured and, the loan accounts being in arrears and demands having issued, the bank appointed receivers over a number of properties. The plaintiff commenced proceedings by plenary summons in September 2012 (accompanied by an affidavit, followed by the delivery of two different statements of claim). The defendants sought an order pursuant to Ord.19 r.28 RSC and/or pursuant to the inherent jurisdiction of the court, striking out the plaintiff's claim on the grounds that the pleadings disclosed no reasonable cause of action and that the proceedings were frivolous, vexatious and bound to fail.

Birmingham J. noted that the court has a power, both pursuant to Ord.19 r.28 RSC and pursuant to its inherent jurisdiction, to strike out proceedings that are frivolous or vexatious, but emphasised that this jurisdiction must not be exercised lightly, and that proceedings should not be dismissed where they are capable of being saved by amendment.

The plaintiff's pleadings were described as diffuse and did not easily lend themselves to being summarised. Each of the plaintiff's pleas was closely considered by Birmingham J., who acceded to the defendants' application to strike out the plaintiff's claim. A notable claim was that "the bank engaged in the illegal creation of currency", which appeared to have been based on the plaintiff's interpretation of an article "Money Creation in the Modern Economy" (Bank of England Quarterly Bulletin, 2014, Q.1) by members of the Bank of England's Monetary Analysis Directorate. Birmingham J. noted that the argument (that a bank did not advance a loan, but created currency) was not a new one and had been considered by Gilligan J. in *Freeman v Bank of Scotland Ireland* [2013] IEHC 371. Birmingham J. observed that the terms "fanciful" and "devoid of merit" (*per* Rooke C.J. in *Meads v Meads* (2012) A.B.Q.B. 571) were appropriate to describe this argument. The same argument (purportedly based on the same Bank of England article) was also closely considered by Hogan J. in *McCarthy v Bank of Scotland plc* [2014] IEHC 340, where the proceedings were struck out pursuant to Ord.19 r.28 RSC on the ground that they were frivolous and vexatious.

Striking out proceedings—"reckless lending" claims It is well-established that no tort of "reckless lending" is known to the law: see Mark Heslin, "A Tort of Reckless Lending?" (2014) 22(7) C.L.P. 164 and Mary Donnelly, "Banking and Security Law Update" 22(4) C.L.P. 107, 110. In *Healy v Stepstone Mortgage Funding Ltd* [2014] IEHC 134, Hogan J. observed that the matter had been put "beyond doubt" by the decisions in *ICS Building v Grant* [2010] IEHC 17 and *McConnon v President of Ireland* [2012] IEHC 184, [2012] I.R. 449 and acceded to an application to strike out the plaintiff's claim (based upon a purported tort of reckless lending) pursuant to the inherent jurisdiction of the court.

Regarding arguments commonly advanced by Freemen on the Land or Organised Pseudolegal Commercial Arguments ("OPCA") litigants, see generally Tomás Keys, "Freemen on the Land and Other Organised Lay Litigant Groups" Part One (2014) 21(10) C.L.P. 230 and Part Two (2014) 21(11) C.L.P. 256.

Isaac Wunder orders In *Quinn v Fennell* [2014] IEHC 20, the defendant sought an order dismissing the proceedings as an abuse of process and/or as *res judicata*, and an Isaac Wunder order against the plaintiffs. It was argued that the issues sought to be litigated in the proceedings were identical to issues which had been determined by order of the High Court (Feeney J.) in earlier proceedings. Birmingham J. expressed the view that the proceedings were "to a very large extent indeed merely a rehash" of the earlier proceedings and, even if any matters raised fell outside the earlier proceedings, they could and should have been litigated in those proceedings and could not be litigated having regard to the rule in *Henderson v Henderson* (1843) 3 Hare 100. Accordingly, Birmingham J. struck out the proceedings, subject to two exceptions relating to new issues (concerning the incarceration of the first plaintiff, and certain complaints regarding the defendant's personal property).

Birmingham J. was also satisfied that (having regard to a number of proceedings) it would be appropriate to make an Isaac Wunder order against the plaintiffs (prohibiting them from issuing any further proceedings against the defendant without the leave of the President of the High Court or his nominee), and would order same unless satisfactory undertakings were given by the plaintiffs.

In *Daire v The Wise Finance Co Ltd* [2014] IEHC 371, an Isaac Wunder order had previously been made against the plaintiff by the High Court (Laffoy J.)

([2013] IEHC 337—see *Annual Review of Irish Law 2013*). The plaintiff issued a motion seeking to set aside the order of Laffoy J., which motion was amended, by agreement, to a motion seeking liberty to commence fresh proceedings. The solicitor for the plaintiff argued that a new point had arisen since the order of Laffoy J., namely that an execution order for possession (which issued on 15 April 2013) was not legally sound, having not been made within six years of the making of the relevant order (an order of the High Court (Dunne J.) for possession made on 31 July 2006) as required by Ord.42 r.23 RSC. Baker J. reviewed the authorities concerning leave to institute proceedings and examined the basis of the proceedings which the plaintiff sought leave to issue. Baker J. expressed the view that the court must ask itself whether the proceedings were sustainable, or whether the plaintiff could "produce a statement of claim, which could be supported by evidence, which would be capable of saving the proceedings." (*per* Laffoy J. at [2013] IEHC 337). Baker J. was satisfied that a new point had been raised, not tested in the previous litigation, and which was not a collateral attack on the order of possession which had already been made. In those circumstances, Baker J. considered whether the proposed proceedings were bound to fail. Closely considering the chronology of the proceedings, Baker J. concluded that "there is no coherent or rational argument that can be made by the plaintiff that the writ of possession was made out of time." Having regard to that view, and taking the plaintiff's case at its height, the plaintiff's case was bound to fail and Baker J. refused to grant the relief sought.

APPEAL

Leave to appeal In *Marie Claire Netherlands B.V. v Controller of Patents, Designs and Trade Marks* [2014] IEHC 362, the plaintiff sought leave to appeal a decision of the High Court pursuant to s.79(3) of the Trade Marks Act 1996 (which provides that such an appeal shall lie to the Supreme Court on a specified point of law). Barrett J. analysed nine purported points of law on which leave to appeal was sought and, finding that none was a point of law, declined leave to appeal.

Re-entry of an appeal to admit new evidence In *Superwood Holdings plc v Sun Alliance and London Insurance plc* [2014] IESC 14, the appellant sought a number of orders in respect of an appeal which had been dismissed by the Supreme Court in 2004, including that the appeal be re-entered and that new evidence be admitted. As part of the proceedings, a re-trial in the High Court had lasted 281 days, "the longest civil hearing in the history of the state" (*per* Fennelly J.). The notice of motion was dismissed in circumstances where it was held by Fennelly J. (with whom McKechnie and Laffoy JJ. concurred) to be misconceived in a number of respects, in particular where, the appeal having been dismissed and no appeal being before the court, the power of the court to admit new evidence under Ord.58 r.8 RSC did not arise.

Death of a plaintiff pending appeal and section 7 of the Civil Liability Act 1961 In *Doyle v Dunne* [2014] IESC 69, the plaintiff had issued personal injury proceedings arising from severe consequences of eye surgery. Damages for pain and suffering were claimed, but no special damages were claimed. In the High Court the plaintiff's claim was dismissed and the plaintiff appealed. The plaintiff was terminally ill and unfortunately died while the appeal (which had been given priority) was part heard. In the Supreme Court, Laffoy J. held that the damages claimed by the plaintiff in the proceedings did not survive her death by reason of s.7 of the Civil Liability Act 1961. There was nothing by way of remedy or relief for the Supreme Court to adjudicate upon, or to remit to the High Court, and accordingly the appeal was dismissed.

APPLICATIONS TO EXTEND TIME WITHIN WHICH TO DELIVER A STATEMENT OF CLAIM

In *Boliden Tara Mines Ltd v Irish Pensions Trust Ltd* [2014] IEHC 488, the plaintiff appealed a decision of the Master of the High Court refusing an application to extend time within which to deliver a statement of claim, and dismissing the proceedings. The parties agreed that the applicable law was that applicable to a motion to dismiss proceedings for want of prosecution. Baker J. held that there was inordinate and inexcusable delay, but that the balance of justice was favoured allowing proceedings to continue, and extended time for the delivery of a statement of claim. It is notable that a letter from the defendant's solicitors which had consented to a short extension of time for the filing of the statement of claim was held to be the "key determining factor" in the exercise of Baker J.'s discretion (having regard to *Comcast International Holdings Corporation Ltd v Minister for Public Enterprise* [2012] IESC 50).

APPLICATIONS TO VACATE A *LIS PENDENS* PURSUANT TO S.123 OF THE LAND AND CONVEYANCING LAW REFORM ACT 2009

A useful and detailed analysis of the principles governing an application to vacate a *lis pendens* is set out in the judgment of Cregan J. in *Tola Capital Management LLC v Linders* [2014] IEHC 324. The defendants sought an order vacating two *lites pendentes* which had been registered against them personally (stating their name, place of residence and description) pursuant to s.123 of the Land and Conveyancing Law Reform Act 2009 ("LCLRA 2009") on two grounds: first, that the *lites pendentes* were not proper *lites* within the meaning of s.121(2)(a) LCLRA 2009 and so should never have been registered; and secondly, that the court could vacate the *lites pendentes* under s.123(b)(ii), where an action was not being prosecuted bona fide. Having regard to the decision in *Quinn v Irish Bank Resolution Corporation Ltd (in special liquidation)*, unreported, High Court, Finlay Geoghegan J., 20 December 2013, Cregan J. held that, even taking the plaintiff's claim at its height, the plaintiff had no claim or interest in the land which was the subject matter of the proceedings. Cregan J. held that the *lites pendentes* ought not to have been registered and should be vacated on this basis. Cregan J. went on to hold that the plaintiff's action was not being prosecuted in a bona fide manner. Accordingly Cregan J. made an order vacating the *lites pendentes* pursuant to s.123(b)(ii) of the LCLRA 2009. Cregan J. observed that the court had an inherent jurisdiction to vacate a *lis pendens* where it was of the view that the *lis* was not properly registrable or that the action was not being prosecuted bona fide, and indicated that he would also have struck out the *lites pendentes* on this basis.

In *Tougher v Tougher's Oil Distributors Ltd* [2014] IEHC 255, the first named defendant sought an order vacating a *lis pendens* pursuant to s.123 of the LCLRA 2009, together with orders dismissing the plaintiff's claim pursuant to Ord.19 r.28 RSC and/or pursuant to the inherent jurisdiction of the court.

Cregan J. held that parts of the plaintiff's claim (for breach of contract) were statable and not bound to fail. However, other parts of the claim (to be legally or beneficially entitled to assets of the first defendant company, of which the plaintiff had been a director) were unstatable and bound to fail, inter alia, having regard to the fundamental principle of company law that shareholders have a right to a share in the company but do not have a direct right to have a share in any of the company's assets (applying the decision in *Quinn*). The *lis pendens* related to these latter parts of the plaintiff's claim. Accordingly, while Cregan J. declined to strike out the plaintiff's claim for breach of contract, he struck out the parts of the plaintiff's claim which related to a claim for a share in the company assets and vacated the *lis pendens*.

Linders was applied in *Togher Management Co Ltd v Coolnaleen Developments Ltd (in receivership)* [2014] IEHC 596, where the court declined to vacate a *lis pendens* pursuant to s.123 of the LCLRA 2009 and to dismiss the plaintiff's claim pursuant to Ord.19 r.28 RSC and/or pursuant to the inherent jurisdiction of the court.

CASE MANAGEMENT

The need for case management In *Talbot v Hermitage Golf Club* [2012] IEHC 372, Herbert J. dismissed the plaintiff's claim for damages for defamation and conspiracy relating to, inter alia, alleged defamation as to the integrity of the plaintiff's golf handicap. The plaintiff appealed, which appeal was dismissed by the Supreme Court (Denham C.J., Charlton J.) at [2014] IESC 57. Aspects of the proceedings were dealt with by the Superior Courts over 83 days, including a 20-day hearing in the High Court. Denham C.J. summarised the development of case management in England and Wales, and in this jurisdiction, and observed that "the Courts would benefit by a further development and use of case management so that the best use may be made of scarce court resources for the benefit of all litigants." See Mr Justice Charlton (writing extra-judicially) and Saoirse Molloy, "Case Management: Fairness for Litigants, Justice for the Parties" (2015) 3 B.R. 59.

Consolidation of proceedings pursuant to Order 49 rule 6 RSC In *James Elliot Construction Ltd v Irish Asphalt Ltd* [2014] IEHC 208, proceedings arose out of the use in construction of filling allegedly contaminated with pyrite (see Arthur Cunningham, "Commercial law Update" (2015) 22(1) C.L.P. 19). The plaintiff (a building contractor) claimed a number of reliefs, including an indemnity in respect of any claim which may be brought by the plaintiff's employer, Ballymun Generation Ltd. Ballymun Generation Ltd had commenced separate proceedings against the same defendants arising out of similar events, and the plaintiff sought an order consolidating the two sets of proceedings pursuant to Ord.49 r.6 RSC.

Having considered Ord.49 r.6 RSC, Ryan J. noted that the parties agreed that the questions to be determined on the application (as stated by the Supreme Court in *Duffy v News Group Newspapers Ltd* [1992] 2 I.R. 369) were the following:

(1) Is there a common question of law or fact of sufficient importance?
(2) Will there be a substantial saving of expense or inconvenience?
(3) Is there a likelihood of confusion or of a miscarriage of justice if the actions are joined or consolidated?

The application was resisted on a number of grounds. It was argued that there was no common issue of law or fact between the proceedings, where different claims (respectively for breach of contract and in negligence) and different reliefs were pleaded. It was argued that consolidation would not lead to a reduction of time or expense. Some defendants proposed that, rather than consolidation, it might be appropriate to have the proceedings heard together.

Ryan J. was satisfied that, applying the test in *Duffy*, the actions ought to be consolidated. He noted that, while the claims advanced were different, there was an "enormous" overlap in the questions of fact to be determined, that consolidation would lead to a substantial reduction in expense or inconvenience, and that there was no rational basis for thinking that consolidation would give rise to a likelihood of confusion or of a miscarriage of justice. Ryan J. also held that there was little merit or advantage in having the proceedings heard together rather than consolidated. Accordingly, Ryan J. granted the relief sought.

CONTEMPT OF COURT

Punishment and civil contempt In *Laois CC v Hanrahan* [2014] 2 I.L.R.M. 141; [2014] IESC 36, the appellant appealed against a High Court order (the "committal order") committing him to prison for contempt of court in failing to comply with a previous High Court order (the "original order") requiring him to remove large volumes of polluting waste from his parents' family farm. The committal order directed that the appellant be committed to prison for a period of six months unless he purged his contempt by complying with the original order.

The Supreme Court allowed the appeal and remitted the matter to the High Court, in circumstances where it held that the committal order unacceptably conflated civil and criminal contempt. Fennelly J. derived from the relevant authorities the following principles affecting the exercise of the jurisdiction to punish in cases of civil contempt:

i) It will normally be a matter for the court to decide of its own motion whether the case is one which justifies the imposition of punishment, which may be a fine or a term of imprisonment, although there may be cases involving matters of purely private interest where the court may be invited to exercise the jurisdiction.
ii) The circumstances justifying the imposition of punishment will almost always include an element relating to the public interest, including the vindication of the authority of the court. The object is punishment, not coercion.
iii) A court should impose committal by way of punishment as a last resort. The contempt must amount to serious misconduct involving flagrant and deliberate breach of a court order. Mere inability to comply will not amount to serious misconduct.

iv) Committal by way of punishment inherently relates to conduct which has already taken place, not to future conduct. A person cannot be punished for his future conduct: that would involve preventative detention.
v) Any imprisonment must be for a fixed term.

Fennelly J. went on to observe that even in cases of purely coercive orders, there is an element of punishment (since it is by committing the contemnor to prison that the court secures the observance of its orders), but that where a term of imprisonment is imposed by way of punishment, the above principles apply. See David P. Boyle, "ILT Digest of Legislation and Superior Court Decisions" (2015) 33 I.L.T. 153.

Breach of undertaking In *Egan v Byrne* [2014] IEHC 538, the defendant sought a number of reliefs (including attachment, committal and sequestration) arising out of alleged breaches of undertakings to the court. The alleged undertakings were recorded in terms of settlement which were handed into court, and parts of which were made orders of court. Donnelly J. was satisfied, as a matter of construction of the settlement agreement and the relevant orders, that no undertaking had been given, and dismissed the application.

COSTS

Costs in complex litigation The courts continued to apply the principles identified in *Veolia Water UK plc v Fingal County Council (No. 2)* [2006] IEHC 240, [2007] 2 I.R. 81 in exercising their discretion as to awards of costs in complex litigation. In *ADM Londis plc v Ranzett Ltd*, a dispute arose out of a franchise agreement. In respect of unpaid invoices, the plaintiff obtained summary judgment against the defendants at a one-day hearing ([2013] IEHC 63). The defendants counterclaimed that the plaintiff had unlawfully terminated the franchise agreement, and succeeded in this counterclaim following a 10-day plenary hearing (damages were assessed at [2014] IEHC 659). Hogan J. dealt with the issue of costs at [2014] IEHC 660. He awarded the plaintiff the costs of the summary judgment application and one half day's costs in respect of the main action. Regarding the counterclaim, Hogan J. awarded the defendants seven days' costs (reflecting the fact that they did not succeed on certain issues which added to the length of the hearing). Hogan J. further directed that the costs awards be set off as against each other.

Costs of proceedings which have become moot *McKillen v Irish Bank Resolution Corporation* [2014] IEHC 190 concerned the costs of the proceedings generally. A number of costs orders were made on consent. An application was made by the Special Liquidators of Irish Bank Resolution Corporation (IBRC) for their costs (relating to the entire proceedings or, in the alternative, to a discovery application at [2014] IEHC 137, discussed below) in circumstances where the proceedings as against them had become moot (the plaintiff having succeeded in acquiring his own loans from the Special Liquidators). Gilligan J. was of the view that all parties were "involved in the very fact that led to the proceedings becoming moot as between them" and, applying the Supreme Court decision in *Cunningham v*

President of the Circuit Court [2012] IESC 69, made no order as to costs. Regarding mootness generally, see M. McMahon, "How Moot is Moot?" (2014) 2 B.R. 44.

DEFAULT JUDGMENT

In *Danske Bank v Meagher* [2013] IEHC 496, Peart J. refused to set aside summary judgment (together with ancillary orders) which had been entered against the defendant in default of his attendance (following service in accordance with an order for substituted service) (see *Annual Review of Irish Law 2013*). The defendant appealed, which appeal was dealt with at [2014] IESC 38. In the Supreme Court, Laffoy J. noted as unfortunate that the court had not been furnished with a transcript (or even an agreed note) of the evidence before Peart J. Laffoy J. held that the substituted service order which was the subject of the appeal ought not be set aside, since: first, there is no requirement (express or implied) in the rules which confer jurisdiction on the Superior Courts to make an order for substituted service that the person sought to be served is within the jurisdiction; secondly, it was reasonable to infer at the time the order was made that the appellant would be put on notice of the proceedings by service pursuant to the order. Laffoy J. noted that the court had no basis on which to depart from Peart J.'s view that the appellant had notice of the proceedings at the material time, and that the summary judgment order was regularly obtained. In addition, the appellant had not even attempted to put on affidavit that he had a defence on the merits with a reasonable prospect of success (a requirement dating at least to *Farden v Richter* (1889) 23 Q.B.D. 124). Accordingly, Laffoy J. dismissed the appeal.

In *Ashbourne Beef and Lamb Ltd v Woods* [2014] IEHC 212, the appellant issued a civil bill in February 2011. No appearance was entered and in March 2011 the appellant entered judgment in default of appearance against the respondent in the Office of the Circuit Court. In April 2013, the respondent issued a motion seeking to set aside the default judgment. He claimed that the proceedings were not served on him and that he was unaware of same until February 2013 when he was served with an equity civil bill in which well charging relief was sought against him. He also denied owing the sums claimed by the plaintiff. An order setting aside the default judgment was made, which order the appellant sought to have set aside.

Kearns P. had regard to the Circuit Court Rules regulating service and default judgment (in particular Ords 14 and 26), and held that service had been effected in the proper manner and judgment validly obtained. He noted that the court had a discretion to set aside the judgment under *Maher v Dixon* [1995] I.L.R.M. 218 and *O'Callaghan v O'Donovan*, unreported, Supreme Court, 13 May 1997 which held that, where a "regular judgment" has been obtained in compliance with the rules, the court may then assess whether the respondent has a reasonable prospect of success (and not simply a statable defence) on the basis of the defence offered, and whether, in the justice of the matter, it would be unfair to allow judgment to be entered without an opportunity to defend the claim. Kearns P. noted that the respondent had not provided a draft defence and had merely made a "bald assertion" that the monies claimed were not due and owing. In those circumstances Kearns P. held that the court could not exercise its discretion to set aside the judgment. Accordingly, Kearns P. vacated the order of the Circuit Court and allowed judgment in default of appearance as against the respondent.

For an example of a default judgment entered in the Central Office of the High Court being set aside in circumstances where the defendant was taken by surprise, see *Stafford v JV Cummins (Supermarkets) Ltd* [2014] IEHC 10.

DELAY AND THE DISMISSAL OF PROCEEDINGS

General comments on judgments delivered in 2014 In dealing with applications based on delay in civil litigation, the courts in 2014 continued to apply the well-established principles (as recently affirmed by the Supreme Court in *Comcast International Holdings Inc v Minister for Public Enterprise* [2012] IESC 50) set out in *Rainsford v Limerick Corporation* [1995] 2 I.L.R.M. 561 and *Primor v Stokes Kennedy Crowley* [1996] 2 I.R. 459, in addition to the principles governing the courts' inherent jurisdiction to strike out for delay as explained in *O'Domhnaill v Merrick* [1984] I.R. 151; [1985] I.L.R.M. 40.

Cases in which proceedings were dismissed on grounds of delay and want of prosecution In *McCormack v Rouse* [2014] IEHC 396, an application was made to strike out proceedings 12 years after commencement, and 15 years after the events in dispute, during which period three witnesses had died. Gilligan J. extensively reviewed the authorities, including a particularly detailed analysis of the Supreme Court decision in *Comcast*. In the circumstances, Gilligan J. was satisfied that the delay was both inordinate and inexcusable, and that the balance of justice favoured dismissing the proceedings.

McClean v Sunday Newspapers Ltd [2014] IEHC 304 concerned defamation proceedings arising out of an article published in the Sunday World newspaper. The plenary summons issued in July 2000, after which proceedings continued at a normal pace until, following an affidavit of discovery by the editor of the Sunday World newspaper in November 2002, nothing occurred until the plaintiff issued a notice of intention to proceed in April 2010 and, in August 2013, the defendant's solicitors requested that the plaintiff serve a notice of discontinuance. When this was not done an application was made for an order pursuant to Ord.122 r.11 RSC staying or dismissing the proceedings for want of prosecution.

Barrett J. noted that regardless of whether the court invokes a jurisdiction to dismiss a claim for want of prosecution under the RSC or by reference to its inherent jurisdiction, it appears that the same principles apply to the court's deliberations. Barrett J. considered the well-established authorities on delay, noting the dictum of Keane C.J. in *Ewins v Independent Newspapers (Ireland) Ltd* [2003] 1 I.R. 583 at 590 that a plaintiff in defamation proceedings is under a particular onus to institute proceedings instantly and without delay.

Barrett J. held that the delay was inordinate. A number of excuses for the delay were proffered by the plaintiff, including that he had suffered from ill health. Barrett J. noted that the plaintiff's unfortunate ill health had not prevented him from taking steps in the proceedings and, during the same period, from commencing fresh defamation litigation against a different newspaper group. Having regard to *Desmond v MGN* [2009] 1 I.R. 737, Barrett J. concluded that "the plaintiff's tactical decision, never communicated to the defendant, to 'let sleeping dogs lie', for the longest of sleeps" led to the conclusion that the delay was also inexcusable. The balance of justice was held to favour striking out the proceedings, and Barrett J. accordingly acceded to the defendant's application.

In *Patton v Rudd* [2014] IEHC 277, the plaintiffs had obtained judgment in July 2002. Following a compromise agreement in June 2006, the judgment was marked as "Satisfied" in March 2008. The plaintiffs claimed that satisfaction was marked without their knowledge and that they only learned of same in January 2012 (when their solicitors sought to execute upon the judgment, and commenced proceedings to reinstate same). The defendants sought to strike out the proceedings on grounds of inordinate and inexcusable pre-commencement delay. Acceding to the application, Hedigan J. was satisfied that the delay was inordinate and inexcusable, and that the balance of justice favoured striking out the proceedings.

The plaintiff in *Kilcoyne v Minister for Defence* [2014] IESC 10 had enlisted in the defence forces in 1981 and served until 1985. His claim (an "army deafness" case) was commenced by plenary summons in 1998. Following the delivery of a statement of claim and a defence in 1998 and 1999, no further steps were taken until 2006 until the defendant (who had resided in Western Australia and appeared to have lost contact with his solicitors) returned to Ireland and instructed a new firm of solicitors. In 2008 the plaintiff's claim was dismissed by order of the High Court (Hedigan J.), pursuant to the inherent jurisdiction of the court, on the grounds of inordinate and inexcusable delay in the prosecution of the proceedings. The plaintiff appealed.

Laffoy J. (with whom Denham C.J. and Murray J. concurred) was satisfied that the delay of almost nine years prior to the order of Hedigan J. was inordinate and inexcusable. Regarding the balance of justice, Laffoy J. held that this favoured dismissing the proceedings, holding that blameworthiness for the delay was primarily attributable to the appellant personally. The appeal was dismissed.

In *Whelan v Lawn* [2014] IESC 75, the Supreme Court dismissed an appeal from an order of the High Court (Charleton J.) in December 2009 whereby the proceedings had been dismissed. In the proceedings it was alleged that the defendant (the plaintiff's grandfather) had committed a number of sexual assaults against the plaintiff between 1989 and 1992. Proceedings were issued in 2009 (by which time the plaintiff's grandmother, a principal witness, had died), and, subsequent to the order dismissing the proceedings, the defendant himself died in 2011, following which the proceedings were reconstituted against the personal representative.

Hardiman J. noted that the defendant's estate was of an amount which would likely be exhausted by the costs of the action. He observed that "the grossest imaginable prejudice is the death of the defendant himself in a case where the basic facts are disputed by one person's word against another's." Hardiman J. also analysed the prejudice consequent upon the death of the plaintiff's grandmother (citing his own judgment in *J.O'C v DPP* [2000] 3 I.R. 478). Having formed the view that the proceedings had "become afflicted with difficulties and prejudice to the defendant 'so…as to be beyond the reach of fair litigation'" (per Henchy J. in *Sheehan v Amond* [1982] I.R. 235 at 239) the Supreme Court dismissed the appeal.

Cases in which delay was held to be inordinate but not inexcusable In *Moffett v O'Hare and McGovern Ltd* [2014] IEHC 368, several defendants applied to strike out the proceedings for want of prosecution, pursuant to the inherent jurisdiction of the court. The proceedings arose out of a construction dispute and commenced in 2002, related arbitration proceedings having been commenced in 2001. Barrett J. was satisfied that the delay (nine years from the delivery of the defence and counterclaim until the plaintiff issued his notice of demand) was inordinate. However, he held that the delay was excusable in circumstances where the plaintiff had signalled its intention to await the outcome of related arbitration, a decision the defendants were aware of and to which they did not materially object. Barrett J. also held that the balance of justice favoured allowing the proceedings to proceed, and dismissed the application.

In *Cassidy v Martin Butterly and Co Ltd* [2014] IEHC 203, proceedings arising out of the plaintiff's employment with one or more of the defendants were commenced in 2000. The first defendant applied to dismiss the proceedings for want of prosecution pursuant to either the inherent jurisdiction of the court or Ord.122 r.2 RSC. Analysing a period of delay of seven years between the filing of a defence and the plaintiff's service of a notice of change of solicitor, Ryan J. held that the delay was inordinate, but not inexcusable in circumstances where the plaintiff had, as a lay litigant, awaited the outcome of an application to the Pensions Board which he had anticipated might affect the proceedings. Ryan J. further held that, had the delay been inordinate and inexcusable, the balance of justice would have favoured allowing the proceedings to continue, and that it was not appropriate in the circumstances to invoke some countervailing principle that would extinguish the equities that operated in the plaintiff's favour. Ryan J. was also satisfied that Ord.122 r.2 RSC did not apply, and that the first defendant had itself delayed in bringing its application. Ryan J. dismissed the application, subject to certain conditions. See David P. Boyle, "ILT Digest of Legislation and Superior Court Decisions" (2015) 33 I.L.T. 121.

In *Vernon v AIBP Ltd* [2014] IEHC 98, the plaintiff issued proceedings in 2001 arising out of an accident at a factory in 1999. After some early steps, nothing occurred in the proceedings between the service of a first (in May 2004) and a second (in November 2012) notice of intention to proceed, a delay which was conceded to be inordinate.

Barrett J. noted that during the period from 2004 to 2012 the plaintiff suffered from a variety of personal and family misfortunes, and had not been in contact with her solicitors. Having regard to the plaintiff's circumstances and authorities including *Guerin v Guerin* [1992] 2 I.R. 287 and *Comcast*, Barrett J. held the delay to be excusable.

The defendant claimed it was generally prejudiced by the effluxion of time, as well as specifically prejudiced by the closure of the factory (the locus of the accident). Barrett J. expressed the view that these difficulties were not such that a fair trial could not be had, and also had regard to the defendant's delay (between service of the first and second notices of intention to proceed). Accordingly, the defendant's application was dismissed.

MC v The Provincialate [2014] IEHC 101 concerned proceedings for physical and sexual abuse allegedly suffered by the plaintiff on the grounds of the Madgdalene Laundry in Donnybrook between 1977 and 1980. Proceedings were issued approximately 30 years later, which the Sisters of Charity sought to strike out on grounds of pre-commencement delay. Barrett J. held that the delay was inordinate but "far from inexcusable" given the nature of the plaintiff's claim and hardships intimately connected to same which she continued to suffer. Regarding the tests in *O'Domhnaill*, Barrett J. noted that, while there were a number of difficulties associated with the prosecution and defence of the proceedings (including the death of the alleged abuser, and of the majority of witnesses), these difficulties did not give rise to a real risk of an unfair trial. Barrett J. dismissed the defendant's application.

In *Shields v Interlink Ireland Ltd* [2014] IEHC 74, the plaintiff issued two plenary summonses in 1998 relating to an allegedly wrongful repudiation of a franchise agreement. In 2013 (following, *inter alia*, the service of several notices of intention to proceed and extensive correspondence relating to discovery) the defendant issued a motion seeking to dismiss the plaintiff's claim for inordinate and inexcusable delay or, in the alternative, seeking an order pursuant to s.390 of the Companies Act 1963 directing the second plaintiff to furnish security for the defendant's costs.

Ryan J. held that the delay was inordinate but not inexcusable (by reference to what was characterised as a "saga of discovery"). Ryan J. also held that the balance of justice favoured the continuation of the proceedings, having regard in particular to the defendant's delay in making the application, the defendant's responsibility for a significant part of the delay, and correspondence from the defendant's solicitors in April 2013 which, inter alia, stated that it would be premature to seek a trial date. The application for security for costs was also dismissed, having regard to the defendant's delay in making the application, and the fact that the second plaintiff's inability to meet an award of costs flowed from the alleged wrongdoing which was the subject of the proceedings.

Cases in which proceedings were allowed to continue notwithstanding inordinate and inexcusable delay In *Costello v Commissioner of An Garda Síochána* [2015] IEHC 681, the plaintiff issued a plenary summons in December 2005 alleging, inter alia, harassment and intimidation by servants and agents of the defendant, and obtained injunctive relief restraining the defendant from entering the plaintiff's property unless under authority of a warrant or at the request of a member of the household. A number of procedural steps occurred, including the delivery of a statement of claim and defence in 2006. In 2013 the defendant issued a motion seeking to dismiss the proceedings for delay. White J. held that the delay was inordinate and, at times, inexcusable. White J. declined to dismiss the proceedings in circumstances where the defendant had considerable resources at its disposal and had not established that it would suffer actual prejudice by reason of the plaintiff's delay in its defence of the claim. However, White J. held that the plaintiff's failure to progress the case expeditiously was an abuse of process, having regard to the injunctive relief obtained in December 2005, and accordingly vacated the injunction.

Permanent TSB Finance Ltd v Orcona Ltd [2014] IEHC 541 concerned an application by the fourth defendant to dismiss summary proceedings in the inherent jurisdiction of the court, on grounds of inordinate and inexcusable delay. It was conceded that the delay (a period of four years during which no step was taken, notwithstanding the filing of a notice of change of solicitor and several notices of intention to proceed) was inordinate.

Three years of the delay related to a period during which the plaintiff sought to obtain (and in fact obtained) judgment in default of appearance against other defendants, while addressing concerns in the Central Office that the papers were not in order. The plaintiff submitted that it was reasonable to await the outcome of this exercise before proceeding with the balance of its claim.

Keane J. rejected the proffered excuse, holding that it was the responsibility of the moving party to rectify or explain any perceived deficiency in its papers. Moreover, having regard to Ord.13 r.8 RSC, Keane J. held that the plaintiff was entitled at all material times to proceed against the fourth defendant, and that it should have done so, at least once it became apparent that there would be some delay in entering judgment against other defendants. Accordingly, this period of delay was held to be inordinate and inexcusable.

The remainder of the delay was sought to be excused by the fact that, on being threatened with a motion for liberty to enter final judgment, the defendant's solicitor actively sought forbearance by indicating an intention to substantively reply to the plaintiff's correspondence (without so replying) and requesting that the plaintiff hold off from issuing a motion. Keane J. held that this period of delay was not inexcusable.

Regarding the balance of justice, Keane J. held that the fourth defendant had failed to establish specific prejudice (notwithstanding health and financial difficulties) or general prejudice, and had acquiesced in the delay. Keane J. held that the balance of justice favoured allowing the proceedings to continue, and dismissed the application.

In *Nolan v Chadwicks* [2014] IEHC 542, an application was made to dismiss proceedings (relating to the supply of allegedly defective bricks) for delay where six years had elapsed since the plenary summons had issued, with no further steps having been taken by the plaintiff. It was agreed that the delay was inordinate.

The plaintiff sought to excuse the delay in preparing a statement of claim by reference to difficulties and delays in obtaining expert reports, which excuse was rejected by Keane J. for the same four reasons identified by Clarke J. in *Stephens v Paul Flynn Ltd* [2005] IEHC 148. First, the plaintiff was under an obligation to move with particular expedition after a lengthy delay in the commencement of the proceedings. Secondly, no explanation had been proffered for why the relevant expert report could not have been obtained sooner. Thirdly, (having regard to the judgment of Hardiman J. in *Gilroy v Flynn* [2004] IESC 98) delay attributable to a professional adviser may be less excusable than might once have been the case, having regard to jurisprudence of the European Court of Human Rights concerning art.6(1) of the European Convention on Human Rights and the recognition of those requirements under the European Convention on Human Rights Act 2003. Fourthly, there is a need to exercise a significant degree of additional scrutiny in assessing excuses put forward to explain or justify delay in civil proceedings. A further excuse relating to the transfer of certain lands was also rejected, and Keane J. held that the delay was inexcusable.

Considering the balance of justice, Keane J. held that no specific prejudice had been made out. Regarding general prejudice, he was satisfied that the proceedings were more an "expert evidence case" and less a "recollection case" (per Laffoy J. in *Manning v National House Building Guarantee Co Ltd* [2011] IEHC 98), in that they would likely be determined by reference to expert evidence as to the quality of the bricks. Reports on the bricks had been prepared and the bricks were available for inspection. In the circumstances, Keane J. held that the balance of justice favoured allowing the proceedings to continue, and dismissed the application.

DISCOVERY AND DISCLOSURE

Relevance and necessity *Ryanair v Somner* [2014] IEHC 634 concerned defamation proceedings in respect of a two-part television programme (also broadcast on the internet) entitled "Mayday Mayday", in the course of which it was alleged that the defendant had made defamatory statements concerning the plaintiff. As part of his defence, the defendant pleaded honest opinion, truth, fair and honest publication on a matter of public interest, and qualified privilege.

The defendant sought discovery of two categories of documents relating to the plaintiff's fuel and pilot hire policies, each of which were alleged to relate to passenger safety and so were relevant to the plea of truth in the defendant's defence. Being satisfied that the discovery sought was relevant and necessary for the full and proper determination of the issues arising from the pleadings, Peart J. ordered discovery of the categories sought (with some modifications).

In *Norris v RTE* [2014] IEHC 84, the plaintiff issued defamation proceedings arising from two "Liveline" interviews broadcast by the first defendant in 2011 concerning inter alia the plaintiff's alleged views regarding paedophilia. The second defendant's defence pleaded, inter alia, truth and honest opinion. The second defendant sought discovery of documents relating to support of, or representations made by, the plaintiff regarding two persons (his former partner, and a poet who had been the subject of a television documentary detailing his relationship with Nepalese teenage boys). Kearns P. dismissed the application, holding that the documents sought were not relevant and necessary to the particulars of material fact in the second defendant's defence, and noting that a number of documents in both categories were in the public domain.

Discovery prior to the closure of pleadings In *Craddock v RTE; Kavanagh v RTE* each plaintiff had issued defamation proceedings arising out of the broadcast, by the defendant, of a programme entitled "A Breach of Trust" which concerned the standards of care in, and regulation of, crèches. The plaintiffs claimed they could not prepare a statement of claim without discovery of recordings shown prior to broadcast to parents of children in the care of a particular crèche. The High Court (Cross J.) ordered discovery in each case of: (a) a recording (and transcript) of the programme shown to the parents of the children cared for at the relevant crèche, and (b) a recording (and transcript) of the programme actually broadcast, discovery to be made in advance of delivery of the statement of claim. The defendant appealed (having agreed to make discovery of category (b)) and both appeals were dealt with by the Supreme Court at [2014] IESC 32.

It was agreed (and apparent from the authorities) that, absent exceptional circumstances, discovery will not be ordered until pleadings have closed. Dismissing the appeals, Fennelly J. (with whom McKechnie and Laffoy JJ. concurred) held that, in circumstances where the plaintiffs had put forward uncontradicted evidence that they had no means (absent discovery) of ascertaining the contents of the relevant recording, and a statement of claim could not be prepared without sight of the relevant recording, such exceptional circumstances had been established.

Discovery where discovery previously ordered in related English proceedings *In re Astrazeneca AB & Patent Acts* [2014] IEHC 189 concerned proceedings relating to the alleged invalidity of an Irish patent granted in respect of an asthma treatment drug. The petitioner sought discovery pursuant to Ord.31 r.12 RSC (as amended). An unusual feature of the application was that "almost equivalent" proceedings had been commenced in England. Barrett J. noted that, while there were substantial similarities between the jurisprudence by reference to which the English and Irish proceedings would ultimately be determined, there was at least one significant difference in procedure, namely the rules governing discovery in each jurisdiction. Barrett J. observed that although the respective discovery rules are directed towards a common end, namely to advance the interests of a fair and proper determination of a hearing between the parties, the Irish rules appear more liberal in terms of what may be discovered. The respondent suggested that, to save time and cost, and to avoid conflicts of evidence between the two sets of proceedings, it would be practical and sensible to confine the discovery process to what had been obtained in England (having suggested in solicitor's correspondence that Ireland should not be used "as some sort of haven for discovery"). Barrett J. rejected this argument and determined the application for discovery in accordance with principles established by Irish jurisprudence.

McKillen v Irish Bank Resolution Corporation [2014] IEHC 137 concerned motions for discovery issued by the plaintiff and several of the defendants. Substantial discovery had previously been ordered in related English proceedings, which were said to concern a battle for control of three of London's leading hotels (Claridge's, the Connaught and the Berkeley). Having reviewed the relevant provisions of the RSC, the Civil Procedure Rules ("CPR") and a number of Irish and English authorities, White J. accepted that the requirements of Ord.31 r.12 RSC are materially different from the CPR. Having regard to the nature of the Irish proceedings (and, in particular, their similarities and differences relative to the English proceedings) White J. directed that certain categories of discovery sought be furnished. It is notable that regard was had to the discovery already made in the English proceedings, which was held to be adequate in relation to a number of categories.

Summary judgment and discovery In *Lombard Ireland Ltd v Kevin Devlin Transport* [2014] IEHC 653 the plaintiff appealed an order of the Master of the High Court striking out its summary summons, and sought an order substituting Vanguard Auto Finance Ltd as plaintiff in the proceedings (or adding same as co-plaintiff). Donnelly J. made the orders sought and adjourned the plaintiff's motion for liberty to enter final judgment to permit the defendant to bring an application for discovery.

Striking out pleadings for failure to comply with an order for discovery In *Quinn v Irish Bank Resolution Corporation* [2014] IEHC 577, the plaintiffs sought an order striking out the first defendant's defence (or, in the alternative, an order for further and better discovery) for an alleged failure to comply with an order for discovery. The discovery orders were made in the course of proceedings which Costello J. characterised as "exceptional in relation to their complexity, the range of issues, both factual and legal, to be determined, the value of the claims and the expected duration of the trial." It was averred on behalf of the first defendant that, in preparing its affidavit of discovery, it had trawled approximately 10,034,000 electronic documents (of which 178,000 were responsive to key word searches and were reviewed), 80 hard copy files and 5,236 audio recordings, over a period of five months and at an approximate cost of €1.55 million. The first defendant accepted that errors had been made in relation to its initial affidavit of discovery, which errors had required to be corrected in subsequent affidavits.

Costello J. observed that discovery is based largely on trust and that the court would not and could not micromanage a discovery exercise. He reviewed the authorities relating to striking out a defence for failure to comply with an order of discovery, noting that the jurisdiction does not exist to punish a defaulter but to facilitate the administration of justice by ensuring compliance with orders of the court, and that an applicant must meet a "very high threshold" before such an order would be made. He viewed as highly relevant that the first defendant had sought and obtained non-party discovery and furnished same to the plaintiffs.

In relation to the discovery of audio recordings (of which 278 had already been discovered), having heard argument on the searchability of such recordings and the likelihood of such recordings being relevant, Costello J. held that to require the first defendant to make the discovery sought would be, both in time and money, "grossly disproportionate to the expected return". He held that neither party had been aware of, or addressed, the potential scope or costs of full audio discovery at the hearing of the initial motion for discovery. He noted that Ord.31 r.12(11) RSC allows for a party to apply to vary an order for discovery where same is unreasonable (having regard to the cost or other burden of providing discovery), and held that the first defendant had made a conscientious attempt to comply with the order for discovery. The first defendant indicated that it would swear a supplemental affidavit dealing with bank statements and documents no longer in its possession.

The plaintiffs also sought an order for inspection, which application was held by Costello J. to be premature and therefore not necessary (having regard to Ord.31 r.18(2) RSC).

In *Green Pastures (Donegal) v Aurivo Co-Operative Society Ltd* [2014] IEHC 209, the plaintiff applied to strike out the first defendant's defence for failure to comply with an order directing further and better discovery. Ryan J. dismissed the application in circumstances where, he held, the first defendant had adequately complied with the order and the plaintiff's notion of what was comprised in the discovery obligation was misconceived.

In *Go2CapeVerde Ltd v Paradise Beach SA* [2014] IEHC 531, the plaintiffs issued proceedings claiming payment of outstanding commissions and damages. The defendant filed a defence and counterclaim arising out of alleged breach of duty on the part of the plaintiffs in the sale of a number of residential units in a development project at Cape Verde. The defendant sought voluntary discovery, and affidavits of discovery were sworn by the plaintiffs and the defendant to the counterclaim. The defendant then issued a motion to dismiss the claim and the defence to the counterclaim, on the grounds of alleged failure to comply with an agreement to make voluntary discovery.

Baker J. held that a three-part test ought to be applied in determining applications pursuant to Ord.31 r.21 RSC to strike out for failure to make discovery. First, the court must determine whether there has been a failure to make discovery. Secondly, the court must consider the reasons for the failure. Thirdly, and even in circumstances where the failure has been deliberate and malicious, the proceedings should only be struck out if the court is satisfied that justice cannot be done between the parties (noting that there must be a substantial risk of injustice which cannot be remedied by the making of an order for further and better discovery and/or costs). Applying the said test and striking out the defence to the counterclaim, Baker J. was satisfied that the failure by the plaintiffs and a defendant to the counterclaim to make discovery was deliberate and malicious, and on the extreme end of the spectrum of culpability.

ENFORCEMENT OF JUDGMENTS

Discovery in aid of execution In *McCann v Trustees of the Victory Christian Fellowship* [2014] IEHC 655, having obtained judgment, the plaintiffs issued two motions seeking disclosure of documentation relating to the defendants' assets and sources of third-party funding. Donnelly J. confirmed, having regard to the decision in *Moorview Developments v First Active plc* [2011] IEHC 117, [2011] 3 I.R. 615, that the court has jurisdiction to direct the discovery of documents prior to examination in aid of execution and made a number of the orders sought.

Appointment of a receiver by way of equitable execution In *Flanagan v Crosby* [2014] IEHC 59, a judgment creditor obtained in the Circuit Court a conditional order, which was subsequently made absolute, appointing a receiver by way of equitable execution over any monies due (both then and in the future) to a judgment debtor (who was a councillor) from Roscommon County Council by way of emoluments. The plaintiff appealed.

Hogan J. expressed the view that if "the matter were to be viewed afresh from the standpoint of first principles, then tradition apart, there seems no reason in principle why an order for the appointment of a receiver by way of equitable execution could not be made in respect of legal as well as equitable interests". However, following *Kadri v Governor of Cloverhill Prison* [2012] IESC 27 and *AG v Residential Institutions Redress Board* [2012] IEHC 492, Hogan J. viewed himself as bound to follow the majority views as expressed by members of the High Court in *National Irish Bank v Graham* [1994] 1 I.R. 215 and *Honniball v Cunningham* [2010] 2 I.R. 1, and, as the judgment debtor had a statutory right to (rather than merely an equitable interest in) the relevant payments, allowed the appeal.

See also *Start Mortgages v Doheny* [2014] IEHC 656 where, having regard to the decision in *Graham*, Donnelly J. declined to make absolute an order appointing a receiver by way of equitable execution over potential proceeds of personal injury litigation.

ORDERS FOR POSSESSION AND THE CODE OF CONDUCT ON MORTGAGE ARREARS 2010 ("CCMA")

In *McGuinness v Allied Irish Banks plc* [2014] IEHC 191, the plaintiff borrower commenced plenary proceedings in which he sought a number of declaratory reliefs arising out of the defendant bank's alleged failure to comply with the CCMA, in particular in relation to the provisions regarding appeals. The plaintiff subsequently sought an interlocutory injunction restraining the defendant from taking enforcement action. Applying the well-established test set out by the Supreme Court in *Campus Oil v Minister for Industry and Energy (No. 2)* [1983] I.R. 88, Gilligan J. refused the plaintiff's application for an interlocutory injunction in circumstances where he held that the plaintiff had not established a fair issue to be tried, that damages would be an appropriate remedy and that the balance of convenience favoured the dismissal of the application.

It is notable that, in *McGuinness*, Gilligan J. accepted that, having regard to the decisions in *Stepstone Mortgage Funding v Fitzell* [2012] IEHC 142 and *Irish Life and Permanent plc v Duff* [2013] IEHC 43, there was an issue as to the legal status of the CCMA which had yet to be authoritatively determined, but held that it was not necessary to determine this issue on the application before him. This issue was further considered by O'Malley J. in *ICS Building Society v Lambert* [2014] IEHC 581. The appellant defendant, who was a solicitor, appealed an order for possession made in the Dublin Circuit Court. Finance had been obtained on the basis that the funds would be used to purchase (and be secured upon) a residential investment. However, the property which was the subject of the proceedings subsequently became the plaintiff's principal private residence.

O'Malley J. noted that "[i]t is apparent that the precise legal status and effect of the Code has yet to be determined", and stated that her analysis on the issue was "tentative." O'Malley J. expressed the view that the CCMA:

> "can be seen as creating an area of discretion, not, ultimately, to defeat a lawful claim by a lender but, perhaps, to adjourn the matter for the purpose of providing to the borrower an opportunity that should have been provided under the Code."

O'Malley J. took the purpose and ambit of the Code as the starting point in a consideration of the exercise of such a discretion, and expressed the following view:

> "It applies only to borrowers whose mortgage is secured on their primary residence. It is thus a protection extended to a borrower's dwelling, not to commercial investments. It imposes obligations on lenders dealing with such borrowers and lays down the process that must be followed before the residence can be repossessed. The objective is, in my view, to bring about a situation whereby borrowers do not lose their homes if a reasonably practicable solution to their indebtedness can be found."

O'Malley J. held that, as the proceedings had issued before the appellant moved into the relevant property, the only provisions of the Code with which the bank had to comply were those as to contact (Provision 50), and the bank had in fact complied with the relevant provisions. O'Malley J. also had regard to the appellant's failure to give the bank adequate information as to his finances. In the circumstances, O'Malley J. dismissed the appeal.

Regarding the consequences of failure to comply with codes of conduct promulgated by the Central Bank, see *Ryan v Danske Bank* [2014] IEHC 236 (analysed by Mary Donnelly, "Banking and Security Law Update" (2014) 21(7) C.L.P. 168, 169) and *Freemen v Bank of Scotland* [2014] IEHC 284.

PARTIES

Applications to substitute a plaintiff In *Irish Bank Resolution Corporation v McCaughey* [2014] IEHC 517, an application was brought pursuant to Ord.17 r.4 RSC to substitute Deutsche Bank AG as plaintiff in proceedings commenced by IBRC (which had assigned the debts and other obligations which were the subject of the proceedings to Deutsche Bank AG). The defendant objected to the order sought, inter alia, on the basis that heavily redacted documents were exhibited to the affidavit grounding the application. Having regard to the ex tempore decision of Kelly J. in *Irish Bank Resolution Corporation v Comer* [2014] IEHC 671 (in which similar arguments were made, with the same result), Costello J. noted that the court's function on the application was not to determine the validity of the assignment, but that the court had to be satisfied on a prima facie basis of the grounds for making the order sought. Being so satisfied, Costello J. made the order sought. A similar order was made in *Irish Bank Resolution Corporation v Morrissey* [2014] IEHC 527.

Applications to join a co-defendant *Persona Digital Telephony Ltd v Minister for Public Enterprise* [2014] IEHC 78 concerned an application under Ord.15 r.13 RSC by a prominent businessman (a third party to the proceedings) to be joined as a co-defendant. The plaintiff argued that an order joining a defendant against the wishes of a plaintiff will only be made in exceptional circumstances. Ryan J. noted that, pursuant to Ord.15 r.13, the court may join a party as plaintiff or defendant in two situations, first where the party ought to have been joined, and secondly where the party's presence before the court is necessary to enable the court to decide all the questions in the case effectually and completely. Ryan J. made the order sought, where he held that both tests in Ord.15 r.13 had been met, in particular where the proceedings involved a claim of conspiracy relating to the proposed co-defendant.

Applications to substitute a party pending an appeal In *Irish Bank Resolution Corporation v Halpin*, proceedings had commenced by summary summons, and summary judgment had been entered in the plaintiff's favour in the sum of €20 million. The balance of the plaintiff's claim had been adjourned to plenary hearing, which resulted in a further judgment being entered in the plaintiff's favour ([2013] IEHC 492). The defendant appealed both judgments, which appeals were transferred to the Court of Appeal ([2014] IECA 3).

The applicant, Kenmare Property Finance Ltd ("Kenmare"), sought an order substituting it for IBRC as plaintiff/respondent (or, in the alternative, adding it as a party to the appeal), in circumstances where it claimed that IBRC's interest in the facilities the subject of the proceedings had been transferred and assigned to Kenmare. It was accepted that Kenmare had no interest in the facilities at the time the judgments under appeal had been entered.

Finlay Geoghegan J. noted that the Court of Appeal has jurisdiction (pursuant to Ord.86 r.2(1)(a) RSC) to make orders which the High Court may make pursuant, inter alia, to Ord.15 r.4 and Ord.17 r.5 RSC, but that it must do so in a manner consistent with its appellate function. Finlay Geoghegan J. noted that, at the time of entering judgment, Kenmare had no interest in the facilities in issue, and where it was sought to uphold judgments which had been obtained by IBRC through placing factual material before the court, such judgments could not be upheld were IBRC released from the proceedings. However, Kenmare had a material interest in the outcome of the two appeals. In the circumstances, the court declined to substitute Kenmare as plaintiff/respondent, but ordered that Kenmare be added as a second plaintiff in the proceedings and as a respondent to the appeal (with a restriction that it may only advance any argument on the appeal capable of being advanced by IBRC).

McKenzie friends and legal representation In *Tougher v Tougher's Oil Distributors Ltd* [2014] IEHC 254, the plaintiff applied for permission for a former solicitor to represent him in an application to strike out proceedings and vacate a *lis pendens* (this latter application, [2014] IEHC 255, is discussed above), not as a "McKenzie friend" but with full rights of representation and unrestricted rights of audience.

Cregan J. noted that the applicable principles are those set out in the Supreme Court decision of *In re Coffey* [2013] IESC 11. Cregan J. noted that, unlike in *Coffey*, the plaintiff's proposed representative was a former solicitor, but observed that "he is not a solicitor who is currently in practice and, therefore, is not a solicitor who is subject to, and bound by, the extensive and detailed codes of professional conduct of the Law Society." Being bound by and applying the decision in *Coffey*, Cregan J. dismissed the plaintiff's application. See generally David Kavanagh, "McKenzie Friends and the Right of Audience Before a Court" (2014) 3 B.R. 50.

Regarding representation of a company by a director, see *McDonald v McCaughey Developments Ltd* [2014] IEHC 455, analysed by Noel McGrath, "Company Law Update" (2015) 22(6) C.L.P. 161.

PLEADINGS AND PARTICULARS

Amendment of pleadings—substitution of entire Statement of Claim In *Rossmore Properties Ltd v Electricity Supply Board* [2014] IEHC 159, proceedings were issued arising out of the alleged restriction by the defendant of development of a corridor of lands in respect of which planning permission had been obtained. After pleadings had closed, the plaintiff sought leave to amend its statement of claim by deleting the original version in its entirety and substituting a completely new wording. Birmingham J. noted that the original statement of claim contained pleas relating to issues not in dispute between the parties, and contained a plea which could be characterised as "at least a nod in the direction of the doctrine of estoppel/legitimate expectation." Legitimate expectation and promissory estoppel were expressly pleaded in several paragraphs of the proposed amended statement of claim. Counsel for the plaintiff derived the following principles from the authorities, which was viewed as helpful and adopted by Birmingham J.:

1. The parties enjoy complete freedom of pleading. This is a reference to the fact that in the ordinary course of events a plaintiff is at large as to how he or she pleads his or her case. Absent pleas that are scandalous or vexatious or the like, the plaintiff cannot be dictated to as to how to formulate and present his or her claim.

2. Order 28 of the Rules of the Superior Courts, which is the rule that deals with amendments, is intended to be applied liberally.
3. Amendments shall be made for the purposes of determining the real questions in controversy between the parties.
4. Amendments should not be permitted when doing so could cause real or actual prejudice to other parties.
5. Amendments should be allowed if all that is present is litigation prejudice which is capable of being dealt with by orders for costs or other directions by way of case management.
6. There is no rule that per se precludes radical amendments.
7. There is no rule against introduction of a new cause of action if it falls within the ambit of the original grievance.

The defendant submitted that it would suffer two kinds of prejudice were the amendments permitted: (i) prejudice through the introduction of statute-barred claims; (ii) logistical prejudice as a result of the lateness and scale of the application (in particular that its ability to make an effective lodgement had been compromised). Birmingham J. noted that it was not clear that certain claims were statute-barred and, in those circumstances, the appropriate course of action was to permit the amendment, while making it clear that the defendant was entitled to rely on the Statute of Limitations and was not in any way to be disadvantaged in that regard by the amendment. Birmingham J. accordingly allowed the amendment, on the condition that the plaintiff discharge any and all of the defendant's costs associated with the amendment, with leave to serve a Calderbank letter within a specified period.

Amendment of pleadings—amplification of claim In *Ulster Bank Ireland Ltd v Sheehan* [2014] IEHC 612, proceedings were commenced by special summons claiming an order directing the defendants to comply with two undertakings, and a further or alternative claim for compensation for failure to so comply. The action was adjourned to plenary hearing with ancillary procedural directions, in compliance with which the plaintiff delivered points of claim. The points of claim amplified the plaintiff's claim relative to that advanced in the special summons and, in particular, claimed damages in the sum of over €1 million (a more than tenfold increase over damages claimed in the special summons). The defendant sought to strike out the points of claim. Hunt J. dismissed the application, holding that the plaintiff was not estopped from advancing the pleas therein and was entitled to put forward all reasonable formulations of its claim in order to ensure that the court will ultimately be in a position to determine the real issues in controversy between the parties.

Regarding amendment of a special summons claiming well charging relief, see *O'Neill v Appelbe* [2014] IESC 31.

Particulars of pleading in defamation proceedings In *Ryanair v Somner* [2014] IEHC 634 (the facts of which are set out above), the plaintiff raised particulars, and further and better particulars, and issued a motion seeking to compel replies to the latter under Ord.19 r.7 RSC. This application was refused in circumstances where Peart J. was satisfied from the pleadings and the replies furnished that the plaintiff knew "not just broadly, but with some particularity" the issues being raised by the defendant in his defence.

Particulars of pleading where fraud is alleged In *James Elliott Construction Ltd v Lagan* [2014] IEHC 547, the plaintiff claimed an indemnity and damages for deceit arising out of the supply of allegedly defective quarried material by the fourth defendant. It was alleged that the fourth defendant had fraudulently represented the quality of its product to the plaintiff while knowing that the stone supplied was defective. Each of the defendants alleged that the claim of fraud and deceit was inadequately particularised. Costello J. had regard to Ord.19 r.5(2) RSC and a number of authorities, deriving the following principles therefrom:

(1) A party is required to be told, as part of the pleading process, not the facts as they may objectively be, but the facts as his opponent alleges them to be.
(2) The particulars of fraud must include the nature and extent of each alleged misrepresentation. They must show by whom and to whom the alleged representations were made and whether orally or in writing and, if in writing, identify the relevant documents.
(3) A party alleging fraud must give the defendant a reasonable picture as to the fraud contended for and so that he knows the case he has to meet.
(4) A party may not by mere invocation of an allegation of fraud become entitled to a widespread discovery.
(5) While particulars may not be ordered prior to the delivery of a defence, a case cannot be allowed to go to trial without detailed particulars and these may be pursued after the provision of discovery if required.

Costello J. had regard to the fact that the plaintiff was in possession of a great deal of information (including information obtained by discovery in related proceedings), and had written an open letter to the defendants (offering to provide additional information on certain terms). In the circumstances, Costello J. directed the provision of a number of the particulars sought.

In *In re Vectone Ireland Ltd (in Liquidation)* [2014] IEHC 185, the applicant had commenced proceedings against a large number of parties alleging, inter alia, fraudulent dispositions of property within a group of companies, reckless trading to which certain directors were knowingly party, and misfeasance and/or breach of duty. The applicant sought a variety of reliefs under the Companies Acts including orders under s.297A of the Companies Act 1963 and s.204 of the Companies Act 1990. After the applicant filed its notice of motion and points of claim, certain respondents delivered a notice for particulars, to which replies were delivered. Further and better particulars were raised and a number of respondents issued a motion seeking an order pursuant to Ord.19 r.7 RSC directing the provision of further and better particulars.

Barrett J. reviewed in details the rules of court and authorities relating to particulars of pleading in fraud cases, including *In the Goods of John Rutledge, Deceased* [1981] I.L.R.M. 198 and *McGee v O'Reilly* [1996] 2 I.R. 229. He derived from the judgment of Clarke J. in the leading decision of *National Educational*

Welfare Board v Ryan [2008] 2 I.R. 816 the following key questions that can be usefully applied where a plaintiff alleges fraud or other wrongdoing:

(1) Is this a case where more than a bare allegation of fraud has been made?
(2) Has the plaintiff gone into some detail as to how the alleged fraud took place?
(3) Has the plaintiff specified in sufficient, albeit general, terms the nature of the alleged fraud?
(4) Has the plaintiff identified the alleged consequences of the fraud?
(5) Is there adequate evidence to support a prima facie or stateable case of fraud?

Barrett J. went on to observe that:

> "If the answer to each of these questions is 'yes', then the judgment in *National Educational Welfare Board* suggests that a defending party should be required to put in a defence, submit to whatever discovery and interrogatories may be appropriate on the facts of the case and then pursue more detailed particulars prior to trial, subject to the caveat that in all instances a defending party must always receive sufficient, but only sufficient, detail to be able to plead its defence."

Barrett J. also observed that the decision in *Ryan* must be viewed in the context of the earlier decisions in *Rutledge* and *McGee*.

Barrett J. concluded that the answer to each of the five questions above was "yes". Having regard to the "potentially ruinous" consequences of the applicant's claim, he went on to consider whether the interests of justice and fairness required that further and better particulars would nevertheless be ordered. Holding that they did not so require, Barrett J. declined to grant the relief sought.

Regarding particulars where conspiracy is alleged, see *O'Flynn v Carbon Finance Ltd* [2014] IEHC 439; [2015] IECA 93.

RENEWAL OF SUMMONSES

In 2014 the courts continued to apply the principles set out in *Chambers v Kenefick* [2007] 3 I.R. 526 to applications to renew or set aside renewal of a summons under Ord.8 r.2 RSC. In *O'Mahoney v Buckley* [2014] IEHC 683, White J. set aside an order renewing a plenary summons in circumstances where no reason had been advanced by the plaintiff for any difficulty in serving the summons in time, and where it was held that the plaintiff had sought to mislead the court on affidavit. The court noted that "[i]t is entirely inappropriate to hold a High Court plenary summons in reserve and then to use it when the plaintiff deems it necessary to do so", holding that this had been the tactic employed by the plaintiff. See also *Byrne v Martin* [2014] IEHC 7, where the plaintiff's explanation for an eight-year delay in serving a plenary summons (namely that he presumed his claim was proceeding towards settlement or trial and had no reason to believe otherwise) was held not to be a good reason to renew the summons, and Peart J. refused to renew same.

In *Managan v Dockery* [2014] IEHC 477, over five years had elapsed between the issue of a personal injury summons and an application to renew the summons. The plaintiff's claim was for serious personal injuries consequent upon hypoxic injury sustained during his birth, by reason of the alleged negligence of the defendant (a consultant obstetrician and gynaecologist). The delay was primarily referable to attempts by the plaintiff's solicitor, on the advice of junior and senior counsel, to obtain a report from a consultant paediatric neurologist. It was accepted that proceedings ought not to be served without obtaining such a report which, Costello J. held, was a distinguishing factor relative to *Bingham v Crowley* [2008] IEHC 453. Costello J. held that there was a good reason (or a potentially good reason) to renew the summons. Considering the balance of justice, Costello J. noted that the plaintiff was a person of unsound mind (not so found) and accordingly, his cause of action was not and could not be statute-barred. He held that the hardship which the defendant would suffer from the proceedings continuing was less than that which the plaintiff would suffer were the proceedings struck out, and accordingly he dismissed the defendant's application to set aside the renewal of the personal injury summons.

SECURITY FOR COSTS

Security for costs —delay In *Interfund Global Services Ltd v Pascarn Services Ltd* [2014] IEHC 164, the defendant (an Irish company) sought security for costs against the plaintiff (a company incorporated under the laws of Nigeria). As the plaintiff was not an Irish registered company, the application was moved under Ord.29 RSC and the defendant submitted that the applicable principles were those relating to applications under s.390 of the Companies Act 1963.

Barr J. held that, in view of the plaintiff's uncontradicted evidence as to its financial position, the defendant had not established that the plaintiff would be unable to pay the defendant's costs if successful at the hearing of the action. Barr J. also observed that it has long been held that delay in seeking security for costs will disentitle a party to the relief sought. Having regard to an almost three-year period between the commencement of the proceedings and the motion seeking security for costs (during which time the plaintiff had issued several motions seeking particulars), Barr J. held that there had been significant delay in bringing the application seeking security for costs and refused the application (under both s.390 and Ord.29) on this ground.

Special circumstances—point of exceptional public importance In *McAdam v ABP Food Group* [2014] IEHC 536, the plaintiffs issued defamation proceedings relating to a press release issued by the defendants. The second plaintiff and the defendant were companies in the beef industry and the relevant press release contained statements regarding the supply of meat contaminated with equine DNA. The defendant applied for security for costs against the second plaintiff pursuant to s.390 of the Companies Act 1963. Kearns P. held that the defendant had a prima facie defence and the second plaintiff was unable to pay the defendant's costs.

The second plaintiff relied on a number of special circumstances as to why the court ought not direct that security for costs be furnished, including that the second plaintiff's inability to pay had been caused by the defendant's actions, and the existence of a natural co-plaintiff. Neither argument was successful. The second plaintiff also argued that the proceedings, which related to an aspect of a pan-European scandal concerning equine DNA in meat products, raised a matter of public importance and that it was seeking to vindicate the public interest. Kearns P. held that the plaintiff's claim was a civil action in defamation which did not of itself raise any issues of wider public importance. He observed that the proceedings involved a company trying to vindicate its own commercial reputation for its own discrete reasons, comparable to a dispute between media celebrities in which the public might be generally interested but which is not otherwise a matter in which the public is impacted. Kearns P. held that the plaintiff's claims did not in any sense raise an issue of "such gravity and importance that it transcends the interests and considerations of the parties actually before the court" (per Morris P. in *Lancefort v An Bord Pleanála* [1998] 2 I.R. 511 at 516) and directed that security for costs be furnished.

STAYS

Stay on execution pending determination of counterclaim In *Stapleford Finance Ltd v Courtney* [2014] IEHC 668, IBRC (formerly Anglo Irish Bank) instituted proceedings by way of summary summons pursuant to certain facilities. The bank's interests were assigned to the plaintiff, which obtained liberty to continue the proceedings as plaintiff, and issued a motion seeking liberty to enter final judgment. The facilities were not in dispute, but the defendant, who appeared in person, argued that he had a bona fide defence and counterclaim relating to Anglo Irish Bank's role in the collapse of the Irish banking system and, more particularly, in the loss of value in Irish bank shares which the defendant had obtained in November 2011. Barton J. was not satisfied that the defendant's assertions were unarguable. Applying *Prendergast v Biddle* (unreported, Supreme Court, Kingsmill Moore J., 31 July 1957) and *Moohan v S. & R. Motors (Donegal) Ltd* (2008) 3 I.R. 650, Barton J. held that the defendant's claims comprised independent cross claims.

Barton J. gave the plaintiff liberty to enter final judgment, but placed a stay on execution which was conditional upon the defendant prosecuting his cross claims against the bank (by way of counterclaim or by separate proceedings) with due diligence, and granted both parties liberty to apply.

Stay on execution pending determination of related proceedings In *National Asset Loan Management Ltd v Crosbie*, the defendant applied for a stay on execution or enforcement of a judgment (delivered at [2014] IEHC 342, described below) pending the determination of related proceedings (in which Mr Crosbie, as plaintiff, claimed declaratory and injunctive reliefs against NALM). NALM applied to strike out the related proceedings (or parts thereof) as having been commenced without statutory leave having been obtained under the relevant legislation. Judgment was delivered by Keane J. at [2014] IEHC 414.

Regarding the related proceedings, Keane J. held that certain remedies sought in Mr Crosbie's originating plenary summons were subject to the requirements of s.182 of the National Asset Management Agency Act 2009 and that, having not obtained leave under s.182(2), Mr Crosbie was not entitled to maintain a claim for any such remedy. Accordingly, Keane J. struck out the relevant provisions of Mr Crosbie's originating plenary summons.

Declining the application for a stay, Keane J. held that to grant such a stay "would be inimical to the appropriate aim of speedy justice under both the summary summons procedure and the rules of the Commercial Court" and would give rise to a risk of injustice.

Stay on execution pending orderly disposition of assets In *AIB v O'Reilly* [2014] IEHC 326, summary judgment had been entered against the defendants, including against the first defendant (a prominent businessman) in a sum of over €22 million, pursuant to facilities in respect of which the bank was also secured. No appeal was contemplated in respect of the judgment. The defendants sought a six-month stay on registration and execution of the judgment insofar as any unencumbered assets of the defendants might be concerned, in order to facilitate an orderly disposition of same to secure equal treatment as between the defendants' creditors.

Kelly J. noted that a creditor who has obtained judgment has a strong prima facie entitlement to immediately execute on foot of it in whatever way the law permits. He noted that, while there is undoubtedly jurisdiction in the court to suspend such an entitlement, the court should exercise particular care before so doing, since such a stay is, in effect, a refusal to allow the judgment creditor to execute the very legal rights which were obtained by obtaining the judgment. Kelly J. noted that the range of circumstances which may be considered by the court on such an application is vast and declined to set out particular rules which regulate the exercise of the court's discretion, but observed that it is the duty of the court to uphold the law and to maintain a fair balance between litigants so as to achieve a fair result. Applying the foregoing principles, Kelly J. refused the application for a stay.

Setting aside a permanent stay on proceedings In *Flynn v Bon Secours Health Systems Ltd* [2014] IEHC 87, an appeal from orders of the Circuit Court (Ó Donnabháin J.) permanently staying three sets of medical negligence proceedings, Hogan J. considered whether the plaintiff's actions for medical negligence should be stayed permanently in circumstances where the plaintiff was unable to produce his own medical report (although at least one of the defendants was in possession of a report which, to some degree, supported the plaintiff's claims). The plaintiff claimed to suffer from an extremely rare condition and the negligence alleged essentially related to diagnosis. One expert report indicated some support for the plaintiff's claim but the plaintiff (who was unemployed, wholly dependent on disability benefit, and not professionally represented) was unable to secure the attendance of said expert as an expert witness on his behalf. Having regard to *Cooke v Cronin* [1999] IESC 54, Hogan J. noted that: the proceedings were against three hospitals (and not against medical professionals as such); it could not be said that there was no appropriate basis for continuing the proceedings; and the order was, in reality, a dismissal of the plaintiff's claim, which was premature in the circumstances. Hogan J. allowed the plaintiff's appeal, but on terms that the plaintiff, if he wished to proceed with the proceedings, must obtain an expert report within 12 months.

SUMMARY JUDGMENT

General comments on judgments delivered in 2014 The courts in 2014 continued to apply the well-established principles governing applications for summary judgment as set out in decisions such as *First National Commercial Bank v Anglin* [1996] 1 I.R. 75, *Aer Rianta cpt v Ryanair Ltd* [2001] 4 I.R. 607 and *Harrisgrange Ltd v Duncan* [2003] 4 I.R. 1. For example, see *National Asset Loan Management Ltd v Coyle* [2014] IESC 27 where Clarke J. (with whom Laffoy and Dunne JJ. concurred) dismissed an appeal from an order of the High Court (McGovern J.)([2013] IEHC 606)—see M. Donnelly, "Banking and Security Law Update" (2014) 21(7) C.L.P. 168.

Regarding summary judgment generally see T. Murphy, "Summary Judgment in the Superior Courts" (2014) 21(8) C.L.P. 175. Regarding considerations particular to summary judgment pursuant to a guarantee, see K. Kaar, "Common Defences to the Enforceability of a Guarantee" (2014) 21(7) C.L.P. 151 and B. Glynn, "Personal Guarantees and the Problems that Arise" (2014) 32 I.L.T. 46.

Cases in which summary judgment was entered In *National Asset Loan Management Ltd v Crosbie* [2014] IEHC 342, NALM sought summary judgment against Mr Crosbie in a sum of over €77 million, together with interest and costs, pursuant to a number of facilities and personal guarantees. Mr Crosbie acknowledged that the sum at issue remained outstanding, but claimed to have a full defence in that he had entered into a written agreement with the plaintiff in August 2012 (reflected, in particular, in a letter written by Mr Crosbie's solicitor), in which it was agreed that, in consideration of Mr Crosbie providing security interests in certain assets to the plaintiff (and divesting himself of other assets), the plaintiff would no longer have recourse to his remaining assets (including his family home, his son's home and a business carried on by his wife).

Applying *McGrath v O'Driscoll* [2007] 1 I.L.R.M. 203 and *Danske Bank a/s v Durkan New Homes* [2010] IESC 22, Keane J. was satisfied that the issue of construction which arose was relatively straightforward and that it could be determined on an application for summary judgment. Applying the test set out in *ICDL v European Computer Driving Licence Foundation* [2012] 3 I.R. 327, and taking the relevant provisions of the agreement at their high-water mark from Mr Crosbie's perspective, Keane J. held that they could be said to include agreements to refrain from taking particular steps (including to seek enforcement against certain specified assets, or to have the defendant declared bankrupt), but could not be said to include an agreement to refrain from obtaining a money judgment against the defendant. Accordingly, Keane J. entered summary judgment.

In *McNamee v Estherfield* [2014] IEHC 205, the plaintiffs sought summary judgment in respect of rent allegedly due pursuant to a lease and licence arrangement. The defendants disputed the amounts claimed, complained of a development by the plaintiffs which they contended would adversely affect their business, and argued that they could not be found liable in the proceedings in respect of rents which became owing after the notice of motion on which the plaintiffs' application was based had issued. Entering summary judgment, Barrett J. held that: the defendants had not met the low threshold required to obtain leave to defend; the plaintiff's entitlement to the rents claimed need not be postponed until the determination of a possible (and unquantified) plenary counterclaim; and, having regard to *Dublin Docklands Development Authority v Jermyn Street Ltd* [2010] IEHC 217 and *Quarryvale Two Ltd v Beere* [2012] IEHC 546, in the interest of procedural efficiency and the avoidance of unnecessary cost, the arrears of rent which had arisen after the notice of motion had issued could be included in the sum awarded.

Leave to defend—construction of relevant documents In *Ulster Bank Ireland Ltd v Fortune* [2014] IEHC 272, the plaintiff appealed a decision of the Master of the High Court where, on a motion for liberty to enter final judgment, the Master struck out the summary summons (which claimed sums due on foot of two facilities, respectively made in April 2004 and April 2006). Both parties agreed that the real issue for determination was whether the plaintiff should be given liberty to enter final judgment or the defendant should be given leave to defend. Barton J. was not satisfied that the defendants had established an arguable defence in respect of sums claimed pursuant to the April 2004 facility. In respect of the April 2006 facility, Barton J. held that there was an issue for determination concerning the construction of the facility letter, which would not be appropriate for the court to determine on an application for summary judgment, and noted that there was an issue as to whether a demand was validly made pursuant to this facility. Accordingly, Barton J. gave leave to defend in respect of the claim based on the April 2006 facility.

In *Irish Bank Resolution Corporation v McCaughey*, the plaintiff sought summary judgment pursuant a number of facilities whereby it had advanced substantial sums to the defendant. The defendant resisted the claim on the basis of an alleged collateral contract (which related to a number of the facilities) which provided that the term of the facilities was to be "for the duration of the funds". The defendant also claimed to have a counterclaim based on his allegation that certain investments were mis-sold in that certain of their features were mis-described.

In the High Court ([2014] IEHC 230), Kelly J. held that having regard to the evidence (and noting the absence of an entire agreement clause in the relevant facilities), a triable issue had been raised as to the possible existence of a collateral contract. Kelly J. noted that the counterclaim was statute-barred (having regard to s.6 of the Statute of Limitations 1957) and held that the defendant had not demonstrated, even on the low threshold of proof required, the basis for a counterclaim. Accordingly, Kelly J. entered summary judgment in respect of certain facilities, granting leave to defend in respect of those facilities affected by the alleged collateral contract.

The defendant/appellant appealed a number of aspects of the order of Kelly J., which appeal was dealt with at [2014] IESC 44. Having regard to new evidence which had been placed before the court, and allowing the appeal in part, Clarke J. (with whom Laffoy and Dunne JJ. concurred) held that there was an arguable basis for the proposition that one of the funds (the New York Hotels Fund) was not at an end, and so leave to defend in respect of this fund ought to be given (based on an alleged collateral contract). However, this leave to defend was limited to the issue of whether the fund was at an end, and leave to defend based on alleged mis-selling was not granted. Leave to defend was not granted in respect of another fund (the Woolgate Fund) in respect of which Kelly J.'s order had also been appealed.

Leave to defend—signature of relevant documents In *ADM Londis plc v Gorman's Supermarket Ltd* [2014] IEHC 95, the plaintiff sought judgment against the second defendant in respect of a personal guarantee, a franchise agreement and a product purchase agreement. The second defendant claimed that the signature on the guarantee was not his, a matter which Barrett J. held the court was not competent to adjudicate upon, and was a factual issue requiring determination at a plenary hearing. Regarding claims on foot of the franchise and product purchase agreements, the defendant claimed not to have understood same when signing them and, having regard to additional factual circumstances, leave to defend was also granted in respect of these agreements.

Leave to defend where defendant is a consumer *Ulster Bank Ireland Ltd v Healy* [2014] IEHC 96 is a notable decision for practitioners. The bank sought summary judgment against the defendant in a sum of approximately €600,000 pursuant to a number of facilities. The purpose of several of the facilities was to enable the defendant to purchase certain investment properties in the United Kingdom, which investment the defendant claimed, on affidavit, to be a long term pension type investment to be realised upon or subsequent to the defendant's retirement, for his benefit or that of his family. The defendant claimed to be a consumer for the purposes of the Consumer Credit Act 1995 (the CCA 1995"). The bank, which had categorised the defendant as a business customer, argued that he was not a consumer for the purposes of CCA 1995.

Barrett J. had regard to s.2(1) CCA 1995 and the decision of Kelly J. in *AIB v Higgins* [2010] IEHC 29. He expressed the view that the borrowings in *Higgins* (in the sum of over €6 million) were both quantitatively and qualitatively different from those of the defendant, whose borrowing could be categorised as seeking to satisfy his individual needs in terms of private consumption (as discussed in the European Court of Justice's decision in *Benincasa v Dentalkit* (C-269/95) [1997] E.C.R. I-03767, which decision was analysed in *Higgins*). Barrett J. noted that the bank's categorisation of the defendant suggested that the CCA 1995 might not have been complied with, and that the consequences of a failure to comply could include rendering a loan unenforceable. In the circumstances, Barrett J. was not satisfied that it was very clear there was no defence, and granted the defendant leave to defend at plenary hearing.

See also *AIB v Fahy* [2014] IEHC 244, where a defendant, who had obtained loans for the purposes of both paying off a mortgage on her principal private residence and for commercial investments, was held not to be a consumer for the purposes of the CCA 1995 (see M. Donnelly, "Banking and Security Law Update" (2014) 21(7) C.L.P. 168 and D. P. Boyle, "ILT Digest of Legislation and Superior Court Decisions" (2015) 33 I.L.T. 137) and *Ryan v Danske Bank* [2014] IEHC 236 where, applying *Healy*, Baker J. held that the plaintiff had made out an arguable case that he was a consumer and entitled to the benefit of the Consumer Protection Code 2012. See generally T. Murphy, "A 'Consumer' or a Professional Investor? An Analysis of the 'Consumer Defence'" Part 1 (2015) 22(5) C.L.P. 127 and Part 2 (2015) 22(6) C.L.P. 147.

THIRD PARTY PROCEDURE

Applications to set aside a third party notice In *Kynes Moycullen Ltd v Whiriskey Refrigeration Co Ltd* [2014] IEHC 348, proceedings were issued in November 2011 after a fire broke out at a premises. The first defendant, who had supplied five condensing units to the plaintiff, served a third party notice on

Refrigeration Distributors Ltd ("RDL"), which had supplied the same units to the first defendant. RDL applied to set aside the third party notice, which application was dismissed by the High Court (O'Neill J.) in December 2012. In October 2013, RDL issued an application for leave to serve a third party notice on Emerson Climate Technologies Ltd. Leave was granted by the High Court (O'Malley J.) in December 2013 and the third party notice was served over the Christmas/New Year period. In February 2014, Emerson sought an order setting aside the third party notice.

O'Neill J. expressed the view that the period with which the court was particularly concerned was between December 2012 (when the court refused to set aside the third party notice, forcing a rethink of RDL's strategy) and October 2013 (when the motion seeking leave to issue and serve a third party notice on Emerson issued), a period of 10 and a half months. O'Neill J. had regard to difficulties in identifying the appropriate party (noting the complexity of Emerson's corporate structure) and that the litigation had generally moved quite slowly. In all the circumstances, O'Neill J. was satisfied that RDL had moved as soon as was reasonably possible to involve Emerson. Accordingly, s.27(1) of the Civil Liability Act 1961 did not provide a basis for setting aside the third party notice, and the application was dismissed.

Service of a notice of indemnity and contribution on a co-defendant who has secured a stay of proceedings pending arbitration *O'Connor v Noel Duffy t/a The Duffy Gaffney Partnership* [2014] IEHC 97 concerned whether a defendant can seek an indemnity and contribution from a co-defendant where that co-defendant has secured a stay of proceedings between itself and the plaintiff pending arbitration. While the relevant order of the High Court (de Valera J.) in fact stayed the entire proceedings, Barrett J. analysed whether an indemnity and contribution might be sought in the circumstances above, concluding that this could be done. Accordingly, Barrett J. adjourned the matter to enable the order of de Valera J. to be varied or substituted, subsequent to which an order allowing the service of a notice of indemnity and contribution might be made.

AMENDMENTS TO THE RULES OF THE SUPERIOR COURTS 1986 IN 2014

S.I. No. 16 of 2014 — Rules of the Superior Courts (Courts and Civil Law (Miscellaneous Provisions) Act 2013) 2014, substituting Ord.4 r.5(2), Ord.99 r.40 and Pt II of Appendix W.

S.I. No. 278 of 2014 — Rules of the Superior Courts (Provision of Transcripts of Sentencing Hearings) 2014, inserting Ord.85 r.13 and Ord.86 r.14(5).

S.I. No. 293 of 2014 — Rules of the Superior Courts (Case Stated) 2014, substituting Ord.62 r.1.

S.I. No. 485 of 2014 — Rules of the Superior Courts (Court of Appeal Act 2014) 2014, making a number of amendments to the rules and forms regulating the procedure to be employed by the Supreme Court and the Court of Appeal of the jurisdiction conferred on those courts by the amendments of the Constitution comprised in the Thirty Third Amendment of the Constitution. See also Practice Directions SC16 – Conduct of Proceedings in the Supreme Court (29 October 2014), CA01 – Expedited appeals and non-compliant notices of appeal (30 October 2014), CA02 – Appeals against sentence and undue leniency applications (30 October 2014), CA03 – Appeals transferred by the Supreme Court pursuant to Article 64 of the Constitution (17 November 2014) and CA04 – Motions and ex-parte applications (5 December 2014). See generally E. Martin, "New Appeals Regime in the Superior Courts" (2015) 22(2) C.L.P. 51.

S.I. No. 539 of 2014 — Rules of the Superior Courts (Supreme Court Forms) 2014, substituting new Forms 3 and 4 in Appendix FF.

S.I. No. 600 of 2014 — Rules of the Superior Courts (Order 76) 2014, amending Ord.76 r.29(1).

Prisons

REMISSION

Remission applies to all sentences, including those of one month or less The Prison (Amendment) Rules 2014 (the "2014 Rules") (S.I. No. 227 of 2014), made under s.35 of the Prisons Act 2007 (*Annual Review of Irish Law 2007*, p.480), replaced r.59(1) of the Prison Rules 2007 (S.I. No. 252 of 2007) (the "2007 Rules") (*Annual Review of Irish Law 2007*, p.480) to provide that a prisoner serving any term of imprisonment, or consecutive terms of imprisonment, shall be eligible, by good conduct, to earn a remission of sentence not exceeding one-quarter of such term or terms, as the case may be. Rule 59(1) of the 2007 Rules had originally provided that remission applied only to sentences "exceeding one month" but this was removed by the 2014 Rules. This followed a challenge to the validity of the exclusion of sentences of one month or less on the grounds that it breached Art.40.1 of the Constitution, which in turn followed the decision in *Byrne v Director of Oberstown School* [2013] IEHC 562 (*Annual Review of Irish Law 2013*, pp.130–132), that the exclusion of persons under 17 years of age from r.59(1) was in breach of Art.40.1. The 2014 Rules came into force on 29 May 2014.

Enhanced remission: criteria prescribed in detail In a series of High Court decisions and one Supreme Court decision in 2014, the basis for granting enhanced remission of up to one third of a sentence under r.59(2) of the Prison Rules 2007 came under critical scrutiny, to the extent that r.59(2) was amended in important respects. For an insightful overview, see Collier, "In Remission" (2014) Gazette, Law Society of Ireland, October 2014, p.34.

In *Ryan v Governor of Midlands Prison* [2014] IEHC 338, [2014] IESC 54, the applicant sought enhanced remission on the basis of participation in authorised structured activities under r.59(2) of the Prison Rules 2007. In the High Court, Barrett J. considered that since these activities had the aim and effect of reducing recidivism and facilitating reintegration into the community, the only conclusion that the Minister for Justice could have reached was that the applicant was less likely to re-offend as a result of his participation and thus better able to reintegrate into the community. Barrett J. accordingly ordered the applicant's immediate release under Art.40.4 of the Constitution. On appeal, the Supreme Court reversed, primarily on the ground that the Art.40 procedure was not suitable to deal with such a case, citing its decision in *State (McDonagh) v Frawley* [1978] I.R. 131. While the Supreme Court did not analyse the basis for the High Court decision, it did not support that analysis either. The High Court decision of Barrett J. was followed by Hogan J. in *Farrell v Governor of Portlaoise Prison* [2014] IEHC 392 and he concluded that as the applicant had successfully participated in structured activities he was entitled to be released under r.59(2).

On the same day as the decision in *Farrell*, Peart J. held, in *Keogh v Governor of Mountjoy Prison* [2014] IEHC 402, that merely because a prisoner signed up for and attended a number of authorised courses ought not lead to the conclusion that he or she was entitled to release under r.59(2). In *Ryan v Governor of Midlands Prison* [2014] IEHC 338, an application for judicial review by the applicant (the procedure recommended by the Supreme Court in *Ryan v Governor of Midlands Prison* [2014] IEHC 338, [2014] IESC 54, above), O'Malley J. also disagreed with the approach to r.59(2) taken by both Barrett J. (in *Ryan*) and by Hogan J. (in *Farrell*) and preferred the analysis of Peart J. (in *Keogh*). The views of Peart J. and O'Malley J. were followed by Kelly J. in *McKevitt v Minister for Justice and Equality* [2014] IEHC 551. Kelly J. stated (at para.71 of his judgment):

> "Whilst participation in authorised structured activity no doubt has as its object a reduction in the prisoner's likelihood of re-offending, it does not follow ipso facto that such object is achieved. It is, in every case, a matter for the Minister to be satisfied that such objective has been achieved as a matter of fact."

While the decisions in *Keogh*, *Ryan (No.2)* and *McKevitt* indicated that the courts were prepared to defer to the Minister's decision-making, by contrast with the views expressed in *Ryan* and *Farrell*, the opportunity was taken in the Prison (Amendment) (No.2) Rules 2014 (S.I. No. 385 of 2014) to amend r.59(2), in particular by prescribing in considerable detail the factors to be taken into account by the Minister in determining whether enhanced remission is to be granted. In this respect, it is worth noting that r.59(2) as originally made in 2007 had read:

> The Minister may grant such greater remission of sentence in excess of one quarter, but not exceeding one third thereof where a prisoner has shown further good conduct by engaging in authorised structured activity and the Minister is satisfied that, as a result, the prisoner is less likely to re-offend and will be better able to reintegrate into the community.

By contrast, r.59(2), as inserted by the 2014 Rules, reads:

> (a) A prisoner who has engaged in authorised structured activity may apply to the Minister for enhanced remission.
> (b) An application shall be made in such form and manner and shall be accompanied by such other information and documentation as may be specified by the Minister.
> (c) An application under subparagraph (a) shall not be made earlier than 6 months prior to the date on which the prisoner would be released if enhanced remission of one third of the prisoners sentence were to be granted to him or her.
> (d) Where the Minister receives an application under subparagraph (a), the Minister shall, as soon as practicable thereafter—
>   (i) if he or she is satisfied that the prisoner, having regard to the matters referred to in subparagraph (f) is less likely to re-offend and better able to re-integrate into the community, notify the prisoner of his or her decision to grant enhanced remission to

the prisoner and the period of enhanced remission of sentence which is to apply, or

(ii) notify the prisoner of his or her decision to refuse the prisoners application and the reasons for the refusal.

(e) A notification referred to in subparagraph (d) shall be in writing and shall be copied to the Governor of the prison in which the prisoner concerned is serving his or her sentence.

(f) The Minister shall, when making a decision in respect of an application under subparagraph (a), have regard to the following matters:

(i) the manner and extent to which the prisoner has engaged constructively in authorised structured activity;

(ii) the manner and extent to which the prisoner has taken steps to address his or her offending behaviour;

(iii) the nature and gravity of the offence to which the sentence of imprisonment being served by the prisoner relates;

(iv) the sentence of imprisonment concerned and any recommendations of the court that imposed that sentence in relation thereto;

(v) the period of the sentence served by the prisoner;

(vi) the potential threat to the safety and security of members of the public (including the victim of the offence to which the sentence of imprisonment being served by the prisoner relates) should the prisoner be released from prison;

(vii) any offence of which the prisoner was convicted before being convicted of the offence to which the sentence of imprisonment being served by him or her relates;

(viii) the conduct of the prisoner while in custody or during a period of temporary release;

(ix) any report of, or recommendation made by—

(I) the Governor of, or person for the time being performing the functions of the Governor in relation to, the prison concerned,

(II) the Garda Síochána,

(III) a probation officer, or

(IV) any other person whom the Minister considers would be of assistance in enabling him or her to make a decision on an application under subparagraph (a).

(g) In this paragraph 'enhanced remission' means such greater remission of sentence in excess of one quarter, but not exceeding one third, as may be determined by the Minister.

It is also worth noting that, in *Doody v Governor of Wheatfield Prison* [2015] IEHC 137, Noonan J. approved the "majority" High Court analysis of Kelly, Peart and O'Malley JJ. as to the correct interpretation of the original version of r.59(2). Noonan J. also noted that, in the *Farrell* case, Hogan J. had considered that the Minister should not have taken account of a report from An Garda Síochána in making her decision under r.59(2); but, as Noonan J. also noted in *Doody*, this was expressly a matter now included in the amended r.59(2) as inserted by the 2014 Rules.

SEGREGATION

Prolonged segregation requires review by Prison Service In *Killeen v Governor of Portlaoise Prison* [2014] IEHC 77, the High Court (Hedigan J.) accepted that the segregation arrangements of the applicant prisoners did not fully conform to r.62 of the Prison Rules 2007 (S.I. No. 252 of 2007) (the "2007 Rules") (*Annual Review of Irish Law 2007*, p.480). While he declined to quash those arrangements on judicial review he nonetheless ordered that they be reviewed by the Director General of the Irish Prison Service.

The applicants were all serving terms of imprisonment at Portlaoise Prison, having been transferred there following security concerns. Since their transfer, a decision had been taken pursuant to r.62 of the 2007 Rules that the applicants could not be accommodated within the general prison population. The applicants were consequently detained together in a self-contained eight-cell unit and precluded from associating with the general prison population or engaging in a number of activities. The applicants sought an order of certiorari either quashing the decision to segregate them or the refusal to transfer them to another prison and the mainstream prison population. They also sought declarations that their segregation and indeterminate close confinement was unlawful and unconstitutional, that their current detention was unlawful, that the respondents were in breach of the 2007 Rules, and that the respondents had failed to perform their functions in a manner consistent with the European Convention on Human Rights (ECHR) in refusing to allow the applicants to engage in authorised structured activities and holding them in solitary confinement.

The applicants also sought injunctive relief transferring them out of segregation and into the general prison population, and allowing them to engage in activities, participate in recreation, avail of facilities, have access to visits and to associate with other prisoners. The respondents opposed the reliefs sought, except that, in light of the decision of the High Court (O'Malley J.) in *Dundon v Governor of Cloverhill Prison* [2013] IEHC 608 (*Annual Review of Irish Law 2013*, pp.149–152), they accepted that the segregation of the applicants from the general prison population from 26 January 2013 to 25 October 2013 had been in breach of r.62 of the 2007 Rules. The High Court (Hedigan J.) essentially accepted the arguments of the respondents and refused the applicants the reliefs sought, with the exception of a declaration that r.62 of the 2007 Rules had not been complied with over the period of time conceded by the respondents.

The court applied the analysis of the High Court (Barrington J.) in *State (Richardson) v Governor of Mountjoy Prison* [1980] I.L.R.M. 82, that it was well established that although some of a prisoner's rights are abrogated or suspended as necessitated by imprisonment, not all of those rights are; that while a prisoner is required to submit to Prison Rules but is also protected by them; and that a prisoner's subsisting rights could often be ascertained from the Prison Rules in light of the Constitution. It might be added that while the *Richardson* case applied this analysis to the Rules for the Government of Prisons 1947 (SR&O No.320 of 1947), a somewhat more rights-focused approach in the 2007 Rules (reflecting the minimum international standards from which the 2007 Rules derived) makes it rather easier to discern such a constitutionally compliant content.

The court, following *Devoy v Governor of Portlaoise Prison* [2009] IEHC 288, accepted that there was a presumption in favour of a prisoner being allowed to have a degree of association subject to the good order of the prison; but that the good order of the prison and the safety of the prisoners may at times require that certain prisoners, notably those of a violent disposition, be segregated from the main body of the prisoners, and that it was for the prison authorities to determine when segregation was required. Where it did, the court added that segregation should be kept under review, and that, because rights were being curtailed, it was clear from the relevant case law, both Irish and ECHR case law, that the principle of proportionality had to be applied. In the event of prolonged segregation, therefore, the court held that judicial review was available to test the necessity and proportionality of the measure.

In the case of the applicants, the court acknowledged that the segregation had been for a protracted period, which was longer than provided for in r.62(9) of the 2007 Rules. The court noted that r.62(9) was in contrast to the detailed provisions in other parts of r.62 concerning short periods of detention. Bearing in mind, however, that the 2007 Rules had to be read in light of the Constitution, this required good reasons and minimum interference with rights and that the interference be proportionate. Just as there was an internal process of review for short periods of isolation, judicial review of the merits and reasons for a prolonged period of isolation was available. In this case, the respondents had set out the risks posed by the applicants, and the court would not assess those risks but rather determine whether they existed and constituted evidence upon which the respondents could rationally base a decision that segregation was an appropriate solution. In that respect, the court was satisfied that there were such reasonable grounds to believe that segregation was necessary in this case and that while it was "a most undesirable measure" it appeared to be the minimum restriction necessary to ensure the safety of the prison and its inhabitants. Applying the classic proportionality test, the court concluded that the decision was rationally based, was clearly connected to the objective pursued, was not arbitrary and was the minimum necessary.

The court then noted that the segregation involved in this case had moved well beyond the maximum 21 days envisaged by r.62(9) of the 2007 Rules, which provided that any further extension had to be authorised in writing by the Director General of the Irish Prisons Service. While no provision was made for review in r.62(9), reading it in a constitutional manner required that some form of review analogous to that provided by r.62(4) had to be read into r.62(9) so as to render lawful any authorisation given under it.

The court therefore held that the Director General should review any removal under r.62(9) at least once every three months or upon request by the prisoner or his legal advisers, providing such requests are not made vexatiously; and that such review had to be carefully recorded and was to comply by analogy with the provisions set out in rr.62(6), (7) and (8). The court also held that the Director General should give the prisoner or his legal advisers the opportunity to consider the grounds advanced for further removal prior to authorising any continuation of their removal, and the prisoner or his legal advisers should be given the opportunity to consider the grounds advanced for further removal prior to authorising any continuation of their removal. The prisoner or his legal adviser was to be notified promptly of his decision, together with the reasons for it. Detailed records of the process should be accurately kept so as to assist the court in any application considering the lawfulness of continuing segregation.

As to review by an independent judicial authority in cases of prolonged isolation in solitary confinement, the court held that such confinement was not in issue here; but that it was, however, open to any prisoner to appeal to the courts for an appropriate declaration and other orders where the terms of imprisonment were not in accordance with constitutional rights.

TRANSFER OF SENTENCED PRISONERS INTERNATIONALLY

In *Sweeney v Governor of Loughan House Open Centre* [2014] IEHC 150, [2014] IESC 42, the Supreme Court, reversing the High Court (Keane J.), accepted the applicant's claim that his continued detention after his transfer from the United Kingdom to the State was in breach of the Transfer of Sentenced Persons Acts 1995 and 1997 (the "1995 and 1997 Acts"). The applicant brought judicial review proceedings claiming that his continued detention beyond 29 March 2014 was ultra vires the 1995 and 1997 Acts. On 7 December 2006, the applicant had been sentenced in the United Kingdom to 16 years' imprisonment, with 252 days on remand taken into consideration. The sentencing rules in the UK provide, pursuant to s.244 of the Criminal Justice Act 2003, that any sentence with a duration exceeding one year has two parts. The first part is the custodial period and the second part is served in the community, where the offender is subject to strict licence conditions. The applicant submitted that the legal nature of his sentence was to serve eight years in prison and a further eight years released on licence. He claimed that his sentence was due to expire on 29 March 2022 and that his conditional release date was 29 March 2014.

The applicant had family ties in Ireland and, therefore, in early 2007 he applied to the relevant authorities in England to be transferred to serve his sentence in Ireland in order to be closer to his family. Prior to approval, the applicant was fully informed that his sentence might be affected in the process of transferring as Ireland's sentencing laws differed from the UK. He was informed that his provisional release date in Ireland was 16 November 2016. The applicant consented in writing to the terms of the transfer and was subsequently transferred to the Loughan House Open Centre on foot of a High Court committal warrant. The warrant recited that the applicant was to serve 16 years' imprisonment with 252 days on remand taken into consideration. Following his transfer, the applicant claimed that the legal nature of his sentence was that he serve eight years in custody and he claimed that, as a result, the State was acting ultra vires the Acts. He further argued that in considering whether to issue a warrant authorising the transfer in 2008, the High Court ought to have adapted his sentence to one of 16 years' imprisonment with eight years of that sentence suspended on conditions designed to mirror the licence conditions in the UK. The applicant claimed that the continued enforcement of his sentence under the warrant amounted to a disproportionate interference with his right to liberty and the security of the person under the European Convention on Human Rights. Finally, the applicant submitted that, upon consenting to the transfer, he understood that the sentence imposed on him in the UK would not be interfered with by virtue of the transfer.

In the High Court, Keane J. refused the application but, on appeal, the Supreme Court (Denham CJ., Murray, Hardiman, Clarke and MacMenamin JJ.) reversed and ordered the applicant's release. Delivering the only judgment, Murray J. noted that, under s.7(4) of the Transfer of Sentenced Persons Act 1995 (the "1995 Act"), the warrant detaining the applicant had the same force and effect as a warrant imposing a sentence following conviction by a court in Ireland, insofar as it authorised the continued enforcement in Ireland of the sentence imposed in England, "with due regard to any remission of sentence accrued in the sentencing State." He considered that this provision referred only to remission already accrued prior to transfer, and had no bearing on any question of remission which might accrue subsequent to the appellant's transfer.

Murray J. held that, as the Convention was given effect to in domestic law by the 1995 Act and as it involved implementing an international convention, it must (as decided by the court in *Bourke v Attorney General* [1972] I.R. 36 and *Crilly v Farrington* [2002] 1 I.L.R.M. 161) be interpreted in light of the provisions of the Convention. He considered that the legal nature and duration of the sentence imposed by the English court was to be determined by reference to English law since the appellant's transfer to prison in this jurisdiction was for the purpose of "continued enforcement" of his English sentence. While the "enforcement" or "administration" of his sentence was governed by the law of the administering State, the sentence enforced could not be longer than the sentence imposed in the sentencing state. As already noted, the sentence imposed in England consisted of one period of imprisonment or "deprivation of liberty", and a second period of liberty under licence. This occurred, Murray J. held, by operation of law, and not by virtue of any remission, discretionary or otherwise, granted by the English authorities. As a matter of English law, therefore, the appellant was entitled to be freed from custody when he had completed eight years of his sentence of imprisonment. He added that the question of his recall to prison could only arise if he was in breach of the terms of his licensed release, but such a sentence could not be characterised as a sentence to a period of loss of liberty of 16 rather than eight years within the meaning of the Convention or the 1995 Act. There was, therefore, no legal basis on which the appellant could be regarded as being required to serve a term of imprisonment in this jurisdiction of 16 years, and as already noted, the court therefore concluded that he was entitled to be released.

Probate and Succession Law

DR ALBERT KEATING, BCL, LLB, LLM, DLitt, BL
Senior Lecturer WIT

INTRODUCTION

In *LC (a minor) v HS* [2014] IEHC 32, Clark J. stated that an order may only be made under s.117 of the Succession Act 1965 (the "1965 Act") on application by or on behalf of the child of a testator "and cannot generally be made if the deceased died intestate", and that "the six month time limit applicable to s.117 applications applies equally to s.121 applications, which can only be sought as a relief in s.117 proceedings in cases where the order is sought in the interest of a child of the deceased." (See *MPD v MD* [1981] I.L.R.M. 179) She also stated that a "disposition" for the purposes of s.121 of the 1965 Act does not include an acquisition or purchase: "an acquisition of property by purchase/gift/inheritance cannot equate to the divesting of the beneficial ownership of property which involves the sale/transfer/gift by will or a *donatio mortis causa*."

In *Mullen v Mullen* [2014] IEHC 407, Cregan J., when construing a will, referred to ss.89, 90, 91 and 99 of the 1965 Act, and to the decision of Laffoy J. in *In Re Rafter* [2012] IEHC 239 where she stated that:

> "The primary duty of the Court in construing a will is to ascertain and give effect to the intention of the testator. In recent years the High Court in this jurisdiction has adopted the guidance on the construction of wills generally given by Lowry LCJ in *Heron v Ulster Bank Ltd* [1974] N.I. 44, as appears from *Howell v Howell* [1992] 1 I.R. 290 (Carroll J.), *Corrigan v Corrigan* [2007] IEHC 367 (McGovern J.), and, most recently, *O'Donohue v O'Donohue* [2011] IEHC 511 (Gilligan J.)."

In *Doyle v Dunne* [2014] IESC 69, Laffoy J. in her judgment for the Supreme Court found that even though the appellant's cause of action survived her death for the benefit of her estate, s.7(2) of the Civil Liability Act 1961 precluded the estate of the appellant from recovering damages for any pain or suffering or personal injury. She stated that:

> "The reality of this case is that the appellant's claim, as pleaded and as pursued in the High Court, whether founded on alleged negligence, breach of duty or trespass to the person, was in its entirety a claim for unliquidated general damages for pain, suffering and personal injury. There is no other component for remedy or relief in the appellant's claim, whether for special damages or otherwise. In the circumstances, when regard is had to the s.7(2) preclusion, there is nothing by way of remedy or relief left in the claim for this Court to adjudicate on or to remit to the High Court."

In *Cavey v Cavey* [2014] IESC 16, Clarke J. in his judgment for the Supreme Court considered whether the appellant's cause of action survived against the deceased person's estate was statute-barred by s.9 of the Civil Liability Act 1961. He found that:

> "[A] significant distinction is made in s.9(2), so far as claims against an estate are concerned, between a cause of action which results from an act or omission of the deceased, on the one hand, and a cause of action which may exist against those in charge of the administration of the estate of the deceased, on the other."

In *In the Estate of O'Connell* [2014] IESC 55, Dunne J. citing Shanley J. in *Re Nevin* [1997] IEHC 209 stated that the court "has an inherent jurisdiction to set aside a caveat where the caveat has been vexatiously lodged", and equally, "the court has jurisdiction to set aside a caveat where the caveator has no interest". Dunne J. also pointed out that:

> "[T]here is a difference between a claim arising under the estate of an individual, either on intestacy or on foot of the will of a deceased person, and a claim against the estate of a deceased person. It is not appropriate for a person with a claim against an estate to lodge a caveat in respect of that estate. Such a person has no interest *in* the estate."

THE INTERACTION BETWEEN SECTIONS 117 AND 121 OF THE SUCCESSION ACT

Section 117(1) of the Succession Act 1965 (the "1965 Act") provides that:

> Where, on application by or on behalf of a child of a testator, the court is of opinion that the testator has failed in his moral duty to make proper provision for the child in accordance with his means, whether by his will or otherwise, the court may order that such provision shall be made for the child out of the estate as the court thinks just.

Section 117(1A)(a) provides that:

> An application made under this section by virtue of Part V of the Status of Children Act, 1987, shall be considered in accordance with subsection (2) irrespective of whether the testator executed his will before or after the commencement of the said Part V.

Section 117(1A)(b) provides that: "Nothing in paragraph (a) shall be construed as referring to a right to apply under this section in respect of a testator who dies before the commencement of the said Part V." However, s.117 applies only to cases where a parent dies testate or partly testate. Even where a deceased parent's will is wholly ineffective due to the predecease of beneficiaries and his or her entire estate devolves as on intestacy, the deceased parent will still be deemed a testator for the purposes of s.117 by virtue of the provisions of s.109 of the 1965 Act. Section

109(1) provides that: "Where, after the commencement of this Act, a person dies wholly or partly testate leaving a spouse or children or both spouse and children, the provisions of this Part shall have effect." In *MPD v MD* [1981] I.L.R.M. 179, Carroll J. when considering the "state of testacy" stated that:

> "The state of testacy does not depend on the effectiveness of the will. It depends on the effectiveness of the execution of the will. If testacy is established, then in my opinion it follows that the person must die wholly or partly testate. There is no third state of testacy – that is, a state of testacy which is neither total nor partial."

Therefore, s.117 does not apply in the case of "a pure intestacy." In *LC (a minor) v HS* [2014] IEHC 32, Clark J. stated that:

> "An order may only be made under Section 117 'on application by or on behalf of the child of a testator' and cannot generally be made if the deceased died intestate."

Section 117(6) of the 1965 Act, as amended by the s.46 of the Family Law (Divorce) Act 1996, provides that the limitation period for making applications to the courts under s.117(1) is six months from the first taking out of representation. It is clear that where a grant of probate or a grant of letters of administration with will annexed has issued from the Probate Office or a District Probate Registry, it will be viewed as the first taking out of representation for the purpose of s.117(6), and also that the limitation period of six months will commence to run from the date of issue, and the same may be said in the case of a grant of letters of administration with the will annexed that issued from the Probate Office or a District Probate Registry in pursuance of a court order under s.27(4) of the 1965 Act. Section 3 of the 1965 Act provides that "representation" means probate or administration. Therefore the context of Pt IX of the 1965 Act requires that "the first taking out of representation of the deceased's estate" for the purposes of s.117(6) must be taken to mean that the limitation period will commence to run from the time a grant of probate or a grant of letters of administration with the will annexed has issued, and this includes a grant of letters of administration with the will annexed that issued pursuant to an order of the court under s.27(4) of the 1965 Act. It may also be noted that s.127 of the 1965 Act which extends the disability provisions of the Statute of Limitations 1957 does not include s.117 applications by children of deceased testators.

Under s.121(2) of the 1965 Act where the court is satisfied that a disposition was made for the purpose of defeating or substantially diminishing the share of his spouse, whether as a legal right or on intestacy, or the intestate share of any of his or her children, or of leaving any of his or her children insufficiently provided for, the disposition may be deemed in whole or in part "to be a devise or bequest made by him by will and to form part of his estate, and to have had no other effect." Section 121 was amended by the Status of Children Act 1987 to include non-marital children and by s.88 of the Civil Partnership and Certain Rights and Obligations of Cohabitants Act 2010 by inserting "or civil partner" after "spouse" wherever it appears. Under s.121(4) of the 1965 Act the court is also empowered to make such further orders as may appear to be just and equitable having regard to the circumstances of the case. An order may be made in the interest of the spouse or civil partner on the application of the spouse or civil partner or personal representative of the deceased within one year from the first taking out of a grant of representation to the estate and in the interest of a child of the deceased on an application under s.117. (s.121(5))

In *LC (a minor) v HS* [2014] IEHC 32, Clark J. referred to the "seminal judgment" of Carroll J. in *MPD v MD* [1981] I.L.R.M. 179 which dealt with the apparent interaction between ss.117 and 121 of the 1965 Act. Clark J. related the facts of that case as follows. It concerned the estate of a man who had two families: (i) his estranged wife and their four marital children who lived in the family home; and, (ii) his partner and their non-marital two children who lived in a house which he had acquired in their joint names. During his lifetime and within three years of his death, his partner acquired a half interest in his business and was joint tenant of their home. A grant of probate of his will issued on 25 September 1978. On 16 October 1979 (i.e. more than 12 months later) his widow issued two summonses against his partner seeking a declaration under s.117 on behalf of the children of his marriage and the other seeking a declaration under s.121 in the interests of the widow and in the interests of her four children. Carroll J. held that the widow was barred from making an application under s.121 in her own interest because the s.121 summons issued outside of the one-year time limit set by s.121(5). She further held at p.181 of her judgment that the success of the s.121 application in the interest of the children was dependent on the success of the s.117 application and accordingly, only one set of proceedings was necessary. The s.117 time limit cannot be extended in the case of a plaintiff who is under a disability such as infancy as it is not a claim under a will or on intestacy or as a legal right, but rather "a claim made independently of the will and against its provisions" (*MPD v MD* [1981] I.L.R.M. 179 at 183). The court had no jurisdiction to make an order under s.117 as the summons issued outside of the then-12 month limitation period. The s.121 application was, therefore, also statute-barred.

In her judgment Clark J. referred with approval to the findings by Carroll J. in *MPD v MD* [1981] I.L.R.M. 179 that the six-month time limit applicable to s.117 applications applies equally to s.121 applications, "which can only be sought as a relief in Section 117 proceedings in cases where the order is sought in the interest of a child of the deceased", and that as one set of proceedings is sufficient to make a claim under ss.117 and 121 is further "recognition of their connection under the Succession Act but is not a licence to use one set of proceedings to stay any statutory time limitations for the other."

LC (a minor) v HS [2014] IEHC 32 concerned an appeal from issues raised in two sets of proceedings instituted in the Circuit Court. The first issue involved s.117 of the 1965 Act and the time limits for making s.117 applications and the interaction between such applications and s.121 applications; the second issue concerned the meaning of a disposition for the purposes of s.121(1). In that case the deceased WS died intestate and was survived by his widow (the defendant), three marital children and three non-marital children including the infant plaintiff. The defendant never denied that the appellant/plaintiff was the child of WS as his six children were noted on the Internal Revenue affidavit. WS died on 18 October 2005. The appellant/plaintiff was born on 7 July 2000. A grant of letters of administration intestate issued to the defendant on 25 May 2006. The estate of WS comprised a net estate of €112,143.32 and under the rules of intestacy each of WS's children was entitled to one-sixth of one-third of the estate making the appellant/plaintiff's share in or around €6,230.18. In February 2006, the appellant/plaintiff commenced her first set of proceedings in the Circuit Court seeking, inter alia, a declaration that she was entitled to a share in the estate of WS under s.117 of the 1965 Act if he died testate or intestate.

The appellant/plaintiff (through her next friend) did not seek relief under s.121 as part of her s.117 application and she did not seek relief under s.121 itself until 31 August 2009 which was long after the expiry of the six-month time limit applicable under s.117(6). In her judgment Clark J. stated that:

> "It is clear from *MPD v MD* that the six month time limit applicable to Section 117 applications applies equally to Section 121 applications, which can only be sought as a relief in Section 117 proceedings in cases where the order is sought in the interest of a child of the deceased."

But she added:

> "That is *not* to say that in an appropriate case, in order to ensure that proper provision has been made for the child of a testator in accordance with Section 117, the Court could not grant an order under Section 121, as part of its inherent jurisdiction to provide just relief, even if no such claim was made. The Court's discretion would clearly depend on a number of pre-conditions being met; i.e. that (1) the Section 117 proceedings were commenced within the statutory time; (2) it would be unjust to ignore the disinheriting disposition; (3) there would otherwise be little or no estate available to provide just provision for the child; and (4) as soon as reasonably possible after becoming aware of the disputed disposition, the Plaintiff put the Defendant on notice that he/she would be seeking to have the disposition treated as a bequest or devise made by will and treated as part of the estate, in the context of the Section 117 proceedings. An order may only be made under Section 117 '*on application by or on behalf of the child of a testator*' and cannot generally be made if the deceased died intestate. However, as previously mentioned, Section 121 is not subject to that limitation and where an order is made under Section 121, the deceased is treated as though he made a bequest or devise by will, which potentially brings Section 117 into play even if the deceased otherwise died intestate (see the judgment of Carroll J. in *MPD v MD*)."

Clark J. concluded that, while it might be unnecessary to expressly seek a declaration under s.121 in s.117 proceedings, "this does not equate to what happened in this case where more than three years elapsed between the time when Plaintiff became aware of the disposition and the date on which the Defendant was first put on notice of the Section 121 claim by way of the 2009 proceedings." Although the s.117 proceedings were brought within time, "they were not appropriate to an intestacy and they did not include a claim under Section 121 nor was any claim brought to amend the pleadings within a reasonable time after the Plaintiff was aware that WS had died intestate and that it had been asserted by the Defendant that his estate did not comprise any real property." In those circumstances, the appellant/plaintiff's claim came under the intestacy rules in s.67 of the 1965 Act "and it would be unconscionable for the Court to exercise its inherent jurisdiction to make an order under Section 121. The Court is satisfied that the action is statute barred."

A DISPOSITION FOR THE PURPOSES OF SECTION 121 OF THE SUCCESSION ACT

Section 121(1) of the Succession Act 1965 (the "1965 Act") applies to "a disposition of property (other than a testamentary disposition or a disposition to a purchaser) under which the beneficial ownership of the property vests in possession in the donee within three years before the death of the person who made it or on his death or later." It follows then that any disposition of property other than by way of a gift by will or a disposition to a purchaser that is made by a person three years before his death for the purpose of defeating or substantially diminishing the share of his spouse or civil partner, whether as a legal right or on intestacy, or the intestate share of any of his or her children, or of leaving any of his or her children insufficiently provided for, may be deemed in whole or in part to be a devise or bequest made by him by will and to form part of his estate, and to have had no other effect. Therefore, the type of disposition envisaged by s.121(1) is a voluntary gift of property that vests in possession in the donee made within a period of three years before the donor's death.

In *LC (a minor) v HS* [2014] IEHC 32, after the plaintiff/appellant became aware that the defendant was a joint owner with WS of lands at locations referred to as "B" and "C" on 31 August 2009 and four years after WS's death issued a second set of proceedings in the Circuit Court entitled a Succession Law Civil Bill claiming inter alia:

> (i) That the deceased had at various stages throughout his life acquired certain properties including (a) the family home and lands at a specified location "B" and (b) farmhouse and lands at a separate specified location "C", which were put in the joint names of the deceased and the Defendant hereto.
> (ii) That upon the death of the deceased the entire beneficial ownership of the said properties vested in the Defendant and as such was a "disposition" of property within the meaning ascribed by s.121 of the Succession Act 1965; and
> (iii) That the effects and purpose of the said dispositions was an attempt to defeat or diminish the Plaintiff's share in the said estates.

The family home and lands of the defendant and the deceased WS at location "B" were purchased in 1985 in the joint names of the defendant and WS as joint tenants, more than 15 years prior to the birth of the appellant/plaintiff. In 2003, the couple entered into a contract to purchase a parcel of land at location "C". The purchase was financed by a loan in the sum of €380,000 and a further private loan from the deceased's brother in the sum of €450,000. The charge of €380 appeared as a burden on the folio when the property was first purchased and when the property was transferred to the defendant following the death of her husband. The purchase was made within three years of the death of WS.

In her judgment Clark J. found that:

> "The only live issue was whether the purchase of the farmhouse and lands at location 'C' in 2003 was a disposition made to defeat the rights of the infant Plaintiff within the meaning of Section 121 of the Succession Act 1965."

When referring to s.121 she stated that:

> "Before any disposition can be made the subject of an order under Section 121 the court must be satisfied that the disposition was made for the purpose of defeating or substantially diminishing the share of the disponer's spouse or civil partner or the intestate share of any of his children, or of leaving any of his children insufficiently provided for. If the Court is so satisfied, it may order that the disposition shall be deemed, for the purposes of Parts VI and IX of the Act of 1965, to be a devise or bequest made by him by will and to form part of his estate, and to have no other effect."

She had to decide whether the purchase or acquisition of the land at location "C" in their joint names and subject to a mortgage was a disposition within the meaning of s.121. She found that by applying the ordinary construction rules, in giving the natural meaning to words, an acquisition or purchase is not a disposition. The two words have opposite meanings and "an acquisition of property by purchase/gift/inheritance cannot equate to the divesting of the beneficial ownership of property which involves the sale/transfer/gift by will or a *donatio mortis causa*." The intention of s.121 "is to prevent the divesting of property in anticipation of death specifically to prevent the surviving spouse and children from enjoying the benefit of the deceased's estate."

Clark J. concluded that "as the acquisition of property is not a disposition, it follows that the acquisition of property at location 'C' in joint names from borrowed funds is not a disposition within the meaning of s.121," and the appellant/plaintiff was not therefore entitled to an order under s.121 of the 1965 Act, and the court "cannot grant an order under Section 117 as the deceased father of the Plaintiff cannot be construed as a testator in the absence of an order under Section 121."

THE CONSTRUCTION OF WILLS

As was stated by Laffoy J. in *In Re Rafter* [2012] IEHC 239:

> "The primary duty of the Court in construing a will is to ascertain and give effect to the intention of the testator."

When attempting to ascertain and give effect to a testator's intention derived from the language used by him or her the court may apply the Lowry Principles as set out in *Heron v Ulster Bank Ltd* [1974] N.I. 44 at 52–53, and admit extrinsic evidence under s.90 of the Succession Act 1965 (the "1965 Act") "to show the intention of the testator and to assist in the construction of, or to explain any contradiction in the will." (*Rowe v Law* [1978] I.R. 55; see also *O'Connell v Bank of Ireland* [1998] 2 I.R. 596)

In *Mullen v Mullen* [2014] IEHC 407 Cregan J., when construing the provisions of a will and in particular the purport of a devise, referred to ss.89, 90, 91 and 99 of the 1965 Act as being the relevant statutory provisions and the decision of Laffoy J. in *In Re Rafter* [2012] IEHC 239 to show how the court seeks to construe a will and to give effect to the intention of the testator by reference to the principles set out by Lowry L.C.J. in *Heron v Ulster Bank Ltd* as follows at para.14:

> "The primary duty of the Court in construing a will is to ascertain and give effect to the intention of the testator. In recent years the High Court in this jurisdiction has adopted the guidance on the construction of wills generally given by Lowry LCJ in *Heron v Ulster Bank Ltd.* [1974] N.I. 44, as appears from *Howell v Howell* [1992] 1 I.R. 290 (Carroll J.), *Corrigan v Corrigan* [2007] IEHC 367 (McGovern J.), and, most recently, *O'Donohue v O'Donohue* [2011] IEHC 511 (Gilligan J.). Lowry LJC stated as follows:
>
> 'I consider that, having read the whole will, one may with advantage adopt the following procedure:
>
> 1. Read the immediately relevant portion of the will as a piece of English and decide, if possible, what it means.
> 2. Look at the other material parts of the will and see whether they tend to confirm the apparently plain meaning of the immediately relevant portion or whether they suggest the need for modification in order to make harmonious sense of the whole, or, alternatively, whether an ambiguity in the immediately relevant portion can be resolved.
> 3. If the ambiguity persists, have regard to the scheme of the will and consider what the testator was trying to do.
> 4. One may at this stage have resort to rules of construction, where applicable, and aids, such as the presumption of early vesting and the presumption against intestacy and in favour of equality.
> 5. Then see whether any rule of law prevents a particular interpretation from being adopted.
> 6. Finally, and, I suggest, not until the disputed passage has been exhaustively studied, one may get help from the opinions of other courts and judges on similar words, rarely as binding precedents, since it has been well said that 'no will has a twin brother'".

Cregan J. also referred to the judgment of Laffoy J. in *In Re Rafter* [2012] IEHC 239 for her comments on s.90 of the 1965 Act and in particular para.11 where she stated that:

> "The main focus of both counsel for the plaintiff and counsel for the defendant in their helpful written and oral submissions was on s.90. The basis on which the Court can admit extrinsic evidence under s.90 is succinctly summarised in the following passage from the judgment of

Keane J., as he then was, with whom the other Judges of the Supreme Court concurred, in *O'Connell v Bank of Ireland* [1998] 2 I.R. 596 (at p. 611):

> 'There are thus two conditions which must be met before such evidence is admissible: it must assist in the construction of the will or resolve a contradiction and it must, in either event, show what the intention, in the particular context, of the testator was.'"

In *Mullen v Mullen* [2014] IEHC 407, the testatrix by her will left various gifts of land to her sons and daughters and a gift of a small plot of land of not more than half an acre to her grandson, James Mullen Jnr, the plaintiff. She died on 24 May 2012 without having altered or revoked her last will. In her will she appointed the defendant James Mullen, her son, to be her executor. A dispute arose between the plaintiff and the executor of the will as to the meaning of the devise to James Mullen Jnr.: James Mullen Jnr. claimed that he was entitled to the property in the gift; the defendant on behalf of the estate claimed that the gift had lapsed and/or had failed.

In his judgment, Cregan J. set out below the terms of the will in full. It was dated 19 July 2004 and it provided as follows:

> "This is the last will and testament of me, Elizabeth Mullen (otherwise Betsy Mullen) of Fahy, Clifden, County Galway. I revoke all former wills and testamentary dispositions heretofore made by me.
>
> I appoint my son James Mullen to be executor of this my will subject to the payment of my lawful debts funeral and testamentary expenses.
>
> I give devise and bequeath as follows:
>
> My house and garden at Fahy, Clifden to my three daughters,
>
> Lily Kane of Dawros Letterfrack
>
> Rita McNamara of Tullyvoheen, Clifden
>
> And Margaret Pride of Letternoosh, Clifden
>
> In equal shares.
>
> The field opposite my house at Fahy, Clifden as to one half thereto to my son, Marty Mullen and as to the other half thereof to my son Thomas. They are each to have the half nearest to their respective houses.
>
> To my executor and son James Mullen the land upon which his house stands at Fahy, Clifden together with the well and water supply servicing same which comes from adjoining lands and also I give devise and bequeath to him the lands running to the sea which he presently occupies.
>
> I also give devise and bequeath to my son, James Mullen the site of the

> house my late husband James Mullen senior was born in which is situated at Fahy, Clifden and is half way between the Low Road and the Sky Road.
>
> I also give, devise and bequeath to James Mullen Junior., son of my son John, a small plot or piece of land of not more than half an acre to make up the site of his proposed new house should he require same.
>
> All the rest, residue and remainder of my property of every nature and kind wheresoever situate I give devise and bequeath to my three sons John, Marty and Thomas in equal shares.
>
> I direct that my executor appoint the firm of Black and Co. Solicitors of 28 South Frederick Street, Dublin 2 to act in the administration of my estate and that they be paid their proper professional fees and expenses for so doing.
>
> In witness whereof I have herewith signed this my last will and testament this 19th day of July, 2004.
>
> Elizabeth Mullen (Betsy)
>
> Signed by the testatrix"

Cregan J. then singled out the devise at issue:

> "I also give devise and bequeath to James Mullen Junior, son of my son John, a small plot or piece of land of not more than half an acre to make up the site of his proposed new house should he require same."

When applying Principle 1 of the Lowry Principles, viz "[r]ead the immediately relevant portion of the will as a piece of English and decide, if possible, what it means", Cregan J. found that the words of the testatrix were clear—she wanted to devise a small piece of land to her grandson, James Mullen Jnr, which was not to exceed half an acre. It was to be available to him if he should require it. The purpose of the bequest was to permit him "to make up the site". Cregan J. had no doubt "that the intention of the testator was, at all times (i.e. at the time of the making of her will and thereafter up until the date of her death), to make a bequest to her grandson of up to half an acre should he require it to make up the site."

According to Principle 2 of the Lowry Principles, one must "[l]ook at the other material parts of the will and see whether they tend to confirm the apparently plain meaning of the immediately relevant portion or whether they suggest the need for modification in order to make harmonious sense of the whole, or, alternatively, whether an ambiguity in the immediately relevant portion can be resolved", and according to Principle 3 of the Lowry Principles, "[i]f the ambiguity persists, have regard to the scheme of the will and consider what the testator was trying to do". The plaintiff submitted that the court should have regard to other provisions in the will and/or the general scheme of the will and that they support the conclusion set out above. By Principle 4 of the Lowry Principles, "[o]ne may at this stage have resort to rules of construction, where applicable, and aids, such as the presumption of early vesting and the presumption against intestacy and in favour of equality". Section 99 of the 1965 Act provides that:

> "If the purport of a devise or bequest admits of more than one interpretation, then, in case of doubt, the interpretation according to which the devise or bequest will be operative shall be preferred."

By reference to the Lowry Principles and s.99 of the 1965 Act, Cregan J. concluded that "the intention of the testator is clear from the words of the will." He stated:

> "However insofar as there is any doubt in the matter, and in particular insofar as the defendant sought to lay considerable emphasis on the ambiguity of the phrases, "proposed new house" and "to make up the site" the consequence of the defendant's interpretation is that the bequest would not be operative. In those circumstances, even if the bequest did admit of more than one interpretation, I am of the view, applying the statutory principle, that the interpretation according to which the bequest would be operative should be preferred. I would therefore conclude that the statutory presumption in favour of the validity of the bequest applies in this case."

Under s.90 of the 1965 Act extrinsic evidence shall be admissible to show the intention of the testator and to assist in the construction of the will.

Cregan J. stated that by virtue of s.90:

> "I can have regard to extrinsic evidence. In my view all the extrinsic evidence in this case, which assists in the construction of the will or which shows the intention of the testator, points to the conclusion that the testatrix intended to devise the small parcel of land (being her garden) to her grandson. This is so because:
>
> a. She lived beside her grandson, his wife and their small children and was aware of his family circumstances.
> b. She was aware of the difficulty of the site and the fact that there was no suitable area on the site for the plaintiff to have a garden.
> c. She gave full consent to the plaintiff to use that part of her land which he did use as a garden for his children. She completely encouraged him in this regard.
> d. She did this in the full knowledge from 2005 until 2012 when she died that the plaintiff's house had been built and was being occupied. She also did so in the full knowledge that the house lacked a garden and that with young children the plaintiff needed a garden for the children to play in safely and without any serious risk that they might suffer an accident."

Therefore, "the bequest to the plaintiff is valid under the will, that the testatrix did intend to confer on the plaintiff the right to select a plot of land of up to half an acre from her lands immediately adjoining those of the plaintiff and that the plaintiff is entitled to a declaration in those terms."

THE SURVIVAL OF CAUSES OF ACTION FOR THE BENEFIT OF A DECEASED PERSON'S ESTATE

The survival of causes of action for the benefit of a deceased person's estate is governed by s.7, which is in Pt II of the Civil Liability Act 1961 (the "1961 Act"). Section 7(1) provides that:

> On the death of a person on or after the date of the passing of this Act all causes of action (other than excepted causes of action) vested in him shall survive for the benefit of his estate.

Section 7(2) provides that:

> Where, by virtue of subsection (1) of this section, a cause of action survives for the benefit of the estate of a deceased person, the damages recoverable for the benefit of the estate of that person shall not include exemplary damages, or damages for any pain or suffering or personal injury or for loss or diminution of expectation of life or happiness.

As regards the "excepted causes of action" in s.7(1) of the 1961 Act, Laffoy J. in *Doyle v Doyle* [2014] IESC 69 stated that:

> "The expression 'excepted causes of action', which appears in subs. (1), is defined in s.6 of the 1961 Act, which has been amended most recently by the Defamation Act 2009. The appellant's cause of action does not come within that definition which, in reality, now only captures an action for seduction."

In *Doyle v Dunne* [2014] IESC 69, Laffoy J. in her judgment for the Supreme Court stated that the primary issue to be determined was whether "the Court has any jurisdiction to adjudicate on the appeal having regard to the nature of the appellant's cause of action and her claim against the respondent."

The appellant sought to set aside the judgment and order of the High Court made on 20 December 2013 and also sought that the Supreme Court should:

> (a) order a new trial on all issues in the High Court, or
> (b) enter judgment for the appellant and assess the damages to which the appellant was entitled.

The appeal was given priority by the court because the appellant was terminally ill but before the case was fully heard she died of her illness. Her death was unrelated to the personal injuries which were alleged to form the basis of her claim in the proceedings.

Laffoy J. in her judgment for the Supreme Court stated that:

> "The position of the respondent at the resumed hearing was not that the appellant's cause of action, such as was vested in her at the date of her death, did not survive for the benefit of her estate in accordance with subs. (1) of s.7. Rather, the position of the respondent was that, having regard

to subs. (2), no damages were recoverable for the benefit of the estate of the appellant, because the only damages claimed in the proceedings were excluded from recoverability by virtue of subs. (2), being damages for pain, suffering and personal injury. In particular, it was emphasised on behalf of the respondent that there was no claim for special damages.

She continued:

> "The situation which has arisen in this case is governed by s.7 of the Act of 1961. By virtue of subs. (1), it is undoubtedly the case that the appellant's cause of action survived her death for the benefit of her estate. However, subs. (2) of s.7 precludes the estate of the appellant from recovering damages for any pain or suffering or personal injury. The reality of this case is that the appellant's claim, as pleaded and as pursued in the High Court, whether founded on alleged negligence, breach of duty or trespass to the person, was in its entirety a claim for unliquidated general damages for pain, suffering and personal injury. There is no other component for remedy or relief in the appellant's claim, whether for special damages or otherwise. In the circumstances, when regard is had to the s.7(2) preclusion, there is nothing by way of remedy or relief left in the claim for this Court to adjudicate on or to remit to the High Court."

Accordingly, applying s.7 of the 1961 Act, Laffoy J. dismissed the appeal.

THE SURVIVAL OF A CAUSE OF ACTION AGAINST A DECEASED PERSON'S ESTATE

Section 8(1) of the Civil Liability Act 1961 (the "1961 Act") provides that on the death of a person on or after the date of the passing of the Act, all causes of action subsisting against him shall survive against his estate. Section 9(2) of the 1961 Act goes on to provide that no proceedings "shall be maintainable in respect of any cause of action whatsoever which has survived against the estate of a deceased person unless either – (a) proceedings against him in respect of that cause of action was commenced within the relevant period and were pending at the date of death, or (b) proceedings are commenced in respect of that action within the relevant period or within the period of two years after his death, whichever period first expires." The relevant period mentioned in s.9(2) means the period of limitation prescribed by the Statute of Limitations 1957. Until the judgment of O'Keeffe J. in *Prendergast v McLaughlin* [2009] IEHC 250, there were two differing views as to whether ss.8 and 9 of the 1961 Act applied to causes of action based in equity for which no period of limitation is prescribed in the Statute of Limitations 1957 (the "1957 Act"), and also, on the point in time at which such causes of action were maintainable and became subject to the period of limitation provided by s.9(2)(b). In *Corrigan v Martin*, unreported, High Court, 13 March 2006, Fennelly J. stated that s.8(1) of the 1961 Act governed all causes of action coming into existence right up to the point of death itself, and when referring to s.9(2)(a) and (b), that an action cannot be maintained unless the plaintiff can bring himself within one of the two sub-paragraphs. This is not affected by the fact that there is no "relevant period" for the purposes of the

Statute of Limitations. He went on to say that he was satisfied that "the correct interpretation of the plaintiff's cause of action in the light of the section is that the obligation of the deceased was to perform the contract during his lifetime and not at the moment of his death. Hence, the cause of action was complete immediately before his death. It is unnecessary to decide how long before his death." Barron J. in *Reidy v McGreevy*, unreported, High Court, 3 December 1986, held the view that whether a cause of action based on a constructive trust is one available against the deceased, and so capable of being barred after the lapse of two years from the date of his death, is dependent upon the facts of the case. But whatever the facts, "the claim could not be maintained until the death of the testator because it could not have been ascertained until then" that he had failed to honour his promise. But he added that if the testator had repudiated his promise in his lifetime, this would have given rise to a cause of action at that stage. O'Keeffe J. in *Prendergast v McLaughlin* had the option of choosing either the analytical approach adopted by Fennelly J. in *Corrigan v Martin* or the equitable approach by Barron J. in *Reidy v McGreevy*, and apparently, he preferred the reasoning of Fennelly J.

In *Prendergast v McLaughlin* [2009] IEHC 250, O'Keeffe J. found that the plaintiff's cause of action was primarily one based in contract or quasi-contract for breach of the deceased's promise to devise the lands to him. The breach could only have occurred during the lifetime of the deceased and the cause of action therefore accrued before the death of the deceased. "I also conclude, based on the agreed facts that the plaintiff's claim can alternatively be based on promissory estoppel or equity. As such it is not a claim arising after the death of the deceased but a claim subsisting at death, namely, the failure of the deceased to execute a will bequeathing the lands to the plaintiff during his lifetime. I do accept that the evidence relating to such cause of action emerged after death, the plaintiff's cause of action in contract, quasi-contract or in equity subsisted during the lifetime of the deceased. I reject the plaintiff's submission to the contrary." He preferred the reasoning of Fennelly J. in *Corrigan v Martin* to that of Barron J. in *Reidy v McGreevy*. In *Corrigan v Martin*, Fennelly J. analysed in detail the interplay between ss.8 and 9 of the Act. There was no such analysis or examination of the two sections in *Reidy v McGreevy*. Referring to s.8(1) which applies to all cause of actions, Fennelly J. stated that: "The Oireachtas intended that provision to apply to all causes of action coming into existence right up to the point of death itself. It is unreal and almost metaphysical to distinguish between causes of action existing immediately prior to the death and those which matured on the death itself." When a cause of action has survived the estate of the deceased, s.9(2) provided two alternative periods in paras (a) and (b), and (a) did not apply as no action was pending the date of death of the deceased. The period provided under s.9(b) is the earlier of the relevant period, being the expiry of the limitation period under the provisions contained in the 1957 Act, or alternatively the period of two years from the date of death of the deceased. As the deceased died on 28 August 2003, proceedings ought to have been issued by 27 August 2005, the period of two years after the death of the deceased. The proceedings did not issue until 25 July 2006, and accordingly, O'Keeffe J. held that the plaintiff's claim whether it arose in contract, quasi-contract or in equity was statute-barred.

In *Cavey v Cavey* [2014] IESC 16, the deceased testator was the father of each of the parties to this appeal who died on the 18 December 2006. The defendants/

respondents were appointed executors in his last will and testament. Probate of the will was granted to the executors on 13 March 2008. The plaintiff/appellant initially commenced a first set of proceedings under s.117 of the Succession Act 1965 on 12 December 2008. The first proceedings were heard by Laffoy J. on 23 April 2009, and were dismissed. The plaintiff/appellant appealed that decision to the Supreme Court but subsequently withdrew his appeal on 23 July 2010. Four days later, on 27 July 2010, he commenced second proceedings. The substance of his claim in the second proceedings arose out of a representation made to him by both of his parents to the effect that he would inherit the family home. He claimed to have acted on that representation and that under the doctrine of promissory estoppel he was entitled to relief.

The executors brought a motion before the High Court seeking to have the proceedings dismissed under alternatively:

(a) an allegation that the proceedings were an abuse of process in accordance with the rule in *Henderson v Henderson* (1843) 3 Hare 100, and/or
(b) that the proceedings must invariably fail as being statute-barred having regard to the provisions of s.9 of the 1961 Act.

Herbert J. held that the proceedings were statute-barred under the provisions of the 1961 Act; that they were, therefore, bound to fail; and that it was appropriate to exercise the court's inherent jurisdiction to dismiss the proceedings on that basis. He did not, in those circumstances, consider it necessary to determine whether the proceedings might also be considered to be an abuse of process under *Henderson v Henderson*. The plaintiff/appellant appealed to the Supreme Court against that decision.

In his judgment for the Supreme Court, Clark J. stated that:

> "Assuming that all the necessary ingredients for a promissory estoppel can be established, then it follows that there was a legal obligation on a person, during their life, to make a will which complies with the promise made. While it is true that the person can make such a will at any time before death, it none the less follows that it is a failure to act during the lifetime of the deceased which gives rise to the cause of action."

Clark J., having referred to *Corrigan v Martin*, unreported, High Court, Fennelly J., 13 March 2006; *Reidy v McGreevy*, unreported, High Court, Barron J., 3 December 1986, and *Prendergast v McLaughlin* [2009] IEHC 250, stated that:

> "It seems to me that a significant distinction is made in s.9(2), so far as claims against an estate are concerned, between a cause of action which results from an act or omission of the deceased, on the one hand, and a cause of action which may exist against those in charge of the administration of the estate of the deceased, on the other. If Mr. Cavey had a cause of action in promissory estoppel at all, it can only be because he might be able to establish that his late father was in breach of a legally enforceable promise in respect of bequeathing the family home to him. If such could be established

> it would be a failure, during his life, on the part of his late father to make an appropriate will to comply with his promise that gives rise to the claim."

He continued:

> "It seems to me that such a claim necessarily comes within the scope of the phrase '*a claim surviving against the estate of the deceased*' even if it is true that a deceased could have avoided such a claim being capable of being brought by complying with their promise to bequeath the relevant property up to the moment before their death."

He concluded:

> "I am, therefore, satisfied that, on a proper interpretation of the effect of s.9 of the 1961 Act, a claim in promissory estoppel arising out of an enforceable promise by a person to leave property by will, is a claim which can properly be characterised as one which survives against the estate of that person in the sense in which that term is used in the section. It follows that the claim brought in these proceedings could only be maintained by Mr. Cavey if it had been commenced within two years of his late father's death. The claim not having been so commenced, it is clearly statute barred. It follows that Mr. Cavey's proceedings are bound to fail on that basis and should be dismissed."

SETTING ASIDE CAVEATS

The court may set aside a caveat where it is shown that the caveator had no interest in the estate of the deceased either under the will or intestacy. (*In the Estate of O' Connell* [2014] IESC 55; see also *Re Nevin* [1997] IEHC 209) In *Re Nevin* [1997] IEHC 209, Shanley J. held that to sustain an allegation that a caveat was entered for a vexatious purpose "the court must be satisfied that the lodgement of a caveat amounted to conduct in all the circumstances no reasonable person could properly treat as bona fide". He stated that:

> "The court has an inherent jurisdiction to set aside a caveat where the caveat has been vexatiously lodged; see the *Goods of Norris* Ir.R. 1 Eq. 334. Equally, the court has jurisdiction to set aside a caveat where the caveator has no interest: see *Nugent v Nugent* 8 Ir. Jur. (n.s.) 52."

The purpose of a caveat is merely to ensure that no grant will issue without notice to the caveator but the entering of one does not restrain the court from making a grant, especially where the caveator has received notice of the application for a grant. Where the court is satisfied that a caveat was not lodged for a vexatious purpose and the person lodging it had an interest in the estate of the deceased, and even though there is some doubt about who will eventually become entitled to a full grant, the court may make an interim limited grant *ad colligenda bona* only for the purpose of preserving the caveator's interest.

In *In the Estate of O'Connell* [2014] IESC 55, the deceased, a retired solicitor, died on 6 March 2008 at the age of 76. At the time of his death, he was a ward of court and had been for a number of years. He executed a will on 1 March 2004 and appointed his nephew as his executor. After making a number of dispositions, the principal beneficiary and residuary legatee under the will was the executor. On the day after the deceased's death, Patrick Reen and Eugene O'Brien lodged caveats in the District Probate Office in Cork in respect of the estate of the deceased. However, neither of them set out his interest in the estate of the deceased, and because of this the executor was successful in his application to the High Court to have the caveats set aside. Both caveators appealed the High Court orders setting aside the caveats. Both appeared in person before the Supreme Court. During the initial stages of the hearing Eugene O'Brien indicated that he would not pursue his appeal against the order setting aside the caveat lodged by him in the estate of the deceased. Patrick Reen pursued his appeal from the order of the High Court setting aside the caveat lodged by him.

In her judgment for the Supreme Court, Dunne J. stated that:

> "Nevertheless, it is important to point out that there is a difference between a claim arising under the estate of an individual, either on intestacy or on foot of the will of a deceased person, and a claim against the estate of a deceased person. It is not appropriate for a person with a claim against an estate to lodge a caveat in respect of that estate. Such a person has no interest *in* the estate. A caveat, as explained by Shanley J. in the decision referred to above, can be lodged in circumstances where the caveator has an interest in the estate of the deceased. Mr. Reen has no interest in the estate of Mr. O'Connell. Accordingly, it is impossible to see any error in the order made by the learned trial judge striking out the caveat in respect of the estate of Mr. O'Connell."

Safety and Health

MANUFACTURING STANDARDS

Batteries and Accumulators The European Union (Batteries and Accumulators) Regulations 2014 (S.I. No. 283 of 2014) (the "2014 Regulations") implemented: (a) Directive 2006/66/EC on batteries and accumulators and waste batteries and accumulators (the "2006 Directive") as amended by Directive 2008/103/EC; and (b) Commission Decision 2009/603 establishing requirements for registration of producers of batteries and accumulators.

Of note is that reg.2 of the 2014 Regulations contains a "general purpose clause", which provides a useful summary of its scope and extent. Regulation 2 provides:

> The purposes for which these Regulations are made include—
>
> (a) the purpose of giving effect to the provisions of European Parliament and Council Directive 2006/66/EC on batteries and accumulators and waste batteries and accumulators as amended by European Parliament and Council Directive 2008/103/EC and Commission Decision 2009/603/EC and having regard to the environmental impact of transport, to take necessary measures to maximise the separate collection of waste batteries and accumulators and to minimise the disposal of batteries and accumulators as mixed municipal waste in order to achieve a high level of recycling for all waste batteries and accumulators,
>
> (b) ensuring that batteries or accumulators—
>
> (i) that do not meet the requirements of the [2006] Directive are not placed on the market on and from 26 September 2008 onwards or, as appropriate,
>
> (ii) placed on the market on and from 26 September 2008 onwards that do not meet the requirements of the Directive are withdrawn from it,
>
> (c) exempting collection points in receipt of waste portable batteries and accumulators from the registration or permit requirements of Directive 2006/12/EC or Council Directive 91/689/EEC of 12 December 1991 on hazardous waste, and
>
> (d) enabling the submission of National Implementation Reports, concerning measures taken to encourage developments affecting the impact of batteries and accumulators on the environment, in particular—
>
> (i) developments, including voluntary steps taken by producers, reducing quantities of heavy metals and other hazardous substances contained in batteries and accumulators,
>
> (ii) new recycling and treatment techniques,

(iii) economic operators' participation in environmental management schemes, and
(iv) measures taken to promote waste prevention, every three years in accordance with the provisions of Article 22 of the Directive.

The 2014 Regulations thus impose obligations on persons who supply batteries to the Irish market, whether as retailers, importers or manufacturers, to ensure that the batteries comply with the manufacturing standards in Directive 2006/66/EC (which repealed and replaced Directive 91/157/EC). They also promote and facilitate the achievement of targets for the collection, treatment, recycling and disposal of waste batteries in an environmentally sound manner in the 2006 Directive. An exemption from these obligations is available to persons who participate in a scheme for the collection, treatment, recycling and disposal of waste batteries in an environmentally sound manner operated by an approved body, such as Repak.

The 2014 Regulations also revoked and replaced (with savings) the Waste Management (Batteries and Accumulators) Regulations 2008 (S.I. No. 268 of 2008), as amended by the Waste Management (Batteries and Accumulators) (Amendment) Regulations 2008 (S.I. No. 556 of 2008) and the European Union (Batteries and Accumulators) (Amendment) Regulations 2012 (S.I. No. 529 of 2012).

The European Union (Batteries and Accumulators) (Amendment) Regulations 2014 (S.I. No. 349 of 2014), which were signed on 24 July 2014, inserted reg.3(3) into the 2014 Regulations (S.I. No. 283 of 2014) so that they came into effect on 30 July 2014. As the 2014 Regulations (S.I. No. 283 of 2014) did not contain any provision on their commencement, they had actually come into effect on the date they had been signed, 14 June 2014, and it is not clear therefore what effect S.I. No. 349 of 2014 purported to have in terms of their enforceability between 14 June 2014 and 30 July 2014. No doubt this is largely a moot point.

Explosives Precursors The European Union (Marketing and Use of Explosives Precursors) Regulations 2014 (S.I. No. 611 of 2014) (the "2014 Regulations") provide for the administrative arrangements required to give effect to Regulation 98/2013 (the "2013 EU Regulation") on the marketing and use of explosives precursors. Explosives precursors are substances or mixtures which can be misused for the illicit manufacture of explosives.

The 2014 Regulations restrict access by the general public, as defined in the 2013 EU Regulation, to certain chemical substances, of certain concentrations, by requiring a Garda Restricted Explosives Precursor Certificate for the introduction into the State, acquisition, possession or use of the substances listed in Annex I to the EU Regulation. The 2014 Regulations also outline the obligations of economic operators if they intend to make these particular substances, above a certain concentration level, available to the general public. The 2014 Regulations also require the reporting of any suspicious transactions, significant disappearances or theft of the substances listed in both Annex I and Annex II of the EU Regulation, to a designated Garda national contact point. They also set out the offences and penalties associated with a breach of the Regulations. The penalties on summary conviction are a class A fine (maximum €5,000 fine) and/or imprisonment for a term not exceeding 12 months. On conviction on indictment, the penalties are a maximum fine of €20,000 and/or imprisonment for a term not exceeding three years.

The 2014 Regulations largely came into force on 31 December 2014. The only exception is reg.5(2) under which a member of the general public shall not possess or use a restricted explosives precursor unless he or she is the holder of a certificate that authorises such possession or, as the case may be, use, which comes into force on 3 March 2016.

Packaging The European Union (Packaging) Regulations 2014 (S.I. No. 282 of 2014) (the "2014 Regulations") implemented Directive 94/62 on packaging and packaging waste, as amended by Directive 2004/12/EC and Directive 2013/2/EC.

The 2014 Regulations provide that a producer may not supply packaging or packaged products to the Irish market unless the packaging concerned complies with specified essential requirements as to its nature and composition. They also provide for limits on the concentration levels of certain heavy metals in packaging.

Although not as extensive as the "general purpose" clause in the European Union (Batteries and Accumulators) Regulations 2014 (S.I. No. 283 of 2014), above, reg.2 of the Packaging Regulations 2014 provide a similar clause to the effect that:

> "The purposes for which these Regulations are made include the purpose of giving effect to provisions of European Parliament and Council Directive 94/62/EC of 20 December 1994 on packaging and packaging waste as amended by European Parliament and Council Directive 2004/12/EC of 11 February 2004 and Commission Directive 2013/2/EU of 7 February 2013 with a view to promoting the recovery and recycling of packaging waste."

The targets for the recovery and recycling of packaging waste that apply from their coming into force are as set out in reg.1(2): (a) a minimum of 60 per cent of packaging waste by weight is recovered; and (b) a minimum of 55 per cent of packaging waste by weight is recycled in total, including material specific recycling targets as follows: (i) 60 per cent by weight for glass, (ii) 60 per cent by weight for paper and board, (iii) 50 per cent by weight for metals, (iv) 22.5 per cent by weight for plastics, and (v) 15 per cent by weight for wood.

An exemption from certain obligations is available to major producers who participate in a packaging waste recovery scheme operated by an approved body, such as Repak.

The 2014 Regulations revoke and replace the Waste Management (Packaging) Regulations 2007 (S.I. No. 798 of 2007), as amended. Regulation 2 provided that the 2014 Regulations "shall come into operation on the day after the date on which notice of their making is published in the *Iris Oifigiúil*." That notice was published in *Iris Oifigiúil* of 20 June 2014.

Storage of human tissues and cells The European Communities (Quality and Safety of Human Tissues and Cells) (Amendment) Regulations 2014 (S.I. No. 209 of 2014) (the "2014 Regulations") amended the European Communities (Quality and Safety of Human Tissues and Cells) Regulations 2006 (S.I. No. 158 of 2006) (the "2006 Regulations") (*Annual Review of Irish Law 2006*, p.513) to give further effect to Regulation 596/2009, which amended Directive 2004/23/EC on setting standards of quality and safety for the donation, procurement, testing, processing, preservation, storage and distribution of human tissues and cells (implemented in the 2006 Regulations). The 2014 Regulations also implemented Directive 2006/17/

EC (the technical implementing Directive for Directive 2004/23/EC), as amended by Directive 2012/39/EC, as regards certain technical requirements for the donation, procurement and testing of human tissues and cells.

RADIOLOGICAL PROTECTION

Dissolution of RPII and transfer of functions to EPA; and ratification of 2005 Amendment to the Convention on the Physical Protection of Nuclear Material The Radiological Protection (Miscellaneous Provisions) Act 2014 (the "2014 Act") had two main objectives: first, to provide for the dissolution of the Radiological Protection Institute of Ireland (RPII) and to transfer its functions to the Environmental Protection Agency (EPA); and, secondly, to introduce the necessary statutory provisions to enable the State to ratify the 2005 Amendment to the Convention on the Physical Protection of Nuclear Material. The 2014 Act also provided for the updating of certain fines under the Radiological Protection Acts, updated the definition of "ionising radiation" to reflect the latest international standard and enabled the EPA, as successor to the RPII, to hold radioactive substances or irradiating apparatus necessary for the fulfilment of their functions without requiring a licence. The 2014 Act came into force generally on 30 July 2014: Radiological Protection (Miscellaneous Provisions) Act 2014 (Commencement) Order 2014 (S.I. No. 354 of 2014).

It was noted during the Oireachtas debates on the 2014 Act that, as part of the comprehensive spending review of all areas of public expenditure, in November 2011 the Government made a decision for the rationalisation of 48 State bodies and agencies and the critical review of another 46. The aim of the agency rationalisation programme was to reduce the number of State bodies. While the savings might not be significant, it was stated that the policy was to follow through on mergers and rationalisations unless there were strong evidence-based reasons for not doing so. The merger of the EPA and the RPII was considered as part of this critical review process. Following completion of the critical review in October 2012, the Minister for Public Expenditure and Reform announced that the EPA and the RPII were to merge, with a target date for the merger of summer 2014. In order to meet this target, the 2014 Act was enacted. It was also stated that there would be no diminution in the functions of either agency, or of the levels of service provided by them, arising from this merger. However, efficiencies following the merger of the EPA and the RPII were expected to give rise to reduction in certain costs over time.

It was concluded that the most efficient and economic means of merging the two bodies was dissolution of one and transfer of all of its functions, staff and assets to the other rather than dissolution of both and the creation of a new entity. This approach required significantly simpler legislation, costs less and ensures the least potential disruption to service delivery. It also made it easier to ensure ongoing maintenance of the functions of both agencies. Accordingly, it was decided to dissolve the RPII and transfer its functions, powers, staff and assets to the EPA, it being the larger of the two organisations.

As well as drafting the requisite enabling legislation in the form of the 2014 Act, extensive preparations and structures had been put in place to ensure a smooth and efficient merger process. These structures included a project management group and a project working group, comprising representatives of both organisations and the Department of the Environment, Community and Local Government. Both groups met on a monthly basis to ensure the merger was progressing, including administration, human resources, financial, accommodation, corporate and the environmental functions and operations of both agencies.

As provided for in the 2014 Act, the merger involved the following. First, on a day appointed by Ministerial Order, the RPII will be dissolved and its functions, powers and staff will transfer to the EPA. It will become a radiological protection office within the EPA, headed up by a director, taking the number of offices in the agency to five. The other four offices are: environmental enforcement; climate, licensing, research and resource use; environmental assessment; and communications and corporate services. The 2014 Act made the necessary repeals and amendments to all relevant enactments and statutory instruments to ensure that the EPA on behalf of the public has the requisite powers to assume the radiological protection role. In this regard, all pre-2014 Act functions of the RPII became functions of the EPA from the date of transfer.

Secondly, the 2014 Act enabled Ireland to ratify the 2005 amendment to the Convention on the Physical Protection of Nuclear Material (CPPNM). The initial CPPNM was signed in March 1980 and included all EU Member States as signatories. Ireland ratified the convention in September 1991, the terms of the treaty being provided for through the Radiological Protection Act 1991 (the "1991 Act"). The original CPPNM required that the international community afford certain levels of physical protection to nuclear materials, including during international transportation. It established a framework for cooperation among states that are party to it for the protection, recovery and return of stolen nuclear material and also set out a range of serious criminal offences for the misappropriation or harmful use of nuclear material, which participating states were to make punishable under national law or in respect of which offenders could be subject to extradition.

In July 2005, the states party to the CPPNM agreed the text of an amending treaty to strengthen its provisions, primarily by extending the provisions to require ratifying states to protect nuclear facilities and materials in peaceful domestic use, storage and transport. It also provides for extended co-operation between and among states to enable rapid measures to locate and recover stolen or smuggled nuclear material and to mitigate any radiological consequences of sabotage. The original CPPNM required that states introduce a series of offences relating to nuclear materials. These included unlawfully obtaining or demanding nuclear materials or using, or threatening to use, such materials in a manner that would cause death or serious injury to a person or substantial damage to property. The 2005 amendment to the CPPNM extended the range of criminal offences to include also offences relating to the sabotage of nuclear facilities, the smuggling of nuclear materials or facilitating, conspiring or directing offences that could lead to deliberate, malicious and dangerous dispersal of nuclear materials or release of radiation from a nuclear facility. It also required ratifying states to make it an offence to engage in any deliberate activity that releases radioactive materials, or radiation through the sabotage of a nuclear facility, in a manner that causes significant harm to the environment.

The 2005 amending treaty, when ratified, will create the Convention on the Physical Protection of Nuclear Material and Nuclear Facilities (CPPNMNF). It is regarded internationally as being significant for nuclear security and is expected to have a major impact in reducing the vulnerability of states to nuclear terrorism. It also increases nuclear security internationally by requiring common high standards of physical protection of nuclear material and facilities and that parties to the convention introduce a range of offences to prevent acts of terrorism involving nuclear material or against nuclear facilities and allows for international co-operation to meet such threats.

It was also noted during the Oireachtas debates on the 2014 Act that Ireland has been a key driver of non-proliferation since the 1960s. The then Minister for External Affairs, Frank Aiken, was the first minister to sign the Nuclear Non-Proliferation Treaty. The 2010 Nuclear Non-Proliferation Treaty (NPT) Review Conference called on all states party to the CPPNM to ratify the amendment to the convention as soon as possible. Ratification of the CPPNMNF is also regarded by the EU as a key element of Europe's nuclear security policy. However, the EU, through the Euratom Treaty, cannot ratify the treaty until all 28 Member States have first ratified it.

Section 3 of the 2014 Act provided for the repeal of those sections of the Radiological Protection Act 1991 (the "1991 Act") which enable the RPII to exist and function.

Part 2 of the 2014 Act provided for the dissolution of the RPII and the transfer of its functions, powers, staff and assets to the EPA. Sections 4 and 5 provided for the setting, by order, of the date of the dissolution of the RPII and that the RPII is formally dissolved on that day. This occurred on 1 August 2014: Radiological Protection (Miscellaneous Provisions) Act 2014 (Dissolution Day) Order 2014 (S.I. No. 360 of 2014). Section 6 transferred all functions of the RPII to the EPA and provided that from the date of dissolution and transfer, all references to the RPII in legislation will be construed as references to the EPA. Section 7 allowed for the transfer of lands and properties to the EPA. Sections 8 and 9 provided for legal continuity, transferring all rights, liabilities, and continuation of leases, licences and permissions granted by the RPII and liability for any legal matters occurring before the dissolution day to the EPA. Section 10 covered the transfer of functions, assets and liabilities to the EPA, put in place transitional measures for actions not completed and allowed for transfers of moneys and other financial assets from the RPII to the EPA. Section 11 provided for the preparation of the final RPII annual report and accounts by the EPA for presentation to the Minister. It required that the final accounts are audited and that the Minister present the final accounts and final report to the Oireachtas.

Sections 12 and 13 made provision for staff transferring from the RPII to the EPA. Section 12 allowed for the transfer of staff to the EPA, preserving their conditions of employment as they relate to remuneration. Section 13 ensured that the terms and conditions of employment of RPII staff relating to superannuation were preserved after transfer to the EPA. It protected the pensions of former staff of the RPII and of An Bord Fuinnimh Núicléigh, which preceded the RPII.

Section 14 provided for appointing the chief executive officer of the RPII as a director of the EPA for a transitional period up to 30 April 2016. Section 15 provided that licences, authorisations, approvals, certificates and codes of practice remain in effect after the dissolution day.

Part 3 of the 2014 Act made various amendments to ensure that the EPA could continue to carry out all of the functions of the RPII without interruption after the RPII was dissolved, and to provide the EPA with the necessary functional authority to do so. It consists of 16 sections and is divided into three chapters. The first chapter made the necessary amendments to the 1991 Act, the second chapter amended the Environmental Protection Agency Act 1992, and the third chapter amended other relevant legislation and statutory instruments.

Section 16 of the 2014 Act amended s.8 of the 1991 Act to ensure that codes of practice concerning radiological protection matters which are completed after the dissolution day comply with the standards laid out in the Environmental Protection Agency Act 1992 (the "1992 Act"). Section 17 amended s.9 of the 1991 Act to ensure that it refers only to radiological functions and not all of the functions of the EPA upon transfer as a consequence of the provisions of s.6 of the 2014 Act. Section 18 amended s.36 of the 1991 Act to remove a potential conflicting duplication between the confidentiality requirements laid out in the 1991 Act and the 1992 Act.

Section 19 of the 2014 Act amended s.3 of the 1992 Act by inserting definitions of "ionising radiation", "radioactive substance" and "radiological protection" for the purposes of the 1992 Act. Section 20 amended s.16 of the 1992 Act to ensure that RPII staff and radiological inspectors are indemnified while undertaking bona fide duties of the EPA upon their transfer. Section 21 amended s.19 of the 1992 Act to provide for a fifth director to be appointed to the EPA. Sections 22 and 23 amended ss.21 and 24 of the 1992 Act, respectively, to allow the Minister to appoint a person with radiological protection expertise to the selection committee that appoints directors to the EPA and that such radiological protection expertise may be a consideration in the appointment of EPA directors by the selection committee. Section 24 amended s.25 of the 1992 Act to ensure that the determination of licences issued under acts or orders dealing with radiological protection may be delegated to staff below director level after the RPII functions transfer to the EPA. Sections 25 and 26 amended ss.27 and 28 of the 1992 Act to allow that radiological protection expertise may be a basis for appointments to be made to the EPA advisory committee and that the advisory committee may provide advice on radiological protection matters.

Section 27 of the 2014 Act amended s.45 of the 1992 Act to disallow the transfer of radiological protection functions from the EPA to other public sector bodies, such as local authorities, using general devolutionary powers under this section available to the EPA in regard to its other functions. Section 28 amended s.53 of the 1992 Act to ensure there is no duplication between the principles and policies laid out in s.53 of the 1991 Act and similar provisions relating to radiological protection functions in the 1991 Act concerning the ability of the Minister to confer additional functions upon the EPA.

Section 29 amended s.55 of the 1992 Act to allow the Minister, other Ministers and the Government to seek advice or recommendations from the EPA in relation to radiological protection functions transferring from the RPII, as well as advice on environmental protection functions as currently provided for within that section. Section 30 amended s.66 of the 1992 Act to extend the entitlement of the EPA to undertake, or seek, quality assurance exercises or guarantees from laboratories undertaking radiological protection work, as well as from those engaging in environmental work as currently allowed by that section. Section 31 amended s.76 of the 1992 Act to ensure that the standards for production of EPA codes of practice apply to codes of practice produced in regard to radiological protection matters after the transfer of functions to the EPA. This does not affect or negate any codes of practice drawn up prior to the transfer and still in operation. Section 32 amended s.79 of the 1992 Act so that the Minister can give general directives on radiological protection matters in addition to environmental matters, as already provided for by s.79 of the 1992 Act.

Section 33 of the 2014 Act amended the Dumping at Sea Act 1996, as amended by the Foreshore and Dumping at Sea (Amendment) Act 2009, to resolve a question over the setting of minimum radiation levels of waste dumped at sea. Section 34 amended various regulations made under s.3 of the European Communities Act 1972 to transpose various EU directives and regulations to remove the RPII as a "public authority" from those under which the EPA was already a designated competent authority, following the dissolution of the RPII.

Part 4 of the 2014 Act put in place the necessary statutory provisions to enable Ireland to ratify the 2005 amendment to the CPPNM. Section 35 amended s.2 of 1991 Act by inserting a series of definitions relevant to the provisions which are necessary to meet the requirements of the amendment to the CPPNM. Section 36 amended s.8 of the 1991 Act to provide the EPA, as successor to the RPII, with responsibility for the exchange of information internationally regarding the protection of nuclear facilities as well as nuclear materials. Section 37 amended s.27 of the 1991 Act to make the EPA, as successor to the RPII, the competent authority for the CPPNM, as amended. Section 38 amended s.29 of the 1991 Act to provide the EPA, as successor to the RPII, with the authority to seek Garda Síochána assistance when making inspections pertaining to quality assurance schemes that relate to the physical security of nuclear materials and facilities.

Section 39 inserted ss.30(4B)–(4E) into the 1991 Act to require that conditions relating to security measures for nuclear materials and facilities are incorporated into the licences issued in respect of them. Section 40 inserted two new sections, ss.34A and 34B, into the 1991 Act. The new s.34A introduced a requirement to prepare contingency plans, setting out the procedures to be implemented in the event of any theft or loss of any nuclear materials in or over the State, or an accident relating to such material. The new s.34B established a quality assurance scheme with a view to providing confidence that specified arrangements necessary for the physical protection of nuclear materials and nuclear facilities are put in place.

Section 41 of the 2014 Act amended s.36 of the 1991 Act to require that individuals maintain the confidentiality of information received from another State under the CPPNMNF, unless duly authorised otherwise by that State. It also requires that any person with knowledge of security arrangements relating to nuclear facilities or nuclear materials should keep it confidential unless duly authorised. A breach of these confidentiality requirements is an offence.

Section 42 amended s.38 of the 1991 Act to incorporate new offences relating to criminal use of nuclear materials or sabotage of nuclear facilities. In particular, it makes criminal deliberate activities intended to cause significant damage to the environment. The new offences include: extending offences relating to nuclear material to include offences relating to the receipt, discharge or emitting of nuclear materials in order to harm people, property or the environment; being reckless as to whether the receipt, possession, use, transfer, alteration, disposal, dispersal, discharge, emission or introduction of nuclear material would harm people, property or the environment; the illegal import or export of nuclear material; sabotage of a nuclear facility in order to release ionising radiation or radioactive substances to cause harm to people, property or the environment; being reckless as to whether sabotage of a nuclear facility could cause such harm; threatening to use nuclear material to damage the environment; or threatening to sabotage a nuclear facility to compel any person, international body or the State to undertake any action.

Section 42 amended s.38 of the 1991 Act to update the definition of the word "steal" to accord with the definition in the Criminal Justice (Theft and Fraud Offences) Act 2001. Section 43 amended s.40 of the 1991 Act to increase the maximum level of fine payable in respect of serious offences, reflecting the provisions of the Fines Act 2010.

Part 5 of the 2014 Act contains a number of miscellaneous provisions. Section 44 amended s.2 of the 1991 Act to update the definition of "ionising radiation" to reflect standard international scientific definitions. Section 45 amended s.7 of the 1991 Act to provide a general function to the RPII to hold, use and dispose of nuclear devices without needing a licence. Section 46 amended s.3 of the Environmental Protection Agency Act 1992 to insert a definition of radioactive substances identical to that in the 1991 Act. Section 47 amended s.52 of the 1992 Act to provide a general function to the EPA to hold, use and dispose of nuclear devices without needing a licence. The Schedule to the 2014 Act contains the text of the 2005 amendment to the CPPNM.

SAFETY, HEALTH AND WELFARE AT WORK

Incorporation into Health and Safety Authority of Irish National Accreditation Board The principal purpose of the Industrial Development (Forfás Dissolution) Act 2014 (as discussed in the Commercial Law chapter, pp.56 and 59, above) was to give effect to the government decision to dissolve Forfás and to integrate its research and policy advisory functions into the Department of Jobs, Enterprise and Innovation. A consequential purpose was to incorporate into the Health and Safety Authority of the Irish National Accreditation Board (INAB) which had been established as a committee of Forfás.

The INAB is the national body with responsibility for the accreditation of laboratories, certification bodies and inspection bodies. Accreditation is the procedure by which an authoritative body gives formal recognition that a body or person is competent to carry out specific tasks. EU Member States have established a network of national accreditation bodies to ensure that the competence of all laboratories, inspection and certification bodies are assessed against the same principles. Accreditation plays an important role in guaranteeing the access of Irish products and services to both EU and worldwide markets. The demand for accreditation has increased significantly in recent times as national regulators continue to rely on conformity assessment as a mechanism to support the implementation of legislation and assure competence.

Prior to the changes effected by the 2014 Act, responsibility for accreditation in Ireland had been vested in Forfás. In practice, the accreditation function had been delegated to the INAB which was a committee of Forfás and had been supported by Forfás staff in the administration of its functions. The 2014 Act provided for the transfer of Forfás's accreditation functions and associated staff to the Health and Safety Authority (HSA) by amending the Safety, Health and Welfare at Work Act 2005 (the "2005 Act") (*Annual Review of Irish Law 2005*, pp.604–618), under which the HSA had been established. As a result, INAB was established as a committee of the HSA, mirroring the pre-2014 Act arrangements that applied to INAB within Forfás.

Part 7 of the 2014 Act deals with the INAB. Section 29 inserted a new s.33A into the 2005 Act, transferring the powers and functions of Forfás relating to accreditation to the Health and Safety Authority.

Section 31 of the 2014 Act provided for the transfer of relevant Forfás staff to the HSA, by inserting a new s.54A after s.54 of the 2005 Act, on terms and conditions of service relating to remuneration and superannuation no less favourable than those applying before the transfer.

Section 32 provides for an amendment to Pt 5 of the 2005 Act, by adding a new Ch.3 and adding a number of new sections, ss.56(A)–56(I). Section 56A provides for the committee established by the board of Forfás, known as the INAB, to become a committee of the HSA and sets out operational procedures for the INAB while the remaining sections deal with administrative arrangements to apply on transfer of functions. Section 56G provides for the HSA to establish an appeals board and related matters. Section 56H sets out the procedures in relation to the making of an appeal against a decision of the accreditation board, or the failure of the accreditation board to make a decision.

Section 36 inserted a new Schedule into the 2005 Act, providing for the INAB and associated procedural matters.

Prevention of Sharps Injuries in Healthcare Sector The European Union (Prevention of Sharps Injuries in the Healthcare Sector) Regulations 2014 (S.I. No. 135 of 2014) (the "2014 Regulations"), which came into force on 14 March 2014 on their signature by the Minister for Jobs, Enterprise and Innovation, implemented the 2010 EU Directive on Sharps, Directive 2010/32/EC (the "2010 Directive").

The 2010 Directive gave the full force of EU law to the 2009 Framework Agreement on Prevention from Sharp Injuries in the Hospital and Healthcare Sector (the "2009 Framework Agreement"). In accordance with art.155(2) of the Treaty on the Functioning of the European Union (TFEU), the 2009 Framework Agreement was adopted by means of a Directive, thus necessitating national transposing legislation. This may be contrasted with an "autonomous" or "soft law" Framework Agreement adopted under art.155 of TFEU, such as the Framework Agreement on Work-Related Stress 2004, which did not require national transposing legislation.

The 2010 Directive was due to be implemented in May 2013, so that under EU law it came into force on that date for all public sector employers to which it applies, notably (given its subject matter) the Health Service Executive (HSE). The effect of the 2014 Regulations therefore is that the 2010 Directive came into effect for all private sector employers to which it applies from 14 March 2014.

Risks from sharps injuries invoke constitutional right to life and to person under Article 40.3 The risks that arise from sharps injuries are one of the most common and serious risks to healthcare workers and have been shown to include actual cases of life-threatening and serious blood-borne infections, such as Hepatitis B and C and HIV. At least four healthcare workers in the UK have died in recent years from needlestick injuries. These real risks are noted in the wide literature in this area, including the HSE's 2012 *Guidelines for the Emergency Management of Injuries from Bloodborne Viruses and Infectious Diseases*, discussed below. The matters dealt with in the 2010 Directive therefore raise legal matters of the highest significance such as the constitutional right to life and to the person, to whose protection the State is committed under Art.40.3 of the Constitution. The right to life is also protected under the EU Charter of Fundamental Rights and the Council of Europe Convention on Human Rights and Fundamental Freedoms. This signifies the importance of the issues raised by the 2010 Directive and the need to ensure its effective transposition in Irish law.

It can be argued that all aspects of safety and health at work raise important issues, but it is notable that EU and national law on occupational safety and health range from dealing with relatively less significant matters such as the size of available workspace or the number of toilets per employee through to matters of medium but high occurrence risk to health such as seating and manual handling, all the way to the occurrence of high risks such as exposure to chemicals and to biological agents such as infectious disease in needles. This is worth noting because the 2010 Directive addresses matters that raise high risks to the right to life and the person that demonstrably have a constitutional dimension.

Overview of 2014 Regulations The 2014 Regulations impose specific risk assessment and control measures to protect employees in healthcare from the hazards and risks posed by sharps. They also require an appropriate response in the event of an incident occurring. The 2014 Regulations complement the general duties in the Safety, Health and Welfare at Work Act 2005 (the "2005 Act") (*Annual Review of Irish Law 2005*, pp.604–618) and the more specific duties on all employers under the Safety, Health and Welfare at Work (Biological Agents) Regulations 2013 (*Annual Review of Irish Law 2013*, pp.529–530). The Health and Safety Authority (HSA) has published a detailed *Guide to the European Union (Prevention of Sharps Injuries in the Healthcare Sector) Regulations 2014*, available at *hsa.ie*.

The 2014 Regulations define sharps as:

> objects or instruments necessary for the exercise of specific healthcare activities, which are able to cut, prick or cause injury or infection.

This includes equipment such as needles, blades (such as scalpels) and other sharp medical instruments.

The 2014 Regulations apply to all employers in the healthcare sector. As to employees this includes:

- cleaners in hospitals and other healthcare facilities such as nursing homes,
- dental nurses,
- dentists,
- home carers,
- medical practitioners (doctors),
- nurses,
- nursing auxiliaries and assistants, and
- paramedics.

The 2014 Regulations apply to students working in healthcare, self-employed persons in healthcare and any employees employed by organisations contracted to provide services for healthcare organisations.

Under the 2014 Regulations, a "healthcare employer" is an employer whose main activity is the managing, organising and provision of healthcare. The 2014 Regulations also apply to other employers who provide services to a healthcare employer, under the authority of a healthcare employer or in a healthcare employer's place of work. The duties on this employer only apply insofar as the employer has control over the relevant activities of their relevant employees.

A healthcare employer must also comply with the 2014 Regulations where any of its employees provide healthcare services in another employer's workplace or in the home of a patient.

Employers whose main activity is not the provision of healthcare but whose employees may work with sharps do not come within the scope of the 2014 Regulations (unless they are working on the premises of a healthcare employer who is subject to the 2014 Regulations). Therefore organisations such as schools and prisons are not subject to the 2014 Regulations even though they might employ medical staff. Those employers remain subject to the general duties in the 2005 Act and to other requirements, such as those in the Safety, Health and Welfare at Work (Biological Agents) Regulations 2013.

2010 Directive should have been implemented under the 2005 Act As already noted, the 2010 Directive was due to have been implemented in May 2013 and that, arising from its "direct effect" under EU law, its provisions have therefore already applied since May 2013 to all public sector healthcare employers in the State. It must be assumed that such employers, including, for example, the HSE, had put in place the arrangements that were proposed in the public consultation documents published prior to 2013. These documents uniformly proposed that the 2010 Directive would be transposed using the regulation-making power in the 2005 Act. Instead, the regulation-making powers in s.3 of the European Communities Act 1972 were used to implement the 2010 Directive.

There are a number of reasons why the 2010 Directive should have been implemented under the 2005 Act. These include that: (a) the 2010 Directive was made by reference to the general framework of EU law on safety and health at work, notably Directive 89/391, the 1989 Framework Directive, and a number of individual Directives under the Framework Directive; (b) the 2005 Act constitutes the national legislative framework on safety and health at work and has been used to date to transpose the EU Directives to which the 2010 Directive refers (see the discussion of s.58(10) of the 2005 Act, below); (c) in accordance with the Government's better regulation principles, the pre-2014 public consultation (including the Regulatory Impact Analysis (RIA)) on the transposition of the 2010 Directive had specified that the 2010 Directive would be transposed using the regulation-making power in the 2005 Act; and (d) pre-2014 Government policy documents had referred to the 2005 Act as the relevant statutory code that addresses the issue dealt with in the 2010 Directive.

As to (b), s.58(10) of the 2005 Act provides:

> The power to make regulations under this section includes power to make provision by regulations to give effect to either—

(*a*) any provision of the treaties of the European Communities, or
(*b*) any act adopted by an institution of the European Communities, which regulates any of the matters set out in Schedule 7.

The regulation-making power in s.58(10) of the 2005 Act therefore specifically includes power to give effect to either any provision of the EU treaties or any act adopted by any institution of the EU, which regulates any matter set out in Sch.7 to the 2005 Act (and which contains a non-exhaustive list of matters on which Regulations can be made). The specific reference to EU obligations in s.58(10) was to ensure that any Regulations which implemented EU Directives in this area (in particular those made under the Safety, Health and Welfare at Work Act 1989 (the "1989 Act") and carried over by s.4(4) of the 2005 Act) complied with the decisions of the Supreme Court in *Browne v Ireland* [2003] IESC 43, [2003] 3 I.R. 205 and *Kennedy v Attorney General* [2005] IESC 36, [2007] 2 I.R. 45. These decisions had held that, in the absence of an express statutory authorisation, Acts such as the 1989 Act could not be used to implement EU Directives. Thus, the 2010 Directive comes within the scope of s.58(10) of the 2005 Act.

The 2005 Act contains a clear and well-understood regulatory framework under which the HSA has been conferred with a set of enforcement powers such as improvement notices, prohibition notices, the ability to seek High Court closure orders and the "last resort" of criminal prosecution. Because the 2010 Directive was not implemented under the 2005 Act, the 2014 Regulations had to include a kind of new parallel set of HSA enforcement powers. Apart from the need to add to the length of the 2014 Regulations that this entailed for the statutory drafter, the details of the enforcement mechanisms varies from their counterparts in the 2005 Act.

Thus, reg.11 of the 2014 Regulations sets out powers of entry and search for HSA inspectors that overlap with those in s.64 of the 2005 Act, but because they are specific to needlestick injuries, they will no doubt require specific attention in order to ensure that the HSA's general protocols on inspection comply with the 2014 Regulations.

Regulation 12 of the 2014 Regulations confers on HSA inspectors the power to issue a "compliance notice." This is remarkably similar to the power to issue an improvement notice under s.66 of the 2005 Act, and it is not clear why a different title was used in the 2014 Regulations. There are also some differences in detail in the 2014 Regulations by comparison with the 2005 Act. For example, the related power in s.65 of the 2005 Act to issue a direction for an improvement plan was not included in the 2014 Regulations. As Regulations, as opposed to Bills that become Acts, are not debated in the Houses of the Oireachtas, we do not have the benefit of a public discussion of these differences between the regulatory regime in the 2005 Act and the regime in the 2014 Regulations.

In addition, the Oireachtas also enacted in s.78 of the 2005 Act a clear set of penalties for breach of safety and health duties, namely a maximum sentence of imprisonment of two years on conviction on indictment and/or a maximum fine of €3 million.

Article 2 of the 2010 Directive provides:

> Member States shall determine what penalties are applicable when national

> provisions enacted pursuant to this Directive are infringed. The penalties shall be effective, proportionate and dissuasive.

This is, of course, a relatively standard provision on penalties. Given as discussed above that the 2010 Directive clearly refers to the constitutional right to life and the person in Art.40.3, it is likely that any "penalties" may be at the higher end of the available spectrum under the 2005 Act.

Because the 2014 Regulations were made under s.3 of the European Communities Act 1972 (the "1972 Act"), as amended in 2007, it was possible for them to provide for a maximum sentence of imprisonment of three years on conviction on indictment and/or a maximum fine of €500,000, and this was done. The maximum term of three years' imprisonment can be argued to reflect that the 2010 Directive raises the right to life and the person under Art.40.3 of the Constitution, but it then raises a question as to whether other EU Directives on safety and health should be implemented under the 1972 Act, given that it provides for up to a 50 per cent greater term of imprisonment on conviction on indictment than the two years possible under s.78 of the 2005 Act. But, by contrast, the maximum fine of €500,000 under the 2014 Regulations is one sixth of the maximum fine of €3 million under s.78 of the 2005 Act. The rationale for these differences has not had the benefit of a public debate. The penalties on summary conviction under the 2014 Regulations are identical to those in the 2005 Act, a class A fine (up to €5,000) and/or a maximum prison term of 12 months.

The 2014 Regulations provide for offences by any "person." In accordance with the Interpretation Act 2005, this includes "corporate persons," such as a limited liability company or the HSE, as well as individual persons. The 2014 Regulations do not, however, include any equivalent of s.80 of the 2005 Act, which deals with the personal criminal liability of directors, managers and other similar officers of undertakings. Again, we do not have the benefit of any public discussion as to why such a provision was not included in the 2014 Regulations.

In accordance with principles of better regulation, as reiterated in the Government's 2013 Policy Statement, *Regulating for a Better Future*, the HSA published a Regulatory Impact Analysis (RIA) in January 2012 which discussed options concerning the transposition of the 2010 Directive. The RIA concluded that this should be done by means of the regulation-making power in the 2005 Act. The RIA was published on the HSA website and was also circulated to relevant stakeholders, including the Department of Jobs, Enterprise and Innovation, the Department of Health and the HSE (see RIA, p.7). There is no published indication that any of the stakeholders put forward an alternative to using the 2005 Act to transpose the 2010 Directive in the consultation period. It is therefore surprising, and difficult to reconcile with the Government's principles of better regulation, that over two years after the RIA was published the 2005 Act was not used to transpose the 2010 Directive.

In addition, because the 2005 Act was not used to implement the 2010 Directive, this may have had the effect of imposing additional administrative and legal burdens on healthcare employers, contrary to the Government's ongoing commitment to reduce administrative burdens, which forms part of the EU's *Action Programme for Reducing Administrative Burdens in the European Union*. Such additional burdens would arise for at least two reasons. First, public sector healthcare organisations, to whom the terms of the 2010 Directive have applied since May 2013, would (presumably) have already integrated the Directive's requirements into their compliance arrangements for the 2005 Act, as specified in the HSE's 2012 *Guidelines for the Emergency Management of Injuries*, discussed below. Any change in such arrangements would likely involve additional administrative burdens. Secondly, other additional burdens arise because the 2005 Act was not used, since both the public sector and private sector have cross-border links with the United Kingdom. In Northern Ireland, the 2010 Directive was implemented using the regulation-making powers in the Health and Safety at Work (Northern Ireland) Order 1978, and in Great Britain it was implemented using the regulation-making powers in the Health and Safety at Work Act 1974. In both instances, this was done following the publication of Impact Assessments (IAs, the equivalent of RIAs) which had concluded that the 2010 Directive should be implemented using the legislative equivalent of the 2005 Act, rather than the UK's European Communities Act 1972. If the 2005 Act had been used to implement the 2010 Directive in this State, both public and private sector healthcare employers would not have been required to ensure that their policies and procedures complied with comparable policies in those UK bodies with whom they have connections because the regulatory arrangements would have been virtually identical.

Thus, if the 2005 Act had been used to implement the 2010 Directive, public sector healthcare employers who had already integrated the Directive's requirements since May 2013 would face no further administrative burdens in 2014; and, equally, public sector and private sector healthcare employers would be more likely to have in place policies that match those to be found in those UK bodies with whom they have connections.

As already mentioned, pre-2014 policy documents that deal with blood borne infection refer to the 2005 Act as the basis on which such matters had been regulated where they arise in the occupational setting, which is the specific subject matter of the 2010 Directive. The most significant such document is the HSE's 2012 *Guidelines for the Emergency Management of Injuries*. It is worth noting that these Guidelines were developed by a wide-ranging expert group and were published in September 2012, after the RIA discussed above was published. The Guidelines state, at p.20, that the "legislation which covers this area is the Safety, Health and Welfare at Work Act 2005 (and 2007 Regulations)" and, at p.65, that needlestick and sharps injuries should be notified to the HSA. This reinforces the view that specific policy prior to the 2014 Regulations was to regard occupational needlestick injuries as falling under the 2005 Act and the Regulations made under it.

Vicarious liability and "reasonably practicable" under the 2005 Act At common law, an employer is vicariously liable for the acts of an employee that occur "in the course of employment." This includes where one employee's negligence causes an injury to another employee. The courts do not usually impose vicarious liability on the employer where an employee assaults another employee because that would be regarded as not having occurred "in the course of employment." But the position is different under the 2005 Act, and in some cases the employer will be held vicariously liable even for assaults committed by one of its employees on another employee. This is illustrated by the decision in *Elmontem v Nethercross Ltd t/a Roganstown Golf and Country Club and Usai* [2014] IEHC 91, which is also discussed in the Torts chapter, pp.659–660, below. The decision also examined in some detail the meaning and effect of the general "reasonably practicable" standard in the 2005 Act.

Briefly, the first defendant had employed the second defendant after he had been dismissed from his previous employment for assaulting another employee. The general manager of the first defendant knew of this incident but did not notify the managing director of the first defendant during the recruitment process. While employed by the first defendant, the second defendant assaulted the plaintiff, also an employee of the first defendant, during a meeting, giving him a black eye, cuts, contusions, swelling and bruising as well as causing him post-traumatic stress. The plaintiff claimed that his employer, the first defendant, was both vicariously liable for the attack and in breach of his duty to provide a safe place of work, so far as is reasonably practicable under the 2005 Act.

The High Court (Herbert J.) found that, at common law, the plaintiff had not established the close connection required between the employment and the assault in order for it to be classified as occurring "in the course of employment" and that to hold otherwise would amount to imposing absolute liability on the first defendant as employer. Therefore, the first defendant was not found to be vicariously liable for the attack.

As regards the claim that the first defendant as employer had failed to provide a safe place of work, so far as is reasonably practicable under the 2005 Act, however, the court held that the first and second defendants were jointly liable. The court considered that, having been aware of the previous assault, the general manager knew or ought to have known that there was a very real risk that the second defendant could become violent: it was therefore reasonably foreseeable that he could be a danger to other employees. The first defendant had thus failed to take steps to protect against the danger of another assault: in particular the court highlighted that there was no policy that identified what conduct would not be accepted. The defendant had also failed to write to the second defendant to notify him that physical violence would not be tolerated in the workplace and would result in dismissal on the grounds of misconduct.

In coming to his conclusions, Herbert J. quoted a number of the general duties on employers in s.8 of the 2005 Act and the definition of "reasonably practicable" in s.2 of the 2005 Act. He quoted from s.8 of the 2005 Act as follows.

First, the general duty in s.8(1) of the 2005 Act:

> Every employer shall ensure, so far as is reasonably practicable, the safety, health and welfare at work of his or her employees.

Secondly, the duty in s.8(2)(b) of the 2005 Act concerning improper conduct and behaviour, which imposes a duty on an employer of

> managing and conducting work activities in such a way as to prevent, so far as is reasonably practicable, any improper conduct or behaviour likely to put the safety, health or welfare at work of his or her employees at risk.

Thirdly, Herbert J. referred to the duty concerning training in s.8(2)(g) of the 2005 Act, which requires an employer to provide information, instruction, training and supervision necessary to ensure, so far as is reasonably practicable, the safety, health, and welfare at work of his or her employees.

Herbert J. then quoted the definition of "reasonably practicable" from s.2(6) of the 2005 Act that an employer:

> has exercised all due care by putting in place the necessary protective and preventive measures, having identified the hazards and assessed the risks to safety and health likely to result in accidents or injury to health at the place of work concerned and where the putting in place of any further measures is grossly disproportionate having regard to the unusual, unforeseeable and exceptional nature of any circumstance or occurrence that may result in an accident at work or injury to health at that place of work.

Herbert J. noted that there is no definition of "improper conduct or behaviour" in the 2005 Act, but he added, at para.17, the following important comment on its scope:

> "I find that it would include such matters as bullying, harassment, rough play, practical joking, racial or other abuse or physical violence."

This assessment of the scope of "improper conduct or behaviour" in the 2005 Act is consistent with the drafting history behind the 2005 Act and with HSA guidance on the 2005 Act.

As already noted, Herbert J. considered that the evidence in the case established that Nethercross/Roganstown, through its general manager, was aware that Mr Usai had on a previous occasion in a fit of temper caused physical injury to a fellow employee in the course of their joint employment. He was also satisfied that the general manager:

> "knew or ought to have known that there was a very real risk, not just a mere possibility, that this could occur again, if for any reason [the second defendant's] temper became aroused and that this exposed his fellow employees, including the plaintiff, to a risk of physical injury. I am satisfied that it was reasonably foreseeable that [the second defendant] was likely to prove a source of danger to other employees of [the first defendant] because of his apparently ungovernable temper." (para.18)

It is worth noting that Herbert J. referred to "a very real risk, not just a mere possibility". This is similar to the approach of the English Court of Appeal in *R v Porter* [2008] EWCA Crim 1271 where the court held that "risk" means a real risk, not a fanciful or hypothetical risk.

Herbert J. also used the "reasonably practicable" test in deciding that the defendant employer was liable. He accepted that it could not be regarded as negligent or a breach of duty, including statutory duty, for the company to have employed the second defendant at all and also noted that the general manager was not aware of any further assaults perpetrated or threatened by the second defendant on fellow employees. Because he had dismissed the second defendant following the previous assault, Herbert J. also accepted that the general manager may have assumed that such an incident was unlikely to recur. However, Herbert J. pointed out that the cause of the previous assault was not a personal antipathy between the second defendant and a particular fellow employee no longer on the scene; rather, it was the second defendant "losing his temper to an almost maniac level with a co-worker over some dispute or perceived grievance in the course of their work." Herbert J. added, at para 19:

> "A real risk of a recurrence therefore remained. In my judgment the making of such an assumption would not and did not excuse the employer from taking no measures whatsoever to prevent a recurrence. *The first defendant did not exercise reasonable care and, certainly did not exercise all due care to put in place measures to prevent or to protect against, such an event. This was not a risk which could be entirely eliminated, but in my judgment was one which could have been adequately controlled without grossly disproportionate or expensive measures.*" (emphasis added)

The last two sentences in this passage echo the definition of "reasonably practicable" in s.2(6) of the 2005 Act, including whether the employer had:

- exercised all due care;
- put in place measures to prevent or to protect against the event that occurred;
- assessed the risk and put in place controls;

without grossly disproportionate or expensive measures.

He added, at para.20, that the defendant as employer

> "took no care to put in place measures to prevent a recurrence of such improper conduct or behaviour on the part of [the second defendant] likely to put the safety and health of other employees at risk. There was no evidence that [the first defendant] had a Safety Statement or a notified policy which identified conduct or behaviour in the workplace that would not be tolerated, conduct such as verbal abuse or physical violence of or towards other workers. There was no evidence that [the general manager] had notified and warned [the second defendant] in writing in clear and definite terms that physical violence towards any other employee would not be tolerated and would result in his being dismissed for gross misconduct."

Herbert J. also took into account that shortly before the assault on the plaintiff by Mr Usai, the managing director had received a complaint from another employee that Mr Usai had made very offensive racist remarks about the wife of that fellow employee (who were both from the same ethnic background). The managing director had immediately investigated this complaint, Mr Usai had apologised to the other employee, and the apology was accepted. Mr Usai had been given a verbal warning about this incident. Herbert J. commented, at para.21, that

> "an incident like this should have clearly brought home to [the first

> defendant] the urgent necessity of having a clear Safety Statement or policy with regard to improper conduct or behaviour at work, especially having regard to the multi ethnic nature of its large workforce."

The *Elmonten* decision reinforces the view that the extent of liability, whether civil or criminal, under the 2005 Act goes beyond what the pre-2005 Act (and pre-1989 Act) common law vicarious liability imposed. In the *Elmonten* case, vicarious liability was imposed on the employer from the criminal assault caused by one employee to another. Usually, such a criminal offence would not, and will not in a future case, involve vicarious liability: the significant factor in the *Elmonten* case was that the employer had known that the second defendant had previously been involved in virtually the same kind of behaviour in the past.

WORKING TIME

Merchant shipping The European Communities (Merchant Shipping) (Organisation of Working Time) (Amendment) Regulations 2014 (S.I. No. 245 of 2014) (the "2014 Regulations") amended the European Communities (Merchant Shipping) (Organisation of Working Time) Regulations 2003 (S.I. No. 532 of 2003) (the "2003 Regulations").

The 2014 Regulations: (a) gave effect to Directive 2009/13/EC, which implemented the Agreement concluded by the European Community Shipowners' Associations (ECSA) and the European Transport Workers' Federation (ETF) on the IMO Maritime Labour Convention 2006; and (b) gave further effect to Council Directive 1999/63/EC concerning the Agreement on the organisation of working time of seafarers concluded by the European Community Shipowners' Association (ECSA) and the Federation of Transport Workers' Unions in the European Union (FST) (as amended by Directive 2009/13/EC); and (c) implemented certain provisions of art.15 of Directive 2008/106/EC on the minimum level of training of seafarers (as amended by Directive 2012/35/EC).

The main effect of the 2014 Regulations is to provide seafarers with an entitlement to specified minimum hours of rest, require records to be kept of seafarers' daily hours of rest and provide for the enforcement of the 2003 Regulations as amended by the 2014 Regulations (by way of summary conviction, which could lead to a class A fine, that is, a maximum fine of €5,000, up from €3,000 under the 2003 Regulations as originally made). They also provide for a minimum age for seafarers working on ships to which the 2003 Regulations apply, set out the conditions under which seafarers under the age of 18 may work at night, and provide for annual leave entitlements for seafarers, as set out in the IMO Maritime Labour Convention 2006 and in Directive 2009/13/EC.

Social Welfare Law

GERRY WHYTE *and* **MEL COUSINS**

CASE LAW

No fewer than nine cases relating to various aspects of the social welfare code were decided by the superior courts in 2014.

Decision making and appeals Five of these cases concerned different aspects of the decision making process and appeals system operated by the Department.

Readers of the 2013 review will recall that in *AM v Minister for Social Protection* [2013] IEHC 524, Hanna J. dismissed an application seeking to quash a refusal to grant the applicant domiciliary care allowance ("DCA") in respect of the applicant's son. In the course of his judgment, Hanna J. indicated, inter alia, that the applicant should have taken an appeal under the Social Welfare (Consolidation) Act 2005 (the "2005 Act") against the decision to refuse payment, rather than seeking to have it quashed by way of judicial review. Following this judgment, the applicant did, in fact, successfully pursue her statutory right of appeal and she was awarded the allowance back-dated to the date of her original application. However, she also lodged an appeal against Hanna J.'s decision and this came before the recently established Court of Appeal. In *Malone v Minister for Social Protection* [2014] IECA 4, the respondent argued that the issue was now moot, following the applicant's successful appeal. The appellant countered by arguing that as the applicant's entitlement to the allowance would be subject to ongoing review likely to occur every two years, the court should take this fact into account in deciding whether the matter was moot. Counsel also contended that the issue in the case concerned the manner in which the deciding officer had exercised his powers under s.300 of the 2005 Act and that this remained of relevance to other potential claimants of domiciliary care allowance. However, the Court of Appeal, per Irvine J., held that the issue between the parties was rendered moot by the applicant's successful appeal. Any controversy that might arise between the parties on foot of a future review of the applicant's claim would be fundamentally different to that which concerned Hanna J. and the applicant's rights would be different at that point in time to those that she enjoyed prior to her successful appeal. Any further review would consider whether there had been a change of circumstances that would affect the applicant's entitlement and so resolving the issues that arose in the instant case could not resolve any such future controversy between the parties. In *O'Brien v Personal Injuries Assessment Board (No. 2)* [2007] 1 I.R. 328; [2007] 1 I.L.R.M. 304, the Supreme Court held that an issue between the parties was not moot because, inter alia, it could arise again in the context of future possible legal proceedings between the parties. However, the Court of Appeal distinguished *O'Brien* on the grounds that *O'Brien* involved the interpretation of a statutory provision that would govern the manner in which one of the parties to the dispute would be obliged to carry out its statutory obligations, whereas the instant case did not. The Court of Appeal also noted that the applicant would not be prejudiced by the dismissal of her appeal and that if any future decision was made that was adverse to her entitlement, she retained her statutory right of appeal and also her right to seek judicial review of any such decision.

In *B v Minister for Social Protection* [2014] 2 I.L.R.M. 290, another case involving DCA, the deciding officer, in rejecting B's application, had relied on the negative opinion of the medical assessor and rejected the evidence of the applicant's medical and multidisciplinary team. It emerged that in over 3,800 applications for DCA, the same deciding officer had—in every case—relied on the medical assessor's decisions and the Department of Social Protection (the "Department") conceded that it would be "highly unusual" for a deciding officer to decide against a medical assessor's opinion on a question of medical eligibility.

It was argued by the applicant that the Department operated a policy whereby the opinions of its medical assessors were "followed slavishly by departmental deciding officers, irrespective of the evidence submitted by claimants such as B" (para.8). The applicant sought a declaration that the Minister's alleged policy of deferring only to, and following, the departmental medical assessor's opinion meant that in this case there has been an abdication of the deciding officer's statutory duty. It was contended that such a policy would unlawfully vitiate and/or void the decision-making process in that the statutorily appointed decision-maker did not, in reality, make the decision and did so only in name, contrary to s.300 of the 2005 Act and contrary to fair procedures and natural and constitutional justice.

The Department of Social Protection did not reassure the court as to the fairness of its approach when, in an affidavit by an assistant principal of the Department, the applicant's medical team were referred to as "advocating on behalf of" the applicant in contrast to the medical assessor whose function was "to provide to the Deciding Officer an independent medical opinion" (para.11). Barrett J. found this view "remarkable" and concluded, at para.12, that

> "the Department apparently adopts a disdainful mind-set [to the applicant's evidence] and prefers instead the desk-top reviews of its own medical assessors who have no personal knowledge of the individual case at hand."

The court was unconvinced by the explanations put forward by the Department as to why deciding officers would be unlikely to disagree with medical assessors, including the medical qualifications of the latter and the possibility of consultation with them.

Section 186C(3) of the 2005 Act provides that in determining whether a child is a qualified child for the purposes of that provision, a deciding officer "shall have regard to" the opinion of the medical assessor. Barrett J. began his consideration of the meaning of this term by pointing out that in *McLoughlin v Minister for Social Welfare* [1958] I.R. 1, the Supreme Court ruled, at 27, that "appeals officers … and equally deciding officers, are, and are required to be, free and unrestricted in discharging their functions under the Act." Having regard to the case law on the meaning of the term "shall have regard to" (and similar provisions), Barrett J. concluded that the requirement that the deciding officer "have regard to" the opinion was not consistent with a situation where the deciding officer appeared invariably to conform with such opinions and the court took the view, at para.23, that

> "a situation may pertain within the Department of Social Protection, or at least in the case of this particular deciding officer, whereby the discretion that a deciding officer enjoys under law … was inappropriately fettered."

Barrett J. concluded, at para.25, that it was

> "not clear that all relevant considerations are taken into account by the departmental decision-maker. The almost disdainful reference in the affidavit of the assistant principal … about the medical evidence supplied by applicants suggests that such evidence is not given the weight that ought to be given by any decision-maker to the honestly held and properly reasoned views of qualified professionals. The department's mind-set as regards such evidence … appears to be that the views of those professionals are necessarily coloured in favour of applicants and hence the views of its own medical experts are invariably to be preferred."

For these reasons, the court ruled, at para.26, that

> "the policy whereby deciding officers generally defer to the opinions of department medical assessors in the manner and circumstances described has yielded a situation in the instant case in which there has been an abdication of statutory duty by the deciding officer who decided B.'s initial application. Indeed the manner of implementation of such policy in the case of the deciding officer who decided B.'s initial application is such that the court finds it has vitiated the decision-making process employed in relation to that application; this is because the deference manifested by this particular deciding officer to the opinion of medical assessors has been proven to be so great that the court concludes that the medical assessor's opinion volunteered in the course of the consideration of B.'s initial application was in fact determinative of that application, thus resulting in a contravention of s.300 of the Social Welfare Consolidation Act, 2005, thereby tainting the decision-making process."

The court therefore ordered that the decision in relation to the claim for DCA be remitted to the Department of Social Protection for fresh consideration.

The court in *B* also considered the issue of the appropriate remedy. The Minister argued that the applicant ought to have pursued an appeal to the Social Welfare Appeals Office rather than bringing an application for judicial review. However, Barrett J. considered

> "this line of argument to be misfounded for the following reason: B. is not in these proceedings seeking a review of the outcome of a decision that issued; she is challenging only the process whereby that decision was formulated and there is no provision in the social welfare code whereby she can challenge the process, as opposed to the outcome, of decision-making."

Hence, the court took the view that it was necessary for B to make application for judicial review (see para.15).

It would appear that following this decision, the practice of appeals officers having regard to medical reports prepared by assessors who had not personally examined the child in respect of whom domiciliary care allowance was claimed was discontinued. See *O'B v Chief Appeals Officer* [2014] IEHC 48 at para.19. This case involved yet another challenge to procedures concerning DCA, this time at appeals level. The applicant had been refused the allowance following medical assessment of her son. She appealed to the appeals office seeking an oral hearing and also requested that the deciding officer and the three medical assessors whose desktop reports were available to the deciding officer at first instance be available at the oral hearing. This was refused by the Chief Appeals Officer (although the precise terms of the refusal are not reported).

The applicant sought judicial review of the failure to direct the attendance of these officers, arguing that fair procedures required that she be permitted to cross examine the deciding officer and/or the medical assessors. It was argued that the absence of the deciding officer and medical assessors would amount to a denial to the applicant of a hearing in compliance with the Social Welfare (Consolidation) Act 2005, the Social Welfare (Appeals) Regulations 1998 (S.I. No. 108 of 1998) as amended (the "Appeals Regulations"), the European Convention on Human Rights Act 2003, fair procedures and natural and constitutional justice.

As already noted, following the *B* ruling, the practice of the Social Welfare Appeals Office in relation to the use of medical reports as evidence in DCA cases had changed. Baker J. stated (at para.19) that

> "the Chief Appeals Officer in the light of that decision [in *B*] took the view that desktop opinions furnished by medical assessors who have not personally examined a child on whose behalf domiciliary care allowance application was made, should as a matter of good practice be excluded from the file on appeal."

The applicant argued that a decision by the Chief Appeals Officer which held that in all cases the medical assessor's reports would be removed from a file would be ultra vires the Chief Appeals Officer. However, the court did not pursue this issue, apparently on the (justifiable) basis that a decision not to rely on negative medical reports could only benefit the applicant.

In relation to the attendance of the medical assessors, the court accepted the assurances that their medical reports would not be before the appeals officer. Therefore, there was no basis to require their attendance. As the court pointed out, at para.27:

> "There is no procedure in our law where a person in an adversarial process can cross-examine evidence which is not before a deciding body."

In relation to the deciding officer, the court pointed out that while art.15(3) of the Appeals Regulations allowed the deciding officer to appear at a hearing, this did not require the deciding officer to attend nor was there anything which required the Chief Appeals Officer to direct the officer's attendance. In addition, the purpose of the deciding officer's attendance was to conduct or process the appeal, not to give evidence on oath as to the reasons for his or her decision. Baker J. also ruled, at para.36, that:

> "The word 'appear' in the Regulation is used in a technical sense as understood in the procedures of courts and means 'attend' not 'give evidence'."

The court concluded, at para.35, that for it

> "to require the attendance of the deciding officer would be akin to a court on appeal requiring that the judge at first instance should make himself or herself available for cross examination on the reasoning that led to a decision."

Finally, in relation to *O'B*, Baker J. pointed out that ss.313 and 314 of the 2005 Act respectively gave an appeals officer the power to administer oaths and to require the presence of any person to give evidence or produce documents. She concluded, at para.36, that for the court to interfere at this stage would be to deny the discretion and jurisdiction of the appeals officer to regulate his or her own procedures.

The companion cases of *LD v Chief Appeals Officer* [2014] IEHC 641 and *Smith v Chief Appeals Officer* [2014] IEHC 633 were both decided by Peart J. and raised the issues of when a decision of an appeals officer can be revised and when an oral hearing may be held as part of the social welfare appeals process. It would appear that the claimants were seeking to establish when an oral hearing *should* be held. However, the Social Welfare Appeals Office ("SWAO")—having originally decided both cases without an oral hearing—proposed to reconsider the appeals *with* an oral hearing after judicial review proceedings were initiated. Thereafter the cases took on a somewhat artificial aspect with the claimants' lawyers arguing that the appeals officer was now functus officio and that the SWAO had no power to hold an oral hearing in such circumstances, while the respondents argued for a flexible approach as to when an oral hearing may be held. Ultimately, Peart J. ruled that oral hearings could be held and, understandably in the circumstances, he did not address the issue of when an oral hearing *should* be held.

Article 14 of the Social Welfare (Appeals) Regulations 1998 (S.I. No. 108 of 1998) provides:

> Where, in the opinion of the appeals officer, a hearing is required he or she shall, as soon as may be, fix a date and place for the hearing, and give reasonable notice of the said hearing to the appellant, the deciding officer … and any other person appearing to the appeals officer to be concerned in the appeal.

Thus, an appeals officer has discretion as to whether to grant an oral hearing or not, but this is not an unlimited discretion. The basic rule is that the claimant should be given an oral hearing unless the case can properly be determined without one. In *Kiely v Minister for Social Welfare (No. 2)* [1977] I.R. 267, the Supreme Court, in interpreting the relevant provisions, stated, at 278, that:

> "An oral hearing is mandatory unless the case is of such a nature that it can be determined without an oral hearing, that is, summarily. An appeal is of such a nature that it can be determined summarily if a determination of the claim can fairly be made on a consideration of the documentary evidence. If however, there are unresolved conflicts in the documentary evidence, as to any matter essential to a ruling of the claim, the intention of the Regulations is that those conflicts shall be resolved by an oral hearing."

In *Galvin v Chief Appeals Officer* [1997] 3 I.R. 240, a case concerning a dispute as to whether social insurance contributions had been paid in the past by the applicant, Costello P. held, at 251, that:

> "There are no hard and fast rules to guide an Appeals Officer ... as to when the dictates of fairness require the holding of an oral hearing. The case (like others) must be decided on the circumstances pertaining, the nature of the inquiry being undertaken by the decision-maker, the rules under which the decision-maker is acting, and the subject matter with which he is dealing and account should also be taken as to whether an oral hearing was requested."

An appeals officer's decision is stated to be final and conclusive (s.320 of the 2005 Act). Nonetheless, an appeals officer may, at any time and from time to time, revise any decision of an appeals officer if the original decision appears to be wrong in light of new evidence or new facts that came to light since the original decision was made or if there has been a relevant change of circumstances (s.317). In addition, the Chief Appeals Officer may, at any time and from time to time, revise the decision of an appeals officer if it appears that the decision was wrong because of a mistake in relation to the law or to the facts (s.318). In *Castleisland v Minister for Social and Family Affairs* [2004] 4 I.R. 150, the Supreme Court commented that this provision did not confer a "double appeal". Rather, what is envisaged is that the Chief Appeals Officer would review the materials before the appeals officer to establish whether there was any error of fact or law.

In *LD*, the applicant was the mother and carer of her son who had been diagnosed with Asperger's Syndrome. She applied to the Department of Social Protection for DCA. The conditions of eligibility require that the child must have a severe disability requiring continual or continuous care and attention substantially in excess of the care and attention normally required by a child of the same age (the disability must be such that the child is likely to require full-time care and attention for at least 12 consecutive months), see s.186C of the 2005 Act (inserted by s.15 of the Social Welfare and Pensions Act 2008). It would appear that limited information was provided in support of the initial application which was refused by a deciding officer on the basis that the evidence did not indicate that the extra care and attention required by LD's son was substantially in excess of that required for a child of the same age who does not suffer from Asperger's Syndrome. The applicant appealed to an appeal officer and provided considerable additional evidence including a detailed letter from the Mater Hospital (from a Consultant Child and Adolescent Psychiatrist and a Senior Speech and Language Therapist) and her own seven page memorandum which set out in a very detailed way her own experience of her child at home and the difficulties which she encounters on a daily basis resulting from his disability.

However, the appeals officer rejected the appeal without holding an oral hearing. The reasons for this decision were stated to be that

> "having examined the evidence available to me in this case, I have concluded that while [LD's son] with his condition, Asperger's, does require extra support [it] has not been established with the evidence provided that he requires substantially more care on a continuous basis, as provided for in Domiciliary Care Legislation."

Peart J. explained, at para.9, that the decision must be taken as meaning that the appeals officer was satisfied that even though LD's son required some extra support because of his diagnosed condition, it was not of a level *substantially* above the level of care and attention usually required by a child of the same age who did not have that diagnosis.

The main issue for determination was whether or not an oral hearing before a new appeals officer could be held in the circumstances of this case. As noted above, once the proceedings commenced, the Chief Appeals Officer proposed to hold an oral hearing before a different appeals officer to hear the additional evidence which the appellant wished to adduce and to consider whether this evidence would warrant a revision of the decision under s.317 of the 2005 Act. However, the applicant's legal team argued that there was no statutory basis for this approach, as the "appeals office" was now functus officio. They argued that the only legal basis upon which that decision could be set aside and an oral hearing granted was if the original decision were to be quashed by the High Court. Peart J. deduced that the applicants' lawyers were anticipating (based on previous experience) that, subsequent to the commencement of judicial review proceedings, the applicant might be offered an oral hearing. They, therefore, sought clarification as to whether there was any lawful basis for such an offer post the determination of the appeal not just for this applicant's case but also for future cases. They argued that there were no new facts or new evidence and that it must follow from the plain and ordinary words in s.317 that the appeals officer has no jurisdiction to re-open the appeal.

The respondents argued that the case was moot since the applicant had now been offered the oral hearing she sought. In addition, they argued that s.317 of the 2005 Act contained an implied power to hold an oral hearing after the decision on the appeal has been made because that section enables an appeals officer to revise any decision of an appeals officer in certain circumstances. It was argued that they were entitled to presume that the appellant would have wished to adduce orally some additional evidence. Finally, they argued that an appeals officer must be entitled to hold an oral hearing, if only to decide whether or not there are any new facts or evidence.

Peart J. accepted that counsel for the applicant was correct when he said that under the scheme of the Act, there is no possibility of a second appeal as such, and that once an appeal has been determined by an appeals officer, the appeal decision is final and conclusive and the appeals officer is functus officio, subject only to, inter alia, any revision of the appeal decision under s.317 of the 2005 Act. Nonetheless, he was satisfied that where a s.317 revision was being held, it was possible to hold an oral hearing as part of this review. His comments on this issue are worth quoting *in extenso*. The court stated, at para.38, that it was important to keep in mind the scheme of the Act.

> "Part 10 thereof is headed 'Decisions, Appeals and Social Welfare Tribunal'. There is no distinct heading called 'Revisions'. Revisions take place within the context of a decision by a deciding officer, or within the context of an appeal decision by the appeal officer (or under s.318 by the Chief Appeals Officer). If a decision or an appeal is revised, it remains a decision or an appeal decision following that revision, albeit one that has been revised. Chapter 1 of Part 10 deals with deciding officers and decisions by deciding officers including any revision of such decisions. Chapter 2 deals with appeals officers, the Chief Appeals Officer and decisions by appeals officers. There is no separate chapter dealing with revisions. In my view it follows that when an appeals officer is dealing [with] a revision of a decision of an appeals officer he/she is nevertheless dealing with the appeal that was lodged by the applicant by virtue of the revision power contained in section 317 of the Act. The revision is a matter arising in the context of such an appeal, and is a 'matter' arising in relation to the appeal. It is a 'matter' arising in relation to something which was referred to the appeals officer under that Part (i.e. an appeal), and is in my view a 'matter' therefore for the purpose of section 313 of the Act, and one therefore in respect of which an appeals officer has the power to take evidence on oath 'at that hearing'. It seems clear therefore that the Act contemplates that a hearing can take place in relation to a revision so that any new facts and new evidence can be adduced and considered."

(Section 313 provides that: "An appeals officer shall, on the hearing of any matter referred to him or her under this Part have power to take evidence on oath and for that purpose may administer oaths to persons attending as witnesses at that hearing".)

According to the judge, at para.38, the Act should "be interpreted as widely as the words reasonably permit in order to reflect the permissive nature of the legislation, and the very detailed procedures laid down for decision-making, and the procedures provided for revision at any time of decisions." It appeared to the court that the clear intention of the Act was that social welfare claimants are provided with different opportunities to put their case, and to do so in a fair manner and comprehensively. Peart J. was satisfied that s.313 of the Act, given the breadth of its terms, provided the necessary power to enable an appeals officer to direct an oral hearing for the purpose, inter alia, of a s.317 revision procedure, whether or not a hearing is requested by the applicant. He concluded, at para.46, that the applicant's request for an oral hearing was responded to appropriately by the appeals officer offering to hold an oral hearing in order to see whether, in the light of whatever it is that the applicant wishes to say, a revision of the appeal decision is warranted. A difficulty with this conclusion, however, is that s.317 only applies where there are new facts or new evidence. Peart J. suggested that it was arguable that a request for an oral hearing could itself constitute a new fact, even if it could not constitute new evidence, thereby enabling an appeals officer to decide *proprio motu* to hold an oral hearing once asked to do so, and to hold it for the purpose of a s.317 revision. However, this is questionable. The new facts or evidence must relate to the original claim for benefit and a request for an oral hearing has nothing to do with this.

Peart J. commented in passing, at para.32, that the new facts or new evidence referred to in s.317(1)(a) of the Act

> "are not confined to matters that may have happened or been generated since the decision, but may consist of material or evidence which, though it existed before the appeal decision was made, was not before the appeals officer at the time the appeal decision was made."

This statement is clearly obiter and Peart J. did not consider whether there were any restrictions on what could be considered to be "new". In *R v Medical Appeal Tribunal (North Midland Region), Ex p. Hubble* [1959] 2 Q.B. 408, [1959] 3 All E.R. 40, the English Court of Appeal considered the meaning of "fresh evidence" in the light of which a decision could be revised. Morris L.J. stated, at 424 and 47, respectively, that this meant

> "some evidence which the claimant was unable to produce before the decision was given or which he could not reasonably be expected to have produced in the circumstances of the case."

The court rejected the argument that "fresh evidence" simply meant some further or additional evidence not presented at the original hearing. In *Iarnród Éireann v Social Welfare Tribunal* [2007] IEHC 406, Murphy J. (again obiter) took a similar approach stating, at para.8.2, that:

> "If new evidence is to be construed as 'fresh evidence' then such a reference in an enactment imports the usual legal meaning of this phrase as evidence which is not merely additional to that adduced on the former occasion but could not be [sic.] reasonably have been expected to be produced then."

In the course of his judgment, Peart J. also commented on the lack of information provided to claimants in relation to oral hearings. In this case, the applicant had not requested an oral hearing. Given his approach to the case, Peart J. did not have to decide if this was significant. However, he noted that the letter from the Department to the applicant notifying her of the refusal of her claim for DCA and of her entitlement to seek a review of that decision, or to appeal to the Chief Appeals Officer, did not refer to the possibility of an oral hearing. He felt that that "must dilute the significance if any of the fact that the applicant never sought to have an oral hearing" (para.14). He did not consider that the applicant should be seen as having acquiesced in a summary decision by not having requested an oral hearing. Peart J. suggested that it would be helpful to claimants, and might avoid unnecessary judicial review proceedings, if the letter informing them of the decision to refuse their claim went on to ask them whether or not they wish to request an oral hearing, and, if so, to state why they considered that an oral hearing should be held. It is worth noting that the standard Notice of Appeal Form (available on the SWAO website) also makes no reference of an oral hearing, although the possibility of an oral hearing is mentioned elsewhere on the site: *http://www.socialwelfareappeals.ie/appeal/Appealprocess.html*.

Given his conclusion that it was open to an appeals officer to hold an oral hearing of a revision of another appeal officer's decision, Peart J. did not have to decide whether the applicant was entitled to an oral hearing prior to the determination of her appeal. It is rather unclear from the judgement whether the court would have been of the view that such a hearing should have been held had it been necessary to decide this issue.

On the one hand, Peart J. stated, at para.20, that

> "since no contrary evidence [to that of the applicant] was considered for the purpose of the appeal, it is no doubt incomprehensible to the applicant how she was deemed ineligible for DCA, and impossible to accept the written submission made in the present proceedings that 'the evidence submitted by the applicant did not establish that her son had a severe disability requiring continual care and attention significantly in excess of that required by a child without that disability'."

This might appear to suggest that the appeal officer should have upheld the appeal, although Peart J. correctly noted this was not a merits appeal and it did not matter whether the court would have come to a different view to the appeals officer.

However, in concluding his judgment, he stated, at para.47, that

> "in so far as it has been asserted that there were clear conflicts arising on the materials put before the appeals officer which needed an oral hearing, I have struggled to identify what those conflicts are, even in the light of the contents of the Medical Assessor's opinions which the appeals officer has stated that she did not have any regard to. I accept that there is a divergence of views as between the applicant on the one hand, and the Assessor, the deciding officer and the appeals officer on the other as to whether her son qualifies for DCA. But that will arise in every case where a negative decision is arrived at by a deciding officer. That is not the sort of conflict or divergence of view that requires an oral hearing, otherwise any appeal which is being refused could not be refused without holding an oral hearing. That is not what is provided by the Act. While the letters from the Mater Hospital and the applicant's GP support the applicant's application, those do not amount to medical evidence as such. They are supportive but do not constitute medical evidence in the sense of stating that her son meets the criteria for DCA (and explaining why) under s.186C of the Act of 2005…."

This passage suggests that not only was the appeals officer entitled to reject the appeal but that she was entitled not to consider an oral hearing necessary.

In the companion case of *Smith v Chief Appeals Officer* [2014] IEHC 633, Peart J. used his reasoning in *LD,* mutatis mutandis, to hold that the Chief Appeals Officer could hold an oral hearing for the purpose of resolving conflicts of evidence when revising the decision of an appeals officer pursuant to s.318 of the 2005 Act.

Eligibility for pro rata State Contributory Pension *Meagher v Minister for*

Social Protection [2014] IEHC 39 concerned the interpretation of regulations governing how different classes of social insurance contributions are to be taken into account for the purpose of determining entitlement to social insurance payments. The applicant had paid 221 Class S contributions as a self-employed contributor and 63 Class A contributions payable in respect of his employment as a county coroner before reaching pensionable age. However, these Class A contributions were paid in respect of a period when the applicant also paid 63 Class S contributions in respect of his self-employment as a solicitor and by virtue of art.23(1) of the Social Welfare (Consolidated Contributions and Insurability) Regulations 1996 (S.I. No. 312 of 1996), the Class A contributions replaced any Class S contributions payable within the same contribution year. Consequently, the applicant was considered to have only 221 contributions in total. He sought to qualify for the pro rata State contributory pension payable to self-employed people who were over the age of 56 when they first entered insurance on 6 April 1988 when compulsory social insurance was extended to the self-employed. To qualify for this pension, a claimant had to have paid at least 260 contributions and to have been over 56 but not yet 62 on or before 6 April 1988. In the instant case, the claimant could not satisfy the requirement of having 260 contributions. Charleton J. held, however, that as this condition was "not entirely illogical", the courts could not interfere with it. Nor did he consider it possible to accede to the argument that the regulations could be interpreted to permit the aggregation of Class A and Class S contributions that had been paid concurrently. Thus he said, at para.9,

> "it seems to me that an intention to make a weekly contribution worth more than a 52nd of a minimum of 260, plain words would be required. The legislation does not mandate that. Similarly, to make any year one in which contributions beyond the number of weeks in the year are possible due to aggregation, the legislature would have to plainly so state. That interpretation is not possible."

(Presumably the first sentence quoted should refer to a weekly contribution being worth more than 1/52 of the total number of contributions made in a year.)

Charleton J.'s decision in *Meagher*, like that of Lynch J. in the earlier, not dissimilar case of *Kingham v Minister for Social Welfare*, unreported, High Court, 25 November 1985, demonstrates that judges are generally not prepared to adopt strained interpretations of technical social welfare provisions, notwithstanding judicial sympathy for the claimant.

An appeal against Charleton J.'s decision was subsequently dismissed by the Supreme Court (see *Meagher v Minister for Social Protection* [2015] IESC 4).

Entitlement to rent supplement In *McCormack v Minister for Social Protection* [2014] IEHC 489, Baker J. rejected as legally erroneous the interpretation by a deciding officer and an appeals officer of the term "qualified child" in s.188 of the Social Welfare (Consolidation) Act 2005 in ruling that the plaintiff was a single person for the purpose of claiming rent supplement which is part of the supplementary welfare allowance scheme. The relevant part of the definition of this term in s.188 was that a qualified child was "in relation to a beneficiary, any child … who is dependent on that beneficiary for support…".

As part of a separation agreement, the plaintiff transferred the family home in rural Ireland into the sole name of his wife, with whom their four children resided. When he applied for rent supplement for his own accommodation in Dublin, he was offered the rate appropriate for a single person on the ground that his children were not dependent on him for support as stipulated by s.188. This meant that he was unable to rent premises capable of accommodating his children when they came to visit him. Baker J. accepted the argument advanced by counsel for the Minister that the support referred to in s.188 was financial support only. However, she held that in transferring the family home to his wife, the plaintiff had, in fact, provided for his children in financial terms and that the deciding officer and appeals officer had erred in law in failing to have regard to that fact. She also held that the children were financially dependent on their father when they visited him in Dublin and that the deciding and appeals officers had also erred in law in concluding that the housing and other basic needs of the children were met by their mother, given that both parents had joint custody. The judge concluded, at para.52, that the decision-making process was flawed as a matter of law given that the decision-makers took an erroneous view of the test to be applied, looking only to the accommodation needs of the applicant himself and failing to have regard to the fact that the accommodation and maintenance needs of the children were met by a capitalised payment in the separation agreement. Accordingly, she quashed the decision and referred it back to the respondents for further consideration.

In the course of her judgment, Baker J. noted that the relevant regulations, the Social Welfare (Consolidated Supplementary Welfare Allowance) Regulations 2007 (S.I. No. 412 of 2007) as amended by the Social Welfare (Consolidated Supplementary Welfare Allowance) (Amendment) (No.2) (Rent Supplement) Regulations 2013 (S.I. No. 215 of 2013), set out in columns the maximum rates of rent supplement for different sizes of household but did not explicitly provide for one parent families with more than three children when prescribing the maximum rate of rent supplement. On that basis, the respondent had argued that the claimant could not qualify for the maximum rate of rent supplement payable to a single parent with three children as he had four children. This was rejected by Baker J. who took the view that in order to avoid an absurd result, the expression "single person with three children" in the Regulations had to be interpreted to mean "a single person with three or more children". She also held that the term "single person" as used in the Regulations referred to a person who lived alone and was not based on his or her marital or civil status.

The applicant had argued that the definition of "qualified child" in s.188 was not applicable to rent supplement, arguing that supplementary welfare allowance and rent supplement were separate and distinct payments. This was rejected by Baker J. who held, at para.34, that the definition of "qualified child" was relevant to all parts of the general scheme of what she referred to as "social assistance" (though she presumably meant "supplementary welfare allowance"). This decision was subsequently buttressed by art.4 of the Social Welfare (Consolidated Supplementary Welfare Allowance) (Amendment) (No.5) (Rent Supplement) Regulations 2014 (S.I. No. 604 of 2014).

Judges tend to be deferential to decisions of the welfare authorities interpreting the provisions of the social welfare code and successful legal challenges to departmental decisions tend to be based on the fact that the authorities applied the wrong legal norm rather than that they misinterpreted the applicable norm. Against that backdrop, *McCormack* is unusual, if not unique, in that a High Court judge was prepared to substitute her judgment for that of administrative officials on the meaning of an aspect of the statutory social welfare code.

Direct Provision Allowance *CA v Minister for Justice and Equality* [2014] IEHC 532 involved a legal challenge to the validity and operation of the extra-statutory Direct Provision Scheme, a largely cashless scheme of support, through the provision of accommodation and meals, for persons seeking asylum or subsidiary protection. People covered by the Direct Provision Scheme cannot seek employment and must comply with detailed rules in the accommodation centres in which they live. Asylum seekers are not entitled to any mainstream social welfare payments (other than discretionary payments made pursuant to ss.201 or 202 of the 2005 Act) by virtue of the operation of the habitual residence requirement in relation to social assistance payments (s.246(7) of the 2005 Act) and by virtue of the fact that they cannot establish a social insurance record that would enable them to claim social insurance payments. The applicants essentially contended that the scheme as operated was unlawful or ultra vires because it infringed various constitutional and Convention rights of the applicants and also because it was in breach of the principle of separation of powers, having regard to Art.15.2 of the Constitution.

Specifically in relation to the payment of Direct Provision Allowance ("DPA"), a modest weekly payment made to people covered by the Direct Provision Scheme, the applicants argued that this allowance was ultra vires the 2005 Act as it was a disguised social welfare payment and therefore made in breach of s.246 of the 2005 Act, as amended, which effectively denies, inter alia, asylum seekers or persons seeking subsidiary protection access to social assistance payments. In the course of dismissing this claim, Mac Eochaidh J. expressed the view that the classification of a payment in the Revised Estimates presented annually by the executive to the Dáil does not establish the legal basis for any payment and that the Revised Estimates cannot amend legislation. He went on to hold that the 2005 Act only prohibited the payment of SWA (apart from payments under ss.201 or 202) to persons in the Direct Provision Scheme and that the State was not prohibited from making cash payments to persons seeking subsidiary protection. In fact, the 2005 Act precludes the payment of any social assistance payment, not just SWA, to persons in direct provision but this does not affect Mac Eochaidh J.'s reasoning on this point. He also held that the applicants had no standing to challenge the legality of DPA as they were not injured by the fact that the payment might be ultra vires. The judge further held that he would refuse relief in the exercise of his discretion in judicial review cases, given that a declaration that the payment was unlawful would have the immediate effect of terminating payment to all claimants and the court should not make an order with such significant negative consequences in the expectation that the Oireachtas would intervene.

Mac Eochaidh J. rejected the various arguments advanced by the applicants that the general Direct Provision Scheme itself was unlawful, though he held that some of the House Rules governing the operation of the reception centres were unlawful as they infringed the applicants' right to privacy and that the complaints handling procedure should be independent of the Reception and Integration Agency which is responsible for the operation of the scheme. For a legal analysis of the

Direct Provision Scheme, see Thornton, "Social Welfare Law and Asylum Seekers in Ireland: An Anatomy of Exclusion" [2013] 20 J.S.S.L. 66.

Miscellaneous Finally, in *O'Loughlin v Minister for Social Protection* [2014] IEHC 672, White J. struck out a special summons issued by the plaintiff whereby he sought to appeal against a decision of an appeals officer on the grounds that the summons disclosed no reasonable cause of action and was frivolous and vexatious.

PRIMARY LEGISLATION

Two Acts were passed in 2014 concerning social welfare law: the Social Welfare and Pensions Act 2014 and the Social Welfare and Pensions (No. 2) Act 2014, though it should also be noted that the Housing (Miscellaneous Provisions) Act 2014 has effected significant changes in relation to the provision of public housing, including the introduction of a new Housing Assistance Payment ("HAP") that will replace rent supplement payable to claimants with long term housing needs. As in past reviews, we have relied on explanatory material provided by the Department of Social Protection in preparing this section of this year's review.

Social Welfare and Pensions Act 2014 Section 3 of the Social Welfare and Pensions Act 2014 facilitates the provision of functions relating to the payment of social welfare and related payment services by way of arrangements with selected payment service providers. Section 4 provides that only gains from share option transactions that result in an employee actually receiving shares will come within the definition of "share-based remuneration" in order to benefit from the exemption from employer PRSI liability. Section 5 provides definitions for the EEA Agreement, the European Economic Area and Member State of the European Economic Area for the purposes of the Social Welfare Acts, while s.6 clarifies the statutory powers of the Minister to make regulations providing for refunds of employer PRSI contributions in the case of certain seafarers employed on board vessels registered in a Member State of the EU or of the European Economic Area and providing scheduled passenger services between ports within those states. Section 7 empowers the Minister to recover debts due from an employer in respect of redundancy lump sum payments from any refund of PRSI contributions to which the employer is entitled, while s.8 amends the definition of "qualified adult" for the purpose of supplementary welfare allowance and further provides that no increases in Jobseeker's Allowance, Preretirement Allowance, Supplementary Welfare Allowance, Disability Allowance or Farm Assist will be paid in respect of a qualified adult who is resident, whether temporarily or permanently, outside the State or is in prison or otherwise detained in legal custody.

Sections 9 and 10 make certain amendments in relation to family income supplement. Section 9 clarifies that where a person is living apart from his or her spouse or civil partner and children, he or she may still claim family income supplement if he or she is maintaining the spouse or civil partner and contributing substantially towards the maintenance of the children and provided that the spouse or civil partner is not claiming any social welfare payments (other than certain prescribed exceptions). Family income supplement is normally paid without change for a period of 52 weeks. However, s.10 now provides that if the claimant seeks to be engaged in remunerative full-time employment, the supplement shall be discontinued immediately. Where the claimant subsequently requalifies for family income supplement before the end of that 52 week period, payment will recommence at the rate payable at the start of the period. Section 10 also empowers the Minister to provide, by way of regulation, for a change in the weekly rate of family income supplement where there is a change in the composition of the family or in the entitlement of members of the family to any benefit or assistance. Finally, this section provides that where a person is included in a family in respect of whom family income supplement is payable, he or she cannot be regarded, for the purpose of this scheme, as a member of any other family during the period of payment.

Section 11 defines "habitual residence" for the purpose of certain social assistance schemes to mean that a person must be habitually resident in the State at the date of making the application for welfare and must remain habitually resident here for his or her entitlement to subsist. A person will also be habitually resident if s/he is a worker or self-employed person covered by art.7 of Directive 2004/38 or a family member of such a person. Where such workers or self-employed persons cease to work or be self-employed, they must be habitually resident in the State at the date of such cessation and must remain habitually resident in the State for their entitlements to subsist. The same requirement applies to their family members. The section also makes certain consequential changes reflecting the promulgation of the European Union (Subsidiary Protection) Regulations 2013 (S.I. No. 426 of 2013) while s.12 provides for a number of consequential changes, following on from the changes in s.11, to uncommenced provisions of the Social Welfare and Pensions Act 2008 relating to the transfer of responsibility for the blind welfare allowance scheme from the HSE to the Department.

Section 13 corrects an incorrect reference in s.320 of the 2005 Act providing that the decision of a deciding officer is, subject to certain exceptions, final and conclusive. Section 14 amends s.333A of the 2005 Act to extend the reference to relevant sections in that provision to include s.341(10) of the 2005 Act, inserted by s.16 of the 2014 Act. Section 333A provides a definition of the terms "benefit" and "assistance" as used in the provisions to which s.333A applies. However, s.341(10) does not use either term. Quaere, whether s.14 should have referred to s.341(9) in this context? Section 15 provides for the termination of appointments of social welfare inspectors and also regulates the position of members of An Garda Síochána seconded to the Minister for the purpose of acting as a social welfare inspector. Section 16 enables the Department to recover overpaid social welfare from certain lump sum payments in respect of refunds of PRSI contributions or made under the Redundancy Payments Act 1967 or the Protection of Employees (Employers' Insolvency) Act 1984 made by the Minister to the person who received the overpaid welfare. Section 17 extends the situations in which overpaid welfare may be recovered by way of notice of attachment to include situations in which the overpaid claimant is entitled to payments from State funds. Section 18 empowers the Minister to discriminate on grounds of age in relation to employment schemes and other schemes and programmes. Section 19 transposes Directive 2010/41 on the application of equal treatment between men and women engaged in self-employment activity by extending liability for PRSI to spouses or civil partners of self-employed contributors who are not business partners or employees where they perform the same or ancillary tasks. Section 20 adds Irish Water to the list of bodies deemed to be specified bodies for the purpose of ss.262–270 of the 2005 Act, s.21 repeals certain uncommenced amendments to the 2005 Act that are no longer deemed necessary, and s.22 makes a number of minor amendments to the 2005 Act.

Social Welfare and Pensions (No. 2) Act 2014 Section 2 of the Social Welfare and Pensions (No. 2) Act 2014 provides for an increase in the rate of child benefit payable in respect of single children to €135 per month. In the case of twins, the rate is increased to €202.50 each per month and in the case of multiple births of three or more children where at least three survive, the monthly rate is €270 each. Section 3 provides for an earnings disregard for a claimant of One-Parent Family Payment of €90 per week together with half the weekly earnings in excess of that amount.

SECONDARY LEGISLATION

Twenty-six statutory instruments pertaining to the social welfare code were promulgated during 2014. As in past reviews, we have relied on explanatory material provided by the Department of Social Protection in preparing this section of this year's review.

Social Welfare (Consolidated Supplementary Welfare Allowance) (Amendment) (No. 1) (Diet Supplement) Regulations 2014 (S.I. No. 36 of 2014) These Regulations provide for the discontinuance of Diet Supplement for new applicants with effect from 1 February 2014. Quaere, whether the Minister's power under s.198(2) of the 2005 Act to prescribe the class of persons to whom weekly or monthly supplements may be paid and the conditions and circumstances under which such payments may be made extends to excluding certain needs completely from the scope of s.198(1) which allows for the payment of weekly or monthly supplements to a person whose means are insufficient to meet his or her needs.

Social Welfare and Pensions Act 2012 (Section 19) (Commencement) Order 2014 (S.I. No. 93 of 2014) This Order commences s.19 of the Social Welfare and Pensions Act 2012 which extends the list of utility companies that may participate in the Department's Household Budgeting facility to include licenced energy companies.

European Union (Transfer of Pension Rights to and from Pension Scheme of European Union's Institutions) Regulations 2014 (S.I. No. 153 of 2014) These Regulations regulate the transfer of existing pension rights to and from the EU and national pension schemes in the case of workers who become officials of any of the institutions, bodies or agencies of the EU or who leave employment in any such bodies.

Social Welfare (Consolidated Contributions and Insurability) (Amendment) (No. 1) (Refunds) Regulations 2014 (S.I. No. 154 of 2014) These Regulations extend the period during which refunds of PRSI contributions may be made to certain employers who employ qualifying seafarers up to 31 December 2014.

Social Welfare (Consolidated Claims, Payments and Control) (Amendment) (No. 1) (Assessment of Means) Regulations 2014 (S.I. No. 155 of 2014) These Regulations exclude payments made to women who worked in Magdalen Laundries and payments made by the Residential Institutions Statutory Fund from the assessment of means for the purposes of social assistance payments, increases for qualified adults and family income supplement.

Social Welfare (Consolidated Supplementary Welfare Allowance) (Amendment) (No. 2) (Assessment of Means) Regulations 2014 (S.I. No. 156 of 2014) These Regulations exclude payments made to women who worked in Magdalen Laundries and payments made by the Residential Institutions Statutory Fund from the assessment of means for the purposes of supplementary welfare allowance.

Social Welfare (Rent Allowance) (Amendment) (No. 1) (Assessment of Means) Regulations 2014 (S.I. No. 157 of 2014) These Regulations exclude payments made to women who worked in Magdalen Laundries, payments made by the Residential Institutions Statutory Fund and compensation awarded by certain Tribunals and Redress Boards from the assessment of means for the purposes of the Rent Allowance payable to tenants of formerly controlled rented dwellings. They also provide for an increase in the amount of weekly means to be disregarded in respect of a qualified child who resides with a claimant of rent allowance.

Social Welfare and Pensions Act 2013 (Sections 13 and 14) (Commencement) Order 2014 (S.I. No. 308 of 2014) This Order commences ss.13 and 14 of the Social Welfare and Pensions Act 2013. Section 13 provides for the recovery of the value of certain illness-related social welfare payments from compensation awards made to persons on foot of personal injuries claims, while s.14 makes consequential amendments to the Personal Injuries Assessment Board Act 2003 in light of s.13.

Social Welfare (Consolidated Claims, Payments and Control) (Amendment) (No. 2) (Recovery of Certain Benefits and Assistance) Regulations 2014 (S.I. No. 332 of 2014) On foot of the activation of ss.13 and 14 of the Social Welfare and Pensions Act 2013, these Regulations prescribe the information to be provided by compensators when applying for a statement of recoverable benefits for the purposes of identifying the injured person and the social welfare benefits that may have been paid to that person. They also prescribe the manner in which an application for a statement of recoverable benefits is to be made. See also S.I. No. 497 of 2014 below.

Social Welfare (Consolidated Contributions and Insurability) (Amendment) (No. 2) (Excepted Emoluments and Income) Regulations 2014 (S.I. No. 333 of 2014) These Regulations specify certain forms of income that are subject to tax but which are not to be regarded as reckonable income or emoluments for the purposes of liability for a PRSI Class S self-employment contribution.

Social Welfare (Consolidated Contributions and Insurability) (Amendment) (No. 3) (Excepted Self Employed Contributors) Regulations 2014 (S.I. No. 347 of 2014) Following on the transposition of Directive 2010/41 by s.19 of the

Social Welfare and Pensions Act 2014, these regulations delete the reference to a husband, wife or civil partner of a self-employed contributor in the list of relatives currently excepted from liability for self-employment contributions.

Social Welfare (Consolidated Claims, Payments and Control) (Amendment) (No. 3) (Discrimination on Grounds of Age) Regulations 2014 (S.I. No. 369 of 2014) Pursuant to s.18 of the Social Welfare and Pensions Act 2014 which authorises the Minister to discriminate on grounds of age in relation to the provision of employment services and support, these Regulations prescribe persons between the ages of 18 and 25 for this purpose.

Social Welfare (Consolidated Supplementary Welfare Allowance) (Amendment) (No. 3) (Rent Supplement) Regulations 2014 (S.I. No. 411 of 2014) On foot of the introduction of the new Housing Assistance Payment ("HAP") by the Housing (Miscellaneous Provisions) Act 2014, these Regulations provide that new applications for rent supplement in areas in which HAP is in operation will only be paid where the claimant has been in rented accommodation, accommodation for homeless persons or in an institution for the period of not less than 183 days during the 12 months immediately preceding the claim or in receipt of rent supplement within that 12 month period. Existing claimants of rent supplement who have been in receipt of the supplement for at least 18 months may also be obliged to apply for a social housing assessment. The Regulations also provide that claimants of rent supplement who change address or who take up employment or work opportunities for short periods will continue to be eligible to apply for this supplement until arrangements for HAP are implemented in full.

Social Welfare (Consolidated Claims, Payments and Control) (Amendment) (No. 4) (Prescribed Employment Schemes) Regulations 2014 (S.I. No. 440 of 2014) These Regulations provide for sanctions to be imposed on claimants of jobseeker's benefit and jobseeker's allowance who fail to participate, without good reason, in the Youth Developmental Internship scheme.

Social Welfare (Consolidated Supplementary Welfare Allowance) (Amendment) (No. 4) (Prescribed Employment Schemes) Regulations 2014 (S.I. No. 441 of 2014) These Regulations provide for sanctions to be imposed on claimants of supplementary welfare allowance who fail to participate, without good reason, in the Youth Developmental Internship scheme.

Social Welfare (Consolidated Claims, Payments and Control) (Amendment) (No. 5) (Recovery of Certain Benefits and Assistance) Regulations 2014 (S.I. No. 497 of 2014) These Regulations extend, with effect from 1 November 2014, the information that must be provided by compensators when applying for a statement of recoverable benefits to include the injured person's PPS number.

Social Welfare (Consolidated Claims, Payments and Control) (Amendment) (No. 6) (Overpayments) Regulations 2014 (S.I. No. 511 of 2014) These Regulations enable the Minister to recover social welfare overpayments by withholding all or part of any refund of PRSI contributions or of lump sum payments made under the Redundancy Payments Act 1967 or the Protection of Employees (Employers' Insolvency) Act 1984.

Social Welfare (Consolidated Contributions and Insurability) (Amendment) (No. 5) (Modifications of Social Insurance) Regulations 2014 (S.I. No. 512 of 2014) These Regulations provide for the continuation of the payment of the public sector modified rate of PRSI contribution by certain employees of An Post transferring to the new National Lottery company, Premier Lotteries Ireland Ltd.

Social Welfare (Consolidated Contributions and Insurability) (Amendment) (No. 4) (Return of Contributions) Regulations 2014 (S.I. No. 513 of 2014) These Regulations faciliate the recovery of overpaid social welfare payments from refunds of PRSI contributions due to the person in receipt of the overpayment.

Social Welfare (Consolidated Contributions and Insurability) (Amendment) (No. 6) (Return of Contributions) Regulations 2014 (S.I. No. 514 of 2014) These Regulations extend the refund arrangements which apply in respect of PRSI contributions paid by contributors in respect of maintenance payments for married persons to cover maintenance payments for civil partners and cohabitants.

Social Welfare (Temporary Provisions) Regulations 2014 (S.I. No. 529 of 2014) These Regulations provide for a payment of a Christmas bonus to claimants of long term social welfare payments and to claimants of domiciliary care allowance. The bonus is worth 25 per cent of the weekly payment made to the claimant, subject to a minimum payment of €20.

Social Welfare and Pensions Act 2014 (Section 6) (Commencement) Order 2014 (S.I. No. 530 of 2014) This Order commences s.6 of the 2014 Act clarifying the powers of the Minister to make regulations providing for the refunding of employer PRSI contributions in the case of certain seafarers.

Social Welfare (Variation of Rate of Living Alone Allowance) Regulations 2014 (S.I. No. 568 of 2014) These Regulations provide for an increase of €1.30 in the weekly living alone allowance payable to claimants of certain welfare schemes.

Social Welfare (Consolidated Claims, Payments and Control) (Amendment) (No. 7) (Homemakers) Regulations 2014 (S.I. No. 569 of 2014) These Regulations extend the time limit within which an application to become a homemaker for the purposes of state pension (contributory) may be made.

Social Welfare (Consolidated Claims, Payments and Control) (Amendment) (No. 8) (Assessment of Means) Regulations 2014 (S.I. No. 595 of 2014) These Regulations provide that income received by way of ex gratia payments from the Lourdes Hospital Redress Scheme, the Lourdes Hospital Payment Scheme and the Surgical Symphysiotomy ex gratia Scheme shall be disregarded in assessing means for social assistance payments, increases for qualified adults and Family Income Supplement.

Social Welfare (Consolidated Supplementary Welfare Allowance) (Amendment) (No. 5) (Rent Supplement) Regulations 2014 (S.I. No. 604 of 2014) These Regulations provide for the continuation of the current maximum rent limits that apply to rent supplement beyond the expiry date of 31 December 2014. They also clarify the meaning of the references to a qualified child contained in Sch.1 to the Social Welfare (Consolidated Supplementary Welfare Allowance) Regulations 2007 (S.I. No. 412 of 2007).

Torts

THE DUTY OF CARE

Conceptual ingredients of the Duty of Care and Economic Loss The decision of the Supreme Court in *Whelan v Allied Irish Banks Plc* [2014] IESC 3 involves the most significant analysis of the nature and scope of the duty of care since *Glencar Explorations Plc v Mayo County Council (No 2)* [2002] 1 I.R. 84. Before examining what it had to say, it may be useful to summarise briefly the effects of *Glencar* on the judicial understanding of the conceptual ingredients of the duty of care.

Prior to *Glencar*, the position was that a plaintiff seeking to establish the existence of a duty of care had to pass two hurdles: that there was a sufficient proximity of relationship between the parties to warrant the imposition of a prima facie duty of care and that there were no policy reasons for not imposing such a duty. *Glencar* altered the test. Keane C.J. stated:

> "There is, in my view, no reason why courts determining whether a duty of care arises should consider themselves obliged to hold that it does in every case where injury or damage to property was reasonably foreseeable and the notoriously difficult and illusive test of 'proximity' or 'neighbourhood' can be said to have been met, unless very powerful public policy considerations dictate otherwise. It seems to me that no injustice will be done if they are required to take the further step of considering whether, in all the circumstances, it is just and reasonable that the law should impose a duty of a given scope on the defendant for the benefit of the plaintiff, as held by Costello J at the first instance in *Ward v McMaster* [1985] I.R. 29, by Brennan J. in *Sutherland Shire Council v Heyman* (1985) 157 C.L.R. 424 and by the House of Lords in *Caparo plc v Dickman* [1990] 2 A.C. 605. As Brennan J. pointed out, there is a significant risk that any other approach will result in what he called a 'massive extension of a *prima facie* duty of care restrained only by undefinable considerations…"

It is not entirely clear how many steps Keane C.J. was prescribing in this passage. The former Chief Justice can be interpreted as requiring four steps: foreseeability, proximity, the absence of countervailing policy considerations and a finding by the court that it would be just and reasonable to impose a duty of care. The case law following *Glencar* is not entirely consistent in its commitment to, or interpretation of, the test proposed by Keane C.J. Some judges have applied four steps. Others have exorcised the step dealing with public policy, generally subsuming it under the requirement of fairness, justice and reasonableness.

An example of the approach generally commanding support is *Beatty v Rent Tribunal* [2006] 1 I.L.R.M. 164, where Fennelly J. considered that the underlying principles of negligence were well established. He stated those to be: "that there is a relationship of such proximity between the parties such as to call for the exercise of care by one party towards the other; that it is reasonably foreseeable that breach of the duty of care will occasion loss to the party to whom the duty is owed; and that it is just and reasonable that the duty should be imposed."

In *Whelan*, the Supreme Court dismissed a claim for negligence, for reasons other than those that had been the basis for Peart J.'s dismissal of the claim. This case involved a solicitor whose instructions had been focused on a specific, somewhat tangential, aspect of a proposed loan facility of €25m for the purchase of lands, which was unconnected with the nature of the facility itself, mistakenly interpreted a communication from the lender as indicating that the loan was of a non-recourse character. Unbeknownst to him, one of the plaintiffs, Mr Lynch, regarded the question as to whether the loan was non-recourse or recourse as critical to his acceptance of the loan. Peart J. declined to impose liability under the *Hedley Byrne* principle, which was integrated into the broader duty of care principle. He stated:

> "In circumstances where [the solicitor] had never been asked to advise on the nature of the facility, was aware that the loan at all times was a recourse loan and had never been told by anybody on the [plaintiff's] side that only a non-recourse loan was acceptable to them, it is hard to see why it would be just and reasonable that his firm should be found to owe a duty of care such that they become liable to the plaintiffs in a sum of €25 million, less anything achieved on a sale of the lands. I would have to be satisfied that as a result of his clients' instructions, or as a result of what he ought reasonably to have known or inferred from those instructions, or even the transaction generally, it was foreseeable that is his answer was incorrect, the plaintiffs would sign up to a loan which he knew or had reason to believe they never intended. I fail to see how that was reasonably foreseeable given the fact that he had never been given the information that a last minute decision had been made that they would not sign up to a recourse facility. I do not believe that when looked at objectively by a reasonable bystander, properly and fully informed of all relevant facts, such a consequence should or could have been foreseen."

Peart J. specifically adverted to the fact that reasonable foreseeability was also a test for remoteness of damage. He explained that, even if he had been satisfied that the solicitor's firm had owed a duty of care to the plaintiffs, he still would not have awarded damages on the basis that they were too remote. Peart J. concluded that "it was not reasonably foreseeable that by acting upon the answer given, the plaintiffs would … sign up to a facility the nature of which they were unwilling to accept, since [the solicitor's firm was] kept in ignorance in that regard."

On appeal, the Supreme Court held that Peart J. had been mistaken to apply the "just and reasonable" test and that a duty of care did arise. (The court also held, however, that Mr Lynch had not in fact communicated an insistence that the loan be non-recourse; thus this claim, albeit for a different reason, was not successful.) O'Donnell J. (Fennelly and McMenamin JJ. concurring) provided a detailed consideration of the duty of care. The best way of analysing his discussion of the subject is first to quote it in its entirety and then to examine its implications. O Donnell J. stated:

"In my opinion the trial judge was quite right to conclude that even though the relevant advice had been given on an occasion, and in relation to a matter outside the original retainer, there was sufficient proximity between the Lynchs and LK Shields to give rise to a duty of care, if all other requirements were satisfied. Similarly, it cannot seriously be doubted that if a duty of care arose, then the firm was in breach of that duty and negligent in advising that the alterations effected on the 7th February meant that the loan was non-recourse to all the borrowers. It is clear, therefore, that the plaintiffs' claim against LK Shields failed because the trial judge considered that it was necessary to take at least one further step and establish that in addition to proximity and the lack of care, it would also be fair and reasonable to impose liability on the defendants. The finding that the damage was not foreseeable was based on essentially the same considerations.

I regret that I cannot agree with the trial judge's approach to the issue of the existence of a duty of care in this case. The cases of *Ward v. McMaster* [1988] I.R. 337 and *Glencar*, particularly when set against the background, in other common law jurisdictions, of cases such as *Donoghue v. Stevenson* [1931] A.C. 562, *Hedley Byrne & Co. Ltd. v. Heller & Partners Ltd.* [1964] A.C. 465 (hereinafter "*Hedley Byrne*"), *Home Office v. Dorset Yacht Co. Ltd.* [1970] A.C. 1004, *Anns v. Merton London Borough Council* [1978] A.C. 728, the decision of the High Court of Australia in *Sutherland* [*Shire Council v Heyman* (1985) 157 C.L.R. 424] and the later decision of the House of Lords in *Caparo* [*Industries Plc v Dickman* [1990] 2 A.C. 60], are probably by now well known to every student of tort, indeed law students more generally, since the emergence of the neighbour principle in *Donoghue v. Stevenson* and its subsequent development and application is a favourite topic in introductory classes on legal systems and methods. Lord Atkin's elegant and memorable speech *in Donoghue v. Stevenson* had the effect of suggesting that there was a single unifying principle which explained why liability arose not just in that famous case, but in other individual cases in which liability had been established in negligence. Thereafter, the question increasingly became whether those areas, where it had hitherto been thought no liability and no duty of care arose or which had not yet been the subject of any decided case, would also succumb to Lord Atkin's unifying principle. Those were areas such as liability for statements rather than actions (*Hedley Byrne*), liability for public law actions of public authorities (*East Suffolk Rivers Catchment Board v. Kent* [1941] A.C. 74 and *Anns v. Merton London Borough Council*), liability for auditors of companies to third party investors (*Caparo*), pure economic loss cases (*Caparo* and *Glencar*), liability for nervous shock, and liability of builders and/or subcontractors to subsequent purchasers of buildings with whom they had no contractual relationship (*Junior Books Ltd. v. Veitchi Co. Ltd.* [1983] 1 A.C. 520), together with other favourite classroom examples such as the potential liability of rescuers.

In *Anns v. Merton London Borough Council* in the United Kingdom and *Ward v. McMaster* in this jurisdiction, the position appeared to have been reached where it was said that liability in negligence in such novel areas could be determined by the application of a two stage test. First, whether, if there was foreseeability of damage owing to the careless act there was sufficient proximity to the parties to establish a duty of care, and second, whether there were any possible policy considerations which should limit or negative the existence of the duty of care, albeit, as McCarthy J. observed in *Ward v. McMaster*, it would require powerful considerations of policy to deprive a plaintiff, who had suffered foreseeable damage as a result of the careless act of a sufficiently proximate wrongdoer, of the damages to which he or she would otherwise be entitled.

In later cases however, and put again perhaps too simply, there emerged a concern that this approach would give rise to a considerable extension of liability, and consequently cost, and make the tort of negligence the dominant vehicle for recovery in any civil action, which would threaten, if not obliterate, the other torts and even recovery in contract and quasi contract. The High Court of Australia in *Shire of Sutherland* pointed out that this approach gave rise to a significant risk of an approach which would result in a massive extension of a *prima facie* duty of care restrained only by some indefinable considerations of policy. This was important because a decision that a duty of care arose in any novel situation controlled not only the instant case, and all similar cases, but also influenced all those cases in which such a situation or some plausible analogy could be advanced, giving rise to a risk of liability which might have to be settled. Parties would have to seek insurance against such potential liability, and furthermore seek to recover that additional cost from their clients and customers, or risk claims and additional costs. In *Shire of Sutherland*, an alternative approach was mooted which was subsequently adopted both in the United Kingdom in *Caparo* and in this jurisdiction in the judgments in *Glencar*. That was where injury or damage was reasonably foreseeable, and there was sufficient proximity between the parties, a duty of care would nevertheless not arise in any such novel area unless the court considered that in all the circumstances it was just and reasonable that the law should impose a duty of care on the defendant.

In the landmark case of *Glencar* this court, through the medium of two comprehensive judgments by Keane C.J. and Fennelly J., with which the other members of the court agreed, reviewed and provided clear guidance in relation to some of the most troublesome areas of the modern law of torts. Thus, the judgments considered the law on the existence of a duty of care, the negligence liability of local authorities for failure to use discretionary powers, the tort of misfeasance of public office, the limits of the tort of breach of statutory duty, and the doctrine of legitimate expectations. In his judgment, Keane C.J. reviewed the development of the law on the existence of a duty of care starting with the famous speech of Lord Atkin in *Donoghue v. Stevenson* and that judgment's treatment of the earlier decision of Lord Esher in *Le Lievre v. Gould* [1893] 1 Q.B. 491. The judgment then traces the development of the law of negligence in England and Ireland and concludes that the oft cited portion of the judgment of McCarthy J. in *Ward v. McMaster*, which appeared to endorse the approach taken by Lord Wilberforce in *Anns v. Merton London Borough Council*, could not be taken to be part of the ratio of the decision in *Glencar* and accordingly, could not be considered to foreclose further consideration of the underlying jurisprudence. Thereafter, in what has become the foundation stone of modern jurisprudence on the tort of negligence, Keane C.J. stated:

> 'There is, in my view, no reason why courts determining whether a duty of care arises should consider themselves obliged to hold that it does in every case where injury or damage to property was reasonably foreseeable and the notoriously difficult and illusive test of "proximity" or "neighbourhood" can be said to have been met, unless very powerful public policy considerations dictate otherwise. It seems to me that no injustice will be done if they are required to take the further step of considering whether, in all the circumstances, it is just and reasonable that the law should impose a duty of a given scope on the defendant for the benefit of the plaintiff, as held by Costello J. at first instance in *Ward v. McMaster* [1985] I.R. 29, by Brennan J. in *Sutherland Shire Council v. Heyman* (1985) 157 C.L.R. 424 and by the House of Lords in *Caparo plc. v. Dickman* [1990] 2 A.C. 605. As Brennan J. pointed out, there is a significant risk that any other approach will result in what he called a massive extension of a *prima facie* duty of care restrained only by undefinable considerations …' (p. 139)

To the casual observer it might appear that there is little difference between an approach which imposes liability where there is *prima facie* a duty of care unless considerations of policy negative the existence of such a duty, and one which imposes a duty of care only when there is sufficient proximity and considerations of policy make it just and reasonable that such a duty should exist. One approach might seem to be merely the negative image of another and to the mathematically minded, five minus two is exactly the same as one plus two. However, there is and has been in practice a very significant difference between the two which might be illustrated by this case. The formulation in *Anns v. Merton London Borough Council* and *Ward v. McMaster* of *prima facie* liability only negatived by considerations of policy loads the balance heavily in favour of finding liability. Furthermore, it tends to ensure that the general issue as to the existence of a duty of care in such circumstances will be addressed in the particular circumstances of the case and the question becomes, almost imperceptibly, whether a plaintiff who has now been found to have been injured by the carelessness of a person whose acts could foreseeably cause damage to the plaintiff, should nevertheless be deprived of damages.

Viewed in this way it is, I think, apparent that the judge's conclusion that the firm of LK Shields owed no duty of care to Mr Lynch when advising as to the nature of the facility agreement because to impose a duty of care in such circumstances would not be just and reasonable cannot be maintained. First, this was not a novel area where liability was being asserted for the first time. The essential components of the plaintiffs' claim were well established. It has been beyond controversy for more than half a century that an advisor may owe a duty of care when making statements which may be relied upon even if there is no contract or retainer covering the advice. It is also well established that a solicitor may owe a duty of care independent of contract, and indeed, owe a duty of care in respect of areas outside the original retainer. None of this is or was in controversy. Second, the just and reasonable test in *Glencar* is also essentially a policy consideration and it has been determined long ago that it is just and reasonable that a solicitor, or indeed any other professional advisor, should owe a duty of care in such circumstances. It is also important that the question must be approached at that level of abstraction. As Lord Browne-Wilkinson observed in *Barrett v. Enfield London Borough Council* [2001] 2 A.C. 550 (pp.559–560):

> '… the decision as to whether it is fair, just and reasonable to impose liability in negligence on a particular class of would-be defendants depends on weighing in the balance the total detriment to the public interest in all cases from holding such class liable in negligence as against the total loss to all would-be plaintiffs if they are not to have a cause of action in respect of the loss they have individually suffered. … Questions of public policy and the question whether it is fair and reasonable to impose liability in negligence are decided as questions of law. Once the decision is taken that, say, company auditors though liable to shareholders for negligent auditing are not liable to those proposing to invest in the company … that decision will apply to all future cases of the same kind. The decision does not depend on weighing the balance between the extent of the damage to the plaintiff and the damage to the public in each particular case.'

The test does not mandate or permit a consideration of each individual case and whether the imposition of a duty of care, and therefore liability, meets some undefined concept of fairness in the particular case. If that were so, then the law would be no more than the application of individual discretion in different facts or circumstances which might well be decided differently from court to court. In such circumstances, the law of negligence would be little more than the wilderness of single instances criticised by Tennyson.

If indeed it is necessary to consider afresh the question of policy then at the appropriate level of abstraction at which that issue must be addressed, it seems clear that the law has consistently and correctly held that an advisor such as a solicitor will owe a duty of care when giving advice to a client on an area within his or her expertise and where the request for the advice, and provision of it, is neither in casual circumstances nor entirely separate from the business then being transacted. It is not necessary that a client make very clear that the advice is critical to any decision which he or she might make, or that it be the sole or decisive factor. The obligation of a professional person is to give advice some of which may be unwelcome. Clients may be slow to appreciate advice, which they are paying for, but which warns them against a course of action which they wish to follow. The practice of law and other professions have developed considerably, and in many cases for the better, but there can be strong pressures on lawyers and other advisors to take a 'commercial' view of matters, and to bring only the good news to a client. It remains very important that advisors give independent advice which, in an appropriate case, may counsel caution. The obligation to give independent and professional advice which is important not just to clients but to society more generally, is reinforced if solicitors and other advisors understand that they have a duty to be careful in the content of the advice which they give to clients. Looked at in reverse, it would be a strange and surely undesirable outcome if it were to be determined that when in the course of a transaction a bank, having been itself advised by its own solicitor, makes changes to a facility letter which may expose individual members of a family to a liability of €25 million, those clients who are paying two firms of solicitors to represent them in the transaction, are not owed any duty of care by either firm in respect of that change. Furthermore if owed no duty of care it would follow that even if advice is given to them by their own solicitors, they cannot complain when it transpires that such advice is clearly incorrect, even if they rely on that advice to their detriment and suffer substantial, even ruinous, loss.

As the trial judge recognised, his analysis of foreseeability relies entirely on the same factors which led to his conclusion on the question of the fairness and reasonableness of the existence of a duty of care. It is, in my view, subject to the same frailties. The question of foreseeability must be addressed at a general level. Is it foreseeable that when advice is given in the context of a transaction and is incorrect, a person to whom that advice is given will suffer damage? Put in this way the question answers itself. The purpose of legal advice when it is sought and given is so that a client can factor that advice into decisions which he or she may take. If that advice is incorrect, it is plainly foreseeable that the client may suffer damage. The trial judge was clearly influenced by the limited retainer which the firm had, and the fact that they were involved late in the day, and perhaps most particularly, the fact that the Lynch family gave no hint as to the overwhelming significance which they now claim to have attached to the question of the recourse of the loans. These are important factors in the case more generally, but they are not decisive on the question of foreseeability. If, for example, there were no issue of the scope of the retainer, and LK Shields had plainly been retained to negotiate and advise upon the facility letter and had given incorrect advice that the loan was now non-recourse, it could scarcely be argued that damage was not *foreseeable*. Accordingly, the conclusion that the firm owed no duty of care to the Lynch family and Mr Lynch when giving advice as to the nature of the facility letter cannot stand and must be set aside.

The setting aside of the finding that the firm owed no duty of care to the plaintiffs in respect of the advice does not mean that the trial judge's strong conviction that it would be unfair to impose liability in full or in part upon the firm in the context of this transaction is by any means irrelevant to the proper resolution of the case. On the contrary, the conclusion of an experienced trial judge who had the merit of observing the parties over an extended period of time in the setting of a trial, are of considerable value. But they may be more relevant to the question of reliance in fact, and therefore causation, and contributory negligence, as indeed the judge himself observed, than the legal issue of the duty of care."

O'Donnell J.'s comprehensive discussion merits close analysis. A number of observations may be made: First, O'Donnell J. at no point seeks to modify the test set out by Keane C.J. in *Glencar*. On the contrary, O'Donnell J. cleaves faithfully to it.

Secondly, it appears that O'Donnell J. interprets Keane C.J.'s test as involving three steps: foreseeability, proximity and a hybrid final step of policy considerations merged with the question whether it is just and reasonable to impose a duty of care: O'Donnell J. observes that "the just and reasonable test in *Glencar* is also essentially a policy consideration…" Perhaps it is reading too much into this phrase to regard O'Donnell J. as having merged the two steps but, if this is not what he meant, it is curious that he should specifically have chosen to characterise the just and reasonable step as a policy consideration.

Thirdly, related to this question, O'Donnell J.'s mathematical analogy is interesting. He regards the *Glencar* test as involving two positive requirements (ignoring foreseeability for a moment): proximity plus considerations of policy that make it just and reasonable that a duty of care should exist. He contrasts this with the *Anns* formulation, which involved a prima facie duty based on proximity qualified by considerations of policy. The *Anns* test, in his view, tended to transform the question, imperceptibly, into whether the plaintiff, an acknowledged victim of negligent conduct causing the victim foreseeable damage, should nonetheless be deprived of compensation. This concern was indeed the one that encouraged the House of Lords in *Caparo* and the Supreme Court in *Glencar* to add the further step, requiring that it be just and reasonable to impose a duty of care. O'Donnell J.'s understanding of policy considerations under the *Glencar* test appears to regard them, not simply as a brake on the prima facie duty of care but as embracing a range of positive possibility. Indeed, on one interpretation of O'Donnell J.'s remarks, a plaintiff would have to show, not only sufficient proximity of relationship to generate a prima facie duty of care, but also, separately, what might be called positive policy considerations making it just and reasonable to impose such a duty. It is true, though rarely judicially acknowledged, that policy considerations can in some cases weigh in favour of expanding the duty of care even though more often they have the opposite effect.

Fourthly, O'Donnell J. points to the fact that the case "was not a novel area where liability was being asserted for the first time" as a factor telling against the invocation of the just and reasonable test to decline imposing a duty of care. Undoubtedly it is sensible that the just and reasonable test should not be regarded as always necessary to address specifically in contexts where courts have long acknowledged that a duty of care arises. It would, for example, be odd in a "running down" case if the trial judge were to take time to address the question whether it is just and reasonable to impose a duty of care on the driver. It is interesting that Peart J. has in at least three cases involving personal injury to plaintiffs made specific reference to the just and reasonable test, though in none of them did Peart J. hold against the plaintiff on the basis that it would not be just and reasonable to impose a duty of care: *Gaffey v Dundalk Town Council* [2006] IEHC 436, *Hackett v Calla Associates* [2004] IEHC 336 and *Keogh v Electricity Supply Board* [2005] IEHC 286. One can envisage situations where the issue of the duty of care is not novel but is nonetheless a live one. A person wishing to assert that a barrister has a duty of care to a client when engaging in advocacy during court proceedings will have to convince an Irish court to depart from older judicial authorities declining to impose such a duty. (The issue has divided common law jurisdictions in the past decade, with the strong tendency towards imposing this duty; the High Court of Australia remains opposed.) One can also envisage cases where a defendant may seek to encourage the court to resile from an earlier authority imposing a duty of care. The tenor of Keane C.J.'s judgment in *Glencar* was hostile to recovery of compensation for negligently caused pure economic loss. While Keane C.J. did not formally repudiate *Junior Books v Veitchi* [1983] 1 A.C. 520 and the imposition of liability for economic loss sustained in protecting people from the risk of physical injury caused by the defendant's negligence, which Costello P. had recognised as appropriate in *Ward v McMaster* [1985] I.R. 29, Keane C.J. certainly cast a dark shadow over their future viability. Thus, the question whether it is just and reasonable to impose a duty of care can arise in contexts where the issue is far from novel.

Fifthly, O'Donnell J.'s discussion of the duty of care in the context of negligently caused pure economic loss is of particular interest because it does not appear to echo Keane C.J.'s hostility. One should not make too much of this point, however, as the issue in *Whelan* arose in the context of a well-established zone of duty based on the principles of professional negligence. Clearly, much of what a solicitor gives advice upon has economic implications and answering the question whether a loan is non-recourse is unquestionably one that is capable of falling within the remit of a solicitor's professional obligation.

Sixthly, O'Donnell J.'s discussion of the *Hedley Byrne* principle is worth noting. He states that "[i]t has been beyond controversy for more than half a century that an advisor may owe a duty of care when making statements which may be relied upon even if there is no contract or retainer concerning the advice". While this statement is not specific as to the contours of the *Hedley Byrne* principle and thus, of itself, does not adopt either a broad or a narrow interpretation of its scope, the tenor of the language, in stark contrast to that of Keane C.J. in *Glencar*, evinces no disposition to constrict the scope of either the *Hedley Byrne* principle or the duty of care for negligently caused pure economic loss generally.

Seventhly, a question of characterisation arises as to a situation involving a professional person – let us assume a solicitor – who has made a representation carelessly in a particular novel context which results in pure economic loss to a client. The court could analyse the issue in one or more of three ways: as an aspect of the *Hedley Byrne* principle (cf. *Doran v Delaney* [1998] 2 I.L.R.M. 1), as an aspect of professional negligence principles or as a distinctive issue under the *Glencar* test. O'Donnell J. is understandably reluctant to require trial judges to wheel out *Glencar* when addressing an aspect of professional negligence that may be considered to fall within the general professional duty of the defendant concerned. The principles relating to professional negligence are unhelpfully broad and lacking in any guidance as to how to deal with previously unexamined fact situations. It is worth noting that O'Donnell J. described the scope of a solicitor's duty of care in terms that leave its precise contours open for debate: "It is … well established that a solicitor *may* owe a duty of care independent of contract, and indeed, may owe a duty of care in respect of areas outside the original retainer" (emphasis added).

Eighthly, O'Donnell J. was anxious that the duty of care should be approached at a higher level of abstraction than each individual case; otherwise the law of negligence will be reduced to the spectre of "the wilderness of single instances". Yet there is a difference between the proposition that the duty of care should not have to be determined uniquely in the light of the totality of circumstances of each individual case and the proposition that a particular case must be resolved in the light of a previous categorical determination relating to the duty of care. O'Donnell J. quotes Lord Browne-Wilkinson's observations in *Barrett v Enfield London Borough Council* to the effect that, once a question of law relating to the duty of care has been determined (such as, for example, that company auditors are not liable to those proposing to invest in the company), "that decision will apply to all future cases of the same kind". While undoubtedly it is true that the decision whether to impose a duty of care in every subsequent case does not depend on weighing the balance between the extent of the damage to the plaintiff and the damage to the public in that particular case, it is not true that the original decision (*Caparo*, as it happens) is beyond reconsideration. A plaintiff is perfectly entitled to try to convince the court that the breadth or the absence of a duty of care as articulated in earlier cases should be modified. Otherwise *Donoghue v Stevenson* would have constituted an illegitimate departure from the licence to manufacturers to produce shoddy and dangerous products afforded by *Winterbottom v Wright* 10 M & W 109, 152 E.R. 402 (1842).

Ninthly, O'Donnell J. was understandably concerned that the foreseeability step should not be applied in a manner that focuses too minutely on the detailed circumstances: "The question of foreseeability must be addressed at a general level". It is worth recognising that O'Donnell J.'s approach in this context, far from being hostile to the imposition of the duty of care, as Keane C.J.'s was, appears positively supportive and certainly not directed towards inevitably defeating claims that otherwise merit the imposition of such a duty through a particularly close parsing of the facts. One is reminded of how the House of Lords in *Hughes v Lord Advocate* [1963] A.C. 837 adopted a similarly robust approach to the issue of reasonable foreseeability in the context of remoteness of damage following the decision of the Privy Council in *Overseas Tankship (UK) Ltd. v Morts Dock and Engineering Co. Ltd. (The Wagon Mound (No 1)* [1961] A.C. 388.

It must be said that an intelligent stranger encountering the law of negligence for the first time would be perplexed by its conceptual incoherence. Reasonable foreseeability is an issue that a court may have to address up to three times in negligence proceedings: as an ingredient in the determination whether a duty of care should be imposed, as part of its determination whether the standard of care has been complied with, and as the determining test for remoteness of damage. How, the stranger might ask, can the same question be relevant to three separate issues? Can it be answered differently, depending on the issue? Does it mean the same for each issue? O'Donnell J. is clearly attempting to temper the impact of the role of reasonable foreseeability in the context of the duty of care question. Still to be resolved is the question whether reasonable foreseeability should be identically interpreted when resolving the other two questions.

The duty of care of stockbrokers The financial crisis that befell Ireland six years ago has generated an avalanche of litigation. In *Haughey v J & E Davy t/a Davy* [2014] IEHC 206, the issue related to contracts for difference but Charleton J. emphasised that the case was "almost entirely fact-dependent", focusing on the character and attributes of the plaintiff. The plaintiff had invested in contracts for difference as a client of the defendant stockbroker. When he went to the stockbroker in 2005 he was a 20 year old student, struggling with his studies, who had inherited a substantial estate from his parents. He was not "a person in the full of his intellectual, physical and mental health", a fact that was "obvious to anyone interacting with him over anything but the briefest of encounters". Much of Charleton J.'s judgment is devoted to examining whether this fact ought to have been apparent to the defendant, Charleton J. coming to the emphatic conclusion in the affirmative. As a result of his investments, some of which had been successful, others seriously not, the plaintiff lost over €2 million. Charleton J. stated:

> "Davy owed a duty of care towards James Haughey. This does not require any deep legal analysis. James Haughey was paying Davy to exercise that care. The duty of care owed arose from the contract but was independently manifested in tort. Davy owed to James Haughey the duty of care that is appropriate to an experienced stockbroker towards the particular client when, pursuant that duty of care, the stockbroker has taken appropriate steps to get to know the client and as to what his or her aims are, what his or her means of knowledge are, what his or her financial circumstances are, what the attitude of the client is to risk and, importantly, judged objectively, whether that level of risk is appropriate to that client. If it is not the client should be advised against and in some circumstances more than that."

Charleton J. likened the stockbroker's duty of care to that which is required of a solicitor to a client:

> "The comparison is appropriate since it is part of the job of the lawyer to ask reasonable questions with a view to ascertaining the true position of the client for the purpose of tailoring the advice accordingly. Here, Davy have continually made the hollow argument that merely taking a pen picture was enough to get to know a client. The implication of the lack of intervention by senior management in authorising James Haughey to trade in CFDs and the failure of the document section to put a stop on the account is that a practice of a sufficient kind was being followed. That is not a discharge of the relevant duty."

Charleton J. considered that, while share transactions invariably involved risk, this did not necessarily absolve a stockbroker of liability on the basis that a client had agreed to risk without "the needs, background and knowledge of that client being first properly probed and the advice tailored appropriately". Charleton J. noted that the defendant's duty to the plaintiff existed concurrently in contract and in tort, and commented: "James Haughey was paying for advice. He had contracted for fees to receive advice based on appropriate analysis of who he was and what his objectives were". In this context, Charleton J. quoted Lord Goff's statement in *Henderson v Merrett Syndicates Ltd.* [1995] 2 A.C. 145 at 193–194 that:

> "[t]he common law is not antipathetic to concurrent liability and [..] there is no sound basis for a rule which automatically restricts the claimant to either a tortious or a contractual remedy. The result may be untidy; but given that the tortious duty is imposed by the general law, and the contractual

> duty is attributable to the will of the parties, I do not find it objectionable that the claimant may be entitled to take advantage of the remedy which is most advantageous to him, subject only to ascertaining whether the tortious duty is so inconsistent with the applicable contract that, in accordance with ordinary principle, the parties may be taken to have agreed that the tortious remedy is to be limited or excluded."

Charleton J. stated his conclusions in frank terms:

> "The Court is bound as a matter of law to accept, and further accepts as a matter of expert opinion, that the correct way to have dealt with James Haughey would have been for Davy, firstly, to get to know him properly. In that context, secondly, if there was a manifest desire coupled with appropriate knowledge to engage in some form of trading in contracts for difference, someone with his background and vulnerability in terms of not having a job and only having inherited wealth should strongly have been advised in writing against any trading in contracts for differences. The correct approach, thirdly, for any investment for this particular client with his particular needs and his special disabilities would be to structure a share portfolio that was spread over time and over investments that would minimise risk; thus providing a reasonable prospect of a steady but conservative return. Had Joe Motley been receiving fees from this client that is indeed what would have happened. It did not happen. That failure represents negligence and manifest breach of contract through deliberate neglect over the relevant period of the relationship.
>
> In summary, Davy manifested an insufficient level of care throughout the entirety of the relationship with James Haughey. Davy failed to provide the service paid for throughout the entirety of the relationship. This was equivalent to, or amounted to, deliberate neglect. This particular client should never have been allowed at any stage of this relationship to engage in contracts for difference either at all or at the level involved. Nor did James Haughey know what he was doing to the degree that he ought to have known prior to being introduced to and while being allowed to speculate with these products. The Court is satisfied that the concept and the ramifications of contracts for difference were never properly explained to James Haughey by Davy. The Court is further satisfied that he remained genuinely mystified in giving evidence as to the full implications and ramifications of these instruments."

Charleton J. awarded damages in the sum of €2,099,621, for the net losses incurred by the plaintiff for the contracts for difference trading accounts, the non-recoverable capital gains tax and the interest cost of funds invested.

The question arises as to whether this case has wider ramifications. The simplest view would be that it does not, as the particular circumstances of the plaintiff are unlikely to be replicated very often. However, the principles stated by Charleton J. and the heavy burden resting on stockbrokers to ensure that their clients are truly suitable for investing in the manner agreed would suggest that the net of liability may well be cast more broadly than had previously been assumed.

Finally, in this context, it is necessary to note Baker J.'s decision in *Ryan v Danske Bank A/S t/a Danske Bank* [2014] IEHC 236. The plaintiff, a borrower, sought to have imported into his contractual relationship with the bank, from which he had borrowed money, an obligation on the part of the bank to behave towards him in a fair and equitable way, as the Consumer Protection Code (the "Code") required. The Code was made by the Central Bank pursuant to the regulatory power contained in s.117 of the Central Bank Act 1989 (the "1989 Act"). Section 117(1) requires the provisions of any such code to be observed by a holder of a bank licence. Failure to comply with a direction given to a licence holder to comply with the provisions of a code constitutes an offence rendering the offender liable to be tried summarily or on indictment. The Central Bank is also given the power to administer administrative sanction for contravention of the Code.

As Baker J. noted, the statutory regime makes no reference to the impact, if any, that a breach of one of the codes might have on the contractual rights of a bank and its customers or on court proceedings for enforcement of those rights. For that reason the legal status of the codes issued by the Central Bank under its statutory regulatory powers had been the subject of what Hogan J. had described in *Irish Life and Permanent v Duff* [2013] IEHC 43 as "cross-currents of judicial opinion".

Baker J. provided a detailed review of the recent case law, concluding that the Central Bank Codes of Conduct might inform a court exercising its discretionary powers in the context of orders for possession and related matters but that such discretion did not, without more, become a ground on which a plaintiff might mount a claim for relief, whether in the form of injunctive relief, declaratory relief or damages. The discretion, Baker J. held, is that of the court, not one imported into the contractual nexus, or one which itself could find a cause of action. The court concluded that the "breach of [a] provision of a code does not in my view offer a borrower a substantive basis on which relief may be sought. It may sound in equity or in defence but it does not offer a justiciable cause of action to a plaintiff at common law."

The plaintiff also argued that the bank owed him a duty of care not to appoint a receiver or seek to enforce its security without giving him an opportunity to be heard and to deal with the arrears. Baker J. rejected this argument, noting that, in *Shamji v Johnson Matthey Bankers Ltd* [1986] B.C.L.C. 278, Hoffman J. had described the issue as follows:

> "The appointment of a receiver seems to me to involve an inherent conflict of interest. The purpose of the power to enable the mortgagee to take the management of the company's property out of the hands of the directors and entrust it to a person of the mortgagee 's choice. That power is granted to the mortgagee by the security documents in completely unqualified terms. It seems to me that a decision by the mortgagee to exercise the power cannot be challenged except perhaps on grounds of bad faith. There is no room for the implication of a term that the mortgagee shall be under a duty to the mortgagor to 'consider all relevant matters' before exercising the power. If no such qualification can be read into the security documents, I do not think that a wider duty can exist in tort ... I might add that Harman J. once remarked that the analogous power of the mortgagee to enter into possession may be exercised 'before the ink is dry on the mortgage'. Certainly there has

> never been any suggestion that the right to exercise the power, as opposed to the way in which the mortgagee deals with mortgage property once he is in possession, is qualified by a duty of care to the mortgagor."

Adopting this analysis Baker J. was "not persuaded that the plaintiff can show that a duty of care arises in the choice by the Bank to appoint a receiver. Certain duties may arise in the receiver or the Bank, as the case may be, if a sale is effected but these duties are not the subject of this application." Baker J. did not expressly deal with an argument that a breach of the Consumer Code generated civil liability in tort for breach of statutory duty, though it seems fair to say that her general analysis evinced little enthusiasm for such an avenue of liability. In order to succeed in an action of this kind, a borrower would have to establish that the statutory provisions were designed to protect a particular class rather than the general public, and the damage he or she sustained was of a kind that the statutory provisions were designed to protect that class against.

Duty of care of Gardaí involved in public order duties In *Fagan v Garda Commissioner* [2014] IEHC 128, Irvine J. provided an important analysis of the issue of the duty of care of members of An Garda Síochána when involved in public order duties. The plaintiff, a 60 year old resident of Gardiner Street, Dublin, was injured when knocked down by a member of An Garda Síochána Public Order Unit deployed to deal with a protest against the visit of Queen Elizabeth II to Dublin in 2011. The incident occurred on the footpath of Dorset Street, close to the Eccles Street junction, as members of the Public Order Unit, in riot gear, on the instructions of their superior officers, started without prior notification to jog forward. Other pedestrians cleared out of the way but not the plaintiff, who was in the course of telephoning his daughter to tell her that he would be unable to meet her at her school on account of the protest, and who was unaware of the sudden advance of the unit. The plaintiff's claim for negligence was met by the following two substantive legal defences:

> "that the defendants did not owe a common law duty of care to the plaintiff as to the manner in which they exercised their public order function; and that, if they did owe such a duty of care to the plaintiff when exercising their function to maintain public order, the standard of proof required by any plaintiff would have to be high–at the level of malice or gross negligence–in order to reflect their operational requirements."

Counsel for the defendants, in support of the former argument, relied, inter alia, on the decisions of the House of Lords in *Hill v Chief Constable of West Yorkshire* [1989] 1 A.C. 53, Kearns P. in *Lockwood v Ireland* [2011] 1 I.R. 374 and Hedigan J. in *L.M v Commissioner of An Garda Síochána* [2012] I.L.R.M. 132, all of which, as Irvine J. acknowledged are "authority for the proposition that members of a police force are immune from actions for negligence in respect of their activities concerning the investigation, prosecution and suppression of crime." Counsel further sought support from the Supreme Court's decision in *Glencar Explorations plc v Mayo County Council (No. 2)* [2002] 1 I.R. 84, to the effect that a public authority could not be sued in negligence in respect of any decision made by it when exercising its statutory functions, unless it could be established that the decision had been made in the context of some wrong or improper motivation.

Counsel for the defendants had not furnished the court with any case law supporting an alleged immunity from suit of members of a police force when involved in public order duties or any written authority to this effect among textbook writers on torts. Moreover, as Irvine J. noted, there was no statutory provision conferring special protections on the Gardaí when exercising such functions. Irvine J. did not consider that *Glencar* afforded protection to the Garda. She stated:

> "In comparing the facts of the present case with those of *Glencar*, the first thing to note is that gardaí when carrying out public order functions, unlike the County Council in *Glencar*, are not acting in pursuance of any statutory obligation. Further, in my view, it cannot be argued that to impose a duty of reasonable care on gardaí when exercising their public order functions would paralyse them in their capacity to achieve public order or would otherwise render them ineffective in carrying out those functions. The public order functions of the gardaí are very wide ranging. In many instances they are carried out in circumstances where there is no significant risk to innocent members of the public or indeed to themselves. If a blanket immunity were to be afforded in respect of the actions of all gardaí when exercising any public order function that would be to give them a latitude extremely disproportionate to their needs. Indeed such immunity could readily be abused by the use of excessive or unnecessary force, something that would not be in the public interest."

This passage provokes a couple of observations. First, the County Council in *Glencar* was acting in the discharge of a statutory function rather than a statutory duty. Second, s.7(1) of the Garda Síochána Act 2005 (the "2005 Act") sets out what it describes as the function of An Garda Siochánά, which is to provide policing and security services for the State with the objective of achieving seven stated goals. Subsection (4) provides that the section does not affect any duties that members of An Garda Síochána have by virtue of any other enactment or at common law. Subsection (5) provides that the section is not to be taken to confer on any person a right in law that he or she would not otherwise have to seek damages for a member's performance of, or failure to perform, a function referred to in the section or to provide a service referred to in the section. Third, it is worth noting that Irvine J. was rightly sensitive to the danger of affording an immunity to the use of force, especially the use of force by agents of the State.

Irvine J. was not willing to apply to the area of public order functions the immunity already recognised by courts for the exercise of prosecutorial and investigative functions: *Hill v Chief Constable of West Yorkshire* [1989] A.C. 53, *Lockwood v Ireland* [2011] 1 I.R. 374, *W. v Ireland (No. 2)* [1997] 2 I.R. 141. In *Hill*, Lord Templeman had stated that, if it were possible to sue the police for negligence in the discharge of its investigative functions;

> "every citizen will be able to require the court to investigate the performance of every policeman. If the policeman concentrates on one crime, he may be accused of neglecting others. If the policeman does not arrest on suspicion

> a suspect with previous convictions, the police force may be held liable for subsequent crimes. The threat of litigation against a police force would not make a policeman more efficient. The necessity for defending proceedings, successfully or unsuccessfully, would distract the policeman from his duties."

Irvine J. did not believe that imposing a duty of care on members of An Garda Síochána when performing their public order functions would involve the same difficulties. She stated:

> "Each case would turn on its own merits and ought to be capable of being dealt with in a relatively straightforward manner such as occurred in the present case. No particular evidential difficulties should arise. Neither can it be stated that the ability of the gardaí to perform their public order duties would be brought to an effective standstill or that their time available to deal other duties would be significantly adversely affected if members of the public had the right to maintain claims for damages for negligence in such circumstances. Further, the threat of such litigation should not, I believe, interfere with their likely efficiency in the conduct of their overall garda duties. Indeed the fact that there is no case law to be found in this jurisdiction dealing with the duty of care owed by gardaí to the public when carrying out even their regular duties would tend to support these conclusions."

Irvine J. went on to note that even drivers of emergency vehicles, who might be exempted from ordinary speed limits, were not exempted in terms of liability for negligence. However, in determining whether due care had been taken, the court was entitled to give the object of the journey due weight. It would make no sense to conclude that Gardaí when performing public order duties could be deemed to be under any less of an obligation in terms of the duty of care which they owed to members of the public.

Neither did Irvine J. favour the option of setting some higher threshold which the plaintiff must establish, such as malice or recklessness, so as to succeed in liability. That again would involve affording a different, albeit lesser, type of immunity than that already rejected by her, which was not provided for by statute and in respect of which no legal authority has been produced.

Instead, Irvine J. preferred the straightforward application of the standard negligence test. The core of the concept of reasonableness was "sufficiently flexible to take into account the interests of the Gardaí and the public alike". Irvine J. identified three factors: the probability of an accident if reasonable care is not used, the gravity of the threatened injury and the social utility of the defendant's conduct at the relevant time. These factors had been recognised in earlier decisions, some of which have also identified a fourth factor: the social or economic cost of preventing the injury. Irvine J. considered that the probability of an accident occurring as a result of a member of the Public Order Unit failing to proceed with due care was "quite small". The members of the unit should have been entitled to assume that, as they were moving along the pavement, anyone there would notice their advance and be able to move out of their way. Moreover, the gravity of any threatened injury to a pedestrian was "likely to be very low". Further, the social utility of the unit's activities was high. It was attempting to maintain public order by reclaiming the streets from protestors whose unlawful violent actions might have potentially caused grave injuries to the members of the public, including the plaintiff, or to visiting dignatories on an official state visit. Irvine J. observed:

> "I believe that if I were to hold the defendants liable for an innocent collision between a member of the riot squad and a man making a phone call, albeit entirely well motivated, who had placed himself between demonstrating rioters and a line of riot squad police officers and who because of that telephone conversation remained oblivious to their advance and was renedered incapable of taking any evasive action, would be grossly unreasonable."

Irvine J. concluded her judgment with some general observations of the plaintiff's contributory negligence—an issue rendered moot by her finding that the Gardaí had not been guilty of any negligence. She did not ascribe a specific percentage to the reduction in the award. She stated:

> "As was clear from the evidence, the plaintiff is clearly a devoted father with a very high sense of parental responsibility. Regrettably it was these latter traits that … led him to take a number of risks with his own safety that he might otherwise not have taken. Every citizen is obliged to take reasonable care in carrying out their day to day activities in public places. The level of care that they must take for their safety clearly depends upon the circumstances in which they find themselves.
>
> When the plaintiff left his home on 17th May, 2011, he certainly knew that there was trouble in the vicinity of Parnell Street. By the time he got to Dorset Street it should have been clear to him that he was walking into a potentially dangerous situation. There were, according to his own statement, hundreds of "thugs" a substantial number of whom were throwing missiles at that junction. As soon as he got past the rioters at the junction of Eccles Street and Dorset Street and started walking towards Bolton Street he should have noticed the line of riot police blocking both the roadway and the footpath and it ought to have been immediately clear to him that he would not be able to get past the cordon. He should have retreated at that stage knowing that as long as he remained between the rioters and their intended target, the riot squad he would be at risk of injury from any number of sources including missiles such as bricks, bottles and fireworks which were being thrown by the protestors at the riot squad and also from any potential escalation in violence between the two adversaries.
>
> I do not think it was reasonable for the plaintiff to conclude that he would be safe just because Dorset Street had not been cordoned off and he had not been advised by the gardaí who were present leave the area. As an intelligent adult, he should have been able to foresee the potential range of dangers to which he was exposing himself.
>
> Regrettably, and again for the most worthy of reasons, the plaintiff decided to make a telephone call from the centre of the footpath. He didn't make his call having sought the protection of a doorway. Neither did he

> stand with his back to the wall, a position which would have allowed him keep any eye out for potential missiles and for any engagement between the protestors and their target, the riot squad. The video and still images establish that the plaintiff was the only member of the public who did not respond to the escalation in the violence and the movement of the riot squad along the footpath. Eight seconds after a barrier was thrown onto the footpath in front of him, the plaintiff is still on his telephone in the middle of that footpath. Every one else managed to retreated to the protection of the wall or elsewhere."

PROFESSIONAL NEGLIGENCE

Medical care In *Foley v Bons Secours Health System t/a Bons Secours Galway* [2014] IEHC 91, Irvine J. imposed liability on a doctor for failing to diagnose a patient's anastomotic leak. Applying the principles stated in *Dunne v National Maternity Hospital* [1989] I.R. 91, Irvine J. observed:

> "I accept [the] evidence that for [the doctor] to have made an incorrect diagnosis of a post operative ileus was not negligent *per se*. However, I accept [the] evidence that, having regard to the patient's post operative history and progress as recorded in the nursing records, the most likely cause for the plaintiff's symptoms at that time was a leak and that it was unacceptable for [the doctor] to fail to consider a leak within his differential diagnosis. The fact that [the doctor] in his own evidence did not consider the patient's symptoms as possibly referable to a leak was to fall short of the standard to be expected of him."

OCCUPIERS' LIABILITY

Duty to visitors In *Deehan v Loughlinstown Inns Ltd t/a The Lough Inn* [2014] IEHC 182, the plaintiff had attended a "Ladies Evening" at the defendant's public house. Payment was required for entry to the event. The plaintiff had consumed "some alcohol". During the evening's entertainment, a spot prize was thrown into the audience. Several people, including the plaintiff, jumped to catch it. In the excitement of the moment, someone pushed against her and she fell, hitting herself on the edge of a loudspeaker on the floor. The plaintiff sued the defendant. Barrett J.'s judgment does not specifically refer to the grounds put forward, although he quotes s.3 of the Occupiers' Liability Act 1995 (the "1995 Act"), which prescribes a "common duty of care" for occupiers to "visitors" relative to damages existing on the premises. The plaintiff also invoked *Coleman v Kelly* (1951) 85 I.L.T.R. 48 and *Rodgers v JACKS Taverns Ltd* [2012] IEHC 314. Barrett J. distilled from these two decisions the following principles:

> "First, the duty of a pub operator is to take all reasonable steps to safeguard patrons against risks and dangers that are foreseeable. Second, a pub operator is not required to guard against improbable or unlikely happenings. Third, the commercial and practical feasibility of such safeguards as might

> be taken by a pub operator is relevant to consideration of whether those safeguards ought to be taken. Fourth, there are dangers that reasonable people expect to encounter, in respect of which they do not expect to be guarded against, and for which they ought not to expect compensation. Fifth, provided a pub operator uses reasonable care and skill to make premises fit for purpose and to operate competitions without risk to attendees, it may be possible to infer a contractual obligation whereby attendees undertake to take reasonable care for their own safety and to accept the dangers inherent to the entertainment."

Applying the principles to the instant case, Barrett J. concluded that it had not been proven that the defendant had failed to take all reasonable steps to safeguard its patrons against risks and dangers that were foreseeable. The proprietors had cleared a space for entertainment taking place in a pub that was more than half-empty, setting aside one alcove for the entertainment and cordoning off another alcove for the disc jockey. The fact that the plaintiff fell to the floor did "not seem an improbable or unlikely event" at a venue where alcohol had been taken and spirits were high and thus reasonable safeguards ought to have been, and were, taken.

It was not clear to Barrett J. what additional safeguards might have been taken to render the pub safer on the evening in question. It had not been proven to the court that the loudspeaker against which the plaintiff had fallen was negligently positioned; on the contrary, the evidence suggested that care had been taken to ensure that it was safely positioned. Moreover, the plaintiff could have fallen anywhere in the pub and the only means of effectively guarding against the risk of such a fall would have been "to swaddle every available surface in the pub in protective material". For the defendant to "accident-proof its premises in such a manner would be both highly expensive and entirely impracticable". To the extent, "if at all", that the matter fell to be treated as one of contract law and not tort, Barrett J. found that the plaintiff had undertaken to take reasonable care of her own safety and to accept the dangers inherent to the party game in which she engaged. Barrett J. observed:

> "[A] person who freely elects to go to a pub, who freely elects to drink alcohol, who freely elects to engage in a party game and who freely elects to jump for a spot prize, can reasonably anticipate that she may fall, cannot reasonably expect that every part of the pub will be proofed so that there can be no injury occasioned if she does fall, and ought not to assume that she will be entitled to compensation when in fact she falls."

The case of *Moore v Westwood Club Ltd* [2014] IEHC 44 is of interest in demonstrating that a safe system of operations will not afford a defence to an occupier if it fails on the fateful occasion. The plaintiff fell when crossing the floor of a restaurant area in the defendant's nightclub and injured her hand when the glass she was carrying fractured. The nightclub was a large one: on the night in question there were 900 people on the premises. Herbert J. was satisfied that the plaintiff was not intoxicated at the time she fell. The nightclub proprietors had chosen floor tiles with good slip resistance. It had consulted companies specialising in assessing and reducing the risk of slippage and had regularly carried out the anti-slip treatment prescribed by one of these companies. Herbert J. was satisfied that the floor on which the plaintiff had fallen, "as maintained by the [nightclub proprietors], provided a safe standing and walking surface for users, including the plaintiff, when dry". As to the position when wet, an expert who gave evidence on behalf of the plaintiff testified that the floor would suffer a "significant decrease" in slip resistance. A safe level of slip resistance depended on ensuring that liquid did not build up in the pores/surfaces roughness valleys which hold, and thereby neutralise the impact of, wetness on the floor. This was consistent with the advice given by the company that had supplied the anti-slip treatment to the nightclub proprietors.

On the night of the accident, there were six trained cleaners stationed at pre-designated locations, with a seventh patrolling the restaurant, bar and dance floor areas. The cleaning stations were well equipped with signs and cleaning equipment. Floor staff and security staff had been instructed to remain at the scene of any breakage or spillage they observed until a cleaner arrived. Herbert J. found that this system of care and maintenance constituted a full and effective discharge by the nightclub of its duty of care to the plaintiff, "provided, of course that the system was in operation on the occasion".

The evidence of the plaintiff and another witness was that the floor was wet. The plaintiff described the floor as being of brown colour. The managing director of the nightclub and the general manager of the restaurant and bar were not in a position to give any evidence as to the actual performance of the cleaners and other staff members on the fateful night. Herbert J. noted that no other witnesses had been called to supply this evidence. Herbert J. concluded that the cleaning and maintenance system "so carefully set up by the defendants", had failed to operate effectively that night. Whether the cleaning and maintenance system had failed under the pressure of the large number of patrons or for some other reason could not be ascertained but there was no evidence to contradict that of the plaintiff and another witness as to the condition of the floor in the restaurant area at the time the plaintiff fell. Herbert J. found that the valleys in the micro-rough surface of the floor tiles that held liquid and therefore controlled slipping had become filled and blocked by a build-up of matter or precipitates from fluids or contaminated water on the surface of the floor. This had the effect of compromising the slip resistance of the floor in the area where the plaintiff fell.

Duty to recreational users In *Ahmed v Longford Town Council* [2014] IESC 46, the Supreme Court affirmed De Valera J.'s dismissal of a claim by a 10 year old boy who had been injured when he fell off a swing in the defendant's playground. He was a recreational user, for the purposes of the 1995 Act, but the defendant, who had provided the swing for his use, had been obliged by s.4(4) to take reasonable care to maintain it in a safe condition. The expert evidence disclosed that the seat of the swing had been placed four fifths of an inch lower than it should have been. De Valera J. found that this did not constitute a breach of the defendant's duty and also that it had not caused he injury. The Supreme Court focused on the issue of causation and concluded that De Valera J. had been entitled to come to the conclusion at which he had arrived.

EMPLOYERS' LIABILITY

Violent co-employee In *Elmontem v Nethercross Ltd* [2014] IEHC 91, a financial controller of a hotel and leisure complex was subjected to an "unexpected and vicious assault" by the head chef during a conversation about the non-receipt by the head chef of a letter regarding the VHI. The details of the assault are set out below, in the section dealing with the issue of vicarious liability, which also arose in the case. Here, it is only necessary to mention that the head chef had been fired from previous employment following an incident when he had thrown a pan at an under chef. The person who fired him had gone on to become general manager at the hotel and leisure complex before the head chef was recruited. He failed to mention the earlier incident when the recruitment was taking place and had recommended him as ideal for the position.

Herbert J. imposed liability on the employer (as well as on the assailant). He considered that every employer had a non-delegable duty of care "to take all reasonable precautions for the safety of each of its employees and not to expose them to a reasonably foreseeable risk of injury: to act as a reasonably careful and prudent employer would in the circumstances". A similar but more extensive duty was placed on employers by the provisions of the Safety Health and Welfare at Work Act 2005 (the "2005 Act"). Section 8(1) of the 2005 Act provides that "every employer shall ensure, so far as is reasonably practicable, the safety, health and welfare at work of his or her employees." Without prejudice to the generality of s.8(1), s.8(2)(b) imposes a duty on an employer of "managing and conducting work activities in such a way as to prevent, so far as is reasonably practicable, any improper conduct or behaviour likely to put the safety, health or welfare at work of his or her employees at risk."

Herbert J. noted that there is no definition in the 2005 Act of "improper conduct or behaviour". He considered that "it would include such matters as bullying, harassment, rough play, practical joking, racial or other abuse or physical violence".

Herbert J. recorded that the evidence had established that the plaintiff's employer, through its general manager, was aware that the head chef had on a previous occasion in a fit of temper caused physical injury to a fellow employee in the course of their joint employment. The general manager knew or ought to have known that there was a very real risk, not just a mere possibility, that this could occur again, if for any reason the head chef's temper became aroused and that this exposed his fellow employees, including the plaintiff, to a risk of physical injury. It was reasonably foreseeable that he was likely to prove a source of danger to other employees because of his apparently ungovernable temper. It had not been submitted, and Herbert J. would not accept, that the plaintiff's employer had been negligent or in breach of statutory duty in employing the head chef at all. The evidence had not established that the general manager was aware of any further assaults perpetrated or threatened by the head chef on fellow employees. He had dismissed him following the previous assault. This might have led the general manager to assume that such an incident was unlikely to recur. However, the cause of the previous assault had not been a personal antipathy between the head chef and a particular fellow employee no longer on the scene:

> "The cause was the [head chef's] losing his temper to an almost maniac

level with a co-worker over some dispute or perceived grievance in the course of their work. A real risk of a recurrence therefore remained. In my judgment the making of such an assumption would not and did not excuse the employer from taking no measures whatsoever to prevent a recurrence. The [employer] did not exercise reasonable care and, certainly did not exercise all due care to put in place measures to prevent or to protect against, such an event. This was not a risk which could be entirely eliminated, but in my judgment was one which could have been adequately controlled without grossly disproportionate or expensive measures.

The [employer], however, took no care to put in place measures to prevent a recurrence of such improper conduct or behaviour on the part of the head chef] likely to put the safety and health of other employees at risk. There was no evidence that the [employer] had a Safety Statement or a notified policy which identified conduct or behaviour in the workplace that would not be tolerated–conduct such as verbal abuse or physical violence of or towards other workers. There was no evidence that [the general manager] had notified and warned the [head chef] in writing in clear and definite terms that physical violence towards any other employee would not be tolerated and would result in his being dismissed for gross misconduct.... The evidence did not establish that the [employer] had security staff or C.C.T.V. monitoring at the complex. This might have had an additional deterrent effect on the [head chef]. However, one cannot lose sight of the fact that the [head chef] perpetrated the assault on the plaintiff in the presence of another employee … and a short distance from the office of [the] managing director … ."

The managing director had given evidence that, prior to the assault on the plaintiff, he had received a complaint from another employee, who was of the same ethnic background as the head chef, that the head chef had made very offensive racist remarks about his wife. The managing director had immediately investigated this complaint. The head chef had apologised to the other employee and the apology had been accepted. The managing director had given a verbal warning to the head chef on that occasion. Far from regarding this as evidence of the employer's discharge of its duty of care to the plaintiff, Herbert J. considered that it strengthened the case against it, noting:

"In my judgment an incident like this should have clearly brought home to the [employer] the urgent necessity of having a clear Safety Statement or policy with regard to improper conduct or behaviour at work, especially having regard to the multi ethnic nature of its large workforce."

Stress and Bullying The courts have recognised three categories of psychological injury that an employee may suffer, each determined by its own distinctive legal principles. These are occupational stress, workplace stress and bullying. In *Glynn v Minister for Justice, Equality and Law Reform* [2014] IEHC 133, Kearns P. observed that each of these categories:

"conceptually at least, are quite different from each other, though on occasion they can overlap and coincide. Occupational stress is not actionable given that occupational stress is something which every employed person may experience at some stage of his or her working life and can occur for reasons quite distinct from and unrelated to bullying. Workplace stress on the other hand may be actionable if certain legal criteria are met. It can be the result of behaviour which falls far short of bullying. It can be the result of negligence where excessive demands are made of an employee or where complaints about shortcomings in the workplace go unheeded. It lacks however that degree of deliberateness which is the hallmark of bullying.

> It follows that the first question that must be asked in every bullying case is whether the behaviour complained of, by reference to an objective test, imports that degree of calibrated inappropriateness and repetition which differentiates bullying from workplace stress or occupational stress."

Kearns P. noted that the legal definition of bullying as recommended by the *Report by the Task Force on the Prevention of Workplace Bullying* (March 2001) is set out in the Industrial Relations Act 1990 (Code of Practice Detailing Procedures for Addressing Bullying in the Workplace) (Declaration) Order 2002 (S.I. No. 17 of 2002) as:

> "repeated inappropriate behaviour, direct or indirect, whether verbal, physical or otherwise, conducted by one or more persons against another or others, at the place of work and/or in the course of employment, which could *reasonably* be regarded as undermining the individual's right to dignity at work. An isolated incident of the behaviour described in this definition may be an affront to dignity at work but, as a once off incident, it is not considered to be bullying." (Kearns P.'s emphasis.)

Kearns P. considered that this wording must be taken as requiring an objective test to determine if bullying has occurred. Any other test "would leave every defendant vulnerable to allegations of bullying based on purely subjective perceptions on the part of a plaintiff who might contend that straightforward situations at work or otherwise were construed by him/her as amounting to bullying". The case involved complaints by a woman who was employed as a civil servant performing clerical duties at a Garda Station. There had been difficulties in the years 1996 and 1997. These had been resolved and she had worked without complaint until 2005 when a further difficulty arose. The plaintiff alleged that she had been "repeatedly hounded and harassed" by the superintendent over a four-day period in May, 2005 in relation to the preparation of monthly accounts and "the need to complete the task quickly and in relation to the issue of the irregular payment to him".

Kearns P. accepted that, insofar as the plaintiff had pursued a case of creating or causing workplace stress, the relevant legal principles had been laid down by the Supreme Court in *Berber v Dunnes Stores* [2009] E.L.R. 61, a decision which had adopted the 'practical propositions' derived by Hale L.J. from case law and set out by her in *Hatton v Sutherland* [2002] 2 All E.R. 1 as follows:

> "1. The ordinary principles of employers' liability apply.
> 2. The threshold question is whether the kind of harm to the particular

employee was reasonably foreseeable: this has two components (a) an injury to health (as distinct from occupational stress) which (b) is attributable to stress at work (as distinct from other factors).

3. Foreseeability depends upon what the employer knows (or ought reasonably to know) about the individual employee. Because of the nature of mental disorder it is harder to foresee than physical injury, but may be easier to foresee in a known individual than in the population at large. An employer is usually entitled to assume that the employee can withstand the normal pressures of the job unless he knows of some particular problem or vulnerability.

4. The employer is generally entitled to take what he is told by his employee (including what he is told by the employee's medical adviser) at face value unless there is good reason to think to the contrary.

5. The indications of impending harm to health arising from stress at work must be plain enough for any reasonable employer to realise that he should do something about it.

6. The employer is only in breach of duty if he has failed to take the steps which are reasonable in the circumstances, bearing in mind the magnitude of the risk of harm occurring, the gravity of the harm which may occur, the cost and practicability of preventing it, and the justifications for running the risk.

7. An employer can only reasonably be expected to take steps which are likely to do some good: the court is likely to need expert evidence on this.

8. If the only reasonable and effective steps would have been to dismiss or demote the employee the employer will not be in breach of duty in allowing a willing employee to continue in the job.

9. In all cases it is necessary to identify the steps which the employer both could and should have taken before finding him in breach of his duty of care.

10. The claimant must show that the breach of duty caused or materially contributed to the harm suffered. It is not enough to show that occupational stress has caused the harm."

Applying this test to the facts of the instant case, Kearns P. held that the plaintiff had not made out her case. Her difficulties in 1996 could be attributed to her sense of injustice at being paid a lower rate for the same work as a male colleague and to the unsatisfactory working conditions in a portacabin which were conducive to work place stress. Kearns P. had "considerable concerns" about certain aspects of the plaintiff's evidence, in particular the plaintiff's unexplained failure to disclose her prior history of depression to either her own medical experts (apart from one, whose report had made no reference to it) or by way of reply to particulars. In a case of this nature, an omission or failure of this sort was "enormously significant", given that so much turned on the credibility of the witnesses on both sides. Kearns P. found the evidence of the superintendent to be both credible and reliable. The plaintiff had portrayed a meeting with him to address her concerns about working with a Garda colleague in the portakabin as one where she was virtually held captive for five hours and denied food or refreshments. Kearns P. preferred the superintendent's account of the meeting, which directly contradicted these allegations. Similarly, Kearns P. considered that telephone calls made by the superintendent to the plaintiff's home had a benign explanation. The superintendent had been perfectly entitled to call her as a concerned senior officer in the station, given that he wished to enquire as to when the plaintiff might be returning to work and whether he could help in any way. On his making the call, the plaintiff had hung up the phone. Her husband then said she had gone out and the superintendent was ultimately obliged to have another officer call the house "to have what most people would regard as a perfectly routine conversation with a work colleague". Kearns P. "totally" rejected any suggestion that these telephone calls constituted harassment or bullying of any kind.

Kearns P. went on to reject the plaintiff's account about an incident in 2005 where she had raised a query about an expenses cheque drawn by the superintendent in his own favour. She claimed that the superintendent had become angry with her when she informed him that she had taken up the matter with the accountant at Garda Headquarters to seek guidance on what she should do with the cheque and that he had thrown the cheque at her across the table in his office. Kearns P. observed:

> "The matter of the Superintendent's cheque was, in the view of this Court, 'a thing of nothing', which certainly could, and should have been, sorted out between the two of them in the garda station, as one would expect normal working colleagues to do. Quite apart from the sheer physical impracticality of 'throwing' a cheque, I do not believe or accept the plaintiff's account in regard to that particular incident, but prefer instead the evidence tendered by [the superintendent], whose calmness and patience under prolonged cross-examination greatly impressed the Court."

Rejecting the plaintiff's claim, Kearns P. noted that:

> "the events upon which the plaintiff relies to mount her claim turn on the events of a few short days in May, 2005, a time span more identifiable with a once-off or single incident rather than the kind of 'repetitive' and 'inappropriate' conduct which constitutes the wrong of workplace bullying or harassment. Even if events were as described by the plaintiff, they are more synonymous with the kind of 'isolated incident' excluded from the definition of bullying by S.I. 17 of 2002."

Ruffley v Board of Management of St Anne's School [2014] IEHC 235 should be a warning to employers of the need to consider the possibility of liability for negligence for bullying or stress in a disciplinary context that, on first view, seems clearly one raising, at worst, the prospect of judicial review proceedings. The plaintiff was a special needs teacher working in a national school catering exclusively for children with physical or intellectual disabilities. In the school there is what was known as the 'Sensory Room'. The purpose and function of this room is to develop the sensory perception of pupils by exposing them to a variety of sensory experiences such as music, vibration, movement, light and colour. It had no windows. Its door could be locked from the inside. In general, only one pupil at a time would be accommodated in the room, although it would appear sometimes there could be more than one pupil there at a given time. To successfully carry out the programme, it was desirable to ensure that there would not be distractions such as the intrusion of others, in particular, pupils coming in to the Sensory Room.

The plaintiff had been employed by the defendants since 1999. She discharged her duties in a satisfactory manner, enjoyed good relations with teachers, other special needs assistants (SNAs) and the principal and had never had any disciplinary issues or grievances. On 14 September 2009, the plaintiff was in the Sensory Room with a young boy after 13.00. Soon after the programme began, and when this pupil lay on a mat or mattress, he fell fast asleep. This was a most unusual occurrence for this pupil who suffered from ADHD, a condition which predisposed him to hyperactivity. When he fell asleep, the plaintiff telephoned the class teacher for instructions. The class teacher instructed her to allow the pupil to continue sleeping for a further period of 20 minutes before bringing him back to the class. In the meantime, the class teacher, being alarmed at this unusual development, rang the principal and asked her to check out the situation. When the principal approached the Sensory Room, she found the door locked. On her third attempt to gain entry, the door was opened by the plaintiff. The question of the door being locked or otherwise was not discussed then. The principal confirmed the instructions given by the class teacher to allow the pupil to continue sleeping for a short period. The plaintiff did this, and in due course brought the pupil back to the classroom in time for departure from school that day.

The following day, the plaintiff was informed by the principal that she was handling the matter in the context of the disciplinary procedure. In the course of a meeting later that day, the plaintiff accepted that she had locked the Sensory Room door and that she had done this over several years. She explained that the reason for doing this was to prevent other children from entering the Sensory Room door whilst she was conducting a session with a pupil and also to prevent a pupil described as "a runner" from running out of the room while the programme equipment was being set up. She explained that she had not been told to lock the door by any teachers, nor had she ever been instructed not to lock the door.

At a further meeting on 18 September between the principal, the plaintiff and a teacher, a process of training was settled for a four-week period, during which the plaintiff, in carrying out the programme of the child who was the "runner", would, on a weekly basis, fill in a form, indicating by a tick, the activities in the Sensory Room which this child accomplished, and at the end of the four-week period, there would be a review. One of the activities that was set for the child was to sit, stand and lie on a swing. The plaintiff initially reported to the teacher that she had not been able to get the child to do this, but later, in the third week of the programme, she told her that she had succeeded in getting the child to sit on the swing. At the end of the four-week period, when the teacher was conducting the anticipated review with the plaintiff, she noticed that the plaintiff had ticked the box on the forms for lying on the swing and she queried this with the plaintiff who promptly confirmed that this was wrong and sought the teacher's permission to change the form so as to make it accurate. The teacher refused to allow her to do this and recorded this result on the review of the plaintiff's performance as a "miscommunication". The principal concluded (as she later testified in evidence) that there had been no improvement during the four weeks and that the inaccurate completion by the plaintiff of the form, which the principal characterised as "falsification", raised an additional disciplinary issue. O'Neill J. found the principal's evidence on this matter:

> "strange, to say the least. Against a background where there was no doubt but that, firstly, there was no question of the door being locked again, and secondly, the child in question was not only participating in his programme so that his tendency to 'run' had not reoccurred, but in fact, had advanced in his programme and was now accomplishing more than had been the case at the start of the four-week programme, the conclusion that there had been no improvement is not only groundless but seems to have wandered into the realm of irrationality.
>
> The treatment of the plaintiff's request .... to change the filling out of the form so as to make it more accurately conform to the undoubted reality, which was never in doubt, as 'falsification', can only be said to be extreme and utterly removed from what right-thinking people would consider to be a reasonable conclusion in that regard."

The principal advised the plaintiff that the matter was going to be raised with the board at its meeting on 23 November. O'Neill J. was critical of the lack of procedural fairness afforded the plaintiff in this regard:

> "The plaintiff was not told by [the principal] any detail whatsoever concerning the material that was to be put before the Board or what proposal, if any, the Board was to be asked to consider or what possible outcome there might be insofar as the plaintiff was concerned. The plaintiff was given no written material concerning what might transpire at the Board meeting. The plaintiff was not told that there might be any adverse disciplinary outcome so far as she was concerned, nor was she told that it was the intention of the Principal to seek a disciplinary sanction against her."

O'Neill J. was satisfied that, in the two months that had elapsed since 15 September 2009, the principal had done nothing to investigate the plaintiff's contention that it was a common practice amongst SNAs to lock the door of the Sensory Room. The evidence established that "there was a general practice amongst many of the SNAs, probably a majority, of locking the Sensory Room door for the same reasons that the plaintiff locked it from time to time." O'Neill J. commented:

> "I would readily accept that it was reasonable of the defendants, both for health and safety reasons and, more probably, for reasons of child protection, to insist on a prohibition on locking the Sensory Room door. It is extraordinary that until 14th September 2009, no issue arose concerning the locking of this door at all. Notwithstanding that the defendants had a comprehensive safety statement prepared with the help of appropriate experts, no-one addressed the locking of this door or the presence on it of a lock on the inside, in the context of health and safety issues or child protection issues, at all. Because no one considered the matter, no instruction was given, either to lock this door or not to lock it. The matter was simply overlooked by the defendants."

When the board met, the majority wanted to dismiss the plaintiff and had to be dissuaded by the principal and chair of the board. Instead, it was agreed that the next most serious sanction should be applied. O'Neill J. stated:

> "The evidence of [the principal] was that she outlined the full history of the matter to the Board. The extreme, if not, downright intemperate, reaction of the Board to whatever they were told, suggests that as a matter of probability, the account given by Ms. Dempsey to the Board of the history of the matter was almost certainly untrue, highly biased [and] coloured, and grossly and unfairly damnified the plaintiff. Whilst I would readily accept that the members of the Board would be hyper-vigilant on all issues relating to child protection, and rightly so, as a group of probably fair-minded people, I do not think they would have reached conclusions so adverse to the plaintiff, unless grossly misled as to the true circumstances prevailing."

O'Neill J. considered that, if the board members had been told the true position, whilst they might well have been shocked that such a practice existed and directed steps to prohibit it, they could not have singled out the plaintiff to suffer punishment for it alone. The manner in which the disciplinary process with regard to the locking of the Sensory Room door had been handled by the principal "was grossly unfair to the plaintiff and utterly denied her the benefit of her constitutional right to natural justice and fair procedures". The conjuring up by the principal of the additional offence of failing to improve during the review process and of the "falsification" of the review forms was "at best, irrational, in the sense of there being a complete lack of any real basis for such conclusions". O'Neill J. found it hard to understand how an educated, sophisticated person, such as the principal, could arrive at such conclusions without an element of bad faith. In O'Neill J.'s view:

> "the plaintiff should not have been subjected to this disciplinary process. When it came to light that the Sensory Room door was locked, and when the plaintiff responded by indicating that other SNAs did it, the appropriate and immediate response of [the Principal] should have been to ascertain the truth or otherwise of the plaintiff's contention. If, having done that, and have ascertained, as she undoubtedly would have if she did conduct an appropriate inquiry, that there was a common practice of doing this, she should have, as she did in October, prohibit the practice, but it would have been entirely unfair and inappropriate to have initiated a disciplinary process against the plaintiff alone. The addition of what might be described as the 'trumped up' charge of failing to improve and the falsification of a form, given the complete lack of any basis for it, was reprehensible, and as this is what led to the matter being brought to the Board, I am quite satisfied that this disciplinary matter should not have been advanced to the Board for the purposes of disciplining the plaintiff.
>
> I am quite satisfied that the treatment of the plaintiff throughout this process by [the Principal] was entirely "inappropriate" within the meaning of the definition of bullying in the workplace."

Over subsequent months, the plaintiff, with the assistance of her union, sought the reversal of the sanction, explaining to the board that there had been a common practice of locking the door in the Sensory Room. The board adhered to its position, O'Neill J. holding that it had failed to give any meaningful consideration to the case being made by the plaintiff. O'Neill J. commented: "The plaintiff's appeal to [the board], insofar as it could be said to be an appeal in the normal sense, as the appeal was to the same decision maker as had made the decision appealed against, thereby demonstrably offending the maxim *Nemo iudex causa suam*, in the event, fell on deaf ears."

Perhaps this particular criticism is a little stern: there is nothing particularly strange about a board being asked to reconsider its position and there is no inevitable obligation that some other forum, or some different personnel, should have to become involved. During this period, the plaintiff began to experience high levels of stress. After her return to school in September 2010, there was a further incident with the principal. The plaintiff then went on certified sick leave. Letters from her solicitor to the board were met with an unsatisfactory response. O'Neill J. concluded as follows:

> "The rejection of the plaintiff's appeal by the Board in May 2010, without any meaningful consideration of the merits of the plaintiff's case, and the subsequent failure or refusal of the Board in the autumn 2010, when given a fresh opportunity, on foot of the correspondence from the plaintiff's solicitor, to at all consider the merits of the plaintiff's case at this late stage when they were aware of the impact that their now erroneous and unjust decision was having on the plaintiff was, in my view, a persistence by them in their unfair and inappropriate treatment of the plaintiff.
>
> Thus, in my opinion, the plaintiff has demonstrated to my satisfaction that the inappropriate behaviour of the defendants was not merely an isolated incident but was persistent over a period of in excess of one year. There can be no doubt but that this persistent, inappropriate behaviour of the defendants wholly undermined the plaintiff's dignity at work."

Evidence was given that the plaintiff suffered a severe anxiety state and depression. O'Neill J. awarded her over €250,000 damages. The judgment is clearly important because it demonstrates that what may appear simply a disciplinary issue may contain within it the covert, insidious ingredients of a tort action for negligence for bullying or stress. It is interesting how O'Neill J.'s judgment uses language usually found in a judicial review.

In a perceptive editorial in (2014) 11(2) Irish Employment Law Journal 34, Claire Bruton BL makes the point that the judgment in *Ruffley*:

> "must be seen to arise in the context of exceptional facts most notably in the context of a finding by the High Court that the disciplinary process against Ms Ruffley was unjustified and unwarranted. It does not, in my view, displace the well-established principle propounded in *Shortt v Royal Liver Assurance Limited* ([2009] E.L.R. 240) that disciplinary action will almost inevitably be accompanied by a certain degree of stress but that such events are encountered in the normal course of management such that ordinarily, stress as a result of a disciplinary process, is not actionable..."

Bruton also mentions that *Ruffley's* approach is similar to that adopted by the High Court of England and Wales in *Yapp v Foreign and Commonwealth Office* [2013] I.R.L.R. 616, where the High Commissioner of Belize, having become the object of false and defamatory allegations of sexual misconduct made by a politician, had been subjected to summary suspension and a lengthy disciplinary process, resulting in his becoming depressed. Cranston J. found that there had been a breach of contract by the defendant as well as a breach of its duty of care to its employee.

Safe system of work In *Madajczyk v Multi-Roofing Systems Ltd* [2014] IEHC 172, Irvine J. rejected, on the evidence, the plaintiff's claim that his employer had negligently operated an unsafe system of work. The plaintiff was a roof and wall cladding operative. He alleged that he had been required to lift, transport, manoeuvre and install panels which were excessively heavy, without adequate assistance. Regardless of the weights of the materials to be installed, he said that no more than two workers were ever deployed to any cladding operation when at times three or four men were required. He further alleged that he had been obliged to carry cladding sheets over uneven terrain and that he had been put under intense pressure in terms of the amount of work that he had to complete on any given day. He maintained finally that he had been given inadequate training and instruction as to how to safely carry out his duties.

The defendant fought the claim strongly. Irvine J. concluded that the plaintiff had not established his case on the balance of probability. She "greatly preferred" the defendant's evidence. The defendant company, over all of the relevant period, had worked as a roofing subcontractor on many major construction projects managed by highly respected building firms such as Walls and Rohan Construction. It had not been in dispute that, on all major construction sites, there would be an on site safety officer. The main contractor's safety officer was responsible for the safety of all personnel on the site regardless of whether they were employed by the main contractor or a subcontractor or were on the site for some other reason. The job of the safety officer included patrolling the site and identifying any unsafe practice. Safety officers had the power to serve warning notices on subcontractors or to direct that work cease on site if they considered any work practice to be dangerous. The defendant had never been cautioned by any safety officer for the manner in which its employees were required to work when installing cladding on any of the sites where the plaintiff worked during his employment. Irvine J. was satisfied that, once detected, any such practices would not have been tolerated by the safety officer:

> "The main contractor has a range of statutory obligations that would make it liable in respect of injury caused by any dangerous practice permitted on site. Also, if such dangerous practices were to be deployed by the defendant, apart from the potential risks thereby generated for its employees and the likely legal consequence of such actions, it would also be putting its professional reputation and its prospects of obtaining further large roofing contracts at real risk."

Irvine J. was satisfied that the plaintiff had been adequately trained such that he ought to have been able to maintain his own safety when deciding whether or not it was possible in any given set of circumstances to safely lift any of the panels or equipment required in the course of his employment. He had been trained to know when he needed additional assistance to safely lift particularly cumbersome panels and had neither complained about the weights of panels he was customarily asked to fit nor requested additional help for such purposes. While it might have been occasionally necessary for the plaintiff and his fellow workers to carry panels over uneven ground, neither he nor the expert witness had given any evidence as to how this might be avoided.

PUBLIC AUTHORITIES

The misfeasance/nonfeasance distinction In *McCabe v South Dublin County Council* [2014] IEHC 529, Hogan J. applied the traditional rules relating to the distinction between misfeasance and nonfeasance of highway authorities. Pursuant to these rules, the highway authority is not liable for injuries resulting from its failure to keep the roads and footpaths in good repair. It is only where it does some positive act negligently that it is legally responsible for the consequential injuries. Section 60 of the Civil Liability Act 1961 (the "1961 Act") prospectively abolishes this distinction but commencement of the section is subject to the Government's making an order that it should come into operation and no such order has been made over the past half century.

In *McCabe*, the plaintiff fell and banged her head when she was walking on the footpath. A stopcock cover was missing and this caused her to trip. The problem of a missing stopcock had been noted, and professedly repaired, by the Council a few months before the plaintiff's accident. Hogan J. considered that this meant that either the repair job had not actually been carried out, through inadvertence or otherwise, or the stopcock had subsequently been removed by vandals. Whichever was the true explanation, the nonfeasance rule would relieve the Council of liability:

> "If the opening was not repaired at all then the Council has no liability by reason of its inaction, even it had intended to repair the opening itself following a notification of the missing stopcock cover. It is true that, as the plaintiff argued, the Council intended to repair the opening. This in itself is not sufficient to take the case outside of the non-feasance rule, since the authorities are at one that there must be actual negligence in the actual repair of the highway before the case comes outside the scope of the nonfeasance immunity.... If, on the other hand, the opening was in fact repaired but it was subsequently removed or tampered with by persons unknown, there is equally no liability on the part of the Council. In that latter situation the most that can be said is that the Council thereafter failed to act when it knew (or ought to have known) that the opening presented a hazard to the public. Nevertheless, even in this situation, the non-feasance rule serves to bar any action in respect of this ground."

Hogan J.'s concluding observations are worth recording:

> "No one can pretend that the non-feasance/misfeasance distinction is perfectly satisfactory or that the rule in this blunt and indiscriminate

form sits easily with general principles of tort law. The rule, after all, has its origins in a decision of the English King's Bench in 1788 (Russell v. Men of Devon (1788) 2 Term Rep. 667) which declined to hold that a statutory duty to repair the highway was enforceable because the local parish (on whom the duty fell) was not a legal entity. Yet the 'illogical distinction' between nonfeasance and misfeasance nonetheless survived the transfer of the statutory duty to repair the highways to local authorities with legal personality who could sue and be sued: see Wade and Forsyth, *Administrative Law* (Oxford, 2000) at 755. Decisions of the Supreme Court describing the rule as either 'anomalous' (see *O'Brien v. Waterford County Council* [1926] I.R. 1, 8, per Murnaghan J.) or 'unsatisfactory' (see *Kelly v. Mayo County Council* [1964] I.R. 315, 324 *per* Kingsmill Moore J.) are of long standing.

These considerations notwithstanding, I must nonetheless apply the law as I find it. This is especially so given that the Oireachtas has, in fact, legislated on this topic. It is often, perhaps, overlooked that the distinction between non-feasance and misfeasance was actually abolished by the enactment of s.60(1) of the Civil Liability Act 1961.... , but over 50 years later the commencement of that sub-section awaits the making of a Government order. That sub-section has never been brought into force by the Government and in *Sheehan* [*State (Sheehan) v Government of Ireland* [1987] IR 550] the Supreme Court rejected the argument that the Government was legally obliged to make such an order. It follows, therefore, that, for the moment, at least, as Cross J. put the matter in *Loughrey v Dun Laoghaire Corporation* [2012] IEHC 502, the distinction still retains 'its ancient purity in this jurisdiction'.

Subject only to some future challenge to its constitutionality (an issue on which I express no view), the rule nonetheless remains embedded in the fabric of the common law which was carried over into our post-Constitution legal system in December 1937 by Article 50.1 of the Constitution, even if–as the Supreme Court pointed out over 90 years ago in O'Brien–the rule can be regarded as anomalous and although the historical underpinning for the rule (such as it ever was) vanished no later than 1898 with the enactment in that year of the Local Government (Ireland) Act 1898 which vested all local authorities with a legal personality.

As such, given its historical vintage and the fact that it has remained undisturbed for over 200 years, the rule now probably lies beyond the capacity of the courts to repair or amend. If, then, the law is considered to be unsatisfactory, the remedy for this lies either with the Government (which could, should it consider it appropriate to do so, make a commencement order in respect of … s.60(1) of the 1961 Act) or with the Oireachtas which could effect further legislative change should it think necessary to do so."

FALSE ARREST

Arrest resulting from impersonation In *Reid v Commissioner of An Garda Síochána* [2014] IEHC 246, Hedigan J. withdrew the case from the jury where the victim of impersonation had been arrested by members of An Garda Síochána on foot of a bench warrant referable to his impersonator. Hedigan J. did not consider that the delay of eight months in executing the warrant rended the arrest unlawful:

> "It is clearly the case that such a warrant is a command by the Court to the gardaí to arrest the person named thereon .... However, ... the issuing of such a warrant need not trigger a national manhunt. There are thousands of such warrants issued every year, and around the country there are warrant officers, just like Garda Joyce herein, whose sole function is the execution of warrants. No legal basis for unlawful arrest arises under this heading."

Neither had the forced entry into the plaintiff's apartment after he had failed to respond to the request to open the door constituted a false arrest:

> "Outside the flat at the time, the gardaí were present with a bench warrant for the plaintiff who lived in that apartment and who was, in fact, present in it. By definition, the bench warrant was in respect of a fugitive from justice i.e. a person in flight from the law. Were the gardaí to tamely withdraw? Hardly. Did they do so, they would have been ignoring a clear command by the Court to arrest the person named on the warrant i.e. the plaintiff and bring him before the Court. In breaking into the apartment, on the plaintiff's own evidence, the gardaí were using the only means open to them to effect an entrance and execute the warrant. No legal basis for unlawful arrest arises in this regard."

Hedigan J. also concluded that the use of handcuffs had not been unlawful:

> "Handcuffs should not be used unless reasonable in all the circumstances. It is for the gardaí present to decide whether to do so or not. See *DPP v. Peter Cullen (Supreme Court.)* 18th February, 2014. The circumstances are the critical test- context, as so often, is all-important. What were the circumstances here? The gardaí, to the best of their knowledge, were attempting to arrest a man in flight from the law. They were unaware of the mistaken identity when they handcuffed him. They only knew that he was the person named on the warrant. He admitted to be. Inklings or suspicions developed only later. He was, indisputably, the man described on the warrant. He had failed to answer their knock. In those circumstances, it cannot, in my judgment, be said that their handcuffing of him was an unreasonable use of force and it would not, in my opinion, be open to a jury to reasonably find otherwise."

Claims for false imprisonment, malicious prosecution and defamation were also withdrawn from the jury.

DEFAMATION

Absolute privilege To what extent does the defence of absolute privilege in defamation extend its protection outwards to defeat claims taken for other torts? That was the question that Barrett J. was called on to resolve in *Jeffery v Minister* *for Equality* [2014] IEHC 99. The plaintiff had been convicted in 2011 at Sligo District Court of certain road traffic offences. Before he was sentenced, a member of An Garda Síochána informed the court that he had previously been convicted of a number of serious offences. In fact, the person who committed those offences was another person by the same name. The plaintiff had no previous convictions. His solicitor indicated to the court that an error had been made and sentencing proceeded without regard to the mistaken information.

The Chief State Solicitor's Office, some considerable time later, issued a letter forwarding a "Statement of Regret" from An Garda Síochána. Barrett J., in proceedings for negligence, breach of duty and misrepresentation taken by the plaintiff, commented in respect of the "Statement of Regret":

> " It might perhaps be contended that this was too little, too late. Certainly the State's continuing refusal to provide a corrective statement before Sligo District Court in the particular circumstances that arose is suggestive of unbecoming obduracy. Indeed there seems no reason why the provision of such a statement might not yet be done or why such a course of action might not in the future be considered where a mistake of the sort in issue in this case leads to the acute embarrassment, anxiety and distress that Mr. Jeffery claims to have suffered."

Barrett J. noted the fact that the plaintiff had not framed his case in defamation. A possible answer was that such an action "would undoubtedly have failed". Section 17(2) of the Defamation Act 2009 (the "2009 Act") established absolute privilege in circumstances where the offending statement was made by a party, witness or legal representative in the course of proceedings presided over by a judge. Prior to this, the Supreme Court, in *Looney v Bank of Ireland and Morey*, unreported, ex-tempore, Supreme Court, 9 May 1997 had recognised this privilege, subject to a possible qualification in cases of "flagrant abuse" (per Barrington J.). The English courts, in *Marrinan v Vibart* [1963] 1 Q.B. 528 and *Evans v London Hospital Medical College and Others* [1981] 1 All E.R. 715, had extended the remit of the immunity to negligent acts preparatory to the court proceedings. Barrett J. observed:

> "In the present case one cannot get around the fact that, regardless of any negligence or breach of duty that occurred, if it occurred, the crux of the issue between the parties derives from what was said in the course of the Sligo District Court proceedings. Consequently, those alternative causes of action must, to paraphrase the Court of Appeal [in *Marrinan v Vibart*], suffer the same fate of being barred by the rule which protects witnesses in their evidence before the courts and in the preparation of that evidence."

Qualified privilege In *Talbot v Hermitage Golf Club* [2014] IESC 57, the Supreme Court affirmed Herbert J.'s dismissal of a claim for defamation taken by a golfer against his club in respect of the communication of an assertion that he had engaged in "handicap building". This occurred when the records of the club were being computerised. A computer programmer from a German firm could read it and thus there had been publication. The assertion was defamatory but the defence of qualified privilege prevailed, in the absence of any malice. Charleton

J. observed that "there was no evidence that malice attended this communication and the dry circumstance of the computerisation of necessary records would make any such idea very unlikely."

Discovery In *Craddock v Radio Telifis Eireann* [2014] IESC 32, RTE broadcast a programme critical of the care afforded children at a crèche where the plaintiffs worked. The plaintiffs sued for defamation. Cross J. ordered discovery of the programme broadcast and of a version of the programme which had been shown to the families of children who went to the crèche but had not been broadcast. The Supreme Court affirmed the decision of the High Court. Fennelly J. (McKechnie and Laffoy JJ. concurring) stated that he had reached this conclusion for two reasons:

> "Firstly, there is uncontradicted evidence on behalf of the plaintiffs that they have no means of knowing what version of the programme was shown to the parents on any of the occasions on which RTE showed it to them... Secondly, and crucially there is a sharp and obvious distinction between written and broadcast material when it comes to drafting a statement of claim. It is unrealistic to expect a solicitor to be able to instruct counsel with sufficient accuracy to enable a clear and cogent pleading to be prepared where the alleged defamation takes the form of a visual and audio recording and the solicitor is not in possession of any recording of what was transmitted. This situation is quite different from the case of written defamation, as in a newspaper. There the solicitor places the text before counsel and instructs him to draft the statement of claim. It is true that, in the present case, the solicitors for both plaintiffs had the benefit of watching the programme as broadcast. However, the crucial fact is that they had no sight of what was shown to the parents."

In *Ryanair Ltd v Somner* [2014] IEHC 634, the plaintiff sued a former pilot for defamation in making allegations during a two-part television programme to the effect that the plaintiff's corporate culture, management structure and the way it dealt with its staff jeopardised the safety of passengers by placing pilots under abnormal stress and pressure. The defendant sought discovery of all documents relating to in-flight fuel-related incidents during a specified period and all documents recording details of the plaintiff's flight fuel policy since 2008, as well as all documents relating to the plaintiff's pilot hire policy for a five-year period. The defendant submitted that these documents were necessary because they would tend to support his claim of truth. Peart J. ordered discovery of the documents. He commented:

> "This application cannot be described as a fishing exercise. The plaintiff has made its case clearly in its Statement of Claim. The defendant has availed of a number of Defences and has clearly nailed his colours to the mast by pleading honest opinion, truth and fair and reasonable comment on matters of public interest. In so far as he is able at this stage to do so, he has given particulars of the basis for these defences. He has not made mere bald assertions. He has provided certain particulars. He has satisfied this Court that the documents sought by way of discovery are relevant and are likely to assist him in mounting his defence to the plaintiff's claim."

In *Ryanair Ltd v Irish Municipal, Public and Civic Trade Union (IMPACT)* [2014] IEHC 594, in litigation relating to somewhat similar claims, O'Malley J., on the plaintiff's application, ordered discovery, as against the three defendants, their spokespersons or agents, of documents relating to allegations or complaints about the plaintiff's fuel or safety policy made by them to any other party connected with the aviation industry within the 12 months prior to the 16 August 2012. O'Malley J.'s detailed judgment also disposed of 27 other categories of documents sought by the plaintiff.

In *Norris v Radio Telifis Eireann* [2014] IEHC 84, Kearns P. declined to order discovery of documents sought by the second named defendant as they were already in the public domain and accessible to him.

Damages The Supreme Court decision in *Leech v Independent Newspapers (Ireland) Ltd* [2014] IESC 79 is important in revealing that court's present valuation of damages in cases of this kind. Ms Leech had been awarded €1,872,000 for defamatory allegations, made in several articles over a period of more than two weeks, that she had had an affair with a Government Minister whereby her career had been advanced. The Supreme Court upheld the appeal on quantum and substituted that amount by an award of €1,250,000. A single judgment was delivered by Dunne J. (Murray and McKechnie JJ. concurring), wherein she noted that the defamation had impugned the plaintiff's character "in every aspect of her life" and had had a real and long lasting impact on her professional and family life. The extent of the loss in terms of her business life had never been quantified and there had been no claim in respect of special damages but it would have been open to the jury to include in an award of general damages an element of damages in respect of loss of business opportunity. Overall, Dunne J. was satisfied that the defamation had been very serious . She observed:

> "Undoubtedly, if one was to place the defamation in this case on a scale of seriousness, it would certainly be towards the higher end of the scale.... Nevertheless, I do not think it could be classed as one of the most serious libels to come before the Courts, such as that in the de Rossa case. That said, the award made to Ms. Leech in this case was one of the highest ever awards made in a case of this kind in this country. Even accepting that this case is one that comes towards the higher end of the scale, I am satisfied that the award made by the jury in this case was excessive and must be set aside."

In *O'Brien v Mirror Group Newspapers Ltd* [2001] 1 I.R. 1, the Supreme Court set aside as excessive a jury award of IR£250,000 in respect of a defamatory allegation that the plaintiff had paid IR£30,000 to a Government Minister by way of a bribe to secure a licence for a radio station and had also secured a licence for ESAT Digifone in circumstances giving rise to a suspicion of bribery. (After a retrial, the jury awarded €750,000.) The Supreme Court in *Leech* appears to have taken a more generous view of damages than it had done in *O'Brien*, even if one has regard to the change in money values over the past 15 years. Dunne J. did not accept that the maximum permitted for general damages in personal injuries litigation, as prescribed in *Sinnott v Quinnsworth Ltd* [1984] I.L.R.M. 523 and its progeny, had any decisive influence over awards in defamation cases, though it would be taken into account in claims for sexual abuse: *MN v SM* [2005] 4 I.R. 461. Dunne J. stated:

> "I think it is apparent that there is a close relationship between an action for personal injuries and an action for damages for assault arising out of sexual abuse such as that described in *M. N. v. S. M.* Both such actions are, in reality, a form of action for damages for personal injuries. There is an obvious correlation between the type of damages that can be awarded in a personal injuries case and in a sexual assault case. It is not so easy to see an obvious correlation between an award in a personal injuries action and an award in an action for defamation....
>
> I have come to the conclusion that the analogy of awards in personal injuries cases may be of some assistance in the area of injuries caused by reason of sexual abuse but is not so useful an analogy in the case of awards in respect of defamation actions for the reasons explained above."

The rejection of the *Sinnott* test in the context of defamation is to be welcomed. It is unfortunate, however, that *Leech* reiterates the proposition that claims for sexual abuse are merely a species of the genus of personal injuries claims. It may be argued that they are quite different and that the violation of dignity that they involve places them in a distinctive category.

Injunctive relief In *ABC v DEF* [2014] IEHC 680, White J. granted an interlocutory injunction preventing the defendant from issuing defamation proceedings which would identify the plaintiff. The plaintiff, when receiving psychiatric care, alleged to a counsellor at the hospital that she had been the victim as a child of sexual abuse by the defendant. The counsellor reported the matter to An Garda Síochána and HSE. The plaintiff gave a written statement to Gardaí. The HSE in turn informed a designated officer appointed to deal with allegations of sexual abuse within the Catholic Church and the defendant was subsequently suspended from active ministry pending the outcome of the complaint. The defendant alleged that this occurred in a manner which disclosed his identity and caused considerable trauma and damage. The defendant's solicitor wrote to the plaintiff seeking a retraction of the allegation and an apology and threatening defamation proceedings if these were not forthcoming. The plaintiff unsuccessfully sought an assurance from the plaintiff that she would not be identified in any such proceedings. She then obtained an interim injunction. During the proceedings seeking an interlocutory injunction, evidence was presented to the court by a consultant psychiatrist. In his affidavit, he swore that:

> "from my recent examination of the plaintiff, it is clear to me that the plaintiff feels that if her name becomes public knowledge in the context of the childhood sexual abuse which she alleges that she suffered at the hands of the defendant, she would not be able to continue with her career and she is convinced that the only course which would be left open to her in those circumstances would be to commit suicide. I say that it is my professional opinion that there is most unfortunately and regrettably a high probability of such an eventuality occurring in the event that the plaintiff's name is

disclosed in the context of the present proceedings or in any defamation proceedings intimated by the defendant against her and I would earnestly appeal on her behalf to this Honourable Court that her name be withheld and not be publicly disclosed in order to prevent, as far as possible such a high probability eventuating or worse still such an occurrence taking place. I further hereby confirm that it is my professional opinion that the plaintiff is currently clinically depressed and that there is now a real and substantial risk to her life if her name and identity are publicly disclosed in these proceedings or in any proceedings for defamation instituted by the defendant."

Granting the interlocutory injunction, White J. observed:

> "In weighing up the balance of convenience it is an important factor that the plaintiff did not seek to publish nor was the plaintiff responsible for the decisions which led to the unnecessary publicity for the defendant. I fully understand the defendant's anger and frustration where innocence is maintained but compromised when suspension from ministry occurred. In the hierarchy of constitutional rights, the undoubted risk to the plaintiff's life takes precedence."

Delay In *Ewins v Independent Newspapers (Ireland) Ltd* [2003] 1 I.R. 583 at 590, Keane C.J. observed that:

> "[a] plaintiff in defamation proceedings, as opposed to many other forms of proceedings, is under a particular onus to institute his proceedings instantly and without delay and, of course, not simply because he will be otherwise met with the response that it cannot have been of such significance to his reputation if he delayed so long to bring the proceedings but also in his own interests in order, at once, to restore the damage that he sees to have been done to his reputation by the offending publication."

In *McClean v Sunday Newspapers Ltd* [2014] IEHC 304, the plaintiff initiated defamation proceedings in 2000. He failed to move matters on over the following decade. In 2010, he issued a notice of intention to proceed. After this, everything stopped again. The defendant sought to have the proceedings dismissed for inordinate and inexcusable delay. Barrett J. acceded to the defendant's motion. He concluded that the actions of the plaintiff in the proceedings were:

> " not consistent with those of a man who is genuinely desirous of defending his good name or seeing a plea of justification defeated. … He has not acted with that special degree of despatch which Keane C.J. in *Ewins* identified as appropriate in defamation proceedings. Conversely, if one looks to the rights of the defendant, there has to come a time when, consistent with the constitutional imperative that the courts put an end to stale claims and the 'reasonable time' requirements in Article 6(1) of the European Convention on Human Rights, the defendant ought not to be subjected to the continuance of the instant proceedings. The court is also conscious in

> this regard of the special importance of the media in our open society. A free press is hardly free if trammelled by litigation that, once commenced, neither proceeds nor ends."

In *Shields v Interlink Ireland Ltd t/a Interlink Express* [2014] IEHC 74, the plaintiff sued the defendant in two claims. In what Ryan J. characterised as "the main claim", he sought a declaration that the defendant had wrongfully repudiated a commercial agreement between the parties, an injunction restraining the defendant from acting in breach, damages for breach of contract, breach of trust, conspiracy to induce breach of contract, misappropriation of confidential information, defamation, injurious falsehood, trespass, detinue, conversion and other reliefs. In what was referred to as " the commission claim", he sought damages for breach of contract, payment of all sums due on foot of accounts owing to him under the agreement and other ancillary reliefs. The facts upon which the two claims were based were similar though the chronology of events in each was slightly different. In determining whether there had been inordinate and inexcusable delay in prosecuting the claims, Ryan J. said that he did not think that the presence of a claim for defamation altered the balance of the equation of justice in the case:

> "Taking the claims made in the main proceedings and in the compensation action together, this is fundamentally an action about the alleged breach of an agreement and the consequences. Although I do not discount the head of defamation, I think it cannot constitute a special reason why a different approach should be taken to the assessment of the respective rights of the parties."

Ryan J. held that, while the delay had been inordinate, it was not in the circumstances inexcusable.

CONSTITUTIONAL TORTS

Rights vindication, false imprisonment and assault In *DF v Garda Commissioner (No 3)* [2014] IEHC 213, the plaintiff, a 28 year old man who was severely autistic, had been arrested, near to his home, under s.12 of the Mental Health Act 2001 (the "2001 Act"). He had been taken to a local Garda station, where he was detained for just under an hour. He was released when his father, a medical practitioner, had attended at the Garda station with the plaintiff's mother and explained the plaintiff's condition. The plaintiff claimed damages for false imprisonment, assault, battery, negligence and breach of duty, breaches of his constitutional rights and breach of his rights under the European Convention Human Rights Act 2003 (the "2003 Act"), as well as breaches of his rights under the Charter of Fundamental Rights of the European Union and the UN Convention on the Rights of Persons with Disabilities 2006. He additionally sought declaratory relief in relation to the alleged illegality of the arrest. The defence was to the effect that the Gardaí had been alerted by a member of the public who had seen the plaintiff chase two women with a dark stick or tree branch; when the Gardaí had arrived on the scene and attempted to speak to the plaintiff, it had become clear that he was suffering from a mental condition as he was unable to provide his name or other personal details. He had been handcuffed in the course of the arrest.

In earlier proceedings, Hogan J. had held that the plaintiff was entitled to a jury trial in respect of the claims, with the proviso that all issues bearing on the legality of the arrest were to be determined by the trial judge, see: *DF v Garda Commissioner (No 1)* [2013] IEHC 5. Hogan J. had also ruled that the proceedings were to be heard in open court, without any restrictions identifying the plaintiff, see: *DF v Garda Commissioner (No 2)* [2013] IEHC 312 (though a stay had subsequently been granted on this latter order by the Supreme Court). The defendants in the instant proceedings applied by motion to have the claims based on breach of constitutional rights, breach of the 2003 Act, breach of the Charter and breach of the UN Convention struck out as either unsustainable in their own right or replicating claims for damages in respect of the torts of assault and false imprisonment. They also contended that it was inappropriate for a court to grant declaratory relief.

Hogan J. first addressed the constitutional claims. He considered that the governing question, in essence, was whether it could be said that these torts provided an adequate or complete mechanism for the vindication of individual rights. Turning to the tort of false imprisonment, Hogan J. considered that Fawsitt J.'s summary of the parameters of that tort in *Dullaghan v Hillen* [1957] Ir. Jur. Rep. 10 at 15 had made it clear that it might "accordingly be regarded as a complete and full vindication of the guarantee of personal liberty in Article 40.4.1". Hogan J. noted further that:

> "[l]iability for false imprisonment is strict and is not based on norms of fault or negligence. By providing a mechanism for the protection of individual liberty in this fashion the common law may thus be said to give full effect to this particular constitutional guarantee.
>
> The claim for damages for breach of the constitutional right to liability accordingly adds nothing to the common law action for false imprisonment. Adapting the language of Baker J in *PR v KC* [2014] IEHC 126, it may be said that the claim for damages [for breach] of the constitutional right to liberty 'is no more than an ancillary claim or another way....of seeking the same relief."

Hogan J. therefore struck out the claim for damages for breach of the constitutional right to liberty as it was "simply another way of claiming the same relief".

While the instant case raised the issue of the constitutional right to liberty in the context of confinement within bounds, and thus might well be considered to replicate the tort of false imprisonment, it is possible to envisage other cases where that tort might not fully replicate a claim for damages for breach of the right to liberty. The constitutional protection of the right to liberty extends further than the prohibition on confinement within bounds. It seems clear enough that a blockage of the exercise of freedom of movement which fell short of confinement could also constitute such a breach—as, for example, where barriers placed on a highway required a person to have to make a huge detour. Such a wrong could generate liability in tort as a public nuisance rather than false imprisonment: *Bird v Jones* 7 Q.B. 742, 115 E.R. 668 (1845). More specifically, it is possible that the Irish courts may develop an expansive understanding of the constitutional right to liberty so as to embrace decisional liberty – the liberty to choose one course of action rather than another, entirely unconnected to freedom of movement. The contemporary understanding of liberty by the United States Supreme Court demonstrates how concepts can expand in their remit over time.

Hogan J. went on to consider whether the torts of battery and assault could be regarded as providing a complete and full mechanism for vindicating the substance of the constitutional guarantees to the person, bodily integrity and privacy. Here, he drew from his jurisprudential analysis in earlier decisions. In *Kinsella v Governor of Mountjoy Prison* [2012] 1 I.R. 467 at 471, he had observed that Art.40.3.2 protects "not simply the integrity of the human body, but also the integrity of the human mind and personality". In *Connolly v Governor of Wheatfield Prison* [2013] IEHC 334, at para.14, he had held that the constitutional protection of the person under Art.40.3.2 must also be understood by reference to the Preamble's objective that the dignity and freedom of the individual may be protected. While accepting that the torts of battery and assault might generally be regarded as a realisation of the constitutional command that "the State must protect and vindicate the person" (*PR v KC* [2014] IEHC 126 (Baker J.)), Hogan J. considered that the question remained as to "whether there are any circumstances at all in which these constitutional guarantees can be called in aid in order to supplement these torts". He answered this question in the affirmative. He identified a limitation on the scope of the tort of assault: it requires that the plaintiff have "a prior apprehension of a battery before it actually takes place…" Hogan J. considered that this specific limitation might be particularly relevant to the instant case, given that with the plaintiff's mental condition it might ultimately transpire at the trial of the action that he lacked the cognitive capacity to have had any understanding of the conduct of the Gardaí in seeking to restrain and arrest him:

> "In these circumstances and in view of this particular limitation on the scope of the tort, the plaintiff might be able to show at the full trial of the action that this nominate tort was, in the words of Henchy J in *Hanrahan v Merck, Sharp & Dohmne Ltd.* [1988] I.L.R.M. 626 at 636, 'basically ineffective' to protect his constitutional rights to the protection of the person and bodily integrity."

In view of the fact that it was "just possible" that the plaintiff might be able to demonstrate at the full hearing that these torts would insufficiently vindicate his constitutional rights, Hogan J. declined to strike out the claims based on the relevant constitutional rights.

Hogan J.'s approach towards the constitutional protection of "the integrity of the human mind and personality" is of particular interest in the context of claims for negligence taken against employers for stress or bullying. Moreover, in *Sullivan v Boylan (No 1)* [2012] IEHC 389 and *Sullivan v Boylan (No 2)* [2013] IEHC 104, Hogan J. interpreted Art.40.3.2°of the Constitution in such a way as to suggest that, in protecting the "person", this provision is capable of protecting personal dignity and a range of rights (to autonomy and privacy, for example), which previously had been identified as falling within Art.40.3.1°. An enterprising litigant in the future may argue that the limitations on claims for bullying—that one incident is not enough—and the limitations on actions for "nervous shock"—that a recognised psychiatric injury must be established and that a secondary victim must generally be closely related to the primary victim and come immediately upon the scene of the accident—are limitations that are inconsistent with the plenitude of protection to mental tranquility and dignity afforded by Art.40.3.2°.

VICARIOUS LIABILITY

The law in relation to vicarious liability has been restated over the past decade and a half in response to the flood of litigation taken by victims of sexual abuse. The old formulation of the test for determining vicarious liability, which enquired whether the wrongful conduct had been done in the course of the employee's employment, simply did not capture the insidious and exploitative abuse of trust of children by those working in religious and educational institutions. A new test emerged, based on proof of a "close connection" between the acts that the employee is engaged to perform and the wrongful conduct in question.

The "close connection" test received the support of Fennelly J., Murray C.J. and Denham J. in *O'Keefe v Hickey* [2009] 2 I.R. 302. Fennelly J. observed:

> "Ultimately, I am satisfied that it is appropriate to adopt a test based on a close connection between the acts which the employee is engaged to perform and which fall truly within the scope of his employment and the tortious act of which complaint is made. That test, as the cases have shown, has enabled liability to be imposed on the solicitor's clerk defrauding the client (*Lloyd v. Grace, Smith and Company* [1912] 1 A.C. 716); the employee stealing the fur stole left in for cleaning (*Morris v. C. W. Martin & Sons Ltd.* [1966] 1 Q.B. 716) and the security officer facilitating thefts from the premises he was guarding (*Johnson & Johnson (Ire.) Ltd. v. C.P. Security Ltd.* [1985] I.R. 362). In each of these cases, the action of the servant was the very antithesis of what he was supposed to be doing. But that action was closely connected with the employment. In *Delahunty v. South Eastern Health Board* [2003] 4 IR 361, O'Higgins J., rightly in my view, held that there was no such close connection. The employee of the orphanage had abused a visitor, not an inmate.
>
> The close connection test is both well established by authority and practical in its content. It is essentially focussed on the facts of the situation. It does not, in principle, exclude vicarious liability for criminal acts or for acts which are intrinsically of a type which would not be authorised by the employer. The law regards it as fair and just to impose liability on the employer rather than to let the loss fall on the injured party. To do otherwise would be to impose the loss on the entirely innocent party who has engaged the employer to perform the service. The employer is, of course, also innocent, but he has, at least, engaged the dishonest servant and has disappointed the expectations of the person to whom he has undertaken to provide the service. There is no reason, in principle, to exclude sexual abuse from this type of liability. That is very far, as I would emphasise, from saying that liability should be automatically imposed. The decision of O'Higgins J. provides an excellent example of the practical and balanced application of the test. All will depend on a careful and balanced analysis of the facts

> of the particular case. In *Bazley v. Curry* (1999) 174 D.L.R. (4th) 45 the employees of the care home were required to provide intimate physical care for the residents. The sexual abuse was held to be closely connected."

In *Hickey v McGowan* [2014] IEHC 19, O'Neill J. gave a comprehensive analysis of the issue. The plaintiff had been subjected to serious sexual abuse over a three-year period from 1969 to 1972, when he was a fourth, fifth and sixth form pupil in St. John's National School in Sligo where the second named defendant, as a member of the Marist Order of Brothers, was a teacher. The first named defendant was the head ("Provincial") of the Marist Brothers in Ireland. He was sued as being vicariously liable for the acts of the second named defendant. All of the academic subjects for the entire three years were taught by the same teacher, the second named defendant. This system was in marked contrast to pupils in the secondary level cycle, who, in general, were taught the different academic subjects by different teachers. O'Neill J. observed that:

> "this meant that, in the 4th, 5th and 6th classes, the teacher had a great deal of contact with pupils, being with them for the entire school day. This necessarily implied that part of the duty of the teacher was to participate in the character formation of pupils, meaning that the teacher would be obliged to correct misbehaviour, to provideinstruction in appropriate or good behaviour where necessary, and generally to assist to ensuring that pupils developed into upright citizens. Given the length of time each day that pupils were in the care of a teacher, probably significantly longer than they were in the care of the parents on a daily basis, it was inevitable that a caring relationship would evolve between teacher and pupils which could also have involved a high level of one-to-one contact with individual pupils. Because of the tender age of the pupils, the teacher was invested with and would have been perceived to have a level of authority over the pupils which, to the pupils, would have seemed, certainly in the years 1969 to 1972, virtually absolute."

O'Neill J. went on to observe that, where a person with paedophile tendencies became a teacher, the teaching arrangements in St. John's National School "not only created a high level of risk of child sexual abuse, but made it a near certainty". O'Neill J. was quite satisfied that the nature of the teaching arrangements in the school "amply" satisfied that part of the "close connection" test, which required that the activity actually being carried on by the abuser be closely connected to the activity that the abuser is engaged to do:

> "By way of contrast to illustrate this, one might say that a gardener engaged to attend the school grounds or a janitor to look after a school building, while having some access to the pupils and therefore opportunity, nonetheless would not have the kind of daily engagement with pupils that a teacher such as the second named defendant would have had with his pupils in his class. By way of further example, there is the decision of O'Higgins J. in *Delahunty v. The South Eastern Health Board* [2003] 4 I.R. 361, in which it was held that the necessary close connection was not established where

> the person abused was a visitor to the institution in question rather than an inmate of it."

It had been submitted on behalf of the Provincial of the Marist Order that vicarious liability should not be imposed because the offending brother's contract of employment as teacher had been with the school rather than the Order. It appeared that the manager of the school who had employed the offending brother had died many years prior to the litigation and that any claim against him would be statute-barred by virtue of s.9(2) of the Civil Liability Act 1961.

O'Neill J. did not accept this argument. He stressed the vows of poverty, chastity and obedience taken by the offending brother, whose salary as a teacher had been surrendered to the Marist congregation. O'Neill J. considered it "clear beyond doubt" that the relationship between the brother and the Marist congregation "was a much closer one than the normal employer/employee relationship". By way of contrast, the employer/employee relationship that the second named defendant had with the manager of the school had gone "no further than the completion of the legal contractual formalities, necessary, no doubt, to entitle the second named defendant to his salary from the Department of Education". The Marist congregation had had full control on a daily basis over the management of the school in Sligo between the years 1969 and 1972. The offending brother had been moved from one school to the school in Sligo and later to another school. All of these moves had been made by the Provincial at the time of the Marist congregation, relying upon his exclusive authority over the second named defendant and without recourse to or consultation with the manager of St. John's National School, save only to the extent of having the formal contractual arrangements completed. The manager of the school in all probability had had no involvement on a day-to-day basis in the running of the school, all of that being left to the Marist brothers. Insofar as any disciplinary issues might have arisen with regard to the second named defendant, these would probably have been dealt with by his superiors in the Marist congregation and the role of the manager would have been confined to formal, contractual arrangements.

O'Neill J. found strong support from the UK Supreme Court decision of *Catholic Child Welfare Society v Various Claimants* [2013] 2 A.C. 1, a decision that has provoked a torrent of analysis: see D. Ryan, (2012/2013) 4(4) *Quarterly Review of Tort Law* 6, C. Fitzgerald, [2013] *Irish Business Law Review* 35, P. Morgan, 129 *Law Quarterly Review* 139 (2013), J. Bell, (2013) 72 *Cambridge Law Journal* 17, N. Bevan, [2013] *Journal of Personal Injury Law* (1)C1 and Lord Hope of Craighead, 129 *Law Quarterly Review* 514 (2013). Apart from the fact that the alleged abuse in the English case had allegedly occurred in a reformatory residential institution, there did not appear to be any material differences between the two cases. There was a similar relationship between the brother teacher and the congregation to which he belonged. This relationship gave to the superiors of the second named defendants in the instant case a high level of control over his life and vocational activities, to which he had voluntarily submitted by taking his vow of obedience. By way of contrast with the facts of *O'Keefe v Hickey* [2009] 2 I.R. 302 the first named defendant against whom a claim of vicarious liability was made had had a high level of control over the teaching activities of the sexual abuser.

The first named defendant had submitted that because the Marist congregation was a non-incorporated association of individuals, there was no basis for a finding of vicarious liability against either the first named defendant as a member of the Marist congregation or of any of the other individual members of the congregation. Referring to the varying circumstances of individual members, past and present, of the Marists, he questioned why any one of these individuals be held to be vicariously liable for the tortious acts of the abusive brother. By way of illustration of this, the position of a Marist brother in Australia was put forward as well as the situations of those who had been members of the marist but had left many years ago, or who had joined the Marist Brothers only in the last few years. O'Neill J. was content to endorse the analysis of Lord Philips in his judgment in *Catholic Child Welfare Society v Various Claimants* [2013] 2 A.C. 1, paras 27–33. Having addressed and not ruled out the possibility of imposing vicarious liability on the religious order at a global level, Lord Philips had stated (at para.33):

> "It seems to me more realistic to view the brothers of the Province from time to time responsible for the area in which Market Weighton lies as members of the relevant unincorporated association rather than the Order as a whole, but I doubt if it makes any difference in principle. Because of the manner in which the Institute carried on its affairs it is appropriate to approach this case as if the Institute were a corporate body existing to perform the function of providing a Christian education to boys, able to own property and, in fact, possessing substantial assets."

O'Neill J. was of opinion that:

> "the foregoing passage from the judgment of Lord Philips, and in particular the last quoted paragraph, could apply with little adaptation to the role of the Marist Brothers in this case. I find the reasoning of Lord Philips in this regard compelling and I adopt it as necessary to arrive at a just outcome of the litigation. To hold otherwise, as submitted on behalf of the first named defendant, that the Marist Brothers were merely an unincorporated band of individuals is to ignore the reality of their true collective identity, to ignore their common purpose, to which each member is committed individually and collectively on behalf of all of the Brothers; to ignore that, for the purposes of carrying out their mission, they necessarily acquire and manage property, no doubt held by trustees for the benefit of the congregation; that in their necessary commercial dealings with the world at large, for example, in employing lay staff, in effecting insurance policies, they must do so under the collective identity or personality of the Marist Congregation, albeit acting through trustees.
>
> Having regard to all of this, is it right, when it comes to the issue of vicarious liability, that the well-known identity of the Marist Congregation can simply disappear into the sands of unincorporated association. I do not think so. In my opinion, the position of the first named defendant as Provincial of the Marists is to be seen, for the purposes of this litigation, as representative of the province of the Marist Congregation in which St. John's National School was located, and I would follow the reasoning of Lord Philips in the *CCWS* case and hold that it is right to approach this case on the basis that the Marist Brothers were a corporate body existing

> to perform the function of providing a Christian education to boys and that the first named defendant is sued as a representative of that body, which is vicariously liable for the tortious acts of the second named defendant."

The fact that the Marist congregation might be liable did not rule out the possibility of dual vicarious liability. This raised the question of the possible vicarious liability of the deceased school manager. If he was so liable, then s.35(1)(i) of the Civil Liability Act 1961 (the "1961 Act") would come into operation as any claim against him was statute-barred. Section 35(1) provides in part as follows:

> For the purpose of determining contributory negligence—
>
> ...
>
> (i) where the plaintiff's damage was caused by concurrent wrongdoers and the plaintiff's claim against one wrongdoer has become barred by the Statute of Limitations or any other limitation enactment, the plaintiff shall be deemed to be responsible for the acts of such wrongdoer ...

By way of contrast, the plaintiff would not have to have his damages reduced to take account of any vicarious liability of deceased or other members of the Marist congregation against whom his claim might be statute-barred. This was on account of O'Neill J.'s holding that the congregation was to be treated as a corporate body, in the instant proceedings represented by the first named defendant.

In estimating the extent of the school manager's vicarious liability, O'Neill J. was satisfied on the evidence that by far the greatest element of control over the teaching activities of the abusing brother had rested with his superiors in the Marist congregation. The manager of the school had had "little or no role to play in any of this". He had, however, retained his residual legal authority over the contractual arrangements between himself and the abusing brother, an authority which could "not be treated as negligible or a nullity". O'Neill J. assessed the liability of the manager at 10 per cent of the overall liability, which was subtracted from the award of damages.

One must have some concerns as to how s.35(1)(i) will operate in future claims for sexual abuse where vicarious liability is in issue. The Statute of Limitations (Amendment) Act 2000 is premised on the fact that sexual abuse can have such a damaging psychological effect as to delay the making of a claim by the victim. In the instant case, the effect had been so strong as to block out all memory of the abuse for decades. If the victim sues Defendant A for vicarious liability and manages to withstand any defence under the Statute of Limitations or under the separate ground of undue delay, he or she will then have to run the gauntlet of Defendant A's producing another defendant—Defendant B—or, worse still, more than one other defendant, now deceased, against whom the plaintiff could, in theory, have taken proceedings and the claim against whom is definitively defeated by s.9(2) of the 1961 Act. The Supreme Court in *Moynihan v Greensmyth* [1977] I.R. 55 upheld the constitutionality of s.9(2) on the basis of the desideratum of winding up the estates of deceased persons with due expedition; but that surely is an easier question than whether it is constitutional to reduce the compensation for victims of sexual abuse during childhood on account of the early demise of their abusers.

Frankly, the present law appears hard to reconcile with fundamental constitutional values relating to dignity, equal treatment, bodily integrity, the right to litigate, property rights and the rights and welfare of children.

As well as the possibility of being held vicariously liable for sexual abuse of a child by one of its congregation, a religious congregation may in some circumstances be held liable for its own negligence in exposing a child to the risk of sexual abuse. This is what happened in *Brennan v Mullan* [2014] IEHC 61. The plaintiff, born in November 1971, sued the representative of a Christian Brothers congregation. While he was a student in a local national school in 1980, his class had been visited by a Christian brother, Brother F. who asked for assistance from a boy to work in the monastery garden which was situate nearby at a Christian Brothers secondary school to which Brother F. was attached. The plaintiff volunteered. He had the support of his parents and family who believed that Brother F. would be a good influence on him. This occurred in 1980 when the plaintiff was approximately eight years old. The plaintiff would call on a regular basis to the monastery and would be admitted by various brothers upon his asking to see Brother F. The plaintiff visited him on almost a daily basis. Brother F, after a period of grooming, began to engage in sexual abuse. Cross J. observed that the sexual abuse suffered by the plaintiff was "of the most extreme that I have seen in my career as a judge or earlier as a barrister". The abuse occurred on almost every occasion the plaintiff visited the monastery. It took place in the brother's bedroom and in areas of the monastery building which were not generally open to members of the public. The abuse continued until at least 1986, when the brother fell ill and was taken to a nursing home in Sutton where the plaintiff visited him there where he was further abused. It later transpired that, in 1960, Brother F had been furnished a formal canonical warning by his superiors on account of his "interfering incorrectly" with boys who had been in his class.

Cross J. held imposed liability on the congregation for its negligent "failure to take any steps whatsoever to supervise Br. F. or to prevent him from access to vulnerable child such as the plaintiff in the full knowledge that Br. F. had been, in the past, guilty of child abuse of young boys". Cross J. fully accepted that, up to reasonably recently, the addictive propensity of abusers to resume their abusive actions had not been widely appreciated. Accordingly, it would be "entirely inappropriate to view any negligence of the defendant with the hindsight of the years since the last decade of the twentieth century". In the instant case, however, as early as 1960, the defendant's predecessors had been aware that Brother F was a person guilty of sexual abuse. In the light of that knowledge, the members of the defendant's congregation had allowed the plaintiff unfettered access to Brother F, members of the congregation had opened the door of the monastery to the plaintiff and "allowed him to wander about the inner sanctum of the monastery and to visit Br. F. in his bedroom unsupervised on a regular basis". Even by the standards of the 1980s, the defendants ought to have put in place a system to watch and monitor Brother F. to ensure that he did not have such access to the plaintiff or to others.

Cross J. concluded that the calling by the plaintiff on a regular basis every day to assist Brother F, in the cultivation of the monastery garden or otherwise, must have been known and must have been remarked upon and ought to have resulted in measures being put in place to watch Brother F. and to prevent him having access to the plaintiff so that he could abuse him on a regular, continuous and sustained basis. There was "absolutely no evidence of any system being put in place by the defendant in relation to Br. F. or any treatment of Br. F. that differentiated him from the vast majority of non-abusive brothers".

O'Keefe v Hickey [2009] 2 I.R. 302 was a case concerned with sexual abuse perpetrated on the plaintiff by the principal of a national school. The Supreme Court, Geoghegan J. dissenting, held that the State was not vicariously liable for the principal's wrongful conduct as, under Ireland's unique constitutional dispensation, the State's obligation was merely to provide "for" primary education, not a direct obligation to provide such education. It is noteworthy that the plaintiff had not sought to sue the manager of the school for its teacher's wrongful conduct.

The plaintiff took the case to the European Court of Human Rights, where, by 11 votes to 6, she was successful in establishing that Ireland had breached arts 3 and 13 of the European Convention on Human Rights: *O'Keefe v Ireland* (Applicaton 35810/09), 28 January 2014. The majority held that Ireland had been under a positive duty to protect the plaintiff from torture or inhuman treatment and that the system of protection in place at the relevant time (the early 1970s) was not sufficiently strong to provide the necessary protection. The majority stated (in paras 168 – 169):

> "The Court has found that it was an inherent positive obligation of government in the 1970s to protect children from ill-treatment. It was, moreover, an obligation of acute importance in a primary education context. That obligation was not fulfilled when the Irish State, which must be considered to have been aware of the sexual abuse of children by adults through, inter alia, its prosecution of such crimes at a significant rate, nevertheless continued to entrust the management of the primary education of the vast majority of young Irish children to non-State actors (National Schools), without putting in place any mechanism of effective State control against the risks of such abuse occurring. On the contrary, potential complainants were directed away from the State authorities and towards the non-State denominational Managers .... The consequences in the present case were the failure by the non-State Manager to act on prior complaints of sexual abuse by [the Principal], the applicant's later abuse by [him] and, more broadly, the prolonged and serious sexual misconduct by [the Principal] against numerous other students in that same National School.
>
> In such circumstances, the State must be considered to have failed to fulfil its positive obligation to protect the present applicant from the sexual abuse to which she was subjected in 1973 whilst a pupil in Dunderrow National School. There has therefore been a violation of her rights under Article 3 of the Convention."

The judgment bases Ireland's breach on principles of direct rather than vicarious responsibility. In the proceedings before the Supreme Court, the plaintiff had not sought to advance a claim based on negligence, which had failed in the High Court. The State argued in Strasbourg that there had thus been a failure to exhaust domestic remedies. The majority rejected this argument but Charleton J. dissented. He considered that the majority had conflated the separate claims. He also was of the view that the majority holding as to breach of art.3 involved the retrospective ascription of knowledge as to the prevention and detection of sexual abuse.

Non-sexual Assaults In *Elmontem v Nethercross Ltd* [2014] IEHC 91 (a decision discussed above, pp.659–660 in the context of employers' liability), Herbert J. was called on to address the issue of vicarious liability where a head chef, employed at a hotel and leisure complex, assaulted the plaintiff, the hotel's financial controller. The head chef had gone to the plaintiff's office to enquire why he had not received a VHI card when other senior employees had received them in the post. During the conversation, the head chef had become increasingly aggressive. The plaintiff advised him that he would telephone the VHI offices as soon as he could. The head chef raised his voice and shouted, "you are always (expletive) busy". The conversation became so heated that the plaintiff pointed his finger to the door and asked him to leave the office. Without warning, the head chef struck the plaintiff, who had remained sitting behind his desk, battering him violently about the face and head with both fists. When the plaintiff tried to get up, the head chef seized him by the neck and pushed him against the wall of the office and continued to punch him about the head and upper body.

The plaintiff sued his employer, as well as his assailant. As to the employer's vicarious liability, Herbert J. considered that he should adopt the "close connection" test. Having quoted from Fennelly J.'s judgment in *O'Keefe v Hickey* [2009] 2 I.R. 302, Herbert J. commented:

> "Whether the actions of the second defendant on the [day of the assault] were closely connected with his employment must be considered in the context of such matters as the nature of the employer's business, whether the risk of the sort of incident which occurred arose because of the nature of that business, the nature of the duties, broadly defined, which the employee was engaged to perform at the time the incident occurred, whether the act could be said to be incidental to or a consequence of anything which the employee was employed to do, whether at the time of the incident the employee could reasonably be said to have been acting, however, mistakenly or excessively in the interests of the employer or was merely pursuing some private end, whether the employee in the course of his duties was expected or encouraged to act aggressively, whether the assault arose out of vengeance or spite, or resentment or intemperate behaviour on the part of the employee and many other similar factors."

Herbert J. concluded that he should not impose vicarious liability on the plaintiff's employer on the basis of the "close connection" test. Even on its most liberal construction, to do so would amount to imposing absolute liability on the employer. To alter the law to that extent would require, in Herbert J.'s view, a clear act of the legislature. The presence of the head chef in the plaintiff's office on the fateful day was in relation to his employment with the employer. His terms of employment had referred to the company health scheme with VHI. The grievance which brought him to the plaintiff as financial controller of the company was therefore connected with his employment. However, what then occurred was, in Herbert J.'s view, "nothing more than a vicious attack on the plaintiff motivated by some personal resentment which ignited an apparently ungovernable temper". This "could not be remotely consistent with the interests of his employer and had no close connection with any acts which fell truly within the scope of his employment as head chef with the [employer]".

Vicarious liability of the State The issue of the vicarious liability of the State, Governmental Ministers and the Attorney General fell for consideration in *Clohessy v Legal Aid Board* [2014] IEHC 72. The background to the case was a protracted land dispute in which the plaintiff's father, represented by the Legal Aid Board, had sued the plaintiff. The plaintiff in the instant proceedings sued the Legal Aid Board as well as nine other defendants. The Minister for Justice and Law Reform was the third named defendant, Ireland the fourth and the Attorney General the fifth named defendant. The pith of the plaintiff's claim was the alleged negligence of the Legal Aid Board in allegedly failing to assess properly the true nature of the claims made against him in the earlier litigation and its alleged failure to take relevant facts into consideration when assessing his father's means.

The Minister, Ireland and the Attorney General sought the dismissal of the proceedings against them on the basis that the plaintiff had neither made out any claim against them nor sought any relief against them.The statement of claim contained the plea that the Minister was appointed by the Government of Ireland and that "its mandated statutory functions are many and varied including the overseeing of the proper lawful functioning of the statutory bodies under its ministerial control which includes the Legal Aid Board its servants and agents, and the employees of the Court Services working within the office of the County Registrar in so far as those functions relate to an executive function of the Government performed by the Courts Services". There was also a plea that "the Attorney General advises the Government in matters of law and legal opinion, parliamentary drafting, statute law revision, and has as part of its office and under its umbrella the office of the Chief State Solicitor whose function includes providing a solicitor service to its principal clients, which are all government departments, the Director of Public Prosecutions, and the Garda Siochana."

It seemed clear to Peart J. that the only justification for including the third, fourth and fifth defendants was "on the basis of some vicarious liability for the actions of the first named defendant". The plaintiff had submitted that ultimately the Legal Aid Board was responsible to, and controlled by, the Minister for Justice and Law Reform, and must ultimately be liable for the actions of the board. However, Peart J. considered it "clear from the Civil Legal Aid Act, 1995 that, while the Minister may, by order, from time to time as occasion requires, issue to the Board such general directives as to policy in relation to legal aid and advice as he or she considers necessary, the Board nevertheless is independent in its functions." In this regard, Peart J. noted that s.3(2) of the Civil Legal Aid Act 1995 (the "1995 Act") provides:

> The Board shall be a body corporate with perpetual succession and an official seal and power to sue and be sued in its corporate name and, with the consent of the Minister, to acquire, hold and dispose of land or an interest in land or rights over or in respect of land and to acquire, hold and dispose of any other property.

In addition, s.7(3) of the 1995 Act provides:

> Nothing in this Act shall be construed as enabling the Minister to exercise any power or control in relation to any particular case with which the Board is or may be concerned.

Peart J. accordingly made an order striking out the proceedings as against the third, fourth and fifth named defendants.

DAMAGES

The Multiplier Cross J.'s decision in *Russell v Health Service Executive* [2014] IEHC 590 is of very considerable significance in the calculation of damages where a plaintiff has been severely injured. Cross J. calculated the discount rate at 1 per cent rather than 3 per cent, which had been the former practice. In *Russell*, the infant plaintiff had suffered catastrophic injuries at birth. Her life expectancy was 45 years. Cross J. emphasised that plaintiffs generally, and this plaintiff in particular, could not be regarded as an ordinary prudent investor, judged by some objective generic test. Greater caution was required than for such a generic hypothetical person. The ILGS available in France and Germany would be likely to be available at the rate for about 20 years but Cross J. considered that for the full period a 1 per cent rate was appropriate. Cross J. awarded over €13 million to the plaintiff.

Dismissal of fraudulent or exaggerated claims All practitioners in the area of personal injuries litigation are familiar with s.26 of the Civil Liability Act 2004 (the "2004 Act"), which requires a court to dismiss a claim where the evidence given by or adduced on behalf of the plaintiff is, to the plaintiff's knowledge false or misleading in any material respect, "unless, for reasons that the court shall state in its decision, the dismissal of the action would result in injustice being done." Over the past decade, s.26 has yielded a rich jurisprudence. What has emerged is that courts are not afraid to dismiss a claim where intentional misrepresentation or exaggeration has occurred but conversely are anxious to protect plaintiffs from unnecessarily strong challenges to their veracity.

In *Daly v Health Service Executive* [2014] IEHC 560, the case involved a challenge to the plaintiff's claim that she had sustained a serious back injury, which prevented her from returning to work. It emerged that her condition prior to the accident had been somewhat more serious than had appeared from the pleadings. Moreover, the plaintiff in evidence had volunteered that, post-accident, she had for a period been regularly attending a gym where she engaged in an extensive programme of exercises, involving what Noonan J. described as "quite vigorous activities such as sit ups, 'crunches', kettle bell weight lifting and 'spinning' using a static exercise bicycle."

The defendant sought a dismissal of the claim, not on the basis of s.26 of the 2004 Act, but rather on the principles articulated in *Shelley-Morris v Bus Atha Cliath* [2003] 1 I.R. 232. Noonan J. refused the defendant's application. He noted that the plaintiff in *Shelley-Morris* had been found to have deliberately lied on oath at the trial in relation to her injuries, and he commented: " I do not think that the plaintiff in this case can in any sense be equated with that. At most it might be said that she had been less than frank about her gym activities with her doctors or perhaps downplayed her pre-accident back pain to a degree but I do not think it elevates the claim to the realm of a total fraud."

In the light of the evidence about these gym activities, Noonan J. held that the plaintiff was in fact capable of returning to work. In an important passage, Noonan J. stated:

> "It is worthy of some note that despite the invitation to the court to dismiss the claim on the basis that it was so tainted by lies as to amount to an abuse of process, the defendant stopped short of reliance on s.26. This might seem at first blush difficult to understand because if that level of dishonesty affected the plaintiff's case, it would seem to follow that a s.26 application must lie. This section was introduced into law not long after the decision of the Supreme Court in Shelley-Morris and .... acts as a very major 'nuclear' deterrent to the mounting of fraudulent and exaggerated claims. It undoubtedly confers litigation advantage on defendants and has long been complained of by plaintiffs' lawyers as violating the principle of 'equality of arms' in personal injury litigation. However, the recent jurisprudence of this court reveals an emerging trend towards a more level playing field by the threat of sanctioning defendants who invoke the section without just cause by way of aggravated or punitive damages …
>
> I have little doubt that the defendants in this case were very conscious of the risk of making a s.26 application were it to prove unsuccessful. Instead they chose to pursue an alternative course which they hoped may achieve the same result without incurring the risk identified. They declined to grasp the nettle.
>
> It would be quite unjust to dismiss the plaintiff's claim on the grounds advanced by the defendant and I decline to do so. Whilst I have said that the claim for special damages is in my view improper, I do not think the court can dismiss the case on that ground alone particularly where the defendants have expressly declined to make a s.26 application."

Noonan J.'s observations provoke a couple of reflections. First, it is difficult to see how the risk for a defendant of being held to have conducted the defence in such a way as to warrant the making of an award of aggravated damages against him or her should be any greater where it invokes s.26 than where it invokes *Shelley-Morris*. Second, the challenge for the defence in seeking a dismissal under the *Shelley-Morris* principles is clearly greater than that facing the defendant who invokes s.26.

In *Looby v Fatalski* [2014] IEHC 564, the plaintiff admitted that he had told lies to his GP on a number of occasions that he could only cycle for one to one and a half hours, when in actual fact he could cycle for up to five hours. The plaintiff admitted that he told these lies in order to get more money in his case. The plaintiff also admitted that he had told lies in order to get more money in his case, that he had told lies to his solicitor for the purpose that he had sworn the affidavit of verification knowing that the reply given at item 11 was not the truth.

Barr J. held that the plaintiff had breached s.26(2) but he was nonetheless satisfied that there would be an injustice if the action were to be dismissed. The doctor had stated that there was not much significance from a clinical point of view between cycling between one and a half hours or for four hours. It did not appear that the doctor had been misled in his diagnosis or treatment as a result of the lies told to him by the plaintiff. Barr J. observed:

> "In the circumstances, I am satisfied that the lies were not of great significance to the plaintiff's overall claim. The injury suffered was an objectively verifiable injury in the form of a fracture of the L1 vertebra. He had required immobilisation in a body brace for three months. Thereafter, he had gradually got back to full fitness. The lies told were not sophisticated and were liable to be found out, as indeed they were by the private investigator. They related to his capacity to pursue his hobby of cycling. As such they did not relate to a central issue in the case ....
>
> The lies related to how much he could engage in his sporting pursuits. He admitted to cycles of up to one and a half hours in duration. This shows that he had attained a reasonable level of fitness. If he had admitted to doing the longer hours, his compensation would not have been much less than on the actual number of hours that he could cycle. It would be an injustice to dismiss the entire claim on account of the lies told in relation to his sporting pursuits."

While the untruths of the plaintiff were not of great significance so far as the quantum of damages was concerned, they were clearly designed to mislead, for financial gain. So far as their intentional character was concerned, there does not appear to have been any mitigating element. It is therefore a little surprising that Barr J. should conclude that dismissal would "result in injustice being done". Perhaps other aspects of the case, not specifically mentioned, had a bearing on this determination.

Transport

MERCHANT SHIPPING

Registration of Ships The Merchant Shipping (Registration of Ships) Act 2014 (the "2014 Act") provided for the updating and modernisation of ship registration legislation and enhanced the safety of ships that operate domestically in Irish waters. It also provided for the repeal and replacement of the Mercantile Marine Act 1955 (the "1995 Act"), as amended, which formed part of a wide-ranging code of maritime legislation that dates from the Merchant Shipping Act 1894, as amended. At the time of writing (July 2015), s.69 was the only provision of the 2014 Act to have come into operation, which it did on the date of enactment, 25 December 2014. The other provisions of the 2014 Act require a Commencement Order or Orders to come into force.

It was noted during the Oireachtas debates on the 2014 Act that international maritime law, in particular the United Nations Convention on the Law of the Sea, requires that every State fix the conditions for the grant of its nationality to ships, registration of ships in its territory and the right to fly its flag. Ship registration is about conferring Irish nationality on ships, allowing them to fly the Irish flag and registering ownership.

Under the provisions of the 1955 Act, as amended in 1998 and 2006, ships wholly owned by an Irish citizen or an Irish body corporate were obliged to register. Exemptions to this obligation included ships not exceeding 15 net tonnes and which navigated in particular areas, sea-fishing boats less than 15m in length overall, and ships owned by Irish citizens not ordinarily resident in the State. As the flag state, Ireland has obligations in respect of ships on its register wherever in the world they travel, including in regard to any serious marine incident in which they may be involved.

It was stated during the Oireachtas debates on the 2014 Act that the need for an updated ship registration system had been growing against a background of international growth in maritime trade, an increase in the use of pleasure craft and an increasing emphasis on safety, security and environmental issues both at EU and international level. The 2014 Act was prepared after a detailed review involving an extensive public consultation process, correspondence and meetings with interested stakeholders, as well as engagement with relevant departments. It had also taken into account standards set by the International Maritime Organisation and the European Union, in particular, to enhance the safety of ships and prevent pollution from ships by addressing the issues of substandard ships and the obligations of states in regard to ships that fly their flag.

Under the 1955 Act, the Department of Transport was the national authority with responsibility for the registration of Irish ships, although the statutory ship registration role is assigned to the Revenue Commissioners. As of 2014, local registrars, who are Revenue officials, administer the registration process in 11 locations throughout the country. Each registrar maintains a register book to record all registration transactions that occur in respect of the port of registry for which he or she is responsible. There were 13 ports of registry designated under the 1955 Act. The local registrars hold all of the original official ship registration records and send details of entries in the register books to the mercantile marine office of the Department of Transport. In 2014, there were more than 3,200 ships registered in Ireland on the national ship register.

The 2014 Act provided for an electronic Irish register of ships which will consist of different parts for the registration of different types of ships and for different registration purposes, such as visitor registration. The electronic register will facilitate easier access to ship registration information and thereby enable the generation of statistical information and reports about the make-up of the Irish fleet. The 2014 Act also addressed gaps in the 1955 Act (which it repealed), such as the absence of a specific power to remove unsafe or unsuitable ships from the register, the absence of ship registration renewal and outdated enforcement and penalty provisions. As well as addressing these gaps, the 2014 Act provided for improvements such as an extension of mandatory ship registration to additional ship categories, including fishing boats less than 15m in length overall, personal watercraft such as jet skis, small fast-powered craft and some small commercial angling boats.

Subject to some exemptions, the 2014 Act requires all ships operating domestically to be on the register or have a current valid registration conferring nationality from another country. The comprehensive legislative framework in the 2014 Act will, as is common in modern legislative codes, be supported by secondary legislation which will provide the detail of the ship registration requirements. This will facilitate further evolution and improvement in the future if the need arises, including a potential to respond quickly to any emerging policy issues of concern at a domestic, EU or international level.

Registration fees Part 1 of the 2014 Act (ss.1 to 8) contains standard provisions, including fees and the making of regulations. Section 3 provides that fees will be based on a scale of charges based on the categorisation, size and use of ships, which will be prescribed in regulations to be made by the Minister for Transport with the consent of the Minister for Public Expenditure and Reform. When the 2014 Act was being debated in the Oireachtas, the Minister for Transport indicated that it was not anticipated that the maximum registration fee levels as of 2014 in the range of €201 to €251 would be exceeded. The registration fee for the ship categories introduced by the 2014 Act, such as personal watercraft or small fast-powered craft, would, the Minister also anticipated, be less than the registration fee for large commercially operating ships, and the Minister envisaged a fee structure under €100 envisaged for smaller vessels. The 2014 Act provides for renewal of registration up to five years after initial registration and up to every 10 years after that. Again, the Minister anticipated that renewal fees would be lower than the initial registration fee, in particular in cases where there were no changes made to the ship in the intervening period. The fee for visitor registration would, the Minister suggested, be a nominal fee, probably under €50, and he noted that the 2014 Act proposed a simplified and straightforward application process in order not to impact negatively on tourism.

Registration of ships Part 2 the 2014 Act (ss.9 to 32) deals with registration of ships. Section 9 provides for the establishment of a modernised central electronic Irish register of ships to replace the primarily paper-based system under the 1955 Act. The detail of the structure of the register and the different registration requirements for each part of the register will be set out in the regulations to be made under the Act, and the register will be established and implemented on a phased basis.

The Minister suggested, during the Oireachtas debates on the 2014 Act, that the structure of the register could consist of five parts. The first part would be for new passenger and commercial ships, existing large passenger and commercial ships 24m in length and greater and the larger recreational craft. A second part would be for licensed sea-fishing boats, a distinction being made between fishing boats over and under 15m in length. A third part would include the registration of existing passenger and commercial ships less than 24m as well as personal watercraft, small fast-powered craft and small commercial angling boats. A fourth part would contain the detail of ships that are the subject of visitor registration or a temporary registration. There would be a fifth part for information on undischarged registered mortgages in respect of ships that have been removed from the register.

The 2014 Act provides for a facility to initiate ship registrations online and that it should be possible to substantially complete many straightforward renewals in this way. However, given the nature of ship registration and some of the documents required, the 2014 Act envisages that it may be necessary to maintain some element of paper documentation in the registration process. The register will be maintained by the Department of Transport and the 2014 Act allows for the designation of officers of the Department, of another Minister and officers of the Revenue Commissioners to be registrars of ships to administer the register.

Section 10 of the 2014 Act provides for service agreements with State agencies to undertake elements of the ship registration administration process, if the need arises in the future. If this happens, officers of the State agency can also be designated as registrars of ships. In light of the State's international responsibilities under the United Nations Convention on the Law of the Sea and the need to retain control over the registration of ships on the Irish flag, the Minister stated that it was not proposed to outsource the entire ship registration process.

Section 11 sets out the ship registration requirements that will apply to ships that operate domestically. Under the 2014 Act, mandatory registration was extended to personal watercraft such as jet skis, small fast-powered craft and all commercial angling boats regardless of size. Other recreational craft less than 24m in load line length, including small angling boats used solely for recreational purposes, are not required to register. However, owners of such vessels may register voluntarily if they so wish. To underpin compliance with safety standards, the 2014 Act also extended registration to fishing boats less than 15m in length overall. When the 2014 Act comes fully into force, therefore, the majority of ships operating domestically in Irish waters will have to be registered.

The extension of mandatory registration to high risk vessels, such as personal watercraft and small fast-powered craft, is a response to the growth in their use in recent years and the need, in the interests of safety, to exercise some degree of control over them. This also implemented recommendations of the Marine Casualty Investigation Board on the registration of jet skis. The Minister noted during the

Oireachtas debates on the 2014 Act that the Irish Coast Guard statistics for 2013 showed that incidents of jet skis requiring assistance were up 189 per cent on 2012. This was attributed in part to the good summer in 2013 but also because of the proliferation of these craft. Registration would act as a support to general maritime law enforcement and make it easier to prosecute offending users through the identification of owners.

The 2014 Act provides for a simple form of registration for personal watercraft and small fast-powered craft operating domestically. A registration requirement will apply to all passenger and commercial ships and boats, recreational craft of 24m and greater in load line length; all fishing boats that hold or are required to hold a sea-fishing boat licence granted under the Fisheries (Amendment) Act 2003; personal watercraft, including jet skis, small fast-powered craft; and all commercial angling boats, including certain small angling boats carrying no more than three passengers that are exempt from the requirement to have a passenger boat licence.

State-owned ships in the relevant categories will be required to be registered but, consistent with international practice, warships continue to be exempt from registration under the 2014 Act. In addition, as noted above, a current valid registration conferring nationality from another state will be an acceptable form of registration.

Section 12 provides that, to be entitled to register, the ship owner must be a qualified person in accordance with s.15 of the 2014 Act and the ship must comply with prescribed conditions or other requirements which may relate to such matters as safety, environment and security, type, age, size, and trading pattern. These provisions reinforce the standards required for registration and allow the State to exercise greater control over the condition of ships that choose to register on the Irish register of ships. All Irish ships will have to have their operations controlled and directed from within the State, although different requirements will apply to the different categories and types of ships.

Section 14 provides that ships that are registered on the pre-2014 register books, when the Irish register of ships is established under the 2014 Act, will be automatically transferred to the appropriate part of the new register free of charge and, subject to compliance with the requirements of the 2014 Act, will be registered for a period of up to five years from the date of transfer. Following this period, they will be subject to a requirement to renew registration at intervals of up to 10 years in duration. To ensure equality of treatment, all ship registrations on the new register will be for a period of up to five years, whether they are registered ships that are transferring to the register under the 2014 Act or ships registering for the first time. The renewal requirement will allow transferred ships that have ceased to exist to be removed from the register when their registration is not renewed and will ensure that such vessels will not remain on the register indefinitely, thus improving the accuracy of the register.

Section 15 provides that "qualified persons" will be entitled to register their ships. These include a ship owner who is an Irish citizen, a national of another EU Member State and certain corporate bodies. Section 16 requires a qualified person who is not resident in the State or who does not have a registered office in the State to appoint a representative person who resides or has a presence in the State.

Registrars of ships will be designated under s.17 which allows for the continuing involvement of the pre-2014 registrars of ships, who are officers of the Revenue Commissioners.

Section 18 provides for the application for and grant of ship registration, including provisional registration where a ship is under construction and non-operative registration to allow for the certification or licensing of a ship, such as for a passenger boat certificate or a sea-fishing boat licence. Section 18 also enables the regulation of a range of matters connected to registration application requirements, including procedures, information, declarations and documentation.

Section 19 provides for the renewal of ship registration which is one of a number of new initiatives being introduced. Renewal acts as a checking mechanism to ensure that ships continue to comply with any relevant safety certification or other requirements that apply to them. Section 20 requires the measurement of ships for the purposes of registration and the issuing of a certificate of measurement.

Section 21 of the 2014 Act involves another innovation, the introduction of a facility to refuse to register a ship and to remove a ship from the register in a range of circumstances, including those relating to safety, pollution prevention, qualified persons and compliance with standards and conditions. These quality-driven measures, along with registration renewal, were introduced in the interests of preserving the integrity and improving the accuracy of the register. An appeal process is provided for in s.22 in specified circumstances.

Section 23 provides for temporary registration of recreational craft less than 24m in load line length. That was intended to accommodate the navigation of such vessels owned by a person normally resident in the State from another country to the State, and will ensure the ship is not detained for not being registered when in foreign waters where ships are required to be registered.

Section 24 of the 2014 Act introduced the new category of visitor registration. That was intended to accommodate ships that are not registered in another state, in particular non-commercial ships that wish to visit Ireland for short periods not exceeding three months, for example, persons on holiday or taking part in sporting events. It will only apply to personal watercraft, recreational craft 24m in load line length and greater, small fast-powered craft and small commercial angling boats. Without visitor registration, such craft would be required to have full registration on the register under s.11. Ships holding a visitor registration will not be known as Irish ships. A simplified registration process with a nominal fee will be set out in regulations to be made under the 2014 Act.

Sections 25 and 26 provide for regulations to set out the requirements for the naming, carving and marking of ships in relation to a range of matters such as the official name or number of the vessel or the port of registry. This reflects the pre-2014 Act situation and common practice internationally. Different carving and marking requirements will apply to different types of ships. Similarly, the regulations on the naming of ships will allow for a variety of ship name requirements, as well as circumstances where a ship name may not be required for practical reasons in the case of particular types or sizes of ship.

Sections 27 to 29 deal with certificates of registry and requirements for carrying documentation on board the ship. It is normal practice for a ship to be registered by reference to a particular port of registry. In Ireland, in 2014 there were 13 such ports and those are retained under s.30 and the associated Sch.3, which lists the ports: Arklow, Cork, Drogheda, Dublin, Dundalk, Galway, Limerick, Skibbereen,

Sligo, Tralee, Waterford, Westport and Wexford. The 2014 Act enables new ports of registry to be prescribed or a port to cease to be a port of registry. Section 30(2) sets out the considerations that would inform such a decision.

Section 31 facilitates the transfer of the port of registry of a ship from one port of registry in the State to another. Historically, ports of registry were chosen because they were the locations of the local registrars. A ship owner may choose a port of registry from any of the 13 ports. However, with the introduction of a central electronic register of ships under the 2014 Act, the ports of registry will continue in name only.

Irish ships, national colour and character Part 3 of the 2014 Act (ss.33 to 38) deals with Irish ships and their national colour and character. It clarifies which ships may be known as Irish ships and the requirements that apply to the flying of flags by such ships. These include prohibitions on hoisting flags other than the national flag, on pretending to be an Irish ship, on concealing Irish character, and on assuming foreign character. The provisions are mainly based on the pre-2014 legislative requirements. Section 37 deals with offences relating to using or assuming Irish national character on a ship that is not Irish.

Enforcement Part 4 of the 2014 Act (ss.39 to 42) deals with enforcement, which includes a number of improvements to the ship registration code under the Mercantile Marine Act 1955 under which enforcement and penalties were limited. To address the situation, a number of changes are included, including an increase in penalty levels, provision for authorised persons for enforcement purposes, the introduction of a system of fixed payments for certain offences involving personal watercraft, small fast-powered craft and small commercial angling boats, and a power of detention for marine surveyors for ship registration related offences.

A range of State personnel who are likely to come across breaches of ship registration requirements in the course of their normal day-to-day activities are designated as authorised persons under s.39 for practical operational reasons. The powers of the authorised persons are set out in s.40. These provisions enable enforcement of the 2014 Act by marine surveyors of the Department of Transport, an officer of the Irish Coast Guard and the Revenue Commissioners, a member of An Garda Síochána, a harbour master or a sea fisheries protection officer, certain Defence Forces personnel and an authorised officer of Inland Fisheries Ireland.

Section 41 introduces powers of detention for marine surveyors in relation to a ship in a port in the State or in Irish waters, or an Irish ship in a foreign port, where breaches of specified sections of the 2014 Act arise relating to registration requirements, the carving and marking of the ship, the certificate of registry of the ship, falsely assuming Irish nationality or intent to conceal Irish national character or assuming a foreign character. The Minister commented during the Oireachtas debates on the 2014 Act that it was not envisaged that this power of detention would be used only in very serious situations.

A system of fixed payments in lieu of prosecution for certain offences is provided for in s.42. That may be used for offences involving failure to register smaller vessels such as personal watercraft, small fast-powered craft and certain small commercial angling boats. Fixed payment notices may be issued by the authorised persons provided for in s.39 and by an authorised person appointed by a local authority under s.17 of the Maritime Safety Act 2005. Similar to the approach in the 2005 Act relating to breaches of safety by-laws or the operation of craft, the fixed payment notice will indicate that the person is alleged to have committed an offence, and if the payment specified in the notice, that is, €150 or such other prescribed amount, is made within 21 days of the date of the notice, court proceedings will not be initiated. Prosecution may be brought by the local authority concerned, Inland Fisheries Ireland (IFI) or the Minister for Transport, depending on who serves the notice.

Evidence and procedure Part 5 of the 2014 Act (ss.43 to 47) deals with a number of evidential and procedural issues that reflect those in the 1955 Act. This includes provisions on the admissibility of documentary evidence and declarations related to ship registration.

Title, ownership etc. Part 6 of the 2014 Act (ss.48 to 62) deals with private law provisions that also reflect those in the 1955 Act. These relate to title, ownership, transfer of ships, and mortgages on ships.

Offences and penalties Part 7 of the 2014 Act (ss.63 to 67) can be linked to the enforcement in Pt 4 of the 2014 Act, above, and includes provisions on proceedings for offences, summary penalties and the liability of both the owner and the master of a ship when certain offences are committed. Section 63 provides for prosecutions, the recovery of prosecution costs and the payment and disposal of fines. Summary prosecution proceedings may be initiated by the Minister for Transport and, in the case of ship registration offences relating to personal watercraft, small fast-powered craft and certain small angling boats, by the local authority concerned or Inland Fisheries Ireland.

Section 64 provides that, on summary conviction (except where provided otherwise in the 2014 Act) a Class A fine applies, that is, under the Fines Act 2010, a maximum fine of €5,000. This contrasts with the maximum penalties under the 1955 Act of €635. Section 65 provides for the prosecution of both the owner and master of a ship in the case of certain specified offences linked to the carrying of a certificate of registry and related documentation, concealing the Irish national character of a ship, or assuming a foreign character. Offences committed by a body corporate are dealt with in ss.66 and 67 deal with service of documents.

Consequential amendments Part 8, comprising s.68 and the associated Sch.4, relates to consequential amendments to ensure that references to the Mercantile Marine Act 1955 in the listed Acts are replaced with references to the 2014 Act.

SOLAS Convention 1978 Part 9, comprising s.69 only, amended s.3(1) of the Merchant Shipping (Safety Convention) Act 1952, by substituting for the definition of "Safety Convention" (inserted by s.6(1)(c) of the Merchant Shipping Act 2010) an updated definition of the 1978 International Convention for the Safety of Life at Sea, SOLAS, to facilitate the transposition and implementation by secondary legislation amendments agreed in May 2012 to the Convention. At the time of writing (July 2015), s.69 was the only provision of the 2014 Act to have come into operation, which it did on the date of enactment, 25 December 2014.

Maritime Labour Convention 2006 A series of regulations made in 2014 gave effect to various elements of the Maritime Labour Convention 2006, which had been adopted at EU level through Directive 2009/13/EC (amending Directive 1999/63/EC), implementing the agreement concluded by the European Community Shipowners' Associations (ECSA) and the European Transport Workers' Federation (ETF) on the Maritime Labour Convention 2006. The regulations referred to below all came into force on 20 August 2014.

Employment agreement The Merchant Shipping (Maritime Labour Convention) (Seafarer Employment Agreement and Wages) Regulations 2014 (S.I. No. 373 of 2014) (the "2014 Regulations") provide that a ship owner of a seagoing Irish ship who employs a seafarer must provide the seafarer with a written agreement in which the terms and conditions of employment of the seafarer are set out. The 2014 Regulations set out the minimum contents of seafarer employment agreements, the duties of ship owners with regard to records of employment, obligations towards seafarers who are not employees and minimum notice periods. The 2014 Regulations also set out provisions relating to the payment of wages.

Accommodation The Merchant Shipping (Maritime Labour Convention) (Accommodation, Recreational Facilities, Food, Catering and Ships' Cooks) Regulations 2014 (S.I. No. 374 of 2014) set out, inter alia, the requirements of the Maritime Labour Convention regarding the provision of accommodation and recreational facilities on all seagoing Irish ships constructed on or after 21 July 2015. They also revoked the Merchant Shipping Act 1906 (Variation of Seamen's Provisions) Order 1941 (S.I. No. 432 of 1941) and the Merchant Shipping (Certification of Ships' Cooks) Regulations 1987 (S.I. No. 276 of 1987). The requirements of the Merchant Shipping (Crew Accommodation on Board Ship) Regulations 1951 (S.I. No. 95 of 1951) continue to apply to pre-2015 ships.

Shipowners' liability and repatriation The Merchant Shipping (Maritime Labour Convention) (Shipowners' Liabilities and Repatriation) Regulations 2014 (S.I. No. 375 of 2014) set out the requirements of the Maritime Labour Convention regarding ship owners' liability and repatriation.

Certification and inspection The Merchant Shipping (Maritime Labour Convention) (Flag State Inspection and Certification) Regulations 2014 (S.I. No. 376 of 2014) set out the requirements of the Maritime Labour Convention regarding flag State responsibilities.

ROAD TRAFFIC

Road safety measures The Road Traffic Act 2014 provided for a series of measures aimed at further contributing to improved road safety. It was noted during the Oireachtas debates on the 2014 Act that, in 2001, there were 415 deaths on the roads but by 2012, this had come down to 162. It was accepted that this involved a combination of various changes in road traffic legislation, a number of initiatives and the work of many people and organisations, and at a time when the number of vehicles on the roads was increasing. However, after a number of years in which the numbers killed on roads were dropping, in 2013 road deaths totalled 190, an increase of 28 on 2012. Serious injuries in 2013 were 468, which was down by 25 on 2012.

Among the legislative reforms in recent years were the creation of the fixed charge and penalty points systems to promote greater awareness of dangerous driving habits. The lowering of legal alcohol limits and the introduction of mandatory alcohol testing checkpoints had also helped to reduce drink driving on the roads. In addition, An Garda Síochána established a dedicated Garda traffic corps to focus on road safety issues and safety cameras were introduced in 2010. The establishment of the Road Safety Authority (RSA), provided for coordination across a range of interrelated policy areas.

During the Oireachtas debates on the 2014 Act, the Minister for Transport acknowledged that there are many factors involved in road safety. Some are physical, such as the standard of vehicles and the quality of the roads. There are also human factors—training, experience and responsible behaviour. The 2014 Act focuses predominantly on the human factors, by dealing with driver licensing, penalty points and the testing of drivers for intoxication. The 2014 Act also amended s.106 of the Road Traffic Act 1961 to deal with "hit-and-run incidents" and it also introduced a new offence of tampering with an odometer, the practice commonly referred to as "clocking" of a vehicle.

Further elements of graduated driver licensing system, GDLS Part 2 of the 2014 Act (ss.3 to 6) deal with the driver licensing regime. It provided for further elements of the graduated driver licensing system, GDLS, which is a multi-step approach to driver learning, by contrast with a "single step" licensing system in which a person gained a full licence with no restrictions once he or she passed the driving test. The GDLS was developed originally in Australia and New Zealand in the 1960s when a provisional licence system was introduced and which has been reformed and updated a number of times since then. It is intended to refocus driver learning away from simply passing a test and onto the acquisition of skills and experience. The general principles of the GDLS have been adopted in many countries, while the precise details vary from one country to another according to what is most appropriate to local circumstances. The Road Safety Authority (RSA), undertook a large programme of study and consultation to develop proposals for a GDLS that would be appropriate to an Irish context. This led to the selection of nine elements of GDLS for Ireland, which were published in 2009: *Graduated Driver Licence Recommendations*, available at <*rsa.ie*>. Of the nine components, three have now been introduced, namely, compulsory basic training with an approved driving instructor; lower alcohol levels for learners and recently qualified drivers; and the reconfiguration of the driver theory test.

The 2014 Act provides for a further three GDLS measures, first, the creation of a new category of novice driver; secondly, the introduction of a lower penalty point disqualification threshold for learners and novices; and, thirdly, the introduction of a requirement for learners to undergo a minimum amount of driving experience before taking a driving test.

Sections 3 and 4 of the 2014 Act create a new category of novice driver, defined as a driver in the first two years of holding a full licence. Novices will be required to display an N plate. A person will be a novice driver only once. If they hold a full licence in one category, they will not revert to being a novice driver if they later qualify in another category. The countdown of the two-year novice period will be frozen during any period in which the driver is disqualified. Section 5 provides that vehicle insurers will have access to endorsements on a person's file on the national vehicle and driver file, NVDF, subject to certain conditions.

Section 6 provides that people taking the driving test must first complete a minimum amount of accompanied driving. The amount of experience required will be set out in regulations. The intention behind this is twofold: at one level it is aimed at ensuring a minimum of experience before drivers take the test; and to promote a culture change in attitudes towards accompanying drivers. International experience shows that accompanying drivers should play an important role in the learning process.

Section 8 provides for a disqualification threshold under the penalty points system of seven points for learners and novices, as opposed to the normal 12-point threshold.

Further reforms of penalty points system Part 3 of the 2014 Act (ss.7 to 10) deal with the penalty points system. It provided for 12 new penalty points offences; provided an opportunity to pay a fixed charge for three offences instead of the offence going straight to court; an increase in penalty points on the payment of a fixed charge for 18 offences, and an increase in the penalty points on conviction in respect of 16 offences. The offences where penalty points were increased include speeding, driving while holding a mobile phone, dangerous overtaking and failure to obey a traffic light. New penalty points offences include the non-display of an L or N plate, contravention of rules on mini-roundabouts, and failure to respect a stop sign.

Part 3 also provided for the repeal and replacement of s.53 of the Road Traffic Act 2010 (the "2010 Act"), which deals with recording penalty points where they cannot be associated with the record of an individual for whatever reason.

The Road Traffic (No.2) Act 2014 dealt with two important and significant difficulties with the general penalty points system which it appeared was noticed when the new penalty points regime in the Road Traffic Act 2014, above, was being brought into force by Ministerial Order. The first difficulty related to the Road Traffic Act 2002 (the "2002 Act"), which first established the fixed charge notice and penalty points system, provided for the endorsement of the relevant number of penalty points on the records of those who made payment on foot of fixed charge notices for offences listed in the Schedule to the 2002 Act. It excluded from this provision those offences which were straight-to-court offences, including using a vehicle without a valid NCT certificate and parking a vehicle in a dangerous position. When the Road Traffic Act 2014, above, was being drafted, these two offences should have been removed from the exclusions contained in the 2002 Act. Due to an oversight, this did not happen and the Road Traffic (No.2) Act 2014 rectified the position.

The second issue addressed in the Road Traffic (No.2) Act 2014 also related to the endorsement of penalty points. Section 2 of the 2002 Act provides the basis on which penalty points can be endorsed on a person's record following the payment of a fixed charge under s.103 of the Road Traffic Act 1961 (the "1961 Act"). Section 8 of the Road Traffic Act 2014, above, amended s.2 of the 2002 Act by substituting a reference to s.37 or 44 of the 2010 Act for s.103 of the 1961 Act. In other words, with the enactment of the Road Traffic Act 2014, above, penalty points would be endorsed on payment of the fixed charge under those sections of the 2010 Act. Section 8 of the Road Traffic Act 2014, above, was commenced with effect from 1 August 2014. Unfortunately, because ss.37 and 44 of the 2010 Act had not yet been commenced, the commencement of s.8 of the Road Traffic Act 2014, above, removed the power to endorse points on the licence record.

Section 2 of the Road Traffic (No.2) Act 2014 sought to address both of these issues. It also provided clarity on a situation where an offence has been committed but the appropriate penalty points associated with the offence have been increased before the fixed charge is paid. Section 2 reflected the pre-existing practice of endorsing the number of penalty points that were applicable on the date the alleged offence took place. The concern that arose when this error was detected was that there might be a question mark over the penalty points endorsed since 1 August following the payment of a fixed charge. During the Oireachtas debates on the Road Traffic (No.2) Act 2014, the Minister for Transport stated that the Department contacted the Office of the Attorney General on this point and received comprehensive advice which pointed out that the legal vacuum caused by the commencement of s.8 of the 2014 Act could not be said to reflect the intention of the Oireachtas, which can be taken to have been that there would be, at all times, some mechanism for endorsing penalty points on the driving licences of persons choosing to make a fixed charge payment in lieu of a potential prosecution. On the basis of this advice, s.3 of the Road Traffic (No.2) Act 2014 provided that penalty points that have been endorsed following the payment of fixed charges should be retained on licence records, including penalty points endorsed since 1 August 2014 following payment of a fixed charge.

Intoxicated driving Part 4 of the 2014 Act (ss.11 to 13) deals with intoxicated driving. Section 11 amended the provisions of the Road Traffic Act 2010 (the "2010 Act") on "preliminary impairment testing" which refers to a range of non-technological cognitive tests such as walking in a straight line or clutching one's nose. The 2010 Act allowed for tests of this kind to be conducted to assist a member of the Gardaí in forming an opinion as to whether a person was intoxicated. It was stated during the Oireachtas debates on the 2014 Act that the evidence for the credibility and robustness of tests of this kind had changed rapidly since 2010 and because they were regarded as outdated they were never commenced. International experience shows that impairment testing of this type can be conducted and recorded to rigorous standards which meet the test of standing up in court as evidence. Section 11 therefore provides for the repeal and replacement of the provisions in the 2010 Act with "intoxication impairment testing", the two key changes being that these tests will be conducted and recorded according to rigorous standards and that the results may be presented as evidence in court. Under the 2014 Act, intoxication impairment tests will assist the Garda concerned in forming the opinion that a driver may be under the influence of an intoxicant. A driver who fails an impairment test may then be arrested, brought to a Garda station where a blood or urine example will be taken for analysis by the Medical Bureau of Road Safety (MBRS). If the case subsequently proceeds to court the impairment test will be used as part of the evidence presented.

Section 12 of the 2014 Act provides for the first time that a specimen of blood may be taken from an incapacitated driver following a road traffic collision subject to medical consent. A specimen of blood may be taken from an incapacitated driver but only in a hospital and only subject to medical consent. Where a specimen is taken, it will be split in two and both parts will be forwarded to the MBRS. The procedure for conscious drivers is that the specimen is split into two parts and one is offered to the driver in order that he or she may have it tested. It was noted during the Oireachtas debates on the 2014 Act that "it is common for drivers to refuse this option, in which case both parts are sent to the MBRS." The MBRS will conduct the necessary analysis of a specimen from an incapacitated driver in exactly the same way as specimens are treated for conscious drivers. This involves tests to determine the presence and concentration of alcohol or the presence of a drug or drugs in the specimen. However, the result will be retained on file by MBRS until the driver regains capacity. If and when the driver regains capacity, he or she will be asked to consent to the release of the result of the test analysis. Refusal to do so will constitute an offence equivalent to that of a driver with capacity refusing to provide a specimen in the first instance. If the driver gives permission for the release of the result, the MBRS will issue a completed certificate of analysis and offer the second part of the sample to the driver. The taking of a specimen from an incapacitated driver could be a basis for future prosecution of the driver if he or she is found to be intoxicated. Equally, it could provide exonerating evidence if he or she were proved not to be intoxicated.

"Clocking" cars an offence Part 5 of the 2014 Act (ss.14 to 26) deals with a wide range of miscellaneous matters. This includes providing, in s.14 of the 2014 Act, a new offence of tampering with a vehicle's odometer, commonly known as "clocking." Prior to the 2014 Act while this kind of activity was covered by the general prohibition on misleading commercial practices in the Consumer Protection Act 2007, which means that it would be an offence for a dealer to sell a vehicle that had been clocked, the act of clocking itself had not been an offence. Section 14 of the 2014 Act provides:

> (1) A person shall not interfere or attempt to interfere with the odometer of a mechanically propelled vehicle.
>
> (2) A person who contravenes, or who procures another person to contravene, subsection (1) commits an offence and is liable on summary conviction to a class C fine or to imprisonment for a term not exceeding 3 months, or to both.
>
> (3) Where a member of the Garda Síochána has reasonable grounds for believing that a person is committing or has committed an offence under this section he or she may arrest the person without warrant.
>
> (4) Where a person is charged with an offence under this section it shall be a defence to show that at the time of the alleged offence the person was acting in good faith in order to test, repair or replace the odometer of the mechanically propelled vehicle.
>
> (5) In this section "odometer", in relation to a mechanically propelled vehicle, means the device that measures and records the distance travelled by the vehicle but does not include an auxiliary device capable of being reset to measure and record individual journeys.

It was noted during the Oireachtas debates on the 2014 Act that this provision had originated in a Private Member's Bill sponsored by Anthony Lawlor TD.

Statutory definition of MIBI Agreement Section 16 of the 2014 Act, which inserted a new s.78B into the Road Traffic Act 1961 (the "1961 Act"), provided for the first time a statutory basis for the MIBI Agreement, the agreement between the Department of Transport and the Motor Insurance Bureau of Ireland on recovering moneys from uninsured drivers. Section 78B of the 1961 Act, as inserted by the 2014 Act, provides that the "MIBI Agreement" means the Agreement on the Compensation of Uninsured Road Accident Victims dated 29 January 2009 between the Minister for Transport and the Motor Insurers' Bureau of Ireland and includes any subsequent agreement which amends or replaces that Agreement.

Duty to assist injured person after traffic collision Section 17 of the 2014 Act made significant amendments to s.106 of the Road Traffic Act 1961 (the "1961 Act") in order to impose positive duties of assistance to an injured person where a person is involved in a traffic collision, non-compliance with which involves in some instances the commission of an indictable offence. During the Oireachtas debates on the 2014 Act it was noted that, like s.14, above, s.17 of the 2014 Act had originated in a Private Member's Bill, in this instance sponsored by Timmy Dooley TD. Section 106 of the 1961 Act, as originally enacted, was confined to providing that where a person is involved in a traffic collision that causes an injury, the driver must stop the vehicle, leave the vehicle at or near the place of the collision, and provide, on request by a member of An Garda Síochána, information related to the collision.

As amended by the 2014 Act, s.106 (which retains the rather innocuous marginal note "Duties on occurrence of accident") adds an important positive duty on a person to provide assistance to an injured person. Section 106, as amended by the 2014 Act, provides that failure to comply with this duty, where it involves "intent to escape civil or criminal liability," is a criminal offence which in some instances is an indictable offence carrying, on conviction, a maximum term of seven years' imprisonment. This rather fundamental reform of s.106 was expressly stated during the Oireachtas debates on the 2014 Act to be intended to deal with those who leave the scene of such a collision, that is, to deal with so-called "hit-and-run incidents." In order to understand the effects of the 2014 Act on s.106, it is useful to set out the text of s.106(1) to (3B), as amended by s.17 of the 2014 Act. The text below is from the Revised Act version of the 1961 Act, one of over 230 Revised Acts (administrative consolidations, the text of Acts as amended) available on the website of the Law Reform Commission, lawreform.ie (the text in square brackets and italics is the text inserted into s.106 by the 2014 Act):

> (1) Where injury is caused to person or property in a public place and a vehicle is involved in the occurrence of the injury (whether the use of the vehicle was or was not the cause of the injury), the following provisions shall have effect:
>
> (a) if the vehicle is not stationary after the occurrence, the driver of the vehicle shall stop the vehicle;
>
> *[(aa) if injury has been caused to any person, or any person appears*

to require assistance, the driver of the vehicle shall offer assistance;]

(b) the driver or other person in charge of the vehicle shall keep the vehicle at or near the place of the occurrence for a period which is reasonable in all the circumstances of the case and having regard to the provisions of this section;

(c) the driver of the vehicle or, if he is killed or incapacitated, the person then in charge of the vehicle shall give on demand the appropriate information to a member of the Garda Síochána or, if no such member is present, to one person entitled under this section to demand such information;

[(d) if—

(i) injury is caused to property other than that of the driver of the vehicle and for any reason he or, if he is killed or incapacitated, the person then in charge of the vehicle does not at the place of the occurrence give the appropriate information to a person entitled under this section to demand it, or

(ii) injury is caused to a person other than the driver of the vehicle,

the driver of the vehicle or, if he is killed or incapacitated, the person then in charge of the vehicle shall, unless he had already given the appropriate information to a member of the Garda Síochána, report the occurrence as soon as possible to such a member and, if necessary, shall go for that purpose to the nearest convenient Garda station and also give on demand the appropriate information to the member.]

(2) Where—

(a) a member of the Garda Síochána has reasonable grounds for believing that an injury has been caused to person or property in a public place and that a vehicle was involved in the occurrence of the injury (whether the use of the vehicle was or was not the cause of the injury), and

(b) the member is not aware of the place where the vehicle is being kept,

the member may require the owner of the vehicle to state to the member where the vehicle is being kept and the owner shall comply with that requirement.

(3) A person who contravenes subsection (1) or subsection (2) of this section shall be guilty of an offence and shall be liable on summary conviction—

(a) in a case in which injury is caused to person, to a fine not exceeding €2,000 or, at the discretion of the court, to imprisonment for any term not exceeding six months or to both such fine and such imprisonment, and

[(aa) in a case in which injury is caused to a person, and the person who contravenes subsection (1) or subsection (2) —

(i) does so with intent to escape civil or criminal liability, and

> (ii) *knows that injury has been caused to a person of such nature as to require medical assistance for the person at that place or that the person be brought to a hospital for medical assistance,*
>
> *on conviction on indictment to a fine not exceeding €10,000 or, at the discretion of the court, to imprisonment for any term not exceeding 7 years or to both such fine and such imprisonment,*
>
> *(ab) in a case where injury is caused to a person, and the person who contravenes subsection (1) or subsection (2) does so with intent to escape civil or criminal liability, and*
>
> (i) *knows that the person to whom injury has been caused is dead, or*
>
> (ii) *knows that injury has been caused to a person and is reckless as to whether the death of the person injured so results, and the death of the person injured so results,*
>
> *on conviction on indictment to a fine not exceeding €20,000 or, at the discretion of the court, to imprisonment for any term not exceeding 10 years or to both such fine and such imprisonment,]*
>
> (b) in any other case, to a fine not exceeding €1,000 or, at the discretion of the court, to imprisonment for any term not exceeding three months or to both such fine and such imprisonment.
>
> *[(3A) A member of the Garda Síochána may arrest without warrant a person who in the member's opinion is committing or has committed an offence under subsection (3) of this section where the contravention involves or, as may be appropriate, involved non-compliance with paragraph (a) or (b) of subsection (1) of this section, injury was caused to person, a mechanically propelled vehicle was involved in the occurrence of the injury and the first-mentioned person is, or as may be appropriate, was in the member's opinion the driver of the vehicle concerned.*
>
> *[(3B) In a prosecution under subsection (3)(aa) or (ab) evidence that an accused failed to stop his or her vehicle, offer assistance, keep the vehicle at or near the place for a reasonable period, or give the appropriate information is, in the absence of evidence to the contrary, proof of an intent to escape civil or criminal liability.]*

The effect of s.106 of the 1961 Act, as amended by the 2014 Act, is to impose a positive legal obligation on those involved in a traffic collision to provide assistance (which is not expressly defined) to an injured person at the scene. It is worth noting that when the Law Reform Commission examined this issue in its 2009 *Report on Civil Liability of Good Samaritans and Volunteers* (LRC 93–2009), it recommended that a *general* duty to assist should not be imposed by legislation and that any extension of the existing, limited, number of positive duties to assist or volunteer, was best left to the Oireachtas to determine on a case-by-case basis. The expansion of s.106 of the 1961 Act made by the 2014 Act can be seen as an example of this approach. The recommendations in the 2009 Report to enact specific legislation on the (limited) civil liability of Good Samaritans and volunteers, that is of those who choose to assist, was implemented in the Civil Law (Miscellaneous Provisions)

Act 2011, which inserted a new Pt IVA into the Civil Liability Act 1961 to effect this (see *Annual Review of Irish Law 2011,* pp.70–71 and 604–505).

Whistleblower Protection

ESTELLE FELDMAN, Trinity College, Dublin

FIRST BE HARMED — PROTECTED DISCLOSURES ACT 2014

No protection, no incentive The publicity surrounding the Protected Disclosures Act 2014 (the "2014 Act") held out the false promise to potential whistleblowers that they will be protected from retaliation if they make a protected disclosure. In common language, protection infers a prevention of harm. However, to avail of the Protected Disclosures legislation a whistleblower will have to prove harm. The actual promise is that if there is retaliation against a whistleblower there may be recourse to redress providing that:

(i) the disclosure was made in strict accordance with the rules in the legislation, and
(ii) following retaliation, the whistleblower has the physical, mental and financial resources to go through the process of some form of employment tribunal and/or court where, if successful, they may be awarded a maximum of five years' salary.

The major whistleblowing story at the time of the passage of the 2014 Act related to two garda whistleblowers, Sergeant Maurice McCabe and Garda John Wilson. Both alleged retaliation and John Wilson alleged that he had been forced out of his employment. In the context of Garda Síochána remuneration, this level of redress may be assessed as follows based on figures on the Department of Justice website (accessed 26 February 2014). A Garda of 17 years' service earns €44,000 per annum, a Sergeant of 12 years' service €55,000, an Inspector of six years' service €57,000, a Superintendent at the top rate €82,000 and a Chief Superintendent at the top rate €101,000 (figures rounded). Consequently, a good faith Garda whistleblower who had suffered retaliation subsequent to making a protected disclosure, depending on rank, might obtain maximum financial redress of between approximately €220,000 and €505,000. Even where there is public acceptance that a whistleblower acted honestly and appropriately, career suicide, destroyed reputation, long-term unemployment, stress-related chronic ill-health and family breakdown are often the inevitable consequences of whistleblowing. The 2014 Act provides that after further conflict in an employment tribunal or court where a causal link between the employer, the retaliation and the harm will have to be proved, there will be a possibility of financial redress. In this context, it is obvious that the possible harm suffered far outweighs €505,000, let alone €220,000.

Thus, the 2014 Act provides neither true protection nor true incentive.

What follows is a broadly based analysis of the 2014 Act rather than a detailed examination.

Making a disclosure The Protected Disclosures Act 2014, which is restricted in application to a "worker", is based on the tiered-model established by the UK Public Interest Disclosure 1998 (PIDA), see *Annual Review of Irish Law 2007*, pp.593–594. Robert G. Vaughn, in his internationally acclaimed *tour de force*, *The Successes and Failure of Whistleblower Laws* (Cheltenham: Edward Elgar, 2012), follows Lewis in describing this as a three-tiered model:

> "The first-tier protections apply to disclosures within the organization for which a whistleblower works. The most lenient standard for protection applies to this first tier. For example, employees need only show that they reasonably believe in good faith that one of the types of misconduct covered by the law has occurred or is threatened. The second tier of protections are applied to disclosures to governmental organizations and law enforcement and regulatory bodies that oversee the institutions contained within the first tier. For example, employees must reasonably believe that the allegations are substantially true. A more strenuous standard applies to these disclosures. All other disclosures, including disclosures to the media, fall within the third tier. These disclosures must satisfy the most demanding standard. For example, employees must meet the standards for tier two disclosures and their disclosures must not be made for personal gain, must be reasonable under the circumstances. In addition, employees must satisfy one of three conditions: (1) reasonable fear of reprisal if disclosure is made internally or to recipients falling under tier two; (2) reasonable belief of the concealment or destruction of evidence relating to the misconduct; or (3) previous disclosure of the misconduct was made to employers or another prescribed recipient and no response has been received or action taken." (p.248)

The Protected Disclosures Act does not require that a disclosure is made "in good faith" but, essentially, the balance of this narrative description applies. The term "reasonable" or "reasonably" is used throughout. There is no indication whether this should be interpreted by a subjective or by an objective test, e.g. is the consideration of whether or not one has a "reasonable belief" to be decided taking account of all the person-specific circumstances or is it to be decided taking account of what a reasonable person might be expected to believe? If the latter, how does it deal with the paranoia often experienced by whistleblowers who believe they are being penalised?

The legislative requirements for a disclosure to be protected are contained in Pt 2 of the 2014 Act. The difficulties facing a putative whistleblower who, untrained in understanding the complexities of Irish legislative drafting, wishes to comply with the law are evidenced by the following:

> **Protected disclosures**
> 5. (1) For the purposes of this Act 'protected disclosure' means, subject to *subsection (6)* and *sections 17 and 18*, a disclosure of relevant information

> (whether before or after the date of the passing of this Act) made by a worker in the manner specified in *section 6, 7, 8, 9 or 10.*

Section 5 includes eight sub-sections of which subss.2 and 3 include two and eight further subsections, respectively. Under s.5(4), "it is immaterial whether a relevant wrongdoing occurred, occurs or would occur in the State or elsewhere and whether the law applying to it is that of the State or that of any other country or territory." This section is so loosely worded that it is unclear whether it is confined to the Irish public service and Irish employers. If not, is the intention that Irish workers are to become the world's conscience and policeman for all wrongdoing everywhere?

Section 5(7) states: "The motivation for making a disclosure is irrelevant to whether or not it is a protected disclosure."

Section 6 refers to a disclosure to an employer or another responsible person:

> (1) A disclosure is made in the manner specified in this section if the worker makes it—
>
> (a) to the worker's employer, or
>
> (b) where the worker reasonably believes that the relevant wrongdoing which the disclosure tends to show relates solely or mainly—
>
> (i) to the conduct of a person other than the worker's employer, or
>
> (ii) to something for which a person other than the worker's employer has legal responsibility, to that other person.
>
> (2) A worker who, in accordance with a procedure the use of which by the worker is authorised by the worker's employer, makes a disclosure to a person other than the employer is to be treated for the purposes of this Act as making the disclosure to the employer.

Section 7(1) on disclosures made to a prescribed person states:

> 7. (1) A disclosure is made in the manner specified in this section if the worker—
>
> (a) makes the disclosure to a person prescribed under subsection (2) (a), and
>
> (b) reasonably believes—
>
> (i) that the relevant wrongdoing falls within the description of matters in respect of which the person is prescribed under subsection (2)(b), and
>
> (ii) that the information disclosed, and any allegation contained in it, are substantially true.

Subsections 2 and 3 describe the manner in which the Minister may prescribe such persons. This has been fulfilled to date by the Protected Disclosures Act 2014 (Section 7(2)) Order 2014 (S.I. No. 339 of 2014). There are a total of 72 prescribed persons by function included in this S.I., for each of whom there is a description of the "relevant wrongdoings" "falling within the description of matters specified" for which they are the prescribed recipient of disclosures. Thus, if someone wished, for instance, to make a protected disclosure in relation to the multibillion euro greyhound racing industry, the prescribed person is the Chief Executive of Bórd na gCon and the matters that may be disclosed are:

> All matters relating to the management and development by Bórd na gCon of the greyhound industry as provided for by the Greyhound Industry Act 1958 (No. 12 of 1958), the Greyhound Industry (Amendment) Act 1993 (No. 37 of 1993), the Horse and Greyhound Racing (Betting Charges and Levies) Act 1999 (No. 24 of 1999) and the Horse and Greyhound Racing Act 2001 (No. 20 of 2001).

On the other hand, if the disclosure is in relation to greyhound coursing, the prescribed person is the Chief Executive of the Irish Coursing Club for all "matters relating to the regulation by the Irish Coursing Club of coursing in the State under the Greyhound Industry Act 1958 (No. 12 of 1958)". Similarly, if someone wished to make a protected disclosure in relation to the far larger multibillion euro horse industry, they should only disclose to the Chief Executive of Horse Racing Ireland for all "matters relating to the control of the operation by Horse Racing Ireland of authorised bookmakers, the totalisator and the Registry Office." The Chief Executive of the Irish Turf Club has been prescribed for all "matters relating to the administration by the Irish Turf Club of the rules of racing for all horse meetings in the State".

Section 8 covers disclosures to a Minister:

> 8. A disclosure is made in the manner specified in this section if—
> (a) the worker is or was employed in a public body, and
> (b) the disclosure is made to a Minister of the Government on whom any function relating to the public body is conferred or imposed by or under any enactment.

This section appears to be simple enough to understand but some public bodies are only public for certain functions and not for others.

Section 9 on disclosures to a legal adviser appears straightforward on first read:

> 9. A disclosure is made in the manner specified in this section if it is made by the worker in the course of obtaining legal advice (including advice relating to the operation of this Act) from a barrister, solicitor, trade union official or official of an excepted body (within the meaning of section 6 of the Trade Union Act 1941).

This raises the question as to when trade union officials became qualified to proffer legal advice. Section 6 of the Trade Union Act 1941 which refers to registering bodies for the negotiation of wages and other conditions of employment is silent on the matter.

Section 10 which deals with disclosures in other cases compounds confusion:

> 10. (1) A disclosure is made in the manner specified in this section if it is made otherwise than in the manner specified in *sections 6 to 9* and—

(a) the worker reasonably believes that the information disclosed, and any allegation contained in it, are substantially true,
(b) the disclosure is not made for personal gain,
(c) any one or more of the conditions in *subsection (2)* is met, and
(d) in all the circumstances of the case, it is reasonable for the worker to make the disclosure.

(2) The conditions referred to in *subsection (1)(c)* are—
(a) that, at the time the worker makes the disclosure, the worker reasonably believes that the worker will be subjected to penalisation by the worker's employer if the worker makes a disclosure in the manner specified in *section 6, 7* or *8*,
(b) that, in a case where no relevant person is prescribed for the purposes of *section 7* in relation to the relevant wrongdoing, the worker reasonably believes that it is likely that evidence relating to the relevant wrongdoing will be concealed or destroyed if the worker makes a disclosure in the manner specified in *section 6*,
(c) that the worker has previously made a disclosure of substantially the same information—
(i) in the manner specified in *section 6,* or
(ii) in the manner specified in *section 7 or 8,*
and
(d) that the relevant wrongdoing is of an exceptionally serious nature.

(3) In determining for the purposes of *subsection (1)(d)* whether it is reasonable for the worker to make the disclosure regard shall be had, in particular, to—
(a) the identity of the person to whom the disclosure is made,
(b) in a case falling within *subsection (2)(a), (b)* or *(c)*, the seriousness of the relevant wrongdoing,
(c) in a case falling within *subsection (2)(a), (b)* or *(c)*, whether the relevant wrongdoing is continuing or is likely to occur in the future,
(d) in a case falling within *subsection (2)(c)*, any action which the employer of the worker or the person to whom the previous disclosure was made has taken or might reasonably be expected to have taken as a result of the previous disclosure,
and
(e) in a case falling within *subsection (2)(c)(i)*, whether in making the disclosure to the employer the worker complied with any procedure the use of which by the worker was authorised by the employer.

(4) For the purposes of this section a subsequent disclosure may be regarded as a disclosure of substantially the same information as that disclosed by a previous disclosure as mentioned in *subsection (2)(c)* even though the subsequent disclosure extends to information about action taken or not taken by any person as a result of the previous disclosure.

(5) In *subsection (1)(b)* "personal gain" excludes any reward payable under or by virtue of any enactment.

Protections None of these provisions will matter in cases where the employer operates sound reporting systems based on best practice in management and administration. In such cases, the likelihood of penalisation is not at issue. Where penalisation is an issue, the likelihood of a person having referred to these provisions and understood their implications in advance of having made a disclosure, protected or otherwise, is negligible. Part 3 of the 2014 Act refers to Protections. If Pt 3 needs to be invoked, the gross inadequacy of the legislation becomes even more apparent as the person making disclosures will have had to have suffered dismissal or some other form of harm in order to avail of the benefits of the Act.

Contradictions As noted above, s.5(7) deems motivation to be irrelevant in relation to making a protected disclosure; yet, in relation to amendments to the Unfair Dismissals Act 1977, s.11(1)(e) inserts the following in s.7 of the Unfair Dismissals Act:

> (2B) Where—
> (a) the dismissal of an employee results wholly or mainly from the employee having made a protected disclosure, and
> (b) *the investigation of the relevant wrongdoing concerned was not the sole or main motivation for making the disclosure*, the amount of compensation that is just and equitable may be up to 25 per cent less than the amount that it would otherwise be. (emphasis added)

Novel tort A much-heralded, novel provision is contained in s.13 which creates a new legal tort:

> **Tort action for suffering detriment because of making protected disclosure**
> (1) If a person causes detriment to another person because the other person or a third person made a protected disclosure, the person to whom the detriment is caused has a right of action in tort against the person by whom the detriment is caused.
> (2) A person may not both—
> (a) pursue a right of action under subsection (1) against a person in respect of a matter, and
> (b) in respect of the same matter make or present against the same person—
> (i) a claim for redress under the Unfair Dismissals Acts 1977 to 2007,
> (ii) a complaint under Schedule 2, or
> (iii) a complaint under section 114 of the Defence Act 1954 or section 6 of the Ombudsman (Defence Forces) Act 2004.
> (3) In subsection (1) "detriment" includes—
> (a) coercion, intimidation or harassment,
> (b) discrimination, disadvantage or adverse treatment in relation to employment (or prospective employment),
> (c) injury, damage or loss, and
> (d) threat of reprisal.

The Explanatory Memorandum states that s.13 "provides that where a third party causes a detriment to a worker who has made a protected disclosure the worker who has suffered the detriment has a right of action in tort against the person who causes the detriment." Due to the way in which the section is worded, it appears to provide a right of action to any person ("A") to whom detriment has been caused by another person ("B") because someone else ("C") has made a protected disclosure. There is no requirement that A and C need to be directly connected. A, therefore, could be a member of the affected family of the harmed whistleblower C, or a friend or a colleague or, indeed, a bystander without any direct link to the events. Whilst the definition in s.(3)(b) of detriment specifies employment, the other subsections are broad and open. Examples of detriment to family could be a child of a whistleblower who alleges poor exam results as a result of the impact of distress at home. A non-connected person could be say a sub-contractor or a customer who acted in reliance on some commitment by a whistleblower who, because of detriment, is no longer able to fulfil that commitment. In such cases, it would be difficult to identify a perpetrator. In addition, the courts will require proof of a causal link between the protected disclosure, the alleged detriment and harm caused. This is, potentially, a floodgates issue, and if pursued is likely to involve the superior courts and consequential costs.

Court costs—wronged employer Another acclaimed provision is in Sch.1, "Interim Relief Pending Determination of Claim for Unfair Dismissal", whereby an application may be made to the Circuit Court for such relief. This further highlights the critical question as to who will pay costs in the event of court action. If it is the general rule of costs following the result, how will an allegedly penalised worker who fails in their action pay their own costs, let alone reimburse a wronged employer? In the case of interim relief, if the allegedly penalised worker wins at the Circuit Court stage but fails in a subsequent appeal the problem is exacerbated. How will a wronged employer recover?

Moreover, as has been indicated many times by the Ombudsman, central government departments and some public bodies are indifferent to the costs incurred by invoking legal procedures and taking legal advice. This places a wronged whistleblower in a very parlous position.

No contracting-out of protections It is unfortunate that one of the most significant provisions in the 2014 Act is not given more prominence but, rather, is included under Pt 5, "Miscellaneous and Supplementary".

> 23. Any provision in an agreement is void in so far as it purports—
> (a) to prohibit or restrict the making of protected disclosures,
> (b) to exclude or limit the operation of any provision of this Act,
> (c) to preclude a person from bringing any proceedings under or by virtue of this Act,
> or
> (d) to preclude a person from bringing proceedings for breach of contract in respect of anything done in consequence of the making of a protected disclosure.

Provision for review Afforded far greater prominence but of little real benefit to either employer or worker is s.2:

> The Minister shall—
> (a) not later than the end of the period of 3 years beginning on the day on which this Act is passed, commence a review of the operation of this Act, and
> (b) not more than 12 months after the end of that period, make a report to each House of the Oireachtas of the findings made on the review and of the conclusions drawn from the findings.

Thus, it might not be until three years after the coming into force of the Act that any review is publicly available. The reasons for this delay are unclear, particularly in light of s.22:

> 22. (1) Every public body shall prepare and publish not later than 30 June in each year a report in relation to the immediately preceding year in a form which does not enable the identification of the persons involved containing information relating to the matters specified in subsection (2).
> (2) Those matters are—
> (a) the number of protected disclosures made to the public body,
> (b) the action (if any) taken in response to those protected disclosures, and
> (c) such other information relating to those protected disclosures and the action taken as may be requested by the Minister from time to time.

In addition, under Sch.3, s.6, the Disclosures Recipient is required to report annually to the Taoiseach starting in year one. The Disclosures Recipient, who is to be a retired High Court judge, is a praiseworthy innovation as the function of this person is to receive protected disclosures which might otherwise be excluded under s.18, "Security, defence, international relations and intelligence".

Section 5 of Sch.3 describes the functions of the Disclosures Recipient as follows.

> 5. Where a protected disclosure is made to the Disclosures Recipient under section 18, the Disclosures Recipient shall consider the relevant information and—
> (a) if he or she considers that the disclosure of relevant information is not one to which section 18 applies, shall give notice to the person by whom the disclosure was made stating that, and
> (b) otherwise, shall make a report—
> (i) referring the relevant information for consideration by the holder of such public office, or such public body, as appears to the Disclosures Recipient to be the most appropriate to consider the relevant information, and
> (ii) including any such recommendations for the taking of action in

> relation to the relevant information as the Disclosures Recipient may consider appropriate.

Consequential amendments Schedule 4 contains amendments of 17 acts and one statutory instrument. It is a blunderbuss instead of a targeted approach which ought to have taken account of the purposes of each act and the one statutory instrument to be amended. There is no differentiation evident in these amendments between the implications of "knowingly false", "reasonable belief" and "motivation".

In *Annual Review of Irish Law 2010*, pp.651–659, we noted the simplicity and clarity with which the Communications Regulation Act 2002, as amended, dealt with disclosures. In fact, we praised the provisions as a model to be followed.

> Protection of whistleblowers.
> 24A.— (1) A person who makes an appropriate disclosure of information to the Commission about the conduct of an undertaking, an associate of an undertaking or an association of undertakings incurs no civil or criminal liability for having done so.
>
> (2) For the purpose of subsection (1), a person makes an appropriate disclosure of information about the conduct of an undertaking, or an associate of an undertaking or an association of undertakings only if—
>
> (a) the conduct relates to the provision of an electronic communications network or service or an associated facility, and
>
> (b) the person—
>
> (i) believes on reasonable grounds that the information is true, or
>
> (ii) not being able to form a belief on reasonable grounds about the truth of the information, believes on reasonable grounds that the information may be true and to be of sufficient significance to justify its disclosure with a view to enabling its truth to be investigated by the Commission or by a law enforcement authority that has a legitimate interest in receiving the information (such as the Garda Síochána).

This eminently sensible provision is now amended by the insertion of:

> (2A) Subsection (1) does not apply where the disclosure is a protected disclosure within the meaning of the Protected Disclosures Act 2013.

Consequently, as a result of this amendment, a person who would otherwise have made an appropriate disclosure and be free of all civil and criminal liability may now be subject to civil liability under the Defamation Act 2009 s.14(1) Protected Disclosures Act 2014 and there is no protection from criminal liability as the Protected Disclosures Act is silent on that topic.

Child abuse However, by far the most perverse of the amendments is to the Protections for Persons Reporting Child Abuse Act 1998. This is a very specific Act which is sui generis. Its purpose was to protect children. It should never have been confused with protecting disclosures. It is not amenable to the generalities of broad sector measures, most particularly of a tiered kind as in the Protected Disclosures

Act 2014. A suspected report of child abuse must go straight to the authorities who are obligated to act immediately. Moreover, a false report of child abuse is clearly far more damaging than a false report in other areas. A false allegation of child abuse has horrendous consequences for anyone wrongly accused, unimaginably worse than false accusations of other wrongdoing.

Commencement date The Protected Disclosures Act 2014 came into effect on 15 July 2014 under the Protected Disclosures Act 2014 (Commencement) Order 2014 (S.I. No. 327 of 2014).

GARDA SÍOCHÁNA

In last year's Annual Review, *Annual Review of Irish Law 2013*, p.587, we noted that at the time of preparing that chapter in early 2014

> "the country was gripped by almost daily revelations regarding Garda whistleblowers and the manner in which they had been treated or mistreated in their attempts to have a fair hearing. As a consequence of the on-going controversy the Garda Confidential Recipient, Oliver Connolly, the Garda Chief Commissioner, Martin Callinan, and the Minister for Justice, Alan Shatter, all lost their positions. The Government announced several inquiries into different aspects of the unfolding revelations."

The revelations and controversy have continued into 2015.

One of the inquiries concluded in May 2014. The primary complaint of the whistleblowers as reported in the media had been in relation to a failure by An Garda Síochána to administer and implement properly the penalty points system in relation to traffic offences, see *Annual Review of Irish Law 2013*, pp.589–590. However, other allegations of failure to investigate criminal and other activities were of a far more serious nature. It was these that were the subject of the 337-page *Report to an Taoiseach, Enda Kenny TD on a Review of the action taken by An Garda Síochána pertaining to certain allegations made by Sergeant Maurice McCabe* conducted by Seán Guerin SC (*The Guerin Report*). Its terms of reference were:

> "1. To conduct an independent review and undertake a thorough examination of the action taken by An Garda Síochána pertaining to certain allegations of grave deficiencies in the investigation and prosecution of crimes, in the County of Cavan and elsewhere, made by Sergeant Maurice McCabe as specified in:
>
> a) the dossier compiled by Sgt Maurice McCabe and furnished to An Taoiseach on the 19th February 2014 and
> b) the letter understood to be from Sgt Maurice McCabe to the Confidential Recipient, Mr Oliver Connolly, dated 23rd January 2012, part of which was furnished to An Taoiseach on the 21st day of February 2014.
>
> 2. To interview Sgt Maurice McCabe and any other such person as may be considered necessary and capable of providing relevant and material assistance to this Review in relation to the aforesaid allegations and to

receive and consider any relevant documentation that may be provided by Sergeant McCabe or such other person.

3. To examine all documentation and data held by An Garda Síochána, the Department of Justice and Equality, and any other entity or public body as is deemed relevant to the allegations set out in the documents at 1 (a) and (b) above.

4. To communicate with An Garda Síochána and any other relevant entity or public body in relation to any relevant documentation and information and to examine what steps, if any, have been taken by them, to investigate and resolve the allegations and complaints contained in the documentation referenced at 1 (a) and (b) above.

5. To review the adequacy of any investigation or inquiry instigated by An Garda Síochána or any other relevant entity or public body into the incidents and events arising from the papers furnished at 1 (a), 1 (b) and 2 above.

6. To consider if, taking into account relevant criminal, civil and disciplinary aspects, there is a sufficient basis for concern as to whether all appropriate steps were taken by An Garda Síochána or any other relevant entity or public body to investigate and address the specified complaints.

7. To advise, arising from this review, what further measures, if any, are warranted in order to address public concerns including whether it is considered desirable in the public interest for the Government to establish a Commission of Investigation pursuant to the Commissions of Investigation Act 2004 and, if so, the matters to be investigated.

8. At the conclusion of the aforesaid review, within eight weeks of 27th February, 2014 or so soon as may be thereafter, to deliver a Report to An Taoiseach on the matters set out at 1, 5, 6, and 7 above."(*The Guerin Report*)

In respect of some of the allegations made by Sergeant McCabe, Mr Guerin found that his complaints had been sufficiently investigated by the Garda authorities. However, there was cause for concern in relation to a number of serious incidents in the Bailieboro District where Sergeant McCabe had served as Sergeant-in-charge for three-and-a-half years.

> "17.1 An analysis of the original Garda investigations in Bailieboro District reveals information which supports the allegation that there were significant deficiencies in the conduct of those investigations. Delay, for whatever reason, is a feature of many of the cases. It is a striking feature, and one common to almost all of these cases, that the original investigations were conducted by inexperienced probationary Gardaí. There is little, and in some cases no, evidence in the papers I have seen of appropriate supervisory and management guidance and, in almost all cases, no clear sense that investigations were being kept under review on an ongoing basis. Even in those cases where there was, at the outset, some guidance or direction given, that direction was not necessarily complied with and the failure to so comply appears either not to have been noticed or, for some reason, not to have led to any consequences internally.
>
> 17.2 That overall assessment of the conduct of those original Garda

> investigations is necessarily an important matter of public concern. Confidence in the effectiveness of the policing service is important not just to encourage a necessary sense of security amongst the public, but also to ensure that there is a measure of public confidence in the likelihood of detection, prosecution and conviction where offences have been committed. The deficiencies identified in the investigations considered in this review, if they were widely replicated, would be a challenge to public confidence in the criminal justice system itself.
>
> 17.3 It is beyond the scope of this review to determine what caused those apparent deficiencies to arise. It must be understood that the opinion that I have arrived at, that the complaints of Sergeant McCabe were not adequately investigated, is not a determination that the allegations he has made are true or that the explanations he identifies for the deficiencies apparent in the investigations are correct. In particular, I wish to emphasise that in expressing the opinion that there were deficiencies in the individual investigations reviewed herein, no finding of fault is made on the part of any individual officer and no criticism is made in that respect." (*The Guerin Report*)

There was some criticism of the manner in which Sergeant McCabe's complaints had been handled.

> "17.7 The conduct of the internal Garda investigation under the direction of Assistant Commissioner Byrne cannot pass without comment. The first and most obvious concern is that, although statements were taken from the individuals in respect of whom Sergeant McCabe had made complaints (and others of course), those statements and the other evidence assembled during the investigation do not appear to have been made available to Sergeant McCabe for comment before the conclusion of the investigation. That appears to be a breach of the policy document under which Sergeant McCabe's complaint was originally made. It appears, equally, to be a breach of the commitment made to him at the outset of the investigation that he would have an opportunity to comment on the evidence assembled.
>
> 17.8 The concern that arises from that approach is aggravated by the impression given by the report which emerged from the investigation that there was, if not an instinctive, at least a routine preference for the evidence of the senior officers in respect of whom complaints had been made. This approach was replicated at the highest level. The Commissioner, when accounting for the investigation to the Minister, described allegations as having been 'answered', in such a way as to suggest that the mere fact that an answer had been given was in some way a substitute for a careful assessment of the reliability of that answer having regard to all the available evidence. Ultimately, it appears that conclusions were arrived at as a result of the investigative process without there ever having been a thorough and searching testing of the evidence.
>
> 17.9 That approach, as previously stated, is reflected in the way in which the outcome of the investigation was communicated to the Minister. It is also reflected in the way in which the outcome of the investigation was

> communicated to other members of the force by the Divisional Officer." (*The Guerin Report*)

The Report then refers to the review conducted of the internal inquiry into Sergeant McCabe's allegations.

> "17.10 The Byrne-McGinn investigation was reviewed by Deputy Commissioner Rice following his appointment to deal with a number of aspects of Sergeant McCabe's complaints after the incident at the Hillgrove Hotel on 11 October 2010. He completed a number of reports reviewing different aspects of the investigation. The report of primary interest is that of 8 March 2011, which reviewed the investigation of most of the incidents considered for the purpose of this review. Deputy Commissioner Rice expressed the view that the Byrne-McGinn investigation was professional, impartial and was carried out with propriety. He was satisfied, in respect of the investigation of most of the specific incidents considered herein, that 'all matters were fully enquired into'. Given the various outstanding issues identified during my review, I cannot share the view that all matters were fully enquired into. Having regard to the apparent failure to give Sergeant McCabe an opportunity to comment on the evidence, and the manner in which the 'answers' of superior officers were accepted without either testing them too rigorously against other available evidence or giving Sergeant McCabe an opportunity to respond to them, I cannot share the generally approving conclusions of Deputy Commissioner Rice's review.
>
> 17.11 He expressed the view that 'some of the blame must rest with Sergeant McCabe' and that many of the issues should have been dealt with by a member of Sergeant rank but he could find no evidence that this occurred.
>
> 17.12 It is a matter of some concern that this conclusion was arrived at in circumstances where I have seen no evidence that it was ever put to Sergeant McCabe to allow him to respond to it. The suggestion was made to Sergeant McCabe at the Hillgrove Hotel on 10 October 2010 but, as previously outlined, it was presented to him at that stage as an outcome of the investigation, not as an allegation to which he had an opportunity to respond. Here again, in Deputy Commissioner Rice's review report, the same view was being presented as a finding, without a response from Sergeant McCabe." (*The Guerin Report*)

Paradigm of the whistleblower This lengthy report concluded with some comments on "the paradigm of the whistleblower" and are, consequently, quoted in full:

> "20.1 In any organization whose members face the significant daily challenges and pressures that must be borne by those whose duty it is to ensure the security of the State and the safety of its citizens, a critical voice is in danger of being heard as a contrary voice. The paradigm of the whistleblower is an unattractive one. The whistle-blower, like the referee from whom he gets his name, is seen as someone who is not on the team.

The challenge of accommodating and learning from legitimate criticism is always going to be a difficult one, especially in a disciplined force.

20.2 But discipline is not merely the absence of insubordination. Discipline is application to the task at hand. The complaints made by Sergeant McCabe all have their origin in what he perceived to be a failure of An Garda Síochána (Confidential Reporting of Corruption or Malpractice) Regulations 2007 in Bailieboro District to apply itself with discipline and determination to the investigation and prosecution of crime.

20.3 While it is beyond the scope of this review to make any determination of the complaints Sergeant McCabe has made, the documentation examined gives cause to share the concern expressed in them and, for the reasons outlined in this report, there is cause for concern as to the adequacy of the investigations that have taken place into those complaints and as to whether all appropriate steps have been taken.

20.4 I should also advert briefly at this point to an issue which has featured extensively in the documents I have examined, but which is beyond the scope of my terms of reference. That is the experience that Sergeant McCabe has had within An Garda Síochána (Confidential Reporting of Corruption or Malpractice) Regulations 2007 since making his complaints, I have seen extensive documentation, including the third volume of the three booklets furnished to the Minister for Justice and Equality by Sergeant McCabe's solicitors in September 2012, which gives cause for concern about the personal and professional consequences for Sergeant McCabe of his having made the complaints examined in this report and other similar complaints. It is not for me to express any view on those matters, except to say that Sergeant McCabe's experience calls for examination.

20.5 It should be recorded here that the Byrne-McGinn report found that:

> 'No malice on the part of Sergeant McCabe is established in the making of his various complaints.'

20.6 The time I have spent with Sergeant McCabe in the course of extensive interviews has led me to no different conclusion. That said, the better view, in any event, is likely to be the testimony of the men and women who worked with Sergeant McCabe in the years before he made the complaints that have been examined in this report."

Resignation of Minister for Justice Within days of the publication of this report in May 2014, the Minister for Justice, Alan Shatter TD, resigned his cabinet post. He subsequently instigated proceedings against Mr Guerin inter alia for failing to afford him constitutional justice and due process. The nub of *The Guerin Report*'s criticism of the Minister appears to be in para.19.60:

"19.59 The letter then concluded:

> 'The Garda Commissioner advises me that, having regard to the outcome of the investigation and review, he is of the view that no evidence was found of any wrongdoing (corruption or malpractice) on the part of the named Superintendent, or Assistant Commissioner Byrne. On the basis of these findings, there is no evidence to support

any further action by me in relation to the allegation made in the confidential report against the Garda Commissioner.'

19.60 This letter is, in effect, a communication of the decision of the Minister on the complaint transmitted to him by the Confidential Recipient. The files that I have received from the Department of Justice, insofar as they relate to the handling of that complaint, consist of the relevant correspondence outlined above. I have not seen any memorandum or submission to the Minister from his departmental staff, to assist him in the exercise of his function under Regulation 8(2) of the Garda Síochána (Confidential Reporting of Corruption or Malpractice) Regulations, 2007. Nor have I seen any internal departmental minute or memorandum of the Minister's decision. On 11 April 2014 I specifically sought internal departmental documents related to the exercise of this function (and other matters). None have been produced relating to this exercise of the Minister's specific function under the Regulations." (*The Guerin Report*)

Commission of Investigation In December 2014, as a consequence of the findings of *The Guerin Report*, a Commission of Investigation was established. O'Higgins J., now retired, has been appointed as sole member of the Commission. The Terms of Reference state:

1. The Commission is directed to investigate the following matters:
   (a) The investigation by An Garda Síochána of a public order incident and possible sexual assault on a bus at Kingscourt, Co Cavan on 25 February 2007;
   (b) The investigation by An Garda Síochána of an assault at the Lakeside Manor Hotel, Virginia, Co Cavan on 14 April 2007;
   (c) The investigation by An Garda Síochána of two incidents in 2007 involving Jerry McGrath, i.e. the assault on Mary Lynch near Virginia, Co Cavan on 30 April 2007 and the abduction of a child during the burglary of a house in Tipperary on 9 October 2007, and the management and coordination by An Garda Síochána of those investigations, in particular in relation to the question of bail;
   (d) The investigation by An Garda Síochána of a public order incident in Cafolla's restaurant, Bailieboro, Co Cavan on 5 August 2007;
   (e) The investigation by An Garda Síochána of an incident of assault and false imprisonment of a girl in Cootehill, Co Cavan on 2 September 2007;
   (f) The investigation by An Garda Síochána of a dangerous driving incident at the Lakeside Manor Hotel, Virigina, Co Cavan on 27 December 2007;
   (g) The investigation by An Garda Síochána of an assault in Crossan's public house in Bailieboro, Co Cavan on 23 May 2007;
   (h) The investigation by An Garda Síochána of sexual offences and child pornography offences in respect of which Michael Molloy was convicted in 2009, having particular regard to the loss of a computer seized during the course of that investigation;
   (i) The investigation by An Garda Síochána of the allegations made

by Sergeant Maurice McCabe of malpractice and corruption in relation to PULSE records seized from him on 11 October 2010 at the Hillgrove Hotel, Monaghan;

(j) The investigation by An Garda Síochána and the Minister for Justice and Equality and Department of Justice and Equality of complaints made by Sergeant Maurice McCabe in relation to matters at (a) to (i);

(k) The investigation by An Garda Síochána and the Garda Síochána Ombudsman Commission of Garda disciplinary issues arising out of the above matters;

(l) The general conduct of policing at Bailieboro Garda District in 2007/2008 with reference to the management and operational structure and resource allocation for Bailieboro Garda District, at the relevant times, including:

- The number of probationary Gardaí assigned to Bailieboro Garda District;
- The number and experience of Sergeants available to supervise and monitor on a daily basis the work of those probationary Gardaí;
- The significance, if any, of the absence of an Inspector permanently allocated to Baileboro Garda Station;
- The stability, continuity, and experience available at District Officer level in Bailieboro District;
- The arrangements in operation for the supervision and monitoring of probationary Gardaí in relation to their operational and, specifically, investigative duties, and
- The standard of accommodation at Bailieboro Garda station and its possible impact on the performance of the policing function.

2. The Commission should exercise discretion in relation to the scope and intensity of the investigation it considers necessary and appropriate having regard to the general objective of the investigation. Commission of Investigation (Certain Matters relative to the Cavan/Monaghan Division of the Garda Síochána) Order 2015 (S.I. No. 38 of 2015).

Confidential Recipient The fault lines that were revealed in this chapter of *Annual Review of Irish Law 2007* in the Garda Síochána (Confidential Reporting of Corruption or Malpractice) Regulations 2007 (S.I. No. 168 of 2007) were not difficult to identify. These Regulations have now been repealed and An Garda Síochána have become subject to the Protected Disclosures Act 2014, which as suggested above is itself unfit for purpose. A core feature of the Regulations was the creation of the position of Confidential Recipient. Sergeant McCabe had made complaints to both incumbents in this position, a position with no investigative role and of such sterility that Mr Guerin "saw no need to make any independent request for documentation to the Office of the Confidential Recipient" (*The Guerin Report,* para.1.11).

During the early days of the Garda whistleblowing controversy, a transcript of a taped conversation between Sergeant McCabe and the second incumbent as Confidential Recipient, Mr Oliver Connolly, appeared in the media. Sergeant McCabe had taped the conversation without Mr Connolly's knowledge. This was raised by the Leader of the Opposition, Mr Micheal Martin, at Leader's Questions in Dáil Éireann:

> "Last week I read elements of the transcript of a conversation between the Garda confidential recipient, Mr. Oliver Connolly, and a Garda whistleblower, Mr. Maurice McCabe, such as how, if the Minister for Justice and Equality, Deputy Alan Shatter, felt the whistleblower was going to screw him, he would be finished. In addition, it was said that if complaints were exposed to the print media, it would make him an angry man and so on. The elements of the conversation were quite shocking in terms of their import. The confidential recipient also spoke about his close proximity to 'Alan' and how he communicated with him on the allegations the whistleblower had put before him. I have since listened to the audiotape of that conversation and can confirm its existence. Every single syllable I articulated last week is on it and, obviously, more. It reveals the frustration of the whistleblower and also the desire of the confidential recipient that at all costs this must not get into the print media, that it must be kept out of the media." Dáil Éireann Debate Unrevised, 19 February 2014, p.18, House of the Oireachtas website.

In his response the Taoiseach, Enda Kenny, advised the House that the Confidential Recipient had been relieved of his post that morning.

Subsequently, Mr Connolly issued a public statement during the course of which he stated:

> "3. *The End Does Not Justify 'Any' Means to Accomplish It*
> I believe that I reached an understanding of many of the concerns of the principal whistleblower and I also believe that I possess some understanding of the principal whistleblower's frustrations. However, for the principal whistleblower to come to what was a statutorily confidential meeting for both parties and proceed to allegedly record our meeting without my notice and then actively seek to publish, in and/or outside Dáil Éireann, an alleged transcription of that recording of our discussion I consider as a very serious breach of confidence.
>
> There is also a personal sense of betrayal in that the principal whistleblower felt it necessary to vindicate his rights by infringing my rights and, by extension, the privacy of my family.
>
> The ends do not always justify any means. One must not become so focused on a goal that it is pursued at all costs. We might accomplish our goal, but in doing so cause unnecessary and regrettable damage to the constitutional rights of others and to the rule of law itself; ironically, the very thing the principal whistleblower seeks to uphold." *Statement of Oliver J Connolly in Respect of Recent Events Concerning the Office of An Garda Síochána Confidential Recipient*, 4 March 2014

Secretive Confidential Reporting Charter In previous *Annual Reviews* we referred to our inability to access the Garda Whistleblower Charter, a Charter that ought to have been a public document. In *Annual Review of Irish Law 2009*, p.770, we reproduced an email from the Garda Press Office in response to our request for sight of the Charter which stated that the "charter has been established but not placed in the public domain." In *Annual Review of Irish Law 2010*, p.660, we commented with the following question: "Does this mean that there is a document which nobody who is not a member of the Garda Síochána may see?" We noted the secrecy yet again in *Annual Review of Irish Law 2011*, p.621, reporting that in a written response to a parliamentary question, on 3 May 2011, the then Minister for Justice, Mr Alan Shatter, advised that the Garda Commissioner has issued a Confidential Reporting Charter to all sworn members and civilian staff of An Garda Síochána. In early 2014, as the failure to act appropriately in relation to Garda whistleblowers was consuming the nation, we attempted to access this document via the good offices of a member of the Oireachtas. Their efforts were eventually rewarded with a letter dated 18 March 2015, almost a year after the initial request by a public representative, advising that the Protected Disclosures Act 2014 had repealed the relevant section in the primary Act, s.124 of the Garda Síochána Act 2005, and had revoked the Garda Síochána (Confidential Reporting of Corruption or Malpractice) Regulations 2007. The letter continued: "Guidelines for the implementation of the Protected Disclosures Act, 2014 by the Public Service are currently being prepared which will be circulated shortly."

The earlier analyses may be found in the chapter on Whistleblower Protection in *Annual Review of Irish Law 2007* to date.

INTERNATIONAL WHISTLEBLOWER DISCLOSURES

Asylum seeker A search of the Courts' Service Judgments database for 2014 has indicated two cases where the term "whistleblower" featured. In the first, *BH v Refugee Appeals Tribunal* [2014] IEHC 163, Barr J. quashed and remitted back a decision of the Refugee Appeals Tribunal inter alia because the Ethiopian asylum seeker had claimed to be a whistleblower.

> "The Tribunal should have considered what fate the applicant would likely meet if repatriated as a deserter from the army, and as a whistleblower in relation to the land allocation and as a failed asylum seeker. It seems to me that these were questions which should have been addressed by the Tribunal before reaching its final decision." (para. 23)

Edward Snowden The second case, *Schrems v Data Protection Commissioner* [2014] IEHC 310, arose as a consequence of the revelations made by the whistleblower, Edward Snowden. This was a judicial review which upheld the decision of the Data Protection Commissioner that the applicant had no sustainable claim in law. However, Hogan J. referred matters at issue to the European Court of Justice pursuant to art.267 TFEU. The applicant had maintained that, as the Snowden disclosures demonstrated that there was no effective data protection regime in the United States, the Data Protection Commissioner ("the Commissioner") should exercise his statutory powers to direct that the transfer of personal data from Facebook Ireland to its parent company in the United States should cease. The substantive issues are considered in the Constitutional Law chapter of this Annual

Review. However, comments of Hogan J. on the implications of Edward Snowden's actions bear repeating in this chapter.

> "4. While it is true that the Snowden disclosures caused—and are still causing—a sensation, only the naïve or the credulous could really have been greatly surprised. The question of transnational data protection and state surveillance is admittedly difficult and sensitive and, subject to fundamental legal protections, a satisfactory via media can in many respects be resolved only at the level of international diplomacy and realpolitik. While a court must naturally be aware of these underlying realities, in resolving issues such as arise in the present case it must nonetheless endeavour to apply neutrally the applicable legal materials.
>
> 5. Yet only the foolish would deny that the United States has, by virtue of its superpower status, either assumed—or, if you prefer, has had cast upon it—far-reaching global security responsibilities. It is probably only world power with a global reach which can effectively monitor the activities of rogue states, advanced terrorist groups and major organised crime, even if the support of allied states such as the United Kingdom is also of great assistance in the discharge of these tasks and responsibilities. The monitoring of global communications—subject, of course, to key safeguards—is accordingly regarded essential if the US is to discharge the mandate which it has thus assumed. These surveillance programmes have undoubtedly saved many lives and have helped to ensure a high level of security, both throughout the Western world and elsewhere. But there may also be a suspicion in some quarters that this type of surveillance has had collateral objects and effects, including the preservation and re-inforcing of American global political and economic power.
>
> 6. One may likewise fairly assume that the Snowden revelations have compromised these important national security programmes. This will certainly hamper entirely legitimate counter-terrorism operations and, by reason of the possibly inadvertent disclosure of personal information, perhaps even the lives of security operatives working overseas have been put at risk: see *Miranda v. Home Secretary* [2014] EWHC Admin 255 where these adverse effects of the Snowden revelations were summarised by Laws L.J. for the English High Court in these terms by reference to evidence tendered in that case by security specialists and operatives.
>
> 7. It would, however, be equally naïve to believe that this sort of surveillance is the preserve of the superpowers. One may fairly assume that even those states—both big and small—who protested loudly in the wake of the Snowden revelations concerning the invasion of the data protection of their citizens would not themselves be above resorting to such irregular espionage (i.e., surveillance and interception of communications which are not provided for by law) where it suited their interests. This might be especially so where these governments could conveniently turn a blind eye to such surveillance and interception activities on the part of their security forces, or, better still, where they could credibly deny that such espionage had ever been officially 'sanctioned.'
>
> 8. On the other hand, the Snowden revelations demonstrate a massive

> overreach on the part of the security authorities, with an almost studied indifference to the privacy interests of ordinary citizens. Their data protection rights have been seriously compromised by mass and largely unsupervised surveillance programmes."

REPUTATIONAL DAMAGE A CONSTITUTIONAL TORT

Two years ago, in the *Annual Review of Irish Law 2012* pp.598–599, reference was made to Hogan J.'s judgment in *Wallace v Irish Aviation Authority* [2012] IEHC 178. Whilst this case was not about a whistleblower we commented as follows:

> "However, it further highlights our concerns noted above that Employment Law is not the appropriate rubric of law in which to found whistleblower protection legislation. The comments of the High Court highlight the relative ease by which damage can be inflicted through employment procedures and the fact that there may be no adequate remedy."

It appears, from a number of cases in 2014, that Hogan J., prior to his elevation to the Court of Appeal, has been laying the ground for a constitutional tort for what might broadly be called psychic injury and, in specific cases, reputational damage. This is based on the "solemn guarantee" contained in Art.40.3.2. which states:

> The State shall, in particular, by its laws protect as best it may from unjust attack and, in the case of injustice done, vindicate the life, person, good name and property rights of every citizen.

This development found fruition in *Ogieriakhi v Minister for Justice and Equality (No.2)* [2014] IEHC 582 in which Hogan J. held that in the special circumstances of the case the plaintiff's constitutional right to a good name was not protected by either employment contract law or by an action for the tort of defamation which he described at para.98 as "the principal remedy provided by law for the vindication of the constitutional right to a good name".

Clearly such a constitutional tort has great significance for a whistleblower who suffers severe retaliation from an employer, injury for which the Protected Disclosures Act 2014 provides no remedy.

Rule in *Addis* ineffective As noted in the Constitutional Law chapter of this Annual Review, Hogan J. observed in *Ogieriakhi* that the common law has traditionally declined to award damages for loss of reputation following dismissal from employment. He cited the classic example of *Addis v Gramophone Co. Ltd.* [1909] A.C. 488, where the House of Lords held (or, at least, appears to have held) that damages are not recoverable in contract for the manner in which an employee has been dismissed from his employment. In that case the plaintiff had been summarily dismissed from his employment in a humiliating manner which had seriously affected his reputation and standing, at para.84. Since the plaintiff's constitutional right to a good name was not protected by employment contract law, Hogan J. held that neither would it be protected by an action for the tort of defamation, the principal statutory remedy for the vindication of the constitutional right to a good name.

> "[98] As the employment cases themselves tacitly recognise, the vindication of the employee's right to a good name following dismissal must normally come through either the mechanism of contract law or not at all. This is because defamatory words or conduct will not normally accompany the act of dismissal and, even if they do, the uttering of such words will generally be protected by privilege in the manner now contemplated by s.18 of the Defamation Act 2009.
>
> 99. It is, moreover, the very act of dismissal which often sends the signal to future employers that the employee is not fit to be re-hired. The gist of the damage to the plaintiff's good name was the immediate and unlawful termination of his contract of employment with An Post. This was not capable of being remedied either by the tort of defamation (for the reasons just stated) or for breach of contract (by reason of the rule in *Addis*). It might have been capable of being remedied by means of proceedings under the Unfair Dismissal Acts 1977 to 2007, but, as we have seen, the Employment Appeals Tribunal rejected the claim that this dismissal was unfair."

Therefore, he held, at para.100, that existing law did not adequately vindicate the plaintiff's constitutional right to a good name, at least in the unusual and special circumstances of the present case.

In *McMahon v Irish Aviation Authority* [2014] IEHC 431, Hogan J. held that an open-ended suspension was invalid. As a statutory body the Irish Aviation Authority was required to exercise fair procedures consistent with constitutional principles. In this case the suspension meant that Mr McMahon was obliged to stand down from a prestigious position which meant everything to him and given that the position has had to have been filled in the meantime, his prospects of being appointed again to that post could not be regarded as high. Hogan J. continued:

> "35. There is equally no doubt but that a suspension of this kind has considerable implications for the good name of the person affected. Many might reasonably think that the Authority imposed the suspension because of concerns that Mr. McMahon had taken a casual or even irresponsible attitude to the vital question of air safety or that he improperly yielded to commercial pressures in allowing flights to take off where the weather conditions for sport parachuting were doubtful or even hazardous. As I pointed out in *Wallace v. Irish Aviation* Authority [2012] IEHC 178, [2012] 2 I.L.R.M. 350, 351, often the 'very fact of suspension is enough, in this valley of squinting windows, to expose the employee to the decidedly unpleasant prospect of calumny and detraction at the hands of the unforgiving and the uncharitable.' Here it must be recalled that Article 40.3.2 of the Constitution requires the State by its laws to protect that right to good name 'as best it may from unjust attack' and in the case 'of injustice done' to vindicate that right."

The constitutional aspects of these cases are more fully analysed in this Annual

Review in the Constitutional Law chapter. The importance of these judgments for whistleblowers can only be realised by a wronged whistleblower including with every claim for redress, a claim for breach of constitutional rights as guaranteed under Arts. 40.3.1 and 40.3.2.

Subject Index